Praise for
THE COLORADO GUIDE

"An informational book—a bible, if you will, compiled with knowledge and affection."　　　**—Claire Walter,** *Denver Post*

"Why not enlist two experts to help you explore the richness of Colorado? This book can multiply your options and significantly enrich your pleasure."　　　　　　　　**—Richard D. Lamm,
former governor of Colorado**

"*The Colorado Guide* is well researched, thorough, and it has a conscience too. Colorado has long needed a comprehensive guide to the state. This book fills the gap."
　　　—Timothy Wirth, former U.S. Senator from Colorado

"*The Colorado Guide* has provided an exhaustive look at the state of Colorado—it's packed with useful facts and anecdotes about every place of interest. I would find it a welcome companion as I traveled the state. It certainly caught the spirit of my hometown, Steamboat Springs."　　　　　　**—Rod Hanna, director,
advertising and public relations,
Steamboat Ski Corporation**

"*The Colorado Guide* is the most extensive escort to our glorious state since the *WPA Guide to 1930s Colorado*."
　　　　　　　　　　　　　**—Mim Swartz, travel editor,
*Rocky Mountain News***

Nominated for
Guidebook of the Year 1990
by *Travel Publishing News*
San Francisco, California

THE COLORADO GUIDE

3rd Edition

THE COLORADO GUIDE

3rd Edition

Bruce Caughey
Dean Winstanley

Fulcrum Publishing
Golden, Colorado

The information in *The Colorado Guide* is accurate as of February 1994. However, prices, hours of
operation, phone numbers and other items change rapidly. If something in the book is incorrect or if
you have ideas for the next edition, please write to the authors at Fulcrum Publishing, 350 Indiana
Street, Suite 350, Golden, CO 80401.

The Colorado Guide provides many safety tips about weather and travel, but good decision making and
sound judgment are the responsibility of the individual.

Library of Congress Cataloging-in-Publication Data

Caughey, Bruce.
    The Colorado guide / Bruce Caughey. Dean Winstanley. — 3rd ed.
        p.   cm.
    Includes index.
    ISBN 1-55591-152-8 (pbk.)
    1. Outdoor recreation—Colorado—Guidebooks. 2. Colorado—Description and travel. 3.
Colorado—Guidebooks. I. Winstanley, Dean, 1960– . II. Title.
GV191.42.C6C37   1994
796.5′09788—dc20   94–4567
                                                       CIP

Printed in the United States of America

0 9 8 7 6 5 4 3 2 1

Fulcrum Publishing
350 Indiana Street, Suite 350
Golden, Colorado 80401-5093

CONTENTS

ACKNOWLEDGMENTS

First off, we must thank our parents who instilled in us the love for Colorado from the beginning. They also helped greatly by encouraging us to go forward with this project, while conducting some of the initial research and reading stacks of chapters.

Naomi deserves our gratitude for coming up with the idea for this project in the first place—and then for prompting two old friends to join forces and work together.

Thanks are due to Vince Bzdek, Mark Eddy, Mark Asimus, Jim Bolick, Ron Catterson, Ricky Lightfoot, Maxine Benson and Sher and Dave Winstanley for providing specific accounts and assistance.

We acknowledge the fine staff at Fulcrum who have supported this book from day one. We greatly appreciate the work of Carmel Huestis and Tammy Ferris in the editorial department and Jay Staten and Patty Maher in the production department. Special thanks to Linda Stark, whose tireless efforts have helped make the first two editions enjoyable and successful. We thank Leslie Jorgensen of Jorgensen Design for creating the extremely functional and attractive maps for this edition.

While we're on the road, we rely and value input from the people who manage our public lands, often working for the National Forest Service, Bureau of Land Management, Colorado State Parks and Division of Wildlife. We also thank the destination chambers of commerce as well as various tourism experts that assisted us in our research. We especially want to thank the many locals who shared secrets about their favorite places.

Finally to Sheila and Naomi, who endured yet a third round of late-night edits and road trips—we know many tasks and responsibilities were juggled your way. We really do appreciate your support, advice and comfort. It helps keep everything in perspective.

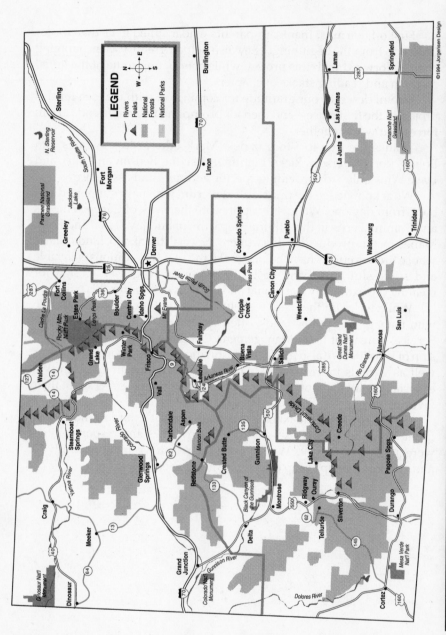

Colorado

INTRODUCTION

BACKGROUND INFORMATION

No one summed up Colorado better than former US President Teddy Roosevelt when he said, "The scenery bankrupts the English language." The Rocky Mountains dominate this striking scenery as they run through the middle of the state, constituting a mountainous area three times as large as the Swiss Alps. Colorado's peaks are legendary—over 1,140 of them are 10,000 feet or higher (54 top off at over 14,000 feet).

The state's colorful history can best be seen at the cliff dwellings of Mesa Verde National Park and in the former mining boomtowns such as Leadville and Silverton. Woven into the historic fabric are the unmistakable impacts of Anglo, Hispanic and Native American culture, all indelibly etched into Colorado's character. Colorado is a rich and varied land; its 3.5 million residents appreciate the healthy mix of recreation and culture, coming together with a dash of the Wild West.

More than 20 million visitors make their way to the state each year, not only for personal adventure and wilderness travel, but also to enjoy some of the best powder skiing in the world. As "Winter Sports Capital of the Country," Colorado offers 26 major ski areas.

With so much to do in Colorado, up-to-date, accurate advice is a precious commodity—this is the main reason for our third revised edition. As native Coloradans, we enjoy sharing tips about the state with friends who come to visit—we hope our guidebook accomplishes the same by capturing the essence and spirit of Colorado for you. With an insider's perspective of Front Range cities, small mountain towns and areas far from civilization, we unlock some of Colorado's best-kept secrets. Included are specifics that guide the way to many popular activities, such as hiking, downhill skiing, fly-fishing and whitewater rafting. We also offer information about luxurious mountain resorts, the arts and museums of towns around the state and the region's many hot springs.

When we first set out to work on this massive project in 1988, we had a feeling that it would strike a chord with our readers. After nine printings and three editions it's safe to say we're on the right track. Even so, keeping this book current requires constant updating—especially all of those restaurant and accommodation write-ups. We have spent the past two years revisiting all of the statewide destinations in the book, with an eye toward improving and expanding our coverage. The result is an even more complete, easy-to-use and accurate guide, which we hope will impart some of the fascination and love we feel for the state. Now get out there and enjoy!

HISTORY

This land called *Colorado*, to which so many people come for rest and relaxation, was anything but that to its first inhabitants. Nomadic hunters of bison and woolly mammoth may have roamed the state as far back as 15,000 years. Archaeologists continue to learn more about these prehistoric residents (Folsom Man) from their stone spear heads and other artifacts. Close on the heels of Folsom Man was the more advanced Anasazi civilization—Colorado's first farmers. They inhabited the mesa tops and cliffs of southwestern Colorado from approximately AD 1 until their mysterious disappearance in AD 1300. The Anasazi are known for their basket making and, in later periods, for pottery and stone masonry (the latter can be witnessed in the stunning cliff-hanging citadels at Mesa Verde National Park—see the **Cortez** chapter).

In centuries following the disappearance of the Anasazi, bands of nomadic Native American tribes (most notably Utes and Comanche in the mountains and Arapaho and Cheyenne on the plains) wandered the state in search of game. To these tribes the buffalo was an integral part of their way of life. By the late 1500s the arrival of Anglos forever changed the Indians' lifestyle in Colorado. These newcomers brought horses, enabling the Indians to travel greater distances and to hunt more effectively.

By many accounts, the first European to enter Colorado was the Spanish explorer Francisco Coronado. In 1540 he and other conquistadors made their way north from Mexico in search of the mythical "Seven Cities of Cibola," where it was said the streets were paved with gold. No such luck for Coronado, who arrived in northern New Mexico only to find Pueblo Indians living in poverty. Probably to get rid of him, the Indians suggested to Coronado that he head to what is now Kansas ... there he would find the riches he sought. Many historians believe he traveled through southeastern Colorado on his way to Kansas. Alas, he never found his gold. At about this time, the Spanish gave Colorado its name, which means "reddish" or "ruddy."

Over the next few hundred years, as the Spanish moved north and settled in the Rio Grande Valley of New Mexico, they played a major role in the history of Colorado. Although they never established any permanent settlements in the state, Spain claimed all the land south of the Arkansas River and west of the Continental Divide. One of the first written accounts of Colorado was provided by the Spanish friars Dominguez and Escalante.

These men left Santa Fe (northern New Mexico) in the summer of 1776, looking for a route to the new Spanish settlement in San Francisco, California. Their journey took them through much of southwestern Colorado. Poor relations with the Indians persisted throughout Spain's colonization of the New World—perhaps stiff taxes and enslavement had something to do with it! This disregard for Native American culture on the part of the Spanish was repeated in later years by Americans.

After the Louisiana Purchase in 1803, the US doubled in size. This largely uncharted land was acquired from Napoleon Bonaparte, ruler of the French empire, in one of the best real estate deals of all time. Expeditions were sent west to explore the new territory, which included northeastern Colorado. In 1806 Lt. Zebulon Pike led the first expedition to Colorado via the Arkansas River. Though a rather inept pathfinder, Pike did manage to explore much of southern Colorado before being captured in Spanish territory along the Rio Grande River in the San Luis Valley (he thought he was on the Red River of Texas).

Another significant expedition was conducted in 1820 by Maj. Stephen H. Long. Entering Colorado on the South Platte River, Long explored much of the Front Range of the Rockies before leaving along the Arkansas River. Unimpressed with the land along the Front Range, Long called it the "Great American Desert" and "unfit for cultivation." He was wrong, though, as eastern Colorado went on to support some of the most productive agricultural land in the western US. Later expeditions in the 1840s by John C. Frémont and in 1853 by Capt. John Gunnison added knowledge about Colorado's complex geography.

In the 1820s the trading and trapping era began, as beaver hats became the rage in Europe and the eastern US. High prices paid for beaver pelts swayed a number of adventurous trappers to venture into the wilds of Colorado. These men were the real pioneers and included Jim Bridger, Jim Beckwourth, Jedediah Smith and Kit Carson. After Mexico achieved independence from Spain in 1821, trade between this new country and the US blossomed. To facilitate trade, the Santa Fe Trail was established between St. Louis, Missouri and Santa Fe. In the late 1820s traders William and Charles Bent and Ceran St. Vrain built Bent's Fort along the Mountain Branch of the Santa Fe Trail that passed through southeastern Colorado. For almost 20 years the fort served as a base for western trade with Mexico and the Pacific Coast.

When beaver hats fell out of fashion in the 1830s, trappers looked around for an alternative income and found it in hunting buffalo. The Plains Indians were concerned, and rightly so, that the buffalo slaughter threatened their way of life. Short-term relations were soothed by trading trinkets, guns and liquor. Even so, within a few short decades the buffalo were almost hunted to extinction.

By 1846 relations between the US and Mexico deteriorated to such a point that the Mexican War broke out. Two years later, Mexico ceded its land in present-day Colorado to US victors in the Treaty of Guadeloupe Hidalgo. The US, however, agreed to honor Mexican land grants in extreme southern Colorado. These grants had been given by the Mexican government to individuals who agreed to establish settlements in remote northern areas of the Mexican frontier. In 1852 Hispanic settlers, moving into what is now southern Colorado, established San Luis, the first permanent town in the state. A number of other settlements followed. Today, this area is still a cradle of Hispanic culture.

Colorado's most notable era kicked into gear in 1858 when William Green Russell and his party from Georgia discovered gold along Dry Creek near present-day Denver. Hundreds of anxious miners made their way to the mining camps of Denver City and Auraria in the Pikes Peak Gold Rush. Many returned east in disgust calling the strike a hoax, but gold strikes by George Jackson near Idaho Springs and by John Gregory near Central City in the spring of 1859 proved the early rush was well founded and thousands more streamed into the territory. Publicity in eastern newspapers also prompted fortune seekers to head west, and in the early 1860s, towns sprang up along the Front Range and in the mountains at Breckenridge, Fairplay and Georgetown, among others. Denver quickly grew as a supply town for the mining camps.

In February 1861 the Colorado Territory was established, which was a step toward statehood and self-rule for the new residents. When the Civil War broke out in 1862, however, the Colorado Territory fell on hard times. Many miners left to fight, and the Plains Indians used this preoccupation with the war to begin a series of raids on new settlers. Angered by the encroachment on their hunting grounds and disregard for Indian culture, Arapaho and Cheyenne intensified their strikes between 1862 and 1864. The conflict reached a bloody climax when over 100 innocent Indians, including women and children, were slaughtered by volunteer troops at the Sand Creek Massacre (see the **Southeast Plains** chapter). Although there were a few more uprisings, Sand Creek was really the death knell for the Indians of Colorado's eastern plains.

By the late 1860s, most of the easily obtainable gold from stream beds in the territory had been snatched up. Miners were now forced to dig shafts into the mountains to get at the gold ore. The problem was that gold proved difficult to extract from the ore—a cheap processing method was badly needed. In 1868 Prof. Nathaniel Hill solved the ore reduction problem and opened his Boston and Colorado smelter in Black Hawk.

In the 1870s and 1880s Colorado mining really boomed. Prospectors pushed further west into the mountains, discovering new mining areas. Silver was mined and soon became more dominant than gold. After

Colorado achieved statehood in 1876, it received the nickname "Silver State." Georgetown and Silver Cliff were large silver mining towns, but nothing could compare to the deposits near Leadville. When silver was discovered in Leadville in 1877, the population soared from less than 100 to more than 24,000 within a few months. Many fortunes were made, including that of H.A.W. Tabor (see the **Leadville** chapter).

The quest for new mining areas created a conflict with another of Colorado's Indian tribes—the Utes. A tough, stocky tribe, the Utes roamed the mountains of Colorado following herds of deer, elk, buffalo and antelope. At first they were friendly with the anglo settlers, especially since these strange-looking newcomers made war on the Arapaho and Cheyenne, the Utes' bitter enemies on the plains. Under the guidance of Chief Ouray, the Utes accepted a series of treaties with the US government, which continued to reduce their territory. Finally, after a band of northern Utes killed Indian agent Nathan Meeker in the Meeker Massacre of 1879 (see the **Meeker** chapter), the tribe was relocated to Utah and a small reservation in southwestern Colorado. Anglo settlers now had reign over the whole state.

Another major factor contributing to Colorado's development was the arrival of the railroads. In 1870 the Denver Pacific spur was completed, connecting Denver to the Union Pacific's transcontinental line at Cheyenne, Wyoming. Soon after, other railroads snaked through the state, including the Denver & Rio Grande Railroad. Well-engineered narrow-gauge railroads chugged along to out-of-the-way mountain mining towns, providing an inexpensive means of shipping ore to the smelters and supplies to the towns. Remnants of these mountain rail lines can be found in many locations throughout the state.

In addition to the mining industry, cattle ranching on the eastern plains helped fuel the state's economy for a couple of decades before homesteaders began farming much of the land. Ambitious irrigation projects turned the arid land along the Lower Arkansas River Valley and the South Platte Valley near Greeley into lush farmland by the late 1880s. This diversification of Colorado's economy came not a moment too soon, as troubling times for the mining industry were just around the corner.

In 1893 the US government abandoned the silver standard, causing silver prices to plummet. Colorado's economy was hit heavily—mines shut down and in a span of a few days, 10 banks closed in Denver. Despite a large gold strike at Cripple Creek that produced through the 1890s and into the 1900s, Colorado's glory days of mining were over. With the new century came an increased emphasis on agriculture and a new industry—tourism.

During the Great Depression of the 1930s, projects by the Civilian Conservation Corps (CCC) and the Works Progress Administration

(WPA) helped develop Colorado's national forest land and highway system, making it easier for visitors to enjoy the state's beauty. Irrigation projects, including the enormous Big Thompson diversion in north central Colorado, brought water from the state's Western Slope (of the Continental Divide) through tunnels in the mountains to the more heavily populated Eastern Slope.

With World War II came an interest in Colorado by the Air Force. High altitude and good weather made Colorado an ideal training area for pilots. Though some bases are slated for closure, numerous military facilities continue to be important in Colorado—most notable is the Air Force Academy in Colorado Springs. Although the extremely cyclical oil and gas industry put a damper on the state's economy in the 1980s, Colorado has rebounded with its steady base in transportation, light manufacturing, ranching, agriculture and high-tech industry. But none of these is as exciting as downhill skiing and other components of the tourism boom.

For more information on Colorado history, contact the **Colorado Historical Society, 1300 Broadway, Denver, CO 80203; (303) 866-2611.**

Suggested Reading—

A *Colorado History* (Pruett, 1988), edited by Carl Ubbelohde, Maxine Benson and Duane Smith, is the best complete history we've been able to find. While driving through the state, carry along James McTighe's well-organized and lively *Roadside History of Colorado* (Johnson, 1984). *The Colorado Book* (Fulcrum, 1993) is an excellent collection of writings on the state by famous authors, celebrities, etc. For an historical travel perspective, it's tough to match *The WPA Guide to 1930s Colorado* (University Press of Kansas, 1987).

GEOGRAPHY AND GEOLOGY

Some residents say if Colorado were to be ironed out, its area would be larger than Texas. This may be an exaggeration, but it does draw attention to Colorado's most distinctive feature—the Rocky Mountains. The Rockies slice north/south through the state with more than 54 peaks rising higher than 14,000 feet, including the highest "14er," Mt. Elbert at 14,433 feet. Covering the eastern third of Colorado, the Great Plains extend east to Kansas and Nebraska and north into Wyoming. On the western side of the Rockies, the Colorado Plateau is characterized by beautiful canyons and valleys.

Along the spine of the Rockies lies the Continental Divide, which acts as a watershed for North America. All waters on the Western Slope drain into the Pacific, while Eastern Slope waters eventually drain into the Gulf of Mexico. Colorado encompasses the headwaters for more than 10 major rivers, including western giants such as the Colorado, Rio Grande, Arkansas and Platte.

Looking at the rugged peaks, deep, beautiful canyons and windswept plains of Colorado, one doesn't have to be a scientist to guess that the state has had a long, active geologic past. This history began 300 million years ago with the uplift of the Ancestral Rockies. These mountains consisted of two ranges similar to the present-day Rockies, located 100 miles west of today's Front Range. After 20 million years, the uplift ceased and erosion began. A million years of exposure to water, wind and ice eroded away the Ancestral Rockies to small hills similar to the Appalachian Mountains of the eastern US. Remnants of these ancient mountains can be seen in the red formations throughout the mountains of Colorado (Red Rocks, Garden of the Gods and the area around Vail are good examples).

During this period of erosion, a shallow inland sea covered most of North America, including Colorado. The water level of this sea varied greatly, causing the formation of huge coastal plains, which, due to a very dry climate, sometimes resembled a desert with windblown sand and dunes. This was especially true in western Colorado.

Later the climate became more humid. Rivers meandered over the coastal plains and the "desert" was transformed into a lush, green, sometimes swampy environment. This period, between 200 and 65 million years ago, was the age of the dinosaurs. Fossils of more than 70 dinosaur species have been found in the Morrison Formation of Colorado, including the bones of the largest Brontosaurus ever excavated. Near the end of this period, the inland sea once again engulfed most of Colorado, depositing thick layers of shale over most of the state.

The present-day Rockies began to form 65 million years ago and continued forming for 20 million years during an event called the Laramide Orogeny. Forces within the earth pushed up the Precambrian "basement" rock by 15,000 to 25,000 feet. The previously deposited layers on top of the much older Precambrian rock folded, buckled and cracked. Today these soft layers have been eroded away to expose the harder, more resistant Precambrian rock. Evidence of this monumental event can be seen throughout Colorado, where layers that had once lain flat have been violently forced up to almost vertical positions.

Forty million years ago in southwestern Colorado, volcanoes erupted over and over again, expelling immense amounts of gas, lava and ash. This period continued for 30 million years. Before some of the magma could reach the surface, it solidified into dikes, sills and laccoliths. Today erosion has exposed these features. Sleeping Ute Mountain near Cortez is a good example of a huge laccolith as are the dikes radiating from the Spanish Peaks near La Veta. This highly volcanic area includes the San Juan Mountains, the West Elk Mountains and the Flat Tops Plateau.

Beginning 28 million years ago (and lasting 23 million years), Colorado land was uplifted by 5,000 feet, yet the overall makeup of the region really didn't change.

From 75,000 to 10,000 years ago, glaciers helped carve and shape the mountains of Colorado. Many glaciers in the higher mountains created cirque valleys, characterized by the U-shaped walls and floor instead of the normal V shape of a stream-formed valley. This U shape forms because the glacier scours out the bottom of the valley.

Suggested Reading—

One of the best sources for geological information is *Roadside Geology of Colorado* (Mountain Press, 1980) by Halka Chronic.

FLORA AND FAUNA

Colorado's varied terrain (grassland, mountains, arid plateaus) provides habitat for diverse plant and animal life. Throughout the book we have tried to include relevant information about the predominant flora and fauna in different parts of the state, but you may want more. The state of Colorado manages more than 250 wildlife areas, which serve as prime observation points, especially for bird watchers. The **Colorado Division of Wildlife** at **6060 Broadway, Denver, CO 80216; (303) 297-1192,** will be happy to answer your questions about Colorado wildlife or to send you brochures and pamphlets. The **US Fish and Wildlife Service, PO Box 25486, Denver Federal Center, Denver, CO 80225; (303) 236-7904,** stands ready with information about a handful of National Wildlife Refuges located throughout the state.

Suggested Reading—

An excellent source for information on the flora and fauna of Colorado is *From Grassland to Glacier: The Natural History of Colorado* (Johnson, 1992) by Cornelia Fleischer Mutel and John C. Emerick. This highly readable book describes various ecosystems of Colorado in easy-to-understand terms. For wildlife lovers, try *Colorado Wildlife Viewing Guide* (Falcon Press, 1992) for suggested locations for catching a glimpse of Colorado wildlife.

CLIMATE

Colorado's weather varies enough to suit anyone's tastes and is therefore tough to generalize. Because the Rocky Mountains cut through the middle of the state, creating their own uncertain weather patterns, forecasting is something of a nightmare. These high peaks attract snow flurries almost any time of year, but once November arrives, large quantities of snow stick around for winter. Thanks to crisp winter weather and powder snow, skiing rules the high country from November through April; Colorado is an outdoor playground for hikers, campers, anglers and sightseers the rest of the year. Snowcover remains at the highest locations until summer when long pleasant days finally melt away winter's residue. Driving in the mountains during or after a snowfall can be treacherous; for **road conditions** call **(303) 639-1111.**

You can count on cool nights even in mid-summer as the thin mountain air loses its heat. The dry climate, however, takes some of the swelter out of summer and some of the bite out of winter, making it a pleasant place despite temperature extremes. Denver, at the eastern foot of the Rockies, almost qualifies as a desert, with merely 15 inches of annual precipitation. Once in a while a heat wave comes through and the temperatures rise over 100 degrees Fahrenheit. The Front Range of the Rockies enjoys more than 300 days of sunshine each year, but afternoon rainshowers are commonplace in summer.

In Colorado you can experience all four seasons in one day, so dressing for unpredictable weather is something of an art—a good rule is to be prepared for anything by wearing layers. In summer be prepared for cool mornings and evenings, hot midday temperatures and afternoon rainstorms. Winter requires a warm jacket, hat and gloves. When you're exploring the high country, summer or winter, be sure to take along sunscreen. For a Denver forecast call **(303) 398-3964;** statewide, **(303) 639-1515.**

VISITOR INFORMATION
GENERAL INFORMATION

For visitor information, the **Colorado Tourism Board** is perhaps the best place to begin. Offering general information about the state, they can also put you in touch with many clubs and organizations for more specifics. Contact them at **1675 Broadway, Suite 320, Denver, CO 80202; (303) 592-5410.** They still operate Welcome Centers at Colorado's major entry points. These centers, located in **Burlington, Cortez, Fruita** and **Trinidad,** are great resources for statewide information and pamphlets.

For information about specific destinations, it's a pretty safe bet to start with each area's chamber of commerce (see the Services section at the end of each chapter). One of the largest organizations offering scattered information about the entire state is the **Denver Metro Convention & Visitors Bureau, 225 W. Colfax; (303) 892-1112.**

TIPS FOR VISITORS

Drinking Laws—To purchase or drink hard liquor, wine or beer, you must be 21 years old. But if you look under 25, have a photo identification ready (a passport is fine). Bars are normally open until 2 am, Mon.–Sat; 12 am on Sun. Colorado strictly enforces laws against drunk driving—do not drive while impaired.

Driving—To rent a car in Colorado, you will need a national driver's license or an International Driver's Permit. Once you're on the road, remember that wearing a seat belt is law in Colorado. One hint for driving in the city: After coming to a complete stop, you are allowed to turn right at a red light when traffic is clear.

Health and Safety—It might be helpful to understand a few common maladies that sometimes plague visitors to Colorado.

Altitude Sickness—If you feel a persistent headache, nausea or dizziness (or in severe cases a buildup of fluid in your lungs), you might be experiencing problems due to a rapid elevation gain. Mountain climbers and skiers especially need to be aware that your body sometimes just needs time to adjust (especially above 8,000 feet). If untreated by an increase in oxygen levels, altitude sickness can be potentially life threatening.

Dehydration—It's important to replace body fluids, especially when engaging in Colorado's many strenuous outdoor activities. If you feel symptoms such as intense thirst, dizziness and higher heart and breath rates, drink lots of fluids.

Giardia—Hikers and backpackers should be sure to purify stream and lake water before taking a single sip. A single-cell parasite called *Giardia lamblia* can make your life miserable (cramps and diarrhea are common symptoms) within a day or two of drinking contaminated water.

Hypothermia—Prolonged exposure to the cold may cause your body temperature to drop, inducing a slowed heart rate, lethargy and confusion—extended hypothermia can cause death. Get immediate medical help and try to get to a warm place.

Sunburn—Colorado's higher elevation provides less protection from the sun's ultraviolet rays—lather up with sunscreen, even if there's cloud cover, or you'll be sorry. Skiers should be really careful because the snow's reflective power increases the intensity of the burning power.

Money—
Credit Cards—Major credit cards (American Express, Mastercard and Visa) are accepted nearly everywhere. You may need one to put a security deposit on a rental car. They are also extremely handy for getting emergency cash from banks and Automated Teller Machines (ATMs).

Travelers Checks—Visitors from abroad should be sure to get travelers checks in US dollar denominations because most banks don't have the capability to exchange foreign currencies.

Student and Senior Discounts—In Colorado seniors can often find discounts at movies, motels and restaurants as well as on buses and airplanes. Students seeking discounts are not quite as well received, but with an International Student Identification Card (ISIC), you may find some price breaks.

Telephones—Two area codes in Colorado serve as prefixes for long-distance telephone numbers; as a general rule the northern region is (303) and the southern region is (719). When dialing long distance, dial 1, the area code and then the seven-digit number. For long-distance directory assistance, call **(303) 555-1212;** within Denver dial **1-411.** The operator will answer if you dial **0.** For emergency assistance, dial **911.**

Time—Mountain Standard Time (Colorado) is two hours earlier than Eastern Standard Time (New York) and one hour later than Pacific Standard Time (California).

Tipping—Porters and bellboys expect at least 50 cents per bag. Taxi drivers, barbers, hairdressers and bartenders expect 15 to 20 percent. Unless you are part of a large group, service charges are not normally included in restaurant bills. When the service has been pleasant, figure a 15 percent (up to 20 percent) tip based on the price of the meal, excluding tax. Many people leave tips for maid service, especially during extended stays.

GETTING THERE

Colorado lies virtually at the geographic center of the United States, and Denver is the largest city in the Rocky Mountain region. Therefore, it's natural for the city to be an important transportation hub. **Denver International Airport (DIA),** lying 23 miles northeast of the downtown area, is the largest (53 square miles) and no doubt one of the busiest airports in the world. Six runways and, ultimately, 260 gates enable daily nonstop flights to 109 cities (1,300 flights), including some in Europe.

From DIA you can make connecting flights to smaller destinations in Colorado, including Aspen, Colorado Springs, Pueblo, Grand Junction, Durango, Steamboat Springs, Telluride, Gunnison and Crested Butte.

The vast concourses, sprawling layout and tentlike architecture of the airport can be intimidating. An underground transit system whisks people from the gate area over to the main terminal where rental cars, taxis, hotel reservations, etc., await. For more specifics, call the main information number at **(303) 270-1000**. To reach DIA from downtown Denver, head east on I-70 past Chambers Rd. and turn north on Peña Blvd.

Trains are no longer a way of life in the West, but the **Amtrak** East Coast to West Coast route, passing through Denver and Glenwood Canyon, is one of the prettiest rides imaginable. For information stop in at downtown Denver's **Union Station** or call **1-800-872-7245**.

From virtually any point in the country, you can take a **Greyhound** bus into Denver. From there you can take a bus to many towns in the state. **1055 19th St., Denver; 1-800-293-6555**.

GETTING AROUND

To really experience the back roads of Colorado away from the major highways, you should have your own vehicle; many rental companies at Denver International Airport can help you. Two reliable companies include: **Budget Rentals; (303) 341-2277** in Denver or **1-800-527-0700** nationally; and **Hertz Rent a Car; 1-800-654-3131**. If you are on a tight budget, consider renting at **Cheap Heap.** These folks will rent you a late-model American car (with snow tires and ski racks if necessary) by the day, week or month. They will pick you up and drop you off at the airport for no extra charge. **6005 E. Colfax Ave., Denver; (303) 393-0028**. A side note: Hitchhiking in Colorado is legal, but rides come v-e-r-y infrequently.

Other ways of getting around include catching a connecting flight from Denver International Airport to mountain resorts. **Greyhound Bus Lines** makes daily runs to many Front Range and mountain towns. Frequent public buses run between the airport, downtown and other locations in the Denver metro area as well as outlying towns. For information and schedules, call **RTD** at **(303) 299-6000**. The **Rio Grande Ski Train** makes runs from Denver to Winter Park Ski Area every Sat.–Sun. in winter. **555 17th St.; (303) 296-ISKI**.

INFORMATION FOR DISABLED VISITORS

Along with the rest of the nation, Colorado is finally reacting to the long-existing needs of disabled travelers by offering improved services. Many organizations throughout the state do exemplary jobs providing outdoor recreation for people with special needs—**Winter Park** has the largest disabled ski program in the country. **Wilderness on Wheels** (see the **South Park and 285 Corridor** chapter) offers a system of wide, wooden boardwalks along a trout-filled creek. The Colorado State Parks, US Forest Service and National Park Service have all worked hard to create more accessible campgrounds, fishing piers, rest rooms and other facilities.

Suggested Reading—

The **Commission on People with Disabilities** in Denver has put together a brief access guide to outdoor recreation and is a great connecting point for learning about the state's resources. **303 W. Colfax, Suite 875, Denver, CO 80204; (303) 575-3056** voice or TDD. A useful source of information is the *National Park Guide for the Handicapped* from the **US Government Printing Office, Washington, DC 20402.**

HOW THE BOOK IS ORGANIZED

"Visitor friendly," *The Colorado Guide* is arranged in six geographic regions: Northwest, North Central, Northeast, Southwest, South Central and Southeast. Each region, with a map pinpointing its location in the state, is divided into "destinations"—40 in all. Background information about each destination sets the scene: general introduction, history and directions. Specific information is then provided on the major attractions, festivals and events, outdoor activities, sightseeing highlights, lodging and camping, restaurants and services.

This introduction generally parallels the arrangement of destination sections. Within each chapter, you will find all you need to plan a terrific trip. The index is an added help.

FESTIVALS AND EVENTS

A full calendar of festivals and events takes place throughout Colorado; from these, we have selected some of the most outstanding to include in each chapter. Many are worth planning your vacation around, while others may merit only a detour. In summer **Telluride** is well known for its wide array of events including, of course, the renowned Bluegrass Festival. Any mention of music must include **Aspen**, which is the best place for a summer's worth. Rodeo is another Rocky Mountain favorite—the National Western Stock Show in **Denver** should not be missed and mountain towns often have their own. Colorado is known for a number of active, sporting events, including marathons, triathlons and bike races. Events are listed each month in *Rocky Mountain Sports Magazine*, available at no charge at sporting goods stores throughout the state; **(303) 440-5111**. Pick up an annual copy of *The Colorado Guide Calendar* (Fulcrum) for our favorite festivals and events each month along with 12 gorgeous full-color photographs.

OUTDOOR ACTIVITIES
BIKING

Mountain Biking—

This extremely popular activity, which many claim originated in Colorado, certainly combines well with the maze of backcountry logging and mining roads found throughout the state. Mountain biking in Colorado really came of age in 1990 when the world championships were held in Durango. Mountain bikes, equipped with 15 to 20 plus gears, a sturdy alloy frame and wide, knobby tires, are perfectly suited for rough rides. More adventurous riders prefer "single-track" trails through the backcountry. Mountain bikers, however, must remember to respect the rights of other trail users; bikes are allowed on national forest land, but remain strictly prohibited in wilderness areas. Since "fat-tire" riding has become so popular, several extensive trail systems have been developed, and rentals are available in many towns. **Crested Butte, Grand Junction, Durango, Winter Park** and **Steamboat Springs** in particular have become well-known centers for the sport. For an extended ride from alpine to desert terrain, consider the San Juan Hut System (see the **Telluride** chapter) between **Telluride** and Moab, Utah.

Touring—

With a good road map you can tour anywhere in the state. Of course, there are some outstanding rides, especially in the Colorado National Monument (see the **Grand Junction** chapter) and along the maintained bike path between Breckenridge and Vail (see the **Summit County** chapter). The **Denver Greenway Trail System**, extending over 100 miles throughout the Denver Metro area is one of the best urban trail systems in the country, suited for both mountain and touring bikes. Excellent maps of trail systems throughout the state are updated annually and available for no charge at **Colorado State Parks, 1313 Sherman St., Room 618, Denver, CO 80203; (303) 866-3437**.

Suggested Reading—

For a selection of mountain bike rides across the state, complete with topographical maps, pick up a copy of William Stoehr's *Bicycling the Backcountry* (Pruett, 1987). You might also try *Mountain Biking Colorado's Historic Mining Districts* (Fulcrum, 1991) by Laura Rossetter. In addition, many books can be found for specific destinations throughout the state.

FISHING

Colorado, with more than 65,000 miles of streams, nearly 2,500 coldwater lakes and reservoirs (and 360 warmwater), provides a kaleidoscope of fishing opportunities. Getting away from it all, clearing your brain of every thought except landing a big brown trout, is what Colorado angling is all about—no matter if you are into fishing with a minuscule dry fly or with a No. 6 hook and a worm. We have carefully selected better-than-average public waters to include in each chapter—but as you know, this is no guarantee of good fishing.

We mention the following special designations throughout: **Gold Medal Water**, the highest-quality trout water in Colorado, offering the greatest potential for catching large numbers of fish, including trophy-sized trout; and **Wild Trout Water**, which supports self-sustaining trout populations. A Colorado fishing license is a must for fishing on all public water; resident and nonresident licenses are available at most sporting goods stores. These stores are also a great source of information—as long as you keep in mind that they would love to sell you armloads of tackle. When buying your license, be sure to pick up a copy of *Colorado Fishing Season Information and Wildlife Property Directory* for specific details on restrictions and regulations throughout the state. For information contact the **Colorado Division of Wildlife (DOW) Central Regional Office, 6060 Broadway, Denver, CO 80216; (303) 297-1192**. The DOW provides up-to-date fishing and stocking reports by region: Denver Metro area, **(303) 291-7535**; Northeast, **(303) 291-7536**; Southeast, **(303) 291-7538**; Northwest, **(303) 291-7537**; Southwest, **(303) 291-7539**; General Information Line, **(303) 291-7533**.

Suggested Reading—

Tim Kelly's Fishing Guide (Hart Publications, 1990) is as complete and well organized an almanac of fishing in Colorado as you'll find. You may also want to call the **Division of Wildlife** and ask about their many publications and videos, **(303) 297-1192**.

FOUR-WHEEL-DRIVE TRIPS

Jeeping in the Colorado Rockies is *big*. Logging and mining roads built as far back as the 1860s provide access to ghost towns and some of the most spectacular scenery in the country. Jeep tour and rental companies are scattered throughout the mountain towns. No matter whether you take to the back roads on a guided trip or are driving your own vehicle, be sure to pack out all your trash. Please don't drive off existing roads, as this promotes erosion; this is especially important above treeline where the fragile alpine tundra will quickly die if driven on. A number of standout four-wheel-drive trips are discussed in the chapters of this book, especially around **Ouray, Telluride, Silverton** and **Creede**.

Information about jeeping on public land is available from the **US Forest Service, PO Box 25127, 740 Simms St., Lakewood, CO, 80225; (303) 275-5350;** or the **US Bureau of Land Management, 2850 Youngfield, Lakewood, CO 80215; (303) 239-3600.**

Suggested Reading—
  One of the best guides to the ghost towns of Colorado is *Jeep Trails to Colorado Ghost Towns* (Caxton, 1963) by Robert L. Brown. For a more in-depth look at the state's ghost towns and mining camps, as seen through the eyes of artist Muriel Sibell Wolle, read her classic, *Stampede to Timberline*, 2nd revised edition (Swallow, 1974).

GOLF

Some of the courses in Colorado rival any in the country for challenge and beautiful scenery. If you plan to play golf in the mountains, practice your putting ahead of time—the difficult break in mountain greens continues to baffle pros and amateurs alike. Also keep in mind that at this high altitude the ball travels *much* farther than at sea level—you may want to club down. Although the mountain courses are open only in summer and early fall, many courses on the Western Slope and along the Front Range (including Denver) are open year-round. Greens fees for 18 holes can vary anywhere from $10 to $50; the mountain resorts tend to charge much more than city courses. Due to the constantly changing fees, we do not list specific prices in this book. But don't worry—we'll warn you if the greens fees are steep.

  A number of celebrity and PGA tournaments take place throughout the state. For specific information about tournaments or anything else connected with golfing in Colorado, contact the **Colorado Golf Association, Suite 101, 5655 S. Yosemite, Englewood, CO 80111; (303) 779-GOLF.**

HIKING AND BACKPACKING

For our money (or lack of it), one of the best ways to experience the varied and beautiful country of Colorado is by getting into the backcountry for a hike. The state is set up for it. Public lands include 11 national forests (comprising a fifth of Colorado), more than 2 dozen wilderness areas, Bureau of Land Management (BLM) land, 2 national parks, 5 national monuments and 40 state parks.

  The national forest land is administered by offices scattered throughout the state. Destinations bordering on national forest land will have the local address for the ranger office. These folks provide a wealth of information for hiking and other outdoor pursuits. They also offer printed material, including the useful *Recreational Opportunity Guide*

(ROG) and forest service maps. For general information about the different national forests in Colorado, contact the **US Forest Service, PO Box 25127, 740 Simms St., Lakewood, CO 80225; (303) 275-5350.**

Wilderness areas, located within the national forests, are so designated to retain their pristine nature. They differ primarily from the rest of the national forest land in that no motorized vehicles or mountain bikes are allowed. Aside from that, a few extra rules apply as well as some very important *wilderness ethics*. Maintaining the unspoiled beauty of these areas is a monumental task; everyone needs to help. Here are a few suggested wilderness practices that you should apply to any outdoor trip, whether it's in a wilderness area or at a roadside picnic table.

1. While hiking, stay on existing trails. Straying off the trails kills vegetation and promotes erosion, especially on the alpine tundra.
2. Camp at least 100 feet from trails, streams and lakes. Choose a site in the woods rather than in an open meadow, for your own privacy as well as that of other hikers.
3. Use existing campsites to protect unused areas.
4. Use gas stoves, especially at high altitudes where firewood is scarce and slow to replenish itself. If you absolutely need a fire, use an existing fire ring.
5. Wash at least 100 feet from water sources; use biodegradable soap.
6. Carry a small shovel or trowel to bury human waste 6 to 8 inches below the ground.
7. Pack out all other trash—don't bury it!
8. Please leave pets at home—they disturb the wildlife.
9. Take only pictures and leave only footprints … leave your camp in better shape than you found it.

In recent years the **Bureau of Land Management**, which oversees an enormous amount of acreage in Colorado, has begun focusing more on use of BLM land for recreation; there are some incredible opportunities, from high alpine climbs to desert canyon hikes. Contact the BLM at **2850 Youngfield, Lakewood, CO 80215; (303) 239-3600.** For information about hiking opportunities at **Colorado State Parks: 1313 Sherman St., Room 618, Denver, CO 80203; (303) 866-3437.**

Colorado's ever-changing weather conditions can be a real problem for unprepared hikers. You should always have warm clothing and waterproof raingear in the high country. Speaking of the high country, altitude sickness (pulmonary edema) can strike anyone, especially those unaccustomed to higher elevations. Take time to adjust to the high altitude—don't go out and climb a 14,000-foot peak the day after arriving from sea level. Afternoon thunderstorms frequent the mountains in summer; lightning strikes above treeline are common. Another precaution involves the hundreds of old abandoned mines scattered throughout the state. It's very likely that you'll come across one or two of them. If you do, *stay out!* They are very dangerous and can contain toxic gases, hidden shafts and rotten timbers, among other hazards.

One of the most exciting things to happen in Colorado in recent years was the opening of the **Colorado Trail** in the summer of 1988. The 469-mile trail stretching from Denver to Durango was 15 years in the making. It crosses national forest and private land, winding through low-lying valleys and over high passes along the Continental Divide. Sections of the trail are mentioned in appropriate chapters throughout the book. If you want more information about this trail or are considering hiking its entire length, contact the US Forest Service. Pick up a copy of the excellent *A Colorado High: The Official Guide to the Colorado Trail* (FreeSolo, 1988) by Randy Jacobs—an official guide (240 pages) complete with maps.

For topographical map quadrangles of Colorado, stop in at sporting goods stores around the state or visit the **US Geological Survey** at the Denver Federal Center located at **PO Box 25046, Denver Federal Center, Mail Stop 504, Denver, CO 80225-0046; (303) 236-5829.**

Suggested Reading—

The Hiker's Guide to Colorado (Falcon, 1984) by Caryn and Peter Boddie offers details on many hikes around the state. *Colorado's Fourteeners* (Fulcrum, 1991) by Gerry Roach provides interesting information about Colorado's highest peaks. The newer *Colorado BLM Wildlands* (Westcliffe, 1992) offers insights into hiking opportunities at lesser-used BLM areas. Newly revised (9th edition), Robert Orms' *Guide to the Colorado Mountains* (Colorado Mountain Club, 1992) is still a great source for background about Colorado's mountains as well as route information up many peaks in the state. A large number of quality hiking books deal with specific regions of the state.

HORSEBACK RIDING

Colorado is horse country, and you'll feel comfortable wearing a cowboy hat and boots in most towns. We have listed stables in each chapter where applicable—most offer trail rides, breakfast rides and overnight pack trips. If you want a chance to ride every day for a week, consider a dude ranch vacation. For more information about horseback riding, you may want to get in touch with the **Colorado Outfitters Association, Inc., PO Box 440021, Aurora, CO 80044; (303) 368-4731;** or the **Colorado Dude and Guest Ranch Association, PO Box 300, Tabernash, CO 80478; (303) 887-3128** or **1-800-441-6060** outside Colorado.

LLAMA TREKKING

In South America llamas have been domesticated beasts of burden for more than 1,000 years; now they've become the rage in Colorado. You can't hop on the back of a llama and ride off into the sunset, but these lovable cousins of the camel can carry up to 100 pounds of gear on their backs. Just drape a tether over your shoulder and start hiking up a trail—your llama will follow wherever you go. It's an exotic way to spend an afternoon or, better yet, a few days of vacation. We have listed many llama packers in destinations around the state. If you need additional information, contact the **Colorado Llama Outfitters and Guides Association, 30361 Rainbow Hill Rd., Golden, CO 80401; (303) 526-0092.**

RIVER FLOATING

There you are, paddling through a stretch of calm water within a beautiful rock-walled canyon. Suddenly you hear the roar of the approaching rapids. Charging furiously down through the white water and maneuvering over a small waterfall, you finally reach calm water once again and have time to catch your breath. If you have the chance, a raft trip down one of Colorado's rivers promises to be an unforgettable part of your vacation, if not the highlight.

From the high Rocky Mountains of Colorado, more major rivers begin their long journeys to the ocean than in any other state in the country. When the snow begins to melt each spring and the water levels in the rivers swell, almost 400,000 rafters and kayakers take to the frigid waters for calm floats and hair-raising runs down some of the most challenging rivers in the world. Desert canyon sections of the **Dolores** and action-filled floats down the **Upper Arkansas, Green** and **Colorado** rivers are definite highlights. Descriptions of rivers and a few outfitters are listed in appropriate chapters of this book.

Although some people take their own rafts down the rivers, most trips are run through private outfitting companies. Outfitters vary greatly, offering different types of trips, so it's important to decide ahead of time what kind of river experience you are looking for. Colorado's rivers offer the full gamut, from leisurely floats (Class I—easy) to demanding (Class IV—very difficult) multiday expeditions. A particularly good source of information about planning a river float is the **American Outdoors, 2133 S. Yarrow St., Lakewood, CO 80227; (303) 377-4811**. They can provide information to help you choose the best river and best outfitter to suit your particular needs. Another source is the **Colorado River Outfitters Association, PO Box 1805, Vail, CO 81658; (303) 369-4632**.

Suggested Reading—

If you are planning to arrange your own rafting or kayak trip or just want further information about rivers in Colorado, we strongly suggest two books: *The Floater's Guide to Colorado* (Falcon, 1983) by Doug Wheat and *The Rivers of Colorado* (Falcon, 1985) by Jeff Rennicke.

SKIING

Cross-Country Skiing—

Gliding across freshly fallen snow, away from crowds and expensive lift tickets, is becoming an attractive alternative for many people. Partly because of this surge in popularity, there has been an increasing number of serious accidents due to avalanches. Before heading into the backcountry, find out about regional avalanche conditions by calling the **Colorado Avalanche Information Center: Denver, (303) 236-9435; Ft. Collins, (303) 482-0457; Colorado Springs, (719) 520-0020; Summit County, (303) 668-0600; Vail, (303) 827-5687; Aspen, (303) 920-1664; Durango, (303) 247-8187.**

There are many groomed trail systems throughout the state that usually charge a small fee. All the mountain resorts have cross-country rental shops, which also can be gold mines of valuable advice. Check the local Forest Service office for additional information, but remember they're usually closed on weekends in winter. Extended backcountry trips can be taken on the 10th Mountain Trail Association Hut System (see the **Aspen** chapter). For more general information, contact the **Colorado Cross-Country Ski Association, PO Box 169, Winter Park, CO 80482; (303) 887-2152.**

Suggested Reading—

For an excellent guide to trails and tours in Colorado's northern mountains, pick up a copy of Brian Litz and Kurt Langford's *Skiing Colorado's Backcountry* (Fulcrum, 1989).

Downhill Skiing—

Very few places in the world can boast the abundance of light powder snow, vertical drop and striking views that Colorado provides. With 26 ski areas to choose from, you should plan your winter getaway with these factors in mind: size and difficulty of the mountain, base village amenities and cost. **Vail** and **Aspen** are world-class resorts in every respect. The four ski areas in **Summit County** are fast approaching that status. If you are in search of a low-key, western atmosphere in a destination with as much mountain as you'd ever desire, make arrangements at **Steamboat Springs, Winter Park, Crested Butte** or **Telluride**. Smaller family areas such as **Ski Cooper, Sunlight** and **Monarch** offer low-cost vacations.

We have written about all the ski areas in the state. With expanded snowmaking capabilities, Colorado's ski season is well underway in November. It peaks during Christmas week and lasts into April (Arapahoe Basin usually stays open until late May). Almost every area offers discounted lift tickets early and late in the season. Quite often, reduced-price tickets can be purchased at Front Range grocery stores and gas stations throughout the season. It's usually less expensive to rent downhill equipment in Denver before heading into the mountains.

Sometimes all-inclusive vacation package deals offered through travel agents are quite a bargain. For more information about downhill skiing, contact **Colorado Ski Country USA, One Civic Center Plaza, 1560 Broadway, Suite 1440, Denver, CO 80202; (303) 837-0793.** Call **(303) 831-SNOW** if you would like a complete snow report; **(303) 639-1111** for mountain road conditions.

SNOWMOBILING

This sport is becoming extremely popular in Colorado. We have not gone into any depth of coverage on snowmobiling because of our emphasis on cross-country skiing (quite often, they compete for the same trails). You might contact the **Colorado Division of Parks and Outdoor Recreation** for more information. **13787 S. Hwy. 85, Littleton, CO 80125; (303) 791-1954.**

SEEING AND DOING
DINOSAURS

More than 60 million years ago, dinosaurs roamed all over Colorado, eating plants and each other. Some of the world's most significant dinosaur fossils have been found in Colorado. It's not that the state had more dinosaurs; it's just that the geologic upheaval that formed the Rockies exposed many dinosaur remains. Some of the best places to learn about dinosaurs are in **Grand Junction, Cañon City, Dinosaur National Monument** and the **Denver Museum of Natural History**.

HOT SPRINGS

The Indians found spiritual well-being in Colorado hot springs. Then came the spas for well-to-do tourists in the late 1800s. Colorado is home to many natural hot springs—some are highly developed, while others present a more natural setting. We have tried to uncover the best places to take a relaxing soak. See Hot Springs in the **Glenwood Springs, Ouray** and **Steamboat Springs** chapters for some great ideas.

MUSEUMS AND GALLERIES

We have included most museums (worth their salt) in the appropriate chapters. With our firsthand descriptions, you should be able to decide if you want to stop by for a visit. As far as galleries are concerned, we have covered only those that are truly outstanding. In places like **Aspen** or **Denver**, it would be absurd to list the scores of possibilities for viewing and buying art. Stop in at the chamber of commerce in each destination. The staff will be happy to help you locate galleries and antique shops.

SCENIC DRIVES

It's tough to avoid beautiful scenery while driving in Colorado. We've still managed to find some atypical routes that offer vibrant scenery and often some historically relevant attractions along the way. Unlike the outings described in the Four-Wheel-Drive Trips sections, all of the drives we include under Scenic Drives can be driven in passenger cars. Over the past few years some of Colorado's more spectacular roadways have been designated as "Scenic and Historic Byways." Anytime you find a distinctive road sign emblazoned with a blue columbine (the state flower), you've managed to find a designated Scenic Byway. Often, local chamber of commerce visitor centers have informational/historical brochures written as accompaniments to drives along these roads. A few of these routes are destined for fame, including our favorite: the San Juan Skyway (see the **Durango** chapter).

WHERE TO STAY
ACCOMMODATIONS

We have gone out of our way to select unique accommodations that you'll remember (fondly, we hope) well into the future. No one has paid for inclusion in the book and, while our narrowed-down list of selections may be subjective, we have given honest evaluations. Each write-up should provide you with enough information to decide whether a particular hotel, motel or bed and breakfast is for you. Whenever possible, we have avoided national chains—not because these places are bad, but simply because most people already know what to expect when checking into a Hilton, Holiday Inn, Best Western or Motel 6. To find the toll-free reservation numbers for these chains, call **1-800-555-1212**. If you would like a complete listing of what is available in an area, give the chamber of commerce a call (listed under Services in each chapter). They will be more than happy to answer your query. The larger resorts offer toll free central reservations numbers (also listed under Services in each chapter).

Because prices are constantly changing, we have used a price guideline throughout the book that shows approximately how much a night's lodging (double occupancy) will cost:

$	less than $25
$$	$25 to $50
$$$	$50 to $100
$$$$	$100 and up

For those of you who have never stayed at a bed and breakfast, it's time to step in from the cold. This European idea has caught on in Colorado, and a number of wonderful "escapes" are scattered throughout the state. Since a bed and breakfast is generally on a smaller scale than other lodging establishments, the owner's personal touch is always evident; you can stay in a small, immaculate Victorian, a sprawling mansion, a fantasyland castle or a rustic lodge. In the morning you'll have the chance to meet and talk with other guests during a complimentary breakfast. A number of organizations represent Colorado's B&Bs; here are a few of the best: **Bed & Breakfast Rocky Mountains, 1-800-825-0225** or **(719) 630-3433; Distinctive Inns of Colorado, 1-800-866-0621; Bed & Breakfast Innkeepers of Colorado, 1102 West Pikes Peak Ave., Colorado Springs, CO 80904.**

Historic hotels provide another unique getaway. During their boom days, many of the mining towns built grandiose hostelries that eventually fell into disrepair. Quite a few have now been beautifully refurbished—for example, you might stay at the Peck House in **Empire**, the Imperial Hotel in **Cripple Creek** or the Hotel Boulderado in **Boulder**. Perhaps the best-known hotel in Colorado is the Brown Palace Hotel in **Denver**. Not quite as many people know about the impressive Strater Hotel in **Durango**, the Hotel Jerome in **Aspen** or the Hotel Colorado in **Glenwood Springs**. You might want to call the **Association of Historic Hotels** at **1-800-626-4886.**

Guest (dude) ranches can be found throughout the state. Normally guests stay for a week and everything (including meals) is provided. If you have ever had a longing for the Wild West (riding horses each day, singing around the campfire ...), but also like sleeping on a firm mattress, you should consider a ranch vacation. Families seem to take very well to the wide list of activities and somewhat structured environment. Some ranches also specialize in fishing, cross-country skiing and outdoor skills vacations. For specific information on some of Colorado's best, turn to the Home Ranch or Vista Verde in the **Steamboat Springs** chapter, Latigo Ranch in the **North Park** chapter, Skyline Ranch in the **Telluride** chapter or the C-Lazy-U in the **Winter Park** chapter. You may also want to contact the **Colorado Dude and Guest Ranch Association, PO Box 300, Tabernash, CO 80478; (303) 887-3128** in **Colorado; 1-800-441-6060** outside Colorado.

When on a budget, there is no better place to find shelter than at a youth hostel. Hostels are also great places to meet other travelers. Sometimes restrictive rules are enforced and a quick morning chore is required, but the price is right. Despite the name, people of all ages are welcome. Though the American Youth Hostel (AYH) system is not as developed as its European counterpart, several accommodations are available in Colorado. For a complete listing and membership information, contact the **American Youth Hostels Rocky Mountain Council, PO Box 2370, Boulder, CO 80306; (303) 442-1166.**

People over 60 years of age (companions 50 or older) may want to inquire about Elderhostel programs, which flourish in Colorado. For a complete brochure, contact **Elderhostel, 75 Federal St., Boston, MA 02110-1941; (617) 426-8056.**

CAMPING

Camping opportunities in Colorado are diverse and numerous. Variations in terrain, amenities and price are all key considerations. Within the chapters of this book, we have listed most campgrounds in the national forests, monuments and parks, state parks and recreation areas as well as many private campgrounds. Most of the listings are designated sites that can be reached by a regular passenger car or RV.

Remember that whether you're camping in the wilderness or just off the highway, minimum impact camping ethics should always be practiced. *Leave your campsite in better shape than you found it.* The following is a brief explanation of possible camping experiences in Colorado.

In the National Forests—

Not everyone realizes this simple fact about camping in the national forest: you can camp anywhere you want to unless it's posted otherwise. Most designated campgrounds charge a fee between $5 and $8 per site per night. Amenities usually include picnic tables, fire pits, pit toilets, pump water and trash cans. Campsites that don't charge a fee usually don't supply drinking water. Most campgrounds have a maximum-stay limit of two weeks; sites are given away on a first-come, first-served basis. Some of the most popular areas of the national forests get extremely crowded in summer—advance reservations are taken for some of these campgrounds at least 10 days in advance through **MISTIX** at **1-800-280-2267**. For more information about camping in the national forests, contact the **US Forest Service, PO Box 25127, 740 Simms St., Lakewood, CO 80225; (303) 275-5350.**

In the National Parks, Monuments and Recreation Areas—

Camping in these areas is usually allowed only at designated sites; most charge a fee and offer the same amenities as national forest campgrounds. An entrance fee to these areas is also required. With the exception of two campgrounds in Rocky Mountain National Park that are available with advance reservations, all campground sites are available on a first-come, first-served basis. For additional information about camping in the national parks, monuments and recreation areas, contact the **National Park Service, PO Box 25287, Denver, CO 80225; (303) 969-2000** or **969-2020**. As in the National Forests, advance reservations can be made through **MISTIX** at **1-800-365-2267**.

In Colorado State Parks—

These areas have some very civilized campgrounds that often include rest rooms with hot showers. An entrance fee is usually required as well as a fee for camping. Reservations can be made at least three days in advance by calling **1-800-678-2267** or **(303) 470-1144**. For further information about camping in the state parks and recreation areas, contact the **Colorado Division of Parks and Outdoor Recreation, 1313 Sherman St., Suite 618, Denver, CO 80203; (303) 866-3437.**

Bureau of Land Management (BLM) Land—

Camping on land supervised by the BLM is possible in many places throughout Colorado. Here and there are some relatively primitive campgrounds that often include picnic tables and outhouses; only a few charge a fee. Some of these campgrounds have been mentioned in the book. For additional information about camping on BLM land, contact the **US Bureau of Land Management, 2850 Youngfield, Lakewood, CO 80215; (303) 239-3600.**

Private Campgrounds and Cabins—

When possible, each camping section ends with a listing of at least one private campground. These are the plush places with all the amenities you could ask for, including shower rooms, laundry facilities and **RV hookups**. If you require further information about private campgrounds in Colorado, try contacting the **Colorado Association of Campgrounds, Cabins and Lodges, 5101 Pennsylvania Ave., Boulder, CO 80303; (303) 499-9343.**

WHERE TO EAT

We narrowed down the list of restaurant choices in each destination by asking countless locals about their favorite places to eat. The restaurants we've listed in each chapter also constitute what we consider to be an accurate representation of price ranges and styles available around the state. We personally visited each of the establishments to see if they were worthy of mention; we accepted no payment for inclusion in the book. If there was a particular specialty in an area, we have given it more play: Mexican food in the San Luis Valley, for instance. You may also notice that we have an aversion to chains—does anyone need to explain what's in store for you under the "golden arches"?

Most people like to know about how much their meal will cost, so we have enacted the following price guideline based on the price of an entrée per person:

$	Under $5
$$	$5 to $10
$$$	$10 to $20
$$$$	$20 and up

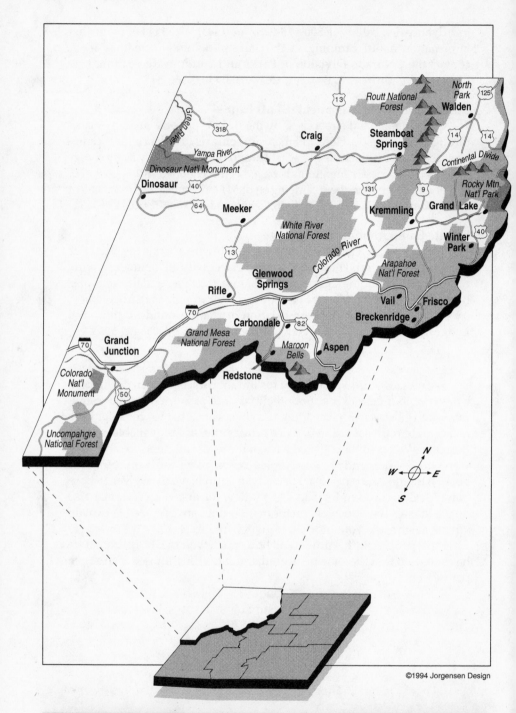

Northwest Region

Routt National Forest
North Park
Walden
125
13
Steamboat Springs
14
14
Craig
Continental Divide
Green River
318
131
9
Rocky Mtn. Nat'l Park
Yampa River
Kremmling
Grand Lake
Dinosaur Nat'l Monument
40
Dinosaur
White River National Forest
Colorado River
Winter Park
40
64
Meeker
13
Arapahoe Nat'l Forest
Glenwood Springs
Rifle
Vail
Frisco
70
Carbondale
Breckenridge
82
Grand Junction
Grand Mesa National Forest
Maroon Bells
Aspen
70
Redstone
Colorado Nat'l Monument
50
Uncompahgre National Forest

N
W E
S

©1994 Jorgensen Design

NORTHWEST REGION

Aspen

Colorado's premier ski resort town, Aspen, sits mountain-locked at the head of the beautiful Roaring Fork Valley. Historic mining town, laid-back mountain retreat, cultural mecca, elitist playground for the super rich: Aspen's images vary greatly, quite often in what would seem to be direct conflict. You don't need to look hard for the town's eccentricities—some might say absurdities—to reveal themselves.

Aspen's allure comes in part from its intriguing and sometimes tumultuous history. Beginning as a remote mining camp in 1879, the town quickly prospered and grew to be one of the richest silver-producing areas in the world, until the crash of the silver market in 1893. Today Aspen's Victorian-era prosperity still makes up a large part of its personality. Reminders of Aspen's past range from the many beautifully restored homes to restaurants and bars named after famous mines and residents.

The visionaries who developed Aspen as a winter ski resort and summer intellectual/cultural retreat in the late 1940s set the tone for what exists today. Winter activities revolve around Aspen's four distinctive ski areas, which uphold an international reputation for fine powder skiing and runs suited to all abilities. Of the four, only Snowmass provides a condo-style planned community right on the ski mountain. Cross-country skiing is excellent in the area, and the range of après-ski partying is unmatched.

In summer the town comes together around the arts: The Aspen Music Festival, theater, ballet and other events attract performers from around the world. With public forest lands and many wilderness areas nearby, hiking, backpacking and fishing opportunities are limitless. In autumn, as far as the eye can see, aspen trees are transformed into burnished coats of gold and red. Aspen quiets down in the spring (mud season) and late fall (after the leaves have fallen), though these can be ideal times for a visit.

Over the years Aspen has drawn a very educated and sophisticated group of residents. Add to this a complex mix of values and lifestyles, and the result is explosive. The vast majority of political issues still hinge on the long-running conflict between development and slow growth. Aspen politics are a heated and fractious part of life for many locals. Recent controversies include an unsuccessful campaign to ban the sale of furs, an attempt to discourage chain stores and fast-food outlets and the continuing fallout over Amendment 2 (the statewide antigay initiative that is currently hung up in the courts).

Aspen's image as a hangout for jet-setters and international celebrities is valid, though it has been blown out of proportion. Money is very important here, especially if you want to stay awhile. The a*verage* house costs over a million dollars. Aspen naturally provides unlimited ways for vacationers to part with large stacks of cash. However, you don't necessarily need to take out a loan to eat at many of the restaurants—budget travelers can actually find some surprisingly affordable vacation options. In summer you can track down deals on hotel rates, many of the festivals are free and you can stay at campgrounds around the area for practically nothing.

HISTORY

In addition to first-rate scenery and great skiing, Aspen draws a lot of people for another reason: its interesting past. Like its beautiful surroundings, Aspen's history has a generous share of peaks and valleys.

For centuries the Roaring Fork Valley had been a prime hunting ground for the Ute Indians, who tenaciously fought to keep the area off limits to settlers. But a treaty in 1868 forced the Utes to move west out of the valley they loved so dearly. It wasn't until more than 10 years later that significant settlement (prospecting) began in the area.

In June 1879 Walter Clark and three others made their way over Independence Pass from Leadville. For more than a year they had studied geologic maps that led them to believe the remote Roaring Fork Valley might contain as much silver ore as the rich Leadville area. They weren't disappointed, as silver was found in abundance. Word of the silver strikes quickly spread, and other anxious miners arrived to stake their claims (mainly on Aspen Mountain) before winter set in. As snow fell that first winter, three camps had already been established: Independence, Ashcroft and Aspen, the latter of which was originally called Ute City. While the first camp leader, H. B. Gillespie, was away in Washington, DC, petitioning for postal service for Ute City, a newcomer named B. Clark Wheeler arrived. Wheeler proceeded to organize the miners and rename the town Aspen.

By the summer of 1880 Aspen boasted a population of more than 1,000. Over time the Mollie Gibson, Chamberlain, Venus and famous

Smuggler mines produced some of the richest silver ore ever found. But one big obstacle remained between the miners and fantastic profits: the lack of a nearby smelter. Transporting the silver ore by pack mules over Independence Pass to the smelters in Leadville, Pueblo and Denver was costly and inconvenient. Aspen needed someone with very deep pockets willing to finance construction of a smelter. In 1883 the answer to the miners' dreams materialized in the form of eastern capitalist Jerome B. Wheeler (no relation to B. Clark Wheeler). This one-time partner in Macy's department store in New York City came to Aspen, bought up some mining claims and built the much-needed smelter. This spurred Aspen's growth, and things started to boom.

The arrival of the Denver & Rio Grande Railroad in 1887 was another milestone. A year later the Colorado Midland Railroad also began service to Aspen. (Unfortunately Colorado Midland's depot location—on brothel-strewn Fanny Hill Street—left a bit to be desired; "nice" women of the town stayed away, thereby saving themselves from the embarrassment of being confused with the "soiled doves.") The railroads provided the vital link with the outside world, thereby helping transform Aspen into a hopping town of 12,000 inhabitants by 1893, the third largest community in the state.

From 1887 to 1893 Aspen was the richest silver mining area in the United States. It boasted six newspapers, two banks, a waterworks, telephone service and the distinction of being one of the first towns in America to run on electricity. During this heyday Jerome Wheeler built the Wheeler Opera House and the magnificent Aspen showpiece, the Hotel Jerome. The hotel opened on Thanksgiving Eve 1889 with Aspen's biggest social event to date. Guests came from as far away as Europe; for perhaps the first time in their lives, miners spruced up with starched shirts and top hats—and bay rum. This soirée helped bring Aspen into the national spotlight, but the attention was short-lived.

In 1893 the demonetization of silver caused prices to plummet. Within a week the mines had closed and people were moving out. The Smuggler II Mine on Smuggler Mountain managed to stay open for a while longer, and in 1894 produced the largest silver nugget in the world, weighing in at over a ton. But not even the richest silver mine in the world could afford to stay open. Aspen was on the skids and would not see the end of economic hard times for decades.

By 1930 the population had dwindled to 700. But before long the Aspen area began to draw attention as a potentially great winter resort. Ironically Aspen Mountain was not the first slope eyed for development. Alpine ski experts initially decided on nearby Ashcroft as the best location for the envisioned resort. On December 26, 1936, Billy Tagert, a local, began charging skiers 50 cents for a sleigh ride up the mountain. But the short run down Little Annie Basin was as close as Ashcroft ever came to being a world-class ski area. In the meantime, the Works Progress Administration (WPA) had constructed a lift on Aspen Mountain in 1936. The lift was actually a 20-person boat tow, consisting of a half-inch cable, two mine hoists and a gas motor. The fee was 10 cents per ride.

World War II put Aspen's ski area development plans on hold. As America was drawn into the war, the 10th Mountain Division ski troops, stationed at Camp Hale, held maneuvers near Aspen. Many fell in love with the town and its skiing, vowing to come back after the war. When the war was over, a number of these men returned to help transform Aspen into a winter resort.

Raising the money needed to develop Aspen into a major ski resort proved difficult. In 1947 Walter Paepcke, founder of Container Corporation of America, arrived with his checkbook open to save the day. Ironically Paepcke was initially drawn to Aspen for the purpose of establishing a summer retreat for business leaders to "revitalize body and soul." He thought the retreat would make money, but was eventually convinced by a local businessman, Austrian Friedl Pfeiffer, that the winter resort idea would be even more lucrative. So Paepcke helped locate investors, and soon Aspen was a year-round attraction.

Very quickly Aspen gained worldwide recognition. The 1949 Goethe bicentennial festival lured more than 2,000 people, including many celebrities. The following winter Aspen Mountain hosted the World Ski Championships and was catapulted into the league of world-class ski resorts. Aspen Highlands Ski Area opened in 1958, soon followed by the opening of Buttermilk, now called Tiehack, the teaching mountain. The last piece fell into place when the Snowmass area opened in 1968.

GETTING THERE

The shortest route from Denver to Aspen (162 miles) can be taken only in summer. Take Interstate 70 west for 79 miles to Copper Mountain, then follow Hwy. 91 south past Leadville to the junction with Hwy. 82. Turn right and drive on the narrow, winding road over Independence Pass to Aspen. (For more information about the pass, see the Scenic Drives section.) In winter you must take a 200-mile route via Interstate 70 to Glenwood Springs and then south on Hwy. 82.

Fly from Denver International Airport (DIA) on a connecting flight to the Aspen/Snowmass Airport. Direct service is available from Los Angeles, Dallas and Chicago. For the 4-mile jaunt into town take a taxi or a shuttle bus (see the Services section). From DIA it's also possible to rent a car, hire a limo or arrange van service. You can also take an Amtrak train into Glenwood Springs (40 miles from Aspen) from Chicago (via Denver) or from San Francisco. Call Amtrak for reservations and information at **1-800-872-7245.**

MAJOR ATTRACTIONS

Maroon Bells Scenic Area

The Maroon Bells, thought to be the most photographed peaks in North America, comprise one of the most beautiful views on the planet. From beautiful Maroon Lake at the end of a scenic, 9-mile road, gaze up at several 14,000-foot peaks that rise within the short span of the Maroon Bells–Snowmass Wilderness Area. The incredible, above-treeline beauty of the peaks attracts so many people to a fragile alpine ecosystem, though, access to the Maroon Creek Valley is restricted by the Forest Service.

No cars are allowed up the Maroon Lake Rd. between 8:30 am and 5 pm in summer (June through Labor Day and September weekends), except for campers with permits and disabled people. Once at the famous Bells, plan on taking a hike on the 100 miles of trails or just simply kick back and enjoy the view. Bring along your fishing pole and camera, too. If you are expecting a man- or woman- in-the-wilderness experience, this is probably not the place. For more information contact the **Aspen Ranger District Office, 806 W. Hallam, Aspen, CO 81611; (303) 925-3445.**

GETTING THERE

Since summer access is restricted, the best way to get a view of the Bells is via the efficient bus system from Aspen. Buses depart from Ruby Park Transit Center every half hour from 9 am–4:30 pm daily. Round-trip fare is extremely reasonable; children under 5 ride free. Once there, stay as long as you wish and take any bus back to Aspen between 9:30 am and 5 pm. Once the snow begins to fall, Maroon Lake Rd. is not plowed above the T-Lazy-7 Ranch due to extreme avalanche danger. For further information call **(303) 925-8484.**

HIKING

Maroon Creek Trail—Several short hikes can be taken from the bus drop off, but this is one of our favorites. Maroon Creek Trail is a 3.25-mile downhill stroll to East Maroon Portal where the bus will pick up hikers at the roadside. Those unaccustomed to the altitude may want to start out on this mellow trail.

Other Hikes—See the Hiking and Backpacking section.

INTERPRETIVE TOURS

The **Aspen Center for Environmental Studies** offers nature tours at Maroon Lake each hour from 10 am–2 pm. In addition a powerful telescope at the lake may help you spot some of the resident elk, deer, bighorn sheep, eagles and other wildlife.

CAMPING

Up Maroon Creek Road—It's very hard to find a campsite in this valley during midsummer. You should definitely make reservations by calling **1-800-283-CAMP.**

Four campgrounds—**Maroon Lake** (44 sites), **Silver Bar** (4 sites), **Silver Bell** (4 sites) and **Silver Queen** (6 sites)—are open from early June until mid-Sept., depending on the snowpack. Private vehicles need to secure a camping permit at the entrance station before heading up the road. Silver Bar and Silver Bell do not accommodate trailers; a fee is charged at all four campgrounds.

FESTIVALS AND EVENTS

Aspen Music Festival
late June through August

For the past four decades music has drifted across the summer hills of Aspen. Styles range from jazz to symphonic, chamber to avant-garde. Music comes not only from formal concerts but from intense rehearsals, informal sessions and private practice. The festival helps provide a perfect learning environment for students at the Aspen Music School. An idyllic summer afternoon at the music tent might feature a famous guest artist such as Itzhak Perlman on violin or James Galway on flute. The concerts are reasonably priced and most people prefer to see as well as hear the musicians; but the unique tent-enclosed setting also allows the music to reach nonpaying patrons seated comfortably on the grass outside. For more information call **(303) 925-3254.**

Snowmass Balloon Festival

late June

Billed as the largest high-altitude balloon festival in the world, the Snowmass Balloon Festival has attracted increasing numbers of spectators since it began in 1975. More than 50 balloonists compete in this series of races and maneuvers. An added attraction for spectators is the champagne breakfast served at the launch site to the accompaniment of classical music. **1-800-421-7145.**

Colorado Mountain Fair in Carbondale

end of July

More than 10,000 people cut loose each summer at this very popular festival in Carbondale, 30 miles northwest of Aspen on Hwy. 82. Since 1971 the fair has offered many kinds of food, music and booths with everything from massage to jewelry making. Music and special contests like log splitting keep the valley locals and outsiders flocking here each summer. For more information call the **Carbondale Chamber of Commerce** at **(303) 963-1890.**

———— OUTDOOR ACTIVITIES ————

BIKING

MOUNTAIN BIKING

Need you ask? When the snow melts off the surrounding mountain trails and jeep roads, locals put away their skis and bring out their mountain bikes. Actually, a few fanatic bikers start riding around town before the snow has even melted. Great trails await riders of all abilities.

Government Trail—

This demanding route traverses the Snowmass Ski Area and eventually leads to the Buttermilk Ski Area. Mountain meadows and panoramic views make it worth the effort. Inquire at Blazing Pedals in Snowmass Village for exact trail directions.

Maroon Lake Road—

This paved road climbs 1,000 feet in 9 miles (18 miles round trip). It's a constant yet gentle uphill ride and the view of the Maroon Bells from Maroon Lake is outstanding. To reach Maroon Lake Rd., take Hwy. 82 out of Aspen for 1 mile north and turn left at the Aspen Highlands sign.

Pearl Pass—

This tough ride shouldn't be considered unless you are in good shape. The 12,700-foot Pearl Pass crosses over into the Crested Butte area to the south. The road was originally built to ship silver from Ashcroft to the nearest railroad downvalley from Crested Butte. To reach the pass, head up Castle Creek Rd. to Ashcroft, 13 miles from Aspen. From Ashcroft, at 9,500 feet, the road follows the river up 3,200 vertical feet and 8 miles to the pass. From the pass you can head back to Aspen or proceed down to Crested Butte 12 miles away.

Rentals and Tours—

Aspen Velo is a longtime favorite for rentals and information. **465 N. Mill St.; (303) 925-1495.** Or try **Blazing Pedals,** which offers downhill bicycle tours as well as rentals. It's a unique option for those who want to enjoy the scenery and the thrill of mountain biking without the huffing and puffing. There are two Blazing Pedals locations: **50 Village Sq., Snowmass Village, CO 81615; (303) 923-4544,** or in Aspen at the **Hyman Ave. Mall; (303) 925-5651.**

DOG SLEDDING

Krabloonik's Kennels—

In 1947 Stuart Mace, who handled sled dogs for the 10th Mountain Division during World War II, began offering sled rides from Toklat, his lodge up in the nearby ghost town of Ashcroft. Raising and training the dogs was a strenuous job. When Mace realized he was getting too old to handle the rigorous routine, he offered 50 dogs as a gift to Dan MacEachen.

Krablooniks offers full- and partial-day sled rides up the valley toward Mt. Daly and the towering 14,130-foot Capitol Peak. Pulled by teams of 13 dogs, the sleds are designed similarly to those made by Eskimos from bone and rawhide. Caution: The rides are quite pricey. Reservations essential (especially around Christmas); full prepayment required. Follow Brush Creek Rd. past the Snowmass Ski Area for about a half mile to the parking lot. **(303) 923-3953.**

FISHING

With long stretches of Gold Medal water on two of Colorado's best trout streams in addition to countless high-country lakes and tributaries, Aspen is a natural destination for anglers. The natural beauty of the area fulfills even if you manage to get skunked. For guided wade trips and float fishing in McKenzie-style boats try **Frying Pan Anglers** at **(303) 927-3441** or **Taylor Creek Angling Services** at **(303) 920-1128.** Here's a rundown of the best fishing in the area.

Fryingpan Lakes—

A 5-mile hike is required to reach the three small lakes at 11,000 feet. The reward is not only the beautiful scenery but a chance at the multitude of small brook trout. This unstocked natural habitat yields many fish from a mere 2 acres of water. From Basalt follow County Rd. 105 along the Fryingpan River until it turns into Forest Rd. 505. From the end of Forest Rd. 505 the trail sets out.

Fryingpan River—

This river is legendary for large browns and rainbows from Ruedi Reservoir down to Basalt. Due to its "legend" status and Gold Medal designation, you can expect competition along the river, especially on weekends. The river never gets muddy, thanks to a controlled water flow from the dam. Use artificial flies or lures only. Catch and release all trout on the Upper Fryingpan (beginning at Ruedi Dam and continuing downstream 4 miles). You can keep two fish over 16 inches on the Lower Fryingpan (beginning at Basalt and continuing upriver 9 miles). For solitude, try fishing the Fryingpan in winter and early spring. Use small (size 18 to 20) green and brown elk hair caddis in spring when the water is still a bit murky and dry flies in summer. In late Aug. lots of top action results from the green drake mayfly hatch.

Hunter Creek—

This smallish creek flows into the Roaring Fork on the northeast edge of Aspen. Catch small brook, brown and cutthroat trout with small flies in the evening hours. Access can be difficult, but a dirt road (Hunter Creek Rd.) from Aspen loosely follows the creek 6 miles to the boundary of the Hunter-Fryingpan Wilderness Area.

Ivanhoe Lake—

To reach this moderately fished lake head 5 miles up the rough dirt road (Forest Rd. 105 and 527) that follows Ivanhoe Creek from east of Ruedi Reservoir. Ivanhoe Lake is pushed up against the Continental Divide in a beautiful setting. The lake is stocked with rainbows, and rainbows are what you'll catch.

Roaring Fork River—

After the spring runoff calms down, fishing within the city limits can be good.

Be aware of the mix of public and private land on the river. Just to the north of town is a good area to catch both rainbow and brown trout. You can fish all the way from Independence Pass down to Glenwood Springs. We tend to focus on the stretch downstream from the Woody Creek Bridge to Carbondale where there's premium trout-fishing water and beautiful scenery.

It's also Gold Medal water from Carbondale, where the Crystal River joins, down to the Roaring Fork's confluence with the Colorado. This heavily fished stretch yields large rainbows, browns and whitefish. Two-fish limit; only artificial lures and flies may be used from Apr.–Oct.

Willow Lake—

This above-treeline lake at 11,705 feet provides good fishing for brook and cutthroat; most are around 12 inches, some much larger. A longtime Aspen fishing expert saw a dozen bighorn ewes on his last trip to this area. Willow Lake is a 5-mile trek from Maroon Bells Lake, high in the Maroon Bells–Snowmass Wilderness Area.

FOUR-WHEEL-DRIVE TRIPS

See the **Gunnison and Crested Butte** and the **Redstone and Crystal River Valley** chapters.

GOLF

Aspen Golf Course—

Although it's a municipal course, unlike the privately owned Snowmass Club course, the Aspen Golf Course has a higher rating and the greens fees are cheaper! It's a fine 18-hole course that poses a pretty good challenge, even to scratch golfers. The holes are laid out fairly flat, making some of the hazards difficult to see. Watch out for irrigation ditches and lakes on this course, as there are more of them than seems fair. If the golf gods will it, snow in the valley clears enough to open the course by May 1. Restaurant and pro shop; carts available. **22475 W. Hwy. 82; (303) 925-2145.**

The Snowmass Club—

If you want to play golf in Snowmass, take a sizable roll of cash or a major credit card. This sculpted course rolls along in the valley down below the ski mountain. Brush Creek runs through the middle of the fairly treeless course. It offers reduced greens fees for guests of the Snowmass Club; guests also have priority on choice tee times. Pro shop, carts and club rentals available. **239 Snowmass Club Cir., Snowmass Village; (303) 923-3148.**

HIKING AND BACKPACKING

White River National Forest surrounds Aspen, tempting lovers of the outdoors with three wilderness areas: Collegiate Peaks, Hunter-Fryingpan, and Maroon Bells–Snowmass. Within the jagged Elk Mountains are no fewer than six 14,000-foot peaks. Mountaineers, backpackers and families wanting to take a stroll converge on Aspen's mountains each summer. Although this creates some congested spots, it is possible to get away from the crowds.

It's difficult to condense a list of the trail opportunities in the Aspen area. For more trail ideas, contact the **Aspen Ranger District, 806 W. Hallam St., Aspen, CO 81611; (303) 925-3445** or the **Sopris Ranger District at 620 Main, PO Box 309, Carbondale, CO 81623; (303) 963-2266.**

For maps, equipment and informed advice, visit the **Ute Mountaineer, 308 S. Mill St., Aspen; (303) 925-2849.** If you want a very detailed, knowledgeable hiking book for the Aspen area, pick up a copy of *Aspen Snowmass Trails: A Hiking Trail Guide* (W. Ohlrich, 1988), by Warren Ohlrich, which provides 30 trail ideas.

American Lake—

This day-long, 7-mile round-trip hike is steep but worth the trouble. The lake is beautiful and the fishing for rainbow trout can be surprisingly good. Views of surrounding peaks are also stunning. Plan on about 5 hours hiking time. Camping is not permitted on the east end of the lake. To reach the trailhead, turn left onto Maroon Creek Rd. from Hwy. 82 just west of Aspen. Take another quick left onto Castle Creek Rd. and drive 10 miles to the trailhead, which is on the right side of the road across from the Elk Creek Lodge.

Braille Trail—

Approximately 2 miles farther up Hwy. 82 from the Grottos turn-off (10 miles east of Aspen), the quarter-mile-long Braille Trail offers blind hikers a chance to experience the natural surroundings. Guided by a nylon cord, hikers can decipher the more than 20 signs, which are in both Braille and print. A miniature tape player and cassette, to enhance the sensory experience, can be borrowed (no charge) from the **Aspen Ranger Station** at **806 W. Hallum St.** The tape was designed specifically for use on the Braille Trail. Look for the turn-off on the right side of Hwy. 82.

Conundrum Creek—

See the Hot Springs section for specifics on this 9-mile (18 miles round trip) hike.

East Maroon Creek Trail—

This trail follows 8.5 miles alongside the creek that fills beautiful Maroon Lake before eventually reaching 11,280-foot East Maroon Pass. It offers great views along the way. In summer the multicolored wildflowers above the lake are stunning; during autumn the golden aspen make for quite a sight, especially when a light snow dusts the Bells.

Four Pass Loop—

This well-known route passes through the heart of the Maroon Bells–Snowmass Wilderness Area. It's a beautiful and demanding 28-mile loop taking you over four major passes (West Maroon, Frigid Air, Trail Rider and Buckskin), all of which are at about 12,500 feet. Allow four to five days for your journey and don't hurry. The loop takes you by Maroon, Crater and Snowmass lakes. The trail begins and ends at Maroon Lake. Parts of the trail are usually snow-covered until July. *Get a topographical map*

for this hike. If you get an urge to bag some of the 14ers along the way remember that many climbers have died on the treacherous slopes of Pyramid Peak and the Maroon Bells—they have been named the "Deadly Bells" by some.

Grottos—

The Grottos are located about 8 miles up Independence Pass (east from Aspen on Hwy. 82), just a short walk along the Roaring Fork River from the parking area. It's a popular picnic and sunning spot in the summer, drawing large numbers. Grottos gets its name from its interesting rock formations, including the granite "ice caves" that were carved out when the river flowed through here. The area is close to town and very scenic. Look for the dirt road on the right side of Hwy. 82 about a half mile past mile-marker 50. A footbridge crosses the river near the parking area. No camping.

Maroon Bells—

See the Major Attractions section for additional information.

Midway Pass to Hunter Creek—

Located in the Hunter-Fryingpan Wilderness, this long hike (allow three days) is less known than the trails in the Maroon Bells–Snowmass Wilderness Area. Both elk and deer make their homes here in summer. Start at about 10,000 feet and enjoy views to Independence Pass as you work your way northwest into the Hunter Creek drainage, which leads back to Aspen. The trail begins 14 miles east of Aspen on Hwy. 82 on the left side of the road across from Lost Creek Campground. There is a fork about half a mile up the trail. Take the left fork up Midway Creek Trail. After crossing Midway Pass, the trail drops and snakes through marshy areas until it intersects Hunter Creek Trail. Take a left onto Hunter Creek Trail and proceed down to the outskirts of Aspen for the completion of this 20-mile route. *Snow remains on the upper part of this trail until July. Get a good map and compass for this hike as the trail is not well marked.*

HORSEBACK RIDING

T-Lazy-7 Ranch—

The T-Lazy-7 has been around for years. Located up Maroon Creek Rd., they rent horses by the hour. Or perhaps you'll want to go on an overnight pack trip. For information about the ranch, see the Sleigh Rides section. **3129 Maroon Creek Rd.; (303) 925-7040** or **(303) 925-4614.** For another idea take a look at the Horseback Riding section of the **Redstone and Crystal River Valley** chapter.

ICE SKATING

The **Ice Garden,** a public indoor ice rink, has skating throughout the week. Special events may preclude public use of the ice. Call to be sure of open ice. Skate rentals for a nominal fee. **233 W. Hyman Ave.; (303) 920-5141.**

LLAMA TREKKING

From July–Sept., **Ashcroft** and the **Pine Creek Cookhouse** offers daily llama treks up into White River National Forest. Treks begin at the cookhouse at 10:30 am and return at 3 pm. The price includes a gourmet lunch. Even so, the treks are a bit pricey. Overnight trips are available on request. Be sure to call for reservations. Located 12 miles up Castle Creek Rd. from Hwy. 82. **PO Box 1572, Aspen, CO 81612; (303) 925-1044, 925-1971.**

RIVER FLOATING

Crystal River—

See the **Redstone and Crystal River Valley** chapter.

Roaring Fork River—

The upper Roaring Fork River is a popular river for kayaking, even though parts of it can be treacherous. This well-named river angrily surges out of the Sawatch Range east of Aspen. Just before reaching town, the river mellows, providing good beginner stretches all the way through Aspen. Above the Maroon Creek convergence (just west of Aspen), expert kayakers put in at Slaughter-house Bridge for a 5-mile stretch down to Woody Creek Bridge that includes a portage around a severe set of waterfalls that have killed a number of people.

From Woody Creek Bridge down to Basalt (12 miles), the water is not so dangerous, but novices are warned to keep out, especially during high water. Kayakers (no rafters) should take warning of the Toothache section near Snowmass Bridge. The 12-mile section below Basalt to Carbondale is much easier. For information about floating downstream from Carbondale, see the River Floating section of the **Glenwood Springs** chapter.

Outfitters—

Aspen Whitewater Adventures—These folks offer trips down the Roaring Fork, Colorado, Crystal and other rivers. Located at the base of the gondola. **555 E. Durant St., Aspen; (303) 925-5405.**

Blazing Paddles—They offer trips on the Roaring Fork, Colorado, Gunnison and Arkansas rivers. At the corner of **Mill St. and Hyman Ave., Aspen; (303) 925-5651.**

SKIING
CROSS-COUNTRY SKIING

Aspen serves as a choice destination not only for downhill skiers but for cross-country skiers as well. This town always has its fingers firmly on the pulse of the winter recreationist. As cross-country skiing has increased in popularity, Aspen has been quick to provide creative opportunities for skiers of all abilities. Everything from extensive groomed trail systems to demanding backcountry trails can be found here. Roughing it overnight in a unique backcountry hut is a peaceful alternative to the town's highly charged atmosphere. For those of you headed off on your own to do some backcountry skiing, remember to call **Avalanche Information** at **(303) 920-1664.** For more backcountry ski ideas and information, contact the **Aspen Ranger District Office, 806 W. Hallam St., Aspen, CO 81611; (303) 925-3445,** or **Ute Mountaineer, 308 S. Mill St., Aspen, CO 81612; (303) 925-2849.**

Backcountry Trails—

Braun Hut System—Colorado's original, this series of six high mountain huts stretches as far south as Pearl Pass and is accessible via Ashcroft (12 miles up Castle Creek Rd. from Aspen). Isolation, difficult trail conditions and avalanche danger make it necessary for skiers to have advanced skills. Guides can be arranged through several companies, including **Aspen Alpine Guides, PO Box 5122, Aspen, CO 81612; (303) 925-6618.**

The Braun huts are a bit more spartan than the 10th Mountain huts (see next entry) and were not truly designed to be skied hut to hut. Built to accommodate from 6 to 18 people, these year-round huts can best be reached via separate trails. Fred Braun, an Austrian ski trooper in the early 1920s, lived in Aspen from 1951 until his recent death. Braun remembered that when he arrived in the US in 1928, he could find skis only in Minnesota and he had to send to Norway for boots! Operated by the United States Ski Association. For more information and reservations, contact the **Braun Hut System, PO Box 7937, Aspen, CO 81602; (303) 925-5775.**

10th Mountain Trail Association Hut System—For more adventurous and experienced skiers, an impressive series of European-style backcountry ski huts stretches between Aspen and the Vail Valley. The 10th Mountain Trail Association (TMTA) operates the hut system. It all started after 10th Mountain Division veteran Fritz Benedict traversed Europe's Haute Route in the Alps. Beginning in 1980, Benedict began working with a group of volunteers to construct a similar hut system in the backcountry between Aspen, Leadville and Vail.

Currently eight overnight huts and four private lodges extend north by northeast through the spectacular Hunter-Fryingpan and Holy Cross wilderness areas along a 250-mile route. You are welcome to ski all or part of the hut system. Future plans include 20 huts forming a continuous backcountry loop.

The huts (each sleeps about 16 people) offer many conveniences and supplies, such as mattresses, pillows, stoves and other kitchen necessities. You will need to bring a sleeping bag, food and emergency gear. Two of the private lodges along the trail (**Diamond J Ranch** and the **Polar Star Inn**) provide more creature comforts, such as running water and saunas. The Diamond J Ranch is a full-blown ski touring resort that can be reached via County Rd. 105 from Basalt.

The 10th Mountain hut system is very popular and attracts people from all over the world who want to experience the beauty of Colorado's high country in winter. Strong intermediate to advanced skills are needed, as well as heavy-duty equipment. Guides and maps are available. To arrange transportation back to your car after a one-way ski, call **Trailhead Transit** at **1-800-634-4813.** Full payment is required when reservations are made. Reserve very early for winter weekends. Open late Nov.–May, depending on conditions. For more information and reservations, contact the **TMTA** at **1280 Ute Ave., Aspen, CO 81611; (303) 925-5775.**

Groomed Trails—

Ashcroft Ski Touring Center—For a relatively remote groomed trail system, try this one, which starts in Ashcroft 12 miles up Castle Creek Rd. south of Aspen. The center offers warming huts and 30 kilometers of groomed trails. How about a gourmet lunch or dinner at the Pine Creek Cookhouse? For details see the Where to Eat section. For more information about the **Ashcroft Ski Touring Center,** call **(303) 925-1971.**

Aspen/Snowmass Nordic Trail System—This fine nordic system offers a 48-mile (80K) network of groomed cross-country trails consolidated within a 15-mile area in the valley. Coordinated by the nonprofit Aspen/Snowmass Nordic Council to facilitate ski connections between the two towns, the free trail system is easily accessible from many points in and around town. Pick up a map of the trail system at the Aspen Visitors

Center in the Wheeler Opera House (see the Services section) or at a sports store. For more information contact the **Aspen Cross Country Ski Center, 39551 W. Hwy. 82, Aspen, CO 81611; (303) 925-2145.**

Telemarking Lessons—

At Tiehack Ski Area, telemark lessons are offered each Tues. and Thurs. during ski season. Classes last from 9 am–noon. For information call **(303) 925-1220, ext. 2288.**

Ski Rentals—

Aspen Cross-Country Center in Aspen has what you need. Half-day to multiple-day rentals are available. Located along the Aspen/Snowmass Nordic Trail System. **22475 W. Hwy. 82, Aspen, CO 81611; (303) 925-2145.** Another choice for equipment, including heavy-duty backcountry gear, is the **Ute Mountaineer, 308 S. Mill St., Aspen, CO 81611; (303) 925-2849.** In Snowmass try the **Snowmass Club Touring Center, 0239 Snowmass Club Cir., Snowmass Village, CO 81615; (303) 923-3148.**

DOWNHILL SKIING

Life in Aspen still revolves around downhill skiing, despite the wealth of peripheral activities. Since 1936, when trees were cut to make room for Roch Run on Aspen Mountain, the ski industry has flourished. Today there are four excellent ski mountains to choose from. Each mountain has a personality of its own and taken together they offer an incredible range of supreme skiing. The key to your enjoyment is to correctly match the mountain with your ability and mood. Now that Aspen Highlands has been purchased by the Aspen Skiing Company tickets for all four areas are interchangeable. All areas offer a range of services including rentals, child care and lessons. For further information contact **Aspen Skiing Co., PO Box 1248 Aspen, CO 81612; (303) 923-1220 and 1-800-525-6200.**

Aspen Highlands—

Aspen Highlands is an all-around ski area with what many consider the ideal division of terrain: half intermediate and the rest split between advanced and beginner—it also has the longest vertical drop (3,800 feet) of any ski area in Colorado. Since it was not a part of the Aspen Skiing Company until recently, it has always been seen as something of a rebel, with its jeans-clad skiers not conforming to the glitzy standards of the neighboring areas. The incredible vertical drop is surpassed at Highlands Bowl—a walk-in, guided, experts-only powder adventure that plunges an amazing 4,300 feet. My favorite attribute of the area still has to be the view as you ride up the Olympic Chairlift: Your eyes follow up Maroon Valley to the impressive 14,000-foot summits of the Maroon Bells and Pyramid Peak.

Aspen Mountain—

This mountain was designed for the enjoyment of expert and strong intermediate skiers. Since there are no "green" runs there should be no worries about novice skiers making tentative tracks across your fall line. Because of the mountain's orientation, skiers may consider taking advantage of the sun. Stick to the eastern flanks in the morning before moving to western exposures later in the day. The Silver Queen gondola whisks skiers from the base to the 11,212-foot summit of Aspen Mountain in a mere 13 minutes. Locals call the mountain Ajax, after a now-defunct silver mine. By whatever name, it is steep, challenging and definitely not for beginners.

Tiehack/Buttermilk—

Two miles west of Aspen, Tiehack is widely known as a great teaching mountain, thanks to endless miles of novice and easy intermediate terrain. Southerly views to Pyramid Peak in the Maroon Bells-Snowmass Wilderness Area make skiing here even more of a pleasure. Families (especially the kids) will enjoy cruising smooth trails; advanced skiers can head for the more difficult Tiehack Parkway and Tiehack Trail runs on powder days. The long, groomed runs are perfect for telemarking—lessons are available.

Snowmass—

A staggering variety of slopes for every ability is just 12 miles from Aspen in a perfect family environment. Four contiguous peaks and more than 2,000 skiable acres eliminate the need to ski the same run twice. Intermediate runs comprise 65 percent of the total. The most notable of these is Big Burn—a mile-wide swath of white space, broken only by occasional stands of evergreen trees. This run down to the base stretches over 4 miles. Supposedly Big Burn is the result of an 1870s' fire set by the Ute Indians to spite white settlers.

Slope names provide more than a hint of what's to come: Take your pick from, say, the steep challenge of Hanging Valley Wall or the gentle incline of Fanny Hill. You can enjoy fine dining on this mountain at Gwyn's. Or, for a truly interesting lunch, make a reservation and ski into Krabloonik's restaurant by way of Dawdler Trail (see the Where to Eat section).

SLEIGH RIDES

The Pine Creek Cookhouse—

Take a mellow, intimate sleigh-ride dinner, ending at the Pine Creek Cookhouse near Ashcroft. See Where to Eat for details.

T-Lazy-7 Ranch—

The T-Lazy-7 offers sleigh rides up the Maroon Creek Valley in winter. Day or evening—you choose. Ask about their popular sleigh ride/dinner dance; try to get reservations far in advance. **Box 858, Aspen, CO 81612; (303) 925-4614.**

SNOWSHOE WALKS

The **Aspen Center for Environmental Studies (ACES)** organizes two-hour walks in the Hallam Lake Wildlife Sanctuary (see the Wildlife section). Learn about the winter ecology from a naturalist-guide. Mon.–Fri.; self-guided tour. Call **(303) 925-5756** for details.

SWIMMING

Iselin Park Complex—

An outdoor swimming pool. Fee charged. **450 Maroon Creek Rd.**

TENNIS

Aspen Meadows Tennis Courts—

Six courts and a pro shop are open to the public for a fee. **25 Meadows Rd.**

Iselin Park Complex—

Four outdoor tennis courts. Fee charged. **450 Maroon Creek Rd.**

WINDSURFING

Aspenites and other folks in the Roaring Fork Valley who windsurf or waterski go to Ruedi Reservoir. Bring a wet suit, because the water in this high-mountain reservoir is cold! Most folks surf from the shore at Freeman's Mesa, located about midlake on the north side. Camping is allowed only at the designated national forest campgrounds. Some sports shops in the valley rent boards by the day. To get to the reservoir from Aspen, head northwest on Hwy. 82 for 18 miles to Basalt. Turn right and drive along the Fryingpan River for about 18 miles to the reservoir.

—————— SEEING AND DOING ——————

BALLOONING

Not every high alpine area is suited to ballooning, but in Aspen it's a popular adventure. The panorama of 14,000-foot peaks takes on a new dimension from the hanging basket of a hot-air balloon. Most ballooning companies depart shortly after sunrise and stay aloft for an hour or two. Balloons accommodate up to eight passengers—just enough for a small wedding party.

Unicorn Balloon Company of Colorado—300B, Aspen Airport Business Center, Aspen, CO 81611; (303) 925-5752 or 1-800-468-2478.

GHOST TOWNS

Ashcroft—

Memories are fading of this ghost town that once rivaled Aspen in importance. In the summer of 1882, Ashcroft had two main streets, three hotels, a jail and a newspaper. Horace Tabor plowed millions of his Leadville silver profits into Ashcroft's Tam O' Shanter and Montezuma mines, with modest success. It is said that when he brought his young bride, Baby Doe, to Ashcroft, a 24-hour holiday ensued, with all drinks on Tabor.

Once Aspen found its place on the map in 1883, Ashcroft started to wane. The transport of silver ore was far easier from Aspen, due to its location in the Roaring Fork Valley. Ashcroft's only route was over Pearl Pass on a rough road to Crested Butte. When the D&RG Railroad puffed into Aspen in 1887, the quiet fate of Ashcroft was secured. Today only nine buildings remain of the town that once boasted a population of 2,500. However, it is still nestled in a beautiful location surrounded by the peaks of the Elk Mountains.

To get to Ashcroft, follow Hwy. 82 west to Castle Creek Rd. Turn left and continue up Castle Creek Rd. for 12 miles until reaching the sign for Toklat gallery. Ashcroft is in the valley east of Toklat.

Independence—

See the Scenic Drives section.

HOT SPRINGS

Conundrum Hot Springs, in the Maroon Bells–Snowmass Wilderness Area, receives visitors year-round. Most people show up in midsummer. To avoid crowds, the best time to make the fairly long (9 miles one way) but not overly steep hike is in spring and fall. Wintertime sees ambitious and skillful cross-country skiers visiting for a quick soak before returning in the afternoon. Beware of avalanche danger in this area.

Conundrum Hot Springs is located on Conundrum Creek, a couple of miles down the valley from Triangle Pass, which leads over into the Gunnison/Crested Butte area. Two pools, one about 3 feet deep and the other 4 feet deep, provide an excellent soaking temperature between 99° and 103° F.

Conundrum is overused, however, and the vegetation directly around the hot springs has been trampled and the tree branches stripped. If you must camp here, remember to do so at designated campsites only. A number of good sites exist, but fires are restricted to a half mile below the springs. To reach the trailhead from Aspen head about 5 miles up Castle Creek Rd. toward Ashcroft. Turn right onto Forest Rd. 128 and drive about a mile to the trailhead parking lot.

MUSEUMS AND GALLERIES

Anderson Ranch Arts Center—

At one time a working ranch, this place has gained quite a reputation in the arts community as a place to come and learn from the best. Each summer photographers, painters, woodworkers and furniture designers, among others, enroll in one- or two-week courses taught by visiting masters. During the rest of the year, the center houses 10 to 15 artists who do work around the ranch in exchange for studio space. The ranch offers self-guided tours of the galleries and grounds between 9 am and 5 pm daily; during weekdays, visits to the studios are permitted after 3 pm. **PO Box 5598, 5263 Owl Creek Rd., 7 Snowmass Village; (303) 923-3181.**

Aspen Art Museum—

This museum features exhibits from local artists as well as nationally acclaimed touring shows. Fine arts, sculpture and crafts are on display. A performing arts series brings in emerging and well-known talent from the fields of music, theater, dance and multimedia performance art. The museum is situated in a park area near the Roaring Fork River, complete with picnic tables and a view to Red and Aspen mountains. It is a great place to stop and relax. Ask about the free lecture series. Open Wed.–Sat. 10 am–6 pm, Thurs. until 8 pm for free tours and a complimentary wine and cheese reception; Sun. 12–6 pm. Closed Mon. **590 N. Mill St.; (303) 925-8050.**

Aspen Galleries—

Paintings, sculpture, Eskimo and Native American art, gemstones, photography, jewelry, pottery, weavings … Aspen's galleries run the gamut. This town is one of the best places to gallery-hop this side of Rodeo Drive. *Aspen* magazine has a rundown of galleries that belong to the Aspen Fine Arts Association. Or check in with the Aspen Visitors Center in the Wheeler Opera House.

Rocky Mountain Institute (RMI) (in Snowmass)—

Amory and Hunter Lovins live in an experimental energy-efficient abode. With the help of more than 100 volunteers they built a 4,000-square-foot, $500,000 research center near Old Snowmass. In keeping with RMI philosophy, their showpiece is built with super insulation and an earth-shelter-ing, passive solar design, but without a conventional heating system. Low-energy appliances are used whenever possible. Showers and toilets are designed to drastically reduce water consumption. The researchers employed at RMI seem to understand the perils of our energy-squandering lifestyles and are out to make a difference. Since construction began in 1982, many of the "radical" ideas originated at RMI have entered the mainstream. A tour of this unique structure, which offers a visual example of renewable energy sources, is highly recommended. Newsletter and publications list available. Small groups are guided around the home on Tues. and Fri. afternoons at 2 pm; or you can take a self-guided tour. For more information contact RMI at **1739 Snowmass Creek Rd., Snowmass, CO 81654; (303) 927-3851.**

Wheeler Stallard House Museum—

The Aspen Historical Society is located in the spacious house Jerome B. Wheeler built in 1888 in a futile effort to entice his wife to Aspen from Manitou Springs. (She never budged.) Inside you'll find authentic Victorian furnishings that have been donated by various families. A re-created living room, dining room and kitchen occupy the main floor. The upstairs features collections of photos, clothing and children's toys. The museum gift shop sells books and other items of interest. The staff is an interesting bunch, adding life to an otherwise quiet and musty museum. On one visit we heard incredible stories about the Aspen of old; Hilder Anderson reminisced about growing up on her ranch in Snowmass: "Back in 1914 a Swedish classmate taught me how to ski. And we took some ribbing at school from kids who said that 'only a dumb Swede would ski'!" The times have changed a bit. Open 1–4 pm daily, in summer and during ski season. Small admission fee. **620 W. Bleeker St.; (303) 925-3721.**

NIGHTLIFE

The nightlife in Aspen is not to be missed. Whether you want a quiet night in a piano bar or an all-night binge, you'll find it here.

Crystal Palace Dinner Theatre—

The Crystal Palace has been an Aspen institution for over three decades, thanks to owner/creator/performer Meade Metcalf. The original cabaret revue, performed by waiters and waitresses, pokes satirical fun at up-to-date subjects. A longtime Aspen resident assured us that the restaurant could "stand on its own" by virtue of its good food alone. Backlit stained glass, a mammoth chandelier and a balcony railing formed from wrought-iron bedsteads whimsically decorate the Crystal Palace. The central bar area is dominated by a 1908 Maxwell and a 1914 Ford Model T. This theater succeeds on the high energy of multitalented performers. Two seatings nightly; reservations strongly recommended. **300 E. Hyman Ave.; (303) 925-1455.**

Double Diamond Club—

Top-notch live music can be heard in this small club setting that seems to have had more names in the past few years than Elizabeth Taylor has had husbands. A well-placed dance floor just in front of the stage draws an energetic and diverse crowd to its feet. The cover charge is usually reasonable. **450 S. Galena St.; (303) 920-6905.**

Explore Booksellers and Coffeehouse—

For dessert and gourmet coffees in a refined Victorian setting this is the choice. Besides the usual espresso and cappuccino, Explore also offers a wide selection of teas, juices and mineral waters. Check out the extensive vegetarian menu. Allow plenty of time to wander around the downstairs bookstore. Open daily 10 am–midnight. **221 E. Main; (303) 925-5336.**

Flying Dog Brew Pub—

See the Where to Eat section.

The J Bar—

Located in the historic Hotel Jerome, built in 1889, this bar goes back a few years. It attracts a diverse crowd of elbow-benders ranging from locals to out-of-towners wealthy enough to stay in the hotel. In Aspen's early ski days, John Wayne brawled here, and playwright Thornton Wilder impressed local ranchers with his legendary drinking capacity. The ceiling is decorated with pressed-tin designs, and there is a great old wooden bar. Belly up to the bar for an après-ski drink, or stop in after dinner when things pick up. Appetizer menu items available. **330 E. Main St.; (303) 920-1000.**

Ultimate Taxi—

You won't forget this ride in an old Checker cab, decked out with a booming sound system, fog machine, spinning disco ball and 160 lights. It's better than a disco. Jon Barnes, owner of the taxi, cranks up the tunes before pulling down a ceiling-mounted microphone and banging away at a couple of keyboards. He mixes the sound, performs and drives you and your friends around creating a scene everywhere he goes. For information call **(303) 925-0361.**

Wheeler Opera House—

Jerome B. Wheeler built this three-story Victorian showpiece in 1889. For many years the opera house languished in disrepair, a burned-out reminder of better days. A multimillion-dollar restoration was completed in 1984, returning the Wheeler to its former glory. Today it is home to Aspen's artistic and cultural community. Natural wood is used lavishly throughout, contrasted by plush velvet stage curtains, red carpeting and gold stars painted on the ceiling; an elegant chandelier dominates the interior. Orchestra or balcony seating and side boxes are available. Today the opera house is much more than a museum—thanks to a year-round program of music, theater, dance and film. Check with the ticket office at **(303) 920-5770** for the performance schedule or an historic tour. **320 E. Hyman Ave.**

Woody Creek Tavern—
For information on this rustic bar/restaurant, see Where to Eat.

SCENIC DRIVES

Independence Pass—
One of the best-known "white knuckle" drives in the state is the narrow paved road over Independence Pass. The winding route, braced on one side by a stone guard rail, provides a bit of excitement for flatlanders unaccustomed to mountain driving. It is unquestionably at its colorful best during autumn and is impassable in winter. The pass, with its barren summit at 12,500 feet on the Continental Divide, provides the best route through the Sawatch Range; when the pass is closed, the drive to Aspen from the east is substantially longer.

The story goes that the pass is named Independence because of a gold strike on July 4, 1879, 4 miles west of the pass. A town quickly grew on that site. In the early 1880s, Independence had daily stage service to Leadville. (Reportedly, the population of only 2,000 supported 10 saloons.) The treacherous road over Independence Pass fell into disuse soon after the arrival of railroads into the lower valleys. Going over the pass required 10 to 25 hours, several changes of horses and payment at three tollgates. Since no railroad ever made its way to Independence, the town was all but a memory by the turn of the century.

An interesting place to pull off is at the Grottos, a series of granite caverns 8 miles east of Aspen (see the Hiking and Backpacking section).

To reach Independence Pass, follow Hwy. 82 east from Aspen. About 15 miles from Aspen, before reaching the summit, look to your right. You will see the remains of Independence down below the road. At the summit you'll find a parking area and a short walking trail. Closed in winter.

WILDLIFE

Aspen Center for Environmental Studies—
In 1968 Elizabeth Paepcke founded this nonprofit foundation to preserve Hallam Lake, on the north edge of town. The Aspen Center for Environmental Studies (ACES) provides environmental programs for local school kids and offers a series of summer programs aimed at enhancing awareness of the environment around Aspen. The ACES facilities at the Hallam Lake Wildlife Sanctuary and the 175-acre Northstar Wildlife Preserve (located just east of Aspen) offer indoor and outdoor classrooms for environmental education. Year-round tours of Hallam Lake and Northstar are available. In winter the tours are made on snowshoe. ACES has programs for everyone, from youngsters to environmentally conscious adults. **PO Box 8777, Aspen, CO 81612; (303) 925-5756.**

—— WHERE TO STAY ——

ACCOMMODATIONS

The array of lodging choices in Aspen runs the gamut from ritzy, full-service hotels to small, European-style ski lodges to luxury condominiums. You will not, however, find many large chain hotels, due to strict zoning requirements. Staying overnight in Aspen is generally more expensive than in other parts of the state, especially in high season when rooms are at a premium. We have listed some of the more outstanding accommodations in Aspen,

geared to suit a variety of tastes and budgets. For a more complete listing, call **Aspen Central Reservations and Travel, 1-800-262-7736** or locally at **(303) 925-9000.** For an interesting new option call **Affordable Aspen 1-800-243-9466,** a small organization dedicated to unearthing value-priced accommodations.

Hotel Jerome—$$$$
Only the Jerome truly reflects the limelight Aspen experienced during its pros-

perous silver boom. After a decades-long slide into disrepair, a major renovation in the mid-1980s put the Jerome back where it belongs—in a league with the finest historic hotels in the country. Layers of paint were stripped, revealing sandstone and beautiful wood that had not seen daylight for the better part of 60 years. Furniture was restored and priceless tile and solid-iron door fixtures were polished for reuse. The end result is a comfortable, plush hotel that's worth a look around even if you aren't spending the night.

Jerome B. Wheeler, the one-time president of Macy's department store in New York City, was Aspen's major benefactor. He donated the land on which the hotel sits and loaned money to the developers. Hopelessly over budget, the developers skipped town after receiving a number of death threats from unpaid workers. Wheeler eventually took over the unfinished project and opened the hotel on Thanksgiving Eve 1889.

Today the resurrected hotel offers 27 luxurious rooms, including 7 guest suites in the original hotel building. The new wing offers an additional 67 guest rooms (no 2 rooms are the same). The original gathering rooms all remain, including the "Ladies' Ordinary." The hotel lobby is marvelously plush with restored antique sofas and chairs. An open core in the center of the building rises three stories to a glass-covered ceiling. The original bar, restaurant and ballroom are worth visiting. For a unique après-ski scene, check out the pool on the west side of the building or head to the J Bar (see Nightlife section). Reserve far in advance for the ski season and the summer music festival. **330 E. Main St., Aspen, CO 81611; (303) 920-1000** locally or **1-800-331-7213.**

Little Nell—$$$

This nearly new, 92-room luxury hotel at the base of Ajax provides the easiest ski-in, ski-out location in town. It takes a while to fully appreciate the muted interior colors, but the logic of this hotel's soothing, contemporary design soon becomes obvious. Besides, after mixing a drink at your own private wet bar, cranking up the gas fireplace and sinking into a down-filled chair, who cares?

All of the spacious rooms and suites come equipped. Hidden away in an armoire lies a remote-controlled TV/VCR. Most rooms have balconies offering views up the mountain and overlooking the year-round heated pool and Jacuzzi. Leave your skis with the ski concierge, who will, for a fee, wax them and sharpen the edges overnight. The oversized marble bathrooms (fitted with brass) have functional spaces to eliminate any tie-ups. Little Nell also features a state-of-the-art exercise facility as well as a quiet bar, a highly regarded restaurant and plush common living room. Though very expensive, Little Nell has no problem booking rooms well in advance. **675 E. Durant St., Aspen, CO 81611; 1-800-525-6200** or **(303) 920-4600** locally.

Ritz Carlton Hotel—$$$$

The Ritz of Aspen, center of controversy since its planning stages in the early 1980s, finally opened its doors in 1991. The luxury hotel offers truly elegant accommodations to those who can afford it. The size by Aspen standards is monolithic—some 257 rooms occupy the horseshoe–shaped structure built to provide mountain views from every room. Despite its newness, the hotel feels like it's been around for a long while thanks to the Colorado red brick exterior and classic design. The Ritz's upper-crust style and round-the-clock service has a place here. The lobby comes off surprisingly warm with its detailed attention to sights, sounds and textures; fresh flowers, lush wood, soft music, fabulous art and sculpture can be found throughout the hotel. Rooms, with every conceivable amenity, include three phones, a safe, a bathroom scale and, of course, a stocked bar and fridge. The beauty salon appears larger than the spa, although there is also an inviting outdoor pool and hot tub. Your choice of restaurants and bars. Reserve rooms far in advance. **315 E. Dean St., Aspen, CO 81611; (303) 920-3300.**

Sardy House—$$$$

Bordered by two towering blue spruces, Sardy House is a beautifully restored Queen Anne Victorian mansion steeped in history. As you pass the red brick Sardy House on Main St., its gables, turrets and balcony will provoke you into taking a second look. Inside, oak staircases lead to well-appointed guest rooms and suites. TVs and VCRs are hidden away in cherry wood armoires. Laura Ashley prints overlay the feather comforters and many of the hardwood ceilings are vaulted and multiangled. White-tiled bathrooms have new fixtures done in the old style and heated towel racks! Don't worry about the driveway icing up; it's heated as well. Outside you'll find a heated swimming pool and a Jacuzzi. Breakfast is included. Downstairs, the Sardy House now serves gourmet dinners ($$$) to the public in a subdued, intimate atmosphere. **128 E. Main St., Aspen, CO 81611; (303) 920-2525.**

Alpine Lodge—$$ to $$$$

This small, family-run gasthaus still represents the best value in Aspen. The owners, Jim and Christina, have carried on in the warm tradition of this Bavarian-style lodge while making welcome upgrades. About half of the comfortable lodge rooms have private baths, as well as balcony views to Aspen Mountain. Though the lodge rooms are rather small, they are homey and immaculately clean. Besides, each guest is made to feel at home in the large downstairs common area. In winter both breakfast and dinner (BYOB) are served for a reasonable extra price. During après ski guests mingle in front of the large ceramic wood stove or, in summer, over a game of outdoor ping-pong. No matter the season, you'll get to know "Bear," the lodge dog.

Adjacent to the lodge, four cottages hem in a carefully tended interior courtyard replete with wildflowers; the redwood deck and large outdoor hot tub get a lot of use in summer and winter. Each unit has a TV, kitchenette and private bathroom.

Unless you reserve far in advance, you'll be lucky to find any space at the Alpine Lodge during high season. Nearly all rooms during ski season are taken for a week at a time. It's a place where guests commonly reserve rooms for next year as they check out. **1240 E. Cooper Ave., Aspen, CO 81611; (303) 925-7351.**

Ambiance Inn (Carbondale)—$$$

Stretch out and enjoy one of the four large, comfortable rooms in this contemporary house just off Main St. in Carbondale. It's an absolute bargain by Aspen standards, and you won't have to deal with the cramped quarters sometimes encountered in renovated Victorians. The huge Aspen Suite with its ski motif and knotty pine walls was our favorite (but we could have skipped the autographed John Denver poster); the Kauai Room, however, has the best single feature: a Jacuzzi tub. All rooms have private baths and are nicely, though not extravagantly, furnished. An excellent full breakfast is provided at the large dining room table downstairs at 8 am sharp. Your hosts Norma and Robert are friendly and nonintrusive; Norma will fix dinner if you give a day's notice. **66 2nd St., Carbondale, CO 81623; (303) 963-3597.**

St. Moritz Lodge—$$ to $$$

This reasonably priced, loud and lively lodge is in financial limbo, but still offers some of the best deals in town. Stay in a dorm room that serves as Aspen's unofficial youth hostel, or sign up for a private lodge room. The well-worn common room looks out onto the deck and small heated pool. Weekly and monthly rentals available. **334 W. Hyman Ave., Aspen, CO 81611; (303) 925-3220.**

In Snowmass—

A number of fine attributes (besides the skiing) entice people to venture to Snowmass, but unique or historic lodging opportunities is not one of them. Condominium rentals dominate the lodging possibilities in the beautiful Brush Creek Valley, reflecting the era of Snowmass' recent boom. Those seeking a full-service resort atmosphere might want to check into the **Snowmass Club Lodge ($$$$)**, which offers plush accommodations along with an athletic club, restaurant, golf course and indoor tennis courts. **PO Box G-2, Snowmass Village, CO 81615; 1-800-525-0710** or **(303) 923-5600** locally.

The burgeoning development at Snowmass has planned for most of the condo buildings to stairstep right up the ski mountain. This ski-in, ski-out accessibility enables you to buckle your ski boots in your living room. The condos are an especially good option for families and people who want to escape the hurly-burly of Aspen. For condominium reservations contact the **Snowmass Central Reservations; 1-800-332-3245** or **(303) 923-2000** locally.

CAMPING

In White River National Forest—

In the Aspen area there are 15 forest service campgrounds equipped with a variety of facilities ranging from primitive to plush. Most campsites are assigned on a first-come, first-served basis. Selected campgrounds in the area accept reservations at least 10 days in advance at **1-800-283-CAMP.** For more information call, write or visit the **Aspen Ranger District Office, 806 W. Hallam St., Aspen, CO 81611; (303) 925-3445.**

Up the Fryingpan River—Although a bit far from Aspen, the drive may be worth it if you seek solitude and great fishing. From Aspen drive northwest on Hwy. 82 for 18 miles to Basalt. From Basalt, head upriver on Fryingpan Rd. (County Rd. 105) to Ruedi Reservoir. Four campgrounds at **Ruedi** charge a fee: **Mollie B** (26 sites), **Little Maud** (22 sites), **Little Mattie** (20 sites) and **Dearhamer** (13 sites). A few miles above the reservoir are two other campgrounds: **Elk Wallow** (8 sites, no pump water, no fee) and **Chapman** (42 sites, fee charged).

Up Maroon Creek Road—See Major Attractions for information.

Toward Independence Pass—Up the valley on Hwy. 82 there are five campgrounds to choose from before you reach the pass. **Difficult Campground,** with 47 sites, is the closest to Aspen (5 miles). Farther up Hwy. 82 you'll find **Weller** (11 sites, fee charged), **Lincoln Gulch** (7 sites, fee charged) and **Lost Man** campgrounds (9 sites, fee charged), located 9 miles, 11 miles and 14.5 miles, respectively, from Aspen. Up Hwy. 82, 11 miles from Aspen, turn south up Lincoln Creek Rd. for 7 miles to reach **Portal Campground** (7 sites, no fee) on Grizzly Reservoir. This road is not maintained and may be tough going for trailers and passenger cars.

Private Campgrounds—

For top-notch RV park facilities in the Aspen area, you need to head down the valley to Basalt. Here's what you'll find:

KOA Campground—20640 Hwy 82, Basalt, CO 81621; (303) 927-3532.

Pan & Fork Trailer Park—23050 Hwy. 82, Basalt, CO 81621; (303) 927-9183.

───── WHERE TO EAT ─────

Of course Aspen fills the demand for top-quality, top-dollar restaurants. But there are also places to get decent food at reasonable prices. More than 100 restaurants, ranging from five-star masterpieces to dive diners, call Aspen home. The town recently added a **Hard Rock Cafe—$$ to $$$, 210 S. Galena St.; (303) 920-1666**—though most locals don't seem thrilled about the arrival of the famous chain. Surprisingly, unlike the revolving door of most resort towns, the Aspen area manages to keep a stable of consistent eateries. Following are some of the best, starting with those in the higher price range.

Chez Grandmère—$$$$

Located in Snowmass, this 19th-century farmhouse is home to the area's finest French cuisine. The atmosphere at this elegant restaurant creates a perfect mood for a special meal. The limited menu changes nightly, always offering meat, fish and poultry dishes. Your elaborate four-course meal comes at one fixed price. Don't worry about being hurried through your dinner because there's only one seating per evening. Reservations are a must. **16 Kearns Rd., Snowmass; (303) 923-2570.**

Pine Creek Cookhouse—$$$$

Imagine a light falling snow under a full moon. Place yourself on cross-country skis or in a horse-drawn sleigh in the Castle Creek Valley, 12 miles from Aspen, and head to an off-beat dining experience. Starting at the ghost town of Ashcroft, the 1.5-mile jaunt through the woods heightens your senses and creates a certain camaraderie among guests. You have a choice of three entrées each evening; Cornish game hen, herbed Rocky Mountain trout and roast leg of lamb were served during our visit. One word of caution for people who ski to the cookhouse and plan on having a few drinks: The downhill trail back can be a bit tricky. The set dinner price includes a guide and cross-country ski rental. A sleigh ride is an extra fee. When skiing at the Ashcroft Touring Center stop in for lunch ($$$), served noon–2:30 pm. In summer it is possible to drive to the cookhouse. One dinner seating each evening; reservations are a must. **Ashcroft Touring Center, Ashcroft; (303) 925-1044.**

Chefy's—$$$ to $$$$

Heading downvalley to Basalt may seem like a pain if you're staying in Aspen, but the food at Chefy's is worth it. Owner/chef Claude Van Horton puts major effort into his cuisine, which ranges from innovative pasta and seafood dishes to perfectly grilled steaks. The delicate sauces, artistic presentation and precision service make special meals a common occurrence. Don't even think about skipping the wild mushroom soup. Though simple, this small restaurant with an outside deck has a pleasant atmosphere that enhances your experience. Couples may want to try reserving a table in the quiet nook behind the bar. Mon.–Fri. lunch served 11:30 am–2:30 pm; cocktails and appetizers served from 2:30–5:30 pm. Open seven nights a week 5:30–9:30 pm for dinner; Sunday brunch served 8:30 am–2:30 pm. **166 Midland Ave., Basalt; (303) 927-4034.**

Krabloonik's—$$$ to $$$$

As a working sled-dog kennel, Krabloonik's has to be one of the most unusual places to dine in the Aspen area, if not in the entire country—due in part to the 300 yipping dogs near the entrance. Located up the road from Snowmass Ski Area, this atmospheric log cabin boasts the honor (?) of being written up in *Sports Illustrated*. Large picture windows offer a spectacular view up the valley to Mt. Daly and 14,130-foot Capitol Peak. The decor is Alaskan rustic, but white tablecloths and fine crystal immediately clue you in to the fact that you are not going to be eating Spam and beans. Krabloonik's fare is indeed gourmet caliber. Wild game selections include moose, caribou, elk and wild boar shipped in from as far away as New Zealand. Choose from more than 200 wines and a European beer list. Open for lunch 11 am–2 pm and dinner from 5:30 pm daily in winter (dinner only in summer). Skiers at Snowmass can reach the restaurant via Dawdler Trail. After lunch ($$$), ski down to the Campground Chairlift. Reservations are essential (months in advance for the peak holiday period). For information about taking a sled-dog ride, see the Dog Sledding section. Located a quarter mile above Snowmass Ski Area on **4250 Divide Rd., Snowmass Village; (303) 923-3953.**

Farfalla—$$ to $$$$

If a restaurant has ever caught on like wildfire in Aspen, it's this one. With locations in Los Angeles and West Hollywood, Farfalla's creative Italian cuisine and contemporary style seem to fit the energetic social style of Aspen. With the freshest ingredients possible, the chefs here prepare a healthful menu with striking combinations, such as asparagus tortellini with a walnut-pesto sauce as well as uncomplicated chicken dishes roasted in a brick oven. You can be pretty much assured of a wait—no reservations unless there are six or more in your party. Delivery and take-out available. Open daily for dinner starting at 6 pm. **415 E. Main; (303) 925-8222.**

Asia—$$ to $$$

An unusual combination: Chinese cuisine served in an old Victorian home. The house features a l00-year-old bar and woodwork throughout. Asia's cuisine is a favorite with Aspen locals (one reason being the free delivery service). The restaurant offers Mandarin and Szechuan menu items with a few Hunan and Cantonese dishes thrown in for good measure. Lily Ko, the manager, came directly to the US from Beijing, so rest assured the Peking duck is done to perfection. Outside seating in summer. Dinner is served 5–11 pm. **132 W. Main St.; (303) 925-5433.**

Flying Dog Brew Pub—$$ to $$$

This place would stand on its own without the in-house brewery, but, ahh, what a plus. With an outdoor courtyard leading to a room accented with heavy wood beams, historic photos and exposed brick walls, Flying Dog feels intimate. The small bar area separated by a wall of glass bricks is a comfortable place to enjoy a Doggie Style (their best-selling brew). The larger restaurant area features classic steak and seafood dinners as well as inexpensive pub food such as fish and chips and brats. Occasional live music; outdoor seating in summer. Open 11:30 am–10 pm daily. Located downstairs on the Cooper Ave. Mall. **424 E. Cooper Ave.; (303) 925-7464.**

La Cocina—$$

Over the years many Aspen eateries have bitten the dust, but La Cocina has been a consistently great place to eat since 1971. A favorite among locals, La Cocina offers creative New Mexican–style food. The owners, Nick and Sarah Lebby, work seven days a week, Sarah in the kitchen and Nick greeting and seating guests. A local in the bar told us Nick never forgets a name. La Cocina's good value makes it a highlight of dining out in Aspen. Menu favorites include the Cocina bean dip appetizer, any enchilada plate and the blue corn tortilla dinner. Don't miss the Chocolate Velvet dessert. The decor is New Mexican, and the atmosphere is friendly and down-to-earth. Hours are 5–10 pm daily. No reservations. **308 E. Hopkins Ave.; (303) 925-9714.**

Little Annie's—$$

Rough wood walls, throwaway antiques and a well-worn floor provide the set for this local stomping ground. The handwritten menu describes a generous assortment of dishes at most reasonable prices (especially considering the quantity of food on every plate). Giant half-pound hamburgers, Greek salads, Poncho's pizza, barbecue ribs and sautéed rainbow trout are only a few of the favorites; nightly specials are also served. By the way, a shot and a beer at Little Annie's is still the cheapest in town! Kitchen open 11:30 am–11:30 pm; bar stays open till 2 am. **517 E. Hyman Ave.; (303) 925-1098.**

The Village Smithy—$ to $$

If you are driving into or out of Aspen, stop in at the Village Smithy. This is without a doubt one of the finest, if not the finest, breakfast place in the valley. Located downvalley from Aspen in Carbondale, this restaurant is, appropriately, housed in an old blacksmith's shop. Eggs Benedict are the house specialty, but the huevos rancheros are a favorite with regulars. Homemade lunch items also keep locals coming back for more. Full bar available. Breakfast and lunch served 7 am–2 pm weekdays; breakfast served until 2 pm on weekends. Located at **3rd and Main in Carbondale; (303) 963-9990.**

Wienerstube—$ to $$

A couple of talented Austrian chefs opened the Wienerstube in 1965. Breakfast at this popular restaurant has become something of an Aspen tradition. A light garden setting is complemented by lots of stained glass. There is even a "stammtisch" table reserved for regular customers. Breakfast choices include traditional bacon and eggs as well as eggs Benedict, crêpes, Belgian waffles with fruit, and homemade Viennese pastries. Open for breakfast 7–11 am. The extensive lunch menu is served from 11 am–2:30 pm. Closed Mon. **633 E. Hyman Ave.; (303) 925-3357.**

Woody Creek Tavern—$ to $$

If the glitz of Aspen starts to get to you, stop in at the Woody Creek Tavern for a game of pool, a burger and a cheap beer on tap. You might ask about the house drink: the Biff. This out-of-the-way spot is a local hangout; occasionally Don Henley or Hunter S. Thompson stops by. Nice patio in summer. Mexican food, burgers and chicken make up the menu— the hot chicken wings are great. Pool table. To get there take Hwy. 82 downvalley from Aspen for a few miles and turn right on Woody Creek Rd. Follow the road across a bridge and turn left at the fork. The tavern is just down the road from there. Serving lunch and dinner 11:30 am– 10 pm. **2 Woody Creek Plaza, Woody Creek; (303) 923-4585.**

Paradise Bakery—$

The Paradise has two major things going for it: a superb assortment of homemade muffins (cinnamon apple spice, pumpkin nut, bran …) and a perfect corner location at Cooper and Galena. Plenty of outside benches are available in the warmer months—ideal for people-watching. Small counter space inside. The bakery also serves cookies, ice cream and freshly squeezed lemonade. Open daily 7 am–midnight. **320 S. Galena St.; (303) 925-7585.**

Popcorn Wagon—$

Calming classical music, crêpes and a nice little outdoor seating area can be found along with inexpensive drinks and, yes, popcorn. It's a great value right in the center of town. The historic wagon, built in Chicago in 1913, has been in operation for 25 years—a long time for any Aspen restaurant. Located across from the Wheeler Opera House on **Hyman Ave. and Mill St.**

SERVICES

Bus Transportation—

Frequent free shuttle buses begin their route at Rubey Park (on Durant Ave. between Mill St. and Galena St.) before whisking skiers to each of the surrounding ski mountains. The buses run every 15 minutes during the morning and afternoon skier rush; during midday the buses operate on a more leisurely schedule, leaving every half hour or so.

In addition to the free shuttle buses, free city buses serve the city of Aspen. The buses run four different routes from 7 am– 1 am. All bus routes originate at Rubey Park. See Major Attractions section for information on buses to the Maroon Bells.

For schedule and route information, call **(303) 925-8484.**

Central Reservations—

Aspen Resort Association—700 S. Aspen St., Aspen, CO 81611; call locally **(303) 925-9000** or **1-800-262-7736** outside Colorado.

Snowmass Resort Association—38 Village Sq., PO Box 5566, Snowmass Village, CO 81615; call **(303) 923-2010** locally or **1-800-332-3245** outside Colorado and **1-800-598-2004.**

Day Care—

Aspen Sprouts, (303) 920-1055; or **Big Burn Bears, (303) 925-1220 ext. 4570, 923-0570.**

Public Parking—

For a reasonable fee you can park in the new, covered lot on N. Mill St. just behind the County Courthouse, near the Hotel Jerome. Another pay lot, closer to the mountain, sits at the corner of Hyman Ave. and Original St.

24-Hour Taxi Service—

High Mountain Taxi—Specializes in luxury four-wheel-drive vehicles and limousine service; **(303) 925-TAXI.**

Visitor Information—

Aspen Visitors Center—Stop in at the Wheeler Opera House for information and advice on what to see and do in the Aspen area. **328 E. Hyman Ave., Aspen, CO 81611;** or call **(303) 925-1940;** or write; **Aspen Chamber of Commerce—425 Rio Grande Place, Attn. Visitors Center, Aspen, CO 81611; (303) 925-5656.**

Basalt Area Chamber of Commerce—PO Box 514, Basalt, CO 81621; (303) 927-4031.

Carbondale Chamber of Commerce—0590 Hwy. 133, Carbondale, CO 81623; (303) 963-1890.

Dinosaur National Monument

Remote and often overlooked, Dinosaur National Monument is a recreationist's mecca and a stunning, beautiful geological exhibit. Located in the unforgiving, arid Colorado Plateau country in the extreme northwestern corner of the state, this three-pronged, 300-square-mile monument straddles the Utah-Colorado border. In its southwestern corner, where an ancient river once flowed, lies the Dinosaur Quarry, representing one of the highest concentrations of Jurassic period fossilized dinosaur bones in the world. Sprawled across the monument, the Uinta Mountains are one of just a few mountain ranges in the western hemisphere that run east-west. At the center of the monument at Echo Park lies the confluence of two of the West's mightiest rivers: the Green and the Yampa.

Dinosaur is a land of rugged plateaus and deep, hidden canyons that are deceptive from a distance. Like other western canyon country, the monument's parks and side gorges are best viewed and discovered from within. By far the best way to see the monument is from the river. Rafters and kayakers spend days floating through the narrow rock canyons, carved as deep as 3,300 feet over millions of years. Tranquil for a few miles, then violent and angry, the river pinches together for steep drops down the narrow rapid sections. Driving the back roads and hiking the backcountry of Dinosaur are other ways to experience the canyons, plateaus and mountains. If you make the effort to reach Dinosaur National Monument, you won't be disappointed.

HISTORY

More than 140 million years ago, during the Jurassic period, dinosaurs and other creatures roamed around the area that today is Dinosaur National Monument. Many of these beasts' bones were covered and preserved over the eons until discovered in August 1909 by paleontologist Earl Douglass. On a search for large fossils for the Carnegie Museum in Pittsburgh, Douglass was excited, to say the least, when he discovered eight Brontosaurus vertebrae imbedded in what was once a sandbar along an ancient river. The dinosaur bones had collected in the silt of the river and had been covered up by accumulating sand and mud.

Over the next 15 years, 350 tons of dinosaur bones and associated rock were excavated from this area and taken to the Carnegie Museum and other institutions around the world. Today 11 different species have been unearthed in what has proven to be one of the world's most prolific dinosaur digs. In 1915 President Woodrow Wilson proclaimed the dinosaur dig and 80 acres around it a national monument. President Franklin Roosevelt expanded the monument land by adding over 300 square miles in 1938.

At least as far back as 7000 BC, primitive humans were making their way over the plateaus and through the canyons of northwestern Colorado. More recently (AD 200–AD 1300), Fremont Man, the prehistoric hunter/gatherer and horticulturist, left marks throughout the area in the form of rock art. Petroglyphs are etched into scores of canyon walls in the form of humans, sheep, lizards and numerous other renderings of life as seen through the eyes of these ancients. Whether these etchings are a form of written language or of art is still not known.

Modern humans' first recorded ventures into the area began in 1776 with the Franciscan friars Dominguez and Escalante, who traveled just south of Dinosaur on their search for a safe route to the West Coast from Santa Fe. When the beaver pelt business was booming in the early 1800s, trappers who fanned out in the Wyoming, Utah and Colorado area met periodically at a rendezvous spot along the Green River called Brown's Park. This area is just north of the monument boundary.

With people entering the area to trap and later to search for gold, it was only a matter of time before they discovered the canyons on the Green and Yampa rivers. In 1825 Gen. William H. Ashley, a fur trader from Missouri, floated through perhaps the most treacherous section of the Green River—Lodore Canyon. The group of men he assembled in Missouri for one of his many trips west read like a Who's Who of mountain men, including Jim Beckwourth, Jim Bridger, John Colter and Jedediah Smith. In 1869 Maj. John Wesley Powell brought news of the Dinosaur area and its river to the world through his compelling journal entries, written during his much-publicized survey and exploration trip west. A few years later, he again floated the upper Green River down through its narrow canyons in northwestern Colorado. These accomplishments become even more significant given the fact that Maj. Powell had only one arm.

Due to Dinosaur's remote location and rough terrain, sections of the area remained wild and unexplored until well into the 1900s. At the turn of the century, some settlers entered the region to homestead the remote canyons and parks. Cattle rustlers, highwaymen and bank robbers also found the remote area a perfect place to hide out between jobs while the heat wore off. Butch Cassidy and his Wild Bunch frequented Brown's Park (then called Brown's Hole).

Dinosaur National Monument has the distinction of being one of the first sites in the country where environmental interests outstripped those of developers. From about 1950 to 1955, intense debates raged over two proposed dams that would have flooded the beautiful canyons and covered up forever a multitude of ancient rock art. Largely due to efforts by the Sierra Club to increase public awareness, the proposed site was canceled. Today the rivers in the northwestern corner of the state remain free-flowing, though there is a dam proposed on the Cross Canyon section of the Yampa, just upriver to the east of Dinosaur National Monument.

FACTS ABOUT THE MONUMENT

Dinosaur Quarry—

Come and visit the place where the first dinosaur bones were discovered in 1909. *This is the only place in the monument to see dinosaur bones!* An enormous structure encloses the quarry, where until recently technicians worked to uncover and extract dinosaur remains. Visible from within the building is an exposed hillside with fossilized remains of at least one Jurassic critter. Visitors can browse through the displays and ask questions of the knowledgeable park ranger on duty. The entrance is 7 miles north of Jensen, Utah. From the parking lot, a shuttle bus, which operates from Memorial Day to Labor Day, takes you up to the quarry; you can drive up yourself during the rest of the year. The quarry visitors center is open 8 am–7 pm daily, early June to early Sept.; 8 am–4:30 pm during the rest of the year. Admission fee is charged. Jensen, Utah, is located 20 miles west of Dinosaur, Colorado, on Hwy. 40; **(801) 789-2115.**

Park Headquarters—

The park headquarters is located 2 miles east of the town of Dinosaur at the intersection of Hwy. 40 and Harper's Corner Rd. There is an audiovisual program as well as exhibits. Free admission. Obtain backcountry camping permits and any other information you need here. Open daily, 8 am–4:30 pm, June–Aug.; Mon.–Fri., 8 am–4:30 pm, the rest of the year; **(303) 374-2216.**

Services—

Gas, food and lodging are not available within Dinosaur National Monument. The towns of Dinosaur and Rangely offer the closest services in Colorado; Jensen (no lodging) and Vernal have what you need on the Utah side.

Weather—

The Dinosaur area is arid, but this doesn't necessarily mean hot. In the summer it can get very hot during the day, but it cools down at night. Thunderstorms are common during June, July and Aug. Snow usually falls by Oct., with cold weather continuing into the spring—temperatures below 32° F are common. Dress accordingly.

GETTING THERE

The two main entrances to the monument are located at Dinosaur, Colorado, and at Jensen, Utah. To reach Dinosaur (295 miles northwest of Denver), head west via Hwy. 40 through northern Colorado. From the south (Grand Junction), head west on Interstate 70 for 16 miles and turn north on Hwy. 139 to Rangely and then northwest on Hwy. 64 to Dinosaur. The northern end of the park at the Gates of Lodore can be reached via Hwy. 318, which heads northwest out of Maybell.

OUTDOOR ACTIVITIES

FOUR-WHEEL-DRIVE TRIPS

Exploring the back roads in the Dinosaur area is a great way to experience the country. But be forewarned that when rain starts to fall in canyon country, some of the roads are not even passable with a four-wheel-drive vehicle. If you get stuck at the bottom of a muddy hill, you may have a long wait while the road dries—or an even longer hike out. Be sure to have plenty of gasoline, food, water and tools along with you.

For road ideas in and around Dinosaur National Monument, visit the rangers at park headquarters near the town of Dinosaur. Bureau of Land Management (BLM) land surrounds practically the entire monument, offering some fascinating country just waiting to be explored. For more information about backroad BLM possibilities, contact the BLM Office in Craig. **Little Snake Resource Area, 1280 Industrial Ave., Craig, CO 81625; (303) 824-4441.**

Crouse Canyon—

Although Crouse Canyon can be driven in a passenger car in good weather, it is a very rough road for the first few miles. The road begins in Colorado, then quickly curves over into Utah for the duration of the 25-mile, dirt road trip. The Crouse Canyon Rd. begins dramatically by crossing a swinging bridge over the Green River. Once across, the road follows the river upstream for awhile, on the southern edge of Brown's Park National Wildlife Refuge. Suddenly the road turns southwest and propels you into a beautiful, narrow canyon. Towering rock walls and a cool stream lined with cottonwood groves await. The road eventually climbs up onto a plateau.

Be on the lookout for some of the most memorable residents of the area, the Mormon crickets. These huge wingless grasshoppers swarm across the road, devouring their comrades who've been tragically crushed under the wheels of passing cars. When the Mormons first settled in Utah, their crops were set upon by these creatures. By "divine intervention," a flock of California seagulls came to the rescue, gorging themselves on these tasty insects. The Mormons were so thankful to the birds that the California seagull was made the state bird of Utah.

To reach Crouse Canyon, head northwest from Maybell on Hwy. 318 for 62 miles to the turn-off to Brown's Park National Wildlife Refuge. Turn left and proceed on the dirt road down to and over the swinging bridge. After 25 miles, you hit a paved road which goes to Vernal, Utah, or to the Dinosaur Quarry.

Yampa Bench Road—

This rough dirt road bumps and bounces its way for 42 miles through the monument and adjacent BLM land. Through canyons and over open country covered with sage, juniper and pinon, Yampa Bench Rd. offers a rugged look at the area. To reach Yampa Bench Rd., head north from park headquarters on Harper's Corner Rd. for 25 miles to Echo Park Rd. Turn right and drive 8 miles down to the fork in the road. The right fork is Yampa Bench Rd. It comes out on Hwy. 40 at Elk Springs, 32 miles northeast of park headquarters.

HIKING AND BACKPACKING

Although the number of established hiking trails within the monument is rather limited, routes into side canyons are endless. Backcountry camping is allowed in the monument, but you need to obtain a free permit issued at either the quarry, park headquarters or some of the field ranger stations. Be very careful if you venture out on your own. Take plenty of water and consult the rangers about the area where you intend to backpack. Below are a few hiking and backpacking ideas.

Irish Canyon—

This is a beautiful, multicolored canyon not more than 150 feet wide. Steep walls with green, red and gray layers tower above the pinon pines in the canyon. An exhibit, petroglyphs and three campsites are at the entrance to the canyon. Side canyons beckon to hikers. Near the north end of the canyon are two natural ponds known as Irish Lakes. You need to bring your own drinking water for camping or hiking in this area. This is a secluded place, even though it is accessible by road. To reach Irish Canyon, head northwest from Maybell on Hwy. 318 for 41 miles and turn right on County Rd. 10N. Proceed 4 miles to the canyon entrance.

Jones Hole—

Follow this 4-mile trail down along Jones Hole Creek into Whirlpool Canyon, one of the few remote parts of the Green River accessible on foot rather than by water. There are plenty of trees and steep rock walls (some with petroglyphs) along the way to keep you somewhat cool in the summer heat. The trailhead is located on the north side of the river, 40 miles east of Vernal. For directions and a map, stop in at park headquarters or the quarry.

Nature Trails—

There are short, interpretive nature trails at the following spots: Split Mountain Campground, Gates of Lodore and Harper's Corner. The trail at Harper's Corner is 2 miles round trip and offers a fantastic view.

Willow Creek Canyon, Skull Creek Canyon and Bull Canyon—

Located in a BLM Wilderness Study Area fairly close to the park headquarters, these three canyons provide spectacular backcountry hiking opportunities without marked trails. Bull Canyon, characterized by many draws, creeks, colorful cliffs and unique rock formations, is accessible from Plug Hat Picnic Area, 4 miles north on Harper's Corner Rd. from park headquarters. Trails into Willow Creek and Skull Creek canyons, located to the northeast of park headquarters, can be accessed from Hwy. 40. The upper reaches of Willow Creek offer intermittent 200-foot waterfalls in early spring. For specific information and maps pertaining to these beautiful, secluded canyons, contact the BLM office in Craig or monument headquarters.

RIVER FLOATING

Some of the best floating in the state can be had on several sections of the Green and Yampa rivers, namely, Cross Mountain and Split Mountain gorges, Whirlpool, Lodore and Yampa River canyons. Each year commercial and private rafters and kayakers submit applications to obtain the limited permits. The best way to experience the monument is definitely from the water. Floating allows access to many places inaccessible by any other means.

Green River—

The Green River flows peacefully into northwestern Colorado below Flaming Gorge, then turns south and enters the magnificent, colorful Gates of Lodore at the northern tip of the monument. It's here that the Green cuts through the Uinta Mountains, exposing 2,300-foot-deep Lodore Canyon. Once inside the 17-mile-long canyon, the river picks up speed, crashing down through the narrow passageway that has frightened and captivated so many boaters over the years. In 1869 Maj. John Wesley Powell described the scenery of Lodore Canyon as "even beyond the power of pen to tell." The Gates of Lodore, like most of the landmarks along the river, was named by Powell. It refers to a passage from a 19th-century poem by Robert Southey that Powell liked to recite to his crew as they started down the rapids in their stiff wooden boats.

Once through Lodore Canyon, the Green is met in Echo Park by the meandering Yampa River from the east. The swollen Green then snakes its way around Steamboat Rock and heads southwest through Whirlpool Canyon and Split Mountain Gorge, before emerging onto the desert plateau.

Yampa River—

Intersecting Hwy. 318 at Sunbeam, 7 miles northwest of Maybell, the Yampa River meanders west for 15 miles until it reaches the treacherous Cross Mountain Gorge. An incredibly demanding stretch of river for kayakers, Cross Mountain Gorge is only for rafters with a death wish. For 3.5 terrible miles, a virtually unending maelstrom eats rafts as it continually scours the rock canyon. The gorge comes out in Lily Park and continues to Deerlodge Park, a put-in point at the east end of Dinosaur National Monument. This is where most rafters put in for the Yampa River trip down through the beautiful Yampa River Canyon. Past alcoves and overhangs of canyon walls rising 1,000 feet, Yampa River Canyon twists and turns its way farther west. Along the banks in sheltered spots

under rock overhangs, ancient campsites still show signs of fire pits, food caches and cryptic rock art. Downriver, Warm Springs Rapids shakes, rattles and rolls river mariners down to the confluence with the Green River at Echo Park. From here on it's a relatively relaxing ride down the Green.

Outfitters—

More than 10 commercial outfitters offer float trips on the Green and Yampa rivers through Dinosaur. Trips vary from one to five days in length. If you just want a day trip through Split Mountain Gorge, check with the park headquarters to see which outfitters have been granted that concession. For extended multiday trips, be sure to book far in advance, because the trips fill up. Listed below are some of the better-known outfitters.

Adrift Adventures—One-, three- and four-day trips down the Green River, as well as five-day trips on the Yampa. **PO Box 192, Jensen, UT 84035; (303) 493-4005** in summer, **1-800-824-0150** year-round.

Don Hatch River Expeditions—First outfitter in the area. Bus Hatch, the father of the current owner, began running trips for "dudes" back in 1936. **PO Box 1150, Vernal, UT 84078; (801) 789-4316, or 1-800-342-8243.**

Holiday River Expeditions—544 E. 3900 S., Salt Lake City, UT 84107; (801) 266-2087, or 1-800-624-6323.

Mountain Sports Kayak School—Barry Smith has begun taking kayakers down the treacherous Cross Mountain Gorge section of the Yampa River. Only advanced intermediate kayakers should consider this trip. **PO Box 1986, Steamboat Springs, CO 80488; (303) 879-8794 or 879-6910.**

Further Information—

For more information about the rivers and obtaining permits, write the superintendent at **Dinosaur National Monument, 4545 Hwy 40, Dinosaur, CO 81610; (303) 374-2216.**

SEEING AND DOING

SCENIC DRIVES

Although some of the dirt roads around the area can be driven in a regular passenger car, if it rains heavily, the desert clay becomes very slick and can make the roads impassable, even for four-wheel-drive vehicles.

Cañon Pintado—

Located in Douglas Creek Valley, just south of Rangely on Hwy. 139, Cañon Pintado is an excellent area for observing the rock art left by ancient cultures. More than 50 sites on the canyon walls in the area display rock art created by the Fremont people who lived here from roughly 600 to 1300 AD. Evidence shows that other humans inhabited the area as far back as 9000 BC!

The canyon gets its Spanish name ("painted canyon" in English) from friars Dominguez and Escalante, who admired the artwork while riding through the canyon. To reach the canyon from Dinosaur, head south 18 miles on Hwy. 64 to Rangely. From Rangely head south into the canyon on Hwy. 139. For more information about the canyon, contact the **BLM White River Resources Office, PO Box 928, Meeker, CO 81641; (303) 878-3601.** A brochure identifying and explaining the rock art sites in the area can be obtained from the **Rangely Chamber of Commerce; (303) 675-5290.**

Cub Creek—

From the entrance to the Dinosaur Quarry 7 miles north of Jensen, Utah, begin this scenic 12-mile drive to Josie Morris's Cabin. Morris moved to this homestead nestled at the foot of Split Mountain in 1914 to raise livestock, vegetable crops and fruit. For 50 years she lived here, visited only occasionally by friends and relatives.

On the drive in, the view of Split Mountain is as spectacular as the rock formations along the way. About 10.5 miles from the entrance, stop and inspect the impressive array of petroglyphs. A small road guide can be purchased at the entrance or at park headquarters.

Echo Park Road—

This is a highlight of the monument, offering beautiful canyons, panoramic views, rock art, history and even a cave. To get there, head north from park headquarters on Harper's Corner Rd. for 25 miles, then turn right on Echo Park Rd. Almost immediately this dirt road begins a steep climb down into the canyons; many rocky side gorges head off from it. This section is impassable when the road is wet. After 8 miles on the dirt road there is a fork. Turn left. After a mile or so you can pull off on the left side of the road to inspect the petroglyphs, which are chiseled into the rock at least 15 feet above the ground. You have to wonder how ancient people were able to get up there, but park rangers are convinced that over the years Pool Creek has eroded the canyon bottom, stranding the petroglyphs high up on the cliff. After another mile or so down the road, there is a turn-off at Whispering Cave. Once inside the arch-shaped entrance, the cool air of the cave may keep you there awhile. A crack in the rock at least a hundred feet high—and just wide enough to squeeze through—extends into the dark for a long distance. Bring a flashlight and see how far you get.

Another 2 miles down the road, you reach the confluence of the Green and Yampa rivers at Echo Park. The park gets its name from Maj. John Wesley Powell, who was the first to notice the incredible echoing qualities of the rock walls. Echo Park was better known at one time as Pat's Hole, named after the old Irish hermit who lived here until the early 1900s. Pat Lynch, who died in 1917 at the ripe old age of 98, was a loner who lived in the caves along the river. According to many stories, Lynch made pets of wild animals in the area, including a mountain lion, which he would screech at—and then get a far-off reply. Perhaps the original conservationist of the

Dinosaur area, Lynch left these words scribbled on a piece of paper found by a local rancher's wife in a nearby cave:

If in these caverns you shelter take
Plais do to them no harm
Lave everything you find around
Hanging up or on the ground

Harper's Corner Road—

The view from the overlook at Harper's Corner is one of the best views into the central canyon area. A 2-mile round-trip

hiking trail follows a knife ridge to an overlook perched 2,500 feet above Echo Park. Harper's Corner is named after a rancher who used to keep his herd in this natural corral. Steep cliffs served to enclose most of the corral, and all he needed was a short stretch of fence to contain his herd. The 31-mile drive on Harper's Corner Rd. begins at park headquarters. At the headquarters be sure to pick up a copy of *Journey Through Time*, a guide to interesting points along the road.

WHERE TO STAY

You can't find lodging within the monument, but there is a small, grotty motel in the town of Dinosaur and a couple of decent ones in Rangely. For a bigger (and better) selection try Vernal, Utah, 13 miles northwest of Jensen, Utah, on Hwy. 40. One worth noting in Vernal is the newly renovated **Best Western Dinosaur Inn ($$ to $$$); 251 E. Main, Vernal, Utah; (801) 789-2660.**

CAMPING

Some great places to camp exist within the monument. All campgrounds are available on a first-come, first-served basis. There is usually no problem finding a site, except on holidays. Although some of these campgrounds provide drinking water (none in the winter months), you should pack in your own to use for washing. RVs can use some of the campgrounds, but there are no hookups. Fires are allowed in designated fire rings only. If you don't want to stay in one of the designated campgrounds, talk to the rangers at park headquarters for other car-camping and backpacking ideas.

Deerlodge Park Campground (8 primitive sites) is located just above the Yampa River Canyon. Most Yampa River floaters put in here for the trip downriver. No water and no fee. To reach Deerlodge

Park, head northeast on Hwy. 40 from park headquarters for 39 miles and turn left on Deerlodge Park Rd. Proceed 14 miles to the campground. From Maybell head southwest on Hwy. 40 for 16 miles and take a right onto Deerlodge Park Rd.

Echo Park Campground (11 sites) is a primitive campground located in Echo Park at the confluence of the Green and Yampa rivers. This small meadow borders the river and is surrounded by sandstone walls and Steamboat Rock, a monstrous fin of sandstone around which the river flows. No fee; drinking water in summer. Echo Park Campground is reached by following Harper's Corner Rd. 25 miles from park headquarters. Take a right onto Echo Park Rd. (dirt) and go 13 miles. Echo Park Rd. is very steep in spots and impassable when wet. Big RVs and trailers should not attempt the drive. For more information about Echo Park see the Scenic Drives section.

Gates of Lodore Campground (17 sites) is located at the north end of the park at the entrance to Lodore Canyon on the Green River. Most rafters put in here for a float down through the monument. To reach the campground from park headquarters, head northeast on Hwy. 40 for 55 miles to Maybell. At Maybell turn northwest on Hwy. 318 and proceed 41 miles to a turn-off, heading left on a dirt road for 10 more miles to the campground. No fee;

drinking water in summer; open year-round.

Rainbow Park Campground (4 sites) and the primitive Ruple Ranch Campground (camping is allowed, but there are no designated sites) are located on the north side of the Green River, 26 miles and 31 miles, respectively, from the Dinosaur Quarry. The road in to these campgrounds is rough and impassable when wet. No fee. Both campgrounds have put-ins for rafters taking day trips through Split Mountain Gorge and the famous S.O.B. Rapids.

Split Mountain Campground (33 sites) and **Green River Campground** (77 sites) are the only modern campgrounds,

located 4 and 5 miles east of the Dinosaur Quarry, respectively. Fee charged. This is where many rafters take out after a trip downriver. Split Mountain itself is quite a geological wonder. The Green River has somehow scoured and scraped away at the rock, splitting the mountain down the middle and baffling geologists at the same time. Green River Campground is open from Memorial Day to Labor Day. NOTICE: As of this edition, Split Mountain Campground is open only in winter (no water or rest rooms; no fee) due to budget cuts; hopefully this will change in the near future and summer visitors can be accommodated.

SERVICES

Park Headquarters—
Superintendent, Dinosaur National Monument, 4545 Hwy 40, Dinosaur, CO 81610; (303) 374-2216.

Glenwood Springs

Indians, prospectors, gamblers, health nuts—throughout the years Glenwood Springs has attracted many types of souls, giving the area a colorful history matched only by the surrounding natural beauty.

Located at the confluence of the Colorado and Roaring Fork rivers, Glenwood Springs is best known for its hot springs pool. Originally used by the Ute Indians, the hot mineral springs began attracting wealthy miners and aristocrats from around the world when the resort was built in the 1880s. These bluebloods who came to "take the waters" received first-class service at the famous Hotel Colorado. For over 100 years, people have come to Glenwood Springs to get out and enjoy the surrounding mountains. Outdoor recreational possibilities here are numerous. Great downhill skiing is nearby at Sunlight and Aspen. The surrounding White River National Forest offers backcountry paradise. The Colorado River running through the spectacular Glenwood Canyon to the east of town has some pretty good whitewater stretches for rafters. The recently completed stretch of Interstate 70 through Glenwood Canyon and the bike trail along the river are extremely impressive (see Major Attractions section). The list goes on.

Today tourism still dominates the local economy. In contrast to its upvalley neighbor, Aspen, Glenwood is a resort town characterized by affordable prices and friendly, down-to-earth people. Noteworthy lodging and memorable dining make Glenwood Springs a highly recommended destination for Coloradans and out-of-staters alike.

HISTORY

Long before the first white settler entered the Glenwood Springs area, the Utes returned to the hot springs each season to bathe in the waters and enjoy the rejuvenating steam of the vapor caves. The Utes called the hot springs *Yampah*, meaning "Big Medicine," and jealously protected them from other tribes. The site held religious significance for the Utes, and they believed the waters had magical healing powers. Isolated from the Anglo settlements to the east, the springs were not officially "discovered" until 1860. Capt. Richard Sopris was in the area to prospect, survey and explore. When a member of his party was hurt in a fall, the Utes welcomed the group to the hot springs and helped nurse the injured man back to health. Sopris named the spot Grand Springs.

It was not until 20 years later that the first permanent settler appeared. In 1880 James Landis, from Leadville, arrived and claimed the hot springs as his property. This took a lot of guts (or stupidity), because, at the time, the Glenwood area was still part of the Ute territory. But the

Utes were soon driven out. The land in the valley was rich and could be easily irrigated. Settlers began to trickle in, as well as frustrated miners from camps in the Flat Tops area. The town's name was changed to Glenwood Springs in honor of an early pioneer's hometown, Glenwood, Iowa.

In 1885 Walter Devereux began his effort to put Glenwood Springs on the map as a hot springs resort. Devereux was an engineer, educated at both Princeton and Columbia universities, who had been sent to Aspen to work for silver magnate and town benefactor Jerome B. Wheeler. He made his fortune quickly in the silver strikes at Aspen and then turned his attention to Glenwood Springs. Devereux incorporated the town and purchased the hot springs along with 320 acres on the south side of the Colorado River. Then, with the help of some English investors, he began to build the resort he hoped would bring a little class and culture to the area.

The influx of big money into Glenwood attracted many questionable characters, and by 1887 there were no less than 22 bars within a two-block area. Among these high-profile low-lifes was Doc Holliday, the card-dealing, gun-toting dentist of Wild West fame.

Development was rapid. In 1887 the Denver & Rio Grande Railroad arrived in Glenwood Springs to much celebration, after blasting its way through the last 20 miles of Glenwood Canyon. The town now had contact with the outside world. By 1888 the world's largest hot springs pool was completed. Measuring 615 feet by 75 feet, the brick-lined pool was created by diverting the Colorado River. This unenviable task was given to the local jail inmates, who pounded away at "jailbird rock" in order to earn meals. The bathhouse was completed in 1890; it featured, among other things, a beautiful casino upstairs (used today as offices).

The icing on the cake was the completion of the Hotel Colorado in 1893, two months before the demonetization of silver and the onset of nationwide economic troubles. However, the hotel did not suffer much, as many of the guests were foreigners or the super-rich Astors and Vanderbilts. For more about Hotel Colorado history, see the Where to Stay section.

In the late 1800s a strange phenomenon developed in Glenwood Springs—the "dude cowboy." Many European aristocrats visited the resort and thought it only fitting to take a trip into the wilderness before returning home. Local cowboys made good money as guides and quite often tried to play tricks on these rich "city slickers." Sometimes the tricks backfired. Al Anderson, a famous local guide, tried to make a fool of his customer, Lord Rathbone, by losing him in the wilderness. Miles from nowhere, Anderson took off on his horse through some impossibly thick brush. To his great surprise, Lord Rathbone kept up with him, saying only, "By jove, that was a lively canter!" Today, of course, dude ranches exist all over the West.

Glenwood Springs was well known for its polo teams at the turn of the century. The Glenwood Polo and Racing Association won the National Championship in 1903, 1904 and 1912. On more than one occasion, however, club members were trounced by a team of local cowboys riding cow ponies instead of thoroughbreds.

After World War I, hot springs resorts went out of fashion and Glenwood's glamorous days faded into a memory. Things weren't necessarily quiet, though. During Prohibition, the town achieved a questionable distinction by becoming a haven for Al Capone and other Chicago mobsters on the run.

History is everywhere in Glenwood Springs, and the town takes great pains to keep historical buildings intact and renovated. With the hot springs, Glenwood remains one of the best places in the state to visit for a relaxing vacation.

GETTING THERE

Glenwood Springs lies conveniently along Interstate 70, 160 miles west of Denver. It is easily accessible by car or train. **Amtrak** trains stop in Glenwood twice a day: one headed east and one headed west. Call Amtrak for more information at **1-800-USA-RAIL. Greyhound Bus Lines (303) 945-8501** has service to Glenwood Springs. Commuter buses run between Aspen and Rifle via **Aspen Limousine (800) 222-2112.**

Aspen's airport, 40 miles up the Roaring Fork Valley, and the Eagle County airport, 30 miles east on Interstate 70, have daily flights from Denver year-round.

———————— MAJOR ATTRACTIONS ————————

Glenwood Canyon

OK, so it's not visible from outer space like the Great Wall of China. But the newly completed 12-mile stretch of four-lane freeway squeezed into the narrow Glenwood Canyon—the final piece in the interstate highway system—is surely an engineering Wonder of the World. Many say it will serve as a prototype for similar highway projects worldwide.

Completed after 13 years of steady work, the Glenwood Canyon project represents an impressive collaboration/compromise between ardent environmentalists and those eager to see the pristine canyon confines tamed by a superhighway. Engineers marvel at the impressive 6 miles of above-ground viaduct and 2 miles of tunnel that lie along the way. "Enviros" point to other facts that project managers faced: any rock blasted away from the 2,000-foot walls needed to be resculpted, revegetated and stained to match the natural surroundings. In addition, trees and other vegetation were purposely worked around and over to avoid any damage. An environmentally sensitive highway?!

Although it's heavily traveled by trains, bikes, rafts and cars, Glenwood Canyon remains one of the most beautiful canyons in the state. This 1,800-foot-high canyon was carved by the Colorado River through layers of sedimentary rock, the oldest being 600-million-year-old Precambrian granite.

The drive through the canyon is spectacular in its own right, but if you have time, head east into the canyon from Glenwood Springs along the cement bike path. The spectacular 20-mile bike path follows the Colorado River through the canyon at river level. It can be reached by continuing east from the Vapor Caves on 6th St.

Glenwood Hot Springs Pool

Completed more than 100 years ago, this facility has been soothing everyone from saddle-sore cowboys to skiers ever since. You'd be foolish not to come and relax at the "world's largest outdoor mineral hot springs pool." (See the History section for more information.) Open year-round, visitors suntan on the grassy area in summer; in winter, the pool provides a steamy haven from the surrounding snow. There are two pools: the large one (which can hold over 1,000 swimmers) is heated to 90° F, and the smaller, therapeutic pool is maintained at 104° F. The hydro-tube water slide is a kick. Towels and swimsuits can be rented. Also accessible are the athletic club, bathing suit shop and restaurant. The pools are closed the second Wed. of each month during Sept. through May. Hours are 9 am–10 pm in winter and 7:30 am–10 pm in summer. Located on the north side of the river. **401 N. River St., Glenwood Springs, CO 81601; (303) 945-7131.**

Yampah Spa and Vapor Caves

For hundreds of years before settlers "discovered" Glenwood Springs, the Utes brought their sick and ailing to partake in the healing qualities of the vapor caves. These caves, formed by hot mineral water percolating up through fissures in the rocks, supposedly have curative powers that alleviate a variety of ailments, from asthma to constipation. The original Ute cave was on the south side of the river. Last used in 1887, it was sealed over and now lies under the railroad tracks. Though such equipment is standard today, the caves were quite luxurious when first developed in the 1880s with marble benches and electric lighting. Back then men and women had separate bathing times and wore linen bags with a drawstring at the neck as suits.

The Vapor Caves were recently renovated by owners who bring their expertise from running spas in Calistoga, California. In addition to enjoying the soothing steam caves so well known by the Utes, today you can opt for other services ranging from private hot tubs to massages to facials to leg waxing. Soothing, new-agey tunes waft throughout the facility. Three separate caves are heated to a piping hot 110° F. Open every day of the year 9 am–9 pm. Located next to the hot springs pool at **709 E. 6th St., Glenwood Springs, CO 81601; (303) 945-0667.**

FACTS ABOUT THE GLENWOOD CANYON HIGHWAY

- 13 years to build
- $500 million spent
- 60 million pounds of steel used
- 400,000 cubic yards of concrete poured (1.62 billion pounds)
- 300,000 cubic yards of dirt and rock moved, but not removed from the canyon
- 150,000 new bushes and trees planted, complete with drip irrigation
- Hanging Lake tunnels lined with 2.5 million ceramic tiles

FESTIVALS AND EVENTS

Strawberry Days

mid-June

Since 1898 the residents of Glenwood Springs and the surrounding area have celebrated what is now the oldest civic festival in the state—Strawberry Days. The festivities have been expanded over the years to include such things as a pony express ride, western band performances, a 5K and 10K footrace and a mountain bike race. One thing that hasn't changed over the years is the free strawberries and ice cream. For more information call **(303) 945-6589.**

OUTDOOR ACTIVITIES

BIKING

MOUNTAIN BIKING

Many of the trails listed as cross-country skiing and hiking routes are also fine for mountain biking. The possibilities are limitless. One area worth checking out is located northwest of Dotsero. Head east 18 miles on Interstate 70 to Dotsero and head north. Two roads, Coffee Pot Rd. and Sweetwater Rd., both head off to the left within a few miles, providing access to the **Flat Tops** area of the White River National Forest. According to an avid Glenwood mountain biker, "The Flat Tops is like a little northern Michigan plopped down at 10,000 feet, man." This translates roughly to "It's a great place to mountain bike." If you do head up to the Flat Tops, remember that no bikes are allowed in the wilderness area.

You might also try a ride up **Red Mountain,** an old ski area located on the end of West 9th St. Bike to the top of the dirt road for a great view of town and the valley. Another nearby possibility is **Red Canyon Rd.** (County Rd. 115) about 2 miles south of town on the west side of Hwy 82. The road climbs steeply for 2 miles and then levels off a bit for the next 1.8 miles to the trailhead for Lookout Mt. Park. Scrub oak dominate the surroundings as do far-off views to Mt. Sopris and the valley south to Aspen.

Other mountain bikers enjoy the trail system up **Four-Mile Rd.** near Ski Sunlight. The road climbs from just below the Sunlight Inn lodge for 4 miles or more up to **Four Mile Park** where you will find a network of roads and single track trails waiting. Here you'll see tons of wildflowers in summer and more than enough aspen for beautiful autumn cruises.

For additional ideas, get a copy of the *Hiking & Biking Trails* brochure that contains information on 19 trails. It's available at the **White River National Forest Office** at **9th and Grand Ave.** or the **Glenwood Springs Chamber Resort Association** at **1102 Grand Ave.**

TOURING

Glenwood Canyon—

See the Major Attractions section.

Rentals and Information—

Alpine Bicycle rents just about everything you need to get going, including mountain bikes, cross bikes and accessories. They can also give trail ideas. Open daily year-round 9 am–6 pm. **51027 Hwy 6, Suite 117; (303) 945-6434.** Information and rentals also available at BSR, **210 7th St.; (303) 945-7317.** Talk to Scratch and the boys.

FISHING

Fishing in the Glenwood Springs vicinity can be excellent. For local information about where the fish are biting, visit **Roaring Fork Anglers, at 2022 Grand Ave., Glenwood Springs, CO 81601; (303) 945-0180.** The guys here also run a fishing guide service that includes float trips down rivers in the state. Here are some places that tend to be consistently good:

Fryingpan River—
Arguably one of the finest stretches of Gold Medal water in the state, the Fryingpan flows into the Roaring Fork River at the small town of Basalt, 24 miles southeast of Glenwood Springs. For more information, see the Fishing section in the **Aspen** chapter.

Rifle Gap Reservoir State Park—
No question that when the water level is up, this is a pretty place to throw a line. Clear blue water is hemmed in by sandstone and shale cliffs. Browns, rainbows, walleyes and bass are all caught here. Keep an eye out for underwater spear fishers, who like this area for the exceptionally clear water. Snagging one of them would not be a pretty sight. To reach Rifle Gap Reservoir from Glenwood Springs, take Interstate 70 west for 26 miles to Rifle. At Rifle, head north on Hwy. 13 for 5 miles to a junction with Hwy. 325. Turn right and continue 5 miles to the state park. For information about how the fish are biting, contact the **Park Office** at **(303) 625-1607.**

FOUR-WHEEL-DRIVE TRIPS

Transfer Trail—
Climbing the mountains toward the Flat Tops to the north of town is Transfer Trail. This extremely rough road (four-wheel-drive only after 2 miles!) was once part of the Ute trail system and then a toll road that at one time crossed the Flat Tops to the Meeker area. The first section of the road provides spectacular views down on Glenwood Springs as well as No Name Canyon. Transfer Trail also connects with other four-wheel-drive roads in the Flat Tops area. From Glenwood Springs drive west on Hwy. 6 toward West Glenwood and turn north (right) onto Transfer Trail (Forest Rd. 6020). An easier route up into the Flat Tops is Coffee Pot Road (Forest Rd. 600) which can be accessed 2 miles north of Dotsero, just east of Glenwood Canyon. Hard cores can eventually reach Coffee Pot Rd. from Transfer Trail and do a loop back to town.

Toward Aspen—
For some spectacular, nearby four-wheel opportunities, see the **Aspen** and the **Redstone and Crystal River Valley** chapters.

GOLF

Glenwood Springs Golf Club—
This mature nine-hole course enjoys a commanding view up the Roaring Fork Valley to Mt. Sopris. Pro shop and restaurant; carts available. **193 Sunny Acres Rd.; (303) 945-7086.**

Johnson Park Miniature Golf—
That's right, miniature golf. This place, boasting two 18-hole putt-putt courses, is definitely worth a visit if you are with the family or just want to kill a couple of hours. Water cascades down a waterfall, winding its way through one of the only naturally landscaped putt-putt courses in the country. Skee-ball, picnic tables and snacks are available. Open Memorial Day to Labor Day, 9 am–10 pm; the months of May and Sept., noon–9 pm; Apr. and Oct., Fri.–Sun., noon–9 pm. **51579 Hwy. 6** (between Glenwood and West Glenwood); **(303) 945-9608.**

Rifle Creek Golf Course—
Avid golfers from around the state rank Rifle Creek high on their list of mountain courses, and with good reason. It's highly scenic, with strange lava dike formations of the Hogback Range running throughout the course. This 18-hole championship course is plenty challenging, especially the hilly front nine, which is characterized by a number of canyons and spectacular elevated tee boxes. The creek comes into play on many of the back nine holes, where you'll also see numerous woolly marmots. A memorable mountain course but, alas, the greens fees are steep! Open Mar.–Nov. Located 5 miles north of Rifle on Hwy. 13, and then right on Hwy. 325 for about 4 miles. **3004 Hwy. 325, Rifle, CO 81650; (303) 625-1093.**

Westbank Ranch Golf Course—

This nine-hole course is located in the Roaring Fork Valley, about 5 miles south of Glenwood, just off Hwy. 82 on Old Hwy. 82. It has a pro shop and restaurant. Par is 70, and the course plays 6,264 yards from the men's tees. **1007 Westbank Rd.; (303) 945-7032.**

HIKING AND BACKPACKING

Up the Roaring Fork Valley from Glenwood Springs no less than four wilderness areas can be reached for day hikes and extended overnight trips within White River and Gunnison national forests. Possible trails in these areas are discussed in the **Aspen** and **Redstone and Crystal River Valley** chapters. Contact the **White River National Forest Headquarters** in Glenwood Springs for maps, trail ideas, etc. **900 Grand Ave., Old Federal Building, Glenwood Springs, CO 81601; (303) 945-2521.** The National Forest Office and the Glenwood Springs Chamber Resort Association Office are also the place to stop in for a free copy of the *Hiking & Bike Trails* brochure which describes 19 trail ideas. **Summit Canyon Mountaineering,** located at **1001 Grand Ave.; (303) 945-6994,** has rental equipment available as well as information you may need.

In the immediate vicinity of Glenwood Springs there are a number of memorable day hikes. Here are a few:

Boy Scout Trail—

This is a relatively short, moderate hike that offers great bird's-eye views of the town, the Roaring Fork Valley and Glenwood Canyon. Near the turn of the century, an observatory was built at the top of the hill, and in 1910 the trail got much use as people flocked to the observatory at night for a view of Halley's Comet. The observatory burned shortly thereafter and was never rebuilt. The 1.5-mile trail begins at the dead end at the east end of 8th St. Follow the signs.

Doc Holliday's Grave—

Just about anyone can take this easy half-mile hike to Linwood Cemetery. Lying on an eastern promontory, the cemetery overlooks town and a large portion of the valley. The second person to be buried here was Doc Holliday, famous gambler and shootist from the Old West. Holliday came to Glenwood Springs in the spring of 1887 to relieve his tuberculosis. It didn't help. Holliday died in November of that year at the young age of 35. Friends pitched in to buy a casket and bury him in this hilltop cemetery. Controversy still rages about whether or not he was really buried in the cemetery or in a plot in town. At any rate, a stone marker in the cemetery commemorates Doc Holliday and says he died in bed, a sentiment Holliday would have been proud of.

Few people know that another famous (infamous, perhaps) character from the Old West is also buried in the cemetery. In the pauper grave section, a stone with the name "Harvey Logan" marks the resting place of Kid Curry. He was a noted bank robber and a one-time member of Butch Cassidy's legendary Hole-in-the-Wall Gang. The trail to the cemetery begins at 12th St. and Palmer Ave. A sign marks the trailhead. The hike takes about 15 minutes.

Hanging Lake—

An extremely popular hiking destination, Hanging Lake is both scenic and easily accessible. It was formed by a geologic fault that caused the lake to drop down from the valley floor above, from where it is currently fed by a series of cascading waterfalls. The 1.2-mile trail, which climbs 930 feet from the floor of Glenwood Canyon, takes about one hour and is definitely worth the climb. Views of the falls and back down Deadhorse Canyon are spectacular. Tip: Be sure also to hike an extra 200 yards above the lake to Spouting Rock, where the full force of the creek shoots directly out of a hole in the cliffside. Hanging Lake's large number of visitors make it important to help preserve the beauty of the surrounding environment by sticking to the designated trails. To reach the trailhead, head east 10 miles into Glenwood Canyon on Interstate 70 from Glenwood Springs. Look for the exit to the parking area.

HORSEBACK RIDING

Canyon Creek Outfitter—
Located just west of Glenwood Springs, this outfitter specializes in breakfast and dinner rides, but also offers hourlong and full-day trips. To reach Canyon Creek Outfitter from Glenwood Springs, head west on Interstate 70 for 7.5 miles to the Canyon Creek exit, and follow the Frontage Road another mile west to the stables. **P.O. Box 862, Glenwood Springs, CO 81601; (303) 984-2000 or 984-2052.**

RIVER FLOATING

Colorado River—
As you probably know by now, the Colorado River flows right through Glenwood Springs, paralleling Interstate 70 on its way west. A 20-mile stretch of river that is very popular for floating begins just below Shoshone Power Plant (in Glenwood Canyon), crashes down through the canyon, through Glenwood Springs and downriver to New Castle. The Glenwood Canyon stretch has some exciting rapids, petering out at the mouth of Grizzly Creek. The calm water down through town offers just a few ripples. Below Glenwood Springs the river enters South Canyon, which offers some exciting rapids for the remainder of the way to New Castle.

Roaring Fork River—
The 13.5-mile stretch from Carbondale on down to Glenwood Springs along the Roaring Fork River is popular with many kayakers, rafters and canoeists. The rapids are fairly mellow (Class I and Class II), but offer a few surprises, especially for people just out for a leisurely float. The river drops an average of 27 feet per mile along this stretch, with many good places to take out on the north end of Glenwood Springs.

Outfitters—
Blue Sky—With its office located on the ground floor of the Hotel Colorado, Blue Sky has been offering trips on the Colorado and Roaring Fork since 1975. Family and group discounts are available. Blue Sky asks that advance reservations be made for both the half- and full-day trips. Located in the Hotel Colorado basement; **(303) 945-6605.**

Rock Gardens—Locals consistently give high praise to Rock Gardens Rafting, which offers trips down the Colorado from Shoshone Power Plant in Glenwood Canyon and along the Roaring Fork. Located just off the No Name exit in Glenwood Canyon at **1308 County Rd. 129; (303) 945-6737.**

SKIING
CROSS-COUNTRY SKIING
As with hiking and mountain biking in the Glenwood Springs area, the crosscountry skiing possibilities are plentiful. Whether it's track skiing or a backcountry adventure, you'll find it close by.

For further information about trail possibilities, maps and avalanche danger, contact the **White River National Forest Headquarters** in Glenwood Springs at **9th and Grand, Glenwood Springs, CO 81601; (303) 945-2521.**

Backcountry Trails—
The **West Elk Creek** area, located about 16 miles northwest of Glenwood Springs, has a number of good trails on White River National Forest land. The trails head north, eventually reaching the Flat Tops Wilderness Area. To get to the trails, head west on Interstate 70 from Glenwood Springs for 11 miles and turn northwest on Elk Creek Rd. at New Castle. Drive a few miles to West Elk Creek Rd. (County Rd. 244) and take a right. Trails leading to the right off this road begin after a mile or so.

Sunlight Peak and **Four Mile Park** trails are two other close possibilities. From the 10,603-foot summit of Sunlight Trail, views up and down the Roaring Fork Valley are fantastic. Four Mile Park trails are well maintained in winter for snowmobile use. If you don't mind sharing the trails with machines, you may like the area. The Four Mile Park trails extend to Grand Mesa, about 30 miles to the west. Both are located near the Ski Sunlight ski area. Take the right fork just below the ski area onto Forest Rd. 300. From the fork go about 2 miles to the Forest Rd. 318 turn-off to the right. Sunlight Trail begins here. About 2 miles farther up Forest Rd. 300, Four Mile Park trails begin.

Groomed Trails—

Ski Sunlight Nordic Center—Located at the ski area, this center has an extensive trail system that is well integrated with the downhill facilities. Cross-country trails can be reached from the Ski Sunlight base, as well as from the top of the Primo and Segundo chair lifts, making this area ideal for telemarking. Equipment rental and cross-country skiing lessons (including telemark) are available. Track fee. Only two thirds of a kilometer down the trail from the parking lot is the **Back Country Cabin ($$)**, available for overnight stays for up to 15 people. **10901 County Rd. 117 (Four Mile Rd.), Glenwood Springs, CO 81601; (303) 945-7491;** toll free **1-800-445-7931.**

Spring Gulch Trail System—This spectacular (and free) brainchild of the Mount Sopris Nordic Council occupies a scenic spot near both the Crystal River and Roaring Fork River valleys. Head south for 12 miles on Hwy. 82 to Carbondale and then west for 7 miles on County Rd. 108. For more information see the Skiing section of the **Redstone and Crystal River Valley** chapter.

Rentals and Information—

Sturdy backcountry cross-country skiing equipment, including telemark skis,

can be rented at **Summit Canyon Mountaineering** in Glenwood Springs at **1001 Grand Ave.; (303) 945-6994.**

DOWNHILL SKIING

Aspen—

Forty-two miles south of Glenwood Springs on Hwy. 82. See the Skiing section of the **Aspen** chapter.

Ski Sunlight—

"We are not high-tech ... we're high-touch," explains Tom Jankovsky, general manager of this family-oriented ski area just 10 miles out of Glenwood Springs. Offering good value in a laid-back atmosphere, Ski Sunlight is a great alternative to the larger resort areas on the Western Slope. Besides, where else can you ski all day and then soak your sore muscles in the world's largest hot springs pool?

Ski Sunlight's vertical drop is 2,010 feet. Runs are primarily intermediate, but there is something for everyone. Free shuttle buses are available from town. Reasonably priced package deals include a lift ticket, lodging in town and a pass to the hot springs pool. Ski Sunlight prides itself on its lesson packages. If you're tired of the glitz and high lift prices at bigger resorts, try Ski Sunlight. **10901 County Rd. 117 (Four Mile Rd.), Glenwood Springs, CO 81601; (303) 945-7491;** toll free **1-800-445-7931.**

Rentals—

In Glenwood, downhill rentals are available at **Ski Sunlight Ski Shop, 1315 Grand Ave.; (303) 945-9425;** and **Blue Sky Ski Rental & Repair; (303) 945-1552,** located in the Hotel Colorado basement.

SWIMMING

Glenwood Hot Springs Pool—

See the Major Attractions section.

——————— SEEING AND DOING ———————

MUSEUMS AND GALLERIES

Frontier Historical Museum—

Actually this is a pretty good place to get a feel for the history of Glenwood Springs and the surrounding area. Information and artifacts about the development of Glenwood's Yampah Hot Springs, coal mining in the area and Teddy Roosevelt's visits highlight the displays. Upstairs in the Tabor Room is a hand-carved bed and dresser that once belonged to H.A.W. and Baby Doe Tabor of Leadville silver-boom fame. Small fee for visitors over 12. Thurs.–Sat. 1–4 pm in winter; Mon.–Sat. 1–4 pm during summer. Located at **1001 Colorado Ave.; (303) 945-4448.**

NIGHTLIFE

The Bayou—

Great live rock and blues music Sun. Fantastic deck in warm-weather months. See the Where to Eat section for more information.

Mother O'Leary's—

Live rock and roll nightly. Pool tables, loud and smoky. **914 Grand Ave.; (303) 945-4078.**

SCENIC DRIVES

Glenwood Canyon—

See the Major Attractions section.

Rifle Falls State Park—

Located 39 miles northwest of Glenwood Springs, Rifle Falls stands out as an oasis in this semi-arid part of the state. At the base of the 50-foot falls, lush green ferns, flowers and moss flourish. It's an attractive place to visit. Below the cliffs from which the falls plummet are a number of limestone caves ideally suited for novices (no pits or brain-twisting labyrinths). Coyote Trail leads to an observation point at the top of the falls.

To reach Rifle Falls State Park from Glenwood Springs, drive west on Interstate 70 for 26 miles to Rifle. At Rifle, head north on Hwy. 13 for 5 miles to a junction with Hwy. 325. Turn right and continue 11 miles (past Rifle Gap Reservoir) to Rifle Falls State Park on the right. The campground has 18 sites; fee charged. You'll find a good map of the area here. Be sure to take the short hike to the falls.

——————— WHERE TO STAY ———————

ACCOMMODATIONS

Glenwood is generally not a place to show up without a lodging reservation; during many times of the year things can get tight. On the north side of town, stretching toward West Glenwood you'll find a lengthy row of motels including a Best Western, Ramada, Affordable Inn, just to name a few. Reservations can be made quickly and easily through the **Glenwood Central Reservations** number at **1-800-221-0098.** Below are a number of suggested standouts that range from the historic to romantic.

Hotel Colorado—$$$ to $$$$

As far as history goes, the Hotel Colorado certainly rivals Colorado's grand hotels for title of "Granddaddy of them all." Since its illustrious opening in June 1893, Hotel Colorado has lodged and entertained notables from all over the world, including six US presidents.

Walter B. Devereux opened the hotel as the final stage of his dream of a world-class spa in the mountains. The hotel, which at the time cost $850,000, was built Italian Renaissance style and rooms went for $5 per night ($200 by today's standards). No detail was overlooked in making this a hotel for royalty.

In 1905 the hotel became the White House of the West when Teddy Roosevelt came and stayed while bear hunting in the surrounding mountains. One day he returned empty-handed from his hunt. The story goes that hotel maids sewed some old rags together and made a stuffed toy resembling a bear which they presented to the president. Newspaper people had a heyday with the bear, as did the public. The result was the birth of the teddy bear. Today the gift shop near the main desk features every kind of teddy bear imaginable.

President William Howard Taft visited the hotel a few years later and greatly enjoyed the accommodations—especially the oversized bathtubs. As the heaviest president, Taft reportedly had gotten stuck in a bathtub at the Brown Palace Hotel in Denver.

As the 20th century pushed on, the hotel relaxed its decorum and admitted the common man, including gangsters of the late 1920s. During World War II the navy turned the hotel into a naval hospital. Wide hallways, therapeutic waters and good rail connections to the coast made it an obvious choice.

Today this 126-room hotel is pushing its centennial. And to mark the occasion, much-needed renovation has greatly improved the appearance of the lower-priced rooms as well as the hallways. If you decide to stay at the hotel, take note: spend a few extra dollars on a deluxe room or suite, which are decorated in antiques and generally are in nice shape. History buffs should ask for Room 230, where both presidents Taft and Roosevelt made speeches to the people in the courtyard below. The Bell Tower Room at the top of the hotel contains a spiral staircase and a sun deck with a commanding view. The hotel also offers dining in the Devereux Room. **526 Pine St., Glenwood Springs, CO 81601; 1-800-544-3998; (303) 945-6511; toll free from Denver, (303) 623-3400.**

Hotel Denver—$$$ to $$$$

The Hotel Denver, built in 1906, is arguably the plushest, most amenity-conscious lodging opportunity you'll find in Glenwood. Located across the street from the Amtrak train station, the hotel offers 60 well-appointed soundproof rooms with special touches like morning papers delivered to your door along with a homemade muffin.

A recent renovation, in an attractive art-deco style, features a three-story glass atrium near the restaurants and front desk. Speaking of restaurants, two on site—the **Daily Bread Too** and the **7th Street Grill**— are worth a visit. The hotel is centrally located, just a short walk from the hot springs pool. Special weekend/low season rates and package rates are plentiful; kids stay free! **402 7th St., Glenwood Springs, CO 81601; 1-800-826-8820 or (303) 945-6565.**

Brettelberg Condominiums—$$ to $$$

Though we normally don't do specific write-ups on condominium complexes, the Brettelberg deserves a mention. Located on the mountain at Ski Sunlight, the Brettelberg provides reasonably priced accommodations ideal for skiers or anyone who appreciates a remote mountain locale. In winter you can ski right from your door; the rest of the year you'll find a lot of peace and quiet with quick access to hiking, mountain biking and other pastimes in the surrounding White River National Forest.

Each of the 47 condos at the Brettelberg comes fully furnished with kitchens, but they are certainly not fancy. Since the units are individually owned, the decor and furnishings vary, reflecting the style of the owners. Condos can be rented by the night or week. Rec room and laundry facilities available. This is definitely a nice alternative to staying in town. **11101 Road 117, Glenwood Springs, CO 81601; (303) 945-7421 or 1-800-634-0481.**

Kaiser House—$$ to $$$

Built in 1902 by Glenwood Springs' first electrician, the restored Kaiser House creates an overall feel that is crisp, clean and comfortable. Current owners Glen and Ingrid Eash gutted the entire house in 1988, keeping the woodwork and rebuilding with a decorating mix of contemporary comfort and antiques. Each of the seven rooms (four upstairs, two in the basement and one in the attic) has a private bath and, of course, an exquisite breakfast is included in the rates. Honeymooners may want to consider a stay in the Turret Room with its valentine motif. A hot tub can be found out back on a nice little patio. No smoking, no pets and no kids under 8. **932 Cooper Ave., Glenwood Springs, CO 81601; (303) 945-8827.**

Glenwood Springs Hostel—$

Offering dormitory-style accommodations and one private room, this AYH hostel provides a friendly alternative to those traveling on a budget. Gary, the owner, is particularly helpful to visitors who want information about what to do in the area. Mountain bike rentals are available. Located at **1021 Grand Ave., Glenwood Springs, CO 81601; (303) 945-8545.**

CAMPING

Rifle Falls State Park—

Located 6 miles beyond Rifle Gap State Park on Hwy. 325. For more information see the Scenic Drives section.

Rifle Gap State Park—

Located northwest of Glenwood Springs. Head west on Interstate 70 for 26 miles to Rifle and then north for 5 miles on Hwy. 13. Turn right on Hwy. 325 and proceed for 5 miles. There are 46 sites, and a fee is charged.

White River National Forest Northeast of Glenwood Springs—

Drive east on Interstate 70 for 18 miles to Dotsero. Head north for 2 miles and take a left on Forest Rd. 600 (Coffee Pot Rd.) and proceed about 16 miles to **Coffee Pot Spring Campground.** Coffee Pot has 15 sites, no water and no fee. On up at the end of the road (another 15 miles) are **Supply Basin Campground** (6 sites), **Kline's Folly Campground** (4 sites) and **Deep Lake Campground** (21 sites). None of these has drinking water or charges fees. Supply Basin and Kline's Folly campgrounds are located on Heart Lake; Deep Lake Campground on the shore of Deep Lake.

About 8 miles north of Dotsero, take a left on Sweetwater Lake Rd. and drive 10 miles to **Sweetwater Lake Campground.** There are 9 sites, drinking water and a fee charged.

White River National Forest Northwest of Glenwood Springs—

About 7 miles north of Rifle Falls State Recreation Area (see Scenic Drives for location) is **Three Forks Campground** (4 sites). No fee.

White River National Forest South of Glenwood Springs—

Many beautiful camping opportunities exist upvalley from Glenwood. For ideas see the Camping sections of the **Aspen** and **Redstone and Crystal River Valley** chapters.

Private Campgrounds—

The Hideout—For cushy camping this place offers close proximity to town, RV hookups and tent sites. Twelve rental cabins ($$ to $$$) with maid service are just the thing for people who can't decide whether they want a weekend in town or one in the woods. Laundry, showers and a store available. Advance reservations during summer are suggested. Open in winter also. **1293 County Rd. 117; (303) 945-5621.**

Rock Gardens—Located along the Colorado River in Glenwood Canyon at No Name Canyon exit, Rock Garden offers both hookups and tent sites. **1308 County Rd. 129; (303) 945-6737.**

WHERE TO EAT

Sopris Restaurant and Lounge—$$$

Perhaps the finest restaurant in the Roaring Fork Valley. Owner and chef Kurt Wigger spent 17 years tickling customers' taste buds at the Red Onion Restaurant in Aspen before opening the Sopris in 1974. Originally from Lucerne, Switzerland, Wigger has professional chef credentials that include membership in the elite *Confrérie de la chaîne des rôtisseurs* of France. After serving celebrities such as Clint Eastwood, George C. Scott, Cybill Shepherd and Vince Bzdek, Wigger surely must have felt his life was complete when Jill St. John announced, "Kurt, I love your crazy cooking." It is impressive fare. Specialties include oysters Rockefeller, lobster Newburg, veal piccata, Milanese and pepper steak flambé. The restaurant is a bit dark, unfortunately, with no view up the valley to Mt. Sopris. The dress code is wide open—some patrons wear jeans, others sport coats or evening dresses. Located about 7 miles south of Glenwood Springs on Hwy. 82. Open 5 pm–midnight daily. **7215 Hwy. 82; (303) 945-7771.**

The Bayou—$$ to $$$

Diving dinosaurs, a monthly calendar of events and a guaranteed overall good time helped this establishment get voted by the *Aspen Times* as "The best place to go down valley." Cajun food (especially seafood and freshwater fish) and wild drinks like the Woo Woo and Blue Bayou keep locals coming back for more. Asked why he came to Glenwood Springs in the first place, owner and New York transplant Steve Beham replied, "Tourist women." The enlarged sun deck is at the perfect angle for afternoon rays. Nonetheless, Beham reminded us, "It's not the size of the deck ... it's how you use it." The Bayou has started offering live music Sun. nights. Be sure to ask for the "abuse room." Open 4–10 pm daily. Look for the giant green frog awning at **52103 Hwys. 6 and 24; (303) 945-1047.**

Florindo's—$$ to $$$

Although initially skeptical toward the local ravings about the fine northern Italian cuisine at Florindo's, we were very impressed with this little place in downtown Glenwood Springs. Opened at the beginning of 1989, Florindo's offers ample portions of seafood, veal, pasta and chicken dishes, preceded by plates of delicious Italian bread. Italian wines dominate the wine list. Italian owner Florindo Gallicchio and his Hungarian-born wife, Roza, have really made an impression here with their food. As our eastern-transplant waitress said, "It's to die for!" Open for lunch Mon.–Fri., 11:30 am–3 pm; dinner Mon.–Sat., 5–10:30 pm; closed Sun. **721 Grand Ave.; (303) 945-1245.**

Italian Underground—$$

Florindo's has the northern Italian but "The Underground" is the place to go for southern Italian. With checkered table cloths, chianti bottles and abundance of marinara sauce you expect to see a Sicilian grandmother busy at work in the kitchen. What you'll find instead is Gregory Durrant (whose grandparents ran a similar restaurant in New Castle years ago) preparing the sausage and all bread and pizza dough from scratch. The Underground is well named, occupying a dimly lit, attractively decorated basement room along Grand Ave. The menu features lasagna, pizza, spaghetti and great homemade cannolis. Each of the main entrées comes with salad, bread and ice cream for dessert; popular with families. Open 5–10 pm daily. Located at **715 Grand Ave; (303) 945-6422.**

Los Desperados—$$

The best all-around Mexican restaurant in town, Los Desperados is very popular, especially at lunchtime. Margaritas are good but not world-class. House specialties include the macho burrito, enchilada plate and relleno royale. It's best to keep Glenwood's Mexican dining opportunities in perspective. When asked where the best Mexican food in town was, more than one person responded, "At my house." Open Tues.–Sat. 11:30 am–10 pm, Sun. 4:30–9:30 pm, Mon. 5–10 pm. **0055 Mel-Rey Rd.; (303) 945-6878.**

Avalon Cafe—$ to $$

This was a genuine pleasant surprise on a recent trip to Glenwood. The Avalon is a small, off-beat cafe with an emphasis on great breakfast dishes and coffee. A number of lunch dishes are mixed in as well. Just relax, sip a cappuccino and listen to music in this attractive, well-lighted place.

Louis Giradot, the owner and chef, whips up excellent, healthful dishes for breakfast, such as the spinach brunch crêpe and killer huevos rancheros. For lunch try chicken souvlaki, a sandwich or salad. Top it off with one of the decadent homemade desserts like pecan fudge pie. Open 8 am–4:30 pm Tues.–Sun.; open at 7 am in summer. Located in the King Mall on **Grand Ave.** near the bridge; **(303) 945-9962.**

Daily Bread Cafe and Bakery—$ to $$

Home-cooked meals with large portions characterize this popular breakfast and lunch spot. Each day all of the breads and delicious pastries are made from scratch. In addition to traditional breakfast fare, creative daily specials are served along with notables like granola and Huevos Extraordinaire. For lunch try their monstrous salads and bowls of homemade soup. Top off your meal with a piece of one of their locally famous pies. Wholesome food and a welcome atmosphere have earned the Daily Bread a very loyal and far-flung clientele. Open Mon.–Fri. 7 am–2 pm, Sat. 8 am–2 pm, Sun. 8 am–12 pm. **729 Grand Ave.; (303) 945-6253.** If you find the place too crowded on the weekend, head over to the Hotel Denver and try the breakfast at the newly opened **Daily Bread Too.** Breakfast items are a bit more upscale with items like artichoke and crabmeat Benedict. The Daily Bread Too is open for breakfast Sat. 8 am–12 pm and until 2 pm on Sun. **402 7th St.; (303) 945-1208.**

19th Street Diner—$

The atmosphere and most of the food is a blast from the past. 19th Street Diner, with its black and white checkered linoleum floors, booths and counter seating, serves up Americana with its blue plate special, chicken-fried steak, honey-dipped southern fried chicken and hamburgers. Updated items such as fettucini Dinaldo and mozzarella sticks please the modern palate. Prices are very reasonable at this casual eatery. Full bar at the back. Dining area open Mon.–Sat. 7 am–10 pm, Sun. 7:30 am–8 pm; bar open Mon.–Sat. 6:30 am–1:30 am, Sun. 7:30 am–8 pm. **1908 Grand Ave.; (303) 945-9133.**

SERVICES

Central Reservations—
Toll free **1-800-221-0098.**

Glenwood Springs Chamber Resort Association—

Staffed during business hours with someone to answer questions; self-serve brochure racks accessible after hours. **1102 Grand Ave., Glenwood Springs, CO 81601; (303) 945-6589.**

Grand Junction

It's difficult to explain why more visitors aren't aware of the Grand Junction area; it has so much to offer. Located in the fertile Grand Valley of western Colorado, Grand Junction is surrounded by diverse, rugged country just waiting to be explored. To the southwest is the stark beauty of Colorado National Monument and the canyon country of the Colorado Plateau. Grand Mesa, with its many forests and lakes, towers to the east. To the north the bleak allure of the Book Cliffs captures your attention.

Exposed strata of the surrounding canyons and buttes attract geologists from around the country—but these layers of shale, sedimentary rock and red slickrock sandstone are so riveting, they catch everyone's eye. From within these layers fossilized dinosaur bones have been unearthed since the turn of the century. Discoveries continue almost daily, giving paleontologists more work than they can handle. The sheer number of significant fossil finds and the popularity of dinosaurs in general have turned Grand Junction into a major dinosaur center; museums, natural sites and on-site digs await those who want to learn more.

To fully appreciate Grand Junction you'll want to get out into the natural surroundings. The whitewater kayaking, rafting and canoeing are outstanding in the area, while the wind- and water-scarred plateau country is perfect for mountain biking and hiking. Driving the many scenic highways and backroads in the area is another excellent way to enjoy your stay in Grand Junction.

All of the enticements listed above, as well as mild winter weather, account for Grand Junction's claim as western Colorado's largest town. With many people continuing to relocate here, Grand Junction's future looks bright.

HISTORY

The Northern Ute Reservation occupied most of the Grand Valley until 1881, when the Utes were forcibly expelled from their lands and pushed into Utah to allow Anglo settlement. Ironically the town of Ute was established in 1881, only three months after the Utes moved west. The town's name soon changed to West Denver—a mere 258-mile commute to downtown Denver. Residents eventually settled on a name taken from the town's location at the junction of the Grand and Gunnison rivers. In 1921 the Grand River was renamed the Colorado, and to this day Grand Junction remains a misnomer.

In 1881 settlers were initially drawn to the valley for the semi-arid land, which was perfect for pasturing cattle. By the end of that year, however, irrigation of the valley caused the rich red soil to spring to life. With new emphasis placed on agriculture, cattle ranchers were soon relegated to the high mesas. The young town began carving a niche as a trade center for western Colorado when the Denver & Rio Grande Railroad's main line started service in 1887.

Over the years apricots, cherries, grapes and peaches have provided an economic mainstay for the town as well as the nearby orchard towns of Palisade and Clifton. Even though the economy has diversified over time, Grand Junction has gone through several boom-bust cycles. In the last 40 years, nearby uranium and oil-shale mining promised to turn Grand Junction into a major city. Hopes and regional pride ran high. (During the uranium boom of the 1950s, one travel writer even referred to the uranium mining as "a radioactive icing" on your "vacation cake.") Neither the uranium nor the oil-shale development, however, panned out. Both went bust, leaving Grand Junction with little more than dreams about what might have been.

These days, a growing tourism industry and reputation as an excellent place to relocate are drawing increasing numbers to this spectacular area of the state.

GETTING THERE

Located on Interstate 70, 258 miles west of Denver, Grand Junction is serviced by Greyhound Bus Lines. Amtrak rolls through Grand Junction on its way to the West and East coasts. Walker Field Airport is becoming popular with out-of-state visitors who are worried about air traffic and snow closures at Denver International Airport. With Grand Junction's fine weather, Walker Field has not had a closure in seven years. Direct flights can be booked from many locations around the country with Continental Airlines and America West Airlines.

—————— MAJOR ATTRACTIONS ——————

Dinosaurs

Grand Junction has quickly developed into a destination for paleontologists and others interested in learning more about these creatures that roamed through western Colorado 150 million years ago. Many significant finds, including a bone from supersaurus—the largest dinosaur yet discovered—have been unearthed in the vicinity. Listed below are some ways that you can get into the action.

Dinosaur Valley—Enter the world of scientifically re-created dinosaurs with moving bodies, roving eyes and terrifying roars. There are six half-sized replicas, including an Iguanodon, a Tyrannosaurus Rex and a Stegosaurus. You'll come face to face with aggressive beasts that ripped their opponents' flesh with knife-edged teeth, as well as more docile vegetarians. Also featured is a dinosaur skeleton in the "death pose" and an interesting display of footprints.

A working paleontological laboratory on the premises shows the painstaking work of scientists and volunteers on recent finds in the area. The lab has worked on some of the world's smallest dinosaurs (about the size of a rugby ball) to some of the world's largest. The Grand Junction vicinity is so rich in fossils that new discoveries come in almost daily. Dinosaur Valley is a special exhibit of the Museum of Western Colorado. Ask here about suggested sites to visit in the area. Open May–Sept. daily 9 am–5:30 pm; open Tues.–Sun. the rest of the year 10 am–4:30 pm. Small admission fee. **362 Main St.; (303) 241-9210.**

Dinamation's Dinosaur Discovery Expeditions—Here's your chance to go out in the field and work at an actual dinosaur dig. Multiday expeditions, some for shooting photos and others for actually participating in a dig, are offered in the Grand Junction area, Dinosaur National Monument, Utah, Wyoming and abroad. Trips are led by professional paleontologists. One option includes a special kid's dinosaur camp, where parents can accompany their kids. For specifics, contact **Dinamation International Society, 325 E. Aspen St., Fruita, CO 81521; 1-800-DIG-DINO.**

Rabbit Valley—Walk down the "Trail Through Time" in Rabbit Valley, located west of Grand Junction. Many sites en route feature uncovered dinosaur bones; several areas nearby are under current excavation by professionals. Pick up a tour brochure at Dinosaur Valley Museum before heading out. Rabbit Valley is located 24 miles west of Grand Junction. Take a marked turn-off north from Interstate 70.

Colorado National Monument

Thousand-foot-deep red canyons and solitary sandstone monoliths characterize this beautiful monument and serve as an example of the force of wind and water erosion. Sheer cliffs and wide vistas have created a unique patchwork of colors, textures and shapes. To fully appreciate the muted contrasts of this national treasure, it's better to visit during low sun—in early morning or late afternoon. Once within the canyons, civilization seems light years away, even though Interstate 70 is only a few miles in the distance.

History—We can thank a dedicated hermit for the creation of Colorado National Monument. For many years in the early 1900s, John Otto lived alone in the canyons while waging a one-man letter-writing campaign urging the creation of a national park. The rest of his time was spent cutting trails and guiding adventurous tourists over the rugged terrain. Many of the trails Otto created are still in use today. Finally, in 1911, President Taft proclaimed the area a national monument, and John Otto was made the first superintendent. Later the same year, he was married at the base of 501-foot-high Independence Monument.

Getting There—To reach the east entrance to the park from the center of Grand Junction, head west on Grand Avenue to Hwy. 340. Follow the signs across the Colorado River and turn left at the first intersection. The west entrance of the monument can be easily reached from Interstate 70 by taking the Fruita exit and following the signs south. Pick up a map of the monument and its hiking trails at either entrance. Open year-round; small entrance fee per car.

Biking—Rim Rock Dr. became known to professional and novice cyclists thanks to professional race classics. It is an ideal touring ride, especially in the early morning when road traffic and heat are at a minimum. The smooth asphalt road draws cyclists fit enough to handle the heat and severe change in elevation—2,300 vertical feet during the 35-mile loop from Grand Junction. For an easier 10-mile ride, start at the visitors center, ride to Artist's Point and return. Off-road mountain biking is not permitted in the park, but several adjoining areas are ideal for it. See the Biking section in Outdoor Activities.

Camping—Saddlehorn Campground, located near the visitors center, has 81 sites and a picnic area. Fee charged from mid-Apr.–Oct.; free the rest of the year. Backcountry camping is permitted throughout the monument; register (no fee) at the visitors center.

Hiking—A hike down into the deep canyons to soak up the sights and sounds of this place is something you will not soon forget. The desert is alive in small ways that require a closer look and more patience than city dwellers are used to. There are many trails snaking their way down into the inner sanctum of Colorado National Monument.

Short trails such as **Coke Ovens, Window Rock** and **John Otto's Trail** offer good views in an hour or less. Especially well suited to families is **Alcove Nature Trail,** across the road from the visitors center. Guide booklets with information about geology, flora and fauna of the monument are available at the visitors center. A hike down popular **Monument Canyon Trail** requires four hours of your time. It is a well-maintained 5.5-mile trail that descends 600 feet and provides a close look at massive cliff walls and looming rock monoliths. Another interesting walk is **Serpent's Trail.** Located near the east entrance, the trail follows an old roadbed around 54 switchbacks in only 2.5 miles. The steep trail allows for sweeping views to Grand Junction and beyond.

Bring your own water for hikes into the canyons. In summer carry at least a gallon per day for each person. Do not drink the water you find in the canyons. No pets or fires are permitted in the backcountry.

Rim Rock Drive—Beginning in the 1930s and, after a couple of lengthy work stoppages, finishing in the 1950s, National Park Service crews, the Civilian Conservation Corps (CCC) and others shoveled dirt and blasted rock for 23 miles through the monument to complete Rim Rock Dr. Today the road offers motorists, bicyclists and even an occasional roller blader dramatic views from the northern edge of the Uncompahgre Plateau. The road, with its many turnouts, descriptive plaques and scenic overlooks, is a worthwhile and easy way to see the broad expanse of desert canyon terrain. There is a 35-mile circuit over Rim Rock Dr. from Grand Junction and back.

Visitors Center—Located 4 miles from the west entrance, the center has exhibits and a slide show on the geology, history, plants and wildlife in the area. Here knowledgeable rangers answer any questions you may have. Rest rooms and water fountains are available. Open daily 8 am–8 pm in summer and until 4:30 pm other times of the year. For more information, contact the **Superintendent of Colorado National Monument, Fruita, CO 81521; (303) 858-3617.**

Grand Mesa

Located east of Grand Junction, 10,000-foot-high Grand Mesa rises more than a mile above the valley floor. Its 53 square miles make it one of the largest plateaus in the country. Lava flows, 400 feet thick, helped form the flat surface and protected the underlying sedimentary rock from the erosion so evident in this area. Dotted with more than 200 lakes and covered with thick pine forests and aspen groves, Grand Mesa attracts a lot of summer visitors. With its magnificent views and many recreational opportunities, it's easy to see why.

The entire mesa is part of Grand Mesa National Forest. Heavy snow in winter closes all roads except Skyway Drive (Hwy 65), which runs north-south across the mesa. In summertime after the snow melts, activity on Grand Mesa reaches "grand" proportions. As one Grand Junction local says, "It turns into one big Winnebago parking lot." Although that's an exaggeration, an autumn visit will avoid crowds while providing a look at the changing aspen.

History—To the Ute Indians, Grand Mesa was known as *Thigunawat*, meaning "Home of Departed Spirits." Ute legend says the many lakes on the mesa were created by vicious thunderbirds that lived along the rim. Apparently, an irate Ute pitched several baby thunderbirds out of their nests and into the waiting jaws of a giant serpent in the valley below. The vengeful thunderbirds reacted by ripping the serpent to pieces and dropping the remains from high over the mesa. These falling chunks of serpent caused indentations, which filled with water and created the lakes. A more scientific explanation suggests the lakes were formed by erosion.

In 1879, following the nearby massacre of Indian Agent Nathan Meeker and some of his men, the Utes took five hostages up onto the mesa. Shortly thereafter, the US Cavalry arrived to negotiate the hostage release. The Utes surrendered and none of the hostages was killed.

In 1881, when significant numbers of settlers began to arrive in the valleys below Grand Mesa, a need for a summer-long water supply led to the building of many reservoirs on the mesa top. Nowadays these reservoirs and lakes not only supply water to the thirsty valley below, but also double as fishing holes. The mesa has developed into a cool summer retreat from the hot, arid valley floor.

Getting There—See the Grand Mesa Scenic & Historic Byway and the Lands End Rd. write-ups in this section.

Visitor Information—Visit the **Grand Junction Ranger District Office, 764 Horizon Dr., Grand Junction, CO 81506; (303) 242-8211.** In summer try the two visitors centers on the mesa; one is located at Carp Lake, and the other is at the edge of the mesa on Land's End Rd.

Fishing—All of the more than 220 lakes and streams on Grand Mesa are actively stocked by the Division of Wildlife. Rainbow trout (up to 18 inches) are the primary fish you'll run across, but brook and cutthroat also swim these waters. The fish begin feeding as soon as the ice melts from the perimeter of the lakes. Unless you fish early or late in the season you will have plenty of company. In winter ice fishing is popular as well as productive.

Hiking—**Crag Crest Trail** is an ideal 10-mile circular trail for short day trips or full-day hikes. The trail winds its way past lakes and through stands of fir, spruce and aspen. The northern section of Crag Crest is the highest part of the trail. On a clear day you'll have great views in all directions: the Book and Roan Cliffs to the north, the West Elk and San Juan Mountains to the south and the La Sal Mountains far to the west in Utah.

Crag Crest Trail is restricted to foot and horse travel. Be sure to bring your own water or a means for purifying what you find along the way. Camping is allowed at least 300 feet off the trail. Be sure to keep a close eye on children when approaching the northern section, as there are a number of sheer drop-offs on both sides. The west trailhead parking lot is located just off Hwy. 65 next to Island Lake; the east trailhead can be reached by taking Forest Rd. 121 from Hwy. 65 near Island Lake and driving to Eggleston Lake (about 5 miles). For maps and more information, go to the visitors center at Carp Lake, which is open in summer 9 am–6 pm daily.

Winter on the Mesa—The mesa virtually closes up in winter. Hwy. 65 (Skyway Dr.) stays open, but Land's End Rd. is closed and doesn't reopen to cars until June. You can cross-country ski on most parts of the mesa, but be warned—snowmobilers love this place. A number of cross-country trail systems are maintained along Hwy. 65. You can park at Skyway (mile-marker 32.5), County Line (mile-marker 30) or Ward Creek (mile-marker 25) to set out on your trips. The trail system at County Line is not groomed. Pick up a trail map, available at the Grand Junction Visitor Center or a Forest Service office. Powderhorn Ski Area offers cross-country as well as downhill skiing (see Skiing section). In winter ice fishing on the lakes is very popular.

Grand Mesa Scenic & Historic Byway— This magnificent 78-mile (one-way) drive takes you from the orchard country of Grand Junction and up across the 11,000-foot high terrain of Grand Mesa. *If you have the time to explore this route, do so!* Starting in Grand Junction, drive 23 miles northeast on Interstate 70 to the Hwy. 65 turn-off at Plateau Canyon. After you have driven 10 miles through the picturesque canyon the road angles south and begins climbing up through the town of Mesa, past Powderhorn Ski Area and eventually onto Grand Mesa. Once on the Mesa, you'll shortly reach an intersection with Lands End Rd. (a nice circle tour back to Grand Junction; see next write-up). Continue across the Mesa on Hwy. 65 and drop down to the end of the byway at the town of Cedaredge. (For information about attractions in Cedaredge see the Black Canyon Country chapter.) To loop back to Grand Junction continue down on Hwy. 65 and then turn right onto Hwy. 92. At Delta head north on Hwy. 50 to Grand Junction. Brochures with byway information and maps can be picked up at the visitors center in Grand Junction.

Land's End Road—In the summertime a drive on Land's End Rd. can be spectacular as well as hair-raising. Land's End is located on the western edge of Grand Mesa, where it snakes its way down a sloping cliff on a series of seemingly endless switchbacks.

To reach the road from Grand Junction, head south on Hwy. 50 about 14 miles and turn left on the road marked as an access to Land's End Rd. The pavement ends after about 7 miles as you reach the Grand Mesa National Forest boundary. Follow the bumpy dirt road as it winds up the side of the mesa. Eventually you'll reach an observation site, just to the left of the road as you reach the rim. From here the view down to the valley floor, thousands of feet below, is dizzying. Once on top of the mesa, continue to the Hwy. 65 intersection.

From Hwy. 65 you can either retrace your 53-mile route back down Land's End Rd. to Grand Junction or turn left and head north across the mesa along the Grand Mesa Scenic & Historic Byway (see previous write-up) and down the north rim. This route takes you past Powderhorn Ski Area, eventually hitting Interstate 70 about 23 miles northeast of Grand Junction. It offers some great views of the Book and Roan cliffs to the northwest and Battlement Mesa to the north. Both routes back to Grand Junction are about the same length.

Lodging—Several lodges occupy the mesa, but most of them are open only during summer and early fall. After seeing a picture of winter snow drifts covering the two-story Grand Mesa Lodge, it's easy to see why. Here are a few possibilities:

Alexander Lake Lodge has six small cabins **($$ to $$$),** three with kitchenettes. Each is furnished with queen-sized beds. The lodge has a restaurant (known for its steaks) and bar, as well as a small store. Open year-round. **PO Box 93, Cedaredge, CO 81413; (303) 856-6700.**

Grand Mesa Lodge ($$) sits beside Island Lake near the northern end of the mesa. Chuck and Jan Harrington run a friendly place with motel units and housekeeping cabins. Rental boats are available for fishing; no restaurant. Pets OK. Closed in winter. **PO Box 49, Cedaredge, CO 81413; (303) 856-3250.**

Spruce Lodge, located on Ward Lake, offers 14 two-room housekeeping cabins **($$ to $$$)** with kitchenettes and double beds. In winter warm up around one of the lodge's three fireplaces or with a cocktail from the bar/restaurant. Open year-round. **PO Box 37, Cedaredge, CO 81413; (303) 856-3210.**

Just down the north rim of the mesa, Powderhorn offers a nice lodging alternative near the ski slopes and closer to town. **Valley View Condominiums ($$ to $$$)** offers fully equipped condos with attractive furnishings and views to the valley or mountain. Cable TV, phone, VCR. Efficiencies have no windows. Sauna and

Jacuzzi available. **PO Box 370, Mesa, CO 81643; 1-800-241-6997.**

Camping—There are 13 campgrounds with more than 250 sites on the mesa equipped with a variety of amenities. Those with more comforts charge a small fee; the more primitive campgrounds without water are free. Some sites are wheelchair accessible. All the campgrounds open in late June and close for the winter on Oct. 15. Reservations for 50 percent of the campsites on the mesa can be obtained by calling **MISTIX** at **1-800-283-CAMP.**

FESTIVALS AND EVENTS

Dinosaur Days
late July
In keeping with the dinosaur fever that hovers over Mesa County, Dinosaur Days takes it a step further. This four-day event is highlighted by a dinosaur lecture, the T-Rex T-Off golf tourney, the Pteranodon Ptrot 5K run, a raft race and dancing to live music at the Stegosaurus Stomp. For information call **(303) 242-3214.**

Colorado Mountain Winefest
late September
The emergence of wineries in the valley has spawned this new festival, held jointly in Grand Junction and the orchard town of Palisade. Great food and music as well as wine tastings dominate the three-day event. Wine-making seminars and winery tours round things out. **(303) 243-8497.**

OUTDOOR ACTIVITIES

BIKING
MOUNTAIN BIKING
The area around Grand Junction is perfect for mountain biking, offering open spaces and unlimited BLM land for exploring. Thanks to a big surge of interest by locals, many trails have been developed in the canyon country over the past few years. For more information about trail possibilities, contact **The Bike Peddler, 710 N. 1st St.; (303) 243-5602** or the **BLM Office** at **2815 H Rd.; (303) 244-3000.**

Kokopelli's Trail—
Officially opened in the summer of 1989, this highly rugged and scenic trail stands as the product of hard work by hundreds of volunteers and cooperation between the BLM offices in Grand Junction and Moab, Utah. Named after the humpbacked flute playing deity familiar to many Native Americans of the Colorado Plateau, Kokopelli stretches 128 miles through canyons and slickrock mesas between Loma (20 miles west of Grand Junction) and Moab.

Though some sections of the trail are quite mellow and flat, a 4,500-vertical-foot climb over the La Sal Mountains does indeed separate the serious pedaler from the novice. Sections of the trail range from single track to well-graded county roads. Those who plan overnight trips along the trail should be familiar with mountain bike ethics and low-impact camping techniques. Important—there is no water available along the trail. Maps can be purchased throughout Grand Junction, including the BLM office. For more information, contact the **Colorado Plateau Mountain Bike Trail Association, PO Box 4602, Grand Junction, CO 81502; (303) 241-9561.**

Little Park Road—
This popular ride, with its canyons and many junipers, attracts riders due to its close proximity to Grand Junction. To reach Little Park Rd., enter Colorado National Monument from the east entrance

and proceed about four miles to the Glade Park Road junction. Turn left and continue a few more miles and take another left onto Little Park Rd. The road loops back toward town.

Tabeguache Trail—

This 142-mile trail, another project of the Colorado Plateau Mountain Bike Trail Association (COPMOBA), winds its way south from Grand Junction through beautiful sections of public land along the Uncompahgre Plateau. Elevations range from 5,500 to just under 10,000 feet. Maps are available at BLM offices in Grand Junction and Montrose. For more information, contact the **BLM Office** in Grand Junction or **COPMOBA** at **PO Box 4602, Grand Junction, CO 81502; (303) 241-9561.**

Rentals—

Try a mountain bike for a half day or a few days. Rentals are available (requiring a $350 deposit) at **Cycle Center, 141 N. 7th St.; (303) 242-2541,** or **The Board & Buckle, 2822 North Ave.; (303) 242-9285** (requiring a $500 deposit). **The Bike Peddler, 710 N. 1st St.; (303) 243-5602,** also offers rentals and information.

Outfitters—

Endless Summer Tours runs shuttles up to the top of Rim Rock Dr. in Colorado National Monument where you are let out to begin your ride. Cruise along the magnificent rim before beginning your "lunar descent." Endless Summer offers other day trips around Grand Junction as well as multiday trips through Colorado and Utah's canyonlands. **202 North Ave., Grand Junction, CO 81501; 1-800-345-3389.**

TOURING
Colorado National Monument—
See the Major Attractions section.

Colorado River Trails—

Since the late 1970s, dedicated folks in Grand Junction have been working hard to create a trail system running along the Colorado River through town. Eventually the trail will extend from Clifton (east of town) to the Loma boat launch, west of Fruita. For now, enjoy a number of trail sections and loops accessible from various locations in town. Great rides are available on the Audubon, Blue Heron, Connected Lakes, Watson Island and Corn Lake trails. For information and a helpful map/brochure, contact the **Colorado River State Park office at Corn Lake, 32 Rd. and the Colorado River; (303) 434-6862.**

FISHING

Even though two of the state's largest rivers converge at Grand Junction, the river fishing is not something you should go out of your way for. Fishing is much better on Grand Mesa (see the Major Attractions section) and upriver in the Gold Medal trout water of Gunnison Gorge (see the Fishing section of the **Black Canyon Country** chapter).

FOUR-WHEEL-DRIVE TRIPS

John Brown Canyon/Moab Loop—

For a mellow day's drive, this is a bit ambitious. But for someone fascinated with the canyon country of the Colorado Plateau, it's time well spent. John Brown Canyon is a remote, steep-walled slickrock canyon that winds its way to the Utah border. This area is closed in winter. Make sure your gas tank is full and that you bring plenty of water; once in the canyon, there are no facilities for car or driver. For the necessary details, visit the **BLM** office in Grand Junction at **2815 H Rd., Grand Junction, CO 81506; (303) 244-3000.** *We strongly recommend that you use BLM and/or USGS topographical maps!*

To reach the canyon from Grand Junction, head south on Hwy. 50 for 9 miles to Whitewater and take a right on Hwy. 141. Drive 44 miles to the town of Gateway and turn left after crossing the Dolores River. The canyon road is just upriver on the right. A four-wheel-drive dirt road leads west into Utah, following the north slope of the La Sal Mountains and providing a dramatic view of the spectacular Wingate sandstone of Fisher Towers to the north. The road eventually comes out on Hwy. 128 along the Colorado River northeast of Moab. Take a left to Moab or just turn right, following alongside the river until rejoining Interstate 70. Turn east on the interstate and return to Grand Junction, about 60 miles down the highway.

Rattlesnake Canyon—

See the Hiking and Backpacking section for details.

GOLF

Grand Junction's mild climate and beautiful views make it a great place for year-round golfing. Winter snowfall is minimal and usually melts quickly. In summertime the town can really heat up, making early-morning tee times a good idea. Here are a few places to play.

Battlement Mesa Golf Club—

Beautiful, expansive views of the surrounding mesas help pass the time at this excellent 18-hole public course, 41 miles northeast of Grand Junction just off Interstate 70. Water, large cottonwoods and treacherous roughs all come into play—unless you want to go through a bag full of balls, keep your shots on the fairway. Located in Parachute (Exit 75); **(303) 285-PAR4.**

Lincoln Park Golf Club—

A mature, nine-hole course with pro shop and driving range. Located in Lincoln Park at 14th St. and Gunnison Ave.; **(303) 242-6394.**

Tiara Rado Golf Course—

This 5,907-yard, 18-hole course is fairly young but challenging. It's located on the west end of town near the entrance to Colorado National Monument. The views are spectacular; all amenities you would expect are available. **2063 S. Broadway; (303) 245-8085.**

HIKING AND BACKPACKING

There's no question about it: the Grand Junction area is the place to come in Colorado for desert canyon hiking and backpacking. Many of these remote canyons of the Colorado Plateau are as beautiful as Canyonlands and Arches national parks in Utah—there are just a lot fewer people. For hiking among pines in a mountain setting try the Crag Crest Trail on Grand Mesa (see the Hiking section for Grand Mesa, under Major Attractions) or dozens of other trails on the Mesa. Listed below are several hiking areas west of Grand Junction in the BLM's vast 72,000-acre Black Ridge Wilderness Study Area. Canyon hiking in the spring and summer is thirsty work and the black gnats can be quite bothersome—*bring lots of water and bug repellent.* Also, keep a lookout for desert bighorn sheep, successfully reintroduced into the area.

Rattlesnake Canyon—

This is one of the best-kept secrets in Colorado. Rattlesnake Canyon offers the second largest concentration of natural rock arches in the world, next to Utah's Arches National Park. At least 12 arches await you, carved by erosion in the Entrada sandstone of the canyon walls. The largest, Rainbow Bridge, is about 80 feet by 120 feet. The canyon's remote location, underdevelopment and intimidating name keep most people away, so if you make the effort you may not see anybody.

From Grand Junction head west on Interstate 70 to Exit 19 (the Fruita exit), then south to the west entrance of Colorado National Monument. Enter the monument and go about 11 miles and turn right (west) on a dirt road marked with the sign Glade Park Store 5 Miles. Proceed 0.2 miles, cross a cattle guard and turn right at the Black Ridge Hunter Access Road sign. From there continue about 8.2 miles to a junction. Turn right, drive 2 miles down the

Old Ute Trail and park your vehicle. *This road, especially the last 2 miles, should be attempted by only four-wheel-drive vehicles with high clearance and only during good weather.* When it rains the road becomes a slippery, muddy mess.

From the parking area a marked half-mile trail leads down to the canyon rim where the southernmost arch, Rainbow Bridge, can be seen. Though a bit tricky for some people, the Lower Arches Trail can be reached quickly by climbing down the slickrock under Rainbow Bridge. Otherwise you must follow the rim .75 miles north and work your way down from there. Rattlesnake Canyon can also be reached by Pollock Canyon Trail (6 miles one way). To reach the Pollock Canyon Trailhead, drive south from Fruita toward the Colorado National Monument entrance and turn right at the marked sign. Proceed 3 miles. For more information and maps, contact the **BLM** office in Grand Junction at **2815 H Rd., Grand Junction, CO 81506; (303) 244-3000.**

Other Canyon Hiking Possibilities—

To many people who have hiked and backpacked in canyon country, the scenery and positive overall experience are unparalleled. However, this deceptive country can quickly turn hostile and deadly to even the most experienced desert rats. The following backpacking trips should be undertaken only by seasoned hikers familiar with desert camping.

Mee Canyon, Knowles Canyon and **Jones Canyon,** located in the BLM's Black Ridge Wilderness Study Area, offer miles of remote hiking. Red sandstone walls and cottonwood groves characterize this desert canyon terrain. The trailhead for Mee Canyon can be reached from the Black Ridge Hunter Access Rd., on the way to Rattlesnake Canyon (see previous hike). Mee Canyon is known for its steep slickrock canyon walls and large 300-foot by 320-foot cave. Knowles and Jones canyons are approached by taking the Glade Park Store Rd. out of Colorado National Monument. Pass the Glade Park Store and continue

west on BS Rd. for 20 to 30 miles. *Obtain topographical maps, directions and other important information from the BLM office in Grand Junction,* **2815 H Rd., Grand Junction, CO 81506; (303) 244-3000.**

RIVER FLOATING

Colorado River—

The stretch of the Colorado River running through Grand Junction is, for the most part, extremely calm. Kayakers, inner tubers, canoeists and rafters cool off in summer by taking leisurely floats west to the Loma take-out.

However, downriver from Loma is a different story. The Colorado turns northwest and enters Horsethief Canyon (9 miles long), then heads southwest through Ruby Canyon (6 miles long) to the Colorado-Utah border. Both of these canyons, rimmed by gigantic slickrock cliffs, have fairly rough water. Look for the Anasazi mochi steps carved in a rock cliff on the north side of the river near the border. This stretch of the Colorado River allows excellent hiking access to spectacular side canyons, including Rattlesnake, Mee and Knowles.

In Utah, Westwater Canyon, stretching almost 30 miles to the take-out at Dewey Bridge, offers one of the wildest stretches on the Colorado River. Included here is the famous Skull Rapid and the nightmarish giant whirlpool known to floaters as the Room of Doom—at high water its outer perimeter can be as high as 3 feet above the vortex. In one section of Westwater, extremely ancient black Precambrian rock is exposed, not to reappear again until the river enters the Grand Canyon hundreds of miles downstream. A permit is required for Westwater Canyon. It may be obtained at the **Moab District BLM Office, PO Box M, Sand Flats Rd., Moab, UT 84532; (801) 259-8193.**

Gunnison River—

The lower Gunnison offers fairly challenging, intensely beautiful stretches of water as it flows northwest to Grand Junction before emptying into the Colorado River. For more information see the River

Floating section of the **Black Canyon Country** chapter.

Outfitters—

For one-day and multiday trips down the Colorado River, including Horsethief, Ruby and Westwater canyons, contact **Adventure Bound, 2392 H Rd., Grand Junction, CO 81505; (303) 241-5633** or **1-800-423-4668.**

Families may want to consider a full-day trip with **Rimrock Adventures,** which combines a half-day of horseback riding near Colorado National Monument with a half-day relaxing river trip on the Colorado. **PO Box 608, Fruita, CO 81521; (303) 858-9555.**

SKIING
CROSS-COUNTRY SKIING

The lifts at Powderhorn take cross-country skiers to the rim of Grand Mesa, where an organized trail system heads into the backcountry. The Powderhorn Nordic Center machine-grooms about 12 kilometers of trails within ski area boundaries. Gentle ski area slopes are excellent for telemark skiing. Rentals and instruction are available. Grand Mesa is a snowmobiler's paradise, but many good cross-country trails exist and are kept fairly separate. For trail locations see Grand Mesa under Major Attractions.

DOWNHILL SKIING
Powderhorn—

Logic would have it that downhill skiing near an area called Grand Mesa would be less than thrilling. Yet, surprisingly, there is a generous vertical drop of 1,650 feet at this ski mountain, only 35 miles east of Grand Junction. If you are looking for an area with a majority of intermediate runs, Powderhorn is perfect. The stunning views you'll see while skiing anywhere on the mountain are completely different from those in any other area in Colorado. The ski area boasts far more trees, primarily spruce and aspen, than either the barren plateau in the distance or the valley below. Ski rentals and lessons are available. Base lodging remains limited, but the Valley View condos are worthy. It is also possible to stay near Powderhorn at lodges and motels, a few of which are on Grand Mesa (see Major Attractions section) and in the town of Mesa. **PO Box 370, Mesa, CO 81643; 1-800-241-6997** or **(303) 268-5700.**

SWIMMING
Island Acres State Park—

Four lakes (gravel ponds, actually) at Island Acres provide swimming opportunities; one is set up exclusively for swimming. Popular with Grand Junction locals. 15 miles northeast of town on Interstate 70. Fee charged. **(303) 464-0548.**

Lincoln Park—

This outdoor pool is open daily from late May until Labor Day 1:30–8 pm (open at 9:30 am on Wed.). Let it be known that the pool now has a 351-foot water slide that is more than welcome on those blistering hot summer days in Grand Junction. Locker rentals available. Small fee charged. 12th St. and Gunnison Ave.; **(303) 244-1548.**

Orchard Mesa—

This indoor pool is open Mon., Wed., Fri. and Sat. 1:30–8 pm; Tues. and Thurs. 1:30–5 pm; Sun. from 1:30–6 pm. Admission fee. Open year-round. **2736 Unaweep Ave.; (303) 244-1485.**

TENNIS
Lincoln Park—

Eight outdoor courts are available on a first-come, first-served basis. No charge. Located in Lincoln Park at **14th St. and Gunnison Ave.**

SEEING AND DOING

MUSEUMS

Cross Orchards Historic Site—

Listed on the National Register of Historic Places, Cross Orchards was a 243-acre working fruit farm from 1896 to 1923. Today it's a great place to learn about the historic importance of the orchards to Grand Junction through daily living history demonstrations. Stroll the grounds and inspect the buildings and orchard. Also of note are the Cross Orchard Country Store, The Swanson Farm, Uintah Railway Exhibit and the collection of antique road-building equipment. Fee charged. Open 10 am–5 pm Tues.–Sat., May 1–Oct. 30. **3073 F (Patterson) Rd., Grand Junction, CO 81504; (303) 434-9814.**

Museum of Western Colorado—

Stop by this excellent museum where you'll learn about the history of western Colorado and, more specifically, of Grand Junction. The history begins with the woolly mammoth–spearing Folsom Man of 15,000 years ago and ranges to the present-day fruit farmers. Other interesting displays are the world's largest unicycle (40 feet) that's actually been ridden and a gun section that includes flintlocks from the early 1800s. The museum also has managed to get most of the pistols used by Mesa County sheriffs dating back to 1883. Exhibits change frequently; fee charged. Open May 1–Sept. 30, Mon.–Sat. 10 am–4:45 pm; open the rest of the year, Tues.–Sat. 10 am–4:45 pm. **4th St. and Ute Ave.; (303) 242-0971.**

NIGHTLIFE

Cancun Saloon—

Located at the Hilton Hotel on Horizon Dr., the Cancun Saloon attracts a younger Grand Junction crowd for dancing to DJ tunes. Belly up to one of the surfboard tables at this Caribbean/beach bar setting, sip a fruity drink and unwind.

Gladstone's—

Although Gladstone's features a reasonably good restaurant ($$ to $$$), it's also a quiet, attractive place to have a drink. The bar section has booths, tables and plenty of barstools. Everything imaginable lines the walls and hangs from the ceiling, including old signs and a kayak. TVs behind the bar. Bar menu available as well as patio seating. **2531 N. 12th St.; (303) 241-6000.**

Wrigley Field—

Local sports fans, including students from nearby Mesa State College, head to Wrigley Field to attack pitchers of beer while watching their favorite team on numerous TVs. In addition to your favorite libation you'll find burgers, sandwiches and daily specials. **1810 N. Ave.; (303) 245-9010.**

SCENIC DRIVES

Grand Mesa Scenic & Historic Byway—

For information about this beautiful drive, as well as a possible trip along the steep, switchbacking Lands End Rd., see the Grand Mesa write-up in the Major Attractions section.

Unaweep/Tabeguache Scenic & Historic Byway—

If you have some time on your hands, this trip is well worth your while. Head south from Grand Junction for 9 miles on Hwy. 50 to the junction of Hwy. 141 at Whitewater. Turn west on Hwy. 141 and head into Unaweep Canyon. It was through Unaweep Canyon (44 miles long and 2,500 feet deep) that the waters of the Gunnison and Colorado rivers once flowed. When the Uncompahgre Plateau began to push up through the shale about 8 million years ago, the water found a new course, leaving Unaweep high and dry. The canyon's steep rock walls and groves of cottonwood and pine make it a pleasant drive.

About 14 miles west of Whitewater, a dirt road (Divide Rd.) heads off to the left, leading up to the rim of the canyon for a good view. Continuing west on Hwy. 141 you'll eventually hit the town of Gateway.

From the town of Gateway, Hwy. 141 takes a swing south and begins winding its way up along the Dolores River in one of the state's most beautiful sandstone canyons. Over the years the Dolores has cut its way down through sedimentary rock, sandstone, mudstone and shale, revealing many-colored layers—a geologist's dream. The looming bulk of the entrada and Wingate sandstone walls is a monument to time and weather.

Twenty-nine miles south of Gateway is a turnout on the right side of the road where you can get a bird's-eye view of the **Hanging Flume.** Constructed from 1889 to 1891, the Hanging Flume was built into the canyon walls to carry water to Mesa Creek Flats for hydraulic gold mining. During construction, workers clung to swinging ropes lowered as much as 400 feet from the canyon rim above. The 6-foot by 4-foot, 6-mile-long flume was an engineering success but a financial disaster.

Continuing south on the highway leads you into uranium country. Beginning in the late 1800s, the world began to see a use for uranium ore. In 1898 an order came from France for several tons of ore, which was then refined into radium by Pierre and Marie Curie. At Uravan, 6 miles south of the Hanging Flume turnout, ore was mined during World War II to supply the Manhattan Project, the US government operation to develop the world's first atomic bomb. Mining boomed in Uravan during the 1950s but died out in 1962, with the town soon following suit. Other abandoned mines can be seen in the vicinity.

From Uravan continue south through Norwood to Placerville and then east on Hwy. 62 to Ridgway. From Ridgway, head north on Hwy. 50 through Montrose and Delta on the way back to Grand Junction. Total round trip mileage is 151. Before heading out on this route, pick up a brochure on the byway at the visitor center in Grand Junction.

The Orchards—

The roads to the east of Grand Junction can be something of a nightmare if you are attempting to follow directions. Road names such as B, C 1/2, F and D 7/8 are common. To reach the graded dirt roads that plot their way into the orchards, head east on F Rd. out of central Grand Junction toward Clifton and Palisade. Driving into the orchards on virtually any secondary road, you will be able to view the rich peach, apricot, grape and cherry orchards. The fields are especially active during the harvest season: mid-July–Aug. Spring is particularly beautiful when the trees are blossoming. Consider stopping in at one of the wineries located in this area (see the Wineries section). You really can't get lost because of the visible landmarks all around. Mt. Garfield and the desolate Book Cliffs lie to the north, Grand Mesa to the east and Colorado National Monument to the west.

Rim Rock Drive—

See the Colorado National Monument write-up in the Major Attractions section.

WINERIES

In Colorado? Yes. The Western Slope of Colorado has proven to have a long, cool growing season and suitable soil, making it fine vineyard country. Though not on a par with the Napa Valley region of California yet, give them time. Currently there are five wineries located in the orchards east of Grand Junction.

Colorado Cellars—

This interesting operation run by Richard and Padte Turley has been producing wine commercially since the late 1970s. Their standout wines include Riesling, Chardonnay and Grand Game. Tours and tastings are available year-round 12–4 pm Mon.–Sat., or by appointment. **3553 E Rd., Palisade, CO 81526; (303) 464-7921.**

Grande Valley Vineyards—

Offers mainly traditional style grape wines including Meritage, Chardonnays and Sauvignon Blanc. They are excellent! **3708 G Rd. #2, PO Box 129, Palisade, CO 81526; (303) 464-5867.**

Plum Creek Cellars—

Located just outside of Palisade; tasting room open Thurs.–Sat., 1–5 pm. Only grape wines. **3708 G Rd. #1, Palisade, CO 81526; (303) 464-PLUM.**

Carlson Vineyards—

This very small winery specializes in peach, cherry, apple and plum wines. Open Wed.–Sun., 12–6 pm in summer, and Fri.–Sun. Check out their dinosaur series. 12–6 pm in winter. **461 35 Rd., Palisade, CO 81526; (303) 464-5554.**

Vail Valley Vinters—

Located just east of Palisade; offers Chardonnay, Cabernet and Reisling wines. Tasting room open 2:30–5:30 on Fri., and Sat. 11 am–5 pm. **363 Troyer Ave.; (303) 464-0559.**

--------- **WHERE TO STAY** ---------

ACCOMMODATIONS

In the early 1880s the two most noteworthy hostelries in Grand Junction were called The Pig's Ear and The Pig's Eye. No wonder they went out of business. Things have come a long way since the early days, and now there are 2,000 motel rooms to choose from. Just off Interstate 70, on Horizon Dr., there are a number of easily identifiable and accessible chain motels and hotels, including the **Grand Junction Hilton,** the **Ramada Inn, Howard Johnson's** and the **Holiday Inn.** To reach most of these establishments from Interstate 70, take the exit for Horizon Dr. or North Ave. Ideas for lodging on Grand Mesa can be found in the Grand Mesa write-up under Major Attractions. Other ideas and phone numbers can be obtained by calling the **Visitor & Convention Bureau** at **1-800-962-2547.** Listed below are a couple of fine bed and breakfast inns.

The Orchard House—$$$

Quiet. If you really want to get away from it all, this is the place. Peach and cherry orchards surround this country home just 20 minutes east of Grand Junction. Get there in Aug. and you may be able to pick fruit from the trees in nearby orchards. Bill and Stephanie Schmid offer accommodations in the rear section of their spacious home, including an upstairs room with a king-sized bed; downstairs are accommodations for approximately another four people. Guests have private kitchen facilities, but with a lavish breakfast included in the room rate, they may not be needed. For an additional charge the Schmids will prepare an excellent dinner, periodically featuring beef tenderloin, fresh salmon, gourmet burgers and succulent rack of lamb. Smokers welcome; reservations necessary. **3573 E 1/2 Rd., Palisade, CO 81526; (303) 464-0529.**

The Gate House—$$ to $$$

Drive under the stone archway and into a sanctuary of comfort, elegance and history. Carefully tended grounds surround the former gate house to Redstone Castle (for more information see the **Redstone and Crystal River Valley** chapter). The Gate House was built as part of the castle by coal baron John Osgood for his wife, Alma (Lady Bountiful), in the early 1900s. Some 40 years later it was moved, stone by stone, to its present location in Grand Junction. In 1988 the large, Tudor-style home was remodeled and given new purpose as a bed and breakfast.

The four guest rooms (two with private baths) are tastefully decorated with many personal touches. Each room is named Abbott and Costello style: are you staying in My room; is she in His room or Her room? You'll understand when you get to Your room at the Gate House. The downstairs common area has a small library, a sofa and chairs and a view out the picture window to the rose garden. A full breakfast is served in the dining room. We had a wonderful concoction of French toast with a cream cheese, peach and pecan filling. They also served fresh fruit, scrambled eggs, coffee cake, bacon, coffee and juice. The atmosphere is light and airy, and the innkeepers will make you feel at home. Children over 10 OK; no smoking inside; reservations recommended. **2502 N. 1st St., Grand Junction, CO 81501; (303) 242-6105.**

On Grand Mesa—

For information about three lodges on Grand Mesa, see the Major Attractions section.

CAMPING

For information on campgrounds at Colorado National Monument and Grand Mesa, see the Major Attractions section.

State Parks—

Highline State Park—Located 7 miles north of Loma, Highline offers 25 grassy campsites for both tents and RVs. Shower building; fee charged. Advance reservations available by calling **1-800-678-CAMP. 1800 11.8**

Rd., Loma, CO 81524; (303) 858-7208.**

Island Acres State Park—Island Acres lies along the Colorado River 15 miles east of Grand Junction on Interstate 70. Thirty-two tent and RV sites available; fee charged. Advance reservations can be arranged by calling **1-800-678-CAMP. Box B, Palisade, CO 81526; (303) 464-0548.**

Private Campgrounds—

Big J Camper Court—This year-round campground has full hookups, a swimming pool, etc. Located 2.5 miles south of the Grand Junction Fairgrounds at **2819 Hwy. 50, Grand Junction, CO 81503; (303) 242-2527.**

KOA Kampground—Has full-service hookups, pool, tent sites, store, trees, etc. Located 3 miles east of Grand Junction at **3238 E. Interstate 70 Business Loop, Clifton, CO 81520; (303) 434-6644.**

WHERE TO EAT

The Winery—$ to $$$$

The Winery is a place where residents go to celebrate special occasions. Low lighting, interior walls of weathered wood and comfortably spaced tables provide an intimate setting. The menu is limited, yet carefully chosen. Dinners of freshly cooked prime rib, shrimp tempura, sirloin steak, mahi-mahi or even lobster are prepared in an open kitchen. Wine is available by the carafe or bottle, though the list is not as extensive as you might expect. Open daily 4:30–10 pm. **642 Main St.; (303) 242-4100.**

Los Reyes—$$

Although sporting a more polished atmosphere since a recent rebuild, Los Reyes' excellent food hasn't changed. Chips with three kinds of salsa (green chile, red chile and chunky red tomato and onion) go perfectly with a cold cerveza Mexicana. Los Reyes offers numerous choices of Mexican beer. The large combination dinners are filling but not cheap. Most menu items may

be ordered à la carte—for something different try a stuffed oro sopapilla. **811 S. 7th St.; (303) 245-8392.**

Sweetwater's Uptown—$$ to $$$

Sweetwater's is a very popular restaurant serving northern Italian cuisine. It's located on the attractive Main Street Mall downtown, which resembles a scaled-down version of Denver's 16th Street Mall. The restaurant offers a small patio facing the mall that attracts a loyal lunchtime and cocktail-hour crowd. Menu items include pasta (especially fettucini), veal and seafood. A full bar features house wine specials and a good selection of bottled and draft beer. Open Mon.–Thurs. 11:30 am–9 pm, Fri. and Sat. until 10 pm. **336 Main St.; (303) 243-3900.**

W W Peppers—$$ to $$$

Innovative Southwestern cuisine is featured at this extremely popular restaurant. Shredded beef or lobster enchiladas,

Santa Fe burritos and chimichangas keep the locals coming back. Also available are sandwiches, burgers and chicken dishes. A word of warning: There is a charge for the chips and salsa. The light southwestern decor is enhanced by skylights and many plants. No reservations are accepted, so be prepared to wait awhile during prime dinner hours. Open Mon.–Fri. 11 am–10 pm, Sat. and Sun. 5–10 pm. No reservations. **759 Horizon Dr.; (303) 245-9251.**

Junct'n Square—$ to $$

Thought the decor is a bit antiseptic, aside from some art on the walls and the trellises over the booths, Junct'n Square serves up some of the best deep-dish pizza we've tasted. Located near the Main Street Mall downtown, this restaurant is hopping at lunchtime when specials are offered in addition to the regular menu items. In addi-tion to the pizza and other Italian specialties such as calzones and antipasto, try the quiche, soups, submarines and salads. Full bar; free delivery. **119 N. 7th; (303) 243-9750.** Also located at **295 27 Rd.; (303) 243-2427.**

Starvin' Arvin's—$ to $$

As you may have guessed by its name, Starvin' Arvin's is the place to deal with serious hunger. The prices are reasonable and the portions ample. Arvin's biscuits and gravy are well known around town. Sandwiches, salads, seafood and steaks are available in addition to breakfast items. Service is speedy, but while you're waiting you can examine the snapshots under the glasstop tables of Arvin's relatives and friends motorcycling, hiking, etc. The restaurant is located just off Interstate 70 on Horizon Dr. Open daily 6 am–10 pm. **752 Horizon Dr.; (303) 241-0430.**

SERVICES

Grand Junction Visitor & Convention Bureau —

740 Horizon Dr., Grand Junction, CO 81506; (303) 244-1480 or 1-800-962-2547.

Tourist Information Center—

Newly opened in 1993, this visitor center offers racks of brochures and information about what to do in the area. Open 9 am–5 pm daily. 759 Horizon Drive, Grand Junction, CO 81506; (303) 243-1001.

Transportation—

Greyhound Bus Lines—230 S. 5th; (303) 242-6012.

Sunshine Taxi Service—1331 Ute; (303) 245-TAXI.

Grand Lake

Wedged between Rocky Mountain National Park and the shores of Colorado's largest natural lake, this alluring mountain village is a vintage throwback to Colorado's past. Creaky wooden boardwalks, rough-hewn summer cabins, false-fronted stores and a well-used hitching post in front of a local bar force you to think about the past while wandering around town. Over the past 100 years, Grand Lake village has been a popular summer retreat. The community of 400 full-time residents swells during the peak summer travel season when each day sees 3,000 visitors pass near town. This surge of visitors has caused too many T-shirt shops and miniature golf courses to sprout up along Grand Ave. Despite Grand Lake's prime location at the west entrance of Rocky Mountain National Park, most people come here unaware of exactly what the area has to offer.

Outdoor recreation is the primary draw: consider the exceptional backcountry trails in Arapaho National Forest or Rocky Mountain National Park, or the fishing, water skiing and boating on Grand Lake, Shadow Mountain Reservoir and Lake Granby. If all that doesn't get your heart pumping, try a round of golf at your choice of two of the top 18-hole public courses in the state. At an elevation of 8,369 feet, Grand Lake's cool summer weather enhances most outdoor activities. When the summer sun fades behind the peaks, an evening of surprisingly good repertory theater can be found in the rustic Community Hall. Or maybe you'd prefer dancing the two-step to live country-western music in a local saloon.

In winter Grand Lake shows an even quieter side when most of the businesses shut down for the season. The closure of Trail Ridge Road, which climbs to 12,183 feet, stops the flow of traffic through Rocky Mountain National Park and turns Grand Lake into a town at the end of the road. A thick blanket of snow transforms the town into its pastoral best attracting many cross-country skiers and snowmobilers. Nearby Winter Park and Silver Creek ski areas make Grand Lake an ideal and inexpensive base for a winter escape, without all the trappings.

HISTORY

Ute Indians living near Grand Lake used trails along the North Inlet and Tonahutu Creek to travel east across the Continental Divide on hunting expeditions. At the same time, the Arapaho and Cheyenne came to Grand Lake from the plains to hunt elk and deer and to fish in the lake. Conflicts between the Utes and these visiting tribes were inevitable. After one legendary fight the Utes began calling the lake "Spirit Lake."

As the story goes, the Utes were camping by the lake when a group of Arapaho attacked them. Greatly outnumbered, the Utes put their women and children on a fishing raft and told them to paddle to the middle of the lake, where they would be safe. During the fight a storm blew off the water, capsizing the makeshift raft and drowning all aboard. The Utes on shore were badly beaten; most were killed. From that time on, the Utes, believing the spirits of their dead haunted the lake, would not camp on its shores. Legend has it that the early morning mists seen rising from the lake are the spirits of the dead Utes.

The first settler in Grand Lake was Joseph (Judge) Wescott, who arrived in 1867. Homesteading 160 acres on the shore of the lake, Wescott made a living by trapping and fishing. Supposedly each morning he caught about 100 trout, which he kept alive in boxes; periodically he packed them off to hotels in Georgetown for sale or traded them for supplies.

Except for an occasional hunting party or band of Utes (with whom he was on friendly terms), Wescott had Grand Lake to himself. In 1877, however, a Denver businessman moved there with his wife and eight children. Several other families soon followed.

In 1879 gold was discovered on the Colorado River about 15 miles north of Grand Lake. To reach the gold fields, well-provisioned prospectors crossed the Continental Divide from the east, along present-day Trail Ridge Rd. Those needing supplies followed a trail into Grand Lake, where they could load up before continuing their search for riches. By the end of 1879 Grand Lake had a hotel, a general store, a sawmill and many commercial buildings and residences. Along with this progress came gambling, prostitution and gunfights. A reputation for lawlessness kept many people away.

The boom was short-lived as the gold soon played out. By fall 1883 mining camps such as Lulu City were almost deserted. In Grand Lake, with bankruptcies the order of the day, only one business and a handful of people remained.

Gradually word spread of the area's beauty and its excellent fishing and hunting. As the 1880s drew to a close, Grand Lake prospered. By 1902 the area was attracting wealthy families from Colorado and surrounding states, who built summer homes along the shores of the lake. In 1905 the highest registered yacht club in the world (at 8,369 feet) was formed.

The biggest boost to tourism came in 1952 when the Colorado–Big Thompson Project was dedicated. The project created a series of dams, reservoirs, channels and a 13.1-mile-long tunnel beneath the Continental Divide to deliver much-needed irrigation water to the eastern plains. In addition to smaller reservoirs, the project created Shadow Mountain Lake and Lake Granby, making the Grand Lake area an ideal water sports playland.

GETTING THERE

Grand Lake is located 100 miles (about two hours) northwest of Denver. Take Interstate 70 west to Hwy. 40 and turn north. Just past Granby head north on Hwy. 34 toward Rocky Mountain National Park. A highly recommended alternative, in summer, is a drive through Rocky Mountain National Park on Trail Ridge Rd. (see the Major Attractions section in the **Estes Park** chapter).

MAJOR ATTRACTIONS

Rocky Mountain National Park

Perhaps the largest number of visitors to the area are drawn to Grand Lake for one reason: close proximity to Rocky Mountain National Park. With beautiful scenery, spectacular hiking and an abundance of wildlife, it's easy to see why. Information about the park has been interspersed at appropriate places throughout this chapter; the lion's share of details and background about the park, however, can be found in the **Estes Park** chapter.

FESTIVALS AND EVENTS

Fireworks Extravaganza
July 4th

Each 4th of July, more than 7,000 visitors jam into Grand Lake for what is billed as the largest fireworks display in western Colorado. At dusk, "ooos" and "ahhs" can be heard for miles around as the brilliant show unfolds over the lake. For this event, deck seating at the **Grand Lake Lodge** (see Where to Eat section) is the place to be. For information, call **(303) 627-3402** and **627-3372**.

Western Days and Buffalo BBQ
mid-July

Patterned after old-time celebrations, the Western Weekend features a buffalo barbecue (held annually since 1947), a 5K run, live music, as well as a parade down the 100-foot-wide Grand Ave. and a lighted boat parade on Grand Lake. For more information call **(303) 627-3402.**

Grand Lake Regatta and Lipton Cup Races
early August

Shortly after the founding of the Grand Lake Yacht Club in 1905, several of the club's members wined and dined English tea baron Sir Thomas Lipton. They convinced him their annual regatta needed a trophy and he donated a solid sterling silver cup. Each year members of the **Grand Lake Yacht Club** compete for the prestigious Lipton Cup while spectators cheer them on. For information call **(303) 627-3402.**

OUTDOOR ACTIVITIES

BIKING
MOUNTAIN BIKING

In summer, a growing number of fat-tire enthusiasts make their way to Grand Lake for leisurely excursions and training rides. Over 100 miles of marked single-track trails and dirt roads provide enough terrain to keep you happy for days. The excellent **Grand Lake Mountain Bike Trail Map** is now available free of charge at the **Sulphur Ranger District Office** on Hwy. 40 in Granby; **(303) 887-3331** and at the **Grand Lake Chamber** visitor center as you enter Grand Lake; **(303) 627-3402.**

In nearby Winter Park there are over 500 miles of marked trails, making it one of the top mountain bike centers in the state. For more information see the Biking section in the **Winter Park** chapter.

Rentals—

Rocky Mountain Sports—Christine, the French owner of this shop, rents mountain bikes, helmets and child carriers if needed. Familiar with the area, she can suggest many good trails and provides trailhead drop-offs if needed. If you own a bike, the shop will watch it while you eat lunch or wander around the village. Open Memorial Day–mid-Sept. **711 Grand Ave., Grand Lake, CO 80447; (303) 627-8124.**

FISHING

The Grand Lake vicinity is famous for its fishing. With **Grand Lake, Shadow Mountain Lake** and **Lake Granby,** the angler has a vast area from which to choose. Arapaho National Recreation Area, which encompasses several lakes, provides 340 overnight campsites as well as public boat access. The recreation area headquarters is located in Granby at **PO Box 10, 62429 Hwy. 40, (303) 887-3331.** Though the Colorado River and many other smaller streams flow nearby, the best fishing is in the lakes. Some experts believe record-breaking fish are cruising the cold depths of these lakes. Majestic views and the possibility of trophy fish make these lakes a paradise. There are several places to buy fishing tackle in Grand Lake.

Colorado River—

The stretch from Granby Dam down to the juncture with the Fraser River offers good fishing for brown and rainbow trout. Some browns up to 15 pounds have been taken in this area, but nearly all of the surrounding land is private.

Grand Lake—

As the largest natural body of water in Colorado, this 300-foot-deep lake offers rainbow trout, kokanee salmon and some of the largest mackinaw in the state. Mackinaws weighing more than 20 pounds are taken almost every year. Because most of the shoreline is private property, a boat is recommended. Rainbows are more active in spring. Trolling and inlet fishing usually produce the best results, especially from early spring through mid-July. Wet flies and lures are good for brown and rainbow while sucker meat can tempt those mackinaw. Spear fishing can also be good, if you don't mind cold (64°F) water. When the lake freezes over in winter, ice fishing rules. Boat rentals are available at **Boaters Choice, 1246 Lake Avenue; (303) 627-9273 or 627-3401.**

Lake Granby—

The largest of the three lakes, Granby offers 41 miles of shoreline when full. Mostly rainbow, kokanee and an occasional big brown trout are caught. Mackinaw fishing has picked up in recent years with lucky trollers catching some over 30 pounds. **Gala Marina** at **928 Grand County Rd. 64; (303) 627-3220** offers fishing boat rentals.

Shadow Mountain Lake—

This shallow reservoir offers rainbow, kokanee and some mackinaw as its prizes. Because of its 20-foot depth, it is often choked with weeds in late summer but the fish are there. The reservoir is best for rainbows and browns through July, with kokanee hitting later in the summer. The most popular areas for fishing are the submerged Colorado River channel and the shoreline. Ice fishing is often good. Boat rentals can be arranged through **Trail Ridge Marina, 12634 Hwy. 34,** 2.5 miles south of Grand Lake; **(303) 627-3586.**

GOLF
Grand Lake Golf Course—
At an altitude of 8,420 feet, this 18-hole course offers a challenge even to the best players. Carved out of aspen and pine forests and surrounded by the rugged peaks along the Continental Divide, the course has tight, tree-lined fairways. An errant shot will leave you with a lost ball, an unplayable lie or little chance of chipping back into play. Leave the driver in the bag at this course and don't expect to putt well the first time out. The break of the greens can be very confusing. From Grand Lake take Hwy. 34 north about a quarter of a mile. Turn left on County Rd. 48 and follow it about a mile to the course. **PO Box 590, Grand Lake, CO 80447; (303) 627-8008.**

Pole Creek Golf Club—
See the **Winter Park** chapter for information on this award-winning public course.

HIKING AND BACKPACKING
Grand Lake, surrounded by Routt and Arapaho national forests and Rocky Mountain National Park, offers some of the most accessible and magnificent hiking in the state.

For more information, backpacking supplies and maps, check with Tim or Marilou Randall at **Never Summer Mountain Products.** Open year-round, daily in summer and Fri.–Mon. in winter. **PO Box 929, 919 Grand Ave., Grand Lake, CO 80447; (303) 627-3642.** Hiking information and maps of hikes in **Rocky Mountain National Park** can be obtained at the **Kawuneeche Visitor Center,** just inside

the park on Hwy. 34; **(303) 627-3471.** The **Sulphur Ranger District Office** can also be of help. **62429 Hwy. 40, Granby, CO 80446; (303) 887-3331.**

Rocky Mountain National Park—
A permit is required for all backcountry overnight stays in the national park. These free permits, limited in number, are available at the West Unit Office all year (located at the west entrance to the park near the Kawuneeche Visitor Center on Hwy. 34). The permits are given out on a first-come basis but may be reserved by writing ahead of time. (See the Major Attractions section of the **Estes Park** chapter.) The following are four standout trails within the national park.

Colorado River Trail—The Colorado River Trail is an easy "up and back" hike that can be as long or as short as desired. It's a 2-mile walk to Shipler Park and 4 miles to Lulu City, an early mining town. When the national park was established, all the structures were removed as part of an effort to restore the area to its natural state. To get to the trailhead from Grand Lake, take Hwy. 34 north 8 miles into the park. Park at the Timber Lake trailhead sign. The Colorado River Trail begins on the left side of the road.

East Inlet Trail—This trail offers the day hiker several alternatives. Those wanting a short hike can stop at Adams Falls (0.75 mile one way). These crashing falls offer beautiful scenery with awesome mountain backdrops. Those who continue along the relatively flat trail another 15 minutes will find themselves in a beautiful high-country meadow. It's a great place to have a picnic and photograph Mt. Baldy. Those who can handle more uphill hiking can take the 4.5-mile trail to Lone Pine Lake, or to Lake Verna, another 0.75 mile. To get to the trailhead from Grand Lake, follow W. Portal Rd. to the end, about a mile and a half from the Grand Ave. junction.

Timber Lake Trail—The 4.8-mile hike to Timber Lake is a little more challenging than the Colorado River Trail. And the trail is well named ... you hike through a thick pine forest for most of the way. After climbing steadily for the first 2 miles (with views to the lofty peaks on the park's western boundary) you reach the Timber Creek drainage. From here the trail contours up the valley on a more level grade. This area is the only place in the US where the Continental Divide forms a horseshoe, thus surrounding the Kawuneeche Valley, including this trail and the Colorado River Trail. For directions to the trailhead, see the Colorado River Trail entry. The Timber Lake trailhead is on the right side of the road.

Tonahutu Creek/North Inlet Loop—A challenging 27-mile, three-day hike (downright difficult in two days) is the Tonahutu Creek/North Inlet Loop, which takes you deep into Rocky Mountain National Park. The best way to hike it is to head east up North Inlet Trail. Proceed over Andrews Pass (in the neighborhood of 12,000 feet) to Ptarmigan Pass and Ptarmigan Point (12,363 feet) through Bighorn Flats to the Tonahutu Creek Trail and then back to the trailhead. The hike from Andrews Pass through Bighorn Flats (all above 11,000 feet) takes you along the Continental Divide for spectacular views. This trip definitely is not for the beginner. Camp in designated areas only. To reach this trailhead, take West Portal Rd. about 0.75 miles to the Shadowcliff Lodge turn-off. Turn left; the road dead-ends at the trailhead in less than a mile.

In Indian Peaks Wilderness Area—
Since the Indian Peaks Wilderness Area receives heavy use from Front Range visitors, a backcountry permit is required for overnight camping. They are available at the Sulphur Ranger District Office in Granby. Call for reservations or check in to see if there are any last-minute permits available. Many trails leave from Monarch Lake into the wilderness area. For more hikes in the Indian Peaks, see the Hiking and Backpacking sections of the **Winter Park** and **Boulder** chapters. Here are two good hikes near Grand Lake.

Buchanan Creek Trail—A 9- to 10-mile hike of intermediate difficulty, the Buchanan Creek Trail parallels the north shore of Monarch Lake, then follows Buchanan and Cascade creeks to Crater Lake. You can camp and fish at Crater Lake, making the trip back the next day. Several opportunities exist for side trips off this trail. If you care to go to the top of the divide you can take Buchanan Pass Trail (veer north at the confluence of Buchanan and Cascade creeks) to 12,304-foot Buchanan Pass. It's about an 8-mile trip (not an easy hike) from the trailhead to the top of the pass. Another way to the top of the divide is Pawnee Pass Trail. Instead of turning south to Crater Lake, continue east 3 miles to the top of the 12,541-foot pass. To get to the trailhead from Grand Lake, take Hwy. 34 south to County Rd. 6. Turn left and follow the road about 10 miles to the trailhead at Monarch Lake.

Arapaho Pass Trail—This relatively easy trail follows Arapaho Creek to the top of the pass (approximately 11,900 feet). It's about 10 miles one way. The first 8 miles are easy hiking, with the last two uphill. This trailhead is also at Monarch Lake (see directions to Buchanan Creek Trail).

HORSEBACK RIDING
Sombrero Stables—
Horses are rented by the hour, day or week for trips into Rocky Mountain National Park. Special breakfast and dinner steak-fry rides are available as well as all-day Continental Divide trips. Reservations are necessary. Pony rides are offered for the kids. Open from the week before Memorial Day–mid-Sept. **304 W. Portal Rd., Grand Lake, CO 80447; (303) 627-3514.**

RIVER FLOATING
Although the headwaters of the Colorado River begin on the Continental Divide just north of Grand Lake, there is really no rafting in the immediate area. Downriver, less than 50 miles away, is one of the most popular trips anywhere. As

many as 40 outfitters make the trip from Pump House to State Bridge on the Colorado. Here are a few ideas for outfitters:

Rapid Transit Rafting—

Rapid Transit Rafting offers trips of moderate difficulty: perfect for the beginner but exciting enough to keep the experienced rafter interested. Though not mandatory, reservations are recommended. **PO Box 1368, Grand Lake, CO, 80447; (303) 627-3062** or **1-800-367-8523.**

Mad Adventures—

Located in Winter Park, they offer beginning to advanced river trips as well as inflatable kayaks, too. Call **1-800-451-4844** or **(303) 726-5060** locally.

Timber Rafting—

For reservations call **1-800-332-3381** or **(303) 887-2141.**

SKIING
CROSS-COUNTRY SKIING

Numerous cross-country trails wind their way into Rocky Mountain National Park and Indian Peaks Wilderness Area and provide serene backcountry opportunities. Trails in Grand Lake are readily accessible along with many other fine trail systems in the Winter Park area. Before heading into the backcountry, be sure to check out the latest snow conditions by calling or visiting the **Sulphur Ranger District Office** in Granby at **(303) 887-3331,** or at **Kawuneeche Visitor Center,** just inside Rocky Mountain National Park on Hwy. 34; **(303) 627-3471.**

Backcountry Trails—

In Rocky Mountain National Park—A ski in to Lulu City on the **Colorado River Trail** (see Hiking and Backpacking section) makes for a pleasant, scenic day trip. In winter, the road (Hwy. 34) is plowed to Timber Lake Trailhead, about 7 miles into the park. From here, a fairly easy ski trip with excellent views is to continue on the snowed in road up to **Milner Pass.**

Another trail idea in the park is **Green Mountain Trail.** For this one-way trail, you may want to use two cars to shuttle between the beginning and ending points. Take one car to the Green Mountain Trail, about 3 miles north of Grand Lake on Hwy. 34 into Rocky Mountain National Park. Ski along Green Mountain Trail east (uphill) about 2 miles. When you hit the Tonahutu Creek Trail, turn right (south) for a nice 4-mile downhill run. Total distance one way is 6 miles. Pick up your other car at the **Tonahutu Creek/North Inlet trailhead.** To reach this trailhead, take West Portal Rd. about 0.75 miles to the Shadowcliff Lodge turn-off. Turn left; the road dead-ends at the trailhead in less than a mile. If you want a longer, more strenuous trip, start at the Tonahutu Creek trailhead and do the trip in reverse and then return (6 miles each way).

Groomed Trails—

Ski Touring Center—Based at the Grand Lake Golf Course, this center features 25 kilometers of groomed and skating trails on and around the course. In addition, a connecting trail leads to Soda Springs Ranch and more trails. Rentals and lessons are available at the pro shop. For information contact the **Metropolitan Recreation District, PO Box 590, Grand Lake, CO 80447; (303) 627-8008.**

Rentals and Information—

Never Summer Mountain Products—Provides rentals and trail information. Open Fri.–Mon., but the owners tend to vary hours and days in winter. **PO Box 929, 919 Grand Ave., Grand Lake, CO 80447; (303) 627-3642.**

DOWNHILL SKIING

See the Outdoor Activities section of the **Winter Park and Middle Park** chapter.

SNOWMOBILING

Come winter, snowmobiles take to the streets of Grand Lake with the same rights as conventional street vehicles—so don't be surprised. Grand Lake boasts the largest groomed trail system in the state with approximately 130 miles of trails, in addition to deep-powder riding. The system provides everything from simple trail riding to hill climbing. Numerous shops in the area that rent snowmobiles can give you information on where to ride. One rental shop to consider is **Spirit Lake Rentals, Inc.,** located on Main St. as you enter town; **(303) 627-9288.**

TENNIS

Grand Lake Golf Course—

The **Metropolitan Recreation District** operates several tennis courts at the Grand Lake Golf Course. No fee; call **(303) 627-8328** for reservations.

WATER SPORTS

In addition to attracting people who like to fish, the lakes also bring in many other water sports enthusiasts. Public boat ramps and marinas are spread out on all major lakes in Grand County, providing access for boaters and waterskiers. Along Hwy. 34 there are numerous rental outfits on the shores of Shadow Mountain Lake and Lake Granby. Lake Granby, with its constant afternoon winds, is a favorite of windsurfers and sailors.

Whale Watch Tour
(Spirit Lake Marina)—

You won't see any whales, but this tour of Grand Lake is still fun. As old-timer guides regale you with tall tales, you'll learn a lot about the history of the area. There's really no other way to see the luxurious but rough-hewn homes built on the lakeshore. Take a sweater because it can get windy and cold. Tours leave daily at 10:30 am and 2 pm. If you want to take off on your own tour, the marina also offers boat rentals. Open from mid-May–mid-Oct. **1244 Lake Ave., Grand Lake, CO 80447; (303) 627-8158.**

———— SEEING AND DOING ————

MUSEUMS

The Kauffman House—

In 1892 Ezra Kauffman built the Kauffman House in downtown Grand Lake and ran it as a hotel until his death in 1921. The restored, two-story log house features displays depicting life in the late 19th and early 20th centuries. Open in summer for free tours. Contact the **Grand Lake Chamber of Commerce** at **(303) 627-3402** for tour information.

NIGHTLIFE

Stagecoach Inn—

Founded in 1923, this rustic bar is one of the local favorites. With a warm, friendly atmosphere, it features live country and western music on summer weekends. The Stagecoach Inn boasts the only dance floor in Grand Lake. Open all year 11 am–2 am. **920 Grand Ave.; (303) 627-9932.**

The Lariat Saloon—

Another local favorite is the Lariat Saloon. Occasionally cowhands ride their horses to town, tie up right in front of the saloon and step in for their favorite drink. The saloon also serves food. Live music on weekends. Open year-round 11 am–2 am; grill 11 am–1 am. **1121 Grand Ave.; (303) 627-9965.**

Rocky Mountain Theater Festival—

A talented cast performs highly acclaimed musical revues and comedy from mid-June–mid-September. These nightly shows (afternoon on Sun.) take place at the **Community Hall** in the park on **Grand Ave.** Advance reservations suggested. Call **(303) 627-SHOW.**

SCENIC DRIVES

Trail Ridge Road—

This incredible 48-mile road through Rocky Mountain National Park crosses the Continental Divide at a lofty 12,183 feet. Driving over during the short summer season is an absolute must! If you do it in early morning or at dusk, watch out for elk on the road as you drive through Kawuneeche Valley. See the Major Attractions section of the **Estes Park** chapter.

———— WHERE TO STAY ————

ACCOMMODATIONS

Grand Lake offers a multitude of places to stay—from rustic cabins and 80-year-old lodges to modern condominiums. For a fairly complete listing of lodging possibilities call **Grand Lake Central Reservations** at **1-800-462-5253.** Those listed below we feel have a special significance, but they are by no means the only good places to stay.

Grand Lake Lodge—$$ to $$$$

Constructed from lodgepole pine in 1925, this historic lodge takes full advantage of its hillside perch. A long porch equipped with swinging wooden loveseats provides soaring views over Grand Lake and Shadow Mountain Lake. Guests can relax and enjoy the stunning views from there or while plunked down in a lounge chair at the best poolside location in the state. The interior of the main lodge building is dominated by a large round fireplace with more swinging seats. Adjacent to the fireplace area is a gift shop with a selection of southwestern art and crafts, and at the other end of the long lobby there's a spacious dining room (see Where to Eat section).

Simple but comfortable two-room cabins are scattered in the woods around the main lodge. Several of the cabins offer kitchenettes. Larger families or groups are invited to stay in a cabin once used by Henry Ford. Henry would still feel at home at the lodge thanks to its small collection of vintage autos. The lodge entrance is located a quarter mile north of the Grand Lake turn-off on Hwy. 34. Follow the signs up a thickly wooded lane to the parking area. Open from the first weekend in June to the second weekend in Sept. For summer reservations contact the **Grand Lake Lodge, PO Box 569, Grand Lake, CO 80447; (303) 627-3967;** or **15500 U.S. Hwy. 34, Grand Lake, CO 80447.** Off-season try **4155 E. Jewell, Suite 104, Denver, CO 80222; (303) 759-5848.**

Lemmon Lodge—$$$ to $$$$

Set on the banks of Grand Lake, this hideaway, excellent for families, offers a private sand beach and 23 cabins on five wooded acres. Each of the cabins is unique: some offer full kitchens and cable TV while others are more spartan (and cheaper to rent). Aside from the usual outdoor activities, the lodge has a playground, horseshoe pit, volleyball court and enough barbecue grills to keep everyone happy. Excellent fishing in North Inlet Stream at the point where it flows into Grand Lake provides motivation for some guests to return year after year. Bring your boat along and slip it into the private dock. Lemmon Lodge has too many good sides to mention and, accordingly, cabins are usually booked a year in advance. Open from the end of May–mid-Sept. For reservations (minimum stay requirement) contact the Lemmon Lodge, **PO Box 514, Grand Lake, CO 80447; (303) 627-3314** in summer and **(303) 725-3511** in winter.

Rapids Lodge—$$ to $$$

Built on the banks of the Tonahutu River around 1910, the Rapids Lodge is the oldest existing lodge in Grand Lake. Owners Lou and Toni Nigro have worked hard to restore the split-pine building in a way that preserves its historic integrity while allowing guests the use of modern conveniences. Highlighted by a warm country decor, each of the six upstairs rooms offers creature comforts such as four-poster beds, thick quilts and color television. Each room has a private bathroom; some feature claw-footed tubs. The rooms vary in size and in price, but each provides much more than just a simple night's rest. Those who enjoy being serenaded by the sounds of rushing water may request streamside rooms. No young kids are allowed at the lodge. Nearby several small cabins and a selection of modern condominiums are available for overnight guests. Open year-round. Located at the east end of town (turn left at the end of Grand Ave.). For reservations contact the **Rapids Lodge, PO Box 1400, 209 Rapids Lane, Grand Lake, CO 80447; (303) 627-3707.**

Shadowcliff Lodge—$ to $$

On a cliff overlooking Grand Lake and North Inlet Stream, Shadowcliff Lodge clings to its spectacular perch. Two large, three-story lodges offer basic, extremely affordable accommodations for the lone traveler as well as families. Most of the lodge rooms feature bunk beds and sleep four to eight people. If you are a couple looking for a romantic getaway, this is not the place. However, for the chance to meet travelers from around the world, there are few better places than the spacious common room in the main lodge. With a small library, games, kids' toys and windows all around, it's a great place to hang out. Many large groups use the lodge for summer retreats; some dorm rooms are set aside for youth hostel members. Several good-sized cabins with full kitchens can be rented for longer stays. To keep their prices low, the owners ask guests staying in cabins to bring their own linens. No pets allowed. Family-style meals available for an extra price. Open June 1–Oct. 1. To get to the lodge from Grand Lake, take W. Portal Rd. north for 0.75 miles (W. Portal Rd. forks away from Grand Ave. directly across from Sombrero Stables in town). Follow the Shadowcliff Lodge signs from there. For reservations contact Shadowcliff Lodge, **PO Box 658, Grand Lake, CO 80447; (303) 627-9220** in the summer.

CAMPING

In Rocky Mountain National Park—

To reach **Timber Creek Campground** from Grand Lake, go north on Hwy. 34 about 7 miles into the park. There are 101 sites and a fee is charged. Some handicap sites available.

In Arapaho National Recreation Area—

Nearly 350 campsites are located within the recreation area and all require a fee. From Grand Lake go south on Hwy. 34 about 3 miles to County Rd. 66. Turn left and go another mile to **Green Ridge Campground** (80 sites) next to Shadow Mountain Lake. **Stillwater Lake Campground** (145 sites) is located 6 miles south of Grand Lake on Hwy. 34, just off the highway on the shores of Lake Granby. Another mile south from Stillwater Lake Campground, turn left on County Rd. 66 and proceed 10 miles to **Arapaho Bay Campground.** Also on the shores of Lake Granby, this campground has 77 sites. To reach **Willow Creek Campground** (35 sites) from Grand Lake, head south on Hwy. 34 for 8 miles and turn right on County Rd. 40. Proceed 3 miles to the shores of Willow Creek Reservoir. Advance reservations for Green Ridge, Stillwater and Arapaho Bay campgrounds can be made by calling **1-800-283-CAMP.**

In Arapaho National Forest—

From Granby head 3 miles northwest on Hwy. 40 and turn right on Hwy. 125. Proceed 10 miles to **Sawmill Gulch Campground** (5 sites); a fee is charged. Another 2 miles up Hwy. 125 leads to **Denver Creek Campground.** It has 25 sites; no fee.

Private Campground—

Elk Creek Campground—Open year round, this place provides RV hookups (summer only) and tent sites. Full facilities available including showers, laundry, groceries etc. Located just off Hwy. 34 north of Grand Lake at the Grand Lake Golf Course Road. **PO Box 549, Grand Lake, CO 80447; (303) 627-8502.**

Winding River Resort Village—Over the years this has developed into quite an operation. Spread out in a beautiful, thickly wooded location adjacent to Rocky Mountain National Park, you'll find 160 campsites, half of which offer full RV hookups. Hot showers, a small country store and laundry facilities are available. You may want to inquire about staying in one of the three extremely plush bed and breakfast rooms ($$$); a couple of small cabins ($$$), each with a private deck, are also available.

The lengthy activity list includes horseback riding, puppet shows, ice cream socials, a western barbecue dinner, volley-ball, hayrides, western movies, fishing and mountain biking. An 18-hole, par 56 Frisbee golf (FOLF) course complete with flags, scorecards and rental Frisbees winds through part of Winding River's 80 acres. (What, no carts?) As Wes puts it, "This is a place where kids can bring their parents for a good time." Entrance to the resort is located on Hwy. 34, across from the Kawuneeche Visitor Center. From here follow the signs for 1.5 miles. Call or write for information and reservations: **Box 629, Grand Lake, CO 80447; (303) 627-3215,** or Denver direct **(303) 623-1121.**

WHERE TO EAT

The Rapids Restaurant—$$$

Part of the historic Rapids Lodge (see Where to Stay section), the Rapids Restaurant offers fine Italian dining with large picture windows looking out to Tonahutu Creek, which is spectacular during runoff. Favorite dishes among patrons include lasagna and manicotti (all pasta is imported from Italy) as well as prime rib of beef. Excellent dessert choices change nightly. Children's menu offered. Open Jan.–late Nov. 5–9:30 pm. **209 Rapids Lane; (303) 627-3707.**

Caroline's Cuisine—$$ to $$$

Popular with locals and return visitors, this comfortable, six-sided restaurant offers fancy haute cuisine. Owners, Jean-Claude and Caroline met while working at the Ritz-Carlton in Boston, and their top-notch training shows through in the food. Start off with an appetizer such as steamed mussels in garlic butter sauce or onion soup au gratin. Entrée highlights include the cônfit of duck with orange sauce, filet mignon and a number of pasta dishes in addition to nightly specials. Be sure to try the decadent desserts. Full bar. Children's menu. Open for dinner Tues.–Sun. starting at 5 pm; Sun. brunch from 10 am–1:30 pm. Located 5 miles south of Grand Lake on Hwy. 34 at the Soda Springs Ranch turn-off; **(303) 627-9404.**

Grand Lake Lodge Restaurant—$$ to $$$

Located in the Grand Lake Lodge (see Where to Stay section), this restaurant offers one of the most spectacular views in Colorado along with fine dining. Look out on Grand Lake, Shadow Lake and the surrounding mountains while enjoying your meal. You may want to reserve a table on the deck in advance, as it gets very crowded for dinner. The restaurant serves breakfast, lunch and dinner as well as a Sun. champagne brunch. A rough-hewn interior and the mesquite-grilled specialties add to the atmosphere. Children's menu offered. In addition to a full bar the lodge has an excellent selection of micro brewery beers on tap. Breakfast served 7:30–10:30 am, lunch 11:30 am–2:30 pm, dinner 5:30–10:30 pm. Sun. champagne brunch served 9:30 am–1:30 pm. Open Memorial Day–Labor Day week. Located just off Hwy. 34 north of Grand Lake; **(303) 627-3967,** or **759-5848** in Denver.

The Mountain Inn—$ to $$$

When the urge hits for a meal like Grandma used to make, head for the Mountain Inn. Locals consider the Mountain Inn one of the best spots in town for down-home, country-style cooking. Specialties include real mashed potatoes, country gravy, chicken-fried steak and biscuits. Top off your meal with a dish of homemade ice cream. Full bar. Open daily all year 11 am– 10 pm. **612 Grand Ave.; (303) 627-3385** or **759-5848** in Denver.

Grand Lake Golf Course Restaurant & Lounge—$ to $$

This spacious restaurant/lounge provides pretty views while serving up tasty sandwiches and Mexican food for a great price. Appetizers are also popular, especially with the ravenous golfers and cross-country skiers who have just come in from a day on the course and trails. Open year-round: breakfast served Mon.–Fri., 8–11 am and Sat.–Sun., 7–11 am; lunches served Mon.–Fri., 11 am–4 pm, until 5 pm Sat.–Sun. See the Golf section for directions; **(303) 627-3922.**

Scandinavian Kaffee House—$ to $$

This small breakfast spot, owned by Ed and Ginger Chadwick, is widely known for its popular specialty—Swedish pancakes with lingonberries. Although primarily a breakfast place, a few lunch items, including sandwiches and Swedish pea soup, are on the menu. Hours are 7 am– 2:30 pm. Open Memorial Day–Labor Day week. **917 Grand Ave.; (303) 627-3298.**

SERVICES

Grand Lake Central Reservations—

P.O. Box 489, Grand Lake, CO 80447; (303) 627-3324 locally, **1-800-462-5253** toll-free or **(303) 443-5391** Denver direct.

Grand Lake Area Chamber of Commerce—

The staffed Chamber of Commerce visitors center is located at the intersection of Grand Ave. and Hwy. 34 as you enter town. **PO Box 57, Grand Lake, CO 80447; 1-800-531-1019** or **(303) 627-3402.**

Meeker

Every autumn hunters crowd into Meeker before setting off into the Flat Tops Wilderness Area to the southeast, their hearts set on bagging some of the area's plentiful game, which includes the largest indigenous herd of elk in the world. During the rest of the year, with the exception of July 4th weekend, this small town in the White River Valley of northwestern Colorado quiets down. The only conceivable traffic jam occurs when ranchers move large herds of cattle and sheep to and from summer ranges by way of local roads. Meeker is an off-beat outdoor lover's vacation destination. Nearby there are several guest ranches where visitors spend much of their time on horseback. Camping, fishing and hiking opportunities are limitless in the White River National Forest and Flat Tops Wilderness Area. Sections of the White River boast as many as 7,000 to 10,000 trout per mile. Also of note is that the national "Wilderness Area" concept was first conceived by a group of visitors enjoying the beauty of nearby Trappers Lake.

Meeker's apparent resistance to change adds to its charm. Most ranchers in this wide valley enjoy a way of life similar to that of previous generations. This continuity, coupled with the fact that Meeker is in a rather remote location, has caused a rich local flavor to emerge. There is no question that residents are proud of their rock-solid community.

HISTORY

Meeker was named after Indian agent Nathan C. Meeker, who was killed on the afternoon of Sept. 29, 1879, during a Ute uprising at the White River Indian agency. The incident was not solely the result of a local problem; rather, it was the culmination of inevitable conflict between Indians and settlers.

Nathan Meeker accepted the job as White River Indian agent in the spring of 1878. An idealist, he had been at various times a Greenwich Village poet, war correspondent, columnist and founder of a Colorado agricultural cooperative (now the town of Greeley). He wanted the Utes to stop their migratory hunting expeditions and to adopt the plow. The Utes, of course, had a different opinion about the sedentary life of farming. Distrust and resentment simmered as Meeker imposed his will during the first growing season. The next year he made a fatal mistake when he ordered an irrigation channel to be built through a field where the Utes raced their horses. He also had some of their best horse pastures plowed under.

War clouds gathered over the White River Indian agency in the late summer of 1879. Meeker finally understood that his safety was in peril when his favorite Ute chief, Johnson, threw him against the wall of his cabin for his offensive suggestion that some of the Utes' ponies be killed to free more farmland. After this assault Meeker sent a formal request for troops. A detachment of army troops, led by Maj. Thomas T. Thornburgh, moved in to support the agency. They were ambushed at Milk Creek by a small band of Utes, who swiftly killed Thornburgh and many of his men.

The Utes' anger turned on Meeker; they felt he was responsible for the advance of troops. In a rage, this small band of Indians descended on the agency later the same day, setting fire to the buildings and killing all of the men at the post. Meeker was found stripped and mutilated. The women, including Meeker's wife, Arvilla, and daughter, Josephine, were kidnapped and held captive for nearly a month on Grand Mesa. During this time they were raped, according to Ute custom, but eventually released. As a result of the White River Ute uprising, all Utes in Colorado suffered: the southern bands were relocated to reservations in extreme southwestern Colorado, while the northern Utes were banished to an area in Utah.

The massacre took place 3 miles west of present-day Meeker by way of Hwy. 64. A roadside marker points the way to the exact location of the White River Indian agency. A military camp was established at the present site of Meeker after the massacre. The army maintained order until 1883, when it closed the post and sold its buildings to settlers coming into the valley.

GETTING THERE

Meeker is 227 miles northwest of Denver. Drive west on Interstate 70 for 185 miles to the Rifle exit. Turn north on Hwy. 13 and continue 42 miles to Meeker.

———— FESTIVAL AND EVENTS ————

Range Call
July 4th weekend
More than a century ago cowboys started competing in the rodeo at Meeker. The annual tradition continues during the July 4th weekend with professionals and local ranch hands. In addition to the rodeo, Range Call offers fireworks, dances, concerts, footraces and, most importantly, the Meeker Massacre pageant—an historical reenactment that illustrates the painful clashing of Indians with the intruding settlers. **(303) 878-5510.**

Meeker Classic
Sheep Dog
Championship Trials
mid-September
Although it has been around only since 1987, the Meeker Classic Sheep Dog Championship Trials has developed quite

a reputation among sheep ranchers, dog lovers and neophytes who just want to see real working sheep dogs in action. Some of the world's best handlers and their dogs compete in a four-day event that pits them against a very challenging course and local

sheep. In addition to the trials, a wool festival features spinning and weaving, sheep-shearing demonstrations and product displays. For specific information about this annual event, contact the **Meeker Chamber of Commerce** at **(303) 878-5510.**

OUTDOOR ACTIVITIES

FISHING

The best fishing in the Meeker area is east of town. Nearly all the lakes and streams discussed in this section are located in the **Flat Tops Wilderness** and other parts of White River National Forest. Meeker offers easy access to the Flat Tops, which encompass some of the finest fishing territory in the state. This 9,600-foot plateau is laced with many high-country lakes and streams. Since there are no roads in the wilderness, getting to the best fishing requires some effort on foot or by horseback. One word of caution: the fish in the Flat Tops are well fed by multitudes of insects that flourish in the waterlogged environment. From spring through fall, be prepared to encounter thick clouds of mosquitos.

We have chosen to include bodies of water that provide relatively good fishing year after year. Remaining are countless fisheries in the backcountry, known only to longtime residents and guides. While many hidden lakes and ponds provide excellent fishing, some are unstocked and others face a yearly winterkill. For up-to-date fishing information call the Colorado Division of Wildlife's stocking report number at **(303) 291-7531** or condition report at **(303) 291-7534;** the division's northwest Colorado office number is **(303) 248-7175.**

Since the terrain is virtually devoid of readily identifiable landmarks, it is easy to get lost or confused. *Maps and a compass are essential.* If you have ever considered hiring a guide or an outfitter, this is the place for one.

The Orvis-endorsed fly fishing masters at **Elk Creek Lodge,** located about 18 miles east of Meeker, offer fishing on over

6 miles of private White River access, 6 miles on Marvine Creek and 100 plus pools along the lodge's 3-mile stretch of Elk Creek. If you tire of the excellent fishing in the area, climb into the lodge's plane for a guided day trip to the Gold Medal water of the Fryingpan River near Basalt, or the trout-infested waters of the Green River below Flaming Gorge in Utah. Steve Herter runs a first-class operation, which includes comfortable accommodations in four units and two cabins. As you may have guessed, Elk Creek Lodge can provide plenty of fond memories, but it ain't cheap. For information contact Steve at **PO Box 130, Meeker, CO 81641; (303) 878-4565.**

Bailey Lake—

If you want a smaller lake in the backcountry, this is an excellent choice. A 5-mile hike from Buford is required to reach Bailey Lake. It is another half mile to **Swede Lake.** Both lakes are considered good fisheries for brook and rainbow trout. To reach the trailhead, take Hwy. 13 for 2 miles east of Meeker. Turn right on River Rd. (County Rd. 8) and head 21 miles to Buford. The trail leads south from the community center in Buford.

Marvine Creeks—

Eight miles northeast of Buford, Marvine Creek flows into the White River on private land. County Rd. 12 follows the creek upstream 7 miles to the Flat Tops Wilderness boundary at Marvine Campground. Below the campground much of the creek flows through private land. Above the campground the creek splits into West, Middle and East forks with good trails following each. The West Fork of Marvine

Creek provides ideal water for catching small brook, rainbow and cutthroat trout on small flies. The Middle Fork is wider and therefore easier to fish. The East Fork can be good, if you can put up with the brush along the narrow banks. From Meeker take Hwy. 13 east for 2 miles. Turn right on River Rd. (County Rd. 8) and continue for 28 miles. Turn right on Marvine Creek Rd. and travel 7 miles to the campground.

South Fork of the White River—

Flowing into the White River near the town of Buford is the South Fork. A road parallels the river for 11 miles to the Flat Tops Wilderness boundary at South Fork Campground. From the boundary a good trail follows the river 16 miles to its origin. The farther you hike, the more beautiful the water and the better the fishing. Though the river is fast, there are many deep pools with lunker cutthroat and rainbows. Six miles of the upper section are limited to flies only. Stop in at the Buford Store and talk with Harry about his selection of small dry flies. He suggested we use a size 24 hook on the upper South Fork. Take Hwy. 13 for 2 miles east of Meeker. Turn right on River Rd. (County Rd. 8) and proceed for 18 miles. Turn right on South Fork Rd. and continue to the campground.

Trappers Lake—

Located near the northeast Flat Tops Wilderness boundary, this beautiful and easily accessible lake remains one of the best fisheries in the state. A pure strain of cutthroat trout reproduces naturally in the deep water of Trappers Lake. Boats without motors are allowed and may be rented at the Trappers Lake Lodge (see the Where to Stay section). Due to heavy fishing pressure, there are some special rules: the inlets (several) and the outlet (only one) to the lake are closed to fishing from Jan. 1 to July 31 to allow native trout to safely spawn; only flies and lures with one hook are allowed; any trout caught between 11 and 16 inches must be released, but you can keep any brook trout you catch. Four

campgrounds with a total of 53 developed units are located near the lake. To get to Trappers Lake, take Hwy. 13 for 2 miles east of Meeker. Turn right onto River Rd. (County Rd. 8) and proceed 39 miles to Trappers Lake Rd., which ends at the lake 10 miles away.

White River—

This river's headwaters are at Trappers Lake (see previous entry), then it flows west through Meeker and eventually into Utah. The upper portion of the river, for 6 miles from Trappers Lake to Himes Peak Campground, offers good fishing for brook, rainbow and cutthroat trout. Big Fish Creek flows into the White River at the campground and can be excellent for small rainbow trout. Below Himes Peak Campground, the river enters a long, narrow swath of private property. The next stretch of public fishing is located on the river near North Fork Campground. West of Meeker, fishing on the White River is poor, and whitefish are the only catch. To reach the upper portion of the White River, take Hwy. 13 for 2 miles east of Meeker. Turn right onto River Rd. (County Rd. 8) and travel 39 miles to Trappers Lake Rd., which ends at the lake 10 miles away.

HIKING AND BACKPACKING

To the east of Meeker is one of the most underrated recreation areas in the state—the northern section of the White River National Forest. If you hope to hike and backpack among the state's tallest peaks, this isn't the place. It's a land of rolling hills surrounding the vast plateau known as the Flat Tops Wilderness Area, which never rises above 12,000 feet. It offers relatively few people, plentiful wildlife, excellent fishing and beautiful scenery. Thick stands of aspen and pine are interspersed with fields of wildflowers.

Just after the turn of the century, Teddy Roosevelt came to the Meeker area on a hunting expedition in country that is still home to herds of deer and elk as well as mountain lion and black bear. If you plan a multiday backpack trip in this area, it would be foolish not to pack a fishing rod. Some of the streams and lakes in the national forest are what fishing dreams are made of.

Vegetation is lush and for a very good reason—it rains a lot here in the summer. Be sure to pack adequate rain gear. The mosquitos and flies can get thick, so bring some effective insect repellent. In autumn this is a popular hunting area, so it would be wise to dress in bright clothing. In addition many sheep graze in the Flat Tops area, so be sure to boil and/or purify all of your drinking water.

Once up on the Flat Tops, the trails crisscross, making route possibilities endless. For more information about trail ideas, contact the **Blanco Ranger District Office, 317 E. Market St., Meeker, CO 81641; (303) 878-4039.**

Chinese Wall Trail—

This trail begins at about 10,000 feet and runs south by southeast for 18 miles along the northwest border of White River National Forest. It then loops back around north for 7 miles to Trappers Lake. Along the way enjoy far-reaching views into the White River drainage to the west and the Williams Fork drainage to the east. The trail winds its way through stands of trees and high plateau meadows. Quite a few trails branch off from the Chinese Wall along the way. *Be sure to bring along a topographical map.* To reach the trailhead from Meeker, drive east 2 miles on Hwy. 13 and turn right on County Rd. 8. Drive 44 miles to the trailhead on the right, 0.2 miles from the summit of Ripple Creek Pass.

Marvine Trail—

This fairly long hike (11.5 miles) gives you a good sample of the Flat Tops Wilderness Area: excellent fishing, the rolling hills of the Flat Tops plateau and lots of pine and aspen groves. The gradual hike up Marvine Creek rises from 8,000 feet up to about 10,800 feet. A couple of stream fords are necessary on the hike, and they can be tricky during spring runoff. This highly popular valley is

also a good place to cross-country ski in wintertime. To reach the trailhead from Meeker, head east 2 miles on Hwy. 13, then turn right onto County Rd. 8 and drive 28 miles to Marvine Creek Rd. (County Rd. 12). Turn right, cross the bridge and take a left; proceed 6 miles to Marvine Campground and the trailhead.

Mirror Lake—

Located in a basin below some 1,000-foot cliffs, Mirror Lake, with its blue water and fantastic brook trout fishing, is one of the best short hikes in the area. The 2.5-mile trail climbs from 8,500 feet up to 10,000 feet, crossing private land in the process (stay on the trail). After about 2 miles you reach a lake with green water. This is Shamrock Lake. Continue on up the trail to Mirror Lake. To reach the trailhead from Meeker, drive east 2 miles on Hwy. 13 and then turn right onto County Rd. 8. Drive 39 miles to Trappers Lake Rd. (Forest Rd. 205). Turn right at Trappers Lake Rd. and drive half a mile to the Mirror Lake Trailhead access road. Turn right and drive a quarter mile to the trailhead.

Peltier Lake Trail—

This 6.5-mile trail (one way) climbs through oak brush and aspen groves as it rises to about 9,000 feet. After 3.5 miles, the trail passes Peltier Lake and continues another 3 miles to Bailey Lake. Both lakes offer good fishing for brookies and rainbow trout. To reach the trailhead from Meeker, head east on Hwy. 13 for 2 miles and then right on County Rd. 8 for 18 miles. Turn right on South Fork Rd. and drive 10 miles to the Peltier Lake Trailhead on the left.

Skinny Fish Lake/McGinnis Lake Trail—

This short 2.5-mile trail (one way) branches to the two lakes half a mile below Skinny Fish Lake. Located in the Flat Tops Wilderness Area, these lakes get heavy use from horse packers and hikers because the fishing is good. Either of the lakes makes for a great day hike, though you must endure many beetle-killed pine trees in the area. Also, be on the lookout for aspen trees that have been written on. In the late 1940s a Greek shepherd named Nick "Theo" Theopolis killed time (and maybe a few trees) by writing a daily diary entry on the aspen. ("Today I saw a coyote—but not a problem—looks like rain.") To reach the trailhead from Meeker, drive east 2 miles on Hwy. 13. Take a right at County Rd. 8 and drive 39 miles to Trappers Lake Rd. (Forest Rd. 205). Turn right and continue 8 miles. Pull in at the Skinny Fish Lake Trailhead parking area on the left. Walk a mile up the Lost Lakes Trail to the Skinny Fish Lake Trail intersection, which heads off to the right.

Spring Cave Trail—

A short half-mile hike from South Fork Campground leads to Spring Cave, the second largest cave in Colorado. Many of its passages are believed to be unexplored. Deep within its recesses is an underground passage known as Thunder Road, which contains one of the largest underground waterways in the United States.

From the campground the trail crosses the White River through blue spruce and climbs into aspen about halfway to the cave. Exploring the cave (spelunking) is definitely not suggested unless you are experienced! It's easy to get lost. To reach the trailhead from Meeker, drive 2 miles east of town on Hwy. 13 and take the right fork onto County Rd. 8. Proceed 18 miles to South Fork Rd. (County Rd. 10) and turn right. Drive 12 miles to the South Fork Campground. The trailhead begins here.

Trappers Lake Trail—

This trail begins at Trappers Lake. It follows the pine forests along Fraser Creek up into the high country of the Flat Tops plateau, about 5.5 miles from the lake. The trail extends about 16 miles (one way), and offers good campsites along most of the way. You can make your trip as long or as short as you want. Numerous trails intersect the Trappers Lake Trail, so a good map of the area can let you play it by ear and take side trips. Fishing in the endless potholes on the plateau can be worth your while. To reach the trailhead from Meeker, drive 2 miles east on Hwy. 13 and turn right onto County Rd. 8. Drive 39 miles to Trappers Lake Rd. (Forest Rd. 205). Turn right and drive 10 miles to Trappers Lake and the trailhead.

HORSEBACK RIDING

White River National Forest has more than 250 miles of maintained trails that are perfect for riding. Many outfitters can take you into the backcountry for hunting and fishing expeditions as well as for shorter rides. Consider staying in a local guest ranch if you want to experience western hospitality and saddle sores. Rental horses are available from each of the following:

Fritzlan's Guest Ranch—

1891 County Rd. 12, Meeker, CO 81641; (303) 878-4845.

Sleepy Cat Guest Ranch—
Trappers Lake Lodge—

Both are described in detail in the Where to Stay section.

SKIING

CROSS-COUNTRY SKIING

For trail ideas see the Hiking and Backpacking section or contact the **Blanco Ranger District Office, 317 Market St., Meeker, CO 81641; (303) 878-4039.**

———— SEEING AND DOING ————

MUSEUMS

White River Museum—

A visit to this museum is far better than climbing up into Grandma's attic. The museum, housed in a former US Cavalry garrison, features a hodgepodge of artifacts and historic memorabilia. The friendly museum curator said truthfully, "We've got a little bit of everything." You'll see a can of carrots from 1938, a bottle collection, a bear coat and a copper still from the 1920s. Prominently displayed is the plow that Nathan Meeker used to destroy the Ute Indians' racetrack. Don't miss the Spanish war ax or the carving in aspen bark of a pretty woman by local sheepherder Pacino Chacon. In the back room are a bright-red fire truck, horse-drawn carriages and a mounted two-headed calf. No fee charged, but donations are accepted. Open daily May 1–Dec. 1, 9 am–5 pm; Dec. 1–May 1, 10 am–4 pm. **565 Park, Box 413, Meeker, CO 81641; (303) 878-9992.**

SCENIC DRIVES

Flat Tops Trail Scenic Byway—
As the name suggests, this drive provides extremely scenic views as it makes its way up the White River Valley from Meeker and then over 10,000-foot Ripple Creek Pass on its way to the town of Yampa. About 40 miles of this 82-mile route are unpaved, but any vehicle can make the trip. It's even open in winter. Along the way are many places to fish, hike and take photos. One of the many worthwhile side trips is Trappers Lake (see the Where to Stay and Fishing sections), 10 miles off the main road on Trappers Lake Road. From Meeker, head 2 miles west on Hwy. 13 and turn right onto County Rd. 8. Continue on this road and follow the signs. Stop by the **Meeker Chamber of Commerce Visitors Center** for a detailed map with information about what to do and see along the way. Check locally for *Come Walk in Their Footsteps— Flat Tops Trail Scenic Byway* by Geri Anderson (Trail Finders Press).

———— WHERE TO STAY ————

ACCOMMODATIONS

Make no mistake … Meeker is a pure outdoor destination, and the best way to enjoy the area is to stay at a guest ranch or small cabin. There are heaps of such places scattered throughout the area. For a fairly complete list of opportunities, contact the **Meeker Chamber of Commerce** at **(303) 878-5510.** Here are a few highlights.

Sleepy Cat Guest Ranch—$$
Located 18 miles east of Meeker in the White River Valley, Sleepy Cat has been putting up families and sportsmen for the last 50 years. Twenty-one cabins with kitchenettes are rented by the night or by the week. The restaurant attracts people from miles away for great food and drink (see the Where to Eat section). Unlike some guest ranches, Sleepy Cat does not have an organized plan of activities for the week. The ranch sits near the edge of the Flat Tops Wilderness Area and offers outstanding fishing, hunting and cross-country skiing. Horses can be rented from an outfitter a half mile away. The people running Sleepy Cat are friendly, and the price is a pittance for what you get. The only drawback, if you want a secluded mountain experience, is that Sleepy Cat is fairly close to a main road. From Meeker take Hwy. 13 east for 2 miles. Turn right on County Rd. 8 and continue for 16 miles to the ranch. **16064 County Rd. 8, Meeker, CO 81641; (303) 878-4413.**

Trappers Lake Lodge—$$
This collection of 14 rustic cabins is located on the banks of one of Colorado's most productive fisheries (see the Fishing section). Though a recent upgrade replaced some of the wood stoves in the cabins with gas stoves and heat, you still must rely on a central bathhouse for rest rooms and hot showers. Other improvements include a new general store and a remodeled lodge building where delicious family-style meals ($$) can be found for an additional price. Trappers Lake Lodge offers guide services, especially for fly-fishing. In addition to the fishing on Trappers Lake, they have a number of fishing camps up on the Flat Tops; catch and release is emphasized. Rowboats,

canoes and horses are available to rent by the hour or by the day. The lodge lies adjacent to the northeast Flat Tops Wilderness boundary. Closed in winter. To get there take Hwy. 13 for 2 miles east of Meeker. Turn right at River Rd. (County Rd. 8) and head 39 miles to Trappers Lake Rd., which ends near the lodge 10 miles away. For more information contact: **7700 Trappers Lake Rd., PO Box 1230, Meeker, CO 81641; (303) 878-4288** or **878-3336**.

Meeker Hotel—$ to $$

Even if you are just passing through, stop off at this old hotel and take a look around the lobby. Once inside, your every move is watched by the beady glass eyes of 15 stuffed elk, buffalo, deer and bighorn sheep heads mounted on the surrounding walls. On one side of the room the Meeker Massacre is depicted by a mural-sized oil painting.

This hotel, built in 1896, once offered high-class accommodations, including a restaurant and a barbershop. Thanks to a recent upgrade, the 25 rooms have been enlarged and modernized; they range from suites with private bathrooms to small rooms with a bath down the hall. You can even stay in the two-room suite where Teddy Roosevelt slept during a visit in 1900 to hunt bear. Closed Dec. 1–May 1. **560 Main St., Meeker, CO 81641; (303) 878-5062.**

CAMPING

In White River National Forest—

Several campgrounds are spread out near the White River Valley east of Meeker.

To reach all of the listed camping areas, drive east on Hwy. 13 for 2 miles. Turn right on River Rd. (County Rd. 8) and proceed to the campground turn-off.

South Fork Campground: drive 18 miles east on River Rd., turn right on South Fork Rd. and head 12 miles over rough road to the campground; 17 sites; fee charged. **East Marvine Campground:** take River Rd. 28 miles east and then turn right onto Marvine Creek Rd. and proceed 6 miles; 7 sites; fee charged. Another mile up Marvine Creek Rd. is **Marvine Campground:** 18 sites; fee charged. **North Fork Campground:** drive 33 miles east on River Rd. (County Rd. 8) to the campground; 40 sites; fee charged. **Himes Peak Campground** is 39 miles down River Rd.; turn right on Trappers Lake Rd. and continue 6 miles to the campground; 9 sites; fee. **Bucks, Shepherds Rim, Trapline and Cutthroat campgrounds** are all located near Trappers Lake; fee charged. To reach the lake, drive 39 miles on River Rd., turn right onto Trappers Lake Rd. and proceed 10 miles. The campgrounds are located past Trappers Lake Lodge.

Private Campground—

Rim Rock Campground—For hearty souls this campground provides full RV hook-ups even in the cold winter months. Twenty tent sites, two rental cabins and five mobile homes are available. From Meeker head west for 2 miles on Hwy. 13 and then a half mile northwest on Hwy 64. **73179 Hwy 64, Meeker, CO 81641; (303) 878-4486.**

———— WHERE TO EAT ————

Sleepy Cat Guest Ranch—$$ to $$$

Nearly everyone we talked with in Meeker raved about the good food and atmosphere at Sleepy Cat. *It's definitely worth the short and scenic trip 18 miles east of town.* The restaurant, located in the recently built hand-hewn log lodge, is divided into several small dining rooms.

Some tables look out over a grassy meadow to the White River. The heavy pine walls of the restaurant are lined with the requisite hunting and fishing trophies. The menu dwells on steaks and chops; on weekends try the rib specials. Some seafood and chicken entrées are served, along with lighter meals ($) such as hamburgers and a salad and soup bar. A separate bar area fills up with ranch hands from the surrounding area and can be a fun place to spend some time before or after a meal. Dancing to tunes from the jukebox or occasional live bands often takes place on weekends. From Meeker take Hwy. 13 east for 2 miles. Turn right on County Rd. 8 and continue 16 miles to the ranch. Open daily Memorial Day–Nov., 8 am for breakfast, 11 am–2 pm for lunch, and 5:30–9 pm for dinner; Fri.–Sat. in winter for dinner only. The bar stays open all day and into the night. **16064 County Rd. 8, Meeker, CO 81641; (303) 878-4413.**

The Last Chance—$ to $$$

The Last Chance is just the kind of place you would hope to find in a small town like Meeker. Locals and folks passing through keep the tables and booths filled while chatting with the very efficient, friendly waitresses. Breakfast, lunch and dinner are served at The Last Chance, but the Mexican food is probably the most notable, especially the fantastic quesadillas. Others may say the BBQ and steaks are the big draw. For those wanting lighter fare here in the land of the beef eater, a surprisingly well-stocked all-you-can-eat salad bar is available. While waiting for your food, page through the menu, which contains newspaper articles of Meeker's more memorable historic moments. Be sure to admire the wall-mounted trophy of one of the area's wily jackalopes. Open Mon.-Thurs. 7 am–9 pm, Fri.-Sat. 7 am–10 pm, Sun. 8 am–3 pm. **975 Market, Meeker, CO 81641; (303) 878-4535.**

Trappers Lake Lodge—$$

Serves three meals daily; the burgers are excellent. Located in a spectacular spot on the banks of Trappers Lake at the Flat Tops Wilderness Area boundary. See the Where to Stay section for more information.

SERVICES

Meeker Chamber of Commerce—

This staffed visitor center provides information and advice on the area. **PO Box 869, 710 Market St., Meeker, CO 81641; (303) 878-5510.**

North Park

This is indeed a special place. While driving through North Park, which essentially follows the Jackson County lines, most visitors are drawn to the lofty peaks which surround the central park basin. The Medicine Bow Range to the east, the Rabbit Ears Range and Never Summer Mountains to the south and the Park Range to the west beckon all who appreciate the natural beauty we visit or live in Colorado for. North Park is reminiscent of Wyoming to the north … big views, a major ranching influence, and just a touch wilder than most areas of the state

Nowhere is this "wild" sense more evident than in the tremendously plentiful and diverse wildlife of North Park. Locals are quick to mention the Gold Medal fishing, excellent hunting and wildlife viewing available throughout North Park. Well-stocked waters of Delaney Butte Lakes and the North Platte River, among others, keep many anglers returning year after year; Colorado's largest concentration of moose (over 600) feed along the willow-covered streams and ponds of North Park.

North Park definitely qualifies as a Colorado backroad destination—instead of a neon cityscape, you look west to an array of peaks rising to over 12,000 feet in the Mt. Zirkel Wilderness Area. An extensive network of trails and dirt roads criss cross public land throughout the entire North Park area, beckoning visitors to explore. Colorado State Forest provides excellent access to such trails and roads along the base and into the Medicine Bow Range.

With a population of less than 1,000, the ranch supply center of Walden is the primary town in North Park offering motel accommodations and meals (though there is a fine restaurant in nearby Gould).

HISTORY

In the first half of the 1800s, Ute Indians would summer in North Park while hunting buffalo and an abundance of other wild game. Beginning in the 1820s, trappers made sojourns into North Park for the easy fur-bearing game. Despite Anglo presence, life for the Native Americans was relatively routine until settlement to the east, near present-day Fort Collins, began. Utes made raids on the new settlements, stealing horses and returning to North Park over Ute Pass in the Medicine Bow Range. The Anglo settlers rarely followed them into the mountains.

When John Frémont visited North Park on his second expedition in 1844, he called it a "paradise to all grazing animals." But it wasn't ranching that drew the first wave of settlement in North Park—it was prospecting. James O. Pinkham, a short Canadian old-timer, began panning for gold in the early 1870s. Other men followed but never struck the rich placer gold

111

they were searching for. By 1880 silver was the draw, and in only two years the new town of Teller City had a population of 1,300. The miners, however, soon learned that transporting the ore was too expensive, and by 1885 Teller City, in the Never Summer Mountains, was deserted. Many of the men who ventured to North Park for mining eventually settled here and began raising livestock. John Fremont had been on the mark back in 1844: the future of the valley was to be found in ranching. Although locals still rely on ranching and lumber for their livelihood, tourism continues to make an ever-increasing impact.

GETTING THERE

The approximate center of North Park is the town of Walden, located about 150 miles northwest from Denver. The most direct route is to drive west on Interstate 70 for 42 miles to Hwy. 40. Follow the highway to Granby before heading north on Hwy. 125 to North Park. Another choice is to follow the Cache La Poudre–North Park Scenic Byway, a picturesque 101-mile drive between Fort Collins and Walden (see the **Fort Collins** chapter).

FESTIVALS AND EVENTS

Never Summer Rodeo & Parade
late June

This annual amateur rodeo draws people in from near and far to Walden. Highlights include a barbecue, dance and parade. **(303) 723-4600.**

North Park Fair
mid-September

This event takes place in Walden over an autumn weekend. Check out the livestock, crafts or the 4-H sale, barbecue or dance. For information call **(303) 723-4298.**

OUTDOOR ACTIVITIES

BIKING
MOUNTAIN BIKING
Colorado State Forest—

With over 110 miles of trails, this is an excellent place for mountain biking. Many routes roll along through stands of lodgepole pine, spruce and aspen. The best way to reach the majority of the riding opportunities is through the main entrance to the forest.

One of the best ways to really experience the biking in the State Forest backcountry without having to carry a lot of extra weight is with an overnight stay along the **Never Summer Nordic Yurt System.** With a State Forest trail map, explore some of the prime trails such as Grass Creek Loop. On this difficult 16-mile round trip, you will pass North Michigan Reservoir and 10,000-foot Gould Mountain before finally coming out on Hwy. 14. Yurts are located in various places along trails throughout the forest. What's a yurt? For an explanation see the Cross-Country Skiing section. For directions, see the Colorado State Forest write-up in the Hiking and Backpacking section.

FISHING

Along with hunting, fishing is the major tourist attraction in North Park. Not only is the angling good on the dozens of streams flowing out of the surrounding mountains, but there are many popular lakes in the bottomland. So take your time and enjoy the mixture of plains and mountains while fishing in North Park. Don't hesitate to pursue some of the smaller tributaries and beaver ponds, for they sometimes offer the best fishing. Although much of the land in the park is privately owned and posted against fishing, miles of streams are open, due to fishing leases with land owners. These areas are marked; if you need more information on public water, stop by **Sportsman's Supply** in Walden, **400 Main St.,** and talk with Russ Bybee. Or call him at **(303) 723-4343** for an update on local conditions.

Delaney Butte Lakes—

Cold spring water feeds this series of three lakes, and ample hatches of insects help the brown, rainbow, and Snake River cutthroat trout grow to the size of small imported sports cars. OK, that's an exaggeration, but they do get big. The fishing is so good that North Delaney Butte Lake has been designated as Gold Medal water. Fishing tends to be better in spring and fall, especially early and late in the day. In Aug. the moss and weeds can get to be a problem for fishermen. Motorboats are allowed at Delaney Butte but cannot be rented. Camping is permitted around the lakes, but it's bleak—there is little to no tree cover or protection from the often gusty wind. To reach the lakes, head west 9 miles from Walden on County Rd. 12W (and then County Rd. 18) until the road reaches a T. Turn right on the well-marked road to Delaney Butte and drive north to the lakes.

Lake John—

A local favorite, this very shallow lake is seemingly full of large-sized cutthroat as well as some brown and rainbow trout. The 550-acre Lake John is easier to fish from a boat. There is camping on the west shore. To reach Lake John from Walden, head west for about 5 miles on County Rd. 12W and then north on the same road for about 7 miles.

Michigan River—

Locals seem to prefer the conditions and setting of the Michigan River to those of the North Platte. About 30 feet wide, the Michigan offers many good holes as it flows north through the park toward its confluence with the North Platte. Many lunker browns can be caught on the Michigan with lightweight fly or spin tackle. Three forks of this river flow into North Park from Colorado State Forest to the east and Routt National Forest to the south. Much of the river southeast of Walden runs parallel to Hwy. 14, providing many access points along the way.

North Platte River—

This meandering Gold Medal stream, flowing north into Wyoming, presents many deep pools and riffles where the predominant population of North Park brown trout feeds. Most of the fish are about a foot long, but some really large ones are pulled from the North Platte every year. Spinners can be effective early in the year, despite muddy water during the spring runoff; casting toward the banks is very good as long as you hunker down low enough to avoid showing yourself to the fish. The North Platte is also excellent for wading with fly-fishing gear. At times in late summer, irrigation demands severely reduce the flow. To get through irrigated plots, be sure to bring your waders and some mosquito repellent. Private land is interspersed with public access fishing. Just north of Walden, below the confluence with the Michigan River, is a good public fishing area. Ten miles north of Walden, a narrow canyon off Hwy. 127 is designated Wild Trout water; 1 mile after crossing the North Platte on Hwy. 127, turn right on a public access road to reach this stretch of river.

FOUR-WHEEL-DRIVE TRIPS

Upper Jack Creek—

This demanding but scenic road along Upper Jack Creek climbs high to the southeast into the **Never Summer Mountains.** Near the upper end of the creek the rough road forks, the right fork leading into the wide open Jack Basin, the other to the Never Summer Wilderness Area boundary and the trailhead to Baker Pass.

There are a couple of ways to reach Upper Jack Creek. From Gould, head south on Forest Road 740 for about 6 miles over Calamity Pass and down to an intersection at the site of Teller City, a thriving mining town in the 1880s. Today only a few remnants of Teller City's log cabins remain. At the intersection, turn left and head up valley. The wilderness boundary is about 5 miles from Teller City. Another way to access the area is to turn east onto County Rd. 21 about 2 miles south of Rand on Hwy 125. Drive about a half mile and turn right (southeast) onto Forest Rd. 740 and proceed about 10 miles to the Teller City.

HIKING AND BACKPACKING

North Park provides seldom-used trail access away from the crowds and into some of Colorado's finest mountain country. Many roads run west out of the park and butt up against the boundary of the Mt. Zirkel Wilderness Area. Encircled by Routt National Forest, this wilderness area offers hikers an expanse of beautiful terrain. Stop by the **Walden District Ranger Office** for information and maps: **612 5th Street, Walden, CO 80480; (303) 723-8204.** For more information on trails from the other side of the Mt. Zirkel Wilderness Area, see the Hiking section of the **Steamboat Springs** chapter.

Colorado State Forest also offers some excellent hikes. With over 70,000 pine-covered acres, this striking 28-mile long strip of remote land extends from the Wyoming border south to the Never Summer Mountains. By far the most popular hikes

in the forest are the ones leading up into the mountain lakes. Numerous trails climb into bowls in the Medicine Bow Range; try trips to **Clear Lake** (5 miles one way), **Kelly Lake** (4 miles), or **Ruby Jewel Lake** (1.5 miles). On the southern end of the forest there are also trails leading past the spectacular **Nokhu Crags** to **Lake Agnes** (1 mile), and the barren summit of Mt. Richtoffen. From here you can also access the seldom-used **Thunder Pass Trail** into the remote north end of Rocky Mountain National Park. Another such trail into the National Park is via **Baker Pass.** The one-mile trail leads to the pass summit for spectacular views into Jack Basin, south into Rocky Mountain National Park, and north into an adjacent drainage and the magnificent peaks of the Never Summer Range. For directions to the trailhead, see the Upper Jack Creek write-up in the Four-Wheel-Drive Trips section.

For further information about Colorado State Forest, drop by the Visitor Center. To get there, go through the main entrance about 20 miles southeast of Walden (2 miles northwest of Gould) along Hwy. 14; the southern entrance is another 5 miles southeast (toward Cameron Pass). **Star Rt., PO Box 91, Walden, CO 80480; (303) 723-8366** or **(303) 866-3437** in Denver.

RIVER FLOATING

See the River Floating section in the **Winter Park and Middle Park** chapter.

SKIING

CROSS-COUNTRY SKIING

Colorado State Forest—

Many miles of the roads and trails in the forest are transformed into excellent cross-country routes when the winter blanket of snow arrives. The park has an extensive network of trails available in winter. For trail ideas, you may want to call or stop in at State Forest headquarters (directions in Hiking and Backpacking section).

Never Summer Nordic Yurt System—

Cross-country skiers, bikers and hikers interested in comfortable huts on a multiday backcountry trip definitely should check out the Never Summer Nordic Yurt System. Actually, they aren't huts ... they are yurts—those portable dome-shaped dwellings used by nomadic Mongols and Turks in central Asia. Located in the State Forest, this yurt system offers great skiing along the Medicine Bow Range and Never Summer Mountains, as well as a fairly comfortable night's stay along the trail. Not quite as rustic as their Asian cousins, these semiplush yurts feature a sun deck and are reinforced to withstand the elements. Each sleeps six and is equipped with bunk beds and foam mattresses, a cook stove, lantern, utensils and firewood. Nightly rates are reasonable, especially during the week. Reservations are a must. For more information contact

Never Summer Nordic, PO Box 1254, Fort Collins, CO 80522; (303) 484-3903.

Upper Michigan Ditch—
Although this trip is very easy if you follow the main trail, side gulches along the way can provide some very challenging downhill runs. Upper Michigan Ditch Trail is located at the top of Cameron Pass. The route contours gradually uphill through the valley, alongside Michigan River. Once you reach the old, rundown cabins you'll have gone a mile and a half. The trail continues up the ditch if you're so inclined. To reach the trailhead from Walden, head 25 miles southeast on Hwy. 14 to the summit of Cameron Pass. Pull into the parking lot on the northwest side of the highway. The trail begins across the highway to the southeast.

—————— SEEING AND DOING ——————

MUSEUMS
North Park Pioneer Museum—
This museum, located west of the courthouse in Walden, keeps going and growing .... Every time we thought we'd seen it all, another room, chock-full of historical items, would open up. Take your time wandering through the Pioneer Museum and you'll gain a better understanding of the ranch heritage of Jackson County. Guns, saddles, carriages, kitchen items and antiques fill the museum. Small fee. Open mid-June through mid-Sept., Tues.–Sun. noon–5 pm; by appointment in winter, call **(303) 723-4711. 365 Logan St.** In Walden follow the signs from Main St. to the courthouse block.

SCENIC DRIVES
Cache La Poudre–North Park Scenic Byway—
This picturesque 101-mile drive between Fort Collins and Walden on Hwy. 14 follows the Cache La Poudre, Colorado's first Wild and Scenic River, and over 10,276-foot Cameron Pass before dropping into North Park. See the **Fort Collins** chapter for more information.

Nearby—
See the **Steamboat Springs** chapter for information on **Buffalo Pass** and **Rabbit Ears Pass,** which cut through Routt National Forest over the Park Range south of the Mt. Zirkel Wilderness Area. This is a beautiful loop trip, especially in fall.

WILDLIFE
Arapaho National Wildlife Refuge—
There are few better spots in Colorado for catching a glimpse of wildlife, especially waterfowl. During migratory months of May and Oct. and Nov., up to 8,000 waterfowl can be found throughout the 18,200-acre refuge. This magnificent, protected wetland habitat is best experienced at dawn and dusk when things can really come to life. In addition to waterfowl, the wildlife you may see practically runs the gamut of Colorado wildlife: golden eagles, great blue herons, owls, red foxes, beavers and, of course, moose.

To reach the refuge from Walden, drive south on Hwy. 125 for 7 miles and turn left (east) at the main entrance sign. Continue on the dirt road to the refuge headquarters; here you can take off on trails or pick up a brochure for the self-guided auto tour. For additional information, contact the **Refuge Manager at PO Box 457, Walden, CO 80480; (303) 723-8202.**

Colorado State Forest—

Wildlife viewing in the State Forest is excellent; if you are patient you can catch a glimpse of deer, elk, raptors and, more recently, moose. Until 24 moose were transplanted to North Park in 1978, Colorado essentially had seen the last of this magnificent animal. Today the North Park herd is flourishing, numbering over 600. The State Forest is home to at least 70 moose. For the best viewing, be out looking at dusk and dawn when the moose tend to spend most of their time in the willow-covered clearings by the streams and ponds. A new moose-watching platform has been built in the forest; stop in at Park Headquarters for directions. (Another great place to see moose in North Park is along the Illinois River, 2 miles south of Rand on Hwy. 125, then left at the Old Homestead Lodge, and 6 miles southeast on Forest Rd. 740.)

WHERE TO STAY

ACCOMMODATIONS

North Park is not a place to find a bed and breakfast or a historic hotel. But if you want to stay in the area, a basic motel room can be found in Walden, Gould or south of the park in Kremmling. For the listing of motels in and around Walden call **(303) 723-4344.** Many camping areas in the surrounding mountains lie in wait. There are, however, a couple of dude/guest ranches ...

Latigo Ranch—$$$$

The heavy woods you drive through on the way to Latigo (northwest of Kremmling) provide no indication of the spectacular open country that awaits at the ranch. With tremendous views of the Indian Peaks and unlimited trails for horseback riding and hiking, this small ranch is a perfect secluded getaway. Riding is emphasized; guests are paired with compatible horses for the duration of their stay. After a week under the instruction of experienced wranglers, your riding skills and horse knowledge should improve greatly. Take off on morning and afternoon trail rides, fish in the private pond or nearby rivers, or just relax by the swimming pool.

The family atmosphere at Latigo encourages people from around the country to get to know one another. One return guest commented, "They make you feel as though you were a guest in their own home." The food is gourmet-ranch style–if there is such a thing. Two entrées are served each evening in the dining room; breakfast and lunch are served buffet-style. Latigo is also open in winter, attracting cross-country skiers and snowmobilers alike. Adjacent to the ranch you'll find more than 30 kilometers of groomed ski trails and some of the best backcountry terrain you'll ever encounter. **PO Box 237-D, Kremmling, CO 80459; 1-800-227-9655** or **(303) 724-9008.**

Whistling Elk Ranch—$$$$

Ride your horse through 6,000 beautiful acres of private land or fish three miles of trout filled stream in one of the most scenic sections of North Park. For over 40 years the Brown family has operated their spacious working ranch. With scads of elk, deer, moose and other wildlife in the vicinity, Whistling Elk has been successfully outfitting hunters for years. But just recently, the ranch opened its gate to visitors who want to horseback ride, mountain bike, fish, cross-country ski, hike and just relax. Guests are also welcome to join in ranch chores such as roundups and fence mending. To each his own, I guess.

Three recently remodeled cabins with two bedrooms sleep up to four people; each comes with a wood-burning stove and a kitchen, which comes in handy as meals are not included. There's also a "secluded" hot tub. Guests can also opt for a backcountry horsepacking trip with camp meals prepared.

Access to this beautiful area is not cheap; horseback riding and fishing on the private stream require an additional charge. Located a few miles north of Rand on County Rd. 27 at **PO Box 2, Rand, CO 80473; (303) 723-8311.**

CAMPING

Colorado State Forest—

The state forest charges a fee not only to access its land but also to stay at one of its four developed campgrounds (104 sites). All of the State Forest's campgrounds are accessible from the north and south entrances to the park along Hwy. 14 near Gould. To reach **North Michigan Reservoir Campground** (24 sites) turn right off Hwy. 14 (2 miles northwest of Gould) at the north entrance to the state park. This is a heavily used campground since boating is permitted at North Michigan Reservoir. To reach **Bockman Campground** (28 sites), continue east for just over a mile on the road past North Michigan Reservoir. At the south end of the park (about 3 miles east of Gould on Hwy. 14) is **Ranger Lakes Campground** (25 sites). Some 4 miles beyond the turnoff to Ranger Lakes, the twisting road to the **Crags Campground** takes off from the right side of the road. Crags has 27 campsites (large rigs may think twice about attempting this steep road).

State Forest also offers rustic cabin rentals ($ to $$). All of the seven cabins (six on the shores of North Michigan Reservoir and one at the Lake Agnes Trailhead) come equipped with wood burning stoves, bunks with mattresses, picnic tables and grills; they do *not* have electricity or running water. To reserve a campsite or cabin in advance, call **(303) 470-1144** in Denver or **1-800-678-CAMP.**

In Routt National Forest—

To reach **Grizzly Creek Campground** from Walden, drive southwest on Hwy. 14 for 13 miles and turn right (west) onto County Rd. 24. Continue 11 miles to the edge of the national forest and this campground, which has 12 sites and a fee. Two miles north of Grizzly Creek on Forest Rd. 615 is **Teal Lake Campground** with 17 sites and a fee. Four miles south of Grizzly Creek Campground on Forest Rd. 20 you'll come to **Hidden Lakes Campground** with 9 sites and a fee. Don't bother fishing in the lakes—it's lousy. **Big Creek Lakes Campground,** on the 400-acre Big Creek Lake at the edge of the Mount Zirkel Wilderness Area, offers 54 sites and charges a fee. Near the Wyoming border, **Big Creek Lakes** can be reached from Walden by heading north on Hwy. 125 to Cowdrey and then west on County Rd. 6 to Pearl. After that, follow the signs southwest on Forest Rd. 600.

Aspen Campground (in the southeast corner of North Park) is 1 mile southwest of Gould on Forest Rd. 740. It has 12 sites and a fee. **Pines Campground** is 2 miles farther south on Forest Rd. 740. It has 11 sites and a fee.

Private Campgrounds—

Lake John RV Park—Located in open country on the south end of Lake John, this place has plenty of RV hookups. Open May–Oct.; 17 miles from Walden. **4521 County Rd. 7A, Star Route, Box 410, Walden, CO 80480; (303) 723-4407** or **723-4533** in the off-season.

North Park KOA Kampground—People who take their RV amenities seriously can rest assured that this KOA has every creature comfort possible. In addition to 27 RV sites, campsites and cabins are available. Located just off Hwy. 14 at the entrance to Colorado State Forest (just outside of Gould). **Star Route, Box 90A, Walden, CO 80480; (303) 723-4310.**

WHERE TO EAT

Cookhouse Dining Room and Lounge—$ to $$$

Situated in the woods of Gould, near the entrance to the Colorado State Forest, the Cookhouse is reminiscent of a rustic roadhouse along the Alaska Highway. An occasional moose even appears in the surrounding forest. Opened in 1978 (the year the state finally paved Cameron Pass), this roadside restaurant offers hearty lunches and dinners in a cozy dining room with an impressive stone fireplace. For lunch try one of the specialty sandwiches, the salad bar or an enormous Wrangler burger; dinners are highlighted by steaks, prime rib and honey-dipped chicken. If you get restless while waiting for your meal, take time to examine the placemat, which features all 92 ranch brands from the North Park area. The bar area is a great place to stop in after a day of hiking or cross-country skiing; 25 brands of beer are available. Open Wed.–Mon. 11 am–9:30 pm and daily during hunting season. Bar is open later. Located along Hwy. 14 in Gould; **Star Rt. Box 95; (303) 723-8339.**

Elk Horn Cafe—$ to $$

The Elk Horn qualifies as one of those places where the locals go to catch up on what's what. And should you forget the topic of many conversations in the cafe, take a gander at the branding iron marks, ropes and other ranching doodads on the surrounding walls. Meals here are homecooked: hearty breakfasts, burger-type lunches and steak, meatloaf and fried chicken for dinner. A pretty decent salad bar is also available. Check out the impressive pie selection. 5:30 am–8:30 pm daily. Located in Walden at **486 Main; (303) 723-9996.**

SERVICES

North Park Chamber of Commerce—

PO Box 68, Walden, CO 80480; (303) 723-4600.

North Park Tourism Information Center—

Staffed for most of the year; plenty of brochures and information. Located on Main in Walden. **PO Box 489TB, Walden, CO 80480; (303) 723-4344.**

Redstone and Crystal River Valley

An ideal mountain retreat, the Crystal River Valley captures the essence of the Rockies. Away from large resort towns, it offers exactly what many people hope to find while visiting Colorado: impressive natural beauty, fascinating history, genuine people and a long list of year-round outdoor activities. This place also offers a welcome contrast to its fast-paced neighbor Aspen—yet Aspen is close enough for visitors to head up the Roaring Fork Valley for great downhill skiing and nightlife.

Hemmed in from the east by peaks reaching above 14,000 feet, the Crystal River flows through this pristine valley. After turning onto Hwy. 133 at the town of Carbondale, the road winds along beside the Crystal River. The lower part of the valley is completely dominated by the broad shoulders of Mt. Sopris (12,953 feet), which looms like a much higher peak. The woods thicken and the scenery becomes more beautiful along the upper reaches, which lie under the prominent Elk and Ragged mountains.

Caught between the Maroon Bells–Snowmass Wilderness and the Raggeds Wilderness, hikers find virtually unlimited access to pristine backcountry. Fishing, kayaking, mountain biking and horseback riding draw others. In winter the focus shifts to cross-country and downhill skiing. In an area of spectacular beauty, the entire valley manages to look its best in fall, when red rocky cliffs are contrasted by broad strokes of golden aspen.

The small towns of Redstone and Marble and the ghost town of Crystal bring an enduring past to light. Ten miles upriver from Carbondale is Redstone, a charming one-street community of about 100 residents. Now many of the miners' homes have been refurbished for summer use. Redstone is also home to a number of fine art galleries and antique shops. At the south end of town, the distinctive Redstone Inn stands much as it did in the early 1900s. Two miles south of town, the magnificent Redstone Castle (Cleveholm) looks like a misplaced storybook fantasy. Further upriver the ramshackle village of Marble, long dependant on its namesake, has found hope again with the reopening of the quarry.

HISTORY

For many hundreds of years nomadic Utes spent summers hunting in the Crystal River Valley. They were later promised by treaty that this land would be theirs forever. However, by 1872 prospectors began trickling over the mountains into the southern end of the secluded valley from Gothic and Crested Butte. The land was officially opened to settlement in 1881 when the Utes were forced to depart for distant reservations in Utah. Small ranches

119

and farms began to flourish, especially in the wide northern end of the valley near the confluence of the Crystal and Roaring Fork rivers.

In 1882 John Osgood, founder of Pueblo's Colorado Fuel & Iron (CF&I), purchased coal claims in the area. Two decades later he founded the model coal village of Redstone with mixed success. In an attempt to avoid the labor problems of other coal towns, Osgood provided each worker with rather luxurious conditions. But the miners resented their loss of independence, as they were forced to join in the community and obey Osgood's many rules. For instance, the men were to shower before appearing on the streets after work, and a "no treating" rule prevented workers from buying drinks for friends.

The Redstone Inn was created as an upscale community hall and bachelor rooming house. Miners with families were put up in small houses, each built slightly different from the next. A couple of miles upvalley Osgood built his opulent $2.5-million, 42-room dream palace called *Cleveholm* (from the first part of his middle name, Cleve, and *holm*, which in Old English means a grassy place with a stream running through it). Rooms were paneled with solid mahogany woodwork, gold leaf, silk brocade and elephant hide; imported chandeliers, rugs and furniture were placed throughout. Osgood entertained industrialists, celebrities and even President Theodore Roosevelt. By 1903 Osgood was virtually forced out of business by economic difficulties and the incursions of eastern tycoons J.P. Morgan and John D. Rockefeller, but he remained a millionaire until his death in 1926.

In the late 1800s marble was quarried with some success at the upper end of the Crystal River Valley. The marble, with its glistening white color veined with pale browns, rivaled the best Italian varieties. With the opening of the Yule Marble Quarry in 1905, the entire valley underwent an economic revival. Trains of 40 mules brought marble to the railhead in the town of Marble until an electric train began service to the quarry in 1908. The town grew quickly and by 1916 boasted a population of over 1,500. The largest piece of marble ever quarried at Marble was a 100-ton block for the Tomb of the Unknown Soldier, which took one year to pare down to 56 tons. The construction of the Lincoln Memorial in Washington, DC, also depended on marble from here. In 1941 a flood and resultant mudslide destroyed much of the town and caused the railroad to stop service. The quarry has recently reopened and now ships marble to markets including Italy!

Over the years many developers have come into the Crystal River Valley with new ideas to promote tourism. But most people seem to come to this isolated valley because it has remained relatively undeveloped.

GETTING THERE

From Denver take Interstate 70 west for 166 miles to Glenwood Springs. Turn onto Hwy. 82 and go 10 miles southeast to Carbondale. Turn right onto Hwy. 133 and head up the Crystal River Valley.

Fly United Express from **Denver International Airport** to the Aspen/Snowmass Airport. (Direct service is available from Los Angeles and San Francisco.) Redstone is located 42 miles from the airport.

For a change of pace, take an Amtrak train into Glenwood Springs from Chicago (via Denver) or from San Francisco. Call **Amtrak** for reservations and information at **1-800-872-7245.** From Glenwood rent a car for the 27-mile ride to Redstone.

———— FESTIVALS AND EVENTS ————

See the Festivals and Events section in the **Aspen** and **Glenwood Springs** chapters for information on nearby happenings.

———— OUTDOOR ACTIVITIES ————

BIKING

MOUNTAIN BIKING

Many jeep roads and single-track trails are ideal for mountain bikes. The best rides leave from Marble. A great 4-mile ride heads up to the historic marble quarry on a recently improved road. Now that the quarry has reopened, you'll encounter more activity along the way. Another favorite is a 5-mile ride up to the ghost town of Crystal (see Four-Wheel-Drive Trips) and its picturesque mill. Adventuresome riders can continue from Crystal over Schofield Pass, eventually dropping into Gothic and Crested Butte.

For rentals and backcountry information, contact **Downhill Don's** in Marble at **(303) 963-0629,** or the **Sopris Ranger District Office** in Carbondale at **620 Main St., Carbondale, CO 81623; (303) 963-2266.**

TOURING

The 31-mile ride up the Crystal River Valley on Hwy. 133 from Carbondale to Marble has long been a favorite of bicyclists. Not only is the scenery fantastic, but the narrow valley protects you from the wind.

FISHING

Beaver Lake—

Located in the town of Marble, this small, heavily fished lake is filled by the Crystal River. Fairly consistent fishing for rainbow and brook trout can largely be attributed to the stocking program. It's a great place for a canoe or a small rowboat, but no motors are allowed.

Crystal River—

At the ghost town of Crystal, the north and south forks converge and the fast-running Crystal River begins its 35-mile tumble down the valley. The river eventually flows into the Roaring Fork River a couple of miles below Carbondale. The heavily stocked river is a good place to catch pan-sized rainbow trout. But because it's easily accessible from the road, this beautiful river can get crowded with anglers. You'll find fewer people as you move upvalley toward Marble, and chances are you'll get more action from brook trout there.

Dinkle Lake—

Rainbow and brook trout are frequent catches at this high-country lake situated near the edge of White River National Forest northeast of Redstone. It's a good place for a leisurely picnic. A 3.5-mile hike from Dinkle Lake, with a 1,600-foot elevation gain, will land you at **Thomas Lakes.** There you'll be challenged by feisty cutthroat trout. The two lakes are about a quarter of a mile apart and have several primitive campsites on their perimeters. The marked turn-off to Dinkle Lake is located a mile south of Carbondale, near the fish hatchery on Hwy. 133.

Gold Medal Waters—

The highly rated **Roaring Fork** and **Fryingpan** rivers are discussed in the **Aspen** chapter.

Yule Creek—

Yule Creek flows into the town of Marble from the south. It's quick and narrow and can provide good fishing for small cutthroats. Cascading over remnants of quarried white marble, the creek takes on a translucence even in some deep spots. The dirt road to the marble quarry parallels the creek for 4 miles through private property. After the quarry a hiking trail follows the creek southeast toward Yule Pass. To reach Yule Creek from Marble, turn right on 3rd St. and drive to a parking area for the mill. Walk or drive across the one-lane bridge for a short distance until you see the little creek by the road.

FOUR-WHEEL-DRIVE TRIPS

Jeep Tours—

Crystal River Jeep Tours offers several different trips in the area, including daily tours to the Yule Marble Quarry and the Crystal Mill. They have jeep rentals, too. All leave from the town of Marble. Call for reservations. **Raspberry Ridge, 200 E. State St., Marble, CO 81623; (303) 963-1991.**

Schofield Pass—

Beginning in Marble, a rough dirt road heads west to the ghost town of Crystal before a treacherous ascent to the top of Schofield Pass (10,707 feet). A mile beyond Marble, turn right on Forest Rd. 314 and continue 4 miles to Crystal. The first man-made structure you will see is the photogenic Sheep Mountain Mill; since 1892 it has been clinging to its rocky perch above the Crystal River. Just beyond the mill, over a slight rise, are the wood-frame houses of "Crystal City." In 1881 Crystal was a bus-

tling town of 650 residents, who used the town as a jumping-off point for prospecting in the area. It had its own newspaper, hotel, general store and post office. Today a dozen original, well-preserved buildings remain as summer homes. The section of the road from Crystal to the top of the pass is suited only to small jeep-type vehicles and experienced drivers.

After Crystal, Forest Rd. 317 leads southwest on a precipitous route toward the pass. At the top of the steep grade a lush meadow marks the site of the abandoned town of Schofield. It was founded in 1879 by a group of miners who didn't seem to care that they were inside Indian territory. After the summit wind down the other side to Gothic and eventually to Crested Butte. If you are staying in Redstone or Marble, try a scenic loop trip from Crested Butte: return over Kebler Pass and McClure Pass, dropping back into the Crystal River Valley.

HIKING AND BACKPACKING

The hiking in this area is surprisingly diverse. There are little-used access points to the Maroon Bells–Snowmass Wilderness Area and hikes into historic locales. You'll always be accompanied by a vista of tall peaks. Since most hikes lead into high elevations of the White River National Forest, beware of altitude sickness. For more information and maps, contact the **Sopris District Office, 620 Main St., Carbondale, CO 81623; (303) 963-2266.**

Avalanche Creek—

This trail leads from Avalanche Campground on a southwestern route into the Maroon Bells–Snowmass Wilderness Area. Hike in as far as you wish for a day trip. This is also a good choice for a two-day backpack trip, since the elevation gain is fairly gradual. The trail merges with East Creek Trail after about 6 miles. East Creek Trail eventually heads west back to Redstone. If you continue on Avalanche Creek Trail, you'll end up in the heart of the Maroon Bells–Snowmass Wilderness Area near Capitol

Peak, Capitol Lake and Avalanche Lake. These are gorgeous hikes, especially when the wildflowers are at their peak, starting in mid-July. Good maps are essential. To reach the trailhead, drive south on Hwy. 133 for 12 miles from Carbondale. Turn left (east) and continue for 3 miles on a rough dirt road to Avalanche Campground.

Crystal—

Bring your camera on this easy 4-mile walk along a jeep road to the ghost town of Crystal. The walk is shaded by aspen and evergreens most of the way. In summer you'll enjoy the cooling effect of walking beside the rushing waters of the Crystal River. Before long you'll see the famous mill, waterfall and the dozen remaining buildings of the old town. See the Four-Wheel-Drive Trips section for more information. To reach the road from Marble, head east from Beaver Lake for a mile to a junction in the road. Park near the junction, unless you have a four-wheel-drive vehicle, and walk down the right fork (Forest Rd. 314) to Crystal.

Thomas Lakes and Mt. Sopris—

From Dinkle Lake the 3.5-mile hike to Thomas Lakes is a beautiful introduction to hiking trails in the area. The two lakes are located on the northwestern side of the massive twin peaks of Mt. Sopris (both reach 12,953 feet). The hike can be done easily in a day; you'll want to bring along your fishing pole. Many hikers spend the night at primitive campsites near the lakes before making the 2,700-foot climb from the lakes to the top of Mt. Sopris. The hike to the summit is nontechnical, but you should be in good shape. The trail leads due south from the southeast side of Thomas Lakes. A mile south of Carbondale near the fish hatchery on Hwy. 133, take the Prince Creek Rd. turn-off to Dinkle Lake. Start walking. *Note: This last stretch of road becomes impassable when wet, so keep your eye on the weather.*

Yule Marble Quarry—

A fascinating but short hike leads from a parking area next to Yule Creek to the actual quarry. See the Scenic Drives section for information.

HORSEBACK RIDING

It doesn't matter what kind of equestrian training you have, because rides for all abilities are provided by **Twin Pines Outfitting** in Marble. You can arrange anything from a five-day wilderness pack trip to an hour's walk on horseback through the woods. George Sever offers breakfast, lunch and barbecue dinner rides. **(303) 963-1220.** Another good option is **Chair Mountain Stables** in Redstone. Located behind the old coke ovens at **17843 Hwy. 133; (303) 963-1232.**

RIVER FLOATING

Crystal River—

The fast-running Crystal is a great river for experienced kayakers with enough sense to portage at a Class VI section known affectionately as the "meatgrinder." The river is free flowing and therefore provides a very high run in June before slacking off in mid- to late summer. To have a successful trip, you must either know the river or spend some time along its banks scouting suitable stretches.

Roaring Fork—

See the **Aspen** chapter.

SKIING
CROSS-COUNTRY SKIING

The Crystal River Valley offers a range of cross-country skiing in fluffy powder snow. Many nordic skiers come to this peaceful valley to make tracks on old forgotten roads, mountain trails and organized trail systems. The only conceivable drawback to skiing in this narrow valley is the short-lived sunshine. Many trails, however, avoid this by climbing high above the valley. For more trail ideas and information on the extensive 10th Mountain Trail Association Hut System, see the Skiing section of the **Aspen** chapter. Check with the **Sopris Ranger District Office** in Carbondale for current avalanche conditions. **620 Main St.; (303) 963-2266.**

Backcountry Trails—
McClure Pass—From the top of McClure Pass (8,755 feet), enjoy spectacular views of the Ragged Mountains and back to the Crystal River Valley. While skiing ungroomed trails far above the valley floor, you'll have a chance to bask in the sun. A moderately easy forest road sets out to the south from the summit. Dogs allowed. To reach McClure Pass drive southwest on Hwy. 133 from Redstone.

Town Trail—Starting at the Redstone Inn, this easy 2-mile round-trip tour tracks along behind town, passing by the old schoolhouse and many former miners' homes. The Town Trail is perfect if you are interested in skiing the flats with the opportunity for a warm cup of hot chocolate at the end of the trail. You can rent skis at the Inn and inquire about other trail possibilities. For information call **(303) 963-2526.**

Groomed Trails—
Spring Gulch Trail System—Near Carbondale a 10-mile nordic system of groomed trails is open to the public at no charge. There are advanced, intermediate and beginner trails. Pick up a map and a descriptive brochure at many locations in Carbondale. Spring Gulch is located 7 miles west of Carbondale on County Rd. 108.

DOWNHILL SKIING
Aspen and Snowmass—
You can ski at any of four world-class mountains in about an hour from Redstone. See the **Aspen** chapter for more information.

Sunlight—
Consider a day of skiing at this uncrowded smaller area. From the Crystal River Valley, Sunlight is a bit closer than Aspen. See the **Glenwood Springs** chapter for more information.

SEEING AND DOING

HOT SPRINGS

Hot Springs Pool at Glenwood Springs—
Only 27 miles away is the world's largest hot springs pool. See the Major Attractions section of the **Glenwood Springs** chapter.

Penny Hot Springs—
Long used by Ute Indians and later by settlers, Penny Hot Springs still bubbles forth. Depending on the water level of the Crystal River and amount of boiling source water, you might enjoy a couple of shallow pools that mix to a good soaking temperature. The springs have been mired in conflict for quite some time. A couple of indecent exposure charges have been filed, and unknown vigilantes keep trying to destroy the pools when no one is looking. Our advice is to ask locally about the status of Penny Hot Springs and, if you decide to soak, wear a suit. The springs are located 1.5 miles north of Redstone on Hwy. 133, hidden down along the river on a wide bend in the road.

MUSEUMS AND GALLERIES

Lined with many fine galleries, Redstone Blvd. is an extremely popular street for window shopping. Among other things you'll see stained glass, original oils and watercolors, and even wearable art. The aesthetically pleasing valley has long inspired artists; well-known painters such as Frank Mechau and Ben Turner have spent time here.

Marble Museum—
This small museum gives you a feeling for the town's good years, when the quarry was operating at full tilt. Artifacts and photos follow the interesting history of Marble from the early 1900s. Donations accepted; open 2–4 pm, Memorial Day to Labor Day. **412 Marble St., Marble.**

Redstone Art Center—
Don't miss this gallery. Nationally known sculptor Eric Johnson works marble into incredible art forms that are displayed

in quantity. He often can be seen transforming huge pieces of local marble into remarkable human forms in an adjacent building to the gallery. Some people might imagine marble as having a certain coldness to it—Johnson somehow creates a softness and warmth from the stone and he encourages you to reach out, touch and feel his work. In addition to sculpted marble you can see other artists' work in pottery, jewelry, woodwork and other media. **0173 Redstone Blvd., Redstone; (303) 963-3790.**

Redstone Museum—

This could be the smallest museum you'll encounter during your Colorado travels. Located in a small log cabin that once housed one of Osgood's offices for the Coal Basin mines, this tiny museum now has an interesting collection of historical memorabilia. Open in summer 10 am-4 pm daily. Located on **Redstone Blvd.** across from the Redstone General Store.

SCENIC DRIVES

Crystal River Valley and Yule Marble Quarry—

You won't be disappointed by the scenery on this drive. Begin by following Hwy. 133 south past the coke ovens of Redstone for 5 miles to a marked turn-off for Marble (Forest Rd. 314). Once in the town of Marble, turn right on 3rd St. and go a block to the remains of the marble mill. At the site are tons of rejected pieces of the gleaming stone and white marble support columns reminiscent of classical Greek ruins.

From the marble mill cross a one-lane bridge over the Crystal River onto a very good dirt road—fit for any vehicle except perhaps a Winnebago. Open in summer only, this road parallels Yule Creek for 4 miles on its southern route toward the slopes of Treasure Mountain (13,462 feet). The pretty drive ends at a small parking lot where a 5-minute walk along the creek will take you to the bottom of an avalanche of refuse marble. Leave grandpa here (unless his name is Jack LaLanne) and take a short but steep 20–30 minute hiking trail to the 100,000-square-foot quarry. The deep pit bears the scars of the process that still removes huge slabs of the crystalline rock. Since the quarry has resumed operations you'll likely be able to see employees sawing and moving chunks of the pure white stone. During the quarry's peak, one "room" could produce 3,000 cubic feet of marble per day. It's a great place to explore, as long as you are aware of the inherent dangers of being around huge chunks of throwaway marble and deep holes in the ground. Please leave all the marble where you find it.

McClure Pass—

Head south on Hwy. 133 past Redstone and toward the top of McClure Pass (8,755 feet); near the summit be sure to pull off and take a long look south to the Ragged Mountains and back north to Mt. Sopris at the head of the valley. The highway eventually drops into the quiet orchards of Paonia. Instead of ending in Paonia, you could easily continue to Crested Butte by way of Kebler Pass (see the **Gunnison and Crested Butte** chapter). Either of these options would be a brilliant choice in autumn.

WHERE TO STAY

ACCOMMODATIONS

Avalanche Ranch—$$$ to $$$$

First off, innkeeper Sharon Mollica knows how to make you (and your family) feel welcome and comfortable at her ranch. The 45-acre spread looks across the Crystal River Valley to the distinctive slopes of Mt. Sopris. Guests have a couple of lodging options: a B&B room in the huge, looming red barn, or a small, efficient cabin. The barn-style farmhouse has four sunny lodge rooms, a large window-encased dining room, a common sitting area and a shop featuring North American antiques and folk art. Each of the simple but comfortable guest rooms is tastefully decorated with antiques. The furnishings may be purchased by guests, which gives the place a new look each time you return. Two of the rooms have private baths, while another two share a bathroom down the hall. All B&B rooms have expansive views over the valley, including the llama pasture. A typical breakfast is homemade granola, yogurt, fruit, hot muffins and coffee or juice. People who choose to stay in one of the 14 cabins can show up for breakfast for an additional charge.

Kids love it here! They can feed pigs, sheep and llamas and go exploring in the apple orchard. There's a tree house and a tire swing, not to mention badminton, horseshoes, fishing and llama trekking. Each cabin has a barbecue pit and a picnic table. The mood and setting of Avalanche Ranch make it a great choice. One rule: absolutely no smoking allowed. **12863 Hwy. 133, Redstone, CO 81623; (303) 963-2846.**

Cleveholm Manor, Historic Redstone Castle—$$$ to $$$$

Though perpetually up for sale, the castle still offers its spacious 42-room interior as a bed and breakfast when groups have not booked the entire place. The $2.5 million castle was built by John Osgood in 1903 to impress his friends and enemies alike. It is said that Osgood and Teddy Roosevelt sat on the front lawn while the gamekeeper let loose captive deer, one at a time, for them to shoot down! Other guests included John D. Rockefeller, J.P. Morgan, Jay Gould and John "Bet a Million" Gates. John Osgood's second wife, Alma, was known as "Lady Bountiful." Each Christmas she asked the children of Redstone to write letters to Santa. She then collected the mail, left on her private railcar for a New York City shopping spree and returned with armloads of presents for the kids.

It's easy to feel the castle's history as you walk around the library, the armory and the main living room with its massive fireplace. The 16 enchanting bedrooms are carefully appointed with antiques; all beds have feather comforters. For a honeymoon few places rival these accommodations, especially the Lady Bountiful Suite. Enjoy the fabulous views across the well-tended

grounds to the Crystal River. Staying in the castle is somewhere between living in a museum and living out your wildest dream. Other ways to experience the castle are to take a tour of the premises or enjoy a leisurely gourmet dinner in the elegant dining room (served most Fri. and Sat. nights). Reservations are essential for an overnight stay as well as for dinner and tours. Located 1 mile south of Redstone at **0058 Redstone Blvd., Redstone, CO 81623; (303) 963-3463.**

Redstone Inn—$$ to $$$

Nestled beside the Crystal River on the south end of town, this distinctive Tudor-style inn is a perfect destination. You can't miss the four-faced clock tower—an exact replica from a Dutch inn in Rotterdam. In 1902 John Osgood built the inn as a place for his unmarried coal workers to live. Today word has spread about the inn, forcing early reservations for summer weekends. If you haven't been here for a few years, you'll be impressed with the many upgrades and improvements. Not only do the rooms sport fresh paint, carpet and wallpaper, but there is also a classy little health spa right on the bank of East Creek.

The rooms vary quite a bit in size, with some on the small side. To ensure a romantic setting, reserve the large bridal suite. People on a tight budget will be glad to know that inexpensive dormer rooms with half-baths are available; showers are down the hall. Furnished tastefully in antiques, all rooms have a classy and subtle decor. A heated lap pool, large outdoor hot tub and tennis courts are available for guests. This Inn has that old European feel: rich, strong colors, a comfortable lobby, reading rooms and a sophisticated bar. You will want to visit the elegant restaurant for breakfast, lunch or dinner. Don't miss the Sun. brunch (see Where to Eat). **0082 Redstone Blvd., Redstone, CO 81623; (303) 963-2526.**

Beaver Lake Lodge in Marble—$$

In the midst of the ramshackle but charming little town of Marble, this two-story lodge offers basic, verging on rough, accommodations. It wouldn't be anything special if not for the friendly owners, the wonderful location and the cheap prices. There are also a few cabins for rent. In winter many people choose this lodge as a base for cross-country excursions in the area. Hank and Pat Kimbrell will also prepare your meals, to be served inside or out depending on the season. **201 E. Silver St., Marble, CO 81623; (303) 963-2504.**

CAMPING

In the White River National Forest—

Bogan Flats Campground enjoys a beautiful setting near the Crystal River south of Redstone. From Redstone, take Hwy. 133 for 5 miles, turn left at the turn-off to Marble (Forest Rd. 314) and continue 1.5 miles to the campground. 37 sites; fee charged.

Janeway Campground is located 12 miles south of Carbondale on Hwy. 133. Turn left (east), cross a bridge and continue for half a mile to the campground. Ten campsites; no water; no fee. It's another 2.5 miles to **Avalanche Campground** along the same dirt road, which is so rough that trailers over 20 feet long are not allowed. Ten sites; fee charged.

Redstone Campground is located a mile north of Redstone. It offers shaded campsites next to the Crystal River and is very popular. Drinking water available; 24 sites; fee charged.

McClure Pass Campground, located southwest on Hwy. 133 from Redstone, offers 19 sites and a fee is charged.

———— WHERE TO EAT ————

There are only a few restaurants in Redstone. If you want to find a better variety in dining, there are many nearby options. A local favorite for breakfast and lunch is in Carbondale, only 10 miles away: the **Village Smithy** at **3rd** and **Main.** Another superb choice for a special meal is **Chefy's** in Basalt. See the **Aspen** chapter for more information on these and other excellent restaurants. Another option is to head downvalley to Glenwood Springs.

Cleveholm Manor, Historic Redstone Castle—$$$$

On most Fri. and Sat. nights Redstone Castle offers gourmet dining in a fabulous setting. One of the regular chefs from Chefy's restaurant in Basalt does the cooking. The castle also offers special dances and wine tastings from time to time. For more information see the Where to Stay section.

Redstone Inn—$$$

The classic setting of the inn matches the excellent food. In the gracious dining room you can enjoy carefully prepared continental cuisine and first-class service. Linens adorn the tables and mouth-watering aromas fill the air. Entrées include roast duckling with an orange and Grand Marnier glaze, coconut shrimp and a tempting filet mignon. Open 5:30–9 pm each evening. The restaurant is also open for breakfast ($) 7:30–11 am and lunch ($$) 11:30 am–2 pm. If you are lucky enough to be staying at the inn over a weekend, make certain you stay for the champagne brunch buffet (Sun. 9 am–2 pm). People from all around the area make a special trip to Redstone for this brunch. Located in the Redstone Inn at the south end of town. **0082 Redstone Blvd., Redstone; (303) 963-2526.**

———— SERVICES ————

Basalt Area Chamber of Commerce—PO Box 514, Basalt, CO 81621; (303) 927-4031.

Carbondale Chamber of Commerce—0590 Hwy. 133, PO Box 427, Carbondale, CO 81623; (303) 963-1890.

Steamboat Springs

Surrounded by sprawling cattle ranches, Steamboat Springs remains a major ranch-supply center in the midst of some of the best skiing in the world. The imposing ski mountain is the reason people flock to Steamboat Springs in winter. It offers what many downhillers consider to be the pinnacle of Colorado skiing: deep powder, aspen glades and the second highest vertical drop in the state. Thanks to the massive mountain and its three-hour drive from Denver, lift lines are usually short.

Lincoln Avenue, the 12-block main street of Old Town, is the perfect place to buy a bridle for your horse or get a hot wax for an old pair of skis. Staid western-wear stores share space with an occasional T-shirt shop. The blending of old and new gives Steamboat a permanence and personality beyond many other ski resorts. Three miles south of the town center, Steamboat Village—a planned development of hotels, condos and boutiques—has sprung up at the base of the ski mountain. A diversity of restaurants and lodging opportunities awaits you both at the mountain and back in town.

Steamboat Springs, now with a population of almost 7,000, has a long tradition of skiing and somehow maintains a competitive advantage over other ski towns. Since the Winter Olympics began in 1924, Steamboat has provided 35 competitors for the US team—seven at the 1992 winter games alone!

Cross-country skiing is less touted here, but no less spectacular. Trails are virtually unlimited in the surrounding valleys, on top of Rabbit Ears Pass and at an organized nordic center beginning near the mountain village. Be sure to take a plunge in the steaming hot spring pools after a day in the cold. The natural Strawberry Park Hot Springs pools lie just a few miles away.

The long days of a Steamboat summer can be filled with any number of activities, and should be—this place lends itself to exploring the surrounding country. Set out on foot, horse or mountain bike. Bring along a picnic lunch or your fishing rod. If you are inclined to take part in a guest ranch vacation, the experience can range from rustic to cushy.

Local tourist magazines talk of the "Yampa Valley Curse." According to local lore, the valley casts a spell over all visitors, compelling them to return year after year. Legend or not, Steamboat Springs does have an indelible allure, making it difficult to stay away—many people have relocated here permanently. And these transplants, not always possessing the same values and beliefs of the Steamboat oldtimers, are increasingly making their presence known. As a matter of fact, a recent town ordinance bestowed a new county bridge with the name James Brown

Soul Center of the Universe Bridge—the "Godfather of Soul" himself showed up at the dedication ceremony sporting an electric-blue jump suit and announced "I feel good!"

HISTORY

With more than 150 hot springs and bountiful game in the Steamboat area, the northern Utes (Yampatika) began summering here as early as the 1300s.

According to most accounts, Steamboat Springs got its name in 1865 when three French trappers riding horseback along the Yampa River heard a chugging sound they thought was a steamboat. It turned out to be a hot spring that continued to chug until 1908 when the railroad blasted out the rock chamber over it.

In 1875 James Crawford, the first settler in the valley, built his homestead. Although a treaty in 1868 took away the land around Steamboat from the Ute Indians, they still made frequent trips to the valley. Soon Crawford was good friends with the Utes. In the summer of 1879, when the Meeker Massacre erupted southwest of Steamboat and the Utes attacked settlers after provocation by the inept Indian Agent, Nathan Meeker, Crawford's homestead remained unscathed. By 1880 the Utes were forced onto a reservation in Utah. This was followed by a sharp increase of homesteaders flocking to the Steamboat area, filling the broad valley with farms and ranches.

At about the same time, a late mining boom was in full swing 30 miles to the north at Hahns Peak. Although the area produced a meager $4 million in gold, eager miners scoured the hillsides and creeks until the early 1900s.

During this period miners and ranchers would converge on Steamboat Springs for a good time. Crawford and other town residents wouldn't allow it, passing an ordinance prohibiting alcohol in town (it lasted until 1940). The rowdy visitors had to go across the river for drinking and hell-raising.

Although the locals relied on skis in winter as a means of transportation, it was not until a wiry Norwegian came to town in 1913 that people started to ski for fun. Carl Howelsen, a champion jumper and cross-country skier from Norway, organized Steamboat Springs' first Winter Carnival, during which he amazed the townsfolk by heaving himself more than 110 feet off a jump he had built. It was not long before locals were trying it themselves. Howelsen Hill, just west of town, became the jumping hill. Occasionally some of the early jumpers would land among a startled herd of wintering elk. By the 1940s, downhill skiing had also become a passion for the townsfolk, so much so that it became part of the school curriculum in 1943. During the late 1940s and into the 1950s, Steamboat Springs produced more downhill champions and Olympic team members than any other town in the country. Among them were Gordy Wren, Skeeter Werner and her brother Buddy Werner.

In the late 1950s, many locals, particularly Jim Temple, began scouting out Storm Peak, the mountain south of town, as a possible site for a new ski area. In January 1963 the mountain opened for business. It was Temple who coined the often-used phrase "champagne powder" to describe Steamboats' light fluffy snow. In 1964, when Buddy Werner died tragically in an avalanche in Switzerland, the mountain was renamed Mt. Werner. Since the early days of the ski area, expansion of the facilities and growth of the town have been dramatic. This growth may even increase in the future if the proposed Lake Catamount ski resort, just a few miles upvalley, begins development.

GETTING THERE

Steamboat Springs is located 157 miles northwest of Denver. Travel time varies depending on the weather, but the drive takes about 3 to 3.5 hours. From Denver head west on Interstate 70 to Silverthorne, north to Kremmling on Hwy. 9 and then northwest over Rabbit Ears Pass on Hwy. 40. **Greyhound Bus Lines** services Steamboat.

About 22 miles from Steamboat Springs, the **Yampa Valley Regional Airport** has nonstop flights from many cities in the country (during ski season only). American Airlines, America West, Northwest, United and Continental all fly into the airport. Closer to town the smaller **Steamboat Airport** accommodates Continental Express, which flies daily from Denver year-round.

———— FESTIVALS AND EVENTS ————

Winter Carnival

early February

Like many snowbound communities that get "cabin fever" about midwinter, Steamboat has a remedy: Winter Carnival. In early Feb. the town lets loose with a week-long celebration highlighted by traditional events such as ice-sculpture competitions, a hockey tournament and ski jumping. Some of the more unusual things happen when snow-covered Lincoln Ave. is blocked off and thrill seekers sit on snow shovels that are pulled down the street by galloping horses as the crowd cheers them on. The Diamond Hitch Parade features the high school band on skis. The famous (at least locally) All Broads Kazoo Band makes an annual appearance. The Winter Carnival dates back to 1914, a tradition that attracts many visitors to town. At night fireworks explode and the "lighted man" skis down Howelsen Hill. After hours the bars are packed and hopping. For more information call the **Steamboat Springs Winter Sports Club** at **(303) 879-0695**, or the **Chamber Resort Association** at **(303) 879-0880**.

Weekly Rodeo
mid-June through Labor Day

Since the late 1800s, Steamboat-area ranch hands have been pitted against one another in rodeo competitions. The tradition continues at the nation's largest weekly pro rodeo. Every Fri. and Sat. night the Steamboat Rodeo Grounds fills up for this genuine exhibition of talent and luck. For more information call **(303) 879-0880.**

Rainbow Weekend
mid-July

A hot-air balloon rodeo and Art in the Park (150 artists) highlight Rainbow Weekend. One of the ballooning events demands that the balloonists negotiate their crafts close enough to a mock steer to rope it. Good luck. Performances by the Strings in the Mountains Chamber Music Ensemble and the Perry-Mansfield Performing Arts Camp also add to the fun. For more specifics call **(303) 879-0880.**

Vintage Auto Race
Labor Day weekend

Imagine over 200 classic automobiles speeding around the 2-mile race course or displayed for close inspection during the Concours d'Elegance. It's a thrill watching vintage race cars such as AC Cobra, Ferrari and Maserati pitted against each other. The weekend is a flash of Monte Carlo in Steamboat! For more information call **(303) 879-0880.**

——— OUTDOOR ACTIVITIES ———

BIKING
MOUNTAIN BIKING

Mountain bikers have found a welcome home in Steamboat. There are an infinite number of ride possibilities spreading out from Steamboat like bent spokes from a hub. Many of the popular rides are on seldom-used dirt roads in the rolling ranch country; some riders, however, seek out the steep slopes of the high mountains. Mountain biking is a perfect way to experience the stunning beauty of the country surrounding Steamboat. For maps and additional information, contact or visit the **Hahns Peak Ranger District, PO Box 771212, 57 10th St., Steamboat Springs, CO 80477; (303) 879-1870.**

Fish Creek Falls—

This rather short ride is a steady 3.5-mile climb up a twisting road to the falls. Once there, the reward is in the beauty of the rushing water and in the knowledge that the return trip is all downhill. From Lincoln Ave. (Hwy. 40), turn north onto Third Ave. and drive one block to the four-way stop at Oak St. Turn right and continue 3 miles until the road ends in the parking area for Fish Creek Falls. For more information see the Hiking and Backpacking section.

Rabbit Ears to Buffalo Pass—

This 20-mile trail through Routt National Forest provides a great look at the beautiful backcountry along the Continental Divide. The elevation gain is less than 800 feet. To reach the trailhead from Steamboat Springs, drive south on Hwy. 40 to Rabbit Ears Pass and park at the **Dumont Lake** parking area. Start from the Rabbit Ears Pass stone marker and head north on Trail No. 311 to Divide Trail. This single track then heads north past **Lake Elmo** and **Round Lake.** Turn left onto the **Percy Lake** Trail and head to **Long Lake.** From there continue north on Trail No. 310 to Buffalo Pass and descend into Steamboat Springs. You may want to get dropped off at the trailhead.

River Road—

This cruising ride is on a fairly flat, improved gravel road that follows the Yampa River south of Steamboat. Great views! You can ride as far as 9 miles from town on the road, or as short a distance as you like. The return is via the same route or on Hwy. 131. To reach River Rd. cross the 5th St. Bridge in town and turn left.

Ski Mountain—

Ride the Silver Bullet gondola up the mountain for rides along the top and, of course, exciting rides down the hill. Helmets required; fee charged. Tickets good for multiple gondola rides; open 10 am–4 pm. Located at the gondola building at the ski area; **(303) 879-6111.**

TOURING
Town Trail System—

Thanks to a recent bond issue, a long-needed paved trail system is complete, making bike travel around town extremely convenient. The trail system, including the **Yampa River Core Trail,** also connects with Forest Service land. For maps and information contact an area bike shop or a **Chamber Resort Association Visitor Center** (see Services).

Rentals and Information—

There are several full-service mountain bike shops in town. Here are a couple of local shops offering repairs, rentals and advice.

Ski Haus—In addition to rentals, Ski Haus also publishes a biking magazine, complete with area maps. Located in front of Safeway at Hwy. 40 and Pine Grove Rd.; **(303) 879-0385.**

Ski Area—Those riding up the gondola may want to rent at the ski area base. Bikes, helmets, etc. **(303) 879-6111.**

Sore Saddle & Cycles—1136 Yampa St.; **(303) 879-1675.**

FISHING
Colorado State Parks—

The following fisheries represent the best flatwater fishing in the Routt County area. For fishing conditions and other information, call **(303) 879-3922.**

Pearl Lake—Only 3 miles east of Steamboat Lake, this smaller lake is well worth the minimal effort of getting there—but it's restricted to flies and lures only. To get here from Steamboat, take County Rd. 129 north 24 miles to the marked right turn for Pearl Lake.

Stagecoach Reservoir—In a short time, Stagecoach Reservoir has already developed quite a reputation for excellent fishing. Let's hope it keeps up. Feisty rainbow trout as well as browns and cutthroats make this 3-mile long fishery on the Yampa River one of Colorado's favorite spots. Two boat ramps available. **Stagecoach Lake Marina** rents fishing boats as well as practically every other craft imaginable. Slips available for rent. Fishing licenses and tackle, groceries and camping supplies available. **(303) 736-8342.** To reach the reservoir from Steamboat, head south on Hwy. 131 for about 5 miles and then turn left onto County Rd. 14 for 5 more miles.

Steamboat Lake—

This popular and scenic fishery is stocked with hundreds of thousands of fingerling rainbow each year. The average size catch is about 12 inches, but much larger fish are taken regularly. Some browns and Snake River cutthroat are also taken. Both shore and boat fishing often result in good catches on the large lake. You may want to talk with the park manager about where the fish are biting. His office is located at the northwest end of the lake. Steamboat Lake is open to fly, lure and bait fishing; a limit of eight fish each is imposed on all fishermen. From Steamboat Springs drive north on County Rd. 129 for 27 miles to reach the lake. **Steamboat Lake Marina** rents fishing, pontoon and paddle boats as well as canoes; they also have fishing supplies and licenses. Located on the northwest shore of Steamboat Lake; **(303) 879-7019.**

Dumont Lake—

Each year plenty of catchable rainbows are stocked at Dumont. The lake offers good fishing and the kind of beauty that makes any fishing trip worthwhile. Your best bet is with bait or spin gear. Dumont Lake is the first in a series of small backcountry lakes that reach north from Rabbit Ears Pass all the way to Fish Creek Reservoir on Buffalo Pass. If you decide to walk to any of the backcountry lakes, be sure to carry along your map and compass. Dumont Lake is located near the top of Rabbit Ears Pass. Take Hwy. 40 east of Steamboat for 24.5 miles and watch for a white sign on the north side.

Elk River—

The Elk flows out of the northwest side of the Mt. Zirkel Wilderness Area, and its upper portions are excellent for small rainbows and some brooks. The best fishing is in late summer when the post-runoff waters are back to lower levels. To reach the upper Elk, take County Rd. 129 north of Steamboat for 18 miles to the small town of Clark. A couple of miles north of Clark turn right on Seedhouse Rd. and parallel the Elk River into Routt National Forest. After turning on Seedhouse Rd., the best fishing is 5 miles upriver between Hinman Campground and Seedhouse Campground.

The smaller tributaries flowing into the Elk River in the Routt National Forest are normally quite good for brooks, rainbows and mountain whitefish. The North Fork of the Elk is brimming with small brook and rainbow trout, especially in its upper portions. From Seedhouse Campground head north on Forest Rd. 431 (four-wheel-drive) along the North Fork to the boundary of the Mt. Zirkel Wilderness Area. Flyfishermen may want to pursue the even smaller creeks flowing into both the North and South forks. Even on the smaller streams the fishing is better in late summer.

Flat Tops Wilderness Area—

A maze of lakes, ponds and streams is spread out over this high plateau only a short distance from Steamboat. The entire area is a superb trout habitat. For more information see the **Meeker** chapter.

Mount Zirkel Wilderness Area—

Remote and wonderfully beautiful are the many backcountry lakes and streams of the Mt. Zirkel Wilderness. The farther you hike, the better the fishing tends to be. A few ideas for backcountry lakes are **Three Island Lake, Mica Lake** and **Gold Creek Lake.** These lakes are not affected by winterkill and tend to offer excellent fishing for small (better eating) brooks and rainbows. *These lakes receive heavy impact; to prevent shoreline damage, don't camp within a quarter of a mile of the lakes.* To reach the Mt. Zirkel Wilderness from Steamboat, travel north on County Rd. 129 for 18 miles to Clark. A mile or so north of Clark, turn right on Seedhouse Rd. and continue until the road forks. A right turn on Forest Rd. 443 takes you to the trailhead for Three Island Lake; continue on Seedhouse Rd. and you'll be at the trailhead for Mica and Gold Creek lakes.

Yampa River—

The Yampa flows east out of the Flat Tops but eventually changes course and passes directly through Steamboat Springs before turning west for its long run to the confluence with the Green River. During the heavy runoff which can extend into July, spin and bait casters do quite well. The fishing near Steamboat has been improved by a kayak course just south of town; pools and eddies provide a good habitat for rainbows, browns, natives and whitefish. Recently there have been a number of large northern pike caught within the town limits.

Outfitters—

Buggywhip's Fish & Float Service—These folks offer guided fishing trips and floats to all of the major rivers in Colorado as well as the Green River in Utah. Located at **435 Lincoln Ave., PO Box 770479, Steamboat Springs, CO 80477; 1-800-759-0343** or **(303) 879-8033.**

Straightline—Provides guide services, rentals, float trips, fly fishing schools, and fishing information. **744 Lincoln Ave., PO Box 4887, Steamboat Springs, CO 80477; (303) 879-7568** in Colorado and **1-800-354-5463 out-of-state.**

GOLF

Sheraton Steamboat Golf Club—

Designed by Robert Trent Jones, Jr., this 18-hole golf course is one of the finest and most challenging mountain courses in the state, with a rating of 71. Groves of aspen and pine combine with far-reaching views of the Yampa River Valley and Mt. Werner. Guests staying at the Sheraton Hotel get a break on the greens fees. This course is first-class and charges accordingly. Walk-ons are welcomed seven days a week, but reservations 24 hours in advance are strongly recommended. Open mid-May to mid-Oct., so long as the weather cooperates. Drive south of town on Hwy. 40, turn left toward the ski area on Mt. Werner Rd. and take another left onto Steamboat Blvd. Turn right onto Clubhouse Dr. and follow the signs. **(303) 879-2220.**

Steamboat Golf Club—

For a course with more down-to-earth prices, try the nine-hole Steamboat Golf Club, located just west of town on Hwy. 40. Greens fees are higher on weekends. **(303) 879-4295.**

HIKING AND BACKPACKING

Tree-covered ridges of aspen, lodgepole pine and spruce, meadows packed with colorful wildflowers, and quiet streams meandering through scenic valleys: these are the characteristics of Routt National Forest near Steamboat. Though it hasn't nearly the rugged terrain or soaring peaks other parts of the state possess, Routt, with its ample wildlife and great fishing, has its own allure. Some of the peaks rise above 12,000 feet, but overall the forests and mountain meadows are closer to 10,000 feet. Within the National Forest, directly east of Steamboat Springs, lies the Park Range. Extending more than 50 miles, this range runs north from Rabbit Ears Pass all the way to the Wyoming border. Straddling the Continental Divide for much of the way, the beautiful Mt. Zirkel Wilderness

Area beckons many hikers and backpackers. Those who take the trouble to hike up to the divide are rewarded with spectacular views of the Yampa River Valley to the west, North Park and the Medicine Bow Range to the east. Many trailheads into the wilderness area branch off from Buffalo Pass Rd., which cuts east from Steamboat over the divide and into North Park.

Topographical maps can be purchased at a number of stores in the Steamboat area, including **Ski Haus,** located in front of Safeway at **1450 S. Lincoln; (303) 879-0385.** Ski Haus also offers camping equipment for rent. In Clark pick up a map at the **Clark General Store; (303) 879-3849.** You can't miss it. When you're at the Clark store be sure to get a "Clark single" ice cream cone. It's the best deal in the state.

For maps and additional information about hiking in the Steamboat area, contact or visit the **Hahns Peak Ranger District, PO Box 1212, 57 10th St., Steamboat Springs, CO 80477; (303) 879-1870.**

Fish Creek Falls—

Fish Creek Falls and the trail heading east from there are good areas for day hikes and extended backpack trips. This has to be the most popular tourist spot in the Steamboat area, and with good reason. Each year thousands of people drive the 3.5 miles up Fish Creek Falls Rd. to the recreation area and look in awe at the 283-foot waterfall. During the late spring and early summer, when the snow melt-off is particularly high, the falls are torrential.

Originally homesteaded in 1901 by the Crawford family, the falls area was aptly named for the whitefish and brook trout spawning here in autumn. The townspeople used to have a picnic each year during the spawn. Using pitchforks, hooks and gunnysacks, they would collect the fish to be salted and stored for winter.

A small footbridge that crosses the creek in front of the falls area can be reached via a quarter-mile trail leading from the parking lot. Picnic tables, restrooms, interpretive signs and handicap accessibility make things easier for visitors.

The upper **Fish Creek Falls Trail** leads to an overlook above the falls and then continues east up to a second set of falls, eventually reaching the Continental Divide. About 5 miles above the lower falls is **Long Lake,** where good campsites can be found. For a longer hike, stay on the trail (No. 1102), which eventually turns southeast, reaching **Dumont Lake Campground** on Rabbit Ears Pass, 10.5 miles from Fish Creek Falls.

To reach Fish Creek Falls from Lincoln Ave. (Hwy. 40) in town, turn north onto Third Ave. and drive one block to the four-way stop at Oak St. Turn right and continue 4 miles on Fish Creek Falls Rd. to the parking lot.

Flat Tops Wilderness Area—

For information about the Flat Tops, see the Hiking and Backpacking section in the **Meeker** chapter.

Luna Lake—

You won't find many people at Luna Lake, as it's a bit secluded in the Mount Zirkel Wilderness Area. And the fishing is pretty good. To reach the lake from town, head north on Hwy. 40 for 2 miles, turn right on Elk River Rd. (County Rd. 129) and proceed to Mad Creek, about 5 miles up the road. Park near the buck and rail fence on the right and hike 7 miles up into Swamp Park near the lake. For an alternate access route, begin at Buffalo Pass and head 6 miles north on the Wyoming Trail to the intersection with Trail No. 1168. Turn left and hike a mile or so to the lake.

Mount Werner (the ski area)—

Many people who visit Steamboat overlook one of the most obvious places to hike in the area: Mt. Werner. Not only are there cut trails and great views, but less ambitious hikers can take a gondola up the mountain. From the top of the gondola you can continue to the top of Storm Peak. A number of trails can get you back down to the bottom of the mountain. Fee charged; open 10 am–4 pm. For ticket information call **(303) 879-6111 ext. 233.**

Seedhouse Road Trails—

Just north of Clark, Seedhouse Rd. (Forest Rd. 400) turns northeast, following the Elk River 13 miles to the old mining camp of Slavonia. From this road many people begin day hikes and backpack trips into the beautiful lakes and craggy mountains of the Mt. Zirkel Wilderness Area. **Gilpin Lake, Gold Creek Lake** and **Three Island Lake** are overused. Backpackers should not camp any closer than a quarter mile from the lakes—day hikes for fishing and sightseeing are a better idea. Up above Gilpin and Gold Creek lakes, Ute Pass crosses the Continental Divide at a low spot that the Utes used to frequent when traveling back and forth between the Yampa Valley and North Park while hunting buffalo and deer.

One good possibility for backpacking in this area is a trip up to **Dome Lake,** about 8 miles up the South Fork of the Elk River. At 10,100 feet the lake is snowed in until July. Directly in back of the lake to the south is the impressive 11,739-foot granite monolith known as the Dome. It can be scrambled up fairly easily from the southwest ridge. To reach the trailhead, head south on Forest Rd. 443 from the intersection on Seedhouse Rd. Continue about 3.5 miles. Allow some extra time for the hike due to a landslide on the trail that takes some effort to walk over.

Wyoming Trail—

Feeling ambitious? How about taking the Wyoming Trail (No. 1101), which follows the Continental Divide for over 40 miles from Buffalo Pass near Summit Lake Campground, north through the Mt. Zirkel Wilderness Area and on up to Medicine Bow National Forest just over the Wyoming border. Views down into North Park and the Yampa River drainage are spectacular from the trail, which is above treeline for much of the way.

The trail can be indistinguishable in many sections and difficult to follow, due to late snowpack and boggy areas. Much of the trail is still used by the local ranchers as a stock driveway. If you just want to hike part of the way, it's possible to get back out on Seedhouse Rd. near Slavonia, about 15 miles from Clark. To reach the trailhead on Buffalo Pass, take Strawberry Park Rd. 4 miles out of Steamboat Springs, turn right on Buffalo Pass Rd. and proceed 9 miles to the pass.

HORSEBACK RIDING

In case you've forgotten, here's a reminder: Steamboat Springs is a great area for horseback riding. The Yampa River Valley and nearby Elk River Valley are packed full of working ranches, guest ranches and some combinations of both. The ranching way of life is vital to the Steamboat area. Even the ski area used to be part of a ranch.

Guest Ranches—

When staying at the **Home Ranch** or **Vista Verde Guest Ranch,** you can ride horses until you can't walk (see Where to Stay). Another nearby ranch is **Latigo** (see Where to Stay in the **North Park** chapter).

All Seasons Ranch—

All Seasons offers a wide array of horseback trips, ranging from breakfast and dinner rides, to full-day fishing trips into Walton Creek Canyon. They can also arrange overnight pack trips into the wilderness. **PO Box 252, Craig, CO 81626; (303) 879-2606** or **824-4526.**

Del's Triangle 3 Ranch—

Del's, located in a secluded area north of Steamboat, offers all of the opportunities you could want from a horsepacker. It is common to spot the many elk that graze in meadows and forests near the ranch. Rides range from one hour to multi-day pack trips into the nearby National Forest. Winter horseback rides are also available. Drive north on Elk River Road about 20 miles to the Clark Store. From there turn left (west) and continue for 2 miles. **PO Box 333, Clark, CO 80428; (303) 879-3495.**

LLAMA TREKKING

Elk River Valley Llama Company—

"Dogs bite, horses kick and, yes, llamas spit," answered Peter Nichols of Elk River Valley Llama Company when asked to verify the stories we had heard about the defense mechanisms of these cousins to the camel. "But llamas spit only if they are severely abused." In 1981 Peter Nichols began offering pack trips with these docile animals as the first commercial outfitter in the state.

The Elk River Valley Llama Company is located near Clark, about 25 miles north of Steamboat Springs near the edge of the Mt. Zirkel Wilderness Area of Routt National Forest. Trips with Nichols's llamas are tailored for guests, whether they want a hard hiking trek, a relaxing one or something in-between. The four- to five-day base camp trips are first-class and include gourmet trail meals, such as steak, jumbo shrimp and grilled halibut steaks. How about a cocktail by the campfire? No problem. The llamas pack in all of the creature comforts. Drop camps, llama leases (no guide) and day trips are also offered. For details, including prices, contact Peter Nichols at **PO Box 674, Clark, CO 80428; (303) 879-7531** or toll free **1-800-562-LAMA.**

RIVER FLOATING

The water in the Steamboat Springs area is primarily of interest to kayakers and inner tubers. Sections with good rapids are located on rivers too small for larger rafts and canoes. The two largest rivers, the Yampa and the Elk, tend to be dominated by gentle stretches that don't give the adrenaline rush so many people look for. In addition, both rivers run through vast acreages of ranch land, quite often owned by hostile characters unwilling to grant permission to float through their property. As a matter of fact, some river floaters have been sent running after being threatened with a shotgun blast of rock salt.

Elk River—

Kayakers flock to the Elk River in late May through June. From Box Canyon Campground down to Glen Eden, 8 miles away, the river drops an average of 70 feet per mile, with mainly Class III rapids. This is a beautiful area located in Routt National

Forest. Thick stands of pine and aspen line the banks. Be sure to take out at Glen Eden, because the river is closed for 10 miles below that point. At a park 2 miles above the town of Mad Creek, a short float through public land featuring Class I and II rapids is possible. Take out at Mad Creek.

Yampa River—

The Yampa River flows through the town of Steamboat Springs before turning west and building steam on its way to the spectacularly carved canyons of Dinosaur National Monument. Originally called Bear River by early settlers, the Yampa got its present name from the potato-like root that grows along its banks. The Utes relied greatly on it as a food source.

In Steamboat Springs local kayakers, canoeists and inner-tubers, with the help of city funds, have fixed up a section of the river. Along stretches through town, boulders have been placed in the river, forming a kayak course. Folks float this stretch all through the late spring and summer.

Outfitters—

Adventures Wild—Based in Steamboat, Adventures Wild offers mild to wild trips on the Yampa (including Cross Mountain Canyon near Dinosaur National Monument) and other rivers in the state. **PO Box 774832, Steamboat Springs, CO 80477; 1-800-825-3989** or locally at **(303) 879-8747.**

Buggywhip's—Buggywhip's offers one-to four-day, guided raft-floating trips on the Yampa, Green, Colorado, North Platte, Arkansas and Eagle rivers. Located at **435 Lincoln Ave., PO Box 770479, Steamboat Springs, CO 80477; (303) 879-8033** or toll free **1-800-759-0343.**

Mountain Sports Kayak School—Barry Smith has been kayaking for years, cultivating a national reputation along the way. Smith led an expedition of disabled people on a first-ever run down a river in Iceland that was filmed for a National Geographic special. So if you want to learn how to kayak, this is the guy to teach you. His company

offers lessons on the river from three hours up to five days. Anyone 8 years and older is welcome. Kayaks and inner-tube rentals are available. Located in **Central Park Plaza, PO Box 1986, Steamboat Plaza, CO 80488; (303) 879-8794** or **879-6910.**

SKIING
CROSS-COUNTRY SKIING

The cross-country skiing in the Steamboat area is ideal from a nordic skier's perspective. Rolling hills make it easy to do circle tours, as opposed to skiing up and down a steep river canyon. Heavy snowfalls make for a long touring season, which attracts the US Olympic nordic team in early fall and late spring.

For years locals have been skiing for sport. People like Sven Wiik, the "Guru of American cross-country skiing," have been instrumental in fueling the enthusiasm for cross-country skiing in the area. Volunteers gather in wintertime to stake out trails in Routt National Forest. Whether you are looking for a groomed trail or a backcountry experience, it's here in Steamboat.

For trail maps and other information, contact the **Hahns Peak Ranger Office, PO Box 1212, 57 10th St., Steamboat Springs, CO 80477; (303) 879-1870** or the **Chamber Resort Visitor Centers** in town.

Backcountry Trails—

Rabbit Ears Pass—People from all around the state who enjoy cross-country skiing are familiar with the Rabbit Ears Pass trail system. Rolling hills at 10,000 feet offer beautiful views and miles of circuitous, marked trails through the pine and aspen. The terrain is great for everything from gliding to telemarking.

Stay on the trails, as it's deceivingly easy to lose your way in the forest, and there are not many distinguishable landmarks. Rabbit Ears Peak, however, with its two crumbly, rose-colored granite spires, is a notable exception. In winter you can ski to the base of the rocks from the top of the pass. All trailheads lie along Hwy. 40 on Rabbit Ears Pass, about 10 miles southeast of Steamboat Springs.

Seedhouse Road—This road follows the path of the Elk River down from the Mt. Zirkel Wilderness in a beautiful mountain valley. Routt National Forest has a marked trail system that begins 4.5 miles northeast of Clark in the Hinman Park area. You may also follow Seedhouse Rd. up from Hinman Park, as it remains unplowed. The trails are mostly of the rolling hill variety, with views to Mt. Zirkel in the distance. For information and maps, contact the forest service office in Steamboat. To reach Seedhouse Rd., take County Rd. 129 north of Steamboat for 18 miles to Clark. A couple of miles north of Clark turn right on Seedhouse Rd. and parallel the Elk River into Routt National Forest. There is also a trail system in and around Clark.

Groomed Trails—
Howelsen Ski Area—About 5 miles of groomed and track trails (2.5 miles lighted) await at the base of Howelsen Hill in town. Rentals not available. **(303) 879-8499.**

Steamboat Ski Touring Center—Over 30 kilometers of trails (both tracked and skating) wind along Fish Creek and the Sheraton Steamboat Golf Club, offering something for beginners to experts. Tickets can be purchased at the clubhouse. Lessons, backcountry guided trips and rentals are available. The Picnic Basket sandwich shop offers warm drinks, Danish open-faced sandwiches, soups and salads. To reach the center, head south from town and turn east on Mt. Werner Rd. Turn left onto Steamboat Blvd. and then right onto Clubhouse Dr. Follow the signs from here. **PO Box 772297, Steamboat Springs, CO 80477; (303) 879-8180.**

Home Ranch—This full-service guest ranch offers public access to 40 kilometers of groomed trails. See the Where to Stay section.

Rentals and Information—
Ski Haus—The Ski Haus rents a full selection of track and backcountry equipment. They can also provide you with good trail ideas. Located in front of Safeway at **Hwy. 40** and **Pine Grove Rd.; (303) 879-0385.**

Straightline Outdoor Sports—Located in town, rents all types of cross-country equipment at reasonable prices. **744 Lincoln Ave.; (303) 879-7568.**

The Clark Store—Located 20 miles north of Steamboat on County Rd. 129, the store rents equipment throughout the winter. There is also a small trail system. **(303) 879-3849.**

DOWNHILL SKIING
Howelsen Ski Area—
Howelsen Ski Area, owned by the town of Steamboat Springs, offers a vertical drop of only 440 feet and is served by a chairlift, a poma lift and a pony tow. In addition to downhill skiing, the hill now has six different ski jumps that are used for Olympic-level qualifying meets and training—it's the largest ski jumping complex in North America. "Eddie the Eagle," the fledgling ski jumper from England who participated in the 1988 Winter Olympics, practiced on the 90-meter Howelsen Hill ski jump just prior to the games in Calgary. The hill is open to the public each day; night skiing also offered til 10 pm nightly. Located across the **5th St. Bridge** from downtown; **(303) 879-8499.**

Steamboat—
From the base of Steamboat, the initial 1,000-foot Christie Peak provides you only an inkling of what kind of skiable terrain lies beyond. But as the eight-passenger gondola carries you swiftly over the first hill, you are on the verge of discovery. Each year an average of 324 inches of Colorado powder drops on 2,500 skiable acres. This ample, light snow has helped Steamboat develop a reputation for superb powder skiing. Spread out among four interconnected mountains, the area offers 3,600 vertical feet (second highest in Colorado) and diverse terrain for all abilities. With its long bump runs, Storm Peak is the choice of many mogul and powder aficionados.

Many advanced skiers are drawn to Priest Creek, where they can pick a run down through the challenging aspen-studded glades of Shadows and Twilight. Incredibly, lift lines still remain short.

The legacy of champions continues as Billy Kidd, 1964 Olympic silver medalist and 1970 world champion, serves as the Director of Skiing at the Steamboat Ski Area. Most days at 1 pm, you can meet Kidd at the top of Thunderhead Mountain for an informal ski clinic and run to the bottom. **2305 Mt. Werner Cir., Steamboat Springs, CO 80487; (303) 879-6111.**

Steamboat Powder Cats—

This is a service for powder lovers (with spare cash) who want to get away from the world of groomed runs and lift lines. Enter a new dimension of skiing by taking a snow cat into the high country near Buffalo Pass and cutting the first tracks. An overnight stay in a secluded cabin is also an option. Contact Jupiter and Barbara Jones at **PO Box 2468, Steamboat Springs, CO 80477; (303) 879-5188.**

SLEIGH RIDES

All Seasons-Ranch—

This company has been offering sleigh rides longer than anyone in the area. Cover up with elk robes while the horses whisk your sleigh up Walton Creek Canyon to a secluded tent where a family-style western meal is served. Departs at 6 and 7:30 pm nightly. Call **(303) 879-2606** for reservations.

Windwalker Elk Tours—

At 1 pm daily Windwalker Ranch loads up its sleighs with passengers and rides near large herds of feeding elk. The photo opportunities are fantastic, so be sure to bring your camera. Allow two hours and dress warmly. Transportation to the sleighs is provided and reservations are required. **(303) 879-8065.**

SWIMMING

Steamboat Springs Health and Recreation Association—

Several large pools and a hydro water slide are available for a fee. See the Hot Springs section for more information. **136 Lincoln Ave.; (303) 879-1828.**

TENNIS

More than 30 tennis courts are available for play in the Steamboat area. Most are located at large hotel or condominium complexes. A couple of options for public courts are at the **Howelsen Hill Recreation Complex** or at the **Steamboat Springs Health and Recreation Association** (see the Hot Springs section).

—— SEEING AND DOING ——

BALLOONING

Pegasus—

Owned and run by Tom and Karen Fox, Pegasus has been providing year-round balloon rides in the Yampa River Valley since 1983. They also offer rides from Hinman Park in the Upper Elk River Valley and a spectacular trip up and over the ski area to the Continental Divide. In summer rides are offered in the morning; winter rides are given both in morning and afternoon. Rides last half an hour or a full hour. It all depends on how much you want to spend. Of course, flights conclude with the traditional champagne toast and a balloonist's prayer. Reservations required. Call toll free **1-800-748-2487** or locally at **(303) 879-9191.**

HOT SPRINGS

Beginning with the Ute Indians, hot springs around Steamboat have been used for medicinal and recreational purposes. Indians believed their strength would be rejuvenated by the Great Spirit who lived below the surface of the earth. In addition to using the mineral springs for health reasons, the Utes may also have used a sulphurous vapor cave across the river for torturing prisoners. Stories indicate that enemies of the Utes, especially captured Arapaho and Cheyenne, were put in the cave and slowly asphyxiated.

In 1875 James Crawford, the first settler in Steamboat, shoveled out a hole in the sand so his family could enjoy a good hot soak at Heart Spring—now the location of the Steamboat Springs Health and Recreation Association. Crawford counted more than 150 springs in the Steamboat vicinity. Though many of the natural springs have disappeared as the town has grown, you'll likely smell an occasional burst of sulphur gas emitted from thermal waters coming up from faults deep in the earth. Iron Spring, Steamboat Spring, Lithia Spring, Soda Spring and Sulphur Spring are the names of a few that still bubble to the surface. A couple of great soaking opportunities remain at year-round swimming holes.

Steamboat Springs Health and Recreation Association—

Starting with James Crawford, many bathers have enjoyed bathhouses and pools at this location. Today there are several concrete and tile pools, a hydro water slide, a snack bar and workout facilities. The hot mineral soaking pool is kept at a steady 100°F. Though this site has been heavily developed, it is a great place for families to come and enjoy an in-town soak. Open year-round 6:30 am–10 pm Mon.–Fri.; 8 am–10 pm on weekends. Fee charged. **136 Lincoln Ave.; (303) 879-1828.**

Strawberry Park Hot Springs—

Longtime Steamboat residents bemoan the recent changes at Strawberry Park Hot Springs. Only a few years ago the springs were known by locals as a great place to ski in to for a private soak. Now the road is plowed in winter and admission is charged, but the rock-lined pools remain a fine place for those in search of a natural location. Three 3-to-5 foot deep hot pools

are fed by source water of 146°F and mixed with cold creek water to an ideal temperature of about 104°F; two colder pools are also available. On hot summer days the water is kept cooler. The important rules are: bring no glass, bring no pets unless you are camping and please wear a bathing suit during daylight hours (optional after dark). There are four cabins ($) for rent and 10 tentsites ($) spread around the property. Open daily 10 am–12 am. To reach Strawberry Park Hot Springs, drive 7 miles north of Steamboat on County Rd. 36 (Strawberry Park Rd.). The road ends at the gate. **PO Box 773332, Steamboat Springs, CO 80477; (303) 879-0342.**

MUSEUMS AND GALLERIES

Depot Art Center—

The historic railroad depot, built in 1906, now serves as a hub for the artistic community. Special dance programs, music programs, plays and continual gallery displays are featured. For more information and a schedule of year-round events, call **(303) 879-4434.** Open Mon.–Fri. 9 am–5 pm; 12–4 pm on weekends. Located across the **12th St. Bridge** from **Lincoln Ave.**

Tread of Pioneers Museum—

With the exception of the small Ute Indian display, nearly all of the items in this museum came from pioneer families in Routt County. It is a worthwhile stop for those interested in the early history of the area. The living room is filled with worn furniture and old photos; check out the piano that was shipped around Cape Horn on a voyage beginning in New York City in 1868 and ending in Steamboat Springs 18 years later. You will gain a new respect for the origins of ski jumping when you look at the heavy leather ski-jumping boots that Carl Howelsen (alias the Flying Norseman) used in the early 1900s. Be sure to look at the rest of the extensive ski memorabilia. Other items of interest include ranch relics and furniture created from the horns of moose, elk and bighorn sheep—illuminating the eccentric waste of the Anglo settlers. Open year round 11 am–5 pm daily. **800 Oak St.; (303) 879-2214.**

NIGHTLIFE

Heavenly Daze Brewery Grill—

In addition to being a beer lovers dream, Heavenly Daze is also worth a visit for the food ($$ to $$$) and great live music. Five different beers are brewed on the premises; my favorites are the Dog's Breath Brown and the Woodchuck Porter. For the serious beer connoisseurs, brewery tours are available a couple of times per week. Walk upstairs at this attractive hand-hewn log pub to the third floor sundeck. Open 11 am–2 am daily; food served until 10 pm. **Ski Time Square; (303) 879-8080.**

The Inferno—

A wild après-ski spot located at the base of the gondola, The Inferno is a great place to unwind after a day on the slopes. Their famous shot wheel is spun periodically (à la Wheel of Fortune) to determine special drink prices for the next few minutes. The Inferno has a reputation for being a "meat market" and is also known for its great live rock music, which can be heard Mon.–Sat. Deck seating, weather permitting. **2305 Mt. Werner Cir.; (303) 879-5111.**

Old Town Pub—

This casual, local hangout with wooden floors and a long bar is a good place for plenty of friendly conversation. It's the people who make the Old Town Pub a great place to visit. The restaurant in the adjacent room serves standard American fare at reasonable prices. Live music, including some great blues, rocks the house, usually on Sun. and Mon. nights. Open daily 10 am–2 am. Located in town at **6th St.** and **Lincoln Ave.; (303) 879-2101.**

The Tugboat—

This local favorite has been around forever and is an integral part of "The Triangle" of popular restaurants and bars at Ski Time Square. The Tugboat is a casual sports bar, offering live music on weekends and big crowds. Skiers flock here for breakfast (best omelette in town), lunch and après ski. For a rowdy night of dancing to rock and blues, try The Tugboat. Après ski 4–7 pm daily; live entertainment 9:30 pm–1:30 am Mon.–Sat. in winter and Thurs.–Sat. in summer. On the mountain at **1864 Mt. Werner Rd. (Ski Time Square); (303) 879-7070.**

SCENIC DRIVES

Buffalo Pass—

This is the only road crossing the Continental Divide through the Park Range just east of Steamboat Springs. It offers great views of the Yampa River basin and North Park. Buffalo Pass gets its name from the time when Ute Indians used to wait in ambush for the herds of buffalo migrating between North Park and the Yampa Valley. In summertime the higher meadows are blanketed with a spectacular and diverse selection of wildflowers, including columbine and Indian paintbrush; autumn offers a memorable golden aspen tour. The dirt road is pretty rough but passenger cars can make it. Snow usually prohibits crossing the pass until after July 4th. Hiking trails branch off to the north of the road into the Mt. Zirkel Wilderness Area. To reach Buffalo Pass, take Strawberry Park Rd. 4 miles out of Steamboat to the intersection of Buffalo Pass Rd. (County Road 38). The summit of the pass is about 12 miles up the road. Continue approximately 16 miles down into North Park to Hwy. 14, turn right and return to Steamboat over Rabbit Ears Pass.

Elk River Valley—

It's hard to match the beauty of this valley as it traces the path of the Elk River down from the Mt. Zirkel Wilderness. In July the wildflowers create a patchwork of colors in the high meadows. Routt National Forest encompasses much of the valley, where you may enjoy camping, fishing and hiking. (See the appropriate sections for more information.) After about 13 miles, at Slavonia, the road ends at a wilderness access point, with views of snowcapped peaks along the Continental Divide. To reach the Elk River Valley, take County Rd. 129 north of Steamboat for 18 miles to Clark. A mile or so north of Clark, turn right on Seedhouse Rd. and proceed into Routt National Forest.

Another excellent option is to continue north on county Rd. 129 to **Steamboat Lake State Park** near the historic mining town of Hahns Peak. Steamboat Lake offers, swimming, boat rentals, camping and picnic sites.

Fish Creek Falls—

This highly scenic 283-foot waterfall, only 4 miles east of Steamboat Springs, provides an excellent bang for your gasoline buck. For history, hiking information, directions and other details, see the Hiking and Backpacking section.

——————— WHERE TO STAY ———————

ACCOMMODATIONS

Accommodations in Steamboat, as in other large resorts in Colorado, are dominated by condominium complexes, many of which boast a ski-in, ski-out location to lifts. The **Sheraton Steamboat** offers a first-class hotel at the base of the Silver Bullet Gondola. All lodging needs can be met by calling **Steamboat Central Reservations** at **1-800-922-2722** or locally at **(303) 879-0740.** Just tell them what you want and they can deliver. Listed below are a few unique places worth noting.

Home Ranch—$$$$

This spacious spread, located in the Elk River Valley at the edge of Routt National Forest 20 miles north of Steamboat, offers guests the chance to enjoy a mountain lifestyle without giving up any comforts. Each cabin, furnished with handmade furniture, Indian rugs and a wood stove, features a private outdoor Jacuzzi. Down comforters overlay the beds and terry cloth robes hang in the closet. In addition to the cabins and six lodge rooms, an enormous 3-room, 3-bath cabin was recently completed, ideal for large families. Daily maid service and a nightly turndown make it feel as though you were staying in a five-star hotel. Carefully prepared, delicious meals are served three times daily. The heated pool is open year-round as a further inducement to guests.

No one is pushed or obligated to do things, but there's plenty to keep you busy. Horseback riding is the emphasis in summer. By the time you leave you'll be able to groom and saddle your own horse. You might also try fly-fishing in their private pond and along the river. In winter cross-country skiing takes over; instruction and rentals are available to guests. Unlimited powder trails fan out on the adjacent public lands, as well as 40 kilometers of groomed tracks on the ranch property. These trails are also open to nonguests. If you're staying at the ranch, you can catch the bus to Steamboat for a day of downhill skiing.

In July and Aug. guests must reserve their stays on a weekly basis, with all meals included. The rest of the year is a bit more flexible but usually requires a three-day minimum stay. For more information write Ken and Cile Jones, **PO Box 822, Clark, CO 80428;** or call **(303) 879-1780.**

Vista Verde Guest & Ski Touring Ranch—$$$$

Winter or summer, this rustic hideaway attracts guests from around the country who enjoy the perfect combination of activities and pure relaxation. Located 25 miles north of Steamboat, John and Suzanne Munn's 500-acre working cattle and horse ranch is bordered by 1.2 million acres of Routt National Forest and the Mt. Zirkel Wilderness Area. In summer, there is an emphasis on horseback riding, though your time may be spent hiking, mountain biking, fishing, whitewater rafting, rock climbing, hot-air ballooning or just enjoying the incredible views. Kids will love feeding and watering the barnyard chickens and gathering freshly laid eggs. In winter the ranch is used as a nordic center, getting 300-plus inches of snow. Miles of groomed trails on the ranch include skating trails and a ski-in cabin; adjacent forest service terrain provides unlimited touring. Bring your own touring equipment. After a day on the trails, enjoy the log-and-glass-enclosed spa with whirlpool, cold plunge, sauna and deck.

Eight hand-hewn cabins spread out among the aspen trees at Vista Verde have recently undergone upgrades, making them even more comfortable and cozy than before. Each cabin retains a rustic feel with pine furniture and a wood stove.

The Munns recently purchased the ranch after enjoying it for years as guests of the previous owners, but the charm that has made Vista Verde so popular over the years remains. By the way, a gourmet chef serves three heaping meals each day at the newly built main lodge; two lodge rooms are now available as well. Meals are included in the weekly summer price; shorter stays can be arranged in winter. **PO Box 465, Steamboat Springs, CO 80477;** toll free **1-800-526-RIDE** or **(303) 879-3858.**

Harbor Hotel—$$$ to $$$$

The Harbor Hotel is something of a landmark, located on Lincoln St. in downtown Steamboat. All 61 rooms in the old hotel have been refurnished, some with wooden and brass bedsteads, armoires, steamer trunks and creaky writing desks. All rooms come with private baths, cable TV and telephones. The honeymoon suite stands above the rest because of its large picture windows and a separate, elegant sitting room. Behind the original hotel, modern condominiums offer additional space. A health spa provides guests the use of two large hot tubs, a sauna and changing room. Continental breakfast available each morning. **703 Lincoln Ave., PO Box 774109, Steamboat Springs, CO 80477; (303) 879-1522;** call toll free **1-800-334-1012** in Colorado or **1-800-543-8888** nationwide.

The Inn at Steamboat Lake—$$$

The Inn at Steamboat is a great option for those who don't want to stay in Steamboat Springs. Built in 1990 on the edge of the historic town of Hahn Peak, the attractive wooden inn provides modern, comfortable rooms; each has a private bath. On the second-floor porch, sit back in a comfortable chair or in the hot tub and enjoy views of nearby Steamboat Lake and the surrounding mountains. You'll also find a TV/sitting room as well as a small kitchen where guests can fix their own meals. Full breakfast is included in the room rate; the Inn's fine restaurant (open to non-guests as well) can provide additional meals to those who are interested. Located 25 miles north of Steamboat Springs. **61276 Rt. County Rd. 129, PO Box 776378. Steamboat Springs, CO 80477-6378; (303) 879-3906.**

Steamboat Bed and Breakfast—$$$ to $$$$

One of the bright spots of a recent trip to Steamboat was the discovery of this spacious and comfortable new bed and breakfast. When lightning struck the Enzoa Church (built in 1891) a few years back and burned half of the roof, the former owner painstakingly undertook a renovation project that lasted two and a half years. The result is an updated version of the church with a perfect layout for a small inn. Each of the seven rooms has a private bath and is decorated with antiques/neo-antiques. Guests can enjoy the "Music Conservatory" and living room, complete with a large fish tank. Breakfast served each morning. Conveniently located and reasonably priced. No smoking. **442 Pine St., PO Box 772058, Steamboat Springs, CO 80477; (303) 879-5724.**

Stephens/Perry Mansfield Log Lodges—$ to $$

Hidden in the pine and aspen trees just northeast of town in Strawberry Park, six cabins await those who want to escape the resort atmosphere of Steamboat. Perry

Mansfield Camp began in 1913 as a performing arts camp for girls. Here the girls would learn not only drama and dance, but also how to handle themselves in the outdoors. Today there is still a six-week summer program for kids in grade school through college, but some cabins can still be booked during this time.

These rustic cabins, which can sleep up to 10 people, are available for very reasonable prices. All contain complete kitchens including utensils and cookware; each has at least one bedroom on the main floor and more sleeping space in a loft. The cabins are winterized. Reservations are a must. **40755 Routt County Road 36, Steamboat Springs, CO 80487; (303) 879-1060.**

CAMPING

In Routt National Forest near Steamboat Springs—

Reservations (up to 10 days in advance) can be made at many of the national forest campgrounds in the area by calling **MISTIX at 1-800-283-CAMP.**

Dry Lake Campground can be reached by heading 4 miles north of Steamboat Springs on Strawberry Park Rd., then east for 3.5 miles on Buffalo Pass Rd. There are 8 sites and no fee. Another 8.5 miles up Buffalo Pass Rd. is **Summit Lake Campground,** located at the summit of the pass. Check to see if the road is open before planning a trip up here. There are 16 sites, and no fee is charged. From the summit of Buffalo Pass, **Granite Campground** can be reached by heading 5 miles south to Fish Creek Reservoir. You'll find 6 sites, and no fee is charged.

Hinman Campground can be reached by driving 18 miles north from Steamboat on Elk River Rd. to Glen Eden. Turn northeast on Seedhouse Rd. (Forest Rd. 400) for 6 miles. This campground on the Elk River has 13 sites, and a fee is charged. **Seedhouse Campground** is just another 3.5 miles up Forest Rd. 400 from the turn-off to Hinman Campground. Seedhouse has 24 sites, and a fee is charged.

Hahn's Peak Lake Campground is located 25 miles north of Steamboat up Elk River Rd. At the sign for the campground, turn left and proceed 2.5 miles on Forest Rd. 486. 25 sites; fee charged.

Heading southeast from Steamboat Springs on Hwy. 40 eventually leads you to **Meadows Campground,** 15 miles from town. It offers 33 sites, and there is a fee. Two miles farther up the road is **Walton Creek Campground,** which has 14 sites; a fee is charged. At the summit of Rabbit Ears Pass (22 miles from Steamboat), head north for a mile on the old Hwy. 40 road to **Dumont Lake Campground,** where 22 sites await; a fee is charged.

For other ideas for camping in Routt National Forest, talk to **Hahns Peak Ranger District Office, 57 10th St., Steamboat Springs, CO 80477; (303) 879-1870.**

State Parks—

Advance reservations at all three state parks listed below can be made at least three days in advance by calling **1-800-678-2267** or in Denver at **(303) 470-1144.**

Pearl Lake—Offers 28 wooded sites (fee charged) near the shores of Pearl Lake. Located in the Elk River Valley 23 miles north of Steamboat. A side road leads 2 miles to the park.

Stagecoach State Park—You'll find 100 modern sites at this popular reservoir state park. Showers available. To reach the park, drive about 5 miles south from Steamboat Springs on Hwy. 131 and then left on County Rd. 14 for 5 miles.

Steamboat Lake State Park—Steamboat Lake, located 25 miles north of Steamboat Springs on Elk River Road, offers a number of camping opportunities; a fee is charged for all sites. **Sunrise Vista Campground,** located on the north side of the lake, offers 103 campsites. **Dutch Hill Campground,** with its 91 sites, is also located on the north side of the lake.

Private Campgrounds—

Ski Town Campground—Located 2 miles west of town on Hwy. 40, Ski Town offers the ultimate in fat camping, including a hot tub, swimming pool and fishing. Cabins, tent sites and RV hookups available. Open all year. **29135 W. Hwy. 40; (303) 879-0273.**

Strawberry Park Hot Springs—Along with the fantastic natural hot springs, four cabins (sleeping bags necessary) and 10 tent sites are available. For further information see the Hot Springs section.

WHERE TO EAT

Hazie's—$$$$

The experience of taking a gondola to the top of Thunderhead Peak for dinner, as well as the starlit return trip, is one to remember. While enjoying a bottle of wine and an elegant meal, gaze out of the picture windows as the sun sets on the Yampa Valley to the west. Although the food (probably the most expensive in Routt County) is inconsistent, quite frankly, not many places can match Hazie's for atmosphere and spectacular views. A full meal and round-trip gondola ticket are included in one package price; in summer the food is à la carte. In winter dinner is served Tues.–Sat.; Fri. and Sat. dinner as well as Sun. brunch served in summer. Reservations required. On the mountain, at the top of the **Silver Bullet Gondola; (303) 879-6111 ext. 465.**

L'Apogee—$$$ to $$$$

Muted pastels in this restaurant's dining room provide an elegant setting for a special night out. A small blackboard menu displays the nightly offerings of traditional and contemporary French cuisine. Thankfully, the staff patiently translates dishes such as entrecôte de boeuf aux trois poivres, côte d'agneau prisianne and canard rôti princesse. L'Apogee has put together an award-winning wine cellar to complement the carefully prepared food of owner/chef Jamie Jenny. The wine list offers 875 choices; more than 38 selections are available by the glass. You may want to ask about their collection of single-malt scotch. Reservations recommended. Open 5:30–10:30 pm nightly. In town, **911 Lincoln Ave.; (303) 879-1919.**

Giovanni's Ristorante—$$$

A proven survivor in Steamboat's topsy-turvy restaurant business, Giovanni's continues to provide delicious Italian cuisine in an intimate atmosphere. Exposed brick, wood paneling, and photos add to the meal. The menu primarily features veal, chicken, and seafood dishes; nightly specials are also a nice option. Giovanni's takes pride in its impressive selection of Italian wines. This is a great place for a romantic dinner for two. Open 5:30–10 pm in winter; 6–9 pm in summer. Reservations recommended. Located at **127 11th St.; (303) 879-4141.**

Harwig's Grill—$$ to $$$

Located next to its swank sister restaurant, L'Apogee, the popular Harwig's offers lighter, more affordable food with an international representation. The all-star lineup of chefs each uses a wide open theme to perfect their own dream dishes. Finger food items on the menu alone could constitute a meal; these range from Shu-mei dim sum to Jamaican jerk chicken. Along with a tasty selection of salads, Harwig's features interesting entrées ranging from Tandoori chicken to Black Forest hunters stew. Be sure to check the nightly specials. Access to L'Apogee's drink selections. Pub atmosphere; highly recommended. Open 5:30–11 pm for dinner; bar open from 5 pm–2 am. **911 Lincoln; (303) 879-1980.**

Old West Steak House—$$$

In cattle country it's a good idea to follow the locals to the best steakhouse in town. The Old West is a no-nonsense eatery specializing in choice cuts of charbroiled beef. Prime rib, filet mignon and top sirloin are served, along with more exotic cuts of buffalo tenderloin and elk steak. If your taste leans toward seafood or chicken, there are several selections. We can attest to the fact that the owners, Barb and Don Silva, personally greet nearly every guest walking into their establishment. You may recognize Don: a few years back he was peering down from billboards across the country as the macho construction worker in a series of Winston cigarette ads. Don is also well traveled. When asked about his prime rib taco night (Wednesday evenings in the bar), he proclaimed, "I've eaten tacos all over the world and mine are the best." And we all know how tough it is to get a good taco in Bangkok. The upstairs bar menu offers a lighter version of the restaurant menu at more affordable prices ($ to $$). Reservations recommended. Dinner served 5–10 pm nightly. A late-night bar menu is served until midnight. In town, **11th St. and Lincoln Ave.; (303) 879-1441.**

La Montaña—$$ to $$$

I would stack La Montaña up against the finest regional restaurants anywhere. The creative award-winning southwestern dishes are superb. This restaurant offers table seating under a peaked solarium with nice views. The light southwestern feel goes well with the food. Unique and spicy concoctions range from elk fajitas and red chili pasta to more traditional enchilada and burrito dinners. You'll love the service. Restaurant hours: 5–10 pm in winter, 5–9 pm in summer. Bar hours: 4:30 pm–midnight. On the mountain at the corner of Après Ski Way and Village Dr. **2500 Village Dr.; (303) 879-5800.**

Chelsea's—$$

An institution in the area? Well, maybe. Chelsea's, located in nearby Oak Creek (22 miles south), has been around since the late 1970s, when the town was enjoying a boom. Although Oak Creek is experiencing hard times these days, Chelsea's remains. Specializing in Szechuan Chinese food, Chelsea's is a small, laid-back place with a lot of character and good food. Named after a previous owner's daughter, the restaurant is decorated with a mishmash of Chinese trinkets, and rock music blasts from ample-sized speakers. The menu is extensive and so is the beer list.

Chelsea's T-shirts get the vote for the most creative design in Routt County. For an escape from Steamboat and a fun meal, you might want to try it. Located on the main street in Oak Creek; **(303) 736-8538.**

Canton Chinese Restaurant—$ to $$

Located in a former Dairy Queen, this building underwent extensive changes when Ney Hoa Cheng and her husband, Siou Cheou, came in. Unfortunately, you can't order a Peanut Buster parfait to go with your Peking duck. Business is booming and for good reason. The Cantonese and Szechuan items are pretty good and affordable. The decor does not evoke China but, hey, the food is the important thing. Try the curried chicken or Hunan beef. Wine and beer (including Tsing-tao) served. Lunch specials served 11:30 am–4 pm Mon.–Fri. Hours are Mon.–Sat. 11:30 am–10 pm, Sun. 5–10 pm. In town, **720 Lincoln Ave.; (303) 879-4480.**

Cugino's—$ to $$

Asked what makes their Philly-style pizza so good, co-owner "Angie" Angelaccio hinted that it has something to do with the dough. Whatever it is, it keeps attracting locals. Cugino's (Italian for "cousin's") is owned by Angie and his cousin Henry. This small, inexpensive restaurant has the feel of an East Coast pizzeria, with Italian travel posters, snapshots of Philadelphia on the wall and bottles of Chianti prominently displayed. The kitchen is easily visible from the tables, and you almost feel as though you are in there with them as they toss the dough and cook the spaghetti. Cugino's does specialize in pizza, but they also are known for their strombolis, calzones and Philly steak sandwiches. A special board changes daily with dishes such as eggplant Parmesan, shrimp Alfredo and sautéed mushrooms with sausage. At lunchtime pizza by the slice is available. Alcohol served. Open daily 11 am–10 pm. Delivery available 5–9:30 pm. In town, **825 Oak St.; (303) 879-5805.**

In-Season Bakery & Deli Cafe—$ to $$

Located just off Lincoln Ave. in town, this gourmet cafe/deli serves fresh-ground coffee and other coffee drinks, Belgian waffles and elegant egg dishes. Although the In-Season is best known for its breakfast items, they also offer great soups, salads, sandwiches and dessert pastries. Outside seating in summer alongside Soda Creek. Open 7:30 am–3:00 pm Mon.–Fri.; til 2 pm on Sat.; til 1 pm on Sun. **131 11th St.; (303) 879-1840.**

The Shack—$ to $$

Breakfast is served all day at this simple and dependable cafe. The Shack has been serving breakfast, under one name or another, for 28 years. It is also a good stop-off for a quick burger at lunch. Open 6 am–2 pm on weekdays, 6:30 am on weekends. In town, **8th St. and Lincoln Ave.; (303) 879-9975.**

Sharon's—$ to $$

Located in a nondescript building along Hwy. 40 in West Steamboat, Sharon's serves up good-sized portions of tasty breakfast and lunch items. Nothing fancy, but the price is right. Breakfasts range from burritos to biscuits and gravy; for lunch choose from a selection of burgers, submarines and hot sandwiches. Open 6 am–2 pm daily. **30058 W. Hwy. 40; (303) 879-9060.**

SERVICES

Day Care—

Grandkids Day Care Center—80 Park Ave., Steamboat Springs, CO 80477; (303) 870-1140.

Steamboat Central Reservations—

Can arrange everything from condominium rentals to ski rentals. **PO Box 774728, 1475 Pine Grove Rd., Suite 202, Steamboat Springs, CO 80477; 1-800-922-2722** or locally at **(303) 879-0740.**

Steamboat Springs Chamber Resort Association—

PO Box 774408, Steamboat Springs, CO 80477; (303) 879-0880 locally or **1-800-332-3204** in Colorado.

Steamboat Springs Information Centers—

There are two places in Steamboat providing information about what to see and do while in the area. One is located at 12th and Lincoln in town; the other is on the east side of the highway as you approach the ski area turn off at the south end of the Steamboat area.

Transportation—

Alpine Taxi-Limousine Inc.—A taxi/limousine service shuttles people back and forth from Denver International Airport and other ski areas and Steamboat. **30475 W. U.S. Hwy. 40, Steamboat Springs, CO 80477; 1-800-343-RIDE** out of state, **(303) 879-2800** locally.

Summit County

Summit County sits high in the mountains 70 miles west of Denver. Taken as a whole, it's the undisputed king of recreation and winter resorts in Colorado. For sheer size and number of visitors, forget Vail and Aspen. Summit County wins the prize with four ski areas and numerous resorts, not to mention the beauty of the surrounding Arapaho National Forest.

The setting is spectacular. Towering mountains along the Continental Divide rim the eastern and southern borders of the county, while the magnificent peaks of the Tenmile and Gore ranges lie to the west. Tenmile Creek, the Blue River and the Snake River all converge from different valleys at the focal point of the county—Dillon Reservoir. The dam that entraps this immense body of water was completed by the Denver Water Board in the early 1960s. From the reservoir the Blue River meanders north to Green Mountain Reservoir, eventually dumping into the Colorado River after 36 miles.

Summit County's first settlements sprang up during the Breckenridge Gold Rush of 1859. Later, silver strikes near Montezuma in 1863 brought even more people to the area. After the mining boom petered out, towns died as people moved out, although some settlements, such as Breckenridge, Dillon and Frisco, hung on. With its unique charm, Breckenridge stands out above the rest. Streets in this Victorian town are lined with attractively restored buildings from its former mining days, earning it a National Historic District designation.

With the development of ski areas and the completion of Dillon Reservoir, Summit County started building its reputation as a great place to get away from it all. When the Eisenhower Tunnel on Interstate 70 was completed in 1973, cutting the driving time from Denver by a half hour, many day visitors from the big city began flocking to Summit County.

Probably best known for its skiing, Summit County boasts four areas, each with its own personality. **Breckenridge** is the largest of the four, with diverse terrain on three separate mountains. The town's authentic Victorian atmosphere adds a great deal of character, more so than the neighboring burgs. Steep runs at **Arapahoe Basin,** one of Colorado's oldest ski areas, complement the terrain at the recently expanded **Keystone,** just a few miles down the road. The planned resort of Keystone stands out particularly for its fine accommodations, restaurants and first-class service. The other true planned resort in Summit County is **Copper Mountain.** Its amenities can't quite match Keystone's, but the ski mountain is superb, considered by many to be one of the best-designed areas in the country. In addition to downhill skiing, a number of nordic centers and dozens of backcountry trails attract many cross-country skiers. When the snow melts and the wildflowers start to bloom, summer activity in Summit County comes close to matching that of the peak winter season. Hiking in the surrounding mountains, mountain biking the back trails, cruising along the outstanding paved Summit County bike trail system, jeeping to old ghost towns and golfing on one of the exceptional courses are just some of the attractions.

About 14,000 full-time residents live in Summit County. During the busy winter and summer seasons the county's population swells with vacationers and seasonal workers. Clustered around Dillon Reservoir, the towns of **Frisco, Dillon** and **Silverthorne** can provide an escape from the resorts and their higher-priced accommodations. If you want a total escape from the adult-Disneyland atmosphere, you might also consider staying in one of the rustic bed and breakfasts near the old mining town of **Montezuma**.

Summit County covers a huge area. Having spent a lot of time there over the years, we've narrowed the chapter down to include what we consider its "best" features. If you want more information, contact the **Summit County Chamber of Commerce** (see the Services section) or drop by their visitors center in Dillon or Frisco and sort through the walls of brochures and pamphlets.

HISTORY

Summit County history started rolling in August 1859 when a small group of prospectors found gold while panning along the Upper Blue River near present-day Breckenridge. Excited by their finds, the miners spread out along the river and up French Gulch, looking for rich veins. Fearing an attack by the local Ute Indians, they built a stockade and named it Fort Meribeh. During that first winter, these prospectors made their first major discovery under 8 feet of snow at Gold Run. Working with just a shovel and a pan, one man could extract up to $500 a day in this gulch.

Word got out and by spring the rush was on. When the town of "Breckinridge" was established that spring, it was the first permanent Colorado settlement on the Western Slope of the Continental Divide. Hoping to get a post office, the town fathers named it in honor of Vice President John C. Breckinridge. When the Civil War broke out, the townspeople were so angered by the vice president's support for the Confederacy that they altered the spelling to *Breckenridge*, changing the first *i* to an *e*.

Over the next 40 years prospectors and mining companies used every conceivable method to extract gold and silver from surrounding streams and mountains, including panning, placer mining, loding and dredging. From 1898 to 1942, large dredging machines tore up miles of streams and rivers while gleaning gold from the sand and leaving ugly piles of rock in their wake (still visible today).

Breckenridge grew quickly, experiencing economic ups and downs along the way. Perhaps the biggest shot in the arm came in 1882 when the Denver South Park & Pacific Railroad arrived in town via Boreas Pass. In 1897 miner Tom Groves unearthed "Tom's Baby," which at 13 pounds was the largest gold nugget ever discovered. (Tom, acting like a doting father, tenderly wrapped it in velvet before showing it off to the townsfolk.)

The town attracted its share of characters. Perhaps the best known was "Father" Dyer, the itinerant Methodist minister who traveled unceasingly to the surrounding mining camps, delivering the mail along with the word of God. His church still stands in Breckenridge. Another local character was "Captain" Sam Adams, who established the ill-fated Breckenridge navy. Adams, a real schemer, convinced the locals to supply him with four boats and a crew of 10 men to float down the Blue River to the Colorado River and eventually to the Pacific Ocean. The attempt failed miserably and Adams was run out of town.

Although Breckenridge was the largest and most successful mining region in Summit County, it was just a matter of time before settlers spread out into other parts of the county. In the 1860s prospectors made rich silver strikes in the Montezuma mining district. Settlements such as Montezuma, Saints John, Peru, Chihuahua and Decatur yielded ore on and off through the turn of the century. In 1873 the town of Frisco got its start due to mining at nearby Mt. Royal. Frisco eventually grew as a central supply link and railroad stop between Georgetown and Leadville. As in other areas of Colorado that relied on mining, the 1900s brought hard times as most mines shut down and populations dwindled. But Summit County was perfectly suited for its 20th-century savior ... skiing.

Skis were used for transportation in Summit County during the early mining days. However, it was not until after 1910 that skiing started being treated as a sport. A group of locals living in Old Dillon (now at the bottom of Dillon Reservoir) built a ski jump on which Anders Haugen, a Norwegian, set a world record in 1919. As downhill skiing caught on in the 1930s, people looked closely at Summit County for its potential ski area development. After World War II, the county's first modern ski area took form at Arapahoe Basin. Trails were cut and a lift installed before the ski area opened for business in 1948. Skiing's popularity increased, and the next area, Breckenridge, opened in 1962. With the completion of the Dillon Reservoir project in the early 1960s, Summit County really started to emerge as an important recreation area. The 1970s saw dramatic growth with the opening of Keystone Resort and Copper Mountain Resort in 1972. With the completion of the Eisenhower Tunnel in 1973, Summit County attracted more visitors than ever.

GETTING THERE

Summit County is located 70 miles west of Denver on Interstate 70. An ample number of van and limousine companies provide regular shuttle service between Denver International Airport and Summit County. Greyhound Bus Lines makes a stop in Silverthorne **(303) 468-1938.**

FESTIVALS AND EVENTS

During winter and summer in Summit County you can usually catch a festival or event. Complete year-round listings can be obtained by contacting individual resorts or the **Summit County Chamber of Commerce** (see the Services section). Here are a few of the best.

Ullr Fest
mid-January

This week-long winter carnival in Breckenridge is one of the Summit County highlights. In celebration of Ullr, the Norse god of winter, people really get into the party spirit. Snow sculptures left over from the **American International Snow Sculpture Championships** (the week preceding Ullr Fest) line the Victorian streets of town. The infamous Ullr parade bonfire and dance can get very rowdy. The festival coincides with the Freestyle World Cup Championship, which includes exciting ballet, mogul and aerial ski competitions. For information contact the **Breckenridge Resort Chamber** at **(303) 453-6018** or toll free **1-800-221-1091.**

Heeney Tick Festival
mid-June

This bizarre festival got its start in 1981 when a Heeney local recovered from a bout with tick fever. Friends decided this called for some sort of celebration. The first year's festivities consisted of miniature floats on a table. Big deal. But the celebration has expanded into a parade (about 10 minutes), a dance, food booths and the crowning of the annual Tick King and Queen. If you have nothing else to do, join in on this unique celebration of summer's arrival to the high country. Located 25 miles north of Silverthorne on Hwy. 9 at Green Mountain Reservoir. For more information call **(303) 724-3812.**

Breckenridge Festival of Music
late June through mid-August

This standout music festival attracts professional classical musicians from around the country who participate in workshops and performances. The highly acclaimed National Repertory Orchestra has now joined the event, which is a move sure to attract even more visitors. Music lovers can purchase tickets for two orchestras, four string quartets, a brass quintet, woodwind quartet and vocal quartet. Other events include workshops, camps and other programs. Some events are free. For schedules and ticket information, contact the **Breckenridge Music Institute, PO Box 1254, Breckenridge, CO 80424; (303) 453-2120.**

No Man's Land Celebration
early August

In the early 1930s the federal government learned that a tract of land, including Breckenridge, had accidentally been left off the map in several historic treaties. To commemorate this oversight, the town has been celebrating the "Kingdom of Brecken-ridge" for more than 50 years. The event is highlighted by a chili cookoff and an old-fashioned firemen's ball. For more information call **(303) 453-6018.**

Dillonfest
early August
The town of Dillon hosts this annual festival, which is highlighted by a 10K run, Colorado's largest sailing regatta, a food fair, fireworks and live music. For more information call **(303) 468-2403.**

Michael Martin Murphey's West Fest
first weekend in September
This popular event, held annually since the mid 1980s, has enjoyed overwhelming success and rave reviews from Summit County residents and visitors alike. This tribute to the art, culture and music of the old and new West is highlighted by a quality display of southwestern art. Concerts also attract many folks. Native American artists come from many states in the region. Still searching for that perfect Navajo rug you've always wanted? This may be the place to look. Located at Copper Mountain. For information call **1-800-458-8386.**

———— OUTDOOR ACTIVITIES ————

BIKING
MOUNTAIN BIKING
Dozens of old jeep roads and single-track trails provide anything from easy cruises to bone-jarring odysseys. The best areas to concentrate on are around Breckenridge and Montezuma. Please remember that the Eagles Nest Wilderness Area, to the west of Frisco and Silverthorne in the Gore Range, is off-limits to bikes. For a complete rundown on various trail ideas in the area, drop by the visitors centers in Frisco and Dillon or the **Dillon Ranger District Office, 680 Blue River Pkwy., Silverthorne, CO 80498; (303) 468-5400;** or call for a recorded message with seasonal information at **(303) 468-5434.**

Bike Trails—
Argentine Pass—If you're looking for the ultimate mountain bike challenge, consider a frightening trip over 13,207-foot Argentine Pass. Needless to say, this extremely difficult trail is for expert bikers only! Back in the 1800s a toll road crossed over Argentine Pass, connecting the Summit County area with Georgetown. The road has deteriorated since then and is only 2 feet wide in spots. As a local biker put it, "One false move and you're hamburger." From

Keystone head up Montezuma Rd. about 3 miles and look for the Peru Gulch trailhead on your left. Park here and begin your ride up the trail, which gets increasingly steep and hazardous. From the summit of Argentine Pass, make your way northeast down to the ruins of Waldorf, an old ghost town from the silver mining days of the late 1800s (see the **Georgetown** chapter). From here the road takes you down to Guanella Pass Rd. and into Georgetown, but a shuttle is necessary to get back. Before attempting this trail, consult with the forest service at the **Dillon Ranger District Office** in Silverthorne. Be sure to carry good maps and supplies. Good luck.

Boreas Pass Road—This is a very easy 10-mile ride to the summit of Boreas Pass from Breckenridge. If you feel energetic you may want to continue down the other side of the pass to the town of Como. In summer car traffic gets heavy. Ride in the morning or early evening to avoid eating dust. For a description and directions, see the Cross-Country Skiing section.

Deer Creek/Webster Pass Loop—This difficult 15-mile trail takes you to the Continental Divide, where you'll have views of the Tenmile and Gore ranges, Grays and

Torreys peaks and sprawling South Park. In midsummer the tundra wildflowers are blooming in full force above 12,000 feet. The trail possibilities in this area are limitless—you may want to get maps and advice at the **Dillon Ranger District Office** before setting out. To get to the trail from Keystone, drive southeast on Montezuma Rd. 2.5 miles past the town of Montezuma. Deer Creek Rd. climbs up to the divide. From here head east over to Radical Hill and down to Webster Pass Rd., which returns to Montezuma.

Georgia Pass—Highly scenic and fairly challenging, Georgia Pass crosses over the mountains southeast of Breckenridge, dropping down into South Park near Jefferson. See the Four-Wheel-Drive Trips section for details.

Peaks Trail—Intermediate riders can negotiate the uphill stretches and stream crossings required on this 9-mile ride along the Tenmile Range between Frisco and Breckenridge. From Frisco head south on the bike path along Hwy. 9 for a mile or so and turn right on Rainbow Lake Rd. Proceed to Rainbow Lake and then south on the trail. You'll come out at the Breckenridge Ski Area.

Saints John—Near Saints John (an old town near Montezuma), a fantastic network of trails awaits. For information see the Saints John write-up in the Cross-Country Skiing section.

Rentals and Information—
Antlers'—Rents both mountain bikes and hybrids. Open 8 am–8 pm daily. **900 N. Summit Blvd., Frisco, CO 80443; (303) 668-3152** and **1-800-755-3152.**

Mountain Cyclery and Ski Exchange—Rents mountain bikes, tandems and touring bikes. Open 9 am–6 pm daily. **112 S. Ridge St., Breckenridge, CO 80424; (303) 453-2201.**

Wilderness Sports—Rents mountain bikes and hybrids. Located across from Wendy's in Silverthorne. **171 Hwy. 9, Silverthorne, CO 80498; (303) 468-8519.**

TOURING
If you are planning a summer vacation in Summit County, strap your touring bike onto the car because the area is a cyclist's dream. Miles of paved bike paths connect most of the towns in Summit County, including the 9-mile **Blue River Bikeway** between Breckenridge and Frisco, the 6-mile **Tenmile Canyon Bikeway** between Frisco and Copper Mountain and the 13.5-mile **Vail Pass Bikeway** between Copper Mountain and Vail. A paved spur also connects Keystone to the rest of the trails. A *Bike the Summit Trail Map* showing the various routes in the area is available at local bike shops, visitors centers and at the **Dillon Ranger District Office** at **680 Blue River Pkwy, Silverthorne, CO 80498; (303) 468-5400.** Additional information on the bikepaths can be obtained at the town halls in Breckenridge, Dillon, Silverthorne and Frisco. This is unquestionably one of the best ways to enjoy Summit County.

A special bikers/hikers-only campground has been set aside at the **Peninsula Recreation Area** on the south end of Dillon Reservoir. No motorized vehicles are allowed; very small fee.

FISHING
With all of the recreational pursuits drawing visitors to Summit County, fishing in one of the area lakes or streams should not be overlooked—you'll find some great water. "Hot spots" do, of course, change with the seasons so you may want to seek up-to-the-minute advice from the **Division of Wildlife's Northwest Region Office** in Grand Junction at **(303) 248-7175.** Visitor centers in Summit County have a couple of brochures with excellent information about area fishing. For local advice, tackle, guided trips and fly fishing lessons, contact **Columbine Outfitters at 502 Main St., Frisco; (303) 668-3704** or **262-0966.**

Blue River—
The Blue River begins its 45-mile run through Summit County (along Hwy. 9)

from Hoosier Pass just south of Breckenridge. A number of small tributaries converge, and by the time the Upper Blue River reaches Breckenridge, the fishing can be pretty good. Downstream from Breckenridge the river runs through an area that was dredged during the mining days, which left large piles of boulders along the banks. You may try early in the season for rainbows and in the fall for browns and brookies. This section (3 miles north of Breckenridge down to Dillon Reservoir) is closed to fishing Oct. 1–Jan. 31. Below Dillon Reservoir the **Lower Blue River** is designated Gold Medal water; catch and release only. Many curse this stretch of the river, complaining that the fish are too hard to catch for it to be designated Gold Medal. There are plenty of places to park along Hwy. 9 as the river moves toward Green Mountain Reservoir. Try to fish the stretches that are as far away as possible from the road. Depending on the hatch, locals have had luck with No. 14 and No. 16 elk hair caddis imitations.

Dillon Reservoir—

Dillon Reservoir is the focal point of Summit County, and many seem content to look no farther for fishing. Casting from along the 24-mile shore is not quite as effective as fishing from a boat, but it can be worthwhile. There are boat launching ramps at **Frisco Bay, Frisco Marina, Blue River Inlet** and **Pine Cove Campground.** Both the **Frisco Marina** and the **Dillon Marina** rent boats. A good time to fish for rainbow trout is in spring just as the ice recedes from the reservoir and after the lake has been stocked. Some four- and five-pounders have been reeled in at this time. A few hog-sized brown trout cruise the waters during the autumn spawn but are hard to catch. The reservoir is also stocked with small kokanee salmon and cutthroat and brook trout. Trolling slowly with a Kastmaster lure has been quite alluring to many species, but, of course, the time-tested worm will also do the trick.

Green Mountain Reservoir—

Although its waters yield many good-sized trout, Green Mountain Reservoir is best known for its excellent kokanee salmon. Among the biggest in the state, the kokanee weigh two pounds and up; snagging is permitted from Sept. 1 through Dec. 31. The water level at Green Mountain Reservoir fluctuates greatly throughout the summer. Boat ramps are available at the south end of the reservoir and at the town of Heeney. Ice fishing is popular in winter. Located 25 miles north of Silverthorne on Hwy. 9.

Mountain Lakes—

Dozens of lakes in Summit County offer good fishing. Some are right beside major roads, while others require a vigorous hike. **Mohawk Lakes** can be reached by heading west on Spruce Creek Rd., 5 miles south of Breckenridge on Hwy. 9. Drive up Spruce Creek Rd. about 3 miles and walk up to the three lakes (about 1 mile to the first lake and another mile to the others). A high-clearance vehicle is required to reach the Mohawk Lakes trailhead. Fairly sizeable cutthroat inhabit these lakes. **Officer's Gulch Pond,** located just off Interstate 70, 4 miles west of Frisco, is stocked with rainbow and brook trout. In the Eagles Nest Wilderness Area, **Salmon Lake** and **Willow Lakes** are 6- and 7-mile hikes, respectively. Although a bit hard to reach, the fishing can be quite good. Ten-inch cutthroats are the common catch with lures and flies. The trailhead begins up in Wilderness, just west of Silverthorne. See the Willow Lakes write-up in the Hiking and Backpacking section for exact directions.

FOUR-WHEEL-DRIVE TRIPS

The rule of thumb for four-wheelers in Colorado is that the more mining activity that went on in an area in the late 1800s, the better the jeeping. Old wagon roads connecting the many mining settlements in Summit County provide great four-wheeling along with spectacular backcountry scenery. No fewer than 11 major roads were built over high mountain passes in the area and many are open for jeepers today. Be sure to stay on the designated jeep roads, especially in the fragile high alpine tundra. Also—don't attempt to cross the Continental Divide roads until at least June, when the snow has had a chance to melt. For other trip ideas visit the **Dillon Ranger District Office** at **135 Hwy. 9, Silverthorne, CO 80498; (303) 468-5400.**

Georgia Pass—

This was one of the first wagon roads built, connecting the Breckenridge mining district with South Park. At 11,598 feet Georgia Pass presents great views of the Tenmile Range, Grays and Torreys peaks and South Park. To reach the pass road from Breckenridge, drive 4 miles north on Hwy. 9 to Tiger Rd. and turn right. Follow the road along Swan River past North Fork Rd. and keep bearing right. Follow the south fork of the river. You will pass through the remains of Parkville, which was the county seat back in the early mining days. One night some residents of Breckenridge snuck into the county hall and stole the county records. Possession being nine-tenths of the law, the county seat was moved to Breckenridge.

The road along the South Fork of the Swan River eventually leads to the summit of Georgia Pass. From the pass the road descends down into South Park along Michigan Creek, eventually reaching Hwy. 285 at the town of Jefferson. From Jefferson you can return to Breckenridge via Boreas Pass or Hoosier Pass (Hwy. 9).

Webster Pass—

Webster Pass is another old wagon road that was heavily used in the late 1800s. It was built to connect the Montezuma mining district with the Eastern Slope of the Continental Divide. The road begins just above the town of Montezuma and heads up 4 fairly easy miles to the pass at 12,108 feet. From the pass the road descends the eastern side down Handcart Gulch into Hall Valley (see the Four-Wheel-Drive Trips section of the **South Park** chapter), but this side of the pass is very steep and extremely tricky to negotiate. To reach the road from Keystone, drive southeast

on Montezuma Rd. through the town of Montezuma. The jeep road begins about 2.5 miles above the town.

Tours and Information—

Tiger Run Jeep Tours—Tiger Run Resort offers rather pricey guided tours from one to three hours in length. Office located in Breckenridge at **128 S. Main St.; (303) 453-2231.**

GOLF

Breckenridge Golf Club—

This young 18-hole course is the only public Jack Nicklaus–designed course in the world. True to the characteristic features of a course designed by Nicklaus, Breckenridge Golf Club is laid out following the natural contours and terrain of its surroundings. It plays through forests, valleys, mountainsides, streams and even beaver ponds. In June the Steve Watson Celebrity Classic offers a chance to see current and former pro football stars hacking up the course. Tee times should be made at least two days in advance. Located just east of Hwy. 9 on Tiger Rd. at **200 Clubhouse Dr., PO Box 7965, Breckenridge, CO 80424; (303) 453-9104.**

Copper Creek Golf Course—

At 9,650 feet this championship 18-hole course boasts the highest altitude of any PGA course in the country. Designed by Perry Dye, the course features great views of the Tenmile Range to the east. Trademark Dye railroad ties bulkhead the tees, lakes and greens. Holes play under the ski area's chair lifts and along Ten Mile Creek. Copper Mountain Resort guests get a break on the greens fees. Fees are reduced after Sept. 7. **122 Wheeler Pl., Copper Mountain, CO 80443; (303) 968-2339** or **(303) 968-2882.**

Eagle's Nest Golf Club—

This challenging 18-hole course has a lot of hills, doglegs and narrow fairways. Set back from the Blue River Valley, it offers incredible views of the valley and the Gore Range. The 15th hole drops 150 feet from the tee to the green. Greens fees are lower before the end of May. Located in Silverthorne, 2 miles north on Hwy. 9 from the Silverthorne exit on Interstate 70. **305 Golden Eagle Rd., Silverthorne, CO 80498; (303) 468-0681.**

Keystone Ranch Golf Club—

Opened in 1980, this outstanding 18-hole course was designed by Robert Trent Jones, Jr., and offers a wide range of terrain and spectacular views. The front nine plays through trees; holes four through eight are patterned after old Scottish courses with lots of sagebrush and streams. The back nine is very open, with water hazards and few trees. The 60-year-old clubhouse (the old ranchhouse) is a beautiful facility with a fine pro shop and restaurant. Carts are required. Resort guests are strongly encouraged to reserve tee times at least four days in advance; space-available only for non-guests; proper dress required. The course opens at the end of May. Guests pay reduced greens fees. Located at Keystone Ranch, near Keystone Resort. **1437 Summit Co. Rd. 150, Box 38, Keystone, CO 80435; (303) 468-4250.**

HIKING AND BACKPACKING

It's hard to justify going to Summit County in summer and not getting onto one of the numerous trails into the backcountry. Hiking through pine and aspen forests, fields of wildflowers or one of the many high alpine basins is one of the best ways to really see the area. Arapaho National Forest encircles the county, offering spectacular walking for the novice and experienced backpacker alike. To the west of Silverthorne, the Eagles Nest Wilderness Area straddles the lofty Gore Range, providing a quick escape from the crowds and condos of the resorts. Residents of the county are quick to share some of their favorite hiking trails. Stop in at the **Dillon Ranger District Office** at **135 Hwy. 9, PO Box 260, Silverthorne, CO 80498; (303)**

468-5400 for additional information. You might want to pick up a copy of Mary Ellen Gilliland's *The Summit Hiker* (Alpenrose Press, 1987). It is an excellent book containing details about dozens of hiking trails in the area as well as some interesting history.

Argentine Pass—

In 1869 workers finally finished the dangerous wagon road over 13,207-foot Argentine Pass. Many lives had been lost in the process, but the much-needed link between the mines in Peru Gulch and Georgetown was complete. This 2.3-mile hike to the summit is difficult but worth the effort. The first part is very steep, but the trail eventually mellows into a steady pitch. The rocky scree and talus slopes require sturdy hiking boots. From the summit on the Continental Divide you'll have views as far west as the Sawatch Range and east to Georgetown and Mt. Evans. To reach the trailhead from Keystone, drive 4.6 miles southeast on Montezuma Rd. and turn left onto Peru Creek Rd. Continue about 5 miles and park at the Shoe Basin Mine building on the right. Hike up the trail 0.3 miles to the Argentine Pass trailhead.

Masontown Trail—

This easy 1.4-mile hike (one way) is great for the whole family. It starts near Frisco and climbs up the lower reaches of Mt. Royal. Along the trail many old mining sites scar the forested slopes. Views of the Blue River Valley and Dillon Reservoir are superb. The trail ends at the battered remains of the old mining camp of Masontown. Local legend has it that on New Year's Eve, just after the turn of the century, Masontown residents were down in Frisco whooping it up when an avalanche roared down the mountain, completely demolishing their small settlement. To reach the trailhead from the west end of Main St. in Frisco (near Interstate 70), head east into Frisco and turn into the public parking lot on the right. Cross the footbridge over Tenmile Creek and turn left onto the paved bike path. After a half-mile hike you'll see the Mt. Royal/Masontown trailhead on the right.

Mohawk Lakes—

This fine 2.8-mile day hike takes you past Mayflower Lakes and beyond to Lower and Upper Mohawk Lakes at 12,100 feet. Mining ruins abound. At Lower Mohawk Lake an old mill site still stands, with an aerial tram leading up the mountain above. Be sure to look for Continental Falls to the north above the old mill. Views from the lakes are spectacular. To reach the trailhead from Breckenridge, drive south on Hwy. 9 for 2.4 miles and turn right into "The Crown" subdivision and then left onto Spruce Creek Rd. Drive 1.2 miles up to the trailhead. There is another trailhead 1.6 miles farther up the road that cuts the hike down to 1.2 miles, but you need a high-clearance vehicle.

Monte Cristo Gulch/Blue Lakes—

Although we suggest hiking through this steep-walled, mining-rich valley, you can cheat and drive almost all the way to the reservoir between Upper and Lower Blue Lakes. On the north side of the valley rises Quandary Peak (14,264 feet). The steep mountainsides are marked with remains of mine shafts and cabins built into seemingly vertical rock walls. It's a wonder the miners were able to get to the sites. For a short 1.1-mile hike, drive along the left fork in the road below the lower lake and park your car. Begin hiking along the trail on the south side of the lake, past a few old mining buildings (now inhabited), including the enormous Arctic Mine. With its five tunnels, tram and stamp mill, the Arctic was one of the biggest gold producers in the area and operated until 1936. The trail follows the lake shore and ends up at a cascading waterfall just below the upper lake.

To reach this valley from Breckenridge, drive south on Hwy. 9 for 7.5 miles and turn right onto Blue Lakes Rd. Drive 2.2 miles to the lower lake.

Mounts Lincoln, Democrat and Bross—

This hike is probably the only one in Colorado in which you can realistically climb three 14,000-foot peaks in one day.

Located just south of Breckenridge over Hoosier Pass. For information see the Hiking and Backpacking section of the **South Park** chapter.

Quandary Peak—

Located near Breckenridge, Quandary Peak (14,264 feet) is one of the most accessible 14,000-foot peaks in the state. Mining was undertaken all over the mountain and many remnants are still visible, even near the summit. A couple of routes can be taken up the mountain, but the easiest is along the wide east ridge. From this approach, the last half mile or so is a fairly steep rock scramble. Enjoy views from the summit to the Blue River Valley, South Park, and Grays and Torreys peaks. To reach the trail from Breckenridge, head south on Hwy. 9 for 7.5 miles and turn right (west) on Blue Lakes Rd. Drive about 0.3 miles and look for a dirt road on the right. Park and begin hiking west and then north for about 0.5 miles, and then head left on a trail that climbs up the east ridge for 2.5 miles to the summit.

Ski Areas—Chairlifts to the Top—

For those uninitiated to the high altitude of Summit County, even a short hike can take your breath away. Breckenridge, Copper Mountain and Keystone ski areas offer chairlift rides in summer. Once at the top of the lift you have a number of options: hike up even farther, hike down to the bottom or enjoy a peaceful lunch and ride the lift back down. At Breckenridge the lift is open late June–early Sept. 10:30 am–3:30 pm daily. Tickets can be purchased at the base of Peak 8. From town head west at the traffic light and up Ski Hill Rd. to the base of Peak 8. At Copper Mountain, E and American Eagle lifts are open daily 10 am–3 pm July–Labor Day, and on fall weekends only. No fee. The gondola at Keystone is open daily throughout the summer 9 am–3 pm. A small fee is charged.

Willow Lakes—

Located high in the Eagles Nest Wilderness Area, Willow Lakes can be a beautiful overnight getaway, but can get quite crowded on weekends and holidays. The 8.5-mile trail leads to a series of four lakes at about 11,400 feet. There is camping at the lakes, and fishing for small cutthroats can be good. The trail begins at Mesa Cortina above Silverthorne and climbs up through dense forests of lodgepole pine. Game is plentiful up here; the last time we hiked this trail we saw a bear paw print. Above the lakes is a very steep, rocky trail to a saddle high in the Gore Range that offers fantastic views over into the Vail area. Firewood is limited, so packing a stove is a good idea. To reach the trailhead from Silverthorne, turn left off Hwy. 9 onto Wildernest Rd. (across from Wendy's). Go a short distance to a fork, turn right and then immediately left onto Royal Buffalo Dr. (No. 1240). Drive less than a mile and turn right onto Lakeview Dr. (No. 1245). Proceed to the fork with Aspen Dr. and turn left, negotiating the curve to the trailhead parking area. The trailhead is marked Mesa Cortina.

HORSEBACK RIDING

Be forewarned. Just because a horse stable happens to be conveniently located next to the visitors center at a resort doesn't mean the ride will be any good. If you want to ride a horse in Summit County, find out where rides are offered away from developed areas. One such company is **Alpine Adventures.** Trail rides begin up near Montezuma in Arapaho National Forest near the Continental Divide. Day-long breakfast and overnight rides are offered, as well as romantic rides in a hay wagon for an evening barbecue. Ride up into the high country and visit old ghost towns in the Montezuma mining district. For information contact **(303) 468-9297.**

ICE SKATING

In winter **Keystone Lake,** in the middle of Keystone Village, is transformed into one of the largest outdoor, groomed skating rinks in the country. Lace up a pair of rental skates and give it a try; lessons also

available. If you prefer the passive approach, sit at one of the nearby cafes and watch the action. A small fee is charged and rental skates are available. Open 10 am–10 pm daily; **(303) 468-2316.** In Breckenridge outdoor skating on **Maggie Pond** on the west side of **Bell Tower Mall** is also a good time, and skates can be rented. Open daily 9 am–9 pm; small fee charged. **West Lake Rink** in the village at Copper Mountain is outdoors, free and open daily 10:30 am–9 pm; **1-800-458-8386.**

RIVER FLOATING

Blue River—

Below Lake Dillon the **Blue River** snakes its way 38 miles north, where it dumps into the Colorado River near Kremmling. The Blue River is not particularly well known to river floaters; Green Mountain Reservoir limits the navigable stretches, and the floating season is very short. The nearby stretches of the **Upper Colorado River** and the **Upper Arkansas River** are worth serious consideration as well. For detailed information about the Arkansas River, see the **Upper Arkansas Valley** chapter.

Joni Ellis River Tours, a Summit County outfit, offers half-day trips on the Blue River and full-day trips on the Upper Colorado and Arkansas rivers. Lunch is provided on the full-day outings. **(303) 468-1028.**

Other companies worth considering include **The Adventure Company,** located in Breckenridge at **(303) 453-0747** and **1-800-497-RAFT,** and **American Adventure Expeditions,** located near Buena Vista at **1-800-288-0675.**

SAILING

With its 26 miles of shoreline and views of the surrounding mountains, Lake Dillon is a great place to sail. There are boat launching ramps at **Frisco Bay, Frisco Marina, Blue River Inlet** and **Pine Cove Campground. Osprey Adventures, 810 Main St., Frisco, (303) 668-5573,** at **Frisco Bay Marina** rents all types of boats. **Dillon**

Marina, recently renovated and expanded, offers an impressive rental fleet of fishing and sailing boats as well as kayaks and pontoon rentals. Dillon Marina also features a sailing school and charter cruises on the lake. For more information about the rental facilities, call **(303) 468-5100.**

SKIING
CROSS-COUNTRY SKIING

Nordic skiers are not neglected in Summit County. In addition to four nordic centers, there are limitless trails into the backcountry at your disposal. If you want to get out on a backcountry trail, obtain information at the **Dillon Ranger District Office, PO Box 620, 135 Hwy. 9, Silverthorne, CO 80498; (303) 468-5400,** or call their recorded message at **(303) 468-5434.** You should also seriously consider calling the avalanche information number for Summit County which is updated twice daily at **(303) 668-0600.**

Backcountry Trails—

Boreas Pass—Beginning just south of Breckenridge, the trail up Boreas Pass follows the old Denver South Park & Pacific Railroad bed, which connected Breckenridge to the outside world back in the mining days. Views of the Tenmile Range from points along the trail are superb. The fairly easy trail follows Boreas Pass Rd. 3.5 miles up to Baker's Tank, which once stored water for railroad locomotives from 1882 to 1937. This is a great place for lunch. Ambitious skiers can continue up the trail another 3.5 miles to the summit of the pass. A settlement on the pass back in the late 1800s included the highest post office in the country. To reach the trailhead from Breckenridge, drive south on Hwy. 9 just past the Breckenridge Inn, then turn left and proceed about 3.5 miles to the end of the plowed road (Forest Rd. 223).

Janet's Cabin—This is the first completed cabin in the Summit Huts & Trails Association's ambitious long-range plans for huts throughout the county. Janet's Cabin provides a perfect backcountry re-treat ... *for overnight guests only.* It's located southwest of Copper Mountain; from Interstate 70 the trail heads 5.5 miles up Guller Gulch to 11,618 feet. The cabin is equipped with many items, including kitchen utensils and mattresses, and accommodates up to 20 people at a time. Janet's Cabin connects with the extremely popular 10th Mountain trail system to the west (see the Skiing section of the **Aspen** chapter for details). For information about booking Janet's Cabin, contact the **10th Mountain Trail Association Hut System, 1280 Ute Ave., Aspen, CO 81611; (303) 925-5775.** For information about future huts planned in the Summit County area, contact **Summit Huts & Trails Association, PO Box 2830, Breckenridge, CO 80424; (303) 453-8583.**

Peru Gulch Trail—Beautiful high alpine views and old mining ruins highlight a trip up heavily used Peru Gulch Trail. It starts out as fairly easy terrain for the first 2 miles and then gradually climbs more steeply for 4 miles to the Pennsylvania Mine. Some skiers continue up from here through the ruins of the ghost town of Decatur and up into Horseshoe Basin, with views to Grays Peak (14,270 feet) and Argentine Pass. The avalanche danger can be high at the upper end of the valley. To reach the trailhead from Keystone, head east 4.6 miles on Montezuma Rd. and look for the trailhead and parking lot on the left.

Quandary Peak—Though the peak is extremely avalanche-prone during the winter, springtime turns the eastern basin of this 14,000-foot peak into a telemarker's dream. For information see the Hiking and Backpacking section.

Saints John Trail—Named for two saints, John the Baptist and John the Evangelist, Saints John is the locale of one of the first major silver discoveries in the Colorado Territory. In 1864 John Coley rigged up a primitive smelter, which was later replaced by a state-of-the-art version made with bricks imported from Wales. The townspeople of Saints John boasted that they had no bars (unheard of for a mining town), but they did maintain a fine library with more than 300 volumes of classics.

Located within the Arapaho National Forest at 11,000 feet elevation, Saints John commands a fantastic view of Grays and Torreys peaks (both over 14,000 feet), Glacier Mountain and a number of nearby (and active!) avalanche chutes. The valley and surrounding peaks and ridges are especially well suited to backcountry skiing. Miles of trails spread out on terrain that includes many narrow downhill stretches. An abandoned cabin at the Wild Irishman Mine, 2 miles above Saints John, is a good place to eat lunch.

To reach Saints John from Keystone, drive 7 miles southeast on Montezuma Rd. to the town of Montezuma and park just off the road, on the right. You'll see the signs and the trail (a road in summer) heading up into the pines. In summer you can drive the remaining 1.4 miles up to the old townsite of Saints John with a four-wheel-drive vehicle. In winter you'll have to ski in.

Webster Pass—This fairly easy 4-mile trail climbs up to the pass at 12,096 feet on the Continental Divide, providing a panorama of jagged peaks and a glimpse down into Hall Valley on the Eastern Slope. To reach the trailhead from Keystone, drive southeast on Montezuma Rd. about 2 miles past the town of Montezuma to where the plowing stops.

Groomed Trails—

Breckenridge Nordic Ski Center—More than 35 kilometers of trails are available for track skiing and skating through the pines. One of the oldest of its kind in Colorado, this center provides everything you need, from rentals to lessons (individual or private). Guided skiing is available for the blind. Telemarking terrain/lessons are available only at the Breckenridge Ski Area. Open daily 9 am–4 pm. Located 1 mile west on Ski Hill Rd. from Main St. in Breckenridge. **PO Box 1776, 1200 Ski Hill Rd., Breckenridge, CO 80424; (303) 453-6855.**

Copper Mountain/Trak Cross-Country Center—This center has a wide reputation as an excellent facility. Owned and operated by Copper Mountain Resort, it has more than 25 kilometers of machine-set tracks, skating lanes and, for more advanced cross-country skiers, rolling hills. The K lift takes skiers uphill for runs down challenging trails. A range of lessons is available, from beginning track skiing to telemarking (telemark lessons are given on the ski mountain). Clinics are offered throughout the winter on skiing techniques, waxing, snow safety and many more subjects. Moonlight tours can be arranged. Rentals available. Hours are 8:30 am–3:30 pm daily. For more information contact the **Copper Mountain/Trak Cross-Country Center** at **PO Box 3001, Copper Mountain, CO 80443; (303) 968-2882 ext. 6342** or **1-800-458-8386 ext. 5.**

Frisco Nordic Center—In a pine forest near the shores of Lake Dillon, skiers can explore 35 kilometers of set trails. The center, designed a few years ago by Olympic silver medalist Bill Koch, provides rentals and lessons. Open daily 9 am–4 pm. Located 2 miles south of Frisco along Hwy. 9; **PO Box 532, Frisco, CO 80443; (303) 668-0866.**

Keystone Cross-Country Center—More than 29 kilometers of set trails provide easy skiing around Keystone Resort. The center has a nordic ski school run by Jana Hlavati, a former US Olympic team member. They even teach telemark techniques at the ski area. Rentals are also available. Mountain Top Trail (intermediate/expert) can be reached via the ski area gondola for a charge. Open 8 am–5 pm daily. Located 2.2 miles east of Keystone on Montezuma Rd., next to **Ski Tip Lodge; PO Box 38, Keystone, CO 80435; (303) 468-4275** or **1-800-451-5930.**

Rentals and Information—

All of the nordic centers have rental equipment available, as do a large number of area shops.

Mountain Cyclery & Ski Exchange—Touring, telemarking and track equipment is available, along with good advice and trail ideas. **112 S. Ridge St., Breckenridge, CO 80424; (303) 453-2201.**

Mountain View Sports—Located 1 mile east of the Keystone stoplight in Keystone; **22869 Hwy. 6** or **PO Box 8965, Keystone, CO 80455; (303) 468-0396.**

Wilderness Sports—Provides a great selection. Located across from Wendy's in Silverthorne. **171 Hwy. 9, Silverthorne, CO 80498; (303) 468-8519.**

DOWNHILL SKIING

Summit County's four ski areas host over three million skiers each winter. More than 4,800 acres of slopes, 60 lifts and 358 trails should have the terrain you are looking for—whether it's easy ballroom skiing or steep, ungroomed mogul runs. Although tickets can be purchased at the individual ski areas, the Lake Dillon Resort Association, among others, offers daily discount tickets as well as four- and six-day Ski the Summit passes. These passes offer great savings and are interchangeable at all of the ski areas in Summit County. For more information contact **Ski the Summit, PO Box 98, Dillon, CO 80435; (303) 468-6607.** Front Range skiers should keep in mind that Summit County ski area tickets are sold at a discount by many outlets along the Front Range, including supermarkets.

Arapahoe Basin—

The top of Arapahoe Basin, perched at a lofty 12,450 feet, is the state's highest ski area summit. This allows it to stay open into June each year, much to the delight of sun-seeking die-hard skiers. Of the four ski areas in Summit County, Arapahoe is the oldest, getting its start back in the 1940s when Max Dercum and a handful of cronies installed the first chairlift. Much of the equipment they used was army surplus, acquired from Camp Hale, near Leadville, where the 10th Mountain Division ski troops trained during World War II. Cables and pulleys were liberated from old mines.

The area has come a long way and now has more than 350 acres of skiable terrain. But it's not the best area for beginners, only 10 percent of the mountain is for novices. However, intermediate and advanced skiers love it. The Pallavicini lift services a slew of black runs on the right side of the mountain—and they are steep! Every 20 minutes a shuttle bus leaves for Keystone. Child care available. Lift tickets are good at both areas. Arapahoe Basin is located a few miles east of Keystone on Hwy. 6, at the western base of Loveland Pass. For information contact **Keystone Resort, Box 38, Keystone, CO 80435; (303) 468-4300 ext. 4332,** or **Arapahoe Basin, (303) 468-0718.**

Breckenridge Ski Area—

The growth of Breckenridge, especially in the past 10 years, has been phenomenal. And the expansion should continue with the recent purchase of the area by Ralston Purina, owner of nearby Keystone Resort. The largest ski area in Summit County, at more than 1,600 acres, Breckenridge comprises three interconnected mountains: Peaks 8, 9 and 10. Together they offer plenty of terrain for skiers of all abilities. The lower part of Peak 8 and most of Peak 9 keep beginners and intermediates happy with well-groomed runs. Advanced skiers usually head to the back bowls of Peak 8 and to the exacting double black diamond bump runs on the North Face of Peak 9. Runs such as Devil's Crotch and Hades are extremely challenging. There are two main bases. The one at the bottom of Peak 9 is accessible right in town; the base at Peak 8 can be reached by a shuttle bus that runs every few minutes. Breckenridge's ample number of lifts, including several high-speed Superchairs, helps keep lift lines relatively short, even during peak season. In addition to open skiing in Imperial bowl, accessible via a half-hour hike to the top of 13,000-foot Peak 8, an additional 200 acres of bowl skiing has been opened on Peak 7. On-mountain restaurants, such as the Vistahaus on Peak 9, have spacious sun decks and spectacular views of the Blue River Valley and the towering mountains to the east. Breckenridge has an excellent teaching program, offering especially good lessons to kids. Child care is also available at the area. If you are interested in snowboarding, Breckenridge is a great place for it. The World Snowboard Championships have been held here. For more information call **(303) 453-5000.**

Copper Mountain Resort—

Not only are the runs at Copper Mountain well designed, but geographically the mountain is a natural. For the most part, beginner, intermediate and advanced terrain are separated into three distinct areas. This provides peace of mind to skiers who don't want to accidentally end up on a run that is either too easy or too difficult. Advanced skiers stick to the left (east) side of the area, which offers challenging bump runs and bowl skiing near the top of the mountain. Runs at the Union Peak side, on the right (west) side of the area, are well-groomed intermediate and beginner terrain. Twenty lifts, including two high-speed quads, provide quick access to the many runs. Because of its fine reputation and 2,760 vertical feet, Copper Mountain receives a lot of day skiers from the Denver area who are willing to drive just a bit farther. Ski school and day care available. Some people grumble about parking facilities at the resort, complaining that you have to walk up to a quarter of a mile. Our advice is to park in the east lot and take the shuttle to the mountain. Located about 6 miles southwest of Frisco on Interstate 70. For more information contact **PO Box 3001, Copper Mountain, CO 80443; (303) 968-2882 or 1-800-458-8386.**

Keystone Resort—

Keystone continues to host more skiers per year than practically any of the other resorts in Colorado. Their award-winning accommodations, facilities and excellent service can take most of the credit. In addition, sophisticated snow-making machines crank up in late September, allowing Keystone to open in October, much earlier than most other areas in the state. The area also offers night skiing on 40 percent of the runs, which keeps the slopes open for more than 13 hours a day.

Keystone has long been a mountain for beginners and intermediates. The well-groomed runs provide worry-free skiing that is especially attractive for families. The teaching programs are first-rate and include the Mahre Training Center. The Mahre twins (Phil and Steve), former world champions and Olympic gold and silver medalists, operate exclusively at Keystone, offering week-long lessons.

During its early years of operation, Keystone drew the wrath of advanced skiers, frustrated with the area's lack of challenging runs. To diversify and attract more advanced and expert skiers, Keystone purchased Arapahoe Basin and developed the challenging North Peak Mountain, accessible from the top of Keystone Mountain. But the best news to advanced skiers was the recent $32 million expansion including a number of high-speed quad lifts, a second gondola (to service North Peak), the impressive 26,000-square-foot Outpost Restaurant, and the opening of the 300-acre demanding "Outback." After a snowstorm, the Outback's advanced and expert terrain provides top-notch tree skiing. Located about 10 miles east of Dillon on Highway 6. **Box 38, Keystone, CO; (303) 468-4300.**

SLEIGH RIDES

Alpine Adventures Inc.—

Located in the out-of-the-way townsite of Montezuma, Alpine Adventures has been offering sleigh ride dinners for years. Dinner is served in miner's style tents and includes homemade cooking whipped up by owner, Donna Papini. Reservations necessary. **5435 Montezuma Rd., Montezuma, CO 80435; (303) 468-9297.**

Dinner in the Woods—

Taking off from Union Creek at Copper Mountain, the sleigh makes its way along a torchlit trail to a tent in the woods where a down-home dinner of brisket, chicken and ribs is served. The meal changes nightly. This is a guaranteed romantic outing—that is, unless you take the kids. Open Tues. through Sun nights. For reservations and information, contact **PO**

Box 3533, Copper Mountain, CO 80443; (303) 968-2882 ext. 6320.

Two Below Zero Sleigh Rides—

Two mule-drawn red oak sleighs depart nightly from the Frisco Nordic Center to a heated tent in the woods near Lake Dillon. Enjoy a combo of top sirloin, chicken breast and marinated shrimp kebobs with all the trimmings; vegetarian dinners are provided with advance notice. Closed Sun. For rates, times and reservations contact **PO Box 845, Frisco, CO 80443; (303) 453-1520.**

SWIMMING

Breckenridge Recreation Center—

See the Recreation section.

TENNIS

Breckenridge Recreation Center—

Two indoor courts and four outdoor accessible for a fee. **880 Airport Rd.** in **Beckenridge; (303) 453-1734.**

Carter Park—

Four outdoor courts and a paddle court. Free; lighted for night play. Located at the extreme south end of High St. in Breckenridge, three blocks east of Main St. There is a sign-up sheet at the park.

Copper Mountain Racquet and Athletic Club—

Year-round courts and lessons available; fee charged. Located at Copper Mountain. Open 6 am–10 pm Mon.–Fri., 8 am–10 pm Sat.–Sun. **(303) 968-2882 ext. 6380.**

Dillon Public Courts—

Four outdoor courts are available at the park in Dillon on La Bonte St. Reservations can be made at Dillon Drug at 103 E. Buffalo. Small fee charged between Memorial Day and Labor Day. For information call **Town Hall** at **(303) 468-2403.**

Keystone Tennis Center—

Open year-round; lessons available; fee charged. **(303) 468-4220.**

———— SEEING AND DOING ————

ALPINE SLIDE

On the **Super Slide** at Breckenridge you can glide down one of two tracks on Peak 8 in your specially designed sled. You control the brake lever so the ride can be as easy or as scary as you want. The sled is big enough for an adult and a small child. No. 5 chairlift takes you to the top of the track. One-ride tickets are available, as well as all-day passes. To reach the lift from the stoplight in town, head west up Ski Hill Rd. for about 1.5 miles. Open daily from mid-June–early Sept., 10 am–5 pm; weekends only in late Sept. Call **(303) 453-5000** for information.

CHAIRLIFT RIDES

During the summer you can ride chairlifts up the mountains at Breckenridge, Copper Mountain and Keystone ski areas. See the Hiking and Backpacking section.

MUSEUMS AND GALLERIES

Frisco Historic Park—

Established in 1982, Frisco Historic Park consists of seven completely restored buildings from Frisco and the surrounding area. The Frisco Schoolhouse Museum, the largest of these, is located on its original site. It was first used as a saloon before becoming a schoolhouse. It now houses artifacts and information about the Ute Indians, mining and Dillon Reservoir. The other buildings include private residences and the old Frisco jail. Open Tues.-Sat. 11 am-4 pm in winter; open through Sun. in summer. No fee. Located at **120 Main St.** in Frisco; **(303) 668-3428.**

Summit Historical Society Tours—

The Summit Historical Society, through local funding, has been able to restore a number of interesting historical sites around the county. Both self-guided tours and tours with a knowledgeable guide are available. For information call **(303) 468-6079** or **(303) 453-9022.** Here are a couple of the more interesting tours.

Located near Breckenridge, the **Washington Mine** operated from 1880 to 1973. Visitors are led into the horizontal shaft with miner's candles. Many artifacts are on display to help you gain a better understanding of gold and silver mining in Colorado. Tours begin June 1, Mon.–Sat. at 1 pm and run through the summer. Small fee. The **Breckenridge Briggle House** is a fine Victorian home built in 1896. Its main attraction is an art collection that includes "hair" art. This unusual medium features small bobbles made from women's hair, which were popular accessories in the Victorian era. The Briggle House tour, along with stops at the **1880 Alice G. Milne House** and the **1875 Edwin Carter Museum,** are offered Wed.–Sat. at 10 am; small fee charged.

NIGHTLIFE

Narrowing down the long list of nightlife options in Summit County is no easy task. Because it contains the largest collection of winter resorts in the country, Summit County offers an abundance of après-ski spots where people dance to live music into the wee hours. Briefly, here are the highlights.

Breckenridge—

For après ski many people converge on the **Village Pub, (303) 453-0369,** located in the Bell Tower Shops at **555 S. Columbine.** Across the street is **Mi Casa, 600 Park, (303) 453-2071,** offering happy hour every day 3–6 pm. For dancing into the night try **Eric's Underworld, 111 S. Main St., (303) 453-8559,** providing great live blues and rock most nights of the week, and **Shamus O'Tooles Roadhouse Saloon, 115 S. Ridge, (303) 453-2004.** How about live theater? **The Backstage Theater, Pond Level** at the **Village at Breckenridge, (303) 453-0199,** gives evening performances in

winter and summer. Call for reservations. Beer lovers should try **Downstairs at Eric's, 111 S. Main St., (303) 453-1401,** where you'll find an incredibly large variety of beer on tap and what some consider to be the area's best pizza. The excellent **Breckenridge Brewery & Pub** provides a welcome new addition to the après-ski and nightlife scene. For more information see the Where to Eat section.

Copper Mountain—

Après ski kicks into high gear at **Farley's, (303) 968-2577,** and **The B lift Pub, (303) 968-2525,** both located at the base of the B lift. **Pesce Fresco** at the Mountain Plaza provides a soothing atmosphere with many drink specialties. **Club Med, (303) 968-2161** (see Where to Stay) has opened up its doors in winter to the public for a dinner buffet and live cabaret performances ... disco then continues until closing.

Frisco—

Along Main St. you'll find the **Moose Jaw, 208 Main, (303) 668-3931,** for cheap beer, burgers and a game of pool. This has been a local favorite for years. **Barkley's Basement Cafe,** at **620 Main, (303) 668-3694,** offers Mexican food, good margaritas and live rock and blues. Happy hour at **Golden Annie's, (303) 668-0345,** attracts a loyal crowd.

Keystone—

The **Snake River Saloon** offers fine dining, and the rowdy bar in the next room often features great live rock music. Built more than 25 years ago and originally called the Loveland Pass Bar, weary travelers, construction workers and miners used to frequent this popular night spot. It still rocks out late into the night. Located at **23074 Hwy. 6; (303) 468-2788.** A recent addition to Keystone nightlife is **Monte-Zuma's,** located right near Keystone Lake, which offers dancing to DJ tunes and live rock and blues bands; they also offer a great selection of locally brewed ales.

Silverthorne—

The **Old Dillon Inn** was an institution in Summit County even before it was moved from the old townsite of Dillon, which was flooded by the reservoir in 1962. Both the restaurant (Mexican food) and bar pack people in like sardines for live music and a few cervezas and margaritas. If you don't mind crowds, then give it a try. **321 Blue River Pkwy. (Hwy. 9); (303) 468-2791.**

SCENIC DRIVES

Boreas Pass/Hoosier Pass—

From the comfort of your Chrysler or Ford, cross two of the most historic passes in the area, which were barely navigable by mule just over a century ago. Boreas Pass Rd. (Forest Rd. 223) begins near Breckenridge and heads southwest along the old Denver South Park & Pacific Railroad bed, which finally laid track to Breckenridge in 1882. The grade was so steep that the engine could pull only three cars at a time. One story has it that P.T. Barnum's circus train was on its way to Breckenridge when it started to stall. The elephants were let out of the cars and helped push the train to the summit. Historic sights along the way include Baker's Tank (a restored water tank) and the remains of a settlement on the 11,482-foot summit. When it was built, this line of train track was the highest in the country. The panorama of the Tenmile Range is spectacular along the way.

From the summit of the pass (10 miles from Breckenridge), continue down the other side of the Continental Divide and take in the views of the wide expanse of South Park. After about 13 miles you'll reach the old town of Como (see the **South Park and 285 Corridor** chapter). From Como turn right on Hwy. 285 and head to Fairplay, then take another right onto Hwy. 9. The road almost immediately begins climbing northward to the 11,541-foot summit of Hoosier Pass. Homesick prospectors from Indiana gave the pass its name around 1860. From the summit return to Breckenridge, about 10 miles north.

Loveland Pass—

It wasn't too many years ago that every motorist driving between Denver and Summit County had to ascend the sky-scraping Loveland Pass. Since the completion of the Eisenhower Tunnel in 1973, people have forgotten how beautiful the views are from the summit of the pass. Granted, the drive takes longer, but at the summit you can get out and walk along ridges of the Continental Divide. Views to both sides are spectacular. Visitors who want to see alpine tundra without having to walk up to it should make this drive. To reach Loveland Pass from Keystone, head east on Hwy. 6 past Arapahoe Basin Ski Area and follow the switchbacks to the summit. Either return the same way or descend the east side of the pass and return via Eisenhower Tunnel.

SHOPPING

Silverthorne Factory Stores —

One of the biggest anomalies in Summit County has been the Silverthorne development of two shopping malls full of well-known retail stores offering reduced prices on merchandise. For those who can't get shopping out of their system (even with the beautiful distractions of the Colorado Rockies), these factory stores are a welcome respite from the premium prices commanded at the nearby resorts. Over 70 stores; open daily. Located just off of Interstate 70 in Silverthorne at **145 Stephens Way; (303) 468-9440.**

WHERE TO STAY

ACCOMMODATIONS
BRECKENRIDGE

The majority of Breckenridge accommodations are deluxe lodges and condominium rentals. At the base of Peak 9 the magnificent **Breckenridge Hilton, Beaver Run Resort** and the **Village at Breckenridge** all offer modern, luxurious rooms right at the ski mountain. Information and reservations for accommodations in Breckenridge can be arranged by calling **Breckenridge Central Reservations** at **1-800-221-1091** or **1-800-800-BREC**.

Allaire Timbers Inn—$$$ to $$$$

It's difficult to find anything not to like at this luxury bed and breakfast inn. Built in 1991 by Jack and Kathy Gumph in a wooded location at the south end of Breckenridge, the Allaire is an attractive wood-and-stone structure, offering 10 guest rooms, each with a private bath and balcony. Named after Colorado mountain passes, each room has a creatively expressed theme. For a special occasion, consider staying in one of the two deluxe suites which include their own fireplace and hot tub. Guests spend a lot of their time in the enormous common room where a full breakfast is served each morning. Take in the view of the Tenmile Range from the Jacuzzi on the large deck. No smoking. **PO Box 4653, 9511 Hwy. 9, Breckenridge, CO 80424; 1-800-624-4904** or **(303) 453-7530.**

The Lodge at Breckenridge—$$$ to $$$$

If you have the financial wherewithal a stay at the Lodge at Breckenridge is recommended for one simple reason—the superb views. Unbelievable views, actually. Large picture windows in most of the 45 rooms and suites look out to Breckenridge ski area and the Tenmile Range, Hoosier Pass or Mt. Baldy. The recently renovated rooms provide spacious, attractive Western decor with comfortable furniture. After a long day of exploring, hiking or skiing, pay a visit to the indoor pool, Jacuzzi, or weight room; facials, body treatments and massages are available for an extra charge at the spa. Breakfast (at a reduced rate for lodge guests) and dinner **($$$ to $$$$)** are served at the **Top of the World** restaurant. Package deals available. When reserving, be sure to ask for a room with a view. Located two miles up Boreas Pass Road from the south end of town. **PO Box 391, 112 Overlook Dr., Breckenridge, CO 80424; 1-800-736-1607** or **(303) 453-9300.**

Ridge Street Inn—$$$

This Victorian-style bed and breakfast has recently undergone a partial renovation, and now enables visitors to chose from six different rooms, all furnished in antiques. For romance try the two new rooms (private baths), done in a country-French motif. Two of the other four rooms share a bath. Families may want to stay in the Parlor Suite with its queen bed, queen pullout and private entrance. Vacationers who enjoy interacting with other guests will like the Ridge Street Inn and the gracious hostess, Carol Brownson. Carol serves up a full breakfast each morning. No smoking or pets; children under six years old are discouraged. **212 N. Ridge St., P.O. Box 2854, Breckenridge, CO 80424; (303) 453-4680.**

Williams House–1885 Bed & Breakfast—$$ to $$$

Beautiful antiques and a historical feel permeate this small mining-era home on N. Main St. in Breckenridge. Completely gutted and restored by owners Diane Jaynes and Fred Kinat, the Williams House dates back to 1885. The three guest rooms (two with private baths) are quite comfortable as are the front parlor and the sun room, which provides a view to peaks 7 and 8. Full breakfast includes fresh-ground coffee, homemade bread and an entrée that varies daily. Connoisseurs of fine bed and breakfasts will enjoy this place. **303 N. Main St., P.O. Box 2454, Breckenridge, CO; (303) 453-2975.**

Fireside Inn—$ to $$$$

Originally built in 1879, this home has been added on to over the years, and the result is a charming, very popular inn. Rates vary quite a bit among the four private rooms with baths and five dorm rooms. American Youth Hostel cards are honored, providing inexpensive lodging. The private rooms, which the new owners have spiffed up a bit, come furnished with some antiques, including brass beds. The Brandywine Suite is the finest room, with one queen bed and a trundle bed. There used to be a decanter of fine brandy in the room, but it was removed after the maid kept getting bombed while cleaning! Downstairs the living room with its cozy fireplace serves as a meeting place for guests. Continental breakfast comes with the room rate in summer; full breakfast is available for a small fee. The hot tub soothes your muscles after a day on the slopes. **PO Box 2252, 114 N. French St., Breckenridge, CO 80424; (303) 453-6456.**

COPPER MOUNTAIN

Accommodations in Copper Mountain are mainly first-class lodge rooms and condominiums. Specific descriptions and prices can be obtained by calling toll free **1-800-458-8386** or **(303) 968-2882.**

Club Med—$$$$

This was the first Club Med in North America. Offering "the antidote to civilization," this glitzy international resort provides week-long vacation packages that include lodging in their lavish hotel, dining, cabaret entertainment and all the skiing you want. The only currency used is bar beads, which can be redeemed for drinks at the bar. Club Med at Copper Mountain is not strictly for swinging singles—programs for kids are provided. Open during winter only. **PO Box 3337, Copper Mountain, CO 80443; (303) 968-2161.**

FRISCO

With its location alongside Interstate 70, Frisco has quite a number of motel chains to choose from. In addition, condominiums and private homes can be rented. Call the **Lake Dillon Resort Association** at **1-800-365-6365** (outside Colorado) toll free, or locally at **(303) 468-6222** for information and reservations.

Galena Street Mountain Inn—$$$ to $$$$

Located just off Main St. in Frisco, this recently completed inn provides comfortable accommodations in 15 spacious rooms. Each room comes complete with a private bathroom, cable TV; the Mission-style furniture, attractive decor and down comforters are the same in each room. For a special occasion, the Tower Room is worth remembering with its turret and large windows. Two common rooms (one with a large selection of books) and a refreshment bar are available to the guests, as are the hot tub and sauna. Breakfast served each morning in the large dining room. No smoking. Located at 1st Ave. and Galena St. **PO Box 417, Frisco, CO 80443; 1-800-248-9138** or **(303) 668-3224.**

Twilight Inn—$$$

Of the many bed and breakfasts in Summit County, the Twilight Inn is a personal favorite. Open since December 1987, this inn continues to receive rave reviews from travel magazines and major newspapers. Each of the 12 rooms is unique and carefully furnished. Eight have private bathrooms, while the others share baths. The largest room sleeps eight people comfortably. The library/TV room is an excellent place to relax and visit with other guests after a day of hiking or skiing. Don't overlook the hot tub and a steam room. The hosts, Rich Ahlquist and Jane Harrington, are great folks. Rich has lived in Summit County for 15 years and can provide a wealth of information about the area. Continental breakfast is included in the price—the zucchini bread is delicious. A comfortable, handsome and reasonably priced place, it's hard not to be impressed with the Twilight Inn. Reservations are recommended during the peak winter months and holidays. **PO Box 397, 308 Main St., Frisco, CO 80443; (303) 668-5009.**

KEYSTONE

Accommodations at Keystone Resort are all handled through a central reservations number. You have three main choices—a room at plush **Keystone Lodge** in the village, a condominium or a luxury home rental. The central reservations number is **1-800-222-0188**. For a charming, historic lodging opportunity, read on.

Ski Tip Lodge—$$$ to $$$$

Those wishing to avoid slick, modern accommodations should think about staying at comfortably rustic Ski Tip Lodge. Located east of the ski area in a relatively isolated pine forest (isolated for Keystone, that is), the lodge, without the distractions of telephones and TVs, is the perfect escape. The log building was a stagecoach stop in the 1880s. When Max and Edna Dercum bought the place in the 1940s, it became the first skiing guest ranch in Colorado. Max, an avid skier, developed Arapahoe Basin Ski Area just up the valley. Hosts and guests alike would ski all day and sit around the stone fireplace at night chatting and getting to know one another. The Dercums sold Ski Tip to the resort in 1983, but the charm lives on.

This lodge is decorated like a Swiss chalet, with colorful flowers blooming in window boxes in summer. Hand-hewn wooden beams and ceilings accent the interior. Fourteen rooms are furnished with antiques, quilts and lace curtains. Some rooms have private baths, while others share. Ski Tip Lodge is famous for its excellent food, and in winter lodging prices include breakfast and a four-course dinner. In summer lodging includes breakfast only. For more information about the restaurant, see the Where to Eat section. In winter bus transportation to Keystone (a mile or so west) is available every half hour. Reservations recommended. **Box 38, Keystone, CO 80435; 1-800-222-0188.**

MONTEZUMA

Paradox Lodge—$$$ to $$$$

Located a mere 5 miles from the bustle of Keystone Resort, Paradox lies tucked away in the woods of Montezuma Valley. Owners George and Connie O'Bleness offer homestays and cabin rentals surrounded by miles of Arapaho National Forest land, including lofty peaks along the Continental Divide. Just across the road from the O'Bleness's 37-acre spread is the Peru Gulch trailhead, providing hiking and mountain biking in summer and cross-country skiing in winter. If you choose to stay in one of the double-occupancy rooms in the cedar lodge, make yourself at home in the living room or perhaps out on the sun deck during summer. Lodge guests receive a filling continental breakfast. A number of private cabins come complete with all the necessities as well as microwave ovens and coffee makers. Be sure to make your way to the wood-fired hot tub. This place is a viable escape from the developed areas of Summit County. **#35 Montezuma Rd., Dillon, CO 80435; (303) 468-9445.**

SILVERTHORNE AND DILLON

For arranging Summit County accommodations not connected with the ski resorts, contact the **Lake Dillon Resort Association** toll free at **1-800-365-6365** or locally at **(303) 468-6222**. You can also write to **Summit County Central Reservations, PO Box 446, Dillon, CO 80435.**

Alpine Hutte—$ to $$

When Fran Colson and her son, Dave, opened their low-cost lodge in the fall of 1987, they let out a sigh of relief—financing had not been easily obtained. As Fran puts it, "The bankers were trying to tell me tourists expected and wanted to spend a lot of money for lodging." Luckily, she convinced one bank otherwise. The result is a European-style lodge offering a startlingly low nightly rate for a bed. The lodge sleeps 66 people in spacious rooms with four to eight bunks each and two large bathrooms on each floor. The only private room has a queen bed but costs three times as much per night.

Downstairs, guests spend time either in the TV room or the main living room with its stone fireplace, dining room table and overstuffed sofas. For a very small fee, breakfast, lunch and dinner are offered; guests may cook their own meals in summer and off-season. The bedrooms are closed for cleaning each day from 9:30 am to 3:30 pm, but the downstairs rooms remain open. There is also an evening curfew. If you don't mind a few regulations, the Alpine Hutte is definitely worthwhile. AYH discount; wheelchair accessible; reservations recommended. **PO Box 919, 471 Rainbow Dr., Silverthorne, CO 80498; (303) 468-6336.**

CAMPING

In Arapaho National Forest—
Lake Dillon—The national forest campgrounds at Lake Dillon are plentiful but extremely crowded during the summer months. Although many sites are available on a first-come, first-served basis, about half can be reserved at least 10 days in advance by calling **MISTIX** at **1-800-283-CAMP.** You might also stop in at the forest service office in Silverthorne to get an idea of where you'll have the best chance to find a site. **Heaton Bay Campground** (72 sites; fee charged), **Peak One Campground** (79 sites; fee charged), **Pine Cove Campground** (50 sites; fee charged) and **Prospector Campground** (107 sites; fee charged) are located along the northwest shore and along Hwy. 9 south of Frisco. Group camping is available at **Windy Point Campground** (72 sites; fee charged). Reservations are required for these group campgrounds.

Blue River Campground (24 sites; fee charged) is located on the Blue River, 9 miles north of Silverthorne on Hwy. 9.

Green Mountain Reservoir—McDonald Flats Campground (13 sites; fee charged), **Prairie Point Campground** (39 sites; fee charged), **Elliot Creek Campground** (primitive camping; no fee) and **Cataract Creek Campground** (4 sites; no fee) are located next to Green Mountain Reservoir, 25 miles north of Silverthorne on Hwy. 9.

Private Campground—
Tiger Run Resort—Believe it or not, as large as Summit County is, only one private RV campground exists. And it's pricey. Tiger Run, one of only a few five-star RV resorts in the country, offers RV sites, tennis courts, a large clubhouse, an indoor swimming pool, a hot tub, a laundry and a game room. Some RVs are available for rent. Tiger Run is located along Hwy. 9 between Frisco and Breckenridge. From Frisco drive south about 6 miles and turn left at the Tiger Run sign. **Tiger Run Resort, PO Box 815, Breckenridge, CO 80424; (303) 453-9690.**

————— WHERE TO EAT —————

BRECKENRIDGE
Briar Rose Restaurant—$$$ to $$$$
In the early 1960s this restaurant was built in tribute to the legacy of good food and drink at the historic Briar Rose Boarding House. Both the fine food and the historic atmosphere make this a really fun place to eat. The dining area is decorated in Victorian style with antiques. The old wooden bar was moved from the Breckenridge Opera House, where for years it helped reluctant operagoers tolerate *Madame Butterfly* a little more easily. Game trophies line the walls, and the portrait of a reclining nude behind the bar seems to fit perfectly.

Menu items range from steak to seafood; occasionally, game dishes such as elk, venison and buffalo are available. The prime rib has a good reputation around town. Pages of the menu are interspersed with an extensive wine selection, featuring straightforward descriptions of each vintage. Reservations re a good idea. Open daily in winter 5–10 pm, 6–10 pm Mon.–Sat. in summer. Located just off Main St. at **109 E. Lincoln St.; (303) 453-9948.**

Breckenridge Brewery & Pub—$$ to $$$

For an outstanding glass of freshly brewed ale and a picture-perfect view of the ski mountain, try to get an upstairs seat at the Breckenridge Brewery. This comfortable place seems to be the new hot spot in town. In addition to six varieties of brew made on the premises (in gigantic steel tanks behind the bar), you can fill up on pub food; lunch and dinner standards include burgers, wings, sandwiches and salads. You might want to order the fresh pasta or fish special in the evening. Locals seem to prefer the India Pale Ale. Open from 11am–2am daily. **600 South Main St.; (303) 453-1550.**

Mi Casa—$$ to $$$

The Mexican food at this very popular Breckenridge restaurant is nothing exceptional, but the atmosphere is lively and the enthusiasm of the wait staff spills over to the customers. The decor reminds you of certain other large Mexican restaurants with its tile floors, white stucco walls and hanging flower baskets. Aside from variations on the standard burrito, enchilada, etc., Mi Casa does offer some fairly interesting chicken dishes as well as a "fish of the day" special. Also—take advantage of the many varieties of salsa, asking for one with a chili rating to suit your taste. Adjacent to the restaurant is the extremely popular Mi Casa bar, which has been an après-ski hangout for years (happy hour 3–6 pm daily). The 16-oz. margaritas here have attracted a loyal following. Restaurant open 5–9:30 pm. **600 Park Place; (303) 453-2071.**

Poirrier's Cajun Cafe—$$ to $$$

Although hundreds of miles from the Bayou country of Louisiana, make no mistake ... the cajun food at Poirrier's is excellent. Cajun artwork/decor, including obligatory pennants of Louisiana sports teams (Geaux Tigers!), and potent Hurricane drinks served during Mardi Gras all get you in the mood. For starters, try some Cajun popcorn: peeled crawfish dipped in corn flour and then deep fried. Entrée standouts include seafood gumbo, poisson hymel and many other seafood dishes. ATTENTION!—do not leave without trying a piece of the exquisite bread pudding, served hot with rum butter sauce and chantilly cream. Open for lunch 11:30 am–2 pm (3 pm in summer); dinner from 5:30–9 pm (til 10 pm in winter). **224 S. Main; (303) 453-1877.**

Blue Moose Restaurant—$ to $$$

Known primarily for its tasty breakfasts, the Blue Moose attracts a loyal local crowd along with vacationers. Sit inside the small restaurant or at a picnic table out front and enjoy breakfast standards such as omelettes, pancakes, or lighter fare including fruit bowls, granola and homemade muffins. Standouts include eggs benedict, huevos rancheros and the breakfast burrito. Lunch and dinner entrées run the gamut from burgers to fresh pasta to chicken Moroccan. Full bar. Open 7 am–2 pm in summer; in winter dinner is served from 5–10 pm. **540 S. Main; (303) 453-4859.**

Cafe Alpine—$ to $$$

Its hard to categorize the cuisine at Cafe Alpine, but international, healthful and delicious all seem to fit. Located off Main St., this popular cafe recently won a number of awards in the "Taste of Breckenridge" competition. Take a seat indoors or at an umbrella table on the outdoor patio and choose from the creative breakfast, lunch and dinner menus. Notables include enormous salads, excellent homemade soups and sandwiches for lunch; dinner entrées range from fresh pasta of the day to spicy Thai prawns and vegetable stir-fry. Daily specials are always worth a try. During ski season, the tapas bar attracts tons of apre skiers who stand five deep at the bar, tasting wine and sampling Spanish mini-meals. Full bar, including an excellent selection of tap beer. Highly recommended. Breakfast served Mon.-Fri. 8–11 am (til 2 pm on weekends); lunch from 11 am–5 pm; dinner starts at 5 pm. **106 E. Adams Ave.; (303) 453-8218.**

Fatty's Pizzeria—$ to $$

If you're looking for a good pizza, look no farther. Fatty's serves up the best pizza in Breckenridge. You have the choice of white or whole wheat dough. This casual restaurant also offers five daily specials, such as beef stroganoff and Mexican dishes. Beer and wine are served. Open daily all year 11 am–10 pm. **106 S. Ridge St.; (303) 453-9802.**

The Gold Pan Restaurant—$ to $$

Once voted by *Ski* magazine as one of the top five restaurants in the country for local flavor, the Gold Pan, built in 1906, oozes history. At one time or another the building housed a nine-pin bowling alley, a funeral home and a buggy repair shop. The current layout features a saloon on one side with an ancient wooden bar. During Prohibition this bar was the only place in the state where a guy could get a drink (with a token purchased up the street). The restaurant decor is basic— wooden walls, tintype photos, mining relics and chairs that have been around since the 1930s. The Gold Pan is famous for its breakfasts, which are served all day. The specialties are the Mexican breakfast dishes with sauces (five kinds), beans, etc., prepared daily. Burgers and sandwiches are also served. Open 6:30 am–10 pm daily. **105 N. Main St.; (303) 453-5499.**

COPPER MOUNTAIN

Farley's—$ to $$$$

An institution in Copper Mountain since 1973, Farley's excels in both its fine food and its après-ski entertainment. The restaurant gets its name from the owner's German shepherd, who's no longer with us. Fireplaces, beer kegs in the walls and vaulted ceilings characterize this comfortable place. Prime rib, steaks and fresh seafood highlight the menu. Appetizers, including barbecue ribs and artichoke parmesan, appease the après-ski crowd. Extensive wine list; margaritas are quite good. Located at the base of the B lift, the tavern opens daily in midafternoon and stays open til 2 am. Restaurant is open 5:30–10 pm daily. **Snowflake Building; (303) 968-2577.**

Rackets Restaurant—$$ to $$$

Located upstairs at the Copper Mountain Racquet & Athletic Club, Rackets provides delicious lunches and dinners with a southwestern flair. The large, comfortable dining area is accented with a stone fireplace and many plants. Lunch specialties include a salad bar, green chile and rotisserie chicken and ribs; for dinner try the house's grilled lamb chops or the mixed mushroom enchiladas served in blue corn tortillas and topped with green chile sauce and cheese. Outside deck seating available. Summit County locals love this place. In summer, lunches served from 11:30 am–2 pm; dinner from 5–10 pm. Only dinner is served in winter; closed in the shoulder seasons. **(303) 968-2882.**

DILLON
Ristorante Al Lago—$$$

Although newcomers to the Summit County area, the Ottoborgo family have wowed locals with their excellent northern Italian cuisine. After their highly praised restaurant in Berthoud Falls burned down a few years ago, the family moved to Dillon and opened Ristorante Al Lago. The father, Alessandro, is from Italy and spends most of his time tending bar. His son, Ivano, studied the culinary arts in Italy for a couple of years and picked up secrets from New York chefs. Ivano prepares everything from scratch and even cuts his own veal and fish. The veal entrées are creative and considered by many locals to be the restaurant's highlight. Also offered are chicken, fresh seafood and a daily special. Delicious bread and desserts round out the meal. The dining room is very comfortable with a stone fireplace, wood beams, brick floors, red tablecloths, candlelight and a spectacular view up to Buffalo Mountain. In the backyard deer and chickens roam (the deer can be fed from the balcony). Open 5–10 pm Tues.– Sun. **240 Lake Dillon Dr.; (303) 468-6111.**

FRISCO

The Blue Spruce Inn—$$$ to $$$$

Strangely enough, this old establishment has traveled through more of Summit County than some vacationers have. Opened 50 years ago as a roadhouse between Old Dillon and Breckenridge, the building was moved to Frisco in the 1960s to avoid the rising waters of the reservoir. It continues to be one of the consistently fine restaurants in Summit County. The Blue Spruce Inn is cozy and intimate, with pine paneling, hanging plants and a lichen-covered stone fireplace. Specialties include slow-roasted prime rib, continental dishes and fresh seafood. Try their daily specials, such as poached salmon with tomato-hollandaise sauce or baked marlin with blackberry-hazelnut butter sauce. Service is superb. Dinners served nightly 5–10 pm; call for reservations. **120 W. Main St.; (303) 668-5900.**

Golden Annie's—$ to $$$

Although Golden Annie's serves a full selection of Mexican dishes, burgers, salads and ribs, the real reason to eat here is the fajitas. Weather permitting, the outside patio is a great place to sit and look out on Mt. Royal. Happy hour from 3–5 pm attracts a large crowd for good prices and appetizers including free hot wings. Lunch served from 11:30 am–3 pm; dinner from 5-10 pm. **603 Main St.; (303) 668-0435.**

The Moose Jaw—$ to $$

Serving heaping baskets of burgers and fries, the Moose Jaw is a great place for a cheap beer and a game of pool. Primarily locals hang out here. It's not fancy, it's just an inexpensive alternative. Open noon–2 am Mon.–Sat.; until midnight on Sun. **208 Main St.; (303) 668-3931.**

GREEN MOUNTAIN RESERVOIR

The Green Mountain Inn—$ to $$$

If you are down at Green Mountain Reservoir and get hungry, you may want to stop in at the Green Mountain Inn. It serves as the meeting place for locals in the Heeney area and leans a bit toward the rustic side. Sit at the counter or in the dining room and listen to music on the old player piano, juke box or wind-up Victrola. Menu items are of the usual steak-and-fried chicken variety, but there are a few house specials you may want to investigate. Open in winter 4:30–9 pm on weekdays, 9 am–9 pm on weekends; summer hours 4:30–9 pm weekdays and 7 am–9 pm weekends. Closed Mon. year-round. Located in Heeney, 23 miles north of Silverthorne on Hwy. 9. **7101 Summit County Rd. 30; (303) 724-3812.**

KEYSTONE

Keystone Ranch—$$$$

When it closed down operations in 1972, Keystone Ranch had been a working cattle ranch for more than 30 years. The restaurant provides beautiful views of the Tenmile and Gore ranges, as well as some of the finest gourmet food in Summit County. The six-course meal changes nightly but always features homemade soups, wild-game dishes and excellent desserts. Enjoy a cocktail in the living room beside the two-story stone fireplace. In summer lunches ($$) are served on the terrace overlooking the golf course. There are two seatings nightly, 5:45–6:45 pm and 8:15–9 pm. Reservations recommended. Three miles from Keystone Village; **1437 Summit County Rd. 150; (303) 468-4161.**

Ski Tip Lodge—$$$$

Located in a rustic cabin east of Keystone Ski Area, Ski Tip Lodge is well known for what many people consider to be the best food in Summit County. A stagecoach stop in the 1880s, the lodge has been operating as a ski lodge and restaurant since the 1940s. Warm yourself by the stone fireplace before being seated in the dining room. Each evening a choice of meat, fowl or fish is offered, with items changing nightly. The sauces are wonderful. Four-course dinners are served 5:45–9 pm nightly with soup, salad and freshly baked bread. Lunches ($$) are served daily in winter 11:30–2 pm and feature all the soup and bread you can eat. In summer Sun. brunch ($$) is served 10 am–1 pm. Reservations required. One mile east on Montezuma Rd. from Keystone; call **(303) 468-4202.**

SILVERTHORNE
Silverheels—$$$

Located in the woods of Wildernest high above Silverthorne, this hacienda-style southwestern restaurant features extremely creative dishes as well as one of the most attractive and romantic dining rooms in Summit County. The appealing decor includes hand-hewn wood beams set in white stucco, with bunches of chilis and Indian corn decorating the walls. Silverheels' menu is really quite something, consisting primarily of steak, seafood and a variety of southwestern specialties, all of which are exquisite in color, presentation and taste. Some entrées entail table-top "Stone Age Cookery" in which customers cook their own meal on a sizzling granite slab. The appetizers are also quite good, especially the crab empanadas, a tasty creation of cheeses and snow crab served with the restaurant's delicious salsa diablo (chili marmalade sauce). Be sure to try for a table in the main dining room for views out the picture windows to the lodgepole pine forest. This is a special place. Reservations highly recommended during peak seasons and on weekends. Open 4:30–10 pm nightly; bar open until 12 am. **81 Buffalo Dr., Silverthorne; (303) 468-2926.**

Old Dillon Inn—$$

The Old Dillon Inn has done its share of moving around. Built in 1869 in Montezuma, it was first moved to Old Dillon piece by piece. When Dillon Reservoir was completed in 1962, the building was loaded on a flatbed and moved to its present location. The owners supposedly had the kegs retapped before the beer had a chance to get warm. The Old Dillon Inn serves tasty New Mexican–style food; the specialty is blue corn crab enchiladas. The nightlife here is locally famous and can get rowdy. Live music (usually country-western) plays Fri.–Sun., and solo artists perform Tues.–Thur. The margaritas are excellent. Although the restaurant gets incredibly crowded, reservations are not accepted. Open for dinner only 4:30–10 pm daily. Along Hwy. 9 in Silverthorne at **311 Blue River Pkwy.; (303) 468-2791.**

SERVICES

BRECKENRIDGE
Central Reservations—

1-800-221-1091 or **1-800-800-BREC** out of state and **1-800-822-5381** in state.

Breckenridge Resort Chamber—

555 S. Columbine, Box 1909, Breckenridge, CO 80424; **(303) 453-6018.**

Copper Mountain Resort—

PO Box 3001, Copper Mountain, CO 80443; **1-800-458-8386.**

Day Care—

Belly Button Bakery and Babies—Day care for kids two months and older. If you want the kids to get ski lessons as well, consider Junior Ranch and Senior Ranch, which provide skiing on a small hill near the center. Reservations required. Located at Copper Mountain; **(303) 968-2882 ext. 6344.**

Breckenridge Children's Centers—The ski area offers a bunch of programs and attractions designed especially for kids. A recently installed pony lift on Peak 9 and the new Kid's Kastle are a couple of examples. **(303) 453-3000.**

Keystone Children's Center—This 8,000-square-foot facility provides day care for infants and children up to 12. Call **(303) 468-4182** for information.

Keystone Resort—

Box 38, Keystone, CO 80435; **1-800-525-1309** out of state, **1-800-222-0188** in Colorado.

Lake Dillon Resort Association—

121 Dillon Mall, Suite 102, PO Box 446, Dillon, CO 80435; (303) 468-6222 locally, or toll free at 1-800-365-6365.

Summit County Chamber of Commerce—

Two visitors centers—one in Frisco and one in Dillon. Mailing address and phone numbers are PO Box 214, Frisco, CO 80443; (303) 468-6205, 668-5800 or 668-0376.

Transportation—

Breckenridge Trolley—Provides daily transport around Breckenridge.

Resort Express—Provides airport shuttles. PO Box 1429, 273 Warren Ave., Silverthorne, CO 80498; (303) 468-7600 or 1-800-334-7433.

Summit Stage—This free public bus system provides year-round transportation between all the resorts and major towns in Summit County. Pick up a schedule at a visitors center or wherever you're staying. For information call (303) 453-1241 or 453-1339.

Vans to Breckenridge/Keystone/Copper Mountain—Offers transportation between Summit County resort destinations and Eagle County Airport and Denver International Airport; 1-800-222-2112.

Vail Valley

Considered by many to be the Colorado ski area with the finest snow conditions and most varied terrain, Vail has made quite a name for itself in a very short period of time. Vail Mountain became king of the ski hills in 1988 when a major expansion made it the biggest ski resort in North America, bigger in fact than the four ski areas in nearby Summit County combined. Located 100 miles west of Denver along Interstate 70, the town, which extends nearly 7 miles through the valley, offers 15 square miles of skiable terrain inside its boundaries. Although established in 1962, Vail really had its coming-of-age party in early 1989, when it played host to the World Alpine Ski Championships. Often called the Alpine Olympics, this biennial competition is the single most important event in alpine skiing. This was only the second time in the 60-year history of the event that it was held in the US.

There couldn't be a more worthy site for the championships than Vail, which was recently voted North America's top resort by readers of *Ski* magazine. Tucked away behind massive Vail Mountain are the legendary back bowls, Colorado's own Shangri-la of schuss. The combination of sun, altitude and dry air on the back bowls is perfect for Dom Perignon powder. A few years ago four new bowls, not as steep as the others, were added, opening the thrill of back-bowl skiing to intermediate skiers.

Beaver Creek, Vail's sister resort 10 miles west, adds over a square mile of skiable terrain to the Vail Valley empire. (Lift tickets between the two areas are interchangeable.) With the addition of the challenging runs on Grouse Mountain, this area now offers a more exciting, well-rounded, skiing experience. Sometimes called the "Last Resort," Beaver Creek is Colorado's swankiest. Exclusive hotels and condo developments, a shopping plaza and an air of European sophistication have developed in a beautiful valley setting. This is a place where even the most trivial, everyday problems are minimized for you—since dogs are prohibited, you don't even have to watch where you step. Nearby towns of **Minturn** and **Redcliff** offer visitors a down-to-earth atmosphere steeped in mining history; a smattering of small businesses, including restaurants and a couple of choice B&Bs, can be found by the curious. Along with **Avon** and **Eagle,** these towns are where most Vail/Beaver Creek employees can still afford to live.

Not to be ignored in all of the skiing hype is the beautiful backcountry of the White River National Forest, complete with two wilderness areas that flank Vail Valley. Within a cross-country run of Vail to the southwest is the popular Holy Cross Wilderness Area. To the north, at the heart of soaring Gore Range, lies Eagles Nest Wilderness Area. Sunsets in the valley turn the craggy range into a spectacular tangerine curtain. This national forest land contains an abundance of trails for hiking, mountain biking and cross-country skiing. Plenty of high mountain lakes and rushing streams await anglers.

Facing this striking alpine scenery in a front-row seat is the quaint Bavarian-style village of Vail itself. Skiers who prefer archrival Aspen call Vail a prefab storybook village with plenty of glitz that lacks the historic charm of Aspen. And even Vail locals admit it can be a mountain Disneyland of sorts. But Disney does have its pluses—convenience, no cars in the center of town and five-star service. Vail entices you with many options for running your gold card to the limit within its Tyrolean labyrinth of shops, lodges and eateries. Those on a tight budget may find Vail a somewhat daunting destination, but be sure that legions of workers have found ways to live well in the valley. Though most are forced to live west of Vail in Avon, Minturn or Edwards, these viable towns provide a welcome contrast and a needed dose of reality.

Even so, behind all of Vail's glamour beats the heart of a real town. There isn't a single stoplight, a fact that makes arriving a bit tricky. The four-way stop sign continues to be one of Vail's major landmarks. Instead of trying to navigate the town in a car, just park in structures at either Vail or Lionshead and walk or take the shuttle bus. Don't panic: the town quickly reveals its meandering logic.

HISTORY

Vail is barely a baby boomer in Colorado history—many of its skiers are older than the three-decades-old area. But the narrow valley was home to the Ute Indians in the 19th century, before gold prospectors prompted their angry exit. Despite their unceremonious ouster, the Utes later helped bring snow to the very back bowls they are so often falsely accused of torching in spite fires. On opening day of the new ski area in 1962, there was one problem: no snow. So the Utes were summoned back. Minnie Cloud led a ceremonial rain dance (renamed a snow dance for the occasion) on the deck of the new lodge at Vail. Within a week a blizzard hit, launching a successful season. By the way, the price of a full-day lift ticket back then was $5.

French trappers and explorers were the first Europeans in the valley. But perhaps the most memorable explorer of all was Lord Gore, a wealthy baronet from Ireland who amassed a hunting party in the mid-1850s for a three-year hunting expedition in the wilds of America. Gore had a veritable hunting army, with nearly 50 men, 100 horses, 50 hunting dogs, 6 wagons, 16 carts, a carpeted silk tent, a fur-lined commode, a few prostitutes and a 3-month supply of trade whiskey (180-proof grain alcohol mixed with red pepper). He took along renowned mountain man Jim Bridger as a guide and the two exchanged stories along the way— Bridger's tales of the frontier for Gore's Shakespearean dramas. When they got into the mountains near Vail, Gore and his party proceeded to shoot every buffalo, deer and elk within range, killing literally thousands of them. Gore took a few trophies and left the rest to rot.

The trip finally came to an end after many misadventures in the Black Hills of South Dakota, when local Indians decided they'd had enough. Bear's Rib, an Uncpapa Sioux, and his war party surrounded Gore and his men, then stripped them of their horses, supplies and all their clothes. Gore was left wandering in the wild until friendly Hidatsa Indians took him in. Later, he quietly made his way back to Ireland. According to historians, Bridger came back later and named a mountain range and creek after Gore. Today the Gore name is attached to many land features in the area.

In 1873 William Henry Jackson brought early fame to the Vail area with his photographs of the long-rumored-to-exist Mount of the Holy Cross. Tales had circulated for years of lost travelers seeing the mountain's snowy cross and suddenly finding their way. One of Jackson's photos of the cross with clouds swirling around it inspired pilgrimages up the mountain, which continue today. Henry Wadsworth Longfellow saw the photo and penned a poem about the mountain. Making the pictures, however, was not easy, given the state of photography at the time. Jackson carried his darkroom with him on mules.

In 1942 more than 15,000 men were stationed at Camp Hale, about 25 miles south of Vail, in preparation for winter fighting in Europe. After WWII, many of these 10th Mountain Division troopers became prime players in Colorado's burgeoning ski industry. Vail's modern history began with Pete Seibert, a 10th Mountain veteran.

Earl Eaton, who had been prospecting for uranium in Vail Valley, had met Seibert in Aspen. Eaton approached Seibert one day in Loveland (where Seibert worked) to tell him about a new prospect: the perfect ski mountain. Seibert took one look at the glorious slopes and agreed. They immediately began soliciting investors and, so as not to tip off anyone, formed the Trans Montane Rod & Gun Club to buy up land. Once permits were cleared and investors found, the ski area was built in a single year.

Vail got its name from Charlie Vail, chief engineer for Colorado's highway department in the late 1930s. Vail originally lent his name to present-day Monarch Pass, but locals who preferred Monarch protested. As a compromise, the moniker was transferred to the unnamed pass that is now Vail Pass.

Vail, which served as Gerald Ford's western White House during his presidency in the 1970s, is approaching middle age in the grand style befitting to Colorado's, and America's, premier ski resort.

GETTING THERE

Vail Valley is 100 miles west of Denver on Interstate 70. Regular and chartered ground transportation is available directly to and from Denver International Airport via bus, taxi, limo and van. The Vail/Beaver Creek Jetport in Eagle can be reached by air from Denver and other major cities. Some shuttle flights add only a nominal charge to the cost of a ticket to Denver International Airport.

FESTIVALS AND EVENTS

There's at least one special event virtually every weekend in Vail. Some of the highlights follow.

American Ski Classic
early March

Pros and amateurs descend on Vail for three events in a short period: the **World Cup**, the **Gerry Ford Invitational Ski Classic** and the **Legends of Skiing**, featuring the sport's greats. For a schedule call **(303) 476-1000**.

Bob Fest
Memorial Day

A few years back, Avon had a contest to name the town's bridge. "Bob" won and Bob Fest has rapidly gained notoriety as the place to be on Memorial Day. Residents square off in a game of Bob Ball, a cross between hockey and basketball—the hoop is only 7 feet high, because, according to one local, "every average guy named Bob has always wanted to jam it." They also have a Bob-B-Que, a Bob-B-Socks dance and, for some reason, a kids petting zoo. Call **(303) 949-5189** for more information.

Fourth of July Celebrations

This area features a concentration of Independence Day celebrations. The festivities include VailAmerica Days, the Vail Hill Climb and a mountaintop fireworks display. Down-valley, the "Salute to the USA" fireworks display in Avon is the biggest and brightest in the valley (well worth the short trip, say locals); the Minturn celebration includes a concert and kayak races. Contact **(303) 476-1000** for more information.

Bravo! Colorado

From early July through the first week in August the Vail valley fills with the sounds of music. Styles range from classical to jazz, but stress the quality of the sounds. Concerts are held variously at the Ford Amphitheater in Vail, the Vail Interfaith Chapel, and in Beaver Creek. For information and schedules call **(303) 479-1385**.

Summer Sporting Events

The **Gerry Ford Invitational Golf Tournament** gets underway in Aug. It attracts a slew of celebrity duffers, as well as some of the top pros on the PGA tour. The tourney is hosted by former president Ford at Vail Golf Club. Yogi Berra and Jack Nicklaus are among the frequent returnees. Call **(303) 479-2260** for more information. In early Aug. the **Eagle County Rodeo** usually kicks off with a bluegrass concert. In addition to events pitting cowhands against animals, you can see horseshoe pitching, draft horse pulling and blindfolded tractor driving competitions. For rodeo information contact **(303) 328-8775**.

—————— OUTDOOR ACTIVITIES ——————

BIKING

MOUNTAIN BIKING

Vail is a good place to two-wheel—good and tough. The steep valley makes for mostly challenging, uphill rides. The *Mountain Biking Guide to Vail, Colorado* by Michael J. Murphy (Alpenrose Press, 1990) is good news for those wanting to explore the rugged trails in the area. Vail and Beaver Creek mountains are also open to mountain biking. Rentals are available at the top of the Lionshead Gondola at Eagles Nest every day during summer. In addition many of the town's ski shops do double duty by offering bike rentals and repair when the snow melts. Cyclists can take the gondola up and ride all the way down to return bikes in Lionshead. Bikes may also be taken up the gondola for a fee. On the way down the mountain, a helmet is a must. It's also a good idea to lower your seat so you won't fly over your handlebars.

Red Sandstone Road—

This is a moderate 12-mile ride north to scenic Piney Lake from Vail. The rocky road starts off steep, then levels out with plenty of downhill stretches sprinkled amid the uphill. Especially fun is a roller coaster set of small hills near the end; the only drawback to this pretty ride is occasionally heavy automobile traffic along the way. At Piney Lake (9,342 feet), you can claim your reward: a dramatic view of the full measure of Gore Range. Also at the end of the trail is Piney River Ranch, where you can rent boats and drop a fishing line. Red Sandstone Rd. (Forest Rd. 700) leaves Vail's N. Frontage Rd. a mile west of the Vail Village exit from Interstate 70.

Shrine Pass Road—

See the Scenic Drives section for information.

Tigiwon Road—

For a taste of what a ride in the lunar rover must have felt like, try this bumpy 6-mile trail. The pitted road leads to the stone Tigiwon Hut south of Minturn and provides excellent views to Vail's back bowls. Most cyclists find this short ride more than enough. Depending on when the road was last graded, however, it's possible to continue another 2.5 miles to the edge of the Holy Cross Wilderness Area. But remember, mountain bikes aren't allowed in wilderness areas. Watch out for heavy truck traffic at the beginning of Tigiwon Rd. due to a mine cleanup operation. To reach Tigiwon Rd. (Forest Rd. 707), drive or ride 2.8 miles south of Minturn on Hwy. 24 and turn right.

10th Mountain Trail Association Hut System—

Just recently this remarkable hut system opened its arms to summer travelers on bike or on foot. For more information see the Cross-Country Skiing section.

Vail Mountain—

A true fat-tire enthusiast will want to ride up the mountain rather than take a relaxing trip up on the gondola or chair lift. A tough two-hour test is the dirt road from Vail Village to mid-Vail. Look for the beginning of the road right behind the Vista Bahn lift. Taking a detour down a section of the ski hill when descending the road is discouraged by Vail officials (but there's nothing quite as frighteningly fun).

Rentals and Information—

Christy Sports—For a varied supply of mountain bikes and 10-speed touring bikes, check this place at **293 Bridge St. in Vail; (303) 476-2244** and **182 Avon Rd. in Avon; 949-0241.**

TOURING

The **Vail Pass Bikeway** from Vail to Frisco has quickly become a favorite with cyclists of all abilities. But why ride a bike up a 10,666-foot pass, enduring a grueling hour or more of hairpin twists and killer inclines? For the thrill of speeding down the other side, of course. Tip: ascending the paved path from the Vail side (elevation gain: 2,206 feet) is a lot tougher than from the Copper Mountain side (elevation gain: 1,400 feet). For more information see the Biking section of the **Summit County** chapter. Another possibility for visitors is to ride the fairly flat recreational trails that connect the lifts along the base of Vail mountain.

FISHING
Eagle River—
Although the once-proud Eagle River seems to be losing the battle to developers, there are still stretches of classic trout fishing to be found. The Eagle flows north through a narrow, scenic canyon near Redcliff, and continues downstream past the contaminated mines and townsite of Gilman. A couple of miles northwest of Minturn, Gore Creek joins the flow. From there Eagle River flows west down the valley between Hwy. 6 and Interstate 70 through ranches and pasture, where it is fed further by Brush and Gypsum creeks. Rainbow and brown in the 10- to 14-inch range can be found in the Eagle on designated public water between Wolcott and Gypsum. The river is easy to get to from Hwy. 6, but stay off private land. Just below the confluence, you can fish on public water for about a mile. The fish seem to be a little bigger downriver near Eagle. Look for pools of deep, flat water. Locals recommend fly-fishing with a 12 to 16 elk hair caddis imitation or perhaps a prince nymph.

Gore Creek—
Gore Creek originates near Red Buffalo Pass in the Eagles Nest Wilderness Area, runs right through Vail and joins the Eagle River 2 miles northwest of Minturn. Although much of it is surrounded by civilization and its trappings, the creek is still swimming with rainbow, brook, brown and cutthroat trout. In fact, within the town's borders (from Red Sandstone Creek to the Eagle River 3 miles downstream) the creek is designated Gold Medal water; flies and lures only. Try fishing just east of the

Vail Golf Course, but do not fish on the course itself. The rushing creek with its large smooth bottom rocks can be tough to wade in places but is usually worth the trouble. Locals highly recommend catch and release fishing. The upper reaches of the creek in Eagles Nest Wilderness Area—north of Gore Creek Campground in East Vail—offer fishing away from the highway and condos.

Homestake Reservoir—
Though steep, rocky banks make fishing tricky, Homestake is a popular spot. Rainbow, brook and cutthroat trout swim in this reservoir adjacent to the Holy Cross Wilderness Area. Controversy over the reservoir and an ongoing sister project, Homestake II, have resulted in lengthy legal battles. Meantime, the fishing's great on the reservoir as well as down below on Homestake Creek, which is stocked and surprisingly uncrowded. From Hwy. 24, 3 miles south of Redcliff, turn right onto Homestake Rd. (Forest Rd. 703) at Blodgett Campground and drive 11 miles up to the 300-acre reservoir.

Mountain Lakes—
Near the summit of Vail Pass are the heavily fished **Black Lakes.** The two lakes, which feed into Black Gore Creek, are generally well stocked with rainbow and are easy to see from Interstate 70. Lost Lake, on the edge of the Eagles Nest Wilderness Area, is a popular lake in a beautiful setting at the headwaters of Red Sandstone Creek. Follow Red Sandstone Road for 6 miles towards Piney Lake. The marked trailhead is on your right just past some private cabins. The upper three of the four **Missouri Lakes** in the Holy Cross Wilderness Area have brook and cutthroat trout. To reach the lakes from Redcliff, drive 3 miles south on Hwy. 24 and turn right on Homestake Rd. to Gold Park Campground. Follow the rough road southwest up Missouri Creek. The lakes are about a 3-mile hike from the end of the road. **Beaver Lake** on the upper reaches of Beaver Creek in the Holy Cross Wilderness Area also has a

good supply of brook and cutthroat. Forest Rd. 738 follows the creek up from the Beaver Creek Ski Area to the wilderness boundary; then it's an easy half-mile hike. **Sylvan Lake State Park** located 16 miles south of Eagle on West Brush Creek Rd. is worth the short trip for the scenery alone. The brook and rainbow trout found in Sylvan Lake are an added bonus and they bite throughout the year. Bring your boat along if you want to catch the big ones in this 40-acre lake.

Piney Lake—

This 60-acre lake about 15 miles north of Vail at the end of Red Sandstone Rd. (Forest Rd. 700) has fair to good brook trout fishing, with good to great views of the Gore Range. On the private, southwest side of the lake is Piney River Ranch which can provide canoes and other small craft for float fishing. Virtually the entire shoreline is open to the public for catching a variety of trout, including native and cutthroat. The ranch also rents rods and waders. Older folks especially love this gentle setting. In winter the ranch opens up to snowmobiling and cross-country skiing. For information, contact **Piney River Ranch, PO Box 7, Vail, CO 81658; (303) 476-3941.**

FOUR-WHEEL-DRIVE TRIPS

Most of the back roads around Vail do triple duty as jeep roads and mountain biking trails in summer and cross-country ski routes in winter. For trip ideas call or visit the **Holy Cross Ranger District Office at 24747 Hwy. 24, Minturn, CO 81645; (303) 827-5715.**

Benchmark Road—

Starting on the maintenance road that leaves from behind the Lodge at Vail, this rugged road ascends through the ski area. Stay to the left as the road passes a gate about a mile up. Keep heading east up to the top of China Bowl and along the China Wall to 360-degree views of the surround-

ing ranges. The real jeeping begins on an old logging road that starts at another gate at about 10,500 feet. Drive until you can't go any farther. In winter the challenging cross-country Commando ski run follows this road down (see the Skiing section). Allow for about a three-hour round trip.

Holy Cross City—

The former stage route from Gold Park Campground to Holy Cross City has a reputation as one of the best, and most difficult, four-wheel-drive roads in the state. It's a particularly challenging drive that requires steady nerves. People from across the country come to navigate the road's coils, which are spiced by plunging chasms below. One negative result of the popularity was a huge bog dug by stuck jeeps near the ghost town. Recently, however, the bog was reclaimed through a massive volunteer effort from 25 jeep clubs. Provided that vehicles stay on the hardened road, the forest service has no plans to close the route. For historical information about Holy Cross City, see the Hiking and Backpacking section. To reach the road from Interstate 70, take the Minturn exit and drive 13 miles south on Hwy. 24. Turn right onto Homestake Rd. (Forest Rd. 703) and go 8 miles to the marked jeep road.

Rentals and Tours—

Timberline Tours—These folks offer guided backcountry trips in custom-built, off-road vehicles. In addition to half- and full-day trips, there are several variations on the theme: night tours, sunrise and sunset tours, and jeeping/caving or jeeping/rafting packages. **PO Box 131, Vail, CO 81658; (303) 476-1414.**

GOLF

Six 18-hole courses provide a good variety of high-altitude (and high-priced) golfing in Vail Valley. Most courses are long, narrow affairs due to the geography of the steep-walled valley. A brand new Hale Irwin-designed course at Cordillera, **(303) 926-2200,** offers tremendous views to the Sawatch and Gore mountain ranges.

The golfing season opens in mid-May and closes in mid-Oct. But spring weather in Vail has on occasion allowed the ultimate recreational day: skiing in the morning and a round of nine in the afternoon.

Beaver Creek Resort Golf Club—

This course, designed by Robert Trent Jones, Jr., is preeminent among the links in the Vail Valley. It twists down the secluded Beaver Creek Valley from the foot of the ski mountain. Though not as long as the other courses in the area, rolling hills, large, irregular traps and undulating, basketball-court-sized greens promise a challenging round. Along the way are great views of the surrounding ranges in the White River National Forest. Many of the resort's multi-million-dollar homes line the fairways and an antique barn stands in the middle of the course. Greens fees are higher for nonguests; public tee times are limited. The course opens in mid-May. Located on the road up to Beaver Creek Ski Area, off the Avon exit on Interstate 70. **103 Offerson Rd., Beaver Creek; (303) 949-7123.**

Eagle-Vail Golf Course—

Designed by PGA pros Bruce Devlin and Bob Van Hagge, Eagle-Vail is a very challenging course wedged in between the Eagle River and White River National Forest. Along with the obvious river hazard, water holes and 60 sand traps wreak havoc upon even the best players. This course, located midway between Vail and Beaver Creek, offers the best deals on golf in the valley, including bargain-rate greens fees during spring and fall. The club features a pool and tennis courts as well as a driving range. Located just off Interstate 70 on Exit 171 at Avon. **0431 Eagle Dr., Avon; (303) 949-5267.**

Singletree Golf Course—

Singletree's location 7 miles downvalley from Beaver Creek allows for a longer season than the other courses in Vail. Opening date in recent years has been Apr. 1. The course's rolling layout was designed in 1980 by Golf Force, formerly a Jack Nicklaus company. Like a Scottish course, there are few trees and many pot-hole-type traps. Tee times should be reserved 48 hours in advance. **1265 Berrycreek Rd., Edwards; (303) 926-3533.**

Vail Golf Club—

This 18-hole municipal course just east of Vail Village is the area's oldest, dating back to 1967, just five years after the ski area opened. Head pro Steve Satterstrom describes it as "a good test of golf," with fairways that dip in and out of the flanks of Vail Mountain and Golden Peak. Gore Creek cuts through the course, coming into play on over half the holes as do a number of sand traps. Nearly every tee has a view of the spectacular Gore Range. Among the several tournaments hosted by the club is the annual Gerry Ford Invitational, presided over by the former president himself, which draws a host of celebrities. Be sure to call for tee times. **1778 Vail Valley Dr.; (303) 479-2260.**

HIKING AND BACKPACKING

Patiently hunched around the glamorous town of Vail is some great hiking country known well by veteran hikers. Not 20 miles from the paparazzi, elk and marmots ply the Eagles Nest and Holy Cross wilderness areas. Holy Cross, which boasts over 100 miles of trails for hikers, is the second-most-used wilderness area in the state. In fact, it used to be a national monument but lost its designation in 1954 because of its poor accessibility and short summer season, according to rangers. Others say it's because the cross on the namesake mountain is crumbling. The enigmatic area remains popular, nonetheless, and the forest service is worried about overuse. Hikers and backpackers are asked to practice low-impact camping by staying on trails and using stoves instead of campfires.

Meanwhile, more and more hikers are discovering the terrain of the Eagles Nest Wilderness Area, which hunters once claimed as their own. Most hikes in this area have the stunning, 600-million-year-old Gore Range hanging above them like a curtain on a stage. For more information stop in at the **Holy Cross Ranger District Office at Dowd Junction** just after turning onto Hwy. 24, **PO Box 190, Minturn, CO 81645; (303) 827-5715.** Or pick up *The Vail Hiker* (Alpenrose Press, 1988) by Mary Ellen Gilliland, the definitive guide for hiking and ski touring in the Vail area. For topographical maps, complete gear and sound advice, stop by **Vail Mountaineering, 500 Lionshead Mall; (303) 476-4223.**

Bighorn Creek—

The 3.5-mile hike to the "Bighorn Hilton," an old homesteader's cabin, is less steep than many hikes near Vail. Wildflowers and a fern grove highlight the early part of this trail in the Eagles Nest Wilderness Area. At mile 2, it's hard to know what to look at first—Bighorn Falls on your left, or downvalley to Vail and Bighorn Creek. From this point the trail climbs quickly up a ridge. Shortly after, a level wooded trail brings you to the cabin. The structure, which serves as a storm shelter, makes a good turnaround point for the day hike. To get to the trailhead, take the East Vail exit off Interstate 70 and drive east on S. Frontage Rd. to Columbine Dr. Turn left and go to the end of the pavement.

Booth Falls Trail—

Sixty-foot Booth Falls is a handsome reward for making this moderate 2-mile hike in the Eagles Nest Wilderness Area. The trail begins steeply, getting into the mountains quickly, but soon levels out to a wildflower meadow with columbines, mariposa lilies, shooting stars and great views back toward Vail. Hikers are treated to an uncountable number of waterfalls and Swiss Alps–like vistas along Booth Creek. Reach the trailhead by taking the East Vail exit off Interstate 70 and turn onto the frontage road on the north side of the highway. Drive a mile west and turn uphill on Booth Falls Rd. The trailhead is at the end of the road near the water gauging station.

Holy Cross City—

History buffs will enjoy this two-hour hike up an old stage route to the remains of Holy Cross City. The ruins of several cabins and other structures mark the treeline ghost town that had boomed and died by 1884. Shaft houses, foundations of two ore mills and skeletons of mines dot the mountainsides. During boom times the Holy Cross Mill was connected to its sister mill in Gold Park by a 2.5-mile flume. From Interstate 70 take the Minturn exit. Follow Hwy. 24 south 13 miles to Homestake Rd. (Forest Rd. 703). Follow this gravel road 8.5 miles west to Forest Rd. 704 and turn right. Drive 2.3 miles to a "T" and turn right again. Go about 2 more miles, keeping to the right, and park in the level area just before the road turns into a very rough four-wheel-drive road. The trail starts on this road, quickly joining the historic Holy Cross City Rd. Look for a signed fork a little over 1.5 miles into the hike. Take the left fork and continue staying to the left to reach the "city."

Mount of the Holy Cross—

Rangers say the climb up Mt. of the Holy Cross is the most popular hike in the Vail area. The trail up this 14er (barely, at 14,005 feet), about 6 miles each way, is usually climbed on an overnight trip. In the 1930s a series of "hanky healing" pilgrimages were made up the mountain. People too ill to make the climb sent their handkerchiefs to a Denver pastor who promised to bless them on the peak and send them back. In 1932 the pastor received over 2,000 hankies, and two rangers had to help him carry them up the mountain. The trail starts off with a rugged, rocky climb to Half Moon Pass; hikers are rewarded by tremendous panoramas of the Gore and Mosquito ranges. The pass alone makes a good day's climb. After crossing the narrow path over the pass, the trail drops down to Cross Creek, which is a great place to see the aspen in fall. Many hikers camp here, so they can finish the ascent up Mt. of the Holy Cross before noon the next day to avoid electrical storms.

When possible, however, the forest service encourages making the climb in a day, because of too many campers in the Cross Creek area. After the trail crosses the creek and follows a series of switchbacks up through the forest, its route becomes obvious: just follow the ragged edge of the Holy Cross Ridge to the summit. Start hiking up Half Moon Pass Trail, just to the right of the Fall Creek trailhead at the end of Tigiwon Rd. (For directions see Notch Mountain below.)

Notch Mountain—

Clergymen still lead pilgrimages up this 5-mile trail to see the giant cross of snow etched in Mt. of the Holy Cross to the west. A stone shelter was built on top of 13,100-foot Notch Mountain in 1924 to accommodate the hundreds of pilgrims. (When I was on the 35th switchback above treeline, it was hard to see how anybody brought materials up for such a structure.) The fairly difficult hike starts off in a shadowy forest that soon opens up to a meadow. From there the trail clings to a steep valley wall until reaching the posted fork for Notch Mountain at mile 2. After the killer switchbacks, the trail has an excellent ending: Mt. of the Holy Cross doesn't reveal itself until the final steps. Then the 1,500-foot-high cross is just sitting there, right in front of you as if on an easel. But alas, the right arm of the cross isn't as prominent as it used to be because of erosion and avalanches. Perhaps a miracle will repair it one day. The best time to see the cross is between June 15 and July 10 when it's filled with snow. To reach the trailhead from Vail, take the Minturn exit off Interstate 70. South of Minturn (2.8 miles) on Hwy. 24, turn right onto Tigiwon Rd. (Forest Rd. 707). Drive 8.5 miles to the end of the road at Half Moon Campground. Take the Fall Creek Trail from there.

Ski Mountains—

Top-of-the-world views can be had without working up a sweat via gondola rides up Vail or Beaver Creek mountains. At the top of the Lionshead Gondola in Vail, seven easy hikes are laid out. The Gore Range Loop is a scenic mile walk to the Eagle's View turnaround and back with no elevation gain at all. Berrypicker Trail is all downhill. Yes, it's lined with all sorts of berries, and it gets hikers back down the mountain to Lionshead in about two hours. Leave the car at the Lionshead parking structure west of Vail Village and walk to the gondola building. Trail maps are available there.

10th Mountain Trail Association Hut System—

See the Cross-Country Skiing section for detailed information.

Two Elk Trail—

This 11-mile hike carries a National Scenic Trail designation, which means some past government official must have really enjoyed it. It's easy to see why: the summit of Two Elk Pass abounds with views of the Gore and Sawatch ranges and the many bowls on Vail Mountain's back side. A little farther along, the trail offers a peek at Mt. of the Holy Cross. But the best reason to hike the trail probably is to see its namesake—the elk. There's always a good chance of spotting some because they are boxed into the area by highways and towns. The best time to hear them bugling is Aug. and Sept. The hike can be done in one day but is best as an overnighter. The trailhead begins in east Vail just south of the Gore Creek Campground on old Hwy. 6 at the closed gate. It ends in Minturn, making a car shuttle necessary. Drive the second car just past the forest service office in Minturn to the bridge over Eagle River. Cross the bridge and drive past the cemetery. Go right at the first fork and left at the second to the mouth of Two Elk Canyon, near the foot of Battle Mountain. The trail begins near Two Elk Creek.

HORSEBACK RIDING

Most trails in White River National Forest are open to horseback riding, so there are plenty of riding opportunities in the Vail Valley.

Beaver Creek Stables—

Here's where riders looking for more elaborate excursions should come. Among the variety of rides Steve Jones and his guides offer are breakfast and lunch rides, rides combined with fishing at Beaver Lake, sunset rides to Beano's Cabin for dinner (see the Where to Eat section), and overnighters to Trapper's Cabin with hiking sidetrips in the alpine meadows of McCoy Park. The stables are at Haymeadow, just above McCoy's restaurant in the Village Hall. **5344 Brush Creek, Eagle, CO 81631; (303) 845-7770.**

Piney River Ranch—

About 15 miles north of Vail, you can really get into the backcountry by riding the trails from the ranch into the Eagles Nest Wilderness Area, with the 13,000-foot Gore Range as a backdrop. Along with horseback rides, the ranch also offers boating, cookouts and fishing on the lake, making it a great destination for a day's getaway from Vail. The road to Piney Lake (Forest Rd. 700) leaves Vail's N. Frontage Rd. a mile west of the Vail Village exit. The ranch is at road's end. **Piney River Ranch, PO Box 7, Vail, CO 81658; (303) 476-3941.**

Spraddle Creek Ranch—

This outfitter is conveniently located just across Interstate 70 from the four-way stop in Vail Village. Horses are available for one- to three-hour rides in the former Ute stomping grounds around Spraddle Creek and the lower reaches of Bald Mountain. The ranch is definitely geared toward families on day outings rather than serious trekkers out for longer trail rides. A pony ring on the ranch is ideal for young children. The ranch can accommodate groups of up to 25 people. **100 N. Frontage Rd. E.; (303) 476-6941.**

ICE SKATING

The John Dobson Ice Arena—

This arena, on the bus route between Vail and Lionshead, holds public skating sessions daily. Children under six are free but must be accompanied by an adult.

Hockey and figure skates are available to rent. **321 E. Lionshead Cir., Vail, CO 81657; (303) 479-2270.**

Outdoor Skating Rinks—

Few things bring out the joy in people more than skating on an outdoor ice rink with beautiful surroundings. Weather permitting, there are several options in the area: at the **Vail Golf Course, (303) 479-2279;** in Avon at **Nottingham Lake, (303) 949-4280;** and a half mile from the entrance of Beaver Creek next to **Beaver Creek Village, (303) 949-9090.**

RIVER FLOATING

Eagle River—

The floating season for the Eagle River is substantially shorter than for many Colorado rafting rivers: mainly during spring runoff (May–July). During that period, however, the Eagle does churn up some pretty exciting white water on its upper reaches. It's one of the few free-flowing rivers left in the state. Families looking for more subdued trips will prefer the rides nearer Eagle on the lower reaches. With the icy-cold water, wet suits are a must in the early float season.

Vail's location near three of Colorado's most popular rafting rivers—the Eagle, the Colorado and the Arkansas—means there are plenty of outfitters to choose from. Here are three quick suggestions of local outfitters with solid reputations:

NOVA Guides—

This widely respected guide service leads raft trips in summer (as well as a variety of winter activities, such as snowmobiling and snowcat tours). They float the Colorado, Arkansas and Eagle rivers and offer float fishing trips on the Roaring Fork and other lakes and streams in the **White River National Forest. PO Box 2018, Vail, CO 81658; (303) 949-4232.**

Raftmeister—

In addition to more ordinary packages, these folks offer a special fly-and-float package, which combines hot-air ballooning and rafting. Meals provided. Located in the Montaneros Building in Lionshead. **PO Box 1805, Vail, CO 81658; (303) 476-RAFT** or **1-800-274-0636.**

Timberline Tours—
Started in 1971, this is Vail's oldest guide service. They float all of the area waters and do a professional job of it. For more info on their various trips contact: **PO Box 131, Vail, CO 81658; (303) 476-1414** or **1-800-831-1414.**

SKIING
CROSS-COUNTRY SKIING
Nordic skiing hasn't gotten lost in the shadow of immense Vail Mountain. Besides two cross-country centers in Vail and one at Beaver Creek, there are a number of great backcountry trails throughout the Vail Valley and surrounding White River National Forest. For information on backcountry trails, contact the **Holy Cross Ranger District Office, PO Box 190, Minturn, CO 81645; (303) 827-5715.** Incidentally, the Ranger's Office, located at Dowd Junction just after turning off Hwy. 24 at Minturn, has a new wildlife viewing station that offers tremendous views of wintering elk.

Backcountry Trails—
Commando Run—This is Colorado's top-rated cross-country tour, a grueling 18 miles for advanced skiers only. Avalanche danger and tough-to-follow trails are only two of the formidable obstacles to completing this day-long trek. Since it's a one-way trail, you must figure out your transportation ahead of time. The best way is to park your car in Vail and take a taxi or have someone drop you off at the Vail Pass rest area. You could also take two cars, leaving one in Vail and driving the other one back to the rest area. The trail begins on the Shrine Pass Rd. and comes in three parts: The Shrine Pass–Lime Creek roads; Bowman's Shortcut to Two Elk Pass; and the descent to the Golden Peak runs at Vail Ski Area. Magnificent views of Gore Range,

Mt. of the Holy Cross, Notch Mountain and the Tenmile and Mosquito ranges will be seen along the way. But it's next to impossible to find the way without a topo map and detailed directions. Take along *Trails Illustrated's* topo map No. 108°–Vail Pass, which has the run marked. It's best to ski it with someone who's done it before. Otherwise, *The Vail Hiker,* by Mary Ellen Gilliland, has the best directions we've seen for the trail.

Shrine Pass—This fairly easy 11-mile trail has a tried-and-true formula: 3 miles up, 8 miles down and margaritas (no pre-mix here) at **Reno's (127 W. Water St.** in Redcliff). No deviations allowed. It's a great day trip, and consequently the Shrine Pass route sees heavy use on weekends from snowmobilers and skiers alike. The best chance for solitude on this ski tour is midweek. Leave one car up Forest Rd. 709 from Redcliff and pile in the other car for the drive up to the rest area at the summit of Vail Pass. The trail starts on Shrine Pass Rd. with a moderate climb to Shrine Pass summit. After reaching the summit, the easy-to-follow road starts downhill to Redcliff, with a great view of Mt. of the Holy Cross along the way. Allow about four to six hours. For more information see the Scenic Drives section.

10th Mountain Trail Association Hut System—The system, organized in 1980 by the 10th Mountain Trail Association, is named in honor of the members of the ski troops who trained in the area and fought in World War II. The trail system encompasses 17 accommodations linked by more than 300 miles of backcountry trails. The Shrine Mountain Inn near the top of Vail Pass is one of the recent additions. On this eastern end, the system extends from Shrine Pass to Tennessee Pass near Leadville. The huts along the way each sleep about 16 and are usually booked to capacity. Basics are supplied. For trail guides (a good idea for most people), see Paragon Guides listed below under Guided Tours. For hut reservations and other details, contact the **10th**

Mountain Trail Association, 1280 Ute Ave., Aspen, CO 81611; (303) 925-5775. Detailed information on the Aspen end of the system can be found in the Skiing section of the **Aspen** chapter.

Tigiwon Trail (Tigiwon Road)—Beginning and intermediate skiers will like this 8-mile run up Tigiwon Rd. to Half Moon Campground. At mile 6 there's a stone hut to warm up in and views of the Gore Range and Vail's back bowls to warm up to. The lodge, built to house pilgrims on their way to Mt. of the Holy Cross, can be reserved for overnight trips by calling the **Holy Cross Ranger District Office** at **(303) 827-5715.** Look for elk on the way since the trail crosses part of their winter range. The full 8 miles can take most of a day, but coming back down should take only a third as long. *Tigiwon* is a Ute word meaning "friends"— ironically, Tigiwon Rd. begins near Battle Mountain, named for a notorious fight between Utes and Arapaho Indians in 1849. Tigiwon Rd. is 2.8 miles south of Minturn off Hwy. 24. Turn right and drive a half mile up the road, park and start skiing.

Groomed Trails—
Cordillera Nordic Ski System—With soaring views to the Upper Eagle Valley and Squaw Creek stretching out in front of you, you will love this upscale retreat. The extensive trail system offers a good variety of loop trails with varying degrees of difficulty. The trails wind in and out of aspen and evergreen forests near future mega-home sites. If you are going to make the short drive to Cordillera, you might as well consider a spa package that offers the benefit of luxurious trappings. Another possibility, depending on when you visit, is the moonlight ski package—starting at 6:30 pm on a full moon. Call **(303) 926-2200** for more information; also see the Where to Stay section.

Golden Peak Center in Vail—Vail's nordic center at the base of Chair 6 on the east side of Vail Village has 20 kilometers of trails. The center, open since 1968, specializes in backcountry tours, as well as short treks on

Vail Golf Course. For the decadent nordic skier, there's the gourmet tour, including hot drinks, three appetizers, three entrées and three desserts served along the way. Reservations for the gourmet tour must be made a day in advance by 4 pm. Equipment rental, group lessons, private lessons and telemark instruction are all available. **(303) 476-3239, ext. 4390.**

McCoy Park at Beaver Creek—The spectacular groomed cross-country trails at the top of Chair 12 are a rarity: track skiing on top of a mountain. The top-of-the-world views make this the best place to ski groomed trails in the area. McCoy Park has 30 kilometers of trails, many named after mining claims made in the area in the late 1800s. Twenty percent of the terrain is beginner, 60 percent intermediate and 20 percent advanced. Telemarking lessons are given at the base of Chair 12. There's also a warming hut with hot drinks and boot lockers at the top of the lift **(303) 845-5313.** If, however, you don't feel like taking the lift to McCoy Park, you might consider slipping onto the Beaver Creek Golf Course right in town.

Vail Nature Center—The nature center has served as a nordic headquarters for East Vail since 1984. An 8-mile track with plenty of loops follows Gore Creek out from Golden Peak. Besides rental equipment and day tours, the center offers snowshoe walks and has exhibits on nordic skiing and natural history. The center is four blocks east of Golden Peak on Vail Valley Dr.–Mar. 9 am–4 pm. **75 S. Frontage Rd., Vail; (303) 479-2291.**

Vail Nordic Center—For track or skate skiing you can't beat the price of the nordic center at the Vail Golf Course: it's free. Try out their 15 kilometers of groomed tracks at the east end of Vail. **1778 Vail Valley Dr.; (303) 476-8366.**

Guided Tours—
Paragon Guides—These folks offer three- to six-day trips on the 10th Mountain Trail

Association Hut System between Vail and Aspen for experienced nordic skiers. See Backcountry Trails for more information. Contact Paragon at **PO Box 130, Vail, CO 81658; (303) 926-5299.**

Rentals and Information—
Vail Mountaineering—Guides for backcountry touring and rentals are available here. **500 East Lionshead Mall, Vail; (303) 476-4223.**

Christy Sports—Located at **293 Bridge St.** in Vail; **(303) 476-2244** and **182 Avon Rd.** in Avon; **949-0241. 182 Avon Rd.; (303) 949-0241.**

DOWNHILL SKIING
Arrowhead—
This ski area is something of a David next to the Goliath of Vail. The upstart can be found 12 miles west of Vail (2 miles west of Beaver Creek Resort). With one high-speed quad lift and 13 runs, Arrowhead complements its giant neighbors. The area is designed for families and those who want less-demanding skiing away from the congestion of larger resorts. And lift tickets aren't such a strain on the wallet. The area also offers slopeside parking, a novelty in Vail Valley.

Recently purchased by Vail Associates, Arrowhead Ski Area is also linked up with a Jack Nicklaus–designed golf course named "Country Club of the Rockies." Even though posh custom homes are springing up alongside the private course, the small ski area remains open to the public. Many locals recommend stopping off for lunch or dinner at **The Bristol ($$ to $$$$)** for its creative American cuisine and wonderful views overlooking the golf course. **PO Box 3418, 676 Sawatch Dr., Edwards, CO 81632; (303) 926-3029** or **1-800-332-3029.**

Beaver Creek Ski Area—
"Like Tiffany's is to jewelry stores, like Gucci is to luggage, like Cadillac is to automobiles, that's what Beaver Creek is going to be to ski areas in this country."

That's the way former Colorado governor Dick Lamm described Beaver Creek at the opening ceremonies in 1980. With something suspiciously like a guard tower on the road leading up to the area, it does feel a little like you're entering a members-only club. Beaver Creek was originally meant as the site for skiing events of the 1976 Olympics, which Colorado subsequently turned down. The area opened anyway in 1980. A computer helped design its ski runs and the town was built after years of studying the best way to combine a resort with nature. Beginning skiers like the area because many of the easiest and most spectacular runs are concentrated at the top of the mountain. Experts prefer the gladed, narrow, double-diamond Birds of Prey, which is tougher than most runs at Vail. The steep pitch of the runs at newly opened Grouse Mountain also call out to expert and advanced skiers. But most of Beaver Creek has an odd fall line that makes you feel like you are skiing at a slant. Generally, the skiers are less aggressive than those at Vail and the lift lines remain shorter for the time being. For more information call **(303) 949-5750.**

Vail—
"There is no comparison" is how master ski filmmaker Warren Miller refers to Vail's back bowls. Now that there are seven back bowls—Sun Down, Sun Up, China, Tea Cup, Siberia, Inner and Outer Mongolia—no other ski area in the region can compare (not even Jackson Hole has more acreage in its vast bowls). Vail's back bowls are totally ungroomed, which can make for a variety of snow conditions. Mornings on fresh-snow days are heaven on skis.

But variety is the key to Vail's appeal, from the broad-faced back bowls to mean moguls and manicured cruising runs on the front side. The mountain is so large and varied that it's always easy to find a new, challenging path down the mountain—no matter your ability. In fact you could ski this area for a week solid and still not be able to cover all of the runs. Stretching over 7 miles of varied terrain, it's bigger than your imagination.

The mountain now has three base areas—**Vail Village, Cascade Village** and **Golden Peak.** With seven quad lifts, Vail can move more skiers an hour over a total of 3,872 acres of skiable terrain. Kids even have their own terrain at Golden Peak (renamed Whippersnapper Mountain). This area is strictly off-limits to adults.

The Vail Ski School is the largest in the world with 450 instructors. Special race classes provide technique evaluation; free "Meet-the-Mountain" tours give skiers a good idea of the immensity of this mountain. For further information contact, **Vail Associates, PO Box 7, Vail, CO 81658; (303) 476-3239.** Also, see the Introduction and History sections of this chapter.

SLEDDING AND TUBING

Head to Meadow Mountain, off Interstate 70 at the Minturn exit. No fee.

SLEIGH RIDES

Steve Jones Sleigh Rides—Nightly rides leave between 4 and 8 pm during winter on Vail Golf Course. **(303) 476-8057.**

Fenno Ranch Sleigh Ride Dinner—If you splurge on this sleigh ride, you'll be treated to a gourmet buffet in a tent after a horse-drawn ride into the backcountry at Cordillera. **(303) 926-2200.**

SWIMMING

Eagle-Vail Swim Club—
A fee is charged at this public pool. **0099 Eagle Dr., Avon, CO 81620; (303) 949-4257.**

Vail Run Resort—
This sports center in Vail has a heated indoor pool open to the public. A fee is charged. **1000 Lionsridge Loop, Vail, CO 81657; (303) 476-1500.**

TENNIS

Of course you can play tennis at many of the resort hotels in Vail and Beaver Creek. Here is a partial listing of some of the public courts in the valley.

Beaver Creek Tennis Courts—
During summers, there are four courts available at the Kiva. The courts are reserved for Beaver Creek Resort guests only. The activities desk can reserve a time for you. **135 Offerson Rd., Beaver Creek; (303) 949-5750 or 845-5781.**

Public Courts in Vail—
In summer there are 24 public courts available in Vail: nine at **Gold Peak;** six at **Ford Park** on S. Frontage Rd. just east of Vail Village; five at **Lionshead;** and four at **Booth Creek** in East Vail. Because it usually cools down too much at night to play, none of the courts are lighted.

——— SEEING AND DOING ———

BALLOONING

For this natural high, call **Camelot Balloons, (303) 476-4743; Mountain Balloon Adventures, (303) 476-2353,** or **Balloon America, (602) 299-7744.**

MUSEUMS
Colorado Ski Museum—
Did you realize that skiing originated 6,000 years ago? You'll learn a lot about skiing when you visit this well-put-together museum (and Colorado Ski Hall of Fame), which focuses on the history of skiing in the state. The museum, founded in 1976, is one of only a handful in the country dedicated to skiing. When Vail was chosen as the site, a few other ski areas grumbled that a history museum didn't belong in a place with no real history of its own. But Vail's central location in Colorado makes it ideal for visitors. One interesting exhibit shows the development of ski equipment over the years. Don't miss the 12-foot-long, 2-inch-thick wood skis that look more like logs. There's also a theater inside that shows

historical and current ski films. A gift shop offers books, posters and other ski stuff. Very small admission fee. Located in the Vail Village Transportation Center on the bus route; open 12–5 pm daily except Mon. Closed during May and Oct. **231 S. Frontage Rd., Vail; (303) 476-1876.**

Vail Nature Center—

This small natural history museum hosts guided nature walks and recreational activities in summer. In winter the nature center becomes a nordic center and the trails become cross-country and snowshoeing treks. Knowledgeable guides run an interpretive center in a renovated farmhouse on the preserve. Inside are seasonal displays on the Vail Valley's flora, fauna and geography. The seven-acre preserve is on the southeast side of Ford Park just east of Vail Village. Open 9 am–5 pm daily June–Sept., 9 am–4 pm Oct. and Dec.–Mar.; closed Apr., May and Nov. Hours vary. **75 S. Frontage Rd., Vail; (303) 479-2291.**

NIGHTLIFE

Beaver Creek—

For après ski folks gather at the **Coyote Cafe, (303) 949-5001.** The cafe specializes in Mexican food. Happy hour lasts from 4:30–6:30 pm. Whereas Vail is known for its nightlife, Beaver Creek is pretty quiet at night. If the serene and sophisticated Beaver Creek scene gets to you, head to Avon and **Cassidy's Hole in the Wall (303) 949-9449.** It's a country and western, beer-swilling hangout with a worn wooden dance floor and a sense of humor (See Where to Eat). Otherwise, you'd better make your way to Vail.

Vail—

For après ski if it's sunny, try the deck at either the **Red Lion (303) 476-7676** or **Pepi's, (303) 476-5626,** at **Gasthof Gramshammer** in Vail Village. Ask for a toe-warming Snuggler—peppermint schnapps and hot chocolate—or a hot buttered rum with a cinnamon stick in it. If it's snowing head for **Cyrano's, (303) 476-5553,** just below the lifts at Vail Village. During ski season the concept of weekend doesn't really exist in Vail—the joints are jumping every night. Each bar seems to have its designated night when it swells in popularity. If staying an entire week, you might try the following rotation:

Mon.: **Vendetta's, (303) 476-5070**—A newer bar upstairs from the restaurant with live music most nights of the week. Its location right in the thick of the village makes it easy to bounce around to several night spots.

Tues.: **Hubcap Brewery, (303) 476-5757**—Vail's very own brewpub. The handcrafted beer can almost substitute for a meal, especially if you sample a few of the darker variations.

Wed.: **Hong Kong Cafe, (303) 476-1818**—This longtime reliable spot of Vail nightlife is still the sentimental favorite of locals. Bahama Mamas here are legendary.

Thur.: **Mickey's, (303) 476-5011 ext. 115**—This Vail institution features the pop and classical music of piano man Mickey Poage in the Lodge at Vail.

Fri.: **Cyrano's, (303) 476-5551**—Usually mentioned first when locals are queried about nightlife, Cyrano's has been the Vail night spot for several years. Rock and roll and blues are featured Tues. through Sat. in an evolved fern bar/Jimmy Buffet lounge lizard sort of setting. During the summer Friday Afternoon Club draws hordes.

Sat.: **The Club, (303) 479-0556**—Loud, young and smoky. Some local live musicians take the stage in the small, basement bar and get the crowd dancing in a hurry. Generally the rowdiest people find their way here.

SCENIC DRIVES

Red Sandstone Road—

Though probably a little rough for OldsmoBuicks and similar cars, this summer-only, 30-mile round trip packs in quite a bit of scenery. And the end result—Piney Lake at the base of the Gore Range—is well worth the bumps. You might also consider taking this beautiful trip on snowmobile in winter. For more details and directions from Vail, see the Biking section.

Shrine Pass Road—

This summer-only route, once temporarily named Holy Cross Trail, was christened for its terrific view of Mt. of the Holy Cross. The route started out as an Indian trail when Utes hunted in the area. Indian campsites unearthed in the vicinity have been carbon-dated to 7,000 years ago. Before the Vail Pass Rd. was built in 1940, this road served as the major route between Denver and Glenwood Springs. Just east of the Vail Pass summit, turn off onto the Shrine Pass dirt road west of the rest area parking lot. The 11,000-foot summit is just 2.3 miles up, with wraparound views of Gore Range to the north, the Sawatch Range to the southwest, the Tenmile Range to the east and the Flat Tops in the far west. Three miles into the drive is the perfect spot for a brief hike to a wonderful lunch or early dinner at the Shrine Mountain Inn (see Where to Eat). Mt. of the Holy Cross can be seen at mile 3.75—look for the sign. The road continues down through the canyon to Redcliff, where it joins up with Hwy. 24 for a pretty drive on pavement past Battle Mountain and Minturn north to Interstate 70. Hwy. 24 south from Redcliff to Leadville makes a nice variation.

WHERE TO STAY

Most people come to stay in Vail for a week or more, so condos and lodges account for many of the rooms. There's also a Radisson, a Holiday Inn and a Days Inn. Perhaps the most impressive chain hotel in Vail is the **Westin, (303) 476-7111.** Located in Cascade Village, this fine hotel features its own ski lift and other luxury amenities, including **Alfredo's,** a highly regarded northern Italian restaurant. You should check into one of the Westin's ski or golf package deals depending on the season.

Vail rates during the summer generally run about half of what they are in winter. For information on hotels, condos and lodges (and last-minute reservations—often at a discount), call the **Vail Valley Tourism and Convention Bureau** at **1-800-525-3875** nationwide or **(303) 476-1000** in Colorado. Renting a private home is another option. For information, contact the Vail Valley Tourism and Convention Bureau (number listed above) or **Kathy Fagan** at **(303) 949-1212.**

Right now virtually all rooms in Beaver Creek are in several self-contained condominium complexes or deluxe lodges. Most of the rooms are available to rent for $100 a night and up, depending on the length of stay. The most extraordinary complex is the **Hyatt Regency** at Beaver Creek (see entry). **The Charter, (303) 949-6660,** nearby, offers condo-style accommodations. You could always get away to **Trapper's Cabin, (303) 845-7900 ext. 102,** where your private chef and cabin keeper will make sure the wilderness isn't too hard on you ($2,000 per night minimum). For information about renting these places, call them direct or contact **Vail Associates Central Reservations, PO Box 915, Avon, CO 81620; 1-800-525-2257** or **(303) 845-5745** locally. There's also plenty of less-expensive lodging in the nearby towns of Avon, Minturn and Redcliff.

The Lodge at Cordillera—$$$$

The contrast is striking. Drive past the mobile home park at Edwards, before heading up Squaw Creek towards this secluded, European-style retreat. After passing muster at the guard station, you will pass massive new homes, a Hale Irwin-designed 18-hole golf course and finally come to the end of the road at the impressive Lodge at Cordillera. Perched amid 3,000 acres of private forest and alpine meadow, the lodge's slate roof, native stone accents and stately Belgian architecture make it a place fit for royalty wannabes. If you want to be pampered, you've come to the right place. At the spa, two hydrotherapy tubs, a state-of-the-art workout room and a staff of personal trainers and masseuses are at your service. In winter nothing beats swimming laps in the indoor pool while surrounded by floor to ceiling windows. Oh, except the hot tub has the same incredible view. The lodge has only 28 rooms, so you won't ever feel lost or neglected. Simple elegance best describes the rooms. Twenty-four of the 28 have balconies or terraces, 15 feature fireplaces, five have lofts (perfect for families) and all have an elegant flair. You don't ever need to leave this privileged preserve, but they do offer shuttles to Beaver Creek and Vail. The natural surroundings and trail system entice you outside in summer (golf, hiking, mountain biking, swimming, tennis) or winter (cross-country skiing on 20 kilometers of groomed track). In the evening you will want to take time for a leisurely meal at the award-winning **Restaurant Picasso ($$$$)**. (Yes, those are genuine Picassos on the wall.) For more information contact **PO Box 1110, Edwards, CO, 81632; (303) 926-2200** or **1-800-877-3529.**

Hyatt Regency at Beaver Creek— $$$$

Most 300-room hotels lose something in intimacy and architectural style. Not so with the Hyatt. Phenomenal attention to detail helps this hotel capture a feeling previously reserved for European aristocracy. Do you know any other hotels that employ a full-time firetender to keep massive stone hearths glowing in common guest areas? There is also a large, round outdoor fireplace that provides a perfect place to sip your toddy after a day on the slopes. Perched dramatically in an exclusive location only steps away from Beaver Creek's slopes, the Hyatt offers plenty of extras, including an indoor/outdoor pool with snow-melt deck and six outdoor whirlpools (the largest, measuring 16 feet in diameter, is lavishly filled by a heated waterfall). The health club and spa offer herbal body wraps and hydraulic workout equipment. "Camp Hyatt" entertains the kids while parents enjoy a real vacation. Three unique restaurants tempt your palate with pizza cooked in a special woodburning oven, a variety of gourmet fondues and, thankfully, deli sandwiches. Prices at the hotel vary dramatically with the seasons—

the same room in May costs three times as much during the peak ski season. For information and reservations contact Hyatt Worldwide at **1-800-233-1234** or the hotel directly at **PO Box 1595, Beaver Creek, CO 81620; (303) 949-1234.**

Black Bear Inn of Vail—$$$ to $$$$

If you're wondering when a unique, quality bed and breakfast will open in Vail, wait no longer. In this immense log structure next to Gore Creek, you'll find twelve rooms and a couple of caring proprietors. Unlike many Vail residents, owners Jessie and David Edeen did not just arrive here from someplace else—and they sound as if they are in business to stay. The large common room has comfortable, overstuffed couches, an antique wood stove and a deck with great views. Watch your step though, or you may trip over Fozzie, a dog that David says, "holds down the carpet." The bedrooms are simple, attractive and comfortable, each with a small private bathroom. Every room has a sleeper sofa and some top-floor rooms connect easily for families traveling together. If you stay in summer, you may want to request a room on the side opposite Interstate 70 because the highway noise isn't totally masked by the creek. Outdoor summer games include horseshoes, bocce ball, croquet and badminton. In addition to a full breakfast of homebaked bread, butter, jam, granola, juice, coffee and fruit, you will get a daily special each morning. Minimum stay requirement, depending on season. Well-behaved kids OK; no smoking inside; no pets. **2405 Elliott Rd., Vail, CO 81657; (303) 476-1304.**

Eagle River Inn—$$$ to $$$$

Sante Fe in ski country? It's not a mountain mirage: this bed and breakfast inn on the bank of the Eagle River in Minturn was indeed reborn in 1987 as an adobe hacienda. Walk through a locally crafted portico and dispel all your doubts. A southwest-style kiva fireplace occupies a corner of the sitting room, which is filled with white-pine furniture. The 12 bedrooms have more of the same southwestern charms, including handcrafted headboards. Try soaking in the outdoor hot tub built into a deck overlooking the Eagle River. The 7-mile drive to Minturn from Vail is just far enough so that it feels like a getaway, but not so far that it's inconvenient. Manager Beverly Rude equals the setting with a breakfast of fresh fruit and homemade yogurt and granola. Wine and cheese are served at 5 pm. **PO Box 100, 145 N. Main St., Minturn, CO 81645; (303) 827-5761 or 1-800-344-1750.**

Gasthof Gramshammer—$$$ to $$$$

Proprietor Pepi Gramshammer is known locally as Mr. Vail; his lodge could just as easily be known as Hotel Vail. The lodge, born the same year as the town, epitomizes all that's good about Vail's transplanted Tyrolean charm. The German word for it is *Gemütlichkeit*, which means something like "friendliness and ambiance." Pepi and his wife, Sheika—both transplanted Austrians—are directly responsible for the cozy inn's charm. Pepi, a former Olympic skier, might turn up to carry your bags, fix your TV or bus your table. Mrs. Gramshammer, an alumna of Mt. Everest, travels to Europe four times a year to find authentic supplies for the lodge. And the family dog, Tasso, Vail's most-arrested canine, makes guests feel right at home.

The 27 European-style rooms and apartments come in color schemes of champagne, blue and rose. All feature fireplaces and down comforters. Warning: the rooms only rent out a week at a time (Sat.–Sun.) during ski season and are usually sold out a year ahead. Most guests are returnees. The hotel's restaurant, the Antlers Room, serves a Bavarian/continental menu, specializing in wild game. The adjacent deck is the best in Vail. **231 E. Gore Creek Dr., Vail, CO 81657; (303) 476-5626.**

Sonnenalp—$$$ to $$$$

The Sonnenalp is a mountain hotel in three parts. The Bavaria Haus, the Austria Haus and the Swiss Chalet are all perched on the sunny side of Gore Creek in Vail Village. The separate houses allow this fairly large hotel to maintain a small-inn atmosphere. And this isn't imitation alpine: the Fassler family created the Sonnenalp idea at its resort near Oberstdorf, West Germany. Fourth-generation innkeepers Rosana and Johannes Fassler continue the tradition in Vail. A giant contingent of Bavarians was staying when we visited, and we were told that 50 to 60 percent of the guests are German, adding to the Bavarian ambience. The favorite of the three houses is the Swiss Chalet with its attention to detail. Second preference is Bavaria. All 178 rooms in the three houses are priced the same. Each features feather comforters and hand-crafted furnishings imported from Germany. The hotel has an elaborate spa even by Vail standards. Among its features are a cold dip—a narrow deep pool to plunge into before heading to the sauna or Jacuzzi—and one "hypotherapy" tub. It's necessary to book rooms at least three months in advance during ski season. **20 Vail Rd., Vail, CO 81657; (303) 476-5081.**

Roost Lodge—$$ to $$$

The Roost is like a Volkswagen bug: it isn't pretty but it's popular and reliable. This A-frame-style lodge has long been a favorite of the budget-conscious—it's the least expensive place to stay in the Vail Village vicinity. During ski season it's about the only place to find a room available on fairly short notice for under $100. The 56 rooms are casually comfortable. Last time we visited, the pool area still doubled as a greenhouse. Roost Lodge is two miles from Vail Ski Area at the West Vail exit. A shuttle bus runs to the ski area hourly from 8 am–midnight. **1783 N. Frontage Rd., Vail, CO 81657; (303) 476-5451.**

Comfort Inn—$$ to $$$

For skiers who like Beaver Creek but don't want to add too much more to their personal budget deficit, Avon's calling. Just a mile from the Beaver Creek Ski

Area, in affordable Avon, is the sturdy Comfort Inn. Inside are 150 good-sized rooms, all with queen- or king-sized beds. Amenities include a pool, Jacuzzi, hospitality suites and free continental breakfast served in the wood-beamed Comfort Clubroom. Folks who have been in Avon in the past will remember this as the Wynfield Inn. It remains the best room deal in the Vail Valley. A bus leaves regularly from in front of the inn bound for both Beaver Creek and Vail. The Beaver Creek bus is free; Vail's charges a nominal fee. From Interstate 70 take Exit 167 and turn right at the light. **PO Box 5510, Avon, CO 81620; (303) 949-5511.**

CAMPING

Sylvan Lake State Park—

Elk Run Campground (30 sites; fee charged) and **Fisherman's Paradise Campground** (20 sites; fee charged) both fit the bill for tents, trailers and campers; there are some pull-through sites for larger units. Located 16 miles south of Eagle on West Brush Creek Rd.

In White River National Forest—

Gore Creek Campground (25 sites, one is wheelchair-accessible; fee charged) is the closest to Vail and therefore the most popular in the area. It's 5 miles east of Vail Village, near the boundary of the Eagles Nest Wilderness Area. Take Exit 180 from East Vail onto Hwy. 6 and head east 2 miles.

Tigiwon Campground (9 sites; no fee) is 6 miles up Tigiwon Rd. off Hwy. 24, 2.8 miles south of Minturn. A stone lodge built as a restover for pilgrimages to Mt. of the Holy Cross is available to groups on a free reservation basis. **Half Moon Campground** (7 sites; no fee) is 2.5 miles farther up Tigiwon Rd. at two trailheads for Holy Cross Wilderness Area.

Hornsilver Campground (12 sites and a fee) is right off Hwy. 24, 1.5 miles south of Redcliff.

Blodgett Campground (6 sites; fee charged) is just off Hwy. 24 on Homestake Rd. (Forest Rd. 703), 12 miles south of Minturn. **Gold Park Campground** (11 sites; fee charged), 10 miles farther up Homestake Rd., used to be an old gold mining camp. Jeep and hiking trails to Holy Cross City ghost town and the Holy Cross Wilderness Area leave from here.

WHERE TO EAT

At last count Vail had more than 70 restaurants, and that's not including the mountain itself. In the past few years Minturn has become a restaurant haven with choices ranging from Mexican to barbecue to cook-your-own steaks. Listed below are a few standouts from throughout the Valley.

Beano's Cabin—$$$$

Taking a moonlit sleigh ride to dinner is probably not something you do every day, so here's your chance. Beano's Cabin is a rustic log cabin in the Larkspur Bowl on Beaver Creek Mountain. Two 42-passenger sleighs leave the Inn at Beaver Creek twice nightly for a sumptuous western-style dinner at the cabin. During summer, guests ride

horses up. Before boarding for either of the two seatings, one at 5:15 pm and another at 7:15 pm, diners are treated to peppermint schnapps and hot chocolate. Be sure to make reservations in advance. Rides leave Wed.–Sun. **(303) 949-9090.**

Mirabelle's—$$$$

This gourmet French restaurant has been referred to not only as the best restaurant at Beaver Creek, but as the best restaurant in the Rockies, period. It's housed in a gorgeous restored farmhouse that dates back to 1898, when it was the biggest residence in Avon. Inside are oak furnishings and etched glass. Entrées include salmon, trout, shrimp provençal, veal, beef and lamb. The selection of wines is palate-boggling. No credit cards accepted. The restaurant is located right across from the reception house on the road up to Beaver Creek. Open for dinner 6–10 pm, Tues.–Sun. **55 Village Rd., Beaver Creek; (303) 949-7728.**

The Left Bank—$$$ to $$$$

A host of restaurants in Vail seems to offer the same exclusive menu of French/continental fare. According to nearly everyone we asked, the Left Bank does it best. Co-chefs Liz and Luc Meyer apprenticed in France, where they also collected the restaurant's French country decor. The Meyers serve a variety of seafood and game, specializing in veal, elk steaks and chicken prepared a different way each day. Though prices are high, The Left Bank is in demand. During ski season reservations are necessary up to two weeks in advance. No credit cards accepted. Open Thur.–Tues. 6–10 pm. Closed Wed. Located in the Sitzmark Lodge at **183 Gore Creek Dr., Vail; (303) 476-3696.**

Shrine Mountain Inn—$$ to $$$

Riding a mountain bike or hiking to lunch to the top of Shrine Pass (11,209 feet) has many rewards. In summer, you can take a 9-mile route from Redcliff, a 3-mile route from the rest area at the top of Vail Pass or a quarter mile jaunt from the parking area. Arriving at the immense log building, you'll have a chance to catch your breath and satiate your appetite with a selection of good foods. If the weather cooperates you'll be able to enjoy the deck for a truly amazing view of the Tenmile Range. The bulk of the lunch menu is made up of hearty soups, salads and sandwiches. More elaborate dinners are available and guests can enjoy a cocktail starting at 6 pm. Open daily in summer for lunch; one seating for dinner between 6:30 and 8:30 pm—for reservations call **(303) 476-6548.** Consider staying overnight summer or winter **(303) 925-5775.** For more information about Shrine Pass Road, see the Skiing section.

Sweet Basil—$$ to $$$

This sunny cafe is a lunch favorite of people who work in the village. One reason is that meals are served quickly, usually in a half hour or less. But speedy service alone doesn't make a successful restaurant. The continental food is also delicious, rated four stars by the *Denver Post*. What struck us most was the variety on the menu, from grilled duck breast sandwiches, to pizza, to chili with cornsticks. The cooks outdo themselves with unusual garnishes, such as pink peppercorn butter and cranberry mayonnaise. Don't leave too soon and miss the Sweet Basil forte—homemade desserts. The breezy interior is all wicker and chrome, and the works of local artists grace the walls. Though best at lunch (served daily 11:30 am–2:30 pm), Sweet Basil also offers dinner 6–10 pm. The Sweet Basil folks also operate a fish restaurant in Lionshead called Montauk. **193 E. Gore Creek Dr., Vail; (303) 476-0125.**

Minturn Country Club—$$

No, it's not really a country club—just a great little restaurant with a good sense of both humor and food. The club truly believes in letting you "Have It Your Way": you're the chef here. Pick a steak, kabob, fish or chicken from a meat case and toss it on the charcoal grill in the dining room. Sidelights include a salad bar, corn on the cob, baked beans, baked potatoes and huge slabs of Texas toast you can swab with garlic butter and throw on the grill. During ski season the club is elbow to elbow for dinner. Don't bother scheduling tee times. The clubhouse is the old Minturn Post Office on Main St. Open daily 5:30–10 pm. **131 Main St., Minturn; (303) 827-4114.**

Cassidy's Hole in the Wall in Avon—$ to $$$

For a solid bite to eat in a down-home atmosphere, stop in at Cassidy's. You'll find locals mixing it up with tourists from Beaver Creek at the bar, or hunched over huge plates of food. The creaky wood floors and stuffed animals on the wall lend a western atmosphere. But it's the live country music (nightly during ski season; otherwise try Fri. and Sat. nights) that really gets the place rolling. As far as the food goes, it's basic but done right: steaks, baby back ribs, burgers, chicken and trout are balanced with lighter dishes, such as salads and sandwiches. Both men and women should have a sense of humor when entering the rest rooms. I won't spoil the laughs here. If you prefer eating a meal in a semi-quiet setting, ask for an up-stairs table. Open every day from 11 am–2 am. **82 East Beaver Creek Blvd., Avon, CO 81620; (303) 949-9449.**

The Gashouse—$ to $$

When you've had a little too much overpriced French food, designer jeans and mink stoles, here's the perfect anti-dote. The only fur you'll see at the Gash-ouse is on the deer heads mounted on the log walls of this Conoco-station-turned-restaurant. This is where many locals run to escape the tourist blitz. Service can be a bit slow and indifferent, but the price is right. The Gashouse is 4 miles west of Beaver Creek on Hwy. 6. Open 11–2 am daily; until midnight on Sun. **34185 Hwy. 6, Edwards; (303) 926-3613.**

SERVICES

Avon-Beaver Creek—
Resort Association—Stop in for informa-tion and advice about what to do in this part of the valley. **PO Box 1437, Avon, CO 81620; (303) 949-5189.**

Central Reservations—
Vail/Beaver Creek Reservations—For res-ervations in Vail and Beaver Creek contact **PO Box 7, Vail, CO 81658; 1-800-525-2257** or **(303) 949-5750** locally.

Vail Valley Tourism and Convention Bureau—Serves as chamber of commerce for Vail, Beaver Creek and Avon, and pro-vides information about the ski areas. Call **1-800-525-3875** nationwide or **(303) 476-1000** locally.

Eagle Valley—
Chamber of Commerce—**PO Box 964, Eagle, CO 81631; (303) 328-5220.**

Day Care—
ABC School Inc.—This preschool located in Vail will care for children 15 months to 5 years old. **149 N. Frontage Rd., Vail, CO 81657; (303) 476-1420.**

Vail Associates—Full-day care for chil-dren aged 2 months to 6 years is provided at Golden Peak in Vail and at Beaver Creek. In Vail call **(303) 476-5601 ext. 5044;** in Beaver Creek **(303) 949-5750 ext. 4325.**

Vail Youth Center—The center serves as a teen hangout, cafe and activity hub for older children. Located in the Lionshead parking structure. **(303) 479-2292.**

Transportation—
Vail's free bus system is second only in volume to downtown Denver's free mall shuttle. For schedule information call **(303) 479-2172.**

Vans to Vail—The name just about sums it up. Try this one for door-to-door transport to and from Denver. **(303) 476-4467** or **1-800-222-2112.**

Airport Transportation Service—Airport shuttles to Vail and Avon/Beaver Creek. **PO Box 4276, Vail, CO 81658; 1-800-247-7074** or **(303) 476-7576.**

Winter Park and Middle Park

As you descend from the 11,315-foot summit of Berthoud Pass on a winding, mostly two-lane highway, you get a true sense of the tall peaks lining the perimeter of the Fraser Valley. Many of these mountains reach above 13,000 feet. A major part of the beauty of this area lies in the million acres of Arapaho National Forest. This huge stretch of public land thankfully preserves undeveloped mountain vistas as you visit the small towns anchored in a narrow procession along the Fraser River.

At the head of the valley is **Winter Park,** a favorite ski destination. A couple of miles downvalley on Hwy. 40 is the neighboring town of **Fraser.** As the river valley widens into what is commonly known as Middle Park, the small towns of **Tabernash, Granby** and **Hot Sulphur Springs** make their entry.

Middle Park, unlike its northern and southern counterparts, offers extremely complex geologic terrain: faults, uplifts and overthrusts have been further altered by volcanic formations and erosion. This activity has created a beautiful variety of mountainous landscape. Once a prized hunting ground of the Indians, today this region is a prized vacationing ground for people from around the country.

With good reason Winter Park is one of the state's most popular ski areas. The combined resort of Winter Park and Mary Jane can accommodate the crush of Front Range skiers that flock here on weekends. Weekday skiing here, with fewer crowds (and fewer "expert" skiers from Colorado), is a great alternative. See the Skiing section for more information.

Once the snow has melted, and "mud season" is declared over (Memorial Day), people stay in the area as a perfect base for hiking, mountain biking, golfing or simply appreciating the gorgeous surroundings. Two miles north of the ski area, the town continues to develop in a haphazard fashion. Numerous mini shopping plazas, restaurants and lodges are spread along both sides of Hwy. 40. Split in half by traffic, Winter Park misses out on some of the intimacy of other ski villages. But what it lacks in city planning, it seems to have gained back in personality.

"The coldest spot in the nation" is a phrase commonly associated with Fraser, Colorado, where the thermometer can dip to more than 50° below zero on winter nights. The ring of tall peaks around the town creates stationary pockets of frigid air. The masochists living here are actually proud of their self-proclaimed designation "Icebox of the Nation." Mayor C.B. Jensen once explained to a reporter, "We don't have logging and railroading anymore, and Eisenhower doesn't fish here anymore ... but, it's colder than hell."

Downvalley, northwest along Hwy. 40, small ranching centers lie beyond the fray of the retail shops and restaurants in Winter Park and Fraser. Hwy. 40 takes you past prime ranchland to the Gold Medal trout water of the upper Colorado River and eventually to quiet Hot Sulphur Springs. Though the hot mineral springs pools are unkempt, the old Riverside Hotel and the Grand County Historical Museum manage to bring some of the history back to life.

HISTORY

Since the mid-1600s Middle Park has been a coveted Indian hunting ground because the large game herds in the valley provided easy prey. Confrontations between Ute and Arapaho hunting parties were commonplace.

When the fur trade was booming in the 1820s, trappers came into the valley. These hardy mountain men had a practical knowledge of the park, but it was not until the expedition of John C. Frémont in 1844 that any maps of Middle Park existed.

Irish nobleman Lord Gore briefly visited Middle Park while on his legendary American hunting expedition, which lasted from 1854 to 1857. Traveling with a huge entourage, Gore single-handedly killed thousands of bison and 40 grizzly bears and lost count of the elk, antelope and deer that he slaughtered. In the evening Lord Gore repaired to his green-striped tents to sip vintage wines and enjoy the company of imported ladies of pleasure.

As the 1870s arrived, a smattering of Anglos had settled in Middle Park. Ute and Arapaho Indians continued to hunt in summer and did not appreciate the intrusion. By the time of the Ute massacre in Meeker on Sept. 29, 1879 (see the **Meeker** chapter), tension was reaching new heights. It was a time of occasional violence and constant concern for the entire valley. A common sentiment of the times was expressed by US Army Gen. Pope, who said the Utes were "worthless, idle vagabonds, who are no more likely to earn a living ... by manual labor than by teaching metaphysics."

After the Indians were expelled from their homeland, sheep and cattle ranching took on primary importance in Middle Park. Many prospectors came into the area but left with little reward for their efforts.

Before the turn of the century, William Byers, owner of the *Rocky Mountain News*, had modest success in trying to lure wealthy vacationers to his latest purchase: Hot Sulphur Springs. Miners and lumberjacks appreciated the soothing vapor waters in greater numbers than the moneyed. Even though the natural springs beside the Colorado River were rumored to have healing powers, Byers's "spa" never really got off the ground. However, by 1911 Hot Sulphur Springs began attracting tourists to skiing events at its first annual Winter Carnival.

Winter has long been a popular season in the Fraser Valley. Skiers have streamed into the Winter Park area since completion of the Moffat Railroad Tunnel in 1927. The train would emerge from underneath the Continental Divide with eager skiers, ready to hike up the mountain with 7-foot wooden skis for a meager two runs per day. The first lift on the Denver-owned watershed was a simple rope tow in 1935.

Today the train still runs on weekends, shuttling skiers from Denver, but the facilities have grown steadily to create a major ski destination. Unlike nearly all ski areas, Winter Park operates as a nonprofit entity under the stewardship of a 15-member board of trustees. Instead of taking on a serious debt load, the resort plows any excess revenues into improvements, while maintaining less expensive tickets.

GETTING THERE

Winter Park is located 67 miles (about 90 minutes) northwest of Denver. By car, the best route from Denver is via Interstate 70, west for 42 miles to Hwy. 40 at Exit 232. Follow Hwy. 40 over Berthoud Pass and drop into Winter Park at the head of the Fraser Valley. After Winter Park come the small communities of Fraser, Tabernash, Granby and Hot Sulphur Springs.

Greyhound Bus Lines **1-800-231-2222** provides daily service to Winter Park from Denver International Airport. Some lines provide service from downtown Denver. You might also try an airport shuttle from **Home James: 1-800-451-4844.**

On winter weekends and for special summer events, perhaps the best way to reach Winter Park from Denver is on the **Rio Grande Ski Train: (303) 290-8497.** The scenery is fantastic as the train winds through South Boulder Canyon and passes under the Continental Divide by way of the historic Moffat Tunnel. The train has recently been refurbished, making the two-hour trip even better. There is also daily **Amtrak** train service, **1-800-USA-RAIL,** to Fraser from Chicago and San Francisco on the California Zephyr.

———— FESTIVALS AND EVENTS ————

Spring Splash

mid-April

The end of the Winter Park ski season is ushered in with a splash. The highlight of the day-long party is a ski race down an obstacle course ending in a 40-foot-long pool of ice-cold water. Costumed skiers try to pick up speed so they can glide over the water, but many lose their momentum about halfway across. For more information call **(303) 726-5514** or **(303) 892-0961** in Denver.

High Country Stampede

Saturday nights from
mid-July to the end of August

At the rodeo grounds just west of Fraser, amateur riders and ropers display their skills (bronc riding, bull riding, calf roping, barrel racing, etc.) in front of an enthusiastic crowd. Most of the contestants are local ranch hands; all ride competitively for their pride and a share of the purse. This popular event coincides with a western barbeque and steak fry that shouldn't be missed. For more information and tickets contact the **Winter Park/Fraser Valley Chamber of Commerce** at **(303) 726-4118** or **(303) 422-0666** in Denver.

American Music and Winter Park Jazz Festivals

Two separate weekends in July

Summertime at the base of Winter Park's ski slopes: lay back on your blanket, enjoy the mountain view and listen to some of the world's top musicians in a natural amphitheater. If you're tired of grumbling about high ticket prices and short concerts, don't worry—while the tickets are not cheap, each festival features more than 10 bands during two distinctive musical weekends. Those into folk and rock music will want to attend the American Music Festival. In past years Bonnie Raitt, Lyle Lovett and Los Lobos have performed for large crowds. The Jazz Festival attracts a talented range of acts from the smooth fusion of David Sanborn to Harry Connick, Jr., and his 15-piece big band. Bring your own food and drink, or browse the veritable tent city of food vendors. For more information contact **Winter Park Resort** at **(303) 726-5514** or **(303) 892-0961** in Denver.

———— OUTDOOR ACTIVITIES ————

BIKING

MOUNTAIN BIKING

Ranchers and loggers in this area have left behind a maze of dirt roads that are ideal for sturdy two-wheelers. Until recently no one really cared about these rough roads; in 1985 the Winter Park Fat Tire Society (FATS) was formed to promote the burgeoning sport of mountain biking. This organization is responsible for a world-class trail system, featuring 600 miles of mapped and marked roads, including a good bit of single-track trails.

The wide Fraser Valley is surrounded by a diversity of terrain that is easily accessible from Winter Park. Trails wind their way through rolling hills, sprawling meadows and dense forests. According to FATS there are enough trails for riders of any skill level to ride for an entire week without ever covering the same terrain. For more information and a free map, write to **Winter Park FATS, PO Box 1337, Winter Park, CO 80482.** Or call the **Winter Park/Fraser Valley Chamber of Commerce** at **(303) 726-4118** or **(303) 422-0666** in Denver.

Another perfect option, especially for those not quite used to high-altitude riding, is to take the Zephyr Express chairlift up (many are equipped with bike racks) and head down the 44 miles of marked trails on the ski mountain. The 6-mile Long Trail is a favorite cruiser. If you want to skip the lift ticket you can, of course, ride up and down the mountain all you want for free.

Rentals and Tours—

This company will take you to the top of Mt. Nystrom or Corona Pass so you can enjoy a continuous downhill ride. For more information call **Mad Mountain Bike Tours; (303) 726-5290.**

There is a proliferation of mountain bike shops in Winter Park, run by enthusiasts who are knowledgeable about the sport and nearby trails. If you plan on renting a bike for a long period of time, be sure to phone in an early reservation.

Ski Depot Sports—Located in Park Plaza Shopping Center on Hwy. 40; **(303) 726-8055** or **1-800-525-6484.**

Sports Stalker—Located in Cooper Creek Square on Hwy. 40; **(303) 726-8873** or **1-800-525-5520.**

Winter Park Sports Shop—Located in Kings Crossing Shopping Center on Hwy. 40; **(303) 726-5554** or **1-800-222-7547.**

FISHING

Arapaho National Recreation Area—

Shadow Mountain Reservoir, Lake Granby, Grand Lake and **Monarch Lake,** all northeast of Granby, offer excellent fishing in a beautiful setting. See the Fishing section of the **Grand Lake** chapter for more information.

Colorado River—

After the Fraser River joins the Colorado River near Granby, the wide river is designated Gold Medal water. It is therefore a pity that, unless you are one of a privileged few, most of the river is off-limits. Only 5 miles of the river between Granby and Kremmling remain unfenced. The river flows through sprawling cattle ranches, and permission to fish is rarely granted. However you might be able to gain access to private water by hiring a local outfitter who has already made arrangements with the landowner. There is a good 2-mile stretch downstream from Hot Sulphur Springs in Byers Canyon. Fishing for large rainbows and browns is popular here, despite the fact that the river is closely paralleled by the road and the embankment is fairly steep. It is easier to wade this stretch than to try to fish it from the riverbank.

Fraser River—

Flowing down from the upper reaches of Berthoud Pass, the Fraser River can be worth your time and persistence. Upper portions of the river, near Winter Park Ski Area, offer a chance at well-stocked rainbows and brooks. The small river flows next to Hwy. 40 for much of its upper run. Access to the lower portions requires walking along the Denver & Rio Grande Railroad tracks north of Tabernash. Get permission to use their right-of-way by calling **(303) 629-5533,** and beware of the many trains still making runs. One mile downstream from Tabernash, until a mile or so above Granby, the river is designated Wild Trout water. As the river enters Fraser Canyon, the fishing for rainbows and browns is rated good. This was President Eisenhower's favorite place to fish. Although there are a few sections of private land, plenty of water remains open to the public. Popular flies include the Royal Wulff and gray caddis imitations on top; Hare's Ear and Stonefly nymphs under the surface. Mepps and Rapala lures tend to produce some bites.

Meadow Creek Reservoir—

As soon as the ice melts from this high mountain reservoir, the fishing gets hot for rainbows and brooks. There are a couple of campgrounds on the north shore. For a smaller, natural lake, try fishing at **Columbine Lake,** a 3-mile hike from above the reservoir. The high lake (11,100 feet) is a sure bet for pan-sized cutthroats. To reach this area, take Hwy. 40 to just east of Tabernash. Turn onto Forest Rt. 129, which winds northeast to the reservoir. Past the campgrounds, at the end of the road, is the trailhead for Columbine Lake.

Williams Fork Reservoir—

This good-sized reservoir is locked between the high peaks of the Williams Fork and Vasquez mountains at an elevation of 7,800 feet. There are a lot of rainbow and brown trout, pike and even kokanee salmon swimming around in what eventually becomes Denver's tap water. Though the water level fluctuates, this can be an excellent place to catch a stringer full of fish. A boat ramp and camping area are located on the west side. To get to the reservoir, take Hwy. 40 west of Hot Sulphur

Springs 4 miles, to a point just east of Parshall. A good road branches south for the last few miles to Williams Fork Reservoir.

FOUR-WHEEL-DRIVE TRIPS

Rentals and Tours—

Mad Adventures—This Winter Park company offers a small selection of guided jeep tours in the area. One three-hour tour goes to the top of Rollins Pass (described below), dwelling on the fascinating point-by-point history of the old railway. Reservations are required 24 hours in advance. **PO Box 650, Winter Park, CO 80482; (303) 726-5290** or **1-800-451-4844** nationwide.

Rollins Pass Road (Corona Pass)—

The tunnel east of the summit of Rollins Pass has caved in, blocking the way for jeeps wanting to continue much beyond the Continental Divide. The drive up the road to the summit is still beautiful, though the status may change in the future. Contact the forest service office in Boulder, **(303) 444-6600**, to find out about current conditions. You can bypass the blockage on foot or by bicycle to complete the trip to Nederland.

The entire route follows the original path of the railway over the divide. Rollins Pass was used for 24 years as the main line of the Denver, Northwestern and Pacific Railway Company until the Moffat Tunnel was completed in 1927. The railway and namesake tunnel were both the brainchild of David H. Moffat. After he made his fortune in banking and mining, he set out to find a shorter passage to Salt Lake City and the West Coast. His idea for a line due west of Denver was a 175-mile shortcut to the established routes. The route over Rollins Pass was intended only as a stop-gap measure until the tunnel was completed. Built from 1923 to 1927, the 6.2-mile tunnel was finally completed at a huge cost: 19 lives and $18 million. At the Continental Divide the tunnel is bored a mile beneath the surface. The completion of the tunnel eliminated 23 miles and cut 2.5 hours of travel time off the "Hill" route.

From Winter Park turn right (east) from Hwy. 40 onto Forest Rd. 149 and stay on the main road. As you continue toward the pass, the condition of the road gets worse. The status of the road, once maintained as a passenger car route, has deteriorated as the result of major rock slides and now the tunnel cave-in.

GOLF

Pole Creek Golf Club—

Highly rated by *Golf Digest* magazine and considered by many to be one of the finest mountain courses in the state, Pole Creek is coming into its own. Built in the early 1980s, the young 18-hole course makes for a very exciting round. Like other mountain courses, lodgepole pines line the fairways on many holes and majestic mountain views can be distracting. Some holes are laid out Scottish-style with few trees and plenty of natural hazards. Veteran golfers say that the manicured greens break slightly toward Pole Creek. Pro shop, range and restaurant; club rentals and motorized carts available. Breakfast and lunch served daily at the Tavern on the Green. Located **11 miles northwest of Winter Park on Hwy. 40; (303) 726-8847.**

HIKING AND BACKPACKING

Arapaho National Forest surrounding the Fraser Valley provides a beautiful expanse for hiking and backpacking. Many backcountry trails weave their way through miles of high country. The popular Indian Peaks Wilderness Area, encompassed within the national forest, straddles both sides of the Continental Divide. Because of heavy use, a permit is required for backcountry camping. Contact the **Boulder District, (303) 444-6600**, or the **Sulphur District** at the south end of Granby, **62429 Hwy. 40, PO Box 10, Granby, CO 80446; (303) 887-3331,** for reservations. If you are unable to plan your trip to the Indian Peaks ahead of time, there are a few last-chance permits issued by the district offices. Wilderness day use is not restricted by permit.

The Vasquez Mountains and the Fraser Experimental Forest are little-used forest areas to the west of Winter Park and Berthoud Pass. The experimental forest is not nearly as sinister as it sounds; new techniques of forest management are applied here. Christmas-tree-cutting permits are available during the Yuletide.

Byers Peak Trail—

This short, steep 2.5-mile hike leads to the top of Byers Peak (12,804 feet). Before reaching treeline the defined trail passes through tall stands of Engelmann spruce in the Fraser Experimental Forest. Nearly constant winds buffet the upper reaches of the peak. There are a couple of small lakes a short distance from the trail that are said to have good fishing. Once at the summit enjoy far-reaching views of the mountains and valleys of northern Colorado. To reach the trailhead, head west on County Rd. 73 (Eisenhower Drive) in Fraser toward St. Louis Creek Campground. After 4 miles take a right at the Byers Peak signpost and continue along the dirt road for 4.5 miles to the Byers Peak Trail parking lot.

Caribou Pass Trail—

This trail offers a fairly difficult 4.4-mile hike to Caribou Pass (11,790 feet) and excellent views of the Indian Peaks. Those seeking a longer backpack trip can continue over Arapaho Pass to Monarch Lake. Be prepared for occasional muddy conditions as you set off on this trail. The first mile is on an old four-wheel-drive road (now closed to vehicles). As the trail tracks beside Meadow Creek, it passes a couple of crumbling log cabins that have seen better days. At a marked trail junction, follow the footpath that heads east from the Columbine Lake Trail (see below) and into a sub-alpine forest. For the next mile, the trail ascends sharply through the trees, interspersed in places with flowering meadows. Caribou Pass is a tiring half-mile hike from treeline. At the top, the panorama to the east is inspiring: Apache Peak (13,441 feet), Navajo Peak (13,409) and down to Caribou Lake at the base of the pass. Another half-

mile hike along the ridge to the north leads to the top of Satanta Peak (11,979 feet). A precarious half-mile cliff walk to the south leads to Lake Dorothy.

To reach the trailhead for Caribou Pass and Columbine Lake trails, take Hwy. 40 northwest almost to Tabernash. A half mile east of town, Forest Rd. 129 heads northeast to Meadow Creek Reservoir. The trailhead for both hikes is located above the reservoir at the parking area for Junco Lake.

Columbine Lake Trail—

This is a great half-day hike despite the fact that your feet may get wet while passing through a low meadow area. The nearly 3-mile trail uses the same route as Caribou Pass Trail (described above) for the first mile and a half. At a marked junction, Columbine Lake Trail continues south into a thick forest before heading to the top of a plateau. The trail passes through a couple of marshy meadows before reaching the lake at treeline. Along the trail the views to Winter Park Ski Area and the Fraser Valley are superb. Columbine Lake (11,060 feet) is a great place for picnicking and a chance at catching cutthroat trout. To reach Columbine Lake Trail, see the directions for Caribou Pass Trail above.

Corona Trail—

There are a couple of ways to reach Corona Trail, but the best is from the top of Rollins Pass at the Continental Divide. From there the spectacular trail follows a level grade atop the divide for 6 miles. Since the trail is entirely above treeline it is wise to carry warm clothing and a full water bottle. Beware of incoming thunder- and snow-storms. Midway along the trail is Devil's Thumb Pass, where the finger-shaped rock of the same name is clearly visible. The thumb is a favorite technical climb. From the pass Devil's Thumb Trail leads to the western and eastern sides of the divide. To reach Rollins Pass from Winter Park, take Forest Rd. 149 east of town. The road can be rough and the forest service does not recommend it for passenger cars, but many make it to the top without any problems.

Another access route to Corona Trail involves climbing 2,000 vertical feet in less than 2.5 miles before reaching the Continental Divide. This trail begins at Devil's Thumb Park at the junction of High Lonesome and Devil's Thumb Trail. Follow Devil's Thumb Trail to the divide. There are good camping spots for backpackers after crossing to the east side of Devil's Thumb Pass, near Devil's Thumb and Jasper lakes. To reach the trailhead requires taking a four-wheel-drive road (Forest Rd. 128) east of Hwy. 40 at Fraser.

Monarch Lake Trailheads—
A number of excellent trails lead into the Indian Peaks Wilderness from Monarch Lake. Some of these hikes are described in the Hiking and Backpacking section of the **Grand Lake** chapter.

HORSEBACK RIDING
High Mountain Lodge at Tally Ho Ranch—
Located near Fraser on County Rd. 50; **1-800-887-2152.**

YMCA Snow Mountain Ranch—
Located 12 miles northwest of Winter Park near Tabernash; **(303) 887-2152.**

RIVER FLOATING
The moderate 14-mile stretch of the Upper Colorado River downstream from Kremmling attracts crowds of floaters on weekends. The periodic rapids and canyon scenery along the way add greatly to the trip. Several other lesser-used stretches of the river downstream from State Bridge offer leisurely floats virtually devoid of people, but without any exciting rapids. Kayaking and canoeing are also great options. As many as 40 commercial outfitters make the trip.

Outfitters—
Mad Adventures—Call for reservations: **(303) 726-5290** in Winter Park or **1-800-451-4844** nationwide.

Timber Rafting—Reservations can be made in Granby at **(303) 887-2141.**

SKIING
CROSS-COUNTRY SKIING
Backcountry Trails—
Berthoud Pass—The top of the pass at the defunct Berthoud Ski Area provides a great set-off point for skiers. However, some of the slopes can be quite difficult and the forest service warns skiers of blasting for avalanches in some areas. *A good map and an awareness of current avalanche conditions are essential for a safe backcountry trip.*

Sevenmile Trail actually is part of the old Berthoud Pass wagon road, a route between Denver and Middle Park. To get the most out of this trail, leave a second car at the fourth switchback on the west side of Berthoud Pass. The trail begins at the top of the pass with a plummeting drop into Hell's Half Acre, which can be avoided by following down along Hwy. 40 to its first switchback. Eventually you will track out by your car on the west side of Berthoud Pass.

Groomed Trails—
Granby—SilverCreek Nordic Center maintains a selection of easy, well-groomed trails just outside of Granby. It has also become a popular place for telemarking on its gentle downhill ski slopes. The trail fee at the Nordic Center includes a couple of rides on certain lifts. Views from the upper trails into Fraser Valley are breathtaking, and a few of the descents will require all of your balance. Rentals, instruction, restaurants and lodging are all available. For more information on the ski area, see below. SilverCreek Nordic Center is located 17 miles north of Winter Park on **Hwy. 40;** **(303) 887-3384.**

Tabernash—YMCA Snow Mountain Ranch/Nordic Center offers a 30-mile public trail system that stretches throughout their property. The Nordic Center has long offered equipment rentals, lessons and passes during its long winter season. Because the snow melts late in the season, the ranch trails are used extensively for training Olympic hopefuls. The employees have a refreshing, professional attitude about the sport. Trails range from beginner to expert. For more information on Snow Mountain Ranch see Where to Stay. Located 12 miles northwest of Winter Park off Hwy. 40; **(303) 887-2152** or in Denver metro area **(303) 443-4743.**

Winter Park—Devil's Thumb/Idlewild Cross-Country Centers, separate but connected ski touring areas, together provide well over 100 kilometers of trails with a balance of expert, intermediate and beginner trails. Skiing between the areas is encouraged. You may want to begin at Idlewild which is higher in elevation, and return on one of the twice-daily shuttles. You will find the terrain at Devil's Thumb offers stunning views of surrounding peaks, while Idlewild is hemmed in by thick woods. However, since Idlewild was once a downhill ski area, there are some wide-open areas for perfecting your telemark turns. Idlewild is located a half mile east of Hwy. 40 from the town of Winter Park; **(303) 726-5564.** To reach Devil's Thumb Ranch, drive 7 miles northeast of Fraser on Hwy. 40 and turn right on County Rd. 83. Follow the signs and be sure to keep right at the fork; **(303) 726-8231**

Devil's Thumb Ranch also features the **Ranch House Restaurant ($$ to $$$),** where many locals go for consistently good food with a wonderful view. Despite some management troubles, you might want to consider staying in a lodge room (thin walls) or reserve one of their well-appointed cabins—for a romantic retreat, reserve the "Fox" cabin ($$$). For reservations and information contact **PO Box 1347, Winter Park, CO 80482; (303) 726-5633.**

DOWNHILL SKIING
SilverCreek—

Colorado skiing took a new turn with the opening of SilverCreek in 1982. This compact ski area was designed with families in mind. It's for people who are looking for a fairly gentle, uncrowded mountain and a reasonably priced ski vacation. Despite the fact that you will see expert slopes at SilverCreek, the black-diamond designation here would indicate intermediate runs at other Colorado areas. Beginners have a separate learning area for making unsteady first turns without the intimidation of snickering experts. SilverCreek is also becoming a destination for cross-country skiers. For more information contact: **PO Box 1110, SilverCreek, CO 80446; (303) 887-3384.**

The base area features a saloon, restaurant, ski-rental shop and nursery. Many condos are springing up at the bottom of the ski mountain. The **Inn at SilverCreek ($$ to $$$,** depending on the season) is a large, 342-room hotel complex with all the amenities just 2 miles away. Open year-round. For reservations call **1-800-926-4FUN.** SilverCreek is located 17 miles north of Winter Park on Hwy. 40. Daily bus service to and from Winter Park each day.

Winter Park Resort—

Since 1940 when Winter Park opened with one T-bar tow, it has grown into a large, technologically equipped resort rivaling the best in the Rockies. Its 1,300 acres of skiable terrain cover four interconnected mountains—Winter Park, Mary Jane, Vasquez Ridge and the newly opened Parsenn Bowl on the slopes of North Cone. Each of the mountains attracts some of the highest snow depths of any major Colorado ski area. Despite Parsenn Bowl's intermediate ranking, its above-timberline location can make conditions on its moderate slopes highly variable (from unbelievable knee-deep powder to tricky crust). Halfway down its wide-open slopes, though, you plunge into the protection of the trees on narrow runs and glades. Advanced skiers will always head for the never-ending challenge of Mary Jane, with its own base facilities and long, deeply carved bump runs. Mary Jane was never meant for beginners, yet it offers quite a few intermediate runs. "Mary Jane's Backside" offers a range of glade skiing and expert chutes.

Most novice and intermediate skiers choose from the wide selection of groomed runs at both Winter Park and Vasquez Ridge. Expert skiers have some limited choices, too. At the top of Winter Park Mountain, stop in at the massive new Lodge at Sunspot for great eats and great views (See Where to Eat). Visible to the northeast are the towering peaks of Rocky Mountain National Park and the nearby Indian Peaks Wilderness Area as the Continental Divide cuts a high route in front of your eyes. Since the area is easily accessible from Denver and a good value, expect longer lift lines on the weekends. The Children's Center at Winter Park offers day care for kids ages 1-8; children over age 3 can participate in a specially designed ski program that takes advantage of the new "Learn to Ski" park. Now with a flexible pricing system skiers can choose how much of the mountain they wish to ski and pay accordingly. Most skiers should still make a note, however, to pick up discounted tickets at gas and grocery outlets before heading up to the hills. For more information contact **PO Box 36, Winter Park, CO 80482; (303) 726-5514** or **892-0961** in Denver.

Winter Park Disabled Skiing—Since Hal O'Leary founded this skiing program in 1970, it has grown to be the largest of its kind. "Downhill skiing enables children and adults with disabilities to experience freedom of movement," says O'Leary. People with all types of disabilities, including blindness, amputation, mental retardation and multiple sclerosis, are given instruction and adaptive equipment at a nominal fee. A racing program, started in 1984, has trained many elite racers in an intense summer and winter training regimen. A volunteer staff of 1,000 gives lessons to more than 2,500 disabled individuals each year. For more information call **(303) 726-5514 ext. 179** or **892-0961** in Denver.

SWIMMING

If you really need to go for a dip, head for the indoor, Olympic-sized pool at the **YMCA Snow Mountain Ranch.** It's located 12 miles northwest of Winter Park on Hwy. 40; **(303) 887-2152.**

TENNIS

There are many courts spread out at lodging facilities in the Winter Park area. A couple of public courts are located at the **Idlewild Lodge** just east of the town of Winter Park. Or try the courts next to the **town hall in Fraser.** For information call **(303) 726-5562.**

TUBING
Fraser Winter Sports—

At the Fraser tubing hill you can enjoy the exhilaration of jumping on a custom-made inner tube and flying down the steep, snow-covered mountain. Kids and adults love the experience equally. A set fee includes the rental of your own tube and as many rides up the rope tow as you can handle. The mountain is well lighted at night, and if it gets too cold you can skip a run and go inside to a crackling fire and a cup of hot chocolate. Located on the south end of Fraser. Open Mon.–Fri. 4–10 pm and 10 am–10 pm on weekends. **(303) 726-5954.**

——————— SEEING AND DOING ———————

ALPINE SLIDE

Unlike the playground-variety slide we all grew up with, the longest slide in Colorado requires a chairlift ride to reach the top. With its high banked curves, the Alpine Slide resembles a luge course in the way it twists down the ski mountain. Fun for a wide range of ages. Open from early June to Labor Day seven days a week 9:30 am–5 pm. Open until 7 pm during most of July and Aug. Fee charged per ride. For more information call **(303) 726-5514** or **892-0961** in Denver.

MUSEUMS
Cozens Ranch House—

William Zane Cozens must have been ready for a serious change of pace in 1874 when he quit his job as the sheriff of Central City and moved to the Fraser Valley. By 1881 he and his family were living in a large ranch complex that included a residence, a small hotel, a stagestop/dining room and the first post office in the valley. The empty Cozens Ranch was gradually falling apart until recently when the Grand County Historical Association undertook an ambitious renovation. Today the ranch displays furniture, clothes and artifacts that reflect the simple quality of life the Cozens family enjoyed. It's worth pulling off the highway for a look around. Small fee. Open daily Memorial Day–Oct. 1 and Dec. 15–Apr. 15 10 am–5 pm; closed during off-season on Mon. and Tues. Look for the sign on the east side of Hwy. 40 between Winter Park and Fraser. **PO Box 165, Hot Sulphur Springs, CO 80451.**

Grand County Historical Museum—

The old Hot Sulphur Springs School, built in 1924, provides a perfect setting for recounting the long history of Grand County. The skiing exhibit provides a choice bit of trivia: Hot Sulphur Springs Ski Area was the first in Colorado. Today it is just a clear swath of snow on the mountainside behind the museum. Looking through the old photos and ski memorabilia in the front room, you realize how much the sport has changed. Another section of the museum displays Indian artifacts from Windy Gap and more recent Indian history.

How many times have you heard the phrase, "... white man's settlement of the West"? The Grand County Museum doesn't forget that pioneer women also played an indispensable role. Other exhibits show the development of towns in Grand County including Fraser, Tabernash, Granby and Kremmling. The helpful staff can answer questions you might have. Free admission, donations are accepted. Open in summer 10 am–5 pm daily. Winter hours are Wed.–Fri. 10 am–5 pm. and the first and third weekends of the month. Located at the east end of Hot Sulphur Springs on Hwy. 40; **(303) 725-3939.**

NIGHTLIFE
Crooked Creek Saloon (in Fraser)—

A young and very local crowd frequents this rowdy mountain bar. The floor starts to shake on weekends when the live rock or blues music begins. A full calendar offers specials to one group or another on every night of the week. The Crooked Creek is a great place to eat hefty fatboy burgers, a plateful of pasta, stir-fry or a 16-ounce T-bone steak. (They even serve full breakfasts, but the bar atmosphere and smoke never quite go away.) Check this place out. It's open every day of the week 7 am–2 am. **Hwy. 40, Fraser; (303) 726-9250.**

The Derailer Bar—

Check out this après-ski scene at the base of Winter Park Ski Area. The Derailer Bar has live music Tues.–Sat. during the season. Appetizers are served. Open until 6:30 pm. **Winter Park base area; (303) 726-5514 ext. 273.**

The Slope—

The partying begins in earnest as soon as the lifts close. Quantity seems the rule with three bars and several levels of mingling space available. The Slope is renowned among locals for its large dance floor and loud bands. Some national acts stop by when on tour. Otherwise, expect high-energy rock and roll, blues and reggae music Tues.–Sat. during ski season and on summer weekends. Located in **Old Town Winter Park; (303) 726-5727.**

SCENIC DRIVES
Rocky Mountain National Park—

It is easy to forget that Rocky Mountain National Park is right around the corner from the Fraser Valley. The west entrance of the park is located north of Granby on Hwy. 34. Before reaching the park you will pass Lake Granby and Shadow Mountain Reservoir. If you have never driven over Trail Ridge Road don't miss this experience; open late-May–mid-Oct. For more information on Rocky Mountain National Park see the **Estes Park** chapter.

—————————— **WHERE TO STAY** ——————————

ACCOMMODATIONS

Most of the accommodations we have chosen are in the vicinity of Winter Park Resort. Even so you may want to consider an inexpensive motel room a little further down valley. You'll find basic rooms at sensible rates along Hwy. 40 between Tabernash and Hot Sulphur Springs—if you prefer a historic, though somewhat tattered hotel, stop in at **The Riverside (303) 725-3589 in Hot Sulpur Springs.** A host of bed and breakfasts have opened up in the area, for information call the **Winter Park/Fraser Valley Chamber of Commerce** at **(303) 726-4118,** or toll free **1-800-722-4118.**

C Lazy U Guest Ranch—$$$$

When a bellboy picks up your luggage at the desk and leads you to your elegant accommodations, you'll know this is no ordinary ranch. The mix of five-star luxury and dude-ranch atmosphere makes this a popular choice among a selective crowd. Rooms can be booked either in spacious individual cabins or in separate lodge buildings. The ranch is geared to horseback riding, and you will have your own horse for the duration of your week's stay. You can also don your C Lazy U robe and find your way to the hot tub. Other options might be to lounge by the pool, try your luck fishing in Willow Creek or play a game of racquetball or tennis. A trained instructor supervises all children's activities. In winter guests take full advantage of 30 miles of groomed cross-country trails. Three meals a day are served family-style in the dining room. Most guests book for a week but some special, shorter packages are available. The C Lazy U is open except for the months of Oct./Nov. and Apr./May. Located north of Granby. Reservations are a must. For information: **PO Box 378B, Granby, CO 80446; (303) 887-3344.**

Iron Horse Resort—$$$ to $$$$

This is what you get when you merge the attributes of a fine hotel with those of a condo. This "condotel" (with a handful of lodge rooms, too) boasts the only true ski-in, ski-out location for Winter Park Resort. With four outdoor hotubs and an indoor/outdoor pool, this place tops our list of Winter Park luxury accommodations. All of the condo-type units feature a working fireplace, a functional kitchen with dining area, balcony or deck as well as a Murphy bed; one- and two-bedroom units are available. The contemporary design and tasteful common areas of the Iron Horse add to the ambiance of its wooded site. The **Rails Restaurant** offers reasonably priced breakfast entrées (**$**) as well as a solid dinner menu. For information and reservations contact **PO Box 1286, Winter Park, CO 80482; 1-800-621-8190.**

Englemann Pines—$$$

With its wooded location just outside of Fraser, this is not the kind of place you are likely to happen onto by chance. But it's worth the short detour. The low-key owners truly enjoy sharing their large, contemporary abode, and you'll love the warm feeling created with the tasteful mix of family heirlooms, beautiful European antiques and sturdy lodge-style furniture. Several common areas divide up the house and encourage mixing with other guests, while offering space to be alone or read. There is even a kitchen for guests' use. The room setup is flexible enough for families; kids of all ages are encouraged. One upstairs suite features a fireplace and a spectacular view glancing across treetops towards the Continental Divide. Four of the six guest rooms have shared bathrooms; two are private. The huge morning meal always includes Bircher Muesli, a tasty Swiss specialty. Two quiet, friendly dogs on the premises; no smoking inside. For reservations contact **Margaret and Heinz Engel, PO Box 1305, Winter Park, CO 80482; (303) 726-4632** or **1-800-992-9512.**

YMCA Snow Mountain Ranch— $ to $$$

In a spectacular mountain setting 14 miles north of Winter Park near Tabernash on Hwy. 40, a range of year-round activities are to be enjoyed by all. This ranch resort maintains a wholesome family environment and provides one of Colorado's best values. Snow Mountain Ranch offers temporary memberships to all guests for the duration of their stay. This membership allows you all the privileges of a full member, except for one very important consideration—full members are given priority over the general public in reserving prime accommodations. Still, there are enough cabins and dorm rooms to take care of everyone for the majority of the year. Perhaps the single most outstanding aspect of the ranch is the extensive trail system stretching throughout the property. The Nordic Center offers equipment rentals, lessons and passes for 30 miles of groomed trails for beginner to expert cross-country skiers. Summer use of the marked trails revolves around hiking, mountain biking or horseback riding. The ranch encourages its guests and members to use its many recreational facilities. A few seasonal activities include indoor swimming, roller skating, basketball, tennis, miniature golf and ice skating. The Aspen Room is open year-round for inexpensive breakfasts and dinners. For more information and reservations: **PO Box 169, Winter Park, CO 80482; (303) 887-2152** or direct Denver line **(303) 443-4743.**

Cabins—$$$

Your best bet for a family vacation is to reserve a reasonably priced two- or three-bedroom cabin (the price goes up on larger cabins). Larger four- to seven-bedroom cabins are available for family reunions. Each well-equipped cabin comes with refrigerator, range and telephone as well as kitchen implements. Gathering before a large mossrock fireplace or out on a wide balcony for views of the Indian Peaks makes each cabin a place for fond family memories.

Dorms—$ to $$

There are inexpensive lodge rooms available for families, groups and individuals in several room designs. Most rooms come with a private bathroom. The lodges are very well kept with large common areas. The drawback of the various lodges is that you never know if you'll be sharing the same lodge with 200 screaming 13-year-olds.

Camping—During summer there are four campgrounds that cater to a segregated smattering of tents and RVs.

American Youth Hostel—$

Without a doubt, this is the cheapest place to stay in Winter Park. It is a great place for basic, clean accommodations in six mobile homes. Rooms have two to four bunks or a double bed for couples (three of these). Each of the trailers has its own kitchen and a common area for guests. Of course, the bathrooms and showers are shared. Reservations are necessary in winter. No curfew; no age restrictions; discount for AYH members. Located across the highway from Cooper Creek Square, behind Dino's restaurant; **PO Box 3323, Winter Park, CO 80482; (303) 726-5356.**

CAMPING

In Arapaho National Forest—

Robbers Roost Campground is located 5 miles south of Winter Park on the east side of Hwy. 40. There are sites for both tents and trailers situated under the shadow of the Continental Divide. Ten sites; small fee.

Smack in the middle of the Fraser Valley is a small piece of national forest land almost entirely occupied by **Tabernash Campground.** The campground is located 3.5 miles northwest of Tabernash on Hwy. 40. It has 30 sites; handicapped facilities; small fee.

Meadow Creek Campground is located 3.5 miles northeast of Fraser on Forest Rd. 129. Five sites; small fee. Another campground of the same name is on up the road at Meadow Creek Reservoir. This is an ideal place to stay while hiking in the area. Both Caribou Pass Trail and Columbine Lake Trail leave from the reservoir.

In Fraser Experimental Forest—

There are many good places to primitive camp throughout the experimental forest. Please try to minimize your impact if you are camping outside of an organized campground. If your preference is a designated camping area, travel 3 miles southwest on Forest Rd. 160 from Fraser to **St. Louis Creek Campground**. There are 18 sites; drinking water; small fee. Another 3.5 miles down the road is **Byers Creek Campground**. Only 6 sites; drinking water; small fee.

Private Campgrounds—
Elk Valley Ranch Campground in Granby—Laundry and showers, yes ... but no pool. There are 30 campsites with full hookups. Located 5 miles southeast of Granby on Hwy. 40; **(303) 887-2380**.

YMCA Snow Mountain Ranch—See Where to Stay for information.

WHERE TO EAT

Gasthouse Eichler—$$$ to $$$$

Hans and Hanna Eichler have a great reputation among locals for their authentic German food. This restaurant should be your first choice for a special meal in a classic European atmosphere. Sit in the bar area before dinner and sip on a German wheat beer (weizen) with a slice of lemon. The German specialties include rindsrouladen, wiener schnitzel, sauerbraten and kassler rippchen. For the gourmet, choose from veal dishes, lobster, scampi or Châteaubriand. Closed mid-Apr.–end of May. Open from 5:30 pm nightly. In **Winter Park on Hwy. 40; (303) 726-5133**.

The Lodge at Sunspot—$$ to $$$$

Few restaurants can compete with the many qualities of this tasteful, new, mountain-top lodge. From a broad picture window at an elevation of 10,700 feet, the view to the Fraser Valley and Continental Divide could hardly be more beautiful. During ski season you can take the lift directly to this 20,000-square-foot monument of timber and stone for a hearty lunch. You have your choice of the Provisioner, a casual food marketplace, or the more formal, upscale Sunspot Dining Room. Try the roasted chicken marinated with a Caribbean barbecue sauce or a broiled elk T-bone steak. On selected evenings, the Sunspot Dining Room features a fixed-price, six-course gourmet meal—getting up to the restaurant by sleigh makes for an especially romantic evening. Open for Sunday Brunch in summer—consider working off the calories by walking or biking down the mountain! For information and reservations call **(303) 726-5514 ext. 373**.

Dinner at the Barn—$$$

Climb into the sleigh under a cozy wool blanket and you're off to a memorable evening with a couple of 2,000-pound draft horses in the lead. Just when the crisp winter air is settling into your bones, the sleigh arrives at the small, heated barn. Hot cider and coffee take the chill off; you might want to bring along something stronger. Soon everyone at your table is digging into a carefully prepared gourmet meal. Knickknacks hang on the old barn wood walls, and the western feel doesn't get much more real than when you have to find your way to the outhouse. It's not your typical evening out—especially when Annie breaks out her guitar and sings upbeat country and western songs. Before you know it, you are simultaneously laughing, clapping and singing along with Annie and her "bang clash." For information and reservations call **(303) 726-4923**.

Crooked Creek Saloon—$ to $$$

See Nightlife section.

Hernando's Pizza Pub—$ to $$

Good pizza is found in abundance in Winter Park, but people tend to agree that Hernando's is the best. For a change of pace try the Roma pizza. Tables are situated near a round fireplace in the center of the room, or you can take out. Served on white or whole wheat crust, with a variety of toppings. Also served are spaghetti, lasagna and antipasto salad. Full bar; free delivery in season. Near **Kings Crossing Center; (303) 726-5409.**

Carver Brothers Bakery—$ to $$

This place is so well known that, despite the hidden, off–Main Street location, there is plenty of business. Choose from a mouth-watering array of freshly baked pastries, including cheese pockets and cinnamon raisin bagels. Take out your order or find a table in the expanded seating area (the whole place was nearly destroyed by a fire in 1991). Reasonably priced full breakfasts include a light and tasty breakfast burrito and an assortment of egg dishes. Lunch items include savory homemade soups, salads, submarine sandwiches and

daily specials. Dinner entrées cover a range from crispy catfish to filet mignon and sautéed pork medallions. Open daily from 7 am; lunch is served 11 am–3 pm in summer, until 5 pm in winter. In winter dinner is served 5–9 pm. Located **directly west behind Cooper Creek Square; (303) 726-8202.**

The Kitchen—$

A small, homey cafe with marvelous breakfasts. Get to this local favorite early or you'll have a long wait. Once inside you will be treated to a real breakfast. Choose from a breakfast burrito, huevos rancheros, eggs Benedict or any number of "dishes for egg haters." No credit cards; smoking OK; no whining. Open 7:30 am–12:30 pm only. Located at the **north end of Winter Park off Hwy. 40; (303) 726-9940.**

——— SERVICES ———

Day Care—
Winter Park Children's Center—Winter Park will take care of your youngster for the day, 8 am–4 pm. Minimum age is 1. Kids 3 to 13 can be taken skiing by specially trained children's instructors. For more information call **(303) 726-5514 ext. 337.**

Fraser Creative Learning Center—**(303) 726-5681**

Information and Reservations—
Winter Park Central Reservations—**(303) 726-5587** in Colorado, **(303) 447-0588** Denver direct or **1-800-453-2525** nationwide.

Winter Park/Fraser Valley Chamber of Commerce—Stop by and talk with one of the helpful staffers about things to see and do in the valley. Located at the south end of town behind the parking structure; follow the visitors center signs. **PO Box 3236, Winter Park, CO 80482; (303) 726-4118,** or **(303) 422-0666** in Denver, or call their toll free reservations number **1-800-722-4118.**

Transportation—
The Lift Bus Service—Winter Park's free shuttle bus provides summer and winter transportation between town and the ski areas. During the peak hours of 8–10 am and 3–5 pm, there are frequent buses stopping throughout town.

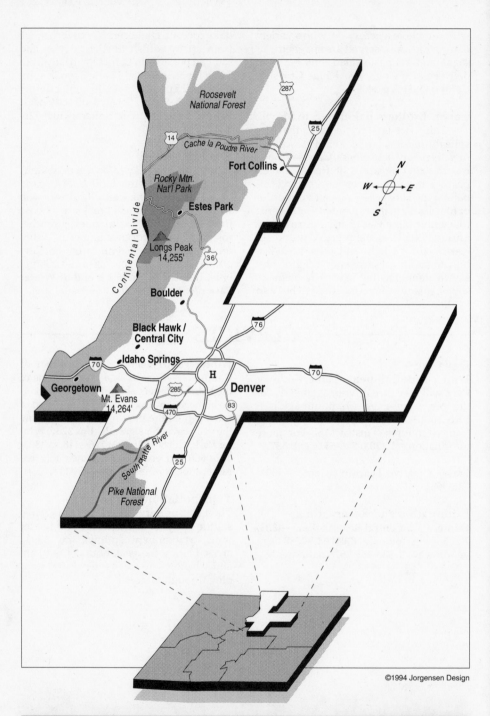

North Central Region

NORTH CENTRAL REGION

Boulder

Though Boulder is only a short 40-minute drive from Denver, you feel like you're entering a different world. From the moment you begin dropping into town from the scenic overlook on the Boulder Turnpike (Hwy. 36), the view forces your attention to the Rocky Mountains shooting up to the west and the plains stretching east toward the horizon. Boulder's supreme location, at the base of the dramatic red rock formations known as the Flatirons, is its major plus.

Many people consider Boulder a type of utopia. *Healthy, young* and *educated* best describe the general mix of the population, and Boulder has managed to retain many 1960s counterculture ideals. Unlike most of the neighboring towns, though, Boulder represents a cosmopolitan rainbow of humanity. Many world-class cyclists, runners and climbers live here while undergoing a high-altitude training regimen. A thriving college community helps Boulder retain the intimacy of a small town.

It's also a major high-tech center, with numerous computer and scientific institutions, often working in tandem on projects spawned at the University of Colorado's main campus. Fewer than 100,000 residents enjoy the quality of life Boulder has to offer, for which they pay a price—having to sustain an upscale economy where everything from groceries to houses costs more.

Boulder doesn't fight its image as an idealistic bastion of free thought. The University of Colorado at Boulder, with more than 25,000 students, is the biggest but certainly not the only place to take classes. Alternative education flourishes at Naropa Institute (America's only Buddhist university), Hakomi Institute, Boulder College, Rolf Institute, Boulder Graduate School and the Boulder School of Massage Therapy. Innovative entrepreneurs have made their mark with landmark businesses such as McGuckins Hardware, Liquor Mart and Celestial Seasonings.

The main thing you'll want to do in Boulder is stay outside—in fact *Outside* magazine has named Boulder the number one spot in the country for outdoor sports. Boulder Mountain Parks and Open Space land preserves spectacular views of the mountains and the wide-open prairies; 33,000 acres are reserved solely for public recreational use. Hiking and mountain biking trails enter the foothills from virtually any street on Boulder's western edge. A half hour further west, Roosevelt National Forest and Indian Peaks Wilderness Area provide virtually unlimited opportunities for hiking, fishing, camping and cross-country skiing.

Exploring former wagon roads is another great way to spend a day in the historic high country of the Front Range. Many twisting canyons lead to old supply towns and mining camps west of Boulder. Nederland, Ward and Gold Hill are still going strong today, and other nearly forgotten towns still provide local color. Cutting across the gorgeous, 55-mile Peak to Peak Highway—one of the state's best autumn drives—should fulfill your highest expectations of the state's new Scenic and Historic Byway program.

In town, music, lectures, theater and dance proliferate. You won't find a place designed to be more conducive to walking or riding bikes and you'll never be far from a cafe or restaurant. A stroll down the Pearl Street Mall or through the beautiful University of Colorado campus shouldn't be missed.

HISTORY

In 1858 Capt. Thomas Aikins, an early prospector, said of the Boulder area: "The mountains looked right for gold and the valleys looked rich for grazing." Other settlers felt the same way. When the first gold strike was made on aptly named Gold Hill a few months later, the town of Boulder City sprang to life. Named for the numerous large rocks in the vicinity, the tag "City" was added in the hope it would actually become one someday.

Early townspeople endured the elements in dirt-floor log cabins built along Pearl St. Occupants used wool blankets to cover furnishings and supplies during rainy periods and slept under leaky roofs on mattresses made with pine needles and hay until enough straw could be grown. The newcomers had virtually no trouble with the Southern Arapaho Indians, who, under the leadership of Chief Niwot (Left Hand), let the settlers stay.

Although the town was built on a pile of rocks in the foothills, Boulder's fortune was not to be found in minerals, which is why it didn't fall victim to the same fate of the boom-and-bust mining towns. Instead, Boulder grew up as a supply and transportation center for the gold, silver and tungsten mining operations dotting the mountains to the west. It later served as a hub for farmers on the plains.

Boulder eventually found its future in education. In 1860 the young town opened the first schoolhouse in Colorado. By the time Colorado achieved statehood in 1876, the original University of Colorado building, Old Main, was under construction. The freshman class consisted of nine men and one woman in 1878.

The arrival of the first railroad in 1879 helped ensure Boulder's continued growth. But its reliance on supply and transportation to the surrounding mining camps gradually diminished as the university grew up with the town. A dramatic leap in enrollment occurred after World War II as returning military took advantage of the GI Bill. Today, as one of four University of Colorado campuses, Boulder attracts top students from every state and 70 foreign countries.

It's hard to believe today, but Boulder was "dry" from 1907 until 1967. Absolutely no liquor was served (legally) until the Catacombs opened in the Hotel Boulderado in 1969. The sixties found Boulder on the same long-hair, barefoot, free-love circuit as progressive campuses in Berkeley and Madison—a kinship that still exists according to some. Since then, however, Boulder has toned down its hippie image and gentrified some of its former hangouts as real estate prices have skyrocketed. Today, a pleasant and diverse mix of night spots, cafes and quality restaurants have opened in town. But despite any changes it's still a place to relax and let your hair down.

GETTING THERE

Boulder is located less than 40 minutes from downtown Denver. To get there drive north on Interstate 25 until you reach the Boulder Turnpike (Hwy. 36), which leads 27 miles northwest to Boulder. Frequent daily **Regional Transportation District (RTD)** buses shuttle between Denver and Boulder.

———— MAJOR ATTRACTIONS ————

Pearl Street Mall

You'll miss the essence of Boulder by neglecting to visit the Pearl Street Mall. It's a place where the pulse of the city is out in the open air. The mall's wide brick walkway is bordered on both sides by restaurants, shops, galleries and bars, most of which occupy turn-of-the-century, two-story buildings. Grassy areas, flowers, sculptures and wooden benches complete the physical environment. But it's the people that electrify the mall's atmosphere, especially on summer evenings when outdoor cafes are packed. While strolling down the mall you'll be sure to catch free performances by jugglers, magicians, acrobats, musicians and mimes. Fashion statements abound. Foreign accents hang in the air. The mood changes with the seasons, but there is always something happening. If you prefer a guided walking tour of Boulder's downtown (or Mapleton Hill neighborhood), contact **Historic Boulder** at **(303) 444-5192;** small fee charged.

OTHER ATTRACTIONS

Celestial Seasonings Tour of Tea

Nineteen-year-old Mo Siegel had a great idea when he started gathering herbs in 1969 in Aspen. Over the years Celestial Seasonings has grown into one of America's best loved companies. They provide a fascinating, free 45-minute tour that includes all of the plant's operations including R&D, marketing, art and the factory floor, where all of the herbs and teas are mixed and packaged (1,000 tea bags per minute). The wonderful aromas you catch are reason enough to take the tour; you won't soon forget the "mint room." The factory gets quite loud so children under 5 are not permitted. Weekdays during the lunch hour stop in for a sandwich, salad or soup at the **Celestial Cafe.** Stop in the emporium for tour tickets, tea tasting and T-shirts. Guided tours are offered on the hour from 10 am–3 pm, Mon.–Sat. Call **(303) 581-1202** for information and directions.

National Center for Atmospheric Research (NCAR)

"Anyone curious about the air, sun and weather will find NCAR a fascinating place," says Rene Munoz, education and tour coordinator. NCAR's scientists work on problems such as lightning, windshear, global warming and climate modeling. There are no classified secrets here. NCAR welcomes the public to take self-guided tours during regular hours. From June to Sept., hour-long guided tours begin at noon Mon.–Sat; once-a-week guided tours are offered from Oct.–May. Don't miss the interactive model of the sun or the two Cray supercomputers that can make nearly a billion calculations per second. A library and a cafeteria are also open to the public.

Lunch is served 11:30 am–1:30 pm. NCAR also has an art gallery on the second floor. A number of hiking trails lead into the Open Space land west of the facility.

Designed by noted architect I.M. Pei, NCAR commands an enviable mesa-top position overlooking Boulder. The unique building resembles the cliff dwellings of Mesa Verde; few modern structures commune in such a beautiful way with a natural setting. If you make the trip to NCAR, you will surely see some deer along the way. Open 8 am–5 pm Mon.–Fri., 9 am–3 pm weekends and holidays. Located at the west end of Table Mesa Dr., **1850 Table Mesa Dr.; (303) 497-1174.** Another stop on the science circuit is the **National Institute of Standards and Technology**, which has a number of lobby displays, the world's most accurate clock and guided tours on Tues. and Thur. at 9:30 am and 1:30 pm. No fee. **325 Broadway, Boulder, CO.**

University of Colorado, Boulder Campus

Right in the heart of Boulder, the University of Colorado is distinguished by both beauty and intellectual energy. Well into its second century, the 600-acre campus reflects a stately maturity. Enormous sandstone buildings with red-tile roofs are separated by open grassy areas and long walkways. The **University Memorial Center (UMC),** with its attractive outdoor fountain, serves as the nucleus of activity—it's one of the most visually appealing campuses in the nation. Inside the UMC students and faculty spend off-time enjoying restaurants, a video game room, pool hall, bowling alley and the all-important University Bookstore. Stop by the **CU Heritage Center** in **Old Main** (open 10 am–4 pm Tues.–Fri.; **(303) 492-6329**) for displays on the history of the University, a pamphlet on some of the campus highlights and guided tours.

FESTIVALS AND EVENTS

Conference on World Affairs
early-April

Everything under the sun is analyzed by the experts who participate in panel discussions on the CU campus every spring. Question-and-answer periods take place after each presentation. You'll be able to mingle with government officials, CIA operatives, witches, cosmonauts, refugees, journalists and radical feminists—something for everyone. For schedule information call **(303) 492-2525.**

Kinetic Conveyance Challenge
early May

This annual spectacle pits outrageous human-powered craft in a race over land and water for a crowd of thousands. Imagine full-grown adults sitting inside a leg-powered toilet or crowded into a huge mud shark, spending a day competing for various titles at Boulder Reservoir. Ridiculous team names range from *A Streetcar Named Perspire* to *Gumby Goes Hawaiian*. The whole event is totally meaningless, which is a big part of what makes it so much fun. Beer and food are served, KBCO radio provides the music and the contestants provide the excuse for having a good time. You might also want to catch the wacky conveyances at a prechallenge parade down the Pearl Street Mall. Don't miss this one! Call **(303) 694-6300** for more information.

Colorado Music Festival
late June through early August

Though not as well known as the Aspen Music Festival, this festival has everything going for it. Classical music concerts take place in the magnificent all-wood **Chautauqua Auditorium,** built in 1898. Under the direction of Giora Bernstein, musicians from symphonies around the world come together to play with renowned guest artists. Pre-concert picnickers cast a cheery array of color across the expansive lawns. If you prefer dining at a table, have dinner on the commodious porch of the **Chautauqua Dining Hall** and enjoy this quintessentially Boulder scene (see Where to Eat). Since 1976 the music festival has been an important part of summertime in Boulder. For more information call **(303) 449-1397.**

Colorado Shakespeare Festival
late June through mid-August

In a beautiful garden setting at the **Mary Rippon Outdoor Theater** on the CU campus, highly entertaining productions of Shakespeare are performed each summer. Talented company members and well-known guest artists play a number of the major roles. This festival has been going strong since 1958 and is now considered one of the best in the country. Whether it is a joyful production of *A Midsummer Night's Dream* or a gruesome rendition of the tragedy *Titus Andronicus*, you will feel the emotions only Shakespeare can evoke. For ticket information (beginning in late May), call **(303) 492-0554.**

Athletic Events
year-round

Boulder not only attracts many world-class athletes to train and live, but the town hosts a large number of athletic events each year. The **CU Buffalos' Big Eight football** games at Folsom Field are always a raucous experience. Each game is preceded by Ralphie (the team's buffalo) making a traditional run around the football field. The **Colorado Buffalos Women's basketball** team has been making waves lately with a top-five national ranking. The university also stages soccer, skiing and ultimate frisbee competitions, among others. Call **(303) 492-8337** for information and tickets. The **Bolder Boulder 10K** race attracts nearly 40,000 runners every Memorial Day making it one of the largest in the world. The finish line can be found inside Folsom stadium as the various classes of runners end the race to the cheers of tens of thousands of spectators. For more information call **(303) 444-RACE**. Attending the **Jose Cuervo Doubles Volleyball Tournament** at the South Boulder Recreation Center is like going to a beach party. Call the **Boulder Chamber of Commerce** at (303) 442-1044 for more information.

———— OUTDOOR ACTIVITIES ————

BIKING
MOUNTAIN BIKING

This sport has actually attracted too many people in the Boulder area. Bikes are prohibited on Boulder Mountain Park trails. In Roosevelt National Forest, however, hundreds of miles of roads and trails remain open to mountain bikes. **Eldora Mountain Resort** has opened up 40 kilometers of cross-country trails to mountain bikers for a fee. Bring your own bike or rent one of theirs. Call **(303) 440-8700** in metro Denver. Many bike shops in town stock the useful "Boulder Mountain Biking Map."

Gold Hill—A ride up to Gold Hill via either Sunshine or Four Mile canyons should satisfy even the most avid riders. It's about a 10-mile uphill ride from the mouth of either canyon to this out-of-the-way hamlet. To get to Sunshine Canyon, ride west on Mapleton Ave.; to reach Four Mile Canyon ride west on Canyon Blvd. (Hwy. 119) for 2 miles, then turn right on County Rd. 118 and right again at the sign for Gold Hill.

Nederland—The area around Nederland is full of possible rides. The ghost town of Caribou lies at the windswept edge of treeline, making a great 5-hour round trip. There are a couple of ways to get to the townsite. The most obvious and direct route follows along the wide dirt Caribou Rd. A rougher, more challenging route, with fewer competing autos, is up the old mining roads along Sherwood Creek. Eventually they funnel out to Caribou Rd. near the once-booming silver camp of Caribou. Riders in really good shape might want to consider an all-day ride over Rollins Pass to Winter Park (see the Four-Wheel-Drive Trips section); have someone meet you there or ride back over the next day.

TOURING

Just park your car and hop on a bike. You're in Boulder, the home of Olympic cycling champions Connie Carpenter-Phinney and Davis Phinney and Tour of Italy winner Andy Hamsten, to name just a few of Boulder's famous cyclist residents. It's easy to get around town, thanks to one of the best bike trail systems in the US. The number of people in Boulder who commute to work on bikes is 10 times the national average. Partly because there are so many bicyclists, laws are especially strict. Please obey the rules and ride safely.

The **Boulder Creek Path** snakes through the city starting from Eben G. Fine Park at the west end of Arapahoe Ave. It leads east along the creek, crossing several bridges and heading quite a way up the canyon. Many riders enjoy the strenuous pull up Flagstaff Mountain (See Scenic Drives for specifics). Other trails and designated bike lanes make up more than 50 miles of well-maintained bikeway. Pick up a trail map at the **Boulder Chamber of Commerce** at **2440 Pearl St.; (303) 442-1044.**

Rentals and Information—
Cycle Logic—**2525 Arapahoe Ave.; (303) 443-0061.**

Full Cycle—This alternative bike shop has a cooperative workshop area where you can repair your own bike or get help if you need it. **1211 13th St. on the Hill; (303) 440-6226.**

University Bicycles—These folks rent 10-speeds, 3-speeds, tandem bikes and mountain bikes. **839 Pearl St.; (303) 444-4196.**

FISHING

Most fishing areas near Boulder receive heavy use. After all, the area's lakes and streams are easily accessible to more than 2 million Front Range residents. A unique attraction in Boulder is the **Fish Observatory,** located on the bike path just behind the Clarion Harvest House Hotel at **1345 28th St.** In a park setting, four round windows are built into a subterranean wall bordering Boulder Creek. The windows provide an underwater view into the natural habitat of brown, brook and cutthroat trout. Look closely enough and you may learn something about their feeding patterns. Here are a few fishing ideas.

Barker Reservoir—

At the east side of Nederland, this popular fishing spot remains a consistent producer for stocked rainbow trout in the 12-inch range. No boats are allowed on the lake, though you may see a few facetious Nederland Yacht Club T-shirts. The water line at Barker Reservoir tends to fluctuate greatly depending on downstream water needs.

Boulder Creek—

Many sections of this small stream prove to be quite productive habitats. South Boulder Creek flows down from the Continental Divide near Rollins Pass. Fishing on the South Fork can be good for smallish cutthroat trout all along Forest Rd. 149 near the East Portal of the Moffat Tunnel. At the tunnel a smattering of small lakes—including Arapaho Lakes, Crater Lakes and Forest Lakes—are accessible by trail. Though these lakes are heavily fished, you can usually have good success for rainbow, brown and cutthroat trout. You can also find excellent, but hard-to-reach, fishing within the steep canyon below Gross Reservoir.

Some good evening fly-fishing can be found within the Boulder city limits on Boulder Creek. It is all catch and release, and some of the trout—brook, brown and cutthroat—grow to large sizes.

Boulder Reservoir—

Fishing for warmwater species including crappie, catfish and largemouth bass can be good at this city-owned water supply. Unless you are a Boulder resident with a permit, boating is prohibited on weekends. For bank fishing try the deep water near the dam embankment. Take the Longmont Diagonal (Hwy. 119) east of Boulder and turn left on 51st St. Travel north for a couple of miles to the gatehouse. Fee charged; open year-round.

Brainard Lake—

Everyone likes to spend Sun. afternoons at Brainard Lake, so you'll have lots of company if you fish here. The lake is in a beautiful setting just a few miles west of Ward. Fishing can be good for pan-sized stocked rainbow and brown trout. A half mile up South St. Vrain Creek lies Long Lake, which is limited to flies and lures. Another mile above Long Lake, a trail leads to Lake Isabelle; flies and lures only.

FOUR-WHEEL DRIVE TRIPS

Rollins Pass Road—

This classic drive was once open to passenger cars. Today a tunnel on the historic route near the top of the pass has caved in, making travel west of the divide impossible. Perhaps the tunnel will be blasted out in the future, but no one is willing to commit to a timetable. For now you can drive to within a mile and a half of the pass, but the route is blocked from there (hikers and mountain bikers can bypass the tunnel and continue down the other side of the pass on the road). For more information on the history of the road, see the Four-Wheel-Drive Trips section of the **Winter Park and Middle Park** chapter. To get to Rollins Pass Rd. from Boulder, drive west on Hwy. 119 to Nederland and then south on Hwy. 72 to Rollinsville. Follow the signs west from

Rollinsville. For current information on the status of the road, contact the **Boulder Ranger District** at **(303) 444-6600.**

Switzerland Trail—

This rough four-wheel-drive road follows the path of the narrow-gauge railroad that once carried rich gold ore from the mines to the smelters. In the early 1900s, excursion trains also made this scenic trip into the high Front Range mountains. To reach this historic route, take Canyon Blvd. (Hwy. 119) west out of Boulder for 3 miles. Turn right on County Rd. 118, which leads into Four Mile Canyon. Stay on County Rd. 118 past Salina and Wallstreet until you reach Sunset, 17 miles from Boulder. From Sunset take a sharp right onto the Switzerland Trail, which climbs uphill, eventually emerging on County Rd. 52. From here you can pass through the old mining town of Gold Hill on the return to Boulder. Another segment of the Switzerland Trail can be reached by taking a left at Sunset. This four-wheel-drive road passes by Glacier Lake before joining Hwy. 72 between Nederland and Ward.

GOLF

Flatirons Golf Course—

This challenging 18 hole course, with many lakes and mature trees, provides exceptionally well-kept greens and unobstructed views of nearby mountains. Consequently, this reasonably priced course is one of the most popular in Boulder. Pro shop. **5706 Arapahoe Ave.; (303) 442-7851.**

Lake Valley Golf Course—

Lake Valley's 18 holes have been challenging golfers since 1965. As the name implies, several lakes and other water hazards come into play. Tee times are taken two days in advance. Located 5 miles north of Boulder on Neva Rd. just east of Hwy. 36; **(303) 444-2114.**

HIKING AND BACKPACKING

Boulder lies flush against the dramatic rocky uplift of the Rocky Mountains. Just west of Boulder, possibilities for hiking and backpacking abound. Many residents can walk from their front doors and be on trails in minutes. Why sit back and just look at the mountains when you are so close? This hiking section could easily be expanded into a book of its own—instead, we have a scaled-back listing of some excellent hiking options in the Boulder Mountain Parks, Roosevelt National Forest and the Indian Peaks Wilderness Area. For more information and maps contact the **Boulder Ranger District Office, 2995 Baseline Rd., Boulder, CO 80303; (303) 444-6600,** or the **City of Boulder Mountain Parks; Ranger Cottage, 9th & Baseline, Boulder, CO 80302; (303) 441-3408.** Topographical maps, rental equipment, supplies and other information can be obtained at **Mountain Sports, 821 Pearl St.; (303) 443-6770.** You may also check at **The Boulder Mountaineer, 1335 Broadway; (303) 442-8355.**

South of Rocky Mountain National Park, the Indian Peaks Wilderness Area straddles both sides of the Continental Divide. Dominant peaks, alpine tundra, colorful wildflowers and a smattering of lakes set a beautiful stage for hikers. The area is so popular that backpacking access is limited by a permit system. Day hikers do not need permits, but one is required for overnight camping June 1–Sept. 15. Permits are available by reservation for a small fee. For more information contact the **Boulder Ranger District Office, 2995 Baseline Rd., Boulder, CO 80303; (303) 444-6600.**

The hikes on the west side of the Continental Divide are discussed in the Hiking and Backpacking section of the **Winter Park and Middle Park** chapter.

Arapaho Glacier—

This strenuous day trip in the Indian Peaks Wilderness Area begins at the same trailhead as hikes in the vicinity of Arapaho Pass (see next entry). Break right from the Arapaho Pass Trail (No. 904) onto Trail No. 905 1 mile after setting out. The 3.5-mile hike tracks along above treeline for most of the way, ending at the glacier at 12,700 feet. Looking up at Arapaho Peak (13,397 feet) from the glacier is irresistible—go ahead and scramble to the top for fabulous views down both sides of the Continental Divide.

Arapaho Pass—

A number of exciting trips for backpackers can be found in the Arapaho Pass area, all of which leave from the Fourth of July trailhead. The steady uphill trail (No. 904) begins at 10,121 feet and climbs 3 miles to the pass at 11,900 feet. It follows an old stagecoach route for part of the way, and close to treeline you'll see the remains of the Fourth of July Mine. From the pass on the Continental Divide, enjoy views to the tall peaks of Rocky Mountain National Park to the north and Middle Park down below to the west. Options from the top of Arapaho Pass include dropping down to the west to Caribou Lake, then continuing southwest over Caribou Pass to Columbine Lake. Another longer trip takes you all the way down to Monarch Lake. Come back over Pawnee Pass, ending at Pawnee Campground, north of where you started out. If you choose this route, you'll need to arrange for transportation back to your vehicle. To reach the Fourth of July trailhead, travel west from Nederland for about 12 miles on County Rd. 107, a rough dirt road.

Boulder Mountain Parks and Open Space—

This sweeping open land virtually encircles Boulder, offering some 100 miles of excellent hiking trails just outside the city. Since 1967 Boulder citizens have been paying a tax to preserve this land from development and to set aside more for the future. This foresight has allowed residents and visitors the luxury of hiking onto the eastern plains and into beautiful mountains to the west of Boulder. For a complete trail map to the Boulder Mountain Parks, drop by the **Boulder Chamber of Commerce, 2440 Pearl St.; (303) 442-1044,** or any local sporting goods store.

Trails lead away from Boulder in clusters from designated trailheads. **Chautauqua Park,** located on the west end of Baseline Rd., has a parking area at the start of a trail leading toward the Flatirons and Bluebell

Shelter. Many trails pass near the stunning red rock strata of the Flatirons. Technical climbers are often seen hanging on these vertical rocks; inexperienced climbers should stick to walking trails to avoid becoming statistics. Other trails lead away from **Sunrise Circle Amphitheater** near the top of Flagstaff Mountain. Still others lead from the National Center for Atmospheric Research (see the Other Attractions section), at the west end of Table Mesa Dr.

Some of the more popular trails include **Mesa Trail,** which leads from just below Bluebell Shelter on a beautiful 6-mile southerly course to Eldorado Springs. Have a car meet you in Eldorado Springs and you won't have to backtrack. The well-defined Mesa Trail provides sweeping views of the Front Range and the Flatirons while tracking through deep woods and grassy meadows. A highly recommended short hike begins on the Mesa Trail in a northerly direction from NCAR. Merge onto **Enchanted Mesa Trail,** which ends at Chautauqua Park in town. Another interesting hike, beginning at the west end of Mapleton Ave. (just past Boulder Memorial Hospital), is **Mt. Sanitas Trail,** which leads to the top of the 6,863-foot mountain. The round-trip hike provides great views of Boulder and can be completed in under two hours. This is a good hike early or late in the year because of its low elevation.

Isabelle Glacier Trail—

Each weekend hundreds of people take this hike—so if you want solitude, look elsewhere. Beginning at the ever-popular Brainard Lake, Trail No. 908 leads gradually uphill to Isabelle Glacier (12,000 feet) in 2 miles. A longer trail (No. 907) goes on up to Pawnee Pass at 12,541 feet. This 4.5-mile hike is particularly steep during the final 2 miles. If you're interested in a longer backpacking loop, head over the Continental Divide to Monarch Lake and return to the east side of the divide via Arapaho Pass (see entry above). To reach Brainard Lake drive just north of Ward on Hwy. 119, turn left and take Brainard Lake Rd. (County Rd. 102) west for about 5 miles.

HORSEBACK RIDING

Bar-A-Stables—
6000 W. Coal Creek Drive, Superior, CO 80027; (303) 499-4464.

LLAMA TREKKING

Timberline Llamas—
Wes and Mary Mauz run a complete llama packing company that will take you on an extraordinary summer excursion. The llamas carry your gear and provide an exotic aspect to your trip, which can last from two days to more than a week. Let the Mauzes know your interests or desires, and they will design a custom backcountry trip. For more information contact **Timberline Llamas** at **30361 Rainbow Hill Rd., Golden, CO 80401; (303) 526-0092.**

SKIING

CROSS-COUNTRY SKIING

Boulder is a jumping-off point for miles upon miles of fantastic cross-country terrain. Whether you prefer a gentle trail or a plunging powder run with opportunities for telemark skiing, you'll find it here. For a map of marked backcountry trails in the Roosevelt National Forest, contact the **Boulder Ranger District Office, 2995 Baseline Rd., Boulder, CO 80303; (303) 444-6600.**

Backcountry Trails—
Brainard Lake Trail System—This area has proven very popular among cross-country skiers, so having tracks to follow is seldom a problem. Thankfully, no snowmobiles are allowed. Fairly difficult marked trails lead to Long Lake and Lake Isabelle, as well as farther north on Blue Lake Trail. Be aware of avalanche areas, especially above Blue Lake and Lake Isabelle. An easy trail is the southern portion of the Walthrop Loop, which is a fairly level 5-mile round trip from Brainard Lake. More experienced skiers can make a hilly loop on Walthrop North Trail. To reach the trailhead, take the Peak to Peak Hwy. just north of Ward to a marked turn-off for Brainard Lake Rd. (County Rd. 102). Turn left and head west as far as possible and park on the side.

Lost Lake Trail—For people with some cross-country experience, this is an excellent half-day trip which leads up an unplowed road from the town of Eldora. The 6-mile round-trip route has an elevation change of 1,000 feet. A mile after setting out, take the left fork and ski up to the townsite of Hesse. Stay on the trail for 1.5 miles and take a left cutoff on Lost Lake Trail. The trail leads south to Lost Lake in just over a half mile. An option to turning left onto Lost Lake Trail is to continue straight on King Lake Trail; there is some avalanche danger as you come within a mile of King Lake. To reach the trailhead from Nederland, drive a half mile south on Hwy. 119. Take the right fork to a parking area at the west end of the town of Eldora.

Rainbow Lakes Road—This easy 4.5-mile trail works its way to Rainbow Lakes. The trail is better after a recent snow because it tends to become windblown and icy in spots. The lakes are half a mile beyond the campground. The gradual downhill return trip provides a chance to stretch out and glide. From Nederland drive 7 miles north on Hwy. 72. Turn left at a sign opposite the Colorado University Mountain Research Station and drive a little less than a mile to the fork in the road. Begin skiing on the unplowed left fork.

Groomed Trails—
Eldora/Rossignol Nordic Center—From the southeast side of the ski area parking lot, 40 kilometers of groomed and backcountry trails take off into the woods. The nordic center offers rentals as well as instruction in skating, telemarking and touring. For a longer trip, inquire about an overnight stay at Tennessee Mountain Cabin, which sleeps up to 12. A trail fee is charged; hours are 9 am–4 pm daily. Located 21 miles west of Boulder. Take Canyon Blvd. (Hwy. 119) west to a mile beyond Nederland and turn left at the Eldora turn-off. For more information call **(303) 440-8700.**

Rentals and Information—
The Boulder Mountaineer—1335 Broadway; (303) 442-8355.

Christy's Sports—2000 30th St.; (303) 442-2493.

Eldora/Rossignol Nordic Center—At Eldora Mountain Resort; (303) 440-8700.

Mountain Sports—821 Pearl St.; (303) 443-6770.

DOWNHILL SKIING
Eldora Mountain Resort—

Only 30 minutes from Boulder, Eldora offers downhill skiing only a short commute away. The modest ski area appears to be on the right track with five double chairlifts, modest lift prices and rarely a wait. Most of the terrain is intermediate, with a smattering of beginner and expert slopes. The expert Corona Bowl, on the back side of the mountain, remains open longer, thanks to strategically placed wind blocks. Advanced skiers love the steep pitch. Wind is the only nemesis at Eldora—toward the top it can get really gusty, though much of the mountain is protected by trees. More than half the mountain is lighted for night skiing, at a bargain price, 3–9:30 pm Wed.–Sat. Snowboarders take note: Eldora features a half pipe. Rentals are available at the base. The lodge serves breakfast, lunch and dinner. Upstairs the Alpenhorn is a great après-ski hangout.

Located 21 miles west of Boulder. Take Canyon Blvd. (Hwy. 119) west to a mile beyond Nederland and turn left at the Eldora turn-off. RTD bus service shuttles skiers five times daily (three times on Sun.) from Boulder. For more information contact: **PO Box 1378, Nederland, CO 80466; (303) 440-8700** in metro Denver.

SLEDDING
Boulder Parks—

The city gives the OK for sledding on the hills at Scott Carpenter and Tantra Parks. Another good spot for a free sledding experience is on the hill near Fairview High School.

SWIMMING
Boulder Reservoir—

It's not the prettiest beach in the world, but in Colorado who's complaining. The "Res" is a fun place to swim and suntan. Many people prefer boating, canoeing and windsurfing, and rentals of many craft are available. Take the Longmont Diagonal (Hwy. 119) east of Boulder and turn left on 51st St. Travel north for 1.5 miles to the gatehouse; open Memorial Day–Labor Day; fee charged. **(303) 441-3468.**

Eldorado Artesian Springs—

Once a famed resort, Eldorado Artesian Springs has slipped a bit over the years. But it has a great setting just outside the entrance to Eldorado Canyon State Park. A day here can include swimming, hiking, picnicking and watching climbers hang on the canyon's sheer rock walls (see the Scenic Drives section). The comfortably warm pool is naturally heated from geothermal waters more than a mile beneath the surface. Located 5.5 miles south of Boulder on Hwy. 93, then west on Hwy. 170 for 3 miles; open Memorial Day–Labor Day; fee charged. **(303) 499-1316.**

Scott Carpenter Pool—

This is a great outdoor pool that also boasts a 150-foot water slide. Open in summer only; small fee charged. **30th St. and Arapahoe Ave.; (303) 441-3427.**

TENNIS
Arapahoe Ridge—

Two courts; **1280 43rd St.**

Chautauqua Park—

One extremely scenic court. Everyone assumes that because there is only one court, it's always full. You'll never know unless you give it a chance. **9th St. and Baseline Rd.**

Martin Park—

Two courts; **36th St. and Dartmouth.**

North Boulder Recreation Center—

Four lighted courts. Fee charged only for reservations and lights. **3170 N. Broadway; (303) 441-3444.**

South Boulder Recreation Center—
Four lighted courts. Fee charged only for reservations and lights. **1360 Gillaspie St.; (303) 441-3448.**

WINDSURFING

Boulder Reservoir—
This is the place to learn how to windsurf or to show off your skills. Condi-tions are usually good, but at times the wind can be fierce. You can arrange lessons and rentals at the reservoir. Take the Longmont Diagonal (Hwy. 119) east of Boulder and turn left on 51st St. Travel north for 1.5 miles to the gatehouse; **(303) 441-3456, 441-3461** or **441-3469** for infor-mation, **(303) 581-9463** for wind conditions.

———— SEEING AND DOING ————

BALLOONING

Air Boulder Champagne Balloon Flights—
3345 15th St., Boulder, CO 80304; (303) 442-5253.

MUSEUMS AND GALLERIES

Boulder is a town of few museums and many galleries. You can find the best and brightest galleries along the Pearl Street Mall. A standout is the **Boulder Arts & Crafts Cooperative,** featuring the works of 72 local artists. It is located at **1421 Pearl St.; (303) 443-3683.** For southwestern art see the **White Horse Gallery** on the Pearl Street Mall; **(303) 443-6116.** For quality western paintings and sculpture, visit the **Leanin' Tree Gallery and Museum of Western Art, 6055 Longbow Drive; (303) 530-1442.** Another recommended stop is the **University Memorial Center** on campus, which features an ever-changing collection of art from nationally recognized artists as well as CU students.

Boulder Historical Society and Museum—
In a wonderful stone mansion on "the Hill" in Boulder, this fine museum houses many artifacts (dating to the 1860s). In fact, because the historical society's collection is so vast, they must rotate their displays sev-eral times a year. The house, replete with its Tiffany stained-glass window and Italian-tiled fireplace, is the perfect setting for old photographs, furniture, toys, clothing and quilts. Don't miss the kitchen with its round icebox and interesting tools. Small donation suggested. Open Tues.–Sat. 12–4 pm. **1206 Euclid Ave.; (303) 449-3464.**

Collage Children's Museum—
Happy shrieks and the patter of feet fill the colorful, fun-filled environment of Boulder's newest museum. Children up to pre-teens will love being told, "yes! please touch." Displays range from a hands-on magnetic sculpture table to a massive soap bubble that children can create with the help of a hula hoop. Your kids will find places for dress-up, experiencing textures inside of a tunnel and, without knowing it, they will undoubtedly learn something. Collage features many special events and performances throughout the year. "Vir-tually the only time you hear a kid crying is when parents attempt to leave this place," remarked Museum Director Alison Moore. Open 10 am–5 pm Thur.–Sat., 1–5 pm on Sun. **2065 30th St.** in Aspen Plaza, **Boulder, CO; (303) 440-9894.**

Fiske Planetarium—
With state-of-the-art equipment, a 65-foot dome and highly regarded on-cam-pus experts, Fiske rivals the best in the world. Friday-evening star talks with CU astronomers point out attributes of the heavens while sharing the most current research with audience members. After the program many people like to go to the observatory for a free peek through one of two large telescopes—16 and 24 inches

respectively—at the real night sky. Other monthly events include multimedia/laser shows geared to the music of groups such as Pink Floyd, R.E.M. and, yes, the Grateful Dead. The children's matinee, science discovery program and other events take place throughout the year. Located on the University of Colorado campus. Call **(303) 492-5001** for a schedule of events.

Mapleton Hill Walking Tour—

See some of Boulder's grandest homes on this fine residential walking tour in a historic neighborhood. Pick up a self-guiding brochure at the **Boulder Chamber of Commerce, 2440 Pearl St.; (303) 442-1044.**

University of Colorado Museum—

This fine museum features subjects ranging from southwest artifacts to paleontology, anthropology and botany. Since the museum was established in 1902, it has grown to include a diversity of exhibits. Lectures, courses and special traveling exhibits are also offered at the museum. Open 9 am–5 pm Mon.–Fri; 9 am–4 pm Sat.; 10 am–4 pm Sun. Located in the Henderson Building on campus at **15th St. and Broadway; (303) 492-6892.**

NIGHTLIFE

Finding nightlife shouldn't be a problem in Boulder. The Pearl Street Mall's (see the Major Attractions section) free summer acts and many bars always draw large crowds. We have listed a few outstanding places, which we hope will stay in business for the foreseeable future. For a more complete listing of area nightlife, check the *Colorado Daily* or the *Boulder Daily Camera* newspapers. The easiest way to get the latest happenings is to call the **KBCO Information Line** at **(303) 444-5226** for a recorded message.

Boulder Dinner Theater—

Since 1976 this dinner theater has provided complete evenings of dining and entertainment. A professional acting troupe with members from around the US puts on Broadway-style shows, including *Cabaret,* *West Side Story, A Chorus Line* and *Evita.* Unlike some dinner theaters, you may choose from a menu—prime rib, spinach lasagna and chicken teriyaki are a few of the entrées—and the performers also wait the tables. There isn't a bad seat in the house, but if you reserve early enough you can request a seat close to the stage. If a performance is sold out, go ahead and stop by. The theater will buy you a drink, and if there are any no-shows, you can buy their tickets. If no tickets become available, at least you've had a free drink. Open Tues.–Sun. **5501 Arapahoe Ave.; (303) 449-6000.**

Hotel Boulderado Mezzanine—

If you want a quiet, classy place to sink back into a comfortable chair and enjoy good conversation with a friend, head for the Mezzanine. On many evenings the Boulderado features pleasant live music in its historic setting. The Mezzanine overlooks the lobby from the second floor and is topped by a magnificent stained-glass ceiling. See the Where to Stay section for more information on the hotel. **13th St. and Spruce; (303) 442-4344.**

Walnut Brewery—

This brewpub hasn't been in existence long, but it already has a loyal following—on weekends lines often form at the entrance. Brewmaster Mark Younquist has the enviable task of preparing the various styles of beer, including bitter, wheat and stout. The beer tasted good, but we were surprised to find the various styles served at the same cold temperature. This popular pub, with high ceilings and window-encased brew vats, is as much restaurant as pub. If it gets a little loud, ask for a table in one of the quieter back dining rooms. **1123 Walnut; (303) 447-1345.**

West End Tavern—

This neighborhood tavern is a great place to hang out. The 100-year-old oak bar—brought to Boulder from Miss Kitty's Saloon in Nebraska—fits into its present home in the tavern with less than a quarter inch to spare. Jazz and blues music in the renovated downstairs section. The upstairs deck offers perfect views of the Flatirons. See the Where to Eat section for more information. Between **9th St. and 10th St. on Pearl St.; (303) 444-3535.**

SCENIC DRIVES

Eldorado Springs—

Just south of Boulder at the base of a narrow, rocky canyon lies the small community of Eldorado Springs. This town enjoyed a heyday in the early 1900s, when it became known as a fashionable spa. Warm artesian spring water was funneled into pools, and guests enjoyed comfortable rooms and a choice of restaurants. Today the spa has lost its glossy image, but it remains a good place to swim (see the Swimming section).

Enter Eldorado Canyon State Park just beyond Eldorado Artesian Springs. After buying an inexpensive parks pass at a self-serve station near the entrance, head into this land of sheer cliffs dotted with climbers from around the world. The technical climbing is some of the state's best, but it's also a great place to hike or relax and watch; bring along a picnic lunch. No camping allowed. To reach Eldorado Springs, take Broadway (Hwy. 93) south of Boulder for 5.5 miles. Turn right on Eldorado Springs Dr. (Hwy. 170) and continue 3 miles.

Flagstaff Mountain—

This quick, winding route up Flagstaff Mountain overlooks Boulder from the west. The paved road has several pull-offs; after a few miles of continuous uphill driving there is a turn-off for the Sunrise Circle Amphitheater. Turn right and continue to a magnificent overlook of Boulder. At the amphitheater there are picnic tables and several hiking trails. At night the lights of Boulder make the drive worthwhile. To reach Flagstaff Mountain, drive west on Baseline Rd. and keep going.

Peak to Peak Highway—

By taking any of the canyons west of Boulder, you'll soon end up on the spectacular Peak to Peak Highway. The road, designated a Scenic and Historic Byway, stretches all the way from Central City north to Estes Park, with beautiful mountain scenery and history along the whole route. In fall shimmering aspen stands provide a show of epic proportions.

A good loop trip from Boulder, taking in a section of the Peak to Peak Hwy., begins at the west end of Canyon Blvd. (Hwy. 119). This old mining road was improved in 1915 by convict labor. After 8.5 miles on the twisting, paved road, there is a parking turnout on the left (south) side for **Boulder Falls.** Cross the highway and after a short distance you'll be face to face with North Boulder Creek cascading over eroded rocks. It's a torrent during spring runoff. After another 8 miles west on Hwy. 119, the road comes out of the canyon at **Nederland.** This small town was born as a supply center to the nearby silver camp of **Caribou** a few miles to the west. In 1873 a few Dutch investors bought the Caribou Mine, which was producing $3 million a year by 1875. The glory years were short-lived, though, because of the silver market crash of 1893. Caribou is a ghost town today, but Nederland (named for the Dutch-owned mine) is still going strong. In town you'll find a couple of restaurants, including the popular Pioneer Bar.

From Nederland turn right on Hwy. 72 (the Peak to Peak Highway), which provides stunning views on the way to **Ward,** 14 miles north. (A left would take you south toward Rollinsville and eventually to Central City.) Ward is an old gold camp that has survived to accommodate a new generation of residents who prefer quiet and solitude. Situated in a narrow canyon, the town is one of the more beautiful near-ghost towns in the state. Fortunately, the schoolhouse and church survived a disastrous fire in 1900. Just north of Ward, a marked turn-off heads west for about 5 miles to **Brainard Lake.** The incredible view of the Indian Peaks from this popular mountain lake make it a worthwhile stop. For more information about some of the trails in the area, see the Hiking and Backpacking section. From Ward continue 27 miles north to **Estes Park** on Hwy. 7 (see the **Estes Park** chapter for more information) and loop back to Boulder on Hwy. 36.

Or drop back toward Boulder via Left Hand Canyon from Ward.

WHERE TO STAY

ACCOMMODATIONS

Hotel Boulderado—$$$ to $$$$

This historic hotel opened with a bash on New Year's Day in 1909. It's a graceful brick hotel built with a style and elegance similar to that of the Brown Palace Hotel in Denver. A stained-glass mezzanine ceiling is clearly visible from the ornate lobby. The hotel thrived from day one, as its luxurious rooms were furnished in the finest style. Many famous guests stayed at the Boulderado, including Teddy Roosevelt (where didn't he stay?), Helen Keller, Louis Armstrong and Robert Frost. Controversial traveling evangelist Billy Sunday, deliverer of hell-fire sermons, also stayed at the Boulderado during its first year. He described the town as "a sinkhole of iniquity, crying for redemption."

The hotel declined dramatically during the 1960s and early 1970s, but was resurrected in the early 1980s. In 1985 a new expansion connected by a walkway added 61 rooms. Both the old and new portions of the hotel are reminiscent of the Victorian era. However, some of the "feel" of an old hotel, with its creaky floors and manual Otis elevator, is lost on the new side. Each of the rooms and suites has a unique personality, but rooms on the upper floors have better views. Staying at the Boulderado entitles guests to a complimentary pass at a nearby full-service health club. Downstairs you'll find three restaurants, three lounges and an oyster bar, and upstairs the Mezzanine for cocktails. Reservations recommended. **2115 13th St., Boulder, CO 80302; (303) 442-4344** or **1-800-433-4344.**

Boulder Victoria—$$$$

In 1891 Colonel Nicholson completed building and furnishing his large, two-story home. Precisely one hundred years later, new owners have spruced up the place into an elegantly appointed, six-room B&B. In a convenient just-off-the-mall location, you will find large guest rooms featuring period antiques and brass beds topped with billowy down comforters. Modern, private bathrooms, telephones and TVs (hidden from sight in a wardrobe) provide the only exceptions to the Victorian atmosphere.

Architectural curiosities and odd angles liven up the guest rooms—especially the Nicholson Room with its archways and covered balcony. Be sure to wander out onto the canopied terrace for prime westerly views of the mountains. The only drawback to staying on the second floor is an extremely steep staircase.

On the main level, you will find three more guest rooms (including a suite) and the main common area, decorated in warm hues of green and rose. Guests are invited to linger, flip through a selection of Colorado picture books, or enjoy a glass of port wine. You can take your continental breakfast—granola, yogurt, baked goods, coffee and fruit—in the adjacent breakfast room or outside on the flagstone patio. They also serve desserts and cappuccino in the evening. **1305 Pine St., Boulder, CO 80302; (303) 938-1300.**

Clarion Harvest House Hotel—$$$ to $$$$

From the outside it doesn't look like anything much. But the interior of the five-story hotel reveals a vast 16-acre garden courtyard with a creekside setting. More than anyplace you might stay in Boulder, this large hotel provides a variety of ways to stay in shape while on the road. Indoor and outdoor pools offer lap lanes or you can soak in the huge whirlpool. Take advantage of StairMasters and weights or, if you prefer, bike or jog on the Boulder Creek Path. Well-appointed rooms provide a mini-refrigerator and complimentary coffee and tea. **The Bistro, (303) 443-3850,** open for breakfast, lunch and dinner, is worth a stop—or try the lounge. In the best Boulder tradition, the Harvest House has the best summer FAC in town with an outdoor stage and plenty to eat and drink. For information and reservations contact: **1345 28th St., Boulder, CO 80302; (303) 443-3850.**

Briar Rose—$$$

Hospitality is a genuine art and Emily Hunter, the owner of the Briar Rose, is a master artist. You will feel right at home in her immaculate 11-room bed and breakfast. The rooms are beautifully furnished in antiques, and the beds are topped with puffy feather comforters. Although it's in the heart of town, the Briar Rose is protected from the outside world by a dense shield of shrubbery and trees. An elegant continental breakfast is served each morning in your room or out on the glass-enclosed sun porch. A common room open to all guests is filled with comfortable couches and chairs arranged around a fireplace; a decanter of sherry stands ready to be poured. Reservations encouraged. **2151 Arapahoe Ave., Boulder, CO 80302; (303) 442-3007.**

The Bluebird Lodge—$$

Built of rough-hewn logs in 1872 to accommodate travelers passing through the booming town of Gold Hill, the Bluebird Lodge now welcomes guests who need a quiet escape. It's a pleasure to enjoy the present-day comforts of the outdoor hot tub and full complimentary breakfast served each morning in the formal dining room. The lodge is furnished with antiques that were stored in the attic for years. Each room features flowered quilts, antique bedframes (new mattresses) and no clutter. Nine rooms share four baths. As Barbara and Frank Finn, owners for the past 26 years, put it, "Our atmosphere is rustic and our ghosts are hospitable." Open in summer only. The Finns also operate the Gold Hill Inn, next door to the lodge (see the Where to Eat section). For information contact the **Gold Hill Inn, Gold Hill, Boulder, CO 80302; (303) 443-6461.**

Foot of the Mountain Motel—$$

This simple motel, with its inordinate amount of charm, sits at the base of the mountains on the outskirts of Boulder. The convenience of the city blends well with unobstructed mountain views. Most rooms have bathtubs that offer spectacular window views up Flagstaff Mountain. The Foot of the Mountain conjures up the feeling of a mountain cabin with its rough bark exterior, bright red paint around the windowsills, blooming flower boxes and all-wood interior. All rooms are equipped with private baths, cable TV and small refrigerators. **200 Arapahoe Ave., Boulder, CO 80302; (303) 442-5688.**

Nederhaus Motel— $

About a half hour west of Boulder in the small mountain community of Nederland you will find the Nederhaus Motel. All of the comfortable motel-style rooms are furnished in antiques. One recent guest said he liked everything about the Nederhaus "except the old furniture." Chances are you'll like something about this place. Located on Hwy. 119 at the Eldora turn-off just 3 miles from Eldora Mountain Resort. **PO Box 478, Nederland, CO 80466; (303) 444-4705 or 1-800-422-4629.**

CAMPING

Boulder Parks and Recreation—

Buckingham/Fourth of July Campground has only 8 tent sites, no water and no fee. Because the small campground usually fills up on weekends, get there as early as possible. It is a primitive campground reached by a rough dirt road. Its proximity to the Indian Peaks Wilderness Area trailheads is a major advantage. To reach the campground from Nederland, travel west on County Rd. 130 past Eldora. After the pavement ends, take the right fork some 5 miles to the campground. (The left fork leads to the Hesse trailhead.)

In Roosevelt National Forest—

Located west of Boulder are a number of first-come, first-served campgrounds.

Some of the campsites, however, can be reserved in advance by calling **MISTIX** at **1-800-283-CAMP.** Three miles south of Nederland on Hwy. 119 is **Kelly-Dahl Campground** with beautiful views of the Continental Divide. There are 48 sites and a fee. Rainbow Lakes Campground is reached by taking Hwy. 72 for 6.5 miles north of Nederland to a sign that reads Mountain Research Station. Turn left and continue on a rough dirt road for 5 miles. There are 18 sites, no drinking water and no fee. **Pawnee Campground** is 5 miles west of Ward on County Rd. 102. This extremely popular area near Brainard Lake has 76 sites and a fee.

To reach **Peaceful Valley Campground,** drive 15 miles west from Lyons on Hwy. 7 to the junction with Hwy. 72. Turn left and continue southwest on Hwy. 72 for 6 miles. There are 15 sites and a fee. **Camp Dick Campground** is located another mile west of Peaceful Valley on a dirt road. There are 34 sites and a fee.

Private Campground—

Boulder Mountain Lodge—Next to a gurgling creek, just five minutes away from Boulder, is a small RV and tent campground with a motel. The motel rooms ($$) are clean and comfortable and some are equipped with kitchenettes. This is a really nice family place located at the former town of Ordell. The office is in the old narrow-gauge train depot. There are mature trees, a small outdoor pool and a year-round hot tub. Kids will love fishing in the private pond. **91 Four Mile Canyon Rd., Boulder, CO 80302; (303) 444-0882 or 1-800-458-0882.**

WHERE TO EAT

Flagstaff House—$$$$

Plan on arriving at Flagstaff House before dark so you can enjoy the commanding view of Boulder as dusk settles slowly over the valley. This restaurant, with tiered decks and glassed-in seating areas, virtually hangs from the side of Flagstaff Mountain. Once darkness takes over, the twinkling lights of Boulder are a beautiful accompaniment to your meal. The menu is not necessarily traditional—more than 40 entrées are served, including grilled rack of Colorado lamb, elk with ginger sauce, Maine lobster and pheasant breast. Flagstaff House is just about the only restaurant in Boulder where you must dress up. Valet parking; reservations requested. Open for dinner from 6 pm Mon.–Sun. (from 5 pm on Sat.). To reach Flagstaff House, head west on Baseline Rd. and continue about halfway up Flagstaff Mountain and look for the sign. **(303) 442-4640.**

John's Restaurant—$$$

Since 1974 John Bizarro has been preparing French, Spanish, Italian and southwestern specialties at his own restaurant. His cooking has received wide acclaim for its balance, presentation and—most importantly—taste. After spending 20 years learning his trade in Italy and the US, he opened this tiny restaurant. It's formal yet comfortable, modeled after intimate European restaurants. Linen tablecloths, oil candles and fresh flowers adorn the tables, but you must request salt and pepper (you really don't need to adjust any flavors here). His dinner specials are unique creations that should be considered before looking at the regular menu. Nightly offerings include shrimp Mediterranean style, filet mignon au poivre and chicken à la moutarde. The wine list is small but carefully chosen, and you might want to top off your meal with brandy. All desserts are made fresh in the kitchen and the selection changes frequently; our favorite was the Chocolate Intensity. Reservations strongly recommended; open each evening from 6 pm. **2328 Pearl St.; (303) 444-5232.**

Gold Hill Inn—$$$

Barbara and Frank Finn operate this inn next door to the Bluebird Lodge in Gold Hill (see the Where to Stay section). Renowned for its delicious fixed-price, six-course dinners, there is a nightly choice of five or six entrées; virtually everything is homemade. Call ahead for special entrées and vegetarian dishes. Dinner by reservation only during the summer months; hours vary. For more information contact Gold Hill Inn, **Gold Hill, Boulder, CO 80302; (303) 443-6461.**

Laudisio—$$$ to $$$$

Tucked into the corner of a small shopping center, you'll find a classic piece of Italy transplanted in Boulder. Fresh ingredients, incredible pasta, premium olive oils and the sights and sounds of cooking permeate the restaurant's open kitchen. One of Boulder's top chefs recommended Laudisio to me as an excellent example of creative Italian cooking—he's right! The daily specials entice you with tastes from all over Italy and the superior staff helps you wade through the choices. A full bar and extensive Italian wine list complement the food as does the artistic setting. End your meal with a cappuccino and a decadent crême brulée. Be sure to get there early or make a dinner reservation. Open for lunch 11:30 am–2:30 pm Mon.–Fri; dinner served daily from 5:30 pm. Located in the Willow Springs Shopping Center, **2785 Iris Ave.; (303) 442-1300.**

Royal Peacock Cuisine of India—$$ to $$$

From the outside of this restaurant, you'd underestimate its comfortable, classy interior. The muted wall colors are interrupted by colorful splashes of India, and the food is authentic. When Bombay resident Rajan Mehta says it's "the best Indian food in the USA," who are we to argue? Dishes such as lamb with lentils and a variety of northwest Indian specialties—tandoor, biryani and chapati—fill the menu. The weekday luncheon buffet gives you the chance to try a number of different items at one sitting. Full bar is available. Open for lunch 11:30 am–2:30 pm Mon.–Fri.; dinner is served each evening 5:30–10:30 pm; open at 5 pm on Sun. **5290 Arapahoe Rd.; (303) 447-1409.**

Narayan's Nepal Restaurant—$$

With bright yellow paint and a few, spare artifacts on the walls, this small square restaurant is a place to focus on the food. While reminiscent of Indian cooking, here you'll find different ingredients and unique combinations. Vegetarians have a dozen excellent choices. Others may wish to sample whole wheat bread stuffed with lamb, chicken curry or steamed dumplings with ground pork and mixed vegetables. All dishes are served with long grain rice. I'd recommend starting your meal with a glass of chia, Nepali spiced tea made with milk (don't worry, no yak butter). No alcohol served. If you are considering a trip to Nepal, stop in and talk with Narayan—he also operates four other businesses including a travel agency. Open daily from 11 am-10 pm. Located at the west end of the mall, **921 Pearl St.; (303) 447-2816.**

Blue Parrot Cafe—$$

The fire that closed the Blue Parrot for most of 1988 didn't alter the spirit of the place. Located in the small community of Louisville (residents pronounce the s), this landmark restaurant has been treasured for its down-home Italian cooking since first opening in 1919. A plateful of thick homemade spaghetti and an extra pot of sauce are the main reasons to eat here; top off your meal with some spumoni. Behind the restaurant the old guard passes time by playing the Italian game of boccie ball. This place is for real. In addition to serving lunch and dinner the casual restaurant is open for breakfast; Italian food diehards will love the option of ordering a side of spaghetti with egg dishes. Open 6:30 am–9 pm Mon.–Thur., 6:30 am–10 pm Fri., 8 am–10 pm Sat., 8 am–8 pm Sun. **640 Main St., Louisville; (303) 666-0677.**

Nancy's—$ to $$$

Nancy's does a wonderful job with breakfast, lunch and dinner—all served in a charming old house with a private outdoor patio. For more than two decades this small restaurant has been a local habit. For breakfast try a blintz, eggs Benedict or a bagel with lox and cream cheese. The lunch menu shifts toward a healthy blend of soups, salads, sandwiches and entrées. Vegetarians also have some choices here. Dinner selections include prime rib, veal picatta, chicken amaretto and tortellini. There is a full bar; fine coffees and espresso are served. Breakfast hours are 7:30–11:30 am Mon.–Fri., 7:30 am–2 pm weekends; lunch hours are 11:30 am–2 pm weekdays only; dinner is served 5:30–9 pm Tues.–Sat. **825 Walnut St.; (303) 449-8402.**

Chautauqua Dining Hall—$ to $$

The atmosphere on the porch of the historic Chautauqua Dining Hall is the main reason to eat here. A wide balcony overlooks grassy Chautauqua Park and offers gorgeous mountain views. It's a good choice for breakfast, lunch and dinner. The food is traditional: omelettes and pancakes for breakfast, sandwiches for lunch and full entrées for dinner. On weekends there is usually a long wait for breakfast, but you can order coffee and banana bread and wait in the park for your turn: it's the most pleasant waiting room in Boulder. Chautauqua is also the perfect place to come for dinner before a festival or event at the drafty, all-wood Chautauqua Auditorium, built in 1898. No reservations. Open in summer only 7 am–2 pm for breakfast, 11:30 am–2 pm for lunch, 5:30–9 pm for dinner. **Chautauqua Park, 900 Baseline Rd.; (303) 440-3776.**

Dot's Diner—$ to $$

This is the ultimate dive restaurant. A gas station with two bays shares space with this funky diner. If you can get a seat at a table or at the counter you'll be treated to a great breakfast burrito, legendary huevos rancheros, homemade muffins or biscuits and gravy. In summer walk around back to a newly opened garden patio with five more tables. Open for breakfast and lunch 7 am–2 pm Mon.–Fri., 8 am–2 pm on weekends. **799 Pearl St.; (303) 449-1323.**

Lucile's—$ to $$

On a side street just off the Boulder Mall is the kind of restaurant you love to happen upon. Lucile's serves breakfast and lunch in the casual confines of an old house. The covered porch is the best place to sit on warm summer mornings; inside, the small rooms create a feeling of intimacy. For breakfast it is hard to imagine a tastier dish than the Cajun Breakfast—red beans, poached eggs topped with hollandaise sauce and served with grits or potatoes and a buttermilk biscuit. Spicy lunch dishes include gumbo, shrimp Creole and blackened red snapper. Don't forget to order the beignets—delicious sopapilla-like donuts. Open 7 am–2 pm weekdays, 8 am–2 pm weekends. **2124 14th St.; (303) 442-4743.**

Rockies Brewing Co./Wilderness Pub—$ to $$

This elite micro brewery has been doing business since 1979, but only recently expanded its kitchen. In the tasting room or out in the beer garden you can enjoy bratwurst simmered in beer. Also served are soups, sandwiches, burgers, pasta, Mexican specialties. Wash your meal down with a two-day-old Buffalo Gold— it rivals the very best! Open 11 am–10 pm Mon.–Sat. Free brewery tours are offered at 11 am, 2 and 5 pm. The tour ends with a free taste of some of the freshest beer you'll ever try. **2880 Wilderness Pl.; (303) 444-8448.**

West End Tavern—$ to $$

"A stiff drink and a good portion of food for a reasonable price is what most people want," according to the owner of the new West End Tavern. The lunch and dinner menu (one and the same) has prices from a decade past. The food is nothing fancy, but it almost always tastes good, and the portions are huge. Choose from barbecue sandwiches, cheeseburgers, special hot dogs from Newark, New Jersey, and Jailhouse Chili with corn chips. When it's warm outside, make your way to the rooftop deck for a terrific view of the Flatirons. The only complaint about sitting inside at the West End is the thick cigarette smoke, otherwise unheard of in Boulder. Open from 11 am daily. Between **9th St.** and **10th St.** on **Pearl St.; (303) 444-3535.**

Tra-Ling's Oriental Cafe—$

This bargain-priced Chinese restaurant offers quick lunches and dinners. You can choose your entrée, rice and noodles from behind glass—we promise, no color photos of selections here. The food is ready before you know it; sit down, take out or have it delivered. Open 11:30 am–9:30 pm Mon.–Fri., Sat.–Sun. 4:30–9:30 pm. **1305 Broadway; (303) 449-0400.**

Assorted Cafes—

An open passageway to Boulder's best bookstore on a prime Pearl Street Mall location sets the **Bookend Cafe (1115 Pearl St. Mall; (303) 440-6699)** apart. The people-watching is good, and, if you can get a table, so are the coffees and fresh pastries. This is an excellent place to lose yourself in a good book and let the afternoon slip by. Open 6:45 am–11 pm daily, until midnight on Fri. and Sat. nights. **Brillig Works Cafe and Bakery (1322 College Ave.; (303) 443-7461)** sits on "the Hill" only a half block from campus. Brillig's has a relaxed, slightly grungy atmosphere perfect for last-minute cramming. Open 7 am–10 pm Mon.–Fri., 8 am–5 pm Sat.–Sun. **Trident Coffee House and Bookstore (940 Pearl St.; (303) 443-3133)** epitomizes a Boulder scene with its eclectic selection of used books and laid-back environment. Stop in to buy a book on one half of the shop and then settle in for a relaxed cup of coffee, espresso or cappuccino on the other side. Open 6:30 am–11 pm Mon.–Fri., 7 am–11 pm Sat., 7:30 am–11 pm Sun.

SERVICES

Boulder Chamber of Commerce—Stop in here for information and advice on the area. **2440 Pearl St., Boulder, CO 80302; (303) 442-1044.**

Day Care—

City of Boulder Child Care Support Center—Information and referrals for child care. **(303) 441-3180.**

YWCA and **YMCA**—Both of these organizations have referral lists of baby-sitters. The YWCA has emergency child care Mon.–Fri. **(303) 442-2778.**

Transportation—

Boulder Airporter—One-way van service to the airport for a reasonable price. **(303) 321-3222.**

Boulder RTD Bus Service—For information on bus service in town and to **Denver International Airport,** call RTD at **(303) 299-6000** or stop by the **Boulder Chamber of Commerce** and pick up a free schedule (see listing above).

Boulder Yellow Cab—(303) 442-2277.

Central City and Black Hawk

As you drive up the mile-long road from Black Hawk to Central City and look at the many old houses perched on the steep mountainsides, it's easy to see how ill-suited the surrounding area is for these two small towns. But early settlers had a very good reason for choosing this location. In the spring of 1859, gold strikes along Gregory Gulch fueled the first big rush to Colorado (at the time called the Kansas Territory). Serving as a catalyst for settlement in Colorado, Central City was also the cultural center for the state and quite nearly became the state capital. The town's tradition for theatre and opera goes back to the 1860s. Many summer visitors to this Victorian mining town still attend the renowned Central City Opera.

When Colorado voters approved limited-stakes gambling in 1990, we said: "... time will tell just how much gaming will change Central City and Black Hawk." Since then, radical, sometimes controversial change has taken hold of these communities. At a glance, the false-fronted towns couldn't look better. Where unkempt, sometimes crumbling buildings and tacky tourist shops once stood, you'll find gleaming new casinos standing behind historic facades. It's an incredible sight, with a price attached.

The historical integrity of the area has been compromised, and locals have left by the dozens, cashing in on hyperinflated land prices. An army of construction workers has transformed both towns into a sort of western theme park. With the exception of a few remaining gift shops (you can't even buy a gallon of gas in Central City or Black Hawk anymore), virtually every available interior space has been filled with slot machines and gaming tables. Time will tell if the towns will get their acts together to provide services visitors expect at a true destination resort. But for now many people are left asking, "How much is enough?"

The towns of Central City and Black Hawk are caught up by a frenzied excitement, and the area's renewed vigor captures the imagination of most visitors. Ringing slots, flashing lights and the rush of coins hitting metal create a charged atmosphere inside most doorways. Dedicated gamblers with coin-blackened fingers—some paying only a nickel per pull—shout and laugh when hitting a jackpot. Others squeeze into a place at the blackjack or poker tables to try to build up their stacks of chips. With a $5 betting limit, though, high rollers should stick to Vegas and Atlantic City. See the Major Attractions section for more specifics on gambling.

If you don't like gambling or opera, don't worry; there are plenty of other things to do. Visit an interesting museum or investigate the hilly neighborhoods surrounding the downtown area. Or drive to some of the neighboring towns—say, Nevadaville or Apex—and to any number of old cemeteries. It's not a good idea to take a hike on the surrounding hills because of hundreds of abandoned mines. A trip to Central City and Black Hawk is still an outstanding way to learn about a fascinating period of Colorado history.

HISTORY

In the spring of 1859, when Georgia prospector John H. Gregory made his way up a side gulch of North Clear Creek, he couldn't possibly have known just how much gold he was about to discover. At a spot between Central City and Black Hawk, he found what he was looking for at a place later named Gregory Gulch. The town of Mountain City grew around Gregory's claim, and by the end of the year thousands of miners were clamoring around the area. Colorado's first major gold rush was on, with the area eventually producing more than a half billion dollars' worth of minerals. Many camps were established, including Black Hawk, Gregory Point, Missouri City, Nevadaville, Hoosier City, Dogtown and, of course, Central City—so named for its central location in the gulch. Out of convenience, miners from the surrounding camps would meet here, and it quickly grew into the main supply center.

Placer strikes continued into the 1860s and many miners became rich. Central City continued to grow and for a few years rivaled Denver as the largest town in the territory. But by the mid-1860s the placer mining began petering out. No one doubted there was still plenty of gold left in the hills, but it was trapped in quartz formations, making it uneconomical to remove. In 1867 Nathaniel P. Hill came to the rescue. Hill, a chemistry professor from Brown University, had studied mining techniques on the East Coast and in Europe. He built the Boston-Colorado Smelter in Black Hawk, which could economically break down the refractory gold ore. That put the mining boom back on its feet. With the smelter and the arrival of the Colorado & Southern Railroad from Denver in 1872, Black Hawk grew into quite a town of its own.

Hardrock mining proceeded at a frenzied pace. On Quartz Hill, between Central City and Nevadaville, the Mammoth vein was discovered, over the years producing millions in gold, silver, lead and copper. The largest mine along the Mammoth vein was the Glory Hole, a highly profitable open-pit mine that helped the area around Quartz Hill to become known as "the richest square mile on Earth."

Aside from mining, Central City is well known for the cultural mark it left on the state. The area drew a diverse group of immigrant miners, including Chinese, Russians, Canadians, Scots and Englishmen. The Cornish miners from England had the greatest influence on the town.

Their mortarless stone walls still characterize both Central City and Black Hawk to a degree. More importantly, they were active supporters of opera and theater. From the beginning the community supported amateur shows performed in makeshift tents. In July 1862 the Montana Theatre opened. Its debut performance went on as planned, despite the fact that on the previous day George W. Harrison, the owner, fired 35 shots into local boxer Charlie Swits. His defense at the trial was that he "didn't like Swits." The jury must have agreed, because Harrison was acquitted. He eventually went on to become a state senator. The Montana Theatre played to packed houses until 1874, when a raging fire wiped out most of the wooden buildings and homes in Central City. Blame was placed on the Chinese, who were accused of allowing their joss sticks and incense to burn out of control during a religious ceremony.

Residents of Central City began to rebuild after the fire, using stone in place of wood to prevent further catastrophes. Evening entertainment resumed in 1875 with the completion of the new Belvidere Theatre, where operatic and theatrical productions received rave reviews statewide. After a performance of *Bohemia Girl* brought down the house, townsfolk began planning a new opera house worthy of such quality performances. In December 1877 the *Rocky Mountain News* reported that the opera house construction was proceeding just fine and promised "the most beautiful auditorium to be found between Chicago and San Francisco." The opera house finally opened in the spring of 1878 to sell-out crowds. Numerous dramas were also performed by famous thespians of the time, such as Sarah Bernhardt and Edwin Booth.

In the 1880s the Central City area experienced a decline in fortunes. With silver prices going up, the central economic focus of Colorado shifted from the dwindling gold fields of Central City to the booming silver town of Leadville. By 1890 many townsfolk had moved on. Along with a loss of local patrons, the Central City Opera House lost business when Tabor's Grand Opera House was built in Denver.

Although some mining continued well into the 1900s, Central City was on its way to becoming another ghost town. Peter McFarlane, who had taken over control of the opera house in 1896, kept it open despite consistent losses. In 1910 he began using the building to show the latest craze—motion pictures. This continued until 1927. Then, after staying closed for more than four years, the opera house experienced a rebirth, when the McFarlane family donated the building to the University of Denver. Funds were raised and restoration began. In the summer of 1932 the opera house reopened with the production of *Camille*, starring Lillian Gish. It was an immediate success and drew large crowds from Denver.

When Coloradans voted to legalize gambling in Central City and Black Hawk, along with Cripple Creek, they changed the course of history. The dramatic pace of change will astound people with pregambling memories of these towns. But then, some 40 years ago gambling was legal, so perhaps some can think of it as a return to better days.

GETTING THERE

Central City is located 30 miles west of Denver. From Golden head west up Clear Creek Canyon on Hwy. 6 and then northwest on Hwy. 119 to Black Hawk. Continue 1 mile west of Black Hawk on Hwy. 279 to reach Central City.

———— MAJOR ATTRACTIONS ————

Gambling

More than 30 new casinos have opened up in Central City and Black Hawk since the new laws went into effect. A few small family-owned places, not much larger than an average living room manage to coexist with dramatic, multimillion-dollar developments. Most casinos have some portion of space for a restaurant, delicatessen or snack bar; getting something to drink is absolutely no problem.

For people staying along the Front Range, many charter bus companies now offer round-trip service from various pick-up points (see the Services section). It sounds like one of the safest bets you can make.

Parking near the casinos has also turned into quite a challenge, particularly if you want to find a space for less than five bucks. Depending on who you ask, the parking situation lies somewhere between a "nightmare" and "no problem." However, if you can't find a parking space in town, you should find success above Central City on the tailings or beyond. Several casinos provide free or inexpensive van service on the 1-mile route between Central City and Black Hawk. Here is a sampling of some of the more unique gambling establishments:

Glory Hole—
Make your way up to the fourth-floor Bottoms Up Bar at this plush casino and

you won't be disappointed. The view over town is tremendous and the decor classy. On the ground floor, perpetual live music jazzes up the atmosphere, and the long walnut bar makes a historic statement. Be sure to ask about the signature wall. This is the place to experience some of the best dining opportunities in town at Emily's fine dining (see Where to Eat). **131 Main St., Central City, CO 80427; (303) 582-1171.**

Lady Luck—
Although this casino has some of the worst ads in the history of television, the historic **Gold Coin Bar** adds some welcome variety and long-standing tradition to the casino-driven landscape. As they have done for many years, patrons still tack dollar bills to the bar's ceiling—"It used to be the locals would take them down and go on a collective binge with them," said the bartender. **120 Main St., Central City, CO 80427; (303) 582-1603**

Long Branch—
The casino somehow maintains a more local feel than most others. Its Western atmosphere comes with bleached cattle skulls and saddle-covered bar stools. **123 Main St., Central City, CO 80427; (303) 582-5896.**

Teller House—
Built in 1872, this stylish place sets the tone for the area's golden history. Even if

you don't feel like gambling, it's worth going inside and asking about a historic tour (see the Museums and Galleries section.) Swiss investors have converted it into an elegant casino complex, and more changes are in the works. The ground floor is split into several separate areas—you can gamble at slots and tables, drink at the long bar (cheap Sam Adams on tap; the faded but visible *Face on the Barroom Floor* nearby), or relax over a cup of espresso at the fancy atrium. With the second-floor renovation, the Teller House has added a restaurant and still more gambling space. **120 Eureka St., Central City, CO 80407; (303) 279-3200.**

FESTIVALS AND EVENTS

Lou Bunch Day
third Saturday in June

Although Central City had very few brothels in comparison with many other Colorado mining towns, each year the town holds a celebration in remembrance of their last known madam—Lou Bunch, who left town in 1916. On Lou Bunch Day, the townsfolk dress up in period costumes (heavy on the garters) and have a brass bed race through town. In the evening the Madams and Miners Ball takes place at the Teller House. All events are free except for the ball. For more information, call **(303) 582-5077.**

Summer Opera Festival
early July through mid-August

Since its grand reopening in 1932, the beautiful, historic Central City Opera House has been thrilling opera and theater lovers with its fine productions. Talented profes-sionals perform in two or three different productions at the oldest summer opera in the country. See the History section for more information on the opera house. For ticket information, contact the **Central City Opera House Association, 621 17th St., Suite 1625, Denver, CO 80293; (303) 292-6700.**

Central City Jazz Festival
third weekend in August

If you're a jazz lover, this international festival shouldn't be missed. Professional musicians (140 last year) from as far away as Europe converge on Central City for a long weekend of performances. With styles ranging from Dixieland to fusion, they play late into the night at local bars. On Sat. there is a parade through town. Expect a crowd if you come—Central City can get gridlocked during the festival. For information about ticket prices, call the Central City Jazz Society at **(303) 582-5563.**

OUTDOOR ACTIVITIES

FOUR-WHEEL-DRIVE TRIPS

Central City to St. Mary's Glacier—
This 10-mile drive takes you west through magnificent country rich in mining history. For detailed directions, see the Four-Wheel-Drive Trips section of the **Georgetown and Idaho Springs** chapter.

HIKING AND BACKPACKING

Taking off on a hike around Central City is not such a good idea. Locals are very careful not to wander off established roads and trails because of the vast number of mine shafts nearby.

Golden Gate Canyon State Park—

This beautiful mountain park offers miles of excellent hiking trails as well as a hut system for backcountry camping. For further information, see the Parks, Gardens, and Recreation Areas section in the **Denver and Environs** chapter.

SEEING AND DOING

CEMETERIES

In the hills around Black Hawk and Central City there are more than 10 cemeteries, complete with ornate Victorian tombstones. That's a lot of cemeteries. A couple of them can be easily reached from Central City by heading west on Eureka St. to the edge of town. You can't miss 'em. Please do not deface or remove any of the tombstones—you'll be slapped with a hefty fine if the locals don't lynch you first. For more information go to **City Hall** at **404 Eureka St.; (303) 582-5251.**

MUSEUMS AND GALLERIES

Central City and Black Hawk are packed with museums and historic buildings. Many of them are open during summer months only. No matter what time of year you visit, be sure to pick up a self-guided map of Central City and take a walking tour. You can pick one up at **City Hall** in Central City and at most restaurants.

Gilpin County Arts Association—

Since 1946 Gilpin County has helped sponsor the oldest juried art show in the state. An impressive display of work by Colorado artists includes everything from watercolor paintings to weavings. There is no admission charge. The art show runs from early June through the second weekend in Sept. Open daily 11 am–5:30 pm. **Box 98, 117 Eureka St., Central City, CO 80427; (303) 582-5952** in summer or **582-5574** in winter.

Gilpin County Historical Museum —

Located in an old stone school building, this museum contains a large historic collection of local memorabilia. The school was built in 1869 and classes were held until 1967. The Gilpin County Historical Society now owns the building and has packed both floors with interesting artifacts. Admission fee charged. Open daily Memorial Day–Labor Day 9 am–5 pm; open on weekends Sept.–Oct. **228 E. High St., PO Box 244, Central City, CO 80427; (303) 582-5283.**

The Lace House—

Built in 1863 by Lucien K. Smith, the Lace House is an excellent example of Carpenter Gothic architecture. Locals refer to it as the Gingerbread House. Ownership changed hands seven times until Evelyn Hume purchased it in 1943, intending to totally restore it. Hume wasn't able to accomplish the task, and after standing empty for a couple of decades, the Lace House was deeded to the town of Black Hawk in 1974. The town restored the Victorian house and furnished it with period antiques. Admission fee is charged. Open Memorial Day–Labor Day 11 am–5 pm; in winter by appointment only. **161 Main St., Black Hawk, CO 80422; (303) 582-5221** or **582-5382** in winter.

Lost Gold Mine—

Although it's somewhat of a tourist trap, complete with a gift shop and a singing ore cart at the entrance, the Lost Gold Mine does have some old mining equipment on display and you can walk 220 feet into the shaft. Part of the old National Bank Lode, the mine produced more than $56 million in gold beginning in 1860. Relics on display include drills, miners' hats and dynamite boxes. A fee is charged. Summer hours are 8 am–8 pm daily; winter hours are 10 am–6 pm daily. **231 Eureka St., Central City, CO 80427; (303) 642-7533** in Denver.

Teller House and Central City Opera House Tour—

When the railroad from Denver finally reached Black Hawk in 1872, construction had already begun on Central City's showpiece hotel—the Teller House. Built with local stone, the four-story masterpiece was furnished exquisitely, including luxurious carpeting in each of the 150 rooms. When President Ulysses S. Grant visited town in 1873, a special walkway was created out of silver bars, leading from his coach to the front door of the Teller House. In later years other celebrities, including Mark Twain and P.T. Barnum, stayed at the hotel.

Because it was built of stone, the Teller House survived the devastating fire in 1874 that ripped through Central City, destroying most of the buildings. When the adjacent opera house reopened in 1932, the Teller House and its famous bar also underwent a restoration. Twelve layers of wallpaper were peeled off the barroom walls, revealing the original murals. It was in 1936 that Denver newspaperman Herndon Davis painted the *Face on the Barroom Floor* while attending the summer opera with a lady friend. The face is still on the floor.

Tours of the Teller House have been sporadic due to a remodeling effort. You can tour the opera house daily throughout the summer for a small fee. **120 Eureka St., Central City, CO 80427; (303) 582-3200.**

Thomas-Billings House—

This well-preserved 1874 Victorian will give you a true sense of what life was like in Central City more than 110 years ago. You'll find everyday stuff in addition to the well-preserved treasures of one prominent local family. Guided tours on the half hour. Small fee. Open 10 am–4 pm Memorial Day–Labor Day. **209 Eureka St., Central City, CO 80427; (303) 582-5283.**

NIGHTLIFE

Since gambling was approved, nightlife has taken on new meaning. For information on casino action, see the Major Attractions section.

Summer Opera—

See the Festivals and Events section.

SCENIC DRIVES

Oh My Gawd Road (Virginia Canyon)—

A drive over Oh My Gawd Road is highly recommended. It leads south from Central City over the mountains to Idaho Springs, 9 miles away. To reach the road, follow Spring St. south past the train station and keep driving. For more information about the road, see the Scenic Drives section in the **Georgetown and Idaho Springs** chapter.

Peak to Peak Highway—

This gorgeous route was recently dedicated as one of Colorado's Scenic and Historic Byways. It begins at Black Hawk and heads north along the Front Range of the mountains for approximately 60 miles to Estes Park. Be sure to pick up a Peak to Peak brochure at the **Central City Hall (117 Eureka St.)** for a mile-by-mile description. For more information see the Scenic Drives section in the **Boulder** chapter.

—— WHERE TO STAY ——

ACCOMMODATIONS

With less than 50 beds in the entire vicinity, someone will likely build a first-class hotel in the near future. For now you have your choice of several small bed and breakfast inns. For information about most of the B&Bs, call the **Gilpin County Chamber** at **(303) 582-5077.** If you want to stay in an inexpensive motel, you might consider venturing to Idaho Springs. Here are a couple of good candidates right in the towns of Blackhawk and Central City:

The Shamrock Inn—$$$

Built more than 125 years ago by a Cornish miner, this small inn has recently been renovated, saving much of the original craftsmanship. Some of the door jambs are crooked, for instance, because the original builder of the house had no square. The inn is decorated with a combination of antiques and newer furnishings. On the main floor are the three smallish guest rooms with private baths; the room farthest from the street (a real plus) looks out on an impressive rock wall. A full complimentary breakfast is served in the main floor dining room. **351 Gregory St., Black Hawk, CO 80422-0137; (303) 582-5513.**

Winfield Scott Guest Quarters—$$$ to $$$$

Overlooking Central City from a beautiful hillside perch, Winfield Scott is an outstanding find—once you find it! The house is built entirely of "Hooper brick," which was used to reconstruct much of Central City after the fire of 1874. Guests have a choice of two well-designed suites in a separate, nearby building. A cozy bedroom, kitchen-in-a-closet, and a living/dining area comprise the tasteful design of the downstairs suite. The larger upstairs suite takes excellent advantage of natural light and has two bedrooms, a fireplace, kitchen and a wonderful deck. Both suites are beautifully furnished and provide a TV/VCR as well as a phone. The hosts have a small movie library and provide guests with a basket of tea, coffee, rolls, fruit and cereal. Gas grill available for outdoor cooking. No smoking; no pets; reservations only. **PO Box 369, Central City, CO 80427-0369; (303) 582-3433.**

CAMPING

In Arapaho National Forest—

The closest campground to Central City is **Columbine Campground,** located 2.1 miles northwest of town on County Rd. 279. It has 47 sites and a fee. From Black Hawk head 3 miles north on Hwy. 119 and 1 mile west to **Pickle Gulch Campground and Picnic Area.** This campground is reserved for groups only. There are 30 sites and no fee. For information call **(303) 567-2901.** Four miles north of Black Hawk on Hwy. 119 is **Cold Springs Campground and Picnic Area** with 47 sites and a fee.

Golden Gate Canyon State Park—

Located 7 miles north of Black Hawk on Hwy. 119 and 2 miles east on Gap Rd., Golden Gate Canyon State Park has 71 sites and a fee. There are also a few primitive campsites (no fee charged).

Private Camping—

KOA Kampground—Just 5.5 miles north of Black Hawk off Colorado 119, you'll find a little camping oasis and the only gas station in Gilpin County. With places for RVs and tents, this campground also features five small cabins. They have a pool, convenience and liquor stores and laundry facilities. **661 Hwy. 46, Black Hawk, CO 80422; (303) 582-9979.**

--- # WHERE TO EAT ---

Dining in Central City and Black Hawk continues to be in a state of total flux. Of the five restaurants we included in the last edition, only one remains: the Black Forest Inn. We can offer suggestions, but please keep in mind that for the most current information, you should inquire locally. To get you inside, most casinos offer some sort of fare—from Cajun to Cantonese—at extremely reasonable prices.

Black Forest Inn—$$ to $$$

Located conspicuously along the road in Black Hawk, this sprawling restaurant has become an institution among loyal locals and regular visitors from the Denver area. Since 1958 Bill Lorenz has been providing standout German cuisine and impeccable service that reflects years of training in his home country. German music, paintings and even a cuckoo clock add to the atmosphere. Aside from the Hungarian goulash, the lunch menu features mainly American-style dishes, including fresh Baja avocado stuffed with assorted seafood, chicken salad, sirloin burgers and steaks. For dinner start off with an appetizer such as a Russian egg—hard-boiled egg halves topped with lox, capers and caviar. Then sink your teeth into wienerschnitzel, sauerbraten, a seafood dish or the game special. Home-baked German sourdough rye bread goes well with all meals. Service at the Black Forest Inn is faultless, and Lorenz often makes the rounds to talk personally with the customers—a really nice touch. A fine, reasonably priced wine list offers selections from Germany, France and the US. Open 11 am–9:30 pm Mon.–Sat.; 11 am–8 pm on Sun. Located in Black Hawk; **(303) 279-2333** or **582-9971**.

Emily's Fine Dining Parlors—$$$

The setting couldn't be more conducive to intimate conversation. Tucked away from the din of the casino on an upper floor of the Glory Hole, you can truly relax in a small, private dining room. Chef Jake oversees the preparation of entrées such as amaretto shrimp, veal scallopini and roast prime rib of beef. The period antiques, low lighting, print wallpaper and historic photos all combine for a very positive dining experience. Wait staff in authentic Victorian costumes, including bustled dresses and plumed hats, complete the picture. Reservations recommended. Open every day during summer 5–10 pm. **131 Main St., Central City, CO 80427; (303) 582-1171.**

——————— SERVICES ———————

Gilpin County Chamber of Commerce—

This organization is looking for a permanent home, so you'll have to ask where they have relocated. The helpful staff should be able to answer your questions; you can also pick up some pamphlets and publications on the area. **(303) 582-5077.**

Transportation—

Van or bus service is perhaps the best way to travel between the Front Range and Central City/Black Hawk. Several casinos offer their own transportation in addition to the companies we have listed.

Ace Express—(303) 433-3613.

Gamblers Express—(303) 288-4170.

Mountain Delivery—(303) 433-2601.

For those who really want to go in style, here are a couple of limousine companies.

Colorado Limousine—1-800-628-6655 or **(303) 832-7155.**

Joker's Limousine Service—(303) 287-0397.

Metro Denver

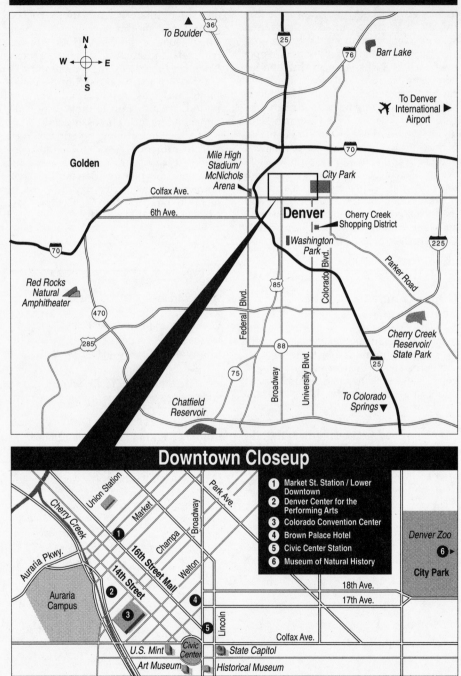

To Boulder

36

25

76

Barr Lake

N
W ← → E
S

To Denver
International ▸
Airport

70

Golden

Colfax Ave.

6th Ave.

Mile High
Stadium/
McNichols
Arena

City Park

Denver

Cherry Creek
Shopping District

Washington
Park

70

I-70

Colorado Blvd.

225

Parker Road

Red Rocks
Natural
Amphitheater

470

285

85

Federal Blvd.

88

75

Broadway

University Blvd.

Cherry Creek
Reservoir/
State Park

25

Chatfield
Reservoir

To Colorado
Springs ▾

Downtown Closeup

Union Station

Cherry Creek

Market

Champa

Park Ave.

Broadway

Welton

16th Street Mall

14th Street

Auraria Pkwy.

Auraria
Campus

1 Market St. Station / Lower
   Downtown
2 Denver Center for the
   Performing Arts
3 Colorado Convention Center
4 Brown Palace Hotel
5 Civic Center Station
6 Museum of Natural History

Denver Zoo

6 ▸

City Park

1

2

3

4

5

Lincoln

18th Ave.

17th Ave.

Colfax Ave.

U.S. Mint

Civic
Center

State Capitol

Art Museum

Historical Museum

Denver and Environs

As a friend once aptly described it, "Denver is a big lawn chair facing the mountains." Looking at most maps of Denver does give you the impression that the Rocky Mountains rise abruptly about 100 yards west of the city. Actually, Denver proper sits 15 to 20 miles from the mountains, located a mile above sea level on the high, arid plains. From many points in the city, though, you can see the hills of the high plains break a bit, then the foothills, followed by mountains towering far in the distance. On summer afternoons, thunderheads mix with the high peaks in a breathtaking display, dwarfing the city's downtown office towers.

Arguably the hub of the Rocky Mountain West, Denver is the largest urban center within a 600-mile radius. Perhaps this is why, over the years, it has been given such grandiose nicknames as the "Queen City of the Plains." Those unfamiliar with Denver tend to view it as either a dusty, riotous cow town or glamorous snow-covered capital of the mountains. Despite occasional dreams of equaling the importance of other urban heavyweights such as Chicago, residents for the most part understand that Denver is both cow town and regional business center; ties to western heritage allow for both high-tech office parks and perhaps the best stock show in the country.

Above all else, Denver is a very livable city with a high quality of life difficult to match elsewhere. One of the best things about living here has to be the balance of a normal work week with weekends at play in the nearby mountains. It's not necessary to head to the hills for a good time outdoors—the Denver area features some excellent parks and what many consider to be one of the finest urban trail systems in the country. With all of this going on, perhaps it's not surprising that the largest sporting goods store in the world (Gart Bros. Sports Castle) is located in Denver. Denver also has the second highest number of college graduates per capita and, for some unknown reason, the highest movie attendance in the US.

Early in 1994, Denver increased its importance as a national transportation center with the opening of the enormous new Denver International Airport. At 53 square miles it's the largest commercial port in the world. Denverites are still coming to grips with the added drive time to get to the new complex, which some joke is so far east from the Metro area it's in Kansas.

Denver hosts a diverse ethnic population. You can find well-established Italian, Jewish, Greek and Japanese communities, usually in particular neighborhoods. The western part of the city reveals Colorado's Hispanic roots in its street names and large Hispanic population. Denver also has a very strong African-American community, centered in the old Five Points area northeast of downtown. The nationally recognized Black American West Museum and Heritage Center, located in this part of the city, brings alive a long-neglected part of American history. Neighborhoods such as Park Hill have about a 50-50 African-American and Anglo mix. Korean, Thai, Laotian and Vietnamese immigrants are building strong communities in the city—the excellent Asian restaurants and markets on S. Federal Blvd. are definitely worth a visit. With its diverse neighborhoods, Denver enjoys a vitality unknown in racially homogeneous cities. Various festivals celebrate ethnic heritages.

The city's cultural diversions might not match those of Chicago, New York or Los Angeles, but there is still plenty to do within the city limits. More than 2,000 restaurants can be found throughout the city, and the Denver Center for the Performing Arts (DCPA), the second largest of its kind in the country, has given the arts community something to sing about. The arrival in 1993 of the Colorado Rockies major league baseball team helped round out an exciting year-round choice of professional Denver sports teams—along with the Denver Broncos and the Denver Nuggets.

There are tried-and-true tourist destinations in Denver—the gold-domed capitol, an impressive granite miniature of the US Capitol; the US Mint with its boullion and machine-gun turrets above a Florentine palace's passageways; or the Molly Brown House with its unusual style of western Victoriana. The abundant museums explain themselves for the most part, and serviceable bus tours leave no obvious stone unturned. Worth noting: Lower Downtown (LoDo), located at the historic north-western edge of downtown, has made a dramatic comeback from skid row to the city's hippest restaurant, entertainment and gallery district. But Denver also has other, hidden enjoyments. Therefore, our mission is to illuminate the unusual corners of Denver—places a Denver cousin would show you only if you never betrayed her to the relatives. Denver's history is intriguing, and many of its lessons are relevant today.

HISTORY

In the spring of 1858, Georgia prospector William Green Russell and 12 companions found gold dust on a tributary of the South Platte River, near present-day Englewood (a suburb of Denver). Though they were only panning $10 each per day and the gold soon ran out, news of a rich strike in the Rockies blew out of proportion and spread east. Enthusiastic miners began making their way west with the slogan "Pikes Peak or Bust."

When the gold played out on the Platte, members of Russell's party moved down the river to a grove of cottonwood trees at the confluence of Cherry Creek and the South Platte and erected a few cabins at Auraria (named after Russell's hometown in Georgia). Across the river from Auraria, the St. Charles Town Company, headed by Charlie Nichols, staked out another town. A group from Leavenworth, Kansas, led by Gen. William Larimer, jumped the St. Charles claim, infuriating Nichols. But Gen. Larimer and his Kansas group held firm, telling Nichols to quit complaining or they would use a noose on him. Since the area at the time was all part of the Kansas Territory, the group named their new town Denver City, after the Kansas territorial governor, James W. Denver. This was done with hopes it would stroke Denver's ego enough to ensure the group's claim to the site. These circumstances surrounding the establishment of Denver angered the residents of Auraria, and an intense rivalry between the two towns lasted for years.

At this time a band of Arapaho Indians remained in the area, observing these strange newcomers who were trespassing on Indian land. Although the land around Denver had been guaranteed to the Arapaho in the Fort Laramie Treaty of 1851, the Indians remained friendly to the settlers for the first couple of years. Historian Thomas Noel recalls, "Arapaho warriors left their women and children in Denver while they made war on the Utes in the mountains. After returning, the Arapaho invited Denverites to their dog feasts and Ute scalp dances."

Miners arriving in 1858 and early 1859 were greeted with outrageously high prices for supplies and found no gold in the streams; many returned east in disgust. In the spring of 1859, however, a rich strike at Central City in the mountains west of Denver rekindled the rush to the area. This time it was real. Denver grew because it was a way station for miners headed to the mountain camps. Those who decided to stay in Denver in these early days comprised a tough, independent group. A noteworthy representative was William Byers, from Omaha, Nebraska, who had written a guidebook to the Pikes Peak region, compiled after hearing stories from miners returning from the Colorado gold fields. When Byers came to Denver, he brought his printing press with him. Quite aware of the feud between Auraria and Denver, Byers set up a newspaper office on the banks of Cherry Creek, between the two towns. His newspaper, the *Rocky Mountain News*, made an immediate impact on Denver when it first appeared on April 23, 1859, gaining a wide readership and fueling further migration of people from the East.

As gold strikes in the mountains increased, Denver continued to grow. In these early years, Denver developed a reputation as a tough, dusty frontier town that disgusted many mannerly visitors. After a trip to early Denver, Horace Greeley, editor of the *New York Tribune*, wrote that in Denver there were "more brawls, more pistol shots with criminal intent than in any other community with equal numbers on Earth."

In the early 1860s relations with the Arapaho and Cheyenne soured when the Indians refused to comply with terms of the new Fort Wise Treaty of 1861. The Indians attacked settlements on the plains and hindered freight shipments to Denver. This clash of Anglo and Indian culture culminated with the brutal massacre of peaceful Arapaho and Cheyenne at Sand Creek in 1864 (see the Southeast Plains chapter). When the territorial troops returned to Denver from the massacre site, the *Rocky Mountain News* reported, "Cheyenne scalps are getting as thick as toads in Egypt—everyone has got one, and is anxious to get another to send east." The Indians retaliated, once again attacking settlements on the plains and cutting off Denver's supply routes for a couple of months before troops squelched the uprisings once and for all.

In the mid-1860s the Union Pacific dealt Denver a severe blow when it chose to lay its transcontinental railroad tracks through Cheyenne, Wyoming, 100 miles to the north. Denverites believed their town was doomed without a railroad. Through the efforts of William Byers and Gov. John Evans, $280,000 was raised by 1867 to finance a railroad spur to the railhead in Cheyenne. The Denver Pacific Railroad was completed in June 1870, followed by the Kansas Pacific, which had laid tracks across the prairie from Kansas. With efficient rail transportation, Denver's population soared from just over 4,000 to 35,000 in one decade. Along with the gold mining towns in the mountains, silver mining districts began thriving—especially Leadville. Times were good in Denver; it was the major supply center not only for the gold mining towns and the metropolis of Leadville, but also for the growing cattle industry of the plains and agricultural towns in the Platte and Arkansas river valleys. In the 1880s many rich miners and cattle barons built mansions in the Capitol Hill area of Denver. Their deep pockets and desire to outdo their neighbors spawned unique sandstone palaces characterized by turrets, bays and leaded-glass windows. Many of these mansions still grace Denver's neighborhoods.

Despite this new money and Denver's development, an unrefined image persisted. The town had, as Walt Whitman described it, "plenty of people, business, modernness—yet not without a certain racy wild smack all its own." This wasn't helped by the town's notorious red-light district on Market St., called "The Row." So seductive was this decadent area that one day, in June 1880, the town council didn't conduct any business—too many council members were attending the grand opening of a new house on "The Row."

In 1893 the price of silver plummeted, and along with it, Denver's fortunes. Many mines closed and 10 Denver banks went under. Denverites were confronted with a grim reality—their future was tied too closely with that of the mining industry. If Denver was to continue to grow and prosper, it needed to diversify its economy. In the second half of the 1890s, a huge gold strike at Cripple Creek gave another boost to the economy, but looking to the future, the town helped finance agricultural research and started to realize how well suited it was for tourism. With constant reminders from a new paper in town—the *Denver Post*—about the town's potential, Denver entered a new era, trying to forget the hard times that had accompanied the mining decline. One of the first things Denver did was to clean up its act. The brothels were closed and, under the direction of Mayor Robert Speer, parks (complete with statues and fountains) were built, streets were laid out and 18,000 trees were planted. When Speer died in 1918, Denver had undergone a remarkable transformation from a dusty cow town to a green, well-planned city.

Of course Denver's growth hasn't been a smooth, easy glide from 1918 to the present. Rather it has been somewhat lurching, sometimes stagnant, but always reflective of Denver's optimism. After World War II, Denver entered a new period of expansion—one that many felt was too fast. The tide turned in 1972 when the state resoundingly voted down a chance for Colorado to host the Winter Olympics. Residents were wary of overdevelopment, higher taxes and a change in their comfortable, uncrowded lifestyle. Times were good for most of the state, with Denver well on its way to becoming a major trade and distribution center. Vast oil and coal reserves attracted hundreds of small firms and many national giants. In the early 1980s new downtown office towers were going up at an incredible rate, with as many as 15 cranes dotting the skyline at once.

Growth seemed to be the mandate as the city teemed with a too-good-to-be-true excitement. After the oil glut in the mid-1980s, the economic vulnerability of Denver was once again exposed. An incredibly high percentage of office buildings stood vacant after the building frenzy ran its course. Today, along with its role as a manufacturing and trade center, the Mile High City has positioned itself as a transportation hub for the country with the recently opened Denver International Airport. The good economic times in Denver are indicative of a recent *Time* magazine cover story: "Boom Time in the Rockies."

GETTING THERE

Although Denver's geographically central location has always made it easy to visit by air, the recent opening of **Denver International Airport** has made traveling here easier still. Daily nonstop flights to 109 cities (1,300 flights), including some in Europe, make the new airport one of the busiest in the world. Flights to many towns and resorts around the state are available as well. Though some locals are grumbling about the long drive to the airport, it's actually only 23 miles from downtown. Head east on Interstate 70 past Interstate 225 and turn north on Pena Blvd. For information call **(303) 342-2000**. **Greyhound Bus Lines** maintains daily bus schedules from all parts of the country to Denver and several of the larger ski resorts. Their main terminal is in downtown Denver. For information about schedules and fares, call **1-800-231-2222**.

Denver's historic **Union Station** is still a railroad hub for **Amtrak**. Six daily arrivals and departures serve Los Angeles, San Francisco, Seattle and Chicago. Trains also make daily stops in Winter Park, Glenwood Springs, Grand Junction and other Colorado towns. For train information call **(303) 297-3000** or toll free **1-800-872-7245**. Denver can also be reached by car from New Mexico to the south and Wyoming to the north via Interstate 25; from Utah to the west and Kansas to the east via Interstate 70; and from Nebraska to the northeast via Interstate 76.

FESTIVALS AND EVENTS

The National Western Stock Show and Rodeo
mid-January

This one is big—really big. For two weeks cattlemen and cattlewomen from around North America attend the largest livestock exhibition in the world. Stetsons and cowboy boots fill the town; horse trailers pull up to the doors of the luxurious Brown Palace Hotel and the doorman doesn't bat an eye. When the stock show is on, all other bets are off. Some of the events include pro and amateur rodeos, livestock judging and horse shows. You can easily spend a few hours roaming the grounds. If you want to stay at a hotel in Denver during the stock show, make your reservations well in advance. For information about the schedule of events and tickets, call **(303) 297-1166**. All shows take place at the recently renovated and improved **Denver Coliseum (4600 Humboldt St.)**, just off Interstate 70 at the Brighton Blvd. exit.

Capitol Hill People's Fair
late May

For one weekend each May over 100,000 Denverites from all walks of life flock to **Civic Center Park** to enjoy the People's Fair. The huge crowd, with a life of its own, ebbs and flows around the statues, past the four music stages and up and down rows of over 500 booths. Everyone walks these aisles, sampling Greek gyros and therapeutic teas, browsing through Krishna cookbooks and tomes on palmistry, signing petitions and greeting members of the Denver Broncos. You can discuss the intricacies of an embroidered dress with a seamstress and the virtues of Libertarianism with a true believer. Virtually every band in Denver spends an hour on a stage. It all happens between the Capitol and the City and County Building. Don't miss it, and bring an umbrella. **(303) 534-6161**.

Cherry Blossom Festival
first weekend in June

Sakura Square, at **19th Ave. and Lawrence St**. downtown, houses several Japanese shops, a Buddhist temple, a tea room and a high-rise apartment building. In early June the Cherry Blossom Festival makes this place as crowded as Tokyo at rush hour. The festival revolves around the Buddhist temple, which contains a large collection of painted Buddhist statues and features several performances of the tea ceremony. The basement houses displays of bonsai, the delicate art of growing and pruning miniature trees, along with several other Japanese arts. In the monastery you will find an incredible array of Japanese foods, including sushi and chicken teriyaki. Music, plays, dances and martial arts demonstrations succeed one another in the square itself. Everything is authentic, especially the enthusiastic welcome you receive from the residents of Sakura Square. For information call **(303) 295-0305.**

Colorado Renaissance Festival (in Larkspur)
weekends in June and July

At this re-creation of medieval England, a costumed lass or lad will ambush you for a kiss. As you approach the wooden fortifications surrounding King Hal's domain, be prepared to pay homage to His Highness as you quaff an ale and devour an enormous drumstick. And beware the fool, who makes quick work of anyone who challenges his wit. A host of merchants vie for your attention with wares from strange lands. The brave engage in feats of strength and the agile balance themselves on rope contraptions. The festival runs on weekends only; fee charged. Drive south on Interstate 25 for 25 miles to the town of Larkspur; **(303) 688-6010.**

Cherry Creek Arts Festival
4th of July weekend

Located amidst the blocks of shops just north of Cherry Creek Shopping Center, one of Denver's newest festivals energizes the city over the long 4th of July weekend. Stop by to see the work of over 200 carefully selected artists, chosen from more than 1,600 applicants. This has quickly developed into one of only a handful of the finest outdoor juried art shows in the nation. Over 250,000 people make their way to the three-day show to get a look at the work of some of the finest artists in the country and listen to excellent live music. The "Creation Station" arts education station for kids has been a big hit. So has the guy who performs his "art attack" by messily painting a canvas to the rhythm of Mozart and Beethoven— infinitely more enjoyable than watching Richard Simmons "Sweat to the Oldies." **(303) 355-2787.**

Festival of Mountain and Plain— A Taste of Colorado
Labor Day weekend

In 1895 Denverites first gathered to celebrate the recovery from the 1893 silver crash and to pay tribute to the strengthening economies of the mountains and plains. The week-long festival, patterned after Mardi Gras, was highlighted by a number of parades. Today the festivities last only a few days but still draw a large crowd—a couple hundred thousand. Scores of arts and crafts booths fill Civic Center Park just west of the State Capitol. The main attraction is the "Taste of Colorado," featuring food from the area's finest restaurants. Live local and nationally known bands perform throughout the festival. For information call **(303) 295-7900 ext. 102.**

Broncomania and Other Sports Phenomena

Each Sunday afternoon in fall, Denver's shopping malls are deserted, streets are empty and the orange sunset over the mountains takes on a slightly brighter hue. What's going on? A **Denver Broncos** football game, what else? Most Denver residents (or Colorado residents for that matter) have their eyes glued to the TV, while the lucky few (75,000) pack into Mile High Stadium to cheer the Broncos and jeer the opponents, creating ear-splitting decibel levels. Without question, Denver fans are the most rabid pro football fans in the country. The games at the stadium have been sold out for years, but people are usually selling extra tickets at the entrance gates.

To the delight of many a hard-core baseball fan, the **Colorado Rockies**, Denver's new major league baseball team, took the field for the first time in spring 1993 ... shattering all single-season attendance records and fielding a very respectable expansion team. The Rockies will continue to entertain fans at Mile High Stadium until their much-touted new stadium (Coors Field) is completed and ready for the 1995 season. For ticket information call **(303) ROCKIES.**

Just south of Mile High Stadium is McNichols Arena, home to the **Denver Nuggets** pro basketball team. Nuggets games run from Nov. to May; tickets are available at the box office, or by calling **(303) 893-3865.**

Other Festivals

There is always some sort of festival in Denver. **Cinco de Mayo** (5th of May) is one of the biggest celebrations in town, especially among the Hispanic community. The **Greeks** have theirs in June on the grounds of the Greek Orthodox Cathedral. **Old South Gaylord Street** celebrates in May, and **Oktoberfest** floods Larimer St. with beer in Sept. In fall the **Denver International Film Festival** draws large crowds, including critics and famous actors. For information and specific dates on these and other festivals, contact the **Denver Metro Convention & Visitors Bureau** at **(303) 892-1112.** Perhaps the best source for week-to-week happenings in Denver is *Westword*, a free newspaper available virtually everywhere in town. Weekend sections of the Friday daily newspapers (the *Denver Post* and *Rocky Mountain News*) are also good sources.

── OUTDOOR ACTIVITIES ──

GOLF

Tee off at well over 35 public golf courses located in the Denver metro area. In winter Denver receives its share of snowfall, but much of it melts off rather quickly. Most courses stay open year-round, weather permitting. Here are a few of our favorites.

Arrowhead Golf Club—

Located among the jutting cathedral-like red rocks near Roxborough Park, this course is an unforgettable golfing experience and, frankly, its beauty can be distracting. Arrowhead was designed in 1970 by Robert Trent Jones, Jr., who considers the course among his favorite six in the world. The interesting layout snakes its way through the rocks and troublesome scrub oak following the natural contours of the land. Its 76 sand traps and six lakes keep golfers challenged. The 13th hole is a standout—a par three that drops 95 feet to the green. Be sure to club down or you'll end up in the lake just behind the green. Reservations a must. Pro shop, driving

range and restaurant. Located southwest of Denver, south of Chatfield Reservoir. **10850 W. Sundown Trail, Littleton, CO 80125; (303) 973-9614.**

Hyland Hills Golf Course—

Hyland Hills is extremely popular, and with good reason. The challenging course is kept in great shape by the greens crew. Holes are long, with lakes and ditches often coming into play. The eighth hole is particularly dangerous—a 526-yard straightaway is lined on the left by a lake, and a ditch crosses the fairway just in front of the green. In addition to an 18-hole course, there is another nine-hole course and two par three courses. **9650 Sheridan Blvd., Westminster, CO 80030; (303) 428-6526.**

Lone Tree—

Once an exclusive private club, this excellent course at the extreme south end of the metro area is now open to the general public. The course is well named; you'll have to contend with very few trees. But ponds, creeks and sand traps all combine to create plenty of challenge. Views from the course to the mountains west of the Denver area are fantastic. **9808 Sunningdale Blvd., Littleton, CO 80124; (303) 799-9940 or 790-0202.**

Meadow Hills Golf Course—

Meadow Hills is one of the finest all-around public courses in the Denver area. The course is very mature, with lots of cottonwood, pine and elms lining the fairways. Greens fees are reasonable to boot. With relatively few sand traps and three lakes, you can score well if you keep to the fairways. The resident Canada geese, however, can be distracting and they don't show much fear. Located in Aurora, just east of Cherry Creek Reservoir. **3609 S. Dawson St., Aurora, CO 80014; (303) 690-2500.**

Riverdale Dunes and Knolls—

Although Riverdale is considered part of the Denver metro area, it feels as if you're out in the country. Don't worry about distracting construction or traffic noise ... there isn't any. Located near Brighton (northeast metro area), the two courses at Riverdale have developed quite a good reputation. A series of irrigation canals characterizes Riverdale's original Knolls course, and water comes into play on 13 holes. The newer Dunes course, finished in 1985, plays like the wide, open Scottish links with rolling hills and natural grass roughs. On the Dunes there are many water hazards; railroad ties border the greens and tee boxes. Located 8 miles southwest of Brighton next to the Adams County Fairgrounds. **13300 Riverdale Dr., Brighton, CO 80601; (303) 659-6700.**

Wellshire Golf Course—

Located in south Denver, Wellshire is another fine, mature course. One of the oldest in the city, it was a country club until Denver purchased it in the 1940s and opened it to the public. Wellshire plays long (6,592 yards), but the small number of lakes and traps helps your score. Trees are everywhere. Views west to the mountains

accompany you on many of the holes. After your round, stop in at the pub or have a meal at the excellent Wellshire Inn restaurant (see the Where to Eat section). Located at the intersection of Hampden Ave. and Colorado Blvd. **3333 S. Colorado Blvd., Denver, CO 80210; (303) 757-1352.**

ICE SKATING

Evergreen Lake—

For decades this lake has been popular for ice skating. At the skating center, you'll find a snack bar, rental skates and shelter from the cold. The lake usually opens for skating by Christmas on a daily basis and remains open afternoons, evenings and weekends after the holidays, weather permitting. Fee charged. To reach Evergreen from Denver, head west on Interstate 70 about 20 miles to the Evergreen Parkway exit. From the exit drive 8 miles southwest on Hwy. 74 to Evergreen. **(303) 674-2677.**

PARKS, GARDENS AND RECREATION AREAS

Cheesman Park—

Cheesman has the most unified and serene landscaping in the city park system, with a wonderful view of the mountains. It's one of the nicest spots within the city to attend a free summer concert. For current schedules, call **(303) 331-4029.** You owe yourself a stroll around the perimeter and a nice rest in the Greek-style pavilion, a remnant of the "City Beautiful" campaign launched early this century. You'll walk past some of Denver's most impressive houses, some of which open directly onto the park. Originally the city cemetery, this land was converted into a park in the 1890s. A massive project to re-inter the remains in other graveyards in town ensued, but sloppy workers desecrated many of the graves. To this day many of the surrounding homes as well as the park itself are believed to be haunted. Cheesman Park is located next to the Denver Botanic Gardens just north of **8th Ave.**, between **Humboldt** and **Race** streets.

Cherry Creek State Park—

The Res' is one of Denver's most popular destinations, especially on scorching summer days. In the summer of 1993 it also proved to be one of the world's most popular destinations as nearly half a million faithful descended on Cherry Creek Reservoir to attend Mass—delivered by Pope John Paul II. Rumor has it he may have blessed the park.

Located on the high plains about 10 miles southeast of downtown Denver, Cherry Creek offers plenty of hiking and, primarily, water sports. Good warmwater fishing (from the bank and from boats), windsurfing, sailing and waterskiing are all very popular. Boat rentals are available at **Cherry Creek Marina (303) 779-6144.** In addition, many people hang out on the meager 250-yard strip of sand (what we in Colorado call a beach) and dip their toes in the water. Families with small kids and bikini-clad teenagers ply the sandy northeast edge of the reservoir under the watchful eye of lifeguards. On summer weekends you start feeling like a human sardine. During the week though, this area can provide a nearby peaceful getaway. Cottonwood trees protect 102 campsites in several designated campgrounds; all charge a fee. The east entrance to Cherry Creek Reservoir is 1 mile south from Interstate 225 on Parker Rd. For more information, contact **Cherry Creek State Park, 4201 S. Parker Rd., Aurora, CO 80014; (303) 690-1166.**

City Park—

The grounds of this large park contain the zoo, Natural History Museum, a golf course and three lakes. When it was completed in 1881, a buggy ride into the country was necessary to reach the park. The designer of the English Gardens in Munich and Hyde Park in London also laid out this Victorian idealization of nature. Statues of Robert Burns and Martin Luther King show how much the park has stretched to contain the changing dynamics of Denver. On the west side people polish their cars, radios blasting, while on the east side you can stroll through a large rose garden. Paddle boats can be rented at one of the lakes. Tall pine trees, grassy areas and views to the mountains make City Park a popular place for many residents. Located north of **17th St.**, between **Colorado Blvd.** and **York St.**

Denver Botanic Gardens—

The Denver Botanic Gardens offer more visual and olfactory pleasures than any other place in the city. You may recognize the futuristic buildings from Woody Allen's movie *Sleeper*. The enormous glass honeycomb of the conservatory dominates your initial view of the grounds. Under the enclosure grows a lush forest of carob, cocoa, banana and hundreds of other trees and shrubs. In winter there is no better place to remember that spring is coming than in the orchid room when it catches the afternoon sun. If you walk to the far western end of the grounds, the Japanese garden, mountain flora path and alpine gardens offer wonderful contours, textures and scents—even in February. On a warm winter day (and such days are common), the goldfish swim below small stone shrines beside the shore of the lake in Shofu-en, the Garden of Pine Wind.

In summer the Japanese garden is the most peaceful spot in Denver. The stream flows under a small wooden bridge, edged with irises in every shade. Bamboo spouts trickle water onto polished gray stones, and a family of ducks fights its way up a small waterfall. On occasion the Japanese tea ceremony is performed in the lovely teahouse near the east gate. The schedule is arcane, but worth inquiring about. A lingering walk through the pine grove brings you to the alpine garden, which is particularly fine in May and early June. This is one of the most important and extensive collections of alpine plants in the world, with colors as vivid as any hybrid created with the gloved hand. You'll also see blossom-laden peonies, extensive rose beds, water lilies, a sensuous garden of the plants of the

Bible, an even more sensuous herb garden, several well-conceived sculptures and fountains and, from late May through July, an explosion of irises.

On many summer nights, KCFR, a local public radio station, hosts concerts in the grassy amphitheater on the grounds. The gift shop has a fine selection of books and a wonderful collection of Chinese and Japanese porcelain. The gardens remain open until dusk on Wed., Sat. and Sun., June – Aug. Otherwise, the hours are 9 am–4:45 pm daily. **909 York St.; (303) 331-4010.**

Denver Greenway Trails —

The South Platte River bursts out of Waterton Canyon southwest of the metro area and winds a slow, meandering course through the heart of Denver. Since 1974 an extensive redevelopment has taken place, and today the river is traced by a well-used cement recreation path. Numerous other recreation trails, over 130 miles total, feed into the Platte trail at various locations throughout the metro area. The core path currently stretches over 20 miles from Chatfield State Park (see write-up in this section) to the northern reaches of the metro area, and will eventually reach Barr Lake State Park (see write-up). Several small parks and even a wildlife sanctuary are situated along its route, as well as historic markers that share interesting tidbits about people and settlements that once occupied the riverbanks. Along the path you'll have pleasant views of the river, interspersed with thick stands of cottonwood and willows (despite ongoing problems with tree-gnawing beavers).

At historic Confluence Park, along the river path in central Denver, is where Cherry Creek and the South Platte merge. It was here that a mining encampment in 1859 grew into a tent city and, eventually, Denver. It's because of the odd northwest angle of Cherry Creek that the downtown grid runs frustratingly askew: The streets were originally laid out to run parallel to the creek, directly facing Longs Peak. At any rate, from Confluence Park an excellent bike path breaks away from the main Platte Trail, tracing Cherry Creek, eventually reaching Cherry Creek State Park (see write-up in this section). For an excellent map of the Denver Greenways, contact the **Colorado Division of Parks and Outdoor Recreation, 1313 Sherman St., Rm. 618, Denver, CO 80203; (303) 866-3437.**

Washington Park—

Springtime brings Denverites outside in eager hordes to this favorite gathering place. Not only is it a beautiful park with mature trees and wide grassy expanses, but it also has a couple of lakes that provide fishing, and the old Denver Canal still flows here. Both kids and adults love all the diversions: recently renovated indoor swimming pool and gym facilities, several tennis courts, jogging paths and two large playgrounds. The playgrounds are wheelchair accessible; one offers a superstructure of ramps and slides, all atop soft wood chips. Though speed limits have been established, bicyclists and rollerbladers whir around and around the park road in their neon lycra.(Cars are prohibited on most of the park's roadways.) Other activities on a warm sunny day range from horseshoes to hackeysack volleyball, ultimate Frisbee to kite flying. On the west side of the park, bordering Downing St., a barrage of flowers blooms in intricate gardens. A replica of George Washington's garden at Mt. Vernon adorns the north bank of Grasmere Lake. The quaint old boathouse with its newly refurbished pavilion is available for most any occasion. What many consider Denver's premiere park lies to the east of **Downing St.** between **Virginia Ave.** and **Louisiana Ave.**

NEARBY

Barr Lake State Park—

Twenty miles northeast of Denver, off Interstate 76, you'll find a haven for birds and birdwatchers. Although the lake once served as a storage lake for Denver area sewage, the South Platte River flooded in 1965, "flushing the reservoir like a toilet." More than 300 species of birds have been spotted at the lake, including herons and cormorants which nest in trees along the lake shore. Other common sightings include owls, falcons, geese and nesting bald eagles. The nature/visitors center provides excellent information.

A 9-mile trail encircles the lake, and boardwalks extend out over the water to strategic birdwatching areas and observation blinds. The gazebo is a great place for a picnic, especially on a weekday when you can have the lake to yourself. Sailboats, hand-propelled craft and boats with electric trolling motors are allowed. Warmwater fishing can be good for perch, bass and an occasional trout. From Denver, drive 20 miles northeast on Interstate 76. Entrance fee charged. **13401 Picadilly Rd., Brighton, CO; (303) 659-6005.**

Castlewood Canyon State Park—

Lying 30 miles south of Denver, this scenic canyon park is a bit of a surprise, contrasting with the surrounding prairie hills. The park is a great place to hike, rock climb, watch for wildlife or just get away from the city. Cherry Creek meanders north through Castlewood Canyon, which is characterized by steep sandstone walls and the remains of an old dam, Castlewood Canyon Dam, built on unstable ground in 1890 for Denver-area water storage, burst in 1933, flooding the Cherry Creek drainage all the way to the Platte River at Denver.

A series of canyon and rim hiking trails take you through ponderosa pine, douglas fir, aspen and gambel oak, providing great views along the way. A recently completed Visitor and Nature Center at the park's south end is worth a stop for maps, information and maybe even a ranger-led walk. To reach the main park entrance from Denver, take Hwy. 83 about 6 miles south of Franktown. The north entrance can be reached by heading a quarter of a mile west from Franktown on Hwy. 86 and then left (south) on County Rd. 51 for 3 miles. Picnic tables; wheelchair accessible. Fee charged. **PO Box 504, Franktown, CO 80116; (303) 688-5242 or 688-5242.**

Chatfield State Park—

This reservoir built along the South Platte River as a flood control effort offers every watersport except surfing. The Army Corps of Engineers didn't foresee how popular it would become with boaters, but today there are over 250 slips for yachts and sailboats. It's also a great place for swimmers, fishermen, scuba divers and windsurfers. Landlubbers enjoy the foothills location for hiking, biking (along the Denver Greenway Trails—see write-up), horseback riding (rentals available), sunbathing and birdwatching. Chatfield is an excellent bird habitat—a veritable holy ground for birdwatchers. The nature trails are very nice, and the arboretum and heron rookery (complete with a newly built observation area) cement this lake's position as one of the best stops in the Denver area. In winter, try the decent ice fishing. You might want to call **B & B Livery** for horseback rides at **(303) 933-3636,** or the **Chatfield Marina, (303) 791-7547.** For those of you prone to urban camping, 153 campsites are located along the shore; all charge a fee. To get here drive south on Interstate 25 to C-470. Take C-470 west to the Wadsworth Blvd. (Hwy. 121) exit and go south on Hwy. 121 beyond the Army Corps of Engineers entrance to the park entrance. **11500 N. Roxborough Park Rd., Littleton, CO 80125; (303) 791-7275.**

Devil's Head—

Located in the Pike National Forest southwest of the Denver metro area, Devil's Head is a beautiful escape for city folk, especially in the fall. Although a lot of people choose to make a weekend out of it, Devil's Head is close enough to town to do in a day. Its craggy profile is easily visible along the Front Range. The main attractions are the huge rocks strewn about the forest, thick aspen groves and the easy 1.5-mile trail up to the Devil's Head Fire Lookout.

The well-marked trail begins at Devil's Head Campground and climbs 948 feet through ponderosa pine and Douglas fir forests. Perched atop a giant granite outcropping at the summit is the fire lookout, an enclosed station that was the last of its kind along Colorado's Front Range. Visitors are welcome to climb the stairway and enjoy the spectacular 360-degree view from the lookout. Be sure to bring your camera.

Devil's Head Campground is a popular weekend destination, with 22 sites; a fee is charged. Some other campgrounds can be found in the area also. To reach Devil's Head from Denver, head south on Hwy. 85 from Littleton for 10 miles to Sedalia. At Sedalia head west on Hwy. 67 for 9 miles and then left (south) on Rampart Range Rd. for 9 miles. Rampart Range Rd. is closed in the winter. For a scenic drive, continue south on Rampart Range Rd. to Woodland Park. From Woodland Park you can return to Denver by heading east on Hwy. 24 to Colorado Springs and then north on Interstate 25.

Golden Gate Canyon State Park—

Within 45 minutes of Denver, you can surround yourself with beautiful, rolling, forested terrain of the Front Range—an ideal year-round escape from the city. Spring brings out a barrage of wildflowers in lush meadows, including columbine; fall is highlighted by golden hillsides of aspen. Roads traverse the outer portions of this 10,550-acre park, while the unspoiled interior can be reached only on foot or horseback. Fishing for rainbow trout on its well-stocked streams can be quite good. Nearly 60 miles of marked hiking trails wind through the park, providing perfect day outings. After winter storms these trails make excellent, meandering cross-country ski routes. Stop by the Visitors Center on Golden Gate Canyon Rd. just inside the southeast entrance for a look at exhibits on the park's ecology, geology and plant life. Open daily 8 am–4:30 pm, year-round. Rangers can help you plan your visit and give you a trail map. In summer a full-time naturalist leads walks and gives campfire talks.

Golden Gate Canyon State Park offers many planned campgrounds. All charge a fee and usually fill up on summer weekends; advance reservations can be made by calling **(303) 470-1144** in Denver or **1-800-678-CAMP** statewide. **Reverends Ridge Campground** (106 sites), in the northwest corner of the park, provides laundry and hot showers to campers. **Aspen Meadows Campground**, with 35 tent sites in the north central portion of the park, is much smaller and less developed. There are 23 backcountry sites (including a number of Appalachian-style log huts) that appeal to hikers who want to get away from camping alongside the road—a permit must be obtained for these sites; no fires are allowed.

We were happy to learn that the state recently acquired 3,600 acres of the adjacent Green Ranch to be set aside exclusively for backcountry use.

To get to the park from Denver, take Interstate 70 west to the Hwy. 58 exit. Stay on Hwy. 58 for 5 miles west to Washington Ave. (Golden exit). Turn right (north) for 1.5 miles to Golden Gate Canyon Rd. Turn left (northwest) and drive 13 miles to the park entrance. The visitors center is inside the park boundary along Ralston Creek. For more information contact **Golden Gate Canyon State Park, 3873 Hwy. 46, Golden, CO 80403; (303) 592-1502.**

Mount Falcon Park—

In the foothills just west of Denver, 1,400-acre Mt. Falcon Park offers easy day hiking and superb mountain biking. Almost 10 miles of hiking trails provide choice views of Denver, Red Rocks Park and Mt. Evans. But the park also has an interesting history, beginning at the turn of the century with the story of wealthy dreamer John Brisben Walker.

The founder of *Cosmopolitan* magazine, Walker owned a 4,000-acre estate that included a stone castle on Mt. Falcon. His grandiose idea was to build a summer White House on Mt. Falcon for presidents to use. One source of funding included 10-cent donations from thousands of Colorado school children. Unfortunately, construction never got beyond the laying of the foundation and cornerstone. World War I caused delays, as did Walker's personal financial problems. The crushing blow came in 1918 when his own home was destroyed by fire. Walker died penniless in 1931 at age 83.

Remnants of his once-impressive home and the "Western White House" can still be seen along the hiking trails in the park. After a big snowstorm, Mt. Falcon is a great place to cross-country ski. To reach the park from Denver, head southwest on Hwy. 285 about 14 miles to the Indian Hills exit (Parmalee Gulch Rd.). Drive north for about 3.5 miles and turn right at the Mt. Falcon Park sign and proceed 1.8 miles to the parking area. For more information about the park, contact **Jefferson County Open Space, 700 Jefferson County Pkwy., Suite 100, Golden, CO 80401; (303) 278-5925.**

Red Rocks Park—

Red Rocks Amphitheater, located in Red Rocks Park just west of Denver near the town of Morrison, is a sight to behold—where else can you see golden and bald eagles perching where the Beatles once performed? This amphitheater, surrounded by towering 400-foot red rocks, was completed in 1941 by George Cranmer, Denver's legendary manager of improvements and parks. Nature had finished about three quarters of the work in this natural bowl, but the 8,000-seat theater left something to be desired acoustically. After a few years of dissonant complaints, Cranmer went to Germany at his own expense to consult with Wolfgang Wagner, son of the great Richard Wagner himself. Cranmer wanted to hear Richard Wagner's operas at Red Rocks, and he wanted to hear them right. Wagner came and adjusted the theater to the acoustic satisfaction of everyone, gallantly refusing to be paid.

These days, rock and roll, country and other popular music concerts pack the place during summer evenings. Both musicians and spectators love the amphitheater for its unique location and the spectacular panoramic view of Denver spreading over the plains. Aside from the summer concerts, the amphitheater remains virtually empty except for the Easter sunrise service (attracts thousands each year) and occasional stray musicians.

A number of fine hiking trails wind through the 2,700-acre park, and it's a great place for a picnic. Although it's tempting to climb around, stay off the rocks—park rangers are quick to dole out stiff fines to anyone challenging this rule. To reach Red Rocks Park from Denver, head west on Interstate 70 to the Morrison exit and drive south to the entrance to the park. Call **(303) 575-2637** for more information.

Roxborough State Park—

Spectacular razor-backed rocks marching along the face of the foothills are the dominant characteristic of Roxborough State Park. Miles of hiking trails take you through lush meadows and between rocks created over millions of years by stream-deposited sand turned reddish from iron compounds. Both prairie and mountain species grow in this unique setting—aspen next to yucca and scrub oak and, in the spring, a diversity of flowers. Bobcats, deer, elk and coyotes roam the hollows, and eagles circle overhead when rainfall is short.

One trail leads you to a small cabin built with hopes of turning this place into a resort four generations ago. Fortunately, the residents of Denver weren't quite up to making the trip on a regular basis. In another instance, a subdivision was planned amid the dramatic rocks, but as luck (and perhaps fate) would have it, the company went bankrupt before any houses could be built. Today everyone can enjoy the miles of nature trails in this dramatic environment; in winter Roxborough is a place of solitude and wonder. After a snowstorm it's best explored on touring skis. The Visitors Center blends perfectly into the landscape—inside you can look at the exhibits and participate in educational programs. Rangers often lead trail hikes and interpretive nature walks. Entrance fee charged. From Denver take Santa Fe Dr. (Hwy. 85) south to Titan Rd. Turn right and proceed 3.5 miles and left (still on Titan Rd.) another 3 miles to a marked entrance to the park. **4751 N. Roxborough Dr., Littleton, CO 80125; (303) 973-3959.**

Waterton Canyon—

This steep canyon, formed by the rushing waters of the South Platte River, has endured a number of major changes. The first was in 1877, when narrow-gauge tracks were laid through the canyon by the **Denver South Park & Pacific Railroad**. Then came Strontia Springs Resort, which catered to Denverites escaping the city for the weekend. The most drastic change occurred in 1983, when a large portion of the canyon was flooded by the Strontia Springs Reservoir. Though the reservoir has forever changed its character, Waterton Canyon remains an excellent recreation area close to the city.

Southwest of Denver a dirt road leads 6 miles to the base of Strontia Springs Dam alongside the South Platte River. Fishing for large rainbow and brown trout in the tailwaters of the dam has been excellent. The road into Waterton Canyon also marks the start of the Colorado Trail, which leads 469 continuous miles to Durango in the southwestern corner of the state. This road ends at the former site of Stevens Gulch at the base of the dam. From here a 10-mile hiking (and horse) trail leads to the confluence of the North and South forks of the South Platte River (near the ghost town of South Platte). Along the way watch for bighorn sheep. To reach the start of Waterton Canyon, drive south on Interstate 25 to C-470; west on C-470 to Wadsworth Blvd. Turn south on Hwy. 121. Continue past Chatfield Reservoir to the start of the service road (near the Martin Marietta plant).

Since the controversial Two Forks plan to dam the river has died out, the South Platte will continue to flow through a beautiful, wide valley while providing some of the finest trout fishing in Colorado. A dirt road follows this fork of the river up Cheesman Canyon to the small town of Deckers; the entire valley is fairly heavily used with a lot of fishing, camping and hiking on public land. Cheesman Canyon and the South Platte River can be reached from Denver by hiking a portion of the Colorado Trail up Waterton Canyon. Or drive south on Hwy. 285 for 32 miles to Pine Junction, then south on County Rd. 126 for 25 miles to Deckers.

SWIMMING

Celebrity Sports Center—

This giant indoor pool also features water slides. For more information see the Amusements section.

Denver Parks and Recreation—

In parks around the metro Denver area, 28 recreation centers are open to the public. The centers don't all have pools, but there are 15 outdoor and eight indoor pools scattered around the city. For information on hours and exact locations, call **(303) 964-2500.** Other city park pool numbers include **Englewood (303) 762-2575, Lakewood (303) 987-7800, Littleton (303) 798-2493, Aurora (303) 695-7200, Thornton (303) 538-7310, Westminster (303) 430-2400,** and **Wheat Ridge (303) 234-5929.**

Water World—

Surfing in Colorado? It's possible at this monstrously large summertime hangout. Hundreds of sun and water worshippers turn out each day for rides down slides, through the innertube rapids and on the waves in the wave pool. This place provides excellent summer fun for kids of all ages. Get into your suit and break out the suntan lotion. Open Memorial Day–Labor Day, **1850 W. 89th Ave., Federal Heights, CO 80221; (303) 427-SURF.**

TENNIS

Free courts can be found at parks throughout Denver. The city puts out a free listing of all public park facilities. For more information on tennis courts in Denver, call **(303) 964-2522.** Here are a few ideas.

City Park—

Six brand-new, lighted courts have been added to the existing six courts. Located at **23rd St. and York.**

Crestmoor Park—

Four courts are located within this quiet park, and they are often open. **E. Center Ave.** at **Monaco Pkwy.**

Huston Lake Park—

Play tennis next to a lake on one of four courts. **W. Kentucky Ave.** at **S. Vallejo St.**

Rosamond Park—

These four courts are usually open. The park is located in the vicinity of the Tech Center at **E. Quincy Ave.** and **S. Tamarac Dr.** If they happen to be full, travel north on Tamarac Dr. for a couple of miles to Bible Park where there are four more courts.

Washington Park—

The 10 lighted courts on the south and west sides of the park are often crowded, but it's a great central location. **E. Louisiana Ave.** at **S. Humboldt St.**

--------- SEEING AND DOING ---------

AMUSEMENTS

Celebrity Sports Center—

This one building houses an 80-lane bowling alley, a billiard parlor, three large rooms filled with video games, three huge water slides, a swimming pool, bars and restaurants. There's probably more, but you get the idea. You'll even find free child care. The whole family can give in to a quarter-spending addiction. You may leave bleary-eyed, blinking at the sun like vampires who have made a dreadful mistake, but the kids will love it. **888 S. Colorado Blvd., Denver, CO 80222; (303) 757-3321.**

Elitch Gardens Amusement Park—

Elitch's has graced Denver since 1890, when the gardens were planted on the high plains northwest of town. Mary Elitch, whose husband died a year after the park opened, is one of Denver's heroines. She kept her prices low and her gardens inviting, offering a vast array of concerts and children's programs for free. She never forgot the children of the poor. For a time in the early 1900s Elitch's was the cultural center of Denver, providing the only access to classical music and light opera. Today all your favorite rides are here, along with islands of flowers and a feeling that this is what amusement parks were meant to be. This is where banjos and straw hats belong. Ride the Twister, rated one of the best roller coaster in the world by roller coaster aficionados. A variety of ticket options are available. It should be noted, however, that a major move and expansion of Elitches is pending—be sure to call ahead. Open weekends April-May, daily from late May-Labor Day. **4620 W. 38th Ave., Denver, CO 80212; (303) 455-4771.**

Lakeside Amusement Park—

Yes, Denver has two very old amusement parks. Smaller than Elitch's, Lakeside has some great attractions, including the Cyclone Coaster and the vintage carousel. They don't make amusement parks like this one any more. Open on weekends in May and then from 6 pm daily June–Labor Day. Look for the high bell tower and the lake just south of Interstate 70 at Sheridan Blvd. **4601 Sheridan Blvd., Denver, CO 80212; (303) 477-1621.**

Tiny Town—

Located on 20 acres in the mountains southwest of Denver, this unique place is just what the name implies—a tiny town. Miniature churches, fire stations, houses and schools line the streets, fascinating children and, yes, adults too. Tiny Town also features a diminutive railroad. Small fee charged. Open 10 am–4 pm on weekends in May and Oct.; 10 am–5 pm daily June–Sept.; limited Dec. hours. From Denver, head southwest on Hwy. 285 about 5 miles past the Morrison exit and turn left onto South Turkey Creek Rd. You'll see the Tiny Town sign from the highway. For more information contact the **Tiny Town Foundation, 6249 S. Turkey Creek Rd., Morrison, CO 80465; (303) 790-9393, 697-6829.**

Water World—

See the Swimming section.

BREWERY TOURS

Coors Brewery Tour—

Each year 350,000 visitors head to Golden for a free, half-hour tour of the world's largest single brewing facility. Small groups of 14 people wander through, looking at the immense 13,000-gallon copper kettles in which the beer is blended, heated and filtered. You'll also get a chance to look at the malting, quality-control and packaging departments. The best part is saved for last: The tour ends in the tasting room where visitors (of age) can sample a fresh, ice-cold glass of free Coors on tap. With advance reservations, tours are available in foreign languages and for those with hearing and mobility limitations. Open 10 am–4 pm Mon.–Sat. **13th St. and Ford St., Golden; (303) 277-BEER.**

Buffalo Herds

Once they numbered in the millions. After settlers made their way west and their 50-year buffalo slaughter ended, barely 1,000 of the furry beasts remained. Luckily, buffalo hunting was finally outlawed. Today their numbers have increased to more than 30,000 throughout the West. A couple of Denver mountain parks contain herds that are usually easy to see. The most accessible place is just off Interstate 70, 20 miles west of Denver at the Genesee Park exit. Daniel's Park, 20 miles south of Denver, has the largest herd. To reach Daniel's Park from Denver, head south on Interstate 25 to County Line Rd. and head west to Daniel's Park Rd. Turn left and proceed to the park.

HISTORIC BUILDINGS

Denver has a cache of historic buildings, hidden away on residential streets and garishly displayed on busy avenues. Organized tours are available at certain times during the year with **Historic Denver Inc., 1330 17th St., Denver, CO 80202; (303) 721-7716.** Pick up a Historic Walking Tour map of Denver at the downtown **Visitors Bureau, 225 W. Colfax.** The *Mile High Trail,* offering directions for six downtown walking tours, is available for a small fee.

Colorado State Capitol—

Modeled after the US Capitol, this venerable building differs from its eastern cousin in its smaller, gold-plated dome and gray granite. Completed in 1908, a full 18 years after the cornerstone was laid, the state capitol sits impressively on a hill overlooking Civic Center Park, commanding an excellent view of the mountains. As well it should—a law forbids high-rise buildings from blocking this view. The 13th step on the west side announces that it is precisely a mile high (a disputed measurement, by a few feet).

Inside, the workmanship is impeccable, with beautiful native marble, brass banisters and vaulted ceilings. Perhaps the most impressive detail is the rose onyx wainscotting throughout the building; so much was needed for the job that the state supply was totally depleted! Above the legislative chambers, stained-glass representations of governors and early settlers illuminate the proceedings. Informative tours begin inside the west entrance and eventually lead you up the spiral staircase from the third floor to the dome for spectacular views of the city and mountains, as well as a dizzying view down into one of the rotundas. But the best show is inside when the legislature is in session (mid-Jan. through mid-May). In small enclosed rooms just off the senate and house floors, lobbyists vie for the attention of legislators. Or you can go into the basement cafeteria where you'll see more of the same politicking in progress. Informative brochures available. Tours are given in summer on the half hour 9:15 am–3:00 pm Mon.–Fri.; 9:30 am–1:30 pm on Sat.; call ahead for winter hours. **1475 Sherman St., Denver, CO; (303) 866-2604.**

Governor's Mansion—

Walter Cheesman, an early settler and Denver's first pharmacist, built this house for his family at the turn of the century. He died before its completion, but not before he had ensured that the grounds were terraced to rival the most innovative gardens in Europe. At one time he owned the site of the future capitol, where he and his neighbors grazed their cattle. Cheesman was an opportunist, however, whose name should not be attached to philanthropy—that was his wife's doing after he died.

Mrs. Cheesman and her daughter lived in the house until 1926, when they sold it to Claude Boettcher. Claude's father, Charles, had the foresight to bring a trunk full of sugar beet seeds home to Colorado after a trip to Europe, thereby founding the sugar beet industry in northern Colorado. From this enterprise he diversified into other businesses with incredible success. When Claude bought the Cheesmans' house, which promptly became known as the Boettcher house, he assured them that it would be maintained and that he would continue to add to the collection of art. He remained true to his word; in addition, the Boettcher family eventually donated the mansion to the state. Most of the house remains as Cheesman designed it, including the large library and lounge off the main hall. Across the hall is an enormous dining room, which now suits the needs of all of Colorado's first families. The house has particularly striking pieces of oriental art. The chandeliers are superb works of crystal and porcelain.

The pride of the house, however, is the 60- by 70-foot Palm Room, added by Boettcher. Its white marble floor, white stone columns and white furniture give the room a feeling of great airiness. Palm trees accent the room; large windows open out to Cheesman's terraced garden. Free limited 20-minute tours of the mansion are given on Tues. afternoons May–Aug. and during the Christmas season; call **(303) 866-3682** for information.

Grant-Humphreys Mansion—

In 1902 James B. Grant, a former governor, completed this 42-room mansion at a cost of $35,000. An Alabama boy, Grant wanted to live in an antebellum mansion. Since he had the money, he went ahead and built it here in Denver. The house is furnished with a billiard room, bowling alley, auditorium and an enormous ballroom. Mahogany ceiling beams adorn rooms up to 60 feet long. When Grant died in 1911, the house came into the hands of another southerner, Albert Humphreys. The new owner's family kept up the proud traditions of the house, though it never became the governor's mansion as Grant had hoped. Today it's all still there, including a grand staircase. Although much of the home is being used for office space, a tour of the mansion is worth your time. The house is open from 10 am–2 pm Tues.–Fri. Admission charged. **770 Pennsylvania St., Denver, CO; (303) 894-2506.**

MUSEUMS AND GALLERIES

Black American West Museum and Heritage Center—

Finally, the story can be told: Nearly one third of all cowboys in the western US were black. This museum, located in the heart of Five Points, tells the history of blacks in the West in various roles as cowboys, doctors, barbers, legislators and teachers. It's a fine place to get a feel for this segment of our history, through artifacts, historic photos and, if you're lucky, through a real live legend. When we visited, Alonzo Pettie strode through the door. A spry 78 years old, decked out in a Levis jacket and cowboy hat, Alonzo told us his story, that of growing up in east Texas and breaking horses on a ranch. He didn't break only horses—while riding in various rodeos he broke his pelvis, shoulder and crushed his knuckle, too. Stop by for a visit. Small admission fee. Open 10 am–2 pm Wed.–Fri.; 12–5 pm on Sat.; 2–5 pm on Sun. **3091 California, Denver, CO 80205; (303) 292-2566.**

Buffalo Bill's Grave and Memorial Museum—

Perched atop Lookout Mountain, just west of Denver, you'll find the final resting place of William F. Cody, better known as "Buffalo Bill." Cody personified the Wild West, having been a pony express rider, scout for the cavalry and quite a buffalo hunter. He got his nickname from the thousands of buffalo he killed. In the late 1800s he achieved international fame with his Wild West show, which toured throughout the US, Canada and Europe. He died at his sister's home in Denver in 1917 and, after a six-month delay, was buried on Lookout Mountain, despite protests from Nebraska and Wyoming claiming Cody had wanted to be buried in their states. To make sure his grave wasn't robbed by miffed residents of either state, it was covered with concrete and reinforced with steel bars. When Cody's wife died, however, workers bashed away at the concrete in order to put Mrs. Cody's coffin on top of her husband's—quite an ironic end for a man who spent much of his life avoiding his wife!

Along with his grave is a museum containing much of Buffalo Bill's memorabilia. An observation deck on top of the museum gives you a great view of the mountains to the west and the Denver area to the east. Small fee charged. To reach the grave and museum from Denver, drive west on Interstate 70 about 15 miles and get off at Exit 256. Follow the signs up Lookout Mountain Rd. to the turn-off. If you continue on Lookout Mountain Rd. for about 7 miles you'll reach Golden. More scenic than the interstate, this road provides a spectacular bird's-eye view of Golden. Open May–Oct. 9 am–5 pm, Nov.–Apr. 9 am–4 pm; closed Mon. in winter. **(303) 526-0747.**

Byers-Evans House—

Historians never second-guess the legendary accomplishments behind the historic names Byers and Evans. The fact that both prominent Denver families occupied the same house is a quirk of fate that does not go unnoticed at this fine museum. Built in 1883 by William N. Byers, founding

editor of the *Rocky Mountain News*, the home was purchased six years later by William Gray Evans, son of Colorado's second Territorial Governor. Kept in the Evans family for three generations, this two-story home recently fell into the caring hands of the Colorado Historical Society, which has restored the home to reflect the 1912–1924 period.

Begin the tour by viewing the 20-minute videotape of Denver's history, an interesting prelude to the home tour. Look around the deceptively large house and you begin to make sense of its many additions. Most of the Evans's furniture remains, including the detailed wooden bookcases in the sitting room. Be sure to notice the parlor's intricately painted ceiling, which was discovered under layers and layers of ordinary house paint. Small admission fee. Open 11 am–3 pm daily except Tues. Located at **1310 Bannock Street** adjacent to the Denver Art Museum; **(303) 620-4933,** or **620-4795.**

The Children's Museum—

If you don't have a child of your own, borrow one and go out for a great time at one of the best museums in town. Displays here are meant to be touched, prodded, pulled and played with, all with the purpose of teaching children (and adults) the inner workings of processes and machines. Shop at the smallest grocery store in the world, complete with automatic price scanner (no coupons accepted). Watch the youngsters shriek with delight while "dry swimming" in two rooms full of plastic balls or spend time in the Three Bears' House. Check out the outdoor playground and ski hill (lessons available). Puppet shows are popular, as are various seasonal exhibits. You'll enjoy the trip as much as the kids will. Open daily 9 am–5 pm; closed Mon. in winter. As you drive by on Interstate 25, you can't miss the museum, across the highway from Mile High Stadium; it's the brilliant green building with a pyramid roof. You may want to consider parking a few blocks away (along the Platte River) and taking the trolley, which passes right by the museum. **2121 Children's Museum Dr., Denver; (303) 433-7444.**

Colorado History Museum—

Colorado's history really comes to life at this fine museum, run by the Colorado Historical Society. The well-organized museum is home to many artifacts and great dioramas depicting Colorado's colorful history—from detailed and accurate Indian gatherings to a display of Denver's disastrous flood in 1864. There are photographs and artifacts of the Indian wars, the massacres, the pioneers and miners, the bars, brothels and early residents. It's as complete a gathering of state history as can be housed under one roof. Take your time and enjoy. Don't miss the fine book shop with a wide selection of Colorado books. Located in the wedge-shaped building just southwest of the State Capitol. Open Mon.–Sat. 10 am–4:30 pm, Sun. noon–4:30 pm. **1300 Broadway; (303) 866-3681.**

Colorado Railroad Museum—

Train buffs will love this large collection of locomotives, cabooses and other railroad cars scattered about a 12-acre yard. Some real gems are kept in this back lot—many of the silent trains are open for anyone to climb aboard and pretend. Take a close look at the D&RG Engine No. 346, the oldest operating locomotive in Colorado, or the Galloping Goose #2, a strange-looking contraption built with various parts from a Buick, Pierce Arrow, Ford truck and a railroad engine. Inside the re-created depot, old photos and exhibits of Colorado's railroad history are displayed. Downstairs, the scale model HO train running through a miniature world is a child's dream. Open daily 9 am–6 pm in summer, 9 am–5 pm in winter. Take exit 265 off Interstate 70 in Golden and follow the signs. **17155 W. 44th Ave., Golden; (303) 279-4591.**

Denver Art Museum—

At first glance, this castle-like structure looks displaced among the office buildings and city hall. A castle it's not, but rather a repository of great artwork, including one of the finest Native American collections in the country. It's also home to fine, recently ugraded displays of Asian, pre-Columbian and Spanish Colonial art collections. The American floor houses Thomas Cole's *Dream of Arcadia,* a masterpiece of the Hudson River School. Several Picassos, Monets and a Klee add strength to the European collection. Beware of *Linda,* resident art critic and patron—she's the lifelike sleeper/statue found on the floor of the contemporary section.

The museum hosts popular Wed. night parties, with music and open exhibits. Fashionable with the city's elite and singles, these gatherings provide a good time. A restaurant ($ to $$) is open for lunch and, though service is not provided at lightning speed, the food is fairly tasty. The gift shop contains some worthwhile items, including a decent book section and merchandise that reflects traveling exhibits. Open Tues.–Sat. 10 am–5 pm, Sun. noon–5 pm; closed Mon. **100 W. 14th Ave. Pkwy.; (303) 575-2793.**

Denver Firefighter's Museum—

One of the best-kept secrets in town, this place is unknown even to many natives. Learn about Denver's history as well as the history of firefighting. The museum houses old fire engines and fire equipment. Don't worry, you don't have to slide down the pole to the exit. Open Mon.–Fri. 11 am–2 pm. **1326 Tremont Pl.; (303) 892-1436.**

Denver Museum of Natural History—

The granddaddy of museums in Denver, this museum is probably best recognized for its traveling exhibits and innovative, extensive dioramas of animals in their natural habitats. This was the first museum to use such displays (some of which were built in the 1930s as WPA projects). It holds the world's largest mammoth fossil, scaring small children and adults alike as they round the corner to a room filled with tusks and teeth. Dinosaur skeletons—especially that of Tyrannosaurus Rex—seem to roar in mid-stride at visitors, and a whale skeleton swims in dry air.

Ornithologists and butterfly enthusiasts will be delighted with the collection of North American birds and butterflies. A walk through the mineral collection mimics a journey into an underground cavern, complete with fluorescent rocks and samples from Colorado's richest mines and mills (be sure to look for "Tom's Baby"). The museum generally hosts several traveling exhibits (check the schedule for current offerings). There is a cafeteria, restaurant and gift shop. Admission fee charged. Open daily 9 am–5 pm. **2001 Colorado Blvd.; (303) 322-7009.** The museum includes two other attractions that can make a visit here exceptional.

The **IMAX Theater,** located at the east entrance of the museum complex, is truly one of those places where the viewer becomes part of the film. The theater features a four-story screen with a state-of-the-art sound system. The screen can become the Grand Canyon, outer space, the stratosphere or Stonehenge. Go where the filmmaker wants to take you, and nobody will get hurt. Call **(303) 370-6300** for prices and show times.

Located on the west side of the building, the **Gates Planetarium** features traditional astronomical displays, including views of the night sky as it appears in all hemispheres and in all seasons. Occasionally, spectacular laser shows get the normally staid planetarium rocking to the music of Pink Floyd, U2, the Beatles or whomever the laser projectionists are moved to feature. Call **(303) 370-6351** for prices and show times.

Forney Transportation Museum—

This large collection of antique cars, motorcycles, trains and planes is housed in the cavernous fairly run-down Denver Tramway Powerhouse Building, built in 1901. Older Denver natives mourn the demise of the trams, much as Brooklynites wish the Dodgers were still home ... but the past can still be seen here at the museum. More than 300 vehicles fill the powerhouse and grounds outside, but the real darling of the collection rests on its own rail spur. The "Big Boy" is one of the few existing examples of the large steam locomotives that opened the West. Open Mon.–Sat. 10 am–5 pm, Sun. 11 am–5 pm. Fee charged. To reach the museum, take Exit 211 off Interstate 25 and turn east on Water St. If you are coming from downtown, take 15th St. west to Platte St. and turn left. **1416 Platte St.; (303) 433-3643 or 433-5896.**

Four Mile Historic Park—

Just a stone's throw from the neon lights and strip joints of the Glendale area, the Four Mile Historic Park provides an interesting look into Denver's past, including the oldest structure in metro Denver. The Four Mile House, built in 1859, operated for years as a stagestop along the Cherry Creek branch of the Smokey Hill Trail. It then went on to become the highly successful ranch/farm of the Booth family. Today 14 acres, including the original house, outbuildings and equipment, serve as a living history museum, representative of the period 1859–1883. Feel free to stroll the farmstead, where you can see draft horses, chickens and crops in the garden. Guides in period costumes add much to the visit and tour of the house. Programs throughout the season encourage children's visits. Also, this has to be the only place in the Denver metro area where you can take a stagecoach ride. Small fee. Open April–Sept. Wed.–Sun. 10 am–4 pm. **715 S. Forest St.; (303) 399-1859.**

Littleton Historical Museum—

Your kids will beg you to return again and again to this wonderful 1860s homestead and farm museum. You'll also find three art galleries featuring changing exhibits. In addition to the farmhouse, look for the schoolhouse, blacksmith shop, smokehouse and a bunch of barnyard animals. No charge. Open 8 am–5 pm Mon.–Fri.; 10 am–5 pm on Sat.; 1–5 pm on Sun. **6028 S. Gallup St., Littleton, CO 80120; (303) 795-3950.**

Mizel Museum of Judaica—

This small museum has a fine reputation for its fascinating changing exhibits.

Anyone interested in Jewish artifacts from around the world should call ahead to see what the museum is showing. Past displays have ranged from ancient Middle Eastern artifacts, to a wonderful collection of hats, to photos from the lost world of the European Jews. Open Mon.–Thurs. 10 am–4 pm, Sun. 10 am–noon. No fee. The entrance is on the east side of the building. **560 S. Monaco Pkwy.; (303) 333-4156.**

Molly Brown House Museum—

Built in 1889 by one of Denver's great architects, William Lang, this Colorado sandstone and lava stone home is a Victorian masterpiece. J.J. Brown, husband of one of the state's most colorful characters, Molly Brown, bought the mansion in 1894 with money made from his famous Little Johnny gold mine.

For years Molly sought acceptance by Denver's high society, but her image as a hell-raising country bumpkin worked against her. Her heroism during the sinking of the Titanic gained her international fame, the nickname "Unsinkable Molly" and, finally, acceptance in Denver. (The gift shop has what must be one of the largest inventories of Titanic memorabilia around.)

Today, tours of the home are given by women dressed in turn-of-the-century costumes. Stone lions guard the entrance, and the interior is decorated in velvet, lace, beautiful dark wood and period furniture. Although the Brown's personal furniture was sold at auction in the 1930s, the museum is buying back much of it. At Christmas time the decorations transform the entire house into something more than a historical landmark. Open Mon.–Sat. 10 am–4 pm, Sun. noon–4 pm; closed Mon. in winter. Fee charged. **1340 Pennsylvania St.; (303) 832-4092.**

Museum of Western Art—

Home to one of the finest Western art collections in the country, this museum is housed downtown in the historic Navarre Building. In the 1890s, its convenient location across the street from the historic

Brown Palace Hotel allowed it to serve beautifully as a high-class bordello and gambling house. Subterranean passageways between the two buildings ensured "discretion in all transactions." The wonderful art includes more than 100 paintings and bronzes by the likes of Bierstadt, Moran, Remington and Georgia O'Keeffe. It's difficult to imagine a better marriage of history and art. Open Tues.–Sat. 10 am–4:30 pm. **1727 Tremont Pl.; (303) 296-1880.**

United States Mint—

This building where US coins are made resembles a Florentine palace inside and out. Inside the mint you'll be treated to a guided tour that explains coin production and also stops before a stack of gold bullion—the mint is the third largest gold repository in the country. Near the end of the tour, the guide might point out the antiquated machine-gun turrets, installed after the stock market crash of 1929 to make sure things didn't get out of hand. Forever afterward you'll check for the little "D" below the date on your pennies. Open daily 8 am–3 pm (Wed. 9 am–5 pm). Located on the corner of **W. Colfax Ave**. and **Cherokee St.; (303) 844-3582.**

NIGHTLIFE

Most visitors do not come to Denver specifically for its late-night and cultural diversions. Some travelers have been quick to decry the lack of big-city lights and late-night (after 2 am) restaurants and bars. But visitors generally will be pleased with Denver's ever-increasing diversity of places to eat, drink and be happy. Downtown Denver is bordered by a couple of areas worth considering: Lower Downtown (LoDo) and the Uptown area along 17th Ave. The jazz scene is flourishing and the Denver Center for the Performing Arts adds a vitality to the cultured side of this so-called "cow town." If you feel like a night of country-western dancing or comedy, there are a number of choices. For a complete listing of events and entertainment in the metro area, pick up a free copy of *Westword*, or consult either the *Rocky*

Mountain News or *Denver Post* Friday editions. Here are a few suggestions.

Arapahoe Park Race Track—

From May–Sept., make the trip to this outlying track for live pari-mutuel horse betting. Year round you can wager on horse and greyhound races which appear via satellite feed from other tracks around the country. For parents with kids that might get antsy watching the races, don't worry...there's a large video arcade. Call ahead for days and post times. **26000 E. Quincy; (303) 690-2400.**

The Boiler Room—

Located in the old Tivoli Brewery, this is a beer lover's dream. Many beers on tap as well as in bottles. Great place to watch TV sports and throw peanut shells on the floor. Ten-minute walk to Mile High Stadium. **901 Larimer; (303) 893-5733.**

Brew Pubs—

Colorado produces more beer than any other state. Along with the Coors and Anheuser-Busch breweries, Denver offers a number of excellent micro breweries/pubs.

Breckenridge Brewery in **Denver** provides good views of its brewing operation from just about every seat in the place. Five tasty house brews on tap; food including appetizers, sandwiches, burritos. Added feature: located across the street from the new Coors Field stadium where the Colorado Rockies will play beginning in 1995. **2220 Blake St.; (303) 297-3644.**

Rock Bottom Brewery is extremely popular with the downtown lunch crowd and for after-work fun. In addition to their great selection of freshly brewed beer, the menu features pretty tasty items (try the chicken potpie). Live jazz Thurs.–Sat. nights; great location on 16th St. Mall; outdoor patio seating, weather permitting. **1001 16th St.; (303) 534-7616.**

Wyncoop Brewing Company has become a Denver institution and remains our favorite of the Mile High City's brew pubs. Housed in the historic J.S. Brown Mercantile

Building in lower downtown, this esteemed and extremely popular brewpub is known not only for its wide selection of home-made brews but also for its relaxing atmosphere. Try the stout, wheat, amber ale or bitter brew. If you can't decide, try a reasonably priced, 6-ounce sample of each. It's a comfortable place to knock down a couple and enjoy a meal of bangers and mashers (traditional English sausage simmered in stout beer and mashed potatoes). Maybe you'd prefer black-bean cakes and brown rice or the spicy green-chile stew. If you enjoy pool, this is the place to be: A second-floor pool hall with at least two dozen tables could be the best place to kill a few hours. Brewery tours on Saturday afternoons. Open Mon.–Sat. 11 am–2 am, Sun. 11 am–12 am. **1634 18th St., Denver; (303) 297-2700.**

Cafes—

The coffee culture has caught up with Denver. In just the past few years, new java joints have been sprouting up all over the city. They offer various atmospheres to fit your mood. The most dense concentration of cafes can be found in Cherry Creek North, amidst Denver's most exclusive shopping district. Stop in at **Starbuck's, 2701 E. 3rd Ave.; (303) 331-9910,** the Seattle-based chain, for its primo blends of rich coffee and classy environment. You might also head a couple of blocks southeast to **Peaberry's, 3031 E. 2nd Ave.; (303) 322-4111,** for a slight change of pace. Both places have indoor and patio seating. Newshounds should head straight to the **Newsstand Cafe, 630 E. 6th Ave.; (303) 778-7070,** for a strong, steaming cup of coffee and a great selection of newspapers and periodicals. If you're wondering where the beret-and-bongo crowd hangs out in Denver, make a beeline for **Muddy's Java House, 2200 Champa St.; (303) 298-1631,** or **Paris on the Platte, 1553 Platte; (303) 455-2451.** These coffee house/used bookstores provide comfortable settings for people to sit and explore the outer limits of their intellect—or at least make it appear that way. **The Market, 1445 Larimer St.; (303) 534-**

5140, in Larimer Square continues to be a popular gathering spot. In the Washington Park area, stop in at **Stella's, 1476 S. Pearl St.; (303) 777-1031.**

Comedy—

If you feel like some laugh therapy, stop by the **Comedy Works,** featuring local acts and national headliners nightly. New talent and improvisation takes the stage on Tues.; closed Mon. Located in Larimer Square at **1226 15th St.; (303) 595-3637.** If you are staying in the Tech Center area or the south part of town, consider the equally funny **George McKelvey's Comedy Club.** Open Tues.–Sun.; new talent and improv on Tues. nights. **10015 E. Hampden Ave.; (303) 368-8900.**

Concerts—

For big-name concerts, Denver has three major venues: **Red Rocks, (303) 640-7334** (see the Parks, Gardens and Recreation Areas section for more information), and **Fiddler's Green, (303) 220-7000,** are outdoor theaters open in summer only; **McNichols Sports Arena, (303) 640-7333,** is open year-round. On a smaller scale, **The Paramount Theatre, (303) 892-7016,** in downtown Denver, and the **Arvada Center for the Arts and Humanities, (303) 431-3080,** both attract national acts. **The Botanic Gardens, (303) 331-4000,** and the **Denver Zoo, (303) 331-4110,** both also host summer concerts ranging from classical to World Beat—they usually sell out. Both locales are gorgeous places to hear music while sipping a glass of wine and polishing off a picnic dinner. Purchase tickets for most major events through **Ticketmaster (303) 290-TIXS,** or stop by the English double-decker **Ticket Bus** on the **16th St. Mall** at **Curtis St.** For more information see the Parks, Gardens and Recreation Areas section.

Country Dinner Playhouse—

Located near the Tech Center, off Interstate 25 at the southern end of the metro area, this dinner playhouse is consistent if not spectacular. A buffet dinner is followed by a full-scale musical production. After the "Barnstormers" perform some country music and square-dance numbers, the stage descends from the ceiling. The acting and choreography are usually good, with some productions excelling each year. This is a great family outing. Reservations recommended. Open Tues.–Sun. nights. **6875 S. Clinton St., Englewood; (303) 799-1410.**

Denver Center for the Performing Arts Complex—

Beautiful and functional, this impressive four-square-block arts center has given Denver a cultural identity. Its nine theaters make it the second largest such complex in the nation, eclipsed only by New York's Lincoln Center. Whether you are interested in theater, music, ballet or opera, this series of architecturally unique buildings in downtown Denver is the place to come. The acoustically acclaimed **Boettcher Concert Hall** is home to the **Colorado Symphony Orchestra, (303) 595-4388.** With the *Phantom of the Opera,* the curtain has risen at the striking, contemporary **Buell Theater;** event hotline **(303) 692-3708.** For traditional and contemporary drama as well as musicals, contact the **Denver Center Theatre Company** at **(303) 893-4100.** National touring shows with huge casts play at the **Auditorium Theatre, (303) 893-4100,** as does the **Colorado Ballet, (303) 837-8888.**

El Chapultepec—

No need to dress formally at this funky jazz dive. Small and unassuming, the smoky bar features some of the best bebop around. So, if you're into upright bass and sultry saxophone, stop by. El Chapultepec ("the grasshopper") is one of those places your mother probably warned you about. But never fear—the crowd won't bite. The Mexican food is hot and the jazz is cool. Open seven nights a week and never a cover. **1962 Market St.; (303) 295-9126.**

Grizzly Rose Saloon & Dance Hall—

With a 5,000-square-foot dance floor, the Grizzly Rose is not only Colorado's largest country-western dance saloon but it's also by far the best place to learn the

Texas Two-Step and other necessary dances. Nightly dance lessons are offered by Bill and Kathy—you'll be struttin' your stuff in no time. Well-known national acts perform on many nights, especially on weekends, when decked out cowboys/girls kick up their heels. The Nashville Network tapes concerts here periodically for national TV. A very entertaining place. **5450 N. Valley Hwy.; (303) 295-1330.**

Herman's Hideaway—

Hot. Dark. Crowded. Smoky. What more could you ask for in a blues/rock club? In this fairly small, informal setting, the music leaps out at you. Unless you want to stand, get here an hour or two before the bands start playing at 9 pm. A recent expansion of the thimble-sized dance floor has been a welcome change for claustrophobics. Great dancing, pool and plenty of general overindulgence here. **1578 S. Broadway; (303) 778-9916.**

NEARBY

The Buck Snort Saloon—

This is a great place for dancing, albeit in crowded quarters, to quality live rock bands on Sat. nights. Located near Pine Junction, about an hour's drive from Denver. See the Where to Eat section for more information.

The Little Bear—

This rustic mountain bar in the town of Evergreen is legendary for providing wild nights of dancing to live music. The Little Bear attracts a diverse crowd—from bikers to bankers—and everyone seems to enjoy the contrast. Top local rock, blues and country-western bands play most often, with national acts frequently making one- and two-night stops. Open nightly until at least midnight. **28075 Hwy. 74, Evergreen, CO; (303) 674-9991.**

Observatory Bar & Cafe—

Live jazz and light rock music are performed at the Observatory (Fri.–Sat. nights). It's especially inviting on summer nights when the roof is rolled back so you can eat and drink under the stars. A large telescope is wheeled out for a closer look at the heavens. Food available. Across from El Rancho restaurant. From Denver take Interstate 70 west 18 miles to the Evergreen Parkway (Exit 252). Cross over to the south side of the highway and look for the sign. **(303) 526-1988.**

SHOPPING

The Denver metro area, isolated from other major cities, attracts people from around the region with its extensive shopping network. More than 25 malls and shopping centers exhibit great appeal, but like any city, there are a few unusually good places to spend, spend, spend ...

Cherry Creek Mall and Surrounding Shops—

Long before the grand opening of the new upscale Cherry Creek Mall in Aug. 1990, it was already the talk of the town. The arrival of such retail heavyweights as Neiman-Marcus, Lord & Taylor and Saks Fifth Avenue has helped Cherry Creek draw shoppers from around the Rocky Mountain region. Cherry Creek has also developed a reputation for its eclectic shops. Classical and operatic melodies waft through the air of the two-level mall as people busily move from shop to shop. Built on the site of the country's first shopping mall, this new one draws attention of its own for such things as automatic bathroom fixtures and valet parking (free to handicapped vehicles).

In addition to all of the stores in the main mall, the surrounding neighborhood is bursting with small shops, art galleries, cafes and restaurants. This is a great place to take a stroll, window shop and peek into some of the city's best small businesses. Located at **E. 1st Ave. and University Blvd.** Of course, no listing of Denver shopping would be complete without mention of what is perhaps the best bookstore in the US.

The Tattered Cover Bookstore—Denver's largest and best-known bookstore puts forth an offering of more than 175,000 books—probably more than were lost at the burning of the library in Alexandria. This is not a used bookstore. Even so, Joyce Meskis, the owner, encourages leisurely browsing and reading. Feel free to plop down in a comfortable armchair and leaf through a few interesting titles. You could easily spend hours wandering through the three-story assortment of books perched on tidy, well-stocked shelves. If you are buying a gift, The Tattered Cover also offers worldwide mailing and free gift wrapping. If they don't have it stocked, and the book is in print on the planet, the helpful staff has the best ability to retrieve it. Also a selection of magazines, calendars, maps, globes and greeting cards. Free parking in the covered lot next to the store. Located in Cherry Creek at **2955 E. 1st Ave. (at Milwaukee), Denver; (303) 322-7727** and **1-800-833-9327** nationwide.

Larimer Square—

In the historic 1400 block of Larimer St., this restored downtown area is a must visit in Denver. Housed in 1880s vintage buildings, a variety of distinctive shops, restaurants and bars line one of Denver's oldest and, at one time, seediest streets. In 1959 Kent Ruth, in his book *Colorado Vacations*, called Larimer St. "pretty much a skid-row slum." Today the mood is both romantic and exuberant, especially in the evening when twinkling tree lights and street globes cast a warm glow on the restored three-story, brick Victorians. During the Oktoberfest celebration, Larimer St. is blocked off and kegs are tapped; brass bands and lederhosen are nearly as common as jeans and T-shirts. Celebrations in Larimer Square mark other occasions as well, including Halloween, St. Patrick's Day and Cinco de Mayo. The architectural integrity has been maintained, even though wares are displayed in a bold, modern manner. From the Market's excellent cappuccino to Williams-Sonoma's exotic cookery utensils, Larimer Square is a treasure to be enjoyed. Northwest of Larimer Square, the historic warehouse district of Lower Downtown (LoDo) houses Denver's most innovative art galleries.

The 16th Street Mall and the Tabor Center—

The tree-lined 16th Street Mall slices through the center of the downtown shopping district. Outdoor cafes, historic buildings, shops and restaurants can be found along its length; free shuttle buses run up and down the mall connecting the Market St. and Civic Center bus stations. The crown jewel of the mall is the Tabor Center, with 65 stores on three levels. This glass-enclosed galleria is home to Brooks Brothers and Sharper Image; a host of unusual items are sold from vendor carts throughout. Stop by for a shoe shine or ride the glass elevator to the third-floor food court, which will entice you with smells from around the world. In summer step on up to the rooftop patio. The Tabor Center is located at **16th and Lawrence streets.**

NEARBY
Castle Rock Factory Stores—

Castle Rock, 20 miles south of Denver, has recently been transformed into a bargain hunter's paradise with the construction of a massive new mall at the northern edge of town. Many of the best-known brands are represented. Complete with a playground for the kids and a large food court, this makes an excellent, scenic side trip, alongside I-25.

WILDLIFE
Rocky Mountain Arsenal Wildlife Refuge—

The US Army and the US Fish and Wildlife Service have teamed up to offer what is these day, perhaps, the unlikeliest combination of visual attractions. This enormous tract of federally owned land in north Denver offers photo opportunities of one of the foulest toxic waste cleanups in the country and an uncanny number of species of Colorado wildlife. Mule deer, coyote and a large assortment of birdlife, including owls and bald eagles, call the arsenal home for at least part of the year. Observation blinds add to the experience. For information about the wildlife bus tours, contact the **US Fish and Wildlife Service** at **(303) 289-0132.**

ZOO

Denver Zoo (City Park)—

Denver's zoo has consistently been one of the city's most popular attractions, with more than one million visitors each year. Generous donations by Denver residents have helped the zoo to continue offering better (not necessarily bigger) exhibits throughout the years. More than 1,300 animal and bird species make their home here. Include a visit to the dall sheep mountain and the "Northern Shores" exhibit where you can view polar bears and sea lions swimming underwater (this is one of the best areas to be during feeding time). Don't miss the new 22,000-square-foot Tropical Discovery complete with hundreds of new animals surrounded by rain forests, rivers and swamps. Among the new exhibit's residents are monitor lizards, venomous snakes, anacondas and vampire bats. The children's zoo allows kids to get close to a few gentle animals; it also offers rides on a small train. Be sure to visit the animal nursery where there is usually a newborn receiving special attention. Many of the animals are fed late morning to mid-afternoon. The zoo is open daily 10 am–6 pm year-round. Fee charged. **E. 23rd St. between York St. and Colorado Blvd.; (303) 331-4110.**

WHERE TO STAY

ACCOMMODATIONS

Denver presents an overwhelming number of lodging opportunities to vacationers. First of all you need to decide which part of the city to stay in: downtown, uptown, the Tech Center area, near the new airport or near Interstate 70 for a quick exit to the nearby mountains. Then there is the question of price and style. The Brown Palace is the best-known Denver hotel—with good reason. For a nonstop row of inexpensive motels, take a cruise down E. Colfax Ave. (it's not the best part of town). You can still find a comfortable night's stay at major hotels near Denver's former airport: Stapleton. Other possibilities include a number of new high-rise hotels, major chain and discount accommodations, bed and breakfast inns and a couple of youth hostels.

We have gone into some depth in picking a range of places to stay in the central area. If, however, you are just passing through or you want to stay in a different part of town, the **Denver Metro Convention and Visitors Bureau, (303) 892-1112,** can help you make a selection. Consider the following unique recommendations.

Queen Anne Inn—$$$$

Since 1987, the Queen Anne has received rave reviews in local and national media for what many consider to be Denver's finest, most romantic bed and breakfast. Built in 1879, this three-story home was designed in the Queen Anne–style by Denver's most famous architect, Frank E. Edbrooke. The neighborhood, located conveniently near downtown Denver, was scheduled for demolition until the previous owner and other preservationists came in and refurbished the grand homes on this historic block, now known as the Clements Historic District.

The Queen Anne is impeccably decorated with fine antiques, fresh-cut flowers and original artwork. Chamber music wafts through the hallways and each of the 10 guest rooms—you can't change the station but you can turn down the volume. Each room has a private bath and unique decor. The Fountain Room on the second floor is the honeymooners' dream, with a queen-sized, four-poster bed, a sunken tub and large picture windows looking out at Benedict fountain across the street. The unusual Aspen Room on the third floor has a turret ceiling with a 360-degree aspen mural painted on the walls. You feel as if you're in an aspen grove. Four plush new "Gallery" suites in the adjacent Roberts House are now available as well. The new owner whips up a full breakfast each morning. **2147 Tremont Pl., Denver, CO 80205;**

(303) 296-6666 or **1-800-432 INNS** outside Colorado.

Brown Palace Hotel—$$$ to $$$$

When the Brown opened in 1892, one year before the silver panic, it put the "Queen City" on the map. The hotel was such a monument to economic good times it helped create the expectations necessary for Denver to survive and flourish into the future. A stunning example of Victorian architecture, the Brown's triangular exterior is built of Colorado red granite and Arizona sandstone; hand-carved Rocky Mountain animals lie in wait above the arched seventh-floor windows. Though the hotel was originally built on the edge of the city, Denver has grown up around the Brown Palace and the hotel now enjoys a downtown location.

Since day one, the magnificent interior lobby has left lasting impressions on visitors. Six stories of wrought iron balconies rise to a stained-glass ceiling; the spacious ground floor retains an intimate feel with red leather sofas and overstuffed chairs, arranged in small groups in the center of the room. Mon.–Fri., from 12–4:30 pm, the lobby hosts an elegant afternoon tea, served with sandwiches, scones and truffles. Around the perimeter of the room, a number of glass cases are filled with historical memorabilia. The hotel may sound a bit stuffy, but really it's not. Stop by during the National Western Stock Show in January and you may see the tables moved aside to accommodate a prize bull. Unless you've got a Stetson and cowboy boots, forget about trying to fit in with the rest of the guests.

Over the years many famous guests have stayed at the Brown. Dwight D. "Ike" Eisenhower used the hotel for his presidential campaign headquarters in 1952. The biggest hubbub the hotel has ever seen was in 1964 when the Beatles stayed at the Brown while performing a concert at Red Rocks. Five thousand screaming fans crowded the streets to catch a glimpse of their favorite musicians. The Brown received hundreds of applications for employment from eager teenage girls. Alas, when the Fab Four arrived, almost none of their fans was aware of the secret back entrance to the hotel.

Each of the 230 rooms and 25 guest suites has its own unique personality, featuring a window view and the finest furnishings possible. Unlike some historic hotels, the Brown Palace is not tattered around the edges. Rather it is a solid, immaculately kept hotel. Many of the bathrooms are decorated in an art deco style and all come with Crabtree and Evelyn toiletries. After bathing, wrap yourself in a thick terry-cloth robe. Indulge in 24-hour room service in your private, luxurious setting.

The Brown is also home to some of Denver's best-known restaurants. Dine at the pub-like Ship Tavern with replicas of American clipper ships. Wear a coat and tie to the formal dining room, the Palace Arms. It's decorated in a Napoleonic theme and contains a set of dueling pistols thought to have belonged to Napoleon. The classy setting of Ellyngton's is popular for all meals, including Sun. champagne brunch. **321 17th St., Denver, CO 80202; 1-800-321-2599** nationwide, **1-800-228-2917** in Colorado, **(303) 297-3111** in Denver.

Castle Marne—$$$ to $$$$

Among Denver's fine historic bed and breakfast inns Castle Marne deserves special mention. Built in 1889, this immense stone structure prominently occupies its corner lot at 16th Ave. and Race St., drawing the admiring attention of passersby. The home was designed by the famous eclectic architect of the time, William Lang, designer of the Molly Brown house (see the Museums section). Current owners, Jim and Diane Peiker, have loving restored the home. Today hand-hewn rhyolite stonework, balconies and an impressive four-story turret dominate the exterior; inside, attention is drawn to the fine woodwork, numerous original ornate fireplaces and the main stairway, which includes an impressive 6-foot-diameter stained-glass peacock above the first-floor landing. Nine rooms of varying sizes (all with private baths) are nicely decorated with antiques and artwork. The third-floor landing features a butterfly display in honor of former owner John Mason, the first curator of the Denver Museum of Natural History. Each morning enjoy a full breakfast. **1572 Race St., Denver, CO 80206; (303) 331-0621** or toll free at **1-800-92-MARNE.**

Cliff House Lodge & Cottages—$$$ to $$$$

Only minutes west of Denver, this quaint little place lies tucked away in the small town of Morrison, just where the foothills of the Rockies begin. This sandstone victorian lodge, built in 1873 by George Morrison, the town's founder, serves largely as a romantic getaway for Denver couples. Both the lodge rooms and cottages are furnished with antiques. Gourmet breakfast served each morning. Walking distance to shops and restaurants (see the Morrison Inn in Where to Eat) and only minutes from Red Rocks Park. Call for reservations. **121 Stone St., Golden, CO 80465; (303) 697-9732.**

The Oxford Alexis Hotel—$$$ to $$$$

To many the Brown Palace Hotel alone represents the grand luxury of historic hotels in Denver. But that's not the case. When completed in 1891 (one year before the Brown Palace), the Oxford Hotel "sported the latest in gadgets and technology as well as Gilded Age opulence." Located next to Union Station, the Oxford stood for years as a standout luxury hotel that catered mainly to train travelers. Since its grand reopening in 1983, after a three-year, $12 million restoration, the hotel has regained its original richness along with all the modern-day conveniences.

Designed by architect Frank E. Edbrooke, who later went on to create his Brown Palace masterpiece, this five-story brick building has had quite a history. The interior, furnished with the finest oriental rugs, woodwork, marble floors and frescoed walls, reflected the profitable silver mining days Colorado was enjoying at the time. Private water closets, along with electric and gas lighting, amazed guests. The Oxford also boasted the first elevator in Denver. When the silver market crashed in 1893 and many Denver businesses went bankrupt, the Oxford pressed on. During the 1930s the Oxford was remodeled and transformed into an art deco showpiece. With its proximity to the train station, troops during World War II packed the hotel from basement to ceiling. Skid row crept into lower downtown Denver in the 1960s and 1970s and the Oxford deteriorated into a run-down flophouse. But many Denverites remember the Oxford for the great jazz, folk music and melodramas that packed the place in the evenings during those hard times.

Today 81 classy rooms, the mezzanine and lobby are furnished with antiques. Rooms range from comfortable singles to palatial suites. In the lobby Baby Doe Tabor's piano sits near the front door, and a fireplace beckons. With **McCormick's Fish House and Bar** you don't even need to leave the building for dining and nightlife. Be sure to visit the **Cruise Room**, a restored art deco bar that opened in the 1930s. Wall carvings, expressing drinking cheers in many languages, were created to celebrate the end of Prohibition.

Health club access for small fee. Special weekend packages offered for couples. **1600 17th St., Denver, CO 80202; (303) 628-5400** or **1-800-228-5838.**

The Westin Hotel—$$$ to $$$$

Part of the Tabor Center in downtown Denver, the Westin is a beautiful art deco hotel. Elegantly decorated, you won't find a harsh shadow in the entire place. If you really want to live the posh life, be sure to get one of the rooms with a TV in the bathroom. Equally popular with investment bankers and rock stars, the Westin is conveniently located in the heart of the city. You'll find a well-equipped health club on the fourth floor. The hotel offers couples a special "indulgence weekend package" that includes a bottle of champagne and dinner for two at the **Augusta Restaurant,** which is rapidly gaining renown as one of Denver's finest. The view is also notable, as the two-tier dining area looks out over the city. Hotel rates are more than half-off on weekends. **1672 Lawrence St., Denver, CO 80202; 1-800-228-3000** toll free out of state or **(303) 572-9100** in Colorado.

Loew's Giorgio Hotel—$$$

From the outside the Giorgio looks amazingly like Darth Vader—you can almost hear it breathe. Don't let the ultra-modern exterior put you off—inside you will find exquisite northern Italian decor with pleasant, immaculate surroundings. Country-villa styling accents the 180 guest rooms and 20 suites. Complimentary continental breakfast and access to the well-appointed Sporting Club are included. The **Tuscany** restaurant features northern Italian cuisine, of course, and very good food at that. The dark one stands at **4150 E. Mississippi, Denver, CO 80222; 1-800-345-9172** outside Colorado or **(303) 782-9300** in Colorado.

Merritt House Bed & Breakfast— $$$

Opened in 1988, this attractive 10-room Victorian B&B provides comfortable accommodations catering mainly to locals and "corporate America." Although each room is unique, all have private baths, cable TV and phones. Since its construction in 1889, the house has been through many uses; prior to the 1986 purchase and renovation by your hosts, Mary and Tom Touris, it served as a union hall for the United Steel Workers of America. Many guests return just for access to the Merritt House restaurant ($$), which is open to the public for breakfast and lunch from 7 am–2 pm daily. Guests, of course, receive a free breakfast. Located close to downtown at **941 E. 17th Ave., Denver, CO 80218; (303) 861-5230.**

Holiday Chalet—$$ to $$$

If you're looking for a unique, historic and generally comfortable place to stay

without spending a fortune, this lodge fits the bill. Built in 1896 as a private residence for the Bohm family, it still retains much of its original charm. The Holiday Chalet is immaculately kept. Many stained-glass windows spread throughout add colorful touches; a Waterford crystal chandelier graces the front entrance, and sunny bed-rooms all have odd little corners. Each of the 10 rooms comes with a kitchenette, telephone and color TV. You'll get used to the pink decor in no time. You may hear some street noise from Colfax Ave., but thanks to 18-inch walls, you certainly won't hear your neighbor snoring. Another reason to stay is because innkeeper Margot Hartman makes you feel right at home—in the same house where she spent many years growing up. She is also extremely knowledgeable about what Denver has to offer and provides restaurant reservations and athletic club discounts. **1820 E. Colfax Ave., Denver, CO 80218; (303) 321-9975 or 1-800-626-4497.**

Denver International Youth Hostel—$

For well under 10 bucks a night you can stay in a dorm at this youth hostel—a chore, however, is required. Check-in must be between 8 and 10 am or 5 and 10:30 pm; doors are locked the rest of the time. For a small deposit you can have a key to the front door. At present there are about 30 beds available as well as kitchen and bath-room facilities. The hostel is located just east of downtown Denver. **630 E. 16th Ave., Denver, CO 80203; (303) 832-9996.**

Melbourne International Hostel—$

Conveniently located downtown, this hostel provides private rooms as well as standard dorm rooms. Each private room has a refrigerator and some have their own baths. A full kitchen and laundry facilities are available. This is a great place for budget travelers to stay and share tips with others about their travels around the region/country. 7 am–midnight check-in; call ahead if checking in after 7 pm. **607 22nd St., Denver, CO 80205; (303) 292-6386.**

—————— WHERE TO EAT ——————

Dining in Denver has never been the same since Louis Ballast invented and patented the cheeseburger at his Denver drive-in restaurant in 1944. This narrowed-down list reflects the favorites of longtime Denverites, as well as some more off-beat eateries. Whether you're in the mood for fine French cuisine, raucous western dining, or an exotic Indian meal, these places are worthwhile. For a more complete listing of restaurants, pick up a free copy of *Westword* newspaper.

AMERICAN

Cliff Young's—$$$$

Cliff Young's philosophy floats between the abstract and the concrete; the sumptuous food is both real and sublime. At the center of one of Denver's finest dining venues, on 17th Ave. just east of downtown, this restaurant manages to outshine other very bright lights. You needn't fear the standard failings of nouvelle cuisine here—the portions are large and the tastes are not forced together into a culinary shotgun wedding. The food looks even better in the classy environment in which it is served. Consider the separate Amethyst Room for a more relaxed atmosphere. For a special meal, Cliff Young's ambience and fine food are the perfect blend. Live piano music and strolling violinist; dancing OK. Reservations recommended; valet parking. Open for lunch 11:30 am–2 pm Mon.–Fri. Dinner is served 6–10 pm Sun.–Thur., 6–11 pm Fri.–Sat. **700 E. 17th Ave.; (303) 831-8900.**

El Rancho—$$$ to $$$$
(near Genesee)

Since 1948 people have been pulling off Interstate 70 at El Rancho restaurant as a matter of tradition. Dinner always begins with a relish tray followed by a basket of homemade cinnamon rolls, salad, soup, entrée and chiffon pie or ice cream. Entrées include rock lobster, buffalo steak, roast prime rib or rocky mountain trout. Don't be discouraged if there is a short wait—just pull up a comfortable chair in one of the lounge areas and have a cocktail. The views from nearly everywhere in El Rancho are spectacular and, in winter, any or all of the seven fireplaces may be burning. Open 7 am–9 pm Mon.–Fri. (til 10 pm on Sat.), 7 am–8 pm on Sun. (brunch until 2 pm). Located 18 miles west of Denver on Interstate 70 at the Evergreen Parkway (Exit 252); **(303) 526-0661.**

The Fort—$$$ to $$$$

The Fort is one of the most popular places near the metro area to go for a special occasion, especially when out-of-town visitors show up. Views of Denver from the dining room are wonderful. The restaurant is a reproduction of Bent's Fort, one of the first trading posts in the Colorado Territory (see the **Southeast Plains** chapter). The atmosphere of Colorado's early days permeates this large restaurant; mandolin-playing musicians rove between the tables on weekends and all employees dress in frontier costumes. And they get into character ... when we visited, one waitress dressed as an Indian maiden whacked the cork out of a champagne bottle with a tomahawk.

Even so, the most unique thing about the Fort is the food. Owners Sam and Carrie Arnold have diligently researched old frontier recipes for food and drink, updated slightly for modern tastes. The fare is made exclusively with ingredients from the American Southwest. Before dinner try some buffalo sausage, Rocky Mountain oysters or buffalo tongue. Entrées include large steaks as well as buffalo, quail, elk and fish. Specialty drinks with names such as the Hailstorm, Jim Bridger and Bear's Blood conjure up images from the early days. Reservations recommended. Open Mon.–Fri. 5:30–10 pm, Sat. 4:30–10 pm, Sun. 4:30–9 pm. Located west of Denver just off Hwy. 285. **19192 Hwy. 8, Morrison; (303) 697-4771.**

The Buckhorn Exchange—$$$ to $$$$

Virtually everyone of any importance in the Old West has eaten here, including

Teddy Roosevelt and Buffalo Bill Cody. It looks much as it did then, complete with over 500 elk, deer, mountain sheep and other animal heads mounted on the walls. This is Denver's oldest continuously operated restaurant, first serving the wild and woolly public in 1895. After all those years, you can be assured that this place is part museum. The Buckhorn features buffalo, elk and alligator appetizers or the inevitable Rocky Mountain oysters (you needn't worry about shelling this particular variety). Their bean soup is legendary as are the steaks. That Denver cousin is almost obligated to take you here. If you just want to stop by for a drink, head to the upstairs bar, one of Denver's friendliest. Open for lunch 11:30 am–2 pm Mon.–Fri. Dinner is served 5:30–10 pm Mon.–Thur., 5–11 pm Fri.–Sat., 4–9 pm on Sun. Located in an obscure off-downtown neighborhood at **1000 Osage St.; (303) 534-9505.**

Denver Buffalo Company—$$ to $$$

This place is quickly becoming a Denver dining landmark. Centrally located, it's popular with business people as well as groups of friends. The southwestern theme works well, from the wonderful Native American art on display, to the main attraction—buffalo dishes. All buffalo is raised on the Denver Buffalo Company Ranch near Kiowa, Colorado. It's served in a wide assortment of dishes from prime rib to Italian buffalo sausage. Menu highlights also include salads, pasta dishes and fresh fish. Be sure not to fill up on too many jalapeño corn bread muffins—they are irresistible.

The sprawling building also houses a trading post with woolen clothing, leather goods, jewelry, and native handcrafts; an art gallery; a coffee house; and a popular deli which features BuffDogs, buffalo pastrami, jerky and more. The main restaurant is open for lunch Mon.–Fri. 11 am–2:30 pm; dinner Mon.–Thurs. 5–9 pm (til 10 on Fri. and Sat.); deli open 7 am–7 pm Mon.–Sat.; closed Sun. **1109 Lincoln St.; (303) 832-0884.**

The Paramount Cafe—$$

It's rock and roll all the way at this stop. In the heart of the 16th Street Mall,

within the historic Paramount Theatre building, this is a high-energy setting. The prices are fair, and the burgers, sandwiches and daily specials are served in generous portions. The diverse beer selection is first-rate, and the people-watching just doesn't get any better. If you can get a table for lunch (after 11 am there is usually a wait), you'll see power ties mingling with Lycra. This is a popular stop for downtown business people, as well as before and after concerts at the classic art deco Paramount Theatre. Open 11 am–2 am Mon.–Sat. **511 16th St.; (303) 893-2000.**

The Buck Snort Saloon—$ to $$$ (near Pine)

In its out-of-the-way location in a narrow canyon near the town of Pine, the Buck Snort has no equal as a backwoods mountain tavern/restaurant. Shoot a game of pool in the front room or have a beer on the back deck, which hangs out over a rocky stream. The Buck Snort's reputation far outpaces its available room—especially on Sat. nights, when live music keeps the place jumping. Menu items include the half-pound Buck Burger, smothered burritos and their wurst sandwich. If you are anywhere close to Pine Junction on Hwy. 285 (some 32 miles southwest of Denver), pull off and make your way 6 miles south to Pine on County Rd. 126. From Pine make your way up Sphinx Park Rd. for 1.5 fairly rough miles. Negotiating the steep rock canyon road should be enough to keep you from drinking too much at the saloon. Open 4 pm till the last person leaves Wed.–Fri., noon–midnight Sat.–Sun. Closed Mon. and Tues. **15921 Elk Creek Rd., Pine; (303) 838-0284.**

Bonnie Brae Tavern—$ to $$

You wouldn't expect great pizza at a tavern with a Scottish name, but the name is based on its location in the Bonnie Brae neighborhood, not the food. Established in 1934 by Carl Dire, this popular spot is now run by his two sons, Mike and Hank. Ever popular with singles, families and University of Denver students, the tavern offers what many consider the best pizza in town. It is a simple place with comfortable, low-slung booths, allowing everyone a good look around the room. A superb minestrone soup and regular specials of American and Italian food help round out the menu. You can expect a wait at this local favorite. Open 10:30 am–11 pm (until 9 pm Sun.); closed Mon. **740 S. University Blvd.; (303) 777-2262.**

Wazee Lounge & Supper Club— $ to $$

The Wazee has been around for years, remaining a fond favorite with many Denverites for its atmosphere, great bar and beer selection, convenient lower downtown location and what just might be the best pizza in Denver. Pull up a chair at one of the numerous tables and have a good time. In addition to pizza, the Wazee also serves sandwiches and salads. Heidi, the muscular waitress sporting the platinum-blonde crewcut, was recently voted "best tough cookie waitress" in Denver by *Westword* magazine. This is a classic. Corner of **Wazee** and **15th St.; (303) 623-9518.**

Coney Island—$ (in Aspen Park)

Located along Hwy. 285 about 20 miles southwest of Denver, the Coney Island is hard to miss. Just look for the giant pink hot dog with all the trimmings. Walk inside this hot dog and order up (you guessed it) a hot dog, Coney Island or corn dog. Hamburgers, fries and ice cream are also available. Tack your business card up on the wall, if you can find any room. Picnic tables out on the sun deck provide the best seating at this unusual place. Vervea Goodwin, the owner, said the building used to sit on Colfax Ave. in Denver until it was moved by flatbed to Aspen Park in 1969. It's now one of the best money-makers in the area. It's worth a visit if you're in the neighborhood. Like we said, you can't miss it. If you have an aversion to greasy food, however, keep driving. Located in Aspen Park; **(303) 838-4210.**

My Brother's Bar—$

For years My Brother's Bar has served as a gathering spot for good friends and lovers of hamburgers. With its exposed brick walls, well-worn wood floors and pressed-tin ceilings this place is nothing fancy—just comfortable. With no TVs or loud music (classical music rules here, including occasional performances), you'll find no distractions from your meal and conversation with friends. The small menu, listed on the wall, features a variety of delicious burgers, including a buffalo burger. The sandwiches are creative and worth a try; a personal favorite is the spicy turkey olé, made with a mixture of turkey, cream cheese and jalapeno peppers. Beer lovers will appreciate the large assortment of fine beers on tap. Great patio seating in summer. Open 11 am–1:30 am Mon.–Sat.; closed Sun. **2376 15th St.; (303) 455-9991.**

BREAKFAST
Dozens—$ to $$

This is a fun place to eat. Specializing in breakfast items (especially egg dishes), Dozens is located in a comfortable Victorian house with wood floors and high ceilings. The creative menu items all have a Denver or Colorado theme. Choose from a large selection of omelettes, scrambled egg dishes or something lighter such as waffles or fresh fruit. Try one of their fresh-baked goods. Dozens attracts its share of business people who appreciate the telephones next to the table and the "power breakfast" option. Lunches feature sandwiches, but you can also order breakfast items. A full bar is available. Hours are 6:30 am–2:30 pm daily. Dozens has two locations. Both are great, but the downtown restaurant has a bit more atmosphere. **13th St.** and **Cherokee St.; (303) 572-0066** and **2180 S. Havana** (in Aurora); **(303) 337-6627.**

Bud's the Workingpeople's Cafe—$

As the name suggests, this is a haven for working people—especially for those rising before the sun each day. Treat yourself to friendly service in a casual setting that consists of a long Formica counter, comfy vinyl booths and plenty of calendars (William "Least Heat" Moon would have loved it here!). Gigantic cinnamon rolls are Bud's trademark, but the egg dishes, pancakes and biscuits with gravy are all delicious. Though lunch and dinner are also served, breakfast is the real reason to come here. Open Mon.–Fri. 4:30 am–8 pm, Sat. 5 am–2 pm. **1701 38th St.; (303) 295-2915.**

CONTINENTAL
Tante Louise—$$$ to $$$$

In a couple of unassuming houses linked together on Colfax Ave. and Cherry St. resides one of the city's better restaurants. Certainly it must be the coziest and perhaps the most romantic restaurant in Denver, with small tables in quaint nooks off the winding passageways and large tables beside roaring hearths. The decor has an Old World charm; the quality of food will have you returning often. Tante Louise, now in its second decade, has always had rave reviews for its fine French cuisine. The prices here are somewhat lower than at the other Denver restaurants of this quality, and the extensive wine list (over 200) is reasonably priced. Open 5:30–10:30 pm Mon.–Sat., lunch on Fri. 11:30 am–2 pm; closed Sun. **4900 E. Colfax Ave.; (303) 355-4488.**

Wellshire Inn—$$ to $$$$

An old English Tudor mansion on the grounds of the Wellshire Municipal Golf Course is home to this appealing restaurant. Unobstructed views of the course and the mountains have made it a favorite among Denverites. One-hundred-year-old imported tapestries and paneling, in addition to leaded stained glass and Tiffany lamps, lend an air of sophistication to the atmosphere. The food has an interesting contemporary continental focus. Renowned chef Leo Goto ensures an excellent dining experience. This is also a good choice for Sun. brunch from 10 am–2 pm (menu rather than buffet). Open for breakfast 7–10 am Mon.–Fri., lunch 11:30 am–2:30 pm Mon.–Sat. Dinner is served 4:30–

10 pm Mon.–Thur., until 11 pm Fri.–Sat.; Sun. 5:30–9 pm. **3333 S. Colorado Blvd.; (303) 759-3333.**

Le Central—$ to $$$

If for no better reason, Le Central deserves a write-up for its great French food and affordability. Their blackboard menu changes daily and features creative variations on pork, beef, chicken and fish. Although new dishes occasionally miss the mark, the restaurant has a strong and loyal following. Thankfully (for some of us) the able wait staff stand at the ready to translate the french explanations of the daily entrées. Enjoy the comfortable, pleasant French country atmosphere while sipping on one of the many modestly priced French wines available. Lunch served 11:30 am–2 pm Mon.–Fri.; dinner from 5:30–10 pm Mon.–Sat. (til 9 on Sun.); Sun. brunch from 11 am–2 pm. **112 E. 8th Ave.; (303) 863-8094.**

EXOTIC/MIDDLE EASTERN
India's—$$$ to $$$$

After a stint as a pilot in the Indian air force, Kris Kapoor did the most logical thing he could think of—he opened a restaurant in Denver. And what a restaurant it is. India's is a special place for vegetarian and meat-eating lovers of fine Indian food. Although authenticity reigns, from the sitar music and extensive list of regional entrées to the stainless steel plates on which they are served, help is available to those yet uninitiated to this exotic cuisine. The menu provides explanations and descriptions, and the waiters take care to gauge your personal spice-meter. Highlights include delicious lamb dishes, especially the spicy Boti Masala. Or try the Ticca Jehangir, a delicious blend of tandoori chicken and shrimp. To top off your meal try one of their fruit lassis, a cool, thirst-quenching combination of yogurt and fruit ice that can be found all over India. Full bar. Open for lunch ($$) 11:30 am–2:30 pm Mon.–Fri. (opens at noon on Sat.); dinner served 5:30–10 pm seven days a week. Reservations are highly recommended. Located at **Tamarac Square, 3333 S. Tamarac Dr.; (303) 755-4284.**

Mataam Fez — $$$

The decor here could be straight out of the tales of 1001 Arabian nights—guests are seated on pillows and cushions in front of short tables and canopied ceilings. Shoes are removed, thick white towels are draped over the diners' shoulders and no utensils are to be found. It's all part of the dining ritual, along with ornately dressed waiters, belly dancers and sword dancers. Typical dishes are chicken with lemon and olives and lamb with apricots; curry dishes and fish are also available. This is a dining experience to be savored over the course of a few hours. Do not schedule a concert or theater performance after the meal, unless you want to watch the midnight show. Open for dinner seven nights a week 6 pm until 9:30 Sun.–Thurs. and 10:30 Sat.–Sun. **4609 E. Colfax Ave.; (303) 399-9282.**

ITALIAN

Little Pepina's—$$ to $$$

Good, plentiful, flavorful Italian food. This is the kind of food that makes you feel fulfilled while you're eating and for a long time afterward. Serves "gourmet" Italian fare as well as classics, but all meals come with soup, salad and side of pasta. The only reason not to visit is if you're on a low-carbohydrate diet. This popular restaurant is located in northwest Denver, the original home of Denver's Italian immigrants. Lunches offered 11:30 am–2 pm Mon.–Fri.; dinner 5–10 pm Sun.–Thurs. and til 11 pm Fri.–Sat.; Sun. brunch 11 am–2 pm. **3400 Osage St.; (303) 477-3335.**

Pagliacci's—$$

You can't miss this restaurant at night, and if you've seen the opera *I Pagliacci*, you'll know why the owners have a lighted neon clown on top of the building. Traditional family-style Italian food has been offered here since 1944. A large wall mural creates the atmosphere of rooftop dining overlooking an Italian city. Featuring homemade pasta and sauces, this busy place is a true classic. Each meal includes all the homemade minestrone and garlic bread you can eat. The food is tasty, plentiful and an excellent value. Service is extremely professional. Dinner served Mon.–Sat. 5–10 pm, Sun. 4–9 pm. **1440 W. 33rd Ave.; (303) 458-0530.**

Pasquini's—$ to $$

Simply put, the food at this place is awesome; so's the loud, friendly atmosphere. Located alongside busy South Broadway, Pasquini's and it's energetic staff crank out some mighty fine pizza, calzones and submarine sandwiches. Everything is characterized by fresh, noticeable spices. The garlic/butter-drenched bread sticks are to die for. Grab a chair at one of the few tables or at the one on the sidewalk where you can watch the cars whiz by while waiting for your food. After your meal (or during) stop in at the Blue Luna Room upstairs for some blues, rock or other live music. Open 11 am–12 am Mon.–Wed., 11 am–2 am Thurs.–Sat., and on Sun. from 4 pm–12 am. **1310 S. Broadway; (303) 744-0917.** For a couple of other great pizza places, check the Bonnie Brae Tavern and Wazee Lounge & Supper Club write-ups.

MEXICAN

Casa Bonita—$$

The decor is so well done, you almost believe that former Disney employees came to Colorado to open a Mexican restaurant. Although the mediocre food will never come close to surpassing the atmosphere or entertainment, a trip to Casa Bonita is still a must for out-of-town guests and families with small children. While you relax over your meal (if that's possible after a wait in line that can be up to an hour), the kids will be turning their heads crazily, trying to see what's going to happen next. Let them roam into the caverns near the pool, where the fake green bats' eyes gleam, or the skeleton of an unfortunate miner awaits discovery in an abandoned shaft. Adults and children alike watch in rapture as cliff divers plunge 30 feet from craggy peaks past waterfalls and into a small pool. Staged gunfights and strolling mariachis provide other entertainment. If you can possibly eat another helping of your all-you-can-eat combo plate or drink a refill of your margarita, just raise the service flag at your table; be sure to save room for a sopapilla. Open Sun.–Thur. 11 am–9:30 pm, Fri.–Sat. 11 am–10 pm. Look for the pink tower at **6715 W. Colfax Ave.; (303) 232-5115.**

Blue Bonnet Cafe & Lounge—$ to $$

Denverites flock to this popular restaurant to put their names on a waiting list for a coveted table in the main cantina area or a nonsmoking seat in the back. Many wait slouched at the small bar, nursing a margarita and cursing themselves for not having arrived at an earlier, perhaps less-crowded time. Once seated, choose from a reasonably priced selection of Tex-Mex items, including a number of house specials such as the El Burro giant burrito and the Chile Relleno Dinner. While waiting for your food, order from a sizeable selection of Mexican beers, listen to the jukebox and peruse the management's collection of flattering newspaper articles that line the south wall. Open 11 am–10 pm Sun.–Thur., 11 am–11 pm Fri.–Sat. **457 S. Broadway;   (303) 778-0147.**

Sabor Latino—$ to $$

If you're in the mood for something a bit different, stop by Sabor Latino and taste some excellent South American cuisine. Dishes from Chile and the Caribbean are the best at this small north Denver restaurant. Try the tasty empanadas, a turnover filled with onions, meat and spices. Other dishes worth a try are the ceviche, Pastel de Choclo (corn pie) and the flan custard for dessert. Your hostess, Maria, is one of the most charming you'll find anywhere. Open Mon.–Sat. 11 am–3 pm and 5–9 pm; closed Sun. **3464 W. 32nd Ave; (303) 455-8664.**

Morrison Inn—$$
(in Morrison)

Simply put, this is a fun place. Located west of Denver at the foot of the mountains in the small community of Morrison, the inn specializes in Mexican food and good times. You'll see the adobe-colored building with green awnings and trim on Main St. Favorite meals include spinach enchiladas, fajitas and pork barbacoa. Don't expect authentic Mexican food—but you should be ready for incredible taste sensations. A major point in the Inn's favor is that no pre-mix is used for the custom-made margaritas. They're great! Open Sun. 10 am–10 pm, Mon.–Thur. 11:00 am–10 pm (11 pm in summer), Fri.–Sat. 11:30 am–11 pm; bar open until 1 or 2 am. Located in the middle of Morrison. **301 Bear Creek Ave.; (303) 697-6650.**

El Noa Noa—$ to $$

It's worth making a special trip for the food at any one of these three traditional Mexican restaurants named after Noah (of ark fame). Sip on a cerveza and pound down a few chips before attacking the ample entrées. El Noa Noa offers up some great lunch specials, including a chicken mole plate that is truly fantastic. All of this and the price is right, too. **722 Santa Fe Dr.; (303) 623-9968,** the north location at **1920 Federal Blvd.; (303) 455-6071,** and the downtown spot at **1543 Champa; (303) 623-5321.**

Las Delicias—$ to $$

If you are one of those people on a continual hunt for an inexpensive and authentic Mexican cafe, then be sure to come here. Unless you are fluent in Spanish, don't even try to pick up the banter between the service staff; even the jukebox offers only Spanish tunes. This is not a contrived place in the least. The real reason to come here is the food—mouth-watering burritos, tacos and enchiladas will keep you utterly happy. "Las D" is a favorite with the downtown crowd for lunch. Full bar available. Open daily 8 am–9 pm. **439 E. 19th Ave.; (303) 839-5675,** LD II at **50 Del Norte; (303) 430-0422,** and LD III just off the 16th St. Mall at **1530 Blake St.; (303) 629-5051.**

ORIENTAL
T-Wa Inn—$ to $$$

A section of S. Federal Blvd. has been transformed into a strip of Vietnamese shops and restaurants. This was one of the first Vietnamese restaurants in town. The food reflects a delicate balance of tastes, borrowing from both Chinese and French cuisines and featuring many traditional specialties. T-Wa boasts an extensive menu of exotic hot and spicy dishes and wonderful seafood. Order something from the excellent selection of appetizers! It has very moderate prices for the quantity and quality of food. Open for lunch and dinner daily from 11 am–10 pm. **555 S. Federal Blvd.; (303) 922-4584.**

Little Shanghai Cafe—$ to $$$

It's difficult to say why more Denverites don't mention Little Shanghai as one of their favorites; in our opinion, it definitely ranks right up there. Amidst very attractive and comfortable tables and booths, the excellent waitstaff hustles with precision to keep the various dishes flowing steadily to the customers. Sit back and sip on a cold Tsing-Tap beer while perusing the fairly extensive (for a Chinese restaurant) menu. Specialties include seafood dishes and an excellent, spicy Kung Pao triple delight. The Chinese dumplings are some of the best we've had in Denver. Lunch specials daily. **460 S. Broadway; (303) 777-9838** or **722-1292.**

Panda Cafe—$ to $$$

The authentic and adventurous cuisine has ensured the success of this extremely popular restaurant. You'll find nothing special about the unobtrusive Chinese restaurant decor, but the excellent food is hard to forget. Spicy (and tasty) inland Hunan and Szechuan dishes such as kung pao have made their way onto the menu, but the real reason to eat at the Panda is for the Cantonese seafood. The chefs get extremely creative with enormous scallops and other seafood, paying more attention to aroma and presentation than most of their fellow oriental restaurants. Anybody doubting the freshness of the fare might try choosing one of the live crabs from the restaurant tank. The Panda Cafe also offers a number of special dishes such as the delicious Eight Treasures Tofu, with scallops, shrimp, mushrooms, pork, beef, tofu, chicken and cuttlefish. This is one of those places that you pray doesn't ever change. Open 10:30 am–9:30 pm Sun.–Thur., 10:30 am–10:30 pm Fri.–Sat. **1098 S. Federal Blvd.; (303) 936-2500.**

Tommy's—$

This small Thai restaurant serves up delicious and surprisingly inexpensive fare. But, perhaps, the best of all is a plate of addictive Phad Thai, a concoction of rice noodles stir-fried with shrimp, chicken, bean sprouts and onion. If you try it you'll definitely be back for more. Also stop in for Tommy's daily lunch special. Open 10:30 am–9 pm Mon.–Fri., Sat. noon–10 pm; closed Sun. **3410 E. Colfax; (303) 377-4244.**

SEAFOOD
The Fresh Fish Company—$$ to $$$

Although Denver has not exactly developed a stellar reputation for fine seafood dining, this casual place continues to improve the town's image. Over 30 varieties of fish are flown in daily for creative preparation. Excellent sourdough bread is served with each of the large entrées. For the lobster lover—don't miss the Sun. evening special. New menu printed daily. Lunch served Mon.–Fri. 11:30 am–2:30 pm, dinners on Mon.-Sat. 5–11 pm (10 pm on Sun.), and Sun brunch from 10 am–2 pm. **7800 E. Hampden; (303) 740-9556.**

VEGETARIAN/HEALTH
Healthy Habits—$$

Riding the wave of popularity that salad bars have had in Denver, Healthy Habits offers your choice of soups, pastas, and an enormous salad bar with a variety of tasty veggies and greens. The pasta bar offers a selection of pastas; soup varieties change daily. Save room on your plate for a large muffin or two—they're excellent. The extensive dessert bar offers end-of-meal treats that don't come readily to mind when thinking about healthy habits. Open daily 11 am–9 pm. **865 S. Colorado Blvd., (303) 733-2105** and **14195 W. Colfax in Golden, (303) 277-9293.**

**The Harvest Restaurant & Bakery—
$ to $$**

What used to be a small Boulder restaurant, called the Good Earth, has changed names and flourishes both there and in Denver. Featuring vegetarian and meat dishes, the Harvest stresses freshness and will not serve food containing additives. Breakfast items include buttermilk pancakes and omelettes. You can't really go wrong for lunch, or dinner either—especially if you enjoy a homemade roll or muffin with a steaming bowl of soup or a fruit shake or smoothie for dessert. Service is fast and the prices are still reasonable. If you're dining alone, you may wish to eat at the community table—where single diners can enjoy a meal together. Open 7–10 pm Sun.–Thurs., Fri.–Sat. 7 am–11 pm. **430 S. Colorado Blvd.; (303) 399-6652.** Also at **7730 E. Belleview Ave., 779-4111.**

SERVICES

**Denver Metro Convention &
Visitors Bureau—**

The visitors center's knowledgeable staff can answer all your questions about attractions, events, shopping, etc. Open in winter Mon.–Fri. 8 am–5 pm, Sat. 9 am–1 pm. Summer hours are Mon.–Fri. 8 am–5 pm, Sat. 9 am–5 pm. **225 W. Colfax Ave., Denver, CO 80202; (303) 892-1112.**

The Greater Denver Chamber of Commerce—

1445 Market St., Denver, CO 80202; (303) 534-8500.

**Transportation—
Cultural Connection Trolley—**This easy-to-spot red and green bus makes runs between some of Denver's best museums and attractions including the Denver Art Museum, Botanic Gardens, Zoo, etc. Buses run on the half hour; $1 for daily pass. Runs 9 am–6 pm. **(303) 299-6000.**

Metro Taxi Company—24-hour service; **(303) 333-3333.**

RTD (Denver metro area bus service)— For maps and route information, call **(303) 299-6000.**

Yellow Cab—24-hour service; **(303) 777-7777.**

Estes Park

Since its settlement over 130 years ago, the Estes Park area has captured the hearts and imaginations of naturalists, photographers and mountaineers from around the world. If you have been here, the logic is obvious—the setting is a classic. Located in the northern Front Range of the Colorado Rockies, the town of Estes Park commands a mountain view to the surrounding craggy peaks of the Continental Divide. Looming nearby is 14,255-foot Longs Peak, one of the most majestic and best-known mountains in the country. Estes Park serves as an eastern sentinel to the immensely popular Rocky Mountain National Park and a conduit for the nearly three million annual park visitors.

Most people coming to this area spend as much time as possible exploring the beautiful high alpine country of the national park, returning to town in the evening for accommodations and meals. As you can imagine, Estes Park can become quite crowded in summer.

Yet, even at the height of the tourist season, after an early evening rain when the low clouds hang around Lumpy Ridge with its strange rock formations, the valley takes on an eerie, almost primordial feel. If you have the option, get a better feel for Estes Park by visiting in the off-peak months of May and Sept., or in winter when it's blissfully quiet. In fall, sounds of bugling elk fill the valley; some of these fascinating giants even wander onto the golf course.

People have definitely made their presence known in this incredibly beautiful area of the state. In and around town, man-made monstrosities such as the large blue sky slide clash harshly with the surrounding natural beauty. But the town has achieved a growing self-awareness, due largely to an environmentally conscious shift by residents. Estes is coming to grips with its appropriate role as complement to and comrade of the wonders of Rocky Mountain National Park.

HISTORY

For centuries before Anglos arrived, Native Americans came to the Estes area from great distances. It's a place that was considered sacred to the Indians—artifacts indicate that Old Man Mountain, located on the west end of town, was a Vision Quest site for braves seeking good fortune for their people. In addition, Arapahos supposedly climbed Longs Peak to set traps for bald eagles. Arapahos laid claim to the territory but when settlers arrived, Utes were occupying the area.

By the time Joel Estes and his family homesteaded the valley in 1860, most of the Indians were long gone. And visitors were few until 1864, when the challenge of climbing Longs Peak attracted William Byers, editor of the *Rocky Mountain News*. Byers and his two companions stayed with the Estes family while attempting to climb the peak. Byers was so enamored with the scenery, he wrote a story in the *News* and proclaimed the area Estes Park, in honor of his host. The Denver newspaperman returned in 1868 and conquered the peak with his companion, Maj. John Wesley Powell (the one-armed explorer of the Colorado River). Byers, of course, wrote another story about his adventure, which prompted many hunters, mountaineers and tourists to come themselves. Griffith Evans, the new owner of the Estes homestead, soon found himself operating a lucrative makeshift hostel. By 1871 Evans added cabins and opened a full-scale dude ranch.

The following year Lord Dunraven (the Fourth Earl of Dunraven, Viscount of Mount Earl and Adare), an Irish nobleman and avid hunter, entered the scene. So impressed with the excellent hunting, Dunraven decided he liked the Estes Park area so much he had to own it—all of it. As a foreigner he was forbidden from homesteading, but Dunraven wasn't going to let little things like laws stand in his way. Through third-party purchases and other shifty methods he gained control of more than 15,000 acres for his private hunting sanctuary.

Though he tried, Dunraven couldn't keep the people away. Famous landscape artist Albert Bierstadt was captivated by the area, and his evocative paintings brought in even more people (one especially fine painting of Longs Peak still hangs in the Western History Department of the Denver Public Library). As an increasing number of settlers streamed in and homesteading opportunities diminished, newly arrived ranchers and homesteaders began contesting the earl's land claims. Dunraven eventually had to give in, leasing large tracts of his beloved land to ranchers.

After Dunraven left, his personal agent, Theodore Whyte, hid the earl's substantial stock of whiskey in a cave for safekeeping. He rolled a boulder in front of the cave, then promptly forgot where it was. The cache may still be there, just waiting for a connoisseur of perfectly aged, single-malt whiskey.

In 1905 the town of Estes Park was platted on John Cleave's land at the confluence of Fall River and the Big Thompson River. Cleave, echoing sentiments of many locals over the years, sold out and moved away, saying he "couldn't stand to see the danged place overrun by tenderfeet tourists."

At about the same time, a man of vision (and inventor of the Stanley Steamer), F.O. Stanley, arrived. He had been diagnosed with tuberculosis, but the dry mountain air seemed to cure him. In 1907 he went into partnership to buy Dunraven's remaining land and built the famous Stanley Hotel (see the Where to Stay section). The hotel opened in 1909 and was booked solid the entire first summer—partly because the inventor used his fleet of Stanley Steamer Mountain Wagons to bring his guests to the hotel from the railhead at Lyons. With his flowing white hair and beard, Stanley became known as the Grand Old Man of Estes Park. He made large contributions to the town and was instrumental in reintroducing herds of elk.

When Congress established Rocky Mountain National Park in 1915, Estes Park was well on its way to becoming a center for visitors to the area. Today Rocky Mountain National Park is the most visited attraction in Colorado. (For more information on the national park, see the Major Attractions section.)

GETTING THERE

From Denver head north on Interstate 25 for about 35 miles and turn west (left) on Hwy. 66. Proceed 16 miles to Lyons and then another 20 miles northwest on Hwy. 36 to Estes Park. The 71-mile drive takes about two hours. An alternate route is via Boulder on Hwy. 36 (the Boulder Turnpike). From Boulder head north on Hwy. 36 to Lyons and then northwest to Estes Park. From the west, Estes Park can be reached via Trail Ridge Rd. (summer only), which crosses the Continental Divide from Grand Lake.

———— MAJOR ATTRACTIONS ————

Rocky Mountin National Park

Rocky Mountain National Park, which straddles the Continental Divide for 40 miles, is without question the showpiece of Colorado's public recreation lands. Each year millions of visitors make their way through the park to see some of the most spectacular high-mountain scenery in the Rockies. Its eastern side is characterized by steep, glaciated valleys and cirque lakes, carved out by the ice floes that once dominated the surroundings. On the western side of the Continental Divide, the land is more gentle, with lush pine forests covering much of the terrain. But the park's 78 peaks over 12,000 feet make up the most dramatic feature. The loftiest of these is famous Longs Peak (14,255 feet), which dominates the Front Range skyline and is visible from more than 100 miles away. The park serves as a sanctuary for many species, including elk, deer, bears, bighorn sheep, mountain lions, otters and raptors such as bald and golden eagles, hawks and peregrine falcons.

Park rangers estimate that 85 to 95 percent of the visitors to the park see it from the car window. The leisurely but dramatically beautiful drive over Trail Ridge Road is a must. For those who are looking for something a bit more active, multi-day backpack trips into the park's remote areas or an all-day hike up Longs Peak provide the challenge.

History—

In the early 1900s, a conservationist movement in Estes Park developed, spearheaded by naturalist and writer Enos Mills. Overuse of land by individuals and businesses in what is now Rocky Mountain National Park galvanized a push to protect this uniquely beautiful area from further damage. Many preservationists were happy when the federal government set aside a large part of the land as a national forest, but others felt that wasn't enough. Another movement to create a national park began, despite opposition from forest service officials who thought they were the best public stewards. Some private landowners also posed opposition, fearing they would lose their property. On Jan. 26, 1915, President Woodrow Wilson ended all the debate by signing a bill creating Rocky Mountain National Park.

Controlled development of the park really started in 1920 when Fall River Rd. opened, helping visitors gain better access to the beautiful areas. By the 1950s the incredible popularity of the park began to work against it—overcrowding and serious damage to the vegetation (especially the high alpine tundra) were apparent. As a result of all this, protective restrictions were imposed, still leaving ample room for all visitors to enjoy the park to its fullest. Today this beautiful area remains much as it was when Joel Estes first settled here in the 1860s. With proper management officials hope to keep it that way.

Getting There—

From the east, Rocky Mountain National Park can be reached via Hwy. 34 or Hwy. 36 from Estes Park. Once inside the park, Hwy. 34 (Trail Ridge Rd.; summer only) crosses the Continental Divide 50 miles to Grand Lake on the Western Slope.

Visitor Information—

If you have questions about the park or its regulations, stop in at one of the visitor centers. **Park Headquarters Visitor Center, (303) 586-3565 ext. 206,** is located just inside the east boundary of the park on Hwy. 36. Visitors entering the park from the west side at Grand Lake can stop in at **Kawuneeche Visitor Center, (303) 627-3471,**

just inside the park boundary. You may also want to stop at the **Alpine Visitor Center,** located at the top of Trail Ridge Rd. Information on both the national park and adjacent Roosevelt National Forest is available at **Lily Lake Visitor Center,** 8 miles south of Estes Park on Hwy. 7. It's open Memorial Day–Labor Day. For additional information any time of year, contact **Rocky Mountain National Park Headquarters, Estes Park, CO 80517-8397; (303) 586-2371.** For information about the west side of the park, see the **Grand Lake** chapter.

RECREATION INFORMATION

Biking—

Mountain Biking—Since off-road biking is not allowed in the park, the mountain bike trail possibilities are limited to the existing roads. For a challenging dirt road, see the Old Fall River Rd. write-up under Scenic Drives below.

Touring—Touring on the roads in Rocky Mountain National Park provides some of the most spectacular high-mountain scenery you'll find anywhere. There are quite a few challenging uphill stretches, so you should be in good physical shape for most of the rides. Most routes are heavily traveled by cars.

Bear Lake Road is a strenuous 10-mile tour that climbs 1,500 feet. For information about the road, see Scenic Drives.

Trail Ridge Road, the 50-mile road between Estes Park and Grand Lake, is one of the toughest and most rewarding bike tours in Colorado. It crosses over the Continental Divide at 12,183 feet and provides incredible, high alpine scenery. If you pedal the entire distance, you'll probably be too tired to return the same day. Stay a night in Grand Lake and return the next day. See Scenic Drives for more information about Trail Ridge Rd.

Fishing—

Successful fishing within Rocky Mountain National Park is fairly sporadic, but still possible. Some of the prime spots require hiking, but there are several lakes and streams alongside the roads. Some of the lakes have paved pathways around them to enable access for disabled anglers. It would be wise to pick up a copy of the park rules. One important rule allows only flies and lures, and many stretches of water are catch and release only, with barbless hooks required. Of special note is the growing population of the greenback cutthroat trout, which must be released immediately if caught.

Big Thompson River—Surrounded by high peaks, this river ambles northeast through the park before flowing to the town of Estes Park and eventually onto the plains. On its upper reaches, you'll find mainly brook trout, with a few browns and rainbows thrown in for good measure. Most of the trout are fairly small, 8- to 10-inch fryers. From Estes Park drive west on Hwy. 36 to the Beaver Meadows Entrance Station. At the first intersection after the entrance, turn left (south) on Bear Lake Rd. After 1 mile turn right (west) onto Moraine Park Rd., which follows the Big Thompson for 2.7 miles to the Fern Lake trailhead. You can either fish the water along the road or follow the rough trail up into the higher country.

Peacock Pool—Plan a day's outing for this combination hiking/fishing trip. Once you complete the 5-mile hike to this little lake, chances are you'll catch many smallish (8-inch) brook trout. The "pool" is filled by a splashing waterfall in a picture-perfect setting at the base of Longs Peak.

The hike, beginning at the East Longs Peak trailhead, is not a cakewalk, so don't attempt it unless you're in pretty good shape. About 4 miles up the trail a spur leads to Peacock Pool (11,360 feet in elevation), offering tremendous views along the way. If you want to complete the hike to **Chasm Lake**—another 1.5 miles from Peacock Pool—you may be able to catch a large cutthroat in that lake's very deep water under the diamond face of Longs Peak. To get to the East Longs Peak trailhead from Estes Park, head 9.2 miles south on Hwy. 7 and turn right at the sign.

Sprague Lake—This shallow, picturesque lake at the east edge of the park yields many pan-sized brook trout. Because it's right next to the road and has a trail all the way around its shore, the lake is used fairly heavy. To get there from Estes Park, drive west on Hwy. 36 to the Beaver Meadows Entrance Station. At the first intersection after the entrance, turn left (south) and continue on Bear Lake Rd. for about 6 miles.

Thunder Lake—Once again the fishing may not be spectacular, but the scenery makes up for it. Fishing here is reasonably good for rainbow and brook trout. For more information see the Thunder Lake/Wild Basin entry below, under Hiking and Backpacking.

West Rocky Mountain National Park—For information about the excellent fishing near the park's western boundary, see the Fishing section of the **Grand Lake** chapter.

Hiking and Backpacking—

Getting into the backcountry is what Rocky Mountain National Park is all about. Most of the park is accessible only by hiking trails. Backcountry permits are required for any overnight stays. These free permits, as well as maps and information, can be picked up at the **Backcountry Office** next to **Park Headquarters** near **Estes Park** or at **Kawuneeche Visitors Center** near **Grand Lake**. During the summer months (June 1–Sept. 30), reserve your permit by writing the **Backcountry Office, Rocky Mountain National Park, Estes Park, CO 80517**, or showing up in person. Reservations can be made for the rest of the year by calling **(303) 586-4459** or writing the Backcountry Office. No pets are allowed on trails, and in most places camping is allowed in designated areas only. Handicamp, a special backcountry camping area, is accessible to wheelchairs. For more information call **(303) 586-4459.**

Bridal Veil Falls—Located in a newly acquired section of the park, Bridal Veil Falls is a fantastic 6-mile round-trip hike. Those who are not looking for a particularly steep and strenuous experience will enjoy this hike with views south to Lumpy Ridge and a plethora of wildflowers in summer. Peregrine falcons and bighorn sheep can often be seen as well. Hikers are rewarded by beautiful 30-foot falls at the end of the trail. To reach the trailhead from Estes Park, head northwest on Devils Gulch Rd. toward Glen Haven. After about 4 miles, bear left on McGraw Ranch Rd., a dirt road marked with yellow gate poles. Proceed on the main branch of this road for 2.2 miles to the Cow Creek/North Boundary trailhead. Begin hiking up the Cow Creek Trail.

Dream Lake Trail—Heading west from Bear Lake, this trail climbs gently up to three lakes—Nymph, Dream and Emerald. It's a popular and easy hike that can be done in a couple of hours. The distances are short (a half mile to Nymph, 1 mile to Dream and just under 2 miles to Emerald) and the scenery, dominated by Hallett Peak, is magnificent.

Fern Lake/Odessa Lake Trail—There are two routes into these lakes, but no matter which trail you take, the scenery is incredible. Perhaps the best starting point is from the trailhead at Bear Lake, which is 1,300 feet above Fern Lake and provides a downhill hike for most of the way. To find the trailhead at Bear Lake, walk up Flattop Trail for about 1.5 miles. At a trail junction you'll find a sign pointing the way to Fern and Odessa lakes. From Bear Lake it's about 4.7 miles to Fern Lake. Along the way you'll pass over a saddle between Joe Mills and Notchtop mountains. The trail, which hugs the mountainside, climbs up to 10,500 feet and affords magnificent views of surrounding peaks offset by deep valleys. From Fern Lake it's another 3.8 miles to the Fern Lake trailhead (located 2.7 miles west on Moraine Park Rd. from Bear Lake Rd.). If you have someone to pick you up, you can start at one trailhead and finish at the other.

Flattop Mountain/North Inlet Trail—If you feel like taking a long hike, you can follow this trail all the way (18.5 miles) to Grand Lake. From Bear Lake climb west about 2.5 miles to the summit of Flattop Mountain (12,324 feet). This mountain is aptly named, having the roomiest summit of any in the park. From there it's a relatively easy 16-mile, downhill hike southwest along North Inlet Trail through pine forests to Grand Lake. This hike (at least the hike to the summit of Flattop) is very popular in summer, so expect to see some other folks. After crossing over the Continental Divide and beginning your descent to Grand Lake, you'll be in pretty remote country until the last few miles.

Longs Peak—This peak has inspired poets, painters and assorted adventurers since explorers first sighted it in the mid-1800s. The challenge of reaching the summit is as exciting today as it was when the 14,255-foot peak was first scaled in 1868 by William Byers and John Wesley Powell. It's not only the tallest and most dominant peak in the park, it's also the northernmost 14er in Colorado (or the Rocky Mountains for that matter).

Following are two hikes up the peak. If you plan to climb Longs Peak, it's recommended that you start very early and try to be off the summit by noon to avoid the all-too-common afternoon lightning storms. Both hikes are considered difficult and are not recommended for novices. If you want to make it an overnighter, there are a few places to camp along the way, but remember that you need a camping permit.

North Longs Peak Trail is reached from the Glacier Gorge trailhead, just before reaching Bear Lake on Bear Lake Rd. It's the longer of the two routes, but it's also less crowded. Start hiking south on Loch Vale Trail. After a mile take the left fork and climb southeast for 5 miles until the trail joins East Longs Peak Trail at the 11,900-foot summit of Granite Pass. From there it's another 2.5 miles to the summit. The round trip takes about 17 hours. To get to the trailhead, drive up Bear Lake Rd. to Glacier Gorge Junction. The marked trailhead is on the left.

East Longs Peak Trail, by far the most popular route up the peak, starts at the

Longs Peak trailhead and climbs 8 miles and 4,850 vertical feet to the summit. The first 6 miles to the Boulderfield ascend through thick pine forests and aspens to treeline, where fantastic views of the area are possible, especially of Longs Peak's magnificent 1,675-foot East Face. From the field the trail climbs to the Keyhole, where the route traverses a steep ledge system across the west face. From there the trail heads up the Trough, then across a dizzying ledge system called the Narrows and finally up the Homestretch to the summit. The route from the Keyhole to the summit is marked with yellow and red bull's-eyes. The round trip from the ranger station at the trailhead takes about 14 hours. To get to the trailhead from Estes Park, head south 9.2 miles on Hwy. 7 to the turn-off for Longs Peak Campground. Turn right and drive about a mile to the trailhead parking lot.

Thunder Lake/Wild Basin—The 7-mile hike to Thunder Lake can be a moderately difficult outing if you decide to do it all in one day. The main trail follows the St. Vrain River, where you'll be treated to lots of waterfalls and cascades. The upper part of the trail moves through the trees to 10,500 feet, breaking out onto promontories overlooking the valley and the Continental Divide—this scenery is all postcard material. Try fishing in the lake and the stream below it for rainbow and brook trout in the 10-inch range.

The hike to Thunder Lake takes four to five hours, and the return trip takes about three and a half hours. To get to the trailhead, take Hwy. 7 south from Estes Park about 13 miles. Turn right and drive a quarter mile to Wild Basin Lodge. Just past the lodge, turn right and follow the road past the ranger station for 2 miles to the trailhead.

Tonahutu Creek—See the Hiking and Backpacking section of the **Grand Lake** chapter.

Horseback Riding—
High Country Stables—Two-hour, half-day and all-day rides are available at High Country's two locations within the park. Both are located close to Estes Park, at Glacier Basin and at Moraine Park. Numbers change from year to year so call Park Headquarters at **(303) 586-3565 ext. 206** for information.

Scenic Drives—
Bear Lake Road—From the Beaver Meadows Entrance Station, it's a 10-mile drive up this heavily traveled, winding road to Bear Lake at 9,475 feet. Along the way you'll have a chance to see deer, elk and other wildlife, as well as views of the surrounding peaks. If you just want to look at the scenery, take one of the free shuttle buses, which leave from Glacier Basin Campground about halfway up the road. At the end of the road, Bear Lake Trail takes you a couple hundred yards to the pine-clad shores of the lake. Chances are you've seen a picture of the often-photographed Bear Lake with its unforgettable mountain backdrop.

Old Fall River Road—This was the first auto route over the Continental Divide in this part of the state, and it played a big part in the park's tourist boom of the early 1920s. The first 2 miles are paved and open to two-way traffic. After that, it's a narrow, one-way gravel road (uphill only!), which climbs 11 miles west before joining Trail Ridge Rd. at the summit of 11,796-foot Old Fall River Pass along the Continental Divide. The route is described by park officials as a "motor nature trail," so stop often to enjoy the scenery as the terrain turns from subalpine forest to alpine tundra. The route doesn't offer the spectacular vistas of Trail Ridge Rd. but does provide shelter from the harsh wind and closer contact with the wilderness. A very popular loop trip is to drive up Old Fall River Rd. and return on Trail Ridge Rd. (both roads closed in winter). To reach Old Fall River Rd. from Estes Park, drive west on Hwy. 34 to the Fall River Entrance Station. Proceed 2 miles from the entrance and turn right onto Old Fall River Rd. Along the way be sure to stop and investigate the enormous Alluvial Fan and its scattered debris that resulted from the Lawn Lake flood in 1982. Trailers and RVs over 25 feet long are prohibited from driving the road due to narrow switchbacks.

Trail Ridge Road (Hwy. 34)—No question about it, a drive over Trail Ridge Rd. is a must for any visitor to the park. You'll see an incredible amount of scenery in a short span of time. The narrow, winding 50-mile ribbon of asphalt stretching between Estes Park and Grand Lake is the highest continuous highway in the US. More than 200 men braved the elements to build Trail Ridge Rd., which opened in 1932. The landscape transition along the way is remarkable. Heading west the road climbs through meadows, spectacular mountain valleys and over the Continental Divide on a 13-mile stretch of alpine tundra that's similar to the arctic. Near the summit on the east side, Forest Canyon Overlook provides dramatic bird's-eye views down on a classic glaciated U-shaped valley and glacial cirque lakes. Forest Canyon Lakes are home to some of the park's black bear. From the 12,183-foot summit, the road drops down the Western Slope of the Continental Divide along the North Fork of the Colorado River through Kawuneeche Valley. Along the drive there are numerous pullouts and informational signs which provide excellent information about the changing ecosystems. Near the top, at the junction with Old Fall River Rd., you'll find the **Alpine Visitors Center**. The center has exhibits on this fragile tundra environment; knowledgeable rangers are on duty to answer your questions. There is also a snack bar and a souvenir shop.

Plan on spending three to four hours on the way to Grand Lake. The road is usually open from mid-May–mid-October, depending on snow conditions. To get to Trail Ridge Rd. (Hwy. 34), enter the park at either Beaver Meadows or Fall River, and follow the signs.

Skiing (Cross-Country)—

The best cross-country skiing in the Estes Park area is in the national park. Due to inconsistent and blowing snow, ski conditions change quickly in this area. Before heading out on a backcountry trip, be sure to check avalanche conditions at Park Headquarters. The rangers can also give you a number of good trail ideas.

Novices will enjoy the easy trails around **Glacier Basin Campground**. The main trail leaves the campground and heads southwest on easy terrain for 1 mile to **Sprague Lake**. There are also a multitude of trails in and around the campground. Glacier Basin Campground is located about 5 miles up Bear Lake Rd. Skiers must park on the west side of the road and walk across to the east side to begin skiing.

Black Lake offers a moderately difficult 8-mile round trip that takes you into some of the most spectacular country in the park. The trip starts at the Glacier Gorge Junction parking lot and follows the signs southwest toward Alberta Falls and Loch Lake. Just past the intersection of Icy Brook and Glacier Creek, turn south and follow Glacier Creek to Mills Lake. After passing Mills and Jewel lakes, continue along the creek through the forested drainage. When you break out of the trees, proceed up the open slope to Black Lake. The view from the lake looks out to Longs Peak to the east, McHenrys Peak to the west and Chiefs Head Peak to the south. This trail is for intermediate to advanced skiers. Glacier Gorge Junction parking lot is located about 9 miles up Bear Lake Rd.

For rentals and information see the Cross-Country Skiing section under Outdoor Activities.

Snowshoeing—

This is perhaps the best way to get around the park in wintertime because you don't have to rely on perfect snow conditions. Throughout the winter **Outdoor World** rents snowshoes. For information contact them at **156 E. Elkhorn Ave.; (303) 586-2114.**

Camping—

Camping is allowed in the park at five designated drive-in campgrounds. All charge a fee. During the summer all offer nightly campfire programs and daily guided nature walks. Advance reservations for **Moraine Park** and **Glacier Basin** campgrounds can be made year-round by calling **MISTIX** at **1-800-365-CAMP.** The other campgrounds are on a first-come, first-served basis. Camping is limited to seven days parkwide from June 1–Sept. 30. **Longs Peak Campground** has a three-day limit. No hookups or showers are available at campgrounds in the park. Camping is also available in the backcountry (see Hiking and Backpacking in this section for more information).

Aspenglen Campground is located 5 miles west of Estes Park off Hwy. 34 just past the Fall River entrance to the park. Fifty-four sites; closed in winter. **Glacier Basin Campground** is located 9 miles west of Estes Park. Enter the park on Hwy. 36 and turn south on Bear Lake Rd. This 150-site campground is closed in winter. **Longs Peak Campground** is a 26-site campground that's set up for tents only. It's located at the Longs Peak trailhead and is open all year. To get there from Estes Park, drive south on Hwy. 7 for 9.2 miles and turn right (west) to the Longs Peak Ranger Station. Follow the road 1 mile to the campground. **Moraine Park Campground** (247 sites) is located 3 miles southwest of Park Headquarters Visitors Center. Drive west into the park, turn left on Bear Lake Rd. and proceed 1.3 miles to Moraine Park Rd. Turn left and proceed to the campground. Open year-round. **Timber Creek Campground,** with 100 sites, is located 7 miles inside the west entrance to the park near Grand Lake. Open year-round.

FESTIVALS AND EVENTS

Rooftop Rodeo and Western Week
mid-July
Estes Park celebrates its western heritage with the Rooftop Rodeo and Western Week. The main draw is the rodeo, which has cowboys competing for various titles. Other events include a parade, a mountain man rendezvous and an arts and crafts fair. This annual rodeo has been going on for more than 60 years, so you can be assured there will always be one next year. For information call **1-800-44-ESTES.**

Longs Peak Scottish-Irish Festival
mid-September
Long, long ago in Scotland, clan members competed in curious contests of strength and stamina to prove themselves as capable soldiers. The ways of the Celts have crossed the Atlantic, and now this annual event in Estes Park provides a weekend of fun and sport. The traditional sporting events include the hammer throw and the caber toss—a caber, by the way, is a tree trunk, averaging 19 feet in length and 120 pounds. Other activities include Scottish bagpipe and drum-major competitions, a highland dance, a parade and sheepdog contests. The highlight of the celebration is the Tattoo, a performance of light and sound that has evolved over 300 years. This festival draws people from all over Colorado and the Rocky Mountain region. Call **(303) 586-6308** or **1-800-44-ESTES** for more information.

OUTDOOR ACTIVITIES

BIKING
MOUNTAIN BIKING

Estes Park offers a number of on- and off-road opportunities, and the local highways offer scenic routes (provided you don't mind cars). Dirt roads and trails in Roosevelt National Forest make for some enjoyable rides. For ideas, see the Four Wheel Drive Trips section. Opportunities in Rocky Mountain National Park are limited to roadways.

Rentals and Information—

For information and maps for rides in **Roosevelt National Forest**, contact the **Estes Park Office at 161 Second St., Estes Park CO 80517; (303) 586-3440.** Larry Wexler, owner of **Colorado Bicycling Adventures**, can set you up with all the equipment you'll need to take off and do some exploring. If you don't feel like taking off on your own, Wexler also provides guided mountain bike tours, including an overnighter in Colorado State Forest. Open year-round. **184 E. Elkhorn Ave., Estes Park, CO 80517; (303) 586-4241.** Rentals are also available at **Colorado Wilderness Sports, 358 E. Elkhorn Ave.; (303) 586-6548.**

TOURING

For information about touring in the national park, see the Major Attractions section.

CLIMBING
Colorado Mountain School—

If you want something a little more challenging than hiking, then you should check out the Colorado Mountain School. Owner Mike Donahue will teach you the ropes. A one-day introductory class will have you ready to take to the field with experienced guides. Everything from one-day climbs to extended international expeditions is offered. If you have an itch to climb a challenging route up Longs Peak, this is your chance. How about learning the finer points of ice climbing? Guided hikes and equipment rentals are also available. Open year-round; reservations requested. **PO Box 2062, 351 Moraine Ave., Estes Park, CO 80517; (303) 586-5758.**

Colorado Mountain Sports—

Offers climbing equipment rentals. **358 E. Elkhorn Ave.; (303) 586-6548.**

FISHING

Several opportunities for angling lie just outside of Estes Park. If you are interested in fishing within Rocky Mountain National Park, see the Major Attractions section. The local fishing authority is Scot Ritchie at **Scot's Sporting Goods**. He can direct you to the hot spots as well as set you up with tackle. Located 1.5 miles west of Estes Park on Hwy. 36 at **870 Moraine Ave., Estes Park, CO 80517; (303) 586-2877.**

Big Thompson River—

After gaining strength in Rocky Mountain National Park, the Big Thompson River flows through spectacular Big Thompson Canyon on its way to the plains. There is a good quality section of river (flies and lures only) starting about 5 miles downstream from Lake Estes. The best spot on this stretch is 8 miles downstream from the lake, just below a place called Grandpa's Retreat. To help nurture the primarily pan-sized rainbow and brown trout that call this stretch home, the Colorado Division of Wildlife and the National Forest Service have created several deep holes. The Big Thompson lies parallel to Hwy. 34 for much of its length, and small parking areas are located along the shoulder. This good stretch of water extends 5 to 9 miles down this heavily traveled, steep-walled canyon. The Forest Service recently developed and installed a barrier-free fishing ramp for wheelchairs. It's hard to realize today, but in 1976 a disastrous flood roared through this area, killing many people.

Lake Estes—

Located on the east side of town, between Hwys. 34 and 36, Lake Estes offers an easy-to-get-to spot for anglers who may not have time to search out more secluded areas. The Colorado Division of Wildlife regularly stocks the lake with 8- to 12-inch rainbows. Though the fishing pressure is heavy, an occasional lunker-sized German brown is caught. For best results use worms or salmon eggs on No. 8 and No. 10 hooks. Mepps lures at a quarter of an ounce or less are also effective. The **Lake Estes Marina** sells fishing tackle and rents boats by the hour. **1770 E. Big Thompson Ave.; (303) 586-2011.**

Marys Lake—

Marys Lake is like Lake Estes in almost every way except for its location. Try fishing the lake's inlet where the fish tend to congregate and feed. Take Hwy. 36 to the west end of Estes Park to Marys Lake Rd. (it's the only stoplight). Turn left and drive 1.5 miles to the small lake.

FOUR-WHEEL-DRIVE TRIPS

If you want to get away from the crowds, a sure way to do it is in a four-wheel-drive vehicle. For more information and maps contact the **Estes Park Office of Roosevelt National Forest** at **161 Second St., Estes Park, CO 80517; (303) 586-3440.**

Johnny Park Road—

This drive offers great views of Big Elk Meadows, North St. Vrain Creek drainage, Mt. Meeker and Longs Peak. From Estes Park, head 10 miles south on Hwy. 7 and turn left onto Big Owl Rd. (County Rd. 82). Continue to the junction with Johnny Park Rd. (Forest Rd. 118). The road eventually comes out at Hwy. 36 just north of Pinewood Springs.

Pole Hill Road—

From Estes Park drive 3 miles southeast on Hwy. 36 to the top of Park Hill. Turn left onto Pole Hill Rd. (Forest Rd. 122) at the sign for Ravencrest Chalet. Drive another mile and enter Roosevelt National Forest. There are numerous loop options

with a variety of terrain in this area. One short circle tour starts when you take the first left after entering the national forest. You'll pass an observation platform in this area referred to as The Notch. The platform affords excellent views of the Estes Valley, the Mummy Range to the north and Flattop Mountain and Hallett Peak west along the Continental Divide.

Pierson Park Road—

This beautiful, 10-mile drive can be taken in a loop from Estes Park. Drive 10 miles south on Hwy. 7 and turn left into the Meeker Park area. After 1.5 miles take another left onto Twin Sisters Rd. Look for the Pierson Park sign. This road takes you through a beautiful valley bordered by Twin Sisters Peaks to the west and House Rock, Pierson Mountain and Lion Head to the east.

Tours—

American Wilderness Tours—With six-wheeled trucks that look like they could go anywhere, these folks will take you to spots you may never see otherwise. Open during the summer season only (specific dates vary) Mon.–Sat. with Sun. tours available by reservation. **481 W. Elkhorn Ave., Estes Park, CO 80517; (303) 586-4237.**

GOLF

Estes Park Golf Club—

Low scores are hard to come by on this difficult mountain course, although it's only 6,000 yards long. Grainy greens make putting a real challenge. Be sure to keep in mind the location of Fish Creek while putting—the ball will invariably break that direction. Several of the par fours are pretty short, but the difficult par three 5th, 10th and 15th holes more than make up for them. The views are tremendous. In early fall elk wander onto the course and even on the greens, where their divots may need some attention. Located about 2 miles south of downtown Estes Park on Hwy. 7. **1080 S. St. Vrain Ave., Estes Park, CO 80517; (303) 586-8146.**

Lake Estes Executive Course—

This relatively flat nine-hole course provides views of the mountains to the west and Twin Owls to the north. Open all year, this challenging course requires complete concentration: Water is a big factor, including the par three 9th hole, which crosses over the Big Thompson River. Next to Lake Estes on Hwy. 34. **690 Big Thompson Ave., Estes Park, CO 80517; (303) 586-8176.**

HIKING AND BACKPACKING

Granted, the scenery from Estes Park is hard to beat, but you owe it to yourself to get out on a trail and escape the crowds, to see deer munching grass in an alpine meadow or the burst of wildflowers as you round a corner. Trails in Rocky Mountain National Park and nearby Roosevelt National Forest cover the spectrum from easy day hikes to challenging high alpine backpacking trips. The **Estes Park Office of Roosevelt National Forest** can provide maps and more information about hiking opportunities in the area; **161 Second St., PO Box 2747, Estes Park, CO 80517; (303) 586-3440.** For hikes in **Rocky Mountain National Park**, see the Major Attractions section.

For topographical maps, equipment and information, talk with the folks at **Colorado Wilderness Sports** at **358 E. Elkhorn Ave., Estes Park, CO 80517; (303) 586-6548.** Open year-round.

Crosier Mountain Trail—

This moderately difficult 8-mile round-trip hike starts at 7,200 feet and ends up at the 9,250-foot summit of Crosier Mountain. From the summit and various vantage points along the trail, you'll have fantastic views of the Continental Divide to the west in Rocky Mountain National Park. On your way to the summit you'll pass through lush aspen groves and meadows with ruins of settlers' homesteads. Keep an eye out for mule deer and take the time to enjoy the abundant and beautiful wildflowers. To get to the trailhead from Estes Park, take Devil's Gulch Rd. north-

east about 8 miles (about a mile beyond Glen Haven). There will be a large gravel cut on the right (south) side of the road. Pull in and park. The trailhead is just up the hill from a gate (please close).

Lily Mountain Trail—

Lily Mountain is a fairly easy 1.5-mile hike near Estes Park. The trail starts at 8,800 feet climbing 986 vertical feet to the summit. Along the way you'll have numerous opportunities for incredible views down to the Estes Valley. From the summit enjoy the panorama of the Mummy Range to the northwest, Longs Peak to the south and the Continental Divide to the west. Many boulders near the top provide challenging scrambling, if you like that kind of thing. The well-marked trail makes an ideal half-day trip. To reach the trailhead from Estes Park, take Hwy. 7 about 6 miles south. Just before mile-marker 6 there is a small turn-off on the right and a parking area by the trailhead sign.

Lion Gulch Trail—

This fairly easy trail starts at 7,360 feet and climbs 1,000 feet, taking you into Homestead Meadows, where remains of homesteaders' ranches dating back to 1889 dot the valley floor. Some ranch houses, corrals, outhouses and other log buildings are still standing. The trails that crisscross the area are readily accessible after you've made the 2.5-mile trip to the meadows on Lion Gulch Trail. You can easily spend an entire day exploring the ruins and perhaps pondering what it would have been like to live in these buildings in the early days. The area is an excellent spot for a picnic and the views won't disappoint you. To reach the trailhead from Estes Park, head southeast on Hwy. 36 to mile-marker 8. The trailhead is on the right side of the road.

Rocky Mountain National Park—

See the Major Attractions section.

HORSEBACK RIDING

Estes Park is home to numerous outfitters offering everything from pony rides for the kids to all-day and overnight rides. Most rides head for trails within Rocky Mountain National Park. Here are a couple of perennial outfitters.

Elkhorn Stables—
Located just west of downtown, they specialize in breakfast steak-fry rides. Reservations requested. **650 W. Elkhorn Ave.; (303) 586-3291** or **586-5225.**

Sombrero Ranch Riding Stables—
Offers one- and two-hour rides, breakfast and dinner trips, and pack trips. Only a couple of miles east of Estes Park on Hwy. 34. **(303) 586-4577** or **586-4517.**

LLAMA TREKKING
Keno's Llama & Guest Ranch—
Keno's offers llama hikes to the top of Teddy's Teeth for a great view. Not only will you be treated to exotic companionship, but you'll learn about the history and flora and fauna of the Estes Park area. Mainly geared for lunch hikes. Call ahead for reservations. Located across from Mary's Lake. **PO Box 2385, Estes Park, CO 80517; (303) 586-2827.**

SKIING
CROSS-COUNTRY SKIING
See Skiing (Cross-Country) under Rocky Mountain National Park.

Rentals and Information—
In addition to equipment and information, **Colorado Wilderness Sports** offers guided backcountry tours. **358 E. Elkhorn Ave., Estes Park, CO 80517; (303) 586-6548.**

Colorado Mountain School is a unique operation that can supply any equipment you need. They also lead backcountry tours and snow school courses. **351 Moraine Ave., Estes Park, CO 80517; (303) 586-5758.**

SWIMMING
Estes Park Aquatic Center—
This indoor/outdoor pool is open all year. Small fee charged. Located just south of Lake Estes at **660 Community Dr.; (303) 586-2340.**

Lake Estes—
There are several beach and picnic areas, but the lake is very cold. The **Lake Estes Marina, (303) 586-2011,** also rents boats, windsurfers and wet suits by the hour. Located just east of downtown on Hwy. 34.

TENNIS
Estes Valley Recreation and Park District—
Six courts are just waiting for you in Stanley Park. Playing is free unless you want to reserve a time. Located on **Community Dr**. just south of Lake Estes.

———— SEEING AND DOING ————

MUSEUMS AND GALLERIES
Estes Park Area Historical Museum—
The emphasis at this museum is the heritage of Estes Park and the surrounding area. Exhibits include a shiny Stanley Steamer automobile and numerous smaller displays relating the noteworthy people who settled Estes Park. Of note is the photo of the Joel Estes family taken in 1859 showing Estes and six of his 13 kids. Out in back next to an old homestead cabin is the original

Park Headquarters building, which houses a changing exhibit. Admission fee charged. Open 10 am–5 pm Mon.–Sat. and 1–5 pm Sun., May–Sept. Check for winter hours. **200 4th St.** (at Hwy. 36), **Estes Park, CO 80517; (303) 586-6256.**

MacGregor Ranch Museum—
In 1872 Alexander MacGregor visited Estes Park on a camping trip and fell in love with the land. That same year the Earl of Dunraven came to the valley and decided he wanted to own every acre.

MacGregor helped lead the fight against Dunraven's claims, and the museum contains all the documents telling the story of the land battle. You can also see ranch equipment, household items from the years 1870 to 1950 and more than 50 paintings by western artists. Check out the collection of antiques, china and silver. Marked walking trails wind around the ranch property. Admission is free. Open 11 am–5 pm Tues.–Sat., Memorial Day–Labor Day. Located half a mile north of Estes Park on Devil's Gulch Rd. at **180 MacGregor Ln., Estes Park, CO 80517; (303) 586-3749.**

NIGHTLIFE

The nightlife in Estes Park is somewhat limited, but with all the activities available while the sun shines, you might look upon this as a blessing. In addition to several bars on Elkhorn Ave. which feature live music, here are a couple of ideas.

Barleen Family Country Music Dinner Theater—

The Barleen family, featuring three generations of singers, musicians and comedians, has been entertaining folks for 14 years. The shows are a blend of country-western favorites along with pop music. Country-style dinner begins at 7 pm with the show following at 8 pm; no booze served. Open June–Sept.; closed on Sun. Half a mile south of the Holiday Inn on Hwy. 7. **Box 2326, 1110 Woodstock Dr.; (303) 586-5749.**

Stanley Hotel Theatre/Fine Arts Series—

Every year the Stanley presents a year-round series of theater and fine arts performances in a great setting, which it boasts is more than any other private property in the western US offers. See the Where to Stay section for more information on this historic hotel. **333 Wonderview Ave.; (303) 586-3371.**

SCENIC DRIVES

Old Fall River Road—

See the Major Attractions section.

Lyons Loop—

After you've driven across Trail Ridge Rd., other scenic drives pale in comparison. Even so, if you are interested in a beautiful 60-mile loop trip from Estes Park, consider this drive to Lyons and back. There are two fine restaurants along the way— **The Fawn Brook Inn** in the town of Allenspark and **La Chaumiere** in the community of Pinewood Springs (see Where to Eat). You may want to start out in the glow of late afternoon and stop for dinner as darkness descends.

The scenery is equally spectacular going either direction on the loop, but you'll start out south on Hwy. 7 under the craggy summits of Battle Mountain, Mt. Meeker, Longs Peak and Horsetooth Peak. By far the most impressive are 14,255-foot Longs Peak and 13,911-foot Mt. Meeker. You'll pass the Twin Sisters and a variety of lower peaks that lie to the east. About 11 miles from Estes Park be sure to stop at the St. Catherine's Chapel or "Chapel on the Rock." This place of worship, built in 1935, looks like it grew out of the massive rock on which it sits. After Allenspark, Hwy. 7 takes an eastern tack and enters a canyon with steep rock walls. The South St. Vrain Creek will be your traveling companion along this part of the drive. More spectacular scenery is in store as you hit Lyons and take Hwy. 36 back to Estes Park.

A highly recommended option, especially in autumn, is located to the south of Allenspark: the Peak to Peak Highway (now a designated Scenic and Historic Byway). To link up with this scenic highway, turn right (south) on Hwy. 72, 4 miles east of Allenspark. For detailed information see the Scenic Drives section of the **Boulder** chapter.

Trail Ridge Road—

Absolutely don't miss this one! See the Major Attractions section.

TRAMWAY

Aerial Tramway—

This tram will take you to the summit of 8,896-foot Prospect Mountain, which is virtually surrounded by the town of Estes Park. From the top you'll have great views of Longs Peak and the Continental Divide. Once at the summit you can stay until the last tram runs back down to town. Yes, they have a souvenir shop and a snack bar available while you are captive atop the mountain. Fee charged. Open mid-May–mid-Sept. **420 E. Riverside Dr., Estes Park, CO 80517; (303) 586-3675.**

WHERE TO STAY

ACCOMMODATIONS

Estes Park sports a multitude of lodging choices, ranging from the historic Stanley Hotel, to a Holiday Inn and right down to the most rustic of log cabins. Bed and breakfast choices in Estes are staggering—honeymooners, anniversary couples and others flock here regularly just for this reason. The **Estes Park Chamber of Commerce, (303) 586-4431** or **1-800-44-ESTES,** is very helpful in narrowing down the lodging choices for you. **Estes Park Central Reservations, 1-800-762-5968,** can actually book accommodations for you, from a limited selection of properties. Here are a few that have something special going for them.

The Anniversary Inn—$$$ to $$$$

This quaint log home, built in 1890, provides an excellent romantic getaway. Including the separate Sweethearts Cottage with its private Jacuzzi, The Anniversary Inn offers five room options (two with private baths). Spend time on the comfortable first floor and mingle with other guests while looking out the windows at deer that make their way onto the wooded property in early morning. A delicious full breakfast is served on the enclosed veranda each morning. Reservations recommended. **1060 Mary's Lake Rd., Moraine Route, Estes Park, CO 80517; (303) 586-6200.**

RiverSong Bed & Breakfast Inn— $$$ to $$$$

Situated on 27 wooded acres alongside the Big Thompson River, the RiverSong is truly an excellent place to get away with someone special. Owners Gary and Sue Mansfield explained that over 80 percent of their business is from birthdays, anniversaries and honeymoons. In addition to stunning views from the living room up to the Continental Divide and Hallet Peak, Gary and Sue really make guests feel at home, and Gary can furnish a wealth of information about the area's hiking trails, flora and fauna. Take a walk on one of the many hiking paths on the property.

Retire to a room decorated with antique furniture, or perhaps one with a private sauna and a huge sunken bathtub. Consider staying in the Cowboy's Delight—a large rustic room in the carriage house with its own deck, wood-burning stove and queen-sized four-poster bed. A recent addition—two duplexes—provides four more exquisite rooms. All of the rooms have unique themes, and 10 of the 12 have private bathrooms.

Wake up at a leisurely hour for a gourmet breakfast, including cream cheese tarts, Eggs Taos and John Wayne casserole. Reservations are essential. Open year-round; kids over 12 are welcome. **PO Box 1910, Estes Park, CO 80517; (303) 586-4666.**

The Stanley Hotel—$$$ to $$$$

At its grand opening in 1909, this elegant hotel, built by inventor F.O. Stanley, was said to rival anything of its size in the world. Horse teams moved supplies 22 miles to the site on roads built especially for the purpose. At its ideal hilltop perch, the hotel is now listed on the National Register of Historic Places.

When patrons arrived by Stanley Steamer from the railhead in Lyons, they walked into a lobby that stretched 80 feet on either side of the main desk. With ornate decor, a golf course, stables and other luxurious features, the hotel was indeed a spectacular establishment for 1909.

Over the years the hotel has played host to many notables, including Stephen

King. King was so taken with the hotel that he drew upon its ambience and history for the setting of his horror classic *The Shining*. Lack of snow, however, prevented the movie from being filmed here.

After a period of poor upkeep in the 1970s, The Stanley has undergone a renaissance that would make F.O. proud. The exterior has been painted white and, wherever possible, the rooms have been completely redone with original furnishings. Some of the elegant rooms once again feature canopied, four-poster beds and claw-foot bathtubs. The corner rooms provide magnificent views of the mountains and town. Meals are served in the still-impressive **MacGregor Room** and **Dunraven Grille**. Be sure to ask about the evening and Sunday-afternoon concert series. The hotel is open year-round. During summer weekends reservations must be made for at least two nights. **333 Wonderview Ave., PO Box 1767, Estes Park, CO 80517; 1-800-ROCKIES or (303) 586-3371.**

Inn of Glen Haven—$$$

For a secluded romantic bed and breakfast the Inn of Glen Haven continues to be a popular choice; many guests return year after year. Located in tiny Glen Haven, 7 miles north of Estes Park on Devil's Gulch Rd., this dark English country inn offers rooms ranging from victorian to colonial motifs. Most of the six rooms have private baths and two feature fireplaces. Two separate cottages are also available. Guests enjoy a continental breakfast at the elegant table on the first floor near the rock fireplace. The inn is also well known for its exquisite gourmet dinners ($$$) served 5:30–9 pm Wed.–Mon. in summer and Fri.–Sat. in winter. Call for reservations. **PO Box 219, Glen Haven, CO 80532; (303) 586-3897.**

Wind River Ranch—$$$

Owners Rob and Jere Irvin have worked hard to preserve the history of this 110-acre ranch homesteaded in 1876. Limited to 55 guests, this is a place where you can get away from the crowds and enjoy the stunning scenery in an unstructured, relaxed atmosphere. Take in the views of Longs Peak and Mt. Meeker from atop a trail-wise horse or from the ranch's heated pool and hot tub. Log cabins create a rustic atmosphere without neglecting the modern comforts. The main living room projects a comfortable atmosphere, with its large stone fireplace, beamed ceilings and walls lined with bookshelves. Sit down and enjoy a chat with other guests. This ranch is noted for its fine buffets, hearty steak dinners and patio picnics. Minimum stay of three days. Open from June through Sept. 10. The ranch is located at the top of Wind River Pass, 7 miles south of Estes Park on Hwy. 7. **PO Box 3410, Estes Park, CO 80517; (303) 586-4212.**

Glacier Lodge—$$ to $$$

Twenty cabins at this resort are nestled along the banks of the Big Thompson River—some are so close to the river you can fish from their front porches. Many of the cabins have fireplaces and all are equipped with full kitchens. Other cabins are located up on the hill, or you can stay in a lodge room. Glacier Lodge lives up to its western atmosphere offering horseback rides, fishing and western cookouts. There is also a heated swimming pool. Kids love the Soda Saloon, where they can meet others of the same age. Closed in winter. Minimum two-day stay, unless they happen to have an opening between reservations. **2166 Hwy. 66, Estes Park, CO 80517; (303) 586-4401.**

YMCA of the Rockies (Estes Park Center)—$$ to $$$

This family-style resort, sprawling over 1,400 forested acres, is virtually a small town. Once you get there, you may decide you don't need to go anywhere else. For those traveling with children, there are a variety of scheduled activities. You can drop off the kids for swimming, roller skating, basketball, tennis, horseshoes, volleyball, miniature golf, horseback riding and hayrides, to name just a few. In winter the sledding hill is an unforgettable experience, and there's always ice skating, snowshoeing and cross-country skiing. A rental shop can take care of all your equipment needs. Also available at this "town" are a church, restaurant, grocery store, library, museum and gift shop.

Most of the 220 cabins have fireplaces and all have refrigerators, stoves, telephones and at least one full bedroom. Some 460 lodge rooms, catering primarily to groups, offer motel-style accommodations. Low-priced YMCA temporary memberships are granted for the duration of your stay. Open year-round. For reservations and information, contact: **Estes Park Center/YMCA, 2515 Tunnel Rd., Estes Park, CO 80511-2550; (303) 586-3341**; Denver metro area **(303) 623-9215.**

Cascade Cottages—$ to $$

These small, spartan cabins, located on 40 acres along Fall River, lie just inside the park and are a great option for those who want to escape the crowds and high prices of Estes. Some of the 15 cabins were built back in the 1920s and have been in the Davis family for over 50 years. All units have heat, bath and kitchen facilities. Evidence of the immensely destructive Lawn Lake flood that roared down Fall River in 1982 can be seen throughout this area. Open Memorial Day–Labor Day. Most cabins are reserved a year in advance. Located one mile inside the park at the Fall River entrance. Summer address is **Fall River Road, Moraine Route, Estes Park, CO 80517.** Wintertime contact is **PO Box 781070, Wichita, KS 67278; (316) 687-6126.**

Colorado Mountain School—$

Known for its excellent climbing school, Colorado Mountain School also offers hostel-type accommodations year-round. Nothing fancy but the price is right. **PO Box 2062, 351 Moraine Ave., Estes Park, CO 80517; (303) 586-5758.**

H Bar G Ranch Hostel—$

The good news about the H Bar G is that it is one of the finest hostels in the country; the bad news is that you have to be a member of a hostel association to stay here. The ranch offers great mountain views with its dorm accommodations and cabin

rentals. Guests are required to do a chore each morning. The host, Lou Livingston, provides rides to and from town. Reservations are strongly suggested. The ranch is located a few miles north on Dry Gulch Road and then right on County Rd. 61. Open from late May–mid-Sept. In summer contact **PO Box 1260, Estes Park, CO 80517; (303) 586-3688;** in winter contact **700 Flagstaff Star Rt., Boulder, CO 80302; (303) 442-7296.**

CAMPING

In Rocky Mountain National Park—

See the Major Attractions section.

In Roosevelt National Forest—

Olive Ridge Campground (56 wooded campsites and a fee) is open all year. Located 13 miles south of Estes Park on Hwy. 7. For campsite reservations at least 10 days in advance, call **MISTIX** at **1-800-283-CAMP.**

Private Campgrounds—

Estes Park Campground—This campground has 65 sites and hot showers, but there are no electrical hookups. It also has a fairly quiet location with views of nearby mountains. Open June–early Sept. To get there from Estes Park, head west on Hwy. 36 and then left for 3 miles on Hwy. 66. **PO Box 3517, Estes Park, CO 80517; (303) 586-4188.**

National Park Resort—In addition to cabins and motel rooms ($$ to $$$), this place at the edge of Rocky Mountain National Park has RV hookups and numerous terraced tent sites spread out among the ponderosa pine on a mountainside with views into the park. Showers are available as well. Open May 1–Sept. 30. Located 4 miles west of Estes Park at **3501 Fall River Rd.-M.R., Estes Park, CO 80517; (303) 586-4563.**

Spruce Lake RV Park—This RV-only campground is open all year with 110 sites. Amenities include a rec room, a swimming pool, a laundry room, etc. Lake and stream fishing are also available. **1050 Marys Lake Rd., PO Box 2497, Estes Park, CO 80517; (303) 586-2889.**

WHERE TO EAT

La Chaumière—$$$$

The rather plain exterior of this small restaurant successfully disguises the excellent food to be had within. Heinz Fricker, your host and chef, specializes in French cuisine, which he considers an art form. He will delight you with masterful entrées such as grilled lamb with rosemary sauce; specials change nightly and entire menu changes every week or so. Be sure not to skip the excellent desserts. Reservations are recommended. Open all year starting at 5:30 pm Tues.–Sat.; at 1 pm on Sun. (2 pm in winter). Located in Pinewood Springs, 12 miles southeast of Estes Park on Hwy. 36; **(303) 823-6521.**

The Fawn Brook Inn—$$$$

Located in the sleepy village of Allenspark, this gourmand's delight is also known for its fine service, intimate atmosphere and excellent views. Sit back in the quaint rustic setting and enjoy a glass of wine or an imported Pauliner or other European beer. Select from a menu that specializes in German preparation of veal, lamb, steak and duck. Start out your meal with a crock of soup. While you're waiting for a table, relax in front of the stone fireplace. Reservations are recommended. Open May 1–mid-Oct. for dinner Tues.– Sat. 5–9 pm; Sun. hours for lunch noon–2 pm and dinner 4–8:30 pm. Open weekends only the rest of the year. To reach the restaurant, drive 15 miles south from Estes Park on the Hwy. 7 business loop in Allenspark; **(303) 747-2556.**

The Dunraven Inn—$$ to $$$

The Dunraven Inn continues to draw loyal patrons, some looking for a beer at the bar, and others seeking the fine Italian cuisine. House specialties include lasagna, eggplant parmigiana marinara and chicken cacciatore. A great selection of Italian wines is available. The walls of the lounge are covered with Mona Lisa wallpaper and dollar bills—tacked up with personal notes by customers. You'd better make reservations

or be ready for a long wait during the summer. Dinner is served 5–10 pm Sun.–Thurs., 5–11 pm Fri. and Sat. Open year-round. **2470 Hwy. 66; (303) 586-6409.**

Orlando's Steak House—$$ to $$$

Let's make it clear—the reason to eat at Orlando's is for the steak. It's located over the rowdy Wheel Bar on Elkhorn Ave. On weekend nights you can hear the shouts of drunks playing pool downstairs. Both the restaurant space and its menu are small. The latter consists of a filet mignon, two sirloin cuts, herbed chicken and a seafood special. A fresh loaf of bread comes with each meal. In addition to the red tablecloths, the cloth napkins rolled up like cowboy bandannas (minus the sweat) provide a nice touch. Open nightly for dinner 5:30–10:30 p.m. Closed Wed. in summer and Tues.–Wed. in winter. **132 E. Elkhorn Ave.; (303) 586-6121.**

La Casa El Centro—$ to $$$

In summer head straight to the pretty outdoor garden at this Mexican/Cajun-style restaurant. The dual cuisines provide excellent blackened shrimp and redfish, voodoo chicken, a spicy beef burrito or the family specialty, the Estorito. Those who can't get enough of Chef Lee's Cajun food can take home a package of his spice or batter mix. La Casa also has a bar area that serves margaritas on tap. It sounds exotic, but be warned—these margs are carbonated and fizzy. Live guitar music nightly. Open 11 am–10 pm year-round. **222 E. Elkhorn Ave.; (303) 586-2807.**

The Baldpate Inn—$$

It's hard to praise the Baldpate Inn enough as a unique, special place to eat. It has all the ingredients: delicious food, charm, a fascinating history and incredible views from the porch. Lois Smith, the co-owner and chef, is a cooking and baking machine in summer, producing incredibly delicious homemade soups, corn bread, pies and cakes which complement the all-you-can-eat salad bar. People flock here from Estes Park as well as from other towns along the Front Range.

This cozy log building, built back in 1917, gets its name from a famous mystery novel of the time—*Seven Keys to Baldpate*. The connection with the novel (which subsequently became a Broadway play and movie) led people to begin leaving keys at the inn or sending them. Today the inn's Key Room has over 15,000 keys, and it's definitely worth a look. The only problem with the Baldpate is that it's not open year-round. Restaurant hours are 11:30 am–7 pm daily in summer and 4–7 pm in Sept. Reservations for the restaurant and a fairly rustic, though charming, 12-room inn ($$$ to $$$$) are highly recommended. **4900 S. Highway 7, PO Box, 4445, Estes Park, CO 80517; (303) 586-6151.**

Ed's Cantina & Grill—$ to $$

Locals flock to Ed's year-round for good food and quick, friendly service for a reasonable price. Start off the morning with a traditional breakfast or one of the Mexican-style specialties; lunch and dinner items also focus on Mexican dishes, but burgers, sandwiches and salads also hold their own. Others head to Ed's to quaff a cold beer at the bar and catch a game on the large TV. Open 7 am–11 pm daily. **362 E. Elkhorn Ave.; (303) 586-2919.**

Johnson's Cafe—$

Located unobtrusively in the upper Stanley Village shopping center, Johnson's Cafe serves up what we think is the best breakfast in town. Bacon, eggs and omelettes are available, but Milt's "wonderful" waffles and Swedish potato pancakes are the real morning specialties. Also try the Arizona hash browns, smothered with jack cheese and salsa. Lunch items include homemade soups, sandwiches, chili and pies. Outside seating is available (weather permitting). Open 7 am–2:30 pm Mon.–Sat. In Upper Stanley Village at **457 E. Wonderview; (303) 586-6624.**

SERVICES

Estes Park Central Reservations—

This office can help you book limited accommodations. **481 W. Elkhorn Ave., Estes Park, CO 80517; 1-800-762-5968** toll free; in Estes Park call **(303) 586-4402** or **(303) 586-4237.**

Estes Park
Chamber of Commerce
and Information Center—

Well staffed with knowledgeable volunteers, this information center is open daily. **500 Big Thompson Ave., Estes Park, CO 80517; (303) 586-4431** or **1-800-44-ESTES.**

Transportation—

Charles Tours & Travel Services—This company provides year-round tours of the area as well as transport to and from Denver International Airport. **PO Box 4373, Estes Park, CO 80517; (303) 586-5151** or **1-800-950-3274; 429 W. Elkhorn, in West Park Shopping Center**

The Estes Park Trolley—Provides easy transportation around town (summer only). Runs 9 am–6 pm daily; fee charged. **PO Box 3111, Estes Park, CO 80517; (303) 586-8866.**

Fort Collins and West

In a fine location between the northeastern plains and the foothills of the Colorado Rockies, Fort Collins residents enjoy a balanced and relaxed lifestyle. Because Fort Collins' economy has always been tied to farming and ranching on the eastern plains, the city lacks some of the drama and excitement of Colorado's well-known mining boomtowns. On the flip side, some 94,000 people have chosen to call Fort Collins home, in part because it has always maintained the heart and friendly attitude of a small town.

The city's downtown area is not much larger than that of some midwestern towns with one third the population. One particularly nostalgic section of Fort Collins is Old Town. The restoration of this original business district in the early 1980s provided a natural linkage for small shops, galleries, restaurants and pubs. Old Town's many businesses have taken up residence in spruced-up brick buildings dating from the 1880s. Highlighted by a quiet pedestrian mall and ample outdoor cafe seating, Old Town is easy to explore on foot.

A large student contingent at Colorado State University (CSU) keeps a youthful edge on the town. University-sponsored programs and sporting events are planned throughout the year, and 20,000 students give the town's nightlife a spark. It may also account for the large number of micro-brewery operations in the area. True to the town's farming roots, CSU still has a highly touted agricultural program, along with other diverse curriculum offerings. Linking high-tech research with agriculture has been a boon to the area economy.

Though Fort Collins provides plenty to do, it is more aptly described as a gateway for vacationers rather than a vacation destination in itself. The town provides easy access to some of Colorado's best recreation lands, which are often overshadowed by nearby Rocky Mountain National Park. Many visitors never hear about the Red Feather Lakes area or the beautiful, granite-walled Cache La Poudre Canyon (now designated a Colorado Scenic and Historic Byway) just west of Fort Collins. The Poudre River barrels out of the mountains through Roosevelt National Forest and its four wilderness areas. Together these lands provide diverse opportunities for hiking, fishing, camping, rafting and cross-country skiing. Outside of the wilderness areas, miles of excellent mountain bike trails lure you into the backcountry. At the doorstep of some of this state's prettiest terrain, Fort Collins uniquely draws together the best attributes of the mountains and plains.

HISTORY

The name of the city notwithstanding, there is no military base here. In fact, there hasn't been a fort in Fort Collins since the 1860s.

The mountainous area west of modern-day Fort Collins was well known to Indians, fur traders and trappers who passed through and camped under tall cottonwoods, long before any permanent settlement was established. Traders and Indians peacefully coexisted in the Cache la Poudre area. The Cache la Poudre ("hide the powder") River receives its name from a party of French trappers who stashed their heavy barrels of gunpowder at the river's edge to make traveling through deep snow less burdensome. In 1844 life there was so good for one trader that he described the area, with its mild climate, rugged landscape and teeming buffalo herds, as "the loveliest spot on earth."

In the late 1850s gold discoveries in the Rockies prompted a number of fortune hunters to pour into the Cache la Poudre area. Few people found any gold to speak of, but some of the discouraged prospectors set up farms and ranches. In 1871 Camp Collins, a short-lived military encampment, was established to protect the Overland Trail and the few farms and ranches nearby, but it was soon abandoned simply because it wasn't needed. A couple of years later lots were offered for sale in an agricultural colony modeled after the successful Union Colony at Greeley, just to the east. No ruffians applied, as the lots were sold only to temperate people of "high moral character."

The survival of Fort Collins was not assured in its early days, as it had a population of only a few hundred people. In September 1879 the Agricultural College of Colorado opened its doors to five students. Experiments at this land grant institution resulted in improved farming and ranching techniques. In the early 1900s the state's sugar beet industry and other agricultural pursuits helped the young town continue a slow but sustained growth. The agricultural college eventually grew into highly respected Colorado State University, the engine that still links the area's past with its future potential. Over the past 15 years, Hewlett-Packard, NCR and other high-tech companies have come to understand the many benefits of locating here.

GETTING THERE

Fort Collins is located 60 miles north of Denver on Interstate 25. It's also 45 miles south of Cheyenne, Wyoming, off Interstate 25. The mountainous area to the west of Fort Collins is accessible almost solely from Hwy. 14. Denver International Airport is well served by shuttle vans to Fort Collins. Contact **Airport Express** in Fort Collins for reservations and information at **(303) 482-0505**. Greyhound Trailways Bus Lines makes five daily trips between Denver and Fort Collins.

———— FESTIVALS AND EVENTS ————

Fort Collins has a number of small festivals. If you happen to be in town you might want to stick around for one of the following:

Fort Collins Flying Festival
late September
This spectator event features everything from kite flying to hot-air balloon races. Since the Fort Collins area is known for excellent wind currents, this is a perfect place for all kinds of aerial sports. For more information contact the **Fort Collins Convention and Visitors Bureau (303) 482-5821** locally or **1-800-274-3678.**

Sculpture in the Park
early August
The town of **Loveland** (a dozen miles south of Ft. Collins) has long been a haven for sculpture. But the main event occurs each summer when 200 sculptors come to Benson Park to sell and display their work for thousands of visitors. Prices range from $400 to $60,000, which makes the nominal admission fee seem like a real bargain. The park also contains 37 permanent sculptures in a collection that grows each year. It makes visiting here worthwhile anytime. From Hwy. 287 head west on 29th St. and follow the signs. For additional information call **(303) 663-2940** or **1-800-551-1752.**

New West Fest
mid-August
Celebrating the city's birthday seems to be a habit in these parts. The city just celebrated number 126 with a huge party that is becoming northern Colorado's largest event. A hodgepodge of musical entertainment and other acts take to stages around the town, and you can be a member of the audience for free. Endless lines of booths offer artsy-craftsy items and lots of tempting, sweet-smelling food. The festival attracts tens of thousands of people over a long summer weekend. Call **(303) 482-5821 locally** or **1-800-274-3678** nationwide for information.

———— OUTDOOR ACTIVITIES ————

BIKING
MOUNTAIN BIKING
The remote and beautiful scenery in the mountains to the west of Fort Collins warrants the extra effort of getting here. A wide range of scenic mountain bike routes can be accessed in the Roosevelt National Forest. For trail ideas stop by the **Redfeather/Estes-Poudre Ranger District Offices** at **1311 S. College, Ft. Collins, CO 80524; (303) 498-1375; 498-2775.** Another excellent possibility is the Colorado State Forest where a network of gravel and four-wheel-drive roads wind together in many loop combinations. Also, within the forest you can bike yurt to yurt on the Never Summer Nordic Yurt System (see the **North Park** chapter).

Horsetooth Mountain Park—
This mountain park, on the western side of Horsetooth Reservoir, and Lory State Park provide miles upon miles of terrific mountain biking trails. See Parks and Recreation Areas for information.

TOURING
An extensive bike trail system winds its way through Fort Collins connecting many points within the city. Bicycle shops in town carry a supply of "Tour de Fort," a free map with 56 miles of local bike trails. One especially nice ride is the snaking trail that runs alongside the Cache la Poudre River in north Fort Collins (see the Scenic Drives section). Not only is it relatively flat and very scenic, but it is accessible from several points in the

city. Here's a longer trip in the mountains to the west of Fort Collins.

Bingham Hill—

To get to Bingham Hill, ride north on Overland Trail Rd., a main north-south artery that lies just west of the city. Once on Overland Trail Rd., continue north past W. Vine Dr. and Lake Lee on the right. About 5.5 miles from downtown Fort Collins, turn left (west) onto Bingham Hill Rd., marked by a sign to Lory State Park. The road is somewhat steep, but you'll enjoy a far-reaching view out to the plains. You'll see many other bicyclists on the Overland Trail and Bingham Hill route.

Rentals and Information—

There's no better place to rent a used bike at extremely reasonable rates than **The Whistlestop, 410 Jefferson; (303) 224-5499.** If you don't want to lose each other on the trail, **Together Tandems** is the absolute safest bet. They rent touring and mountain tandems, and child trailers, too. **2030 S. College Ave.; (303) 224-0330.**

FISHING

The Fort Collins area presents an unusual combination of stream trout fishing and warmwater lake fishing. In addition, an abundance of tributaries, small lakes and beaver ponds in the high country west of Fort Collins have trout. This water often presents challenging, uncrowded fly-fishing for smallish (8- to 10-inch) brook trout or cutthroats. Stop by any local fishing store for information about current conditions. Fly-fishermen interested in arranging guided wade or float fishing trips, renting equipment or just shooting the bull should check in at **St. Peters Fly Shop, 202 Remington St.; (303) 498-8968.**

Big Thompson River—

See the **Estes Park** chapter.

Cache la Poudre River—

The Poudre offers long stretches of accessible water along its journey east from the high reaches of Rocky Mountain National Park. Much of the river parallels Hwy. 14 as it flows easterly toward Fort Collins. Though the Poudre has a predominant brown and rainbow trout population (averaging about 11 inches), it's also home to a number of ugly whitefish. Actually, the whitefish are strong fighters and surprisingly good to eat. Fly-fishing is the most effective way to take Poudre River trout, but fishermen occasionally do well with lures, worms or salmon eggs. One warning for bait anglers and encouraging news for fly-fishermen: The Poudre has two Wild Trout sections in which bait is not allowed. These well-marked sections are located between mile 28.1 to 31.4 and 35.1 to 40.2. Others are farther upstream near the town of Rustic. The Poudre River is scenic, easy to reach from Fort Collins and, as a result, heavily fished. There are campgrounds, picnic grounds, resorts and frequent turn-offs along Hwy. 14. Try fishing the Poudre in the area near Long Draw Reservoir where the river comes out of Rocky Mountain National Park. To get there from Fort Collins, head 10 miles northwest on Hwy. 287 and then 53 miles west on Hwy. 14. Turn left (south) on Long Draw Reservoir Rd. (Forest Rd. 156). The best time to fish the Poudre is from mid-July and prior to runoff in the spring. If you take only one fly along to fish the Poudre, make sure it's a Hare's Ear nymph (size 8 to 14 hook).

Horsetooth Reservoir—

See the Parks and Recreation Areas section for fishing information.

Laramie River—

In the Chambers Lake area, the Laramie can be good fishing for small brook and cutthroat trout. The narrow stream flows north through the Laramie River Valley, and eventually into Wyoming with many beaver ponds along the way. To get here from Fort Collins, drive northwest on Hwy. 287 for 10 miles and then west on Hwy. 14 for 52 miles. Turn right (north) on Laramie River Rd. (County Rd. 103).

Red Feather Lakes—

Red Feather Lake is only one of 14 lakes in the Red Feather region, about 50 miles northwest of Fort Collins. Six of the lakes are open to public recreation with fishing as the main attraction. The fishing can be good whether you're in a boat or fishing from the shore. You can use flies, lures or bait, except on Parvin Lake, which is restricted to flies and lures only. Red Feather Lakes can be reached from Fort Collins by taking Hwy. 287 northwest for 22 miles. Turn left onto Red Feather Lakes Rd. (the old North Park freight trail) at the Forks Cafe and continue about 25 miles to the lakes. Red Feather Lakes are also accessible from Poudre Canyon (Hwy. 14) via County Rd. 69 at Rustic. At Goodell Corner, turn left onto County Rd. 162 and continue to the lakes.

Watson Lake/Poudre River—

Watson Lake, which has plenty of parking and some picnic tables, is stocked regularly with trout. The Poudre flows by Watson and is also stocked. Fishing pressure on both Watson Lake and this section of the Poudre River is pretty heavy. If you come up empty, however, you can always stop by the hatchery on the way out and see thousands of trout. Watson Lake is about 8 miles northwest of Fort Collins. To get here take Hwy. 287 a mile past La Porte and, at the junction, turn left onto Rist Canyon Rd. (at a marked turn for the Bellvue Fish Hatchery). Continue about a mile to the lake.

FOUR-WHEEL-DRIVE TRIPS

Green Ridge Trail—

This scenic, moderately difficult 17-mile round-trip drive includes several narrow and challenging sections of road. The drive starts at about 9,400 feet and passes Lake Laramie and Twin Lakes before ending at Deadman Rd. (10,200 feet). Just before reaching Deadman Rd., the trail goes through thick stands of lodgepole pine to Nunn Creek Basin. To the west from Nunn Creek Basin are sweeping views of the Medicine Bow Range. To reach Green Ridge Trail, take Hwy. 14 up Poudre Canyon for 52 miles. Turn right on Laramie River Rd. (County Rd. 103) and drive about 1.5 miles to Lost Lake parking lot. The trail, marked with a sign, starts at the north end of the parking lot.

Kelly Flats—

This rugged, seldom-used road has steep hills and some challenging stream crossings—good ground clearance is a must. The 9-mile round trip leads to the top of Wintersteen Mesa, which provides a panorama of Poudre Canyon and parts of Rocky Mountain National Park to the south. Continue west to Manhattan Rd., which runs north and south between the town of Rustic and Red Feather Lakes. To reach the road, take Hwy. 14 west up Poudre Canyon for 20 miles to Kelly Flats Campground. Turn right off Hwy. 14, just past the campground, and head north. The first 1.5 miles is a steep climb which drops off into a drainage, then climbs for another 2 miles before leveling off in a grassy meadow. At the end of the road, return to Poudre Canyon via County Rd. 69.

GOLF

Collindale Golf Course—

This fine 18-hole course is the first choice of locals. Characterized by many mature cottonwood trees, a number of creeks and carefully maintained fairways, Collindale is open all year, weather permitting. Unless there has been a lot of rain, the greens are usually very fast. So that you don't end up breaking your fairway wood across your knee on the very first hole, be forewarned: There is a large hidden lake to the front right of green No. 1. Full service. **1441 E. Horsetooth Rd.; (303) 221-6651.**

Ptarmigan Golf and Country Club—

Though this is a fairly new course, you can be sure of having a memorable and challenging round—it was designed by Jack Nicklaus. In true Nicklaus fashion, the course follows the natural contour of the rolling terrain, rather than trying to dominate it. And it's tough. Long water hazards, lots of trees and monstrously large sand traps come into play on just about every hole. One of the sand traps is as expansive as a California beach, complete with a grass island in the middle. The back nine is considerably more hilly than the front. Currently Ptarmigan is rounding up enough memberships so they can go private—so don't waste any time. Call two days in advance for a tee time unless you happen to be a member. Located southeast of Fort Collins, just east of the Windsor exit off Interstate 25. **5412 Vardon Wy.; (303) 226-6600.**

HIKING AND BACKPACKING

Within the Roosevelt National Forest to the west of Fort Collins, four wilderness areas including the Cache la Poudre, Neota, Comanche Peak and Rawah provide varied terrain ranging from easy, low-altitude hikes to multi-day backpack trips. Two of the most spectacular areas are Rawah and Comanche Peak with pine forests, alpine tundra, barren rock formations, high peaks, cirque lakes and moraines, trout streams and an abundance of wildlife. Both have extensive, interconnecting trail systems. These areas deserve more than just a peek.

For more specific details about the wilderness areas and other parts of Roosevelt National Forest, stop in at the **Redfeather/Estes-Poudre Ranger District Offices** at **1311 S. College, Ft. Collins, CO 80524; (719) 498-1375.** They can supply you with pamphlets and maps of the forest area. In summer two forest service visitors centers can give you tips: at the Arrowhead Lodge, 3 miles west of Rustic on Hwy. 14, and at the old ranger station in the Red Feather Lakes area on Dowdy Lake Rd. Open Space and Trails Guide, a pamphlet offered free of charge by the city of Fort Collins, shows short hikes in town and the foothills. Further information, maps and rental equipment may be picked up at **The Mountain Shop at 632 S. Mason; (303) 493-5720.**

Browns Lake Trail—

This beautiful 4-mile (one way) hike in the Comanche Peak Wilderness Area, at altitudes between 10,000 and 12,000 feet, illustrates up close what the term "treeline" means. Though much of the trail is rather barren, it eventually drops down to Browns Lake in a heavily wooded area. In summer many colorful wildflowers line the trail. To reach the trailhead, head up Poudre Canyon on Hwy. 14 for 26 miles to Pingree Park Rd. (Forest Rd. 131) and turn left. Take Pingree Park Rd. 4 miles and keep right at Crown Point Rd. (Forest Rd. 139) for another 12 miles. The trail is on the left.

Cache la Poudre Wilderness Area—

This small wilderness area ranges in altitude from a little more than 6,000 feet to 8,600 feet, but it does not have the overwhelming beauty of some of the higher mountain areas. The trade-off is that the steep, rugged terrain is seldom traveled. Mt. McConnel Trail is the only maintained trail in the wilderness area. It's a 5-mile loop climbing through juniper, fir and pine to the summit. Once there, eat lunch at the flat rock while enjoying the views. Other parts of the wilderness area are accessible, if you don't mind bushwhacking. Your efforts will be rewarded with solitude, thick forests and a chance to glimpse some of Colorado's more exotic fauna—bear, mountain lion and the endangered peregrine falcon. The South Fork of the Cache la Poudre River flows through the west central part of the wilderness, so there is a chance for fishing as well. From Fort Collins head northwest on Hwy. 287 for 10 miles and then west on Hwy. 14 for 22 miles to Mountain Park Campground. The wilderness area is south of the river (you'll see the Mt. McConnel trailhead).

Greyrock Trail—

Greyrock is perhaps the best known and one of the most often recommended day hikes in the Fort Collins area. It's a fairly steep 3-mile (one way) hike but the reward comes at the 7,500-foot summit where you'll have views west to higher mountains and east to the plains and Fort

Collins. You might even catch sight of a bobcat or a black Abert's squirrel. Local hikers rate Greyrock as a much better experience during spring or fall, when it is less crowded and cooler, than in summertime. The Greyrock Trailhead is located 9 miles west up Poudre Canyon on Hwy. 14. A parking lot is provided opposite the trail, which begins by crossing a footbridge. You might consider Meadows and Dadd Gulch trails, a couple of longer, but extremely scenic options within the same area.

Lory State Park—

More than 30 miles of hiking trails attract many people to this nearby park, only 20 minutes from Fort Collins. The elevation is low enough that you can hike all year, though there are a few snowstorms in winter. One suggested hike is Arthur's Rock. Trail maps are available at the park entrance. See the Parks and Recreation Areas section for directions.

Mirror Lake—

The trail to this high alpine lake at 11,000 feet takes you through a beautiful section of Rocky Mountain National Park. It's a tough, 7-mile hike over steep terrain through pine and fir to the glacial moraine that holds Mirror Lake. You'll also pass a waterfall on the way. There are two forks along the trail: At the first fork, head right and keep left at the second one. To reach the trailhead from Fort Collins, head northwest on Hwy. 287 for 10 miles and then west on Hwy. 14 for 53 miles. Turn left on Long Draw Reservoir Rd. (Forest Rd. 156). Continue for 8 miles and look for the parking area on the left side of the road. The trail begins by following Corral Creek.

Rawah Lakes Trail—

This 10-mile hike into the heart of the Rawah Wilderness Area makes a great overnighter. It's a fairly steep hike, climbing 2,100 feet through aspen and pine forests, eventually giving way to spruce and fir. From Rawah Lakes there are spectacular views of surrounding peaks in the Medicine Bow and Mummy ranges. The lakes even yield an occasional trout. To reach the trailhead from Fort Collins, drive 10 miles northwest on Hwy. 287 and then 52 miles west on Hwy. 14. Turn right (north) on Laramie River Rd. (County Rd. 103). Continue about 12 miles to the trailhead near Rawah Ranch. Start hiking west.

HORSEBACK RIDING

Fort Collins has a long tradition of interest in horses. Indeed, as far back as the 1880s, the town was home to a two-story livery stable. Today CSU has a nationally known equine sciences program and Fort Collins is undeniably western in its outlook.

Double Diamond Stables—

Located within Lory State Park west of town, Double Diamond offers miles of uncrowded trails over rolling terrain. They rent mainly Tennessee walkers that are easy on the back if you haven't been on a horse in a while. Double Diamond also has breakfast and dinner rides, hayride parties, western entertainment and guided tours. During winter sleigh rides are offered. Call ahead for reservations and information. **(303) 224-4200.**

Sno-Cap Stables—

These stables also offer hayrides, guided trips and mountain horses for hunting and fishing expeditions. Sno-Cap Stables can be found at Livermore, about 35 miles northwest of Fort Collins on Hwy. 287. Call **(303) 482-4784** for information.

ICE SKATING

Edora Pool Ice Center—

Skate year-round at this excellent indoor arena. Rentals, changing room, lessons and a snack bar are all available. **1801 Riverside Dr.; (303) 221-6679.**

PARKS AND RECREATION AREAS

Horsetooth Reservoir—

Named after a nearby rock that looks vaguely like a horse's tooth, this body of water just west of town attracts hordes of people for water recreation as well as hiking, mountain biking and horseback riding. Many dirt roads and trails wind through the land surrounding Horsetooth Reservoir providing scenic, hilly tours on foot or mountain bike. Horsetooth Mountain Park and Lory State Park, adjacent to the reservoir, offer wide stretches of public land. Horsetooth Reservoir has almost 4,000 acres of water and attracts people from much of northern Colorado. There are picnic and camping areas as well as several marinas. Horsetooth sometimes gets very crowded with swimmers, boaters, waterskiers, windsurfers, etc.

Horsetooth Reservoir is the first choice of many fishermen in this area who come for kokanee salmon, various species of trout (including Mackinaw up to 30 pounds), bass and walleye. You can fish Horsetooth by boat, but because the shoreline drops off quickly, it's possible to fish very deep water from the bank. The problem is that most of the shoreline is composed of large boulders and smaller rocks that make moving around kind of tough. Horsetooth has a reputation of being either hot or very slow. Fish can be taken with lures or bait. A map of the reservoir put together by HydroSurveys Inc. (available at area sporting goods stores) is extremely handy because it shows water depth as well as other pertinent information.

More information about Horsetooth is available from the **Larimer County Parks Department** at **(303) 226-4517**. To get to the reservoir from downtown Fort Collins, drive west on virtually any road until you reach Overland Trail Rd. at the edge of town. Turn left (south) and drive to County Rd. 42C at the south end of town. Then turn right (west) and continue to the reservoir.

Lory State Park—

Lory State Park borders the west side of Horsetooth Reservoir in an area between the prairie and foothills. The transitional environment is remarkably rugged and scenic, featuring rolling hills, tall grasses, wide sculpted valleys and sharply uplifted rock formations to the west. With its close proximity to town, the park attracts people for its 30 miles of hiking trails, backcountry camping, rock climbing, picnicking, horseback riding (**Double Diamond Stables, 303-224-4200**) and mountain biking. An easy gravel road travels through the center of the park. Fishing in the coves from the west shore of Horsetooth Reservoir can be quite good. In winter, after a snowstorm, it's an ideal place for cross-country skiing.

Visitors frequently spot deer, rabbits and many birds; occasional sightings of prairie rattlesnakes, bear and bobcat occur as well. To reach the park from town drive west to Overland Trail Rd. Turn right (north) and continue past W. Vine Dr. and Lake Lee on the right. Turn left (west) onto Bingham Hill Rd., marked by a sign, to Lory State Park. Turn left again at the T intersection leading 3 miles to the park entrance. Stop by the park office just 300 yards beyond the entrance for information, maps and advice. **708 Lodgepole Dr., Bellvue, CO 80512; (303) 493-1623.**

RIVER FLOATING

For river floating in the Fort Collins vicinity the choice is obvious—the **Cache la Poudre**. It's definitely one of the state's hot spots for both rafters and kayakers. The river starts high in Rocky Mountain National Park and works its way 25 miles northeast before turning abruptly east. For the next 40 miles the Poudre twists down a deep canyon that it has slowly scoured out of the granite. Spilling out onto the plains, it loses its fight and flows gently into the South Platte River.

Kayakers are particularly attracted to the Poudre; it offers some serious whitewater stretches rating up to Class IV and Class V. The problem is that the river can only be run in short sections, due to water diversions and a number of suicidal boulder-clogged rapids that are feared by even the finest rafters and kayakers. The Poudre Canyon stretch can be easily scouted from Hwy. 14, which follows alongside; a number of picnic areas and campgrounds provide easy access. If you are going to arrange your own raft or kayak trip, be sure to check with the forest service or an outdoor shop in Fort Collins about the dangerous sections and how to avoid them. If you want to leave the worries to an experienced guide, then contact one of the following.

Rocky Mountain Adventures—This outfitter specializes in half-day family runs down the Poudre on paddle rafts. Advance reservations are a must. **1816 Orchard Pl., Fort Collins, CO 80521; (303) 493-4005.**

Wildwater Inc.—Although they offer trips around the state, their Poudre runs are definitely the most popular. The "Poudre Wildwater" trip is a half-day run that anyone can handle, while the "Poudre Wild and Scenic" offers some very tough whitewater stretches. Trips run from May into Aug. Call for reservations and details. **317 Stover St., Fort Collins, CO 80524; (303) 224-3379.**

SKIING
CROSS-COUNTRY SKIING

Although Fort Collins is a long way from the major downhill skiing areas, locals get their skiing fix on a multitude of cross-country ski trails. Opportunities abound. Whenever there is enough snow, skiers take to nearby areas, such as Fort Collins City Park or Lory State Park. But cross-country skiers from Fort Collins most often head for the high country. Cameron Pass is perhaps the most popular area. For information and maps stop by the **Redfeather/Estes-Poudre Ranger District Offices** at **1311 S. College, Ft. Collins, CO 80524; (719) 498-1375.**

Backcountry Trails—
Blue Lake and Long Draw Trails—Blue Lake is a moderately difficult 6.5-mile trail offering very diverse terrain, from steep, uphill sections to level glides through meadows. The trail climbs steadily uphill from 9,500 feet to 10,800 feet. Panoramic views of the Mummy Range and Rocky Mountain National Park await you at the

lake, but there is plenty of scenery along the way. To reach the trailhead from Fort Collins, drive 10 miles northwest on Hwy. 287 and then 53 miles west on Hwy. 14 to the trail parking lot. The trail begins on the left side of the highway, east of Long Draw Reservoir Rd. (Forest Rd. 156). Beginner and intermediate skiers enjoy Long Draw Trail, which begins at the same trailhead. This gradual trail parallels Long Draw Reservoir Rd., actually joining the road at Box Canyon.

Never Summer Nordic Yurt System—Cross-country skiers interested in comfortable huts on a multi-day backcountry trip definitely should check out Never Summer Nordic (see the **North Park** chapter for information).

Zimmerman Lake Trail—This very popular, well-marked trail is moderately difficult. It climbs a mile and a half up along an old logging road to Zimmerman Lake. Once at the lake, you can enjoy plenty of off-trail skiing. Winter is indeed a great time to be at the lake—the views of the Medicine Bow Range and Poudre Canyon are spectacular. This high-altitude trail starts at 10,000 feet and climbs to almost 10,500 feet. To reach the trail from Fort Collins, head northwest on Hwy. 287 for 10 miles and then west on Hwy. 14 for 58 miles. The parking lot is on the left, just past Joe Wright Reservoir.

Groomed Trails—
Beaver Meadows—This resort has more than 20 miles of maintained trails, some of which are groomed. Terrain varies enough to challenge even the best nordic skiers. Located northwest of Red Feather Lakes, Beaver Meadows' trails are on national forest and private land. The ski shop on the premises provides rentals and lessons. In addition to cross-country skiing, there are a variety of other winter activities as well as fine accommodations (see the Where to Stay section). To reach Beaver Meadows from Fort Collins, drive northwest on Hwy. 287 for 22 miles and turn left on the Red Feather Lakes Rd. Drive to Red Feather Lakes and

turn north on Creedmore Rd. Proceed 6 miles to the Beaver Meadows sign. For more information call **(303) 482-1845.**

Rentals and Information—
The Mountain Shop—This shop rents equipment for any kind of cross-country skiing, whether it is for groomed trails or backcountry telemarking. **632 S. Mason; (303) 493-5720.**

Adventure Outfitters—514 S. College Ave.; (303) 224-2460.

SWIMMING
Edora Pool Ice Center—
This facility offers a large indoor pool that has a wheelchair ramp. **1801 Riverside Dr.; (303) 221-6679.**

Mulberry Pool—
Open year-round. Call for times. **424 W. Mulberry; (303) 221-6659.**

TENNIS
Rolland Moore Racquet Center—
There are eight lighted courts at this outdoor complex, which is open Apr.–Nov. For reservations during prime times (4–10 pm Mon.–Fri.), call ahead. **2201 S. Shields; (303) 221-6667.**

Warren Park—
Five courts with lights are located at this park. **Lemay St. and Horsetooth Rd.**

WINDSURFING
Horsetooth Reservoir is the obvious place for this sport. Beware however: Horsetooth can get very crowded with speedboats. For more information on the reservoir see the Parks and Recreation Areas section. For information, rentals, lessons and supplies, check in with **Outpost Sunsport** at **622 S. College, Fort Collins; (303) 482-1069.**

SEEING AND DOING

BALLOONING AND OTHER AERIAL PURSUITS
Aviation Adventures Aloft—
Since 1979. Call **(303) 493-4959** for information and reservations. **3508 Dixon Cove Dr., Ft. Collins, CO 80526.**

Dragon Fire Ltd.—
With their 14 years of experience, you'll feel comfortable heading up into the sky with this company. **(303) 226-4465.**

BREWERY TOUR
Anheuser-Busch Brewery—
A relatively new attraction on the outskirts of Fort Collins, Anheuser-Busch has built what is currently the fastest-producing brewery in the world, with a top capacity of 2,200 cans of beer per minute. The brewery's hospitality center offers free hour-long tours of the huge facility, including a stop at the Clydesdale Hamlet (stables), where you can get a close-up look at these 2,300-pound horses. Your tour ends with a glass of ice-cold beer inside a window-enclosed room looking out over the manicured grounds to the mountains. If you must have that Anheuser-Busch mug, towel or T-shirt, the gift shop will gladly take your money. In summer you may have to wait up to an hour; it's better to arrive before noon. Located north of Fort Collins (Exit 271 from Interstate 25), on **Busch Dr., PO Box 20000, Fort Collins, CO 80522; (303) 490-4500.**

MUSEUMS AND GALLERIES
Colorado State University has five art galleries that feature a variety of media styles. All of these are free and open to the public. Contact the information desk at Lory Student Center for information. **(303) 491-6444.**

The Fort Collins Museum—

This rather small museum specializes in displays focused on Fort Collins history. The museum complex also includes restored and preserved buildings from early Fort Collins. Perhaps its real claim to fame is one of the most extensive collections of Folsom points outside the Smithsonian Institution in Washington, DC. These prehistoric spear points were collected in the 1920s and 1930s at the Lindenmeier site, near the Wyoming border north of Fort Collins. Open Tues.–Sat. 10 am–5 pm, Sun. 12–5 pm. **200 Mathews St.; (303) 221-6738.**

Historic Buildings—

An interesting tour of the town's historic buildings is highlighted by the **Avery House** at **328 W. Mountain Ave.** This elegant, custom-built Victorian home also hosts many special events, including a Christmas open house in early Dec.; Victorian-style Christmas wrapping paper, ornaments, note paper and cookies are for sale. For more information on the Avery House, call **(303) 221-0533.** A brochure that outlines a tour of other historic buildings in Fort Collins is free at the **Visitors Bureau** in **Old Town.**

Sweatsville Zoo—

It's amazing what can happen when people have a little time on their hands. In this case Bill Sweat created Puff the Two-headed Dragon, Harry the Hitchhiker, Penny the Dimetrodon and about 70 other sculptures out of old car parts, farm machinery and scrap metal. On the outskirts of Fort Collins, these creatures rear up from the surrounding farmland like a weird mirage. Anyone can come by to enjoy these fantasy creatures for free ("donations are appreciated," he says). In addition miniature steam railcars ply a 3/4-mile route beside the Poudre River. Located just south of Ft. Collins, on the east side of I-25 at the Harmony Rd. exit 265. **4801 E. Harmony Rd., Ft. Collins, CO 80525.**

NIGHTLIFE

Coopersmith's Pub and Brewing—

This is the cream of the three micro breweries in Fort Collins. See Where to Eat.

Fort Ram—

Where do the college students go? They head directly to the largest dance floor and, as you may have guessed, the cheapest drinks. This is a great place to meet people and dance to rock and roll. **450 N. Linden St.; (303) 482-5026.** Another good bet for live rock and roll or blues music is **Lindens** at **214 Linden; (303) 482-9291.**

Lincoln Center—

As the city's performing and visual arts complex, Lincoln Center plays host to live theater, concerts, the Fort Collins Symphony, Larimer Chorale and art exhibits. Some of the more unique features include a mini-theater, with its intimate stage, and The Terrace, a sculpture and performance area complete with flower gardens and plants. Step across the street to the **Magnolia Café,** a restaurant that caters to the arts crowd and others who like homemade soups and desserts; **(303) 484-6744.** The Lincoln Center is at **417 W. Magnolia St.; (303) 221-6735,** box office **(303) 221-6730.**

Mishawaka Inn—

Located about 25 miles from Fort Collins, this bar and restaurant really gets shaking on weekends to live country rock music. The old place was built in 1901 with the help of convict labor. Nationally known musicians, such as Jerry Jeff Walker and Commander Cody, often play on summer weekends. You might also want to stay for a juicy steak or rainbow trout. Sometimes the view from the deck includes bighorn sheep that come down to drink in the Poudre. Open Nov.–Feb. Thur.–Sun., Mar.–Oct. seven days a week. To get here from Fort Collins drive 10 miles northwest on Hwy. 287 and then 15 miles west on Hwy. 14. **13714 Poudre Canyon Hwy.; (303) 482-4420.**

Wine Cellar—

Come here for good drinks, a great selection of wine by the glass and live jazz in an intimate atmosphere. **3400 S. College Ave.; (303) 226-4413.**

SCENIC DRIVES

Poudre Canyon—

This 101-mile trip along a recently designated Scenic and Historic Byway will take you into beautiful mountainous country west of Fort Collins. Start by heading northwest for 10 miles out of Fort Collins on Hwy. 287 and turn west on Hwy. 14. This highway proceeds into a narrow rocky canyon next to the Cache la Poudre River. The river's name means "hide the powder."

As you're driving upriver, you can almost feel the intense force of the water, especially during spring runoff. The exceptional Poudre is the last free-flowing river along the Front Range, hence the bumper stickers reading, "Don't Damn the Poudre." Today the age-old conflict of growth versus environment remains. The Poudre is Colorado's first National Wild and Scenic River, which, we hope, should keep it from being dammed.

Take twisting and turning Hwy. 14 through Poudre Canyon keeping your eyes peeled for Rocky Mountain bighorn sheep, deer and elk. The incredibly scenic drive takes you past resorts, campgrounds and interesting geological formations cut by thousands of years of wind and water erosion. One mile past the summit of Cameron Pass, stop for a few moments to appreciate the dramatic rocky tops of the Nokhu Crags, which lie at the tip of the Never Summer Range. The road continues to skirt the northern edge of Rocky Mountain National Park allowing tremendous mountain views before coming in sight of the flat expanse of **North Park** (see the **North Park** chapter). This scenic trip ends in the center of the park at the town of **Walden**.

WHERE TO STAY

ACCOMMODATIONS

Most national chains have motels here—Holiday Inn, Ramada Inn, Motel 6 and several others are located in a convenient conglomeration at the intersection of Hwy. 14 and Interstate 25 (at the main Fort Collins exit). In the mountains west of town, however, a number of cabins and resorts provide a special atmosphere along the banks of the Poudre River and in more secluded areas such as Red Feather Lakes. Following are a few highlights:

Beaver Meadows Ranch Resort—$$$

Located 55 miles northwest of Fort Collins in the Red Feather Lakes area, this ranch/resort is well known for its cross-country skiing and easy access to 20 miles of marked trails, some of which are groomed. Along the backcountry trails, you are invited to stop in a warming hut for snacks and spirits. During the summer Beaver Meadows features horseback riding, mountain biking, a kids' fishing pond and, for more serious anglers, fishing in the North Fork of the Poudre. Accommodations are in condos, mountain homes or cabins; all come equipped with kitchens. If you don't feel like cooking, stop by the restaurant (open daily). Live entertainment is featured on Fri. and Sat. nights. No minimum stay, but weekly packages are offered. For reservations, contact **PO Box 178, Red Feather Lakes, CO 80545; (303) 881-2450.**

Helmshire Inn—$$$

The Helmshire Inn is actually a hybrid, produced by crossing a bed and breakfast concept with a small hotel. Inside are 26 rather large and well-decorated rooms, each with a unique, almost contemporary feel. All have private bathrooms as well as the convenience of a refrigerator and microwave. A complimentary breakfast is served from 7 to 9 am in the newly decorated dining area. Since the Helmshire is located just across the street from the CSU campus, you are likely to run into students' families and visiting professors. For an especially quiet night's sleep, you may want to request a room away from busy College Ave. **1204 S. College Ave., Fort Collins, CO 80524; (303) 493-4683.**

Sylvan Dale Ranch—$$ to $$$$

Located 7 miles west of Loveland (15 miles south of Fort Collins on Hwy. 287) this working ranch draws you into the actual operation: Stack hay or brush the horses. You are free to participate as much as you want. All of the accommodations have private bathrooms; nine cottages are also available. Enjoy the luxury of the heated pool or play a set of tennis. Stay over July 4th weekend and you can get involved in the cattle drive. There are no telephones or TVs here. The Jessup family has been operating this ranch for more than 40 years. For an extra charge you can sign up on the full American plan and savor wonderful, country-style meals. In the summer, you need to book a minimum six-night stay. During off-season (Labor Day through Memorial Day), the ranch offers a "bunk and breakfast" arrangement. Groups of up to 12 should consider renting Mama J's Guest House. Kids love the activities and the change of being out in the country. **2939 N. County Rd. 31 D, Loveland, CO 80538; (303) 667-3915.**

Elizabeth Street Guest House—$$

Staying at this charming three-room bed and breakfast is akin to being welcomed into a friend's home. The comfortable rooms all have their own sink, but bathrooms are shared. A homey atmosphere is created by plentiful antiques, old quilts, handmade items, leaded windows and oak woodwork. Breakfast, served as late as 10 am, may include homemade pastries or a unique specialty called "Scotch eggs"—we won't spoil the surprise, but they are delicious. All breakfasts come with juice, tea or coffee. A beautiful, small patio garden in back of the house is a great place to read a book or just hang out. A big plus is the excellent location of this four-square, brick-style home, just one block from the university. **202 E. Elizabeth St., Fort Collins, CO 80524; (303) 493-2337.**

CAMPING

In Colorado State Forest —

See the **North Park** chapter for information.

In Roosevelt National Forest—

The Poudre River has a cache of campgrounds conveniently located just off Hwy. 14 west of Fort Collins. Access to the stream from each of these campgrounds is easy, but the campsites often fill up by early afternoon and even earlier on weekends and holidays. Reservations are accepted for **Mountain Park, Dowdy, West Lake and Chambers campgrounds** by calling **MISTIX** at **1-800-283-CAMP.** Seven campgrounds are bunched together within about a 15-mile stretch between Poudre Park and Kelly Flats. The first is **Ansel Watrous Campground** (19 sites; fee charged), which is about 23 miles west of Fort Collins. **Stove Prairie Campground** is 3 miles farther west offering 7 sites and no fee. A mile beyond, you'll reach **Upper Landing Campground** with 5 sites and no fee. Virtually next door is **Stevens Gulch Campground** with 4 sites and no fee. Three miles west is the **Narrows Cooperative** with 4 units and no fee. **Mountain Park Campground** is 3 miles down the road with 45 sites and a fee, followed by **Kelly Flats Campground** 2 miles farther (23 sites; fee charged). **Kelly Flats and Stevens Gulch campgrounds** have handicapped facilities.

Still rolling west on Hwy. 14, 49 miles west of Fort Collins you will arrive at **Big Bend Campground** with 9 sites and a fee. Travel another 4 miles to **Sleeping Elephant Campground** with 15 sites and a fee.

Four public campgrounds are located in the vicinity of Red Feather Lakes. To get here from Fort Collins drive 22 miles northwest on Hwy. 287 to the Forks Cafe. Turn left and drive 30 miles west on Red Feather Lakes Rd. **Dowdy Lake Campground** (66 sites; fee charged) is located 1.5 miles east of Red Feather Lakes Village on Forest Rd. 218. Dowdy has campsites designed for handicapped use. **West Lake Campground** (29 sites; fee charged) is 2 miles east of the village on Forest Rd. 200. To reach **Bellaire Lake Campground** (7 sites; fee charged) take Forest Rd. 162, 5 miles south of the village toward Rustic. **North Fork Poudre Campground** (9 sites; no fee) is located 6.5 miles west of Red Feather Lakes Village on County Rd. 162.

From Fort Collins, drive 10 miles northwest on Hwy. 287 and then 52 miles west on Hwy. 14. Turn right on Laramie River Rd. (County Rd. 103). There are two campgrounds along this road. **Tunnel Campground** (49 sites; fee charged) is another 5.5 miles north on Laramie River Rd. And **Brown's Park** (28 sites; no fee) is 14.5 miles north near Glendevey.

A couple of other campgrounds are located on the northern edge of Rocky Mountain National Park. To reach **Long Draw Campground** (31 sites; no fee) drive 10 miles northwest of Fort Collins on Hwy. 287 and then west on Hwy. 14 for 53 miles to just past Chambers Lake. Then turn left onto Long Draw Rd. (Forest Rd. 156) and continue 9 miles to the campground. Continue another

4 miles on Forest Rd. 156 and you'll arrive at **Grand View Campground** (8 sites; no fee).

Private Campgrounds—

Glen Echo Resort—Located in Poudre Canyon with good fishing available. To get here drive 41 miles west of Fort Collins on Hwy. 14. **31503 Poudre Canyon Dr., Bellvue, CO 80512; (303) 881-2208.**

KOA Mile High—With a swimming pool and full hookups this campground gets plenty of use. To get here drive 10 miles northwest of Fort Collins on Hwy. 287, just opposite the turn-off for Hwy. 14. **6670 Hwy. 287N, PO Box 600, La Porte, CO 80535; (303) 493-9758.**

WHERE TO EAT

Cuisine! Cuisine!—$$$

This is one of the consistently better restaurants in Fort Collins. It features regional American as well as international specialties for lunch and dinner. The diverse menu, which is posted daily on an outdoor chalkboard, gives you a chance to sample different cuisines, including southwestern, Cajun, French, nouvelle … it's the perfect place to come when you are part of a group that can't decide what to eat. Also known for its excellent desserts. Open for lunch 11 am–3 pm on Fri. only; dinner is served 5–9 pm Mon.–Sat. Closed Sun. **130 S. Mason St.,** across from the courthouse; **(303) 221-0399.**

Bisetti's—$$ to $$$

As soon as you enter this small, family-owned Italian restaurant, the fresh smell of garlic, basil and oregano pleases your senses. Empty Chianti bottles hang from every conceivable nook—you may want to empty one yourself while eating a meal of fettuccine, rigatoni, manicotti or pasta pesto. All pasta is made fresh daily on the premises and you can really tell the difference. You can't leave without trying a slice of Bisetti's house specialty: cheesecake. Open for lunch 11 am–2 pm Mon.–Fri.;

dinner 5–9 pm Sun.–Thur., until 10 pm Fri.–Sat. **120 S. College Ave.; (303) 493-0086.**

Charco Broiler—$$ to $$$

Feel like having a slab of steak cooked to perfection over an open flame? Fort Collins locals go straight to the Charco Broiler's lived-in setting. You'll know why it's crowded nearly all the time as soon as your meal arrives. Try to save some room for a slice of homemade pie. This is also a good choice for your basic American breakfast and bottomless cup of coffee. Open Mon.–Thur. 6 am–11 pm, Fri–Sat. 6 am–midnight, Sun. 11 am–10 pm. **1716 E. Mulberry (Hwy. 14, east of Fort Collins); (303) 482-1472.**

Rio Grande—$$

Scoring high on the local's approval meter and low (for a Mexican restaurant) on the calorie/cholesterol meter is the Rio Grande. This restaurant features fresh ingredients and is known for its standout black beans, fajitas and other Tex-Mex specialties. Giant margaritas and a large selection of Mexican beers are available. Since the restaurant doesn't take reservations, you may have to wait. Kids menu available.

Lunch served 11 am–2 pm Mon.–Fri., til 2:30 pm on Sat.–Sun.; dinner 5–9 pm daily. Downtown at **143 W. Mountain Ave.; (303) 224-5428.**

Young's Cafe—$ to $$$

Don't let the name fool you. Young's is much more than an ordinary "cafe." With outstanding Vietnamese cuisine, this restaurant has a loyal following. The atmosphere is elegant, and carefully prepared meals tease tastebuds you never knew existed. The house specialties are highly recommended as are their Vietnamese "creations," in which you select your favorite seafood or meat to go with a special sauce. Young's is also a good choice for vegetarians and places a strong emphasis on fresh ingredients. Lunch is a bargain. Carry-out is available. Open 11:30 am–3 pm weekdays; dinner 4:30–9:30 pm Mon.–Thur., 4:40–10:30 pm Fri.–Sat., 4:40–9:30 pm Sun. In the Crystal Gardens at **3307 S. College Ave.; (303) 223-8000.**

Coopersmith's Pub and Brewing— $ to $$

The real reason to eat at Coopersmith's is to be able to wash down your food with one of the brewpub's beers. In a unique restored building with exposed brick walls and a wonderful patio area, Coopersmith's serves up creative pub food. Menu items include everything from grilled mahi sandwiches, to salads, to a bratwurst simmered in ale. The cheese and artichoke dip is decadent and worth every calorie. Of five beers being brewed in large tanks on the premises, our favorite was the subtly sweet Nut Brown Ale. The beer may take a while for Bud drinkers to get used to, but it's worth the effort. Happy hour prices 4–6 pm daily. Non-beer drinkers may be interested in trying one of the brewery's homemade sodas: rootbeer, ginger ale or cream soda. Open 11 am–2 am Mon.–Sat, until midnight on Sun. **#5 Old Town Square; (303) 498-0483.**

Silver Grill Cafe—$

Since 1933 this well-known breakfast spot has provided good food at reasonable prices. It retains some of the feel of old Fort Collins, even though it has recently been remodeled. Busy counter and booth seating indicates this restaurant is still a local favorite. Their claims to fame are the giant cinnamon rolls for $1.25 each and the cinnamon roll toast. They also serve up all of the other breakfast standards. The homestyle cooking spills over into lunch when burgers, sandwiches and daily specials fill the menu. Open daily 6 am–2 pm, Sun. 7 am–1 pm. **218 Walnut St. in Old Town; (303) 484-4656.**

Vern's Place—$

If you are anywhere near La Porte, stop in for a tank of gas and one of Vern's famous cinnamon rolls. Located 9 miles northwest of Fort Collins just off Hwy. 287. **4120 County Rd. G, LaPorte; (303) 482-5511.**

NEARBY

Bruce's—$ to $$$

East of Fort Collins, in the almost empty town of Severance, a totally unique dining experience awaits. Fort Collins residents often make a special trip here when entertaining out-of-town guests. For detailed information on Bruce's, see Where to Eat in the **Northeast Plains** chapter.

SERVICES

Fort Collins
Chamber of Commerce—

Located at **225 S. Meldrum St., Fort Collins, CO 80521; (303) 482-3746.**

Fort Collins Convention and
Visitors Bureau—

If you're going to be around the area for a few days, be sure to contact these helpful folks. Located in the **Carriage House Building** at **420 South Howes St., Suite 101, PO Box 1998, Fort Collins, CO 80522; (303) 482-5821** locally or **1-800-274-FORT** nationwide.

Transportation—

Buses—Transfort, the Fort Collins bus system, serves most of the major areas of the city from 6:30 am to 6:30 pm. Schedules are widely available. **6570 Portner Rd.; (303) 221-6620.**

Taxi—Call **Shamrock Taxi (303) 224-2222.**

Trolley—It doesn't go very far, or very often, but if you're in Fort Collins from May–Sept., check out the trolley. It runs from City Park to W. Mountain Ave. and back, from noon to 6 pm Sat., Sun. and holidays, weather permitting. A small fee is charged.

Georgetown and Idaho Springs

About 30 miles west of Denver, Interstate 70 drops down from Floyd Hill and makes its way along Upper Clear Creek through one of the oldest historic areas in the state. Gold strikes in 1859 brought thousands of fortune hunters to this high mountain valley rimmed by soaring rocky peaks. Even if you are just driving through in a car, views from the highway suggest the mining legacy that's so deeply entrenched in this area. Old mine shafts and tailing piles on nearby mountainsides and the long-established towns of **Georgetown, Idaho Springs** and **Silver Plume** all serve as reminders of the days when throngs of optimistic miners scoured the area. Although Idaho Springs was the first settlement in the valley, Georgetown and Silver Plume evoke the most vivid image of the mining days. Once the third-largest town in Colorado, Georgetown is full of impeccably restored Victorian homes and buildings, making it an exceptional National Historic District. History also accompanies you on a trip along the refurbished Georgetown Loop Railroad. This engineering wonder snakes its way up to nearby Silver Plume, offering a ride as memorable today as it was 100 years ago.

With easy access to these towns along Interstate 70, many skiers and summer visitors stop in Georgetown and Idaho Springs for a look around or to have a meal at one of the many fine restaurants. By the time this edition comes out, the Georgetown factory outlet stores should be open and attracting many shoppers (check with the **Georgetown Visitor Center** at **(303) 569-2555** for an update). But don't let the accessibility lead you to believe the area is overdeveloped—lots of remote country surrounds the valley and it's common to catch a glimpse of a bighorn sheep among the rocky crags. Visit the "Watchable Wildlife" viewing station along the Interstate 70 frontage road at Georgetown Lake—you can spend time looking for bighorns without having to worry about rear-ending the car ahead.

Ghost towns and old mine ruins are scattered throughout the canyons and mountains in the Georgetown and Idaho Springs area. Many old mining roads, including Waldorf Rd. and the precipitous Oh My Gawd Rd., cut through backwoods sites once teeming with miners. Another road not to be missed is Mt. Evans Hwy., one of the world's highest paved roads. It climbs 14 miles up 14,264-foot Mt. Evans, providing views of the plains and surrounding mountain ranges that are hard to match.

Encompassing most of this area, heavily used Arapaho National Forest attracts many outdoor enthusiasts, especially for its great hiking and cross-country skiing. In winter many cross-country skiers converge on the area and fan out on the snow-covered roads and trails. Loveland ski area, 10 miles west of Silver Plume on Interstate 70, attracts many day skiers, especially from Denver, with its relatively inexpensive lift tickets, variety of terrain and light powder snow.

HISTORY

In January 1859 George Jackson, a prospector on a hunting trip, made his way to what is now Idaho Springs. The story goes that as he trudged through the snow over a hill, he saw haze in the distance that he believed to be smoke from an Indian camp. What he found instead were natural hot springs. More importantly, just up the valley near the confluence of Clear Creek and Chicago Creek, he found some rocks that he thought contained gold. Returning the next spring, Jackson and a few comrades panned and placered $1,500 in gold the first week. Soon, thousands of miners and merchants poured into the site known as Jackson's Diggins. Eventually the name was changed to Idaho Springs, due largely to the importance of the hot springs, which later lured many visitors for medicinal purposes.

Shortly after Jackson's big discovery, two brothers, George and David Griffith, made a historic strike. After leaving their home in Kentucky and heading west to Denver in 1858, the two brothers followed the masses up to Central City. Since most of the good mining claims were taken, they set off to explore Upper Clear Creek Canyon upstream from Jackson's Diggins. Quickly they struck rich gold ore, established their claims and built a cabin. Other miners followed, and before long the mining camp was named Georgetown, after the elder Griffith brother. Although Georgetown miners were initially drawn to the gold, by the mid-1860s it was apparent that silver ore abounded in the mountains around Georgetown and its sister mining camp, Silver Plume, 2 miles up the valley. Soon more silver was being produced here than in any other district in the world until the great Leadville strike in 1878. It's estimated that more than $200 million in silver was mined near Georgetown during these early days.

Georgetown boomed and by the 1870s had more than 5,000 residents. Unlike other mining towns in Colorado, Georgetown was settled by families with relatively upstanding morals. Many fine and substantial homes were built, showing off a variety of architectural styles popular in that era. Georgetown was very proud of its volunteer fire department, which kept the town from burning down (the fate of most other towns during this period). Thanks to the fire department's commitment, more than 200 of Georgetown's original buildings still stand today.

As mines in the valley and surrounding mountains grew in number, locals anxiously awaited the Colorado Central Railroad, which eventually reached Georgetown in 1877. But it was not until 1884 that the famous Georgetown Loop Railroad, stretching from Georgetown to Silver Plume, was finished (see the Major Attractions section). When the Argentine Central Railroad was built from Silver Plume to the mines up near Waldorf, silver ore could be more economically shipped to the mills and smelters.

When the silver market crashed in 1893, most of the mines around Georgetown and Silver Plume closed, and the mining population began to dwindle. Although some mines continued to produce gold, copper and other minerals, the boom days were over. By 1910 the 22,000-foot Argo Tunnel was completed from Idaho Springs under the mountains to Central City. The Argo connected many existing tunnels and provided easy access between the two mining towns. In 1913 the Argo Gold Mill was completed in Idaho Springs. The finest mill of its kind in the country, it supplied much of the gold for the Denver Mint. Due to increased mining costs, most of the area's mines are closed these days. Plenty of gold and silver still remain in the hills around Idaho Springs and Georgetown, but until mining becomes more profitable, the minerals will remain in the ground.

GETTING THERE

Idaho Springs is located 32 miles west of Denver on Interstate 70. A more scenic route is up Lower Clear Creek Canyon from Golden on Hwy. 6, which follows the old Colorado Central Railroad bed. Georgetown is located 14 miles west of Idaho Springs along the interstate.

MAJOR ATTRACTIONS

Georgetown Historic District

What separates Georgetown from many other historic mining districts in Colorado is the sheer number of old Victorian homes still standing and the heartfelt dedication of its citizens to preserving and restoring these buildings. The Georgetown Society (a local historical preservation group) has spearheaded the painstaking restoration of many homes, buildings and shop fronts. Visitors need only walk or ride through the streets of town to get a feel for the way things were a century ago.

Many buildings in town are on the National Register of Historic Places, including two museums, the **Hamill House** and **the Hotel de Paris** (see the Museums and Galleries section for details). One of the finest examples of residential architecture is the **Maxwell House**, stunningly painted in shades of pink and cream. It is, however, a private home. Stop by the Episcopal church, which houses the oldest pipe organ in the state. You can still see the bell tower that blew off with the roof in a big wind of 1867, the year the church was built. During summer pick up a historical buildings map at the Community Center on 6th St. (across from the post office) and take a self-guided walking or driving tour.

Georgetown Loop Railroad

If you want to get from Georgetown to Silver Plume, everyone knows that the 2-mile stretch of Interstate 70 will whisk you there in a matter of minutes. But what's the fun of that? If you climb aboard the Georgetown Loop narrow-gauge railroad the trip to Silver Plume takes on a whole new meaning. This historic 3-mile stretch of tracks, once called the "Scenic Wonder of the West," was quite an engineering feat when built more than a century ago.

History—

During the booming silver mining days in Upper Clear Creek Canyon, getting the ore down out of the mines to the mills by wagon was extremely difficult. A railroad line to the upper end of the valley was greatly needed. Building a railroad to Georgetown presented the usual construction problems, but extending the tracks to Silver Plume was a real nightmare. The situation seemed insurmountable—Silver Plume was only 2 miles away, but stood a full 700 feet above Georgetown. Conventional railroad locomotives would not be able to climb the 6 percent grade.

An engineer for the Union Pacific Railroad, Jacob Blickensderfer, spent a couple of years studying the problem. His innovative solution required building a system of curves and bridges that would reduce the average grade to 3 percent. The planned route included three hairpin curves and four bridges. At Devil's Gate, the valley's narrowest spot, the track looped over itself by a 300-foot-long bridge that passed 75 feet above the track below. The Georgetown Loop was completed in 1884. From Silver Plume, tracks were laid on up the valley to Greymont and Bakerville.

After silver prices crashed in 1893, the railway shifted its focus to tourists. The engineering feats of the Georgetown Loop were known throughout the world, and soon as many as seven trains a day made the trip between Georgetown and Silver Plume. Passengers seeking further adventure opted for a trip up from Silver Plume to Pavilion Point on the Argentine Central Railroad. Later, as automobile routes were built into the mountains, train travel began losing its glamour. In 1939 the railroad tracks on the Georgetown Loop were torn up and sold for scrap. But the story has a happy ending. Thanks to help from the Colorado Historical Society and generous benefactors, the Georgetown Loop was restored and reopened in 1984, 100 years after its inception.

Facts—

Today the Georgetown Loop Railroad offers trips from the station at the west edge of Georgetown to the restored Silver Plume Depot up the valley. Both depots offer free slide shows and ticket servicing. The Silver Plume Depot also has a number of railroad exhibits. Trips on the railroad begin from either end. The round-trip ride takes about an hour, but we recommend you stop along the way to take a tour of the 1870s **Lebanon Mine**, accessible only by train (for a small additional charge). Put on a hard hat and enter the old silver mine with a guide who will fill you in on its history and explain early mining techniques.

The train makes frequent daily runs from Memorial Day through Labor Day; through Sept. the train runs on weekends only. The Lebanon mine tour is available Memorial Day–Labor Day. For information contact **Georgetown Loop Railroad, C/O/ Old Georgetown Station, 1106 Rose St., PO Box 217, Georgetown, CO 80444.** For reservations call **(303) 569-2403** or in Denver at **(303) 670-1686.**

FESTIVALS AND EVENTS

The Silver Plume Melodrama
weekends in April

Each April the **Plume Players** perform melodramas to raise money for historic preservation in Silver Plume. Encore performances are given on one weekend in May and on July 3. The shows are great fun and usually receive good reviews. A sandwich buffet and dessert are served; B.Y.O.B. Reservations should be made well ahead of time. Call **(303) 569-2023** or in Denver at **(303) 893-2333**.

Christmas Market
first two weekends in December

The Christmas season gets into full swing at Georgetown's Christmas Market in Strousse Park. Food booths offer home-baked goods from many nations of the world and homemade crafts are also on display. Folk singers, dancers and carolers provide the entertainment. The shops in town are decorated for the occasion. Open 10 am–5 pm. Contact **Historic Georgetown Inc.** at **(303) 569-2840** or in Denver at **(303) 674-2625.**

OUTDOOR ACTIVITIES

BIKING
MOUNTAIN BIKING

Plenty of hiking trails and old mining roads provide exciting mountain bike rides in the Clear Creek area. Check the Hiking and Backpacking, Scenic Drives and Four-Wheel-Drive Trips sections for ideas, or stop in at the **Clear Creek Ranger District Office**, one block south of Interstate 70 on Hwy. 103, in Idaho Springs. **PO Box 3307, Idaho Springs, CO 80452; (303) 567-2901.**

If you want to rent a mountain bike for half or full days, stop in at **Mountain & Road Bicycle Repair**. The shop also repairs bikes and sells bikes and accessories. They are located at **1514 Miner St., Idaho Springs, CO 80452; (303) 567-4666.**

Barbour Forks—

Situated just south of Idaho Springs, Barbour Forks provides a fine, somewhat challenging ride up through a high valley and meadows. Eventually you'll reach a ridge (4.7 miles from Idaho Springs) that offers views down into Devil's Canyon. To reach the trail from Idaho Springs, head south on Soda Lakes Rd. past Indian Hot Springs for 3 miles and then up Forest Rd. 194 for 1.7 miles.

Devil's Canyon—

This excellent 2.5-mile ride winds up into the Arapaho National Forest. The canyon, site of a fire a number of years ago, is currently filled with small saplings. To reach this dirt road from Idaho Springs, head south for 10 miles on Hwy. 103 and turn left after the curve at Ponder Point onto Forest Rd. 246.

FISHING

There are many places to fish in the Georgetown and Idaho Springs area but, overall, the fishing is not much to speak of. Mine runoff has made fish in some of the streams unfit to eat; overfishing has also taken its toll. Following are some of the better opportunities.

Fall River Reservoir—

This is not a bad place to catch brook, brown and cutthroat trout, but the reservoir is very heavily fished. To reach the reservoir, take the Fall River Rd. exit on Interstate 70 (about 2 miles west of Idaho Springs). Follow the road 5.5 miles and turn left onto the dirt road just at the base of a steep switchback. Follow the dirt road 3 miles, keeping to the right.

Georgetown Lake—

Located at the east end of Georgetown along Interstate 70, Georgetown Lake is well stocked with rainbow and cutthroat trout. Though the pressure is heavy, fishing can be rewarding.

Silver Dollar Lake—

To reach this high mountain lake from Georgetown, head 8.5 miles south on Guanella Pass Rd. just beyond Guanella Campground and turn right at the sign to Silver Dollar Lake Trail. The rough road climbs steeply for a mile to the trailhead for Silver Dollar Lake. The hike into the lake is about a mile, and fishing can be good for 12-inch cutthroat trout.

FOUR-WHEEL-DRIVE TRIPS

St. Mary's Glacier to Central City—

The backcountry between Silver Lake (near St. Mary's Glacier) and Central City is a great place for jeeping, but a few words of advice are necessary. Many four-wheel-drive roads crisscross the area, and a patchwork of private mining claims prevents access to many of them. Be sure to have a topographical map of the area and follow the brown forest service markers. When you get up on the high alpine meadows, don't create your own road—this kills the fragile plant life and promotes erosion, requiring decades for recovery. This 10-mile (one way) drive offers beautiful alpine scenery, wildflowers, historic mines and old cemeteries.

To reach the road from Idaho Springs, head west on Interstate 70 for about 2 miles and get off at the Fall River Rd. exit. Drive 9 miles to the end of Fall River Rd. at Silver Lake. Turn right and after a short distance turn left on Forest Rd. 175 up a hill to Yankee Hill. Stick to this route for about 4.5 miles and you'll reach Pisgah Lake. Another mile past the lake brings you to the junction with Forest Rd. 273.1. Turn left here and proceed 2 miles to Bald Mountain Cemetery. From the eastern end, turn left (north) and follow the road to Boodle Mill just west of Central City.

Saxon Mountain—

Saxon Mountain, which rises to the east of Georgetown, saw its share of miners during the gold and silver era. Many old mines dot the road on the mountain and the others in the vicinity. For folks with four-wheel drives with HIGH CLEARANCE, exploring the road network on and around Saxon Mountain is hard to beat. It also has to be the most seldom-used route between Idaho Springs and Georgetown.

Most of the roads lie on Arapaho National forest land; the access from Georgetown starts on BLM land. To reach the road system from Georgetown, head north on Main St. until it turns into Saxon Mountain Rd. The rough, steep road climbs 6.5 miles to the summit of the mountain. From there, you can make your way down roads to Ute Creek and Cascade Creek, eventually coming out on Hwy. 103 just a few miles southwest of Idaho Springs. To find the road from the Idaho Springs side, head southwest on Hwy. 103 about 5 miles to Ute Creek Rd. or another 1/2 mile to Cascade Creek Rd. (unmarked). For more information, check with the **Clear Creek Ranger District Office** in Idaho Springs.

HIKING AND BACKPACKING

The territory covered in this chapter offers an excellent array of alpine hikes. Although a large number of hikers from Denver invade this area in summer, the beauty of the country overrides the sometimes-crowded trails. A vast majority of the land is within Arapaho National Forest, including a large part of the 74,000-acre Mt. Evans Wilderness Area south of Idaho Springs. Many of the hikes around Idaho Springs, Georgetown and Silver Plume are accented by old ghost towns and mining sites. We must caution you to not explore the old mines ... they are extremely dangerous! For hiking ideas and information about Arapaho National Forest, visit the **Clear Creek Ranger District Office**, one block south on Hwy. 103 from Interstate 70 in Idaho Springs, **PO Box 3307, Idaho**

Springs, CO 80452; (303) 567-2901 or in Denver at (303) 460-0325. For equipment purchase, maps, and advice, visit **Chicken-head Mountain Sports, 1435 Miner St., Idaho Springs, CO 80452; (303) 567-9404** or in Denver at **(303) 825-8314.**

Chicago Lakes Trail—

This 4-mile trail, which leads up to Chicago Lakes in the Mt. Evans vicinity, gets quite a bit of hiking traffic, but it scores a 9 on the scenic meter. The trail begins at heavily used Echo Lake. It winds around to the south end of the lake, where badly trampled ground makes it difficult to follow the main trail—look for blazes on the trees. From the lake the trail heads southwest for 1.7 miles to Idaho Springs Reservoir and then up through the Chicago Lakes Burn, where 400 acres went up in flames in 1978. Though the trees are not much to look at, the wildflowers are beautiful. Eventually you reach the spectacular Chicago Lakes Basin, which is surrounded by the looming cliffs of the Mt. Evans massif. To reach the trailhead at Echo Lake, drive 14 miles south from Idaho Springs on Hwy. 103 and park just inside Echo Lake Campground. Walk across the Mt. Evans Hwy. (Hwy. 5) and look for the trailhead under the power lines.

Grays and Torreys Peaks Trail—

These twin peaks, called the Ant Hills by the Ute Indians, are anything but. Standing 14,270 feet and 14,267 feet, respectively, Grays and Torreys were at one time as well known as Longs Peak and Pikes Peak. When Georgetown and Idaho Springs were booming back in the late 1800s, it was very fashionable to hike the 4.5-mile trail to the summit of Grays and traverse the half-mile ridge over to Torreys. Even Victorian ladies, delicate creatures that they were, would adjust their skirts and ride horses sidesaddle up the mountains.

These days the beautiful hike, with spectacular views from the top of the peaks, is still very popular. Beginning at 11,200 feet, the trail crosses Quayle Creek and heads up the valley to the southwest, eventually

beginning a steep ascent up Grays Peak. Be sure to take a camera, as this is an excellent area to spot mountain goats. To reach the trailhead from Georgetown, head west on Interstate 70 for 6.5 miles and get off at Bakerville (Exit 221). From Bakerville proceed south up Stevens Gulch Rd. for 4 miles to the parking area near Stevens Mine.

Herman Gulch Trail—

Each day thousands of people whiz by this trailhead alongside Interstate 70 with no idea that a beautiful, secluded valley lies just a short hike away. This fairly steep 2.5-mile trail climbs almost 2,000 feet up through thick stands of pine, eventually coming out into an alpine meadow where wildflowers (especially columbine) grow abundantly in mid-July. The trail heads up to Herman Lake at 12,000 feet, which is a good place for lunch. If you still have the drive, climb the saddle above the lake for views south to the east portal of the Eisenhower Tunnel. To reach the trailhead from Georgetown, head west on Interstate 70 for 9.5 miles to Exit 218. Park on the south side of the highway, walk over to the north side and then head east a couple of hundred yards to the trailhead near the highway department sandpiles.

Mount Bierstadt Climb—

This 14,060-foot peak, Mt. Bierstadt, deserves mention for its spectacular high-altitude beauty and easy accessibility (the trail to the summit is a mere 2.5-mile climb). From the top of Guanella Pass the mountain and its long jagged north ridge tower to the east. It's an impressive sight and quite often you'll find a painter or two sitting by the road getting the scene down on canvas. Routes to the summit of Mt. Bierstadt are numerous, but take this hard-earned advice … begin the hike by heading just to the right of the lake to avoid the boggy meadow and a bushwhack through wet willow bushes. You don't want to be soaking wet during the climb. After getting around most of the bushes and the bog, head southeast up to the gradual ridge and then to the summit. To reach the trailhead at the summit of Guanella

Pass Rd., drive south 11 miles from Georgetown. Actually begin the hike about 200 yards down from the summit (north).

Mount Evans (Rest House Trail and Summit Lake Trail)—

Yes, we know, you can drive to the summit, but that's not quite as rewarding as doing it the old-fashioned way. This 12-mile (one way) route from Echo Lake Campground to the summit is challenging, beautiful and, at times, even eerie. The trail winds through a number of burn areas complete with charred pine trees, which can make parts of the hike look like a forest out of The Wizard of Oz.

From Echo Lake Campground, begin hiking southeast on Rest House Trail (Forest Service No. 57). This 6.5-mile section of the trail crosses over a couple of ridges before entering an area of forest near Lincoln Lake that burned in 1968. After 5 miles you'll reach a fork in the trail—the right fork leads 1 mile to Lincoln Lake. This lake lies just below Mt. Evans Rd. (6 miles up from Echo Lake Campground). If you want to knock a few miles off the hike to the summit, consider beginning the hike from the road at Lincoln Lake. Meanwhile, back at the fork, continue on the left trail another 1.5 miles to the remains of the Mt. Evans Shelter House, which burned in 1962. There are a number of good campsites in this area, but be sure to bring a stove, as firewood is scarce. From here you'll need to head right, connecting with the Summit Lake Trail (Forest Service No. 82), which climbs 4.7-miles to Summit Lake at 12,830 feet. The last 2 miles of this stretch can be wet and sloppy in early to mid-summer, so consider yourself forewarned. From Summit Lake you'll have to scramble the remaining distance (less than a mile) to the summit unless you want to hitch a ride along the road. To reach the trailhead at Echo Lake Campground, drive 14 miles south from Idaho Springs on Hwy. 103.

Pavilion Point—

This is more of a historic walk than an actual hike. A short trail (1 mile, tops) follows a section of the old Argentine Central Railroad bed to Pavilion Point. When the railroad was built in 1905 to transport ore from the Argentine Mining District at Waldorf down to Silver Plume, it was the highest steam railroad track in the country and remained so until it was dismantled in 1920. Hordes of visitors would board at Silver Plume and ride up to Pavilion Point for picnics and memorable bird's-eye views down to Silver Plume and Georgetown. (For information about the Argentine Central Railroad, see the Waldorf Rd. write-up in the Scenic Drives section.)

These days a stone chimney is all that remains of the pavilion, but in summer, with good timing, you can look down on the Georgetown Loop train as it chugs up the valley to Silver Plume. To reach the trail from Georgetown, drive south on Guanella Pass Rd. for 2.5 miles to Waldorf Junction (Forest Rd. 248). Turn right and proceed 1.2 miles to the fourth switchback and park your car. The unmarked trail heads off to the north. An alternate route begins in Silver Plume on the south side of Interstate 70. After heading under the highway bridge, turn right, park, and continue walking on the frontage road for a couple hundred yards. The road turns south up the old Argentine Central rail bed for a gentle 3-mile walk to the old pavilion site.

St. Mary's Glacier—

See the Fall River Rd. description in the Scenic Drives section.

SKIING
CROSS-COUNTRY SKIING

When snow falls on the mountains and in the valleys around the Georgetown and Idaho Springs area, summertime jeep roads and hiking trails are transformed into wonderful trails for cross-country skiing. The forest service has done a good job marking many trails and providing information and maps for skiers. Snow conditions and trail ideas are available at the **Clear Creek Ranger District Office** (closed on weekends in winter). **PO Box 3307, Idaho Springs, CO 80452; (303) 567-2901.**

Backcountry Trails—

Butler Gulch—This 3-mile trail (one way) leads up into a snow-covered bowl just below the Continental Divide. Due to its quick access from Denver, many skiers come here on weekends. The trail begins next to the Henderson Mine property up the Jones Pass Rd. After about a quarter mile, take the left fork over a good bridge and start your climb through the forested valley. The skiing along most of the trail is fairly easy, but there is a steep, narrow section about halfway up that can be a bit tricky for beginners. When you reach a series of switchbacks, the pine trees begin to thin out. Once up in the high open area you can choose your own trail, but be sure to stay clear of the avalanche chutes along the steep walls to the left. Return on the same trail or choose your own route down through the steep, dense forests along the gulch.

To reach the trailhead from Idaho Springs, head west on Interstate 70 to the Hwy. 40 turn-off. From Empire drive along Hwy. 40 about 7.5 miles to the Henderson Mine turn-off on the left. Proceed about a mile and a half along this road to the ski parking area next to the mine.

Chicago Lakes Trail—This is a moderately difficult trail. See the Hiking and Backpacking section for details.

Loveland Pass—If you don't want to spend time skiing uphill, consider a few runs down Loveland Pass. This is a great place to practice telemark turns. You need to shuttle cars between the pass and Loveland Valley Ski Area. From the summit of the pass, pull off to the right side of the road and ski along the contour to the west into a wide open bowl and start skiing down the steep drainage heading north. After a half mile, you'll run into Hwy. 6. Cross the road and continue skiing down the drainage on easier terrain, where you'll meet up with the runs at Loveland Valley Ski Area. You can't beat the price.

Mount Evans Road—Beginning at Echo Lake, the gradual 14-mile-long road up Mt. Evans (Hwy. 5) provides a scenic ski trip. On the way down you may want to bypass some of the switchbacks near the bottom by breaking your own trail through the pine glades. The powder can be exceptionally light. For details about the Mt. Evans Rd. see the Scenic Drives section.

Waldorf Road—Located just 2.5 miles south of Georgetown on Guanella Pass Rd., this 7-mile trail leads along Forest Rd. 248 to the old ghost town of Waldorf. This is a fantastic beginner to intermediate route. For information see the Scenic Drives section.

DOWNHILL SKIING

Loveland—

Nestled just below the Continental Divide 12 miles west of Georgetown on Interstate 70, Loveland is primarily a day ski area. The majority of visitors come from the Denver metro area and enjoy Loveland's excellent, reasonably-priced skiing without the extraneous trappings of a major resort. Two connected ski areas, the easy rolling Loveland Valley and the larger, more challenging Loveland Basin, provide a wide variety of terrain and snow conditions.

Loveland Valley is connected to the main base at **Loveland Basin** by the long Chair 5. It's an excellent place for novices and is very popular with families. Six lifts service Loveland Basin, whisking skiers up to mostly intermediate and advanced runs. The diversity of runs—including glade skiing, bowl skiing and steep bump runs—provide a big part of Loveland's appeal.

With a top elevation of 12,280 feet, the area has become well known for its fluffy powder. Most of the runs have a protected northern exposure, but some of the snow on the south-facing slopes can turn into heavy slop after a few hours in the sun. Winds often kick up, blasting snow off some of the higher slopes (this is the Continental Divide, after all). Loveland is also quite well known for its long season, running from mid-Oct. to mid-May.

The base facilities include a restaurant, bar, nursery/day care, rental shop and ski school. **PO Box 899, Georgetown, CO 80444; (303) 569-3203** or in Denver at **(303) 571-5580.**

St. Mary's Glacier—
Those who just can't quite pack enough skiing into eight months bring their rock skis up to St. Mary's Glacier in the summer. Mary holds claim to being the southernmost glacier in North America, a tidbit that all geographers should be sure to file away for future use. Skiing St. Mary's is for the hearty and knowledgeable, and for good reason.

The 3/4-mile trail to the glacier is rocky and uphill; "snow" on the glacier more often than not maintains the consistency of ice … unless your turns are precise and your edges freshly sharpened you could end up tangled on the rocks below the snow line. For directions, see the Fall River Rd. write-up in the Scenic Drives section.

SEEING AND DOING

CEMETERIES

Alvarado Cemetery—
Take time to visit the old Alvarado Cemetery, located 3.5 miles east of Georgetown on the Interstate 70 frontage road. Ornate Victorian-era tombstones dot this burial ground, including that of Louis Dupuy, founder of the Hotel de Paris.

HOT SPRINGS

Indian Springs Resort—
After a long day on the ski slopes, some skiers returning to Denver on winter weekends avoid the traffic jam by stopping in at Indian Springs until the traffic dies down. Indians, who first used the springs, had a unique arrangement—the springs were a no man's land where all tribes could enjoy the hot water. Supposedly, after George Jackson discovered the springs in 1859, local miners enjoyed the luxury of soaking after their long workdays. By the late 1860s the first resort development began. Touted as the Saratoga of the Rocky Mountains, Indian Springs attracted quite a few famous visitors, including Walt Whitman and Teddy Roosevelt.

Today this sprawling resort offers a number of spa experiences that might turn some people off—the facilities are a bit grimy and rundown not to mention overpriced. The swimming pool is covered by a translucent bubble and surrounded by a botanic garden of ferns, palms and other tropical plants—a bizarre sight in winter. Downstairs, hot mineral baths and vapor caves are accessible from the men's and women's locker rooms. For an extra price, try a massage or a dip in Club Mud, an 8-foot-square by 1-foot-deep pool of mud. Hey, it's supposed to be good for you!

Overnight accommodations, though not recommended, are available in the 120-year-old lodge (bathrooms down the hall) and newer motel units across the road (private baths and TVs). The lodge rooms ($$) are very dingy, but if you're just too relaxed after a soak it may not matter. Indian Springs also has a lounge and a restaurant ($ to $$$), serving breakfast, lunch and dinner. The complex is located about 100 yards up Soda Creek Rd. from Miner St. in Idaho Springs. **PO Box 1990, 302 Soda Creek Rd., Idaho Springs, CO 80452; (303) 567-2191** or in Denver at **(303) 623-2050.**

MINE TOURS

The Edgar Experimental Mine—
In the 1870s this hardrock mine produced large amounts of silver, gold, lead and copper. Today it serves as a research area and classroom facility for future mining engineers from the Colorado School of Mines in Golden. Students use the latest in high-tech mining equipment on-site to gain the valuable experience they'll use after graduation. For a small fee, the general public can take a tour lasting 45 minutes to an hour. From mid-June—late Aug. no advance warning is necessary … just show up for a tour. Open daily in summer 9 am–4 pm. During the rest of the year, reservations are necessary. From Idaho Springs head north for a quarter of a mile on 8th St.

and follow the signs to the mine. **(303) 567-2911.**

Lebanon Mine Tour—

This fascinating tour is accessible only by the Georgetown Loop Railroad. See the Major Attractions section for details.

The Phoenix Mine—

This place is definitely a must see! Open just a few years, the Phoenix Mine gives you a glimpse into an actual working hardrock mine. What really makes this tour is the owner, Al Mosch, and the others who lead tours through the mine discussing history and mining techniques. Visitors may even get the chance to swing a pickaxe themselves. Al captivates the crowd with his stories; however, public employees be warned—he doesn't like bureaucrats. Be sure to touch the "lucky bucket." Open daily 10 am–sundown. Located 1 mile west of Idaho Springs on the Interstate 70 Frontage Rd., and then south on Trail Creek Rd. for three-quarters of a mile. **Box 751, Idaho Springs, CO 80452**; or call the **Idaho Springs Information Center** at **(303) 277-0129.**

MUSEUM AND GALLERIES

Argo Gold Mill and Museum (in Idaho Springs)—

Opened for business in 1913, the Argo Gold Mill processed rich ore from mines in the area, much of it delivered via the 22,000-foot Argo Tunnel. The mill was shut down in 1943 and has since been added to the National Register of Historic Places. Currently it processes tourists instead of ore. A section of the old mill with much of its original machinery intact is open for self-guided tours (for a rather hefty price). Mining relics, such as ore cars and parts of a stamp mill, are strewn about the grounds. Adjacent to the mill, gunfights (don't worry folks, they're only blanks) take place four times daily at a re-created Old West town. For an additional charge, you can take a

jeep tour up a nearby mountain to the Double Eagle Gold Mine. Open May through mid-Oct., 9 am to 30 minutes before sundown. Located in Idaho Springs on the north side of Clear Creek at **2350 Riverside Dr.; (303) 567-2421.**

George Rowe Museum (in Silver Plume)—

Located in an old schoolhouse built in 1894 and used until 1959, this museum contains a number of interesting historical artifacts, as well as a completely restored old-time schoolroom. Highlights include historic photos, clothes and a hand-pump fire wagon purchased by the town after a major fire in 1884. The museum is worth a look if you're in town. Local history books and other information are available here. Open daily Memorial Day–Labor Day 10 am–4 pm and weekends in Sept. Fee charged. **95 Main St.; (303) 569-2562.**

Georgetown Galleries—

The restored buildings lining the streets of Georgetown house many shops and galleries. **Saxon Mountain Gallery** at **408 6th St., Georgetown, CO 80444; (303) 569-3186** or in **Denver** at **(303) 674-0353,** was opened by the recently deceased Bill Alexander, nationally known for his impressive watercolors of mountain snow scenes (especially downhill skiers). The gallery has a large display of his prints and paintings, along with artwork by over 40 other regional artists.

Georgetown Gallery at **614 6th St., Georgetown, CO 80444; (303) 569-2218,** is a cooperative with works from various Colorado artists and craftsmen. It features watercolors, oils and pastels as well as pottery.

Hamill House—

Completed in 1879 this elegant Victorian mansion was home to William Hamill, a local silver magnate, politician and civic leader. At the time it was considered one of the finest homes in the state. Although today it's missing a bit of the original furniture, the exquisite interior serves as a reminder of just how much money some of the mine owners made. Marble fireplaces, walnut and maple woodwork, a curved-glass conservatory and diamond-dust mirrors show off the superb craftsmanship of the era. Be sure to pay a visit to the elegant, three-seat, cupola-covered outhouse. Catch a glimpse of how the upper crust used to live. A fee is charged. Summer hours (Memorial Day–late Sept.) are 10 am–5 pm daily; winter hours are noon–4 pm Sat.–Sun. **305 Argentine St., Georgetown, CO 80444; (303) 569-2840** or in Denver at **(303) 674-2625.**

Hotel de Paris—

Perhaps the most famous of Georgetown's grand old buildings, the Hotel de Paris served for years as the social center of town and was the talk of the nation. The hotel was built in 1875 by Louis Dupuy, "the mysterious Frenchman," so called because locals disagreed over just who he was, where he came from and, perhaps more importantly, what, if anything, he might be hiding about his past. But evidence suggests he was a French army deserter. Guests at this magnificent two-story hotel were attracted by discussions about art and literature with Dupuy, who was a philosopher and a scholar as well as a gourmet cook. But without a doubt, this plush hotel's main attractions were the fine furnishings, the cuisine and the French wines.

Today the hotel has been faithfully restored by the National Society of Colonial Dames of America, and tours are offered. The stone and stucco building is complete with cast-iron decorations and pressed-metal trim. The original furnishings and decorative art objects fill the hotel. The formal dining room and well-equipped kitchen with its antique stove and accessories highlight the tour. Open daily late May–late Sept. 9 am–5 pm; winter hours are Tues.–Sun. noon–4 pm. Located at **Taos St.** and **6th St.** in Georgetown, **409 6th St.; (303) 569-2840** or in Denver at **(303) 674-2625.**

Silver Plume Depot—

This is the restored, original depot for the historic Georgetown Loop Railroad. It serves as a ticket office for the train and has a number of original rooms, including a telegraph office. The railroad yard displays a number of engines and cars. There is also a gift shop and a free slide show about the train. For more information see the Major Attractions section. The depot is located on the south side of Interstate 70 at Exit 228 (Silver Plume).

Underhill Museum (in Idaho Springs)—

This small mining museum is especially interesting because it's located in the old town assay office. Assayers were a vital element in the mining communities–they analyzed the ore to determine its mineral content. Assaying equipment as well as other artifacts are on display. Small fee charged. Open Memorial Day–Labor Day. **1416 Miner St.** in Idaho Springs; **(303) 567-4709.**

NIGHTLIFE

Buffalo Bar (in Idaho Springs)—

See the Where to Eat section.

Plume Saloon (in Silver Plume)—

Locals crowd into this extremely rustic night spot for a bite to eat and a drink to take the edge off. Over the mantelpiece of the stone fireplace hangs a portrait of Frances Willard, president of the Women's Christian Temperance Union at the turn of the century. Devilish locals are fond of toasting her as they quaff their drinks. Open year-round Wed.–Fri. 4 pm–midnight, Sat.–Sun. 11 am–midnight. Located next to the Brewery Inn in Silver Plume. **776 Main St.; (303) 569-2277.**

SCENIC DRIVES

Fall River Road (St. Mary's Glacier)—

Drive up this 9-mile road along the Fall River through aspen and pine. Enormous rock outcroppings hang from the valley walls. About 7.5 miles up the road is a turn-off to the ghost town of Alice. If you continue ahead on Fall River Rd. for about a mile, you'll see the trailhead for the short half-mile hike to St. Mary's Glacier. A beautiful lake awaits, as well as the glacier. To reach Fall River Rd. from Idaho Springs, head west on Interstate 70 for about 2 miles and look for Fall River Rd. (Exit 238).

Guanella Pass Road—

Guanella Pass, a Scenic and Historic Byway, is a perennial favorite and for good reason. Pine forests and shimmering aspen line the road most of the way. At the 11,669-foot summit, the above-treeline view east to Mt. Bierstadt is quite a sight. The road is open year-round, but the best time to go is in early fall when the aspen are turning. Begin the trip from Georgetown by driving south on Guanella Pass Rd. (Hwy. 118). Be sure to pick up a brochure at the Georgetown Information Center which provides historic and other insights about the Guanella Pass Route. It's about 12 miles to the summit. From here you drop south over the pass about 15 miles to the intersection with Hwy. 285 at the town of Grant. Along the way you'll find a couple of campgrounds and plenty of trailheads, including many into the Mt. Evans Wilderness Area.

Loveland Pass—

The pass is located 11 miles west of Georgetown on Interstate 70. Instead of driving through the Eisenhower Tunnel, turn left onto Loveland Pass Rd. (Hwy. 6) for a fantastic drive over the top of the Continental Divide. See the Scenic Drives section of the **Summit County** chapter for more details.

Mount Evans Road—

This has to be one of the most underrated attractions in Colorado. The paved Mt. Evans Rd. snakes its way 14 miles to the summit of Mt. Evans (14,264 feet). Although only 35 miles from Denver, this road remains unknown to many city dwellers.

Mt. Evans was first named Mt. Rosalie by the famous landscape painter Albert Bierstadt, in honor of his wife. In 1863 he was also the first person on record to climb the peak. In 1870 the peak was renamed in honor of the second governor of the Colorado Territory. A primitive road was built up the mountain in the early 1930s and was improved for regular passenger cars in 1939. The road begins at Echo Lake, 14 miles south of Idaho Springs on Hwy. 103. It climbs up to treeline after about 3 miles and eventually leads to Summit Lake, where picnic tables and restrooms are available. There is also a short trail, which climbs about 600 vertical feet to the summit. If you continue on the road from Summit Lake, a tight series of switchbacks will lead you to a parking area just below the summit. Along the way you'll probably catch a glimpse of a mountain goat—the Mt. Evans herd is one of the largest in the state. You'll also see the Denver Cosmic Ray Research Lab, built in 1936, which attracts famous scientists from around the country for atmospheric research. The 360-degree view from the summit is something you'll just have to see for yourself. Be sure to watch out for approaching lightning storms and get to your car if you spot one. Mt. Evans Rd. (Hwy. 5) is open in summer only; the stretch up to Summit Lake is usually open by Memorial Day.

Oh My Gawd Road—

Although there are a couple of steep drop-offs, this drive up Virginia Canyon isn't nearly as intimidating as the name implies. The 9-mile road connects Idaho Springs with Central City and is open year-round to all vehicles. Mine shafts and building remnants dating back to the 1860s can be seen along the road. There are superb views to the south across Clear Creek Canyon to Chief Mountain and Squaw Mountain. Once over the top of the hill, descend through the remains of the Russell Gulch townsite and into Central City. This drive begins in Idaho Springs at the intersection of Canyon St. and Placer St. and heads north on Virginia Canyon Rd. Stay on the main road or you may have the same nightmare that a recent visitor had—he drove off on a side road and plunged his new Blazer into an abandoned mine shaft! For a self-guided map, stop in at the **visitors center** (open daily) in Idaho Springs at **2200 Miner St.**

Waldorf Road—

Although this road is not bad enough to require four-wheel drive, your vehicle should have good ground clearance (RVs can forget it). Located near Georgetown, the road leads up to the old ghost town of Waldorf, which was quite a booming silver and gold mining area when rich ore was found in the 1860s. Just southwest of Waldorf, a stage route crossed over 13,207-foot Argentine Pass, providing transportation to the early mining camps in Summit County. In 1905 Edward John Wilcox, owner of the prosperous Waldorf Mining & Milling Company, built a 16-mile stretch of railroad track connecting mines in the area with Silver Plume in the valley far below. The Argentine Central Railroad ended up making much more on tourism than it ever did hauling ore. Until ceasing service in 1920, it was the highest railroad in the world. Part of the road to Waldorf follows along the old rail bed. Not much is left of the town, as scavengers have stripped the buildings down to the foundations, but with a vivid imagination you can picture what life must have been like for the hundreds of miners who lived there. To reach Waldorf from Georgetown, head south on Guanella Pass Rd. for 2.5 miles and turn right at the hairpin curve onto Waldorf Rd. (Forest Rd. 248). Continue about 6 miles to Waldorf.

WILDLIFE

Georgetown Wildlife Viewing Area—

The first of its kind in the state, this is truly one of your surest bets for a close-up view of Colorado's animal—the bighorn sheep. Of the 6,000 animals roaming the state, the herd near Georgetown numbers over 175. Early and late in the day are the best time for viewing; from Nov.–Jan. be sure to listen and watch for rams clashing horns in a battle for the herd harem. The viewing station, fully equipped with viewing scopes and a wheelchair accessible ramp, is located next to Georgetown Lake along Interstate 70 on old Hwy. 6. To reach it from the Interstate, take the Georgetown exit (Exit 228).

WHERE TO STAY

There are a number of motels located along Miner Street in Idaho Springs. Call **1-800-685-7785** for specifics. For unique accommodations, read on.

ACCOMMODATIONS

Georgetown/Baehler Resort Service— $$$ to $$$$ (rates based per home)

Perhaps the most intriguing lodging possibility in Georgetown is to rent a historic Victorian home. Working through the Georgetown Resort Service, choose from 14 of Georgetown's fine homes, ranging from gingerbread victorians to swiss-style chalets to cozy miners' cabins. A minimum stay of two nights is necessary, and some require a stay of one week. Advance reservations are required. This can be a great mountain rendezvous for two, but family reunions, celebrations and large meeting groups are also encouraged. If you are interested, Odette Baehler, the charming proprietor of the service, provides a wealth of historic information and is available to give tours of town and the immediate area. **PO Box 247, Georgetown, CO 80444; (303) 569-2665.**

The Peck House—$$$

James Peck was a successful Chicago merchant who came west in the Pikes Peak gold rush of 1859. A year later he built the Peck House as his private home in the little town of Empire. It wasn't until 1872 that Mrs. Peck opened her doors to overnight guests, and soon the home became a regular stagecoach stop for travelers over Berthoud Pass. As the oldest hotel in Colorado, the Peck House still carries on in a grand Victorian tradition.

A wide veranda stretches along the front of the building, with views across the valley. Inside, the mood is created by a large parlor with comfortable antique furniture, historic photos, red velvet curtains and plenty of books available to guests. The owners, Gary and Sally St. Clair, have done a tremendous job in catering to all of your wants. A hot tub and downstairs ski lockers are a couple of nice touches. Eleven smallish rooms are elegantly appointed with period antiques and a constant supply of fresh flowers; nine of the rooms have private bathrooms. Let it be known, however, that the undersized antique beds don't suit everyone. The Peck House is well known for its fine dining and Sun. brunch (see the Where to Eat section). Located along Hwy. 40, 2 miles from Interstate 70. **83 Sunny Ave., PO Box 428, Empire, CO 80438; (303) 569-9870** or reservation service at **1-800-626-4886.**

Alpendorf on the Lake—$$ to $$$

The secluded setting atop Guanella Pass is hard to beat. On a private lake nonetheless! Alpendorf is truly a lodge worth noting. Bill and Julie Holms recently began offering their two chalets and two rustic trappers cabins for overnight stays. The accommodations aren't fancy, but then again, that's not why you go to the Alpendorf. For a nominal additional charge, guests may fish private Duck Lake which teems with greenback and native cutthroat trout. In winter, enjoy cross-country skiing around the lake or into the spectacular nearby backcountry. Let's hope this gem remains open for a long time to come. Reservations required. **PO Box 819, Georgetown, CO 80444; (303) 569-2681.**

Brewery Inn—$$ to $$$

If you want to stay in Silver Plume, this is the place—it's also the only place. This Victorian bed and breakfast was built in the 1890s and is filled with antiques. The house sits on the site of the old Boche Brewery,

which burned in 1889 and should not be confused with the Busch Brewery in St. Louis. You'll find no Clydesdale horses around, but if you look up on the rocky cliffs north of town, chances are good that you'll see a bighorn sheep. The old spring pump house, which was the water source for the brewery, still operates, and the water flows by the house, under the gazebo in the backyard and down to nearby Clear Creek. The first-floor suite has a private bath; three upstairs rooms all share a bathroom downstairs. A continental breakfast is included. Advance reservations are recommended, especially during ski season. **PO Box 473, Silver Plume, CO 80476; (303) 674-5565.**

The Hardy House—$$ to $$$

Relax in this red Victorian home which was built in 1877 by Georgetown's blacksmith. The four guest rooms at the inn are the Ruby Room, the Loui-Ans Suite (two-room suite with hall bath), the romantic Victoria Suite, which features a private bath and a potbellied stove, and the second-floor Peak Room with (you guessed it) a view of the nearby peaks. The Hardy House's comfortable 19th-century furnishings add a real charm; spend some time in the parlor by the potbellied stove. Full breakfast is served each morning. Reservations necessary. **PO Box 0156, 605 Brownell St., Georgetown, CO 80444; (303) 569-3388.**

Indian Springs Resort—$$

This Idaho Springs resort offers fairly rundown accommodations, but the hot springs are a big plus. See the Hot Springs section for details.

CAMPING

In Arapaho National Forest—

From Georgetown there are two national forest campgrounds located up Guanella Pass Rd. Drive south on Guanella Pass Rd. (Forest Rd. 118) about 4 miles to **Clear Lake Campground.** There are 10 sites and a fee. Another 4 miles south of Clear Lake Campground is **Guanella Campground** with 17 sites and a fee.

About 8 miles west of Empire on Hwy. 40 toward Berthoud Pass is **Mizpaw Campground**. It has 10 sites and a fee.

Southwest of Idaho Springs are two other campgrounds. From Idaho Springs drive southwest on Hwy. 103 to the intersection with Forest Rd. 188. Turn right onto Forest Rd. 188 and proceed to **West Chicago Creek Campground** (12 miles from Idaho Springs). It has 11 sites and a fee. If you continue on Hwy. 103 for 14 miles from Idaho Springs you'll reach **Echo Lake Campground** with 17 sites and a fee.

Private Campgrounds—
Indian Springs Resort—Full hookups right next to the hot springs pool (as well as the road). Located 100 yards up Soda Creek Rd. from Idaho Springs. **PO Box 1990, 302 Soda Creek Rd., Idaho Springs, CO 80452; (303) 567-2191** or **623-2050** in Denver.

Mountain Meadow Campground—This place offers plenty of RV hookups and tent sites. Located about 2 miles west of Empire on Hwy. 40. **PO Box 2, Empire, CO 80438; (303) 569-2424.**

WHERE TO EAT

The Peck House—$$ to $$$

The ambience of the Peck House, built in 1860, is only part of the dining experience—the fine food is the real attraction. Located in Empire, this restaurant serves up lunch, dinner and a well-attended Sun. brunch. Within the Victorian confines of a cozy inn (see the Where to Stay section), the ground-floor dining room is set with red linen tablecloths, and a crackling fire is often burning. Dinner prepared by owner Gary St. Clair is a tasty menu of steaks, fowl and seafood selections; nightly specials during our visit included baked, stuffed rainbow trout. Also offered is an extensive wine list. On Sun. the champagne brunch features menu items such as quail and eggs, eggs Benedict and salmon Napoleon. In summer the covered porch with pleasant mountain views is open for meals. Lunch hours are 11 am–4 pm Mon.–Sat. June–Sept.; Sat. only Oct.–May. Dinner hours year-round are 4–9 pm Sun.–Thur., 4–10 pm Fri–Sat. Sun. brunch is served year-round 10 am–2 pm. **83 Sunny Ave., Empire; (303) 569-9870.**

The Renaissance—$$ to $$$

It's not the atmosphere and decor that draw the large clientele to this Georgetown restaurant ... it's the exquisite northern Italian cuisine. Czechoslovakian chef/owner Poul Dufka meticulously and lovingly whips these up back in the kitchen. The dishes are accented by Dufka's delicate sauces and fresh ingredients. For dinner, veal, chicken, fish, beef and wild game dishes come with soup, Caesar salad, homemade bread and a side of pasta. Take a look at the fine wine list. Be sure to show up with a large appetite–you'll probably still leave with a doggie bag. Reservations recommended. Open Wed.–Sun. 11:30 am–4 pm (lunch), 4–10 pm (dinner), closed Mon.–Tues.; in winter lunches served only on weekends. **1025 Rose St., Georgetown; (303) 569-3336.**

Buffalo Bar—$ to $$$

Located in a brick building on Miner St. that's been a watering hole since 1885, the Buffalo Bar in Idaho Springs reeks of history (except for the large-screen televisions). The layout is very inviting, with its wooden bar and mirror, exposed brick, high ceilings and the buffalo head on the wall. The Buffalo Bar opens its doors early in the morning when it starts serving its famous breakfast, which includes trout and eggs, breakfast burritos and numerous omelettes. The lunch and dinner menus offer specialty sandwiches, buffalo burgers, steaks, seafood and popular Italian calzones. The nightlife here gets hopping during the summer and during winter ski season. To accommodate more people, **The Other Bar** is open adjacent to the Buffalo. Open year-round Sun. 8 am–11 pm, Mon.

11 am–midnight, Tues.–Thur. 8 am–midnight, Fri.–Sat. 7 am–2 am. **1617 Miner St., Idaho Springs; (303) 567-2729 or 595-9018 in Denver.**

Beau Jo's—$ to $$

Beau Jo's is probably better known for its pizza than any other restaurant in Colorado. That's quite a statement, but true nonetheless. In the early 1970s this Idaho Springs restaurant got its start with a seating area for 15 customers; today they can seat 300. The reason for their huge success is the creative pizzas they prepare with a mind-boggling array of choices. Select from five thicknesses of crust (made with sesame wheat, whole wheat, white or butter white) and 25 toppings. The thick-crust mountain pies come with honey to use on the leftover crust for dessert. Specialty pizzas include Thai pie made with curried chicken and sweet-and-sour sauce and tofu pizza (that's right, tofu). Beau Jo's also serves sandwiches, but to order one would be a sin. The restaurant has a comfortable wood decor and a wild napkin art display near the entrance. Open daily 11 am–9 pm Sun.–Thur. and until 9:30 pm Fri.–Sat. **1517 Miner St., Idaho Springs; (303) 567-4376 or in Denver at 573-6924.**

The Happy Cooker—$ to $$

Located in an old, restored Victorian home set back off 6th St. in Georgetown, The Happy Cooker serves up some of the tastiest and most creative breakfast and lunch items around. This upbeat place is decorated with turn-of-the-century antiques, and the walls are covered with artwork for sale from the Georgetown Gallery. Menu favorites are quiches, Belgian waffles, homemade bread and soups. If you are on your way to the ski slopes, stop in for a hearty breakfast and a cup of tea. During good weather the patio is a fantastic place to enjoy a meal. Open daily in winter 8 am–4 pm, in summer Mon.–Fri. 8 am–5 pm and Sat.–Sun. 8 am–6 pm. **412 6th St., Georgetown; (303) 569-3166.**

Pittsburg Mine Company—$ to $$

Considering how good the pizza is at the Pittsburg, it would be a crime to only mention Beau Jo's. Like its better known competitor, the Pittsburg is located on Miner Street in Idaho Springs. This sports bar (11 TVs) and live-music nightspot serves burgers, daily specials and an incredibly tasty thin-crust pizza. Open daily. **1600 Miner St., Idaho Springs; (303) 567-4591.**

KP Cafe—$ to $$

Historical eras blend and wholesome food permeates the KP. Occupying one of the historic mining buildings on Main St. in Silver Plume, this restaurant is reminiscent of a soda shoppe from the 1940s or 1950s. Four dated tables, counter seating and an old soda fountain in the corner all add to the atmosphere. Open for breakfast and lunch, the KP offers standard menu items like omelettes and burgers and sandwiches, but their vegetarian specialties are excellent. Try their Machu Picchu Burrito, loaded with black beans, quinoa and jack cheese. Also worth noting are their homemade soups and pies. If you try the KP, don't expect fast food. Open 7am–4pm Wed.–Sun. in summer, 7am–4pm Thurs.–Sun. in winter. Located on the corner of **Main St.** and **Silver St.** in Silver Plume; **(303) 569-2054.**

SERVICES

Georgetown Chamber of Commerce—

PO Box 444, Georgetown, CO 80444; (303) 569-2888.

Georgetown Information Center—

Located at **404 6th St.** across from the post office; **(303) 569-2888.** Open Memorial Day–Labor Day.

Historic Georgetown Inc.—

This group is involved in the historic preservation of Georgetown. They offer information about tours and events. **305 Argentine, PO Box 667, Georgetown, CO 80444; (303) 569-2840** or in Denver, **(303) 674-2625.**

Idaho Springs Information—

For information on Idaho Springs, stop by the visitors center at **2200 Miner St.** (next to the statue of Steve Canyon). Or contact **PO Box 97, Idaho Springs, CO 80452; 1-800-685-7785, (303) 567-4382** or **567-4844.**

Silver Plume Information—

In the summer months, information is available at the **George Rowe Museum** in Silver Plume at **95 Main St; (303) 569-2562.** Also try the **Silver Plume Town Hall** at **360 Main St., Silver Plume, CO 80476; (303) 569-2363.**

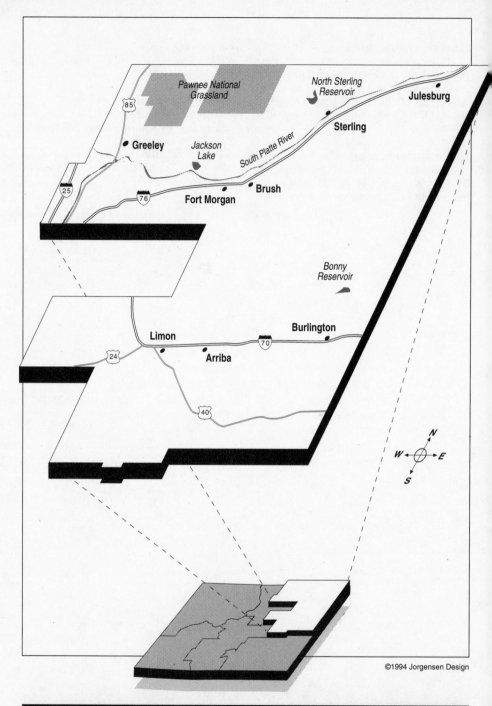

Northeast Region

©1994 Jorgensen Design

NORTHEAST REGION

Northeast Plains

The image of Colorado's plains, dominated by immense rolling grasslands, plotted dirt roads, irrigated fields, oil pumps and an occasional town has its problems. While not the vision of Colorado most tourists hold, the plains have their own brand of subtle beauty.

A fascinating history can be found along the routes of trappers, traders and homesteaders in the northeast plains; several towns preserve this history in excellent museums. You may also want to keep your eyes posted for antique shops (great bargains!) in many small eastern Colorado towns. Other attractions are usually passed, but they provide the essence of the "Other Colorado." Jackson, North Sterling and Bonny reservoirs entice large numbers of people who like to fish, boat and camp. Consider a ride on the turn-of-the-century carousel in Burlington, which will make you appreciate the craftsmanship of another era.

One of the major influences in the settling of the northeast plains was (and still is) the accessibility of water flowing down from the Rocky Mountains. The South Platte, the largest and most crucial river in northeastern Colorado, marked a route for explorers and was life-sustaining to settlers. In its own right, however, it wasn't very impressive—especially compared to the Mississippi. When Mark Twain saw the South Platte, he wrote in *Roughing It*, it's "a melancholy stream straggling through the center of the enormous flat plain, and only saved from being impossible to find with the naked eye by its sentinel rank of scattering trees standing on either bank … the Platte was 'up' they said which make me wish I could see it when it was down, if it could look any sicker and sorrier."

Homesteads over a century old can be recognized by sudden, dense clumps of trees on the barren prairie. Some homesteads thrive today, while many others have faded or disappeared altogether. Most residents of northeastern Colorado still work on large farms and ranches. It's these people, more than the landscape, that make this corner of Colorado an interesting place. Close-knit communities are situated along historic migration routes, now paved highways. Their sense of community is strong, but unless you catch a high school football game or town festival, you probably won't see it.

A vast diversity of birdlife draws many people to northeastern Colorado. Audubon Society members enjoy gazing quietly into binoculars and identifying species, while hunters prefer bagging low-flying pheasants and species of waterfowl. No one, however, will pull a trigger at frequently sighted white pelicans or blue herons. Keep your eyes peeled for a glimpse of these large birds while driving down those long straightaways—and consider taking some side roads, especially during the spring and fall migrations.

HISTORY

When Major Stephen Long passed through Colorado's northeastern plains in 1820, he proclaimed that the region "would never be fit for human habitation other than by the nomad races." He also reported, it "should forever remain the unmolested haunt of the native hunter, bison and jackal." We're sure the predominant Arapaho and Cheyenne Indians who lived on the plains would have agreed, but by the 1820s traders and trappers began trickling through in search of beaver; soon trading posts were springing up along the South Platte corridor. At one time there were four trading posts (Fort Lupton, Fort Vasquez, Fort Jackson and Fort St. Vrain) within a 15-mile radius. These well-fortified posts did a thriving trade with Anglos as well as Indians, especially when inhibitions loosened after a few swigs of potent "Taos Lightning."

Just when trading had almost dried up, the 1859 gold strikes in the Colorado mountains lured a new wave of people across the plains. The vast majority were passing through, but some discouraged miners settled near the South Platte River, taking advantage of the fertile bottomland.

Almost coinciding with the gold strikes, the short-lived Pony Express established a mail stop in Julesburg, in the far northeastern corner of the state. (It wasn't until 1862, however, that mail was carried regularly along the South Platte route to the burgeoning town of Denver.) A transcontinental railroad was the next big step. Union Pacific rails reached Julesburg from the east in 1867, causing a population explosion and earning this wild town the nickname, "wickedest city in the West." Four thousand gamblers, speculators, prostitutes, outlaws and road agents poured into Julesburg, forming a ramshackle village that featured 22 saloons and five dance halls. At this stage of development, there was no law and order—murder by six-shooter occurred at the least provocation. Though the first railroad across America stopped in Julesburg, it passed for the most part above present-day Colorado.

The influx of new settlers wreaked havoc on the Indians' way of life, especially their hunting. The Indians began to strike back as a last resort when the herds of buffalo were depleted. The inevitable conflict culminated with the Sand Creek Massacre (see the History section of the **Southeast Plains** chapter). The final engagement, however, came a year later at the Battle of Summit Springs (located between Sterling and Akron).

The open range had been used for years as pasture, but a long drive was necessary to get the beef to the railheads. With the Indians removed and the arrival of trains to Colorado, cattle barons were enjoying their zenith. John Iliff was the biggest of them all, owning much of the northeastern part of the state. Sheep ranching was to follow, but cattlemen never liked the woolly beasts—one line of a poem recalls, "A sheep just oozes out a stink, that drives a cowman to drink!" Or was that just an excuse?

In the spring of 1870 the Union Colony agricultural cooperative, under the steadfast direction of Nathan C. Meeker, founded a town named after Meeker's boss, Horace Greeley (owner of the *New York Tribune*). This group of greenhorn easterners came west with inflated expectations of paradise—including waterfalls, which were not to be found on the barren prairie of northeastern Colorado. Water, however, was plentiful, and the town of Greeley was platted at the confluence of the South Platte and Cache La Poudre rivers. With the help of irrigation canals, the fertile soil produced successful crops. The newcomers had their share of problems, but liquor wasn't one of them—Meeker had brought only temperate colonists. One of the enforced rules of the young town was, "Thou shall not sell liquid damnation within the lines of the Union Colony." This rule prompted the success of several small establishments that sold booze just outside the city limits.

One nagging problem in Greeley was the trampling of crops by roaming cattle; settlers solved it by stringing up a 50-mile-long, $20,000 fence around the crops. Their neighbors scoffed at them, saying the fence was erected to keep out "godless" cowmen. But it worked and the town achieved unprecedented agricultural success. Just when things were going well, Meeker was forced by money matters to leave Greeley and take a job at the White River Indian agency in northwestern Colorado. Meeker went down in history in 1879 when he was murdered by Ute Indians who didn't appreciate his efforts to transform them into farmers. The Meeker Massacre caused the entire tribe to be removed to distant reservations (see the History section in the **Meeker** chapter).

In retrospect it seems not much has changed in terms of the plains economy: Crops are more diverse and methods for planting and picking have been modernized, but agriculture and ranching remain the mainstays. Though a flurry of activity in the 1970s caused oil wells to sprout up, much of the prehistoric-looking machinery now lies dormant.

Interstate 76 and Interstate 70—

Since the northeast plains is not a destination as such, we have organized this chapter based on attractions along the major interstates, focusing on interesting diversions along the way. The main arterial roads passing through the northeast plains from the east are Interstate 76 and Interstate 70. Most people will be coming into the state on these roads. If you happen to be traveling from west to east, work through the chapter backward.

INTERSTATE 76

This highway leads into the extreme northeast corner of Colorado from Nebraska, ending in north Denver in about 200 miles. Just inside the Nebraska border you'll come to Julesberg, home to the **Northeast Colorado Information Center, (303) 474-3504.** However, we are fudging the borders a bit to let you know about a beautiful diversion just before coming into Colorado from the east.

OGALLALA, NEBRASKA

Lake McConaughy—

The North Platte River used to meander through this sparse farm and ranchland before Kingsly Dam was completed in 1941. But the river was never as enticing as manmade Lake McConaughy, which boasts 105 miles of gorgeous, white sand beaches. Attracting legions of recreationists from as far away as Denver, Lake McConaughy makes you feel as though you are on the coast. There is enough shoreline for everyone to stake a claim and break out the toys: volleyball, Frisbee, inflatable raft, catamaran, windsurfer, or waterskis. Cool breezes come off the long, slender reservoir and groves of cottonwoods provide comfortably shaded camping spots. Don't forget your fishing gear—this lake has produced record catches of striped bass, coho salmon, kokanee

salmon, walleye and tiger muskie. Many folks simply come here equipped with lawn chair and cooler for some "power lounging." Located 30 miles over the Nebraska border from extreme northeastern Colorado, Lake McConaughy is definitely worth a detour. For more information contact **Ogallala/Keith County Chamber of Commerce, PO Box 628, Ogallala, NE 69153; 1-800-658-4390** and **(303) 284-4066.**

STERLING

The small town of Sterling, in the midst of irrigated farm country, is an attractive regional hub. It's a good place to pull off the road for a quick meal at one of a dozen fast-food places on Main St. or to spend the night at one of many AAA-rated motels. While driving about, keep your eyes open for "living trees" sculptures. These detailed works of art include a clump of giraffes, a mermaid and a golfer. By the way, there are four golf courses here. Jumbo, North Sterling and Prewitt reservoirs provide good warmwater fishing and boating. A number of campsites can be found at water's edge. If you're just dying for a change of scenery, drive north on N. 7th Ave. to County Rd. 70 and then west for 8 miles to Chimney Canyons with its 250-foot chalk cliffs. For more information on Sterling, stop in at the **Overland Trail Museum's Visitor Information Center** (see entry below for directions).

Overland Trail Museum—

Stop and take a look inside this excellent regional museum, named for the well-trod route pioneers followed on westerly journeys. The grounds offer shaded picnic tables; a large plot is planted with several types of prairie grasses, identified by small markers. The museum is housed inside a stone reproduction of Fort Sedgewick, established on the Overland Trail in the early 1860s to quell Indian problems. Once inside, take a leisurely look at the branding iron collection, horse-drawn machinery, the one-room schoolhouse and geological displays. Wildlife exhibits include rattlesnakes and a buffalo. Lots of interesting stuff can be found here—and it's free. Open from May to Sept. 30. Mon.–Sat. 9 am–5 pm, Sun. 10 am–5 pm. Located conveniently at the intersection of Interstate 76 and Hwy. 6 just east of Sterling; **(303) 522-3895.**

BRUSH

In the 1860s John Iliff and Jared Brush contracted to sell beef to Army troops; thus began a cattle empire reaching from Julesburg to Greeley. In the early 1900s farmers were given incentives to plant sugar beets. Today the beets are such an important crop that the high school football team goes by the name "Beetdiggers." With its wide, tree-lined streets Brush still serves as a key agricultural and ranching center. If you are passing through Brush on July 4th weekend stop in for the Brush Rodeo. The long tradition of rodeo continues as 450 top amateur cowboys and cowgirls compete. Other events include wild cow milking and a 5K run. On Independence Day the town comes out for a pancake breakfast, a parade and, when it gets dark, a fireworks display. Free camping (with hookups, picnic tables, etc.) can be found at the Brush City Campground; a motel or two is also available in town.

Drovers Restaurant—$ to $$

If you grew up in rural America, Drovers will be like a homecoming; to confirmed city dwellers, though, it's an eye-opener. Because of its 1950s prices, genuinely friendly waitresses and a unique setting amid thousands of penned-up cattle, it's worth going a few miles out of your way. Sit at the counter or find an unoccupied table. Most of the clientele comes in from outlying ranches to do some business or to meet with friends over a cup of coffee (it only costs a dime) and a slice of lemon meringue or cherry pie. The menu varies from traditional breakfasts to burgers, barbecue beef sandwiches and T-bone steaks. Open 5:30 am–8 pm daily. **28601 Hwy. 34; (303) 842-4218.**

Across the hallway from the restaurant is the sale barn: a small auction house with spittoons placed all about for the bidding, tobacco-chewing ranchers. If you show up on a Thurs. or Fri., you can witness an auction (lasting from noon into the night). The western-wear store in the same building is one of the best places around to buy a pair of cowboy boots, a hat or a plaid shirt at fair prices.

FORT MORGAN

As the Morgan County seat, this agricultural and ranching center is a small but important hub with several attractions worth checking out. Downtown Fort Morgan has a few standard motels for those wishing to spend the night.

Fort Morgan Museum—

The displays of this tidy museum cover the history of Morgan County. Permanent exhibits include information on the life of Glenn Miller (who attended high school here) and an old soda fountain from the Hillrose Drugstore. Unfortunately, cold drinks or ice cream are not served at the fountain any longer. (However, in Akron, 32 miles west of Fort Morgan, you can visit a similar working fountain right on Main St.) Also displayed is a collection of Plains Indian artifacts. A large room is reserved for traveling exhibits that change every two to three months. Check out the excellent collection of Charles Russell's western paintings and sculptures as well as some of his personal letters. Open year-round, Mon.–Fri. 10 am–5 pm, Sat. 1:30–4:30 pm.

404 Main St., Fort Morgan, CO 80701;
(303) 867-6331.

Jackson Lake State Park—

Just northeast of Fort Morgan is Jackson Reservoir, with its excellent warmwater fishing in the spring and early summer. Along the western shore you'll find a boatlaunch and clean sandy swimming beaches; the warm water makes for ideal waterskiing and windsurfing conditions. Jackson Lake offers wind-protected picnic tables with grills and 180 shoreline campsites with showers, toilets and drinking water (fee charged). To reserve a campsite call **(303) 470-1144** in Denver or **1-800-678-CAMP.** On the way to the lake, stop in at the very local **Squeek's Corner** in **Goodrich** for a hand-patted hamburger and a piece of cherry pie.

Pawnee Buttes—

These two 300-foot-tall sandstone towers provide relief to a landscape virtually devoid of unique features. Once called White Buttes, these primitive monuments rise from the expanse of the Pawnee National Grasslands, having withstood the erosion that affected the surrounding landscape. Get out of your car and take a walk or ride your mountain bike on 4-mile Pawnee Buttes Trail. It's like revisiting the Old West while letting your senses adjust to the solitude and comfort of the prairie. Silence is interrupted only by the wind and a surprising number of songbirds and raptors. Stories of rattlesnakes hold some truth, so be aware of where you sit down for a break or a picnic. The best times to visit Pawnee Buttes are in spring and fall when the scorching heat isn't so intense, or in early morning or evening when shadows lengthen and a colorful sky brings added contrasts to the sandstone monoliths.

To reach the trailhead from Fort Morgan, drive north on Hwy. 52 for 25 miles to Raymer. Turn left onto Hwy. 14 and continue about 10 miles to County Rd. 390. Turn right, proceed north for 14 miles and then turn right again onto County Rd. 112. Drive east for 6.5 miles to a T intersection where you'll take a left on a marked road leading shortly to the Pawnee Buttes Trail. The parking area is located next to a large windmill. For more information contact the **Pawnee National Grasslands Office** on the north side of town, **660 "O" St., Greeley, CO 80631; (303) 353-5004**

GREELEY

Founded by the Union Colonists in 1870, Greeley has enjoyed steady, sustained growth. Today, it's the largest town in this part of the state, with a population of 70,000. The town's wide streets are shaded by trees, many of which were planted by settlers in the 1870s; cattle and crops are still the moving forces behind the town's economy. History is perhaps the reason to come to Greeley. James Michener lived here while writing *Centennial*. You can visit several excellent museum collections in town.

Centered in Greeley, the University of Northern Colorado is well known for its education and music programs. The town has a brand-new performing arts center, **Union Colony Civic Center, (303) 356-5555,** that hosts a number of plays and concerts. Its schedule includes an impressive line-up of local and national talent. Another Greeley attraction is the **Denver Broncos Training Camp.** You can watch practices and scrimmages each July and Aug. as the Broncos prepare for yet another NFL season. Quite a number of hotels, motels, restaurants and bars are available if you are passing through. For more information contact the **Greeley Convention and Visitors Bureau, 1407 8th Ave., Greeley, CO 80631; (303) 352-3566.**

Centennial Village—

Centennial Village vividly tells plains history through the chronological reconstruction of buildings from the years 1860–1920. Knowledgeable guides provide hour-long tours through the Centennial Village grounds and the various homes constructed of rock, wood, adobe and sod. Some highlights along the way include the wagon house (built in 1917, the predecessor to the modern-day Winnebago) and a Swedish-American Stuga home. At the end of the tour, a firehouse and a blacksmith's shop prove especially fascinating for kids. If you visit only one museum on the northeastern plains, it should probably be this one. Open Memorial Day–Labor Day, Mon.–Fri. 10 am–5 pm, Sat.–Sun. 1–5 pm. The last tour leaves one hour before closing time. Reduced hours from mid-Oct.–mid-Apr. **1475 A St., Greeley, CO; (303) 350-9224.**

Fort Vasquez—

Built in 1835 by a few hard-core mountain men, Fort Vasquez capitalized on the trade routes along the South Platte River. Twelve-foot-high adobe walls contained rifle ports and two corner towers. An ill-fated attempt was once made to ship 700 buffalo robes and 400 buffalo tongues from Fort Vasquez to St. Louis via the South Platte River. After 69 days of pushing, pulling and occasionally floating a flat-bottomed boat, the tired crew arrived in St. Louis with the news that the South Platte was not a navigable stream.

Fort Vasquez crumbled to the ground many years ago, but the WPA reconstructed an identical structure in the 1930s. Today the State Historical Society runs a visitors center next to the fort with information and displays on the fur trade and Plains Indians. Staffers are extremely knowledgeable about the history of the area. Walking around Fort Vasquez provides a glimpse of frontier life—except for the cars zooming by on the nearby highway. Open Memorial Day–Labor Day, Mon.–Sat. 10 am–5 pm, Sun. 1–5 pm. Located 17 miles south of Greeley (1 mile south of Platteville) on Hwy. 85; **(303) 785-2832.**

Meeker Home Museum—

Nathan Meeker, founder of the Union Colony at Greeley, was a fascinating man. You can visit his well-preserved two-story adobe home that has survived the past 100-plus years in good stead. Filled with many of the Meeker family's personal artifacts, it gives an excellent idea of life in the 1870s. If you want to learn every conceivable detail about Meeker's life, you'll find the information here. For casual visitors, however, the personal tour can be too in-depth and, therefore, lengthy. As it stands now, the museum is open Memorial Day–Labor Day, Mon.–Sat. 10 am–5 pm. **1324 9th Ave.; (303) 350-9221.**

WHERE TO STAY

Plenty of motels are spread throughout Greeley, including most of the national chains. For above-average accommodations with lots of amenities and a southwestern feel, try reserving a room at the **Ramkota Inn ($$$ to $$$$), 701 8th St., Greeley, CO 80631; (303) 353-8444.** For a unique night's lodging, try these places:

Heritage Inn—$$$$

This sort of Disneyland for lovers will take you worlds away from the surrounding farmland. Snuggle up on a large bed placed inside a pink 1959 Cadillac (it's much more comfortable than the back seat). Have you ever wondered what it would be like to wake up inside an igloo surrounded by ice blue mirrors? Stay in the Northern Lights. The Sherwood Forest entices you with a unique pedestal bed and a waterfall crashing down into a large whirlpool tub. Head to ancient Rome, climb to another orbit in the Gemini Space Capsule, or drift to sleep under the stars in The Jungle's exotic octagonal water bed. Though each of the 14 immaculately clean FantaSuites has a different theme, all prominently feature a whirlpool spa. If you just want to look at the suites, take a free afternoon tour on weekends. Besides the special suites, you can also ask for a "normal" room ($$ to $$$). Outdoor pool and restaurant available on the premises. Located south of Greeley just off Hwy. 85 at **3301 W. Service Rd., Evans, CO 80620; (303) 339-5900.**

Sterling House Bed and Breakfast—$$$

The Sterling House, built in 1886, has only two rooms, but they are sunny and fresh with 12-foot ceilings, fresh flowers by the beds and spacious private baths. You'll enjoy the Victorian elegance (no TVs) and being surrounded by antiques. The parlor, with its gold-print wallpaper and antique furniture, is centered around a porcelain-tile fireplace. The woodwork throughout the old house is stunning. Full breakfasts are served on china at a linen-draped dining room table; specialties are apple pancakes and crêpes. Dinners may be arranged by request. Why not rent both rooms with some friends and have the whole house to yourselves? No children under 10; smoking on the enclosed porch is OK. Reservations recommended. **818 12th St., Greeley, CO 80631; (303) 351-8805.**

WHERE TO EAT
Bruce's—$ to $$$

Located in Severance, about 10 miles north of Greeley, this restaurant has an unusual theme. An outside mural has bulls standing up on two legs with various picket signs saying "unfair," "very unfair" and "you don't know how unfair." Bruce's specialty is Rocky Mountain oysters, also known as bull fries, swinging steaks and prairie oysters. In a recent *Rocky Mountain News*: story, Co-owner, Betty Schott said: " ... come to Severance and have a ball." Tender turkey oysters, steaks and seafood are also served. You can get a juicy hamburger for almost the same price as a fast-food joint. The former Severance Recreation Hall has a casual feel with four long tables, each seating about 20 people and booths running down both sides of the room. On weekends live country and western bands play from 8 pm–closing. Open

seven days a week: 10 am–10 pm Mon.–Thur., 10–2 am Fri.–Sat., and 10 am –midnight on Sun. Located in Severance; **(303) 686-2320.**

Lucky Star—$ to $$$

This seems to be the locals choice for steak, as well as huge portions of virtually any non-healthmark type of food. The restaurant almost never closes, so stop by regardless of what time it is for breakfast, lunch or dinner. You'll be mixing primarily with the over-the-road trucker crowd as you'll see by the huge rigs parked out front. The Sat. night all-you-can-eat prime rib buffet is an unbelievable value. Next to the family restaurant is an extremely popular bar, which features live country music most nights. Open 24 hours Tues.–Sat., until 10 pm on Sun., 5 am–10 pm Mon. Located 3 miles north of Greeley on Hwy. 85 in Lucerne; **(303) 351-8000.**

Rosi's European Cafe—$ to $$

When you're tired of eating corn-fed beef, it's time to head for Rosi's. For lunch, this restaurant has a wonderful selection of serve-yourself salad, soup and pasta as well as deli sandwiches and tempting desserts. For breakfast try the excellent pastries, crépes or omelets. This efficient restaurant in the heart of downtown Greeley keeps a healthy outlook by promising smoke-free dining. In summer try to find a seat at one of the outdoor tables on the walking mall. Breakfast 7–10 am, lunch 11 am–2 pm Mon.–Fri.; Sun. brunch 8 am–2 pm. **809 9th St.; (303) 352-1126.**

INTERSTATE 70

Interstate 70 is the most heavily used route into Colorado, entering from Kansas in the east central part of the state. Along the way many restaurants and lodges are available to weary travelers. The highway passes several interesting and historic places as it makes a beeline west. Another more scenic route to Denver and the mountains is to follow Hwy. 86 from west of

Limon via the towns of Kiowa, Elizabeth, Franktown and Castle Rock.

BURLINGTON

The first thing to do when arriving at Burlington is stop in at the **State Welcome Center,** just off Interstate 70; **(719) 346-5554.** The center, staffed by volunteer travel counselors, can help you plan your Colorado vacation, and you can pick up armloads of brochures from around Colorado. Burlington offers many fast-food restaurants and inexpensive places to spend the night.

Kit Carson County Carousel—

This fully restored, handcarved wooden merry-go-round, built in 1905, is a designated National Historic Landmark. Climb onto one of several life-sized horses or the more exotic camel, zebra, giraffe, deer or lion. Take a while to observe the incredible detail of the snake curling around the giraffe's neck and the various prancing positions of each animal. These proud animal figures march to the music of a 1909 Wurlitzer Monster Military Band Organ— one of only two of this particular vintage in existence today. On the outer rim of the carousel, three tiers of oil paintings portray various subjects of the time. Quarter admission for a ride and tour. Open from late May through mid-Sept. afternoons and evenings. Located on the County Fairgrounds in Burlington, **15th St. and Lincoln Ave., Burlington; (719) 348-5562.**

Old Town—

This collection of 1900s-era buildings, with rooms full of antiques and exhibits, re-creates a historic atmosphere. Tour guides patiently explain the implements of the blacksmith, newspaper and harness shops. The spacious grounds also feature a western saloon, where you can witness cancan shows and staged gunfights, but you can't buy a beer. Special on-site craft demonstrations are continuous. Be sure to take a wagon ride from Old Town to the Kit Carson County Carousel (see previous entry). In a large red barn with a 45-foot-high roof, a troupe performs melodramas for the whole family. Melodramas are staged from June through mid-Aug. at 7

pm nightly (except Mon.); they are free of charge with a tour ticket. Old Town is open year-round: Memorial Day–Labor Day 9 am–9 pm; the rest of the year 9 am–5 pm. **420 S. 14 St., Burlington, CO 80807; (719) 346-7382.**

Bonny State Recreation Area—

About 22 miles north of town on Hwy. 385, Bonny boasts great warmwater fishing, windsurfing, boating and bird-watching in a pleasant setting. Four campgrounds with more than 200 sites (fee charged) can be found among the cottonwood trees on the lake shore. The campgrounds can accommodate tents, trailers and motor homes. Only 35 sites come equipped with electrical hookups, but Foster Grove and Wagon Wheel campgrounds offer showers in addition to toilets. To reserve a campsite call **(303) 470-1144** in Denver or **1-800-678-CAMP.**

GENOA

Genoa Tower—

If you're into two-headed calves and oddball things from Grandma's attic, then you'll probably get a kick out of the Genoa Tower. Like a bad commercial, it makes itself known from the interstate. Actually, after a long drive across the high plains, this is a good place to stretch your legs. The place has a haphazard collection of stuff, including: Indian artifacts, hundreds of branding irons, antique guns, mutated animals—the list goes on. Locals warned us not to believe everything we encountered, but of course, the jackalopes are authentic. The rock tower got a mention in *Ripley's Believe It or Not* due to a claim that you can see into six states from its perch— NOT! Modest admission fee. Open year-round 8 am–8 pm. Located in Genoa, **just off Interstate 70 at Exit 371; (719) 763-2309.**

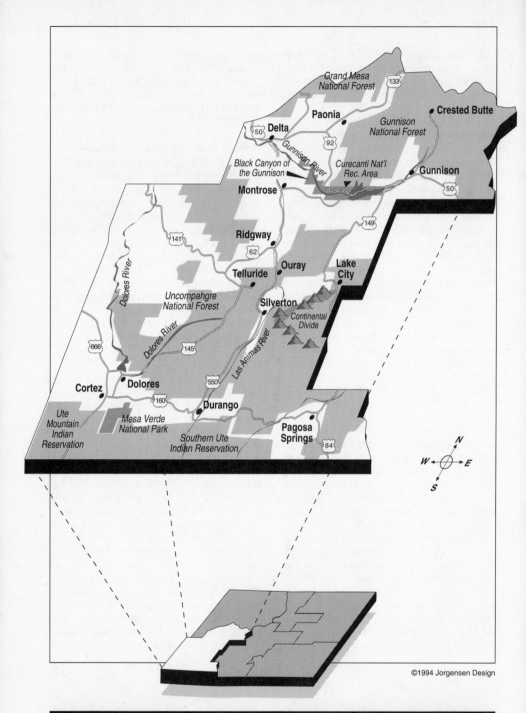

Grand Mesa
National Forest

133

Paonia

Crested Butte

50 Delta

92

Gunnison
National Forest

Gunnison River

Black Canyon of
the Gunnison

Curecanti Nat'l
Rec. Area

Gunnison

Montrose

50

149

141

Ridgway

62

Dolores River

Ouray

Lake
City

Telluride

Uncompahgre
National Forest

Silverton

Continental
Divide

Dolores River

145

Las Animas River

666

550

Cortez

Dolores

160

Durango

Mesa Verde
National Park

Pagosa
Springs

84

Ute
Mountain
Indian
Reservation

Southern Ute
Indian Reservation

N

W ⊕ E

S

©1994 Jorgensen Design

Southwest Region

SOUTHWEST REGION

Black Canyon Country

This intriguing area of western Colorado, which we refer to as Black Canyon country, is seldom seen by residents, let alone out-of-state visitors. That it is overlooked and underdeveloped is a major part of its appeal. Black Canyon country encompasses a large area with deep canyons, lush fertile valleys, towering mountains and far-reaching views.

The focal point is the **Black Canyon of the Gunnison National Monument,** one of the most magnificent canyons in the world. As deep as 2,900 feet and as narrow as 1,300 feet, this snaking 50-mile-long chasm draws hundreds of thousands of visitors each year, many of whom take a brief look and then move along to another part of the state. But the Black Canyon is not something to see in a hurry. So take the time to camp overnight or to do some hiking, perhaps down one of the steep trails to the river far below.

The waters of the Gunnison River flow north, eventually emerging from the Black Canyon and Gunnison Gorge to be joined by the North Fork of the Gunnison, which flows out of the beautiful North Fork Valley to the east. Ranches and fruit orchards are spread throughout the valley; Grand Mesa to the north and the West Elk Mountains to the southeast provide an unbelievably picturesque setting. The small towns of **Crawford, Hotchkiss** and **Paonia** are great jumping-off places for fishing, hiking and river floating. Or you may want to just sit around and enjoy the views.

West of the Black Canyon lies the Uncompahgre Plateau and the fairly large towns of **Montrose** and **Delta.** Both towns (bitter rivals according to some locals) are good way stations located 20 miles apart along Hwy. 50. Wide main streets, comfortable neighborhoods and stable communities provide Montrose and Delta with a similar Midwestern appeal. Both towns provide plenty of roadside motels and also happen to be within driving distance of some of the most beautiful, diverse country in Colorado. One especially pleasant aspect of Delta is

345

the newly completed Confluence Park, complete with a 70-acre fishing lake, picnic sites and a living history museum.

Though you may not want to spend your entire vacation here, Black Canyon country offers a pleasant alternative (and cheaper prices) to the nearby resort communities.

HISTORY

Into the 1880s Ute Indians hunted plentiful game and foraged in the area around the Black Canyon and the North Fork Valley. The Ute council tree, an ancient cottonwood tree that still stands in Delta, was a famous meeting place for the Indians.

The first Europeans in the area were probably Friars Dominguez and Escalante, who passed through in 1776. Hwy. 92, between Delta and Hotchkiss, is lined with numerous historical markers where the two men camped. Trappers entered the area in the 1820s, but did not leave much of a record of their findings. French trapper Antoine Roubidoux built a trading post just west of Delta in 1830 and named it Fort Uncompahgre. (To learn more about a reconstruction of this fort, see the Museums section.) Roubidoux was successful until the Utes burned it down in 1844.

By 1880 Anglo desire for the mineral-rich country of the nearby San Juans became too great—soon the Utes were pushed off their land, which included Black Canyon country. Following the miners were cattlemen and farmers, who quickly began to settle the land from Montrose north to Delta and up the North Fork Valley. The original ranchers moved their herds from Gunnison to the hills just north of Crawford, which is still a cattle town. Today, a trip along Hwy. 92 near Crawford may be interrupted by a cattle drive.

Early settlers introduced fruit trees to the North Fork Valley. For years the produce of the valley consistently won competitions at the World's Fair. Although a vicious frost in 1912 killed most of the productive orchards in Hotchkiss, today the fruit has made a comeback. Paonia, 10 miles up the valley from Hotchkiss, was spared the devastation of 1912 because of its "Million Dollar Wind," which blows in early morning and late afternoon, preventing serious frost damage. Today Paonia is famous for its sweet cherries as well as pears, peaches, apricots, plums and grapes. Paonia once made it into *Ripley's Believe It or Not* for having more churches per capita than any other place in the country.

GETTING THERE

From Denver, Black Canyon country can be reached several ways. The quickest is to head 250 miles west on Interstate 70 to Grand Junction and then south on Hwy. 50 for 40 miles to Delta. A scenic alternative from

Denver is to turn south (left) off Interstate 70 at Glenwood Springs onto Hwy. 82 and drive 12 miles to Carbondale. At Carbondale turn onto Hwy. 133, which takes you up the Crystal River Valley past Redstone, over McClure Pass and down into the Upper North Fork Valley above Paonia. The Montrose County Airport has daily flights from Denver and, just before landing, passengers get an incredible view into the Black Canyon of the Gunnison.

—————— MAJOR ATTRACTIONS ——————

Black Canyon of the Gunnison National Monument

Wallace Hanson, a US geologist who surveyed the Black Canyon in the 1950s, had this to say:

Several Western canyons exceed the Black Canyon in overall size. Some are larger; some are deeper; some are narrower; and a few have walls as steep. But no other canyon in North America combines the depth, narrowness, sheerness and somber countenance of the Black Canyon.

Most visitors to the Black Canyon would agree with these sentiments. The unassuming 6-mile drive from Hwy. 50 to the south rim gives no indication of what awaits. Suddenly you're peering down into the yawning chasm of the Black Canyon. Sheer, shadowy rock walls drop more than a half mile down to the Gunnison River, one of the last protected stretches of river in Colorado. Entering the deep, narrow passage to the east, the river snakes its way northwest for more than 50 miles before making its way to open country.

Along the deepest, most spectacular 12 miles of this canyon, the Black Canyon of the Gunnison National Monument allows visitors a glimpse at one of the most awesome geologic sites in the world. You can visit the canyon from either the south rim or the north rim. Most people choose the easily accessible (and often crowded) south rim, though some prefer the more remote and less-developed north rim.

Geology—

Many people who see the Black Canyon wonder how it could ever have been sliced through the surrounding gentle countryside. The answer is erosion. More than two million years ago, volcanic debris from the West Elk Mountains to the east and the San Juan Mountains to the south accumulated in the Black Canyon area. The ancient Gunnison River, making its way west, began cutting through the soft debris, eventually hitting the harder and much older rock of the Gunnison uplift. Since the river's course and steep banks had already been established, all it could do was wear away at the harder, underlying rock.

History—

The Ute Indians dared not enter the Black Canyon of the Gunnison. Calling the area *Tomichi*, meaning "land of high cliffs and plenty water," they preferred instead a view from the rim. Game was plentiful, and the Utes hunted buffalo and deer by driving them into traps or over some smaller cliffs in the area. On the north rim of the Black Canyon some of these old traps and pits can still be found. The first documentation of the river was given in 1853 by the Gunnison party, which was scouting a transcontinental railroad route. In the 1880s a survey crew for the Denver & Rio Grande Railroad initiated an intriguing possibility—diverting some of the water from the Gunnison River to irrigate the arid Uncompahgre Valley to the west by tunneling through the rock.

With this idea in mind, people began to talk of its possibilities, though most thought it was absurd. In order to irrigate the valley, a 6-mile tunnel would have to be drilled with pinpoint accuracy through solid rock. If the dream were to become reality, an accurate survey of the "impassable" canyon would be necessary.

In September 1900 William W. Torrence and four other men set off in two wooden boats on a 30-mile journey through the canyon, expecting to emerge four or five days later. Wrong. The second day out they lost one of the boats, which contained most of their food and survey equipment. After three long weeks the weary crew had made it only 14 miles. Finally they reached a narrow section of the canyon where 60-foot-high boulders and cascading waterfalls blocked their way. Unable to portage around the boulders or to turn back, they were forced to climb the dangerous 2,000-foot-high cliffs. After 12 hair-raising hours they reached the rim, but Torrence was more determined than ever to complete his mission. The next year he returned with A.L. Fellows. The two men set out in rubber rafts. The accounts of this voyage are intriguing. At one point they had lost the last of their food but somehow managed to corner a mountain goat; Torrence held onto it while Fellows killed it. Finally they made it through the canyon, and Fellows's notes provided the information needed to begin the routing of the diversion tunnel. The project began in 1903, but it was not easy—workers cursed the dense rock, staggering heat, scalding hot springs and poisonous gas pockets. Not surprisingly, everyone cheered when the tunnel was completed in 1909. President Taft presided over the opening ceremony.

In 1933 President Hoover declared the most spectacular 12 miles of the canyon a national monument. Although three dams—Blue Mesa, Morrow Point and Crystal (see Major Attractions in the **Gunnison and Crested Butte** chapter)—have reduced the flow of the mighty Gunnison through the canyon, it is a compelling, pristine area that should not be missed.

Getting There—

To reach the south rim from Montrose, head east on Hwy. 50 for 6 miles and turn left. Drive the 6-mile paved road (Hwy. 347) to the monument boundary. The north rim can be reached from Hotchkiss by heading southeast on Hwy. 92 for 13 miles to Crawford Reservoir. Turn right at the sign and continue 11 miles on the dirt road. You can also get there from the town of Crawford. The North Rim Rd. is closed in winter.

RECREATION INFORMATION
Camping—

South Rim Campground has 102 sites, including many that are accessible to disabled people. This campground rarely if ever fills up according to the Park Service. **East Portal Campground,** along the river at the bottom of East Portal Rd., has 12 tent sites. **North Rim Campground** has 13 sites. A fee is charged at each of these campgrounds; first-come, first-served only; all are closed in winter.

Fishing—

Lower Gunnison River—From both the north and south rims, several difficult trails descend sharply to the Gunnison River far below (see Hiking and Backpacking in the next section). If you can make it down to the river's edge, chances are you'll be rewarded. Deep pools and large trout, many in the five-pound range, are lurking within the canyon—and because the river is so hard to reach, the fishing pressure is fairly light. In some places there is room to pitch a tent and fish for a few days at the bottom of the spectacular canyon. Flies and lures only. Try a large, weighted wet fly or nymph: Stone Fly, Woolly Worm or Muddler Minnow; on top a 12 to 16 Royal Wulff or an Adams are local favorites. The Panther Martin lure works wonders.

Just south of the monument boundary on the south rim, the steep and twisting East Portal Rd. leads down to the river's edge below Crystal Reservoir. It's good fishing from the bank, and there is a small campground (no RVs). Fishing in the Gold

Medal water downstream from the monument can be great (page over to the main Fishing section).

Hiking and Backpacking—

Into the Canyon—Anyone thinking about hiking down to the river from the rim should keep this in mind—the trails are very rough and tiring and can be dangerous. It's also easy to lose your way as the trails are not well marked. Campsites along the river are very limited, but the fishing is superb. In summer be on the lookout for tall poison ivy plants, which are found along most of the trails and beside the river. Backpackers heading down one of the trails need to register with the park ranger. Listed below are the trails from the south rim:

Tomichi Trail drops 1,800 feet and takes about one hour (ascent is three hours). Two campsites are available along a half-mile stretch of river. **Gunnison Point Trail** drops 1,800 feet and takes an hour and a half to descend (ascent is three hours). Three campsites are located along a 0.75-mile stretch of the river. **Warner Point Trail**, the longest route to the inner canyon in the park, drops 2,660 feet and takes two and a half hours (ascent is five hours). Five campsites are located along a 1.5-mile stretch of river.

Trails accessible from the north rim are as follows: well-named **S.O.B. Draw** drops 1,800 feet, taking two hours (ascent is four hours). There are six campsites along a 2-mile stretch of the river. **Long Draw** is a straight shot, 1,800-foot drop, taking one and a half hours (three-hour ascent) with many loose rocks and large boulders along the way. There is only one campsite on a quarter-mile stretch of the river. **Slide Draw** drops 1,600 feet, takes one and a half hours (ascent is four and a half hours) and has two campsites along a 0.75-mile stretch of the river.

On the Rim—Stop in at the visitors center at the south rim for a map of several short hiking trails that provide great views of the canyon. (After a snowstorm, these marked trails also provide good cross-country skiing.) On the north rim, the one-third-mile **Chasm View Trail** heads from the campground to a great canyon observation point. **North Vista Trail,** a newly built 3.5-mile trail by Volunteers for Outdoor Colorado sets out from the North Rim Ranger Station. Take the time for a hike—it's the best way to see the wildlife of the canyon. Golden eagles, mule deer, mountain lions and even black bears make their home here.

Scenic Drives—

In the Monument—The roads running along both the south and north rims within the monument offer great views of the canyon and the surrounding area. **South Rim Dr.** has 12 pull-offs with views from Tomichi Point and a spectacular view across the canyon to Painted Wall, the highest rock cliff in the state. If you look closely you may see climbers on the wall, making their way very slowly to the top. Just outside of the southern monument boundary, a very steep paved road winds its way down to the East Portal of the irrigation tunnel, just at Crystal Dam. No RVs are allowed on the road and regular cars should have good brakes. **North Rim Dr.** also provides a number of excellent views.

Scenic Highway 92—From the north side of the Black Canyon, consider this long but spectacular drive along Hwy. 92, via the **West Elk Scenic Byway.** This length of highway puts you in the middle of a wilderness experience with many options for longer connecting routes. From Hotchkiss head southeast on Hwy. 92 alongside the canyon and Curecanti National Recreation Area, keeping a lookout for scenic pullouts and wildlife along the way. The road extends 52 miles, providing great views of the West Elk Range, the San Juan Mountains and Curecanti Needle before joining Hwy. 50 at Blue Mesa Reservoir. From the junction at Hwy. 50 you can head west to Montrose and then north to Delta and east on Hwy. 92 back to Hotchkiss to complete the loop.

Visitors Center—
Located at the south rim, the visitors center is open Memorial Day–Labor Day. Take a look at the interesting exhibits on the history, flora, fauna and geology of the canyon. Campfire programs, guided walks and demonstrations are given. Open Memorial Day–mid-Sept., 8 am–7 pm daily.

Open intermittently in spring and fall; closed in winter.

For More Information—
Contact the Park Superintendent at **Black Canyon of the Gunnison, 2233 E. Main St., Montrose, CO 81401; (303) 249-7036.**

FESTIVALS AND EVENTS

Crazy River Raft Race
mid-June
This wild event causes normally sane people to build "crazy" rafts and float them down a 7-mile stretch of the Gunnison River below the Black Canyon. Dozens of prizes are given out to the contestants, but most people come for a good party. Festivities kick off with a Saturday morning parade of the crews and their rafts. For more information contact the **Delta Chamber of Commerce, 301 Main St., Delta, CO 81416; (303) 874-8616** or **(303) 874-8616.**

Paonia Cherry Days
early July
This three-day festival, celebrating the cherry harvest, has been a tradition for years. A parade, a barbecue, a talent show, crafts,

games, fireworks and the crowning of the Cherry Day Queen pack people in from miles around. And, of course, there are plenty of cherries and cherry pies to eat. Call **(303) 527-3886** for more information.

Native American Lifeways
late September
This fascinating two-day event celebrates Native American traditions, such as story telling, basket weaving, crafts and dance. Fry bread, buffalo burgers and soft drinks are sold. Held on the shaded grounds of the **Ute Indian Museum** (see the Museum section); the museum is free on both days. Located at the southern end of Montrose, just off Hwy. 550. **17253 Chipeta Dr., Montrose, CO 81401; (303) 249-3098.**

OUTDOOR ACTIVITIES

BIKING
MOUNTAIN BIKING
Mountain biking is making its presence known in this part of the state in a big way. With the opening of the 142-mile **Tabeguache Trail** connecting Montrose with Grand Junction, and the 128-mile **Kokopelli's Trail** from Grand Junction to Moab, Utah, the sport now has a number of great rides spreading over the Colorado Plateau (see the **Grand Junction** chapter for information on these and other rides). More specifically, just west of Montrose the Uncompahgre Plateau offers hundreds of miles of excellent mountain bike routes.

For detailed information about a multitude of area trails, we recommend picking up a copy of Bill Harris's book entitled *Bicycling the Uncompahgre Plateau* (Wayfinder Press, 1988). You can also check with the **Delta Forest Service, (303) 874-7691**, or the **Paonia Ranger District Office, (303) 527-4131.**

FISHING
Crawford Reservoir—
This popular state park has good fishing for 10-inch rainbows and some warmwater species, especially perch. If you are lucky enough to hook into one, the

catfish here can get really big—some over 15 pounds. This large reservoir also has a campground, a swimming beach and boat ramps. Entrance fee charged. Located a mile south of Crawford on Hwy. 92.

Curecanti National Recreation Area—

Curecanti encompasses the reservoirs on the Gunnison, upriver from the national monument. Fishing on Blue Mesa, Morrow Point and Crystal reservoirs can be very good. For more information see the Major Attractions section in the **Gunnison and Crested Butte** chapter.

Lower Gunnison River—

Don't miss fishing this Gold Medal stretch of the Lower Gunnison as it flows out of the Black Canyon of the Gunnison National Monument down to the confluence with the North Fork. It's quite simply some of the finest trout water in Colorado. Recently a Division of Wildlife employee estimated there were more than 10,000 trout larger than 6 inches in each mile of the Lower Gunnison. A good road provides fairly easy access to the river from the north. From Delta drive 14 miles east on Hwy. 92 to a sign marked Gunnison Forks Wildlife Management Area River Access. Turn right and head a mile south to the confluence of the North Fork and the Gunnison River. Cross the North Fork on a footbridge and walk up the Gunnison River on a 4-mile trail leading up to the Smith Fork. The fishing all along this stretch is excellent for large trout. Since this is the easiest access to this prime portion of the river, the fishing pressure is fairly heavy.

It is possible to reach the Gunnison River above the Smith Fork, but getting there is involved. The more than 15 miles of water just below the monument in the Gunnison Gorge is best fished from a boat with a guide. Several companies offer this service. The one with the most experience is Hank Hotze of **Gunnison River Expeditions, PO Box 315, Montrose, CO 81402; (303) 249-4441.** If you want to head down on your own to try some bank fishing or

wading, there are four trails leading to the water's edge from the plateau on the west side of the river. It takes a high-clearance vehicle to reach the trailheads. For more information on the specific routes, see the Gunnison Gorge Trails in the Hiking and Backpacking section.

Lower Gunnison River within the National Monument—

See the Major Attractions section.

Sweitzer Lake—

Fishing for warm-water species can be good at this state park, but the fish are inedible due to a high selenium content. To reach the reservoir head 1.5 miles south from Delta on Hwy. 50 and then east for a half mile on Park Entrance Rd.

HIKING AND BACKPACKING

Trails leading down into the Black Canyon and the Gunnison Gorge provide access to excellent fishing and a unique river ecosystem. To the east of the Black Canyon, Gunnison National Forest offers pine and aspen forests as well as high alpine scenery. For more information about hiking and backpacking opportunities in the area contact the **Delta Forest Service** at **2250 Hwy. 50, Delta, CO 81416; (303) 874-7691,** or the **Paonia Ranger District Office** at **PO Box 1030, N. Rio Grande Ave., Paonia, CO 81428; (303) 527-4131.**

Black Canyon of the Gunnison National Monument Trails—

See the Major Attractions section.

Gunnison Gorge Trails—

Located just downriver (north) of the monument boundary, this section of the Gunnison River offers beautiful scenery and Gold Medal fishing. There are four trails leading down to the river from the west rim. Be on the lookout for river otters and bighorn sheep, which were recently reintroduced into this area. Access to the trails is possible from Hwy. 50 between Montrose and Delta. From Montrose head north on Hwy. 50 for 6 miles and turn right on Falcon Rd. Proceed 3.6 miles to Peach Valley Rd. and turn northeast. From Peach Valley Rd. there are four roads (four-wheel-drive vehicle highly recommended) that break off to the east, leading to four trailheads.

After 1.5 miles the first access road heads right for 10 miles down to the **Chukar Trail** trailhead. Chukar Trail drops 500 feet in a 1-mile hike to the river.

Another 2.1 miles down Peach Valley Rd. the second access road turns right and heads a mile and a half to **Bobcat Trail.** Bobcat Trail drops 800 feet to the river in 1 mile.

Following Peach Valley Rd. for another 1.4 miles leads you to the third access road on the right, which winds 2 miles to **Duncan Trail.** This steep 1-mile trail drops 900 feet to the river.

Two more miles along Peach Valley Rd. lead you to the last access road, heading right and continuing 2.5 miles to Ute Trail. Ute Trail descends 1,200 feet to the river in 4.5 miles.

Gunnison National Forest—
Curecanti Trail—This 10.5-mile trail heads up Curecanti Creek through aspen, spruce and fir, eventually reaching the mountain grasslands of the West Elk Wilderness Area. The creek has created a canyon with many unusual rock formations and spires. After an elevation gain of 1,600 feet, the trail emerges on Curecanti Pass. From Crawford head south on Hwy. 92 for 25 miles to the Curecanti Creek crossing, turn left onto Forest Rd. 720 and proceed 8 miles to the trailhead.

Three Lakes Trail—This easy 3-mile loop takes you to a waterfall and provides impressive views into the West Elk Wilderness Area. As the name indicates, there are also three lakes along the way with pretty good fishing. To reach the trailhead from Paonia, head northeast on Hwy. 133 and then right on Hwy. 12. Drive about 14 miles to Forest Rd. 706 and turn right. Proceed 2 miles to the trailhead at Lost Lake Campground.

HORSEBACK RIDING
Needle Rock Ranch—
Located on the western boundary of the West Elk Wilderness Area, Needle Rock Ranch provides good trail horses and access to the wilderness area. Full- and half-day rides are offered Mon.–Sat. during the summer and into the fall. To reach the ranch from Crawford, head east on the road between the church and the post office, then follow the signs. **4389 F Rd., PO Box 305, Crawford, CO 81415; (303) 921-3050.**

LLAMA TREKKING
Backcountry Llamas—
One great way to experience the beauty of the West Elk Wilderness Area of Gunnison National Forest is by taking a llama trek with Backcountry Llamas. Working out of Paonia, Paul and Fran Cranor run trips into the wilderness area from a number of trailheads. Hike along the trails while the llamas carry most of your supplies. Treks from a half day to four nights are offered. Be sure to set up a trek well in advance, as there are a limited number each season. Special dietary requirements are no problem. Contact Paul and Fran Cranor at **PO Box 1287, Paonia, CO 81428; (303) 527-3844.**

Cedars' Edge Llamas Bed and Breakfast—
Consider staying at this new B&B in Cedaredge and spending time with more than a dozen of these friendly creatures. See Where to Stay for more information.

RIVER FLOATING
The Lower Gunnison—
Although it's hard to believe, there are some expert kayakers who run the river through the 12-mile stretch of the Black Canyon of the Gunnison National Monument. This is the canyon the Utes feared and early settlers said could never be navigated. Nonetheless, each year determined kayakers run the Class IV and Class V rapids, portaging around drop-offs as high

as 17 feet. A lot of planning is necessary for this section. Most kayakers put in at the East Portal, which they reach via the steep road just outside of the monument boundary on the south rim.

Below the monument the canyon opens up a bit into the Gunnison Gorge, a stretch of river that offers excellent floating. This section of the river is home to many species of birds, including golden eagles, red-tailed hawks, prairie falcons and great horned owls. There are no roads into this 16-mile stretch of the river down to the North Fork confluence—most boaters carry their crafts in on the 1-mile Chukar Trail. For directions to Chukar Trail see the Hiking and Backpacking section. Rafters take out at the campground next to Hwy. 92 at the Gunnison–North Fork confluence. From here down through Delta the river is calm.

Below the confluence with the Uncompahgre River at Delta, the Gunnison cuts through the maroon and purple Morrison strata, eventually reaching the exposed red sandstone of Dominguez Canyon. Within the canyon walls are many unusual rock formations—one resembles a profile of Richard Nixon. This 39-mile stretch between Delta and Whitewater is fairly calm but beautiful.

Outfitters—

Gunnison River Expeditions—Hank Hotze began running river trips down the Gunnison River in the 1970s, and today his operation has been outfitting river runners longer than any other in the area. The main stretch he runs is the Gunnison Gorge, which combines great rafting, Gold Medal fishing and plentiful wildlife. For more information contact Hotze at **PO Box 315, Montrose, CO 81402; (303) 249-4441.**

Dvorak's Kayak & Rafting Expeditions—Offers multi-day expeditions on the Gunnison and other Colorado rivers. **1-800-824-3795** toll free.

Mind Body River Adventures—This may be your only chance to combine yoga, tai chi and chi kung on a multi-day raft trip. This unique company run by a couple of experienced (and experiential) river rats offers many trip combinations. Vegetarian meals unless otherwise requested. **PO Box 863, Hotchkiss, CO; (303) 921-3455.**

SEEING AND DOING

FISH HATCHERY

Hotchkiss National Fish Hatchery—
Located 3 miles southwest of Hotchkiss (1 mile south of the small town of Lazear), the Hotchkiss National Fish Hatchery is a main supplier of rainbow trout for reservoirs in western Colorado and New Mexico. Millions of eggs are hatched in controlled ponds, and when hatchlings are the right size (3–9 inches) they are shipped to various reservoirs in special trucks resembling aquariums on wheels. The public can tour the facility year-round from 7:30 am to 4 pm daily, free of charge. There are a few picnic tables nearby. From Hotchkiss head west on Hwy. 92 for 2 miles and turn left (south) to Lazear. **(303) 872-3170.**

MUSEUMS

Delta County Historical Museum (Delta)—
Though the Delta County Historical Society was established back in 1964, it never really had an appropriate home for all of its artifacts. Now with the opening of a museum in a beautifully restored firehouse, the large collection gets its due. The Jones Gallery, with many important dinosaur finds from the nearby Uncompahgre Plateau, is fascinating. The museum also houses Delta's first jail, a huge butterfly collection, guns, appliances, cameras and historic black and white photos. This museum has better descriptions on their "stuff" than most museums we've seen. Small entrance fee. Open May–Sept., 10 am–4 pm Tues.–Fri. and 10 am–1 pm Sat. **251 Meeker St.**

Fort Uncompahgre (Delta)—

In Confluence Park (with its worth-while 3-mile walking trail) near the center of Delta, the tall wooden gates of a trading post look slightly out of place. But even that didn't prepare us for the surprise of finding buckskin-clad, heavily bearded, tough-looking mountain men walking around the compound. Several wooden huts with sod roofs line the perimeter of the fort. A couple of hides (complete with musket holes) could be seen stretched tightly on racks, drying in the breeze. A blacksmith shop, with double bellows, makes all of the horseshoes and metal implements for this fort. Look around and examine the detail. You won't see any-thing that could be bought, borrowed or stolen outside the years 1826–1844. Every year Fort Uncompahgre hosts an encamp-ment, but it's really set up primarily to educate visitors about life during the trad-ing and trapping era. Open 10 am–5 pm Wed.–Sun. in Mar.-Aug.; Thur.-Sun. in Sept.-Oct.; Thurs.-Sat. in Nov.-Dec. Located at the end of Gunnison River Dr. in Confluence Park (behind Gibson's). Call the **Delta Chamber of Commerce** for in-formation: **(303) 874-8616.**

Montrose County Historical Museum (Montrose)—

In the original Denver & Rio Grande Depot, this museum focuses most of its attention on early-day settlers. You are welcome to look through a complete col-lection of Montrose newspapers dating from 1896. A homesteader's cabin and country store can be seen outfitted with original furnishings. Open May–Oct.; **11 North First St.; (303) 249-2085.**

Montrose Children's Museum (Montrose)—

For the past decade this small mu-seum has offered exhibits, classes and other learning experiences for the younger set. Since they are planning to move, please call **(303) 240-4833** for information. **PO Box 3044, Montrose, CO 81402.**

Pioneer Town (Cedaredge)—

It's truly worthwhile to stop off at the authentic Coalby Store, Girling Mercan-tile, Lizard Head Saloon, Cedaredge Town Jail and other historic buildings collected here at the foot of Grand Mesa. Check out the antiques, clothes and historic memora-bilia from the past 100 years. While this collection has been put together fairly re-cently, its magnitude is impressive. No admission fee, but donations are accepted. Stop by Pioneer Town (signs direct you from Hwy. 65) between Memorial Day weekend and Labor Day weekend; 10 am–4 pm Mon.-Sat. and 1–4 pm on Sun. For more information contact the **Surface Val-ley Historical Society, PO Box 906, Cedaredge, CO 81413.**

Ute Indian Museum (Montrose)—

Dedicated to Ouray, chief of the Southern Utes, and his wife, Chipeta, this museum provides information and dis-plays about the Ute Indians of Colorado. Artifacts (many of which belonged to fa-mous Utes such as Ouray, Ignacio, Colorow and Buckskin Charlie), diora-mas and other information help you gain insight into traditional Ute culture, which ended so tragically. A large collection of ceremonial and traditional artifacts was provided by Thomas McKee, a local pho-tographer who lived with the Utes begin-ning in the 1880s. Next to the museum building is Chipeta's grave. A fee is charged. Open Memorial Day–Labor Day, Mon.–Sat. 10 am–5 pm, Sun. 1–5 pm; shorter hours during Sept. Located at the southern end of Montrose, just off Hwy. 550. **17253 Chipeta Dr., Montrose, CO 81401; (303) 249-3098.**

NIGHTLIFE

Montrose Pavilion (Montrose)—

You probably wouldn't imagine a world-class arts facility in a town the size of Montrose. But after years of effort and many thousands of dollars in donations, plays, music and lectures can all be found here on various nights. Located at the south end of town a quarter mile off Hwy. 550—check in at **1800 Pavilion Dr., Montrose, 81401; (303) 249-7015** for more information and a current schedule of events.

Thunder Mountain Lives Tonight! (Delta)—

If the kids get restless consider taking them to "the greatest outdoor show west of the Mississippi." *Thunder Mountain Lives Tonight!* is an extravaganza spiced with music, humor and a cast of 60 people. It recreates many historical episodes of Delta County, with Thunder Mountain (Grand Mesa) in the distance. Started in 1986 to help out the faltering local economy, the show has received rave reviews from magazines, newspapers and even NBC's "Today Show." It's an entertaining way to learn about Indian culture and the life of pioneers in the area. There is a fee charged. The show runs from July 4 until Labor day, Tues.–Sat. 6–8 pm. Located in Confluence Park at the end of Gunnison River Dr. (behind Gibson's). For reservations and information contact the **Delta Chamber of Commerce** at **301 Main St., Delta, CO 81416; 1-800-228-7009** toll free or **(303) 874-8616.**

SCENIC DRIVES

Black Canyon of the Gunnison—

For information see the Major Attractions section.

Escalante Canyon—

Located northwest of Delta, this starkly beautiful and historic canyon drive is worth a look. From Hwy. 50 the well-marked road follows Escalante Creek up toward the Uncompahgre Plateau. Within easy access are a couple of rocks displaying Ute petroglyphs and an area where dinosaur digs have been conducted. Many old homesteads remain in the area. One in particular is very interesting—Capt. Smith's Cabin. In 1907 Capt. H.A. Smith, at the age of 67, moved into the canyon and built an unusual stone house. One wall is built into a solid slab of rock while the other three were made from rough-cut stones. This ex-Union Army officer was a skilled stonemason who claimed to have learned his techniques from Indians. In the cabin a 6-foot-long sleeping area was cut into the rock, as well as a small niche for a bedside pistol. Remember, this was the Wild West.

To reach Escalante Canyon, head northwest from Delta on Hwy. 50 toward Grand Junction and turn left onto County Rd. 650. Follow the road down to the river and across the bridge. There are a number of side trips you can make from here. A well-marked signpost gives directions and information about the different sites. If you need more information about this area, visit the **Delta Chamber of Commerce, 301 Main St., Delta, CO 81416; (303) 874-8616.**

Kebler Pass—

See the **Gunnison and Crested Butte** chapter.

———— WHERE TO STAY ————

ACCOMMODATIONS

Both Montrose and Delta are large towns with plenty of motels along the main thoroughfares. If you need lodging information contact the chamber of commerce numbers listed in the Services section at the end of this chapter. The unique lodging opportunities listed here are located up the North Fork of the Gunnison and near Grand Mesa. These are definite "blue highway" destinations: off the beaten track but worth the effort.

The Last Frontier—$$$

Overlooking Crawford Reservoir from a spectacular perch not far from the north rim of the Black Canyon, The Last Frontier is a one-of-a-kind destination. "It's somewhere between rustic and crude—and I built it myself just a few years ago," said Claire Hicks, the rugged, good-natured cowboy who runs this out-of-the-way lodge with his wife Nola. If you want to leave your worldly cares behind, a few days here could be ideal. This place is not for everyone—for solitude or luxury, go someplace else.

The nine smallish guest rooms—some adjoin for the convenience of families—are located upstairs in the main house; all are decorated simply and tastefully and have private bathrooms. Southern facing rooms feature balconies. The expansive, window encased common room opens to a wide terrace with a great view of Needle Rock. Three meals a day are included here for about the price of a basic hotel room in the city. We're talking huge ranch-style meals, such as ribs, steaks and roasts for dinner (excellent between-meal snacks, too). You'll get to know the other guests over meals or perhaps when you hit the trail on one of their horses. Lots of fishing nearby. Claire and Nola have a real knack for making everyone feel comfortable and cared for during their stay. Kids welcome (those under five stay free). Open year-round. Call for reservations: **(303) 921-6363.**

Cedars' Edge Llamas Bed and Breakfast—$$ to $$$

Get away to this unique, peaceful setting at the base of Grand Mesa and you'll have the chance to learn more about llamas. Ray and Gail Record not only breed and raise llamas, but also run a two-bedroom B&B out of their large, solar-heated home. Each bedroom features a private bathroom and southerly views from secluded decks overlooking the llama pastures. A full breakfast is served either in your room or, weather permitting, on the deck. Guests are invited to share the Records' living room in the evening. Located 5 miles outside of Cedaredge. **2169 Hwy. 65, Cedaredge, CO 81413; (303) 856-6836.**

Saddle Mountain Guest Ranch—$$ to $$$

Located 6 miles east of Crawford and surrounded by Gunnison National Forest,

Saddle Mountain enjoys a prime location. Sleeping quarters are nothing more than a room with a bed; three rustic cabins can be rented on a space available basis at the same rate. But you didn't come all this way to stay inside anyway. Explore the pretty area on horseback for an hourly charge. A large lake on the property is stocked with rainbow, brown and cutthroat trout, and the Smith Fork River, which runs through the property, is also stocked. In winter you can cross-country ski in the rolling hills around the ranch and then relax in the hot tub on the deck. The dining hall serves up good, down-home meals for a reasonable charge. Be sure to call the ranch for reservations. From Hotchkiss, head 11 miles southeast on Hwy. 92 to Crawford and turn left on the road between the church and the post office. Drive 3 miles, turn right and proceed another 3 miles to the ranch. **4536 E. 50 Dr., Crawford, CO 81415; (303) 921-6321.**

CAMPING

Black Canyon of the Gunnison National Monument—

For information on camping on the north and south rims of the Black Canyon, see the Major Attractions section.

Crawford State Park—

Located a mile south of Crawford on Hwy. 92 at Crawford Reservoir. There are 61 sites and a fee is charged. Open all year.

In Gunnison National Forest—

Smith Fork Picnic Ground offers dispersed camping with minimal facilities and no fee. To reach it head southeast from Hotchkiss on Hwy. 92 to Crawford and turn left onto Forest Rd. 712. Proceed about 7 miles east to the picnic ground. **Erickson Springs Campground** is located in the upper North Fork Valley. From Paonia head northeast on Hwy. 133 for about 12 miles and turn right on County Rd. 12. Proceed 6 miles to the campground. There are 18 sites and a fee is charged. From Erickson Springs Campground head up Hwy. 12 another 7 miles to Forest Rd. 706, turn right and proceed about 2 miles to **Lost Lake Camp-**

ground. This campground has heavy use in summer; there are 15 sites and no fee is charged. **McClure Campground** is located on McClure Pass, 12 miles north of Paonia Reservoir on Hwy. 133. There are 19 sites and a fee is charged. Some sites in Gunnison National Forest can be reserved by calling **1-800-283-CAMP.**

Paonia State Park—

Located about 16 miles northeast of Paonia on Hwy. 133 at Paonia Reservoir. There are 10 sites and a fee is charged.

Private Campgrounds—

Crystal Meadows Ranch—Crystal Meadows Ranch, with its gorgeous location at the base of Kebler Pass, has plenty of RV hookups and tent sites. Other attractions include a fishing lake, laundry facilities, a restaurant (locals rave about the steaks here) and showers (extra charge). Located just out of Somerset in the North Fork Valley. From Hotchkiss drive 17 miles northeast on Hwy. 133. 30682 **County Rd. 12, Somerset, CO 81434; (303) 929-5656.**

Delta/Grand Mesa KOA Campground— This is one of the best-equipped RV campgrounds available, with complete RV hookups and tent sites. Full amenities include showers, a store and even a swimming pool. Located a mile east of Delta on Hwy. 92. **1675 Hwy. 92, Delta, CO 81416; (303) 874-3918.**

Gunnison River Pleasure Park—Fishermen, rafters and others appreciate staying overnight at this prime location along the Gunnison River. In addition to RV and tent campsites, they also have cabins, a restaurant and other services. Located 14 miles north of Delta on Hwy. 92; **(303) 872-2525.**

The Hangin' Tree RV Park—RV hookups, tent sites, showers and everything else you could possibly expect to find at an RV park. Located 2 miles south of Montrose on Hwy. 550 (across from the Ute Indian Museum). **17250 Hwy. 550 S., Montrose, CO 81401; (303) 249-9966.**

—————————— WHERE TO EAT ——————————

The Glenn Eyrie Restaurant (in Montrose)—$$ to $$$

Located in an old farmhouse surrounded by stately trees, the Glenn Eyrie was a pleasant surprise when we last visited. Inside the atmosphere is very comfortable and homey. Dinners are served at tables out on the lawn or inside in a more formal atmosphere. The food is excellent. Owner and chef Johannes "Steve" Schwathe is from Austria, where he studied in Vienna under the watchful eye of a master chef. The ambitious menu selection is impressive, with entrées ranging from lamb kebab and Châteaubriand Bouquetière to Steak Diane. An entrée with a local twist is the crab-stuffed Colorado trout. The fine wine list is reasonably priced. Reservations are recommended. Great Sunday brunch now offered from 11:30 am–2 pm. Open for dinner 5–9 pm Tues.–Sun. **2351 S. Townsend Ave.; (303) 249-9263.**

The Red Barn (in Montrose)—$$ to $$$

With a bull on the sign, you can be sure this local favorite is the place for tender steaks, good burgers. But the Red Barn also offers several chicken and fresh fish dishes as well as a large salad bar. Real barnwood walls, low lighting and pleasant service help finish off the comfortable atmosphere. Separate lounge area with TV sports emphasis. Lunch served Mon.–Fri. 11 am–3 pm. Open every night for dinner 3–10:30 pm. Sun. brunch 9 am–3 pm. **1413 E. Main; (303) 249-9202.**

Sakura (in Montrose)—$$ to $$$

Yayoi Corder has lived in Montrose for more than 20 years and when she opened this restaurant in 1985 people thought she was crazy. A Japanese restaurant in Montrose?! You bet, and it's a good one, too. People from as far away as Telluride rave about it and make the long drive for a plate of her sushi or tempura. The decor is very Japanese, including an intimate tatami room. Great lunch specials and dinners are served. Try the teriyaki chicken or beef. The green tea ice cream is delicious. Imported Japanese beer and saki, as well as a full bar, are available. Lunch is served Mon.–Fri. 11 am–2 pm, dinner Mon.–Sat. 5–9 pm; closed Sun. **411 N. Townsend Ave.; (303) 249-8230.**

Zack's Trading Post (in Hotchkiss)—$$ to $$$

Zack's is known throughout the area for its succulent barbecued ribs, beef, chicken and ham. Breakfasts are also served. Open 6:30 am–9 pm in summer, 6:30 am–8 pm in winter. Located at the east end of **Bridge St.** in Hotchkiss; **(303) 872-3199.**

Little's Restaurant (in Paonia)—$$

Little's has been through a transition, but the quality of its food is back. The chef doesn't specialize in just one type of cuisine—you can order a steak, burrito, pasta plate or sandwich. Leave enough room for a slice of their specialty: cheesecake. Little's main room, with its hand-hewn wooden ceiling beams and a huge round fireplace, is the most comfortable place to kick back. Other settings in the restaurant include the tropical room (complete with waterfall), the library and a great deck. Open daily 11 am–10 pm. Just west of Paonia on **Hwy. 133; (303) 527-6141.**

Boardwalk Restaurant and Lounge (in Crawford)—$ to $$

With its home-cooked meals at very reasonable prices, the Boardwalk deserves a special mention. This restaurant serves great breakfasts and dinners, including inexpensive T-bone steaks. Homemade baked goods including their special wheat bread are served with all meals. Dinners come with potato or rice and salad bar or vegetable of the day; fresh bread and rolls are also served. Open 7:30 am–8 pm Thur.–Tues., closed Wed. Located on the main street in Crawford; 64 Hwy. 92; **(303) 921-4905.**

The Daily Bread (Montrose)—$

For fresh bread, wonderful sandwiches, filling breakfasts and a mouthwatering array of pastries, cookies and pies—all at a decent price—stop here. This corner restaurant has an inordinate amount of charm. Take out, too. **346 Main St., Montrose; (303) 249-8444.**

SERVICES

Delta Chamber of Commerce—

301 Main St., Delta, CO 81416; (303) 874-8616.

Hotchkiss Chamber of Commerce—

PO Box 727, Hotchkiss, CO 81419; (303) 872-3226.

Montrose County Chamber of Commerce—

Stop by the excellent visitors information center as you enter (or exit town). **550 N. Townsend Ave., Montrose, CO 81401; 1-800-872-0244** nationwide and **(303) 249-5515** locally.

Paonia Chamber of Commerce—

PO Box 366, Paonia, CO 81428; (303) 527-3886.

Cortez

Extreme southwest Colorado is marked by a unique juxtaposition of terrain, as the soaring peaks and lush forests of the San Juans loosen their grasp to the desert canyons and high mesas of the Colorado Plateau. Once home to thousands of *Anasazi*—a Navajo word meaning "Ancient Ones," or "Ancient Enemies"—this entire area was alive with Anasazi settlements. Today this beautiful corner of Colorado continues to be an important location for exploration, excavation, study and interpretation of these remarkable people who vanished mysteriously from Colorado about AD 1300.

Anyone interested in learning more about the culture of the Anasazi should plan on spending a lot of time in the Four Corners area. Most visitors blast their way directly to Mesa Verde National Park, which has an international reputation for its magnificent cliff dwellings. Spending a day or an afternoon at Mesa Verde is an absolute must. We are quick to stress, however, that many other lesser-known sites and museums encourage a larger range of archaeological and personal discovery. Consider lingering in the area for a few days to understand more about the Anasazi far off the beaten track.

At the hub of activity, Cortez (population 8,000) provides a welcome base for a mind-bending exploration of Colorado's past. Though basically a sleepy agricultural center, Cortez is awakening to a tourism boom. Today an array of lodging and dining possibilities awaits visitors, but during the peak summer season rooms can get booked solid. Ties to Native American cultures also run deep in Cortez. During summer evenings you can listen to stories and flute songs by a Ute Mountain Indian, watch an Indian dancer or see a Navajo sand painter at work (see Cortez Center in the Major Attractions section).

The surrounding area is as diverse as it is beautiful, offering a wide range of outdoor experiences. You'll never be far from the outline of Sleeping Ute Mountain (9,884 feet), which lies to the southwest of Cortez. Enshrouded in Ute legend, the prominent slopes of this mountain clearly show the outline of a sleeping Indian with his arms folded across his chest. It is said that the sleeping Ute is a great warrior god who fought a fierce battle with the powers of evil. Once he lay down to rest, the blood pouring from his wounds turned into water for all creatures to drink.

Just 11 miles north of Cortez, the hamlet of **Dolores** takes a position near the recently filled McPhee Reservoir. This reservoir has created a number of recreational opportunities, from water skiing to fishing to canoeing. The reservoir's constant supply of irrigation water means that pinto beans and a few other crops can better survive the long, dry summers, but the pristine Dolores River Canyon and a multitude of Anasazi artifacts have been lost forever. But due to mitigation from the McPhee project, a fascinating collection of artifacts can now be seen at the Anasazi Heritage Center (see Major Attractions).

PREHISTORY

Thousands of years before the arrival of the pueblo-dwelling Anasazi, nomadic hunters and gatherers roamed southwestern Colorado in search of food. These nomadic people left little behind and, consequently, what is known about them today is sketchy and speculative. Archaeologists agree, however, that near the time of Christ, people began settling in southwest Colorado's mesa lands. Instead of roaming far afield for their food, they started building shallow pit houses and cultivating beans, corn and squash in the rich red soil of the valleys. These early inhabitants did not make pottery but instead wove exquisite, coiled baskets, which were often found perfectly preserved in their dwellings. Archaeologists were moved to name these people Basket Makers. Only a handful of sites in Colorado date to this Anasazi period (Basket Maker II).

By AD 550 (Basket Maker III) the Anasazi also learned how to make pottery and experienced dramatic cultural advancements. Soon the bow and arrow replaced the primitive atlatl spear thrower, and the Anasazi began relying on stored food to get them through the winter. Settlements from this period consist of single-family farms with small storage rooms scattered around a single pit house. Many very large pit structures called "great kivas" were built. Evidence suggests that these impressive round rooms and other smaller kivas were used for religious and social purposes. Many Colorado sites, including some near Mesa Verde and the Dolores River Valley, can be traced to this period.

Around AD 750 (Pueblo I), the Anasazi started coming together in multifamily villages. In some cases several hundred families lived in close proximity to one another. But by AD 900 these large villages lay abandoned, and the Anasazi dispersed for the next 100 years.

Between the years AD 1000–1300 (Pueblo II), the Anasazi reached their peak in terms of architectural, political and economic advancements. Many rich and varied cultural traits can be traced to this period. Mesa-top homes built of stone and masonry replaced the subterranean pit houses. Cotton weaving and fire-resistant pottery also improved the quality of life. The entire Anasazi region was connected by a network of roads. A complex, integrated lifestyle can be seen in the region's "great kivas" (Lowry Pueblo and Chimney Rock in Colorado) and "great houses" (best exemplified by Chaco Canyon National Park, New Mexico).

By AD 1200 (Pueblo III), the Anasazi gradually sought refuge beneath overhanging cliffs, including the ones we know as Mesa Verde. Reasons for this move are unclear, but the settlements appear to be built in easily defendable positions. Many archaeologists believe these ancient people wanted to be closer to a water source; some of the walled compounds dating to this period enclose natural springs. Other groups near Mesa Verde chose to remain closer to their fields by living atop the mesas. For the first time many Anasazi built towers, which can now be seen in the area straddling the Utah-Colorado border at Hovenweep National Monument. This final period of development featured fine pottery craftsmanship.

By AD 1300 the Anasazi had deserted Mesa Verde and the Four Corners area for reasons that have never been fully explained. It was not a spontaneous exodus, but rather a gradual migration over the course of many years. Like gypsies, the Anasazi spread out in small groups, eventually losing their cultural identity. The generally accepted theory is that the Anasazi left because of a prolonged drought. Evidence also suggests that a cooling of the climate, a lack of burnable wood, and soil depletion after hundreds of years of intensive farming may have contributed to their abandonment of the area. After their departure, the Anasazi cliff houses and mesa-top communities stood empty. Nearly two hundred years passed before the area was inhabited again, this time by Ute tribes.

GETTING THERE

Located in southwestern Colorado near the Four Corners, where Utah, Colorado, Arizona and New Mexico converge, Cortez acts as a gateway to traffic coming into the state from the south on Hwys. 160 and 666. From Denver (377 miles to the northeast), Cortez can be reached via Interstate 25 south to Walsenburg and then west on Hwy. 160. Cortez also has a small airport with daily flights coming in from Denver on United.

———— MAJOR ATTRACTIONS ————

Mesa Verde National Park

Mesa Verde is the most dramatic introduction to the ancient Anasazi culture imaginable. With its twisting canyons, panoramic views and outstanding archaeological remains, Mesa Verde continues to fascinate visitors from the US and abroad. As one of the largest archeological preserves in America, Mesa Verde has more

than earned its rank of World Heritage Cultural Site.

History—

During the period between AD 1190 and 1300, advances in masonry skills enabled the Anasazi to build huge 100- to 200-room cliff houses, some four stories high. Hundreds of years after the Anasazi disappeared, Ute Indians moved into the Mesa Verde area. They knew about the empty cliff dwellings but kept away, believing the ancient cities to be haunted. Spanish explorers and settlers looked around the area for many years before trappers, prospectors and settlers entered the region, but they never saw the ruins.

Abandoned for almost 600 years, the interconnected settlements at Mesa Verde were finally rediscovered in December 1888. While looking for stray cattle during a snowstorm, ranchers Richard Wetherill and Charlie Mason stumbled upon Cliff Palace, the largest site in Mesa Verde, with more than 200 rooms and 23 kivas. In the 1890s many people flocked to the area to collect artifacts. In 1906, after persistent lobbying by some Coloradans, the US Congress passed a bill creating Mesa Verde National Park. It was this unusual foresight that helped create the first park in the country set aside exclusively for the preservation of archaeological artifacts.

Getting There—

The entrance to the park is located 10 miles east of Cortez on Hwy. 160, halfway to Mancos. From there a narrow paved road snakes its way up the mesa to the south for about 21 miles to the Far View Visitor Center. From there you will need to make a choice between Chapin and Wetherill mesas.

Facts About the Park—

Since the ruins are located in two main areas—Chapin and Wetherill mesas—you will need to decide where to begin. The highly popular Cliff Palace, as well as the dramatic dwellings at Spruce Tree House and Balcony House, entice most visitors directly to Chapin Mesa. If you have only a few hours it's probably best to stick with Chapin Mesa. Only a fraction of the park's visitors make the twisting 12-mile drive from the Far View Visitor Center to Weatherill Mesa. Once there you board a small tram (get here early to avoid a wait), which drives to various trailheads for ranger-guided walks. The most dramatic ruin and primary attraction on Weatherill Mesa is Long House, Mesa Verde's second

largest cliff dwelling, once home to 150 Anasazi.

Mesa Verde National Park is well maintained and equipped with facilities to make your visit convenient and comfortable. There are five short designated hiking trails in the park. Due to the large number of visitors each year and the potential damage to the artifacts and the environment, straying off the trails is forbidden. A guidebook for disabled visitors can be found at the visitor center and museum.

The park is open year-round, but some of the sites are closed during the winter months. Weatherill Mesa is open during summer only between 8 am-4:30 pm. For more information contact **Mesa Verde National Park, CO 81330; (303) 529-4465 or (303) 529-4475.**

Archaeological Museum—

A visit to the Archaeological Museum will begin unraveling the fascinating history of the Anasazi Indians. Allow enough time to take in this museum before going to look at the major cliff dwellings. In addition to a bookstore, it contains many Anasazi exhibits and artifacts. The museum is open daily May–Sept. 8 am–6:30 pm. Hours the rest of the year are 8 am–5 pm. Free admission.

Lodging and Camping—

The park is close enough to Durango and Cortez to be a day trip, but consider an overnight stay. Waking in the early morning to the intense colors of the rock walls makes it well worth your time. There are two options for staying in the park.

The rooms at the comfortable **Far View Lodge** feature balcony views of the park and the far-off mountains. All of the rooms have recently been remodeled. The lodge also has a restaurant and a lounge. Advance reservations are highly recommended. Closed from mid-Oct.–mid-April. For reservations and information write **Far View Lodge, Mesa Verde, c/o PO Box 277, Mancos, CO 81328; (303) 529-4421.**

Located 4 miles from the park entrance, **Morefield Campground,** with its

490 sites (showers available; fee charged), offers the only camping in the park. No reservations are necessary, but camping is on a first-come, first-served basis. Nearby is a general store, a gas station, a gift shop, a snack bar and laundry and shower facilities.

Visitor's Center—

Fifteen miles from the park entrance a visitor center offers information, maps and modern southwestern Indian exhibits. Open May–Sept. only; 8 am–5 pm daily.

Other Anasazi Culture Sites

In addition to the spectacular cliff dwellings at Mesa Verde, several other places beckon you to visit for a more complete understanding of the Anasazi culture—without the frustration of crowds. Gaining a more complete picture of what this peaceful culture was all about takes patience and curiosity.

Anasazi Heritage Center—

This fine archaeological museum, which opened in the summer of 1988, provides an excellent background for understanding the ancient Anasazi culture. Ironically, the highly controversial McPhee Dam and reservoir project is the reason the Anasazi Heritage Center exists at all.

In 1977 the Dolores Archaeological Program got underway, discovering 1,600 Anasazi sites, only 125 of which were extensively excavated, sampled and tested. The museum houses more than two million artifacts from these digs, with some of the most outstanding pieces displayed for the public. The "discovery" section of the display room gives people a chance to learn about the Anasazi through hands-on experience: you can grind corn, examine grains with a microscope and watch a weaver using a loom. Traveling exhibits (some from the Smithsonian) change at least yearly. Be sure to see the eerie three-stage hologram depicting what these ancient people looked like. Open year-round, admission is free. Mon.–Sat. 9 am–5 pm,

Sun. 10 am–5 pm. Located just west of the town of Dolores. **27501 Hwy. 184, Dolores, CO 81323; (303) 882-4811.**

Take a minute to look at the **Dominguez** and **Escalante** ruins located a half-mile from the museum and named for the Franciscan friars who passed through the area in 1776. They were the first to document Anasazi ruins in Colorado.

Cortez Center—

The University of Colorado initiated this nonprofit center in 1987 to help preserve the Anasazi heritage of the Cortez area. The recently refurbished facility has a small museum displaying artifacts from Yellow Jacket and other nearby sites. In summer the museum hosts free evening sessions on a range of subjects, including archaeology, astronomy, art and Native American culture. The demonstration of Navajo sand painting is fascinating for its artistic quality and insight into Navajo beliefs. Adjacent to the center, the Bufort Wayt Cultural Park has Native American families-in-residence. Activities include craft demonstrations, native foods, storytelling and dancing. Open 10 am–9 pm Mon.–Sat. in summer; and 10 am–5 pm Mon.–Fri. during the rest of the year. Free admission. **25 N. Market St., PO Box 1326, Cortez, CO 81321; (303) 565-1151.**

Crow Canyon Archaeological Center—

People from all walks of life come together here for an intensive week of on-site digging, sweating and learning under the guidance of trained archaeologists. After some classroom training, participants lay out grids and remove dirt inch by inch with trowels, chisels, toothbrushes, buckets and brooms. Crow Canyon also offers a less intensive summer day program that includes examining artifacts, throwing a spear with an atlatl and taking a tour of the laboratory and a working site. Weaving, jewelry making and other classes are offered in the off season.

To preserve the ruins under the soil for future archaeological study, Crow Canyon currently uses a random grid system.

This enables them to learn as much as possible about many different sites without exposing them entirely to the elements. All full participants receive one week of lodging (shared quarters) and meals. For prices and more information, contact **Crow Canyon Archaeological Center, 23390 County Rd. K, Cortez, CO 81321; 1-800-422-8975 or (303) 565-8975.**

Hovenweep National Monument—

Established as a national monument in 1923, Hovenweep (a Ute word meaning "deserted valley") stands as one of the most impressive Anasazi ruins in the Four Corners area. Although the culture of the Hovenweep people was similar to that at Mesa Verde, the structures at Hovenweep are different—characterized by tall stone towers, some as high as 20 feet.

Looking out across the inhospitable landscape at Hovenweep, it's hard to imagine that prior to AD 1300 the inhabitants planted terraced fields in this dry, rocky landscape. Near the end of their habitation here, they moved from smaller scattered pueblos to larger settlements at the heads of canyons. It is thought they did this to protect their water sources and fend off invaders.

Facts About the Monument—Hovenweep National Monument straddles the Colorado–Utah border west of Cortez. There are six main sites—**Square Tower** and **Cajon** ruins in Utah, and **Holly, Hackberry Canyon, Cutthroat Castle** and **Goodman Point** ruins in Colorado. Square Tower Ruins is the best preserved of the six sites and the only one that can be reached by car. The others involve a hike. But if you enjoy desert canyon hiking, Hovenweep should not be missed. The square, oval and circular towers are especially spectacular at sunset, and this shadow-encrusted lighting makes for great photos.

A ranger station and a campground are set up near Square Tower Ruins on the Utah side of the border. The campground has no water; fee charged. The monument and the campground are open year-round.

If you are staying in the Cortez area, a scenic driving loop with stops at Hovenweep and Lowry Pueblo (see below) is highly recommended. From Cortez head southwest of town for 3 miles on Hwy. 666 and turn right on McElmo Canyon Rd. Drive up this beautiful slickrock canyon over the border into Utah, following the signs to Hovenweep. After 39 miles you arrive at the monument headquarters, where the ranger station, the campground and Square Tower Ruins are located. After spending all the time you want here, drive northeast 25 miles, back into Colorado. This road brings you near Lowry Pueblo and back to Hwy. 666, 20 miles northwest of Cortez. Along the way you have panoramic views of many Four Corners landmarks—Sleeping Ute Mountain, Mesa Verde Plateau and the La Sal Mountains in Utah. Be sure to inquire locally about road conditions because these rough dirt roads can be impassable after storms.

For more information about Hovenweep, contact the park superintendent at **Mesa Verde National Park, CO 81330; (303) 529-4465.**

Lowry Pueblo—

Lowry Pueblo, located northwest of Cortez, was built about AD 1000 and inhabited by 100 Indians. It is best known for its great kiva, one of the biggest yet discovered in the American Southwest. The ruins were first excavated in 1928, restored in 1965 and dedicated as a National Historic Landmark in 1967. To reach Lowry Pueblo from Cortez, drive northwest on Hwy. 666 for 20 miles to the town of Pleasant View. Turn left (west) and proceed 9 miles to the site.

Ute Mountain Tribal Park

A greater sense of discovery accompanies you while walking down a dusty trail with your Ute escort in this isolated setting just south of Mesa Verde National Park. Undeveloped and relatively undisturbed, the extraordinary Anasazi cliff houses, kivas and storerooms seem to gain a spirit and importance of their own.

The Ute Mountain Tribal Park was set up by the tribe to preserve the culture of the Anasazi. Stretching over 125,000 acres along a 25-mile stretch of the Mancos River, a strong emphasis is placed on experiencing Anasazi ruins within a natural setting. No developed amenities exist in the backcountry. You must therefore come prepared and have the stamina to handle at least a few hours of backcountry hiking. One- to four-day guided backpacking trips are also available. The fee for this unforgettable experience is nominal. For more information about the Ute Mountain Tribal Park, contact **Ernest House** at the **Ute Mountain Tribal Park, Towaoc, CO 81334; (303) 565-3751** or **1-800-847-5485.**

Overnight Camping—

Primitive campsites are available in the park, down by the banks of the Mancos River. One thing is certain: if you are allowed to camp overnight in the park, you'll need a permit. Check with the tribe for details.

Tour Information—

Because the Anasazi ruins cannot be reached by road, good weather is essential for an enjoyable hike. Tours are usually available by June 1 and continue into autumn on a limited basis, depending on the weather. The tribe asks that visitors to the park make reservations at least three days in advance. All tours are led by an Indian guide and start at the Ute Mountain Tribal Headquarters, 20 miles south of Cortez at the intersection of Hwy. 160 and Hwy. 666. A full-day tour begins each morning at approximately 8 am. Be sure to call and reconfirm your tour and what time it begins! You need to bring your own lunch, water and car.

EVENTS

Indian Dancing
summer

During June, July and Aug., Indian dancers perform every evening at 7 pm at the Cortez City Park; no fee charged. For more information call the **Cortez Visitors Center** at **(303) 565-3414.**

OUTDOOR ACTIVITIES

BIKING
MOUNTAIN BIKING

The plateau and canyon country surrounding Cortez is perfect for mountain bikers. Less known than its neighbors at Moab, Utah, and Grand Junction, Colorado, this area is just beginning to be discovered. Stop by and talk to Randy Adair at **Southwest Bicycles** for trail ideas, rentals and repair. **450 E. Main St., Cortez; (303) 565-3717.** The **Colorado Welcome Center** in Cortez also has information and maps on rides in the vicinity. **928 E. Main, Cortez; (303) 565-3414.**

Cannonball Mesa—

This fairly easy 10-mile circle tour combines great scenery with the opportunity to explore Anasazi ruins. It's marked by bicycle emblem signs the entire way. To get to the trailhead, drive 3 miles south of Cortez on **Hwy. 666** to the intersection of **McElmo Canyon Rd.** (at the M&M Cafe). Turn right and travel precisely 20.4 miles west to an unmarked county road that heads off from your right. Park immediately at the cattleguard at a sign reading "Keep Vehicle on the Road," and begin your ride. After riding 1.5 miles north, take a left fork onto a road that switchbacks up Cannonball Mesa. After 2 miles on top of the flat top, take the right fork which eventually ends at Cannonball Mesa Ruin and offers excellent views over McElmo Canyon.

Ute Mountain Tribal Park—

Mountain bike tours may be arranged by contacting the **Ute Mountain Tribal Park, Towaoc, CO 81334; (303) 565-3751** or **1-800-847-5485**. See the Major Attractions section for more information.

FISHING

For fly fishing information as well as tackle, supplies and bait, visit **The Outfitter Sporting Goods** in Dolores. **410 Railroad Ave.; (303) 882-7740.**

Disappointment Creek—

Need we say more?

Dolores River—

Even though the Dolores experienced a setback due to a recent three-year drought, it's still a good-producing area for rainbow, cutthroat and brown trout (not too many lunkers, though). Of course, the catch and release designation for the 12-mile stretch downstream from the dam to Bradfield Bridge is meant to keep it that way. Whatever your opinion of McPhee Reservoir, which controls the level of the Dolores River, fish seem to thrive in the nutrient-rich tailwaters from the dam. And, because of the controlled water flow, the river no longer totally dries up in late summer. From Cortez head north on Hwy. 666 for 21 miles to just beyond Pleasant View, then turn right (east) onto County Rd. DD. Drive 1 mile to County Rd. 16, then 3 miles north to an access road for Bradfield Bridge. Once there take Lone Dome Rd. (County Rd. 504), which follows along the Dolores River for 12 miles southeast to the dam. A couple of campgrounds have opened up in the Lone Dome area.

Groundhog Reservoir—

Some fishermen seem to have forgotten about 670-acre Groundhog Reservoir, but the fishing can be excellent for 12- to 14-inch trout—especially from a boat. The reservoir has an assortment of brown, brook, rainbow and cutthroat trout. Cabins and boats available for rent; a convenience store near the lake also sells tackle. To reach the lake from Dolores, take 11th St. (which turns into Forest Rd. 526) north for 27 miles until the road splits. Take the right fork and continue 5 miles on Forest Rd. 533 to the reservoir.

McPhee Reservoir—

Filled completely for the first time in 1987, McPhee Reservoir is now one of the largest bodies of water in the state. The sloping, timbered shoreline creates an interesting vista and the fishing can be superb. However, it can also be a bit inconsistent due to severe water level fluctuations. The Colorado Division of Wildlife has been very active in stocking this reservoir with hundreds of thousands of 3- to 5-inch McConaughy-strain rainbows. While this is the main thrust of the stocking program, large- and smallmouth bass, bluegills and crappies can be found in abundance. This could become one of the best lakes in the state for catching kokanee salmon. At McPhee fishing is better from a boat. At the upper end of the lake are two boat ramps. See the Camping section for more information about staying overnight near the lake. To reach McPhee Reservoir from Cortez drive 8 miles north on Hwy. 145, then 4 miles northeast on Hwy. 184. There is a marked access road from there.

West Fork of the Dolores River—

Angling for small rainbow, brown and cutthroat trout is normally quite good on the West Fork. Some 8 miles of the river are posted against fishing, but there is still plenty of public water. The small stream is paralleled for 30 miles by a well-maintained gravel road in an exceptionally beautiful, thickly wooded area in the San Juans. The drive is incredible in late Sept. when the scrub oak and aspen change colors. To reach the West Fork of the Dolores River from the town of Dolores drive 15 miles northeast on Hwy. 145 to a marked turnoff for Dunton Rd. (Forest Rd. 535). The road follows the stream for 30 miles, ending up back on Hwy. 145 north of the town of Rico.

GOLF

Conquistador Golf Course—

This 18-hole public course offers great views of the surrounding peaks and mesas in the Cortez area. Green fees are reasonable. The course is open from mid-Mar. to mid-Nov. Located in northeast Cortez just off Hwy 145. **2018 N. Dolores Rd., Cortez, CO 81321; (303) 565-9208.**

HIKING AND BACKPACKING

Hiking near Anasazi sites in the canyons and along the mesas in the Cortez area is hard to beat. Hiking trails at Mesa Verde, Hovenweep and the Ute Mountain Tribal Park take you through juniper and pinon pine and over slickrock to Anasazi ruins. See the Major Attractions section for more information.

From Hwy. 145, east of Dolores, excellent and seldom used high country lies waiting to be explored. Fourteen-thousand-foot peaks, fields of wildflowers, abandoned mine buildings and abundant wildlife characterize the alpine country of the San Juan and Uncompahgre national forests accessible from the Upper Dolores River area. For more information, contact the helpful folks at the **Dolores Ranger District Office, PO Box 210, 100 N. 6th St., Dolores, CO 81323; (303) 882-7296.** Other great hiking areas lie east of Cortez, closer to Mancos. For information on this area, contact the **Mancos Ranger District** at **PO Box 330, 41595 E. Hwy. 160, Mancos, CO 81328; (303) 533-7716.**

Calico/Fall Creek/Winter Trail Loop—

This 14-mile loop begins at the new Calico trailhead, above the small town of Dunton. Calico Trail climbs southwest, following a ridge between the Dolores River and the West Fork of the Dolores. Along the route you have spectacular 360-degree views of the surrounding mountains. The trail begins in a vast mountain meadow and rises through Engelmann spruce and

subalpine fir before reaching treeline and, eventually, the summit of 11,866-foot Papoose Peak. The trail then drops down to the intersection with Fall Creek Trail, 6 miles from the trailhead. Turn right and follow Fall Creek Trail for 4 miles to Dunton at 8,800 feet. From Dunton turn northeast (right) onto Winter Trail to complete the loop. Winter Trail is an old wagon road used to move supplies between Rico and Dunton in the early 1900s. Mail was delivered over this road in winter by skiing mailmen. The 4-mile trail climbs sharply the first mile and then levels off for the remainder.

To reach the trailhead from Dolores drive east on Hwy. 145 for 12.5 miles and turn left onto West Fork Rd. (Forest Rd. 535). Drive about 25 miles to an area called the Meadows above Dunton, then turn right onto Forest Rd. 471. Drive to the trailhead.

Geyser Spring Trail—

This easy 1.25-mile trail ends up at a small pool of water fed by the only true geyser in the state of Colorado. The frequency of eruptions varies, but one usually occurs about every half hour. It's not exactly Old Faithful, but the geyser bubbles for about 15 minutes, emitting a strong-smelling sulfur gas. The trail begins 2.2 miles south of Dunton. From Dolores drive east on Hwy. 145 for 12.5 miles and turn left onto Forest Rd. 535. Follow this road for 23.3 miles (a half mile beyond Paradise Hot Spring, which is closed to the public) and look for the trailhead on the right. The gradual hike up to the geyser takes you through aspen forests and small meadows.

Mesa Verde Trails—

Five short designated hiking trails can be found in the park. For more information on Mesa Verde see the Major Attractions section.

Navajo Trail—

Navajo Trail, which begins about 2 miles north of Dunton on Forest Rd. 535, takes you into the heart of the Lizard Head

Wilderness. From the trailhead, follow the trail 5 miles up steep switchbacks through open meadows and forests to Navajo Lake in Navajo Basin. This is the source of the headwaters of the West Fork of the Dolores River. Navajo Basin is also a good place to be if you like to climb 14ers—El Diente, Mt. Wilson and Wilson Peak are all within striking distance. This is the most heavily used area in the West Dolores area—so if you don't want to run into other hikers, try another area.

Ute Mountain Tribal Park Trails—

A Ute Indian guide must accompany you on any hikes into the park. For more information on the Anasazi ruins see the Major Attractions section.

RIVER FLOATING

Dolores River—

One of the most beautiful rivers in the west, the Dolores is especially suited for an overnight trip. With its sandstone canyons and Anasazi artifacts, it features more of a desert Southwest feeling than do most of the other major rivers in Colorado. Plan an early trip (mid- to late Apr. through June), because the Dolores peaks sooner than almost any other river in the state. The actual river running season is only three to four weeks each year. Some recent lean water years suggest that you should be sure to check on current flow conditions.

The Upper Dolores, a 37-mile stretch from Rico down to the town of Dolores, drops an average of 50 feet per mile through shady pine forests and ranch property. Kayaks are the best bet for this section.

Aside from the already apparent reduction of water flow on the desert canyon section of the Dolores, other long-term effects of the McPhee Reservoir remain to be seen. Running this 171-mile section of the river can be done in one week, but a lot of people choose leisurely weekend snippets. Highlights of this section include Ponderosa Gorge, Dolores Canyon (offering wild rapids including the famous Snaggletooth, which many prudent rafters choose to portage), Little Glen Canyon, Slick Rock Canyon, Paradox Canyon, Mesa Canyon and Gateway Canyon. For up-to-date flow information or other questions about the river, call the **Bedrock Store, Bedrock, CO 81411; (303) 859-7395.**

Dvorak's Kayak & Rafting Expeditions— One of the state's most respected outfitters, offering extended day trips down the Dolores. **1-800-824-3795.**

SKIING
CROSS-COUNTRY SKIING

Many wonderful ski-touring options are available in this extreme southwest corner of the state. In the transition zone between alpine and desert, many suitable trails exist. The **Colorado Welcome Center** in Cortez will be glad to provide you with more information. **928 E. Main; (303) 565-3414.** For more trail ideas, contact the **Dolores Ranger District Office, PO Box 210, 100 N. 6th St., Dolores, CO 81323; (303) 882-7296.**

Groomed Trails—

Mancos–Chicken Creek Area—Head out on 32 miles of groomed track in this gorgeous location east of Cortez. The main trail plugs along for 20 miles, offering several loops and a spur trail for varied abilities. It's all free! From Cortez drive 17 miles east on Hwy. 160 to Mancos. Turn north on Hwy. 184 and continue to Chicken Creek Rd. (County Rd. 141), which leads 3 miles to the parking area and trailhead.

Backcountry Trails—

Dunton—Too bad the hot springs at Dunton continue to be closed to the public, because a hot soak would be just the thing after a day of cross-country skiing. Nonetheless, Dunton still offers excellent intermediate touring with wide-open views.

Just above Dunton the road is not plowed. A mile after setting out on skis, you'll reach the fork of Forest Rds. 611 (left) and 535 (right). The left fork leads up through aspen and eventually a meadow, coming out at Groundhog Stock Driveway, 2 miles from the fork. This is a good area for telemarking. The right fork (Forest Rd. 535) leads up past Burro Bridge Campground, over Burro Bridge and past the Navajo Lake trailhead. After about 5 miles, the trail leads into high meadows with good views of Mt. Wilson, Wilson Peak and El Diente Peak to the northeast. This route is not for beginners.

The trailhead is located 12.5 miles east of Dolores on Hwy. 145 and then 20 miles up West Fork Rd. (Forest Rd. 535). Take note, the West Fork Rd. into Dunton can be very slippery—four-wheel-drive vehicles are suggested. Check road conditions before the trip.

Lizard Head Pass—A bit farther up Hwy. 145 from Dolores (47 miles) is 10,250-foot Lizard Head Pass, which attracts heavy snows. With open meadows and great views of surrounding peaks (especially Lizard Head Peak to the north), this is an especially popular area with nordic skiers. From the summit of the pass there are a number of directions in which to ski. Try the south side of the highway and ski southwest for 2 miles down fairly easy slopes, in and out of trees. On the north side of the highway, many advanced skiers head north toward Lizard Head Peak and the Lizard Head Wilderness Area for some great tree skiing. Trails can be difficult to follow in winter, so topographical maps and a compass are recommended. Be sure to stay clear of avalanche-prone areas.

Mesa Verde National Park—Inside the park the eastern loop of Ruins Rd. is not plowed in winter. Although it's usually only skiable for a few days after a snowfall, it can be one of the most memorable ski tours you'll ever take. Like the men who first discovered Mesa Verde during a snowstorm in 1888, you'll be awed by the haunting dwellings at Cliff Palace and other sites along the way. The east loop is an easy, 6-mile ski trail. Be sure to check on snow conditions at the park before driving up there. If they give you the thumbs up, drive 10 miles east from Cortez on Hwy. 160 to the park entrance and turn right (south). Drive 20 miles to the intersection of Ruins Rd. Please park well off the road. For more information about skiing, contact the park superintendent at **Mesa Verde National Park, CO 81330; (303) 529-4465** or **(303) 529-4475.**

SWIMMING

There is a 50-meter municipal swimming pool open to the public in **City Park.** Small fee. Open Memorial Day–Labor Day. Located in Cortez, next to the visitors center. **830 E. Montezuma Ave; (303) 565-7877.**

TENNIS

Four lighted courts are open to the public in **City Park;** no fee. Located in Cortez, next to the visitors center.

—————— SEEING AND DOING ——————

GAMBLING

Ute Mountain Casino—

This newly opened attraction lies just 11 miles south of Cortez on Hwy. 160/666. The large, ground-floor gambling complex houses 300 slots as well as video poker; for small stakes you can also try the live blackjack and poker games. Up to 500 frothing bingo players sometimes pack a special back room to vie for prizes as large as $10,000. With no alcohol served (free pop and coffee) and no drunken brawls, this casino takes on a much more wholesome atmosphere than most. A restaurant, called **Kuchu's,** serves food 20 hours a day. The casino itself seems to fly in the face of important beliefs of the Ute Indians. But with extremely high unemployment and few available jobs in the Tribal Park, it seems to be serving a useful purpose. Open 8 am–4 pm daily. For more information call **(303) 565-8800** or **1-800-258-8007.**

MUSEUMS AND GALLERIES

Anasazi Museums—

See the Major Attractions section.

Galleries and Shops—

A proliferation of Indian pottery shops and the like has sprouted on the main streets of Cortez. Some of them offer carefully worked Indian crafts, while others have cheap (but often pretty) imitations. A gallery of note is the **Ute Mountain Pottery Plant,** located on the Ute Mountain Indian Reservation 15 miles south of Cortez on **Hwy. 160 S.; (303) 565-8548.**

SCENIC DRIVES

Cortez/Hovenweep Loop—

See Hovenweep in the Major Attractions section.

San Juan Skyway—

See the Scenic Drives section of the Durango chapter for information about this remarkable 236-mile route.

STAGE COACH

Mesa Verde Stage Line—

Will Stone operates a stage coach line in Mancos with dinner rides, half-day to three-day adventures and custom trips. He also builds and restores wagons for a living. Families and groups (eight person minimum) should consider climbing into a Conestoga wagon and heading into colorful Weber Canyon. All wagons are pulled by mules; "More miles per bale," says Stone. Even if you don't sign up for a trip, stop by and take a look at his wagons lined up on Main St. For more information and reservations contact **PO Box 346, Mancos, CO 81328; (303) 533-7264**

WHERE TO STAY

ACCOMMODATIONS

For the most part, lodging opportunities in Cortez are predictable, but in the outlying country, you'll find many opportunities for more unique accommodations. The main street through Cortez is lined with motels ranging from mid to low end. Major motel chains are present as well as many independent motels, including several with Indian themes such as the Arrow Motel and Tomahawk Lodge. During the summer it's highly recommended to make reservations in advance because lodging gets surprisingly tight. In winter look for special "ski Telluride" packages. For information and help securing motel reservations, contact the **Cortez Visitors Center, 928 E. Main St., PO Box 968, Cortez, CO 81321; (303) 565-3414.**

Blue Lake Ranch—$$$ to $$$$

Located near Hesperus, this plush B&B is worth a little driving time. See the **Durango** chapter for details.

Lost Canyon Lake Ranch—$$$

The wrap-around porch with its peaceful view over Lost Lake is reason enough to spend a night or two at this secluded hideaway just southeast of Dolores. Owner Beth Newman (who also doubles as an intensive care nurse) and her physician husband ensure you are well looked after—this could be the safest place in the state to choke on your food. Five good-sized guest rooms (with private bathrooms) each with unique decor, range from white wicker to contemporary southwest. A large common room has an open, airy feel thanks to a wall of windows; a huge moss rock mantle dominates one side. One caution to those with allergies: lots of cats and dogs roam the property, thanks to Beth's weakness for animals. It is extremely clean, though, and well tended. Breakfast is simple and substantial with a hot entree each day. Smoking outside only; well behaved kids (and pets) OK. Call ahead for reservations and directions. **PO Box 1289, Dolores, CO 81323; (303) 882-4913.**

Holiday Inn Express—$$ to $$$

This hotel could be the place for the most comfortable night's sleep in Cortez. Though fairly standard, the rooms are new, spacious and clean. In addition to the expected amenities, the Holiday Inn Express also features an indoor pool, hot tub, sauna and 24-hour front desk service. Continental breakfast provided. **2121 E. Main, Cortez, CO 81321; 1-800-626-5652 or (303) 565-6000.**

Kelly Place—$$

Located on 100 acres in beautiful McElmo Canyon about 15 miles west of Cortez, Kelly Place not only offers unique, affordable lodging, but also involves visitors in the archaeology and early history of the area. Operated primarily for group visits, Kelly Place also opens its doors to occasional overnight guests. Smack dab in the middle of Anasazi country, the Kelly property offers a hands-on approach, helping guests acquire an appreciation for Anasazi prehistory. Five simple rooms each sleep up to six people and have their own bathroom. Groups of up to 24 people can be accommodated. Kelly Place accepts reservations only. **14663 County Rd. G, Cortez, CO 81321; (303) 565-3125.**

Jersey Jim Lookout Tower—$

For solitude, space and a four-state, 360-degree view, make early reservations at Jersey Jim, a former fire lookout tower near Mancos. The sun setting behind prominent Sleeping Ute Mountain absolutely can't be beat. But Jersey Jim isn't for those who balk at a bathroom down the hall—here you'll encounter an outhouse down a 55 foot ladder! The crude but functional pulley system helps you bring up your essentials: food, water and bedding. Once inside the 15-square-foot room (windows all around) limited luxuries include a propane-powered heater, lamp and refrigerator; a twin bed, chairs and a few other sticks of furniture round out the furnishings. The space is comfortable for couples though an occasional family of four rents the tower. Open June 1-late Sept. For information and reservations contact the **Jersey Jim Foundation** at **PO Box 1032, Mancos, CO 81328; (303) 533-7255.**

CAMPING

Near Dolores—

McPhee Reservoir—McPhee Recreation Complex has 73 sites and a fee. From Dolores head west on Hwy. 145 for 5 miles and turn right at the reservoir entrance. Drive 1 mile to the campground. **House Creek Campground,** with 58 sites and a fee, can be reached by driving about 1 mile east from Dolores on Hwy. 145 and turning left onto Forest Rd. 526. Drive 6 miles and turn left onto Forest Rd. 528 and proceed 5 miles to the campground. To reserve a campsite near McPhee Reservoir call **1-800-283-CAMP.**

Lone Dome—Three new campgrounds have opened up along the Dolores River below McPhee Reservoir. For the protection of wildlife the road is closed Dec. 1–Mar. 31. From Cortez head north on Hwy. 666 for 21 miles to just beyond Pleasant View, then turn right (east) onto County Rd. DD. Drive 1 mile to County Rd. 16, then 3 miles north to an access road for Bradfield Bridge. **Bradfield Ranch Campground** (18 sites; fee charged) is located a half mile below the bridge. Four miles up the Dolores from Bradfield Bridge is **Cabin Canyon Campground** (11 riverside sites; fee charged); another 5 miles upriver brings you to **Ferris Canyon Campground** (6 sites; fee charged). This access road follows up along the Dolores (southeast) for a total of 12 miles from Bradfield Bridge to the dam.

Anasazi Areas—

Mesa Verde—See the Major Attractions section.

Ute Mountain Tribal Park—See Ute Mountain Tribal Park in the Major Attractions section.

In San Juan National Forest—

There are a number of campgrounds east of Dolores. **Mavreeso Campground** (14 sites), **West Dolores Campground** (13 sites) and **Burro Bridge Campground** (15 sites) are located up the beautiful West Fork Rd. (Forest Rd. 535) along the West Fork of the Dolores River. Each campground has a fee.

To get there, head east from Dolores on Hwy. 145 for 12.5 miles and turn left onto Forest Rd. 535. **Mavreeso, West Dolores** and **Burro Bridge** campgrounds are 5, 7 and 24 miles up the road.

From the junction of Hwy. 145 and Forest Rd. 535 (12.5 miles east of Dolores) head east on Hwy. 145 for 41 miles to **Cayton Campground** up near Lizard Head Pass. It has 27 sites and a fee.

Heading east on Hwy. 160 from Cortez, there are a few campgrounds. **Transfer Campground** is located 9 miles north of Mancos on Forest Rd. 561. It has 13 sites and a fee. It's less than a mile walk from here to the West Mancos River. **Target Tree Campground** is located along Hwy. 160, 7 miles east of Mancos. There are 51 sites and a fee. About 16 miles east of Mancos off Hwy. 160 take Forest Rd. 571 to **Kroeger Campground** (10 sites, fee charged) near the La Plata River.

Mancos Lake State Park—

This relatively new park with superb views of the La Plata Mountains offers 26 campsites (fee charged). Take Hwy. 184 just northeast of Mancos and then follow the signs for 5 miles to the park. By the way you'll find free camping right in Mancos at Boyle Park.

Private Campgrounds—

Cortez KOA Campground—Plenty of RV hookups, laundry facilities, showers, etc. Located just east of Cortez on Hwy. 160. **PO Box 1257, 27432 Hwy. 160, Cortez, CO 81321; (303) 565-9301.**

Dolores River RV Park—Situated along the Dolores River, 2.5 miles east of Dolores on Hwy. 145, this place has hookups, tent sites and everything else you could possibly need. **18680 Hwy. 145, Dolores, CO 81323; (303) 882-7761.**

Priest Gulch Ranchcamp—Located 35 miles northeast of Cortez on Hwy. 145. Full hookups and tent sites. Laundry, store, playground, etc. **26750 Hwy. 145, Dolores, CO 81323; (303) 562-3810.**

WHERE TO EAT

Nero's Italian Restaurant — $$ to $$$

It's tough to believe Cortez is home to one of the better Italian restaurants around, but Nero's linguini with clam sauce makes a convincing argument. Nero's also features seafood, chicken and many other pasta dishes. The whole experience is made better by the wonderful aromas, soft music, paintings and candlelight though the small restaurant is slightly cramped for interior space (shall we say cozy). Now that Nero's has added a deck, you can enjoy summer evenings outside. They offer a choice selection of Italian wines. Open from 4:30 pm nightly in summer; closed Sun. the rest of the year. Reservations accepted. **303 W. Main; (303) 565-7366.**

Old Germany Restaurant in Dolores—$$ to $$$

Many people in the surrounding communities make their way to Dolores for Jim Blound's authentic German cooking. He's not German but his wife, Rita, from northern Bavaria, makes sure the food stays on track. Inside the simple, homey restaurant, you can start the meal with a different sort of beer: light or dark Pauliner on tap, or perhaps a glass of wheat beer with a lemon wedge. The dinner specialties include sauerbraten and paprika schnitzel that taste straight out of Bavaria. For what you get, this restaurant is very reasonably priced. Open 4–9 pm Tues.–Sun. Located at the east end of Dolores on Hwy. 145; **(303) 882-7549.**

Line Camp in Dolores—$$

Considering all you get for your dining dollar, Line Camp is an excellent choice for the entire family. Get here early and pitch some horseshoes, play volleyball, fish in the Dolores River (license required) or look around the small museum. Dinner is served promptly at 7:30 pm inside a large pavilion with open-air walls. After a tasty homemade supper that includes cake and coffee or lemonade, the entertainment begins. A one-hour western show with live music and comedy from "The Trailhands," brings the entire audience along for a good time. Open Memorial Day to Labor Day; reservations required; no credit cards. Located 9 miles northeast of Dolores on Hwy. 145. **(303) 882-4158.**

Francisca's—$ to $$

Excellent Mexican food is served at reasonable prices at Francisca's. Try the stacked enchiladas, stuffed sopapilla, chile rellenos or a chimichanga. For those not hungry for Mexican food there are a few burgers and steaks. When we asked the owner, Pedro, if we could take a menu for reference, he immediately thought we were spies from another restaurant—his food probably is the best! Thanks to a couple of large white gazebos and many hanging plants, the restaurant always feels like an outdoor patio in summer. Open 11 am–10 pm Mon.–Sat. **125 E. Main St.; (303) 565-4093.**

M&M Truckstop and Restaurant—$

With rows of Phillips 66 gas pumps out front, this full-service restaurant is a great place for sandwiches, burgers, steaks and tacos. But their best meal of the day is undoubtedly breakfast (served 24 hours a day). The coffee keeps coming just as soon as you find a seat, pancakes are piled five high and the service is fast and friendly. In this part of the state, refried beans are an option with your eggs. When we asked people in town where they go for breakfast, there was a unanimous reply, "M&M's." Open 24 hours a day, seven days a week. **7006 Hwy. 160; (303) 565-6511.**

SERVICES

Cortez Welcome Center—

This should be your first stop when coming into Cortez. Helpful volunteers have information about the immediate area as well as all points in Colorado. **PO Box 968, 928 E. Main St., Cortez, CO 81321; 1-800-346-6525** outside of Colorado, **(303) 565-3414** in Colorado.

Dolores Visitors Center—

Stop by and check out the Galloping Goose Museum and speak with someone about the area inside the replica of the Dolores Railroad Depot, originally built in 1900. It's located in the town center at Hwy. 145 and 5th St. If you need information by mail, contact the **Dolores Chamber of Commerce** at **PO Box 602, Dolores, CO 81323; (303) 882-4018.**

Mesa Verde–Cortez Visitor Information Bureau—

PO Drawer HH, Cortez, CO 81321; 1-800-253-1616.

Ute Mountain Tribal Park Visitor Center—

All trips into the park depart from here. Small museum on the premises. Located 22 miles south of Cortez on Hwy. 666 at the junction with Hwy. 160.

Durango

Tucked between reddish sandstone bluffs, Durango occupies a spectacular position in the wide Animas River Valley close to the sharply uplifted peaks of the San Juans. It's southwest Colorado's largest town, with a steadily growing population of more than 12,500. Durango could be the perfect place to base a trip to the Four Corners area due to its location, history and charm.

An aura of 19th-century prosperity is embedded in this town, which once had visions of surpassing Denver as the wealthiest city in the state. Durango has managed to preserve many of its important historic landmarks; the town encompasses two National Historic Districts as well as the famous Durango & Silverton Narrow Gauge Railroad (D&SNG). When you're visiting here, a journey upriver to Silverton on the restored train is practically required. Another "must see" is Mesa Verde National Park, just 37 miles away (see the **Cortez** chapter for details).

El Rio de las Animas Perdidas, "the River of Lost Souls," flows right through the middle of town, adding another welcome element, especially to rafters, kayakers and fishermen. The river is bordered by more than two million acres of the awesome beauty of the San Juan National Forest. Vallecito Lake, with 22 miles of wooded and secluded shoreline, serves as a popular water sports playground (see the Fishing section).

Without question Durango is one of the world's top mountain biking centers, home to hundreds of miles of backcountry trails and a fanatic local population. Local riders took home four gold medals and one silver at the 1990 World Mountain Bike Championships. For backpackers and hikers who want to avoid running into bikes on the trail, consider a trip into the Weminuche Wilderness Area, where bikes are strictly forbidden. Summer highlights absolutely include golfing, hiking, fishing or taking a drive along the San Juan Skyway.

When it comes to year-round recreation, the changing seasons prove this to be a region of infinite variety. In late September brilliant stands of Aspen contrast with the reddish soil and barren, snow-dusted summits. Soon the snow begins to pile up, making winter a time for heading to Purgatory-Durango Ski Resort—thirty minutes to the north. This low-key resort offers a true Colorado experience for those who are in search of a great ski mountain. Few destinations feature better cross-country skiing than the abundant National Forest lands in the Durango vicinity.

If all this sounds too good to be true, you can be sure that during the peak summer season you may encounter a scramble for rooms and rather congested traffic in the center of town. The crush of visitors can be a little distracting, but it also ensures lodging, dining and high-caliber shopping—

in the form of 22 factory outlet stores as well as local shops and galleries. And because Durango is surrounded by mountains, it's never a problem to find solitude. Underneath it all Durango is a stable town, with a good mix of residents who certainly benefit from tourism but don't live solely for it.

HISTORY

In 1868 the United States government granted Chief Ouray and the Ute Indians a tract of southwestern Colorado that encompassed nearly a quarter of the territory. Almost as soon as this huge tract of land was assigned, rich gold and silver strikes in the San Juan Mountains drew a legion of miners into the area. Terms of the 1868 treaty should have provided governmental protection to the Utes against the intruding prospectors. The mood of the day, however, ensured only the miners' "destiny" and, by 1873, Ouray had relinquished 6,000 square miles of mineral-rich land.

The Meeker Massacre of 1879 in northwestern Colorado (see the Meeker chapter) provided the excuse to remove the Southern Ute Indians to a reservation in southern Colorado and New Mexico. This removal coincided conveniently with the early growth of a railroad center named Durango.

A great need for efficient transport of the tons of ore generated by the mines prompted the Denver & Rio Grande Railroad to extend its tracks from the eastern plains to the Animas River Valley. The logical location for a new railroad center was the small farming community of Animas City (2 miles north of present-day Durango). But the town declined the railroad's offer, refusing to have its solitude destroyed. By snubbing the railroad, Animas City sealed its destiny as one more western ghost town. A group of investors formed the Durango Trust to provide money for a new townsite and railroad center. In 1880 Durango sprang into being, with the railroad providing the basis for prolonged future growth.

By 1881 the mining boom was in full swing in the nearby mountains, and so were the related problems of public drunkenness, prostitution and gambling. Not far from Durango's thriving saloons and brothels were the spires of one lonely church. For one year during this period of reckless growth, Durango was home to a streetcar line, which was discontinued because "... the crews were abusive and insulting to patrons." Most of the growing pains, however, subsided as Durango came into its own. The largest industry of the decade was the smoke-belching smelter that refined the rich ore transported from the nearby mines.

When mine production began to wane in the early 1900s, Durango fell on hard times. Over the years, though, large numbers of cottage industries and small retail shops have flourished as the scope of the local economy has shifted to a diverse base of tourism and education. The latter came in 1956 with the founding of Ft. Lewis College atop a high mesa near town. The college has had no trouble attracting students to its prime location at the base of the San Juans.

GETTING THERE

To reach Durango from Denver, take Hwy. 285 southwest to Monte Vista and then head west on Hwy. 160. It's a very scenic 332-mile drive. The other route requires going south on Interstate 25 to Walsenburg and then west to Durango via Hwy. 160.

Several airlines offer daily service to Durango from various parts of the country, with the majority of flights connecting in Denver. Air access has closed the time gap between Denver and Durango, making short trips possible from the Front Range without the long drive.

———————— MAJOR ATTRACTIONS ————————

Mesa Verde National Park and Other Anasazi Culture Sites

Mesa Verde National Park, site of the world's largest Anasazi cliff dwellings, lies within an hour's drive of west Durango via Hwy. 160—whatever your itinerary, don't miss it. Check the Major Attractions section in the **Cortez** chapter for detailed information on this and other Anasazi culture sites.

Durango & Silverton Narrow-Gauge Railroad

During the summer season in Durango (early May to late Oct.) the tranquillity of town is broken by the lonesome blast of a locomotive whistle. You can't miss it—this marvelous sound becomes part of your psyche during any stay. For almost as long as Durango has existed, the smoke-belching locomotive and bright yellow passenger cars have been making a 45-mile trip north to the well-preserved mining town of **Silverton** (see the **Silverton** chapter).

Each year more than 210,000 passengers pile on board the daily trains to enjoy a trip that hugs hair-raising cliffs while crossing and recrossing the raging Animas River. To experience the unique beauty and history of the San Juans, nothing beats a trip along these tracks.

History—

In the fall of 1881 the Denver & Rio Grande Railroad (D&RG) broke ground for a stretch of track linking the remote mining boom town of Silverton to the eastern plains. The route was completed the following summer and was used for shuttling passengers and supplies. More important, it transported an estimated $300 million in gold and silver out of this rich mining town. In 1921 the D&RG emerged from receivership as the Denver & Rio Grand Western (D&RGW). In the late 1960s, the tracks between Antonito and Durango were abandoned, cutting off Durango and Silverton from the rest of the present-day D&RGW rail system.

The railroad between Durango and Silverton was purchased by a Florida orange grower who changed the name to the

Durango & Silverton Narrow Gauge Railroad Co. (D&SNG). Stressing authenticity, he poured money into refurbishing the train, including open and closed coach cars and the old Alamosa parlor car. The Alamosa, built in 1880, is a first-class, 28-passenger car equipped with an ash wood bar serving the only liquor on the train.

Everyone had a scare in the winter of 1989 when fire consumed the D&SNG roundhouse with all operable locomotives inside. Heroic efforts of the firemen somehow saved the engines from all but minor damage. The roundhouse has since been completely rebuilt.

Further Information—

A round trip on the D&SNG takes eight hours (three hours getting to Silverton, two hours in town and three hours back to Durango). For handicapped visitors, one train each day is equipped with lifts (advance reservations necessary). Many passengers, young and old alike, who have ridden the full-day round trip suffer from track burnout. Although most people do make the round-trip journey in one day, and fully appreciate the trip, we should note some options. You can stay a night or two in Silverton before returning to Durango. Bus transportation is also available between the two towns, making it possible to take the train one way and to return via Hwy. 550 over scenic Molas Pass. Daily 45-minute yard tours are a perfect option for those who cannot spend an entire day on the train.

Reservations—

Reservations for a trip on the D&SNG are strongly recommended. Advance purchases must be made 30 days prior to the date of the train's departure, but you may be able to buy tickets just by showing up (the more time in advance, the better). When the train sells out, sign up on the waiting list; we're told some people are able to get on board at the last minute. No credit cards; personal checks accepted only with a check guarantee card. Although groups can be accommodated, there are no group rates. For additional information contact **Durango & Silverton Narrow Gauge Railroad Co., 479 Main Ave., Durango, CO 81301; (303) 247-2733.**

RailCamp—

Billed as a "wilderness recreational vehicle," RailCamp functions as an RV on train tracks to bring small groups into Cascade Canyon near the remote Weminuche Wilderness Area of San Juan National Forest. It is offered for people who wish to camp out (and perhaps do some fishing) far away from civilization, while still enjoying the creature comforts of home. RailCamp is a beautifully refurbished box car equipped with sliding glass doors, four bunk beds, a bath, running water, a kitchen with a propane stove, refrigerator, utensils and cooking necessities. What, no cable TV?! RailCamp rents by the week (Mon.–Fri.) from late May through late Sept. Reservations are required. For further information contact **Durango & Silverton Narrow Gauge Railroad Co., 479 Main Ave., Durango, CO 81301; (303) 247-2733.**

Wilderness Access—

The D&SNG train makes daily stops to trailheads leading into the Weminuche Wilderness Area at Needleton and Elk Park. Backpackers may get on and off the train at these points. For more information see the Hiking and Backpacking section.

Winter Holiday Train—

From Late Nov. through the first of the new year (excluding Dec. 24 and 25), a steam locomotive departs from Durango and travels 26 miles to the wilderness of Cascade Canyon. The five-hour trip, through peaceful, snow covered terrain is tough to match. The train also has a brief two-week run during the second half of April.

FESTIVALS AND EVENTS

Iron Horse Bicycle Classic

Memorial Day weekend

World-class cyclists are pitted in a grueling road race against the Durango & Silverton Narrow Gauge train. Taking place during **Narrow-Gauge Days,** this 47-mile race ends in Silverton and is a unique tribute to the long history of the train. Throughout the long weekend there are several other touring and mountain bike races. For more information call **(303) 247-0312.**

Animas River Days

last weekend in June

Whitewater enthusiasts from around the country converge on Durango for a weekend of competitions on the Animas River. Watch as participants maneuver canoes, rafts and kayaks through specially designed courses. One highlight is the all-out race down a swift 4-mile stretch. In addition, there are several instructional clinics. For more information call **(303) 259-3893.**

Durango Pro Rodeo

mid-June to late August

Every Tues. and Wed. night, get a dose of the real West at the La Plata County Fairgrounds. Saddle bronc riding, bull dogging, roping and trick riding are only part of the evening's activities: a western barbecue begins at 6 pm, the rodeo starts at 7:30 pm. Every Labor Day weekend the Ghost Dancer Rodeo attracts Indian riders from throughout the western U.S. Located at **25th and Main** in **Durango; (303) 247-1666.**

Colorfest

mid-September to mid-October

The Four Corners area celebrates the arrival of autumn's colors with a variety of events. Each year from mid-Sept. through mid-Oct., when the aspen turn gold and red, Colorfest happenings fill the calendar. The area's brilliant colors highlight a vintage automobile show, workshops, art shows, fishing contests, raft races, hang gliding and more. For information call **(303) 247-0312.**

OUTDOOR ACTIVITIES

BIKING

MOUNTAIN BIKING

While there are some excellent touring routes around Durango, the area has become much better known as a hub for mountain biking. Mountain bike enthusiasts have found trail possibilities endless. Recently the town attracted 1,000 of the world's top mountain bike riders for the first-ever World Mountain Bike Championships. Turning the area into a neon blaze of Lycra shorts and jerseys, the riders competed on a grueling downhill course and a long cross-country track at Purgatory/Durango Ski Area.

If you didn't bring a bike, don't sweat it. There are several local shops with rentals, tour recommendations and maps. For further information and advice you might also check in at the **Animas Ranger District Office, 701 Camino del Rio, Room 301, Durango, CO 81301; (303) 247-4874.**

Colorado Trail—

For more experienced riders, a great two-day ride in the San Juan National Forest leaves from Little Molas Lake climbing 1,700 feet in the first 10 miles. The single track ventures above timberline for long stretches, before dropping back down Hotel Draw—a good place to camp for the night. The next day you can complete the final 36-miles (6–10 hours) back into Durango. Be sure to take a detailed map and to be prepared for weather. See the Hiking and Backpacking section for more information on the Colorado Trail. To reach the trailhead go north on Hwy. 550 for 41 miles.

Hermosa Creek Trail—

This has become one of the more popular day-long rides in the Durango area. It's a fairly advanced 21-mile ride with a couple of bridge crossings and a 2,000-foot decline in elevation. The rough trail passes through beautiful wooded terrain near Hermosa Creek—bring your fishing equipment along. Most people prefer a one-way route. This requires leaving a car at the lower trailhead located 11 miles north of Durango on Hwy. 550 and a mile up County Rd. 201. The upper trailhead where you will begin the ride is near Purgatory/Durango Ski Area, 28 miles north of Durango on Hwy. 550. From the ski area parking lot, stay right and follow the signs west on Forest Rd. 528 to Sig Creek Campground. Continue for 2 miles past the campground and turn left on a road that leads to the trailhead. Be sure to take a map along.

La Plata Canyon Road—

A maze of dirt roads dotted with remains of old mining camps provides a great day of mountain biking. For more information see the Four-Wheel-Drive Trips section.

Lime Creek Road—

Just north of Purgatory lies perhaps the best moderate ride you'll ever find. The 12-mile trail follows an old stagecoach route through incredible aspen groves and great views of the Needles. Leave a car at the lower trailhead near Purgatory/Durango Ski Resort and the ride will be almost exclusively downhill. Otherwise you may want to do a longer loop ride via Hwy. 550 from the ski area. The upper access point can be found on Hwy. 550, just 4 miles south of Molas Pass.

Purgatory/Durango Ski Area—

Take your bike up the specially equipped chairlift before setting out on more than 36 miles of marked trails that wind through spruce and aspen covered slopes. All abilities can enjoy the range of trails that set out from nearly 10,000 feet in elevation. Rentals available at the base area. For more information contact **(303) 247-9000.**

TOURING

Animas Valley Loop—

This easy, relatively flat 30-mile ride follows the path of the Animas River (a shorter 15-mile route can also be taken if you loop back at Kimo's Store). Leave Main Ave. in Durango and head east on 32nd street to a stop sign. Turn left onto on E. Animas Rd. (County Rd. 250), past prime ranchland to the northern end of the ride at Baker's Bridge—remember the cliff jumping scene from *Butch Cassidy and the Sundance Kid*? Continue past the one-lane bridge on the only serious uphill pull, and ride until you meet Hwy. 550. Head south on Hwy. 550 down to Hermosa, where you will turn right and catch County Rd. 203 just after the railroad crossing. NOTE: 6 miles before reaching Durango, you'll come to Trimble Hot Springs (see the Hot Springs section). It's a perfect place to stop for a soak before continuing on into town.

Rentals and Information—

Durango Cyclery—A good bet for mountain and touring rentals. **143 E. 13th St.; (303) 247-0747.**

Hassle Free Sports—The knowledgeable people at this shop rent mountain bikes on a per day basis, with discounts for longer terms. Open Mon.–Sat. 8:30 am–6 pm. **2615 Main Ave.; (303) 259-3874.**

Mountain Bike Specialists—Not only does this store offer rentals and trail information, but they arrange half-day to multi-day bike tours—ask about tours to Anasazi ruins. **949 Main Ave.; (303) 247-4066.**

FISHING

Because of its central location to many trout streams and high mountain lakes, Durango is a top-notch destination for people who like to fish. Listed below are some of the better public-access fishing areas. Several private lakes and streams may also be fished by arrangement with outfitters and guest ranches in the area. For further fishing information and supplies, call on **Duranglers Fly Shop, 801-B Main Ave., Durango, CO 81301; (303) 385-4081.**

Animas River—

This is a highly fished river, but rest assured that large trout (including a former record brown trout) can be pulled from inside the Durango city limits. You can try a novel fishing trip by taking the D&SNG train to Elk Park or Needleton and then fishing the Animas and its many drainages before catching the train back to town. Generally, however, the best fishing is south of town, on intermittent stretches of public water, all the way down to the Southern Ute Indian Reservation.

Dolores River—

This has been called the best public-access trout stream in the state. It is worth the trek from Durango to fish the water between the McPhee Dam (10 miles north of Dolores) north to Bradfield Bridge. See the Fishing section of the **Cortez** chapter for more information.

McPhee Reservoir—

See the Fishing section of the **Cortez** chapter.

Piedra River—

See the Fishing section of the **Pagosa Springs** chapter for more information.

Vallecito Reservoir—

The surrounding snowcapped peaks of San Juan National Forest help attract visitors to this heavily used reservoir. Spring and fall are the best times to catch good-sized rainbow and German brown trout and kokanee salmon. Documented catches of northern pike surpass 4 feet in length—you may not want to dangle your toes in the water! There are several boat ramps and docks along the 22-mile shoreline. Boat rentals and fishing supplies are available. Located 23 miles northeast of Durango, Vallecito Reservoir provides developed campgrounds, motels and lodges. The **Wit's End Guest Ranch and Resort (303) 884-4113** offers many deluxe cabins as well as restaurant meals in its historic lodge. Call the **Vallecito Lake Chamber of Commerce** for other options: **(303) 259-3966** and **884-9782.**

Take County Rd. 240 east out of Durango. Stay to the right on 240 at the junction with County Rd. 243. Turn left on County Rd. 501 and continue along the Los Pinos River to the lake.

FOUR-WHEEL-DRIVE TRIPS

Durango is close to Silverton and Ouray, often touted as the greatest jeeping area in the world. Serious jeepers can take day trips on these scenic and treacherous roads by heading north out of Durango on Hwy. 550 over Molas Pass. See the Four-Wheel-Drive Trips section of the **Silverton** chapter for more information. The area immediately surrounding Durango is not known as a jeeper's mecca, but there are some interesting ghost towns and old mining roads nearby.

Durango Ghosts—

A great day trip combining remnants of old mining towns and a far-reaching view of the La Plata Mountains is up La Plata Canyon, just west of Durango. Head west on Hwy. 160 to the town of **Hesperus,** then north on La Plata County Rd. The road is paved up to the small community of **Mayday,** near the site of **Parrott City.** Once a gold placer camp and miner's supply town, Parrott City was the county seat in 1876. A cluster of old white frame buildings with red trim stands out on the west side of the main street. The first is the old saloon brought down from La Plata City by Billy and Olga Little. Twenty-seven bullet holes were found in the wall behind the bar—must have been a pretty wild place on Saturday nights!

From Mayday/Parrott City the road turns to dirt and is rough going without a four-wheel-drive vehicle. Four miles up the road is what's left of La Plata City, an old mining camp. You will pass the old schoolhouse on the west side of the road. Continue to the end of the road at the 12,000-foot mountain summit for great views of the La Plata Mountains, Junction Creek Canyon, the Animas River Valley and Durango.

GOLF

Dalton Ranch and Golf Club—

Opened in July 1993, this Scottish links course on the outskirts of Durango provides plenty of challenge. While the greens are still immature, the surroundings are not. Tall trees line some of the fairly flat fairways and views to cliffs in the surrounding Animas River Valley brings about a sense of permanence. "There are absolutely no easy holes!" exclaimed one local when I inquired about the young course. Indeed some type of sand or water obstacle comes into play on every hole. Fairly reasonable greens fees; pro shop; semiprivate; nonmembers need to reserve within 48 hours of tee time. Located 6 miles north of Durango on Hwy. 550. Turn right on Trimble Lane across from the hot springs. **PO Box 2705, Durango, CO 81302; (303) 247-8774.**

Hillcrest Golf Course—

This well-kept, 18-hole course offers a far-reaching view of the La Plata Mountains. On the Fort Lewis College mesa, east of town; **2300 Rim Dr.; (303) 247-1499.**

Tamarron Resort Golf Course—

Doubtless one of Colorado's finest resorts, Tamarron lies etched in a once-wild cross-section of thick ponderosa woodland beneath the sharp 10,000-foot Hermosa Cliffs. Guests and members staying at Tamarron have first choice of tee times on this classic 18-hole course, which features 72 bunkers, eight water holes and stunning views along its entire 6,885 yards. Non-lodging golfers cannot reserve advance tee times, making play in the peak summer season close to impossible. Green fees are expensive but worth it. Located 18 miles north of Durango on Hwy. 550; **40292 Hwy. 550 N; (303) 259-2000, ext. 422.**

HIKING AND BACKPACKING

There are few places better than the Durango area for experiencing Colorado's outdoors. Whether you are interested in a half-day hike in the La Plata Mountains near town or a week-long trip deep into the Weminuche Wilderness Area, your satisfaction is assured.

Snowfall in the San Juans is heavy. During normal years snow cover remains at the higher elevations (above 11,000 feet) until July. Many folks choose to take backcountry trips in early fall when the aspen are turning color. This is a spectacular time to see the San Juans, but be prepared for snow, as storms are not uncommon in Sept.

Forest service maps, brochures and advice about hiking in the Durango area can be obtained at local sporting goods stores or at the **Animas Ranger District Office, 701 Camino del Rio, Room 301, Durango, CO 81301; (303) 247-4874.**

Animas Overlook—

This half-hour, interpretive nature walk offers terrific views over the entire Animas Valley. It's perfect for families with young children or those wanting a picnic site with a grill. Handicapped accessible. To reach the trailhead, head west on 25th St. from north Main Ave. in Durango and into the San Juan National Forest. Continue 8 miles from where the pavement ends to the well-marked trailhead.

Colorado Trail (Junction Creek)—

For hikers interested in exploring the southwest end of the 469-mile Colorado Trail, this is the place. To reach the trailhead, head west on 25th St. from north Main Ave. in Durango. At a cattle guard about 3.5 miles up the road is the San Juan National Forest boundary. Proceed from here about 100 feet and look for the trailhead on the left. This well-maintained trail heads up into some of the most beautiful high country surrounding Durango. For more information about the Colorado Trail, check in at the Animas Ranger District office in Durango. Complete maps and a book on the Colorado Trail can usually be found at sporting goods stores.

Goulding Creek Trail—

Another good day hike, the Goulding Creek Trail is especially nice in Sept. and

Oct. when the aspen groves are shimmering gold. It's a moderately difficult 6-mile round-trip hike that climbs up above Hermosa Cliffs near Tamarron. Three miles up the trail is a spot that offers a view into the secluded Hermosa Creek Roadless Area, one of the best elk summering grounds in southwestern Colorado. The trail begins 17 miles north of Durango on the west side of Hwy. 550, a half-mile north of the main entrance to Tamarron Resort.

Twin Buttes—

From the top of Twin Buttes (7,737 feet) the view of the surrounding La Plata Mountains is beautiful. It is an easy 4-mile round-trip hike that can often be done in winter, depending on snowfall. To reach the trailhead, take Hwy. 160 to a road 1.3 miles west of the Animas River Bridge (south end of Durango). Turn right and follow the road as it winds north and then west to where it starts climbing a steep hill. You can park there and begin the walk.

Weminuche Wilderness Area—

Deep valleys, jagged peaks, beautiful blue lakes and raging rivers characterize the Weminuche. Named for the band of Ute Indians that once inhabited the area, the Weminuche was granted wilderness designation by President Ford in 1975, making it the largest wilderness area in Colorado. Here are some ways to gain trail access to the area.

Via the Narrow-Gauge Railroad—One of the most exciting backpacking adventures possible is a trip into the Weminuche Wilderness Area via the narrow-gauge railroad. Starting each day from both Durango and Silverton, as many as 20 to 40 backpackers ride the train to and from the isolated stops at Elk Park and Needleton. From these locations they begin their trips up the extensive trail system. The quick transition from the civilized world of the train to primitive wilderness is striking. One minute you are surrounded by laughing, shouting passengers drinking Pepsi and eating potato chips; the next minute

they have traveled on and you are left standing by the train track, miles from the nearest road, with no sounds but the crashing water of the Animas River and the wind in the pines.

Needle Creek Trail, starting in Needleton, heads up into the breathtaking Chicago Basin, home to Mt. Eolus (14,084 feet), Sunlight Peak (14,059 feet) and Windom Peak (14,087 feet). Elk Creek Trail begins in Elk Park and climbs east up into the Elk Creek River Valley and eventually to the Continental Divide.

Backpacking into the Weminuche via the narrow-gauge railroad has become very popular. Unfortunately, signs of heavy use are apparent. The forest service has been forced to consider limiting use of the area. By practicing no-trace camping (no fires, use of gas stoves, packing out all trash and staying on designated trails), visitors can ensure that this plan of action does not become a reality. For Durango & Silverton Narrow Gauge Railroad information see the Major Attractions section.

Via Vallecito Reservoir—Both the Vallecito Trail and the Pine River Trail are heavily used and provide access to the Weminuche Wilderness Area. They are fine for both day hikes and extended trips. This is a popular access for horseback riders. See the Camping section for directions.

Via Purgatory Campground—Located 26 miles north of Durango on Hwy. 550. On the east side of the highway Cascade Creek Trail begins, crossing Purgatory Flats before dropping 4 miles down to the Animas River. From there you can hike another 7 miles upriver on the Animas River Trail to Needleton for access to the wilderness area. Many people find the 8-mile hike down to the river and back a good day trip.

HORSEBACK RIDING

One of the best ways to enjoy the astounding beauty of the San Juans is from the saddle of a horse. Several local outfitters offer a variety of long and short trips.

Purgatory Resort—
Call to arrange from several local out-fitters at **(303) 247-9000.**

RAPP Guide Service—
For a unique, custom-designed itin-erary into the San Juan National Forest, Ute Mountain Tribal Park or Weminuche Wilderness Area, consider hiring this trusted outfitter. With many years of ex-perience, they know what they're doing. For a historical and personal perspective of the area contact **Jerry and Anne Rapp, 47 Electra Lake Rd., Durango, CO 81301; (303) 247-8923.**

Southfork Riding Stables—
Six miles east at **28481 Hwy. 160; (303) 259-4871.**

RIVER FLOATING

"Water is God in southwestern Colo-rado," said Walt Werner, former ranger with the National Forest Service in Durango. Diverting the water is necessary in this arid landscape, but this "progress" has certainly taken a toll on the natural flow of area rivers. Despite a more con-trolled spring runoff, the swollen rivers still offer some exceptionally hair-raising rapid rides.

Animas River—
Many a kayaker and rafter has won-dered if the *River of Lost Souls* wasn't a name conjured up for those crazy enough to float the 28-mile stretch of the **Upper Animas.** From Silverton down to Rockwood, the river drops an average of 85 feet per mile offering water that is isolated and beautiful, rugged and dangerous. To attempt this section of the river you should be in good physical shape and an expert kayaker. Be sure to get out at Tacoma because the river then enters a boxed-in, churning chasm lasting 3 miles. Floating this section would have an effect on your body not unlike what the average car-rot experiences going through the puree cycle in a Cuisinart.

Closer to Durango, beginning near Trimble Hot Springs (6 miles north of

Durango off Hwy. 550), a tranquil 10-mile stretch of the river drops only 5 feet per mile. This section is best for canoes and those who shuddered while reading the previous paragraph.

Downstream from Durango, the **Lower Animas** has some good rapids but is a bit more sedate. Especially exciting for novices and intermediates, the **Lower Animas** winds its way 20 miles south through the Southern Ute Indian Reserva-tion. The river drops an average of 24 feet per mile and can be floated by kayaks, rafts and canoes. The Lower Animas can be floated into autumn. Permits are needed to enter the Indian reservation.

Piedra River—
Intersecting Hwy. 160 between Durango and Pagosa Springs, this is a river that more and more serious whitewater enthusiasts are discovering. See the River Floating section of the **Pagosa Springs** chapter for more information.

Outfitters—
Durango suffers no shortage of raft-ing outfitters offering guides, equipment, supplies and transportation to the rivers. Listed below are a couple of good ones.

Durango Rivertrippers—Promising "miles of smiles," these folks offer safe trips for the family. Located at **720 Main Ave., Durango, CO 81301; (303) 259-0289.**

Mountain Water Rafting—Experienced and highly regarded. **108 W. 6th; (303) 259-4191.**

SKIING
CROSS-COUNTRY SKIING
Due to the abundant snowfall in the San Juans, the ski season here is lengthy, but avalanche danger can run high. Backcountry skiers should use good judg-ment. To find the best snow consider the higher elevations to the north of Durango off Hwy. 550. Take a glance at the Hiking and Backpacking section for some more trail ideas.

Backcountry Trails—
Haviland Lake—Several easy routes take off from Haviland Lake Campground, 17 miles north of Durango via Hwy. 550. After a recent snow, this is an excellent area to come for the day. Beginners can practice by skiing around the unplowed campground on gentle terrain.

A 3-mile route follows a roller coaster trail on an old wagon road from the campground. The route is marked by blue signs with a distinctive "XC." The trail eventually comes out on Forest Rd. 166 (Chris Park Rd.). Look for a historical marker at this point before you complete the loop to Haviland Lake Campground. Another marked 2-mile loop begins just after turning off Hwy. 550 toward Haviland Lake. The trail heads into the forest to the right (south) just before you reach Forest Rd. 166, which leads to Chris Park Campground.

Molas Pass—See the **Silverton** chapter.

Groomed Trails—
Purgatory Ski Touring Center—This established cross-country trail system is ideal, thanks to a great location in the San Juan National Forest. More than 15 kilometers of trails accommodate all abilities. Instructors are available for touring and Telemark lessons. Rental equipment; small trail fee. Located across the highway from Purgatory Ski Area on Hwy. 550; **(303) 247-9000.**

Ski Rentals and Information—
Pine Needle Mountaineering—Anything you want to rent. **835 Main Ave.; (303) 247-8728.**

DOWNHILL SKIING
Purgatory/Durango Ski Area—
Almost invisible off Hwy. 550 between Durango and Silverton are the numerous runs of Purgatory/Durango Ski Area. An average of 300 inches of dry powder snow and abundant sunshine come together for unusually good conditions. Purgatory features a mix of runs,

heavy on the intermediate, and a generous vertical drop of 2,029 feet. More than some areas, Purgatory is geared to families. Experts, however, will find more than enough surprises on steep, narrow runs that challenge reaction time.

Located 28 miles north of Durango, the area has a convenient base village which, though small, is coming into its own. Ample lodging, a few restaurants and close proximity to the lifts make it extremely attractive. **Cascade Village,** another condo and lodge development, can be found 1 mile north of the ski area; **(303) 259-3500** in Colorado, **1-800-525-0896** nationwide. Many people, however, prefer staying in Durango and taking the frequent **Durango Lift** bus service to and from the area. For more information contact: **PO Box 666, Durango, CO 81302; (303) 247-9000.**

SWIMMING
Durango Municipal Swimming Pool—
A public outdoor pool located at 2400 Main Ave. next to Durango High School. Open daily in the summer 1:30–6 pm. A small fee is charged.

Fort Lewis College Natatorium—
An indoor pool located on campus. Open to the public 7–9 pm Mon.–Fri., 1–5 pm Sat. and Sun. A small fee is charged.

Trimble Hot Springs—
For information see the Hot Springs section.

TENNIS
Durango High School—
2390 Main Ave. Six outdoor courts.

Fort Lewis College—
Overlooking Durango from the mesa. Twelve courts are open unless scheduled for lessons or tournaments.

Mason School—
12th St. and E. 3rd Ave. Two outdoor courts.

SEEING AND DOING

ALPINE SLIDE

It's similar to a icy luge course, but there's not a snowflake to be seen. Summertime brings out riders of all ages who climb inside plastic toboggans and plunge down the mountainside on dual tracks, banking countless curves before finally coming to a breathless halt at the bottom. Time to head up the chairlift again. Note: ride in the morning to avoid possible afternoon thunderstorms. Located at Durango/Purgatory Ski Area 26 miles north of town on Hwy. 550; **(303) 247-9000.**

GAMBLING

Sky Ute Casino—

The Southern Utes have just opened a new $5 million gambling parlor with high-tech, bill-eating slot machines, poker tables and blackjack. The $5 limit hopefully will keep you from losing your shirt. Wine and beer are served in the adjacent dining room only if you are in the casino you'll need to stick to the nonalcoholic beer, pop or mineral water. Located a half-hour southeast of Durango in Ignacio; **(303) 382-2267.**

HOT SPRINGS

Trimble Hot Springs—

With the help of owner Ruedi Bear, Trimble Hot Springs has been restored again with a new bathhouse, snack bar, nursery and locker rooms. The main attractions are the Olympic-sized outdoor pool (150 feet x 50 feet), a smaller outdoor pool with massage jets, and two private tubs. The source water, heated far beneath the La Plata Mountains, emerges through a fault at Trimble at a piping hot 119° F before being mixed to a more tolerable temperature. Behind the pools is a landscaped park with picnic tables, outdoor grills and a volleyball court. Open in summer 7 am–10 pm daily; 8 am–11 pm in winter. Admission fee. Located just 6 miles north of Durango via Hwy. 550. **6475 County Rd. 203, Durango, CO 81301; (303) 247-0111.**

MUSEUMS AND GALLERIES

Animas School Museum—

Time stops as you enter a turn-of-the-century schoolroom furnished with small wooden desks, heavy blackboards and a faded 46-star flag. Can you name the last four states to join the Union? Upstairs is a photographic history of Animas City and Durango. Also displayed are artifacts from the Basket Maker Anasazi Indians and opium pipes found below a once-active(!) Chinese laundry in the area. Anyone interested in the history of Durango will enjoy spending a few moments in this small museum. Open in summer 10 am–6 pm. **31st St. and W. 2nd Ave.; (303) 259-2402.**

Southern Ute Indian Cultural Center—

Only 25 miles southeast from Durango lies the world of the Southern Utes. The history, culture and art of the Ute Indians, as well as 700-year-old Anasazi remains, are all on display in this small but interesting collection. Wonderful artistry is especially evident in the Ute bead and leatherwork, some from the 19th century. Open 9 am–6 pm Mon.–Sat. and 10 am–3 pm Sun. Adjacent gift shop. Located in **Ignacio; (303) 563-4649.**

NIGHTLIFE

Now Magazine, a supplement to the Thursday *Durango Herald*, provides current information about nightlife and leisure pursuits on a weekly basis. To learn about nocturnal happenings such as live music, theater presentations and dancing, pick up a free copy around town. Listed are a few of the more unique night spots.

Diamond Circle Theatre at the Strater Hotel—

Hiss-s-s-s the villain and cheer the hero during a Victorian melodrama presentation. The whole family will enjoy this entertainment in a period setting of red velvet curtains, checkered tablecloths and brass chandeliers. During a break in the show, the actors and actresses serve refreshments from the bar. **699 Main Ave.; (303) 247-4431.**

Farquahrts—

Live rock and roll or blues music is the rule for the lively crowd at this popular spot. The small dance floor in front of the stage encourages rubbing elbows while enjoying a great view of the band. (See the Where to Eat section.) **725 Main Ave.; (303) 247-5440.**

Bar-D Chuckwagon—

If you're looking for an evening of family fun and frontier-style food, the Bar-D has it all. "It's hokey and it's fun—a great place to take the kids or people from out of state," says one Durango local. After supper the Bar-D Wranglers take to the stage with songs, stories and comedy. You can also ride the Bar-D train and browse the half-dozen gift shops. Open nightly Memorial Day–Labor Day. Reservations required. Located 9 miles north of Durango on **County Rd. 250; (303) 247-5753.**

SCENIC DRIVES

San Juan Skyway—

It's difficult not to use superlatives when describing this drive through time. At every turn the landscape is transformed by some greater force. You'll see high mountain lakes, deep valleys, rocky summits, virgin wilderness and colorful plateau country with its desert canyons and weirdly eroded buttes. Man-made impressions come in the form of Anasazi cliff dwellings, historic mining towns and ski areas.

The San Juan Skyway is a 236-mile, nationally designated route that you can pack into one day or stretch into a much longer trip. It's marked by columbine road signs the entire way; you may easily start this circle tour at any point. Our description begins in Durango. Please flip to the

appropriate sections in the book for an in-depth look at major destinations along the way.

Before getting into specifics on the route, credit should be given to Otto Mears, pioneering roadbuilder of the San Juans. Mears, born in Russia in 1841, emigrated to San Francisco with his parents as a young teenager. After the outbreak of the Civil War he joined the First California Volunteers and served his adopted country with Kit Carson in the Indian campaign. By 1867 Mears settled in Colorado's San Luis Valley but was faced with the problem of getting his product (flour) to lucrative markets. Never one to sit back and brood, Mears set out to build a toll road over Poncha Pass. His most impressive accomplishment was completing 450 miles of roads over forbidding mountain passes in the San Juans, including sections of this scenic byway.

From **Durango,** driving north on Hwy. 550, the route roughly parallels the D&SNG route through the Animas Valley. However, the auto route splits off and heads over Coal Bank and Molas passes. Both passes top out at over 10,000 feet revealing delicate alpine beauty beside the crests of the Needles Mountains.

The well-preserved, Victorian town of **Silverton,** end of the line for the D&SNG Railroad, is the first destination. Hwy. 550 then continues its northerly course over Red Mountain Pass (11,075 feet), before descending into **Ouray.** This twisting stretch over the "Million Dollar Highway" into the soul of the San Juans will rivet your attention.

Ouray, one of the most popular destinations on the route, features many natural hot springs. If your neck muscles are tightening up from all of this driving, it's obviously time for a soak. From Ouray continue north on Hwy. 550 to the small town of **Ridgway** and turn left (southwest) on Hwy. 62. Soon the view is beautifully transformed by the 13,000- and 14,000-foot peaks seen from Dallas Divide. A left turn on Hwy. 145 leads you southeast towards **Telluride.**

Beautifully situated at the base of a towering box canyon, the historic mining town of Telluride is an easy place to linger for days. Continue southwest from Telluride on Hwy. 145 and enjoy the striking views of Wilson Peak and Mt. Wilson. Keep your bearings past magnificent Trout Lake and over Lizard Head Pass, as the road winds past little **Rico**. Rocky peaks give way to high, reddish bluffs as you approach the small town of **Dolores**, site of the Anasazi Heritage Center and McPhee Reservoir.

Continue south down Hwy. 145 to **Cortez**, located at the epicenter of Anasazi culture and Mesa Verde. From Cortez, Hwy. 160 makes its way east past **Mancos** and **Hesperus** to complete the scenic loop back to **Durango**.

Vallecito Reservoir—

The rocky crags of the San Juan National Forest serve as a beautiful backdrop to Vallecito Lake (see the Fishing section) and the 23-mile drive isn't too shabby either. Take County Rd. 240 east out of Durango. Stay to the right on 240 at the junction with County Rd. 243. Turn left on County Rd. 501 and continue along the Los Pinos River to the lake.

SOARING

Val-Air Soaring—

The tow plane eases off the grass runway with you and your experienced pilot not far behind encased in the glider's glass cockpit. Once at an acceptable altitude you are cut loose to ride the thermals and look out over the Animas River Valley. It's an unforgettable experience and Val-Air Soaring has never, knock on wood, had an accident. The airstrip is located 2 miles north of Durango on Hwy. 550. For information and reservations call **(303) 247-9037**.

WHERE TO STAY

ACCOMMODATIONS

For inexpensive motel accommodations simply follow Main Ave. to the north end of town. Both sides of the street offer ample lodging choices, but in the summer high season, neon No Vacancy signs begin flickering in early evening. In winter, however, it's usually no problem finding a room. In addition to economy accommodations you'll also find a Holiday Inn, a Comfort Inn and a couple of Best Westerns. For a quick rundown of local options call **Purgatory/Durango Central Reservations** at **1-800-525-0892**. Here are a few more ideas for a memorable night's stay in the Durango vicinity.

Blue Lake Ranch—$$$ to $$$$

To soothe the soul and plunge into pure relaxation, consider taking a break amidst the sculpted gardens of this exclusive 100-acre retreat. Located down the road from Hesperus, Blue Lake Ranch occupies a lonesome, flower-covered plain with fabulous views of the La Platas. Owners Shirley and David Alford both have an innate sense of how to make people feel comfortable. The main house has a European feel, especially now that a couple of California artists have added wall glazing and touches of decorative artwork. Without feeling the slightest bit contrived, each of the four rooms has a mood of its own. The immense Garden Room with expansive views has a king-sized bed covered with a lace spread and a working fireplace. Push aside French doors, walk outside and enter another room—this one created by an ingenious landscape mix of trees, shrubs and flowers. "I'm obsessed with gardening," David Alford admits. While staying here be sure to allow plenty of extra time to hang out on the deck (in an Adirondack chair, or in the hot tub) and enjoy this special setting—the peacocks won't mind.

There are several other lodging arrangements: a comfortable three-bedroom "cabin" with a large deck overlooking Blue Lake; a "cottage in the woods, or, perhaps, the very private "river house" a half mile away. No smoking. Call for reservations and directions. Discount in winter. Highly recommended. **16919 Hwy. 140, Hesperus, Durango, CO 81326; (303) 385-4537.**

The General Palmer Hotel—$$$ to $$$$

This hotel, built in 1898 and named for the cavalry general who was farsighted enough to push for railroad service into southern Colorado, successfully blends Victorian elegance with modern conveniences. Enjoyable personal touches include chocolates by the bed and a toiletry basket in the bath. Complimentary fresh muffins are served with juice and coffee each morning in the meeting room. Adjacent is the Old Muldoon Saloon with plush velvet couches and a long bar. Reservations essential. **567 Main Ave., Durango, CO 81301; 1-800-523-3358 nationwide, or (303) 247-4747 locally.**

Tamarron Resort—$$$ to $$$$

This three-story lodge built of stone sits perched on a sandstone bluff overlooking its well-known 18-hole golf course. Larger than you might expect, the rooms allow for excellent views. Townhouses with a number of options, some with full kitchens, may also be rented. This self-sufficient resort offers the discriminating visitor a choice of several restaurants, boutiques, a lounge and a healthy variety of recreational opportunities. The deck of the indoor/outdoor pool enjoys one of the best views anywhere. Take advantage of the health spa, tennis courts, platform tennis courts and, of course, the golf course, which is always ranked among Colorado's finest. Tamarron is also an ideal place to stay in winter because it's close to the Purgatory/Durango Ski Area. Tamarron offers enticing packages for guests in the off-season. Located 18 miles north of Durango on Hwy. 550. **PO Box 3131, 40292 Hwy. 550 N., Durango, CO 81302-3131; 1-800-678-1000 or (303) 259-2000.**

The Jarvis Suite Hotel—$$$

This historic hotel, built inside the 100-year-old Gem Theater, was converted into 22 contemporary suites with skylights, kitchens and modern furnishings. It's a welcome experiment in contrasts of style, form and function. Prices vary considerably, depending on season and room design. Located in a convenient downtown location. **125 W. 10th St., Durango, CO 81301; 1-800-824-1024 nationwide** or **(303) 259-6190 locally.**

The Strater Hotel—$$$

Some 100 years ago at the seemingly exorbitant cost of $70,000, Henry H. Strater built the hotel that was to become his legacy. Durango was in need of a first-class operation to demonstrate that the burgeoning community was worthy of the title "Denver of the West." The 93 rooms are tastefully decorated in restored antiques; each is different and has its own bath. Despite modern amenities, the authentic Victorian feel of the red brick hotel is retained by antique walnut furniture, lace curtains and old-time light fixtures.

Located within shouting distance of the comfortable hotel lobby are Henry's Restaurant, the Diamond Belle Saloon and the Diamond Circle Theatre with its outstanding melodrama. Room rates vary according to season. **699 Main Ave., Durango, CO 81301; 1-800-247-4431 nationwide, or (303) 247-4431 locally.**

Edelweiss Motel—$$

A good bet when staying in Durango is to book a room at the Edelweiss. The friendly owners will treat you right and you won't part with too many dollars. Located in a quiet setting a couple of miles north of town, the motel still has easy access to Durango. Along with clean, basic rooms it also features a jacuzzi and sauna. One corner of the small 20-room complex is occupied by a good German restaurant—although when we visited, it was Cajun night. **689 Animas View Drive, Durango, CO 80301; (303) 247-5685.**

Durango Hostel International—$

OK, so it's slightly rundown. But this AYH-approved house is the cheapest place to stay in town. Open 7–10 am, 5–10 pm;

doors closed at all other times. Use back entrance. **543 E. 2nd Ave., Durango, CO 81301; (303) 247-9905.**

CAMPING

In San Juan National Forest—
The closest campground to Durango is **Junction Creek Campground,** located about 4 miles away. Thirty-four sites; fee charged. Head west on 25th St. from north Main Ave. and follow the road up into the national forest.

Lemon Reservoir—Located 17 miles northeast of Durango. Follow County Rd. 240 out of town. Turn north on County Rd. 243 and follow it to the reservoir. There are three campgrounds: two located north of the reservoir and one on the east shore. Fee charged; total of 62 sites.

North toward Purgatory—Traveling north out of town on Hwy. 550 leads you to **Haviland Lake Campground** just north of Tamarron. 45 sites; fee charged. Stay on Hwy. 550 north for another 7 miles to reach **Purgatory Campground;** 14 sites; fee charged. For a more remote location try **Sig Creek Campground.** Nine sites; small fee. Situated 28 miles northwest of Durango on Hermosa Park Rd. From Hwy. 550 turn into the ski area and stay right above the parking lot. Just follow the signs.

Vallecito Reservoir—This popular area, located 23 miles northeast of Durango, can be reached by taking County Rd. 240 out of town. Stay to the right on 240 at the junction of County Rd. 243. Turn left on County Rd. 501. Vallecito Reservoir boasts five campgrounds with 111 sites by the reservoir and one (Vallecito Campground, 80 sites) just to the north on Vallecito Creek. Fee charged.

Private Campground—
KOA Campground—For folks looking for electrical and water hookups, showers and the like, the KOA Campground is located **5 miles east of Durango city limits** at **30090 Hwy. 160, Durango, CO 81301; (303) 247-0783.**

WHERE TO EAT

Ariano's—$$$
The owner and chef, Vince Ferraro, has created a menu loaded with northern Italian specialties. He assured us that his pastas and ravioli are made fresh daily in the restaurant. Milk-fed veal, ginger shrimp, steaks and specials round out the menu. An extensive Italian wine list complements the full bar. In the words of one longtime Durango resident, "If I could go to any restaurant in Durango, it would definitely be Ariano's." Open nightly from 5:30 pm. **150 College Dr.; (303) 247-8146.**

Red Snapper—$$ to $$$$
The hexagonal fish tank in the entry way of this popular restaurant should be your first clue: try the fish. Many other large saltwater aquariums line the room. Variations on red snapper and a special daily catch are among the menu items. You may want to start out with a trip to the oyster bar. All seafood is flown in daily, but the restaurant also features "landfood," including steaks and prime rib. Top your meal off with Death by Chocolate. Extensive wine list. **144 E. 9th St.; (303) 259-3417.**

The Edgewater Dining Room at the Red Lion Inn—$$ to $$$
Look out the large picture windows from your table to the rushing Animas River below as ecstatic rafters float by. A trip to the Edgewater's extensive salad bar can be a complete lunch. Or come by in the evening for more elaborate and expensive ($$$) fare. The dinner menu includes a good selection of steaks and seafoods. The soups and appetizers will make your mouth water: baked French onion soup, brie soup, stuffed mushrooms, escargot or oysters casino. Their Sun. brunch ($$) is considered by many locals to be the best in town.

Open Mon.–Sat. 6 am–2 pm, 5–10 pm; Sun. 6–10 am, 10 am– 2 pm (brunch) and 5–10 pm. **501 Camino del Rio; (303) 259-6580.**

The Ore House—$$ to $$$

Nothing too fancy graces the menu of Durango's most popular steakhouse, but I can almost guarantee you will want to savor each bite. All of the beef at the Ore House is aged in an on-premises cooler and hand-cut daily; try a generous rib-eye cut or a 16-oz. T-bone steak. Also offered are fresh seafood items ranging from scallops to Australian lobster. The decor is rustic with barn-wood walls and old mining implements throughout. Consistently voted "best steakhouse" in a local restaurant poll. Good wine cellar. Bar open at 5 pm; restaurant open 5:30–11 pm nightly. **147 6th St.; (303) 247-5707.**

Olde Tymers Cafe—$ to $$$

For a burger and an ice cold beer this is the place. The bar area packs them in during happy hour; in summer be sure to head out back to the shaded brick patio. In winter find a booth and choose from the selection of salads, soups, pasta and Mexican dishes. Nightly specials. Open daily from 11 am–10 pm. **1000 Main Ave.; (303) 259-2990.**

Carvers Bakery Cafe/Brew Pub—$ to $$

An odd cohabitation of a bakery and brewpub under one roof makes you wonder if this schizo place is any good. It's definitely worth a try. In the morning pick up a loaf of bread, giant pastry or bagel for take-out. You may want to take a seat (weekend waits are common) to enjoy a steaming cup of coffee with your favorite egg dish— the eggs, chorizo and hash browns couldn't have been better. The solid breakfasts are the highlight, but Carvers also offers a creative selection of lunches and dinners. In the evening slip around to a small backroom to sample their various beers, brewed on the premises in large vats. Open Mon.–Sat. 7 am–10 pm, Sun. 7 am–2 pm. **1022 Main Avenue; (303) 259-2545.**

Farquahrts—$ to $$

Voted the best pizza in town, but there is much more. The interior decor is rustic and inviting; a turn-of-the-century portrait of a nude woman gazes down upon a long bar at one end of the room. Antique signs form a shield of armor on the walls, and ceiling fans are forever circling overhead. It tends to attract a college-age crowd, especially after 9 pm when live rock and roll or blues begins. Open 11 am–10 pm Mon.–Sat., 4–11 pm on Sun. **725 Main Ave.; (303) 247-5440.**

The Durango Diner—$

A sure sign of value is the large number of locals rubbing elbows at the long counter in this unpretentious diner. Huge portions are served up as you catch the latest goings-on around town. Hash browns are a standout favorite of the house; large peeled potatoes are shaved onto the grill and may be smothered with melted cheddar cheese and green chilis. Other breakfast specialties include flapjacks, biscuits and gravy, and omelettes. Lunch items are added to the menu and served until closing at 2 pm. Open Mon.–Sat. from 6 am, Sun. from 7 am. **957 Main Ave.; (303) 247-9889.**

Griego's—$

The only drive-in Mexican restaurant in Durango is housed in a former A&W franchise. The likeness is obvious until you bite into a smothered burrito, taco or combination plate. Order anything smothered in green chili. Remember though, no alcoholic beverages are served to help you cool down. Top off your authentic meal with a homemade sopapilla dipped in honey. Open 10 am–9 pm Mon.–Sat. **2603 Main Ave.; (303) 259-3558.**

The Meeting Place—$

Creative homemade foods and smoke-free dining are the obvious attributes of the Meeting Place. Traditional omelette and egg varieties share the menu with whole wheat pancakes, breakfast shakes and homemade bread. Lunches feature crêpes and brown rice, which share the menu with a variety of soups, salads and pasta dishes. Alcohol-free beverages are served.

Open daily 7 am–2 pm, closed Tues. and Wed. 6th St. and 7th Ave.; **(303) 247-5322.**

SERVICES

Day Care—
Peter Pan Pre-School—750 E. 4th Ave., Durango, CO 81301; (303) 247-5954.

Transportation—
The **Durango Lift** provides daily bus service to and from Purgatory during ski season from several pickup spots in Durango; reservations recommended. Bus service is also available in and around Durango for a small fee. Sightseers may want to take a one-hour historic Durango mini-tour. Check with your hotel/motel for more information, or call **259-LIFT.** A new, open-air trolley runs up and down Main Ave. in Durango from 6:30 am–10 pm daily.

Visitor Information—
Durango Area Chamber Resort Association—Stop by this excellent visitors center right in the midst of a riverside park on the Animas. In addition to information about area businesses, the National Forest Service staffs a booth. Call for reservations. **PO Box 2587, 111 S. Camino del Rio, Durango, CO 81302; (303) 247-0312** or **1-800-525-8855.**

Purgatory/Durango Central Reservations—Call nationwide **1-800-525-0892.**

Vallecito Chamber of Commerce—PO Box 804, Bayfield, CO 81122; (303) 884-9782.

Gunnison
and Crested Butte

The Gunnison area is quintessentially western, its character having been molded by Indians, miners, ranchers and railroads. Located in the fertile Gunnison Valley at the confluence of the Gunnison River and Tomichi Creek, Gunnison is one of the most purely outdoor-oriented destinations in this book. The snowcapped Elk Mountains and Taylor Park lie to the north; to the east you'll see the Sawatch Range and the Continental Divide. West of Gunnison, Curecanti National Recreation Area, which encompasses Blue Mesa Reservoir, and the spectacular Black Canyon of the Gunnison continue to be major draws.

In the midst of a sought-after preserve of outdoor activity, Gunnison serves as an ideal jumping-off point for vacationers. With 1.6 million acres of the Gunnison National Forest surrounding the town, finding a remote backcountry escape is no problem. Prime hiking, mountain biking, skiing and hunting can be found in abundance. More than 750 miles of trout streams and a number of productive reservoirs attract legions of avid fishermen every year. In addition, exploring the back roads and ghost towns in the Gunnison area can comprise a whole vacation in itself.

Gunnison locals appear proud of the fact that chilling winter temperatures in the Gunnison Valley are often the coldest in the country. Up at **Crested Butte,** about 30 miles north of town, the temperatures are a bit warmer and the skiing is hot. During winter exceptional powder snow challenges downhill skiers on a wide variety of terrain, including some of the best extreme skiing in North America.

Crested Butte is widely considered the mountain biking capital of the planet; you will see more bikes there than cars when the snow melts. In summer high mountain meadows burst into a barrage of colors as wildflowers reach and maintain their apex. Fall brings another welcome change when mountainsides of golden aspen come into the picture. As long as you are willing to treat the fragile surroundings with the utmost respect, laid-back Crested Butte locals seem perfectly willing to share their version of paradise.

Driving up the pastoral valley from Gunnison to Crested Butte, you experience a memorable feeling of isolation and natural beauty. Vast stretches of ranchland dominate the immediate surroundings, while four nearby wilderness areas and the Gunnison National Forest occupy the higher elevations. Emerging in an alpine basin, you'll be awed by the scene: Mount Crested Butte and other high, rocky peaks, virtually encircling the century-old town mining town of Crested Butte.

With humble beginnings primarily in coal mining and supplies, the old town has maintained much of its original western simplicity. Crested Butte has an understated personality that doesn't aspire to become like its more glamorous neighbor, Aspen. Brightly painted false-fronted business establishments and weathered miners' shacks make up the bulk of the town's buildings. The National Historic District designation helps to preserve Crested Butte's intriguing history while scrutinizing any proposed renovation or new construction. The main thoroughfare, Elk Ave., offers a large number of shops, restaurants and bars housed creatively in old buildings. Unlike some ski resorts, dining out here doesn't require an increase in your credit card limits.

The old and the new come together at Crested Butte without colliding, thanks in part to the 3-mile distance between the old town and the modern ski resort at Mount Crested Butte. This short distance has alleviated many conflicts by separating the luxury condos and multi-level hotels from the historic district. Each locale complements the other without crowding or creating aesthetic confrontations. Most accommodations are located conveniently at the base of the ski slopes at Mount Crested Butte. A frequent shuttle plies the route between the resort and the old town, allowing you to leave your car parked for the duration of your stay.

HISTORY

As early as the mid-1600s, the Gunnison area was a primary Ute hunting ground for buffalo, deer and other game. In 1853 a famous expedition, led by Capt. John W. Gunnison, passed through the area in an attempt to find a suitable transcontinental railroad route. Gunnison and his men had a very successful expedition until they reached Utah, where all but four members of the party were brutally killed by a band of Paiute Indians. Capt. Gunnison was shot with 15 arrows before his arms, tongue and heart were removed. The least that could be done was to name a town after the man.

After the Ute treaty of 1868, an Indian agency in the Gunnison area opened at Los Piños. Under treaty, the Utes had to move west, vacating the Gunnison valleys. It wasn't long before settlers began arriving. Some prospectors pushed their luck by venturing into the Elk Mountains of Ute territory, usually with severe consequences. But rich mineral strikes further to the west in the San Juan Mountains put pressure on the Utes to renegotiate the treaty, further reducing their territory. The resulting Brunot Treaty in 1873 forced the Utes to cede more land to the US and relocate in the Uncompahgre area to the west.

In 1874 the town of Gunnison got its start when farmers and cattle ranchers settled in the valleys. Five years later miners struck rich gold and silver deposits and the Gunnison area came to life. Gold and silver strikes up Tomichi and Quartz creeks, in Taylor Park and in the Elk Mountains spurred the growth of many mining towns such as Pitkin, Tincup and Gothic. With the mining boom in full swing, Gunnison became a very important place to come for supplies and a little hell-raising. The town also became a crucial transportation center. Demand from mining towns in the area and from cattle ranchers eager to send their stock to outside markets prompted both the Denver & Rio Grande Railroad (D&RG) and the Denver South Park and Pacific Railroad (DSP&P) to extend service to Gunnison in the early 1880s.

In 1893, as in so many other mining areas across the state, the demonetization of silver proved catastrophic to these boom towns. Many became ghost towns immediately, while others lingered on, dying slow deaths. The town of Gunnison, with its cattle industry and role as supply center for the area, emerged unscathed from this period of economic upheaval. So did another nearby town—Crested Butte.

During the mining boom of the early 1880s, Crested Butte provided its rich neighbors with supplies and cut lumber. Soon Crested Butte residents discovered they were living on top of a huge deposit of high-grade coal. In 1881 the Denver Rio & Grande Railroad connected Crested Butte to the outside world and within three years was transporting 1,000 tons of coal per month.

Coal fueled the economy in Crested Butte, and by the 1890s the young town boasted 1,000 residents, 13 saloons and one minister. As the boom towns in the nearby Elk Mountains began to wither away, Crested Butte became a company town under the guiding hand of Colorado Fuel & Iron (CF&I). The town prospered until 1952, when the Big Mine finally closed. In 1953 the *Denver Post* published a fallacious article on Colorado's "newest ghost town."

Only 10 years later many skiers began challenging the slopes of Crested Butte Mountain (12,162 feet). Resort developers were on target when they started cutting runs and building a planned community at the base area. The ski industry resuscitated Crested Butte at just the right moment, allowing the delightful town to escape "ghost town" classification.

GETTING THERE

Gunnison—Located 196 miles southwest of Denver, Gunnison can be reached on Hwy. 285 and Hwy. 24 to Poncha Springs, then west over Monarch Pass on Hwy. 50. Monarch Pass can be slow going in the winter. TNM&O Bus Lines services Gunnison from points east and west. Getting to Gunnison by air is easy. In winter daily direct flights are available from Dallas and Chicago among other major cities as well as connecting flights from Denver International.

Crested Butte—Located 30 miles north of Gunnison on Hwy. 135. It takes about 40 minutes to make the trip from Gunnison to Crested Butte. For optional summer route to Crested Butte consider the trip over Cottonwood Pass (see the **Upper Arkansas Valley** chapter). Van service between Gunnison and Crested Butte is available.

———————— MAJOR ATTRACTIONS ————————

Curecanti National Recreation Area

Blue Mesa Reservoir and much of the **Black Canyon** of the Gunnison are encompassed by Curecanti National Recreation Area and its breathtaking scenery. A series of dams have altered the natural path of the Gunnison River on its course through the ancient Precambrian stone of the Black Canyon. Blue Mesa Dam, at the head of the Black Canyon, created the first and largest of three reservoirs. It has transformed the semi-arid landscape into an area especially well suited to boating, fishing and windsurfing.

Downstream from Blue Mesa you'll come across the dramatic beauty of Morrow Point and Crystal reservoirs; the mixture of jutting rock and calm water in the abyss of the canyon is as close as Colorado can come to the Norwegian fjords. Below Crystal Dam the Gunnison River flows freely through the deepest and narrowest section of the Black Canyon of the Gunnison. This area has been preserved as a national monument (see Major Attractions in the **Black Canyon Country** chapter).

History—

The namesake of Curecanti is former Ute Chief Curecata, who was known for directing the Ute Bear Dance with his twin brother, Kanneatche. The Ute Indians once hunted wild game in the dry hills around the Gunnison River, staying away from the Black Canyon. When trappers and traders began exploring the area in the mid-1800s, the rugged canyon terrain was still viewed as an obstacle. Nonetheless, in 1882 the Denver & Rio Grande Railroad somehow completed its narrow-gauge "Scenic Line

of the World" through the upper part of the canyon, which left lasting impressions on its passengers. In 1899 English author Rudyard Kipling wrote the following description about the passage:

We seemed to be running into the bowels of the earth at the invitation of an irresponsible stream. The solid rock would open up and disclose a curve of awful twistfulness. Then the driver put on all steam, and we would go round that curve on one wheel chiefly, the Gunnison River gnashing its teeth below.

The route climbed out of the canyon in the vicinity of Crystal Reservoir and continued to Cimarron and Montrose. The railroad operated until 1949. Today the track bed lies submerged by Morrow Point and Blue Mesa reservoirs.

Facts About the Recreation Area—

Blue Mesa Reservoir is 20 miles long, offering a wide expanse of clear water for sailing, windsurfing and fishing. Narrow arms reach out from the main body of water, making boat exploration the best way to get into remote areas. The two other smaller reservoirs are more difficult to reach, but the beauty of the canyon makes it worth a hike. Hwy. 92 follows the northern rim of the Black Canyon, offering several dramatic overlooks down to Morrow Point and Crystal reservoirs. Several hiking trails wind their way down to water level; only hand-carried watercraft are allowed on the smaller reservoirs.

Elk Creek Marina—

Tackle, gas, a convenience store, boat rentals and tours can all be found here. Located off Hwy. 50 on the north shore near the midpoint of the **Blue Mesa Reservoir. (303) 641-0707.**

Visitor Information—

Elk Creek Visitor Center—A good place to begin your visit to the recreation area is at the park headquarters/visitors center. Several exhibits, a slide presentation and printed information tell the story of the Curecanti area. Rangers will inform you of any interpretive programs and of the area's many recreational possibilities. Open from mid-May–late Sept. Located on the north side of Blue Mesa Reservoir off Hwy. 50. For more information contact **Superintendent, Curecanti National Recreation Area, National Park Service, 102 Elk Creek, Gunnison, CO 81230; (303) 641-2337.**

Other Information—Check in at the Lake Fork, Cimarron and East Portal information centers and talk to the ranger on duty.

Fishing—

Curecanti National Recreation Area provides excellent fishing on Blue Mesa, Morrow Point and Crystal reservoirs. Blue Mesa is by far the largest, most popular and most accessible (the other reservoirs require a hike), with 96 miles of shoreline. It accommodates heavy use from both bank and boat anglers. Shore fishing is best when the water level is low. More than 30 streams flow into Blue Mesa, providing numerous channels and inlets. Rainbows are the most frequent catch, although brown, mackinaw and brook trout and kokanee salmon are also caught in quantity. The reservoir is stocked with hundreds of thousands of trout and kokanee salmon each year. The best fishing is early and late in the day. In winter many fishermen drive out onto the ice from the boat ramps around the reservoir. Iola Basin is a favorite for ice fishing.

Handicapped Access—

The East Elk Creek Visitors Center, as well as the Lake Fork, Cimarron and East Portal information centers are all wheelchair accessible. Most of the campgrounds can accommodate handicapped persons.

Hiking—

A number of hiking trails leave the roadside and twist their way down inside the Black Canyon. The half-mile **Neversink Trail,** at the eastern tip of Blue Mesa Reservoir, goes through a lush bird habitat. Several other trails leave the north side of the reservoirs from Hwy. 92 and offer dramatic views.

For a water-level view of Morrow Point Reservoir and the Curecanti Needle, try **Curecanti Creek Trail.** This 2-mile trail rapidly descends 1,000 feet from the rim of the Black Canyon of the Gunnison down to the water level of Morrow Point Reservoir. It would be wise to save some time and energy for the walk back up. The well-maintained trail crosses bridges and even has a few steps in places. The route follows the path of turbulent Curecanti Creek, which looks more like a waterfall than a creek due to the steep grade. Once at the bottom, the view up the canyon walls and across the water to Curecanti Needle is fantastic. There is room for a couple of tents on a sandy bank at the bottom of the trail. Fishing is usually good in the deep water where Curecanti Creek flows into the reservoir.

Morrow Point Reservoir Boat Tours—

From within the deep canyon walls you will find a new appreciation for the beauty of the Black Canyon. On the small tour boat, an interpreter relates the history of the lake as you ride toward a water-level view of the Curecanti Needle. Before embarking on a boat tour, you must first take a mile-long hike down Pine Creek Trail. For reservations and more information call the **Elk Creek Marina; (303) 641-5387.**

Water Sports—

Sailing, motorboating and windsurfing are popular activities on Blue Mesa Reservoir. Many boat ramps are situated around Blue Mesa for easy entry into the water. Windsurfers prefer the warmer waters of The Bay of Chickens. Morrow Point and Crystal reservoirs are limited to hand-carried craft due to the surrounding canyon walls. Fluctuating water levels at the two smaller reservoirs cause some boating hazards. Check with rangers at the Cimarron Information Center for information and advice.

Camping—

A number of developed campgrounds are situated, for the most part, around the perimeter of Blue Mesa Reservoir. The major campgrounds are at **Elk Creek, Lake Fork, Cimarron** and **Stevens Creek.** For a smaller, less developed area, try camping among the cottonwoods at **Red Creek** or **Gateview.** All campgrounds are first come, first served. There are more than 350 sites; all charge a fee. For information on camping closer to the Black Canyon see the Major Attractions section of the **Black Canyon Country** chapter.

———— FESTIVALS AND EVENTS ————

Cattlemen's Days
mid-July

Gunnison cuts loose each year during Cattlemen's Days, the state's oldest rodeo, celebrating the ranching heritage of the area. Held annually since 1901, the rodeo features stock shows, horse races, a barbecue and pro rodeo events. If you want to get a good feel for the area and its people, work this event into your schedule. Call the **Gunnison County Chamber of Commerce** for more information at **(303) 641-1501.**

Fat Tire Bike Week
mid-July

This Crested Butte celebration originated in 1975 when a few locals decided to ride one-speed Schwinn klunkers over 12,705-foot Pearl Pass to Aspen. The hapless riders made the trek, but only by pushing their bikes most of the way. Today, riders have mountain bikes equipped with 18 gears, lightweight alloy frames and cantilever brakes to assist them. Fat Tire Bike Week mingles pro racing events with tours for riders of all abilities. The Pearl Pass Classic is the perfect culmination of the festivities. Hundreds of riders camp below Pearl Pass for a night of music, bonfires, food and fermented hops. At first light everyone heads over the rough pass to Aspen in a boisterous reenactment of the first ride in 1975. For more information call **(303) 349-6438.**

Aerial Weekend
last weekend of July

For nearly two decades this ultimate spectator event has filled Crested Butte's skies with a colorful rainbow of hot-air balloons. As many as 50 balloons participate in the annual event. The graceful balloons are visible from practically anywhere in the wide valley. The aerial excitement also includes sky divers, hang gliders, a stunt pilot and games in the town park. For more information call **(303) 349-6438.**

Vinotok
mid-September

This spirited annual fall festival brings hoards of Crested Butte locals out to celebrate the harvest in Slavic tradition. If you happen to be in town, it's a great time. The festival kicks off with a crazed parade down Elk Ave. Chanting revelers, many wearing wild costumes, progress down the street towards the park, where a huge bonfire lights the evening sky. The crowd works into a pitch before a huge papier-mâché "grump" is thrown on the fire. The burning "grump" removes the town's collective worries, and before long everyone is back in the bars. For information call **(303) 349-6438.**

———— OUTDOOR ACTIVITIES ————

BIKING

MOUNTAIN BIKING

It's tough to overstate the importance of mountain biking in Crested Butte. With only one paved road leading into town, it's obvious why the locals' favorite mode of travel is on sturdy mountain bikes. If you have never tried a mountain bike, take one for a spin. Single-track trails and jeep roads provide varied terrain for all abilities. Because Crested Butte has so many backcountry trails, few conflicts exist among hikers, horseback riders and mountain bikers. Just be sure to respect your surroundings and other trail users. For additional information, visit the **Taylor River/Cebolla District Forest Service Office, 216 N. Colorado St., Gunnison, CO 81230; (303) 641-0471.**

Aspen via Pearl Pass—

Advanced riders love this rough, high-altitude ride over Pearl Pass (12,705 feet). If you have the stamina to consider a steep (at times) 39-mile, one-way ride, then keep reading. To get to the road over Pearl Pass, take Hwy. 135 south from Crested Butte for 2 miles to the Skyland turn-off. Go left and follow Brush Creek Rd. for 6 miles to a fork in the road. Take the right fork up Middle Brush Rd. to the stream crossing. The trail proceeds just downstream from that point. After the Dead End sign, follow along the old road grade before merging back up with Middle Brush Rd. After passing some rolling meadows, the ride pushes on to the summit of the pass. From there it's mostly downhill to the townsite of Ashcroft, where the pavement begins for the final 13 miles to Aspen. If you'd like some company for this ride, come to Crested Butte during Fat Tire Bike Week (see Festivals and Events).

Cement Creek Trails—

A country dirt road passes 12 miles through the valley next to Cement Creek. You can take this road all the way to the base of Italian Mountain or turn off on one of the many trails snaking up the sloping valley walls. Walrod Gulch is a steep four-wheel-drive road. For single tracking on a rough trail, try Trail 409, leading the way to Farris Creek Rd. and a loop back to Crested Butte. For access to Cement Creek, see the Hiking and Backpacking section.

Crested Butte to Marble—

You can't use this route until mid-to late summer due to the heavy snowpack. It's a long ride unless you have arranged for someone with a vehicle to pick you up in Marble. Maybe you like long rides? Anyway, this arduous route passes through Gothic (which in itself is a great 7-mile one-way trip), over 10,707-foot Schofield Pass, past the Devil's Punchbowl, on through the pristine ghost town of Crystal, finally ending in Marble. Once in Marble you can either turn around and return to Crested Butte or ride an exhausting loop over McClure and Kebler passes.

Gothic Trails—

Several excellent trails possibilities converge on the ghost town of Gothic, just 7 miles north of Crested Butte. Forest Service Trail #401 is one of the favorites. It leaves from Gothic and soon heads above timberline with views of Baldy, Gothic and Crested Butte mountains along its 6-mile route to the top of Schofield Pass. Loop back to Gothic on the jeep road. Catch the trail a half mile upstream from Gothic at the Judd Falls trailhead or via a spur from Avery Campground (see Camping).

Rentals and Information—

Before heading out on a fat-tire bike excursion, check with one of the many mountain bike shops for trail maps, advice and rentals. Here are a couple of ideas:

The Alpineer—419 6th St., PO Box 208, Crested Butte, CO 81224; (303) 349-5210.

The TuneUp—222 N. Main St., Gunnison, CO 81230; (303) 641-0285.

FISHING

No question about it: the Gunnison and Crested Butte area could be one of the top fishing destinations in Colorado. Stop by local sporting goods stores or the Chamber of Commerce and pick up a free copy of the detailed *Gunnison Country Angling Guide*. If you need advice or tackle, drop in at **Gene Taylor's Sporting Goods in Gunnison: 201 W. Tomichi Ave.; (303) 641-1845.**

Blue Mesa Reservoir—
See the Major Attractions section.

East River—
Unfortunately, much of the East River below its headwaters at Emerald Lake flows through private land. Permission to fish some of the best stretches requires an OK from landowners. Some good public water can be found adjacent to the Roaring Judy Hatchery, 13 miles downstream on Hwy. 135. The water above and below the hatchery bridge is designated wild trout water. You have an excellent chance of hooking a large rainbow, brown, brook or cutthroat on this section. Only flies are permitted; catch and release all trout over 12 inches.

Emerald Lake—
This high-country lake at an elevation of 10,445 feet is best known for its rainbow trout and a beautiful location just below Schofield Pass. The fishing can be a bit sporadic, though the trip is worthwhile. Located at the headwaters of the East River. Emerald Lake can be reached by heading north from Crested Butte for 9 miles to Gothic. From there head on up the Schofield Pass Rd. (Forest Rd. 317) for 4.5 miles to Emerald Lake. Great picnic spot!

Gunnison River—
At the town of Almont, where the East and Taylor rivers join, the Gunnison River is born. Stretches of this legendary trout stream are easily considered some of the very best in the state.

For 3 miles downstream from Almont, you will find plenty of good fishing in public water. Beyond that point the river flows through mostly private property until passing the Neversink Picnic Area a couple of miles below the town of Gunnison. From Neversink down to the inlet of Blue Mesa Reservoir is a popular public fishing area. The length of the free-flowing section below Neversink fluctuates between 5 miles and a half mile, depending on the water level of the reservoir. Try a weighted Hare's Ear, a Stone Fly or a Woolly Worm in the deep pools near the banks; Mepps and Rapala lures are favorites.

As you follow downstream, the Gunnison flows into a series of three reservoirs: **Blue Mesa, Morrow Point** and **Crystal.**

The **Lower Gunnison River** below Crystal Reservoir is difficult to reach, but worth it. Below this final reservoir, the Gunnison surpasses all other rivers in the state for sheer numbers of trout per mile. See the **Black Canyon Country** chapter for more information on this Gold Medal water.

Roaring Judy Ponds—
Don't be too skeptical about your chances of pulling trophy-sized fish from a couple of small ponds beside the East River. Alan Schneider, a student at Western State College in Gunnison, pulled a record 30 lb., 8 oz. brown trout from one of the ponds in March 1988. The ponds are connected by drainages to the hatchery, but the state wildlife officer swears the record-breaking fish did not come from there. At any rate, the ponds are fed by warm spring water and do not freeze during winter. Fishing for small rainbows is generally quite good. From Crested Butte head about 13 miles south on Hwy. 135. At the Roaring Judy Hatchery, cross over the East River and follow the signs.

Taylor Park Reservoir—
If a beautiful location is any consideration, you should definitely try fishing here. And the tremendous views are not all: you can catch ample numbers of good-sized rainbows, browns, mackinaws and even kokanee salmon at this superb Colorado

fishery. Located in the shadow of the jagged Sawatch Range, the enormous Taylor Park Reservoir is best early or late in the day. If you are fishing from the shore, your best bet will be to try in early spring when the fish seek out shallow, ice-free water. Rental boats, fishing supplies and licenses can be found at the **Taylor Park Boat House;** call ahead for information and advice on current fishing conditions **(303) 641-2922.**

Taylor River—

Runoff from the Elk and Sawatch mountains is stored in Taylor Park Reservoir and escapes ice-cold from the bottom of the dam. Above the reservoir the Taylor teems with rainbows, brooks and browns to 10 inches. Forest Rd. 742 follows the Taylor upstream for 22 miles. Below the reservoir difficult wading requires concentration, because the river bottom consists of smooth, round rocks and sudden, deep pools. Be sure to watch for private property markings. Even so, more than half of the water remains open to the public and nine forest service campgrounds lie next to some of the best stretches. Fishing for browns, brooks and rainbows can be good with large nymphs and select lures. Try throwing a line in the large pools near the bridge just below Taylor Park Dam.

FOUR-WHEEL-DRIVE TRIPS

Schofield Pass—

See the **Redstone and Crystal River Valley** chapter.

Taylor Pass—

For a quick, highly scenic trip over to Aspen and the Roaring Fork Valley you might try this treacherous route. It can be snow-covered into the summer, so be sure to get updated conditions from the National Forest Service.

Taylor Pass, at 12,400 feet, was built as an important supply route to the booming Aspen area in the 1880s. Now the connection is less important, but the views north to the Roaring Fork Valley and Hunter

Fryingpan Wilderness Area are far reaching. Did we forget to mention the tremendous view south into Taylor Park?

To reach the pass from Gunnison, head north on Hwy. 135 for 11 miles to Almont and then turn left on County Rd. 742, which heads up the Taylor River. Follow the road to Taylor Park Reservoir. A mile or so beyond Lakeview Campground, turn left, following the reservoir shoreline and heading upriver all the way to Dorchester Campground. The road gets rough from here. Once to the summit of Taylor Pass, follow Express Creek to Ashcroft in the Castle Creek Valley. Head down the road about 15 miles to Hwy. 82 near Aspen. For a scenic return to Gunnison, turn left on Hwy. 82, and proceed to Carbondale, then head up the Crystal River over McClure and Kebler passes (see the Scenic Drive section) to Crested Butte and back to Gunnison.

Tincup Pass—

If you want to cross over the Sawatch Range on this early stagecoach route, see the Four-Wheel-Drive Trips section of the **Upper Arkansas Valley** chapter.

GOLF

Dos Rios Golf Club—

Located in a great setting, this semi-private club at the confluence of the Taylor River and Tomichi Creek provides far-reaching views. Water is the key to this course— it comes into play on 17 holes. Especially tough is the relatively young front nine, which still needs some maturity. Open to the general public in summer. Moderate greens fees. Pro shop, carts and club rentals. Located 2 miles west of Gunnison, just south off Hwy. 50; **(303) 641-1482.**

Skyland Resort—

Designed by Robert Trent Jones, Jr., this fine 18-hole course has a short history and a long reputation. Open since 1984, Skyland has already been judged among the top mountain courses in the nation. Enjoy the spectacular mountain views from its position at the base of Mount Crested

Butte. If you're able to stay out of the numerous sand traps, you may be able to enjoy the scenery. Besides a pro shop and a restaurant, Skyland features a full health club with indoor tennis and racquetball facilities. **Country Club Dr. #1, Mount Crested Butte, CO 81224; (303) 349-6129.**

HIKING AND BACKPACKING

Deep canyons, lush meadows, streams, lakes and ghost towns can be easily found in **Gunnison National Forest** and nearby wilderness areas. Narrowing down the long list of hiking possibilities is especially difficult, simply because there are good trails crisscrossing virtually the entire county. Huge quantities of public land can be easily accessed from both Gunnison and Crested Butte. For maps and further information, visit the **Taylor River/Cebolla District Forest Service Office, 216 N. Colorado St., Gunnison, CO 81230; (303) 641-0471.**

Cement Creek Trail—

A veritable trail system leads away from different points along Cement Creek and into the mountains of this little-known mountain valley. The one we have chosen is an excellent, short hiking loop that begins on Trail 409, only a mile up the Cement Creek Valley. The trail leads quickly uphill toward a large rock outcropping with a couple of deep caves. Just above the caves, the trail splits in two. The left branch of the trail continues uphill to an aspen-cloaked ridge and a number of longer trail possibilities. The right fork leads east across the forested mountainside, eventually reaching Walrod Gulch. Walrod is a seldom-driven four-wheel-drive road that heads back down to Cement Creek a couple of miles upstream from your starting point.

Cement Creek is located 7 miles south of Crested Butte off Hwy. 135. Turn east onto Cement Creek Rd., which leads up the valley to a number of trail access points and a shaded campground. Trail 409 begins directly across from the Cement Creek Guard Station, 1 mile from Hwy. 135.

Copper Creek and Conundrum Trails—

These trails have it all: beautiful scenery, a ghost town, natural hot springs and, consequently, heavy use. If your goal is to get away from other humans, try someplace else. Don't underestimate these strenuous backcountry hikes. An overnight stay is the best way to experience Conundrum Trail. It's also quite possible to hike to Conundrum Hot Springs one day and on to Aspen the next. To reach the trail, drive to Crested Butte Ski Area and continue 7 miles north to the ghost town of Gothic (see the Scenic Drives section). A half-mile upstream from Gothic catch the Judd Falls/Copper Creek trailhead. After the overlook to the falls and a short rest on the bench dedicated to Judd, follow about 8 miles northeast up Copper Creek Trail to a junction just before Copper Lake. The right fork is Conundrum Trail; the left fork heads over East Maroon Pass toward Colorado's best-known mountains. See the Hot Springs section of the **Aspen** chapter for more information.

Curecanti Creek Trail—

See the Hiking section under Major Attractions.

Forest Service Trail #401—

This trail leaves from north of Crested Butte—at Gothic—and soon offers tremendous above-timberline views along its 6-mile route to the top of Schofield Pass. Leave a car near Gothic and take a one-way hike. For more information see Gothic Trails write-up in the Mountain Biking section.

Mill Creek Trail—

This short 1.5-mile trail cuts between steep valley walls and through a thick conifer forest before ending in a grassy meadow at the edge of the West Elk Wilderness Area. The watery sounds of Mill Creek provide a soothing background for a picnic or a nap. Bring along your fishing pole, too.

For serious backcountry exploration of the West Elk Wilderness Area, the Mill Creek Trail provides a little-used access. The trail continues from the wilderness boundary into a scenic area, with views to the volcanically formed Castles and to West Elk Peak (13,035 feet). A 14-mile route takes you over Storm Pass (12,440 feet), which is steep going on both sides. On an autumn hike you'll be able to enjoy the changing colors, but wear bright clothing and beware of hunters. From Gunnison drive 17 miles north up the Ohio Creek Valley on County Rd. 730 to the Mill Creek turn-off. Turn left and follow Mill Creek 4 miles on a fairly good dirt road (Forest Rd. 727; two-wheel-drive vehicles are fine) until reaching a dead end where the trail begins.

Timberline Trail—

Enjoy superb views of Taylor Park Reservoir while hiking on a level contour averaging over 10,000 feet in elevation, just beneath the snow-streaked peaks of the Sawatch Range. This is a perfect trail for extended trips. The trail is fairly easy and passes many small but fishable lakes and streams along its route. Timberline Trail traverses several roads and has a number of marked access points. From Taylor Park Reservoir take Cumberland Pass Rd. southeast to the ghost town of Tincup. Follow E. Willow Creek Rd. 2 miles east to Mirror Lake. The trailhead begins just below Mirror Lake Campground. Another good idea would be to pick up Timberline Trail as it crosses Cottonwood Pass Rd.

HORSEBACK RIDING

Fantasy Ranch—

Custom horseback adventures can be arranged for all abilities and time frames. Try a "get acquainted" ride, or a breakfast or dinner ride. Their specialty is a three-day ride over Pearl Pass to Aspen. Three locations in town and on the outskirts. For information contact **PO Box 236, Crested Butte, CO 81224; (303) 349-5425.**

RIVER FLOATING

The character of the rivers flowing into the Gunnison Basin has been altered forever by several monolithic reservoirs. Nonetheless, excellent stretches still entice rafters and kayakers for short runs. A couple of river outfitters in the area will take you on a quiet family float or a whitewater odyssey.

Lower Gunnison—

This stretch of water below the national monument will take you into remote sections of the Gunnison Gorge. See the **Black Canyon Country** chapter.

Upper Gunnison—

One mile downstream from Almont, open canoes, rafts and kayaks put in for the fairly gentle trip downriver. The wide river flows unobstructed through the town of Gunnison, all the way to the fringe of Blue Mesa Reservoir. The only rapids in this mild stretch result from the spring thaw. The river passes through a rural setting of pasturelands and country homes. Unfortunately for river enthusiasts, the free-flowing water doesn't last long enough. Beginning 5 miles below the town of Gunnison, large dams force the water into lakes for the next 45 miles.

Taylor River—

The water rushing out of Taylor Park Dam tumbles downstream through the deep canyon. The fast water is ideal for experienced kayakers who can handle Class II to Class V water. The path of the river is followed by Hwy. 306; many developed campgrounds and access points can be found along its entire run from the dam to Almont. The dam tends to lengthen the season by holding water back during runoff and slowly releasing it into the fall.

Outfitters—

C.B. Rafting—309 Gothic Rd., Crested Butte; (303) 349-7423.

Scenic River Tours—703 W. Tomichi Ave., Gunnison; (303) 641-3131.

SKIING
CROSS-COUNTRY SKIING

Whether you are into telemarking or just gliding along in solitude, any number of trail choices entice you into the backcountry. Mount Crested Butte is known for its throngs of devoted telemark skiers. Several broad alpine valleys leading from Crested Butte provide safe and easy passage. More adventuresome skiers can test their limits on the ridges and slopes. For maps and further information, visit the **Taylor River/Cebolla District Forest Service Office, 216 N. Colorado St., Gunnison, CO 81230; (303) 641-0471.**

Backcountry Trails—

Gothic—Tracks are set each year to the ghost town of Gothic (see the Scenic Drives section). It's an easy 7-mile tour from Crested Butte, with tremendous views along the way. Ski tracks usually continue beyond Gothic and into the upper valley.

Pearl Pass—Skiing over Pearl Pass to Aspen has long been a favorite of experienced skiers. This route is strenuous, isolated, dangerous and exceptionally beautiful. The Braun Hut System allows for a warm overnight stay during the long trek (see the **Aspen** chapter). Check with the folks at the Alpineer in Crested Butte for more information.

Groomed Trails—

Crested Butte Nordic Ski Center—Located at the Crested Butte Athletic Club in the downtown historic district, this complete facility offers rentals, lessons, advice, a 20-kilometer groomed track and, most important, a hot tub and sauna. Open daily 9 am–4 pm. **2nd and Whiterock Ave.; (303) 349-1707.**

Ski Rentals—

The Alpineer—419 6th St., Crested Butte; (303) 349-5210.

DOWNHILL SKIING

Crested Butte —

Soaring above its namesake town, Crested Butte Mountain appears as an intimidating pinnacle. It's only after you take your first chairlift ride that the mountain begins to reveal its true diversity. Just enough gentle, rolling terrain makes this a wonderful place to learn the sport. With more than half the groomed trails rated blue, the area is especially suited to intermediate skiers. This a great place to perfect your turns, before even thinking about extreme skiing.

Without a doubt, only true experts can take advantage of the entire mountain. As one local said, "Crested Butte has all the expert terrain that a sane person needs." Experts flock to the double black diamonds of the North Face, which offer some of the best "steep and deep" powder anywhere. Untamed and ungroomed, this 400-acre preserve provides a place for radical skiers to find some adventure—that means chutes, powder bowls, cliffs and glades. The North Face ventures very close to a helicopter skiing experience. A unique early ski season promotion provides free lift tickets for all skiers! Ask about this. For more information contact **Crested Butte Mountain Resort, 12 Snowmass Rd., PO Box A, Crested Butte, CO 81225; (303) 349-2333.**

SNOWCAT/HELI SKIING

Two thousand feet of untracked powder await you on the ridge behind the Irwin Lodge (see Where to Stay).

SWIMMING

Dos Rios Golf and Swim Club—

Pool, restaurant, bar and golf course are open to all visitors during summer. Follow the signs from Hwy. 50 just west of Gunnison; **(303) 641-1482.**

Gunnison Sport and Fitness—

A large pool is open to the public. Located a half mile north of Gunnison off Hwy. 135; **(303) 641-3751.**

TENNIS

Crested Butte—

In the center of the **town park** there are three outdoor courts. No lights; no fee.

Gunnison—

Check out the courts at **Char Mar Park.** No lights; no fee.

--------- **SEEING AND DOING** ---------

MUSEUMS

The Pioneer Museum in Gunnison—

One thing to be said about this museum is that there are a lot of big exhibits. Big, you ask? Yeah, big. How about the first post office in Gunnison, a schoolhouse built in 1909, the Denver & Rio Grande Railroad depot, Narrow Gauge Railroad Engine #268 and the old Mears Junction water tank. The Pioneer Museum also displays old photos, furniture and other artifacts that sufficiently convey pioneer life in the valley. Open Memorial Day–Labor Day, Mon.–Sat. 9 am–5 pm, closed Sun. Located at the **east end of Gunnison on Hwy. 50; (303) 641-4530.**

NIGHTLIFE

Idle Spur—

This popular hangout features a spacious log-encased room, long bar, varieties of freshly brewed beer and unpretentious atmosphere. It all seems to fit perfectly in this town. Lunch and dinner served. **226 Elk Ave., Crested Butte; (303) 349-5026.**

Kochevar's—

It's tough to beat Kochevar's for a lively crowd, good bands and reasonable prices. And besides, with pool tables, dart boards and a shuffleboard table, there is something for everyone. This place has enjoyed a long history of illicit entertainment—the upstairs was once a notorious bordello. Bar menu served. **127 Elk Ave., Crested Butte; (303) 349-6745.**

The Rafters—

Don't miss the great après ski scene that starts just as the lifts begin closing. On sunny days the deck stays packed from lunch till dusk. During ski season live bands get the house rockin'. Located in Mt. Crested Butte right at the base of the ski area in the upper level of the **Gothic Building, Crested Butte; (303) 349-2299.**

SCENIC DRIVES

Alpine Tunnel—

The Alpine Tunnel, constructed by the Denver South Park & Pacific Railroad (DSP&P) in 1881, is an engineering marvel. The 1,800-foot-long tunnel was bored through the Continental Divide in a race with the Denver & Rio Grande Railroad to provide railroad service to the Gunnison area. Working conditions were miserable, and the labor turnover was rumored to have totaled more than 10,000 men. Once completed, the tunnel proved very expensive to maintain, prompting the DSP&P to abandon the line in 1910. Even though the west portal of the tunnel caved in a number of years ago, remnants of many buildings and a water tower remain along the drive. Just above the water tank is what's left of Woodstock, a train workers' boardinghouse destroyed in an 1884 avalanche that killed 13 people.

To reach the Alpine Tunnel from Gunnison, head east on Hwy. 50 for 12 miles to Parlin. Turn left, heading north up along Quartz Creek to Ohio City and then Pitkin. About 3 miles beyond Pitkin, the marked road to the Alpine Tunnel turns off to the right. Follow this rough dirt road about 10 miles up to the west portal of the tunnel. A passenger car with good ground clearance can make the trip.

Black Canyon of the Gunnison—

See the **Black Canyon Country** chapter.

Cottonwood Pass—

See the **Upper Arkansas Valley** chapter.

Cumberland Pass/Taylor Park Loop—

For a firsthand look at Gunnison area history and some outrageous scenery, take this drive. You'll visit Quartz Creek, Tincup and Taylor Park mining districts, all of which brought settlers into the area in the late 1870s. Cumberland Pass, at just over 12,000 feet, is one of the highest dirt roads in the state and can be easily driven in a passenger vehicle.

The loop starts from Gunnison and can be done in one day, but you may want to take a few days and camp along the way. Head east on Hwy. 50 from Gunnison for 12 miles to Parlin, then north on the road leading up Quartz Creek. The first big area of interest is along Quartz Creek. **Ohio City** and **Pitkin** were centers for two large silver strikes in 1879 and 1880. Cumberland Pass Rd. begins climbing north out of Pitkin to its orange-colored summit. Built as a pack trail in 1880 to connect Tincup with the Quartz Creek camps, the pass has seen a lot of use over the years. From the summit you can look out on the massive, steep mountains of the Sawatch Range to the east and beyond Taylor Park to the north.

When you've seen enough, head down the pass to **Tincup.** Now a peaceful summer residence for a lucky few, Tincup was once a rough mining town that saw seven sheriffs killed within a period of a few months. The origin of Tincup's name is not completely clear, but many believe it comes from one of the original miners here who sifted through the gold-flaked gravel of the stream with his tin cup. People began prospecting here as early as 1859, but things didn't get hopping until 1879 when Tincup became the leading silver producer in the area.

Continuing north from Tincup, the road leads to **Taylor Park Reservoir** in Taylor Park. You can, however, head over the Sawatch Range on rugged Tincup Pass Rd. (see the Four-Wheel-Drive Trips section of the **Upper Arkansas River** chapter). There are plenty of campgrounds in the area and the trout fishing in the creeks and reservoir can be great. From the reservoir follow the Taylor River southwest through Taylor Canyon, eventually intersecting Hwy. 135, 11 miles north of Gunnison at Almont.

Gothic—

A trip to Gothic is easily worth the minimal effort it takes to get there. Located 7 miles north of Mount Crested Butte, this silver camp once boasted a population of thousands. Rich pockets of silver created much excitement but small returns. In 1880 the town received a visit from President Grant, who wanted a firsthand look at some Rocky Mountain mining camps. He traveled with Gov. Frederick Pitkin and ex-Gov. John Routt by mule team from Gunnison. Grant distrusted mule drivers and therefore insisted on holding the reins for most of the trip. By 1885 the Sylvanite Mine could no longer stay open and Gothic began to wither away. Most of the old buildings are gone, but the site receives a lot of use in summer and fall from students of the Rocky Mountain Biological Laboratory. Gothic is also a jumping-off point for many popular hikes in the Maroon Bells–Snowmass Wilderness Area. To reach Gothic drive to Mount Crested Butte and continue north on scenic Forest Rd. 327 above the East River.

Kebler Pass—

In fall this ultimate foliage drive is highlighted by mountainsides of golden aspen. A graded dirt road winds past alpine meadows covered with wildflowers and dense forests; the West Elk Mountains and the Raggeds rise all around. With an elevation of about 10,000 feet, Kebler Pass never rises above treeline, but the views are far-reaching at times. About 7 miles after reaching the summit, a left turn onto Forest Rd. 706 will land you at Lost Lake. The road can be rough, but is passable by all vehicles. Lost Lake is ideal for a lazy afternoon picnic or an overnight stay at the small campground.

To reach Kebler Pass from Crested Butte, take County Rd. 12 from the west end of town. The road continues for about 24 miles before intersecting Hwy. 133 at Paonia Reservoir. From here you can take a right and drive over McClure Pass (8,755 feet) before dropping into the beautiful Crystal River Valley.

Lake City—

The 55-mile drive south to Lake City on Hwy. 149 gets progressively more beautiful after you pass through the barren hills near Blue Mesa Reservoir. Soon the San Juan Mountains introduce themselves dramatically as the road continues beside the Lake Fork of the Gunnison. Situated in the narrow river valley is the small town of Lake City, named for its setting only 2 miles from spectacular Lake San Cristobal. The area is better known for the grotesque antics of cannibal Alferd Packer. For more information see the Lake City section in the **Creede** chapter.

Marshall Pass—

One of the lowest passes over the Continental Divide, Marshall Pass was the route the Denver and Rio Grande Railroad chose when extending service to the Western Slope. Tracks were laid over this 10,846-foot pass in 1881. A train robbery took place at the pass in 1902. The inept outlaws couldn't blow open the safe (they blew up just about everything else), so they robbed the passengers, though not before the travelers were able to hide most of their valuables under seats and in petticoats. The railroad is long gone, but the dirt road follows the railroad grade up and over the pass.

From Gunnison head east on Hwy. 50 for 32 miles to Sargents. An old stagecoach stop, Sargents was later a railroad depot for cattle and ore from mines in the area. Just east of the town's gas station, the Marshall Pass road turns right. Once at the summit of the pass, continue on the road past O'Haver Lake to Hwy. 285. Turn left at the highway, heading north over Poncha Pass to the intersection with Hwy. 50 at Poncha Springs. From here turn left on Hwy. 50 and head over Monarch Pass back to Gunnison.

—————— WHERE TO STAY ——————

ACCOMMODATIONS
CRESTED BUTTE

Crested Butte offers a wide choice of accommodations, from spiffy condos to a variety of bed and breakfasts. You'll also find a large number of cabin rentals favored by fishermen and rafters, at Almont, halfway between Gunnison and Crested Butte where the East and Taylor rivers merge to form the mighty Gunnison. Try the cabins at **Three Rivers Resort ($$$); (303) 641-1303.** If you want to stay in a deluxe hotel right on the ski mountain try the **Grande Butte Hotel ($$$ to $$$$)** at **(303) 349-4000. Crested Butte Mountain Resort** can reserve rooms at about 90% of area properties: **1-800-544-8448.**

Crested Butte Club—$$$ to $$$$

Reserve one of the seven bedrooms at this exclusive inn and you will enjoy modern comfort and Victorian style during your entire stay. This National Historic Landmark, built in 1886 as the Croatian Social Club, has more than its share of history. The false-fronted inn in old Crested Butte belies the plush interior. All of the spacious rooms at the Club are filled with high-quality antiques or reproductions—each features a sitting area with a fireplace. One suite is dominated by a brass chandelier, which casts a romantic glow over a four-poster bed. All of the elegant rooms also feature conveniences such as deluxe private bathrooms with his and her pedestal sinks, cable TV with remote control and phones. Guests have free access to the on-site athletic club with weight machines, indoor lap pool, whirlpools and steam rooms; guests receive discounts on spa services, such as massages. No smoking; children discouraged; some minimum stay requirements. **512 Second St., PO Drawer 309, Crested Butte, CO 81224; (303) 349-6655.**

Christiana Guesthaus Bed and Breakfast—$$$

A casual atmosphere pervades this 20-room European-style ski lodge. Built with comfort in mind, there are many common areas to enjoy. English owners Rosie and Martin Catmur have made some nice upgrades to all the Cristiana's rooms—each has a private bath. Perhaps the best feature of the lodge is the outdoor hot tub with views to Mount Crested Butte. A hearty breakfast is served each morning. **621 Maroon Ave., PO Box 427, Crested Butte, CO 81224; 1-800-824-7899 or (303) 349-5326.**

Irwin Lodge—$$$

This 22-room self-contained lodge offers a perfect means to experience the isolated beauty of the Elk Mountains. Located a scant 12 miles from Crested Butte, it remains a world away. Irwin Lodge is a year-round destination offering as much to guests in summer as in winter. But winter, when an average year drops over 30 feet of snow, is the time for spectacular downhill skiing on the ridge behind the lodge. Since the nearest plowed road is 10 miles away, the only way to reach Irwin Lodge in winter is by snowcat, snowmobile or skis. Take the lodge's snowcat to the ridge for the chance of a lifetime: 2,000 vertical feet of virgin powder. A maximum of 40 skiers at a time take runs down various bowls suited primarily to intermediate and expert skiers. Cross-country trails start at the front door.

Once at the lodge you'll enjoy the open feeling of the lobby with its massive fireplace and heavy wooden beams. The small lodge rooms are pretty basic, but you didn't come to Irwin to stay locked in a room. A family-style restaurant, a bar and a hot tub round out the lodge amenities. For reservations and information: **PO Box 457, Crested Butte, CO 81224; (303) 349-5308.**

The Nordic Inn—$$ to $$$

At the base of the ski mountain this 25-room inn aptly reflects the warmth of the owners. Each room has two double beds, cable TV and a private bathroom. The common room really shines at this Norwegian-style lodge. Chairs are grouped around the fireplace, providing a relaxing après-ski environment. Kids stay free. **PO Box 939, Crested Butte, CO 81224; (303) 349-5542.**

GUNNISON

The Inn at Arrowhead—$$$ to $$$$

In a beautiful, secluded location between Cimarron and Lake City, you will find this exclusive preserve, surrounded by vast stretches of public forest land. This Inn combines the best attributes of a plush hotel with all the activities of a dude ranch. Those who appreciate a quiet setting with just-out-the-door access to cross-country skiing, hiking, horseback riding, mountain biking and fishing will love this place. Snowmobiling is big here, too—some guests like to ride to Lake City for the day. In summer Lake City can be reached along a rough four-wheel-drive road. The first-class rooms in the contemporary, solidly built lodge all have southwestern touches, fireplaces, private baths and ample space. Check out the sundeck balcony with its hot tub. Downstairs you'll find a large screen TV, bar and an excellent on-site restaurant (breakfast included in the room rate). Call for directions and reservations. **21401 Alpine Plateau Rd., Cimarron, CO 81220; 1-800-654-3048 or (303) 249-5634.**

The Mary Lawrence Inn—$$$

This B&B is worth telling your friends about. Located in a prime location just off the Western State College campus, the Mary Lawrence Inn provides natural warmth and chemistry. The huge, stately looking house looks like a bed and breakfast from the minute you drive up. Built in 1885, it seems appropriate that its four rooms (plus one suite) are filled with antiques. After a good night's sleep, you won't be disappointed by a full breakfast in the common dining room. The back porch of the B&B leads to a small yard and wood deck. Children welcome; no smoking. **601 North Taylor, Gunnison, CO 81230; (303) 641-3343.**

Gold Creek Inn—$$ to $$$

See Where to Eat for more information about this Ohio City restaurant and B&B.

Comfort Inn Water Wheel—$$

There are 65 rooms at this comfortable motel. Half of the rooms have air conditioning; all have cable movies. Tennis court and exercise room. Take Hwy. 50 west of town for 1.5 miles. **PO Box 882, Gunnison, CO 81230; (303) 641-1650.**

Cattlemen Inn—$

If you are on a tight budget and just want a place to sleep, try the low-cost rooms at the Cattlemen Inn. The rooms are simple, small and stuffy. With the money you save, you can buy a tender steak at the restaurant just down the hall. **301 W. Tomichi Ave., Gunnison, CO 81230; (303) 641-1061.**

CAMPING

In Gunnison National Forest—

Crested Butte Area—Cement Creek Campground can be reached by heading 7 miles south of Crested Butte on Hwy. 135. Turn east onto Cement Creek Rd. and travel 4 miles up the valley to the shaded campground. Thirteen sites; no fee. **Irwin Campground** enjoys a beautiful location west of Crested Butte. Take Hwy. 2 for 7 miles west of Crested Butte to the Lake Irwin turn-off and proceed north on Forest Rd. 826. There are 32 tent and trailer sites; no fee. **Avery Peak Campground** is located just north of Gothic, 7.4 miles north of Crested Butte by Forest Rd. 317. Ten sites; no fee. **Gothic Campground** is another half mile up the road. Four sites; no fee.

Lake Fork of the Gunnison—Campgrounds south of Hwy. 50 get much less use than those areas to the north. To reach **Red Bridge** and **Gateview** campgrounds drive 25 miles south on Hwy. 149 from the eastern end of Blue Mesa Reservoir to a turn-off with a sign noting Red Bridge 2 miles. Keep an eye peeled for bighorn sheep during the short drive. **Red Bridge Campground** has 12 sites and no fee. Another 5 miles down a rough dirt road through a narrow canyon is **Gateview Campground.** There are 7 well-placed tent sites above the road and no fee.

Taylor River Area—North of Gunnison there are a dozen popular campgrounds from Almont, upstream on Taylor River Rd., to Taylor Park Reservoir. Well known among trailer and RV campers, these areas fill up early; fee charged. The camping areas are scattered along the shaded river banks and up above the reservoir.

Curecanti National Recreation Area—

See the Major Attractions section.

Private Campgrounds—

The Gunnison area offers six private campgrounds with hookups, showers, etc. There are no private campgrounds in Crested Butte.

KOA Gunnison—Get comfortable at this cushy campground near the Gunnison River. One mile west of Gunnison on Hwy. 50, turn south and follow the signs for a half mile. **(303) 641-1358.**

WHERE TO EAT

CRESTED BUTTE

The small, historic district of Crested Butte has a surprising number of excellent restaurants that have been here for years. They usually stay open year-round, excluding the spring mud season and late fall when many close for a few weeks.

Soupçon—$$$$

High expectations should accompany you upon entering this small log cabin on a back alley behind Kochevar's. Once inside, you will join a lucky group of people about to sample exceptional French food. The casual atmosphere belies the careful preparation in the kitchen. The menu is spelled out on a chalkboard; innovative poultry, lamb, beef and fish entrées are offered. On our visit a sampling of appetizers included duckling mousse, escargots Monaco and fresh scallops in caviar cream. This smoke-free restaurant is open nightly 6–10 pm. Reservations are a must. In the alley just behind Kochevar's Bar at **2nd St. and Elk Ave.; (303) 349-5448.**

Le Bosquet—$$$ to $$$$

For 11 years this fine French restaurant has served consistently excellent food with polished service. Le Bosquet is the place to enjoy a special meal in an elegant setting. The featured entrées come with complex and creative sauces. Some examples of the tempting dishes offered are grilled duck breast in a minted raspberry sauce, elk filets in a Bordelaise sauce, veal with a Roquefort basil sauce, and fresh salmon with a ginger glaze. A selection of appetizers and salads is also available. Reservations requested. Luncheon menu 11:30 am–2 pm during summer; dinner served nightly from 5:30 pm. **2nd St. and Elk Ave.; (303) 349-5808.**

Angello's—$$

Pizza, pasta, meatball sandwiches and antipasto salads are the order of the day at Angello's. Most locals agree that for inexpensive and great-tasting Italian food, Angello's is the place. The restaurant has recently expanded into the shop next door to satisfy even more hungry customers. In summer the outside deck offers a pleasing place to linger over lunch. The dinners come in full and half portions, including salad and homemade bread. Garlic bread with melted cheese is the perfect appetizer. The small bar area features TV sports. Delivery during winter. Open daily 5–9 pm. **501 Elk Ave.; (303) 349-5351.**

Donita's Cantina—$$

At the slightest craving for Mexican food, you should head straight to Donita's. Your hunger will be satisfied with enormous portions of spicy fare. If you're not very hungry, order à la carte. Specials of the house include beef or chicken fajitas; dinner quesadillas with shredded beef, chicken or veggies; and camarones (Gulf shrimp) sautéed in butter and garlic. Everything, including the sauces and salsa, is made fresh daily. The margaritas are excellent. Open seven nights a week 4:30–9:30 pm. Reservations not accepted. **330 Elk Ave.; (303) 349-6674.**

Karolina's Kitchen—$$

Though the restaurant is newer, the Kochevar building has enough history to fill this book. Take a look around the dining room at the various antique contraptions, including the still used to provide jugs of moonshine during Prohibition. Large sandwiches, salads and homemade soups make up the bulk of the menu. Also served: pork chops, peel-and-eat shrimp, knockwurst and sauerkraut, and a 24-oz. rustler's T-bone ($$$$). Open daily 11 am–midnight. **127 Elk Ave.; (303) 349-6756.**

The Bakery Cafe—$

Select from a long list of fresh-baked goods for a quick take-out, or enjoy a leisurely cappuccino while poring over the morning paper. You'll also find quiches, delicious homemade soups and sandwiches. This corner cafe gets hectic during the lunch rush in winter, but the food is worth the wait. Open daily 7:30 am–5 pm and until 8:30 pm during ski season. **308 Elk Ave.; (303) 349-7280.**

GUNNISON
The Gold Creek Inn—$$$ to $$$$

You wouldn't expect to find a five-star gourmet restaurant in a community of 44 people, but that's exactly what awaits in **Ohio City** (24 miles east of Gunnison). Built in an 1890s general store, the Gold Creek Inn has a tiny, fireside dining room. Chef/owner Joe Benge was trained at the prestigious Culinary Arts Institute in Hyde Park, New York—and you can watch him work his magic. Because fresh ingredients are emphasized, daily specials appear on a chalkboard menu. In the cozy atmosphere of the restaurant, the succulent food seems to taste even better.

This restaurant is worth going out of your way for—but be sure to reserve well in advance because Joe is often booked solid. Dinner is served 5:30–10 pm Tues.–Sat. from May–Oct. As a quiet bed and breakfast alternative, consider staying overnight in one of his two guest rooms ($$ to $$$). It's quite nice. To get here from Gunnison, drive 12 miles east on Hwy. 50

to Parlin. Turn left and follow Quartz Creek Rd. 12 miles to Ohio City. **Box HH, Ohio City, CO 81237; (303) 641-2086.**

The Trough—$$$

As you may have gathered by the name, this is the place in Gunnison to "pig out" during the long summer months. This spacious, rustically tasteful restaurant and bar is known for monstrous slabs of prime rib, steak and beef ribs. Kevin Brown, the manager, assures us the large variety of seafood is flown in every other day. Try the pork Hawaiian, the shrimp and other surf and turf items. The not-so-ugly-duckling is served with The Trough's special orange glaze. Open May–Oct. only; 5:30–10:30 pm during the week and 5:30–11 pm on Fri. and Sat. One mile west of Gunnison on Hwy. 50.

Mario's Pizza—$ to $$

Mario's serves great pizza on white or whole wheat, thick or thin crust. You'll probably end up with enough left over for breakfast. The kitchen also prepares pasta dishes, calzones and a long list of reasonably priced sandwiches. Eat in the restaurant or take advantage of free delivery. Open seven days a week 11 am–11 pm. **213 W. Tomichi Ave.; (303) 641-1374.**

The Sidewalk Cafe—$

With breakfast and lunch items at reasonable prices, the seats are usually filled at this attractive little cafe. Lots of windows, plants and an outdoor wooden deck add considerably to the meal. For breakfast, egg dishes as well as "giant" pancakes are the specialties; sandwiches and burgers for lunch. Open Mon.–Fri. 5 am–3:30 pm, Sat. 5 am–2 pm, closed Sun. **113 W. Tomichi Ave.; (303) 641-4130.**

———————— SERVICES ————————

Central Reservations—
Crested Butte Central Reservations—Box A, Mount Crested Butte, CO 81225; 1-800-544-8448.

Crested Butte Chamber of Commerce—
The Old Town Hall, PO Box 1288, Crested Butte, CO 81224; (303) 349-6438.

Day Care—
Butteopia Children's Program—They will take care of kids from ages 6 months to 6 years while you are on the slopes. A baby-sitting referral list is available. Located in

the Wetstone Building, PO Box A, Crested Butte, CO 81225; (303) 349-2209.

Gunnison County Chamber of Commerce—
Right next to the town park you'll find a helpful visitors center with information and advice on the entire area. **500 E. Tomichi Ave., PO Box 36, Gunnison CO 81230; 1-800-323-2453 or (303) 641-1501.**

Taxi—
Just Horsin' Around—29 Whiterock Ave., Crested Butte, CO 81224; (303) 349-9822.

Ouray

To get out and see the rugged, beautiful country around Ouray, the town's former mayor, Bill Fries (better known as country-western singer C.W. McCall), lays out three possibilities: "You can hike it if you've got the legs, ride it if you've got the horse, and jeep it if you have the nerve." One look at the mountains around town and you'll know what Fries is talking about.

Ouray is a quiet little Victorian community wedged tightly into a nook of the Uncompahgre River Valley. To the east and the west, colorful rock walls shoot hundreds of feet skyward; to the south, the famous Million Dollar Highway clings to a cliff high above the river, snaking its way up to Red Mountain Pass. This gravity-defying road makes up the most famous, and most nerve-wracking, stretch of the 236-mile San Juan Skyway, one of the western United States' scenic and historic drives (see the **Durango** chapter for more information).

Ouray's roots go back to the discovery of gold and silver deposits in the 1870s. Hardrock miners have left behind more than 10,000 tunnels, cuts and abandoned shafts within a 10-mile radius of Ouray. Dozens of old wagon roads lead to many of the mines, giving rise to another of Ouray's more recent claims to fame: fantastic jeeping. Drives over narrow, rough roads such as Engineer Pass, Imogene Pass and Black Bear Pass are not soon forgotten.

Summer is the big tourist season for Ouray, and a number of curio and souvenir shops on the main street suggest as much. Many colorful homes from the late 1800s have been carefully preserved; as a result, the town is a designated National Historic District. Hiking and camping in the nearby Uncompahgre National Forest are big draws. During the winter, when a heavy blanket of snow covers the San Juans, most shops in Ouray close and the day-to-day pace winds down. But winter is a great time to be in Ouray. Cross-country skiing on Red Mountain Pass is hard to beat, especially when followed by the activity Ouray is perhaps best known for—soaking in a hot springs pool. The town's many hot springs are soothing any time of year, but in winter, when steam rises from the water, it's just a bit more relaxing.

For its small size, Ouray offers plenty of great lodging. Unfortunately, though, it looks like the enormous old Beaumont Hotel, built in 1887, will stay boarded up forever. Even so, several well-kept Victorian homes have been converted into bed and breakfasts, and other places to stay are generally very pleasant.

Just 10 miles downriver from Ouray the Uncompahgre Valley widens and the San Juans serve as a dramatic backdrop. Here lies the historic

411

ranch supply and railroad center of Ridgway. This small town has a determined survival instinct despite many lean years and a 1950s plan to build a dam that would have completely submerged it. Today though, thanks to the opening of nearby Ridgway State Park, and a developer induced real-estate boom, Ridgway is thriving. Among the many transplants who now call the Ridgway area home are Ralph Lauren and Dennis Weaver (who has built an ecologically sound home—he calls it the "Earth Ship"—from scrapped tires, aluminum cans, beetle-killed wood, rocks and mud).

HISTORY

Long before prospectors led their heavily laden mules into Ouray, the Ute Indians cherished this spot on the Uncompahgre River for its hot springs. The town's namesake, Chief Ouray, spent much time here. Settlers named the town in honor of this great Ute who almost single-handedly averted inestimable bloodshed between Anglos and Utes during the twilight of the tribe's claim to western Colorado.

Mineral strikes in the Ouray area began in 1875. Although most of these early mines produced silver, one, called the Mineral Farm, yielded large chunks of gold, which were said to have been extracted from the ground using nothing more than hoes and shovels. The very first building in town was a saloon that did a hopping business. As with other mining settlements in the San Juans, Ouray's growth was hampered by its isolated location and the astronomical cost of transporting the ore. This problem was solved when Otto Mears built a cliff-hanging toll road (now called the Million Dollar Highway) up the wall of Uncompahgre Canyon to Red Mountain Pass south of town, connecting Ouray with Silverton. Wagons replaced mules for transporting ore, and Ouray began to boom. The first railroad arrived in Dec. 1887, further reducing shipping costs. Ouray became a crucial trading and transportation center for the surrounding mining camps and even then was attracting tourists. One of the town newspapers, the *Solid Muldoon,* was widely read and frequently quoted around the state. Its unusual format and sarcasm prompted even Queen Victoria of England to send for a subscription!

When the silver crash hit in 1893 and many mines closed down, Ouray lost its stride. But in 1896 an Irishman by the name of Thomas Walsh put Ouray-area mining back on track. Walsh had arrived in Ouray after suffering a huge loss in Leadville a few years earlier. He began to inspect the discarded piles of rock at local silver mines and discovered they were full of gold. This "dump grabber," as he was known to some, bought up a number of claims near Yankee Boy Basin, west of Ouray, and named them Camp Bird. Camp Bird went on to produce $20 million in gold before Walsh sold it in 1902 to an English group. Walsh then moved to Washington, DC, and gradually became part of the high society. His daughter, Evalyn Walsh McLean, talked her father into buying her the famous (but cursed) Hope diamond. The diamond's curse proved true when McLean lost her 9-year-old son in an auto accident and her 25-year-old daughter to a drug overdose. On top of all these tragedies, her husband was an adulterous alcoholic who eventually went insane. But we digress.

In the past mining, ranching and tourism have successfully sustained Ouray's economy. The silver crash in the early 1980s, brought on by the efforts of Texas' Hunt brothers to corner the market, prompted one former miner to tell us his one big wish is to see these brothers lynched. And with the closure of the Camp Bird, the last remaining mine in the area, all Ouray miners now find themselves forced to find other lines of work. Even so, the local economy seems to be perking along at a steady pace as more people learn of the beauty and serenity that can be found in the small town of Ouray.

GETTING THERE

Ouray is located 320 miles southwest of Denver. Travel west on Interstate 70 to Grand Junction, then south on Hwy. 50 to Montrose. Continue south on Hwy. 550 past Ridgway to Ouray. Another more scenic though slightly longer route is via Hwy. 285 south from Denver to Poncha Springs and then west on Hwy. 50. At Montrose head south on Hwy. 550 to Ouray.

———— FESTIVALS AND EVENTS ————

Cabin Fever Days
Presidents Day Weekend

A fun way to shake off the winter blahs is to join the Ouray locals for this homegrown festival. One of the highlights is the Chili Cookoff. Anyone can enter a favorite recipe, to be judged by an expert panel of chili connoisseurs. Recipes are rated on the basis of aroma, appearance, flavor and afterburn. Kids' events are held at the local ski hill, and there is usually a cross-country ski race for adults. For more information call **1-800-228-1876.**

Ouray Jeep Jamboree
late September

Maybe you'll feel a bit better about heading out on Ouray's many four-wheel-drive road as part of an organized caravan. During the peak of fall colors, this annual event provides a large number of outdoor adventures for individuals, families and groups. For information write **Jeep Jamboree USA, PO Box 1601, Georgetown, CA 95634** or the **Ouray Chamber** at **1-800-228-1876.**

OUTDOOR ACTIVITIES

BIKING
MOUNTAIN BIKING

Many old mining roads with beautiful scenery await your tracks. See the Four-Wheel-Drive Trips section for more ideas. A terrific ride for the entire family is **River Road,** a 10-mile dirt road with a mild gradient from Ouray to Ridgway along the basic path of the Uncompahgre. Have lunch or a snack in Ridgway and make the trip back. In Ouray, take 7th Ave. west and head north just after crossing the river. You can rent a bike, purchase a mountain biking map of the area and talk trails with Ed Carr, at **Downhill Biking, 722 Main; (303) 325-4284.**

FISHING

The streams near Ouray rush out of the mountains and join the Uncompahgre River on its way north. Between Ouray and Montrose the river flows through private land, but much of the fishing there is slow anyway. Some good high-country lakes are discussed in the **Silverton** chapter. You might try **Silver Jack Reservoir** northeast of Ouray. Silver Jack provides pretty good fishing for rainbow, particularly in the spring and fall. No motorized boats are allowed on the water. Take Hwy. 550 for 12 miles north turning east on Owl Creek Rd. (Forest Rd. 858) a couple of miles north of Ridgway. Continue about 20 miles to Silver Jack. The reservoir catches water from the West, Middle and East forks of the **Cimarron River,** all of which can be good for brook, cutthroat and rainbow trout. Some of the best fishing in the area, however, can be found at the recently opened **Ridgway State Park,** described below.

Ridgway State Park—

Located 10 miles north of Ouray next to Hwy. 550, this state park is widely considered the jewel of 'em all. Newly opened in the fall of 1989, Ridgway State Park offers spectacular views in the southern sky toward Dallas Divide. The reservoir's thickly forested shores provide a secluded mountain setting despite the nearby highway. Several developed state-of-the-art campgrounds are available (see Camping).

The entire project centers on water sports, including fishing, boating, windsurfing and swimming. Some people worry that heavy minerals carried by the Uncompahgre River might taint the fish in the reservoir. But, for the time being, the Division of Wildlife maintains that the fish are perfectly safe and any dangerous minerals have settled. Due to an intense stocking program and nitrogen-rich water, many rainbows have grown quickly to the 14- to 18-inch range. Along with the stockers, lunker browns from the Uncompahgre River have found a new home at the deep reservoir. If you still have questions, stop in at the visitors center or call **(303) 626-5822.**

FOUR-WHEEL-DRIVE TRIPS

"Ouray is to jeepers what Oahu is to surfers" states a newspaper article tacked to the wall of a local jeep tour office. And how true it is. For visitors to Ouray, especially those coming for the first time, a jeep trip on the network of old mining roads is a must. Via these exciting roads, often cut into cliffs with sheer drops of hundreds of feet, the area's mining history comes to the forefront. For those with steady nerves nothing can compare with the excitement, beauty and history of a trip over Black Bear and Engineer passes.

Black Bear Pass—

See the Four-Wheel-Drive Trips section in the **Silverton** chapter.

Corkscrew Road—

Drive south from Ouray on Hwy. 550 up to Ironton just before the summit of Red Mountain Pass. Turn left and follow the road south as it starts up Corkscrew Gulch. The narrow road winds up to the summit, which is covered with the same rocky red soil as nearby Red Mountain. From the summit you can return on the same road, or work your way east and then south near the ghost town of Gladstone and along Cement Creek Rd. (County Rd. 110), ending in Silverton. Return to Ouray on Hwy. 550.

Engineer Pass—

This incredible pass is part of the Alpine Loop Scenic and Historic Byway. See the Four-Wheel-Drive Trips in the **Creede, South Fork and Lake City** chapter.

Imogene Pass—

See the Four-Wheel-Drive Trips section in the **Telluride** chapter and the Yankee Boy Basin/Governor Basin write-up.

Ophir Pass—

See the Four-Wheel-Drive Trips section in the **Silverton** chapter.

Poughkeepsie Gulch—

Drive south from Ouray on Hwy. 550 for 4 miles and turn left on Engineer Mountain Rd. Three miles up the road, turn right and drive up through a basin. It would be wise to stop before the road crosses a treacherous rockslide.

Yankee Boy Basin/Governor Basin—

This is one of the best drives in the area, as it goes by mines, towering mountains and fields of wildflowers. The road begins just south of town on Camp Bird Rd. (County Rd. 361). Follow the road southwest up the valley through aspen and pine. After about 4 miles the road takes a frightening curve along a ledge blasted out of the canyon's rock wall. Another mile up the road, the famous Camp Bird Mine can be seen on the left (see the History section for more information). Follow the dirt road up to the old townsite of Sneffels. There is a fork here: the left road heads over Imogene Pass to Telluride (see the Four-Wheel-Drive Trips section in the **Telluride** chapter). Stay right past the Sneffels townsite and follow the steep, winding road up past Twin Falls and into immense

Yankee Boy Basin. In summer this wildflower-covered basin is transformed into a riot of color. Mt. Sneffels lies directly to the north and can be climbed via the ridge on its east side.

From Yankee Boy Basin a road heads off to the left, up a set of tight switchbacks into Governor Basin, site of the well-known Virginius Mine. The dramatic spires of St. Sophia Ridge are just to the southwest.

Rentals and Tours—

San Juan Scenic Jeep Tours—In business for more than 40 years, these folks are the ones to do your driving if you aren't up for it. They offer half- and full-day trips on some of the toughest roads around. For reservations and information, contact the office at **PO Box 290W, 480 Main St., Ouray, CO 81427; (303) 325-4444 or 1-800-325-0350.**

Switzerland of America Jeep Rentals—If you have four-wheel-drive experience and want to rent a jeep, contact Switzerland of America. They have jeeps seating from two to five people. Jeeps may be picked up the night before you set out. This company also offers Historic District tours, rafting, horseback rides and snowmobile rentals. **PO Box 780, 226 7th Ave., Ouray, CO 81427-0780; (303) 325-4484 or 1-800-432-5337.**

HIKING AND BACKPACKING

Rugged trails, wide-open mountain meadows, towering peaks, aspen glades, beautiful waterfalls and crashing streams can all be found near Ouray. Uncompahgre National Forest encircles town. Mountains rise to the west, leading into the Mt. Sneffels Wilderness Area. To the east, the Big Blue Wilderness Area offers beautiful hikes in valleys seldom used by other hikers. South of town, trails climb up into the heart of the old mining country. Many shafts, buildings and even an occasional aerial tram indicate the extent of activity that took place here 100 years ago. *As in other areas of the San Juans, use caution and PLEASE stay out of the mines!*

A good map of hiking trails in the Ouray area can be picked up at the visitors center next to the Ouray Hot Springs Pool. Topographical maps of the area can be purchased at **Big Horn Mercantile** at **609 Main St.; (303) 325-4257.** For additional information stop by the **Ouray Ranger District Office, 2505 S. Townsend Ave., Montrose, CO 81401; (303) 249-3711.**

Bear Creek Trail—

This is one of our all-time favorite trails. It begins south of town and heads east up along Bear Creek, on an old road that was built by miners with diggings in the area. The trail cuts into the steep canyon's rock wall high above the raging water. Mining history is so pervasive along the trail that you almost expect to see a miner coming around the next corner leading a burro weighted down with a load of ore. Volcanic intrusions are also visible from the trail.

After some initial switchbacks, the trail traverses high above the creek. Grizzly Bear Mine is visible after 2.5 miles and Yellow Jacket Mine after 4.2 miles. At Yellow Jacket Mine the trail forks, the left heading up to American Flats where you can take Horsethief Trail northwest, eventually ending up north of Ouray near the Bachelor-Syracuse Mine. The right fork heads up Bear Creek for 3 miles to the summit of Engineer Pass. From here you can turn around or try to bum a ride from a jeeper.

Parents should think twice about taking this trail with small children—the dropoffs to the creek along the first few miles of the trail are substantial, so why tempt fate? To reach the trailhead, drive 4 miles south on Hwy. 550 to the first tunnel. The trail begins on top of the tunnel.

Blue Lakes Trail—

This 4-mile trail to Blue Lakes leads into the beautiful Mt. Sneffels Wilderness Area and can be approached from two directions. Perhaps the most popular route is from Dallas Divide. From Ouray drive north to Ridgway and turn left onto Hwy. 62. Proceed about 5 miles and turn left onto East Dallas Creek Rd. (County Rd. 7). Go almost 9 miles to the gate at the wilderness area boundary and begin hiking south. A sign marks the trailhead.

The other approach is just south of town on the road to Camp Bird Mine. You can drive up to the mine with a regular passenger car, but if you have a four-wheel-drive vehicle it's possible to continue an additional 3 miles up into Yankee Boy Basin. From there hike up the basin to the northeast for 2 miles to the lakes.

Box Canyon Falls and Park—

Off Hwy. 550 just southwest of Ouray a torrent of water falls 285 feet into a narrow box canyon. This short trail provides views of the magnificent falls rushing through a fault in the quartzite rock. A rickety wooden pathway provides easy access to a misty viewpoint near the base of the falls. Allow about 15 minutes for a short but steep walk to a rocky overlook from a 1900s-era steel bridge spanning a narrow gap high above the waterfall. The view from atop the falls is wonderful. The city owns the land and access to this unusual geologic showpiece. Covered picnic tables and restrooms are available, but no overnight camping is allowed. Small fee. Open officially from mid-May–mid-Oct. For more information call **(303) 325-4464.**

Lower Cascade Falls Trail—

For people not yet used to the high altitude of Ouray, this half-mile trail provides an easy introduction. Starting at the east end of 8th Ave., the trail climbs gradually up to the base of the impressive Lower Cascade Falls, where water has cut deep into the mountain's sandstone wall. There are a couple of picnic tables along the way.

Upper Cascade Falls Trail—

Beginning at Amphitheater Campground just south of town, this trail (No. 213) heads 2.5 miles and 1,500 vertical feet up a series of switchbacks. The last half mile traverses the rock walls east of town, eventually crossing over Cascade Creek just below the falls. Just beyond the falls are the remains of the Chief Ouray Mine's boardinghouse and machine shop. The last mile or so is very steep, but the views down onto town and of the surrounding mountains are worthwhile. To reach the trailhead, drive south on Hwy. 550 to the entrance to Amphitheater Campground. A sign marks the trailhead.

Wetterhorn Basin Trail—

Located in the heart of the Big Blue Wilderness Area, Wetterhorn Basin Trail is a 5-mile hike that stays above treeline most of the time. The wide-open views to Wetterhorn Peak (14,015 feet) and Coxcomb Peak (13,656 feet) make this hike worth the effort.

To reach the trailhead from Ouray, head north on Hwy. 550 a couple of miles past Ridgway and turn right on Owl Creek Pass Rd. After crossing the summit of Owl Creek Pass, turn right on Forest Rd. 860 and proceed 5 miles to the trailhead (you will need a four-wheel-drive or high-clearance pickup truck for the last 1.5 miles).

ICE CLIMBING

When the many waterfalls in the Ouray area freeze in winter, out of the woodwork appear droves of that strange breed of winter recreationist ... ice climbers. Converging on the Ouray area, these serious thrill seekers search for an iced-over waterfall and, with pterodactyl-like axes in each hand and ice screws on their belts, they start their ascents. It's exciting to watch; if you want a lesson, inquire at the visitors center in Ouray or contact the **International Alpine School, Box 434, Ridgway, CO 81432; (303) 626-5722.**

ICE SKATING

A large 75- by 160-foot skating rink is set up each winter at the Box Canyon Falls & Park off Hwy. 550 just southwest of Ouray. Lights come on in early evening to make this an enchanting stop, day or night, for the entire family. Skates may be rented at the Ouray Hot Springs Pool. Rink hours: 8 am–10:30 pm. For information call **(303) 325-4464.**

SKIING
CROSS-COUNTRY SKIING

The magnificent backcountry skiing around Ouray is becoming better known each year. West of town toward the Mt. Sneffels Wilderness Area, a number of fine trails offer good views and very few people. Although avalanches are a serious consideration, the basins around Red Mountain Pass provide an almost limitless amount of ski terrain. As one Ouray local puts it, "Backcountry skiing around Red Mountain Pass is like playing on a 1,000-hole golf course—every hole is different, so just tee off and enjoy." If you are unfamiliar with the area and want to try skiing on Red Mountain Pass, be sure to inquire locally about avalanche danger or go out with an experienced trail guide. You can also call **(303) 247-8187** for current avalanche information in the San Juan Mountains.

Backcountry Trails—
East Dallas Creek Trail—This easy trail heads south, winding its way up 7 miles to the northern boundary of the Mt. Sneffels Wilderness Area. The lofty summit of Mt. Sneffels (14,150 feet) is laid out in front of you while you ski in through piñon, juniper and eventually spruce and fir forests. Private property lines the road for the first 5 miles, so stay on the trail. To reach East Dallas Creek Trail from Ouray, head north on Hwy. 550 for 10 miles to Ridgway and turn left on Hwy. 62. Drive about 5 miles, turn left again onto County Rd. 7 and follow the signs to Uncompahgre National Forest. Start skiing where the plowing stops.

Miller Mesa Trail—A good route for beginners to intermediates, Miller Mesa Trail rises above Ridgway, providing views of both the Sneffels Range and the Uncompahgre Valley. The trail heads south and then east up the mesa for 5 miles. From Ouray drive north on Hwy. 550 to Ridgway and turn left on Hwy. 62. At the west end of Ridgway turn left onto County Rd. 5, marked by a sign to the Girl Scout Camp. After a quarter mile, turn right and drive about 5 miles to Elk Meadows. Park where the plowing stops.

Red Mountain Pass—At the summit of the pass many people choose to ski the trees on the west side of the road. However, on the east side, US Basin offers what one local termed "the best backcountry skiing with road access in the country." In an isolated and dramatic setting near the basin, Chris and Donna George run the unique St. Paul Lodge. Chris, an avalanche expert, offers cross-country ski lessons along with his rugged accommodations. For more information about the lodge and other skiing opportunities on Red Mountain Pass, see the Outdoor Activities section in the **Silverton** chapter.

Groomed Trails—
Red Mountain/Ironton Park—On a shelf 4 miles below the top of Red Mountain Pass, the Ouray County Nordic Council has developed a marked trail system perfect for beginner and intermediate skiers. Nine miles south of Ouray on Hwy. 550, three trailheads leave the highway on a number of connecting loop trips. Trails wind through an historic mining area with signs identifying important sites. Local merchants carry a trail map to the area, or send a stamped envelope to the **Ouray County Nordic Council, PO Box 468, Ouray, CO 81427**

Rentals and Information—
Big Horn Mercantile—A large assortment of cross-country skis, boots and poles, including telemark equipment, can be rented here. **609 Main St.; (303) 325-4257.**

Downhill Biking—Despite its name, this place is a good bet for cross-country rentals and information. **722 Main; (303) 325-4284.**

TENNIS

Two public courts are located at the northwest end of town, adjacent to the hot springs pool. No lights and no fee.

———— SEEING AND DOING ————

BALLOONING

In Ridgway call **San Juan Balloon Adventures** at **(303) 626-5495.**

HOT SPRINGS

The healing waters of the area's natural hot springs were well known to Chief Ouray for their spiritual and medicinal qualities. After Chief Ouray and the Utes left the area, the town became known for its "radioactive" hot springs. Don't worry, the water isn't really radioactive, but geothermal waters continue to boil to the surface from deep inside the earth. You can't walk up Canyon Creek for a soak in a natural hot pot any longer, but four lodges in town have hot springs facilities; the large town pool offers an outdoor soak with spectacular views. Nine miles downriver in **Ridgway**, Orvis Hot Springs features a more natural environment.

Orvis Hot Springs—

Originally known for the Orvis Plunge pool built in 1916, Orvis Hot Springs now offers an exceptional variety of settings for enjoying the natural springs. The large outdoor pool with its sandy bottom and perfect water temperature has an added bonus: unobstructed views to the Sneffels Range. Filled by a cascade of steaming hot water, this pool is definitely the highlight; bathing suits are optional. If you are interested in soaking in hot water (on the verge of scalding), ease into the smaller stone tub. Inside there are four private tub rooms. Most families prefer splashing around in the wonderfully constructed indoor pool (bathing suits required). Massage therapists are available. If you want to spend the night, six spacious but simple rooms share two bathrooms ($$). Tent sites available for a small fee. Overnight guests do not pay extra for use of the hot springs. The pools are open to the public daily 10 am–10 pm; no curfew for overnight guests. Located 9 miles north of Ouray on Hwy. 550 (1.3 miles south of Ridgway). **1585 County Rd. 3, Ridgway, CO 81432; (303) 626-5324.**

Ouray Hot Springs Pool—

Life somehow makes sense while you're soaking in this hot spring's shallow 104° F pool and gazing up at the surrounding peaks. For swimming laps or cooling off, dive into the larger of the two pools. In winter large snowflakes fill the air and steam billows off the water, creating an almost mystical atmosphere. The hot springs entrance fee is good for the whole day, provided you get a hand stamp. After a fire in 1988, a complete workout room and new locker rooms were built. Some cool water pools have been added for your summer comfort. Also available are picnic tables, a playground and a running track. Kids love searching in the murky goldfish pond for crawdads. Open 10 am–10 pm Tues.–Sat. and 10 am–8 pm Sun. in summer; 12 am–9 pm Mon.–Fri. (except Tues. when the pool closes) and 10–9 pm, Sat.-Sun. in winter. Located on the north end of town just off **Hwy. 550; (303) 325-4638.**

Wiesbaden Hot Springs—

This well-known spa features a private outdoor tub with a roomy deck, enclosed by a redwood fence. Natural hot water cascades over a gentle rock waterfall before reaching the contoured Fiberglas tub. Day or night, it is a complete escape from the rest of humanity—unless of course you'd like to go there with a special friend. This tub is reserved by the hour; significant discount for Wiesbaden guests. See the Where to Stay section for more information. Located at the corner of **6th Ave. and 5th St., PO Box 349; (303) 325-4347.**

MINE TOUR

Bachelor-Syracuse Mine Tour—

A sure-fire way to get a feel for what brought people to the San Juan area more than 100 years ago is to take a tour of the Bachelor-Syracuse gold and silver mine. Featured in National Geographic, this mine tour could easily be the best in the state. Ride the "trammer" 3,350 feet back into this hardrock mine, first worked in 1884 by three bachelors. Closed after the silver crash in the early 1980s, the mine now offers daily tours during the summer months. A real miner acting as tour guide accompanies you deep into the mountain.

Actually, the hour-long tour is fascinating. You stop at a work site where the guide describes the whole hardrock mining process, from drilling dynamite holes to hauling ore out of the mine by trammer. He also compares today's sophisticated mining to the rudimentary methods and extremely dangerous conditions endured by miners in the 1800s. The tunnel is well lighted and ventilated. Be sure to bring a coat, as the temperature in the mine is a brisk 52° F. The mine site also offers a gift shop, gold panning and the "miner's outdoor cafe." A fee is charged. Be sure to take the tour before silver prices go back up and the mine reopens for the real thing. Open daily mid-May to mid-Sept.; closed July 4; hourly tours. To reach the mine, drive a mile or so north from Ouray on Hwy. 550. Turn right onto County Rd. 14 and follow the signs. **PO Drawer 380W, Ouray, CO 81427; (303) 325-4500.**

MUSEUMS AND GALLERIES

Ouray Historical Museum—

There is a lot to do in Ouray without heading inside to the confines of a museum. This special place, however, can give you a historical perspective as you visit room after room of quality displays. Victorian-era items rekindle the town's heyday: guns and bullets from the 1890s, Edison phonographs, bar tokens and hotel log books—even a piano with worn ivory keys from the Gold Belt Theatre. Since the ivory is worn through only in the key of C, it can be assumed that most patrons played by ear.

Upstairs you'll find several re-created hospital rooms, a general store and a legal office. Downstairs a fine collection of mining tools, including bellows, an ore train and tongs, is displayed next to the assayer's office. The museum is located inside the former St. Joseph's Hospital, which opened in 1887. Open daily 9 am–5 pm year-round. Minimal admission fee. **5th St. and 6th Ave.; (303) 325-4576.**

NIGHTLIFE

Chipita Opry Company—

A la Branson, Mo. this live musical stageshow with a bent for country, gospel and even rock-n-roll music, provides good clean fun for the whole family. No booze and no smoking inside the theater—"and no depressing songs," says owner and Elvis impersonator Gary Davis. The fast moving show lasts two hours. You'll love America by the time you leave. One show nightly; open from Memorial Day–October 15. **630 Main Street, Ouray, CO 81427; (303) 325-7354 and 1-800-356-8729.**

San Juan Odyssey—

If you are looking for something to do in Ouray at night, consider the San Juan Odyssey. It's an impressive computerized slide show of the San Juan Mountains done with 15 projectors, five screens and surround-sound. The London Symphony Orchestra performs the soundtrack. The show was put together by former Ouray mayor and country singer C.W. McCall (best known for "Convoy"). Most of the inspiring photos were taken by McCall and his family on their many trips around the San Juans. There are two shows nightly; a fee is charged. The box office is at the old Ouray Opera House at **5th St. and Main St.** in Ouray where the show is held. For information about group rates or special showings call **(303) 325-4746.**

SCENIC DRIVES

Dallas Divide—

This 25-mile stretch of road between Ridgway and Placerville is one of the most photographed in Colorado. From the top of the 8,970-foot divide, views to the Sneffels Range (high point: 14,150-foot Mt. Sneffels) and Uncompahgre and Wetterhorn peaks are stunning. To reach Dallas Divide from Ouray, head north on Hwy. 550 to Ridgway and turn left onto Hwy. 62 and continue for about 10 miles.

Million Dollar Highway—

Try as you will, there is absolutely no better vantage point for an auto trip deep into the San Juans than the Million Dollar Highway. This road winds up a glacial valley past once-thriving mines to the 12,217-foot summit of Red Mountain Pass. Towering peaks, elephantine mountain slopes, sheer cliff walls and thick stands of aspen and pine dominate the scenery.

The road was the result of Otto Mears's foresight. He understood that most counties were too poor to build roads to provide crucial economic links between the mining towns. Mears took it upon himself to build this road to connect Ouray with Ironton Park in 1883, and in time completed the route over Red Mountain Pass to Silverton. The narrow road had a tollgate located atop Bear Falls, which charged $3.75 per vehicle and $.75 per horse. (A mile and a half south of Ouray is a turnout to view the 227-foot waterfall.)

Debate continues over the origin of the name Million Dollar Highway. It is true that gold tailings were used in the original construction, but certainly not a million dollars' worth. Though the highway is said to have originally cost $40,000 per mile to build, a million-dollar price tag for the entire project would be too high. Another possibility involves a woman who traveled the road by stagecoach back in its early days. She exclaimed, "I wouldn't go back over that road for a million dollars!" Lastly ... the most probable and least colorful explanation is that it cost approximately $1 million to improve the road for automobile use.

The stagecoach is long out of service, but the Million Dollar Highway remains a breathtaking adventure. Take the 22-mile drive south on Hwy. 550 out of Ouray to the top of Red Mountain Pass, which eventually drops into historic Silverton. The entire route is easily completed in a passenger car.

San Juan Skyway—

This National Scenic and Historic Byway encompasses the most beautiful part of southwest Colorado. The Million Dollar Highway is just a part of the 236-mile route. For more information see the Scenic Drive section of the **Durango** chapter.

WHERE TO STAY

ACCOMMODATIONS

With its abundance of large Victorian homes and steady stream of visitors, Ouray may be the perfect place for people to operate bed and breakfasts. Here are a couple of top choices that are open year-round:

The **Manor ($$$)**, is a centrally located and beautifully renovated Georgian Victorian hybrid with a place on the National Historic Register. Your hosts, Joel and Diane, will make your stay a pleasant one. Their charming, three-story house features seven individually decorated guest rooms with private baths. **317 2nd St., Ouray, CO 81427; (303) 325-4574.** So you want southern hospitality and a generous breakfast to start your day? Joyce and Mike Manley offer eight rooms at **The Damn Yankee ($$$ to $$$$)**, their well-appointed, chalet style B&B with all the conveniences. All rooms have private entrances and bathrooms (telephones and cable TV, too). Check out the incredible view of the surrounding peaks from the third-floor sitting room. **100 Sixth Ave., Ouray, CO 81427; 1-800-845-7512.**

San Juan Guest Ranch—$$$$

Set in the Uncompahgre Valley just 4 miles north of Ouray, this small ranch is steeped in western tradition. The intimacy of the ranch is its highlight. Located in the midst of working ranches, the San Juan Guest Ranch fits in well with the rest. All of the buildings appear weathered and well used from the outside, but comfortably modern from within. Horseback riding on spectacular trails in the San Juan Mountains is the underlying emphasis at this ranch. You'll also be treated to a balloon ride, jeep tour and soak in the Ouray Hot Springs Pool. Consider staying here for a fall photo workshop or for cross-country skiing in winter. Meals included. **2882 Hwy. 23, Ridgway, CO 81432; (303) 626-5360.**

Mainstreet Bed and Breakfasts—$$$

Located on the east end of town at the start of the Million Dollar Highway, you'll find two B&Bs side by side. Lee and Kathy Bates had owned the 1898 House for years before purchasing the Mainstreet house next door. Both two-story houses have been thoroughly and lovingly renovated; now they are filled with antiques and offer a surprising number of choices for couples and families. All rooms have private bathrooms. Between the houses you'll find a courtyard and children's playground. A couple of highlights: the romantic Lilac Room with its private deck and incredible view of Twin Peaks; and, the Oak Creek Suite, which features a sunroom, kitchen and private deck. Families—up to six members—might also want to consider renting the self-sufficient southwestern style Chipeta Cottage out back. All are open May 15–Oct. 15. For reservations contact the Mainstreet B&Bs, **PO Box 641, Ouray, CO 81427; (303) 325-4871,** in winter call **(816) 665-0277.**

Wiesbaden Hot Springs Spa and Lodgings—$$$

Follow a stairway from the glass-enclosed lobby into the geothermal wonders of a hot mineral water vapor cave below. Guests receive free, unlimited use of the vapor cave, hot mineral outdoor pool, sauna and universal weight room. Available for guests at reduced fees is a private outdoor tub (see the Hot Springs section) and services such as professional massage, reflexology, acupressure treatment and facials. The rooms in the L-shaped motel are fairly standard, though some are equipped with kitchenettes; rooms in the main lodge building take on fanciful designs. The central lobby has a common seating room and free coffee and tea. For a special retreat ask about renting the rustic cabin on the hill above the lodge. It is heated by a wood stove, and the small porch offers a spectacular panorama of the surrounding mountains. The Wiesbaden offers special winter discounts. **Box 349, Ouray, CO 81427; (303) 325-4347.**

St. Elmo Hotel—$$ to $$$

Built by Kitty Heit in 1898 as a boardinghouse for miners, the St. Elmo has been transformed into a first-class bed and breakfast. The turn-of-the-century ambiance is tastefully preserved in each of the nine uniquely furnished rooms. Period antiques, touches of polished brass and stained glass are in abundance throughout the hotel. Some rooms come with elegantly appointed sitting rooms; families may reserve separate sleeping rooms linked by a common bath; for special occasions, the genteel refinement of the presidential suite is at your disposal. Light breakfasts are served in the sunny Kitty Heit Room. The caring attitudes of Sandy and Dan Lingenfelter are warmly reflected in their well-run hotel. **426 Main St., PO Box 667, Ouray, CO 81427; (303) 325-4951.**

Orvis Hot Springs—$$

See the Hot Springs section for information.

The Adobe Inn—$$

This small lodge is well named. Tile floors, adobe-style archways and wooden ceilings and furniture give the Adobe Inn a distinctive southwestern feel. Passive solar helps heat the place. Three rooms are available, with either bunk beds or a queen-sized bed in a room with views up the valley. Bathrooms are shared by all guests. Opened in 1987 by Joyce and Terre Bucknam, the Adobe Inn is a good value. Continental breakfast is served each morning. See the Where to Eat section for details about this fine restaurant. Located 10 miles north of Ouray in Ridgway. **651 Liddell Dr., Ridgway, CO 81432; (303) 626-5939.**

CAMPING

In Ridgway State Park—

High above Ridgway Reservoir, the **Dutch Charlie** area is dotted with low-lying pinon pine and sage. Spread out along driving loops are two highly developed campgrounds with nearly 200 sites (fee charged, hookups, flush toilets, showers and laundry facilities). According to Ranger Riddle, 144 sites are fully accessible for disabled people. About a dozen sites are reserved for tents. Campers at Dutch Charlie have easy access to a six-lane boat ramp and a separate swimming area along a sandy beach. An additional 100 developed sites can be found below the dam in the **Cow Creek** area. For reservations call **1-800-678-CAMP.**

In Uncompahgre National Forest—

Just a mile south of Ouray on Hwy. 550 is the turn-off for one of the most popular national forest campgrounds in the state—**Amphitheater Campground.** With fantastic views of the Sneffels Range and the Uncompahgre Valley, people don't want to leave. There is a seven-day limit and a fee is charged; 30 sites.

The other national forest campgrounds in the Ouray area are located quite a few miles northeast, near Silver Jack Reservoir. Drive about 2 miles north of Ridgway on Hwy. 550 and turn right on Owl Creek Pass Rd. (Forest Rd. 858). After crossing the pass, follow the road north along the Cimarron River to **Silver Jack Campground** at Silver Jack Reservoir. There are 60 sites and a fee is charged. Handicapped facilities are available. Continuing north on Forest Rd. 858 for 1 mile brings you to **Beaver Lake Campground** with 11 sites and a fee. Another half mile north is **Big Cimarron Campground** with 16 sites and no fee.

Private Campgrounds—

KOA Ouray—Located away from town in a quiet setting, KOA Ouray offers RV hookups, tent sites, a store and even jeep rentals. Open during summer only. To reach the campground from Ouray, drive 4 miles north on Hwy. 550 and turn left onto County Rd. 23. **Box J, Ouray, CO 81427; (303) 325-4736.**

Polly's Campground—Operating in conjunction with a motel, this campground offers all of your favorite amenities. Located just north of town on Hwy. 550. **Box 342, Ouray, CO 81427; (303) 325-4061.**

WHERE TO EAT

Bon Ton Restaurant—$$$

Carefully prepared northern Italian cuisine is the specialty of this highly regarded restaurant. The inception of the Bon Ton Restaurant dates back to the 1880s. The long history is still evident in the Victorian atmosphere of its intimate surroundings. Cut-glass booth dividers and exposed brick walls create personal spaces for all diners. You won't be disappointed by indulging in a rich pasta entrée. House specialties include beef Wellington and a selection of veal dishes. Try out the Bon Ton's Sun. champagne brunch ($$) beginning at 10 am; dinner is served each evening from 5 pm. Reservations are recommended. **426 Main St.; (303) 325-4951.**

The Adobe Inn—$$$

Joyce and Terre Bucknam serve up some of the most delicious and creative Mexican food you'll find anywhere in Colorado. Southwestern decor and South American music add rich atmosphere as you look out the windows at the surrounding mountains. Entrées include enchiladas served six different ways and superior chimichangas. Each dinner comes with chips and salsa, refried beans and tomal en elote (corn casserole). The Adobe Inn also has excellent margaritas and a selection of Mexican beers; a recently expanded bar area makes coming in for a cold one even more enticing. Dinner served 5:30–9:30 pm. Open year-round. Located 10 miles north of Ouray in Ridgway. **651 Liddell Dr., Ridgway; (303) 626-5939.**

The Outlaw—$$ to $$$

When the overpowering urge to savor a perfectly cooked steak comes over you, as it does with alarming frequency in the San Juans, head to the Outlaw. Choice cuts of aged Colorado beef are charbroiled and accompanied by salad, hot rolls, baked potatoes, seasonal vegetable and your choice of coffee or tea. This place also serves up a good selection of fish. Hefty portions are dished out in a casual western atmosphere with red checkered tablecloths, antique junk hanging on the walls and a pressed-tin ceiling. Hats hang everywhere—it all started when John Wayne left his here after a day of filming True Grit. The Outlaw offers a special outdoor chuckwagon barbecue cookout during the summer for a limited number of reservations. Lunch from 11:30 am–2 pm in summer only; dinner served nightly from 5 pm. **610 Main St.; (303) 325-4366.**

Pricco's—$

A classy yet casual feel invades this popular lunch and breakfast spot. The same family has owned the historic Pricco building since the late 1800s. Today the exposed brick is juxtaposed with an airy skylight and dark green tablecloths. A large selection of omelettes and egg dishes stands out on the breakfast menu. For lunch try a hoagie sandwich, Philly cheese steak, and/or homemade soup topped off with a fresh dessert. Beer and wine are served. Breakfast served daily 8–11 am, lunch 11 am–4 pm. **736 Main St.; (303) 325-4040.**

Silver Nugget Cafe—$

Each mountain town has a cafe that attracts a local crowd by worrying about the quality of the food and the friendliness of the staff. The recently remodeled Silver Nugget has an open kitchen and counter seating, as well as table service. The country-style food is served in generous portions for breakfast, lunch and dinner. Open year-round 6 am–9 pm daily. Closed at 8 pm in winter. **940 Main St.; (303) 325-4100.**

SERVICES

Ouray County Chamber of Commerce–

An excellent visitors center is located next to the Ouray Hot Springs Pool at the north end of town. **Box 145, Ouray, CO 81427; Call 1-800-228-1876** nationwide; **(303) 325-4746** locally.

Pagosa Springs

An author who visited Pagosa Springs in 1924 called the area a "Shangri-la ... a great retreat from the speakeasies, jazz and stock market of the real world." Today the stress factors of the "real world" are somewhat different (except for the stock market), but the sentiments still ring true.

Pagosa, a Ute word meaning "healing waters," gets its name from the hot mineral springs that were long coveted by the Indians. In addition to a unique collection of small pools in the town center, Pagosa uses geothermal water to heat many of its buildings.

The San Juan River crashes down from the Continental Divide to the northeast, making its way through Pagosa Springs and then down to Navajo Reservoir on the New Mexico border. A city park right in the town center features a pleasant river walk in addition to a playground and picnic area. The strongest plus of Pagosa Springs, however, has to be its exceptional mountain views and easy backcountry access.

San Juan National Forest near Pagosa Springs offers many outdoor recreational opportunities, including some great mountain bike and horseback rides. The fishing and hunting are outstanding. Countless hiking trails crisscross their way through low valleys and up into the high country of the Weminuche Wilderness Area and along the Continental Divide. In winter rolling, forested hills are ideal for cross-country skiing. Wolf Creek Ski Area has reached legendary status for its short lift lines and heavy snowfall, quite often the deepest of any ski area in the state. The fascinating Anasazi ruins at Chimney Rock (see the Anasazi Ruins section in this chapter) provide yet another major draw to the area.

Once again Pagosa Springs has entered a real estate boom phase, and land-sale offices litter the town's entry points offering "incredible bargains." Somehow this low-key, one stoplight town remains generally unaffected by the surge of newcomers.

Most people familiar with Pagosa Springs still think of it as a place they pass through on their way to somewhere else. If you want to spend a vacation visiting exceptional museums and enjoying a hopping nightlife, Pagosa is not the place. But to escape hectic schedules—and, for that matter, hectic vacation spots—keep Pagosa Springs firmly in mind.

HISTORY

In 1859 when Capt. J.N. Macomb, a surveyor for the US government, arrived at Pagosa Springs, he described the location as "... the most beautiful hot springs in the world. There is scarcely a more beautiful place on the face of the earth." The Utes and Navajos probably agreed with these sentiments, as they sporadically fought with each other for

424

control of the springs. The largest spring (Great Pagosa) measured 75 feet across, and even today its water emerges from the rocks at a scalding 153° F. More than one Indian brave attempted to show his courage by trying to swim across this seething cauldron; the results were grim.

In 1866 the Utes and Navajos agreed to decide once and for all which tribe would lay sole claim to the coveted springs. One brave from each tribe was to be chosen for mortal combat, and the winner would claim the springs for his people. Unexpectedly, the Utes chose a white man, Col. Albert Pfeiffer, an Indian fighter and friend of Kit Carson. Pfeiffer, a short, stocky Dutchman, was haunted by the murder of his wife by Indians in New Mexico. He had spent a few years with Kit Carson's battalion, fighting Apaches and Navajos. Pfeiffer had gained respect from the Utes and was honored to be chosen by them for the chance to do in another Navajo. Pfeiffer chose knives as the weapon for the fight. Close accounts of this showdown indicate that both men ran toward each other, then Pfeiffer stopped, raised his knife and threw it into the Navajo's heart, killing him instantly. The Utes finally had possession of the springs.

But the possession was short-lived, as Anglo settlers, miners and lumbermen began crowding into the area. In 1878 Fort Lewis was established to deal with the growing controversy between the settlers and the Utes. In 1891 the town was established and the Utes were pushed aside. Not long after, the Denver & Rio Grande Railroad arrived when it extended service to the nearby San Juan mining district. Ranches and lumbermills sprang up. At one time the Pagosa Springs area was the largest lumber-producing area in the state, but it didn't take long before much of the good timberland was destroyed. Although a number of spas were started, none really took hold. A travel brochure from the early 1900s pushed the town as "a wonderful place to recuperate." Perhaps the image of dozens of sickly people sitting in the hot springs kept many vacationers away. Though the springs have never achieved the notoriety of resorts such as Glenwood Springs and Ouray, they are finally being recognized for their potential commercial success.

GETTING THERE

Pagosa Springs is situated along Hwy. 160 in the southwestern part of the state, 60 miles east of Durango. From Denver Pagosa Springs is 265 miles southwest via Interstate 25 south to Walsenburg, then west on Hwy. 160 over Wolf Creek Pass.

OUTDOOR ACTIVITIES

BIKING
MOUNTAIN BIKING

Located in the midst of rolling terrain cut by miles of jeep roads and single-track hiking trails, Pagosa Springs is rapidly becoming a popular mountain bike destination. The San Juan Forest Association publishes a booklet of recommended rides throughout the national forest (available at shops, bookstores and the Pagosa Ranger District Office).

To talk face to face with an expert on rides in the area, stop by San Juan Sports Center. In addition to free advice, John Steinert and his crew offer quality rental bikes maps and guided tours for all abilities. Their location directly across from the hot springs pools (see the Hot Springs section) is an added bonus, especially when returning bikes after a day on the trail. Incidentally, all tours include a soak. **155 Hot Springs Blvd., Pagosa Springs, CO 81147; (303) 264-4730 or 1-800-955-0273.**

Trails—

Try this 16-mile loop ride beginning at the Red Ryder Rodeo Grounds at the east side of Pagosa Springs on Hwy. 84. Head north on Hwy. 84 before turning right on Hwy. 160, then continue 3 miles toward Wolf Creek Pass to the graveled Fawn Gulch Rd. Turn right and continue uphill for about a mile past two cattle guards. Just past the second cattle guard, turn right on an unmarked two-track dirt road. The road leads generally downhill through Willow Draw on a southerly course, with stunning views of the San Juan Mountains. You may need to ford Mill Creek. After crossing turn right onto the gravel Mill Creek Rd. and ride east (downhill!) into town.

FISHING
Echo Lake—

"It's the most underrated lake in Colorado," says one Pagosa resident. The lake is well stocked with rainbow trout, largemouth bass and yellow perch. Many rainbows over 5 pounds have been taken from the deep, unassuming lake. Trout take lures, flies and the sure-fire worm; bass rise to surface lures; catfish respond to cut bait. Echo Lake is known to have good ice fishing for trout and bass. Located 4 miles south of Pagosa Springs on Hwy. 84.

Lake Capote—

Good-sized rainbow and cutthroat trout are regularly pulled from this spring-fed lake on the Southern Ute Indian Reservation. Fishing the lake does not require a Colorado fishing license, but you must obtain a permit from the tribe (four-fish limit). Lake Capote is regularly stocked with catchable trout in the 12- to 14-inch range. At the lake there are boat rentals, a store and a campground with 25 sites (fee). Lake Capote is located 17 miles west of Pagosa Springs at the junction of Hwys. 160 and 151.

Navajo Reservoir—

The northern third of Navajo Reservoir is located in Colorado, while the remainder of this large body of water lies in northern New Mexico. The reservoir, located within a state park, contains both warm- and coldwater species. Millions of rainbow trout, kokanee salmon and largemouth bass have been stocked since the dam was dedicated in 1962. Pike, catfish, crappie and perch can also be caught. To fish the Colorado side of the reservoir, only a Colorado license is required. If you cross the border to fish, you'll need a New Mexico fishing license. The state park near Arboles has a visitors center, campground (70 sites, fee charge, flush toilets) and a large boat ramp/marina. The reservoir can be reached by taking Hwy. 160 west from Pagosa Springs for 17 miles and then going south on Hwy. 151 for 35 miles.

Piedra River—

With its headwaters in the Weminuche Wilderness Area and its lower waters on the Southern Ute Indian Reservation, the

Piedra River has 40 miles of good trout water in between. The upper tributaries that flow into the Piedra are quite good for small cutthroat trout. Below these upper tributaries, in the stretch of water from First Fork down to Lower Piedra Campground (just north of Hwy. 160), only artificial flies or lures may be used. Try gray and brown nymphs below the surface, or the current hatch on top. Travel upstream (north) from Hwy. 160, 22 miles west of Pagosa Springs. Turn right and follow Forest Rd. 622 just east of the river into a box canyon. The farther upstream you go, the better the fishing.

San Juan River—

Ten miles north of Pagosa Springs, the East and West forks of the San Juan River join. Working downriver from here you'll find many stretches of public water, loaded with small rainbow and brown trout. The river flows through Pagosa Springs; below town there are rumored to be larger trout. The fish habitat has been improved due to a restoration project that has placed large boulders along the waterway. Eventually the San Juan flows into the Southern Ute Indian Reservation and Navajo Reservoir.

Below the reservoir the San Juan River has many posted rules, and a New Mexico fishing license is required. Fishing is allowed only with artificial lures and flies with barbless hooks; you may keep only one trout over 20 inches.

North of Pagosa Springs, the West Fork of the San Juan can be reached by driving a mile on a rough dirt road from West Fork Campground (see the Camping section) to Born's Lake. From there a trail follows the river for a dozen miles up into the Weminuche Wilderness Area. Stretches of the river flow through a canyon with deep pools and some hard-to-reach places. The West Fork is wadeable except during runoff, although several bridges have recently been built. When the river calms down in July, the fishing really picks up. The East Fork of the San Juan flows out of Crater Lake (good fishing for cutthroat) and is paralleled for most of its 10-mile run

by Forest Rd. 667. To reach Forest Rd. 667, take Hwy. 160 for 10 miles northeast of Pagosa Springs and turn right. The East Fork has mostly pan-sized rainbow. The river remains murky until early July and after heavy rains. Quartz Creek flows into the East Fork about 8 miles upstream from East Fork Campground and is paralleled for 5 miles by a rather steep trail. The creek is known for fairly large cutthroat trout.

GOLF

Fairfield Pagosa—

West of Pagosa Springs at the plush Fairfield Pagosa Resort, you'll find the 18-hole **Pines** and nine-hole **Meadows** courses. At an elevation of 7,300 ft., both courses lie in a beautiful setting among the pines. Watch your hook: the newer nine-hole course has six holes bordering water. The golf course recently changed its policy and now is open to the public. The fees are reasonable considering the excellent couse design, impeccable greens and wonderful views. Golf shop, lounge, carts and lessons. Fairfield Pagosa Resort is located 3.5 miles west of Pagosa Springs on Hwy. 160. For more information call **(303) 731-4755.**

HIKING AND BACKPACKING

For information, maps and trail ideas in the Pagosa Springs area, stop in at the **Pagosa Ranger District Office** at the corner of **2nd and Pagosa St., PO Box 310, Pagosa Springs, CO 81147; (303) 264-2268.** They have wilderness maps available. If you are interested in getting more in-depth information about hiking possibilities in the Weminuche Wilderness Area, consider picking up a copy of the fine *Backpacking Guide to the Weminuche Wilderness Area* by Dennis Gebhardt (Basin Reproduction Co., 1976), available at bookstores in Pagosa.

Fourmile Falls—

This is an easy 3-mile hike (one way) that follows Fourmile Creek up between Pagosa Peak and Eagle Mountain, both over 12,000 feet. The falls are on the left. From there you can take the trail up another 4 miles to Fourmile Lake. After about 2 miles there is a fork in the trail; the left fork goes to the lake and the right fork goes on to Turkey Creek Lake and over the Continental Divide into the Creede area. To reach Fourmile Falls Trail from Pagosa Springs, head north out of town on Fourmile Rd. (Forest Rd. 645) and drive to the end of the road about 14 miles from town. The trailhead is at the end of the road.

Poison Park Trail—

Poison Park Trail, located near Williams Creek Reservoir, gets pretty heavy horse traffic, but it leads into the spectacular Weminuche Wilderness Area, where you can branch off in many directions. Talk to the folks at the Pagosa Ranger District Office for trail ideas via Poison Park Trail. The Weminuche Wilderness Area has few equals for extended backpacking trips. Towering peaks, crystal clear mountain lakes, wildflowers and thick forests await. To reach Poison Park Trail from Pagosa Springs, head west 2.5 miles on Hwy. 160 and turn right on Piedra Rd. Drive 22 miles and turn right on Williams Creek Reservoir Rd. (Forest Rd. 640). Drive in a few miles and turn left on Forest Rd. 644 and follow it to the end. The Poison Park Trail heads off to the northwest.

Treasure Pass—

Treasure Pass is located up near the summit of Wolf Creek Pass. The wildflowers and views are incredible. To reach the trailhead from Pagosa Springs, head northeast on Hwy. 160 to the summit of Wolf Creek Pass. A trail heads south to the top of a bowl. From there Treasure Mountain is on the right. You need to head for the saddle on the left side of Treasure Mountain. From the saddle you can return to Hwy. 160 on Wolf Creek Rd. (Forest Rd. 725) or continue southwest on Treasure Mountain Trail for about 4 miles and take the right fork onto Windy Pass Trail, which continues for 3 miles to Hwy. 160 near Treasure Falls. If you choose this route, a car shuttle or hitchhiking is necessary unless you want to hike back up the pass to your car.

HORSEBACK RIDING

San Juan National Forest north of Pagosa Springs is beautiful country for horseback riding. There are a number of outfitters who can take you out for an hour-long trail ride or a 10-day pack trip.

Sundown Outfitters—

David and Jane Cordray provide just about every horse-related service imaginable. They specialize in extended fishing and hunting trips up into San Juan National Forest but also offer trail rides. Drop camps or full-service camps are available. For more information contact **PO Box 261, Pagosa Springs, CO 81147; (303) 264-2869.**

Wolf Creek Outfitters—

Working out of the Bruce Spruce Ranch, Wolf Creek Outfitters provides mainly short rides on an hourly basis, but they also offer full-day and overnight pack trips. They are open into the fall for rides up in the golden aspen glades. Located 15 miles northeast of Pagosa Springs on Hwy. 160; **(303) 264-5332.**

RIVER FLOATING

Piedra River—

Increasing numbers of whitewater enthusiasts are discovering this river, which intersects Hwy. 160 between Durango and Pagosa Springs. The Piedra offers challenging, steep rapids as well as tame, meandering sections. The difficult 20-mile section of the Upper Piedra begins at the Piedra Rd. Bridge 10 miles north of Pagosa Springs on Piedra Rd. This stretch ends at Hwy. 160. This narrow, deep river runs through canyons with steep rock walls that can make portages impossible. The Upper Piedra, recommended for upper intermediate and expert kayakers, peaks early and should be run in May and June. The Lower Piedra, a 10-mile section, is navigable by rafters, kayakers and canoers of all abilities. It winds its way through cottonwood trees and ranches, dropping 20 feet per mile before reaching Navajo Reservoir.

San Juan River—

The headwaters of the San Juan River are just northeast of Pagosa Springs. By the time the river gets to town, there is enough water during runoff for kayaking and raft trips. Inner-tubing is also possible, but the water is very cold. The San Juan River is not particularly difficult to float and is very relaxing.

Outfitters—

Pagosa Rafting Outfitters—These folks offer trips down the San Juan and Piedra rivers for a half day to three days. For information and reservations call **(303) 731-4081.**

SKIING

CROSS-COUNTRY SKIING

Pagosa draws a lot of cross-country skiers in winter because the terrain is so varied. Just out of town, mellow, fairly level trails please beginners and novices. On the other end of the spectrum, backcountry skiers enjoy challenging, steep trails, excellent snow conditions and inspiring views—especially in the Wolf Creek Pass area. Rentals are available at the Pagosa Pines Touring Center. (See the Groomed Trails write-up in this section.) For maps and avalanche information, contact the **Pagosa Ranger District Office** at **(303) 264-2268.** Also, for backcountry rentals and advice, check in at the Ski and Bow Rack at the east end of Pagosa Springs, **(303) 264-2370.**

Backcountry Trails—

Chimney Rock—This is an excellent 3-mile ski up to the Chimney Rock Archaeological Area. This easy trail can be an excellent place to see elk and deer as well as peregrine falcons and a bald eagle or two. To reach the trailhead, drive 17 miles west from Pagosa Springs on Hwy. 160 to Hwy. 151 and turn left. Drive about 3.5 miles and be looking for the snowed-in road up to Chimney Rock on the right. It may be hard to find a place to park off the road. The snowed-in road winds its way up through pine and aspen, eventually terminating just below the summit of Chimney Rock. Make your way up to the summit from

here. Please look at the Anasazi ruins but don't climb around on them or remove any artifacts. For more information about Chimney Rock see the Anasazi Ruins section.

Williams Creek Reservoir—This beautiful and fairly easy trail winds its way through pines and meadows with mountain views all around. To reach the trailhead from Pagosa Springs, drive 2.5 miles west on Hwy. 160 to Piedra Rd. and turn right. Follow Piedra Rd. for 22 miles to Williams Creek Reservoir Rd. and park the car. Begin skiing on the snowed-in road. You will pass Williams Creek Campground and then Teal Campground after about 2 miles. From here it's another 3 miles up to Cimarrona Campground.

Wolf Creek Road—This 4-mile trail is not for beginners. From the summit sign at the top of Wolf Creek Pass on Hwy. 160, look to the south. You should see an open bowl. Begin skiing toward its summit (11,600 feet) through the trees. Be sure to stay to the right, as the left side can be struck by avalanches. From the summit traverse down, heading south and slightly west. On your left is the Continental Divide and to the right is Treasure Mountain. You need to get to the saddle between them. Once at the saddle, you are on Wolf Creek Rd. From here turn right and ski 2.5 miles back to Hwy. 160, about 2 miles below the pass. Hitch a ride or leave one car here and one at the trailhead. Topographical maps are highly recommended.

Groomed Trails—

Pagosa Pines Touring Center—Located on the golf course at the Fairfield Pagosa Resort west of town is a well-maintained 12-kilometer trail system. Perfect for beginners to intermediates, the trails offer clear views of the Continental Divide. The touring center rents and sells cross-country equipment. Fee charged. Open from Nov. 1 to the end of Mar. Head west on Hwy. 160 from Pagosa Springs for 3 miles and turn right onto Piñon Causeway just past the Fairfield Lodge. Continue on to Pines Club Place and look for the clubhouse on the right. **PO Box 2520,**

Pagosa Springs, CO 81147; (303) 731-4141 ext. 2021.

DOWNHILL SKIING
Wolf Creek Ski Area—

The daily snow reports in the newspaper provide ample proof: Wolf Creek has the highest average snowfall in the state. The ski area receives about 38 feet—or 465 inches—of snow in a normal year! There is no better place to learn to ski powder, because the mountain rarely gets "skied off." Besides great snow Wolf Creek still features one of the least expensive lift tickets in the state. The base area sits at 10,600 feet, atop the Continental Divide, and rises to 11,775 feet at the summit. As one of the oldest ski areas in Colorado, Wolf Creek has had a rope tow in place since 1938. Expansion has been gradual. Even though the vertical drop at Wolf Creek is nothing spectacular, the skiing is. And there is more than enough skiing for all abilities.

Wolf Creek is remote, with no resort development at the base—just a cafeteria and a rental shop. If you want to stay in the area, the closest pillow is in Pagosa Springs or on the other side of the pass at South Fork. Wolf Creek is located about 20 miles northeast of Pagosa Springs on Hwy. 160. For more information contact **PO Box 2800, Pagosa Springs, CO 81147; (303) 731-5605.**

SNOWCAT SKIING
The Water Fall area at Wolf Creek Ski Area will be serviced by lift in the future, but for now this expert terrain is accessible only by snowcat. The deep powder is tough to beat, and only a few skiers at a time are lucky enough to be in the area. A snowcat will shuttle you out from the bottom of the sparse pine forest. Sign up at the top of the Treasure Triple Chairlift. Snowcat skiing is not included in the price of a lift ticket. Contact **Wolf Creek at PO Box 1036, Pagosa Springs, CO 81147; (303) 731-5605.**

——————— SEEING AND DOING ———————

ANASAZI RUINS
Chimney Rock Archaeological Area—

Chimney Rock, with its towering structure and mountain setting, ever so slightly resembles Machu Picchu, the lost city of the Incas. Occupied 1,000 years ago by as many as 2,000 Anasazi, Chimney Rock was supposedly the northernmost outpost of the Chaco Canyon Anasazi, who were mostly concentrated to the south in New Mexico. The Anasazi at Chimney Rock were farmers who lived in pueblo villages on ridges along the Piedra River and on the high mesa tops. The most impressive remnants of this ancient culture are the large pueblo ruins located just below the two rock pinnacles at the summit.

Chimney Rock Archaeological Area came into being in 1970 when the federal government set aside more than 3,000 acres under the watchful eye of the National Forest Service. The area is also home to the peregrine falcon, which is protected in its natural habitat. Other wildlife, including

elk and deer, also thrive here. Visitors are allowed to enter the site only with guided tours. From May 1 to Sept. 15 (weather permitting) rangers lead four walking tours each day lasting about two hours each. The tour includes walks to two main sites and a Forest Service fire lookout. Tours begin at the Chimney Rock entrance, located 17 miles west of Pagosa Springs on Hwy. 160 and about 3.5 miles south on Hwy. 151. Small fee for those over the age of 12. For more information about the tours contact **(303) 883-2442** or **(303) 264-2268.**

HOT SPRINGS
In Town—

In a prime location next to the San Juan River, in a mystic, made-to-look-natural setting you can soak in a number of outdoor tubs. The natural spring water has a high mineral content that many locals swear has certain healing qualities. The tubs interconnecect, so that you can find one with just the right temperature and view. A wooden fence wraps around the tubs, with lounge chairs and a few tables spread out on an adjacent concrete deck. You can soak for free as a guest of the Spring Inn (see the Where to Stay section), or pay for privileges.

MUSEUMS AND GALLERIES

Fred Harmon Art Museum—

This museum captures the lifework of one man from Pagosa Springs: Fred Harmon. Not everyone remembers his comic strip, Red Ryder and Little Beaver, but at one time the strip appeared in more than 750 newspapers on three continents. Later, Red Ryder and his buddy Little Beaver were seen in films. Fred Harmon was a gifted artist who never had any formal training. He once said, "I wasn't a born artist—I was born with a husky pair of lungs and a liking for hair and rawhide." In his later years, Harmon devoted his life to capturing the spirit of the West with oil on canvas. Small fee charged. Open 10:30 am–5 pm Mon.-Sat., 12–4 pm Sun. Two miles west of Pagosa Springs on **Hwy. 160; (303) 731-5785.**

Rocky Mountain Wildlife Park—

As the clock ticks toward the end of your vacation, the realization sets in—the only wildlife you've seen on this vacation has been road-kill. Fantasies of elk grazing in a meadow, bears frolicking in a mating ritual and a bobcat slinking among craggy rocks are diminishing rapidly. The Rocky Mountain Wildlife Park, essentially a zoo, might just be the place for you to actually get a look at some wildlife. Open daily from 9 am–6 pm; feedings usually take place at 2 pm. Located 5 miles south of Pagosa Springs on **Hwy. 84; (303) 264-5546.**

San Juan Historical Museum—

Inside this false-fronted museum building, you'll be treated to an array of historical knickknacks. The many displays include items such as Angora goat chaps, worn saddles, a one-horse open sleigh and an old barber's chair; there is also a re-created blacksmith shop and a schoolroom (circa 1900). Since the historical society is located in the same building, chances are you will be able to talk with a knowledgeable person about the area. No fee, but donations are accepted. Open Memorial Day–Labor Day, Mon.–Sat. 10 am–5 pm. **1st St. and Pagosa St.; (303) 264-4424.**

NIGHTLIFE

As we mentioned in the intro, Pagosa Springs certainly doesn't conjure up images of flashy nightlife. However if you get the urge to drink a couple of cold ones someplace that captures the essence of Pagosa. ... **Hogs Breath** features "foot-stompin" country and rock music on weekends in a classier environment than the name implies. This place also has a solid lunch and dinner (ribs, Mexican, steaks) menu and a comfortable long wooden bar. Open 11 am–2 am daily. Located just off of **North Pagosa Blvd.; (303) 731-2626.**

TOURS

The Pagosa Springs Area Chamber of Commerce has organized a variety of area tours given on a daily basis. The two-hour tours are led by local volunteers who introduce visitors to everything from alpine wildflowers to the workings of a sawmill. The tours are free and can be very interesting. For more information contact the **Chamber of Commerce** at **1-800-252-2204** or **(303) 264-2360.**

—————— WHERE TO STAY ——————

ACCOMMODATIONS

Pagosa Lodge—$$$

Anyone visiting Pagosa Springs will inevitably hear about or see the sprawling Fairfield Resort just west of town. It functions primarily as a retirement community interspersed with time-share condominiums and sprawling executive style homes, but the complex also features a large 100-room lodge. The resort is particularly suited to families, as it provides a large number of activities. A fine 27-hole golf course, indoor swimming pool, game room, tennis facilities and many other diversions make it tempting to never leave the grounds during your stay. If you like the self-enclosed, all-inclusive type of resort vacation, you'll like the Pagosa Lodge.

Comfortable if not luxurious accommodations are complemented by a natural setting beside Piñon Lake and incredible views to the San Juans. Try the **Great Divide** restaurant on the premesis. Located 3.5 miles west of Pagosa Springs on Hwy. 160. **PO Box 2050, Pagosa Springs, CO 81147; 1-800-523-7704** or **(303) 731-4141.**

Spring Inn—$$ to $$$

This basic but comfortable 20-room motel allows guests unlimited free use of four outdoor mineral baths next to the San Juan River. This ultimate amenity provides a relaxing end to a day exploring the area. Massage and exercise facility nearby. Located just across the bridge on Hot Springs Blvd., **PO Box 1799, Pagosa Springs, CO 81147; (303) 264-4168** or **1-800-225-0934.**

Echo Manor Inn—$$ to $$$

Echo Manor Inn, referred to as "the castle" by the locals, looks very out of place in Pagosa Springs. It's so unusual that many people driving by actually slam on their brakes and stare at the extraordinary structure. Ginny and Sandy Northcutt, the owners, recall one day when an entire busload of people was outside taking pictures of their place.

With more than 10,000 square feet of space, the sprawling inn enjoys a setting with a spectacular view to Wolf Creek Pass. Although the structure was originally a small A-frame, the first owner, upon returning from Disneyland, began building additions that were inspired by Fantasyland. The Manor features six rooms with private bathrooms and four with shared. Each of the comfortable rooms is individually named and decorated. The romantic Royal Suite has a great view from the bed. The Safari room with its dark wood and gun cases might be your choice. In addition, the "Courtyard" apartment can comfortably accommodate up to 12 people.

Guests not staying in the Courtyard are treated to Ginny's enormous breakfast, which will keep you full for most of the day. The breakfast table, set with 100-year-old crystal, offers great views. Be sure to make time for the hot tub on the back porch, and check out Sandy's Game Room, where he has a large collection of game trophies mounted on the walls. Located 3 miles south of Pagosa Springs on Hwy. 84 on the left side of the road across from Echo Lake. You can't miss it. **3366 Hwy. 84, Pagosa Springs, CO 81147; (303) 264-5646.**

Davidson's Country Inn—$$

Staying at Davidson's will provide a simple, country experience that is particularly well suited to families. The three-story log inn has 10 individually decorated rooms with country touches and a Christian motif that will appeal to many. Except for the Mountain Man Room (with a waterbed and a glass rifle case), the rooms are of the dainty sort. Kids will love the solarium filled with pint-sized toys; anyone can make use of the pool and ping-pong tables, horseshoes and table games. Evelyn and Gilbert Davidson will make you feel right at home as soon as you walk in the door. Evelyn loves to bake and she'll make a box lunch for anyone heading out on a hike or a fishing trip. Full homemade breakfast included; no smoking. Located 2 miles northeast of Pagosa Springs on Hwy. 160. **PO Box 87, Pagosa Springs, CO 81147; (303) 264-5863.**

CAMPING

In San Juan National Forest—

Camping opportunities are numerous in the San Juan National Forest around Pagosa Springs.

Blanco River Campground, located 13 miles south of Pagosa Springs on Hwy. 84 and 2 miles east on Forest Rd. 656, has 6 sites and a fee. **East Fork Campground, Wolf Creek Campground** and **West Fork Campground** are located about 12 miles northeast of Pagosa Springs on Hwy. 160 heading toward Wolf Creek Pass. They have between 25 and 28 sites each and a fee is charged. **Bridge Campground** is 17 miles northwest of Pagosa Springs on Piedra Rd. (Forest Rd. 631). It has 19 sites and a fee. Another 2.5 miles up the road brings you to **Williams Creek Campground** with 66 sites and a fee. **Teal Campground** (16 sites) and **Cimarrona Campground** (21 sites) are a couple more miles up Piedra Rd. A fee is charged at both. Heading west on Hwy. 160 from Pagosa Springs to the Piedra River and then north a mile on Forest Rd. 621 brings you to **Lower Piedra Campground,** with 17 sites, no fee and no drinking water.

Navajo State Park—

Seventy campsites await you at Navajo Reservoir. This state-run area also offers showers. A fee is charged. From Pagosa Springs drive 17 miles west on Hwy. 160 and turn left on Hwy. 151. Proceed about 15 miles, turn left on County Rd. 982 and drive 2 miles.

Private Campgrounds—

The Pagosa area has more than its share of private RV campgrounds equipped with everything from showers to laundry facilities. The ones with the best surroundings are located east of town on Hwy. 160 toward Wolf Creek Pass. Here are a few of them.

Bruce Spruce Ranch—Located 16 miles northeast of Pagosa Springs on Hwy. 160, this place offers cabins and a trailer park. Closed in winter. **PO Box 296, Pagosa Springs, CO 81147; (303) 264-5374.**

Elk Meadows Campground—Located 5 miles east of town, Elk Meadows entices visitors by its alluring invitation, "Sleep to the sound of the ol' San Juan River!" We wondered, "What about the sound of the ol' Hwy. 160." Open from June–Nov. **PO Box 238, Pagosa Springs, CO 81147; (303) 264-5482.**

Pagosa Riverside—Open year-round and located in a nice setting just 1.5 miles east of Pagosa on Hwy. 160. **PO Box 268, Pagosa Springs, CO 81147; (303) 264-5874.**

WHERE TO EAT

The Greenhouse—$$ to $$$

With its beautiful views and ample portions, this restaurant is always worth a visit. The menu covers the gamut from moist barbecue ribs to Châteaubriand for two served at tableside. You won't go away hungry: every dinner starts with a relish tray, bread, soup and salad. The Greenhouse also features nightly dinner specials. Arrive early and enjoy a spectacular sunset from the enclosed patio area. Cocktails served in the dining room or in the separate

bar area. Call for reservations. Open nightly 4–10 pm. Located just north of Pagosa Springs on **Piedra Rd.; (303) 731-2021.**

Old Miner's Steakhouse—$$ to $$$

The weathered barnwood walls create the feeling of a mine shaft, and privacy is guaranteed by low lighting and tables that are tastefully partitioned from one another. Even the waiting room is something special—so comfortably appointed that it's as though you are waiting in the owner's living room. The food gets rave reviews. Most of the entrées are char-broiled steaks, but there are also seafood, pork and chicken dishes. The menu also promises "Grub served with hot bread and your 'pickins' from the salad bar." No alcohol is served and no smoking is allowed. Open for lunch 11:30 am–1:30 pm Mon.–Fri., dinner from 5:30 pm Mon.–Sat.; call for winter hours. Three and a half miles northeast of town on **Hwy. 160; (303) 264-5981.**

The Elkhorn Cafe—$

For a great Mexican-style breakfast, lunch or dinner, stop in at the Elkhorn Cafe. Located downtown, this one-room Mexican restaurant opens early, serving both Mexican and American entrées. For breakfast try the huevos rancheros or the green chili cheese omelette. Lunch and dinner specialties include the Elkhorn stuffed sopapilla and the combination plate. Select from several varieties of Mexican and American beer. The Elkhorn opens at 6 am Mon.–Sat., 7 am Sun., and closes at 9 pm daily. **438C Main St.; (303) 264-2146.**

SERVICES

Pagosa Central Reservations—

For condo and home rentals. **PO Box 900, Pagosa Springs, CO 81147; (303) 731-2215.**

Pagosa Springs Area Chamber of Commerce—

The Chamber just moved into a new facility next to the San Juan River. Stop by for information and advice on the entire area. Located in a distinctive building across the bridge from the only stoplight in downtown Pagosa Springs. **PO Box 787, Pagosa Springs, CO 81147; (303) 264-2360.**

Silverton

The ornate Victorian buildings in Silverton are a true reflection of the millions of dollars in gold and silver brought up during the mining heyday of the late 1800s. The town, designated a National Historic Landmark, appears as if it were frozen at the turn of the century thanks to the opulent, many-windowed Grand Imperial Hotel, the pretentious gold-domed courthouse, false-fronted buildings, magnificent Victorian homes and small, restored miners' cabins. Silverton once played host to as many as 32 gambling halls, saloons and what were affectionately known as the Blair St. "sporting houses."

Sealed off in a high mountain valley at 9,318 feet, Silverton exists solely due to its proximity to the rich gold and silver mines in the San Juan Mountains. Now that mining no longer plays a part in the area economy, the town has dwindled to five hundred hardy souls who live in this movie-set world, surrounded by four towering peaks (Kendall, Anvil, Boulder and Sultan). The two major auto routes into Silverton require crossing spectacular, sometimes treacherous Red Mountain or Molas passes. In the midst of hundreds of square miles of the San Juan, Uncompahgre and Rio Grande national forests, isolation and supreme natural beauty make Silverton an excellent springboard for backpacking trips. Another popular pastime is jeeping to ghostly mining camps, as well as to nearby towns such as Ouray, Telluride and Lake City.

In summer the historic Durango & Silverton Narrow Gauge Railroad pulls into Silverton several times a day, enabling its passengers to poke around town for a couple of hours. The spawning of t-shirt, candle and curio shops attests to the forced speed of most purchases by the train crowd. Understandably the locals are glad to have the train travelers as a captive audience during high season, but it's a love-hate relationship. As one restaurant worker put it, "We've got four trains and two thousand people and two hours to get rid of them." Two hours is really not enough time to get acquainted with Silverton. If you arrive on the train, consider spending a night or two. The town and its residents take on a more genuine and relaxed personality after the last train of the day departs for the journey back to Durango. Besides, to get a complete picture of the area's rich history, you should do some further exploring.

The boundaries of San Juan County do not contain one acre of tillable land. Rhubarb is the one garden crop that survives a growing season rumored to last only "14 days … and not 14 in a row." Winter is undoubtedly the longest season at this altitude. It's a beautifully quiet time when Silverton goes into semi-hibernation and the town takes on a pristine, totally unique feel. Although most of the town's shops, lodging establishments and restaurants close, just enough businesses remain open to keep things interesting. Many people don't realize that Silverton lies in close proximity to some of the best cross-country and downhill skiing anywhere; many others like to snowmobile. An added plus: the quick 24-mile trip south to the Purgatory/Durango Ski Area (see the **Durango** chapter) rarely sees any winter traffic.

HISTORY

The commonly accepted legend is that Silverton got its name from an early miner who bragged, "We may not have gold here, but we have silver by the ton." The first attempt at prospecting came in 1860 when Charles Baker led a party of men over the Continental Divide to the site of Silverton. Despite meager finds, he kept returning to the Upper Animas River vicinity (referred to at that time as Baker's Park). After a short stint in the Confederate Army, Baker returned to the area in 1865, only to be killed by Ute Indians.

Once the exclusive domain of Utes, land including all of San Juan County was officially granted to them in an 1868 treaty. Gold fever set in a few years later and, despite the treaty, a steady stream of miners poured into the area. A short, bitter struggle for the land ensued, and the Utes, under the direction of Chief Ouray, soon surrendered 3 million acres of mineral-rich mountains to the US government.

With the "Indian trouble" resolved, Silverton boomed in a hurry. Settlement began in earnest in 1875 when a crude mountain road connected Durango and Silverton. That same year a newspaper known today as the *Silverton Standard and The Miner* printed its first issue. Soon Otto Mears connected Silverton to his system of toll roads in the San Juans including the route from Silverton to Ouray over the "Million Dollar Highway." Since transportation of supplies, mail and tons of high-grade ore was crucial for the town's survival, everyone celebrated when the Denver & Rio Grande Railroad pulled into Silverton in 1882. Over the next decade Silverton's population grew to more than 2,000 residents and the young town became the terminus of three other railroads. From 1880 until the end of the century, nearby mines took minerals worth millions every year from the surrounding mountains.

Growing pains accompanied the early years. Vigilante groups took care of law enforcement and did fairly well at keeping the local peace. After a police force evolved, it was sometimes used as a tool for ethnic suppression. White merchants, tired of the proliferation of Chinese businesses, called on the police to "raid the Mongolians." In 1891 a Chinese Endeavor Society was formed to "convert the Chinese and to induce them to handle soiled linen and red checks with more Christian charity," according to an article in the *Silverton Standard*.

The demonetization of silver in 1893 and, later, the nationwide financial panic of 1907 effectively stopped the growth of the town. Mining was still the bread-and-butter industry, but tourism and occasional moviemaking gradually entered the fray. However since the Sunnyside Mine shut down operations in 1991, the "mining town that wouldn't quit," now must rely primarily on tourism for sustenance. Today Silverton remains a snapshot of another era with merely one fourth the number of year-round residents as it had at the turn of the century.

GETTING THERE

Silverton is located 343 miles southwest of Denver. Those arriving from the southwest should take Hwy. 550 north from Durango for 49 miles over Coal Bank and Molas passes. Many people who visit Silverton do so by riding the Durango & Silverton Narrow Gauge Railroad from Durango (see the Major Attractions section of the **Durango** chapter). From Ouray it is an unforgettable 22-mile drive over Red Mountain Pass on the Million Dollar Highway. (See the Scenic Drives section of the **Ouray** chapter.)

MAJOR ATTRACTIONS

Durango & Silverton Narrow Gauge Railroad

Riding the Durango & Silverton Narrow Gauge Railroad is the best way to relive the history of the area. On its 45-mile route to Durango, the vintage steam-powered train passes through some of the most beautiful terrain imaginable. Package trips include one-way ridership with bus return, and layovers in Durango or Silverton. See the Major Attractions section of the **Durango** chapter for more information. Call **(303) 247-2733** in Durango for information and reservations.

FESTIVALS AND EVENTS

Gunfight
summer
Each day at 5:30 pm, the notorious corner of Blair St. and 12th St. is the stage for the reenactment of a Wild West gunfight. Running around shooting blanks at each other, the actors have as much fun as the visiting crowd.

Hardrockers Holidays
mid-August
When people first hear of Hardrockers Holidays, they sometimes have the wrong impression. Instead of blaring rock music, this event draws gold and silver miners from across the state to prove their mettle (so to speak) in events ranging from machine drilling to mucking. It's fascinating to learn more about what normally goes on deep in the mines. The miners also create an exciting atmosphere in town. For more information call **(303) 387-5654.**

Brass Band Festival
third weekend in August
Since 1981 musicians from around the world have converged on Silverton to make music at the Great Western Rocky Mountain Brass Band Festival. Melodic strains of John Philip Sousa music fill the thin mountain air. Outdoor concerts held in Memorial Park are free (donation bucket) and open to the public. For more information call **(303) 387-5654.**

OUTDOOR ACTIVITIES

BIKING
MOUNTAIN BIKING

If you are an advanced mountain biker you will appreciate the Silverton vicinity's selection of long and grueling trips over rough jeep roads. One thing should be remembered: there are only two directions to go from Silverton—up or down. It is not a good area for mellow rides, unless you limit yourself to staying in the valley. At present no place in town rents bikes, so you have to bring your own.

Trails—

One lengthy loop tour from Silverton involves riding over Ophir Pass and on to Telluride. Spend the night there and cross over Imogene Pass to Ouray the next day. You might want to spend a day recovering and soaking in the hot springs pool before considering a route back to Silverton. Consult the Four-Wheel-Drive Trips section for information on routes in the area.

FISHING

Fast currents and high mineral content prevent good angling in the streams near Silverton. The Durango area offers a number of fishing possibilities only a short distance away.

High lakes near Silverton, however, are hopping with small but feisty trout. Just 6 miles south of Silverton on Hwy. 550 you'll find three popular lakes: **Molas, Little Molas** and **Andrews.** Another area abounding with small alpine lakes can be reached by taking Hwy. 550 northwest for 2 miles and then going 5 miles southwest on Forest Rd. 585. At South Mineral Campground a good trail follows the South Fork of Mineral Creek to **Ice Lake, Little Ice Lake, Fuller Lake** and **Island Lake.** The fishing for cutthroat is usually good. Since access is on foot, the fishing pressure is usually minimal. You can also take Forest Rd. 815 (four-wheel-drive) from the campground for about 2 miles to **Clear Lake,** which is also a good place to catch cutthroat trout.

FOUR-WHEEL-DRIVE TRIPS

Silverton was the first mining area worked in the San Juan boom of the late 1800s. As a result, it's connected by a web of incredible jeep roads to other mining towns, including **Lake City, Creede, Ouray** and **Telluride.**

The Alpine Loop Backcountry Byway—

Engineer and Cinnamon passes, located northeast of Silverton, connect with both Ouray and Lake City. The historic sites of Animas Forks, Mineral Point, Rose's Cabin, Capitol City and Sherman lie along the way. High alpine views of the surrounding peaks and basins attract a large number of jeepers each year. To reach these two roads from Silverton, head east from town on County Rd. 110 along the Animas River. For more information see Four-Wheel-Drive Trips in the **Creede, South Fork and Lake City** chapter.

Black Bear Pass—

This is probably the most frightening and dangerous pass in the state and perhaps in the country. Still interested? Black Bear Pass Rd. begins near the summit of Red Mountain Pass (between Silverton and Ouray on Hwy. 550) and heads west up to the 12,840-foot summit of Black Bear Pass— visible to the north is the old Black Bear Mine. The road was built to deliver ore from the mine to Ouray and Silverton via the Million Dollar Highway. (See the Scenic Drives section of the Ouray chapter.) From the summit of Black Bear Pass, the knife-edged road gets rougher and the views get better. The switchbacks descending the mountain are so tight that they require three-point turns. Easing the clutch out without slipping forever over a rocky cliff requires total concentration—this is the point where passengers tend to get out and direct from the road. Below the worst of the switchbacks, the road arrives at the hydro station on top of Bridal Veil Falls. This is a good place to stop, collect your thoughts and let your adrenaline level return to normal. From the falls drive down the remainder of the road past the Liberty Bell Mine and into Telluride. From Telluride return to Silverton via Imogene (or Ophir) Pass or drive around to Ridgway and Ouray on the highway.

Cement Creek/Corkscrew Road—

See the Four-Wheel-Drive Trips section in the **Ouray** chapter.

Ophir Pass—

As far as four-wheel-drive roads go, Ophir Pass can be a bit hairy in spots. From the 11,750-foot summit, enjoy great views of the peaks around Red Mountain Pass to the east. To the west a spectacular view awaits of Mt. Wilson, Wilson Peak and El Diente Peak, as well as the deep Ophir Valley. According to some old-timers, the name Ophir came from an early resident of the area, Lt. Howard, who stumbled upon a huge cave and exclaimed, "O fer God's sake, lookit that hole!" However, in all probability the name is a biblical reference to King Solomon's mines. A toll road was built by Otto Mears over Ophir Pass in 1881, connecting Telluride with Silverton.

To reach the pass road from Silverton, drive 5 miles north on Hwy. 550 toward Red Mountain Pass and turn left onto the Ophir Pass Rd. Follow the road as it drops down over a bridge before climbing about 4 miles to the pass. From the pass the road descends sharply on a shelf road that cuts across a massive rock slide. It eventually enters a forest of spruce, fir and aspen just above Old Ophir. Before reaching Old Ophir, you may want to visit the old cemetery up the hill on the right. Old Ophir, 3.5 miles from the pass, was once a thriving mining town. Today people still live there, braving the monstrous avalanches that thunder down steep chutes and pummel the valley floor in winter. About 2.5 miles below Old Ophir you will arrive at the remains of New Ophir, established mainly as a stop for the Rio Grande Southern Railroad next to the Ophir Loop. From here you can return to Silverton by heading north on Hwy. 145 to Telluride and over Imogene Pass, or just continue

northwest around to Ridgway, Ouray and over Red Mountain Pass.

Stony Pass—

The road over Stony Pass was built as a crucial supply route between Silverton and settlements to the east in the San Luis Valley. This very rough road crosses over the Continental Divide, dropping into the Rio Grande drainage at the headwaters of the Rio Grande. It passes by Rio Grande Reservoir and eventually comes out on Hwy. 149 on the Silver Thread Scenic and Historic Byway between Creede and Lake City. To reach the road from Silverton, head east on County Rd. 110 to Howardsville. In its day Howardsville was quite a town; it was once the county seat and the residents supported many saloons, a livery stable and a meat market. Turn right at Howardsville and up Cunningham Gulch Rd. Drive about 2 miles and look for Stony Pass Rd. on the left.

Rentals and Tours—

Silverton Lakes Campground Jeep Rentals— Located on the northeast end of town, this campground rents jeeps for half- and full-day trips. Reservations are strongly urged in July and Aug. **PO Box 126, Silverton, CO 81433; (303) 387-5721.**

Triangle Service Station Jeep Rentals— Open-top Jeep Wranglers and four-door Jeep Cherokees rent for full or half days. **864 Greene St., Silverton, CO 81433; (303) 387-9990.**

HIKING AND BACKPACKING

Silverton is surrounded by vast stretches of BLM land as well as three national forests; to the north the Uncompahgre, to the west the San Juan and to the east the Rio Grande. No matter which direction you choose, high mountains, raging rivers and ghost towns await, providing great hiking and backpacking. The area on the Continental Divide to the east of town provides excellent hiking on rolling hills once you're up on top. For hiking information try the visitors center, **PO Box 565, Silverton, CO 81433, (303) 387-5654,** on the west end of town, but your best bet is to stop at the **San**

Juan National Forest Headquarters in Durango at **701 Camino del Rio, Room 301, Durango, CO 81301; (303) 247-4874.**

The Durango & Silverton Narrow Gauge Railroad offers a unique service to hikers by making stops along a remote section of the Animas River (for information see the Hiking and Backpacking section of the **Durango** chapter).

Continental Divide Trail—

Silverton is an excellent jumping-off point for hikes in the Weminuche Wilderness Area. South of town the Weminuche straddles the San Juan and Rio Grande national forests, providing access to miles of trails and dozens of rugged peaks. Many sheep graze here, so be sure to treat your water. The Continental Divide runs through the wilderness area. A trail along the divide opens up many possible trips. To reach the Continental Divide Trail, follow the directions to Highland Mary Lakes (see below). From Highland Mary Lakes, hike southeast and then south along the divide. About 4 miles south on the divide, a trail switchbacks down into the Elk Creek Valley to the right (west). There is a mine shack just down from the divide that makes a fine place to spend the night. If you follow the trail down Elk Creek for 9 miles, you'll end up in Elk Park, where you can catch the train back into Silverton.

Many hiking trails take off from the Continental Divide Trail (see the Hiking and Backpacking section of the **Creede, South Fork and Lake City** chapter). Obtain some topographical maps (the Storm King Peak, Howardsville, Rio Grande Pyramid and Needle Mountains quadrangles) to devise your own route.

Highland Mary Lakes Trail—

This fine day hike takes you into the upper reaches of Cunningham Gulch, a heavily mined area with many fascinating relics still in place. Near the trailhead the famous Highland Mary Mine can be seen high up on the right. The trail heads due south, climbing up along Cunningham Creek for 2.5 miles to the lakes. To reach the trailhead from Silverton, drive east for 5 miles to Howardsville, then turn right on Cunningham Gulch Rd. Proceed about 4.5 miles to the end of the road. Along the drive you will see many mine sites complete with aerial trams and rusty cables hanging hundreds of feet above the valley floor.

Ice Lake Trail—

Beginning at South Mineral Creek Campground, this trail climbs west up the valley for 3 miles to Ice Lake. Along the way you will see a waterfall, ruins of old mining camp buildings and fields of wildflowers. Just north of Ice Lake is U.S. Grant Peak. A nice side trip is Island Lake, about a half mile northeast of Ice Lake. Some people try to reach the island in the center of the lake by hopping over the ice floes that remain until late summer, but this is not recommended. To reach the trailhead from Silverton, drive 2 miles northwest on Hwy. 550 toward Ouray and turn left onto Forest Rd. 585. Proceed 5 miles, until just past the campground, and look for the trailhead climbing into the forest on the right.

Molas Pass Trail—

Although only a 3-mile hike, this trail drops over a thousand feet on its way down to Elk Park, along the Animas River. It's very steep and you should have on a good pair of tightly laced boots to prevent blisters. The trail begins beside Molas Lake, about 5 miles south of Silverton on Hwy. 550. Park at the lake. As the trail drops through spruce and fir forests it provides intermittent views of the rocky west wall of the river valley. Stunning views southeast to the Grenadier Range in the Weminuche Wilderness Area highlight this hike. Once down to the river, the trail runs parallel to the water and then crosses a bridge. Just downriver from here along the train tracks is a fine camping area. Be sure to bring along a stove and leave no traces. The train stops here each morning on its way to Silverton if you want to catch a ride.

ICE SKATING

The ballfield at the southwest end of town is flooded during winter, forming a town ice rink. The public library has a small supply of rental skates.

RIVER FLOATING

Expert kayakers consider the Upper Animas an excellent but treacherous stretch of whitewater. See the River Floating section of the **Durango** chapter.

SKIING

CROSS-COUNTRY SKIING

No question about it, the Silverton area is a great place to strap on skinny skis and head into the backcountry. Numerous trails extend into nearby valleys and basins from town. The terrain can be quite difficult and avalanche-prone, but knowledgeable and experienced skiers have unlimited routes. Mountaineering skiing is an especially appropriate method here. Anyone wishing to learn more about avalanche safety should consider a three-day workshop at Silverton Avalanche School. The course is attended by ski-patrol members, highway workers and recreational skiers. For more information contact the **Silverton Chamber of Commerce** at **418 Greene St., Silverton, CO 81433; 1-800-752-4494** nationwide or **(303) 387-5654** locally.

Backcountry Trails—
Molas Pass—The top of Molas Pass (10,910 feet) allows for unimaginably beautiful views to the rocky spires of the Needles and to the summit of Snowdon Peak (13,077 feet). Many easy backcountry routes can be taken across rolling hills that were cleared by a forest fire over a century ago. Sparse groves of lodgepole and spruce are the result of a reforestation effort. Skiers wanting to sample a few short downhill runs can find many opportunities in deep, untracked powder. The avalanche danger is low in most of the area. A number of routes leave from points along Hwy. 550, near the top of the pass. Little Molas Lake is a bit over a half mile from the highway. The route begins on the west side of Hwy. 550, just before reaching the summit of Molas Pass, some 6 miles south of Silverton. Andrews Lake Rd. is an easy climb from the left side of the highway, about a mile after crossing Molas Pass. The snow-covered road reaches Andrews Lake in a half mile; more challenging terrain lies beyond the lake. One route makes a steep ascent to the top of a knoll (11,290 feet) from the west end of Andrews Lake.

Ophir Pass—Intermediate and advanced skiers may want to ski up the eastern side of the pass (a 1,700-foot gain in elevation) and return on the same route from the 11,789-foot summit. A ski down the other side to the town of Ophir would be foolish because of high avalanche danger. As it is you'll be crossing several avalanche slide paths; the 9-mile route should not be attempted during avalanche warnings. To reach the Ophir Pass Rd. take Hwy. 550 northwest for 4.6 miles, to a marked forest road (No. 679) on the left.

Red Mountain Pass—See the Skiing section of the **Ouray** chapter and the St. Paul Lodge (see Where to Stay).

South Mineral Creek—This easy half-day excursion involves skiing along a level forest road in a wind-protected valley. Oftentimes there are tracks leading the way. The area is fairly safe, but some avalanche danger exists. You should inquire about snow conditions before setting out. Head northwest on Hwy. 550 for 2 miles and park at the head of the valley. Forest Rd. 585 leads about 5 miles southwest, ending at South Mineral Campground.

Groomed Trails—
Purgatory/Durango Ski Touring Center—See the Skiing section of the **Durango** chapter.

Rentals and Information—
The French Bakery—This full-service bakery undergoes a metamorphosis in winter, when it turns into a full-service cross-country ski rental shop. The people there can give you a quick rundown of trails in the area. **1250 Greene St.; (303) 387-5423.**

DOWNHILL SKIING
Purgatory/Durango Ski Area—
This respected downhill resort is situated midway between Durango and Silverton. Staying in Silverton would be a pleasant alternative while skiing Purgatory.

For more information see the Skiing section of the **Durango** chapter.

TENNIS

A couple of public courts are located in Memorial Park on the northeast end of Silverton.

———— SEEING AND DOING ————

HOT SPRINGS

The Ouray hot springs are only a short distance away, although the route can be treacherous in winter. See the **Ouray** chapter for more information.

MUSEUMS
Old Hundred Gold Mine Tour—

Pull on a yellow rain slicker (you'll need it) and a white hard hat before lurching into a damp mining tunnel on a narrow, topless railcar. The railcar takes you 1,500 feet underground into an actual 1960s mining operation. The continuously dripping water gives you a sense of the miserable working conditions. Our guide explained a variety of mining techniques and pointed out ore veins as we walked inside the dimly lit tunnel. The entrance fee seemed a bit much for the hour-long tour— indeed our guide commented, "The only thing we mine now is tourists." Located 5 miles east of Silverton on Hwy. 110 (turn right at Howardsville and follow the signs). Open June–Sept. **PO Box 430, Silverton, CO 81433; 1-800-872-3009.**

San Juan County Historical Museum—

Located in the old San Juan County Jail, this museum provides historical information and interesting relics from surrounding mining camps. The jail operated from 1902 to 1931, serving as home to the sheriff and his family (one of the sheriff's

babies was born in the women's cell). Open 9 am–5 pm daily from June 1–mid-Sept., 10 am–3 pm daily until mid-Oct. Small fee. Located next to the courthouse on **1567 Greene St.; (303) 387-5838.**

NIGHTLIFE
A Theatre Group—

This community-based theatre group has a loyal following because the actors put their hearts into each play. Climb the stairs to the historic Miners Union Theatre (above the old Miner's Union Hall) and, for a reasonable admission fee, you too can catch a live performance. Thanks to an intimate and historic setting you almost feel a part of the action on stage. In summer plays generally run on Wed.–Sun. evenings; call ahead during other times of year for the schedule. Curtain time is 8 pm. **1069 Greene St., Silverton, CO 81433; (303) 387-5337 or (303) (303) 387-5654.**

SCENIC DRIVES

Because Silverton is locked in a high valley, you can't drive anywhere from the town without encountering heart-stopping views. The **Million Dollar Highway** is a beautiful and historically fascinating drive (see the Scenic Drives section of the **Ouray** chapter for more information). The outstanding trip along the **San Juan Skyway** can be taken in part or whole from Silverton (see the Scenic Drives section of the **Durango** chapter).

———— WHERE TO STAY ————

ACCOMMODATIONS
St. Paul Lodge—$$$

From the summit of Red Mountain

Pass, a cross-country ski trail works its way up to the rustic confines of the St. Paul Lodge at 11,400 feet. Since 1974 Chris and Donna George have been housing groups of skiers in an old tipple house, originally built in the 1880s over the main shaft of the St. Paul Mine, where the ore was cleaned and loaded into carts. Using an eclectic hodgepodge of recycled materials, including lumber from abandoned mine buildings and solid oak paneling from a Denver church, the couple has created a warm environment for up to 22 skiers at a time. The lodge is not for everyone: "I don't need slick California skiers that want to run 20 kilometers of track and drink martinis," George said with a wry smile. For the most part it's rough and basic. Small dormitory rooms and an indoor outhouse can turn off some people, but the lodge also features a redwood sauna and hot showers. Enjoy kerosene light, woodstove heat and unique access to some of the best high alpine skiing anywhere.

The rustic lodge, which sits at an elevation of 11,400 feet, provides ski touring equipment as well as tours guided by avalanche expert Chris George. Though George is unchallenged by the telemark turn, he swears he can "teach you to telemark in 20 minutes." This technique is extremely useful for the terrain and conditions in US Basin and on McMillan Peak. Choose from gentle routes as well as steep, wide-open slopes. Staying at the lodge includes three meals a day; Chris is a trained chef and former Outward Bound instructor. Open in winter only. **PO Box 463, Silverton, CO 81433; (303) 387-5494.**

Grand Imperial Hotel—$$$ to $$$$

With new owners taking the helm of this landmark hotel it's a pleasure to finally be able to recommend it. Built in 1882, it's a fine example of Victorian architecture, and the rooms are comfortable if not grand. All rooms facing the outside offer excellent views. For a special occasion reserve one of the large, classy corner rooms with arching windows. The floral print wallpaper, antique reproductions and gravity flush toilets really send you back to the hotel's heyday. Though the hotel is not yet up to the standards of its historic cousins in downtown Durango, the owners are extremely helpful and are making improvements every day. Look around the gorgeous lobby,

with its fine leather couches, pressed-tin ceiling and portrait of the town sweetheart, Lillian Russell, over the piano. Adjacent to the lobby is the **Gold King Dining Room** (at $ to $$$, a good value for breakfast, lunch and dinner) and the Hub Saloon featuring a stunning backbar made of heavy cherry wood columns with intricate carvings and even a bullet hole. Open year-round. **1219 Greene St., Silverton, CO 81433; (303) 387-5527.**

The Wyman Hotel—$$$

If you feel like an "Accidental Tourist," this should definitely be your choice for lodging. Yes, each large, clean room has a Beautyrest mattress, fitted percale sheets, a clock radio by the bed and a private bathroom with individually wrapped Neutrogena soap. Owners Don and Jolene Stott really know how to take care of their guests in their totally renovated, historic corner building. All of the tastefully decorated rooms come equipped with a VCR, and you may choose a couple of movies each night from a video library. No smoking allowed. **14th and Greene St., PO Box 780, Silverton, CO 81433; (303) 387-5372** in season, **(303) 249-4646** off season.

Teller House Hotel—$$

The smell of baking bread wafts into open windows at the Teller House, located atop the French Bakery restaurant. Full breakfast at the bakery is included in the price of your room. Once a boardinghouse for hardrock miners, the Teller House still has a lot of character. The nine rooms are situated around the outside of the upper floor, with windows facing both inside to a common area and out. The simple rooms have high ceilings and are furnished with oak dressers. Four rooms have private bathrooms; five others share large, clean bathrooms down the hall. The Teller House is an inexpensive and enjoyable lodging alternative. **1250 Greene St., Silverton, CO 81433; (303) 387-5423.**

CAMPING

One of the most beautiful areas to camp near Silverton is **South Mineral**

Campground. To get there head north-west on Hwy. 550 for 2 miles, and then southwest on Forest Rd. 585 for 5 miles. There are 23 sites; a fee is charged. To reach **Sig Creek Campground** take Hwy. 550 for 21 miles southwest of Silverton and then proceed 6 miles west on Forest Rd. 578. There are 9 sites; small fee.

Private Campgrounds—
Silverton Lakes Campground—Just north-east of town, not far from the Animas River, is this full-service campground. Hookups, groceries, laundry, hot showers and jeep rentals are available. **PO Box 126, Silverton, CO 81433; (303) 387-5721.**

WHERE TO EAT

Romero's—$$

More than 20 years ago, George Romero came out of the mines and opened up this small Mexican restaurant on Silverton's main street. The narrow room has a mural down one long wall and metal mine tools, irons and general knickknacks ominously hanging on the other. The fam-ily-run institution is known equally for its smothered burritos and silky smooth margaritas. George makes 150 margaritas each day (more than 1,000 per week) dur-ing the summer rush. The special blend is a family secret—you won't see any pre-mix here. George's semiretirement means summer hours only from 10 am–10 pm daily. **1151 Greene St.**

The Pickle Barrel—$ to $$$

Built in 1880 as the Sherwin and Houghton General Store, this historic brick building has been a favorite local hangout since 1971. Run by Fritz Klinke and Loren Lew, The Pickle Barrel is a great spot for lunch, featuring deli sandwiches and burgers. More elaborate dinners include a selection of steak and seafood dishes. Full bar with good selection of beers. Open daily in summer from 7 am for breakfast, lunch and dinner. **1304 Greene St.; (303) 387-5713 or 387-5432.**

The French Bakery Restaurant— $ to $$

Opened in 1917, this distinctive glass-fronted building was once a meat market and grocery store. The ground floor level of the Teller House Hotel is now an enjoy-able full-service restaurant. As the name implies, the bakery on the premises makes fresh goodies daily. For breakfast standard eggs and bacon or omelette dishes are cooked to perfection. Starting mid-morn-ing consider picking something from a large variety of baked goods lining the glass case. In winter the bakery side of the restaurant converts to a ski rental shop. Open in summer only 7–11 am for break-fast, 11 am–3 pm for lunch. **1250 Greene St.; (303) 387-5423.**

SERVICES

Silverton Chamber of Commerce—

Stop by the new chamber headquarters as you enter town and pick up some advice on how to spend your time in Silverton. The staff members can help you wade through the brochures; be sure to ask for a historical walking tour map. Open year-round. **PO Box 565, Silverton, CO 81433; 1-800-752-4494** nationwide or **(303) 387-5654** locally.

The Silverton Standard and Miner—

Since 1875 this local newspaper has been telling people what's happening in Silverton. Pick up a copy and check out their excellent selection of books and maga-zines. Ask to see their Hoe Cylinder Press, which dates clear back to 1830. Located at **1257 Greene St., PO Box 8, Silverton, CO 81433; (303) 387-5477.**

Telluride

Whether you are looking for a plush ski vacation and nights out at fine restaurants or a week of backpacking in the high mountains of the San Juans, we highly recommend Telluride. Squeezed into a box canyon along the San Miguel River, Telluride could easily be the most beautiful spot in Colorado. Surrounding this growing Victorian town of more than 1,300 full-time residents are lofty, jagged peaks—many approaching 14,000 feet in elevation.

The mining legacy of Telluride is one of great wealth and prosperity—60 million in gold and silver was mined in the first 30 years alone. But slowed by steadily declining profits in the 1900s, the mines began closing one by one. Today abandoned mine shafts and buildings lie scattered throughout the nearby mountains, and Telluride's focus has completely shifted to year-round tourism, especially world-class skiing.

Some locals claim that Telluride's skiing really started back in the mining days. On payday at the Tomboy Mine, located 3,000 feet above Telluride, the Finns and the Swedes would beat their co-workers to the brothels in town by skiing down from the site. Today skiers take advantage of 1,105 pristine acres of groomed slopes at Telluride Ski Area—including the Plunge, the longest, steepest mogul run in the US.

During summer the surrounding Uncompahgre National Forest offers some of the state's best and most beautiful opportunities for exploring nature. Supreme hiking and mountain biking trails and hundreds of miles of bone-jarring jeep roads justify spending an extended period of time here. An additional summer drawing card is the town's numerous festivals. The excellent Bluegrass, Jazz, Wild Mushroom, Film and Hang Gliding festivals, among others, attract many people who come for the event and leave infatuated with the area.

Telluride is very concerned about its future. Because of its obvious appeal, debates rage on between developers and those wanting slow growth. You'll hear talk about million-dollar real estate deals and movie stars—indeed most workers have been forced to find more affordable digs downvalley in places like Sawpit and Placerville. Nearly everyone who lives in the area, from an unemployed miner to a commuting worker to John Naisbitt, author of *Megatrends*, has his or her own vision of the town's future.

Some of the pressure to build in historic Telluride has been siphoned off by the rapid pace of development 5 miles away at the sleek Mountain Village. Already the site of many new lodges, condos and homes, the ski-in, ski-out Mountain Village also features an 18-hole golf course and a brand new gondola connection to the old town.

In the meantime, Telluride somehow retains its very authentic Victorian charm. Downtown Telluride has been declared a National Historic District, and any building plans in that area are closely scrutinized by an architectural review committee. Though land values have risen out of the realm of ordinary incomes and people are quick to make comparisons to Aspen, Telluride still manages to avoid becoming another mega-resort.

HISTORY

A handful of eager prospectors first climbed into Telluride from over the towering mountains to the east in 1875. Their efforts were rewarded when they found rich deposits of gold and silver, causing a rush to the area. Successful mines include the Liberty Bell, the Union, the Tomboy, the Pandora and the Gold King. In 1876 J.B. Ingram discovered through careful research that two adjacent mines had overextended their claims by 500 feet. He filed a claim and set up shop between the two mines, naming his the Smuggler. The Smuggler was sitting on a rich silver vein. Ingram went on to expand his operation, which eventually became one of the richest mines in the state.

In the 1880s Telluride, originally known as Columbia, underwent a name change after a rare sulfurous element, tellurium, turned up in local gold deposits. Isolation plagued Telluride through the 1880s. The high cost of transporting ore to faraway smelters and mills prevented an all-out mining boom. A solution appeared in 1890 when Otto Mears's amazing pathfinding skills brought the Rio Grande Southern Railroad into town, connecting the mines with the outside world. The boom was interrupted briefly in 1893 when the silver market crashed. But rich gold strikes soon brought the town back to life.

From the beginning Telluride had a reputation as a hell-raising mining town, with an infamous gambling and red-light district on Pacific Ave. By 1891 the 4,000 residents supported 26 saloons and 12 bordellos. Supposedly this immoral section of town and the harsh natural conditions prompted warnings of "to-hell-u-ride" to people bound for this area. Decent people turned a blind eye to the decadence; bordellos were fined $250 weekly, which is said to have almost singlehandedly financed the town government!

During the 1890s Telluride prospered. In 1895 the New Sheridan Hotel was built, rivaling the finest hotels in Denver with its accommodations and gourmet dining. But at the turn of the century, the boom days began to wane. Intense labor wars at the mines began in 1901 when union miners struck, protesting a new contract that had decreased their wages substantially. Scab labor was brought in and violence erupted. A brief, uneasy peace hung over the valley until 1903, when heightened tensions brought the national guard to town in the winter of 1903–1904 (see Imogene Pass in the Four-Wheel-Drive Trips section). Decreasing profits from mining, coupled with labor problems, brought the mining industry in Telluride to its knees, never to fully recover. Most of the mines as well as the Bank of Telluride had closed by 1930, and the population dwindled to 500. Telluride was saved from becoming a complete ghost town when the Idarado Mining Company bought up the existing mines in the area in 1953 and connected all of the mines with a 350-mile network of tunnels. One tunnel extends 5 miles through the mountains to a point just south of Ouray. Idarado mined millions of dollars worth of copper, lead, zinc, silver and gold before closing in 1978.

During the slow decline of mining in the area, the idea of turning Telluride into a ski resort was kicked around by a few locals. In 1945 a rope tow was constructed at Town Park, but it operated for only two years. It was brought back to life in 1958, when $5 season passes were offered. But in 1971 when ground was broken for the Telluride Ski Area, no one could have predicted the success that would follow. Continued prosperous times are on the horizon for a town that the *Denver Post* once called "doomed."

GETTING THERE

The shortest (327 miles) route from Denver to Telluride is via Hwy. 285 to Poncha Springs; then drive west on Hwy. 50 to Montrose, south on Hwy. 550 to Ridgway, west on Hwy. 62 to Placerville and southeast on Hwy. 145 to Telluride. Now that construction through Glenwood Canyon is complete, a route (several are possible) via Interstate 70 takes about the same amount of time. The Telluride Regional Airport, located 5 miles west of town, is serviced year-round, as is Montrose County Airport 68 miles away. Many flights into Telluride arrive from Denver, Los Angeles and Albuquerque, in addition to other points. Rental cars and taxi transport are available from the airport into town. Now that a gondola has debuted, the easiest, safest and most scenic transport between Telluride and the Mountain Village is over 10,540 foot Coonskin Ridge.

———— FESTIVALS AND EVENTS ————

Every summer a diverse procession of festivals attracts people to the area—many are yearly events with loyal followings. For more information and a complete schedule of events, call the festival hotline at **(303) 728-6079.**

Telluride Bluegrass Festival
late June

Esquire magazine proclaimed that "Telluride has established itself as the country's premier progressive bluegrass event," and after experiencing a few of them we have to agree. Each summer the town gears up for its biggest event, which runs Wed. through Sun. Since 1973 the country's best bluegrass musicians have been performing at the festival, including Bela Fleck, David Bromberg and Sam Bush. Amateur mandolin, banjo, flat-picking guitar and band contests begin on Wed. and run through Fri. morning. The main acts play Fri.–Sun. night. All concerts take place at Town Park. On the weekend some of the musicians play until the wee hours of the morning at local bars. Workshops for those interested in everything from banjo picking to clogging are offered. **1-800-624-2422.**

Telluride Jazz Celebration
early August

The outdoor stage in Telluride's Town Park provides a 360-degree view of the scenery—a perfect accompaniment to a weekend of cool jazz. Since 1976 the festival has attracted both well-known and somewhat obscure musicians in mostly mainstream, traditional jazz styles. After the sun sets, the music comes indoors to local bars and the Sheridan Opera House. **(303) 728-7009.**

Telluride Film Festival
early September

Whether you are a filmmaker or a film lover, this late-summer event will appeal to your cinematic tastes. Since 1973 the film festival has been attracting attention as a lesser-known American counterpart to Cannes. Free showings of premieres and foreign films take place nightly in an outdoor theater. Animation and innovation are topics at daily seminars, and private showings around town are hot tickets. **(303) 728-6079.**

Telluride Hang Gliding Festival
mid-September

Just as the chill of fall enters the high country, professional hang gliders send more chills through the crowd by performing high-altitude acrobatics. There are also competitions between some of the top-ranked hang gliders in the world. It's a quiet and colorful time of year to come to Telluride for this incredible spectator event. **(303) 728-6079.**

OUTDOOR ACTIVITIES

BIKING
MOUNTAIN BIKING

From Telluride you can leave town on a mountain bike and enter another dimension in about five minutes—a dimension without cars, houses and people. Mountain biking is catching on in Telluride in a big way. The terrain is perfect for riders of all abilities and there is even a hut-to-hut system available for an extended ride from Telluride to Moab, Utah (see San Juan Hut Systems in this section).

Bear Creek Trail—
A quick morning or evening ride up to Bear Creek Falls can be taken right out of town. See the Hiking and Backpacking section for more information.

Ophir Pass—
Known to many as a great four-wheel-drive shortcut from Telluride to Silverton, the Ophir Pass road also offers an interesting road for mountain bikes. But be prepared for riding on a sometimes steep, scree-covered road. See the Four-Wheel-Drive Trips section in the **Silverton** chapter for more information.

Rentals, Tours and Information—
Olympic Sports—150 W. Colorado Ave.; (303) 728-4477.

Paragon Ski & Sport—213 W. Colorado Ave.; (303) 728-4525.

San Juan Hut Systems—This first-of-its-kind operation will sound compelling to anyone fit enough to appreciate seven days' riding through beautifully diverse back-country. Beginning in Telluride the 207-mile, self-guided ride starts in the alpine environment near Telluride gradually working down to the Uncompahgre Plateau and eventually into Utah's canyon country, ending at Moab. Spending each night in a provisioned hut takes a weighty burden off your mountain bike.

Advanced mountain bikers can leave the main route and take single tracks over more difficult terrain. But the route is intended for any intermediate rider to complete. The huts are spaced far enough apart for a good five hours of riding each day. They are basic, yet have everything you'll need, including three basic meals, a couple of wool blankets, a sleeping pad and wood stoves. You might also think about doing a two- or three-day stage of the route. **San Juan Hut Systems, Box 1663, Telluride, CO 81435; (303) 728-6935.**

FISHING

The fishing around Telluride can be good, and when the conditions are right it can get downright hot. You may want to take a guided trip or enroll in fly-fishing school. For information contact **Scott Guides** at **Telluride Outside, PO Box 685, 666 W. Colorado Ave., Telluride, CO 81434; 1-800-828-7547.** Otherwise here are a few ideas:

Dolores River—
This Gold Medal river can be one of the state's best, depending on the release levels from McPhee Reservoir. See the Fishing section of the **Cortez** chapter.

San Miguel River—
This fast-moving river is stocked with rainbow trout up to about 12 inches. While catching trout in the San Miguel below Telluride, remember that the water has become mineralized from all of the mining operations: we recommend that you catch and release all fish. After heavy summer rains, the river becomes a useless, muddy flow; when the water is clear, try fishing in

the morning and evening with small, brightly colored dry flies. Fishing with black caddis and Hare's Ear nymphs is also recommended. The San Miguel River below the town of Norwood offers poor fishing.

Kids Fishing Pond—
Kids 12 and under can fish in the pond at the Town Park located at the east end of town. They love it and can usually catch trout on whatever bait they use.

Trout Lake—
If beautiful scenery is part of the fishing experience for you, then make the effort to drive to Trout Lake. Though inconsistent, the fishing can be quite good for smallish rainbows and brooks. Boat rentals are available, and there is even a gazebo for picnicking. Trout Lake is located about 12 miles south of Telluride on Hwy. 145.

Woods Lake—
Nestled at the base of three 14,000-foot peaks (Mt. Wilson and El Diente and Wilson peaks), Woods Lake enjoys a spectacular location away from any major roads. Only artificial flies and lures are permitted. The lake is well stocked with rainbow trout, and an occasional brook or cutthroat can be caught. To get to Woods Lake take Hwy. 145 northwest for 10 miles (just beyond the town of Sawpit). Turn left and head south on Fall Creek Rd. (Forest Rd. 618), which winds its way to Woods Lake in 9 miles.

FOUR-WHEEL-DRIVE TRIPS

Today those with courage (in some cases, stupidity) and a reliable four-wheel-drive vehicle can navigate the historic mining roads around Telluride.

Black Bear Pass—
Black Bear Pass is etched into the west side of Ingram Peak at the east end of the valley above Telluride. Visible from town, the road zigzags up what seems to be a vertical wall. Locals strongly urge that only

experienced drivers attempt this dangerous road. Black Bear is a one-way road that begins near the summit of Red Mountain Pass and heads west, eventually ending in Telluride. For specifics see the Four-Wheel-Drive Trips section of the **Silverton** chapter.

Imogene Pass—

Built back in the 1870s to transport ore from the Tomboy Mine over to Ouray, Imogene Pass is one of the toughest jeep roads in Colorado. The view from the summit will make the drive worthwhile, except for vertigo-prone passengers. Imogene begins in Telluride. From the north end of N. Oak St., turn right onto the pass road (Forest Rd. 869). As the road climbs, it offers a great view of Telluride and the east end of the valley, including Ingram Falls, Black Bear Pass Rd. and Bridal Veil Falls. Five miles up the road you'll arrive at the Tomboy Mine site. When the Tomboy was in full operation during the late 1890s, hundreds of men living at the mine camp enjoyed such unusual luxuries as tennis courts, a bowling alley and a YMCA. Today the Tomboy is nothing but ruins. Above the mine it's another 1.5 miles of tough switchbacks to the summit at 13,509 feet.

Just after the turn of the century, Telluride mines were hit with serious labor disputes that eventually built up into a long strike in 1903. The national guard was called in. They loaded the union "agitators" on a train and shipped them out of town with orders never to return. Just to make sure they didn't return via the "back door" to Telluride, the guardsmen erected Ft. Peabody on the summit of Imogene Pass and manned it through the winter of 1903–1904.

On the other (east) side of the pass, the road winds down a steep section into Imogene Basin. From the pass it's about 11 miles to Ouray. For more information about the Ouray side of the pass, see the Four-Wheel-Drive Trips section in the **Ouray** chapter. From Ouray you can return to Telluride via Ridgway and Dallas Divide or over another jeep road such as Ophir Pass.

Ophir Pass—

This fairly mild four-wheel-drive road can be reached just south of Telluride. Head south on Hwy. 145 for about 10 miles and turn left to the pass on Forest Rd. 630. *The road is very narrow and vehicles traveling uphill have the right of way.* For more information about the pass from the Silverton side see the Four-Wheel-Drive Trips section in the **Silverton** chapter.

Tours and Rentals—

Telluride Outside—Take a full-day or a half-day trip on some of the wild roads near Telluride. Trips depart daily in the summer. Rentals are also available if you want to drive yourself. Jeeps can be rented for half or full days. You can pick up your vehicle the night before. **PO Box 685, 666 W. Colorado Ave., Telluride, CO 81435; (303) 728-3895** or **1-800-831-6230.**

GOLF

Telluride Golf Club—

This brand new 6,733 yard, par 71 championship course at the Mountain Village will challenge your senses and your patience (it's still a bit rough). The 18-hole course winds amidst massive homes while offering stop-in-your-tracks views to the surrounding peaks. Watch out for deer and elk on the fairways. The signature on this course may be the unique high tee on the par 3, 17th hole. Your ball will fly 15% further at this elevation (close to 10,000 feet) than sea level, so remember to club down. Open to the public with the exception of certain weekend tee times. Reasonable green fees for the time being. Located at the **Resort at the Mountain Village; (303) 728-6366.**

HIKING AND BACKPACKING

It's difficult not to use superlatives when talking about hiking and backpacking opportunities in the Telluride area. Just out of town beautiful forests and high alpine basins covered with wildflowers await. *But by all means, stay out of the mine tunnels—they can be death traps!*

West of Telluride, **Lizard Head Wilderness Area** in Uncompahgre National Forest straddles the San Miguel Mountains. It's characterized by many glacial cirque lakes, roaring streams, spruce and fir forests and several 14,000-foot peaks.

The **visitors center** in Telluride **(666 W. Colorado Ave.)** has very good information concerning trails in the area. Topographical maps and information can be found at **Olympic Sports,** with three locations—Oak St. Lift, Coonskin Base and the **Mountain Village; (303) 728-4477.** The nearest forest service office for the Telluride area is located 33 miles northwest on Hwy. 145: **Norwood Ranger District Office, 1760 Grand Ave., PO Box 388, Norwood, CO 81423; (303) 327-4261.**

Bear Creek Trail—

This beautiful 2-mile hike starts in town and leads south, uphill to an impressive waterfall. The trail through this deep valley offers great views of the surrounding craggy peaks. At one point it crosses over an avalanche slide area, showing vividly why cross-country skiers avoid the valley in winter. The trailhead begins at the south end of Pine St.

Bridal Veil Falls—

This short, steep hike can catch the unacclimated by surprise. If you are new to the high altitude, take it slow and easy. From Telluride drive up to the end of the box canyon and begin hiking up the jeep road. Views of Ingram Falls on the left and Bridal Veil Falls—Colorado's longest at 325 feet—on the right make this a highly recommended 1-mile hike. At the top of the falls, hanging over the impressive cliff, is the recently restored old Smuggler-Union hydroelectric plant. This National Historic Landmark, built in 1904, offers stunning views back down the valley to Telluride.

Hope Lake Trail—

From the Hope Lake trailhead, this gradual 3-mile hike leads up to 12,500 feet. Many families like this hike, which offers impressive views. Fishing is usually poor.

Hope Lake is located above Trout Lake and was built as a reservoir for the Ames hydroelectric plant. To reach the trailhead from Telluride, head south about 12 miles on Hwy. 145 to Trout Lake. Turn left onto Trestle Rd. (Forest Rd. 626) and drive 1 mile to the intersection with Hidden Lake Rd. (Forest Rd. 627). Turn left again and drive to the parking area 2.5 miles up the road.

Silver Pick Basin/Navajo Basin Loop—

This exciting and beautiful backpacking trip is marked with old mine buildings, snowfields and rugged mountains. The trail (No. 408) begins on the north side of Lizard Head Wilderness Area and heads south into Silver Pick Basin. It climbs out of the forest and up into a rocky area where a lot of old mining claims dot the mountainside. At the top of the basin a saddle allows access to Navajo Basin to the southwest. From the saddle Wilson Peak, Gladstone Peak, Mt. Wilson and El Diente Peak loom from left to right. Wilson Peak is a fairly easy climb but the others are very difficult. If you decide to attempt El Diente (it's possible to climb Wilson and El Diente in one day) just be sure to bring a helmet and go up carefully with some friends. Just below the south side of the saddle is an old building that many hikers sleep in.

If you drop down from the saddle into Navajo Basin and follow the drainage west, you will come to Navajo Lake. Below the lake the trail splits. The left fork (Navajo Lake Trail) heads toward Dunton and Woods Lake (see the Hiking and Backpacking section of the **Cortez** chapter). The right fork climbs northwest and then down to another fork. From this new fork, head to the right on Trail No. 407, which will take you back to the start of the loop. To reach the trailhead from Telluride, head northwest on Hwy. 145 for about 7 miles and turn left onto Big Bear Rd. (Forest Rd. 622). Follow the road south for 5.5 miles and begin hiking up the jeep road to the wilderness area boundary.

Ski Mountain—

The mountain at Telluride Ski Area is a very popular hiking spot with spectacular views. The Coonskin Chairlift is open in summer Thur.–Mon. 10 am–2 pm. For a small fee you can ride to the top and hike down. Another option is to get off at the midway point on the new gondola. If you're feeling ambitious and are in excellent shape, forget the lifts and hike to the top. Be sure to call **(303) 728-3041** for information. Located on the west end of town.

Wasatch Trail—

Starting from town, this 10-mile loop trail is one of the most scenic in the Telluride area. Many people hike it in a day, but it also makes a good overnighter. The trail follows Bear Creek up to the falls and then climbs up to 13,000 feet at a divide between Bear Creek and Bridal Veil Creek. From Telluride follow the trail from the south end of Pine St. up to the falls and look for the Wasatch Trail (No. 414) on the right. It climbs steeply for the first mile to La Junta Basin and then gradually climbs to the divide. Follow the trail northeast as it drops down to Bridal Veil Creek, then follow the trail down past Bridal Veil Falls and back into town.

HORSEBACK RIDING

Olympic Sports—

This outfit offers one-hour, full-day and cowboy breakfast or dinner rides. Ride with Roudy, a cowboy you won't soon forget: **(303) 728-4477** or **1-800-828-7547**.

RIVER FLOATING

San Miguel River—

Much like the Upper Dolores, the San Miguel River flows west out of the San Juans, cutting a deep valley and exposing red rock walls. From Telluride the river meanders west for about 3 miles before plunging 400 feet in a half mile, then flowing into the South Fork. From here down to the bridge at Naturita (54 miles) the floating can be good in May through June, depending on the runoff. At high water

this section of the San Miguel can be dangerous due to huge waves. Be careful.

Upper Dolores River—

See the River Floating section in the **Cortez** chapter.

Outfitters—

Telluride Outside—Experienced river guides lead one- to six-night trips on the San Miguel, Gunnison, Dolores and Colorado rivers. They can also cook a pretty mean river meal. For information contact them at **666 W. Colorado Ave., Box 685, Telluride, CO 81435; (303) 728-3895** or **1-800-831-6230**.

SKIING
CROSS-COUNTRY SKIING

One word of caution: with its heavy snows and steep mountains you need to be knowledgeable, aware and prepared for avalanche danger. We don't want to scare you off completely, because there are many beautiful cross country trails, but please use your head.

Backcountry Trails—

Lizard Head Pass—See the **Cortez** chapter.

San Juan Hut Systems—Take off from Telluride on old mine roads and backcountry trails for 7 miles a day with a cozy mountain hut waiting at the end. Or, just reserve one of the huts and make loop trips back to your home base. The five huts in this system extend between Telluride and Ouray. The trails, designed for intermediate to expert skiers, wind through spectacular territory in Uncompahgre National Forest with views of the Sneffels Range. All skiers should have a basic knowledge of changing mountain weather conditions and preparedness. The basic huts all have wood stoves, a wood supply, bedding and food. San Juan Hut Systems, **117 N. Willow St., Box 1663, Telluride, CO 81435; (303) 728-6935**.

Groomed Trails—

Telluride Nordic Center—About 50 kilometers of groomed trails meander through aspen groves and open meadows with fabulous views to the nearby peaks. The Telluride Nordic Center offers terrain that varies from easy to moderately challenging in three main areas: on the mile-long Town Trail, at the golf course in the Mountain Village and up in the Prospect Basin area. Guided backcountry trips, telemark skiing and skating are all options. Rentals and lessons available at the Mountain Village's Meadows Base. **(303) 728-5989.**

Town Trail—This informal, mile-long trail is popular among locals wanting to stretch out a bit. Located along the south edge of town, the trail loosely follows the course of the San Miguel River.

Rentals and Information—

There are numerous places to rent skis in town. All of the shops in town and at the Mountain Village should have current knowledge of avalanche conditions in the area.

DOWNHILL SKIING

Telluride Ski Area—

It takes some determination to get to Telluride, but once there you'll be greeted by short lift lines and some of the best conditions imaginable. Not only is the skiing great, but the views to the 14,000-foot summits of the San Miguel Mountains, the odd rock of Lizard Head Peak and the distant La Sal Mountains in Utah will halt you in your tracks. Telluride Ski Area has a wide reputation for having some of the longest, steepest, nastiest bump runs in the country. It's all true, but there is also a gentle, more sunny side to the mountain that towers over town. The back side of Telluride, with its southern exposure, is a paradise for nonexpert skiers.

But Telluride is still the consummate expert mountain. The shaded front side of the mountain usually offers soft snow since it hardly ever melts and refreezes. The Spiral Stairs run has a 40-degree slope near the top and keeps going for what seems like forever. From the expert front side of the mountain, the dramatic view down into town and around the edge of the box canyon will take your breath away—as if that's what you need at 11,000 feet! If the tremendous 3,145-foot vertical drop of the mountain isn't long enough, there are walk-up runs from the top of Gold Hill (400 acres of additional expert skiing). Someday the steep slopes of Bear Creek and Delta Bowl, known to a select group of expert skiers, will be serviced by lift.

The ski mountain is accessible both from town and from the Mountain Village. For information contact **Telluride Ski Resort, Box 11155, 562 Mountain Village Blvd., Telluride, CO 81435; (303) 728-3856.**

Telluride Helitrax—

Nothing compares to the exhilaration of cutting down through virgin powder in remote unfolding basins. Getting away from ski lifts, though, requires climbing into a Helitrax helicopter—an alternative for people with very deep pockets. For information call **(303) 728-4904.**

TENNIS

There are two free tennis courts at **Town Park,** located at the east end of town.

--------------- **SEEING AND DOING** ---------------

CHAIRLIFT RIDES

In summer rides up the **Coonskin Chairlift** are available Wed.–Sat. 10 am–2 pm. From the top of the mountain at 10,500 feet, enjoy spectacular views of the surrounding peaks, including the La Sal Mountains in Utah. Food is available at a snack bar, or bring your own picnic lunch. A small fee is charged, but children under 6 ride free if accompanied by an adult. Located at the west end of town. For more information call **(303) 728-3856.**

HOT SPRINGS

See the **Ouray** chapter.

MUSEUMS AND GALLERIES

Telluride Historical Museum—

Take some time to wander around the interesting collection at this small historical museum. All of the objects, when taken together, create a fine reflection of life in early Telluride. Old black and white photos of a raucous saloon are displayed with beer tokens, old pool balls and gaming tables. A barber's chair with leather handstraps represents a time when barbers were the ones to pull teeth or do minor surgery. In the kitchen you'll find handwritten cookbooks, old calendars and an assortment of gadgets for the time. Small fee. Open from Memorial Day to mid-Oct. 10 am–5 pm daily; winter hours, 12–5 pm Mon.–Fri. **217 N. Fir St.; (303) 728-3344.**

NIGHTLIFE

Fly Me to the Moon Saloon—

This is the most consistent venue for live music in Telluride. It's also the best place to meet some of the local blond-haired, Rastafarian/Dead Heads. Downstairs in a narrow underground room is a stage, a spring-loaded dance floor that absorbs shocks from frantic dancing and a well-stocked bar. The bands usually play danceable rock, reggae or blues. It's Telluride custom to just start dancing regardless of whether or not you have a partner. During ski season or large festivals, Fly Me to the Moon can get packed. Cover charge when there is a live band. **132 E. Colorado Ave.; (303) 728-6666.**

Last Dollar—

This local hangout is a good place to go for a cold beer and a game of pool or darts. A stone fireplace keeps things warm in the winter months. Open until 2 am (midnight on Sun.). Located at the corner of Pine St. and Colorado Ave.; **(303) 728-4800.**

Mountain Splendor—

The changing seasons in the San Juans are brought to life in Jack Pera's well-done computer-synchronized slide show. Pera, a Telluride native, speaks before the slide show, which features 25 years' worth of his wildlife and wildflower slides taken in the San Juan area. A photo gallery of Pera's work is displayed in the lobby; framed photos are available for purchase. Mountain Splendor is shown at 8:30 pm nightly in the Masonic Lodge Hall. The box office opens at 8:10 pm; fee charged. **200 E. Colorado Ave.; (303) 728-3632** or **728-4132.**

San Juan Brewing Company—

Telluride's brewpub is a hit. See Where to Eat for more information.

Sheridan Bar—

There is no better place to imagine how Telluride looked and felt at the beginning of the century. After all, in 1889 Butch Cassidy made his very first unauthorized bank withdrawal only a block away. Located just off the lobby of the New Sheridan Hotel, this bar is a happening spot for locals and visitors. This casual place has a stamped-tin ceiling and well-worn hardwood floors. The massive, cherry wood backbar is stocked to the hilt. If you need to test your motor skills, check out the darts and foosball games. Open daily until 2 am (midnight on Sun.). **225 W. Colorado Ave.; (303) 728-3911.**

SCENIC DRIVES

Alta—

Located a short 12 miles from Telluride, Alta provides great views of Ophir Needles to the south, Lizard Head Peak, Mt. Wilson, and Wilson and El Diente peaks to the west. The development of the rich Gold King Mine in 1877 enabled the mining community of Alta to boom into the 1890s. Mining in the Alta area produced gold, silver, copper and lead, and continued sporadically until the mid-1940s. Today a few buildings remain, including the old boardinghouse for Gold King miners. The site is privately owned by a mining company, but visitors are allowed as long as you stay out of the buildings and don't destroy anything. To reach Alta from Telluride, head south on Hwy. 145 for about 5 miles to Boomerang Rd. (Forest Rd. 632) on the left. From here continue 4 miles to Alta.

Last Dollar Road—

This dirt road travels past old ranch properties with weathered buildings and provides excellent views to the west end of the Sneffels Range. Last Dollar Rd. heads north from Telluride and comes out near Dallas Divide on Hwy. 62. The road traverses Hastings Mesa and is a good shortcut between Telluride and Ouray. Passenger cars can drive Last Dollar Rd. when it's dry, but it would be a good idea to inquire locally before heading off. To reach the road from Telluride, drive west 3 miles and look for Last Dollar Rd. (Forest Rd. 638) on the right.

Lizard Head Pass—

Lizard Head Pass is only about 15 miles from Telluride, but a lot of spectacular scenery is packed into this short drive. Heading south on Hwy. 145 takes you by the town of Ophir (about 10 miles from Telluride). This was the location of the legendary Ophir Loop, an impressive 100-foot-high trestle for the Rio Grande Southern Railroad. The railroad, built by Otto Mears, connected Telluride with the smelters in Durango and the rest of the outside world via Lizard Head Pass. Continuing on the highway from Ophir for another 3 miles takes you to Trout Lake, one of the most beautiful settings in the state. Towering above the lake to the south are Yellow Mountain, Vermillion Peak and Sheep Mountain. Although the lake is privately owned, fishing is allowed.

Trout Lake was built as a reservoir for the historic power plant downriver at Ames, which in 1891 generated the world's first commercial AC power. At the south end of the lake, an old, rickety Rio Grande Southern Railroad trestle appears ready to topple any day. See it while you can. From Trout Lake continue on Hwy. 145 up to the summit of Lizard Head Pass for views west to the Upper Dolores River Valley and north to the eerie-looking Lizard Head Peak. From the top of an already-tall peak, this 400-foot spire of crumbly rock is an inspiring sight, as well as what many rock climbers consider to be the most difficult technical climb in the state.

San Juan Skyway—

Telluride is but one stop on this 236-mile nationally designated route. For more information about this dramatic drive see the Scenic Drives section of the **Durango** chapter.

—————— WHERE TO STAY ——————

ACCOMMODATIONS

Telluride has a lot to offer when it comes to accommodations. If you would like to stay in a historic hotel or guest ranch, there are a number of choices. In addition, a cache of top-notch bed and breakfast inns have opened in town. Well heeled guests may want to consider staying at the plush 177-room **The Peaks at Telluride ($$$$)** though many locals say it resembles a mental institution. Whatever the outside looks like, the spa facilities inside are first-class, and it's about the only place for round-the-clock service. For information call **(303) 728-6800.**

If you prefer a modern condominium with all the amenities, call **Telluride Central Reservations** at **1-800-525-3455** or **(303) 728-4431.**

Pennington's Mountain Village Inn—$$$$

The term "bed and breakfast" once connoted simple, affordable places to stay. Pennington's, a deluxe B&B at the Mountain Village, destroys that conception with its luxurious accommodations. Each of Pennington's 12 spacious guest rooms has a private deck, and takes advantage of a spectacular ridgetop perch. Few places in the world rival this dramatic location. Inside, the French Country decor looks right out of a glossy decorator magazine, but Innkeepers Michael and Judy McClean put a warm, human touch on the place. Common areas include a formal sunken library/lounge, a window-encased jacuzzi room and an elaborate downstairs game room. Gorge yourself on a large, full breakfast served in the sunny dining room or, if you prefer, in your own bedroom. Call for reservations. **100 Pennington Ct., PO Box 2428, Telluride Mountain Village, CO 81435; 1-800-543-1437** or **(303) 728-5337.**

Bear Creek Bed and Breakfast—$$$ to $$$$

Several special features set this small, contemporary B&B apart: 1) the large upper rooms have walls of windows with unbelievable mountain views; 2) even if your room doesn't feature such a view, the rooftop deck has a dramatic 360 degree panorama; 3) the convenient Colorado Ave. location close to the Town Park is perfect for summer festivals, and; 4) the sauna and steamroom make great places to relax after a day on the slopes. While Bear Creek doesn't have the street appeal or historic charm of some accommodations, its personalized approach will appeal to many. All 10 well-appointed rooms have private baths, cable TV and daily maid service. **PO Box 2369, Telluride, CO 81435; 1-800-338-7064** or **(303) 728-6681.**

Skyline Guest Ranch—$$$ to $$$$

Just 8 miles south of Telluride off Hwy. 145, Skyline Guest Ranch sits on what could very possibly be the most beautiful property in the Colorado Rockies. Nestled at 9,600 feet in a mountain meadow, the ranch faces towering peaks, most notably Mt. Wilson and Wilson Peak (both over 14,000 feet) just to the west. Summer wildflowers cover the meadows with every color under the sun. In fall colorful aspen compel visitors to snap roll after roll of pictures.

Longtime owners and hosts Dave and Sherry Farney go out of their way to help guests get the most out of their stay—whether they want to go climb a mountain or just lounge around the ranch. The easy-going atmosphere encourages everyone to get to know one another. Up the hill from the main lodge is a lake stocked with brown, brook and Tasmanian rainbow trout. A string of excellent horses allows you to ride to your heart's content. After a day of hiking you can relax with a cold beer or head to the sauna and the wood-fired hot tub.

Accommodations at the ranch include 10 guest rooms in the main lodge and half a dozen private cabins nearby. Exquisite meals served in the main lodge include the famous "Sherry" bread. Those staying in the cabins can opt to cook their own meals. Open June to Oct. and from Thanksgiving to Apr. A week-long minimum stay is required in summer. In winter, cabins and rooms in the lodge ($$$) are available and rates are figured on a daily basis. **Box 67, Telluride, CO 81435; (303) 728-3757.**

New Sheridan Hotel—$$ to $$$

In 1895 two enterprising men, Gus Brickman and Max Hippler, decided to stop their search for riches in the mountains around Telluride and build a fine hotel for the town. Despite a burgeoning population of 2,000, Telluride lacked quality accommodations. The hotel's place in history was assured when, in 1902, perennial presidential hopeful William Jennings Bryan made a speech from a large wooden stage erected at the front of the landmark three-story hotel. But as the mining town declined, the hotel followed, eventually closing in 1925. The resilient hotel reopened years later and after extensive renovations is back in the limelight.

Rooms range from the merely comfortable to the plush William Jennings Bryan Suite, with its expansive views and period antique furniture. Most rooms are not equipped with private baths, but the "club" baths are clean and numerous enough. All rooms have color TVs and phones. This could be the best lodging value in town. Just off the first floor lobby, check out the Sheridan Bar (see the Nightlife section) and Sheridan Opera House. **231 W. Colorado Ave., Telluride, CO 81435; (303) 728-4351.**

CAMPING

Town Park Campground, on the east end of town, is very popular in the summer. It has 28 sites, restrooms and shower facilities. During summer festivals sites are taken quickly. The campground's beautiful location in the trees along the San Miguel River and its proximity to town make it a great spot. No RV hookups; a fee is charged.

In Uncompahgre National Forest—
Sunshine Campground possesses what is certainly one of the most spectacular views of any national forest campground in the state. Located 8 miles southwest of Telluride on Hwy. 145, Sunshine has a larger-than-life view west to Mt. Wilson and Wilson Peak in the Lizard Head Wilderness Area. There are 15 sites and a fee is charged. Two miles farther southwest on Hwy. 145 is **Matterhorn Campground** with 24 sites and a standout view; fee charged.

A few nearby primitive camping areas are free of charge (no pump water). On Hwy. 145 between Sunshine and Matterhorn campgrounds, Boomerang Rd. (Forest Rd. 632) heads east for 3 miles to **Alta Lakes,** where there are some places to camp. Camping at **Woods Lake** is also possible. It's located 17 miles west of Telluride—drive northwest on Hwy. 145 past Sawpit and turn left on Fall Creek Rd. (Forest Rd. 618). Follow the road south to Woods Lake. Campsites are also available along **Illium Valley Rd.** (Forest Rd. 625) just west of Telluride. The road can be reached from Telluride by driving northwest on Hwy. 145 for about 5 miles. Look for the turn-off for Illium Valley Rd. on the left.

WHERE TO EAT

La Marmotte—$$$
La Marmotte receives consistently high praise from its toughest critics: the locals. It's a special place for classic and country-style French cuisine. Owners Bertrand and Noelle Lepel-Cointet have hit on a restaurant formula that works well. La Marmotte is located in the old town icehouse down in the warehouse district. Exposed brick and weathered wood dominate the decor of this small, intimate place. The menu offers entrées ranging from pasta to steak du jour. A fine selection of French and California wines can be ordered. Sun. brunch is also served at the restaurant (not a buffet). Reservations recommended during the busy winter months. Open year-round 6–10 pm nightly; Sun. brunch 10 am–2 pm in summer only. **150 W. San Juan Ave.; (303) 728-6232.**

Leimgrubers Bierstube & Restaurant—$$ to $$$
Christal Leimgruber brings a genuine warmth and lively spirit to her Bavarian restaurant. Raised in East Berlin, Leimgruber made it across the border to the West just two years before the construction of what used to be the Berlin Wall. She has brought the Old World to Telluride, and local support has been tremendous. The small restaurant, with its friendly service, generous portions and good beer, keeps people coming back. Menu entrées include bratwurst, wienerschnitzel and Kässler—smoked pork tenderloin with champagne sauerkraut. Choose from a wide selection of German beer, including three different shades of draft Pauliner and wheat beer, as well as a good selection of wines and liquors by the glass. Bavarian music and a collection of beer steins give the restaurant a distinctly European feel. There is also deck seating. Leimgrubers serves breakfast in winter and gets packed and wild for après ski. Open for dinner 5:30–9:30 pm Tues.–Sat. during summer; open in winter 3–10 pm daily. **573 W. Pacific Ave.; (303) 728-4663.**

San Juan Brewing Company— $$ to $$$

Someone finally fixed up the historic Rio Grande Southern train depot. The 100-year-old structure hadn't been used regularly since the last run of the "Galloping Goose," back in 1951. Now it's been transformed into a great brewpub. The U-shaped mahogany bar with cut-glass etchings overhead attracts a good mix of locals and visitors. The taps are conveniently located next to the massive copper brew kettles filled with handcrafted beer. The favorite seems to be Black Bear Porter. Try the simple bar menu with burgers, "vegeburgers," soups (try the beer cheese soup) and sandwiches. Or step inside an adjacent dining room that serves up steaks and seafood in a quiet, elegant atmosphere. In summer the back deck, right next to the San Miguel River, is a top draw. Open daily from 11:30 am–2 am. **300 S. Townsend; (303) 728-0100.**

Sofios—$$ to $$$

Mexican food with a southwestern slant fills the menu at this busy eatery. Enchiladas, burritos and tacos come in traditional and jazzed-up versions. Smaller appetites may order à la carte ($) from the varied menu. You'll be served in a two-tiered room with exposed brick walls, white stucco archways and a pressed-tin ceiling. Sofios also serves egg dishes, pancakes and waffles for breakfast. Breakfast served daily 7–11:30 am (noon on Sun.), dinner 5:30–10 pm. **110 E. Colorado Ave.; (303) 728-4882.**

The Excelsior Cafe—$ to $$$

Located in a building that was a bowling alley in the 1890s, the charming Excelsior Cafe features exposed brick walls, pressed tin ceilings and a spiral staircase leading to upstairs seating. We're taking a chance with the new owners and new Mediterranean Italian cuisine featured at the Excelsior for two main reasons: its great atmosphere and the creative, well-balanced menu (locals consistently rave about the food). The cook has a prominent place at an open grill near the front of the restaurant so customers can watch. Enter at the dinner hour and you'll smell a sweet, but not overpowering garlic in the air. The small copper bar area is a perfect place to order a glass of wine, eat some olives and watch Telluride go by on the sidewalk. Also an Italian deli for take out and bulk purchases. Open daily 7:30 am–2:30 pm for breakfast and lunch; 6–10:30 pm for dinner. **200 W. Colorado Ave.; (303) 728-4250.**

Eddie's—$ to $$

Eddie's has one of the best sun decks in town—and definitely the best pizza. From your table you have great views of the ski mountain and up and down the valley. In addition to pizzas made with the usual toppings, specialty pizzas with ingredients such as capers, calamari and artichoke hearts can satisfy even the most adventuresome. Pasta specials, sandwiches and appetizers round out the menu. Eddie's sister restaurant in Moab ships its microbrewed beer to Telluride—try the raspberry wheat. Orders to go and deliveries are available. Open 11 am–11 pm daily. Located on **Colorado Ave. next to Elk's Park; (303) 728-5335.**

Baked in Telluride—$

A mouth-watering array of croissants (various fruit, meat and cheese combinations), rolls, donuts, bagels and brownies keep people coming back to this full-service bakery. There is also fast counter service for deli sandwiches and pizza by the slice. Now they serve beer brewed on site, too. Find an outside bench on the small covered porch or bring your food up on the first chairlift ride in winter. Also a few inside tables. Open 5:30 am–10 pm daily. **127 S. Fir St.; (303) 728-4775.** Those of you who want an alternative should try **Gregor's Bakery & Cafe ($ to $$)** with its great baked goods and creative vegetarian cooking (excellent "no huevos" rancheros and pizza du jour). Open 6:30 am–9 pm Mon.–Sat.; til noon on Sun. **217 E. Colorado, (303) 728-3334.**

——————— SERVICES ———————

Telluride Central Reservations—

This is the only number that covers all of Telluride. Call **1-800-525-3455** or **(303) 728-4431.**

Telluride Chamber Resort Association Visitors Center—

Be sure to stop in at the visitors center at the west end of town for advice, happenings and loads of printed information on the area. They also have a touch screen with 24-hour computerized information. Located at **666 W. Colorado Ave., Box 653, Telluride, CO 81435; (303) 728-3041.**

Transportation—

Skip's Taxi and Shuttle Service of Telluride—Twenty-four hour taxi service is available at **(303) 728-6667.**

Telluride Transit—Chartered bus/van transportation to and from the Telluride, Montrose and Grand Junction airports can be arranged 24 hours in advance by calling **(303) 728-6000.**

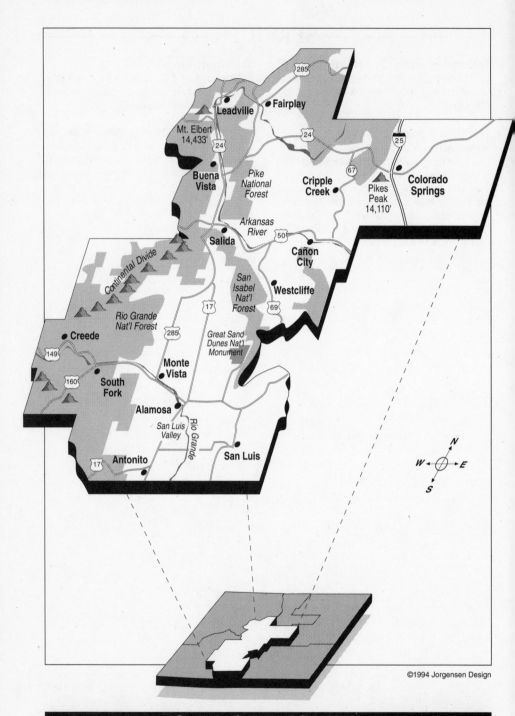

South Central Region

©1994 Jorgensen Design

SOUTH CENTRAL REGION

Cañon City

Cañon City doesn't claim to stand alone as a vacation destination. But the small, historic town, with a population of 15,000, truly enjoys a great location in the midst of spectacular surroundings. The Royal Gorge has long been the best-known attraction in the area, bringing in more than half a million visitors each year. Some 1,000 feet deep and 8 miles long, the gorge is an awesome sight, especially when viewed from the world's highest suspension bridge: examples of nature and human engineering at their best. Unfortunately, just a couple of miles from the wonderment of the Gorge, you find yourself under siege by huge, tacky billboards trying to get you to pull off the road for one thing or another.

Rafting might be the perfect way to experience the beauty of the Arkansas River and the fascinating geology of the area around Cañon City. A float trip might be a mellow family excursion or a rough ride through the intense rapids within the Gorge itself. A number of little-known mountain parks in the surrounding foothills and thousands of acres of national forests make Cañon City a perfect setting-off point for hikers, mountain bikers and sightseers. To get a feel for the importance of gold in the mountains to the north spend a half-day (minimum) on the Gold Belt Tour (see the Scenic Drive section), which leads you to Cripple Creek, among other interesting stops.

Cañon City's residents enjoy a protected, natural setting that buffers the town from harsh weather. A well-preserved five-block stretch of Main Street has been named to the National Register of Historic Places. But Cañon City is best known as the home of the state penitentiary. In fact Cañon City and Florence, its neighbor just to the east, together lay claim to 14 state and federal correctional facilities. No doubt it's the foundation of the area economy. Though the prison system is not open to the general public, the Territorial Prison Museum is a fascinating and disturbing way to get a feeling for life on the inside. Aside from all the stone walls and guard towers, Cañon City remains a quiet town with an intriguing history.

461

HISTORY

Cañon City was a favorite camping area for Ute Indians, but it also served as a war line between the mountainous domain of the Utes and the territory of the eastern plains Indians. Sporadic tribal fighting kept permanent settlers away in the early 1800s. Several US Army explorations headed by the well-known soldiers Lt. Zebulon Pike and Maj. Stephen Long passed through the area. Their travels in the early 1800s helped chart the territory acquired in the Louisiana Purchase of 1803.

It was the gold rush that eventually brought settlers to Cañon City in 1859. People came not for mining per se, but to build a trading center for supplies and provisions needed by miners in the mountains to the west. The town grew quickly and within two years there were 900 residents.

Cañon City hit the skids by 1863 as the men rode wagons east to join sides in fighting the Civil War. The Anson Rudd family was nearly the only one to stay behind. By autumn of 1864 a few families returned to occupy vacant homes and begin a town revival.

In 1868 Golden and Denver were vying to be named the seat of the territorial government. Just as the heated political battle appeared deadlocked, Cañon City lined up the support of a block of southern Colorado legislators to name Cañon City as the capital. Even though Cañon City had no possibility of winning, it now had enough clout to make a deal. During some backroom wheeling and dealing, Denver enlisted the support of Cañon City. Soon Denver was named the capital and, in return, Cañon City was given the chance to build the territorial penitentiary. The secure prison walls began keeping prisoners from the general population in 1871, just five years before Colorado was to become a state.

In the early 1900s Cañon City was a prime location for movie making. Spectacular scenery provided the backdrop for local cowboy Tom Mix, the hero of many silent Westerns. But the spotlight was short-lived. Grace McCue, a popular leading lady of the times, was swept away and drowned in the Arkansas River during filming, and the tragedy provoked damage suits that forced the Colorado Motion Picture Co. into bankruptcy. Other films such as *Cat Ballou*, *Continental Divide* and *The Dutchess and the Dirtwater Fox* were also made in the Cañon City vicinity.

Cañon City had the dubious honor of being state headquarters for the Ku Klux Klan in the mid-1920s. The Klan published a small newspaper and eventually controlled many county and civic offices as well as the school board. They even operated a Klan bank in the Hotel St. Cloud for five years. Thankfully, the hateful ideals of the Klan were short-lived.

Due in large part to the prison system, slow, steady growth has provided residents with jobs over the years, without depriving them of small-town status. Most residents will tell you that having the prison actually makes it one of the safest towns in the country. In addition, its mild climate and lack of many big-city problems have made Cañon City into a favored place to retire.

GETTING THERE

Cañon City is located 115 miles south of Denver, or 38 miles west of Pueblo. To get there from Denver, drive south on Interstate 25 for 68 miles to Colorado Springs. Angle southwest on Hwy. 115 for 36 miles, then turn right (west) on Hwy. 50 for the last 11 miles into town.

———— MAJOR ATTRACTIONS ————

Royal Gorge

For three million years the Arkansas River has cut through solid granite to form this spectacular 1,053-foot-deep chasm. Known to early explorers as the Grand Canyon of the Arkansas, the Royal Gorge has astonished travelers for generations. Despite overcommercialization, the gorge remains a magnificent sight to anyone willing to look over its edge.

History—

In 1806 Lt. Zebulon Montgomery Pike camped near the eastern portal of the canyon, but his scouting party determined that it would be impossible to get through the gorge. It took 70 years and the promise of profits from the silver boom to inspire the railroads to chisel a way through the narrow canyon. When the Leadville silver rush was in full force, two railroad companies started laying tracks in different sections of the gorge, and a bitter right-of-way struggle ensued. There was room in the narrow canyon for only one track, and both companies desperately wanted the route. By 1878 the "war" between the Denver & Rio Grande (D&RG) and Santa Fe railroads escalated to the point of gunfire and frequent sabotage. Somehow, no one was ever killed. Ultimately a lease through the gorge was granted to the D&RG by the courts.

In 1929 the world's highest suspension bridge was built across the Royal Gorge 1,053 feet above the Arkansas River. The bridge is still the best way to get an unobstructed view of the river—that is, unless you attach yourself to an extra long bungee cord and hurl yourself over the edge, as four daredevils did in 1980. Other reasonable ways to experience the gorge here are via the aerial tramway, the steep-incline railway to the bottom or a 26-minute "multimedia slide presentation." All of this costs money: an all-inclusive ticket to the highlights runs about ten bucks per adult. Also available are several restaurants and, of course, curios by the armload. Open during daylight hours year-round. **(719) 275-7507.**

It doesn't cost a thing if you simply want a view of the gorge and bridge from afar. Drive along the road toward the north rim toll booth. Pull a U-turn at the booth, park off to the side and walk over to the rim. The view is a little sweeter without the entrance fee.

Getting There—

The gorge is located 8 miles west of Cañon City, off Hwy. 50. Beware of tame deer on the winding road as you near the entrance. Unfortunately, during the short drive from Cañon City to the gorge entrance, you can't avoid numerous massive billboards spouting all manner of means for lightening your wallet. For an unspoiled alternative route to the gorge via the south rim, see the Temple Canyon description in the Scenic Drives section.

FESTIVALS

Music and Blossom Festival
first weekend in May

The biggest event in Cañon City attracts thousands to a colorful spring get-together. For 50 years Fremont County residents and visitors have gathered to celebrate the cherry and apple blossoms in the surrounding orchards. High school marching bands come from across the country to parade down historic Main St. alongside many floats. The weekend features an art show, a car show, a craft fair and carnival rides. For more information call **(719) 275-2305.**

OUTDOOR ACTIVITIES

BIKING
MOUNTAIN BIKING

Mountain biking is the best way to go in this area due to rough road conditions on most of the scenic routes. The Scenic Drives section provides many ideas near Cañon City that are perfect for sturdy two-wheelers. Here's an easy ride that shouldn't be passed up:

Tunnel Drive—

This short ride winds through three tunnels in what was originally intended to be a water project. Convict labor blasted through solid granite to create this interesting road that dead-ends overlooking the Arkansas River only a short distance from the Royal Gorge. Catch Tunnel Dr. opposite the penitentiary on the west end of town. Tunnel Dr. begins near the banks of the Arkansas as Hwy. 50 rounds a large bend and heads north. Until very recently this road was open to cars.

FISHING

Want to hear the latest on fishing in the Cañon City area? Talk with Jimmy at **Jimmy's Sport Shop** on Main St. He has been handing out advice and selling tackle, bait and licenses for over four decades. **311 Main St.; (719) 275-3685.**

Arkansas River—

It's possible to catch trout within the Cañon City limits, but the best fishing on the Arkansas is west of town. Actually, for a great day of fishing on the Arkansas, head to the Gold Medal trout water below Salida (see the Fishing section of the **Upper Arkansas Valley** chapter). Large brown trout can be pulled from the roily water. The river is not wadable, forcing most fishermen to approach from the highway side.

Texas Creek—

Twenty-six miles west of Cañon City, Texas Creek flows into the Arkansas River. Next to the creek, Hwy. 69 follows south into the high country along the east side of the Sangre de Cristo Mountains. This road provides access to a number of small streams and lakes. Fishing can be good for brown trout in Texas Creek.

GOLF
Shadow Hills Golf Course and Country Club—

This nine-hole, 36-par golf course has been here since 1949. Two sets of tees help to make the "back nine" marginally different from the front. Shadow Hills is a mature course with great views and, as the name implies, lots of rolling hills. The course is open to the public with a couple of exceptions. Before 3 pm on weekends you must play with a member to get on the course. At other times you may play without a member, but for a slightly higher greens fee. Advance tee times are required. The course is just south of town on 4th St. **1232 County Rd. 143; (719) 275-0603.**

HIKING

Cañon City is a good area for short hikes and picnics. **Red Canyon Park, Temple Canyon** and the **Royal Gorge** provide miles of trails for easy walks. Close to town you might try walking along the 4 mile long riverwalk (access along the Arkansas River from Mackenzie or Raynolds avenues). Another excellent outing is the 1.1 mile Tunnel Drive Trail (see the Biking section for directions). For longer, more strenuous backcountry trips in the area, we suggest reading the Hiking section in the **Wet Mountain Valley** chapter.

HORSEBACK RIDING

Indian Springs Ranch—
Ride at this 2,500-acre ranch for surprisingly reasonable fees and you'll get the added bonuses of beautiful country, historic sites and 450-million-year-old fossil areas. See the Camping section for more information. Call ahead for directions: **(719) 372-3907.**

RIVER FLOATING

Arkansas River—
Along with the Royal Gorge Bridge, the biggest draw to the Cañon City area is the Arkansas River with its scenic canyons and treacherous rapids. Raft and kayak trips along the Upper Arkansas offer, according to many serious river floaters, perhaps the best water in the state. The Royal Gorge section is one of the hairiest rapid stretches in the West. In addition to exciting floating, the river is very accessible as Hwy. 50 snakes alongside all the way to Salida, 44 miles upriver.

Downriver from Salida to the Royal Gorge entrance, the river travels through the Arkansas River Canyon, past cottonwoods and rock walls, offering nothing too difficult. Just below Texas Creek there is a rapid rated Class III. Just beyond that, Spike Buck and The Tube rate Class IV and Class III, respectively. *Warning: unless you know what you're doing, be sure to take out above Parkdale or you will end up entering Royal Gorge!*

The Royal Gorge section, beginning at Parkdale, is a 7-mile journey of churning, dangerous rapids varying in severity depending on the water flow. Enclosed within the towering rock walls, the river sees sunlight only during a short period each day. This stretch of river has killed many people over the years. If you are not an expert rafter or kayaker, sign up with an outfitter to do this stretch.

For information about the Upper Arkansas River from Salida upriver to Granite, see the River Floating section of the **Upper Arkansas Valley** chapter.

Outfitters—
Upriver, along Hwy. 50 from Cañon City to Salida, dozens of raft outfitters have hung up signs and are peddling their expertise and guided trips down the river. Outfitters are open for business from May through Sept., but the fastest water is, of course, during the spring runoff. The following are a few reputable outfitters that have been doing business for quite a while.

Arkansas Adventures—PO Box 1359, Cañon City, CO 81212; (719) 269-3700.

Echo Canyon River Expeditions Inc.— Established in 1978, Echo Canyon offers half-day, full-day and overnight trips. **45000 Hwy. 50 West, Cañon City, CO 80212; 1-800-748-2953.**

Lazy J Rafting, Inc.—PO Box 109, Coaldale, CO 81222; (719) 942-4274.

SEEING AND DOING

AMUSEMENTS

Buckskin Joe Theme Park—

You won't miss the signs for Buckskin Joe's on the drive to the Royal Gorge. It is a re-creation of an Old West town, made of 100-year-old log buildings from ghost towns around the state. Used frequently as a movie set, it has a print shop, blacksmith shop, livery stable, barn and H.A.W. Tabor's general store. If you want to feel totally off-kilter, don't skip the mystery house. Gunfights on Main Street are acted out eleven times a day! If you're "lucky" you might even catch a hanging. There are also many shops, a few saloons and the Gold Nugget restaurant (try the buffalo burger)—fun for families and for burned-out parents who want to drink a yard of beer. Admission fee; kids under 4 are free. Open May–Oct. 9 am–dusk. **PO Box 1387, Cañon City, CO 80215; (719) 275-5149.**

GOLD PANNING

Stop by or call the Bureau of Land Management (BLM) office to learn about recreational gold panning or sluicing opportunities near town. **3170 E. Main St., Cañon City, CO 81212; (719) 275-0631.**

MUSEUMS

Cañon City Municipal Museum—

This museum features displays of Indian artifacts and big-game trophies. Anson Rudd's small stone house, built in 1860, is just behind the museum; inside are furnishings of the late 1800s. Look for the bear trap, handmade by the blacksmith in the nearby town of Silver Cliff. Free admission. Open daily, May–Aug. 8 am–5 pm, Sept.–Apr. 1–5 pm. In the municipal building at **6th St. and Royal Gorge Blvd.**

Indian Museum in the Holy Cross Abbey—

In the unlikely location of a Benedictine Abbey, Father William, a monk since 1939, showed us around the small basement Indian museum. He told us of the days when 92 monks roamed the old Tudor-gothic–style building; today only 16 monks remain. Father William will be glad to show off the collection of axes, arrowheads, pots, wicker, etc. He tries to keep the museum open every afternoon. The Abbey is located 2 miles east of town on **Hwy. 50; (719) 275-8631.**

Colorado Territorial Prison Museum—

Under the shadow of guard towers at the Colorado State Penitentiary, a pathway leads through a steel gate to cell house #4 that used to hold many of the state's women prisoners. Now it holds only the tragic residue of prison life in Colorado.

Most of us have a morbid curiosity about life in the "big house" and this museum leaves a lasting impression. A long hallway leads between dozens of cell doors; each one exhibits a different aspect of prison life. You will see convict attire, disciplinary paraphernalia, historical photos and display cases of homemade, but lethal, "shivs." There is even a scale model of the gas chamber. The gift shop sells a variety of convict-made arts and crafts. Open daily in summer 8:30 am–5 pm; winter 10 am–5 pm. 1st and Macon Ave., **PO Box 1229, Cañon City, CO 81215-1229; (719) 269-3015.**

Steam Train and Antique Car Museum—

This little gem can be found at the back of the complex that houses Buckskin Joe, assorted curio shops and the little railway that carries you to the edge of the gorge. Inside a warehouse you'll see rows of vintage automobiles, including a 1915 Model T Highboy Speedster, a 1929 Model A pickup and, my personal favorite, a turquoise 1956 T-Bird. Also on display is a collection of steam trains built to scale. Open in summer. **PO Box 1387, Cañon City, CO 80215; (719) 275-5149.**

SCENIC DRIVES

The Cañon City area is beautiful, relatively undiscovered and perfect for taking scenic backcountry drives. With a little effort, you can be cruising along in a surprising number of completely different natural settings. Most of the roads are dirt, but well graded. Two-wheel drive and steady nerves are all that is required.

Gold Belt Tour—

This designated National Back Country Byway pulls together the area's best scenic drives into an eventful three-hour to three-day circle tour. There's absolutely no reason to hurry along the twisting dirt roads—roads that follow abandoned railroad and stage routes to the former boom towns of **Cripple Creek** and **Victor**. The Gold Belt Tour threads a path between the eerie rock walls of **Phantom Canyon**, returning along the confining, one-lane Shelf Road or, for those too timid (or acrophobic), on the meandering **High Park Road**. Stop by the Cañon City Chamber of Commerce or the BLM office to pick up a brochure that explains the informational road markers along the way. Otherwise you can follow the light blue signs emblazoned with the state flower.

You can begin or end the tour wherever you please. For practical purposes we will start in Cañon City and travel east on Hwy. 50 for 8 miles to the Hwy. 67 cutoff (option: turn off on Hwy. 115 just east of Cañon City to visit the quiet, tree-lined streets of Florence). Phantom Canyon Road follows the railroad line north, which began somewhat inauspiciously in 1894 with financing from David Moffatt. The second day of operation was greeted with a massive train wreck. Soon, though, three trains daily made the winding journey from the gold mines at Cripple Creek and Victor down to the ore reduction mills in Florence. The name "Phantom Canyon" came about thanks to a sharp railroad PR guy who felt he could improve on the original: Eightmile Creek Canyon. As you drive into the mine-scarred hamlet of Victor, a 4,500-foot elevation gain, the history of the area is unavoidable (see the **Cripple Creek and Victor** chapter).

There are a couple of options for the return trip to Cañon City. For those who are skittish about heights, High Park Road begins 9 miles northwest of Cripple Creek on County Rd. 1, providing a relaxing drive through rolling hills ending with a fabulous view of the Royal Gorge Bridge. The recommended route back to Cañon City, however, requires traversing a narrow shelf perched high above a streambed. To reach the well-marked **Shelf Road**, head west off Hwy. 67 just south of Cripple Creek. The narrow road passes by the Shelf Road Climbing Area where thrill seekers cling to limestone cliffs. Also of interest is Red Canyon Park (see the write-up in this section) and the **Garden Park Fossil Area**.

While you can't see much at Garden Park, most people have a special appreciation for the important discoveries of complete skeletons of Camarasaurus, Allosaurus, Diplodocus and other dinosaurs. Excavations from Garden Park have resulted in displays at the Smithsonian as well as the Carnegie, Denver and Cleveland museums of natural history. The Garden Park Paleontological Society has ambitious future plans for a visitors center. From mid-May to mid-Sept. a slide show and tour of the fossil area are held; contact the **Cañon City Chamber of Commerce** for information at **(719) 285-2331**.

Oak Creek Grade (County Rd. 143)—

Heading southwest from Cañon City, this spectacular road leads toward the Wet Mountain Valley. After you cross over the hump of a small pass, the panorama of the Sangre de Cristo Mountains will take your breath away. Crestone Needles, Kit Carson and Humboldt peaks are only a few of the 14ers in this dramatic range. Stay right at the major forks and the dirt road will take you to Silver Cliff/Westcliffe in the Wet Mountain Valley. (See the **Wet Mountain Valley** chapter.) To reach County Rd. 143 from Royal Gorge Blvd. turn south on 4th St. and cross over the Arkansas River. Keep going.

Phantom Canyon Road—
See the Gold Belt Tour write-up above.

Red Canyon Park—
Red sandstone rocks shoot up the valley in dramatic formations. The contrast of immense red rocks against the lush green of the pine forests is striking. This beautiful park is a hidden gem, well worth the short drive from Cañon City. Many hiking trails provide access to secluded portions of the park. There are several designated picnic areas with grills and tables. To reach Red Canyon Park, head north on Field Ave. until you reach the park 12 miles north of Cañon City.

Skyline Drive—
This one-way lane threads its way along the narrow spine of the hogback northwest of Cañon City. Look down on the town and prison from 800 feet above. The 3-mile drive was built by convict labor in 1906. It takes a strong stomach and a steady hand on the wheel to negotiate this road. You've never seen one like it before. To reach Skyline Dr., head west on Hwy. 50 out of town. About 3 miles after the highway turns north, you'll see the sign for Skyline Dr. Turn right, pass under a rock archway on the east side of the highway and head on up the hill.

WHERE TO STAY

ACCOMMODATIONS

Best Western Royal Gorge Motel— $$$
This 68-room motor inn has a trout pond and an outdoor heated pool (not one and the same!). The gazebo-covered Jacuzzi is a perfect place to soak weary muscles. While it's your basic motor inn, all rooms are spotless and extremely well maintained, with air conditioning, cable TV and movies. Catch a trout in the pond and have it cooked up at the on-site restaurant. They'll even furnish you with a fishing pole! One mile east of downtown Cañon City on **Hwy. 50; (719) 275-3377** or toll free **1-800-231-7317.**

Cañon Inn—$$ to $$$
The recently remodeled Cañon Inn boasts 103 rooms with queen- and king-sized beds. Thirty poolside rooms vie for your reservation; the outdoor heated pool is open year-round as is an airy solarium with six large hot tubs. If that's not enough, try the putting green or switch on cable TV in your air-conditioned room. There are two dining rooms, and the lounge features live acoustic entertainment on weekends. Reduced winter rates. Two miles east of downtown Cañon City on **Hwy. 50; (719) 275-8676.**

CAMPING

Although very few "designated" campsites exist on public land near Cañon City, you can find many excellent car camping areas along the Gold Belt Tour (see the Scenic Drive section).

In San Isabel National Forest—
Oak Creek Campground is located 15 miles southwest of Cañon City. For directions see Scenic Drives: Oak Creek Grade. Only 6 sites; no drinking water at the campground and no fee. Forest Service phone: **(719) 275-4119.**

Private Campgrounds—
Indian Springs Ranch—This 2,500-acre working ranch, located in a Colorado Natural Area, is a perfect place to camp out and explore the surroundings. Take a tour of the fossil areas with small vertebrates dating from 450 million years ago and the outlaw cabin of "Wild Bill" McKinney (registered National Historic Landmark). Heated pool, showers, hookups and unlimited backcountry tent sites. Horseback riding for a reasonable fee on the premises. Located on Phantom Canyon Rd. 6 miles off Hwy. 50. Open Apr.–Sept. **PO Box 404, Canon City, CO 81212; (719) 372-3907.**

Royal Gorge KOA Kampground—Full and partial hookups with tent sites. Signs will direct you from Royal Gorge Rd. west of town. **(719) 275-6116.**

Royal View Campground—Many secluded tent sites and 31 RV hookups. Go 1.5 miles west of the Royal Gorge exit on Hwy. 50. **(719) 275-1900.**

WHERE TO EAT

Merlino's Belvedere—$$ to $$$

Opened in 1946, this restaurant has a solid reputation that goes far beyond the borders of Cañon City. A fire recently destroyed Merlino's, but you can once again get great Italian dinners at their new home. All Italian dishes come from family recipes—try the ravioli, cavatelli, manicotti or spaghetti and you won't be disappointed. If you are not in the mood for fresh pasta, order from a long list of steak, seafood or chicken dinners. Sandwiches and soup are available. Open Mon.–Sat. 5–11 pm, Sun. noon–9 pm. Expect a wait (sometimes lengthy) if you show up at the dinner hour. Reservations available for groups of 12 or more. Located at **2305 Elm; (719) 275-5558.**

Janey's Chili Wagon—$ to $$

Janey Workman came to Cañon City in 1967 with $750 in her pocket and dreams of opening a restaurant. Her tenacity and "rags to riches" success recently earned her a profile in the *National Enquirer*. Despite three locations over the years, she has developed a loyal clientele for her excellent, homemade Mexican cuisine. "I cater to the local people who are still here when the winter comes and the tourists are long gone," she once said. The Chili Wagon's most recent home is practically a local landmark. Try the massive "El-Burrito" or a combination plate with your choice of Janey's tasty red or green (or half red and half green) chili. The restaurant is light and airy with neon accents around the doorways. Full bar; carryout available. Open 11 am–8:30 pm Tues.–Sat, closed Sun. and Mon. **807 Cyanide; (719) 275-4885.**

The Owl Cigar Store—$

This old bar/restaurant has a simple formula for success: a good selection of cold beer, pool tables and a little hamburger grill behind the bar. "Ask anybody, they're the best hamburgers in town," said our helpful bartender/cook. The best part is that the burgers cost less than a dollar. They also serve up old fashioned shakes and malts. The Owl has been in the same family for decades and remains a great place to unwind after a long day on the road. Eat in or take out. Open at 11 am daily. **626 Main; (719) 275-9946.**

Waffle Wagon Restaurant—$

Go where the locals go for a full breakfast. Homemade biscuits and gravy, breakfast burritos, pecan and blueberry waffles and egg dishes are among the choices at this crowded restaurant. Closed Mon. and Tues., open at 6 am Wed.–Fri., open at 6:30 am weekends. Open for lunch 11 am–2 pm Wed.–Sat. **315 Royal Gorge Blvd.; (719) 269-3428.**

SERVICES

Cañon City Chamber of Commerce—

If you want advice on the area, it's a good bet to stop in here. The new chamber office is located in the historic former home of Governor James Peabody. They have lots of brochures and ideas about what to see and do. **401 Royal Gorge Blvd., Cañon City, CO 81212; (719) 275-2331.**

Florence Chamber of Commerce—

Rialto Theatre Bldg., PO Box 145, Florence, CO 81226; (719) 784-3544.

Colorado Springs

When Katharine Lee Bates wrote "America the Beautiful," she was looking out upon Colorado Springs, and the "purple mountain majesties" in the anthem refer to the perch that inspired her: Pikes Peak. It's quite a legacy to live up to, but Colorado Springs and its famous mountain manage to do so beautifully.

Colorado's second largest urban center sits on a high plateau right in the shadow of the 14,110-foot peak. Crammed into the area are a lion's share of the state's most popular attractions. In addition to Pikes Peak are the red sandstone towers of Garden of the Gods, Seven Falls, the popular Cave of the Winds and scenic Cheyenne Canyon. But nature doesn't get all the credit: the Pikes Peak area is also home to the US Air Force Academy, the renowned Broadmoor Hotel resort, quaint Manitou Springs, the Olympic Training Center and the country's only mountain zoo. Nearby are Florissant Fossil Beds National Monument and the mining-town relics of Cripple Creek (now a gambling boom town) and Victor. In a few years Colorado Springs will also be home to the Olympic Hall of Fame.

The concentration of manmade and natural treasures and the city's central location make Colorado Springs one of America's most popular vacation destinations. In that lies a pair of warnings—squadrons of people in touring formation sweep through each summer, and there's plenty of fool's gold in them thar hills. Some of the scores of area attractions, though amazingly popular, stretch the imagination in terms of audacity and sheer cheesiness. For example: cliff dwellings have been moved here 350 miles from their natural home, and the North Pole now rests at the foot of Pikes Peak.

But Colorado Springs does have it all. And with a little forethought and a bit of extra effort, ways can be found to see the worthwhile sights far from the mad-dashing crowd.

HISTORY

Years before Zebulon Pike spotted his namesake peak in 1806, the Ute Indians hunted the area below what they called "The Long One." Pike first saw the peak from near present-day Las Animas, where he recorded, "it appeared like a small blue cloud." Pike tried to christen it Grand Peak or Blue Peak, but his name stuck.

Fifty years later, in 1859, the mountain gained its enduring place in history thanks to the gold rush: thousands of fortune hunters headed west in Conestoga wagons with Pikes Peak or Bust emblazoned on the sides. Although in those early years most of the gold actually was found

100 miles to the north, near Central City, Pikes Peak proved to be a magnet for would-be millionaires.

That same year, prospectors staked out a town named El Dorado (now known as Colorado City) at the base of the Ute Pass Trail. Wedged between Colorado Springs and Manitou Springs, this area served as the territorial capital of Colorado before Denver's rise.

The city of Colorado Springs was conjured up by a lovestruck general for his thankless queen in the early 1870s. The general was William Jackson Palmer, a Civil War hero who founded several southern Colorado cities as part of his Denver & Rio Grande Railroad empire. Colorado Springs was to be the posh resort home for his blue-blood bride, Queen Mellen, complete with a castle of her own. But she stayed at the estate only a year, running home to the safe civility of the East and, later, of England. It's ironic that many of the attractions that draw visitors to Colorado Springs today went unappreciated by the person for whom they were intended.

Palmer's vision was to make the town a genteel place for well-to-do people. The name Colorado Springs was chosen by an early publicist because of its "rich eastern spa sound," as historian Marshall Sprague puts it. The actual springs referred to are the ones at Manitou Springs.

The city soon became better known as "Little London" because of the number of Englishmen and other tea drinkers brought in by Palmer. The resort didn't really take off until a second gold rush in 1891, this time closer by in Cripple Creek (see the **Cripple Creek** chapter). By 1900 the population of the region had swelled to over 50,000. Over the next 10 years, thanks to tycoons who had invested in Cripple Creek mines, Colorado Springs was the richest city per capita in the country.

Guided and goaded by tycoons such as Spencer Penrose, founder of the Broadmoor Hotel, Colorado Springs thrived for the next few decades as a tourist and retirement center. During World War II the military's omnipresence began. In 1942 Camp Carson, now Fort Carson, was built, followed quickly by Peterson Air Force Base and later by the North American Aerospace Defense Command (NORAD). In 1955 Colorado Springs struck gold again, this time by landing the US Air Force Academy. It's one of the state's most popular manmade tourist attractions. Today the area is home to almost as many generals as the Pentagon. Recently Colorado Springs became headquarters for the US Space Command, which will oversee all space-based defense activities, including the Consolidated Space Operations Center (CSOC) now being built east of the city. CSOC will control all military space missions. With stars in their eyes, some city officials predict Colorado Springs will soon surpass Houston as a space center. Perhaps astronauts will be signing off with a "Roger Colorado" before long.

GETTING THERE

Colorado Springs is located 65 miles south of Denver on Interstate 25. The town is a major bus hub; **Greyhound Bus Lines, (719) 635-1505,** serves Colorado Springs with frequent runs to Denver.

Colorado Springs Airport handles over 100 direct flights per day and is served by most major carriers, including American Airlines, America West, Continental, Delta, TWA, United and Mesa. Other airlines connect out of Denver. The **Airporter, (719) 578-5232,** offers shuttle service between airports in Denver and Colorado Springs.

———— MAJOR ATTRACTIONS ————

Air Force Academy

The US Air Force Academy, training center for America's future air force officers, receives more than a million visitors annually, making it Colorado's third most popular attraction after Rocky Mountain National Park and Denver's Museum of Natural History. The Academy's beautiful location is one reason why in 1954 it was chosen over 580 other proposed sites around the country. Although much of the stunning 18,000-acre campus at the foot of the Rampart Range is off limits, most of the manmade facilities are free and open to the public. An easy way to see the grounds is to take a self-guided tour using the "Follow the Falcon" brochure available at the **Barry Goldwater Visitor Center.** This facility, open daily 9 am–5 pm, features an enormous gift shop, displays about cadet life and films on the history of the Air Force.

A short nature trail from the visitors center leads to the chapel, which is not to be missed. The soaring 17-spire **Cadet Chapel** is an engineering and architectural masterpiece that took five years to design and four years to build. Tours are given Mon.–Sat. 9 am–5 pm, and Sun. 1–5 pm. Just below the chapel is the great square where you can see Colorado's version of the changing of the guard. At 12:10 pm Mon.–Fri. during the academic year, most of the 4,400 cadets parade across the square to lunch. Many visitors to the Academy

enjoy the planetarium (program schedule is available at the visitors center). The campus is also a game refuge, so watch for deer and wild turkeys by the road.

Golf—

Retired or active military are invited to play the two excellent and challenging 18-hole courses at the academy. The Blue is a Robert Trent Jones course with long, narrow fairways, and The Silver is a mountainous course with shorter holes demanding a bit more precision. The courses lie directly across from the cemetery on Parade Loop. Call one day in advance for tee times. **(719) 472-3456.**

Hiking—

The Academy offers a number of scenic hiking trails around the grounds as well as access to the adjacent **Pike National Forest** located in the foothills just to the west. Stop in at the visitors center for maps and information about the 12-mile **Falcon Trail** and the shorter hike to **Stanley Canyon Reservoir.**

Getting There—

The South Entrance can be reached from Colorado Springs by heading north on Interstate 25 to Exit 150B (Academy Boulevard). The North Entrance is located a few miles further north on Interstate 25 at exit 156B; **(719) 472-4040.**

Garden of the Gods

Red sandstone formations that jut out at wild angles, thousand-year-old juniper trees, twisting needles of rock sculpted by wind—all these make this Colorado Springs city park truly a "garden fit for the gods."

Dedicated in 1909, the 1,350-acre park at the foot of Pikes Peak has since become a Registered National Landmark. Most visitors take a quick drive through the park—maybe with a stop to pretend to hold up Balanced Rock—then leave and think they've seen it all. A better way is to park your car and take a walk on one of the many trails, several of which are accessible to the handicapped. Take time to watch the technical climbers who can usually be found negotiating the treacherous Over the Rainbow route on the Gateway Rocks near Hidden Inn. Those tempted to try some rock scrambling of their own should be warned that climbing in the park (unless you obtain a permit) is prohibited, and zealous rangers enforce the rules. Picnicking and guided horseback riding are also popular (see the Horseback Riding section).

Geology—

A half day in Garden of the Gods is probably the equivalent of a semester of geology. About 300 million years ago, Frontrangia, part of the ancestral Rocky Mountains 30 to 50 miles west of the modern-day Rockies, stopped growing. Ancient rivers began to carry rocks and debris from the shrinking mountains, spreading them out over the Colorado Springs area in hundred-foot-thick alluvial fans. Balanced Rock and Steamboat Rock are evidence of these deposits. A great sea covered Colorado for the next 150 million years; then, about 60 million years ago, the Rockies began to rise again. As a massive dome grew at the site of Pikes Peak, it vertically tilted the horizontal rock layers along its edges. Wind and water finished the job, stripping away the less resistant rocks while carving the tougher ones into the towers and spires that make up Garden of the Gods.

The formations are as whimsical as their names: Three Graces, Kissing Camels, Weeping Indian, Rocking Chair. An early publicist for the area, W. E. Parbor, lost his job when he dubbed one formation "Seal Making Love to a Nun." The name was changed to Seal and Bear.

Getting There—

The south entrance to the Garden of the Gods can be reached by taking Hwy. 24 west from Interstate 25 to the Ridge Rd. exit; the northeast entrance is reached from Interstate 25 by heading west on Garden of the Gods Rd. (exit 146) to 30th St., turning left and proceeding about a mile.

HIDDEN INN

Right in the center of things, the Hidden Inn has a free lookout tower for photographers, snack bar, gift shop, maps and information. It's usually packed with tourists. Hours are 8:30 am–7 pm in summer; 9 am–5:30 pm in winter. **(719) 632-2303.**

HIGH POINT

The best vantage point in the park. There's also a gift shop and a "camera obscura" here—a 16th-century invention that provides a 360-degree panoramic view from inside a darkened chamber. Located on Ridge Rd. near the south entrance to the park. Closed in winter; open 9 am–4 pm in summer. **(719) 632-9768.**

TRADING POST

Built in the late 1920s to resemble the home of Pueblo Indians, the post is the largest gift shop in the Pikes Peak region. It includes a Southwest Indian art gallery with paintings, rugs, crafts, pottery and jewelry. Located near Balanced Rock on the west edge of the park. Also has patio dining. Open year-round with extended hours in summer; **(719) 685-9045.**

VISITORS CENTER

Located on the park's southeast boundary, the visitors center is a good place to start and usually not as crowded as the Hidden Inn. Hours are 9 am–5 pm in summer; 10 am–4 pm in winter. **S.E. 3500 Ridge Rd.; (719) 578-6939.**

Pikes Peak

Pikes Peak, at 14,110 feet, is America's Mountain, the best-known peak in the country. This isn't because it's the highest (30 other peaks surpass it in Colorado alone) or the most beautiful, but because it rears out of the plains apart and alone, dominating the landscape around it. Those who take the time to reach its summit are rewarded on clear days with dramatic and unobstructed views of many mountain ranges and the eastern plains.

History—

A small expedition headed by Lt. Zebulon Pike came to within 15 miles of the summit on Nov. 27, 1806, when Pike declared "I believe no human being could have ascended to its pinnacle." The first ascent came just 14 years later, by Dr. Edwin James, a botanist with the Long expedition. In 1929 a Texan, Bill Williams, pushed a peanut to the top with his nose. He wore out 170 pairs of pants during the 20-day trek. Today there's a cog railroad and a toll road to the summit.

In 1873 the US Army Signal Corps built a weather observatory on the summit, which was manned year-round by a lone enlisted man. The most notorious of these early weathermen had to be Sgt. John O'Keefe. He collaborated with journalist Eliphalet Price to concoct stories about what was then the most remote, intriguing spot in the country. His most infamous tall tale told of man-eating rats. As the story goes, rats devoured O'Keefe's baby, "leaving nothing but the peeled and mumbled skull." The Denver papers picked up the yarn, and consequently it ran in papers as far away as Turkey. O'Keefe appeared in a photo beside a tiny headstone with little Erin O'Keefe's name on it. In truth, however, O'Keefe had neither wife nor child—his black cat was named Erin. He received a reprimand from army headquarters for the stunt.

A whale was reported on the summit in 1923. When journalists investigated, they found a 40-foot wooden frame with a notorious public relations man inside spraying seltzer through a blowhole.

Today die-hard runners race up and down the peak every August in one of the most rigorous marathons on the planet. It's also the nation's second oldest. In winter a local club trudges up through the snow to set off midnight fireworks marking the New Year.

Facts About Pikes Peak—

The view from the summit is well worth the trip. From there you can look straight down on Colorado Springs, see Denver 70 miles to the north, the Spanish Peaks and spiny Sangre de Cristo Mountains to the south, and the snowcapped Sawatch and Mosquito ranges to the west. The summit itself is windswept and barren, except for the summit house, and anywhere from 10° to 30° colder than Colorado Springs. Take a coat. The summit house features a gift shop, snack bar and incredibly good hot chocolate and donuts. Ask one of the workers to tell you stories about living on the summit (especially during lightning storms).

Getting There—

To reach the Pikes Peak Hwy. from Colorado Springs, head west for 10 miles on Hwy. 24. At the town of Cascade, look for the marked exit to the left.

HIKING THE PEAK

There are several hiking routes to the summit of Pikes Peak, and **Barr Trail** is the most commonly used. The trail, about 13 miles each way, starts just off Ruxton Ave. above Manitou Springs, near the cog railway station. Fred Barr built the trail between the years 1921 and 1923 with a pick, shovel and dynamite. The trail has since made Pikes Peak one of the state's longest but easiest 14ers, and its most-ascended. Probably the best way to make the hike is a two-day trip with a stopover at the Barr Camp 6.8 miles up. At treeline (about 8.5 miles up) is a lean-to that can also be used as a stopover. For a one-day trip, it's possible to take the cog railway or hitchhike to the summit and hike down. A shorter and, perhaps, more remote and scenic route is possible from the northwest side of the peak via The Crags (see the Hiking section of the **Cripple Creek and Victor** chapter). For information on other routes, call **(719) 578-6640 (Parks and Recreation).**

PIKES PEAK COG RAILWAY

Zalmon A. Simmons decided to build a cog railroad up Pikes Peak after a painful ride to the top on a mule. His goal, says historian Marshall Sprague, was no less than "to alleviate the suffering of the soft-bottomed human race." The railroad, which first made it to the top in 1891, is still a quick and easy way up the mountain. Swiss-made diesel trains have long since replaced the old angled steam engines, but one relic still sits at the station. Trains depart regularly from the depot. Round trip is three hours. Advance reservations are advised. Open May through Oct., but trains don't always make it all the way up in May because of snow. Located at 515 Ruxton Ave. in Manitou Springs. For fares and other information, contact **PO Box 351, Manitou Springs, CO 80829; (719) 685-5401.**

PIKES PEAK HIGHWAY

Although Pikes Peak has been tamed by a highway, the road itself is anything but tame. The 38-mile round trip is said to take six months off the life of your car. The drive includes 156 often harrowing turns along a nearly 7,000-foot climb. The original carriage road was built in 1868–88 and the first car reached the summit in 1901. The present highway, built in 1915–16, provides awesome panoramas of the Continental Divide. You might even spot big-horn sheep, deer or elk. The road is paved for the first 7 miles and improved dirt the rest of the way. Open seasonally, May through Oct. Toll fee is charged. For information contact **Dept. of Public Works, PO Box 1575, Colorado Springs, CO 80901; Colorado Springs Convention and Visitors Bureau, (719) 635-7506** or **684-9383.**

PIKES PEAK HILL CLIMB

For information on this spectacular car race to the summit of Pikes Peak, see the Festivals and Events section.

OTHER ATTRACTIONS

Cave of the Winds

Although it has sacrificed something to commercialization, such as rocks that sing in the parking lot, a nightly laser light show that illuminates the canyon and colored lights that enhance the formations' natural beauty, Cave of the Winds is still worth seeing. Discovered by children in 1880, the mile-long cavern gets its name from winds that used to blow through it. Alas, the magical sound has since been silenced by the need for a new entrance.

The cave is known for its dazzling samples of stalactites and stalagmites. (OK, which one hangs from the ceiling?) A new 60-foot-long, 40-foot-wide, 35-foot-tall room was added to the tour in 1988, lit up by 10,000 more watts of colored lights.

The 40-minute guided tour on paved walkways can make you feel a bit like you're on a conveyor belt. For a true taste of spelunking, call ahead to make reservations for the so-called "wild tour" of the Grand Caverns. This is a muddy two-and-a-half-hour plunge into the deepest pockets of the cave. One highlight is crawling on your belly under Fat Man's Misery, where Gen. Palmer, on his first visit, was said to have gotten stuck and ordered part of the ledge to be sawed off. On the "wild tour," old clothes and a flashlight are required. Light jacket recommended for all tours. Admission fee charged. The cave is located 6 miles west of Colorado Springs off Hwy. 24 above Manitou Springs. Open 9 am–9 pm in summer; 10 am–5 pm in winter. For "wild tour" reservations and other information, contact **PO Box 826, Manitou Springs, CO 80829; (719) 685-5444.**

Cheyenne Mountain Zoo

Clinging to the side of Cheyenne Mountain, this zoo's setting has to be one of the greatest. What the zoo lacks in size it makes up for in unique animal habitats. It's also a bastion for endangered species, more than 100 of which are represented among the over 800 animals at the zoo. These include orangutans, snow leopards, Asian lions and a huge collection of giraffes. Some of the better exhibits are the birds of prey and the monkey house.

Just above the zoo stands the **Will Rogers Shrine of the Sun**, a tribute to the famed American humorist as well as the final resting place for Spencer Penrose, developer of the Broadmoor Hotel. Admission to the zoo also includes the shrine, which is worth a quick drive. Open year-round, the winter months are less crowded. Hours are 9 am–5 pm in summer, 9 am–4 pm in winter. To reach the zoo from Interstate 25, head south on Nevada Ave. (which turns into Hwy. 155). Turn right on Lake Ave. and proceed to the Broadmoor. Then turn right and follow Mirada Rd. up to the zoo. **4250 Cheyenne Mt. Zoo Rd., Colorado Springs, CO 80906-5728; (719) 475-9555.**

Glen Eyrie

Colorado Springs' own castle, Glen Eyrie, is a well-kept secret mainly bypassed by most summer visitors. Privately owned by the Navigators, a Christian group, Glen Eyrie is primarily a conference center but limited tours are given.

Built by Gen. Palmer in 1904 for his wife, the Tudor-style castle testifies to Palmer's European tastes and high standards of architecture. It includes 24 fireplaces, some of which were brought over from cathedrals and castles in Europe. Mrs. Palmer eventually spurned the nest, though it's difficult to see why. The estate is practically a city unto itself, with greenhouses, stables, nine reservoirs, a dairy, schoolhouse, pool, bowling alley and Turkish bath. Listed on the National Register of Historic Places, the castle sits amidst many of the same stunning rock formations found in Garden of the Gods.

Be sure to call ahead for information about tours. Located just north of Garden of the Gods on 30th St. **PO Box 6000, Colorado Springs, CO 80934; (719) 598-1212.**

Manitou Springs

Colorado Springs was named for the mineral springs that are actually located in Manitou Springs. Ute Indians used this area on the west edge of Colorado Springs as one of their favorite hunting grounds. They probably used the springs for their medicinal value. Manitou is in fact an Indian word meaning "Great Spirit," but the town's name actually comes from a reference to a spirit in Longfellow's poem "Hiawatha."

Manitou became nationally known in 1877 for "the water cure," said to remedy almost any illness. Later, as hospitals began to take over its role, this Victorian town evolved into a tourist center and has been designated a National Historic District. The 26 springs still bubble, and samples are available in many restaurants and stores.

Today Manitou is home to artists, crafts people and even a couple of witches' covens. Many knickknacks, antiques and original works of art can be found in the quaint shops crammed into a few blocks. There's also a charming outdoor arcade, including what has to be one of the few penny arcades left in the country.

Most visitors to the Pikes Peak area end up in Manitou because of its proximity to many of the most popular attractions. If you do find yourself here for a day, get off the main road and walk through the Queen Anne homes that crawl up either side of the canyon. There are plenty of the expected tourist amusements in Manitou, like a combination mini-golf/water park. For lodging and restaurant information see the Where to Stay and Where to Eat sections.

Miramont Castle

Stair-stepping up Mt. Manitou is the eccentric castle Father Jean Baptiste

Francolon had built for his mother and himself in 1895. Its name means "look at the mountain." The structure is a fantastic (though a bit run down), rambling hodgepodge of nine different styles of architecture, from Byzantine to Romanesque. Inside the 46 rooms, a Victorian Life Museum, a miniature model of Colorado Springs in the 1888 "Little London" days and, as sort of an added bonus near the end, a model railroad display highlight the tour. The castle was built by Francolon after he was sent to Manitou to avail himself of the mineral waters for his health. Over the years it has been a sanatorium run by the Sisters of Mercy and an apartment complex in which banisters and furniture are said to have been used by apartment dwellers as firewood before the castle was added to the National Register of Historic Places in 1977. Today it is operated by the Manitou Springs Historical Society. Admission fee charged. Open daily Memorial Day through Labor Day, 10 am–5 pm; tea room and soda fountain, 11 am–4 pm; Sept.–May, 12–3 pm daily; weekends only in Jan. Located at **9 Capitol Hill Ave., Manitou Springs, CO 80829; (719) 685-1011.**

NORAD

The North American Aerospace Defense Command, though not exactly open to the public, does host some tours. A visit to the underground fortress is unforgettable. Buried deep inside Cheyenne Mountain behind 25-foot-thick doors, NORAD is an entire city on metal springs, built to withstand nuclear attack. Within the complex sharp, serious GIs keep watch over the world's airspace. About 20 times per month the Air Force takes people through. The tours are usually booked 6 months in advance, so call the taped phone message for specific instructions about getting reservations. For information contact **Headquarters, NORAD/PAK, 1 NORAD Road, Suite 128, Colorado Springs, CO 80914; (719) 554-2241 ext. 2239.**

US Olympic Complex

Each year this 37-acre complex plays host to thousands of athletes training for the Olympics in the thin mountain air of Colorado Springs. The complex, home to 14 of the 44 national governing bodies for amateur athletics, is the headquarters of the US Olympic Committee. The attractive facilities house nine permanent national teams. The visitors center features a gift shop and an Olympic video. One-hour tours of the complex are offered on the hour in winter and every half hour in summer. In summer open Mon.–Sat. 9 am–5 pm, Sun. 10 am–5 pm; winter hours are Mon.–Sat. 9 am–4 pm, Sun. 12–4 pm. **1 Olympic Plaza, 1750 E. Boulder St., Colorado Springs, CO 80909; (719) 578-4618, Tour Hotline at (719) 578-4644.**

Seven Falls

Billed as "The Grandest Mile of Scenery in Colorado," the concentration of beauty in Seven Falls and South Cheyenne Canyon is both a blessing and a curse. Indian tribes used to trap animals in the box canyon by stampeding them into its dead end. Although truly spectacular, this area can still feel like a trap as some 300,000 visitors a year cram in.

Seven distinct but connected falls splash 300 feet down a black granite wall and are accessible by two sets of stairs. One set leads to Eagles Nest platform, which offers a good view of the falls; another goes to a mile-long trail ending at an overlook of the city. Eagles Nest is now accessible via elevator(!) by those unable or unwilling to attack the stairs. But for another great view of the falls, consider going up North Cheyenne Canyon, rather than south, and walking up the never-crowded Mt. Cutler Trail. It's an easy 2-mile round trip and it's free.

Admission fee charged. The falls are open year-round; from mid-May–mid-Sept. the canyon is illuminated by over 1,000 multicolored lights. Supposedly it's the only completely lighted canyon in the world. Located at the west end of Cheyenne Blvd. in southwestern Colorado Springs. Open daily 9 am–4:15 pm year-round; 8 am–11:15 pm. May 15–Sept. 15. **P.O. Box 118, Colorado Springs, CO 80901; (719) 632-0741.**

FESTIVALS AND EVENTS

Aside from the highlights listed below, you can get an update of weekly events by calling **(719) 635-1723.**

Springspree Street Festival

late June

Many locals turn out for this festival, which features a 10K run and bed races down Pikes Peak Ave. (the Air Force Academy team always wins). Music and merriment spread throughout downtown and in adjoining Monument Valley Park. **(719) 635-1551.**

Colorado Opera Festival

summer

Many of the country's best directors and artists are in residence in Colorado Springs for this annual summer series. Operas are always in English and range from rare to contemporary. **(719) 473-0073.**

Pikes Peak Hill Climb

July 4th

Every summer race-car drivers take to the highway in the Race to the Clouds. It's the second oldest auto race in America and without a doubt the most grueling. Bobby and Al Unser, Mario Andretti and Rick and Roger Mears have all won the event. The best vantage points include Devil's Playground or Crystal Creek; Halfway Picnic Grounds and Glen Cove aren't bad either. Many people drive up the night before and stake out a camping site near the best viewing areas. There is a charge for both camping and the race. For more information contact **Pikes Peak Hill Climb Association, 135 Manitou Ave., Manitou Springs, CO 80829; (719) 685-4400.**

Pikes Peak or Bust Rodeo

early August

As the state's largest outdoor rodeo, this event attracts the country's best professional cowboys and cowgirls. The city kicks things off with a free pancake breakfast downtown and a parade. Both rodeos are held at Penrose Stadium. Call the visitors bureau for information; **(719) 635-1632** or **1-800-88-VISIT.**

Theatreworks Shakespeare Festival

August

Considered by many to be one of the best small Shakespeare festivals in the country, Theatreworks puts on nightly productions (except Mon.) through Aug. Located in a tent in Monument Valley Park; some seats reserved for a fee, the rest are free. **(719) 593-3232.**

International Balloon Classic

Labor Day weekend

More than a hundred hot-air balloons take off from Memorial Park at sunrise each of the three days, making for spectacular photo opportunities. Accompanied by parachuting displays and other aerial events, the classic seems to increase in popularity every year. Worth waking up for. **(719) 635-1632** or **1-800-88-VISIT.**

Athletic Competitions—

Several national and international events are hosted yearly in the Colorado Springs area, many at the **Olympic Training Center.** Call for schedules. **(719) 578-4644.** Also, if you love baseball, check out a **Sky Sox** game, the AAA farm team for the Colorado Rockies. For that special occasion, you can watch the game from a hot tub! Call **(719) 597-3000** for tickets and schedule of games.

———— OUTDOOR ACTIVITIES ————

BIKING
MOUNTAIN BIKING

With Colorado Springs' close proximity to the mountains, there are plenty of scenic and challenging rides just west of town in the Rampart Range. Mountain bike rentals are available at a number of places, including **Backeddy Boating** at **1310 S. 21st St.; (719) 520-0066.** Maps and information about trails in the Pike National Forest can be obtained at **Pikes Peak Ranger District Office, 601 S. Weber St., Colorado Springs, CO 80903; (719) 636-1602. Criterium Bike Shop** also offers maps, trail ideas, and repairs. You'll find them a few blocks south of **Colorado College at 326 N. Tejon St.; (719) 475-0149.**

Gold Camp Rd. and trails branching off from it offer many popular rides of varying difficulty. Gold Camp and a number of other roads listed in the Scenic Drives section make for worthwhile scenic rides.

Old Ute Trail, St. Mary's Trail, the challenging **Barr Trail** and **Waldo Canyon,** all listed in the Hiking and Backpacking section, are also excellent mountain bike trails. In town try the trails (specifically the old jeep trail) that run through Palmer Park. It can be accessed in town just off Maizeland Road between Chelton Rd. and Academy Blvd.

TOURING

Bicycling has taken off in Colorado Springs, which recently was the first US city to host the World Cycling Championships. Most of the races were held at the new Velodrome in Memorial Park, where speed records continue to be set, thanks in part to the area's thin air. A popular trail right in the heart of the city follows Monument Creek through Monument Valley Park. Other destinations for longer rides include Garden of the Gods, Air Force Academy, Black Forest and Woodland Park.

FISHING
Elevenmile Canyon and Reservoir—
See the **Cripple Creek** chapter.

Manitou Lake—
Locals suggest using salmon eggs and worms to land the rainbow trout at this ideal family spot. Seven miles north of Woodland Park on Hwy. 67.

Rampart Reservoir—
This out-of-the-way reservoir provides 10 miles of excellent shoreline for fishing. The difficulty of getting to this reservoir means the angling is usually uncrowded. No fishing is allowed Dec. 2–Apr. 30. Rampart Reservoir is located 8 miles east of Woodland Park on Rampart Range Rd.

South Platte River—
For information about fishing the South Platte, see the Waterton Canyon write-up in the Parks, Gardens and Recreation Areas section of the **Denver** chapter. Located 28 miles north of Woodland Park on Hwy. 67.

GOLF
PRIVATE COURSES
Air Force Academy—
Two beautiful 18-hole courses are open to active and retired military only. See Major Attractions section for information.

Broadmoor Golf Club—
The courses at the Broadmoor are considered by many to be some of the finest in the state. This is where Jack Nicklaus got his start with a win in the US Amateur. The three 18-hole courses provide three good reasons to stay at the Broadmoor Hotel, since they're reserved for members and hotel guests only. Pines and scrub oak dot the rolling fairways, which all have Cheyenne Mountain as their backdrop. Greens fees are moderately expensive if you are a guest and pricey for friends of hotel guests. Cart required. **(719) 634-7711.**

PUBLIC COURSES
Patty Jewett Golf Course—
Built in 1898, this course was the first set of links west of the Mississippi. The tall

trees and mature greens make Patty Jewett one of the best public courses in Colorado Springs. Its 27 holes allow clear views of Pikes Peak from central Colorado Springs. **900 E. Española St.; (719) 578-6825.**

Pine Creek Golf Club—

Though still a bit of a youngster, this 18-hole public course, located on the high prairie grasslands about 10 miles northeast of the downtown area, offers fantastic views of Pikes Peak and the mountains to the west. Over 70 sand traps provide a formidable challenge; so does the strong wind, which tends to pick up later in the day. Full facilities. Take Exit 151 (Briargate) from Interstate 25, just north of town, and follow the signs about 3 miles east. **9850 Divot Tr.; (719) 594-9999.**

Valley Hi Municipal Golf Course—

This 18-hole course has one distinctive draw: great views of Cheyenne Mountain and Pikes Peak from every hole. The 30-year-old par 71 is relatively flat with plenty of lakes. **610 S. Chelton Rd. in east Colorado Springs; (719) 578-6351.**

HIKING AND BACKPACKING

Colorado Springs' city mountain parks are full of great hikes. The treks range from hour-long strolls to two-day climbs up Pikes Peak. The visitors bureau provides a reasonably good list of hiking trails in the area. For more detailed information about hikes in nearby Pike National Forest, contact **Pikes Peak Ranger District Office, 601 S. Weber St., Colorado Springs, CO 80903; (719) 636-1602.**

Bear Creek Regional Park—

Five miles of easy trails, with access for the handicapped. An ecologist's dream, the park also contains a nature center that can guide and educate. Bear Creek Rd. in west Colorado Springs. **(719) 520-6387.**

The Crags—

See the Hiking and Backpacking section in the **Cripple Creek and Victor** chapter.

Mount Cutler Trail—

See the Seven Falls entry in the Other Attractions section.

North Cheyenne Canyon Trail—

This 5-mile loop has an easy grade, passes three springs and provides widespread views of the canyon and down to Colorado Springs. To reach Cheyenne Canyon, head west on Cheyenne Blvd. from Colorado Springs. The trail begins just past the entrance to the canyon, on the left side of the road.

Old Ute Trail—

Centuries old, this 4-mile trail was first used by the Ute Indians and later traveled by miners and trappers. The trailhead begins near the Mt. Manitou Incline on Ruxton Ave. and ends up on Hwy. 24 near Cascade. Easy grades.

Pikes Peak—

See the Pikes Peak entry in the Major Attractions section.

St. Mary's Falls Trail—

This 4-mile trail begins at the top of Helen Hunt Falls and leads to St. Mary's Falls. Cross the bridge and follow the path on the far side of the stream. Expect a half day there and back. Bring a lunch and enjoy great glimpses of Colorado Springs. To reach the trailhead at the far western end of North Cheyenne Canyon, head west on Cheyenne Blvd. from Colorado Springs.

HORSEBACK RIDING

Academy Riding Stables—

This stable rents horses for one- and two-hour guided tours through Garden of the Gods. Seeing the park from a saddle is a good way to avoid the many carloads of visitors. Riders must be at least 8 years old. Reservations urged. **4 El Paso Blvd., Colorado Springs, CO 80904; (719) 633-5667.**

The Mark Reyner Stables—

Horses are rented by the hour in Palmer Park. Ride in this relatively unspoiled natural area surrounded by the city in northeast Colorado Springs. **3254 Paseo Rd., Colorado Springs, CO 80909; (719) 634-4173.**

ICE SKATING

Plaza Ice Chalet—
Downtown in the Plaza of the Rockies, this urban rink is surrounded by shops in an enclosed atrium. Small fee charged; lessons offered. Open for public skating 10 am–5 pm and 7–10 pm. **111 S. Tejon St.; (719) 633-2423.**

SKIING

CROSS-COUNTRY SKIING

The Crags and Mueller State Park—
The best cross-country skiing in the Pikes Peak area lies about 30 miles away at The Crags and Mueller State Park. See the Outdoor Activities section in the **Cripple Creek and Victor** chapter.

Rampart Reservoir—
Located about 8 miles east of Woodland Park on Rampart Range Rd. The 13-mile Lakeshore Trail around the lake makes for a good day of cross-country skiing. Although it's possible to drive all the way from Colorado Springs to the reservoir on Rampart Range Rd., the dirt road is often blocked in winter. It is wiser to take Hwy. 24 west to Woodland Park and then backtrack 8 miles to the reservoir.

Rentals and Information—
Mountain Chalet—This shop in downtown Colorado Springs rents touring equipment and can point skiers in the right direction. **226 N. Tejon St.; (719) 633-0732.**

SWIMMING

Manitou Springs Public Swimming Pool—
This indoor pool is open year-round. **202 Manitou Ave., Manitou Springs; (719) 685-9735.**

Monument Valley—
Open only during summer. Set in a beautiful park next to Monument Creek. **(719) 578-6636.**

Portal Park—
Open in summer daily, 11 am–1 pm, 1:30–3:30 pm, 4–6 pm. **3535 N. Hancock; (719) 578-6679.**

Prospect Lake Beach—
This roped-off swimming area is open only during summer in the lake adjacent to Memorial Park. Located in central Colorado Springs. **(719) 578-6637.**

TENNIS

Bear Creek Park—
Eight new, lighted courts are set right in the foothills. At the corner of **Argus and 21st streets.**

Memorial Park Tennis Center—
Twelve new courts (eight lighted) and a club house. The park hosts several tourneys during summer. East Pikes Peak Ave. and Hancock St.; **(719) 578-6676.**

Monument Valley Park—
Eight courts (six lighted) within walking distance of downtown. Courts are located near Cache La Poudre Ave., next to Monument Creek.

—————————— **SEEING AND DOING** ——————————

AMUSEMENTS

North Pole/Santa's Workshop—

Most people probably don't realize it, but the North Pole isn't on some remote ice floe above the Arctic Circle; it's perched conveniently on the flank of Pikes Peak. It's always Christmas at the region's only amusement park, where you'll find brightly garbed elves, reindeer, plenty of rides, magic shows, Christmas gift shops and of course Santa himself (real beard). Kids who still believe love the place. Open mid-May through Christmas Eve. Summer hours are 9:30 am–6 pm. Closed Thurs. in May, and Wed. and Thurs. Sept.–Dec. Located 10 miles west of Colorado Springs on Hwy. 24 at the entrance to the Pikes Peak Hwy. **(719) 684-9432.**

MUSEUMS AND GALLERIES

American Numismatic Museum—

Numismatic is probably a word only coin collectors know, and this is a museum probably only coin collectors will love. Operations for the American Numismatic Association are headquartered here, so this is the big time of coin collecting. The museum houses one of the most extensive collections of coins, paper money, tokens and medals in the United States. Open Mon.–Fri. 8:30 am–4 pm (Sat. after Memorial Day). Free entrance. Just south of Colorado College at **818 N. Cascade Ave., Colorado Springs, CO 80903-3279; (719) 632-2646.**

Colorado Springs Fine Arts Center—

This marvelous facility is housed in an art deco masterpiece built in 1937 and listed on the National Historic Register. A museum, theater, library, art school and shop make up of the Colorado Springs Fine Arts Center. Of specific note is the Taylor Museum for Southwest Studies, which houses a fabulous collection of Native American works and Hispanic art including its well-known collection of santos. Six traveling exhibits are showcased annually. Theater activities include repertory theater, three film series and various performances. In summer enjoy lunch on the balcony looking out to Pikes Peak. Open Tues.–Fri. 9 am–5 pm; Sat. 10 am–5 pm; Sun. 1–5 pm. **30 W. Dale; (719) 634-5581.**

Hall of Presidents—

This museum contains more than a million dollars' worth of wax figures from the renowned studio of Madame Tussaud of London. All of the presidents except Bush and Clinton are among the 100 figures from American history. Each one, with real hair and dentures, is posed in a historical diorama. Highlights include Thomas Jefferson writing the Declaration of Independence, Lincoln on his deathbed and Teddy Roosevelt charging up San Juan Hill with dead soldiers strewn about. This all sets the stage for a bizarre transition smack dab in the middle of the historical scenes—a fairyland display with storybook figures such as Snow White (see her heart actually beat), Pinocchio and Peter Pan. The lifesize Pat Nixon may haunt you after you leave. Admission fee charged. Summer hours are 9 am–9 pm daily; 10 am–5 pm in winter. **1050 S. 21st St.** just south of Hwy. 24; **(719) 635-3553.**

Manitou Cliff Dwellings Museum—

If you want to see Indian cliff dwellings in their natural setting, you'll have to go to Mesa Verde in southwestern Colorado. None of the cliff dwellers lived within 350 miles of Manitou Springs. The 40-room dwelling here is a reconstruction of prehistoric Basket Maker apartment houses under a convenient sandstone overhang above Manitou. It was built in 1906 after the stones were hauled from a private ranch near Mesa Verde. The museum pales in comparison to the real thing. Admission fee charged. Hours are 9 am–8 pm during summer; 10 am–6 pm in May, Sept., Oct. and Nov.; **(719) 685-5242.**

May Natural History Museum—

The giant hercules beetle outside welcomes visitors to one of the world's outstanding collections of arthropods. Bugs, that is. Some 8,000 of them are on display, collected by James May over a period of 63 years. The entire collection includes over 100,000 critters. Don't miss the tarantula locked in a death grip with a humming-bird, and the Colombian beetles so big they are said to have knocked people over with speeds of 40 miles per hour. The center also has 5 miles of nature trails and a new National Museum of Photography. Take the Hercules turn off Hwy. 115, 9 miles south of Colorado Springs. Admission fee charged. Open 8 am–6 pm May–Sept. 30; by appointment in fall and spring; closed in winter. **710 Rock Creek Canyon Rd.; (719) 576-0450.**

McAllister House—

Maj. Henry McAllister, "born friend" of Colorado Springs founder Gen. William Jackson Palmer, came out to Colorado Springs in 1872. He built the first brick house in Colorado Springs. After one of the area's infamous chinook winds blew a train off its tracks, McAllister ordered 20-inch-thick walls to withstand all the elements. His unique house opened as a museum in 1961. Guided tours give a taste of Colorado Springs in its "Little London" era. Summer hours are 10 am–4 pm Wed.-Sat., noon–4 pm Sun.; winter hours are 10 am–4 pm Thurs.-Sat. Admission fee. **423 N. Cascade Ave., near downtown; (719) 635-7925.**

Michael Garman Galleries—

Even if you're not planning to buy sculpture, this gallery is worth a stop. The studio is dominated by "Court and Darby Street," a miniature 24-foot-long city scene, and contains other of Garman's unique urban miniatures and realistic figures. Garman makes originals for the figures out of sculptor's wax. Then a mold is made of latex rubber, and the pieces are cast out of a type of cement. A variety of pieces are for sale at reasonable prices. **2418 W. Colorado Ave.; (719) 471-1600.**

Pioneer's Museum—

To see the way Colorado Springs was, visit this museum in the old El Paso County Courthouse. The building, a registered National Historic Landmark, is worth the stop in itself. Inside, among other things, is the house and furnishings of writer and poet Helen Hunt Jackson. Other tidbits of Pikes Peak history include historic photos (such as William Henry Jackson photos), antique toys and Indian artifacts. Hours are 10 am–5 pm Mon.–Sat., 1–5 pm Sun. Free admission. **215 S. Tejon St.; (719) 578-6650.**

ProRodeo Hall of Fame—

This is the rodeo hall of fame. The young, well-designed museum is also a monument to the legacy of the American cowboy. A visit begins with two multimedia shows: one on the history of the Old West, another that recreates the feel of being a cowboy. After that, Heritage Hall traces the development of cowboy gear. The Hall of Champions showcases the trophies, belt buckles and other paraphernalia of the rodeo greats. Where do Brahma bulls retire? Right here at the mini-rodeo arena—at least one especially mean-looking one has. Open 9 am–4:30 pm year-round; closed Mon. during winter. Admission fee. Take exit 147 west off Interstate 25; **(719) 593-8847.**

Space Command Museum—

Exhibits on the history of flying in Colorado Springs, concentrating on the Air Force and space. Aviation, art, historic uniforms and model aircraft make it the perfect museum for aviation buffs. It features a fascinating film on the history of the North American Aerospace Defense Command and a sample of 3.9-billion-year-old moon rock. An accompanying air park is brimming with aerial hardware. Admission is free. Hours are 9 am–5 pm Mon.–Fri., 10 am–5 pm Sat. Closed Tues. from Dec. 1–Feb. 28. Located on Peterson Air Force Base in east Colorado Springs.

Western Museum of Mining and Industry—

Before heading to the mining country up around Cripple Creek and Victor, think about stopping by this gem of a museum. Visitors can learn how the mines were worked and what to look for when sightseeing. See a host of mining machines in operation and learn how to pan for gold. Tours include a multimedia show, a blacksmith shop and a reconstructed mine. Admission fee. Open 9 am–4 pm Mon.–Sat., 12–4 pm Sun. Take the Gleneagle Dr. exit (156-A) off Interstate 25 at the North Gate to the Air Force Academy; **(719) 488-0880.**

World Figure Skating Hall of Fame and Museum—

Displays memorabilia of skating champions, including the Broadmoor's own Peggy Fleming, and a history of the sport. The museum includes what is billed as the finest collection of skating art in the world and also has a gift shop. Free admission. Located at the Broadmoor at **20 First St.; (719) 635-5200.**

NIGHTLIFE

For a full list of nighttime activities, consult an issue of *Springs* magazine or a *Gazette-Telegraph* "Scene" section on Fridays. Also call the Events Line at **(719) 635-1723** for weekly happenings around town.

Cruising—

Depending on your mood, Nevada Ave. on Friday and Saturday nights could be a good place to take a drive back in time. Or it could be a place to avoid at all costs. The approximately 10-block-long section of the parkway that cuts through downtown has to be one of the last great cruising strips in the West. Hundreds of "cherried-out" cars, from vintage Chevys to low riders and the latest sports cars, extend bumper to bumper along Nevada Ave. Most cruisers drive a loop that starts around Colorado Ave. to the south, eventually wrapping around the statue of Gen. Palmer to the north. But if you are in a hurry to get somewhere, take Cascade Ave. or Interstate 25.

The Golden Bee—

Walking into the Golden Bee, the curators like to say, is like pulling on a familiar sweater—you feel right at home. The Bee is an authentic English pub brought over from London and reassembled in the basement of the International Center at the Broadmoor. The infectious piano tunes and wide variety of English ales make this small room one of the best night spots in Colorado Springs. The entire pub sings along to the ragtime piano music, often led by a baritone named Gary. But don't worry about knowing the words—the Bee has its own hymnal. Another tradition that shouldn't be missed is the quaffing of a 38-oz. yard of ale. The record for polishing off a full yard stands at about seven seconds. Warning: waiting in line is often part of visiting the Bee, but there is a tangible reward—nary a patron is allowed to leave without a woven bee stuck to his or her lapel. Beef and kidney pies are served, as well other menu items and complimentary cheese and crackers. Located at the Broadmoor; 11:30 am–2 am daily. Across from the Broadmoor at **1 Lake Ave.; (719) 577-5776.**

The Iron Springs Chateau—

The emphasis is on audience participation at this comedy melodrama. Things get under way at 6 pm with an all-you-can-eat meal of barbecue beef and country-fried chicken. The curtain goes up at 8:30 pm, with ample opportunity for cheers and jeers. A rousing sing-along olio and dancing in the lounge round out an entertaining night. Open Wed.–Sun.; dinner served 6–7 pm. Reservations necessary. Located in Manitou Springs across from the Cog Railway Station at **444 Ruxton Ave.; (719) 685-5104** or **685-5572.**

Jeff Valdez' Comedy Corner—

Local and national stand-up comics perform here Wed.–Sun. nights. Call for reservations. **1305 N. Academy Blvd.; (719) 591-0707.**

Judge Baldwin's Brewing Company—

Located next to the Antlers Doubletree Hotel, Judge Baldwin's was the first brewpub to open in the Springs and the only one that brews beer on-site. Pull up a chair and try one of their four tasty brews while perusing the menu; the two-fisted burger is a highlight. Judge Baldwin's is usually pretty crowded with plenty to keep your attention including TV sports, karaoke, and live music on Saturday nights. **4 S. Cascade Ave.; (719) 473-5600.**

Meadow Muffins—

With walls covered with memorabilia, Meadow Muffins has become a Springs institution attracting a younger crowd. Its dance floor features pop and rock. Theme nights every night. Cheap beer and free popcorn. Mon.–Sat. 11 am–2 am; Sun. 11 am–midnight. **2432 W. Colorado Ave.; (719) 633-0583.**

Pine Gables Tavern—

Classic rowdy mountain bar that is well known for its live rock and roll, cheap beer and great Bloody Marys. Located about 10 miles west of Colorado Springs off Hwy. 24 at **10530 Ute Pass Ave., Green Mountain Falls; (719) 684-2555.**

The Ritz Grill—

Currently many young professionals and/or urban sophisticates frequent this art deco gathering place in downtown Colorado Springs. Live music (predominantly jazz and R&B) attracts many, as do the evening happy hours which last from 4:30–6:30 pm. The decor features high ceilings with fans and track lighting; of note is the oval bar. The Ritz serves plenty of appetizers as well as full meals. Open 11 am–11 pm Mon.–Wed.; 11 am–1 am Thurs.–Sat. **15 S. Tejon St.; (719) 635-8484.**

SCENIC DRIVES
ROADS TO CRIPPLE CREEK AND VICTOR

Three scenic drives lead from Colorado Springs to the historic mining towns of Cripple Creek and Victor. A combination of two makes for a great 70-mile round trip.

Through Florissant—

This route works best for stops at **Florissant Fossil Beds National Monument**. Take Hwy. 24 to Florissant, turn south on County Rd. 1 for a couple of miles and look for the monument entrance on the right (west). About 5 miles past the monument the road turns to dirt, climbs up past Mt. Pisgah and then descends into the Cripple Creek basin. For more information about the fossil beds, see the Major Attractions section of the **Cripple Creek** and **Victor** chapter.

Gold Camp Road—

Teddy Roosevelt traveled by train along Gold Camp Rd. back at the turn of the century. But even without the tracks the scenery is just as stunning. The sometimes harrowing drive is open late spring to early fall. It's quite a show in late September when the aspen are turning.

Go up North Cheyenne Canyon and follow the signs on the left for Gold Camp Rd. On the way to Cripple Creek the dirt road wraps around Cheyenne Mountain, with views of Colorado Springs, then plunges through seven tunnels still etched with the soot from Short Line (of Monopoly fame) locomotives. Since the road is often in poor condition and very narrow, the 30-mile trip can take hours. Attention: A tunnel cave-in a couple of years ago eliminated a section of Gold Camp Rd. near Colorado Springs. A detour, however, is possible by beginning the drive to Cripple Creek on the Old Stage Rd. located near the Broadmoor Hotel on the way to Cheyenne Mt. Zoo. For information on the detour, contact the **Pikes Peak Ranger District Office** at **(719) 636-1602.** RVs and trailers are not recommended.

Highway 67—

This is the most traveled and fastest route to Cripple Creek, but that doesn't mean the drive is any scenery slouch. After winding up Ute Pass to the town of Divide on Hwy. 24, take Hwy. 67 south through great stands of aspen and a one-way tunnel. You might consider this paved route for a speedy return trip.

HIGH DRIVE

A quick, cliff-hugging drive with a tremendous panorama of the Broadmoor, Cheyenne Canyon and Colorado Springs. Drive up North Cheyenne Canyon to the end of the pavement at the Gold Camp Rd. crossroads. Follow the signs to the right for High Dr. or Lower Gold Camp Rd., both of which eventually feed into Hwy. 24, without ever really having left the city.

PIKES PEAK HIGHWAY

See the Pikes Peak entry in the Major Attractions section.

RAMPART RANGE ROAD

The scenery along this road starts off auspiciously in Garden of the Gods and never really quits. The road actually goes north through Pike National Forest and all the way to Hwy. 67 northwest of Castle Rock, but the Woodland Park turn-off is usually far enough for the shock absorbers of most vehicles—(and riders). Beware of boulders in the middle of this roller-coaster dirt road. Taking Hwy. 24 back to Colorado Springs from Woodland Park makes for an adventurous half-day trip.

———— WHERE TO STAY ————

ACCOMMODATIONS

Colorado Springs is home to plenty of well-known first-rate hotels. There's also a healthy representation of national bargain chains, many campgrounds, and a sprinkling of bed and breakfast inns, dude ranches and cabin-type motels. It's easiest to find a bed by calling the **Colorado Springs Visitors Center** at **1-800-DO-VISIT** during business hours Mon.–Fri. 8 am–5 pm (weekend also in summer). Below are some of the more unique and indigenous places to stay in the area.

The Broadmoor—$$$$ and up

A destination in itself—worth visiting even if you're not staying. This resort at the foot of Cheyenne Mountain is one of only eight in America to be awarded Mobil's five-star rating. The complex contains three hotels, three championship golf courses, 16 tennis courts, a carriage museum, several excellent restaurants (see Where to Eat), three spring-fed pools, a shooting grounds, a "Fifth Avenue" row of shops and an ice arena where Olympic figure skaters train. Separating the modern Broadmoor West from the two older hotels is an idyllic lake graced by a variety of waterfowl. Don't miss the black swans, which are native only to Australia. One of the most pleasant ways to spend an hour in Colorado Springs is to stroll around the shoreline path.

A casino originally stood where the main hotel now stands. After it burned down, Spencer Penrose, who had made his fortune in gold and copper, bought the property in 1916 and opened the luxury resort two years later.

Staying here can be an expensive proposition. Room prices start at a little over $100 a night and go all the way up to $1,000. **1 Lake Ave., Colorado Springs, CO 80906; (719) 634-7711.**

Cheyenne Mountain Conference Resort—$$$$

This luxury resort holds its own against the formidable competition from the nearby Broadmoor resort by offering many modern amenities. And the views west to Cheyenne Mountain and surrounding mountains are spectacular. The inn's 278 rooms are spread throughout several buildings. The room design resembles that of most hotels, yet they are spacious, plush and modern. The resort also has its own 18-hole golf course (greens fees extra), three swimming pools and a nearby lake with fishing and sailing. Its two restaurants include five-star **Remington's**. This hotel was built for conferences but offers weekend packages for those not in a large group. **3225 Broadmoor Valley Rd., Colorado Springs, CO 80906; (719) 576-4600.**

Antlers Doubletree Hotel—$$$ to $$$$

Located in downtown Colorado Springs, the refurbished Antlers Doubletree provides 290 rooms for those who want a downtown location. All rooms and suites come with turn down service and cable TV. Other amenities include a fitness room, indoor pool and whirlpool. Downstairs, **Palmer's Restaurant** and **Judge Baldwin's Brewing Company** (see Nightlife) provide the food and entertainment. **4 S. Cascade, Colorado Springs, CO 80903; (719) 473-5600.**

Hearthstone Inn—$$$ to $$$$

This has to be one of the premier country inns in Colorado. The inn, listed on the National Register of Historic Places, is actually two sister Victorians in a row of similar mansions on serene Cascade Ave. near downtown Colorado Springs. Inside are three floors of 25 sumptuous, sometimes eccentric rooms. Each chamber has its own theme, such as the Gable Room, the Author's Den and the Billiard Room. Most have baths or showers, some have antique fireplaces and one boasts its own breakfast terrace. But none has a TV or telephone, as it should be in this 19th-century setting.

Half the fun of staying at the Hearthstone is exploring the other rooms. Puzzles, games and a piano in the homey lobby encourage guests to revive the art of conversation. Just behind the inn is Monument Valley Park, with a jogging trail, tennis courts and swimming pool. The gourmet breakfast is easy to miss at 8 am, but don't. **506 N. Cascade Ave., Colorado Springs, CO 80903; (719) 473-4413.**

Red Crags B&B—$$$ to $$$$

Located on two acres with great views to Pikes Peak, the Red Crags has quickly become popular with the honeymoon, anniversary and Valentine's Day couples. Each of the seven rooms comes with a private bath, queen- or king-size bed and a fireplace or pot bellied stove. The Teddy Roosevelt Room features great views and a private sun deck. That's right, TR himself stayed here. He seems to have visited practically every old hotel in Colorado that is still standing! Proof positive awaits the skeptical—check out the picture next to the living room fireplace of TR atop his horse in front of the Red Crags. Carrie, the owner and recent Texas transplant, is a wonderful cook and often incorporates the fresh herbs and vegetables she grows into the morning meal. **302 El Paso Blvd., Manitou Springs, CO 80829; (719) 685-1920.**

Holden House—$$$

This restored 1902 Victorian offers all the comforts of home without any dishes to do. Sallie and Welling Clark have filled (more like jammed) the home with family heirlooms, including a tremendous quilt made by Sallie's great-grandmother. There are seven rooms—two guest rooms, three suites and two recently added carriage house suites out back. The Cripple Creek room has a view of Pikes Peak. Sunday's champagne breakfast on the veranda is worth the stay in itself. No pets allowed (probably out of respect for the resident cat's territory); children aren't encouraged. The home is located in a shady residential neighborhood near Old Colorado City at the corner of 11th St. and Pikes Peak Ave. **1102 W. Pikes Peak Ave., Colorado Springs, CO 80904; (719) 471-3980.**

Two Sisters Inn—$$$

Like other B&Bs in Manitou, this nicely restored bungalow overlooks town. The four bedrooms at Two Sisters (two with shared bath) are appointed with antiques and fresh flowers. The "Honeymoon Cottage" out back, which used to be an old wagon shop for the town livery stable, has its own kitchenette. Your hosts, Wendy and Sharon, used to be in the catering business so rest assured, you'll have plenty to eat, especially at breakfast. Both Wendy and Sharon are enthusiastic about Manitou and the surrounding area and can be a great source of information about where to go and what to see. **Ten Otoe Pl., Manitou Springs, CO 80829; (719) 685-9684.**

Outlook Lodge—$$ to $$$

This former parsonage for travelling Congregationalist ministers sits on a steep hill 15 miles west of Colorado springs in Green Mountain Falls. And things are definitely quiet here. New owners Pat and Hayley Moran have done a great job with the Outlook as is witnessed by many who have stayed there recently. The Outlook offers three rooms with shared baths and two suites with private baths. Guests share the parlor area and sunny breakfast room. The Morans have recently started murder mystery weekends, which you may want to ask about. Located of Hwy 24 at **PO Box 5, Green Mountain Falls, CO 80819; (719) 684-2303.**

American Youth Hostel—$

The Colorado Springs AYH shares facilities with Garden of the Gods Campground near Manitou Springs. Each of the 12 cabins has four bunk beds. No restrooms in cabins, but campground facilities are accessible. It's a good idea to call ahead. Swimming pool and hot tub. Open May–Oct. only. **3704 W. Colorado Ave., Colorado Springs, CO 80904; (719) 475-9450.**

CAMPING

In Pike National Forest—

North of Woodland Park via Hwy. 67 are several good campgrounds. The first campground, 5.8 miles north of Woodland Park, is **South Meadows Campground** with 56 sites; fee charged. Another mile up the road is **Colorado Campground** with 63 sites; fee charged. Farther up the road are **Big Turkey Campground** (10 sites and fee charged), **Painted Rocks Campground** (15 sites and fee charged) and **Trail Creek Campground** (7 sites and fee charged). They're usually filled by early afternoon in summer. If you want to make reservations for a camp site at least 10 days in advance, contact **MISTIX** at **1-800-952-7442.**

For more information, maps and campground vacancies, stop by the Pike's Peak Ranger District Office in Colorado Springs at **601 S. Weber St.; (719) 636-1602.**

Private Campgrounds—

Garden of the Gods Campground—Conveniently located near the south entrance to Garden of the Gods, this RV heaven includes 250 campsites, complete with heated pool, Jacuzzi and grocery store. Tours and jeeps available as well. Open Apr. 15–Oct. 15. **3704 W. Colorado Ave.; (719) 475-9450** or **1-800-345-8197.**

Lone Duck Campground—Located about 10 miles west of Colorado Springs in Cascade, this place offers 75 RV hookups, a heated pool, tent sites, lounge, etc. Seasonal. **8855 W. Hwy. 24, Cascade, CO 80809; (719) 684-9907.**

WHERE TO EAT

The Briarhurst Manor—$$$$

Although there are occasional complaints about poor service, the Briarhurst Manor continues to be one of the best places in town to go for a special dinner. In 1975 chef and proprietor Sigi Krauss opened for business, serving excellent continental cuisine. Born in Leipzig, Germany, chef Sigi's many credentials include membership in the *Confrérie de la chaîne des rôtisseurs*. The impressive stone manor, built in 1876, allows dinner to be served in its various intimate rooms and occasionally on the sprawling patio. It is difficult to isolate certain dishes as standouts but the Colorado rack of lamb, roasted with garlic and thyme and then baked, is exquisite. Stop by at the end of August when up to 2,000 people per day visit the Briarhurst's Oktoberfest celebration out on the lawn. Make sure you dress up for dinner; reservations suggested. Open Mon.–Sat. 6–10:30 pm. **404 Manitou Ave.; (719) 685-1864.**

Charles Court at the Broadmoor—$$$$

This elegant restaurant decorated in the style of an English country manor is perhaps the Broadmoor's best and Colorado Springs' most exclusive. The continental and southwestern food is superlative, but the prices are even more stunning. Charles Court is in the modern Broadmoor West and has a wonderful lake view. If for no other reason, sup at Charles Court for the awesome wine selection (650 choices!) and the knowledge displayed by the wine steward. He does everything to educate you about your bottle short of producing the vintner in person. We were told that over 100,000 bottles of wine are stored in the Broadmoor complex wine cellar. Serving breakfast, Sun. brunch and dinner. Sun. brunch is unsurpassed in the Springs. Reservations recommended. Dinners served 6:30–9:30 pm Mon.–Fri., 6–9:30 pm Sat.; hours for breakfast and lunch vary. Coat and tie required, dresses or suits for women. **1 Lake Ave.; (719) 577-5774.**

Craftwood Inn—$$$ to $$$$

This fine restaurant is the place in town to go for three main reasons: romantic atmosphere, fine selection of wild game dishes, and creativity. Located in a beautiful English Tudor style home built in 1912, the Craftwood Inn offers a warm atmosphere with a stone fireplace in one room and soft music playing throughout. Cris Pulos, the talented chef and owner, has put together an incredible menu. Start off your meal with an unusual appetizer such as black bean ravioli or artichoke hearts wrapped with venison. Entree choices include variations on fish, poultry, and, especially, meat. Wild game specialties range from grilled Colorado boar and sautéed caribou to mixed game bird including pheasant sausage. Vegetarians should not shy away—the salads are tasty as well as the veggie platter served with wild rice. Desserts are exceptional and also difficult to choose from. I recommend the prickly pear sorbet or the Jalapeño white chocolate mousse. Full bar. Open nightly 5–10 pm. Located in Manitou Springs at **404 El Paso Blvd.; (719) 685-9000.**

Flying W Ranch—$$$

This working cattle and horse ranch north of Garden of the Gods is part restaurant, part tourist attraction. Keep a tight rein on your travelers checks, pardner, as you visit 14 different museum buildings and gift shops. All kidding aside, it can be a lot of fun, especially for out-of-state visitors and families. All meals include the campfire western show featuring the Flying W Wranglers, a cowboy band that's been around since the 1950s. Chuckwagon suppers are held mid-May–mid-Sept. Dinners are served inside during the winter months. Dinner served 7:15 pm with show at 8:30 pm daily during summer, dinner and show at 5 pm and 8 pm Fri. and Sat. in winter. Reservations are necessary. As many as 1,400 can be seated. Take Garden of the Gods Rd. west off Interstate 25 to 30th St. and turn right. Follow the signs. **3330 Chuckwagon Rd.; 1-800-232-3599** or **(719) 598-4000.**

Zeb's—$$$

Named after Zebulon Pike, this restaurant lives up to its name with Pikes Peak–sized portions. Prime rib is a sure bet, as are the well-known BBQ baby back pork ribs, which are baked during the day, then put on the grill at night. Dinner is served with a great view of the mountains. Open Sun.–Thurs. 6–10 pm, Fri.–Sat. 5:30–11 pm. **945 S. 8th St.** in south central Colorado Springs; **(719) 473-9999.**

The Pampered Palate—$$ to $$$

For over 10 years the Pampered Palate has packed people in for their creative menu which changes monthly to feature cuisine from a different country or theme. Cuisine ranges from Indian to Greek to "Cuisine de Halloween." Lunches in this comfortable restaurant include fresh bread and soup or salad; dinners include the same with complimentary appetizers and side dishes. Full bar. Be sure to call ahead for reservations and to find out the theme of the month. Lunch served Mon.–Sat. 11:30 am–2:30 pm; dinner Mon.–Sat. 5:30–9:30 pm. **2625 W. Colorado Ave.; (719) 632-9299.**

Giuseppe's Old Depot—$$

This restored Denver & Rio Grande train station specializes in spaghetti and other Italian dishes. Great salad bar, too. Families love this place. Relax at the comfortable tables and watch the freight trains go by. Meals arrive on plates rimmed with train track. Kids who are into model trains go ape. Open Sun.–Thurs. 11 am–10 pm, Fri. and Sat. 11 am–11:45 pm. **10 S. Sierra Madre; (719) 635-3111.**

Mission Bell Inn—$$

This highly regarded Mexican restaurant located in Manitou Springs is named for the immense iron bell and thick oak front door that were moved to it from an old mission in Mexico. The Masias family has been operating the restaurant since 1962. Along with the standard Mexican fare such as chalupas, flautas and enchiladas, try a norteno (a green pepper stuffed with ground beef and onions smothered with green chili cheese sauce). Open 5–10 pm Tues.–Sun.; closed Mon. Located in Manitou Springs at **178 Crystal Park Rd.; (719) 685-9089** or **685-9983.**

Adam's Mountain Cafe—$ to $$

Repeatedly chosen by *Springs Magazine* readers as the best natural food restaurant, Adam's should not be missed for a number of reasons. This cozy little cafe in Manitou is best known for its excellent breakfasts, delicious homemade soups and salads and Mexican entrees. The atmosphere is relaxed, with hanging plants, art work and soft music in the background. Be sure not to miss their tasty "gourmet" desserts. Open Mon.–Sat. 7:30 am–3 pm and 5–9 pm; Sun. from 7:30 am–3 pm. **733 Manitou Ave.; (719) 685-1430.**

D.A.M. Good Pizza—$ to $$

Yes, yes, there is an immense salad bar, pasta bar and other pasta specialties, but the real reason to come here is for homemade pizza (especially the "Pikes Peak Heap"). Try the patio during good weather; the bar area offers satellite sports and plenty of happy hours. Open 11 am–10 pm on weekdays, 11 am–11 pm weekends. Located 2 miles south of Interstate 25 on Academy Blvd. at **1840 Dominion Wy.; (719) 548-8787.**

Dale Street Cafe—$ to $$

Located in an old home north of the downtown area, this small cafe serves up truly fine lunches and dinners with a European flair. When weather permits, sit at one of the tables in the front yard and peruse the fine wine and beer list. Standout menu items include salads (Caesar, spinach, etc.), pasta dishes and a number of Mediterranean pizzas. When I was there the Marghuerite pizza with mozzarella, parmesan, tomato and basil was just light enough to leave room for a slice of their superb key lime pie. The Dale Street is highly recommended. Open Mon.–Thur. 11:30 am–9 pm; Fri.–Sat. 11:30 am–9:30 pm; closed Sun. **115 E. Dale St.; (719) 578-9898.**

The Olive Branch Restaurant—$ to $$

The Olive Branch is extremely popular for its breakfasts and healthy food. The downtown location has an attractive open cafe feel, with hanging plants, exposed brick and skylights. Start off with a coffee drink and a breakfast skillet or honey yogurt pancakes. Lunches range from tasty soups and salads to entrees such as stir frys and the Olive Branch pot pie. Dinners (served only at the north location) include Mexican dishes and pasta. Open for breakfast 6:30–11 am; lunch from 11 am–3 pm (dinner until 9 pm at the north location); Sun. brunch from 9 am–2 pm. Located at the Agora Mall, **333 N. Tejon; (719) 475-1199.** The north location is at **2140 Vickers Dr.; (719) 593-9522.**

Michelle's—$

The Micopolous family makes its own ice cream in the basement, then serves it in style upstairs, where pastoral Greek scenes adorn the walls of this vintage soda fountain. Once featured in *Life* magazine, Michelle's serves about 24 flavors of ice cream and frozen yogurt and scores of candies. The truffles are delicious. Special coffees. The Believe-It-or-Not sundae serves 22 people and sells for about $75. Sandwiches and gourmet burgers are also served, as well as Greek food. Open 9 am–

11 pm Sun.–Thur., 9 am–12 pm Fri.–Sat. Two locations, but go to the one at **122 N. Tejon St.; (719) 633-5089.**

Red Top—$

This Colorado Springs institution made its name with larger-than-life burgers—6 inches in diameter and weighing half a pound. One of these hamburgers is, as the owners say, indeed a meal. And the malts here are like the unforgettable, rich, thick ones of the 1950s (the campy decor is 1950s-like, too). Red Top has expanded to three locations, but the south Nevada Ave. restaurant is the one with the 1950s ambience. Open Sun.–Thurs. 11 am–9 pm; Fri.–Sat. 11 am–9:30 pm. **1520 S. Nevada Ave.; (719) 633-2444.** Two other locations are **910 N. Circle** and **3589 N. Carefree.**

Sunday Brunch —

The Springs is a great place to be if you're in the mood for an all you can eat Sunday brunch. Truly decadent spreads that are guaranteed to put on a few pounds are listed below. **Charles Court ($$$)** at the Broadmoor is exquisite (see above write-up). **The Lake Terrace at the Broadmoor ($$$)** serves from 9:30 am–1 pm. Complete with ice sculptures, veggie and omelette chefs and great mimosas, the buffet at the **Antlers Doubletree ($$$)** is excellent. Another choice, with great views out toward Cheyenne Mountain is the well-named **Mountain View Dining Room** at the **Cheyenne Mountain Conference Center ($$$).**

———————— SERVICES ————————

Colorado Springs Convention and Visitors Bureau—

Provides information and brochures during regular business hours. **104 S. Cascade Ave.; (719) 635-1632** or **1-800-DO-VISIT.**

Colorado Springs Chamber of Commerce—

PO Drawer B, Colorado Springs, CO 80901; (719) 635-1551.

Manitou Springs Chamber of Commerce—

Walls of brochures and someone to talk to about Manitou. **354 Manitou Ave., Manitou Springs, CO 80829; (719) 685-5089.**

Pikes Peak Country Attractions Association—

354 Manitou Ave., Manitou Springs, CO 80829; (719) 685-5854.

Taxi—

Yellow Cab—(719) 635-9907.

Creede, South Fork and Lake City

A diverse and beautiful 75-mile stretch of Hwy. 149, recently renamed the Silver Thread—a National Scenic and Historic Byway—strings together the three communities of **South Fork, Creede and Lake City.** In addition to proximity, these towns have other things in common: millions of acres of public lands, hundreds of miles of productive trout streams and a far-reaching network of breathtaking two- and four-wheel-drive roads. Both Creede and Lake City have also been named National Historic Areas.

The Uncompahgre, Rio Grande, Gunnison and San Juan national forests as well as several wilderness areas provide enticements for people who like to explore the backcountry without crowds. If you have the time, take a hike to the stunning formations at the Wheeler Geologic Natural Area. In winter, after the hunters have left, locals reclaim a sense of solitude. Very few visitors come through Lake City and Creed after the snow has fallen, but cross-country skiing and snowmobiling remain excellent ways to enjoy the suuroundings.

Many alpine lakes and popular Rio Grande and Lake Fork of the Gunnison rivers lure fishermen to the area. Jeep roads connect with the popular destinations of Silverton, Telluride and Ouray. Your regular passenger car can also take you to some pretty incredible scenery: Lake San Cristobal, Slumgullion Earthflow and the Silver Thread itself to name a few.

Isolated and strikingly pictuesque, **Creede** lies nestled in a compact side canyon of the Rio Grande Valley. With few of the trappings of a full service resort, Creede is a place that snaps you back to the wide-open history of a century ago. Historic Main St., lined with galleries, shops and a few restaurants, leads directly into a sharply cut ravine behind town. Continuing into the ravine, this road works its way near the town's original settlement, which is now called North Creede, soon arriving at the mines that have pulled out 80 million troy ounces of silver in the past century. Outside of Creede, in the Upper Rio Grande Valley, a large number of guest ranches cater to people searching for rustic vacations.

An independent spirit lives on in Creede, though the once mighty Homestake Mine is closed. Fortunately, Creede is in no danger of becoming a ghost town because a dramatically beautiful environment and low-key atmosphere has drawn a unique brand of people together who choose to call Creede home. They make the town a special place, without the cookie cutter sameness so evident in some areas. A perfect example of Creede's resourcefulness lies in the town's nationally acclaimed repertory theater (see Nightlife for details).

Lake City sports an entirely different history (including one of Colorado's most bizarre chapters) yet remains a charming little community deep in the San Juan Mountains northwest of Creede. The colossal peaks of the San Juans dwarf this already little town to even smaller proportions. Unlike Creede more than a handful of 14ers tower nearby.

Tucked into a grassy canyon at the confluence of Henson Creek and the Lake Fork of the Gunnison, Lake City remains a Colorado original that relatively few Coloradans know about. In the 1920s and 1930s, when Lake City was on the verge of becoming a ghost town, a rash of visitors from the south discovered its air-conditioned summer weather at 8,663 feet. Many Lake City visitors are Texans and Oklahomans who have been coming here for generations.

Since the late 1800s, **South Fork** (to the southeast) has developed primarily as a logging and lumbering community though it has grown to serve the needs of visitors. Located at the foot of Wolf Creek Pass, and due to its proximity of year-round recreational possibilities, it offers a decent mix of restaurants and motels. South Fork and Pagosa Springs (see the **Pagosa Springs** chapter) are the two most convenient places to stay while skiing the deep powder at Wolf Creek Ski Area atop the Continental Divide.

CREEDE HISTORY

"Holy Moses!" shouted Nicholas C. Creede when he discovered the area's first silver lode in 1889. Within a few months, the Holy Moses, Ethel, Amethyst and Last Chance mines were producing fantastic quantities of high-grade ore. A latecomer to the silver boom, the new town of Creede was soon attracting 300 newcomers a day and nearing a population of 10,000. During this time a mass of humanity became locked in a struggle for huge stakes. With land selling for exorbitant prices, some new arrivals built shanties on wooden supports laid across Willow Creek; later, outhouses were built across the creek, which "flushed" away the sewage. This reckless growth contributed to Creede's reputation for nonstop nightlife. In 1892 Cy Wyman penned a famous poem about the town—the last verse reads, "It's day all day in the daytime, and there is no night in Creede."

Soapy Smith, a strongman con artist from Denver, ran nearly all of the gambling in town from his Orleans Club. Smith once claimed he found a petrified man in the mud near town at Farmer's Creek. He cleaned it for display at the Vaughn Hotel and charged a quarter admission. Soon enough, however, the so-called petrified man's cement skin began to flake off, and the scam was forced to move to a new location. Smith eventually resurfaced in Skagway, Alaska, where he was gunned down in 1898.

Boomtown status attracted a special breed of men and women whose names have survived the passage of time. Bat Masterson was the marshal of Creede for a short while. Bob Ford was another of Creede's residents—famous only because he killed Jesse James with a shot to the back. Ford operated a saloon in Creede until Ed O'Kelly gunned him down with a double-barreled shotgun. Champagne, wine and song flowed freely at Ford's funeral. He will be forever remembered in a ballad as "the dirty little coward." The flourishing trade of ladies of the night had a queen named Slanting Annie. Calamity Jane and her friend Poker Alice Tubbs were a couple of other well-known locals.

Though Creede was once the leading producer of silver in the state, the repeal of the Silver Act in 1893 caused the area economy to collapse. Boom had turned to bust in less than five years. On top of that came catastrophic fires in 1892, 1895, 1902 and 1936. A number of flash floods nearly completed the picture of destruction, and today many of the town's grand old buildings are only memories.

Even with all this adversity, the town has always been able to rebuild, and, over the years, it has attracted an eclectic bunch of locals. For a while a volatile combination of hippies and rednecks flocked to the area—very gradually the distinction has become blurred. Today the town is a relaxed haven for writers and artists as much as for retirees and outdoorsmen.

LAKE CITY HISTORY

Many years before Creede hit its heyday in the late 1880s, this San Juan mining camp had already gone through a few booms and busts. Before 1874 Ute Indians prevented any permanent settlements from cropping up in the Lake City area. But after pressure from the government, the Utes ceded most of the San Juan territory, and rumors of gold inspired prospectors to come into the area. When Enos Hotchkiss made a major strike in 1874, a rush of prospectors started arriving. Within two years the young town of Lake City had a population of 1,000 and supported two banks, five blacksmith shops, seven saloons, two breweries, the *Silver World* newspaper and four Chinese laundries. The first church on the Western Slope of Colorado was built at Lake City in 1876. Today this pretty, white-framed church still stands at 5th St. and Gunnison Ave.

Because it was difficult to get ore out of this hard-to-reach valley, Lake City's initial boom died down by 1880. The town experienced periods of exaltation and discouragement until 1889, when the Denver & Rio Grande Railroad laid 38 miles of track from Sapinero (north of town) to Lake City. The railroad became a stabilizing force in the economy for years to come.

Compared with other mining towns, Lake City stayed a rather calm place to live. There were a few lynchings and, of course, the requisite bordello district (called Hell's Acres), but most hoodlums moved on to other camps.

One particularly gruesome exception to law and order occurred the winter before Lake City was established. In January 1874, when Alferd

Packer and some companions showed up at a Ute encampment near present-day Delta, they were warned not to continue because of deep snow and severe weather. Though Packer knew nothing of the San Juans, he claimed expertise, and five eager prospectors hired him as their guide. They set out on the dangerous passage into the snow-covered mountains with only enough provisions to last 10 days. Six weeks later Packer showed up at the Los Piños Indian Agency 76 miles northeast of Lake City—all alone, with a beard and long hair, but appearing well-fed.

He claimed to have endured the below-zero weather by eating rose pods and roots. Packer then stupidly turned down something to eat and soon went on a drinking binge in Saguache, paying for drinks with money from several wallets. This suspicious behavior raised a few eyebrows, especially when Indians, walking along the same trail Packer had taken, found strips of human flesh. It wasn't until late summer that five partially decomposed bodies were discovered a few miles south of Lake City on the northeast side of Lake San Cristobal (the area is now called Cannibal Plateau). Four of the men had been murdered in their sleep with an axe to the head and the fifth, found nearby, was shot to death. Chunks of flesh had been cut from the men's chests and thighs.

Packer sensed something was awry and managed to escape from detention in a Saguache jail. Nine years later he was discovered in Wyoming living under the assumed name of John Schwartz. On April 13, 1883, Packer was sentenced to hang at the Lake City courthouse. The embellished version of the sentencing, which is now folk history, was actually made up by an Irish barkeep in Lake City. According to his story, presiding Judge Melville Gerry shouted, "Packer, ye man-eatin' son of a bitch, they was seven dimmycrats in Hinsdale County and ye eat five of 'em, God damn ye! I sentins ye to be hanged by the neck until ye're dead, dead, dead ... ."

Gallows were constructed, but because of a technicality, Packer's trial was declared unconstitutional. He was given a new trial, convicted of manslaughter and sentenced to 45 years of hard labor at the Cañon City Penitentiary. However, as his last act, Colorado Gov. Charles Thomas pardoned Packer, who was released after serving only five years. He died of natural causes in 1907 and is buried in Littleton under the misspelled name Alfred Packer.

GETTING THERE

Creede is located between South Fork and Lake City on Hwy. 149. The town is about 300 miles southwest of Denver. The easiest route from Denver is to take Interstate 25 south for 160 miles to Walsenburg, then head west on Hwy. 160 for 120 miles to South Fork. Turn right onto Hwy. 149 for the remaining 22 miles to Creede. A more scenic route from Denver is via Hwy. 285. Lake City is located 53 miles northwest of Creede on Hwy. 149; it's also 55 miles southwest of Gunnison via Hwy. 149.

FESTIVALS AND EVENTS

Rio Grande Raft Races
early June

Since 1959 wild raft races on the Rio Grande, between Creede and South Fork, have been a summer highlight. Various race categories provide a weekend of excitement, including money and prizes for contestants. The Hooligan Race is definitely the most fun to watch, because all of the crafts are judged on originality. Entries may be anything that floats, except for boats. The Elks Lodge in Creede puts on a Sat. night dance as this small town kicks into high gear. For more information contact the **Creede/Mineral County Chamber of Commerce, PO Box 580, Creede, CO 81130; (719) 658-2374.**

Creede Repertory Theater
mid June to Labor Day

Actors from across the country converge on the Rio Grande Valley each summer and the Creede Opera House takes on a life of its own. See the Nightlife section for more information.

Days of '92
Fourth of July weekend

Creede's Main St. turns into an open market as vendors sell snake oil, jewelry and crafts. Everyone turns out for the parade complete with a kazoo band (more marchers than spectators), and soon afterward the mining contests get underway. Fiercely competitive miners test their skills in events such as single-jack drilling, machine drilling and hand mucking. At the end of the festivities, an impressive fireworks display lights up the sky. For more information call **(719) 658-2374.**

Alferd Packer Jeep Tour and Memorial Barbecue
mid-September

This annual autumn tribute to the gruesome antics of Alferd Packer features a jeep tour, arts and crafts and the all important barbeque. The public is welcome to stop by and clean some ribs—pork or beef we hope. For more information call **(303) 944-2527.**

OUTDOOR ACTIVITIES

BIKING
MOUNTAIN BIKING

The Creede area offers as much good terrain for biking as you could ever explore in an entire summer of riding. And quality rental bikes are available at **San Juan Sports** on Creede Ave.; **(719) 658-2359.** Check with the folks at this shop for trail ideas and maps, or consider some of the roads in the Four-Wheel-Drive Trips and Scenic Drives sections. A highly recommended ride is on the rough, seldom-traveled road to the stunning formations at Wheeler Geologic Natural Area (see the Hiking and Backpacking section).

FISHING

If vast opportunities for good fishing in spectacular scenery mean anything to you, come to the Creede/South Fork area. We've outlined a few of the better possibilities, but there are literally hundreds of miles of streams and dozens of brimming lakes and reservoirs in this part of the state. For more information on local conditions, stop by the **Ramble House** on **Creede Ave.; (719) 658-2482.** Talk with Alton Cole and take a look at his excellent selection of flies and lures.

High-Country Lakes—

In the mountains around Creede and South Fork, innumerable lakes situated in gorgeous locations provide excellent fishing. Spend a morning on the trail and an afternoon throwing a line. Fern Creek Trail (see the Hiking and Backpacking section) leads into the Weminuche Wilderness Area west of Creede. After a few miles, the trail comes out at **Little Ruby Lake, Fuchs Reservoir** and **Ruby Lake.** Of the three, Ruby Lake is the deepest and most consistent. The most common catch is pan-sized rainbow and brook trout. You can take refuge in a few tumble-down cabins on the lakeshore. If you continue up the trail toward the Continental Divide, you will reach Trout Lake. This high lake can be good for cutthroat trout, especially in midsummer and fall.

Rio Grande Reservoir—

Thirty miles west of Creede, this long reservoir offers good fishing for trout from boats and from the shore. This is the place to skewer a worm and wait for a tug on your line while enjoying the scenery. The northern shore is traced by Forest Rd. 520, while the steep southern shore is the boundary for the **Weminuche Wilderness Area.** Several campgrounds and picnic areas are available near the reservoir. To get there from Creede, drive west on Hwy. 149 for 21 miles and then turn left on Forest Rd. 520, which reaches the reservoir in 9 miles.

Lake Fork of the Gunnison—

The Lake Fork headwaters begin in the mountains far above Lake San Cristobal. Some good public fishing for smallish rainbow and brook trout can be found in a mile-long stretch, 1.5 miles below Lake San Cristobal. The water, accessible from Hwy. 149, offers some nice riffles for dry fly-fishing. This little-known area receives relatively light use.

Within Lake City town limits, some good holes attract many anglers in the summer months. The water is stocked, and occasionally some very large trout are pulled out on nymphs, flies and lures. Below Lake City the river flows through mostly private property until reaching Gateview. Below Gateview, at Red Bridge Campground, the river is entirely public, offering some prime trout water. With waders this 30-foot-wide stream can be easily fished. Along the stretch between Gateview Campground and Blue Mesa Reservoir, the water and the bank are strewn with debris from the reservoir, making the area unattractive and difficult to fish.

Lake San Cristobal—

The second largest natural lake in Colorado, Lake San Cristobal was formed about 800 years ago when the Slumgullion Earthflow blocked the valley. It is rimmed by high, snowcapped peaks, and in fall the area becomes a golden carpet of aspen. Primarily rainbows and browns prowl the depths, but every now and then someone pulls out a 20-pound Mackinaw. In spring, just as the ice recedes from the banks, you'll have your best shot at catching one of these hogs. Bank fishing and boat casting are both popular at this crowded, easy-to-reach destination. The mossy upper end of the lake is the best place to fly-fish from the bank. Many people do very well by throwing lures or baiting with eggs, cheese or worms. To get there drive 2 miles south of town on Hwy. 149, turn right on County Rd. 30 and proceed 1.5 miles to the lake.

Rio Grande River—

The Rio Grande headwaters lie 30 miles to the west of Creede above Rio Grande Reservoir. Fed by a number of tributaries, the river gains strength as it flows east. From the reservoir down to Creede, several patches of public water offer excellent fishing for German brown trout as well as a few rainbows and brooks. The runoff usually calms down in early July. Twelve miles east of Creede (6 miles west of South Fork), a 15-mile stretch of Gold Medal water, beginning at Collier Bridge, entices anglers. Many lunker trout can be caught on flies and lures. The land along this stretch is mostly public, arranged through a series of leases and buyouts. Please observe and obey posted signs. The Gold Medal water is easily wadable, with many of the larger trout staying low near the banks.

Rio Grande Tributaries—

Between Creede and South Fork an incredible number of productive tributaries flow into the Rio Grande from the nearby mountains. A wide variety of fishing challenges can be found on national forest land. Starting at the west end of Rio Grande Reservoir, a trail follows **Ute Creek** into the Weminuche Wilderness Area. This small creek is a good place to catch small cutthroat; a large brook trout population inhabits the higher elevations. About 6 miles from the reservoir, Ute Creek forks into **West, Middle** and **East Ute creeks;** trails follow each tributary to popular high-country lakes with good-sized cutthroat and rainbow trout. Just below the east end of Rio Grande Reservoir, **Little Squaw Creek** flows down from the Weminuche Wilderness Area, entering the Rio Grande at River Hill Campground. This creek is small, but boasts a population of large cutthroat trout. There is no good trail along the lower portions, but you can fight your way upstream. Fern Creek Trail (No. 815) provides good access to the upper reaches of Little Squaw Creek. The trailhead is at Thirtymile Campground at the east end of the reservoir.

Road Canyon Reservoir—

Just 5 miles east of Rio Grande Reservoir, this smaller fishery offers a chance for big fish—meaning up to 6-pound rainbow trout and 2-pound brookies. The long, western shore of Road Canyon Reservoir is easily accessible for bank fishing. Boats at wakeless speeds are allowed. Road Canyon Campground is located at the southwest end of the reservoir. Follow the directions to Rio Grande Reservoir (see above) and you'll pass Road Canyon Reservoir 4 miles after turning off Hwy. 149.

South Fork of the Rio Grande—

The South Fork of the Rio Grande converges with the Rio Grande at the community of South Fork, 22 miles southeast of Creede. A major tributary of the Rio Grande, the South Fork is about 18 feet wide and is paralleled for many miles by Hwy. 160. The stream is pretty good for brown, rainbow and brook trout. A trail from Big Meadows Campground (14 miles southwest of the town of South Fork) follows the upper reaches of the South Fork to some small lakes near the Continental Divide.

FOUR-WHEEL DRIVE TRIPS

More than most parts of Colorado, this mineral-rich district provides great four-wheel-drive routes. Lake city is a natural hub to other San Juan mining towns—Silerton, Telluride and Ouray to name a few. If you have time for just one adventure, don't miss the Alpine Loop National Back Country Byway, which goes over Engineer and Cinnamon passes.

Alpine Loop—

This spectacular 49-mile round trip, recently dedicated as a Back Country Byway, is only one of the many four-wheel-drive routes in the area. From this loop trip various forays into the San Juans can be taken. This particilar drive can be taken just as easily in either direction, but we will start out by heading west over Engineer Pass. From the south end of Lake City, a green sign directs you toward Engineer Pass. The road soon climbs uphill alongside Henderson Creek, reaching a T intersection at Capitol City after 9 miles. This ghost town was named in an attempt to compete with Denver for the state capital—good thing it lost! Turn left and drive 4.5 miles over fairly rough road to Rose's Cabin, which is a good place to shift into four-wheel. Bear right here at the sign indicating Ouray/Silverton (unless you want to make a detour to Silverton) and in a half mile take another right. This road leads above treeline to the summit of Engineer Pass(13,100 feet), which offers fantastic views of the San Juans.

The main road the drops over the other side of the pass and comes around the west side of Engineer Mountain before descending into a valley. (A couple of miles after the pass, Mineral Point Rd. leads off to the right for 7 miles to the Million Dollar Highway—Hwy. 550— just south of Ouray.) Some 5.5 miles after the summit, you arrive at a marked turn-off for Cinnamon Pass, a moderately steep jeep road that breaks off to the left. This road goes over the pass and then winds downhill, passing many mine ruins along the way and reaching Lake City in 24 miles. Back at the marked turn-off for Cinnamon Pass, consider going straight (past the ghost town of Animas Forks) for 13 miles to Silverton.

East Willow Creek Loop—

The beautiful aspen-cloaked mountains north of Creede are strewn with mine remnants. Drive through this area on an easy four-wheel-drive road that makes a 7-mile loop. Drive north on Main St. into the sharp ravine at the end of town. After 0.6 miles, turn right at the fork leading to North Creede. Thousands of miners lived here in 1890, but today North Creede is home to only a few hardy souls who love its isolation and beauty. Follow the road up the west wall to the vicinity of the top-producing Solomon–Holy Moses vein. Both sides of the road are littered with old mine buildings and shafts. The road switches back down to West Willow Creek, a hiking trail leads up into the unspoiled Phoenix Park area. Take West Willow Rd. back down to Creede or continue past the Midwest Mine to Bachelor (see the Scenic Drives section for more information).

Stony Pass—

This is a stunning ride over a rough and, as you may have guessed, stony road. Take time to enjoy the scenery as you angle toward the Continental Divide among high 13,000-foot peaks. To reach Stony Pass Rd., drive west on Hwy. 149 for 21 miles. Turn left onto Forest Rd. 520, which passes Rio Grande Reservoir and circumvents Pole Creek Mountain (13,716 feet) on the 30-mile route to the summit of Stony Pass. Once there, enjoy the views before continuing down the other side. The road eventually leads down Cunningham Gulch, ending at a T intersection at County Rd. 110. A left turn will land you in the National Historic District of Silverton (see the Four-Wheel-Drive Trips section of the **Silverton** chapter for more information on the history of this area and for connecting routes). From Creede to Silverton takes about four hours. A right turn on County Rd. 110 takes you through Animas Forks and over Cinnamon Pass (see the Major Attractions section) to Lake City. Return to Creede on Hwy. 149.

Rentals—

So you feel like negotiating the spine-tingling roads yourself? **Rocky Mountain Jeep Rental in Lake City** is the place to rent your own jeep and to find out about routes in the area. For reservations, call **(303) 944-2262.**

HIKING AND BACKPACKING

Sandwiched by Rio Grande National Forest and the La Garita and Weminuche wilderness areas, Creede offers a slew of remote hiking options. You'll be satisfied with the area whether you are interested in hiking for days along the high reaches of the Continental Divide or are looking for a shorter day hike near town. Since wilderness areas in this vicinity receive relatively little use, it isn't difficult to get away from crowds. It is horse country, though, and you will find traces wherever you go. For additional information on hiking in the area, consult the **Ouray, Silverton** and **Gunnison and Crested Butte** chapters. For more trail information contact the **Creede Ranger District, PO Box 270, Creede, CO 81130; (719) 658-2556.** For topographical maps, advice and supplies, stop by **San Juan Sports** on **Main St.** in **Creede; (719) 658-2359.**

Whenever you are in the backcountry, beware of remnants of old mine buildings, mine shafts and pits. Besides being privately owned, the mines are often filled with "bad air," rotten timbers and unstable soil—stay out of them!

Continental Divide Trail (in the Weminuche Wilderness Area)—

Along the 80-mile length of the Continental Divide Trail from Stony Pass to Wolf Creek Pass, you'll find some incredibly beautiful backcountry. But this underused area offers a special set of considerations for avid hikers. For one thing, most of the trail is above treeline, making hikers susceptible to lightning strikes. Pick up topographical maps, because the trail can be difficult to find—especially between Stony Pass and Weminuche Pass—and you may need to change your route at the last minute. Despite all the necessary precautions, this is a prime route that we highly recommend. There isn't enough room here to detail the passage along the Continental Divide. If you want a good description of the route, pick up a copy of *A Backpacking Guide to the Weminuche Wilderness* by Dennis Gebhardt (Basin Reproduction Co., 1976).

Fern Creek Trail—

This may not be the most beautiful trail in the wilderness, but its destination at the shores of Little Ruby Lake, Fuchs Reservoir and Ruby Lake is enticing. As an added bonus, the fishing can be quite good at Ruby Lake and the reservoir. At Ruby Lake some people make use of a couple of drafty, abandoned cabins for overnight shelter. Often used as a stock driveway, the 3.5 mile Fern Creek Trail climbs steadily to the lakes. In early summer, fields of wild iris take over the grassy meadows, providing a pretty purple haze. To reach the trailhead from Creede, take Hwy. 149 southwest for 17.5 miles to Fern Creek Rd. (Forest Rd. 522). Turn left and drive for about 2 miles to the trailhead.

Rio Grande Pyramid—

In 1874 when the Wheeler Survey came through the area, William Marshall called the then-unnamed Rio Grande Pyramid "one of the handsomest and most symmetrical cones in Colorado." It hasn't changed much since then. A hike to the 13,821-foot summit is an invigorating experience. In a day it's a daunting 20-mile round-trip hike with a 4,500-foot elevation gain. In two days you'll be able to stop and smell the flowers: columbine, Indian paintbrush and alpine sunflowers, among others. Many picture-perfect campsites can be found at the midpoint near Weminuche Pass.

The trail begins at Rio Grande Reservoir and reaches the summit of Weminuche Pass after about 5 miles. From the pass, which sits atop the Continental Divide, continue south for a mile to a split in the trail. Take the right fork up Ricon La Vaca ("Valley of the Cow"). In a short while the trail emerges above treeline, with an awesome view to the landmark Rio Grande Pyramid and, just south of the summit, the window—a 150-foot-deep cut in the ridge. Shepherds used to call it the devil's gateway. Stay on the trail until it veers sharply

south away from the peak. From here the trail disappears, but the obvious route up the east flank of the peak is square in front of you. From the top it's hard to imagine a better view of the San Juans.

To reach the trailhead from Creede, drive west on Hwy. 149 for 21 miles and then turn left on Forest Rd. 520, which leads to Thirtymile Campground (at the eastern end of Rio Grande Reservoir) after 9 miles. The forest service trail (No. 818) heads west along the southern shore of the reservoir before turning south to Weminuche Pass.

Wheeler Geologic Natural Area—

Reminiscent of Bryce Canyon, Utah, the unusual rock formations at Wheeler Geologic Natural Area will fascinate you with their variety and beauty. The oddly beautiful geology has been created by wind and water erosion of piles of volcanic tuff (ash). Outcast Ute Indians used the area as a hideout, camping out among the eerie rock spires, canyons and domes. Once designated a national monument, this remote site could not be reached by passenger car, so its designation was changed in 1933. The site can be reached on foot in three to four hours over a gentle 7-mile trail. To reach the trailhead, drive east of Creede on Hwy. 149 for 7.3 miles. Turn left on Pool Table Rd. (Forest Rd. 600) and proceed 10 miles to a sign marking what's left of Hanson's Mill. Park your car and start walking on the jeep road.

Try this shortcut: a quarter mile after setting out, take the left (west) fork and continue for a mile down to East Bellows Creek. Ford the small creek and pick up the trail on the other side. In 4 miles the trail rejoins the jeep road leading to the formations.

HORSEBACK RIDING

Broadacres Guest Ranch—

These folks have the largest stable near Creede. If you are considering a trail ride or an overnight pack trip, they would be the best ones to contact. **PO Box 39, Creede, CO 81130; (719) 658-2291.**

Lakeview Resort—

For guided horseback rides to high mountain lakes or a sunset supper in the backcountry contact **PO Box 1000, Lake City, CO 81235; (303) 944-2401** or **1-800-456-0170.**

LLAMA TREKKING
Lost Trails Ranch—
Carol Ann Getz and her son Bob raise llamas at their ranch 30 miles west of Creede near Rio Grande Reservoir. Contact them for a scenic, tailor-made trip into the wilderness without the burden of a heavy pack. **H. C70, Box 7, Creede, CO 81144; (719) 378-2610,** or **5224 E. 3 South Rd., Monte Vista, CO 81144; (719) 852-2036.**

RIVER FLOATING
Floating on the Rio Grande has long been a pastime of residents—especially during the maniacal annual raft races from Creede to South Fork. Many good stretches of water can be found on the "Grand River from the North," and several professional outfitters can make your trip a pleasant one. If you sometimes dream about fishing and floating at the same time, this is an ideal place.

Rio Grande—
The Rio Grande begins its nearly 2,000-mile journey to the Gulf of Mexico above Rio Grande Reservoir in the mountains west of Creede. The water exits the dam and rushes into a narrow canyon accessible only by boat. The fishing in this 5-mile stretch is excellent and there are many secluded campsites along the way. Since the river drops fairly rapidly, rafters will find good Class III and Class IV rapids. After the river emerges from the canyon, it meanders into the wide Rio Grande Valley. The best put-in for a trip into the canyon is a couple of miles below Rio Grande Reservoir at River Hill Campground (see the Camping section). Take out at the Fern Creek Rd. Bridge.

Down below Wagon Wheel Gap, southeast of Creede, is the most popular of all Rio Grande runs. Good fishing and a few rapids make this float down to South Fork a memorable one. Good places to put in along Hwy. 149 include Phipps Bridge and Goose Creek Rd. Bridge. Soon after setting out, beware of the steel bridge with

rather closely spaced supports (dangerous to rafters). Otherwise, enjoy the ride!

Outfitters—
Mountain Man Rafting Tours—Take a guided float down the Upper Rio Grande or just rent all the gear you need and go by yourself. This established company is run locally by Greg Coln—you can trust his advice and experience. He can also arrange a kayak run down the tumbling waters of the Lake Fork of the Gunnison. Contact him at **Mountain Man Rafting Tours at Box 11, Eagles Nest, Creede, CO 81130; (719) 658-2663** or **658-2843.**

Scenic River Tours—This company has been running the Lake Fork of the Gunnison for 15 years during the season (May–July). Make contact at the **Tackle Box** in **Lake City** or by calling **(303) 944-2306.**

SKIING
CROSS-COUNTRY SKIING
When the snow comes down, most of the people in the Rio Grande Valley are long gone, with the exception of a few hardy locals and travelers who can appreciate the change of seasons. The higher elevations always have enough snow and, at times, even the valley floor can be a good place to ski. Some people prefer snowmobiling, but with so few people and so much space, you will not come across them often while skiing. For trail and avalanche information, contact the **Creede Ranger District, PO Box 270, Creede, CO 81130; (719) 658-2556.**

Backcountry Trails—
Spar City Trail—This well-marked, 5-mile loop is one of the best tours in the valley. Working its way on an easy grade to the ghost town of Spar City, this trail is usually well packed, except after recent storms. In 1892, 300 people lived in Spar City while working the nearby silver mines. The town once had a host of buildings, including a jail, a dance hall, a newspaper office (the *Spar City Candle*), a sawmill and a lumberyard. On the way to the townsite, the trail offers great views to the Bristol Head Cliffs

before heading deeper into a mixed forest of pine and aspen. To reach the trailhead, drive south and west of Creede on Hwy. 149 for 7 miles to Sevenmile Bridge (at Marshall Park Campground). Turn left and continue to the trailhead.

West Willow Canyon—Beginning at the northern edge of town, this 11-mile loop trip heads up to the townsite of Bachelor (see the Scenic Drives section). The scenic route follows a road over varying terrain, which is not recommended for beginners. If you want an even more difficult and longer trip, head up past the Equity Mine and to the Continental Divide. This route follows a jeep trail up West Willow Creek from a sharp switchback at the northern extreme of the loop. To reach the trailhead, drive, walk or ski north from Creede until the road is no longer plowed (see the Scenic Drives for specific directions). If the mines are being worked, the plowing may stop further up the road.

Wheeler Geologic Natural Area—This four-wheel-drive road that winds its way to this former national monument makes a great ski trip. Though the route is maintained by local snowmobilers, on weekdays you can often find solitude. There are also many places to take shortcuts or different routes altogether. See the Hiking and Backpacking section for more specifics and directions to the trailhead.

Guided Tours—
Lost Trails Ranch—Bob Getz will take you on guided backcountry ski tours in the Weminuche Wilderness Area above Rio Grande Reservoir. He also specializes in winter survival courses for those hardy enough to stand the bitter cold at this high elevation. While on a tour, you can also take up residence in one of the ranch's winterized cabins, which are heated but have no running water. Reservations required. For reservations and information contact **Getz** at **5224 E. 3 South Rd., Monte Vista, CO 81144; (719) 852-2036.**

Rentals and Information—
San Juan Sports—Before setting out into the backcountry, stop by this full-service shop for trail ideas, topographical maps and the latest on avalanche conditions. The shop stocks rentals for touring and mountaineering skiing, as well as incidental items such as gaiters. Located in the Elks Building on **Creede Ave.; (719) 658-2359.**

DOWNHILL SKIING
Wolf Creek—
This rather small ski area is renowned for the huge quantity of light powder snow it receives each year. It is located about halfway between Pagosa Springs and South Fork at the summit of Wolf Creek Pass along Hwy. 160. For more information on Wolf Creek Pass see the Skiing section of the **Pagosa Springs** chapter.

——— SEEING AND DOING ———

MUSEUMS AND GALLERIES
Creede Underground Mining Museum—
What makes this underground experience so compelling is not that it goes into a real mine (it doesn't), but that a true hardrock miner takes you through. Chuck Fairchild, our miner/guide, explained in the evolution of mining tools and techniques used over the past century inside a large U-shaped tunnel that resembles a

real mine. During our one-hour tour (shorter tours available for children), our small group gained a better understanding of the pains, joys and dangers of going inside for a shift. The exibits and personal approach make this museum a true learning experience. Bring along a sweater or light jacket: The underground temperature remains at a constant 55°F. Gift shop with core samples, hats and T-shirts as you exit. Small fee charged. Open daily in summer from 10 am–4:30 pm; check sign at entrance in winter. Take Main St. north into the ravine at the end of town; the museum is **located adjacent to the underground firehouse.**

Galleries—

Artisans must be attracted to the picturesque natural setting of Creede and Lake City. The number of galleries per capita is astounding. Without making too many judgments, here are a few of the best. On Main St. in Creede check out: **Baskay, Quiller, Abbey Lane** and **Rare Things** galleries. In Lake City, stop by the **Adobe, Higher Elevations, Gwendolyn's** and **Nice Woodworks**. Both towns are great places to stroll around and poke into stores no matter what they carry.

NIGHTLIFE

Creede Repertory Theater—

Since 1966 the old Creede Opera House has been a perfect setting for popular musicals, historical dramas and light comedies. The plays are performed on a rotating schedule throughout the summer. It's a fun evening for people who come from miles around to enjoy the energy and excitement of the show. Since performers expand their repertoire you can see six plays performed in four days by late summer. The nonprofit theater recruits performers from across the country to its remote downtown Creede location. Last year more than 700 individuals sought auditions for a mere 30 jobs. Patrons have a chance to meet the actors after each performance. Check this place out! Reservations neccessary; many plays are sold out early in the season. **Main St. in downtown Creed; PO Box 269, Creede, CO 81130; (719) 658-2540.**

SCENIC DRIVES

Bachelor Historic Tour—

This circle tour, a little over 11 miles long, takes you past some famous mines in a beautiful area north of Creede. Head into the aspen-covered hills by driving north from Main St. into the narrow canyon. The first notable sight is Creede's fire house—or should we say fire cave?—blasted 120 feet back into a solid rock wall and, right next door, the Underground Mining Museum (see Museums and Galleries). A half mile after setting out, the road splits. Take the left fork up West Willow Rd. Very soon after the fork, on your left, is the stone foundation to the Humphry's Mill, which was a large gravity ore concentrator. The road follows the creek up to the Commodore Mine along a steep 2.5-mile stretch called the Black Pitch. (If your car has trouble up steel inclines, consider starting your trip at the other end of the road.) The Commodore Mine tapped the southern portion of a huge amethyst silver vein. A mile farther along the road are the stables for the sturdy mules that once carred the heavy ore. When the road practically doubles back on itself at the Midwest Mine, be sure to stay left. Keep left again as the road crosses Willow Creek.

The road eventually passes the Bachelor townsite. Now only a deserted meadow with a few foundations, it was once home to 1,000 people. In 1893 the town was booming with mines such as the Bachelor, the Spar, the Cleopatra and the Sunnyside, all located on Bachelor Mountain. It also supported as many as a dozen saloons. The views from the road down to the Rio Grande Valley are tremendous. On the way back to Creede the road passes the Sunnyside Cemetry, the gravestones dating back to the 1880s. The Creede Ranger District and Creed Chamber of Commerce have created a detailed booklet on the entire route.

Silver Thread—

The 75-mile drive on Hwy. 149 from South Fork—through Creede—to Lake City recently received proper recognition as an official Scenic and Historic Byway. The journey, once a stage route, takes in many interesting natural and manmade sites along its beautiful route. The paved road crosses the Continental Divide at Spring Creek Pass before heading over 11,361-foot Slumgullion Pass with a close-up view to the odd-looking mud flow. Most unique natural features and places of historical significance have interpretive signs and are covered elsewhere in this chapter.

WHERE TO STAY

ACCOMMODATIONS

The Rio Grande Valley is home to a quantity of guest ranches and lodging establishments. Many families from Texas, Oklahoma and other southern states flock to the higher elevations of southern Colorado during the summer to escape the oppressive heat of their homelands. No matter where you're from, an extended stay is recommended. Right in the town of Creede the choices are extremely limited; South Fork hosts a number of motels and is a convenient home base while skiing at Wolf Creek Ski Area. For a more complete listing of accommodations, contact the **Creede/Mineral County Chamber of Commerce** at **PO Box 580, Creede, CO 81130; (719) 658-2374.**

The Inn at Arrowhead—$$$ to $$$$

As the crow flies, this deluxe, out-of-the-way inn and restaurant is probably closer to Lake City than anyplace else. But because the only way to the Inn from Lake City requires navigation of a four-wheel-drive road, we have decided to include it in the **Gunnison and Crested Butte** chapter (see Where to Stay for information).

Creede Hotel—$$

In 1890 there were 100 places to stay in Creede. Today this five-room bed and breakfast is virtually the only option. The Creede Hotel is not for everyone, but if you appreciate rustic charm and owners who are low-key and friendly, stop by. Rich and Cathy Ormsby are constantly renovating this historic hotel. It's still not finished but the place has character! Each room is sparsely furnished with an iron bedframe, a dresser and a chair. Breakfast is always a wonderful homemade concoction: it may be an egg and sausage casserole, salsa eggs or creamy oatmeal with homemade muffins. The hotel is officially open in summer only; if you want to stay in winter, be sure to call ahead because the owners might not be around. See the Where to Eat section for information on the restaurant. **PO Box 284, Creede, CO 81130; (719) 658-2608.**

The Crystal Lodge—$$$

A couple of miles south of Lake City, not far from Lake San Cristobal, this exceptional lodge caters to all guests' needs. Built of wood and decorated in natural colors, it blends in well with the surroundings. Nine smallish rooms, five apartments and four small cottages are available. All have private bathrooms but no TVs. But who needs the drone of a TV here? Fishing on the Lake Fork of the Gunnison is only steps away. Outside you'll find an inviting heated pool and a wide deck. The home-cooked food at the restaurant is a "cross between country and gourmet" according to the new owners, Ann and Gale Udell. Open year-round. Located 2 miles south of Lake City on Hwy. 149. **PO Box 246, Lake City, CO 81235; (303) 944-2201.**

The Old Firehouse No. 1 B&B—$$$

What used to be a dumpy fire station has been carefully upgraded into a classy B&B, with a Victorian ice cream parlor and restaurant on the main floor. Upstairs you'll find four nicely decorated rooms with high ceilings, transoms and private, modern bathrooms. Some historic accents remain and all rooms have been furnished carefully in antiques or reproductions. R. Katherine Brennand, the owner, is also a partner in the Abbey Lane Gallery just down the street. Continental breakfast served in an upstairs eating area separate from the restaurant. Open year-round. **PO Box 603, Creede, CO 81130-0603; (719) 658-0212.**

Wason Ranch—$$ to $$$

Just 2 miles southeast of Creede on the banks of the Rio Grande, Wason Ranch rents modern cabins of various sizes. The ranch owns 4 miles of riverfront property with excellent fishing (guests only) for good-sized German browns. Cabins come equipped with kitchenettes, furnishings and baseboard heat; larger three-bedroom cottages down by the river come with fully loaded kitchens, fireplaces and, most important, unobstructed views out picture windows. In summer guided river trips are available; in winter the ranch hosts a large number of skiers and snowmobilers. Very reasonable prices; discounts for longer stays. For reservations contact **Rod and Marilyn Wintz, Box 220, Creede, CO 81130; (719) 658-2413.**

Wolf Creek Ski Lodge and Motel— $$ to $$$

Located in South Fork, this small motel offers easy access to the slopes at Wolf Creek. The owners are friendly and the rooms clean—what more do you want? OK, they've got a hot tub, too. Also on the premises, a good restaurant serves up breakfast and dinner. **Box 283, 31042 W. Hwy. 160, South Fork, CO 81154; (719) 873-5547.**

CAMPING

In Rio Grande National Forest—

There are several nice campgrounds near the town of South Fork. To reach **Beaver Creek Campground** (20 sites; fee charged) and **Upper Beaver Campground** (12 sites; fee charged) drive 2.5 miles southwest from South Fork on Hwy. 160. Turn left on Forest Rd. 360 and continue for 3 and 4 miles respectively. From **Upper Beaver Campground** drive another 2 miles on Forest Rd. 360 to **Cross Creek Campground**, where there are 9 sites and fee.

Five miles southwest of South Fork on Hwy. 160 is **Highway Springs Campground** with 11 sites and a fee. **Park Creek Campground** (10 sites; fee charged) is located 9 miles southwest of South Fork on Hwy. 160. Ten miles northwest of South Fork on Hwy. 149 is **Palisade Campground** with 13 sites and a fee.

Closer to Creede, a number of campgrounds await. **Marshall Park Campground** is located 6 miles southwest of Creede on Hwy. 149. There are 15 sites and a fee. To reach **Rio Grande Campground** from Creede drive 10 miles southwest on Hwy. 149. It has 4 campsites and a fee.

A grouping of campgrounds is located farther southwest of Creede via Hwy. 149. To reach **South Clear Creek Campground** drive 23 miles southwest of Creede on Hwy. 149. Turn right on Forest Rd. 510 and continue for 0.3 mile. There are 11 sites and a fee. **North Clear Creek Campground**, with 22 sites and a fee, is located another 1.8 miles up Forest Rd. 510. **South Clear Creek Falls Campground** is located 24.5 miles southwest of Creede on Hwy. 149. It has 11 sites and a fee.

To get to **Road Canyon Campground** (5 sites; no fee), drive 21 miles southwest of Creede on Hwy. 149 and turn left on Forest Rd. 520. The campground is located on the southern end of Road Canyon Reservoir. Another 3.5 miles down Forest Rd. 520 will take you to **River Hill Campground,** with 20 sites and a fee. Continue another 1.5 miles to **Thirtymile Campground** on the eastern end of Rio Grande Reservoir. There are 33 sites and a fee. **Lost Trail Campground** is located on the northwestern end of the reservoir another 5.5 miles down Forest Rd. 520. It has 7 sites and a fee.

Camping in Gunnison National Forest—

South of Lake City, not far from Lake San Cristobal, are a couple of prime campgrounds. Drive 2 miles south of Lake City on Hwy. 149, turn right and continue 6 miles to reach **Williams Creek Campground** (25 sites; fee charged).

Slumgullion Campground (21 sites; fee charged) is located 6.5 miles southeast of Lake City on Hwy. 149. From just west of the campground, Forest Rd. 788 heads northwest from Hwy. 149 to a number of campgrounds. After turning, drive 2.5 miles to **Deer Lakes Campground** (12 sites; fee charged). In another 4.3 miles you'll come to **Hidden Valley Campground** with 6 sites and no fee. Continue another 1.5 miles to **Spruce Campground** (8 sites; fee charged) and soon after, Cebolla Campground (five sites; fee charged).

Big Blue Campground is located 10 miles north of Lake City on Hwy. 149, then 10 miles northwest on rough Forest Rd. 868. It has 11 sites and no fee.

Private Campgrounds—

This remote area of Colorado is truly RV heaven. Here are just a few ideas from the many choices available.

Broadacres Travelin' Tepee—This ranch/trailer park has 20 full hookups on a prime location beside the Rio Grande (and away from the highway). Bring your fishing pole! Located 5 miles southwest of Creede on **Hwy. 149. PO Box 39, Creede, CO 81130; (719) 658-2291.**

KOA South Fork/Rio Grande—This is one big campground. More than 100 sites are nestled in a tree-lined meadow between the Rio Grande and the highway. Full hookups are offered at a third of the sites. In summer free movies are shown in the laundry/recreation room. Located just east of South Fork. **26359 W. Hwy. 160, Del Norte, CO 81132; (719) 873-5500.**

Riverbend Resort RV Park—Just over 50 sites are available, some with full hookups. This RV park is located along a 1-mile stretch of the South Fork of the Rio Grande. To get there from South Fork, drive 3 miles southwest on Hwy. 160. **PO Box 129, South Fork, CO 81154; (719) 873-5344.**

Woodlake Campground has shaded, grassy campsites and RV hookups. It also offers fishing on its private stretch of river. Located just 2.5 miles south of Lake City on Hwy. 149. Contact **Latella Smith** at **PO Box 400, Lake City, CO 81235; (303) 944-2283.**

WHERE TO EAT

There are several restaurants in Lake City. Nothing really struck us as being worthy of special mention—but this isn't to say you should starve yourself. You may wish to stop by the **Crystal Lodge** (see the Where to Stay section above) 2 miles south of Lake City on Hwy. 149. Many of the restaurants in Lake City and Creede close up during the off-season. If you are vacationing near Creede, check out the following places.

The Bristol Inn—$$$

Located in an out-of-the-way corner of the woods southwest of Creede, the Bristol Inn has a loyal following. The casual yet elegant atmosphere complements the kitchen, where only the freshest ingredients are used; the homemade bread is made from fresh stone-ground flour. Chicken, beef and fish entrées are served with a professional flair, even though tips are not accepted. From Mother's Day

through the end of Sept. the restaurant stays open for dinner 5–9 pm Wed.–Sat.; their famous Sun. buffet runs 11 am–3 pm and should not be missed. The restaurant also houses an art gallery, so you'll be able to browse before or after your meal. Reservations strongly recommended. Located 18 miles southwest of Creede on Hwy. 149; **(719) 658-2455.**

Creede Hotel—$$

With no set menu and only two entrée selections each evening, you can be assured the chef uses the freshest quality ingredients. Special dishes include grilled tamari honey chicken and mouth-watering lasagna. This small, homey restaurant tends to fill up before plays next door at the Creede Repertory Theater. If you would like to stay at the Creede Hotel, see the Where to Stay section for more information. Creede Ave. in downtown Creede; **(719) 658-2608.**

SERVICES

Creede/Mineral County Chamber of Commerce—
PO Box 580, Creede, CO 81130; (719) 658-2374.

Lake City Chamber of Commerce—
PO Box 430, Lake City, CO 81235; (303) 944-2527.

South Fork Chamber of Commerce—
PO Box 116, South Fork, CO 81154; (719) 873-5512.

═ Cripple Creek and Victor ═

Although not known to many Americans these days, the gold-hearted mining town of Cripple Creek was once a household word throughout the country. The Cripple Creek district has produced more than $600 million in gold—more than any other single geological deposit on earth. That's 12 billion in today's dollars. The streets in Cripple Creek are literally paved with gold—gold ore, that is. A very low grade.

Cripple Creek sits in the crater of an extinct volcano, which created the gold fields. And the gold isn't gone. Some local miners say 80 percent of the gold in the area is untapped. But today international companies own most of the claims and plan to keep the mines dormant until gold prices go up.

Although the district is scarred by mine remnants and nearly barren of trees, it's ringed by tremendous mountains, including Pikes Peak to the northeast and the Sangre de Cristos to the southwest. Nearby, Mueller State Park provides a gorgeous wooded setting with some of the region's best mountain biking, cross-country skiing and wildlife viewing. Another thing to do in Cripple Creek is mingle among its ghosts and mine skeletons to get a sense of its glorious past. But a word of caution: *Most of the mine shafts in the district are death traps just waiting to happen. Stay on the roads.*

After relying on its gold mining history to attract tourists, Cripple Creek is currently caught up in the early stages of a new rush—legalized gambling. Colorado voters gave the go-ahead in 1990 for businesses in Cripple Creek (as well as Central City and Black Hawk) to begin limited stakes gaming (maximum $5 bets). Since the first casinos opened the following year, the town's character has changed dramatically. Time will tell if gambling will truly rejuvenate the local economy without sacrificing the integrity of Cripple Creek's historic buildings and driving out long time townsfolk. Other historic Colorado mining towns are keeping a close eye on gambling's effect on Cripple Creek, wondering if they too should take a spin with games of chance.

Although the visitors and locals place the historical mining focus on Cripple Creek, most of the gold mining actually took place at nearby Victor; its hills and yards are perforated with famous mines like the Ajax, the Independence and the Portland. The town is named after an early settler, Victor Adams, but its most famous resident was Lowell Thomas, one of the world's first news commentators. Victor, once known as the "City of Gold," remains much more like it was originally than does Cripple Creek. And since gambling began, Victor has become more attractive as a quiet place to escape the frenzied casino atmosphere of Cripple Creek.

HISTORY

According to a local miner, the town was named the day an early settler's son fell off the house they were building and broke a limb. That same day a calf broke its leg jumping over a high-banked stream nearby. The settler's comment: "This sho is some Cripple Creek."

It took drunken cowpoke and erstwhile rancher Bob Womack (known as "Crazy Bob") to transform a barren cow pasture he called "Poverty Gulch" into "the world's greatest gold camp." There was no reason for people to believe his claims of riches: the geology was all wrong, and the man drank himself into a stupor regularly. In fact, Womack could lean down from his saddle while riding at full gallop and scoop up a bottle of whiskey.

The beginning of the country's last major gold rush was delayed even further by false reports. In 1884, two charlatans salted a vein with gold in Cripple Creek. Hundreds of prospectors rushed to the area, only to discover the hoax after about a month of digging. In 1891, however, Womack finally convinced a few people to believe him, and gold fever rose faster and higher than ever before. Unfortunately, Womack was left out: soon after he found his first gold, he got drunk again and sold his claim for $500. The mine went on to produce hundreds of thousands of dollars of the precious metal.

Within a year of the find, 2,500 people were living in Cripple Creek. Just as the first train reached town in 1894, Cripple Creek installed its own nickel-a-ride trolley. That same year, three stock exchanges were trading in Colorado Springs thanks to the influx of Cripple Creek gold.

The rush made millionaires out of at least 30 people, and the town got a taste of fame. The Wright brothers won an auto race from Cripple Creek to Colorado Springs, and Groucho Marx delivered groceries between Cripple Creek and Victor for a while. Boxer Jack Dempsey even lived in Cripple Creek, mining during the day and boxing at night.

In April 1896, fire broke out in a Cripple Creek dance hall and burned down most of the town. Another blaze five days later nearly finished the job, leaving 5,000 people homeless. But Colorado Springs and Victor came to the rescue with a trainload of supplies. Within days the town was rebuilding, with brick this time. Three years later an eerily similar fire destroyed 12 blocks and 200 buildings in Victor.

By 1900, 25,000 people lived in Cripple Creek, making it the state's fourth largest city at the time. The district boasted 150 saloons (70 on notorious Myers Ave. alone), 90 doctors, 34 churches and 15 newspapers (priorities were in order). At the height of the rush the Continental Hotel was so busy the silverware at the restaurant wasn't washed between meals.

Myers Ave. was also home to plenty of brothels, or "pleasure palaces," as they were known. Some of the more illustrious ones in the district were: Bucket of Blood, Crapper Jack's Great View, Iron Clad and the Red Onion.

Labor strife broke out in 1903, leading to sabotage and several murders. In one period, 400 to 500 miners just disappeared off the streets. The violence came to a head in 1904 when a railroad station at Independence (just north of Victor) was dynamited, killing 13 non-union workers and maiming many more. Riots followed, and the state militia finally came in and broke the union by deporting members to Kansas and New Mexico.

As gold prices fell, the boom declined as quickly as it had surged. By 1912, most of Cripple Creek's 475 mining companies had folded. Eight years later only 40 of the original 500 mines were working. Bob Womack, the spark of the rush, died penniless in Colorado Springs. The beginning of gold mining in the town of Victor had ironic origins. Two promoters, Frank and Harry Woods, advertised the town in 1893 by saying that on every lot was a gold mine. The promotional gimmick turned out to be true as homesteaders began pulling gold out of their backyards. When grading for a hotel, the Woodses discovered an 18-inch vein and decided to build a mine there instead. Within a year, the Gold Coin Mine was turning out $50,000 a month. Frank, who had a penchant for luxury, built stained-glass windows in the mine's shaft house, lined it with marble and laid down carpeting.

Lowell Thomas is remembered everywhere in Victor. The author, radio announcer and lecturer began his journalism career as a paper boy for the Victor *Record* and went on to travel around the world. The Lowell Thomas Museum tells his story and is worth a brief stop.

GETTING THERE

From Denver, drive 65 miles south on Interstate 25 to Colorado Springs and then west for 25 miles on Hwy. 24 to the town of Divide. From Divide, drive south (left) on Hwy. 67 for 20 miles to Cripple Creek. Since gambling began in Cripple Creek, traffic on Highway 67 has increased 300 percent and DUI arrests are up 85 percent! If you have time, you may want to consider one of the alternative routes listed in the Scenic Drives section.

MAJOR ATTRACTIONS

Gambling

Since its legalization in 1990, limited stakes gambling has definitely become the town's number one attraction, and has brought with it many changes. Past visitors who have yet to see the "new" Cripple Creek may be a bit taken aback by the town's metamorphosis—historic buildings lining Cripple Creek's Bennett Ave. sport new faces, interiors and flashy signs; live music, hordes of optimistic (and beaten) gamblers, and lot after lot of cars all contribute to the town's neo-boom. To date, 25 gambling establishments have sprung up along or near Bennett Ave., with still others either under construction or in the planning stages. The transition continues.

Casinos—

After visiting enough of them, you'll notice that the casinos begin to blend together. Rows of slot and video poker machines, a few black jack tables and full bar service generally appear everywhere; other attractions such as live music, in-house restaurants, TV sports and ice cream shops/video games for the kids are evident as well. Even still, the casinos have begun to develop reputation for certain features. A few of the highlights are listed below. Most of the casinos are open from 8 am–2 am daily.

Aspen Mine & Casino—With its Disneyland-like props, this mega-buck casino is worth a stop. Featuring an old mine theme, the Aspen sports artificial rocks and tree work throughout the two-story casino; kids may be diverted by the working slough and live trout pond (indoor no less) long enough for you to slip a few bucks worth of quarters into one of the 200+ slot machines. **The Columbine Cafe** offers eats with views of the surrounding hills out the large glass windows. Live country and blues combos play on weekends. **166 E. Bennett Ave.; (719) 689-0770.**

Bronco Billy's Sports Bar & Casino—Along with gambling, Bronco Billy's is known for its 13 TVs airing sports programs. Locals also tout the food at the "historic" **Home Cafe**, which serves standard fare along with daily specials and a 99-cent breakfast. **233 E. Bennett Ave.; (719) 689-2142.**

Gold Rush Hotel & Casino—The rather spacious Gold Rush provides the **Golden Grille Restaurant** (mesquite specialties) at the rear as well as an ice cream parlor and video arcade for the kids. **209 E. Bennett Ave.; 1-800-235-8239.**

Imperial Hotel & Casino—One of the most historic places in town, the immense Imperial establishment offers a three-level gaming parlor, dining in the old dining rooms (see the Where to Eat section), a well-known melodrama (see Nightlife), and rooms at the historic hotel (see Where to Stay).

Midnight Rose Casino—On the second floor you'll find an all-you-can eat buffet as well as live rhythm and blues bands; espresso bar on main floor; arcade and **Wendy's Restaurant** in basement. **256 E. Bennett Ave.**

Old Chicago Restaurant & Casino—This franchise pizza and beer establishment, familiar to many folks, really packs in the crowds. Along with gaming diversions, you'll find sports on TV (including baseball memorabilia on walls), 21 beers on tap and 100 in bottles, Old Chicago's trademark deep-dish and stuffed pizza. Some locals gripe that the restaurant ($$ to $$$) still struggles with perfecting the deep-dish crust at this high altitude, but I found it tasted just fine. Restaurant open 11 am-10 pm daily (11 pm on weekends). **419 E. Bennett Ave.; (719) 689-7880.**

Parking—

Parking lots are located at the east end of Bennett Ave. as you enter town near the Cripple Creek–Victor Narrow Gauge Railroad station. You'll also find one at the west end of town, as well as a few smaller lots scattered through town. When these lots get full, a parking area a few miles northeast of town along Hwy. 67 is available with free shuttle buses making regular runs to town. If you don't want to drive to Cripple Creek, many tour companies provide buses and vans from Colorado Springs. For more specifics on transportation, see the Services section at the end of this chapter.

Florissant Fossil Beds National Monument

Palm trees in Colorado? Once upon a time—about 36 million years ago—yes. Also thriving in the Florissant area were enormous redwoods, a thousand species of insects, including tsetse flies common to South Africa, giant katydids and an incredible variety of plants and animals. Thanks to a once-raging volcano field nearby and tons of ash, these remnants of the Oligocene epoch have been preserved better than any other ancient ecosystem in the world.

The fossil bed formed when volcanic eruptions sent lava and mud into the Florissant Basin, creating a large lake. Continued eruptions sent more ash and dust over the lake, taking insects, leaves and fish to the bottom with it. Over a 500,000-year period the sediment formed shales. Mud flows eventually covered and protected these future fossil beds, and recent erosion led to their discovery.

Facts About the Monument—

Florissant ("flowering" or "blooming") was named for the abundant wildflowers in the area. But the rest of the scenery is subtle. Stop by the visitors center for an introduction to spotting fossils. The Petrified Forest Loop (1 mile) is the best. Don't miss the Trio (three petrified redwood trunks sharing a root system) and Rex Arborae ("King of the Forest"), a petrified stump 14 feet tall and 74 feet around. Scientists guess the tree once towered 250 to 280 feet—one of the biggest sequoias

ever found. Admission fee charged. Open daily in summer 8 am–7 pm; during the rest of the year 8 am–4:30 pm. **PO Box 185, Florissant, CO 80816; (719) 748-3253.**

Getting There—

To get to the fossil beds, take Hwy. 24 west from Colorado Springs for 35 miles to Florissant. Turn south on County Rd. 1. The monument entrance is about 2.5 miles up the road on the right (west). From Cripple Creek, head northwest on County Rd. 1 for 16 miles to the monument entrance.

Mueller State Park

Located just off Highway 67 between Cripple Creek and Divide, the recently opened Mueller State Park provides an exciting addition to outdoor recreation in the Pikes Peak Region. Mueller, with its 12,103 acres of pine-covered hills, mountain meadows and dramatic granite formations, such as the enormous Dome Rock, has already begun to attract a large number of visitors.

Wildlife here is thick. Thanks to protection when the property was run as a ranch, elk, bighorn sheep, mule deer, eagles, hawks and even bears, bobcats and mountain lions are plentiful.

Trails—

Many Mueller visitors are excited about the park's extensive network of recreation trails—over 90 miles of them! These trails provide access into remote parts of the park for hikers, mountain bikers, horseback riders, cross-country skiers and snowshoers. Spectacular views of Pikes Peak and the Sangre de Cristo Range await you along many trail sections. Trail maps are available at the entrance station and park headquarters. For access to some of the more remote trails in the southern section of the park, drive to the day use area 8 miles north of Cripple Creek via Hwy. 67 and County Rd. 63 (Fourmile Rd.).

Camping—

Mueller boasts 90 campsites, including 78 with electric hookups and 12 walk-in tent sites. Fees vary according to the services provided at the sites. Restrooms, hot showers and laundry facilities available. For reservations, call **(303) 470-1144** from Denver or **1-800-678-CAMP.**

Other Information—
Mueller is located 15 miles north of Cripple Creek along Highway 67. At the park entrance, turn west. Information and trail maps can be obtained at the entrance station or at park headquarters. **PO Box 49, Divide, CO 80814; (719) 687-2366.**

─────── **FESTIVALS AND EVENTS** ───────

Donkey Derby Days
last weekend in June
As the major event of the summer, Cripple Creek's Donkey Derby Days packs in tourists drawn to town for a parade, donkey races, live music, etc. For information, call **(719) 689-2169.**

Fall Aspen Leaf Tours
last two weekends in Sept. and first in Oct.
For those of you without four-wheel drive vehicles, the Fall Aspen Leaf Tours is worth investigating. Free jeep rides on the surrounding roads provide excellent views of the surrounding mountains and the golden aspen. For information, call **(719) 689-2169.**

─────── **OUTDOOR ACTIVITIES** ───────

BIKING
MOUNTAIN BIKING
With hidden mine shafts sunk all over the area, Cripple Creek is definitely not a place for off-road ventures. If you want to ride in this area, stay on the roads listed in the Scenic Drives section. But perhaps the best opportunity is the extensive trail system available at Mueller State Park. For information, see the Major Attractions section.

FISHING
Elevenmile Canyon—
Plenty of brown and rainbow trout inhabit the tumbling waters of the South Platte River in this narrow, scenic canyon about 40 miles west of Colorado Springs. This regularly stocked river comes out of Elevenmile dam and flows northeast through the canyon for 10 miles. Since the water flow exiting the dam fluctuates, so does the quality of the fishing. To reach Elevenmile Canyon from Cripple Creek, head northwest on County Rd. 1 to Hwy. 24 at Florissant and turn left. Drive to Lake George and look for the canyon turn-off on the left.

Elevenmile Reservoir—
Located within Elevenmile State Park 11 miles southwest of Lake George, this reservoir is known for its bountiful rainbow and brown trout, kokanee salmon and pike. The largest kokanee (up to 5 pounds) in Colorado are often caught at Elevenmile Reservoir. Elevenmile's 3,400 surface acres provide good results from both boats and shore. From Cripple Creek, head north on County Rd. 1 to Florissant and turn left on Hwy. 24. Drive to Lake George and look for the road sign to the reservoir on County Road 92 at the west edge of the town. Ironically, the reservoir can't be reached from Elevenmile Canyon.

Spinney Mountain Reservoir—
One of Colorado's most productive fisheries. For details, see the Fishing section in the **South Park** chapter.

HIKING AND BACKPACKING
The Crags—
Located on the northwest slope of Pikes Peak, this is a relatively undiscovered

hiking area. Trails spread out over the back side of Pike Peak and through the immense granite formations that give the area its name. From Cripple Creek, head north on Hwy. 67 about 14 miles and turn right (east) onto County Road 62 (Forest Rd. 383). Drive 3.5 miles to the trailhead at the end of the turnaround near the Crags Campground.

To reach The Crags from Colorado Springs, head west 25 miles on Hwy. 24 to Divide and turn left onto Hwy. 67. Drive about 4 miles and turn left onto County Road 62 (Forest Rd. 383).

Mueller State Park—

Mueller provides 90 miles of excellent trails with chances to view wildlife and surrounding mountains. For details, see the Major Attractions section.

Pikes Peak (via The Crags)—

On a clear day, the 6.5-mile hike up Pikes Peak from The Crags Campground is one of the most scenic in the state (and much easier than Barr Trail on the east side of the mountain). This trail climbs 4,100 vertical feet through pine and aspen, across an alpine bowl covered with wildflowers, and on to the rocky upper reaches of the peak. Once you make your way out of the trees, enjoy the stunning views of the Spanish Peaks to the south, Mt. Evans to the north, and the several mountain ranges in between.

This is a great route up the peak, but it requires a topographical map and careful attention along the way. From The Crags Campground (see the Camping section under Where to Stay), start up the trail to The Crags. After about 200 yards, you will come to a spot where the creek on the south side of the trail forks. Here you must leave The Crags Trail and cross the closer of the two creeks (so that you are in between the two), and follow the old logging road up to

the southeast. After about 1.5 miles the road comes to an old area just below tree line where there are many stumps. Just after the trail swings north, be looking for a trail going off to the right and take it. Eventually you climb up over a saddle to timberline where you have a view of the summit to the southeast. Continuing on you reach the Pikes Peak Highway at a place called Devil's Playground, named for the way lightning bounces off of the rocks when it hits in the vicinity! From here, cross the road and make your way to the top.

SKIING
CROSS-COUNTRY SKIING
The Crags—

The Crags continues to be one of the best areas to go near Cripple Creek for good winter touring trails, from beginner to advanced. For information, see the Hiking and Backpacking section.

Florissant Fossil Beds National Monument—

Open to the public year round, the national monument provides miles of easy terrain for cross-country skiers. Serving as hiking trails most of the year, these tracks may provide you with views of petrified trees (if the snow isn't too deep). The visitors center provides trail maps and even loans out snowshoes to those who are interested. For more information, see the Florissant Fossil Beds National Monument write up in the Major Attractions section.

Mueller State Park—

Mueller, witih its 90 miles of trail, has quickly become the most popular location in the Cripple Creek area for cross-country skiers. For more information, see the Major Attractions section.

SEEING AND DOING

MUSEUMS

Cripple Creek District Museum—

All small historic mining towns should have a museum like the Cripple Creek District Museum. The museum houses tons of antiques and paraphernalia from the boom days. Rooms in the main three-story building have specific themes such as mining and assaying. Be sure to inspect the fascinating 3-D engineers map of the Portland Mine. Two other buildings house a natural history collection and an assay office where someone is usually on hand to demonstrate how ores are tested. Open 10 am–5 pm daily, Memorial Day–Sept.; open weekends the rest of the year, 12–4 pm. Located at the west end of Bennett Ave., **Box 475, Cripple Creek, CO 80813; (719) 689-2634.**

Victor–Lowell Thomas Museum—

This interesting museum is worth a quick look if you're in town. The main floor displays relics of Victor's early days, including mining equipment, antique furniture and even a slot machine. The upstairs floor is devoted exclusively to Victor's most famous son—Lowell Thomas (the first news commentator as well as a prolific writer). Thomas memorabilia, re-creations of rooms in his house and all of his books are displayed. Open daily 10 am–5 pm, May 1–mid-Oct. Located in Victor at **3rd and Victor; (719) 689-3211.**

NIGHTLIFE

With the explosion of gambling in Cripple Creek, the casinos and bars are where you'll find most of the action. You can find everything from live music to comedy at the casinos (see Major Attractions). But for a Cripple Creek tradition and a good time, the Imperial Melodrama Theatre is hard to beat.

Imperial Melodrama Theatre—

One of the main attractions at the Imperial Hotel is the melodrama theatre—the nation's oldest, established in 1948. *Time* magazine has called the thespians here the "Old Vic" of modern melodrama. Whether you go to the show with your kids or on a date, you'll really have a good time. Start off upstairs with dinner in one of the Imperial Hotel's historic dining rooms. Open June–Labor Day; show times are 2 and 8:30 pm Tues.–Sat., 1 and 4:30 pm Sun. **PO Box 869, Cripple Creek, CO 80813; (719) 689-2922.**

RAILROADS

Cripple Creek & Victor Narrow-Gauge Railroad—

Ride this train and get a literal feel for the Old West—by the seat of your pants. A 15-ton engine follows the 3-foot-wide narrow-gauge tracks of the Old Midland Terminal Railroad on a 4-mile round trip past some great mountain scenery, historical sites and mines. Along the way you'll stop to take plenty of photos and hear a bit about Cripple Creek's history, in which narrow-gauge trains played a huge role. Fifty-five locomotives used to stop in Cripple Creek daily, hauling ore out and passengers in. The ride's great fun for kids. Open Memorial Day–mid-Oct., 10 am–5 pm. The train leaves every 45 minutes from Midland Station at the end of Bennett Ave., next to the Cripple Creek Museum, at the north end of town. **PO Box 459, Cripple Creek, CO 80813; (719) 689-2640.**

SCENIC DRIVES

Take a self-guided car tour on some of the district's back roads, using the helpful ghost town map available at most shops in town.

Cripple Creek/Victor—

From Cripple Creek make sure to drive to Victor along Hwy. 67, which goes past some of the larger mines in the region. Also consider driving half of this 12-mile round trip via **Range View Rd.** This dirt road leaves Cripple Creek just north of the Molly

Kathleen Mine, climbs around Battle Mountain and connects with Diamond Ave. in Victor.

Gold Camp Road—

This beautiful and historic back road follows the path of the railroad, which used to connect Cripple Creek with Colorado Springs. An excellent drive. See Gold Camp Rd. in the Scenic Drives section of the **Colorado Springs** chapter.

Phantom Canyon—

This road, part of the Bureau of Land Management's recently designated Gold Belt Tour, begins in Victor and snakes its way through a narrow canyon to the south along an old stagecoach line. For information, see the Scenic Drives section of the **Cañon City** chapter.

Shelf Road—

Like Phantom Canyon, Shelf Road (part of The Gold Belt Tour) is an old stagecoach road that runs between Cripple Creek and Cañon City. The scenery along the way is wonderful. For information, see the Scenic Drives section of the **Cañon City** chapter.

TOURS

Molly Kathleen Mine—

For those who have never been down into a hardrock mine, this tour is highly recommended. Ride the "skip" down 1,000 feet into the Molly Kathleen Mine for a taste of the subterranean insides of a mountain. Although it looks touristy from the outside, don't be put off: this is a full-fledged tour led by miners through the inner workings of an actual mine, which clearly explains why people flocked to Cripple Creek in the first place. The Molly operated from 1892 until 1961. Open 9 am–5 pm, May–Oct. Admission fee charged. The Molly's just north of town off Hwy 67; **PO Box 339, Cripple Creek, CO 80813; (719) 689-2465,** or **(719) 689-2466.**

———— WHERE TO STAY ————

ACCOMMODATIONS

With all of the recent building in Cripple Creek, its surprising that there are so few places to spend the night. You may want to consider staying elsewhere (such as Colorado Springs or Woodland Park) and just spending the day in Cripple Creek. But if you want to stick around, here are a few recommendations.

Holiday Inn Express—$$$

With a bird's eye view of Cripple Creek and the surrounding mountains, this brand-spanking new hotel is a nice option for those who don't want to stray too far from town. Sixty-seven comfortable rooms with queen beds and TV await; continental breakfast provided. Free shuttle service into town. **601 E. Galena Ave., Cripple Creek, CO 80813; 1-800-HOLIDAY or (719) 689-2600.**

The Victor Hotel—$$$

Built in 1899 and operated for years as a bank, this historic building serves nicely as a quiet bed & breakfast getaway. With many of the other original buildings in various stages of dilapidation, the Victor Hotel, flush from its $1.25 million renovation, stands out like a rich cousin. From the fine, period decor in the lobby to the 30 comfortable rooms, the dollars have worked magic. Ride up to your room in the original cage elevator. The rooms represent a tasteful blend of old and new—exposed brick and original steam registers blend with queen beds, private baths, cable TV and phones. Two rooms are completely handicap accessible. Continental breakfast served each morning. A continental-style restaurant ($$ to $$$) in the hotel is just getting up and running; it could be worth trying if you don't want to make the drive to Cripple Creek. **4th St. and Victor Ave., Victor, CO 80860; (719) 689-3553.**

The Imperial Hotel—$$

One of Cripple Creek's original brick hotels, The Imperial stands as a reminder of the town's mining boom days. Most of its furniture dates to the rich Victorian period, as do the antiques and paintings. The clawfoot tubs in some rooms provide privacy while others rely on bathrooms down the hall. All 30 rooms are reasonably priced. Other highlights include the **Red Rooster Bar**, just off the hotel lobby, which is packed with roosters of all kinds—stone, wood, metal, etc. Customers have been bringing them here from around the country. The Imperial also offers a three-level gaming parlor in the adjacent building. Reservations recommended. **123 N. 3rd St., PO Box 869, Cripple Creek, CO 80813; (719) 689-2922 or (800) 235-2922.**

Travel Park & Hospitality House— $$ to $$$

Although newly renovated to keep pace with the times, the Hospitality House still offers a night's stay that is, let's say, a bit unusual. Located in the old county hospital, built in 1901, 18 rooms (9 with private bath) are offered to guests. Many of the remnants from the old hospital days (including wheelchairs, etc.) decorate the building, and the rooms, though newly furnished, are still referred to according to their previous function (Maternity Room, Operating Room). The property also provides 60 RV and 20 tent sites. Continental breakfast served each morning. Some rooms handicap accessible. **600 N. B St, PO Box 957, Cripple Creek, CO 80813; (719) 689-2513.**

CAMPING

In Pike National Forest—

The Crags—Located on the west side of Pikes Peak, The Crags Campground has 17 sites; fee charged. Take Hwy. 67 north from Cripple Creek for 13.5 miles, then turn right (east) on Forest Rd. 383 (County Rd. 62). Drive 3.5 miles to the campground.

Elevenmile Canyon—This scenic canyon has six campgrounds with a total of 91 campsites (fee charged). The road in the canyon is slim and twisting, so large trailers and RVs are advised to stay near the entrance. To get to the canyon take Hwy. 24 west out of Colorado Springs to the Elevenmile Canyon turn-off (Forest Rd. 245) to the left (south) at the town of Lake George. Great fishing.

State Parks—

Elevenmile State Park—The 265 campsites can be reached from Hwy. 24 at the west end of Lake George. Turn left off County Rd. 92 and drive 11 miles. Fee charged. Some sites available on the reservoir shore. Advance reservations available by calling **(303) 470-1144** from Denver, or **1-800-678-CAMP.**

Mueller State Park—For details on Mueller's 90 campsites, see the Major Attractions section.

Private Campground—

Lost Burro—Wilderness camping with modern conveniences, claims the Lost Burro. They offer RV hookups, tent sites, restrooms, showers and picnic tables. Located 4 miles northwest of Cripple Creek on County Rd. 1. **PO Box 614, Cripple Creek, CO 80813; (719) 689-2345.**

Travel Park & Hospitality House—See write-up under Accommodations.

WHERE TO EAT

Although scads of casino restaurants have popped up claiming to offer the full spectrum of culinary "specialties," casino dining is a bit inconsistent. Given time, certain places will eventually rise to the top. For ideas about casino dining (especially Old Chicago) see the casino write ups in the Major Attractions section. But here are a couple of places that have been around for years.

The Imperial Hotel—$$ to $$$

The dining rooms at the Imperial Hotel are best known for their buffet-style dinner items, highlighted by prime rib and chicken curry. Leave enough room for chocolate mousse or any of the other rich desserts. The Imperial is open daily year-round. Breakfast buffet ($) is served 7–10 am daily except Mon.; lunch from 11 am–3 pm; dinner from 5–8:30 pm. 123 N. 3rd St., **PO Box 869, Cripple Creek, CO 80813; (719) 689-2922.**

Zeke's—$ to $$$

Although once known wide and far for its chili and crusty mining bar atmosphere, Zeke's has changed a bit. The atmosphere is about the same but an expanded menu (including good barbecue) and outside patio seating have smoothed the edges. Like many buildings in Victor, this one has a colorful history; once it was expanded to incorporate an area once used as a house of ill repute. Open year-round, 7–2 am (until midnight on Sun.) serving breakfast, lunch and dinner. **108 S. 3rd St.,** between Victor and Portland aves., in **Victor. (719) 689-2109.**

SERVICES

Cripple Creek Chamber of Commerce—

PO Box 650, Cripple Creek, CO 80813; (719) 689-2169.

Transportation—

Colorado Gamblers Express—Provides charter van service from the Colorado Springs area. **(719) 578-8203.**

Johnny Nolan's Casino Fun Bus—Free transportation between Colorado Springs and Cripple Creek. **1-800-366-2946.**

My Chauffeur Limousine—Located in Colorado Springs, offers van and limo service by the hour. **(719) 597-4822.**

Leadville

In 1880 Leadville was the second largest city in Colorado, bursting with a population of more than 24,000. Today a quiet mountain community of 3,000 maintains Leadville's profound sense of history in a low-profile atmosphere. Not much mining takes place anymore, but residents have managed to preserve and protect many of the town's opulent Victorian-era buildings. Designated a National Historic District, few places rival Leadville for the preservation of Colorado's mining heritage.

One of the most highly mineralized areas in the world, Leadville has produced gold, silver, zinc, molybdenum, manganese and turquoise. Just east of town, hundreds of mines at California Gulch and Carbonate, Fryer and Iron hills provided the source of Leadville's livelihood for many decades. The town's mining fortunes have long since been squandered, but more than a handful of local museums have rescued the legacy of the area's mining history.

Stopping off in Leadville for an hour or two hardly cracks the door on this town's past. Try booking a room in one of many historic accommodations. Staying a couple of days (or longer) allows a chance to fully enjoy the town and its intensely beautiful surroundings.

Located high in the Arkansas Valley at an elevation of 10,152 feet, Leadville is hemmed in by the Sawatch Range to the west and the Mosquito Range to the east. Colorado's two highest peaks, Elbert (14,433 feet) and Massive (14,421 feet), absolutely dominate the view from town. The Colorado Trail tracks along the base of these peaks and other trails wind to their summits—literally at the top of Colorado (see the Hiking and Backpacking section). Fishing and camping opportunities also help make this area a sort of outdoor paradise.

Though anything but a winter resort, Leadville lies at a ski crossroads: you can be on the slopes at Ski Cooper in 20 minutes and at six other major downhill areas in less than an hour. Cross-country skiers appreciate the expanse of well-suited terrain—especially near the summit of Tennessee Pass, where the US Army trained its elite ski troops for World War II. For a quiet, less expensive and historic change of pace, Leadville makes an ideal winter base.

HISTORY

Leadville's history is mirrored by the twists and turns of H.A.W. Tabor, who came west with his wife, Augusta, during the Pikes Peak gold rush of 1859. After many years of chasing his fortune from one Colorado gold camp to another, Tabor eventually settled in Oro City (2.5 miles from present-day Leadville), where he hoped somehow to strike it rich. Not long before Tabor arrived, Oro City had boomed when gold deposits were discovered in California Gulch in 1860. But the deposits were not big producers and a heavy black sand made it difficult to isolate the gold ore.

It wasn't until 1875 that William Stevens and his partner, A.B. Wood, a metallurgist, reworked some of the abandoned mines and discovered that the heavy black sand clogging the gold sluicing operations had a high silver content. Working quietly to discover the source, Stevens and Wood staked out claims that eventually netted them millions. After this initial success, miners began prospecting to the north and west on Iron and Carbonate hills. But when George Fryer discovered a rich body of ore on what is now called Fryer Hill, Leadville sprang to life.

Tabor, sensing that Oro City was losing ground to Leadville, moved down the road a couple of miles to this fledgling town. Soon after he opened the doors of his general store, he was hounded by two poor German shoemakers with no money or mining experience. To get rid of them he grubstaked George Hook and August Riche in return for a one-third interest in their claim on Fryer Hill. As luck would have it, the inexperienced miners soon hit a 30-foot-thick silver vein, some 29 feet below the surface. A month later their Little Pittsburg Mine was producing $50,000 worth of ore per month.

Tabor became the talk of the state and was soon commissioned to purchase a claim for a Denver wholesaler. Hearing of Tabor's commission, a man named Chicken Bill salted one of his unproductive claims with silver dust and duped Tabor into buying the mine. Tabor didn't get paid for the "worthless" claim. Although he was the laughingstock of the town, somehow he felt lucky enough to continue mining at the site. He hired a group of miners to deepen the shaft and soon discovered the famous Chrysolite lode. In less than two years, the former stonecutter was Leadville's first multimillionaire.

By 1880 Leadville had gone from a camp of 200 to a rip-roaring city of 24,000. The mines were producing nearly $12 million of silver a year and trains regularly made their way to the valley. As the area flooded with fortune hunters, a quarter mile of saloons, brothels, wine-theaters and gambling halls sprang up along State St. (now Second St.), giving Leadville an uninhibited atmosphere. The *Leadville Herald-Democrat* described a chaotic street scene:

On all sides was a conglomerate mass of diversified humanity—men of education and culture, graduates of Harvard and Yale and Princeton, mingling with ignorant and uncouth Bull-whackers ... representatives of the better element in all the callings of life—hopelessly entangled in throngs of gamblers, burro-steerers, thugs, bullies, drunkards, escaped convicts, dead beats and the "scum of the earth" generally.

It wasn't long before Tabor and the other bonanza kings attempted to civilize the city with gracious Victorian homes, hotels and even the Tabor Opera House. Many who got their start in Leadville are well remembered today, such as Meyer Guggenheim, Marshall Field and David May (May D&F). Sidewalks lined the gaslit streets, and Harrison Ave. was paved with black slag. (Today, a huge mound of slag—not coal—is piled next to the highway at the south end of town.) The mountains around Leadville were left bald from the frenzied construction of mine shafts as well as the extraction of charcoal for the smelters and city buildings.

In the scandal of the era, H.A.W. Tabor divorced his stoic wife, Augusta, to marry the young divorcee, Elizabeth "Baby Doe" McCourt, who shared his passion for a flamboyant lifestyle. He married Baby Doe in a lavish Washington, DC, ceremony attended by President Chester Arthur.

The glory days ended in 1893 when the Sherman Silver Purchase Act was repealed. The price of silver plummeted during the ensuing panic and Leadville's glory days were over.

Tabor's fortunes continued to mirror those of Leadville as he lost virtually everything he owned. Though he eventually moved to Denver and pushed his way into political office as high as US Senator, Tabor died a penniless postmaster in 1899. While on his deathbed, he told Baby Doe to "hang on to the Matchless," the mine which he believed would make her rich again. For 36 years Baby Doe lived in a cabin next to the Matchless Mine above Leadville, until she froze to death one winter evening. With the irony of a Greek tragedy, only Tabor's first wife, Augusta, who preferred to live simply, died a millionaire.

Just before the turn of the century, James J. Brown (husband of the Titanic heroine, "unsinkable" Molly Brown) sank a deep shaft into the Little Johnny Mine just east of the city and discovered a huge gold vein. This discovery revitalized Leadville enough for it to be established as a permanent mining town.

Up until 1900 zinc was thought to be a worthless byproduct that had clogged the silver sluicing operations. After the turn of the century its value became known and much of the metal was taken from the abandoned silver mines. Lead and manganese deposits were also worked profitably. A huge body of molybdenum was discovered in 1918 at Fremont Pass. Until fairly recently when synthetic replacements were discovered, the Climax Mine near Leadville accounted for as much as 80 percent of the total world production of this steel-hardening mineral. At present Climax is closed except for reclamation of the tailings ponds. With the closing of Climax, another chapter has closed on Leadville's mining era.

In 1942, 15,000 men in the 10th Mountain Division were stationed at Camp Hale, 18 miles north of Leadville just over Tennessee Pass. In white camouflage uniforms, the army troops practiced alpine combat maneuvers before heading to Europe for battle. Camp Hale was nicknamed Camp Hell by men forced to endure the high altitude, harsh weather and rigorous training regimen. Near the summit of Tennessee Pass, a 20-foot high slab of granite is etched with the names of nearly 1,000 of these men who lost their lives in World War II. A number of their fellow veterans went on to make a huge impact on the ski industry in Colorado. Locally, Ski Cooper is a direct result of efforts by former 10th Mountain members.

GETTING THERE

Leadville is located 103 miles southwest of Denver. To get there take Interstate 70 west to Copper Mountain. Turn south on Hwy. 91 and continue 24 miles to Leadville.

FESTIVALS AND EVENTS

Oro City

summer weekends
from late June to mid-July

In April 1860 Oro City sprang up near present-day Leadville, and by July of the same year there were 5,000 inhabitants. More than 120 years later, an annual re-creation of this mining camp includes tents, false-front buildings and log cabins manned by a bunch of locals dressed up in period clothes. They provide demonstrations of gunsmithing, gold panning, sluicing and even breadmaking. As the saloon becomes filled with camera-laden tourists, it gets a little tough to imagine the Wild West. Nonetheless, Oro City can be a lot of fun. Admission fee. For more information call **(719) 486-3900.**

Boom Days

early August

During Leadville's main summer bash, you'll have no trouble imagining what the town was like during the real silver boom. The streets once again fill with tough-looking hardrock miners, dancing girls, brass bands and burros. The weekend kicks off with a parade down Harrison Ave. and ends with a burro race over Mosquito Pass. In between there are mining events such as hand mucking (loading broken rock by hand) and jackleg drilling (drilling with a jackhammer). Carnival rides accompany the carnival atmosphere. The Lions Club sets up a traditional beer garden every year. For more information call the **Leadville/Lake County Chamber of Commerce** at **(719) 486-3900.**

Leadville 100

late August

Each year this grueling 100 mile race heads up into the Sawatch range crossing above 12,000-foot elevations at times. It takes a rare breed of runner to somehow enjoy this punishing annual event. Recently, two Tarahumara Indian runners from Mexico finished far ahead of the pack wearing handstitched sandals made from discarded tires. The winner was 55 years old! Hundreds of spectators join hundreds of runners for the exciting 4 am start. Most runners return to Leadville 20 to 30 hours later. For more information call **(719) 486-3900.**

OUTDOOR ACTIVITIES

BIKING

MOUNTAIN BIKING

Leadville is starting to become recognized as a premier location for mountain bike enthusiasts. The maze of old mining roads right around town provides a limitless area for exploring. Some particularly good roads are just east of town on heavily mined Fryer Hill. An extremely tough ride is up and over Mosquito Pass, ending in South Park (see the Four-Wheel-Drive Trips section). Riders who want to find single-track trails might set off from the western side of Tennessee Pass on a number of marked cross-country ski trails. Here are a couple of favorites:

Turquoise Lake Trail—

This fairly easy 6.5-mile trail winds along the beautiful, forested shoreline of Turquoise Lake. Start at any of the campgrounds or picnic areas along the perimeter of the lake and complete a loop trip back to your cooler. Don't forget your fishing pole! See the Fishing section for directions to the lake.

Weston Pass—

From the beginning of Weston Pass Rd. ride 10 gradual miles to the top of the pass. Turn around or continue on to South Park. For more information and directions see the Scenic Drives section.

Rentals and Tours—

Bill's Sport Shop—A small selection of good rental mountain bikes and local topo maps. Ask Paul Copper for advice on local trails. **225 Harrison Ave.; (719) 486-0739.**

Mosquito Pass Tours—To get a real feel for Leadville's mining history, we recommend taking one of these two-hour to all-day guided mountain bike rides. For reservations and information call **(719) 486-0570.**

FISHING

Arkansas River—

The heavily mined mountains around Leadville have created a toxic imbalance in the Arkansas River near Leadville. The fishing, however, improves markedly below Clear Creek Reservoir (see the Fishing section of the **Upper Arkansas Valley** chapter).

Crystal Lakes—

Stocked with rainbow and cutthroat trout, these lakes are usually hopping with feeding trout in early evening. From the shore small dry flies are effective on top; many fishermen cast hardware and bait into the middle where larger trout swim the deep water. This easy-access fishing area is only 3.5 miles south of Leadville on Hwy. 24.

Halfmoon Creek—

Directly beneath the tallest peaks in Colorado, Halfmoon Creek offers many pools and eddies to the diligent angler. It is stocked with rainbow trout, but browns and brookies can also be caught. To reach Halfmoon Creek travel west on Hwy. 24 for about 2 miles. Continue west on Hwy. 300 instead of following Hwy. 24 around a wide bend in the road. Stay on Hwy. 300 for a mile before turning south on Halfmoon Creek Rd. (Forest Rd. 110). After a couple of miles the creek parallels the dirt road for 4 miles to Halfmoon Campground. Upstream from Halfmoon Campground, a jeep road parallels the creek eventually narrowing into a trail. It is possible to hike all the way up to North Halfmoon Creek, which is good for small brook trout.

Turquoise Lake—

At nearly 10,000 feet in elevation, this large lake offers some of the best fishing in the Leadville area—only 3 miles west of town. Good fishing combined with a beautiful location make it a heavily used recreation area; eight campgrounds are located around the lake. Fishing from a boat or from the shore will yield brown, rainbow and cutthroat trout. There are other species in the lake, including stocked kokanee salmon. Turquoise Lake is known for its excellent ice fishing. Hiking trails lead from Turquoise Lake to high alpine lakes, including several good producers just inside the Holy Cross Wilderness: **Timberline Lake, Galena Lake** and **Bear Lake**. To reach Turquoise Lake, drive west on 6th St. to the edge of town. Turn right (northwest) on Turquoise Lake Rd. and continue 3 miles.

Twin Lakes Reservoir—

So, you want to catch a mackinaw (lake trout) in the 30-pound range? Twin Lakes, at the foot of Independence Pass, will give you the chance. But you can keep only one and it must exceed 20 inches. In addition to large lake trout, Twin Lakes Reservoir is stocked with rainbow and cutthroat trout. Although shore fishing can be good, many fishermen prefer trolling for mackinaw; boat ramps are located on the north side of the lake. Several picnic and camping areas make this lake an extremely popular destination. From Leadville follow Hwy. 24 south for 14 miles until reaching Hwy. 82. Turn right and head west on Hwy. 82, which follows along the north shore. Be sure to stop off Hwy. 82 between the lakes, at the **visitors center** and power plant. There you can get information on the area and see an interesting scale model of the water storage system. The tiny community of Twin Lakes, lies along Hwy. 82; several accommodations and campgrounds can be found (see Where to Stay).

FOUR-WHEEL-DRIVE TRIPS

There are untold numbers of four-wheel-drive roads in the mountains around Leadville. This is a great place to explore because the mines have left so many visible traces. If you don't have a jeep, contact **Sugar Loafin' Campground** at **(719) 486-1031** for information on their group tours.

Hagerman Pass—

This fairly mild road manages to slip through a gap along the Continental Divide

between Leadville and Basalt. Just to the west of the summit, a four-wheel-drive vehicle is needed for a rough stretch, but lower elevations on both sides of the pass can be negotiated by most passenger cars. The views from the open summit stretch back to Leadville and the Arkansas Valley; you can't help but enjoy the western view down to Ivanhoe Lake and the Upper Fryingpan Valley. (Bring your fishing pole!) See the Fishing section of the **Aspen** chapter for information.

The historic route plunges into the impressive Sawatch Range along the defunct Colorado Midland Railroad bed. Along the way you can stop off to see two tunnels, bored so the trains could make their way to Aspen and the Roaring Fork Valley. In 1886 trains began passing through Hagerman Tunnel, bored out of solid rock at 11,500 feet. Due to high maintenance costs, the Carlton Tunnel was constructed 800 feet lower in elevation.

From Leadville drive west on 6th St. to the edge of town. Turn right on Turquoise Lake Rd. and follow along to the dam. Check your odometer, and 3.5 miles west of the dam turn left on an unlikely side road, which continues over the pass. The easy hiking trail to the abandoned Hagerman Tunnel is marked, just below the summit on the east side of the pass.

Mosquito Pass—

At 13,188 feet the road over Mosquito Pass is the highest through road in North America. Built as a wagon road in 1879, it connected Leadville with the mining camps of South Park. Heavy traffic over the pass was short-lived as trains arrived the following year. Today this difficult four-wheel-drive road offers great views of many Colorado mountain ranges.

At the summit a stone marker commemorates the mail-carrying Father John Dyer, known as the "snowshoe itinerant." He not only held services for many mining camps, but also carried the mail over several high passes on 10-foot wooden skis. Every August during Boom Days, a 23-mile pack burro race takes place on Mosquito Pass.

From Leadville take 7th St. east from Harrison Ave. The road leads into the Fryer Hill mining district as it follows Evans Gulch up toward the pass. Stay on the main road past the Matchless Mine. About 4.5 miles after starting out, Mosquito Pass Rd. breaks off to the left. From here, the road leads 18 miles over the summit and down to the town of Fairplay. Instead of returning on the same route, come back to Leadville via Weston Pass, located 5 miles south of Fairplay on Hwy. 285 (see the Scenic Drives section).

GOLF

Mount Massive Golf Club—

At 10,200 feet this nine-hole course is billed as the highest in the world. The claim is disputed, but the beauty of the course is not. The well-maintained greens are located along gentle slopes at the base of Mt. Massive (14,421 feet). Since the course is surrounded by a thick forest of lodgepole pines, it is not uncommon to see deer and elk wander onto the links. Advance tee times are normally unnecessary. Located 3.5 miles west of town on **Turquoise Lake Rd. (County Rd. 4); (719) 486-2176.**

HIKING AND BACKPACKING

The Leadville area offers some of the most spectacular mountain terrain imaginable—and hiking is perhaps the best way to get out and enjoy it. The town is surrounded on three sides by San Isabel National Forest, including Colorado's two highest peaks to the west: Mt. Elbert (14,433 feet) and Mt. Massive (14,421 feet). At lower elevations a web of trails meanders through ponderosa forests, wildflowers, meadows and crumbling remnants of the mining boom. Several great hikes near the Leadville area are discussed in the **Vail** and **Upper Arkansas Valley** chapters. For trail information and maps, contact the **Leadville Ranger District Office, 2015 N. Poplar St.; (719) 486-0749.** For topographical maps and outdoor equipment try **Bill's Sport Shop** at **225 Harrison Ave.; (719) 486-0739,** or **Buckhorn Sporting Goods** at **616 Harrison Ave.; (719) 486-3944.**

Colorado Trail—

Passing just to the west of Leadville, the 469-mile Colorado Trail offers access to spectacular scenery: thick woods, trout streams and historic mining areas. Consider leaving a second car at a pickup point near the trail and taking a one-way backpacking trip for a few days. The stretch near Leadville between Tennessee Pass and Twin Lakes is absolutely gorgeous. A sidetrip up Mt. Elbert or Mt. Massive could be easily taken from the Colorado Trail.

Interlaken Trail—

This 2-mile, one-way trail leads due west along the gentle shoreline of the eastern Twin Lake, eventually reaching the ghost town of Interlaken; the round-trip hike takes about 2.5 hours. True to its name, Interlaken—a few cabins and other boarded up buildings—lies directly between the Twin Lakes. From Leadville take Hwy. 24 south for 14 miles until reaching Hwy. 82. Turn right and head west on Hwy. 82 for about 3 miles to the tip of the eastern lake. Just before crossing a bridge, turn left on a gravel road which passes below the dam and intersects shortly with the Colorado Trail.

Leadville National Fish Hatchery—

Beginning near the teeming cement fish tanks of this hatchery is a nature trail with 15 numbered stations along its 1-mile route. The walk takes about an hour and is in a beautiful area near the base of Mt. Massive. At a midpoint between the three Evergreen Lakes is a picnic area. Pick up a trail guide at the visitors center. To reach the hatchery take Hwy. 24 west of Leadville for 2 miles to Hwy. 300. Turn right (west) and drive a couple more miles to the historic hatchery, built in 1899.

Mount Elbert—

A hike up Colorado's tallest peak (14,433 feet) requires a degree of strength, stamina and common sense. This is a popular hike that can be done in one day. The first part of the hike is heavily wooded and provides the best chance for sighting mule deer and other wildlife. After you leave the trees behind, colorful alpine tundra takes over the ground. Please stay on the trail, as this plant life is easily damaged. In early summer the trail passes over snowfields close to the top. When you make it to the summit, the views are astounding in all directions.

North Mt. Elbert Trail begins at an elevation of 10,100 feet and climbs 4.5 miles to the summit. Although the shortest route, it's steeper than the South Trail. To reach the trailhead from Leadville, head west on Hwy. 24 for about 2 miles. Continue west on Hwy. 300 instead of following Hwy. 24 as it turns south around a wide bend. Stay on Hwy. 300 for a mile before turning south on Halfmoon Creek Rd. (Forest Rd. 110). Continue 6 miles on the dirt road to Halfmoon Campground. The trail leaves from just above the campground parking area.

South Mt. Elbert Trail is longer, but receives more use thanks to its more gradual incline. The trail begins at 9,600 feet and climbs 6 miles to the summit. The trailhead is located at Lake View Campground near Twin Lakes (see Camping)

Yet another approach to the summit of Mt. Elbert is on **Black Cloud Trail**. This is the least used of all the routes and is a truly beautiful way to the top. Even if you don't have the urge to conquer a 14er, this can be an excellent short hike—just return when you feel like it. The trail gains nearly 5,000 feet in 5.5 miles, but the steady uphill pull is rewarded by the view from the top. To reach the trailhead travel south on Hwy. 24 for 14 miles to Hwy. 82. Turn right and drive past Twin Lakes to a half mile beyond Twin Peaks Campground. The trail leaves from the north side of the highway.

Mount Massive Trail—

Even though Mt. Massive is 12 feet shorter than Mt. Elbert, its trail is quite a bit longer—from Halfmoon Campground it is 7 miles to the summit, with an elevation gain of almost 4,500 feet. This long day hike is fantastic if you're in good shape. The trail begins on the Colorado Trail and tracks north along the base of the peak for 3 miles. At a marked junction with Mt. Massive Trail you take the left fork and head sharply uphill toward treeline. Once above the trees, views to Leadville and Mt. Elbert are incredible. It gets even better once you are on the summit! To reach the trailhead see the entry on North Mt. Elbert Trail. Both hikes begin just above Halfmoon Campground.

HORSEBACK RIDING

Leadville Stables—

What could be better than having a friendly Leadville native take you on a guided horseback ride through the historic mining district? Take a one-, two-, half-day or longer trip with an expert on the area. The breakfast rides feature hot biscuits and sausage gravy. Located at the northern edge of town. **181 N. Hwy. 91; (719) 486-1497.**

Pa and Ma's Guest Ranch—

Sign up for an all-you-can-eat breakfast or dinner ride—or rent a horse by the hour. The ranch also runs historical tours of Leadville in a horse-drawn surrey, beginning in front of the **Leadville/Lake County Chamber of Commerce** at **809 Harrison Ave.** Open Memorial Day–Labor Day. Located 4 miles west of town on **Hwy. 24 at E. Tennessee Rd.; (719) 486-3900.**

RIVER FLOATING

The Upper Arkansas River is renowned for giving rafters thrilling, whitewater rides. A slew of outfitters make the run, but most are based downriver near the towns of Buena Vista and Salida. The Upper Arkansas River, including Brown's Canyon, is discussed in detail in the River Floating section of the **Upper Arkansas Valley** chapter. For a local outfitter, try **Twin Lakes Expeditions** at **PO Box 70, Twin Lakes, CO 81251; 1-800-288-0497** or **(719) 486-3928.**

SKIING
CROSS-COUNTRY SKIING

Leadville lies at the center of a cross-country skier's paradise. Miles of back-country trails weave through the lower reaches of the Sawatch mountains. In addition, groomed trail systems leave from the base of Ski Cooper on Tennessee Pass and from the Colorado Mountain College campus. All in all, the snow conditions at this altitude are excellent, the views are beautiful and avalanche danger is low. For maps and information about trails in San Isabel National Forest, contact the **Leadville Ranger District Office, 2015 N. Poplar St.; (719) 486-0749.**

Backcountry Trails—
Leadville National Fish Hatchery—A marked system of looping trails for various abilities leads away from the fish hatchery at the base of Mt. Massive. The area is stunning in its natural beauty. A good half-day trip is on the Highline Trail Loop or the more difficult Kearney Park Loop. More information is posted at the hatchery. To get there see the Hiking and Backpacking section.

Silver City Trail—Skiing through Leadville's historic mining district is one of the best ways to get a feeling for the lifestyle of the miners. Back when the mines were operating year-round, however, men working in the mines in winter never saw the sun. Today miles of unplowed mining roads weave past the abandoned mine buildings that litter the countryside. Dangerous pits and holes abound off the roads. A map with a key to the markers on the "routes of the silver kings" is available at the **Leadville/Lake County Chamber of Commerce, 809 Harrison Ave.; (719) 486-3900.**

Twin Lakes Trails—
A number of trails lead off from Twin Lakes, 22 miles south of Leadville. You might ski across the frozen lakes to the ghost town of Interlaken or head up Independence Pass on the road that closes for winter. From Leadville take Hwy. 24 south for 14 miles until reaching Hwy. 82. Turn right and head 8 miles west on Hwy. 82. For information, advice and rentals stop in at the Nordic Inn on Hwy. 82, **Twin Lakes, CO 81251; 1-800-626-7812 or (719) 486-1830.**

Tenth Mountain Trail Association Hut System—Over 250 miles of trails stretch into the beautiful backcountry between Leadville, Aspen and Vail with huts along the way. For detailed information see the Skiing section of the **Aspen** chapter.

Tennessee Pass—Just west of the summit of Tennessee Pass on Hwy. 24, a number of trails head off into the woods. Some of the trails follow the old Denver & Rio Grande Railroad beds. The **Mitchell Creek Loop** begins on the fairly level grade of a railroad bed for 2.5 miles before getting a bit tougher. The entire loop is slightly over 7 miles long. More difficult tours include the **Powder Hound Loop** and the **Treeline Loop**. Views of old mine buildings accompany nearly every tour. This is the area where the 10th Mountain Division trained before heading off to Europe in World War II. All of the trails are marked; maps are available from the **Leadville Ranger District Office, 2015 N. Poplar St.; (719) 486-0749.**

Groomed Trails—
Ski Cooper Nordic Center—Thirty-five kilometers of maintained trails leave from the base of Ski Cooper on Tennessee Pass. Many of the trails are loops of varying length and difficulty. Reasonable trail fees make the terrain accessible to all skiers. Cross-country rentals and instruction can be arranged at the nordic center. For those interested in telemark skiing, 302 acres of lift-served slopes at the ski mountain are perfect (telemark clinics and rentals available). Located 10 miles north of Leadville on Hwy. 24; **(719) 486-2277.**

Rentals and Information—
Ski Cooper Nordic Center—The Nordic Center offers excellent telemark and cross-country equipment. See the entry above for information. Located 10 miles north of Leadville on Hwy. 24; **(719) 486-2277.**

Bill's Sport Shop—This place has equipment, maps and advice for cross-country skiers. **225 Harrison Ave., Leadville; (719) 486-0739.**

DOWNHILL SKIING

You won't find condo developments or a large, well-known hotel in its low-key setting, but about 20 minutes you can be on the slopes at **Ski Cooper;** In under an hour you can reach **Copper Mountain, Breckenridge, Vail, Beaver Creek** and **Keystone/ Arapahoe Basin.**

Ski Cooper—

One of Colorado's best-kept secrets is located astride the Continental Divide at the summit of Tennessee Pass. Low-priced lift tickets (half the price of some resorts!), no lines, good snow and a casual atmosphere are trademarks at Ski Cooper. The lift-serviced mountain does not have the intimidating runs of some larger areas, making it perfect for most families. Since the base elevation is at 10,500 feet, the snowfall (260-inch average) is normally dry and powdery.

Since the opening of the bowls, chutes and glades of **Chicago Ridge**, advanced intermediate and expert skiers now have a place to ski challenging, ungroomed runs. Snowcats load up with 18 skiers at a time and head up above timberline to 1,600-acres of spectacular scenery and excellent skiing. Be sure to call ahead for snowcat reservations; extra fee. The base lodge has a cafeteria, a rental shop and a nursery, but no overnight accommodations are available at the ski area. Located 10 miles north of Leadville on **Hwy. 24; (719) 486-2277.**

SWIMMING

Lake County Intermediate School Recreation Complex—

An indoor Olympic-sized pool, full gym facilities and a 22-person whirlpool spa are all open to the public for reasonable fees. Hours vary daily, so call for information. **6th St. and McWethy Dr.; (719) 486-2564.**

TENNIS

Four public courts are located at **City Park** just west of **W. 5th St. and Leiter Ave.**

———— SEEING AND DOING ————

MUSEUMS

"The Earth Runs Silver," a multi-image slide show with narration, is also a good place to get an overall view of Leadville before heading to your museum of choice. In summer the show runs on the hour, inside the old church next door to the **Leadville/Lake County Chamber of Commerce.** For tickets and information stop by **809 Harrison Ave.; (719) 486-3900.** We have listed the museum highlights.

Healy House and Dexter Cabin—

The Healy House, an elaborate Victorian built in 1878, was originally a single-family residence but served as a boarding house from 1897 to 1902. Five of the residents in 1898 were female schoolteachers. In those days schoolteachers were required to wear seven undergarments at all times

and take examinations twice a year. For their troubles they were paid $40 per month; $30 was for the rental of cramped quarters in the Healy House.

Dexter Cabin looks like any primitive log cabin, until you get inside. The builder of the small structure was James Dexter, who made a pile of money in mining and investments. Dexter Cabin was never used as a residence; rather, it was for members of an exclusive poker club. The cabin's interior, furnished with the finest woods, is an example of pure luxury. The museum complex is open from Memorial Day–Labor Day, 10 am–4:30 pm Mon.–Sat., 1–4:30 pm Sun.; shorter hours in Sept. Fee charged. **912 Harrison Ave.; (719) 486-0487.**

Heritage Museum—

The Carnegie Library, built in 1904, was turned into a historical museum in

1977. Inside you'll find mining implements, dioramas of mining activity and placards describing the exciting history of the area. Upstairs are museum exhibits from Leadville's heyday as well as a gallery featuring the work of Colorado artists. Small admission fee. Open 9 am–6 pm Memorial Day through Labor Day; 10 am–5 pm from Labor Day–end of Oct.; winter hours are limited. **102 E. 9th St.; (719) 486-1878.**

Matchless Mine—

The headlines around the country screamed "Queen of Colorado's Silver Boom Perishes" and "Baby Doe Freezes To Death While On Guard At Matchless Mine." It was a tragic end to the life of Baby Doe Tabor, second wife of mining magnate H.A.W. Tabor. On his deathbed Horace Tabor whispered to Baby Doe, "Hang on to the Matchless." Baby Doe moved into a shack at the mine and became a recluse. She died in squalor in 1935 after a 36-year vigil. The Matchless has been preserved, and tours of the property are given, including the exterior workings of the mine. Follow E. 7th St. east of town for 1 mile to the mine entrance. Small admission fee. Open June–Labor Day 9 am–5 pm.

National Mining Hall of Fame—

There couldn't be a more appropriate place for a national mining museum than Leadville, Colorado. Housed in a four-story Victorian shell of the former junior high school, the large museum is a showcase for mining methods and technologies—both historical and futuristic. It's a great place to learn about the hardships and engineering feats of miners. Exhibits include a model of ancient mines with elaborate pulley systems operated by teams of horses. The highlight is a fascinating walk-through replica of an actual working underground mine. Venture into space by gazing at Fred Haberlin's imaginative mural of mining on the moon. The Smithsonian's mineral exhibit demonstrates that wealth can be found in many colors. Walk through room after room of idle heavy equipment, exhibit cases and colorful murals telling the interesting story of mining in the United States. Upstairs, individuals who have "achieved lasting greatness in mining" are commemorated on plaques. The museum charges a reasonable admission fee; gift shop. Open daily 9 am–5 pm, May–Oct.; 9 am–2 pm, Mon.–Fri., Nov.–Apr. **120 West Ninth St., PO Box 981, Leadville, CO 80461; (719) 486-1229.**

Tabor Opera House—

Built in 1879 by H.A.W. Tabor to provide Leadville with culture and entertainment, this opera house is a dazzling relic, with its original stage, dressing rooms and wrought-iron seats upholstered in red velvet. Originally the theater was a complex with retail stores on the ground level, a saloon in the rear and a five-room suite on the upper floor. The adjacent Claredon Hotel was joined by a walkway on the upper level so the Tabors and other hotel guests could enjoy private access. Baby Doe and Horace had a private curtained booth close to the stage.

For quite a time, the Tabor Opera House was touted as the best theater west of the Mississippi. Several of the greats appeared on its stage, including John Philip Sousa, Harry Houdini (note the trap door on the stage), Lillian Russell and Oscar Wilde. In all, the theater still provides an intimate setting, with good acoustics from its original canvas ceiling (see the Nightlife section for more information). For a small fee, self-guided, tape-narrated tours can be taken in summer 9 am–5:30 pm Sun.–Fri. **815 Harrison Ave.**

NIGHTLIFE

Silver Dollar Saloon—

Very few saloons in Colorado are entering their second century of operation. The Silver Dollar is one of them. The first drink was pushed across the bar in 1879 when it opened under the name Board of Trade. The stunning white oak backbar was shipped by wagon from St. Louis, Missouri. It is a remarkable piece of work, inlaid with a 0.75-inch-thick diamond-dust mirror. There is also an oak windbreak as you enter the bar; some say it was placed there to protect men from the prying eyes of their wives. During Prohibition the bar remained active, with a trap door mounted beneath the bar for quick disposal of moonshine. Today the bar retains the feel of boomtown Leadville. **315 Harrison Ave.; (719) 486-9914.**

Tabor Opera House—

An Icicle Pickle, or How to Stay Cool as a Cucumber While Your Frozen Assets Thaw was the title of a recent theater production at the Tabor Opera House. The melodramatic comedy was based on events surrounding the 1896 Leadville Ice Palace. Every year a new play by the Crystal Comedy Company breathes life back into the historic theater. And what a setting! (For more information see the Museums section.) The reasonably priced family entertainment starts in mid-June and lasts through Labor Day. Shows only on Wed., Thur. and Sat. nights at 8 pm. Tickets may be purchased the day of the show. The Tabor Opera House is located at **815 Harrison Ave.**

RAILROADS

Leadville, Colorado & Southern Railroad—

In 1988, after a 50-year silence, a passenger train once again began arriving and departing from Leadville. Pulled by a strong locomotive, the open passenger cars on the standard-gauge railroad provide expansive views during the entire traverse up to treeline. The scenic ride ends at a roundhouse near the Climax Mine at an elevation of over 11,000 feet. Stephanie and Ken Olsen found the bargain of a century when they purchased two 1,750-horsepower engines, eight flatcars, five cabooses, 13 miles of track and a roundhouse for $10—less than it costs for a ticket to ride the train today. However, they have poured a lot of money, sweat and effort into the operation to make it a worthwhile venture. The train departs from the Leadville depot two times daily, Memorial Day through Labor Day; weekend trips continue until the fall colors are gone. The ride takes about two and a half hours, including a short break at the water tower. Reduced rates for children. **326 E. 7th St., PO Box 916, Leadville, CO 80461; (719) 486-3936.**

SCENIC DRIVES

Independence Pass (Hwy. 82)—

During the summer and fall, this beautiful drive leads to Aspen over a narrow, twisting road. For more information see the Scenic Drives section of the **Aspen** chapter.

Routes of the Silver Kings—

Driving among the decaying wooden mine structures and piles of yellowed tailings is a fascinating way to get a true picture of the once-booming industry. Good dirt roads thread their way between famous mines on Fryer Hill and California Gulch. Several round-trip auto tours leave from Leadville and climb into the mountains. Along the roads numbered route markers are placed at points of historical interest. Each marker corresponds with a description in a booklet that can be purchased at the **Leadville/Lake County Chamber of Commerce, 809 Harrison Ave.**

Weston Pass—

This old wagon road, which crosses the Mosquito Range south of Leadville, connects the Upper Arkansas Valley with South Park. The dirt road will shake your car, but high clearance is not necessary to complete the scenic trip. Following the South Fork of the South Platte River, the road winds its way up to an elevation of 11,921 feet. The route goes between Weston Peak (13,572 feet) to the north and Marmott Peak (13,326 feet) to the south. To reach Weston Pass Rd. from Leadville take Hwy. 24 for 6 miles south to the marked turn-off. Turn left and drive east over the pass, eventually reaching Hwy. 285 south of Fairplay.

WHERE TO STAY

ACCOMMODATIONS

Delaware Hotel—$$$ to $$$$

By 1886 the Delaware Block was completed, with 50 upstairs offices and bedrooms. Named for the first owners' home state, the Delaware Hotel originally featured the conveniences of steam heat and hot and cold water, but had only four bathrooms for the entire complex. The exterior similarities between the Delaware and renovated Tabor Grand/Vendome Hotel across the street can be attributed to a common architect—George E. King. For a long time the venerable Delaware operated as the Crew Beggs Dry Goods Company, but it has been back in service as a hotel for quite some time.

Climb the stairway from the newly renovated lobby area and you'll get a feel for this classy, historic hotel. The careful renovation is not overdone or cutesy. Each room at the Delaware Hotel is slightly different, with uneven floors and furniture from the late Victorian period; some have the nice touches of exposed brick and brass beds. All have plush carpet and private bathrooms. With the exception of the suites, the rooms are on the small side—shall we say cozy? The two-room suites are a bargain for four people—a personal favorite was the suite tucked into the western corner on the third floor with a gorgeous mountain view. The recent addition of a hot tub makes staying here even more enjoyable. A night's stay in any room at the Delaware includes a full breakfast. High quality breakfast, lunch and dinner are served at **Calloway's ($ to $$$)** on the main floor. **700 Harrison Ave., PO Box 960, Leadville, CO 80461; (719) 486-1418.**

Leadville Country Inn—$$$ to $$$$

Sid and Judy Clemmer run this textbook example of a successful country inn/bed and breakfast in a beautifully restored 1893 Queen Anne Victorian and its carriage house. Ten uniquely decorated rooms vie for your attention. Polly's Room, deco-rated with a canopied brass bed, also has a small private sitting room. This adjacent room, with windows on three sides, could accommodate two children on trundle beds. Each of the rooms features a private bathroom. But only Maggie's Room has an antique copper tub laid into a polished wooden frame at a perfect angle for a long soak. Maggie's king-sized bed provides for a picture-perfect view out to Colorado's highest peaks. A favorite is Sophie's Attic with its private entrance, rich textured walls, four poster bed, antique loft and a decadent bathroom with a jacuzzi tub built for two. The entire inn is decorated in a blend of styles the innkeepers refer to as "Country Victorian." A full breakfast can be taken in the large common room or, if you prefer, in your own bedroom. Try the **Tea Room** for an intimate light lunch ($$) to strains of classical music. Did I forget to mention the gazebo encased outdoor hot tub? Contact the inn for reservations and more information. **127 E. 8th St., Leadville, CO 80461; 1-800-748-2354 or (719) 486-2354.**

Nordic Inn—$$ to $$$

Constructed in 1879 as a stagecoach stop, the Nordic Inn enjoys a pristine mountain location in the tiny community of **Twin Lakes** (year-round population 20). It finds itself at the end of a dead-end road when Independence Pass closes in winter, shutting off the 39-mile route to Aspen. Summer or winter (cross-country ski rentals available) the Nordic Inn finds itself amidst the stunning San Isabel National Forest, offering easy access to those who love the outdoors but don't necessarily feel like camping out. The inn itself offers a unique, reasonably priced night's stay in the funky former brothel and historic landmark. It has been fixed up over the years in a haphazard way—but honestly, that's part of the charm. Choose a video and watch it in the small common room or, snatch a good book from the library and head upstairs to your puffy featherbed. Most of the small-ish rooms share baths, but two feature private baths. There's an excellent restaurant downstairs if you feel like breakfast, lunch or dinner (see Where to Eat). Adventuresome souls may wish to reserve a room during the annual Hooker's Ball in mid-Oct. (costumes required). Closed in mud season: early spring and late fall. Located 22 miles south of Leadville on Hwy. 82, **Twin Lakes, CO 81251; 1-800-626-7812** or **(719) 486-1830.**

Matchless Properties—$$ to $$$

This property management company can rent you a Victorian house or even a cabin. The completely furnished homes can accommodate large or small groups. **700 Harrison Ave., PO Box 971, Leadville, CO 80461; (719) 486-3030.**

Club Lead—$$

Club Lead offers rough, inexpensive dorm-style accommodations to individuals and groups. Breakfast is included in the price. Owner Jay Jones is perpetually fixing the place up. Geared to the active, budget traveler, Club Lead can arrange everything from whitewater rafting to mountain biking to cross-country skiing. **500 E. 7th St., Leadville, CO 80461; (719) 486-2202.**

CAMPING

In San Isabel National Forest—

Eight campgrounds (368 campsites) are situated around the perimeter of Turquoise Lake. This heavily wooded area offers hiking, fishing and boating. The **Belle of Colorado Campground,** on the east end of the lake, is the only walk-in campground and is limited to tents. All campgrounds charge a fee and have water and toilets. Turquoise Lake is located 3 miles west of Leadville. Many of these campgrounds may

be reserved by calling **1-800-280-CAMP.**

South of Leadville, under the towering summits of Mt. Elbert and Mt. Massive, are the nicely wooded **Halfmoon** (24 sites) and **Elbert Creek** (17 sites) campgrounds. A fee is charged at both. Since a trailhead for climbing Elbert and Massive takes off from the area, use is heavy, especially on weekends. To reach the campgrounds travel west from town on Hwy. 24 for about 2 miles. Continue west on Hwy. 300 instead of following Hwy. 24 as it turns south around a big bend. Stay on Hwy. 300 for a mile before turning south on Halfmoon Creek Rd. (Forest Rd. 110). Continue 6 miles on the dirt road to the campgrounds.

In the Twin Lakes area there are five large campgrounds. From Leadville follow Hwy. 24 south for 14 miles until reaching Hwy. 82. Turn right and head west on Hwy. 82, which skirts the north side of the reservoir. After 3 miles you'll reach **Dexter Point Campground** beside the lake. There are 26 sites, and a fee is charged. Another 2 miles down Hwy. 82, turn right onto Forest Rd. 125 and continue to **Lake View Campground.** As the name suggests, the view to Twin Lakes is beautiful. There are 59 sites and a fee is charged. **Past Lake View Campground** you can proceed west along Hwy. 82 to **White Star** (64 sites), **Perry Peak** (26 sites) and **Twin Peaks** (37 sites) campgrounds. All charge a fee.

Private Campgrounds—

Sugar Loafin' Campground—Not far from Turquoise Lake, this scenic campground offers full RV hookups and tent sites. Amenities include hot showers, laundry and, listen up—ice cream socials! Located 3.5 miles northwest of Leadville on County Rd. 4; **(719) 486-1031.**

WHERE TO EAT

The Prospector—$$$

Leadville residents frequently take the short 3-mile trip out of town to this special restaurant. The excellent food makes it well worth the trip. From the outside it

looks as if it were someone's log cabin. Walk past mining implements, through the stone entryway and once inside you'll be treated to a friendly, family atmosphere. A large picture window offers a beautiful mountain view to the south. Full portions of steak, lamb, poultry and seafood take up most of the menu. Start off with the full salad bar and soup tureen. When we visited in Aug., the fresh peach pie in a crumbly homemade shell was delicious. Open 5–10 pm Tues.–Sat., Sun. brunch 10 am–3 pm, Sun. dinner 4–7 pm. Closed Mon. Located 3.5 miles north of Leadville on Hwy. 91; **(719) 486-2117.**

Nordic Inn—$ to $$$

The alpine setting in the town of Twin Lakes simply cannot be matched. A wall of small windowpanes in this cozy restaurant opens up to one of the finest mountain views imaginable. The warm wooden insides of this historic stage coach stop are filled with old skis, books and other cool collectibles. A roaring fire and small bar area (over 50 bottled beers) can really fit the bill in winter. You'll find standards for breakfast and lunch. German dinner specialties include wienerschnitzel and sauerbraten; veal and poultry dishes are prepared with care.

Open daily 7 am–11 am for breakfast; 11 am–3 pm for lunch and 5–9 pm for dinner. Closed for several weeks in spring and after the leaves have fallen. For information on the inn see Where to Stay. Located 22 miles south of Leadville on Hwy. 82, **Twin Lakes, CO 81251; 1-800-626-7812** or **(719) 486-1830.**

Casa Blanca—$ to $$

It's tough to single out the best Mexican restaurant in Leadville, partly because there are several good ones. Local opinion though seems to have shifted to Casa Blanca as the best, thanks to consistently good food, quick service and reasonable prices. The small, spare restaurant offers a few window tables—grab one if you can. Owners Cleo and Tony Mascarenaz do a terrific job with the crispy chile rellenos as well as large combination dinners. You can order à la carte, too. Good selection of Mexican beers; they also serve wine. Open Tues.– Sun. 11:30 am–8 pm. Closed Mon. **118 E. 2nd. Ave.; (719) 486-9969.**

SERVICES

Leadville/Lake County Chamber of Commerce—

PO Box 861, 809 Harrison Ave., Leadville, CO 80461; (719) 486-3900.

San Luis Valley

High in the mountains of southern Colorado lies an often overlooked, oval-shaped treasure—the San Luis Valley. Its rich and fascinating cultural heritage and extensive history combine with natural surroundings as beautiful as any in the state, making the region worth considering for an extended stay. Ranging in elevation from 7,000 feet on the valley floor to the 14,345-foot summit of Blanca Peak, the geography is impressive. At 125 miles long and 50 miles wide, it's one of the largest valley basins in the world. To the east and south, the valley is bounded by the mighty Sangre de Cristo (Blood of Christ) Range, which is dominated by the Sierra Blanca Massif. Nestled up against these mountains are the ever-shifting Great Sand Dunes, perhaps the most unusual (and popular) geographical feature in the valley. To the north and west, the valley is enclosed by the San Juan, La Garita and Conejos-Brazos mountains. The Rio Grande originates in the nearby mountains and flows southeast through most of the valley on its way to New Mexico.

Long a frontier between New World colonial settlements, the valley has a history spiced with Indian, Anglo and particularly Spanish influences. The Hispanic culture is etched deeply in the valley even today; examples surface frequently in Spanish architecture (such as the Catholic churches), arts and crafts, local folklore and the Castilian dialect, which has changed little since the 16th century. Most of the towns, rivers, peaks and valleys have Spanish names.

The people in the San Luis Valley are some of the friendliest in the state. You'll find few pretensions, a lot of wholesome values and a relaxed attitude toward everyday life. The town of Alamosa is set in the approximate center of the valley and, mainly for this reason, it's the area's largest community. It has served as a main shipping point for valley products (including well-known valley potatoes) to outside markets since its founding in 1878, when the Denver & Rio Grande Railroad arrived. Adams State College is located here, boasting an outstanding cross-country running team. From Alamosa, communities in the valley spread out in all directions.

Northeast of Alamosa, situated against the jutting Sangre de Cristo Range, lies the intriguing little settlement of **Crestone**. Originally a stage stop and mining area, the town has long been a summer getaway. More recently it has become a haven for the spiritual community. Apparently, Crestone was once a sacred Indian site where lines of planetary energy are said to converge. Today many groups, from Tibetan monks and Zen Buddhists to New Agers, are snapping up real estate in the area.

West of Alamosa lie **Monte Vista** and **Del Norte**; both were early stage stops and trading towns and are agricultural areas today. To the

533

east, the **Fort Garland Museum** remains a vivid example of life in frontier Colorado.

The vibrant Hispanic community of Colorado's oldest town, San Luis, evokes an atmosphere reminiscent of John Nichols's *Milagro Beanfield War*. Located in the southern part of the valley at the foot of 14,047-foot Culebra Peak, this town has one of the last commons (*vegas*) in the country outside of the Boston area. The San Luis *vega*, an 860-acre tract of land, is used by the entire community for grazing and crops. Culturally, the people of San Luis and the neighboring villages of adobe structures seem more connected to New Mexico than to Colorado.

West of San Luis, the small town of **Manassa** was settled by Mormons who thought the local Indians were descendants of Manasseh, son of Joseph. It's also the birthplace of ex-heavyweight boxing champion Jack Dempsey (a.k.a. the "Manassa Mauler"). At the extreme south end of the valley, near the New Mexico border, **Antonito** home to the depot of the **Cumbres and Toltec Scenic Railroad,** one of the best narrow-gauge railroad trips in the country. Antonito was a railroad town built to house Anglos who were less than willing to assimilate into the much older Hispanic settlement of **Conejos**, just north of town. Our Lady of Guadalupe Church in Conejos is considered to be the oldest in the state, although residents of San Acacio beg to differ.

HISTORY

The Ute Indians controlled the San Luis Valley for hundreds of years before Europeans ever set foot in the area. Called the *Blue Sky People* by other tribes, the Utes followed herds and hunted throughout this territory.

Although some speculate that Spanish explorer Francisco Coronado entered the San Luis Valley in 1540, the first recorded European visit to the valley was by another Spaniard, Don Diego de Vargas, in 1694. Eighty-five years later the governor of New Mexico, Juan Bautista de Anza, passed through the San Luis Valley on a vengeful search for Comanche Indians who had raided northern New Mexico settlements. De Anza noted both the Rio Grande and Cochetopa Pass, a well-traveled crossing over the Continental Divide in the northwest section of the valley.

In the winter of 1806–1807, Lt. Zebulon Pike and his men came west into the valley at the sand dunes before making their way south to what Pike thought was the Red River of Texas. They built a stockade nearby, raised the American flag and settled in for the remainder of the winter. However, Pike, the Inspector Clouseau of American explorers, had made a major navigational error—what he thought was the Red River was really the Rio Grande. He had raised the American flag on Spanish soil. It was not long before a detachment of Spanish troops arrived, arrested Pike and his men, and escorted them to Santa Fe and then all the way down to Chihuahua. Pike and his men were eventually released at the US border with the promise that they would never set foot in Mexico (New Spain) again.

In the first half of the 1800s, Mexican government officials were anxious for settlers to populate what was then the Mexican frontier. They awarded large sections of land (known as land grants), much of it in what is now northern New Mexico and southern Colorado, to men who planned to develop the area. However, it was not until after the Mexican War that the first permanent settlement appeared in the valley. In 1851 a group established the town of San Luis. A number of Hispanic settlements soon followed San Luis' lead. By that time the US had gained possession of southern Colorado, and one of the responsibilities that beset the new government was protecting these frontier settlements from marauding Utes and other Indians from the south. In 1852 Fort Massachusetts was built, then replaced six years later by Fort Garland, which helped stabilize the valley until the fort was abandoned in 1883.

Rich mineral strikes in the valley at Summitville and Kerber Creek and in the San Juan mining district to the west helped bring about a rail connection with the Front Range by way of La Veta Pass in 1878. Alamosa, a railroad town and former stage stop, literally sprang up in a few days when most of the buildings were shipped in by flatcar as the railroad arrived. Aptly named, Alamosa means "cottonwood grove" in Spanish. A particularly large tree by the Rio Grande served as the town gallows; early train passengers were occasionally greeted by a corpse swinging from this giant cottonwood.

During the 1880s much of the valley along the Rio Grande was irrigated by canals, turning the naturally arid land into rich farmland especially suited to growing potatoes. Today the valley is used primarily for farming and ranching. And as unlikely as it seems, this arid valley sits on top of a deep, enormous aquifer. Seeing the aquifer as vital to the valley's agriculture, residents have successfuly banded together to prevent outside sources from pumping the water out and using it to irrigate lawns in the suburbs of some far-off city.

GETTING THERE

The San Luis Valley is located in south central Colorado. Alamosa is located 212 miles from Denver via Interstate 25 south to Walsenburg, then west on Hwy. 160 over La Veta Pass. The valley can also be reached via Hwy. 285 from the Upper Arkansas River Valley to the north. Buses service some towns in the valley with more frequent stops in Alamosa.

United flies into the Alamosa Municipal Airport from Denver. Call **(303) 398-4141** for information and reservations.

MAJOR ATTRACTIONS

Cumbres and Toltec Scenic Railroad

The wail of the whistle, hiss of the steam and pungent aroma of coal smoke make this narrow-gauge train irresistible. An added bonus is the lush, rolling countryside and inspiring rock formations along the way. The Cumbres and Toltec, America's longest and highest narrow-gauge railroad, begins its 64-mile journey to Chama, New Mexico, from the small burg of Antonito, Colorado. Its serpentine path takes you through Toltec Gorge of the Los Piños River and up to the 10,015-foot summit of Cumbres Pass, once used by the Spanish to enter the San Luis Valley as early as the 16th century. From the summit the train drops down a steep 4-percent grade into Chama. Along the way the train crosses the Colorado–New Mexico border seven times! This scenic railroad, now a National Historic Site, should not be missed if you are spending any time in the San Luis Valley.

History—

Tracks between Antonito and Chama were originally laid down in 1880 by the Denver & Rio Grande Railroad to connect their line to the productive mining camps of southwestern Colorado. After the gold and silver mining petered out in the San Juans, the need for the train fizzled, and eventually the route was discontinued. In the late 1960s, a determined group from Colorado and New Mexico set out to fix the track. Volunteer gangs and train crews worked more than 2,000 hours fixing tracks and clearing obstacles. In September 1970 the refurbished track from Antonito to Chama was opened, and the train made its run.

Facts About the Train—

The Cumbres and Toltec Scenic Railroad is jointly owned by the states of Colorado and New Mexico. The train runs daily from Memorial Day weekend through mid-Oct. The trip to Chama takes all day, stopping at the halfway point (Osier), where lunch is served for an extra charge. Afterward, many people take the train that returns to Antonito, while others push on to Chama and return to Antonito by van (the return takes about an hour and a half).

Reservations are highly recommended. Overnight lodging packages in either Chama or Antonito can also be arranged. Group rates are available, and the caboose can be reserved for special parties. Wheelchair accessible; provide at least seven days notice. **PO Box 668, Antonito, CO 81120; (719) 376-5483.** In Chama, **PO Box 789, Chama, NM 87520; (505) 756-2151.**

Great Sand Dunes National Monument

Like a piece of the Sahara Desert grafted onto the side of the snowcapped Sangre de Cristo Mountains, Great Sand Dunes National Monument looks out of place—almost inappropriate. Never ceasing to amaze visitors, the 39 square miles of dunes rise as high as 700 feet and are one of the state's most popular places during summer. Thanks to the hard work of valley residents, the Great Sand Dunes were proclaimed a National Monument by President Hoover in 1932.

Providing all of the information you need for a stay at the monument, the visitors center has exhibits explaining the natural and human history of the area. Ask about walks, talks and campfire programs with rangers in the summer months. There is also a good bookstore here. Open Memorial Day–Labor Day 8 am–7 pm, winter 8 am–5 pm.

Getting There—

From Alamosa head east on Hwy. 160 for 14 miles to Hwy. 150. Turn left (north) and drive 16 miles to the monument entrance. The monument can also be reached from Hwy. 17 north of Alamosa by driving east from Mosca. **Great Sand Dunes National Monument, 11999 Hwy. 150, Mosca, CO 81146; (719) 378-2312.**

Geology—

There are many colorful explanations as to why the sand dunes exist, but the real reason is not nearly so interesting. Water and wind scour the surrounding mountains, breaking much of the rock down into sand. The sand is blown or carried by rivers down into the valley. Once in the valley, prevailing winds carry the sand northeast to where the Sangre de Cristos rise 4,000 feet from the valley floor. Acting as a natural trap, these mountains create such a high barrier that the wind loses its punch, dropping the sand and thus forming the dunes.

Camping

Piñon Flats Campground (88 sites) is the only camping area within the monument. It's open from Apr.–Oct. on a first-come, first-served basis. Fee charged. In winter, water is not available. **Great Sand Dunes Oasis and RV Park,** located just outside the monument entrance, offers hookups, showers, etc. Additional camping (50 sites) is available at **San Luis Lakes State Park,** about 10 miles west of the monument entrance on Sixmile Rd. (See the Camping section for more information.)

Four-Wheel-Drive Trips

Medano Primitive Rd. follows Medano Creek up along the edge of the dunes for a few miles. Four-wheel-drive vehicles can follow the road but are not allowed to drive off it. Because the sand creates traction difficulties, air needs to be let out of the tires; this prevents most from continuing over Medano Pass to the Wet Mountain Valley (east). Near the campground there is an air hose for refilling tires. The road is open from May–Sept. Trips are offered by the **Great Sand Dunes Oasis Campground and RV Park** located just outside the monument entrance. Contact **Great Sand Dunes Oasis, Mosca, CO 81146; (719) 378-2222.**

Hiking and Backpacking

The sand dunes' location next to the Sangre de Cristos makes for some unique hiking and backpacking opportunities. Permits are free but required for all backcountry camping within the monument. Pick them up at the visitors center. No backcountry fires are permitted. For additional information contact the visitors center.

On the Dunes—

The beckoning power of the dunes is amazing. As soon as many people pull into the parking lot, an overpowering desire to conquer the sand overtakes them. During the midst of tourist season, visitors dressed in Bermuda shorts wade across Medano Creek and scamper all over the dunes, lost in their own thoughts about Lawrence of Arabia and the French Foreign Legion. From the top of the dunes, spectacular views of the San Juan Mountains to the west and the Sangre de Cristos to the east transfix visitors even by moonlight. By day, dune trekking is hot and thirsty work, *so bring lots of water, and don't forget shoes, sunscreen and a hat.* Even worse, many people don't realize how vulnerable they are up on the dunes. The dunes occasionally endure violent thunder and hail storms: proof positive is on display at the visitors center, where you can see exhibits of sand that has been fused into big globs by lightning. Where do you hide from pelting hailstones when you are on the dunes? Maybe you can bury your head in the sand like an ostrich.

Along Medano Creek—

Flowing out of the Sangre de Cristos from the east, Medano Creek makes its way down a river valley and runs into the dunes. The creek then angles left, paralleling the edge of the dunes all the way past the picnic area and campground, eventually disappearing into the dry soil of the San Luis Valley.

When you approach Medano Creek during spring and summer you will notice a rather unusual phenomenon—waves come down the creek about every 30 seconds. These "bores" are created by sand build-up on the bottom of the creek, forming antidunes. The water pressure builds up, the antidunes break and water comes gushing downstream.

A primitive road follows the creek upstream along the dunes and then up into Rio Grande National Forest, passing numerous old log cabins along the way. Eventually the road reaches Medano Pass, where views back down to the dunes are spectacular, as are those of the Wet Mountain Valley to the east.

Mosca Pass—
A 3.5-mile trail heads up to the summit of Mosca Pass, providing great views of the San Luis Valley and the Wet Mountain Valley. This is supposedly the pass Lt. Zebulon Pike used when he crossed over into the San Luis Valley for the first time in 1807. The trail follows Mosca Creek up through juniper and pinon pine. Look for the trailhead on the east side of the road near the first picnic area.

FESTIVALS AND EVENTS

Crane Festival
mid-March
Each spring as hundreds of bird species make their way north on the valley's main flyway, many outside observers converge on Monte Vista to witness the flurry of avian activity at the nearby national wildlife refuge. Guests of honor are the thousands of sandhill and extremely rare whooping cranes. Many activities take place in town, including wildlife art exhibits, wetland educational seminars, photo contests and a banquet. Free buses leave Ski-Hi Park each morning at 7:30 am for the wildlife refuge. There is a reason that this area is referred to as "The Valley of the Cranes." For information contact the **Visitor Center** at **1-800-835-7254.**

Ski-Hi Stampede
end of July
An annual event, this three-day pro rodeo has been a tradition since 1921. Chuck wagon dinner, carnival and rodeo events. **835 1st Ave., Monte Vista; (719) 852-2055.**

San Luis Valley Mountain Man Rendezvous
early August
In the tradition of the mountain men of the early 1800s, modern men (and women) don their buckskin outfits and coonskin caps and head for the rendezvous in Del Norte. Modern-day Jim Bridgers compete in muzzle loading and knife and tomahawk throwing. Fiddlers encourage people to dance around the fire; booths display cottage industry crafts and offer "mountain man" food. Camp out and enjoy the activities at a festival you definitely won't find in New Jersey. For information call **(719) 657-2845.**

OUTDOOR ACTIVITIES

BIKING
MOUNTAIN BIKING
Public land in the San Luis Valley, including the surrounding Rio Grande National Forest and BLM land. Some good trails can be found in the southwestern section of the forest (west of Antonito in the Cumbres Pass area and up the Conejos River). Other National Forest riding ideas

include the road into **Natural Arch** (see Scenic Drives), **Taylor Gulch** and **Sawatch Park** near Sawatch. For more information contact: **Rio Grande National Forest Headquarters, 1803 W. Hwy. 160, Monte Vista, CO 81144; (719) 852-5941**, or the **Bureau of Land Management, San Luis Resource Area Office, 1921 State St., Alamosa, CO 81101; (719) 589-4975.**

For trail information, go to **Kristi Mountain Sports** and ask for Eric Burt. **7565 Hwy. 160, Alamosa; (719) 589-9759.**

FISHING

It would be like opening a can of worms to effectively cover all of the noteworthy fishing holes in the San Luis Valley area. OK, the pun is weak, but it's true given the large number of fishable streams, lakes and reservoirs in the valley. For up-to-date fishing conditions as well as an excellent booklet on fishing opportunities in the valley, contact the **San Luis Valley Office of the Colorado Division of Wildlife, 722 South Rd. 1 E., Monte Vista, CO 81144; (719) 852-4783.**

Conejos River—

Meaning "rabbits" in Spanish, this river flows southeast through the beautiful Conejos Valley from Platoro Reservoir (good fishing, boat rentals available) to Antonito, eventually merging with the Rio Grande southeast of Alamosa. The best and most scenic water is in Rio Grande National Forest and can be reached via Forest Rd. 250 about 18 miles west of Antonito. The Conejos can reach a width of 50 feet and is best fished with chest waders. On the upper Conejos you'll catch good-sized brown trout for the most part; the lower areas east of Antonito are flanked by cottonwoods and can be good for rainbows, browns and even an occasional northern pike. After runoff this stream clears up, providing excellent fly-fishing (many stretches are restricted to flies and lures only). When it is running murky your best bet is a caddis fly or stone fly imitation. Many productive tributaries flow into the upper Conejos from the west and south-

west. Trails provide good access to Elk Creek and the South Fork of the Conejos and on up to high lakes near the Continental Divide.

La Jara Reservoir—

Several small streams flow into La Jara Reservoir, helping it maintain a population of small, pan-sized brook trout. Motorboats are allowed on the rather large reservoir and provide the best way to get around. No rentals; primitive campsites. La Jara Reservoir is located 13 miles south of Alamosa on Hwy. 285.

Rio Grande—

The Rio Grande, at 1,887 miles long, is the second longest river in the country. It is also a diverse river system, offering good fishing during its flow through Colorado. The stretch from just above the town of South Fork downstream to Del Norte has been given a Gold Medal designation. Only one-third of this 22.5-mile stretch is open to the public. It can be the inspiration for a good float trip, with large brown trout feeding near the banks. Current restrictions on this stretch of the river include a limit of two fish 16 inches or over, and fishing by flies and lures only. For more information about this stretch, see the Creede Fishing section. Farther downriver, between Monte Vista and Alamosa, a large population of northern pike provides a lot of excitement if offered the right lure. They like the slow water near weeds and other obstructions.

Sanchez Reservoir—

This reservoir, 5 miles south of the town of San Luis, has been gaining the respect of many skeptics. The fishing has improved markedly in recent years, most notably for 30- to 40-pound northern pike. Check out the freezer at Alamosa Sporting Goods for a firsthand look at some recent catches. There are also some sizeable walleye and yellow perch, but the trout are few and far between. Boat ramp available; primitive camping by the shore.

FOUR-WHEEL-DRIVE TRIPS

Although the valley is not well known for four-wheel-drive roads, there is a worthwhile route in **Great Sand Dunes National Monument** (see the Major Attractions section). Also, see the **Creede** chapter for some great nearby routes.

GOLF

Great Sand Dunes Golf Course—

Located about five miles south of the Great Sand Dunes National Monument, the setting of this challenging 18-hole course is hard to match. It's laid out on an old ranch spread and reportedly plays like both a Scottish and mountain course. Although this is a young course, the mature cottonwood trees come into play on most of the holes. A couple of lakes and a meandering stream also make things interesting. The fourth hole was nicknamed Bison Run by the pro after he saw a herd of the ranch's buffalo stampede across the fairway. (There are 2,000 of the hairy beasts scattered throughout the ranch.) For information about the excellent restaurant and inn at Great Sand Dunes, see the Where to Eat and the Where to Stay sections. **5303 Hwy. 150, Masca, CO 81146; (719) 378-2356** or **1-800-284-9213.**

HIKING AND BACKPACKING

Surrounding the valley, Rio Grande National Forest boasts a diverse landscape of 14,000-foot peaks, rolling hills, river canyons and thick forests of pine and aspen. The Continental Divide forms the western edge of the forest, with San Juan National Forest just over the divide. Access to the under-used South San Juan Wilderness Area is fairly easy from the Rio Grande side of the divide. For more information about trail possibilities, contact **Rio Grande National Forest Headquarters, 1803 W. Hwy. 160, Monte Vista, CO 81144; (719) 852-5941,** the **Conejos Peak Ranger District Office** at PO Box 420, La Jara, CO 81140; (719) 274-8971, the **Del Norte Ranger District Office, 13308 W. Hwy. 160, Del Norte, CO 81132; (719) 657-3321,** or the **Saguache Ranger District Office, 46525 Hwy. 114, Saguache, CO 81149; (719) 655-2553.**

Blanca Peak—

The Mount Blanca Massif, located in the Sangre de Cristo Range northeast of Alamosa, is the dominant feature in the San Luis Valley. Without many foothills around it, the mountain shoots up thousands of feet from the valley floor, providing a view that has held Indians, Hispanics and Anglos spellbound for centuries. Blanca Peak is such a big mountain, at 14,345 feet, that it's hard to believe it is only the fourth tallest in the state.

The actual climb up the peak is not that difficult for an average person, but the trail takes a bit of effort to reach. Unless you have a good four-wheel-drive vehicle and a full day, you will need to camp along the way. From Alamosa head east on Hwy. 160 for 14 miles and turn left (north) on Hwy. 150. Proceed about 3.2 miles to a dirt road heading off to the right (east), up into the mountains. Turn onto the dirt road and drive about 1.5 miles northeast to a parking area. Passenger cars should park here—the road ahead is not maintained and is extremely punishing even for four-wheel-drive vehicles. From the parking area it's about 4.5 miles up to Lake Como. From Lake Como the easy trail crosses alpine tundra to Blue Lakes and then to Crater Lake, just a half mile above Blue Lakes. From Crater Lake the trail starts climbing a rocky slope up to the saddle between Ellingwood Point and Blanca Peak. From the saddle head straight up to the 14,345-foot summit of Blanca Peak. Hike early to avoid afternoon thunderstorms.

Crater Lake—

Although this 3.5-mile trail, which crosses west over the Continental Divide from the southern Rio Grande National Forest, is trod by every manner of off-road machine and four-hoofed pack animal, the sweeping panoramas and colorful wildflowers are hard to beat. The trail (No. 707) begins on the side of Forest Rd. 380, about a mile south of Elwood Pass, and climbs up through Douglas fir before reaching treeline after about three-quarters of a mile. Another half mile brings you to the 12,200-foot summit of the divide. The scenery here is BIG. Two options await: first is to descend the west side to Crater Lake where rainbow and cutthroat trout await; second is to head south on the Continental Divide Trail across the immense alpine meadow. The Divide Trail eventually leads you to the beautiful South San Juan Wilderness Area and the New Mexico border. Wildlife inhabiting the area include elk, black bear, bald eagles and the dreaded San Juan range maggot (sheep). *Don't drink the water.* To reach the trailhead from Monte Vista, head south for 12 miles on Hwy. 15 and turn west onto Forest Rd. 250 for 32 miles to Forest Rd. 380. Continue west another 7 miles to the trailhead.

Crestone Trails—

To explore the northeastern part of Rio Grande National Forest in the Sangre de Cristo Range, the town of Crestone is the best jumping-off point. From town head north for a mile, then northeast on the dirt Forest Rd. 950 past North Crestone Creek Campground and begin hiking up along the creek. After a couple of miles there is a fork in the road. The left fork heads up to Groundhog Basin and Venable Pass for views of the San Luis Valley and east down into the Wet Mountain Valley. The right fork (Trail No. 744) turns southeast and heads about 3 miles up to North Crestone Lake. To the south 13,900-foot Mt. Adams blocks the view of Crestone Peak and Crestone Needle, two of the most treacherous 14,000-foot peaks in the state.

Sand Dunes National Monument—

For information about hiking on the dunes, up Medano Creek to Medano Pass and up Mosca Pass, see the Major Attractions section.

Stations of the Cross—

See the Religious Shrines section.

RIVER FLOATING

The upper Rio Grande offers some floating. See the River Floating section in the **Creede** chapter for more information.

SKIING
CROSS-COUNTRY SKIING

For the most part, the San Luis Valley offers much less in the way of organized cross-country trail systems than do many other parts of the state. Though this is not the best place to plan a cross-country ski vacation, there are some trails that can be good, depending on the snow.

Cumbres Pass—

From Antonito, Hwy. 17 snakes its way 39 miles over La Manga and Cumbres passes to the New Mexico border, offering some good areas to cross-country ski. The adequate snowfall and pretty scenery sustain the interest of skiers from northern New Mexico and southern Colorado. The terrain between the two passes is perfect for ski touring, made especially good as a result of a forest fire in 1879 that left the area open and now dotted with spruce trees. *Avalanches can be a problem so use extreme care.* Trujillo Meadows is an excellent area to focus on; see Camping section. For maps and trail information, contact the **Conejos Peak Ranger District Office, PO Box 420, La Jana, CO 81140; (719) 234-8971.**

Rentals and Information—

Kristi Mountain Sports rents cross-country equipment. **7565 Hwy. 160, Alamosa; (719) 589-9759.**

DOWNHILL SKIING

For information on the nearby **Wolf Creek Ski Area,** see the **Pagosa Springs** chapter.

SWIMMING
Splashland—

Though it resembles a regular pool found in Anytown, USA, Splashland is actually fed by geothermal water. This water flows continuously through the pool, providing a complete changeover every eight hours. Showers, rental suits and towels are available. Wading pool for the kids. This is a great place to cool off after a trip to the sand dunes. Small fee. Opens in mid-May. Sun. 12–6 pm, Mon.–Tues. 10 am–6:30 pm, Wed. closed, Thurs.–Sat. 10 am–6:30 pm. One mile north of Alamosa on Hwy. 17. **(719) 589-5151.**

SEEING AND DOING

HOT SPRINGS
Valley View Hot Springs—
During weekdays this series of natural mineral pools provides a relaxing soak to anyone interested (members only on weekends—all day Sat., Sun. until 3 pm—and holidays). Locals in the valley rave about it, but the bashful should be warned: bathing suits are optional and seem to be the exception rather than the norm. Valley View Hot Springs is located in the upper end of the valley, northeast of the now-defunct Mineral Hot Springs. At one time a going concern of its own, Mineral Hot Springs supposedly had a curse put on it by the Ute Indians, who forewarned that the springs would never make any money. The springs have since dried up. Let's hope a similar fate does not await Valley View, with its prime location against the west slope of the Sangre de Cristo Range. You can soak in the developed pool or hike up the mountainside to four smaller natural rock pools. Overnight accommodations ($) are available in dorm rooms, private cabins, or tent and RV sites. Bring your own sleeping bag. From Alamosa, drive 50 miles north on Hwy. 17 to where it meets Hwy. 285. At this junction turn right on the dirt road and head east toward the mountains for 8 miles. Small fee charged. Open 7 am–11 pm daily. **PO Box 175, Villa Grove, CO 81155; (719) 256-4315.**

MUSEUMS AND GALLERIES
It seems as if the valley has always had its fair share of museums. Now the number of art galleries is growing rapidly. Many of the traditional arts and pioneer Spanish crafts of the San Luis Valley are in danger of dying out. Do your part to preserve this priceless aspect of the valley's cultural heritage by visiting a gallery or two. In addition to traditional arts and crafts, many galleries carry contemporary works and/or a blend of new and old. Pick up a copy of the *San Luis Valley Guide to Arts and Culture* at any valley chamber of commerce for a complete listing of the galleries. Listed below are a few notables.

ALAMOSA
Firedworks Gallery—
This interesting gallery, once tucked away on a side alley, has blossomed into an expanded main street location. Carol Mondragon and Mike Cavaliere show striking paintings, pottery, jewelry and other fine collectibles, mostly from local artists, including photographer, J.D. Marston. Carol, herself a fine potter, admits that she has been too busy recently selling other people's work to do enough of her own. Open 10 am–6 pm daily. **608 Main St., Alamosa, CO 81101; (719) 589-6064.**

DEL NORTE
Rio Grande County Museum and Cultural Center—
The Del Norte Museum houses some fine historic relics. A highlight is the display of Indian rock art as well as a recently added exhibit (including artifacts) on John Charles Fremont's fourth and final expedition in the winter of 1848–49 entitled "Of Ice and Men." Looking for a railroad route, the party froze and starved to death just north of Del Norte in the La Garita Mountains. Throughout the summer months, regional and local artists are in residence; every two weeks lectures are given on the valley's wildlife and social history. Open

10 am–5 pm Mon.–Sat., May–Sept.; 11 am–4 pm, Mon.–Fri. the rest of the year. **580 Oak St., PO Box 430, Del Norte, CO 81132; (719) 657-2847.**

FORT GARLAND
Fort Garland Museum—

Twenty-six miles east of Alamosa on Hwy. 160 sits Fort Garland, one of the most famous outposts on the frontier and now a museum run by the Colorado Historical Society. It should not be missed.

As settlers pushed into the San Luis Valley from the south, protection from the Indians and a strong military presence in the area became priorities of the US military. In 1852 Fort Massachusetts was built a few miles north of the present site of Fort Garland. Fort Massachusetts proved vulnerable to attack, and the swampy area it occupied made many soldiers ill, so in 1858 Fort Garland was built.

During the Civil War, Union soldiers from Fort Garland were sent south into New Mexico, where they had a bloody battle with Confederate troops at Glorieta Pass. The Union side won, and their victory essentially eliminated any serious threat to the American West by the rebels.

Life in the valley became difficult for the settlers in 1863 when two Mexican brothers, the "Bloody Espinozas," began a murderous reign of terror. Supposedly, the older of the two brothers was inspired by the Virgin Mary in a dream to go out and make life hell for the "gringos." A $1,500 reward was offered to put an end to the killings. Tom Tobin, a local army guide and mountain man, along with a few soldiers, set out from the fort and in no time tracked down and killed the older Espinoza brother and his cousin (the younger brother had already been killed). Feeling a need for proof of his kill, Tobin cut off Espinoza's head, took it back to the fort and threw it at the feet of the commander. When informed that he needed to wait until the Colorado Territorial Legislature reconvened in order to collect his reward, Tobin put the head in a jar of alcohol so it would keep. Thirty years went by before Tobin finally collected his reward.

Following the Civil War, only a volunteer regiment was retained at the fort. Kit Carson commanded the fort in 1866, but left only a year later. The fort continued to play a crucial stabilizing role in Colorado's history until 1883, by which time the Utes had been relocated to reservations in southwestern Colorado and northeastern Utah.

Today the reconstructed fort is a fascinating place to visit and get a feel for Colorado history. Anglo, Indian and Hispanic artifacts fill the many rooms, much as they did during the days when the fort was considered the Siberia of US Army outposts. One visitor to the fort in the 1860s said he was "struck with commiseration for all the unfortunate officers and men condemned to live in so desolate a place." Believe me, it's not that bad now. Be sure to check out the old stagecoach and the list of rules posted by the Barlow and Sanderson stage company that serviced the San Luis Valley before the train arrived. Tips like "spit with the wind, not against it" and "no hogging the buffalo robes" prove that some people in the Wild West cared about manners.

Open April 1 to Labor Day, 9 am–5 pm daily; in winter from 8 am–4 pm. Small fee charged. **PO Box 368, Hwy. 159, Fort Garland, CO 81133; (719) 379-3512.**

MANASSA
Jack Dempsey Museum—

Every little town in America dreams of a local boy (or girl) going out into the world and making good, putting the town on the map. A local boy from Manassa did just that. Jack Dempsey, born in Manassa in 1895, went on to become the heavyweight boxing champion of the world. At age 14, Jack began fighting at mining camps under the name "Kid Blackie." When he was 24, he took the heavyweight crown from Jess Willard. In 1950 the Associated Press voted the "Manassa Mauler" the best heavyweight of the first half of the 20th century. Until Jack's death in 1983, he kept in close touch with his family and friends in Manassa.

The pride of the community shows itself in the Jack Dempsey Museum, a one-room log cabin sitting near the spot where Jack grew up. Boxing mementos and pictures donated by locals and the Dempsey family are on display. Be sure to take a look at the old postcards (of the jackalope and fur-bearing trout variety) that have been on the display rack since the place opened in the mid-1960s. Located in downtown Manassa, across the street from the post office. Open Memorial Day–Labor Day, Mon.–Sat., 9 am–5 pm. **406 Main St., PO Box 130, Manassa, CO 81141; (719) 843-5207.**

SAGUACHE
Saguache County Museum—
If you are passing through Saguache, you should visit this museum. It houses a little of everything, including what is said to be one of the largest Indian arrowhead collections in the country. Established in 1959, this National Historic Site is sprawled out in the old town jail and the schoolhouse next door. The jail cell holds the Alferd E. Packer display, in honor of this notorious cannibalistic Coloradan who was held briefly in Saguache in 1874. Small fee. Open Memorial Day–Labor Day, 10 am–5 pm daily. Located 35 miles north of Monte Vista. **Hwy. 285, Saguache, CO 81149; (719) 655-2557.**

SAN LUIS
Centro Artesano—
This gallery, located within the El Convento Bed & Breakfast, features handmade traditional and cultural pieces of over 70 local artists. Open 11 am–5 pm Mon.–Sat., 11 am–3 pm Sun. You should call ahead to double-check. **512 Church Place, San Luis, CO 81152; (719) 672-4223.**

San Luis Museum, Cultural and Commercial Center—
Hispanic culture of southern Colorado comes to life in this excellent museum in Colorado's oldest town. The building's 17th-century New World Spanish architecture blends with solar technology as an example of old ways coming together with new. The museum contains a wonderful collection of *santos* (Hispanic religious items), including wood carvings and, most notably, a *morada* (where the Penitentes gathered for meetings and worship). Downstairs the award-winning exhibit La Cultura Constante de San Luis vividly conveys the Hispanic culture of southern Colorado, especially that of the San Luis Valley. Open Memorial Day–Labor Day Mon.–Fri. 8:30 am–4:30 pm, Sat.–Sun. 10 am–4 pm; open Mon.–Fri., 8 am–4:30 pm the rest of the year. **PO Box 619, 402 Church St., San Luis, CO 81152; (719) 672-3611.**

RELIGIOUS SHRINES
Stations of the Cross—
Nothing has more properly marked the economic revitalization and deep faith of the people of San Luis than the recent dedication of the Stations of the Cross. The shrine, which is laid out along a 1.4-mile round-trip path winding its way up the mesa at the edge of town, features spectacular bronze statues that depict the suffering and death of Jesus Christ. Father Pat Valdez, pastor of the local Catholic church, headed the project, which required the work of countless volunteers, including Huberto Maestas, the local sculptor who created the 14 nearly life-sized bronze statues.

On the mesa top, the final depiction of Christ's crucifixion commands an impressive position with a view down on town, the valley and across to nearby Culebra Peak (14,047 feet). The trailhead for the shrine is located at the corner of Hwy. 142 and Hwy. 159 in San Luis.

ROCK ART
Ancient Indians left their mark in a number of places throughout the San Luis Valley. Although much of this rock art lies on private property, it is often accessible. An impressive wall of pictographs located on La Garita (L-Cross) Ranch is worth a look. If you are interested, the gate key and directions to the ranch can be obtained at La Garita Store in, as you may have guessed, La Garita. By the way, the store serves great hamburgers. North of Monte Vista, **(719) 754-3755.**

SCENIC DRIVES

Alamosa–Monte Vista National Wildlife Refuge—

See the Wildlife section.

Cochetopa Pass—

Used by Indians, mountain men and early settlers as an easy crossing of the Continental Divide, Cochetopa Pass can be driven today by passenger cars. Cochetopa (an Indian word meaning "buffalo crossing") rises to 10,022 feet, crossing to the west, then eventually branching north to Gunnison or southwest over Los Piños Pass to Lake City. Capt. John Gunnison crossed Cochetopa Pass in 1853 on his expedition to search for a transcontinental railroad route. The Los Piños Indian agency was established on the west side of the pass in 1868 and for years served as the central government post for dealing with the Utes. To reach Cochetopa Pass from Alamosa, drive 17 miles northwest on Hwy. 160 to Monte Vista, then head north on Hwy. 285 for 35 miles to Saguache. From Saguache head west on Hwy. 114 (North Pass Rd.) until you see the sign for the Cochetopa Pass turn-off on the left. Open in summer only.

La Garita Arch—

This 5-mile (one way) drive up Forest Rd. 660 provides great views of the surrounding rolling hills, wildlife viewing (especially antelope), and something for geology buffs, too. La Garita Arch, located at the end of the road is an enormous eroded hole in a lava dyke (over 100 feet tall). The maintained dirt road and surrounding trails also make an excellent mountain bike trip. Head northeast from Del Norte on Hwy. 112 for 3 miles and then left at the La Garita Ranch sign and continue north for about 6 miles. You'll see Forest Rd. 660 on the left (west) side of the road.

Los Caminos Antiguos Scenic and Historic Byway—

Los Caminos Antiguos, which means "the ancient roads," explores the rich cultural heritage of the San Luis Valley by retracing the settlement of the valley and its unique blend of Native American, Hispanic and Anglo cultures.

The 170-mile route begins on the New Mexico border on Hwy. 17, roughly following the route of the **Cumbres** and **Toltec Scenic Railroad** (see Major Attractions) over Cumbres Pass. It's a beautiful drive, especially in the fall when the aspen turn. The road passes through rolling hills and the Conejos River Valley for 39 miles to the town of Antonito. Just north of **Antonito** on Hwy. 285 you'll pass by **Conejos** (1 mile off the road, site of Colorado's oldest church. A bit further north, turn right (east) at **Romeo** and continue through the the towns of **Manassa** and **San Acacio** to Colorado's oldest town, **San Luis**. From here, head north on Hwy. 159 to **Ft. Garland** for a tour of the museum (see the Museums and Galleries section).

If you still have the stamina, head west on Hwy. 160 for 12 miles and then north on Hwy. 150 toward the Great Sand Dunes. After about 13 miles look for a road on the right that heads up to **Zapata Falls**, offering great views out to the valley. A short trail leads to 60-foot-high Zapata Falls. Continuing a few miles north on Hwy. 150 leads you to **Great Sand Dunes National Monument** (see Major Attractions). The tour makes its final turn and heads about 15 miles west on Sixmile Lane to Hwy. 17, 14 miles north of Alamosa. Birders may want to stop along Sixmile Lane for a visit to **San Luis Lakes State Park**.

Southern Rio Grande National Forest—

This highly scenic 57-mile backcountry trip through the valleys and mountains of the southern Rio Grande National Forest is worth the late summer washboard bumps and dust. Early summer when the wildflowers are in bloom, or autumn when the aspen turn would be the best times to head down here. The first section of this route begins at Antonito and follows the Conejos River west along Hwy. 17 for 20 miles to Forest Rd. 250. From here turn right and follow the river up the beautiful Conejos

River Valley, lined by tall mountains and impressive cliffs. The fishing along this section of the Conejos is excellent (see the Fishing section). After 23 miles up Forest Rd. 250 you'll reach the old town of Platoro where you'll find the reservoir and a number of lodges, including Sky Line Lodge (stop here for one of their Golden Bonanza cheeseburgers). In winter the road is not plowed beyond this point. In summer, however, continue over Stunner Pass and stay left on Forest Rd. 380 when you approach Alvarado Campground. From here the road climbs up near the Continental Divide and eventually continues down to Hwy. 160, a few miles west of South Fork.

WILDLIFE

In addition to the ideas listed below, you may want to pick up an excellent Watchable Wildlife brochure from the **San Luis Valley Office of the Colorado Division of Wildlife, 722 South Rd. 1 E., Monte Vista, CO 81144; (719) 852-4783.**

Alamosa–Monte Vista National Wildlife Refuge—

Birders will be glad to know that the San Luis Valley is an incredibly rich bird habitat. Canals and marshland near the Rio Grande make this area a popular place for many migratory birds, such as whooping cranes, sandhill cranes, avocets and teals. In winter many hawks, bald eagles and golden eagles make their home here.

The US Fish and Wildlife Service, which oversees two large tracts of land, offers a self-guiding loop drive through the refuge complex during winter, spring and summer. Headquarters are located at the Alamosa unit, 3 miles east of Alamosa on Hwy. 160 and 2 miles south on El Rancho Ln. The Monte Vista unit is located 6 miles south of Monte Vista on Hwy. 15. For more information contact **Refuge Manager, Alamosa–Monte Vista National Wildlife Refuge, 9383 El Rancho Ln, Alamosa, CO 81101; (719) 589-4021.**

San Luis Lakes State Park—

Opened in the spring of 1993, San Luis Lakes provides spectacular views of the nearby Sagre de Cristo Range and the Great Sand Dunes. And the bird life at the park is exceptional; even non-birders will be amazed at the variety which ranges from grebes to great blue herons. Many birds can be seen at San Luis Lake, even with boaters plying the waters. To increase your chances for sightings you may want to drive or walk north to Head Lake or a couple of other small bodies of water; be sure to ask if the ranger is leading any nature hikes. This north area is closed to vehilces during duck nesting season (mid-Feb. through the end of August). San Luis Lakes has a campground with electric hook-ups (51 sites), water and a shower building. Small fee. Located 8 miles east of Mosca on Six Mile Rd.; **PO Box 175, Mosca, CO 81146; (719) 378-2020.**

San Luis Valley Alligator Farm—

A stop at the alligator farm is a must. Seeing alligators and the other warm water squirmers in a 7,500-foot mountain valley is not only a novelty, it's downright bizzarre! How do they survive? As proprietor, Erwin Young explains, geothermal water seeps from the ground at a constant 87 degrees, providing a perfect environment for this unique Colorado livestock.

You'll be led back to at least one of the large aquarium buildings to see first-hand what Erwin and his employees are raising. Many fish species, incluiding the Rocky Mountain White Tilapia, swim in the tanks and through the many canals.

Outside, in a large lagoon you'll find gator central. Separated from you by only a low chain link fence, almost 100 alligators sun on the banks and lie in the water waiting to be fed. And when they are fed (gator chow pellets made from vegetable protein) their enthusiasm is frightening. Erwin allowed that he had to stop feeding them red meat a few years ago because the gators kept maiming each other in the ensuing feeding frenzy. Open daily 9 am–5 pm. Located north of Alamosa between Mosca and Hooper on Hwy. 17. **PO Box 1052, Alamosa, CO 81101; (719) 589-3032.**

WHERE TO STAY

ACCOMMODATIONS

ALAMOSA

Alamosa is by far the largest town in the valley and serves as a major intersection for traffic heading to all four points on the compass. So, naturally, there are quite a few motels to choose from. If the suggestion below doesn't turn your crank, then contact the **Alamosa Chamber of Commerce** at **(719) 589-3681** for other ideas, or call **1-800-BLU-SKYS**.

The Cottonwood Inn—$$$

Found while poking around Alamosa, this charming bed and breakfast was a welcome surprise. Owners Julie Mordecai and George Sellman opened for business in the summer of 1988 after painstakingly refurbishing this fine old corner-lot home. The handsome wood trim, local art and tasteful antiques all accent the comfortable feel inside. There are currently four rooms available, two of which have private baths. In addition, two larger attractively decorated apartment-style accommodations provide more privacy. Julie and George, both teachers, are quite knowledgeable about the San Luis Valley and can offer very good advice. Delicious full breakfasts made from local products are health-oriented or traditional. The Cottonwood also doubles as a small art gallery; much of the art throughout the house is for sale as well as local crafts which are on display. The gallery is open to the public from 4-9 pm daily. No smoking or pets. Ten percent discount for bicyclists, seniors and groups. **123 San Juan Ave., Alamosa, CO 81101; (719) 589-3882** or **1-800-955-2623**.

ANTONITO

Conejos River Guest Ranch—$$$

Located along the scenic Conejos River about 10 miles west of Antonito on Hwy. 17, Conejos River Guest Ranch is a scenic, quiet place. Owners Clancy and Rosie Spicer have done an admirable job renovating and redecorating the ranch, part of which is 100 years old. Each lodge room has its own private bathroom and decor theme; some have better views than others. The cabins are a bit more rustic.

There is plenty to do at the 14-acre ranch, including fishing along the ranch's private section of the river, horseback riding (extra charge), horeshoes, or just sitting on the fantastic sundeck taking in the scenery.

Lodge guests receive a full country breakfast—you may also want to try the ranch for a steak or trout dinner ($$ to $$$). Open May–Dec. **PO Box 175, Conejos, CO 81129; (719) 376-2464**.

GREAT SAND DUNES

Great Sand Dunes Country Inn at Zapata Ranch—$$$$

The Great Sand Dunes Country Inn possesses more than its share of allure. The Inn's land stretches over 100,000 acres at the edge of the Great Sand Dunes National Monument, encompassing the old Zapata and Medano ranch spreads. Hisa, one of the owners, is fond of taking guests out to remote parts of the ranch to see some of the 2,000 bison that are raised here.

The Inn consists of 15 rooms, spread out among the refurbished Zapata ranch house, bunk house and nearby home. Each room is extremely plush and decorated tastefully with handcarved wood furniture and thick quilts on the beds. The honeymoon suite features an adjacent sitting room and a picture view of the sand dunes from the king-sized bed.

Other attractions at the ranch include the gourmet restaurant (see Where to Eat), outdoor pool, sauna, jacuzzi, a health spa, and, oh yeah, an 18-hole championship golf course (see Golfing). Complimentary breakfast is included. Reservations recommended. Open May 1 through Oct. 31 only. Located about 3 miles south of the great Sand Dunes National Monument entrance on Hwy. 150. **5303 Hwy. 150, Mosca, CO 81146; (719) 378-2356** or **1-800-284-9213**.

LA GARITA

Wild Iris Inn at La Garita Creek Ranch—$$ to $$$

One of the more remote, attractive and peaceful stays in the San Luis Valley has to be the Wild Iris Inn. Located at La Garita Creek Ranch, adjacent to the Rio Grande National Forest, the inn provides quick access for hiking, nearby rock climbing and mountain biking.

Jeff Wilkin, the manager, knows the area well and often leads guests on hikes. A tennis court, pool and hot tub provide activities if you don't want to leave the property.

Accommodations include the comfortable lodge, where country breakfasts are served each morning (free to guests). There are 8 rooms in the lodge, some with private bath. The "deluxe cabin" nearby is really a duplex; each unit comes with two queen beds, a private bath and a fireplace. The "family cabin" offers 2 bedrooms (3 queen beds), 2 baths, a kitchen and a woodburning stove. Located 10 miles north of Del Norte (3.5 miles soutwest of La Garita); **38145 Rd. E-39, Del Norte, CO 81132; (719) 754-2533.**

MONTE VISTA

Monte Villa Inn—$$ to $$$

Squeaky clean, Monte Villa Inn offers spotless (though somewhat drab) rooms for reasonable prices. Built in 1929, this restored, 40-room hotel features rooms with king-, queen- and double-sized beds, each room a little different in size and color. Be sure to ride the original cage elevator. Downstairs there is a breakfast room/dining room (see Where to Eat) and lounge. **925 First Ave., Monte Vista, CO 81144; (719) 852-5166.**

Movie Manor—$$

Ever enjoyed a drive-in movie from the comfort of your own motel room? We didn't think so. George Kelloff's Movie Manor is Americana gone crazy. "It's the only one of its kind in the world," George beamed. So unique is it that it was included in a PBS special. Two and a half miles west of Monte Vista, Kelloff's Drive-

In has been showing movies on its big screen since 1955. Back in the early days, when the Kelloff family lived over the snack bar, George and his wife would tuck the kids in and scoot their beds over to the window so they could see the movie. As George explained, "I started thinking, hey! Why not build a motel at the back of the drive-in so everybody can do this?" The rest is history.

The first addition of this two-story motel was completed in 1964 and has been added on to more than once since then. The rooms are comfortable (Best Western Motel), and every window looks out at the big screen. A speaker is built into the ceiling and it's free with the room. Unfortunately, double features ceased a few years ago because, as George put it, "The locals (watching the movies from their cars) got a little liquored up and this disturbed the guests." Movies are not shown in winter. There is also a lounge and a dining room on the premises. If unique is what you seek, look no further. **2830 W. Hwy. 160, Monte Vista, CO 81144; (719) 852-5921** or toll free at **1-800-528-1234.**

SAN LUIS

El Convento Bed & Breakfast— $$ to $$$

Built in 1905 as a school and then used as a convent, this building has recently undergone a complete restoration and is open for business as an intriguing new bed and breakfast. Under the direction of Father Pat Valdez of the Sangre de Cristo Catholic Church, *El Convento* ("the convent") offers four upstairs bedrooms with kiva fireplaces in two of the rooms. Thick adobe walls, 10-foot-high ceilings and handcarved furniture give the place a homey and roomy feel. Downstairs is Centro Artesano, where local artisans practice and sell their works. A delicious, homemade breakfast is served in the dining room each morning. For a quiet, slightly different overnight experience in the state's oldest town, try a night at El Convento. **512 Church Pl., San Luis, CO 81152; (719) 672-4223.**

CAMPING
In Rio Grande National Forest—
In the southwest section of the national forest there are a number of campgrounds. Forest Rd. 250, which is the major access road to this area, heads west along the Alamosa River 12 miles south of Monte Vista from Hwy. 15. Thirteen miles up Forest Rd. 250, just past Terrace Reservoir, is **Alamosa Campground** at 8,600 feet, with 10 sites and no fee. Another 21 miles up the road is **Stunner Campground** at 10,000 feet, with 10 sites and no fee charged.

From Antonito head west into Rio Grande National Forest on Hwy. 17 for 13 miles to **Mogote Campground** at 8,300 feet, with 41 sites (fee charged). Two miles farther west is **Aspen Glade Campground** with 34 sites and a fee. Six miles farther up Hwy. 17 is where Forest Rd. 250 heads off to the right (northwest), reaching **Elk Creek Campground** at 8,700 feet. There are 44 sites (16 without picnic table or fireplace), and a fee is charged. Five more miles up Forest Rd. 250 is **Spectacle Lake Campground**, with 24 sites and a fee charged. Another mile will take you to **Conejos Campground**, with 16 sites and a fee. **Lake Fork Campground** is yet another 9 miles up Forest Rd. 250. At 9,500 feet it has 19 sites and charges a fee. **Mix Lake Campground** at Platoro Reservoir is another 5.5 miles up the road. Boats are available. There are 22 sites, and a fee is charged.

Near the top of Cumbres Pass (about 35 miles west of Antonito on Hwy. 17), turn right onto the Trujillo Meadows Rd. and proceed about 4 miles to the **Trujillo Meadows Campground**. There are 50 sites; a fee is charged. Trujillo Meadows Reservoir has a boat ramp.

Two miles south of Monte Vista on Hwy. 15, and then right on Forest Rd. 265 for 13.5 miles, will lead you to **Rock Creek Campground** and **Comstock Campground**, offering 13 sites and 8 sites, respectively. No fee.

From the Del Norte Ranger Station, head about 9 miles west on Hwy. 160 and turn north on Embargo Creek Forest Access Road for 12 miles to **Cathedral Campground**; no fee.

Up in the northeastern part of the valley near Crestone is **North Crestone Campground**. There are 14 sites, and a fee is charged. From Crestone head 1.5 miles northeast on Forest Rd. 950. This is a great place to watch for bighorn sheep. They have been reintroduced to various parts of Rio Grande National Forest and are doing well. Look for them up on top of the rocky canyon walls.

Many of these National Forest campsites can be reserved in advance by calling **1-800-283-CAMP.**

Great Sand Dunes National Monument—
See Major Attractions.

Private Campgrounds—
Located 21 miles east of Alamosa on Hwy. 160, **Blanca RV Park** has 20 full hookup sites and 6 tent sites; showers and a laundromat also available. Located at the east end of Blanca; **(719) 379-3201.**

Located just outside the entrance to Great Sand Dunes National Monument, **Great Sand Dunes Oasis and RV Park** offers RV hookups, cabins, showers and other services, including four-wheel-drive trips into the monument. **Sand Dunes Rd., Hwy. 150; (719) 378-2222.**

———— WHERE TO EAT ————

ALAMOSA
True Grits—$$ to $$$
Somewhat of an institution in Alamosa, True Grits is THE place to go for a great steak. And the decor is what you'd expect: spacious, somewhat smoky and dark, country music in the background, brown wood everywhere and pictures of John Wayne staring at you from the walls. Along with nightly specials, the dinner menu continues the Wayne theme with the Sons of Katie Elder filet mignon, Rooster Cogburn

country fried steak, the Little Pilgrim childrens meals, etc. Lunch offers slightly lighter fare. Full bar with margaritas as the house specialty. This place does "The Duke" proud. Open 11 am–10 pm daily. Located at the corner of Hwys. 17 & 160. **100 Santa Fe Ave., (719) 589-9954.**

St. Ives Pub & Eatery—$ to $$

Most everything in this cafe and pub is as green as the Notre Dame leprechaun. Extremely popular, the St. Ives serves up fantastic burgers, sandwiches and salads. The atmosphere is open and airy with rough-hewn wood walls. A full bar features cable sports and there's an upstairs lounge in the back. Open 9 am–midnight Mon.–Sat., closed Sun. Located at **719 Main St.; (719) 589-0711.**

Bauer's Campus Pancake House and Restaurant—$

This is the breakfast hangout for the locals. There are no frills at the Campus— just good pancakes, waffles, gigantic cinnamon rolls and egg dishes smothered with green chili. If you are accustomed to saying grace before eating, you can choose from among three prayers printed on the menu. Locals meet for breakfast and sit around for an hour or two, chatting at their tables as the ceiling fans slowly rotate above. Discounts for seniors. Open daily 5 am–2 pm. **435 Poncha Ave., Alamosa; (719) 589-4202.**

El Charro Cafe—$

El Charro Cafe is a standout Mexican restaurant in an area with many to choose from. It's a small, intimate place with quick service. Neon lights around the windowsills, small orange booths and a jukebox are about the only adornments. You get the feeling from the food and the people who run the place that they really take pride in what they do and what they serve. For over 50 years Ike Lucero's family has run El Charro Cafe, and they have it down to a science. The chili rellenos are delicious and HOT! Also consider the chorizo Mexicano con huevos or an enchilada. Alcohol is not served here. For a margarita or a cold cerveza you'll have to look elsewhere. Hours are Sun. and Tues.–Thurs. 11 am–10 pm, Fri.–Sat. 11 am–2:30 am. **421 6th St., Alamosa; (719) 589-2262.**

CRESTONE
Road Kill Cafe—$

With what has to be one of the most unsavory restaurant names, the Road Kill Cafe follows the old Smucker's jam slogan: "With a name like that, it has to be good." And the food is. Located along the main street in Crestone, the Road Kill offers up standard but healthful fare made with fresh ingredients. The simple decor includes pine walls and floors with both counter and booth seating. You'll find the menu on the chalkboard; specialties include breakfast burritos, hamburgers, salads, soups and stews, and the chicken chili (not for the meek!). Be sure to save room for a slice of homemade pie. Open Wed.–Sun. 6:30 am– 6 pm, til 8 pm on Fri. and Sat. **115 S. Alder, Crestone, CO; (719) 256-4975.**

GRAND SAND DUNES
Great Sand Dunes Country Club & Inn—$$ to $$$

This restaurant, perhaps the finest in the San Luis Valley, is located in the refurbished Zapata Ranch house near the Great Sand Dunes National Monument. Part of a luxurious golf course and country inn (see Where to Stay), it features creative, healthy and delicious cuisine. The decor includes wood beams, a stone fireplace and southwestern art. Danish chef Charlotte Dudek, who used to cook for the Danish Ambassador, has created lunch and dinner dishes especially for the ranch. Charlotte uses as many local ingredients as possible, including local produce, grains (such as quinoa), trout and buffalo; produce also comes from the ranch's organically grown garden. Dinner items change nightly, but always include a bison dish, representing the finest of the ranch's herd. Be sure to try Charlotte's potato pancakes and one of her decadent desserts. For lunch you'll find sandwiches, salads, soups and, of course, bison-beer stew and a bisonburger. The full bar includes an American wine list and a nice choice of micro brewery beers. Reservations are a good idea. Lunch is served 11:30–2:30 pm, dinner 6–9 pm; limited bar menu served on and off 11 am–10 pm. **5303 Hwy. 150, Mosca, CO 81146; (719) 378-2356.**

MONTE VISTA
Monte Villa Inn—$$ to $$$

No one raves about the food here more than Doris Hunt, the owner. But she has good reason. Good steaks, Mexican food and fettucini are the highlights. The comfortable dining room is open year-round and usually has a number of locals eating (a telltale sign). Full bar. Open 5–9 pm Mon.–Sat.; at 6 pm in summer. The coffee shop ($ to $$) is open 6 am–5 pm. **925 First Ave., Monte Vista; (719) 852-5166.**

ROMEO
Abe's Cafe—$

Put a tune on the jukebox and enjoy an authentic Mexican meal at Abe's. On one side is a restaurant, on the other a bar (food is served at both). The menu is not fancy, but neither are the prices. Abe, a miner by trade, got into the restaurant business a number of years back. He's very easy-going and makes this an enjoyable alternative to eating in Alamosa. So play some pool, eat a couple of chili rellenos and relax. Open daily 9 am–10 pm. Sunflower mural on the outside of the building. **110 Main St., Romeo; (719) 843-9902.**

SAN LUIS
Emma's Hacienda—$ to $$

Keep in mind that even though you can count the places to eat in San Luis on

COLORADO PROFILE—PENITENTES

One of the most fascinating and mysterious sects of the Christian faith once thrived in southern Colorado, playing an integral part in the history and culture of the Hispanic communities. The Penitentes began as an offshoot of Catholicism in 13th-century Europe as a society honoring St. Francis of Assisi. Members practiced self-flagellation as a way to prove their devotion, but eventually the practice died out everywhere in Europe except for Spain. It is commonly believed that when the conquistadors came to New Mexico, the Penitentes (*los Hermanos*) came with them. Beginning about 1810 in the isolated communities of northern New Mexico, the Penitentes thrived and eventually spread north into southern Colorado. Since many of the small villages did not have a regular priest, the Penitentes filled a spiritual void and satisfied a desire for ritual.

Many men in the communities joined los Hermanos and met at their *moradas* or lodges. Self-torture was a part of their practice, but more important, the men quite often helped bind together the community, taking on charitable work that no one would do. The Penitentes continued to obey the Catholic church, adhering to all of its precepts except during Holy Week. During this time, the brothers dressed in black hoods and white breechcloths and re-enacted Christ's capture, trial and crucifixion. Whipping themselves with cactus leaves, they climbed a hill on which one of the members was tied (and, some say, even nailed) to a cross and left until he fainted. Because of the high number of injuries and the mock crucifixions, the Catholic church finally outlawed the Penitentes. The Penitentes did not disband, but instead became secretive and did not allow outsiders to visit their *moradas* or witness their rituals.

Well into the 1900s there were still hundreds of practicing *moradas* spread throughout southern Colorado. Today, however, these numbers have dwindled to just a few, but many deserted *moradas* can still be seen in and around the small Hispanic villages of southern Colorado.

one hand, Emma's standout Mexican food would get rave reviews no matter where it was located. In business since 1949, Emma still oversees the restaurant and personally takes orders. Menu notables include Emma's Special (a little of everything), enchiladas and the S.O.B. burger smoth-ered with green or red chili. Try a slice of homemade pie for dessert. It seems fitting that in this laid-back town the restaurant should keep nonspecific hours. But it's *usually* open for business 10 am–8 pm (how's that for vague?). **(719) 672-9902.**

SERVICES

Alamosa Chamber of Commerce—
This visitor center provides printed information and advice from the staff. **Cole Park, Alamosa, CO 81101; (719) 589-3681,** or call **1-800-BLU-SKYS.**

Del Norte Chamber of Commerce—
PO Box 148, 1160 Grand Ave., Del Norte, CO 81132; (719) 657-2845.

Monte Vista Chamber of Commerce—
1035 Park Ave., Monte Vista, CO 81144; (719) 852-2731.

San Luis Visitor Center—
PO Box 9, San Luis, CO 81152; (719) 672-3355.

South Park and 285 Corridor

At the center of Colorado, the high grassland basin of South Park and its surrounding peaks lies relatively undiscovered. Displaying its beauty in a different way than mountain resorts, the entire 30- by 40-mile park is virtually devoid of commercialism. Partly because of this lack of development, many people drive through South Park without slowing to enjoy the scenery and outdoor activities. You won't have a chance to be slowed by a stoplight either—there isn't one in the entire county.

Fairplay, the largest town in South Park, appeals to many with its obvious ties to history. At an elevation of almost 10,000 feet, this one-time gold mining camp is now home to only 450 permanent residents. Of particular interest is the South Park City Museum, a reconstructed 19th-century mining town. Some 30 buildings, containing more than 50,000 historic objects, were carted here from around Colorado. A new attraction at Fairplay is "The Beach." It's a great place to stop for the day and picnic, fish in a well-stocked lake, pan for gold or take a walk. Fairplay also has two historic hotels, several local restaurants and a patrol car with a very active radar gun (the speed limit is 25).

Around the perimeter of the park, the Mosquito, Park and Tarryall mountain ranges offer unlimited terrain for hiking, mountain biking and cross-country skiing. Hundreds of thousands of acres are set aside for public use in Pike National Forest, including Lost Creek Wilderness Area. The aspen-cloaked mountains are dotted with ghost towns and weathered remnants of gold mines; when exploring away from designated roads or trails, beware of open shafts and pits. At the base of several 14,000-foot peaks north of Fairplay, the Bristlecone Pine Scenic Area boasts 1,000-year-old trees growing in beautiful wind-twisted forms. Gushing tributaries from the surrounding mountains form the headwaters of the South Platte River, then find their way to the valley floor, which is laced with miles of streams and many reservoirs. Anglers consider these waters some of the finest in Colorado.

Hwy. 285 leads to South Park from Denver. Originally established by Ute Indians, this route has been used by covered wagons, the narrow-gauge Denver South Park & Pacific Railroad (DSP&P) and cars. Today this smooth, paved road plies a winding route past the communities of Bailey, Shawnee and Grant before angling southwest over Kenosha Pass (10,001 feet) and dropping into South Park. The area included in this chapter, from Bailey to the top of Kenosha Pass, we refer to as the 285 Corridor. This time-honored route follows the North Fork of the South

Platte River up through a pine-clad valley on its southwestern voyage. The memory of the far-reaching view into South Park from the summit of Kenosha Pass will stick with you for years.

HISTORY

Long before Spanish explorers came to South Park, Ute Indians were ensconced in the area. Plentiful game provided the Utes easy hunting for herds of deer, elk, antelope and buffalo. Other tribes learned about the fine hunting and came to South Park. Because the area was worth fighting for, frequent skirmishes erupted.

One notable battle, in the spring of 1852, was not the usual spontaneous ambush, but a carefully organized challenge for control over the park between the Utes and the Comanches. With a stream as the dividing line between the warring tribes, one tribe would be declared victorious if it could force the other back to a nearby ridge. Kit Carson witnessed the fight and very wisely decided not to take sides. Soon after the war cries sounded, blood started flowing and scalps were claimed. Volleys of arrows and hand-to-hand combat inflicted heavy losses on both tribes. After three exhausting days (both tribes would break for dinner and a night's rest), the Comanches managed to push the Utes back to the ridge. The Utes left after the fight but never fully relinquished South Park. It wasn't long, though, until the Anglo influx wrested control over the park from all tribes.

Trappers were attracted to the park, primarily for beaver but also for the boundless game. It wasn't until the gold rush in 1859 that settlement of towns began. In July of that year, a few straggling prospectors crossed Georgia Pass and started prospecting north of present-day Como at the north end of the park. Their gold pans revealed an exciting strike and, within two weeks, hundreds of prospectors were staking out claims. After only a couple of months, the town of Tarryall ("Let's tarry, all," said one early miner) was in place and all of the claims had been taken. Disgruntled late arrivals dubbed the town Graball and founded a new town called Fair Play on the banks of the South Platte River. Prospecting fell into a deep freeze with the arrival of winter. But by the summer of 1860, 11,000 miners were swarming over the surrounding hills and establishing gold camps with names like Buckskin Joe, Hamilton, Montgomery and Sacramento.

South Park was known to many as "Bayou Salado" because of its plentiful natural salt springs. In 1864 the Colorado Salt Works, located just north of Antero Junction on Hwy. 285, started evaporating brine into usable salt. To accomplish this task, the company imported 18 cast-iron kettles and heated them over a fire. When the saltworks were operating at capacity, 4,000 pounds of salt could be recovered in 24 hours. The salt was used primarily for refining gold ore, but it also found a place on many dinner tables. The saltworks operated successfully for three years until other suppliers came into the area.

Silver Heels is a name that conjures up images of South Park's heyday. As the legend goes, Silver Heels was the most beautiful woman ever seen at Buckskin Joe ... a dance-hall girl whose beauty went far beneath her skin, to the depths of her soul. When a terrible smallpox epidemic broke out, the people who had not contracted the disease left immediately. Silver Heels, however, stayed behind to help stricken miners, and eventually she too became sick. When the epidemic had run its course, she mysteriously disappeared. Many years later, a silent woman was seen visiting the cemetery in Alma, paying her respects to victims of the disease. She always wore a veil over her face, it was said, to hide pockmarks; the townsfolk seemed to know who the mystery lady was. Grateful miners honored her by naming the beautiful Mt. Silverheels (13,822 feet) in her memory, sometime before 1870.

By 1879 the Denver South Park & Pacific Railroad finally completed the route from Denver to Como. A tent city with more than a thousand residents sprang up at the Como terminus of the railroad, where a roundhouse was built. From Como people often transferred onto a stagecoach to complete the trip west over Mosquito Pass to the booming town of Leadville. Eventually the rail line was completed over Boreas Pass to Breckenridge and on to Leadville. In the 1880s Como became known for its coal reserves, and lumbering began in the vast forests around South Park. Ranchers fenced in the prime grazing land, and it wasn't long before large herds of sheep and cattle flourished.

The trains provided exciting weekend excursions for people from Denver as well as a means to move goods. But due to limited demand, the railroad was abandoned in 1938. Without the train Como began to decline, while the rest of the park remained aloof from much of the development happening in other parts of the state. With mixed blessings South Park remains a quiet place—much as it was decades ago.

GETTING THERE

The town of Fairplay, situated in the middle of South Park, is located 80 miles southwest of Denver on Hwy. 285.

FESTIVALS AND EVENTS

Burro Days
last weekend in July

You don't want to miss the "world championship" pack burro race. This fun event has contestants racing to the top of Mosquito Pass (13,188 ft.) and back to Fairplay. Determined men and women are pitted not only against the pass, but also against the iron wills of their burros. When the racers are out of town, you'll have time to concentrate on food booths and arts and crafts displays in town. The new pack llama race is a sign of the times. Stick around for a parade and dancing into the night. For more information contact **Park County Tourism Office, Box 220; (719) 836-4274; or PO Box 411, Fairplay, CO 80440.**

Mountain Man Rendezvous
summer

Modern-day mountain men converge on South Park each summer to hone skills such as ax throwing, black powder shooting and flint-knapping. In keeping with the mood of the early 1800s, participants wear heavy buckskin jackets instead of Gore-Tex, and sleep in primitive tents and tepees. A traders row completes the strange visual picture of the rendezvous. One thing is for sure, everyone involved seems to have a great time. Three rendezvous take place in South Park each summer: **Bayou Salado Rendezvous** in Fairplay, **(719) 481-4291; Rocky Mountain College Rendezvous** near Jefferson, **(303) 336-3647; Como Mountain Man Rendezvous,** call Booshway Jack Portice at **(719) 836-2403.**

OUTDOOR ACTIVITIES

BIKING
MOUNTAIN BIKING

With varied terrain in South Park and the surrounding mountains, this area attracts many mountain bikers. Since there are no places to rent bikes, though, you must bring your own. Mining roads and hiking trails provide hundreds of miles of possibilities throughout the area. Take a close look at the Four-Wheel-Drive Trips and Hiking and Backpacking sections for trail ideas. For more information contact the **South Park Ranger District Office** at the junction of Hwys. 285 and 9, **PO Box 219, Fairplay, CO 80440; (719) 836-2031.** Here are a few ideas to challenge all skill levels:

Buffalo Creek Area—

Just southeast of Bailey on County Rd. 68, this area has been designated as a national mountain bike trail system by the U.S. Forest Service. The area's 11 rides range from 1-10 miles in duration and provide an interesting mix of terrain. For more information about the rides, contact the **South Park Ranger District Office** in Fairplay; **(719) 836-2031.**

Fairplay State Snowmobile Trail System—

A good option for mountain bikers is to ply the routes taken by snowmobiles in winter. Virtually unknown outside of the local community, this 35-mile network of marked (look for orange diamonds) trails provides unique challenges at higher elevations (10,400 to 11,800 feet). Each of the seven rides on this network loops back around to a central starting point. The trail system is located 2.5 miles north of Fairplay on Forest Rd. 659 (Beaver Creek Rd.).

Boreas Pass/Georgia Pass Loop—

This popular and historic ride will challenge your stamina (see the Biking section of the **Summit County** chapter for information and directions).

TOURING

Many riders from Denver make the arduous (one could say dangerous) journey up narrow Hwy. 285 to South Park. The park itself is a wonderful, flat expanse, but it invariably seems as if you are working against a headwind.

DISABLED RECREATION

Wilderness on Wheels—

For people confined to wheelchairs, this is a totally accessible wilderness area designed for special needs. A mile-long, wooden boardwalk, wide enough to allow two wheelchairs to pass, has been constructed along the banks of Kenosha Creek. Campsites, prime fishing spots and a nature trail are just the beginning. Campsite reservations can be made by calling ahead; no fee is charged. Restroom and shower facilities are available. In addition, a 7-mile trail to the summit of Twin Peaks (12,300 feet) is currently in the works. Volunteer labor and donated lumber have made this excellent program possible. Many more hours are needed to complete ambitious future plans. For more information on the area and how you can help out, contact **7125 W. Jefferson Ave., Suite 155, Lakewood, CO 80235; (303) 988-2212.** Wilderness on Wheels is located 15 miles west of Bailey on Hwy. 285.

FISHING

Elevenmile Reservoir—

For catching trophy-sized trout, the reservoir at Elevenmile State Park, at the south end of the park, is an excellent choice. For specific fishing information, take a look at the Fishing section of the **Cripple Creek and Victor** chapter.

Jefferson Lake—

At the headwaters of Jefferson Creek northwest of Kenosha Pass, this popular lake provides quality fishing. Early and late in the day, fly-fishing for rainbows can be excellent from the northeast side. Many boaters ply the water for Mackinaw, brook and rainbow trout. Jefferson Lake receives heavy fishing pressure but is also frequently stocked. From the small town of Jefferson in the northwest corner of South Park, head

north and west on County Rd. 35. After a couple of miles, turn right (north) on County Rd. 37, which leads to the campgrounds and to the lake within Pike National Forest.

South Platte River—

Each fork of the South Platte offers a variety of fishing. The headwaters lie northwest of Fairplay in the Mosquito Range. Most of the land surrounding the South Platte as it runs through the park is private. (The best public fishing is actually in the Deckers area and below Cheesman Reservoir.) For some good public water closer to South Park, try fishing the Middle Fork of the South Platte above the Montgomery Reservoir inlet (on Hwy. 9 north of Fairplay). With the recent Division of Wildlife acquisition of 28 river miles above Hartsel, the Middle and South Forks of the South Platte River constitute the longest "Gold Medal" trout stream (40 miles) in the state. This means you'll have a much improved chance for catching big fish. The Middle Fork flows south from the reservoir to Fairplay between piles of river rock displaced by dredging operations, but can still be good for small rainbow and brown trout. The South Fork of the South Platte merges with the Middle Fork just above the town of Hartsel in the center of South Park, creating the South Platte River.

The North Fork of the South Platte flows east from Kenosha Pass toward Denver. Located right next to Hwy. 285, the river is heavily fished with fair results.

Spinney Mountain Reservoir—

This reservoir has only been open for public fishing since 1983, and those who appreciate feisty cutthroat trout keep returning. Spinney Mountain is famous for producing large trout, especially in the spring as ice recedes from the shoreline. You'll have to pay a small fee to fish the nitrogen-rich water of this state park. The South Fork of the South Platte fills the reservoir, and the land upstream from Spinney Mountain is now open to the public; downstream can be good, but it is closed from Sept. through Nov. On the north shore, a boat ramp and a small picnic area are available. From Fairplay, drive 23 miles south on Hwy. 9 to the entrance points.

Tarryall Creek—

On the east side of South Park, Tarryall Creek exits from Tarryall Reservoir. A challenging and often good stretch of water for brook and rainbow trout exists between the reservoir and Lake George. A few miles of water above the confluence with the South Platte are designated Wild Trout water. Though the creek is fairly narrow, the fish often grow to lunker sizes. To reach the creek from Jefferson (northeast corner of the park), take County Rd. 77 southeast for about 20 miles.

FOUR-WHEEL-DRIVE TRIPS

Mosquito Pass—

This classic four-wheel-drive road is the highest road over a pass in the North America. It leads west over the Mosquito Range to Leadville, through an area saturated in mining history. For details see the Four-Wheel-Drive Trips section of the **Leadville** chapter.

Webster Pass—

A narrow, rough road leads up beautiful Hall Valley from the east side of Kenosha Pass. After passing Handcart and Hall Valley campgrounds, the road gets extremely rough and steep as it heads through thick groves of aspen to the summit of Webster Pass (12,108 feet). Try this four-wheel-drive tour in autumn and you'll be treated to quite a show. On the opposite side of the pass, the former wagon road switchbacks down to Montezuma (see the **Summit County** chapter for more information). To reach the road from the town of Grant, drive 3 miles southwest on Hwy. 285. Turn right and head basically west on County Rd. 60.

HIKING AND BACKPACKING

The varied terrain of the mountains around South Park is perfect for long backpacking trips and short walkabouts. Miners have left traces of their work all around, but instead of appearing as ugly scars, the kingdom of abandoned mines and mining camps leaves the hiker with a profound sense of history. If you visit in fall, a barrage of colors, unequaled on Colorado's Eastern Slope of the Continental Divide, will make your backcountry experience even better. For more information on hiking and backpacking, including the Lost Creek Wilderness Area contact the **South Park Ranger District Office** at the junction of Hwys. 285 and 9, **PO Box 219, Fairplay, CO 80440; (719) 836-2031.**

Colorado Trail—

From South Park and the 285 corridor, it's easy to reach the Colorado Trail. The moderately steep trail offers hikes as long or short as you wish through beautiful and surprisingly uncrowded terrain. Plan a two- or three-day backpacking trip by leaving a vehicle at a prearranged point along the trail. A good access point lies just south of the town of Bailey on Forest Rd. 560 near Wellington Lake. Another easy place to start or stop a hike is at **Kenosha Pass Campground** on Hwy. 285. From Kenosha Pass the well-defined trail heads west past the **Jefferson Creek Recreation Area** and then over Georgia Pass toward Breckenridge. Several campgrounds are near the route; primitive camping can be done anywhere except in the Jefferson Creek area, where designated campgrounds are the rule.

Limber Grove Trail—

This nice 1-mile round-trip hike heads into the woods only to emerge on a rocky slope above treeline. The trail leads to one of the best areas for viewing gnarled bristlecone and limber pine groves. Some of the bristlecone trees date back 1,000 years, and the views of the Mosquito Range and South Park are tremendous. Limber Grove Trail begins at Horseshoe Campground (see the Camping section for directions).

Lost Creek Wilderness Area—

Within the Tarryall Range to the east

of South Park, the Lost Creek Wilderness Area offers spectacular scenery with easy access. The wilderness is known for its unearthly rock formations and grottos. As the name implies, the creek disappears for a mile or so as it works its way under a rocky hill. There's an excellent trail system, including a 25-mile loop, which circles through the southern section of the wilderness. Lost Creek is a very popular area and can get quite crowded in the summer. Since most of the trails are below 10,000 feet, you can hike in early spring and well into the fall. Here are a few of the trailheads.

From Hwy. 285, 1 mile northeast of Jefferson, turn east onto Lost Park Rd. (County Rd. 56). The dirt road leads to Lost Park Campground in 20 miles. The campground serves as a trailhead for the **Brookside-McCurdy Trail** (No. 607) and the **Wigwam Trail** (No. 609). Ranchers have grazing rights around this section of the wilderness, so you'll probably see some cattle. Be sure to purify your drinking water. Another trailhead can be reached by driving southeast from Jefferson on Tarryall Rd. (County Rd. 77) for about 20 miles to Tarryall Reservoir. Continue another 4 miles to the **Ute Creek Trail** on the left (northeast) side of the road. The trailhead is marked, and there is a parking area.

Perhaps the most popular access to the wilderness area is **Goose Creek Trail.** This section of the wilderness area features some of the most beautiful rock formations. Fishing for small trout along Lost Creek is not bad either. It can be reached by continuing about 16 miles southwest on County Rd. 77 from the Ute Creek Trailhead to Forest Rd. 211. Turn left (northeast) on Forest Rd. 211 and follow it 12 miles to Forest Rd. 558. Turn left and continue about 1 mile to the trailhead.

Mounts Democrat, Lincoln and Bross—

Bagging three 14ers in a long day of hiking is ambitious but entirely possible in the Mosquito Range towering just above Alma. And for that reason you will undoubtedly encounter many hikers in the area. The mountains' proximity and connecting saddles make it relatively easy to climb all three together. All in all, the elevation gain is about 3,600 feet on the 6-mile loop trail. Of course, hiking to the summit of the first mountain (14,148-foot Democrat) is enough for many hikers. The trail to Democrat leads northwest from Kite Lake, which is above treeline, passing some exposed mining shacks on the way to the summit. From the top, views to the Sawatch, Gore, Tenmile and Elk ranges are tremendous.

If you are still energetic enough to continue, walk back down to the saddle between Democrat and Lincoln. The trail leads 2 miles northeast to the summit of Lincoln (14,286 feet), passing Mt. Cameron along the way. Mt. Cameron is a mountain in its own right, but it's actually considered a part of Mt. Lincoln. From Lincoln head back down to Cameron and then hike 1 mile southeast to the broad summit of Mt. Bross (14,169 feet). Hiking down the scree slope from Bross to Kite Lake can be a bit tricky, but very doable.

To reach the trailhead from Fairplay, follow Hwy. 9 northwest for 7 miles to the town of Alma. In Alma turn left on Buckskin Gulch Rd. (County Rd. 8) that breaks away from Main St. across from the Texaco station. Follow the rough dirt road 7 miles up Buckskin Gulch to Kite Lake. Don't try this last bit in a passenger car if it has been raining. High-clearance vehicles are better suited to this road in all types of weather. The road passes many old mines along the way to the trailhead at Kite Lake.

HORSEBACK RIDING
Wade's Stables—

For an hourly ride on a meandering trail, pull off Hwy. 285, 2.5 miles west of Bailey; **(303) 838-7993.**

Western Safari Ranch—

A wide variety of rides, including pony rides for the kids, breakfast rides and overnight trips, can be arranged here. **PO Box 128, Fairplay, CO 80440; (719) 836-2431.**

SKIING

Fairplay is located on heavily used Hwy. 9, a half hour away from several popular Summit County ski areas. Many people blast through Fairplay without a second glance on their way to the slopes at Breckenridge, Keystone, Arapahoe Basin and Copper Mountain. Why not consider stopping off for a less-expensive night in Fairplay?

CROSS-COUNTRY SKIING

Many avid cross-country skiers are discovering the wealth of backcountry trails in the South Park area. With 20 kilometers of groomed trails at **Fairplay Nordic Center,** this is fast becoming a touring oasis. For more information on backcountry skiing, contact the **Park County Tourism Office** on Main St. in Fairplay at **(719) 836-4279,** or the **South Park Ranger District Office** in Fairplay at the intersection of Hwys. 285 and 9; **(719) 836-2031.**

Backcountry Trails—

Boreas Pass—Stretching between Como and Breckenridge, the Boreas Pass Rd. peaks out at 11,481 feet. It's a popular cross-country route. Follow the signs west from Como on County Rd. 33, and drive as far as the road is plowed before setting out on skis. Enjoy the great views of Mt. Silverheels along the way. Roads following the drainages of Taryall and North Taryall creeks branch off the main Boreas Pass route before reaching the high point of the pass. See the Skiing section of the **Summit County** chapter for more information on the west side of the pass.

Bristlecone Pine Scenic Area—This 7-mile round trip is a backcountry highlight. Allow about six hours round trip, over varied terrain, to complete this beautiful and historic tour. There is little avalanche danger as the trail follows a road to nearly 12,000 feet in elevation—a gain of 700 feet. The trail passes mining sites from the 1860s, ending on a ridge among bristlecone pine trees. To reach the trail from Fairplay, drive 7 miles northwest on Hwy. 9. Turn left (west) in Alma at the Texaco station and continue on the road for 3 miles to the Paris Mill. The road isn't plowed beyond this point—begin skiing here, taking the first road on the right (Windy Ridge Rd.) beyond the Paris Mill.

Tie Hack Trail—This 5.5-mile ski loop is well marked by forest service blazes. It follows a fairly difficult route that is best skied after a snowstorm. Tie Hack Trail is steeped in history: the trail follows an old stage road to the defunct mining camps of Sacramento and Horseshoe, passing through aspen groves and wide-open meadows. Several stretches of downhill cruising help make this a fun tour. By the way, tie hacks were men who cut timber and worked it into usable railroad ties. To reach the trailhead from Fairplay, drive south on Hwy. 285 for a quarter mile to County Rd. 18, marked by a Forest Access sign. Turn right (west) and drive 3.5 miles to the trail, which follows a jeep road from the right side of the road.

Groomed Trails—

Fairplay Nordic Center—Even though South Park can get very windy, the Fairplay Nordic Center enjoys a protected setting with 20 kilometers of groomed trails. In fact, it is on the lee side of a ridge and the wind sometimes drops powder on the trails, even on sunny days. This new center is experiencing rapid growth under the direction of its owner, Gary Nichols. Not only does the center offer touring lessons and rentals, but there is a series of lectures and seminars on relevant topics throughout the winter. This is a beautiful area of the state, so stretch out and try the trails before they become known to all. Ask about bed and breakfast ski packages. To get to the center, turn north on Fourth St. in Fairplay (at the Fairplay Country Store) and continue north for four blocks to Bogue St. Turn left and continue on a gravel road 1.8 miles. **PO Box 701, Fairplay, CO 80440; (719) 836-2658.**

Rentals and Information—

Fairplay Nordic Center—The only place to rent skis without having to go over Hoosier Pass. Talk with owner Gary Nichols about backcountry skiing routes and avalanche conditions (see entry under Groomed Trails).

SEEING AND DOING

MUSEUMS

South Park City—

South Park City puts history in context. More than 30 buildings from crumbling mining towns in the area have been moved to this central location where a period town—circa 1870–1900—has been re-created. Filled with room settings, dioramas and exhibits, this museum vividly shows how life was a century ago. South Park City has been open since 1959, attracting thousands of visitors each year. You'll see a simple trapper's cabin, a mercantile, the South Park Lager Beer Brewery, the old Bank of Alma and a stagestop from the top of Mosquito Pass. One display shows the heavy equipment used in hydraulic and hardrock mining; in front of the railway station lies a narrow-gauge engine with several cars and a caboose. A slide show on the history of South Park is shown daily on the half hour from 10:30 am to 3:30 pm at the stone brewery building.

After two fascinating hours of walking into creaky old buildings, we learned South Park City is anything but a tourist trap. Admission fee charged. Open May 15–Oct. 15: 9 am–7 pm Memorial Day – Labor Day; 9 am–5 pm from May 15–Memorial Day and from Labor Day–Oct. 15. Follow the signs from the center of Fairplay; (719) 836-2387.

SCENIC DRIVES

Boreas Pass/Hoosier Pass—

The connecting routes between the mines in South Park and Summit County provide both history and beauty. Hwy. 9 over Hoosier Pass can be taken right out of Fairplay to Breckenridge; Boreas Pass is a graded dirt road heading north from Como with spectacular scenery on the route to Breckenridge. For more information on Boreas Pass, see the Scenic Drives section of the **Summit County** chapter.

Bristlecone Pine Scenic Area—

This short drive leads into one of the few areas in Colorado where ancient, wind-twisted bristlecone pines can be seen. This type of tree is believed to be the world's oldest living thing—one tree in Nevada is thought to be 4,500 years old. New branches grow only on the leeward side of trees, as new buds are quickly blown off the windy side. The trees somehow survive at exposed elevations as high as 12,000 feet. This scenic area, at the foot of 14,169-foot Mt. Bross, can be seen from a car. From Fairplay drive 7 miles northwest on Hwy. 9. Turn left (west) in Alma at the Texaco station and continue up Buckskin Gulch until reaching a marked turn-off.

Guanella Pass—

For an exciting drive with a beautiful view of Mt. Bierstadt from the summit, head north on Guanella Pass Rd. from Hwy. 285 at Grant. This trip is a designated National Scenic and Historic Byway. For details see the Scenic Drives section of the **Georgetown** chapter.

Weston Pass—

This road, which crosses the Mosquito Range, can get pretty rough, but it should be OK in the family car. Originally an Indian trail, the road became a wagon route crossing the 11,945-foot pass in 1860. The road still provides exceptional scenery and colorful wildflowers during summer. On the west side of the pass, it descends south of Leadville. To reach Weston Pass Rd. from Fairplay, drive 5 miles south on Hwy. 285 to the marked turn-off. Take a right on County Rd. 22 and begin the odyssey.

WHERE TO STAY

ACCOMMODATIONS

Como Depot—$$

The restored Como Depot used to fill up with guests when the narrow-gauge train made its runs from Denver to South Park in the early 1900s. After the train stopped service, the hotel shut down until 1978, when it was reopened by Jo and Keith Hodges (Como's first going business in 25 years). Four upstairs rooms are simple, clean reminders of the past. One room, decorated in pastel blues, sleeps three to four guests and has a fireplace. All rooms share a bathroom down the hall, equipped with a claw-foot bathtub. It's nothing fancy, but this friendly place exudes the colorful history of Como. There are no TVs or telephones. The downstairs restaurant has an excellent reputation among locals in Como and Fairplay and is open from 8 am–8 pm daily, except Tues. (See the Where to Eat section.) For more information or reservations, contact **Como Depot, Box 648, Como, CO 80432; (719) 836-2594.**

Fairplay Hotel—$$

Twenty-six basic rooms are spread out on the upper floor of the historic Fairplay Hotel. About half of the rooms come with a private bathroom. There is a comfortable lobby area with couches situated around a stone mantel adorned with a huge elk trophy. One word of advice … unless you plan on staying up til 2 am, request a room that is not above the raucous Silver Heels Bar. **Box 639, 500 Main St., Fairplay, CO 80440; (719) 836-2565.**

Glen Isle Resort—$$

Since 1900 Glen Isle has been a rustic retreat. Now it has made its way onto the National Register of Historic Places. It is located halfway between Bailey and Grant on Hwy. 285. The first guests arrived on the narrow-gauge Denver, South Park and Pacific train. Thankfully, few changes have been made to the outward appearance of Glen Isle over the years. And the sure-fire hospitality of the owners is as strong as ever. A large doll and artifact collection adds to the character; don't miss the octagonal fish tank (made in 1875) in the dining room with live trout inside!

Cabins for two to eight people are available, as well as comfortable lodge rooms with a bathroom down the hall. During the summer season, Glen Isle operates as a resort with three meals a day (optional) and activities during the week. You may want to participate in the all-day picnic or the chuckwagon dinner and square dance. Kids love fishing in the private pond (an ice rink in winter), and the resort is hemmed in by plenty of national forest terrain. Though Glen Isle doesn't have any horses, you can rent by the hour at a stable a quarter mile up the road. For families this is a low-priced alternative to guest ranches; the minimum stay is two nights. Reserve early for summer visits, because by June most of the best times are taken. In winter the lodge and restaurant are closed, but the cabins remain open. Gordon and Barbara Tripp, **PO Box 128, Bailey, CO 80421; (303) 838-5461.**

CAMPING

In Pike National Forest—

Beginning on the east side of Kenosha Pass on Hwy. 285 at the town of Grant, take Guanella Pass Rd. (County Rd. 62) north. After 2.5 miles you'll reach **Whiteside Campground** (5 sites; no fee). Another 2.5 miles up the road is **Burning Bear Campground** (13 sites; fee charged). Continue 2 miles to reach **Geneva Park Campground** (26 sites; fee charged).

Take Hwy. 285 west of Grant for 3 miles to the Hall Valley turn-off. Head northwest on rough and narrow County Rd. 60 for 5 miles to reach **Handcart Campground** (10 sites; no fee). Virtually at the same point on the road is **Hall Valley Campground** (9 sites; fee charged). After the campgrounds this road gets even rougher as it leads over Webster Pass (see the Four-Wheel-Drive Trips section).

Popular **Kenosha Pass Campground** is at the top of Kenosha Pass on Hwy. 285, between Grant and Jefferson (25 sites; fee).

On Hwy. 285 west of Kenosha Pass, turn northwest on County Rd. 35 at Jefferson. Continue 2 miles and turn right (north) on County Rd. 37. After 1.5 miles you'll come to a succession of campgrounds. The first one is **Lodgepole Campground** (35 sites; fee charged), followed by **Aspen Campground** (12 sites; fee charged) and **Jefferson Creek Campground** (17 sites; fee charged). Bring your fishing pole along and try your luck at Jefferson Lake. If you continue on County Rd. 35 for 6 miles from Jefferson, you will reach **Michigan Creek Campground** (13 sites; fee charged).

From 1 mile northeast of Jefferson along Hwy. 285, head southeast on County Rd. 56 for about 20 miles. This will take you to the edge of the Lost Creek Wilderness Area and **Lost Park Campground** (10 sites; no fee). Back in Jefferson take County Rd. 77 south for approximately 30 miles to **Spruce Grove Campground** (28 sites; fee charged).

From Como, take Boreas Pass Rd. (County Rd. 33) northwest for 7 miles to a turn-off for **Selkirk Campground** (15 sites; no fee).

Beaver Creek Campground (3 sites; no fee) is located 4 miles north of Fairplay on Forest Rd. 659.

To reach **Kite Lake Campground** (7 sites; no fee) from Fairplay, follow Hwy. 9 northwest for 7 miles to Alma. In Alma turn left on an County Rd. 8 that breaks away from Main St. across from the Texaco station. Follow the rough dirt road 7 miles up Buckskin Gulch to Kite Lake, which is above treeline. The road is especially rough for the last mile. You may want to walk, unless you have a jeep.

From Fairplay you can easily reach **Fourmile** (14 sites; no fee) and **Horseshoe** (7 sites; no fee) **campgrounds**. Drive south on Hwy. 285 for 1.5 miles, turn right (west) on Forest Rd. 421 and continue for 7 miles.

Five miles south of Fairplay on Hwy. 285 is a turn-off for Weston Pass Rd. Turn right (southwest) and drive 11 miles to **Weston Pass Campground** (14 sites; no fee). Fifteen miles south of Fairplay on Hwy. 285, take a right turn (west on Forest Rd. 431) and drive for 0.5 miles to **Buffalo Springs Campground** (17 sites; no fee).

WHERE TO EAT

Como Depot—$ to $$$

Gather around the fireplace at this local favorite and enjoy a down-home meal. This historic hotel located in the town of Como has a relaxed setting and excellent food. The menu will satisfy your desires for anything from a simple quarter-pound hamburger to 14 ounces of prime rib or a salmon steak. Try their Mexican specialties. The Como Depot is also open for breakfast, offering pancakes, chicken-fried steak and eggs as well as sweet rolls. Open 8 am–8 pm daily except Tues. For information on staying at the Como Depot, see the Where to Stay section. Located in Como; **(719) 836-2594.**

Fairplay Hotel—$ to $$$

This has long been the restaurant of choice for a filling breakfast before heading out for a day of skiing. The cozy dining room of the hotel has a warm ambiance. It's open for all meals, but breakfast is the standout: omelettes, eggs, home fries and, especially, gigantic cinnamon rolls. For lunch try a burger, fried chicken or a bowl of homemade soup. Dinners include reasonably priced fish, chicken and beef dishes. For more information on the Fairplay Hotel, see the Where to Stay section. Open daily 7 am–9 pm Sun.–Thur., until 10 pm on Fri. and Sat. nights. (The restaurant closes one hour earlier in winter.) **500 Main St., Fairplay; (719) 836-2565.**

SERVICES

Park County Tourism Office—
Contact **Gary Nichols, PO Box 220, Fairplay, CO 80440; (719) 826-4279.**

═══ Upper Arkansas Valley ═══

Throughout the earlier years of its settlement, the Upper Arkansas Valley, stretching 45 miles north from Salida to the small town of Granite, hosted people "just passing through." Early on, wagon roads and rail lines crisscrossed the valley, providing routes over the Continental Divide to the west, over Poncha Pass to the south, across Trout Creek Pass to South Park and alongside the Arkansas River. Today things have changed—for a variety of reasons, the Upper Arkansas Valley has evolved into one of Colorado's best outdoors destinations.

The Arkansas River, one of the longest in North America, flows through the entire valley before entering Upper Arkansas Canyon on its way to the eastern plains at Pueblo. In recent years the river has attracted huge numbers of rafters and kayakers (well over 130,000 per year) who seek the thrill of shooting some great rapids. Runs through The Numbers and Browns Canyon have helped the Arkansas to become the most popular river floating area in the country!

Along the western edge of the valley, the lofty Sawatch mountain range angles skyward, providing a memorable view, especially to first-time visitors. More 14,000-foot peaks are packed into this small area than anywhere else in North America. The Sawatch, within San Isabel National Forest, offers fantastic recreational possibilities, especially if you like to climb peaks. Monarch, at the southern end of the range, is a fine small ski area.

Mining history can be relived by a visit to one of the many ghost towns in the region. Though some require a four-wheel-drive vehicle, many others can be reached in the family car. But the ghost towns are not the only places to get a sense of the Upper Arkansas Valley history. **Salida**, located in the southern end of the valley, still reflects its railroad legacy. The turn-of-the-century brick buildings in downtown Salida make up a very large National Historic District. This town of 4,600 residents, along with smaller **Buena Vista** (half of Salida's population), located 25 miles up-valley, offers the majority of accommodations, restaurants and other services. Though there is not a lot to do in Buena Vista (called "BYOONIE" by the locals), it does enjoy quick access to the adjacent Sawatch mountains and the put-in spots for the popular river runs on the Arkansas.

HISTORY

Before settlers entered the scene, the Upper Arkansas area was the domain of Indian tribes, especially the Utes. Semipermanent villages were occupied by the Utes along the Arkansas River near Buena Vista and, farther upriver, by the Comanche. When the Indians began using horses and could travel much farther to hunt, habitation in the valley declined. Lt. Zebulon Pike, who passed through the area in 1806, found an old Indian camp in which he believed 3,000 natives had once lived. By the time settlers entered the area in the 1860s, few Indian villages were in evidence, though curious, friendly Utes made occasional visits.

It was mining that first drew large numbers of settlers to the Upper Arkansas. In 1860 gold was discovered at Kelly's Bar near Granite, 20 miles upriver from Buena Vista. Eager to strike it rich, placer miners spread out along the Arkansas and up the side valleys and gulches. Though some decent mines were worked in the 1860s and 1870s, this area paled in comparison to strikes upriver at Oro City, near present-day Leadville. By the 1880s better roads and improved mining techniques contributed to successful mines throughout the area, including those up Clear Creek Canyon and Chalk Creek Canyon. Vibrant towns like Winfield, Vicksburg and St. Elmo grew and prospered along with the mines in these two canyons.

Meanwhile, down along the Arkansas River, hay farmers and ranchers moved in. By the end of the 1870s, cattle were grazing on most of the land throughout the valley. Buena Vista grew as a supply town for the mines and ranches, as well as a transportation center for those making their way upriver to Leadville (Oro City). By 1880 Buena Vista had grown large enough to be voted the new county seat. Townsfolk in Granite, the prior county seat, did not take kindly to the news, refusing to relinquish the county records. Buena Vista residents took matters into their own hands by sneaking into the courthouse in Granite late one night and stealing all the county records. The next day, county business went on as usual, but from Buena Vista.

The railroads finally came to the Upper Arkansas Valley in 1880, when Gen. Palmer's Denver & Rio Grande Railroad made its way upriver to South Arkansas (later named Salida). This town grew quickly as a rail hub and smelting and supply center, much to the consternation of residents of Cleora, a couple of miles downriver. Miffed that the Denver & Rio Grande did not choose their town as a rail center, the townsfolk fired off a protest letter to the governor in Denver. He quickly replied, "God Almighty made some townsites and Salida is one of them!" Though these words from the governor were not popular in Cleora, they settled things once and for all. From Salida the Denver & Rio Grande extended tracks up the valley through Buena Vista and on to Leadville. They also ran a line up Poncha Pass and over Marshall Pass to the Western Slope near Gunnison. Shortly thereafter, the Denver South Park & Pacific Railroad arrived in the valley. Its major achievement was the

Alpine Tunnel at the upper end of Chalk Creek, which was bored through the Continental Divide in a race with the Denver & Rio Grande to reach Gunnison. When the Colorado Midland Railroad reached the valley in 1887, both Salida and Buena Vista were rip-roaring towns. Buena Vista was especially rowdy, with 36 bars and a hanging judge, who was responsible for stringing up outlaws. Two of Colorado's most notorious madams operated in these towns. Cockeyed Liz ran her "Palace of Joy" in Buena Vista for years until marrying at the age of 40. Laura Evans, who lived to the ripe old age of 90, ran a bordello in Salida from 1896 until 1950.

With the demise of the mining industry and railroads, most area residents make their living ranching, farming or in tourism related businesses. The latter has become extremely important, especially with the incredible growth of commercial rafting on the mighty Arkansas River during summer months. Dedicated in 1990, the Arkansas Headwaters Recreation Area will help ensure that floaters, fishermen and other visitors to the valley can enjoy the river to its fullest.

GETTING THERE

Buena Vista is located 117 miles southwest of Denver via Hwy. 285. Another approach from the east is up the Arkansas River from Pueblo to Salida—a 97-mile trip on Hwy. 50 that includes a beautiful canyon section. Greyhound bus service is available to Salida.

———— FESTIVALS AND EVENTS ————

FIBArk
mid-June

FIBArk (meaning First In Boating on the Arkansas) brings many visitors to Salida for a long weekend of good fun. Music, craft booths, a bed race, a parade and many boat races provide the entertainment. The featured event is the 26-mile kayak race from Salida down to Cotopaxi, touted as the oldest and longest whitewater kayak race in North America. Some nuts even swim this stretch of the river! For more information write **FIBArk, PO Box 762, Salida, CO 81201; (719) 539-7254.**

——————— OUTDOOR ACTIVITIES ———————

BIKING
MOUNTAIN BIKING

The Upper Arkansas area has quickly become extremely popular among mountain biking. One reason for this is the diversity of terrain. Trails through the hills on the east side of the valley tend to be a bit more mellow than those that wind into the lofty Sawatch Range to the west. For maps and other trail ideas, visit the **Salida Ranger District Office, 325 W. Rainbow, Salida, CO 81201; (719) 539-3591.** You should also check with area visitor centers and bike shops.

Alpine Tunnel Trail—

For a scenic and relatively mellow ride up to the old Alpine Tunnel see the Tunnel Lake Trail write-up in the Hiking and Backpacking section.

Midland Trail—

This highly recommended intermediate trail runs for about 14 miles between Trout Creek Pass and the outskirts of Buena Vista. For the most part, the trail follows the grade of the defunct Midland Railroad. Along the way you'll see remnants of the railroad days and enjoy great views west to the Sawatch Range. If you choose to only travel one way, start at the Trout Creek Pass end. To reach the trailhead from Buena Vista, head east on Hwy. 285/24 for about 9 miles to County Rd. 309. Begin riding here. After 1.4 miles, turn left onto County Rd. 376.2. after about 3 more miles turn left onto Shields Gulch Rd. (County Rd. 315). Proceed for just over 2 miles and turn right onto the Midland Trail. After a few miles you'll hit a one lane road which you take west until you see the Barbara Whipple Trail on the left. This trail descends to the bridge over the Arkansas at Buena Vista's Recreational River Park.

Rainbow Trail—

Beginning up at the Continental Divide, southwest of Poncha Springs, the well-maintained Rainbow Trail (Trail No. 1336) stretches 100 miles along the north and east side of the Sangre de Cristo Range, ending in the Wet Mountain Valley. The trail travels through a wide variety of terrain from flat open meadows to steep, forested stretches. Many other side trails lead off from the main one, providing unlimited exploring if you're up for it. Access points to the trail are numerous; many lie along Hwy. 50, southeast of Poncha Springs. Visit the Forest Service office in Salida for maps.

Rentals and Information—

Capricorn Sports—Rentals, maps and information. **123 Main St., Salida; (719) 539-3971.**

Headwaters Outdoor Equipment—Rentals and excellent information about where to ride. **F St. and Bridge, Salida; (719) 4506.**

The Trailhead—Supplies trail ideas, maps and rental mountain bikes. **707 N. Hwy. 24, Buena Vista, CO 81211; (719) 395-8001.**

High Valley Center—Provides rental mountain bikes. **310 S. Main, Poncha Springs, CO 81242; (719) 539-6089.**

FISHING

For many years the Upper Arkansas Valley has been well known for its excellent fishing. Countless anglers have reeled in lunker browns and other trout from stretches along the Arkansas River. The multitude of streams and lakes in the mountains to the west has yielded ample numbers of smaller brookies, cutthroats and rainbows. Many of these can only be reached by hiking trail or four-wheel-drive road. Tributaries along the Arkansas and high lakes provide worthwhile fishing. If you plan to fish in the area, your best bet is to consult with locals for up-to-date information on where the fish are biting. **Homestead Sports Center, 444 Hwy. 50, Poncha Springs; (719) 539-7507** or **1-800-539-7507,** sells tackle and offers advice on good fishing spots. You might also try visiting the **Division of Wildlife Office** in Salida at **7405 Hwy. 50; (719) 539-3529.** Listed below are some of the better spots in the area.

Arkansas River—

The Arkansas is still one of the best spots to land a fat brown trout, especially during the spring caddis fly hatch. During this hatch, which usually lasts from three to four weeks, fly-fishermen should try the elk hair caddis. Snow runoff from mid-May through the end of July normally inhibits good fly-fishing, but you might try spin casting with a Mepps or Panther Martin. Also, those planning to fish during runoff should be warned that this is when the Arkansas is thick with rafters and kayakers. In August (or when the river flow finally drops below 600 c.p.s.) decent fly-fishing can return, with anglers successfully using black wooly buggers, pheasant tail nymphs and grasshopper patterns.

Generally speaking, the fishing on the Arkansas is good all the way from Granite down through Texas Creek. Although a fish kill back in 1988 affected the fishing along this stretch, rest assured that things are back to normal. Some of the better access spots include the lower section of Brown's Canyon (Hecla Junction), Ruby Mountain (via Fisherman's Bridge), and the 7.5-mile section from the bridge below Salida down to Badger Creek. This last spot is flies and lures only; fishermen can keep only two fish over 16 inches.

Clear Creek Reservoir—

Though the level of this 400-acre (when full) reservoir fluctuates greatly, making for inconsistent fishing, the Division of Wildlife stocks plenty of rainbows, browns and brookies. Fish from shore or launch a boat from the north shore ramp. Clear Creek Reservoir is located 16 miles north of Buena Vista on Hwy. 24 and then 1 mile west on Clear Creek Canyon Rd. (County Rd. 390). Upriver from the reservoir, above Winfield, four-wheel-drive vehicles and hikers can reach upper Clear Creek to fish for cutthroats.

Twin Lakes—

Home to huge Mackinaw and other trout. See the Fishing section in the **Leadville** chapter for information.

Cottonwood Lake—

Located off the Cottonwood Pass road, this small wooded lake at 9,600 feet offers bank fishing for rainbows up to two pounds. No motor boats allowed. Handicap fishing dock and trail. Head west from Buena Vista on County Rd. 306 for about 12 miles and turn left at the sign.

FOUR-WHEEL-DRIVE TRIPS

Aspen Ridge/Bassam Park—

Located in the rolling Arkansas Hills on the east side of the Arkansas River, this route runs 30 miles north/south between Buena Vista and Salida. With thick stands of aspen trees and occasional views west to the magnificent Sawatch Range, this drive wins our recommendation, especially in autumn. Much of the route, including the popular picnic area at Bassam Park, is accessible by regular passenger cars, but if you drive the entire way you'll need a four-wheel-drive vehicle.

To reach the road from Salida, head northwest on Hwy. 291, 1 mile past the traffic light at First and F streets. Turn right onto County Rd. 153, cross the river and turn right on County Rd. 175 (Ute Trail). About 7.5 miles from the highway, bear left onto County Rd. 185. After a while the aspen get thick. A few miles down the road you'll pass through Calumet, an old Colorado Fuel & Iron Co. town and mine. When you reach the intersection after 20 miles turn left and proceed 4 miles to Bassam Park, where it joins up with County Rd. 187. Keep going north on County Rd. 187 until reaching the junction with County Rd. 307 after a total of 29 miles. Turn left and proceed 1.4 miles to Hwy. 285/24 (at the Trout City Inn), about 7 miles east of Johnson Village.

Hayden Pass—

This challenging, punishing road crosses over the Sangre de Cristo Range, southeast of Salida, dropping into the upper San Luis Valley near the town of Villa Grove. The extremely rough road offers fairly decent views of the San Luis Valley and surrounding mountains, but trees obstruct the view from the summit. To reach the pass from Salida, drive southeast along Hwy. 50 for 20 miles to Coaldale and turn right on County Rd. 06. After 4 miles you'll reach Hayden Creek Campground. From here the road gets brutal and climbs sharply for 4 miles to the pass at 10,709 feet. From the pass descend into the San Luis Valley and continue to Villa Grove, along Hwy. 285 (about 7 miles from the summit of Hayden Pass). Return to Salida by turning right at Villa Grove on Hwy. 285.

Tincup Pass—

Stretching from St. Elmo over the Continental Divide to the ghost town of Tincup, this rugged road provides sweeping views from its 12,154-foot summit. To the west the West Elk Mountains are an impressive backdrop to Taylor Park. Before the Denver South Park & Pacific Railroad built the Alpine Tunnel under the divide, Tincup Pass was an important stagecoach and freight supply route for settlements such as Gunnison and Tincup on the Western Slope. To reach this road from St. Elmo, cross the bridge in town and turn left. Tincup Pass Rd. starts climbing through a thick aspen forest and eventually opens into an enormous bowl before reaching the pass 8 miles up the road. Enjoy the fantastic views from the summit, or take a 1.5-mile hike up 13,124 ft. Fitzpatrick Peak. From the summit descend about 7 miles, past Mirror Lake to Tincup. For information about Tincup, see the Scenic Drives section of the **Gunnison and Crested Butte** chapter. From Tincup an interesting return trip to the Upper Arkansas area is over Cottonwood Pass. Drive north from Tincup to Taylor Park Reservoir and then east over Cottonwood Pass to Buena Vista. For more information about Cottonwood Pass, see the Scenic Drives section.

Jeep Tours—

Fun Time Jeep Tours—Offers tours from one hour to all day. Located at the Little River Ranch Motel in Salida. **7870 W. Hwy. 50, Salida; (719) 539-7607** or **1-800-727-0525.**

GOLF

Collegiate Peaks Golf Course—

This nine-hole course offers great views of Mt. Princeton and other mountains in the Sawatch Range. Large cottonwood trees dot the course, with a creek and several small lakes coming into play. The fairways are in pretty rough shape. To reach the course from the center of Buena Vista, turn west at the stoplight and continue 1.3 miles. Turn right at the green-and-white sign for the golf course. **28775 Fairway Dr., PO Box 533, Buena Vista, CO 81211; (719) 395-8189.**

Salida Golf Club—

Built in the 1920s, the nine-hole course at the Salida Golf Club offers a challenging round to even the best golfers. With narrow fairways on many of the holes, accuracy is necessary to avoid the thick, troublesome roughs. The par three eighth hole is particularly difficult with a pond guarding its elevated green. West-facing tees provide wide views of the Sawatch Range (particularly Mt. Shavano). Located at the corner of **Crestone St. and Grant St.** in Salida; **(719) 539-6373.**

HIKING AND BACKPACKING

If you enjoy putting on a pack and getting out into the backcountry (especially high alpine country), the Upper Arkansas Valley region is for you. When you get your first glimpse of the towering Sawatch Range, you'll know why. There are many trails, from easy mile-long jaunts to long, steep ascents of 14,000-foot peaks. In the Upper Arkansas area, twelve 14ers are easily accessible, but not necessarily easy to climb. They are La Plata Peak, Huron Peak, Missouri Mountain, Mt. Belford, Mt. Tabeguache, Mt. Shavano, Mt. Antero and the Collegiate peaks—Oxford, Yale, Princeton, Harvard and Columbia. If you plan to hike in the high country, remember to get an early start to avoid frequent afternoon thunderstorms.

Information for many hiking trails can be obtained at the **Salida Ranger District Office, 325 W. Rainbow, Salida, CO 81201; (719) 539-3591.** Trail maps, equipment rental, information or whatever you need can be supplied by **Trailhead Ventures, 707 N. Hwy. 24, Buena Vista, CO 81211; (719) 395-8001.** Also try **Headwaters Outdoor Equipment** in Salida at F St. and the Bridge; **(719) 539-4506.**

Brown's Creek Trail (Mount Antero)—

This 11-mile trail begins in the valley at 9,000 feet and climbs west along Brown's Creek, eventually reaching the summit of 14,269-foot Mt. Antero. It provides outstanding scenery, from mountain meadows and spruce forests to the far-reaching views from the summit of Mt. Antero. Except for the final push up the peak, the trail climbs gradually. To reach the trailhead from Hwy. 285 between Buena Vista and Poncha Springs, head west on County Rd. 270 for 1.5 miles and then straight on County Rd. 272 for 2 miles. At the intersection turn left and proceed 1.5 miles to the trailhead.

A much shorter route up Mt. Antero can also be accessed via a four-wheel-drive road that begins on Chalk Creek Rd. (County Rd. 162). From Nathrop drive west up Chalk Creek about 11 miles and turn left on the Baldwin Gulch Rd. This rocky road takes you about 6 miles, up near the gem field, about a mile south of the Mt. Antero summit.

The Colorado Trail—

The 469-mile Colorado Trail, stretching from Denver to Durango, makes its way through the Upper Arkansas area, skirting the eastern edge of the Sawatch Range. Terrain varies from relatively low-altitude sections through ponderosa pine groves to high alpine meadows. Access to the trail is possible from numerous roads that head west from Hwy. 285 (between Poncha Pass and Buena Vista) and from Hwy. 24 (north of Buena Vista).

Fitzpatrick Peak—

A fairly steep 1.5-mile hike leads to the summit of this 13,124-foot peak, offering fantastic 360-degree views to most ranges in southern and central Colorado, including the far-off San Juans. The trail begins at the summit of Tincup Pass and heads off to the southwest where the summit of the peak is visible. For information about Tincup Pass, see the Four-Wheel-Drive section.

Mount Tabeguache/Mount Shavano Trail—

This fairly difficult day hike climbs up the southwest ridge of 14,155-foot Mt. Tabeguache and then follows a saddle over to the summit of 14,249-foot Mt. Shavano. On Shavano's east side, an unusual snow formation known as the "Angel of Shavano" is visible in May and early June, depending on the snowfall. Many legends exist concerning the "angel"—one explains that a mischievous Indian princess so angered the gods that they turned her into ice and put her on the mountain. When a drought struck the valley below, the princess redeemed herself by crying. Her tears became the melted snow, which ended the drought.

Begin the 5-mile hike to Tabeguache's summit by going north along Jennings Creek and then angling northeast to the ridge on Tabeguache's southwestern side. Follow the ridge up to the summit. Cross over to Shavano's summit and then return by traversing below the summit of Tabeguache. A topographical map is suggested for this hike. To reach the trailhead from Poncha Springs, drive west on Hwy. 50 for 6 miles and turn right onto County Rd. 240. Drive about 3.8 miles to Angel of Shavano Campground and continue 1.7 miles up the road to the trailhead at Jennings Creek.

Ptarmigan Lake Trail—

Beautiful Ptarmigan Lake is a popular destination for hikers. Fishing at the 11-acre lake has been very good for small cutthroats. Views of the surrounding peaks are perhaps the biggest attraction. The moderately difficult 3.3-mile trail begins at 10,670 feet and climbs to 12,132 feet. The Forest Service asks that you camp and collect firewood well away from the lake. To reach the trailhead from Buena Vista, drive about 14 miles west on Cottonwood Pass Rd. (County Rd. 306). The trailhead is on the left side of the road.

Rainbow Trail—

See the Biking section.

Tunnel Lake Trail—

This trail traverses the Continental Divide beginning at the east portal of the Alpine Tunnel (see the Scenic Drives section in the Gunnison and Crested Butte chapter for information). The 7.5-mile trail begins at the Hancock townsite, an old settlement that serviced area mines and housed Alpine Tunnel workers. Hike 3.5 miles along the old railroad grade to the caved-in portal of the Alpine Tunnel. This first section of the trail is very easy and provides great views of the surrounding valleys and mountains. On top of the tunnel (another half mile), the trail (No. 1439) heads north through alpine meadows and willow fields. The wildflowers in mid-summer are awesome! Alpine Lake can be seen below. The trail intersects Tincup Pass Rd., 4 miles above St. Elmo. To reach the trailhead, turn left (south) off of County Rd. 162 onto County Rd. 295 just before reaching St. Elmo. Continue about 5.5 miles to the ghost town of Hancock.

HORSEBACK RIDING

With a rich ranching history in the valley and a vast amount of nearby public land, horseback riding is very popular in this part of the state.

Gunn's Livery Stables—

Guided trail rides head into San Isabel National Forest, BLM land and the old Hutchison Homestead, one of the original ranches in the valley. Gunn's also features breakfast and dinner wagon rides, certainly a unique option to a cafe in town. Located just east of Poncha Springs at **5560 E. Hwy.**

50. PO Box 171, Poncha Springs, CO 81242; (719) 539-3213.

Horn Fork Guides—

Horn Fork is the company to contact if you're looking for an extended pack trip into the remote mountains of San Isabel National Forest. Fishing and hunting expeditions are their specialty. Contact Joe Boucher in Buena Vista at **(719) 395-2081.**

Mount Princeton Riding Stables—

Located up Chalk Creek Rd. above Mt. Princeton Hot Springs Resort, these folks offer trail rides up into the surrounding mountains of the Sawatch Range. **15870 County Rd. 162, Nathrop, CO 81236; (719) 395-6498.**

RIVER FLOATING

Of the many large rivers originating in Colorado, none is run by more rafters, kayakers and canoers than the Upper Arkansas River. Due to easy access and abundant stretches of rapids, the river receives heavy use. When the spring runoff begins, river rats flock to the area; scores of outfitters offer exciting float trips throughout the summer.

Upper Arkansas River—

Forty-seven miles of the Upper Arkansas, from Granite down to Salida, provide a full range of water. Running parallel to Hwy. 24 between Granite and Buena Vista, the infamous "Numbers" rapids, rated Class IV to Class V, are too treacherous for many river runners. This is perhaps the most technical stretch on the Arkansas. Below Buena Vista, at Ruby Mountain, boaters put in for the most popular river run in the state—Brown's Canyon. From Ruby Mountain, the first 2 miles are relatively mild until the river drops into the granite canyon. Boulder fields abound during low water; they are transformed into standing waves at high water. Most rafters and kayakers conclude this exciting section by taking out at Hecla Junction to avoid the nasty Seidel's Suckhole (a churning spot a half mile downriver that flips many boats). Below Seidel's Suckhole the river flows 12 miles to Salida, offering less hair-raising water.

Below Salida the river enters the narrow Arkansas River Canyon and eventually the exhilarating Royal Gorge, 44 miles downstream. Along the way are numerous put-ins and even a campground at Five Points (between Texas Creek and Parkdale). For information about this part of the river, see the River Floating section of the **Cañon City** chapter.

River users got a boost in 1990 with the dedication of the **Arkansas Headwaters Recreation Area** (AHRA). In the works for a number of years, AHRA represents a unique partnership between state and federal agencies that has helped beef up facilities and access along the river for recreational purposes. This linear park extends 148 miles, essentially from Leadville to Pueblo. Along the way you'll find numerous river access points, changing rooms, camping and picnic sites etc.

Boaters should check with AHRA for any requirements. Private property occupies 60 percent of the land along the river, so please respect landowners' rights. Maps of the river showing put-in and take-out spots are available at many river companies in the valley and at the chamber of commerce visitor centers in Salida and Buena Vista. For an excellent mile-by-mile description of the river including geology, wildlife and a compelling history, pick up the *Upper Arkansas River* by Frank Staub (Fulcrum, 1988). For more information contact the **Arkansas Headwaters Recreation Area** office at **PO Box 126, Salida, CO 81201; (719) 539-7289.**

Outfitters—

Almost 100 licensed commercial river outfitters run the Upper Arkansas River; you can't help but run across them if you're anywhere near the river. The outfitters vary in quality and type of service provided. The following are a few of the most reputable businesses in the area. For a more complete listing, consider contacting the **Colorado River Outfitters Association** at PO Box 1622, Buena Vista, CO 81211.

American Adventure Expeditions—Located in Johnson Village, 2 miles south of Buena Vista, American Adventure Expeditions offers anything from half-day trips to overnighters on the Arkansas. Their expeditions include runs down all major sections of the Upper Arkansas River. **PO Box 1549, 12844 E. Hwy. 24/285, Buena Vista, CO 81211; 1-800-288-0675.**

Arkansas Valley Expeditions—Billy Mansheim has been running the Arkansas longer than most other outfitters in the area. He specializes in exciting day trips with an emphasis on having a good time. Take a float on relatively calm water or more challenging runs through the Numbers, Brown's Canyon and the Royal Gorge. For a first time on the river, these folks are highly recommended. **(719) 539-6669** or toll free at **1-800-833-RAFT.**

Dvorak's Kayak & Rafting Expeditions—One of the longest operating outfitters in Colorado, Dvorak's specializes in expedition-type boating. In addition to trips down the Arkansas, they run extended trips on other major rivers in Colorado (including the Gunnison and Dolores rivers) and in other states. Fishing expeditions and kayak lessons offered as well. **17921-A Hwy. 285, Nathrop, CO 81236; (719) 539-6851** or **1-800-824-3795** toll free.

Moondance River Expeditions—These folks offer moonlight floats and quarter-day to five-day trips down the Arkansas. Their trips are more suited for people looking for a rafting vacation and an outdoorsy/camping experience. Unique to Moondance are their Russian paddle-catamarans ... ask for information. Contact Nonny and Bear Dyer at **310 W. First St., Salida, CO 81201; (719) 539-2113.**

ROCKHOUNDING

Attention geologists and weekend rockhounds! Rock formations in the Upper Arkansas River area yield a fairly diverse assortment of minerals and gems.

Armed with rock hammers, hordes of people scour the mountains and valleys each year, but plenty of specimens still lie unclaimed. Be sure to stay off private land unless you have permission from the landowner. Two popular places to look are Mt. Antero and Ruby Mountain. For information on these and other spots, check with the **Greater Buena Vista Area Chamber of Commerce Visitors Center** (see Services).

SKIING
CROSS-COUNTRY SKIING

Although snowmobiles compete for many of the area's trails, you can find secluded areas away from the whine of their engines. Valley locals and the San Isabel National Forest Headquarters have done plenty to accommodate cross-country skiers by marking trails and providing services in the towns. For avalanche information, maps, etc., contact the **Salida Ranger District Office, 325 W. Rainbow, Salida, CO 81201; (719) 539-3591** or **The Trailhead, 707 N. Hwy. 24, PO Box 2023, Buena Vista, CO 81211; (719) 395-8001.**

Backcountry Trails—
Cottonwood Pass Road—From the trailhead near Rainbow Lake follow the easy grade of Cottonwood Pass Rd. for 10 miles to the summit at 12,126 feet on the Continental Divide. Pine and aspen line the road up to treeline. On a clear day you'll have views west to Taylor Park, the Elk Mountains and other mountain ranges. To reach the trailhead from Buena Vista, head west on County Rd. 306 for about 9 miles to where the plowing ends just past Rainbow Lake at the Avalanche parking lot.

Old Monarch Pass Road—Located just west of the Monarch Ski Area on Hwy. 50, Old Monarch Pass Rd. takes off to the right. The first 1.5 miles to the summit have set tracks. From the summit of the pass, take time to enjoy the views of the surrounding mountains. The trail descends to the west for 7 miles through pine forests. Be sure to save enough energy for the return trip.

Tincup Pass Road—The road up to the summit of Tincup Pass at 12,154 feet makes a fantastic ski trip, but it can receive heavy snowmobile traffic on weekends. This intermediate trail starts at St. Elmo. Cross the bridge over Chalk Creek, turn left and begin skiing up the trail through the trees. It's steep for the first half mile but gradually mellows for the remaining 7.5 miles to the summit. To reach the trailhead from Buena Vista, drive south on Hwy. 285 for about 10 miles and turn right on Chalk Creek Rd. (County Rd. 162). Drive about 15 miles to St. Elmo.

Groomed Trails—
Monarch Ski Area—For no charge, you are welcome to ski a number of groomed trails at Monarch Ski Area. The nearby Old Monarch Pass Rd. is also groomed for 1.5 miles to its summit on the Continental Divide. Rentals and cross-country lessons are available. To reach the ski area from Salida, drive west on Hwy. 50 for 21 miles.

Rentals and Information—
Trailhead Ventures—This shop rents everything from telemark skis to gaiters. **707 N. Hwy. 24, PO Box 2023, Buena Vista, CO 81211; (719) 395-8001.**

Monarch Ski Area—The shop at the ski area rents cross-country and telemark equipment. **(719) 539-3573.**

DOWNHILL SKIING
Monarch Ski Area—

Major ski magazines and other national ski area reviewers have long sung the praises of Monarch. Located along the Continental Divide near the summit of Monarch Pass, the ski mountain is a natural. A basin traps more than 350 inches of light, fluffy powder snow each winter—who needs snowmaking machines? The runs are laid out so you can practically reach any one of the four lifts from any place on the mountain. A major attraction here is Monarch's diversity of terrain—beginners, intermediate skiers and experts can find challenging runs from the top of all the lifts. This is especially appealing to families: one parent can take the kids down an easy bunny slope while the other hits the mogul run; everyone can meet at the bottom for another ride up the lift. Although the vertical drop is only 1,100 feet, you'll get as much skiing in (if not more) than at a much larger area. Monarch's appeal to many skiers is its laid-back atmosphere. Lift-ticket rates are reasonable to boot. Diehard powder hounds with extra cash to spend may want to investigate the Great Divide Snow Tours which provide excellent backcountry skiing via snowcat.

The day lodge at the base offers a cafeteria and the Sidewinder Saloon for après ski. Day care, ski school and rentals are also available. Three miles down the road you can stay at the reasonably priced Monarch Mountain Lodge (see the Where to Stay section). Located 16 miles west of Poncha Springs on Hwy. 50. **#1 Powder Place, Monarch, CO 81227-1100; 1-800-332-3668** or **(719) 539-2581.**

SWIMMING

Salida Hot Springs—
See the **Hot Springs** section.

TENNIS

Centennial Park Courts—
In Salida there are four courts at Centennial Park, next to the Chamber of Commerce Visitors Center. Reservations are not taken.

Town Park Court—
One court is located in the park on the west side of Hwy. 24 at the traffic light in Buena Vista. Just show up and play.

--------- SEEING AND DOING ---------

FISH HATCHERY

Mt. Shavano Trout Hatchery and Rearing Unit—
Those who enjoy aquariums will love this sizeable trout hatchery—where else can you see a million fish at one time? Annually, the facility hatches six million eggs of species such as rainbow, brown, brook and cutthroat trout, kokanee salmon and arctic grayling. After raising the fish to stocking size, they are transferred to other facilities or released in rivers, streams, lakes and reservoirs around the state. Many of these fish end up in southeastern Colorado waterways. That doesn't include, of course, the elusive Colorado fur-bearing trout of the high mountain streams. Open daily 8 am–4:30 pm. Located 1/2 mile northwest of Salida on Hwy. 291. **7725 County Rd. 154, Salida, CO 81201; (719) 539-6877.**

HOT SPRINGS

Mount Princeton Hot Springs Resort—
Don't miss a soak in one of the two large swimming pools or one of many rock pools down along Chalk Creek. Suits required. Open 9 am–10 pm Sun.–Thurs.; 9 am–midnight Fri. and Sat. For additional information see the Where to Stay section.

Salida Hot Springs—
Hot mineral water is piped from 8 miles away to Salida Hot Springs Pool, the largest indoor hot springs pool in Colorado. Built as a WPA project in 1937, this well-maintained facility is worth a stop. Take a swim in the 25-meter lap pool or a hot soak in the 18-inch wading pool or 4-foot-deep shallow pool. Private hot tubs are available for an additional charge. Summer hours: Mon.–Sun. 12–9 pm. Winter hours: Tues.–Fri. 4–9 pm and Sat.–Sun. 1:30–9 pm. Located next to the **Chamber of Commerce** at **Centennial Park. 410 W. Rainbow Blvd., Salida, CO 81201; (719) 539-6738.**

MUSEUMS

Buena Vista Heritage Museum—
Located in the old Chaffee County Courthouse, built in 1882, this museum features period clothing displays, a school-

room and a mining and ranch room with a number of historical artifacts. Railroad buffs will be particularly interested in the scale layout of historic valley sites and the three major narrow-gauge railroads that chugged their way through the Upper Arkansas Valley in the 1880s. Rotating art exhibits offered throughout the summer months. Open daily Memorial Day–Labor Day, 9 am–5 pm. Fee charged. **511 E. Main St., Buena Vista; (719) 395-8458.**

Salida Museum—

The Salida Museum is packed with the usual mining, railroad, pioneer and Indian artifacts as well as the unusual. Displayed prominently is a horse-skin coat made by an early Salida resident after his favorite horse died—what a tribute! It's worth a visit. Open Memorial Day–Labor Day, 11 am–7 pm. Small fee charged. Located next to the Chamber of Commerce at **406 W. Rainbow Blvd.**

Winfield School Museum—

If you drive up Clear Creek Canyon to the ghost town of Winfield, visit the museum located in the old school building. Old worn desks and other memorabilia are on display. Maintained by the Clear Creek Canyon Historical Society. Open in summer only. To reach Winfield from Buena Vista, drive 16 miles north on Hwy. 24 to Clear Creek Canyon Rd. (County Rd. 390) and turn left. Drive about 13 miles. No fee charged.

NIGHTLIFE

You must be kidding. For the most part, sidewalks roll up by 9 pm in Buena Vista and Salida throughout the year. During the ski season Monarch Lodge and the lounge at Monarch Ski Area are hopping. Here are a couple of places to try in Salida:

Powerhouse Players—

Since 1990, the Powerhouse Players have been delighting audiences with their melodramas, performed at the old Salida Steam Plant Building. Each performance starts off with a singalong and concludes with a musical revue. Shows run from late June–August; Mon.–Sat. at 8 pm and 2 pm matinee. For information and tickets, contact **PO Box 1317, 200 W. Sackett, Salida, CO 81201; (719) 539-2455.**

Victoria Hotel & Tavern—

Very popular among Salida locals, the Vic is a great place to unwind and listen to live rock and blues music. Open Sun. noon–midnight, Mon.–Sat. noon–2 am. **143 N. F St., Salida; (719) 539-4891.**

SCENIC DRIVES

Clear Creek Canyon Road—

A drive up Clear Creek Canyon is highly recommended for its beautiful scenery and history. Beginning in 1867, prospectors made their way up this canyon and surrounding gulches while looking for gold and silver. Known as the La Plata Mining District, many successful mines led to the founding of a number of settlements, including Beaver City, Vicksburg and Winfield, by the 1880s. The largest of these towns was **Winfield**, which had a population of more than 1,500 by 1890. Today quite a few buildings remain at these sites—many are used as summer homes. Winfield Cemetery serves as the final resting place for more than 25 of the early residents, many of whom died from gunfights, avalanches, fire and lightning.

Clear Creek Canyon serves as a jumping-off point for trails up many of the 14,000-foot peaks in the area, including Mt. Oxford, Mt. Belford and Missouri Mountain. To reach the road from Buena Vista, drive about 16 miles north on Hwy. 24 and turn left on County Rd. 390. A few cabins remain at Vicksburg, 8 miles up the road. You'll reach Winfield in another 4 miles.

Cottonwood Pass—

Before Independence Pass Rd. was built, the route over 12,126-foot Cottonwood Pass served as a vital supply link not only to the mining camps of Tincup and Pitkin in Taylor Park on the west side of the Continental Divide, but also to Ashcroft and Aspen via Taylor Pass (see the **Gunnison and Crested**

Butte chapter). Built as a toll road in 1880, the road (paved to the summit) climbs through pine forests, aspen groves and eventually into alpine tundra where wildflowers, especially columbine, can be seen flourishing into mid-August.

Be sure to stop on the summit for great views in all directions, especially west down to Taylor Park and north to the Three Apostles. There is good camping along the way, with plenty of side roads to explore. Cottonwood Pass Rd. (closed in winter) can be easily driven in a regular car.

To reach the pass from Buena Vista, head west for 28 miles up Cottonwood Creek on County Rd. 306. From the summit continue down the west side 12 miles to Taylor Park Reservoir. At the reservoir return to Buena Vista along the same route or via Gunnison or Tincup (see the Four-Wheel-Drive section) and Cumberland Pass, eventually heading back east over Monarch Pass on Hwy. 285.

Marshall Pass—

See the Scenic Drives section of the **Gunnison and Crested Butte** chapter.

Midland Tunnels Road—

If you are heading north from Buena Vista, consider taking a scenic alternative to Hwy. 24. This road parallels the Arkansas River on the east side for about 10 miles before rejoining Hwy. 24. From the stoplight in Buena Vista, head east on Main St. for a couple of blocks and turn left at the Colorado Transportation Department building. This road takes you north out of town. You'll drive through a series of four rock tunnels, blasted out of the mountainside over 100 years ago by the Colorado Midland Railroad. Since the Denver & Rio Grande already had its tracks laid down by the river, the Colorado Midland had no alternative but to blast the tunnels through this narrow section of the valley. A local claims this was the only stretch of railroad track on which one train could be in four tunnels at once. After making your way through the tunnels, be on the lookout for Elephant Rock, which is hard to miss.

St. Elmo—

St. Elmo is the typical Old West ghost town. Weathered false-front buildings line the main street, resembling a Western movie set. Originally settled in 1880, St. Elmo served as a supply center and hell-raising Sat. night town for the mines around the area. The biggest mine, the Mary Murphy, produced millions in gold until closing in 1926. In 1881 the Denver South Park & Pacific Railroad started construction of the Alpine Tunnel just a few miles above town (for information see the Scenic Drives section of the **Gunnison and Crested Butte** chapter). By the mid-1880s, St. Elmo was home to more than 2,000 residents, but by 1890 its inevitable decline began. A fire in 1890 destroyed the two main blocks in town, including the post office. The postmaster valiantly saved the mail from going up in flames but was harassed for failing to rescue the liquor and cigar supply.

To reach St. Elmo from Nathrop (8 miles south of Buena Vista), head west up Chalk Creek on County Rd. 162. St. Elmo lies about 15 miles up the valley. Along the way you'll notice the white Chalk Cliffs to the right on the south side of Mt. Princeton. A popular legend claims that Spanish conquistadors stashed two bags of gold and silver at the base of the cliffs while being chased by Indians. Many treasure hunters have lost their lives over the years climbing these limestone cliffs looking for the booty. Keep your eyes peeled for the herd of bighorn sheep that is frequently spotted near the cliffs. The scenery is especially striking when the aspen turn colors in fall.

TRAMWAY

Monarch Aerial Tramway—

Take a ride up to an observation tower on the Continental Divide for incredible views of the surrounding Colorado mountain ranges. The experience is a bit sedentary but at least your lungs can get a workout at 12,000 feet. Located near the summit of Monarch Pass, the tram runs from May 15–Oct. 15; open daily 9 am–5 pm. From Poncha Springs drive west on Hwy. 50 for 16 miles. Call **(719) 539-4789.**

WHERE TO STAY

ACCOMMODATIONS

Although the Upper Arkansas area lends itself to the outdoors and camping, a number of unique lodging opportunities have popped up, including interesting bed and breakfasts. If in Salida, you may want to check out **Castillo de Caballeros ($$ to $$$)** with its 37 acres adjacent to the National Forest; **PO Box 89, 6720 Paradise Rd., Salida, CO 81201; (719) 539-2002.** Or try the **Gazebo Country Inn ($$ to $$$)**, an attractive Victorian home near the downtown area; **507 E. 3rd, Salida, CO 81201; (719) 539-7806. The Thomas House ($$ to $$$)** provides affordable B&B accommodations in Salida as well; **307 E. 1st, Salida, CO 81201; (719) 539-7104.** In addition, many motels line the main streets, especially in Buena Vista and Salida. The following are what we consider to be the valley standouts.

Monarch Mountain Lodge—$$$

Located just 3 miles down the road from Monarch Ski Area, Monarch Mountain Lodge offers comfortable year-round accommodations. Each of the 100 rooms has modern furnishings, a bathroom and a TV. If you want to cook your own meals, choose one of the 16 rooms that come with a kitchenette. Balconies look out to the South Arkansas River and the surrounding forest (if you get a room on the south side). Recent renovations to the lodge have added bunk beds for student groups and numerous cosmetic flourishes, including shutters and Bavarian window boxes.

The lodge's additional features include an excellent fitness center with Nautilus machines, tennis and racquetball courts, a heated pool, jacuzzi and sauna. There's also a restaurant and lounge. Free shuttle buses run between the lodge and ski area in winter. Located in Garfield, 13 miles west of Poncha Springs on **Hwy. 50 West, Monarch, CO 81227; 1-800-332-3668.**

Mount Princeton Hot Springs Resort—$$$

Sandwiched between Mt. Princeton and Mt. Antero along Chalk Creek Gulch, this resort has three outstanding features: comfortable accommodations, pretty good dining and, of course, hot springs pools. Early settlers wasted no time in constructing bath houses by the 1870s. Improvements continued, climaxing with the completion of the imposing Antero Hotel in 1917. This elegant four-story resort, with its large veranda, served as host to the rich and famous until the stock market crash of 1929 prompted a slow decline. A newer lodge has since been built featuring nine rooms in the main lodge and 40 spacious, modern motel units just across the road.

The biggest draw at the lodge are its hot springs, including three large outdoor swimming pools, a couple of private indoor hot tubs and numerous rock pools down by the creek. The rock pools were built in 1987 by a group of 70 guests who stayed at the resort for a week during the Harmonic Convergence. All guests of the lodge have free use of the hot springs; a reasonable fee is charged to others.

The restaurant in the main lodge with its expansive outdoor deck is popular with locals (see the Where to Eat section). From Buena Vista drive south on Hwy. 24/285 to Nathrop and turn west on County Rd. 162. Proceed 5 miles to the lodge. **15870 County Rd. 162, Nathrop, CO 81236; (719) 395-2447.**

Streamside Bed and Breakfast—$$$

Location, location, location ... it certainly figures significantly at this quaint B&B located up Chalk Creek Rd. on the way to St. Elmo. Denny and Kathy Claveau offer three comfortable rooms (private baths and queen beds) and streamside lounging as well as a fine breakfast served each morning. Your hosts love the outdoors and are eager to help you choose a perfect day hike or cross-country ski trip. Since Denny works at the Monarch Ski School, he may steer you toward the slopes as well. **18820 County Rd. 162, Nathrop, CO 81236; (719) 395-2553.**

The Adobe Inn—$$ to $$$

The Adobe Inn looks a bit out of place in Buena Vista; its distinct Southwestern style is something you'd expect to find in Santa Fe. Paul and Marjorie Knox remodeled this old building and it barely resembles its former self. A solarium with Mexican tiles, a large adobe fireplace and southern-facing windows make for a cozy place to relax and read or chat with other guests. Three guest rooms, each with a private bath, represent the cultures of the Southwest. In an adjacent house, the tastefully furnished Wicker and Mediterranean suites provide additional sleeping space for larger groups. Breakfast is served each morning, quite often including eggs with chili, fruit and coffee or Mexican hot chocolate.

You may also want to get into the Southwestern spirit by eating lunch or dinner at the Knoxes—excellent Casa del Sol restaurant, located adjacent to the inn (see Where to Eat). **303 N. Hwy. 24, PO Box 1560, Buena Vista, CO 81211; (719) 395-6340.**

Vista Court—$$ to $$$

The cluster of cabins that comprise Vista Court allows for privacy at a reasonable price. Each of the eight cabins has a private bath, kitchenette and cable TV. Four of the cabins have two bedrooms. The recently built lodge with its southwestern motif features 5 rooms with private baths and a great railed in porch for kicking back. Relax in the jacuzzi on the front lawn while looking off at Mt. Princeton. The current owners, Ginger and Grover Horst, have put extensive work into the place and are eager to make your stay enjoyable. A good lodging choice any time of year; great for kids. Located a half mile west of the traffic light in Buena Vista on Main St. **1004 W. Main St., PO Box 3056, Buena Vista, CO 81211; (719) 395-6557.**

The Poor Farm Country Inn— $$ to $$$

When the Chaffee County Poor Farm was built in 1892, little did anyone know that one day visitors would flock happily to its doors (or that it would achieve a listing on the National Historic Register). Until 1945 the Poor Farm provided housing to those who were out of both luck and money. The current owners, Herb and Dottie Hostetler, first saw the three-story brick structure in 1982, when they decided to buy it and turn it into a bed and breakfast. What a task that was. The building had been abandoned for 20 years and was a mess—the front room on the main floor had even been used as a chicken coop!

The second floor has five separate bedrooms (two with private baths). Up on the third floor, 12 dorm-style bunks provide inexpensive accommodations for individuals and groups on a budget. Downstairs a library and TV room is open to guests. Gather round the breakfast table for fruit, coffee or tea and Dottie's special Belgian waffles. The Poor Farm sits in the country outside of Salida with fantastic views west to the Sawatch Range. An added feature for anglers ... The Poor Farm offers private fishing on their stretch of the Arkansas River, with public water on either side. Call ahead for directions and reservations. Children under 5 stay free. **8495 County Rd. 160, Salida, CO 81201; (719) 539-3818.**

Trout City Inn—$$

Some people take their history very seriously—Juel and Irene Kjeldsen, the owners of the Trout City Inn, are two examples. At a spot near the summit of Trout Creek Pass, about 10 miles east of Buena Vista, their unique inn sits where the Denver South Park & Pacific Narrow Gauge Railroad had a station, water tank and Western Union telegraph office in the 1880s. Today the Kjeldsens have reconstructed the station and offer four guest rooms, including two within the train cars that sit out back. The Pullman car is decorated with velvet curtains, Persian rugs and brass-trimmed lights and mirror, and have pull-down pullman beds; the less formal caboose provides a great kids' room. Victorian decor and antiques can be found in the depot, where a full breakfast is served each morning by the hosts dressed in period costumes. The Trout City Inn also features a trout stream and a westerly view to Mt. Princeton, perfectly framed by the valley walls. Stay here if you want a dose of history as well as suggestions for day trips around the valley. Open June–mid-Sept. Located about 8 miles southeast of Buena vista on Hwy. 24/285 at the County Rd. 307 turn-off. **Box 431, Hwy. 24/285, Buena Vista, CO 81211; (719) 395-8433** in summer, **(719) 495-0348** in winter.

CAMPING

The vast majority of visitors to the Upper Arkansas Valley choose to camp out. Plenty of campgrounds in San Isabel National Forest as well as private campgrounds meet these needs. Although you should be able to find a spot at one of the National Forest campgrounds, reservations can be made at most of them (at least 10 days in advance) by calling at **1-800-283-CAMP.**

Arkansas Headwaters Recreation Area—

About 9 miles north of Poncha Springs on Hwy. 285, turn right (east) on County Rd. 194 and proceed about 3 miles to **Hecla Junction**, along the Arkansas River. This is a popular take-out spot for rafters and kayakers coming out of Brown's Canyon. There are a number of campsites. Fee charged.

About 5.7 miles south of Buena Vista on Hwy. 285, turn left at Fisherman's Bridge, drive a half mile, turn right and proceed another 2.5 miles to **Ruby Mountain**. This scenic spot down along the Arkansas River offers a number of campsites as well as put-ins for floats down through Brown's Canyon. Fee charged. For reservations (at least three days in advance) call **(303) 470-1144** in Denver or **1-800-678-CAMP.**

In San Isabel National Forest—

Driving 7 miles west from Buena Vista along Cottonwood Pass Rd. (County Rd. 306) and then south on County Rd. 344 leads to **Cottonwood Lake Campground.** Located along the shores of beautiful Cottonwood Lake, this campground offers 28 sites; a fee is charged. Another 4 miles west on Cottonwood Pass Rd. leads to **Collegiate Peaks Campground,** with 56 sites; a fee is charged.

From Nathrop (8 miles south of Buena Vista on Hwy. 285), Chalk Creek Rd. (County Rd. 162) heads west to four campgrounds; all charge a fee. Driving 7 miles up Chalk Creek Rd. leads to **Mt. Princeton Campground** with 17 sites. Another mile up the road is **Chalk Lake Campground** with 21 sites. Still another mile up the road is **Cascade Campground** with 23 sites. **Iron City Campground,** located 15 miles west of Nathrop on County Rd. 162, offers 17 sites.

Heading west from Poncha Springs on Hwy. 50 toward Monarch Pass will take you to four more campgrounds. Six miles west of Poncha Springs at Maysville, turn right on County Rd. 240 and proceed 4 miles to **Angel of Shavano Campground** with 20 sites; a fee is charged. Another 6 miles up County Rd. 240 is **North Fork Reservoir Campground** with 8 sites and no fee. Thirteen miles west of Poncha Springs on Hwy. 50 is **Garfield Campground** with 11 sites; a fee is charged. Another 2 miles west on Hwy. 50 brings you to **Monarch Park Campground** with 38 sites; a fee is charged.

O'Haver Lake Campground, located southwest of Poncha Springs, has 30 sites; a fee is charged. To reach the campground from Poncha Springs, head south on Hwy. 285 for 5 miles and turn right (west) on County Rd. 200 for 2.3 miles and then right on County Rd. 202 for 1.5 miles. Handicap accessible.

About 20 miles east of Salida on Hwy. 50 and right (southwest) for 3 miles on County Rd. 06 leads to **Coaldale Campground.** It offers 11 sites and no fee is charged. One mile farther up County Rd. 06 is **Hayden Creek Campground** with 11 sites and no fee.

If you just want to primitive camp on National Forest land, drive up Clear Creek

Canyon Rd. (County Rd. 390). To reach the road from Buena Vista, head north on Hwy. 24 for about 16 miles and turn left on County Rd. 390 toward Clear Creek Reservoir. Along the road, which continues 12 miles to Winfield, there are plenty of places to camp.

Private Campgrounds—

Buena Vista Family Campground and Resort—Located 2.5 miles southeast of Buena Vista on Hwy. 24, this well-equipped (though a bit arid) RV campground offers, among other things, a large recreation room and free movies nightly. "Yuppies" not welcome. Tent sites are also available. **27700 County Rd. 303, Buena Vista, CO 81211; (719) 395-8318.**

Four Seasons Campground—Amenities include a laundromat. Tent sites are available as well as hookups for RVs. Located 1.5 miles east of Salida. **4305 E. Hwy. 50, Salida, CO 81201; (719) 539-3084 or 539-9950.**

Heart of the Rockies Campground—Heart of the Rockies offers plenty of RV sites, many with full hookups. Tent sites available down by the river. Heated swimming pool, groceries, other activities. Located 5 miles west of Poncha Springs on Hwy. 50. **16105 Hwy. 50, Salida, CO 81201; 1-800-496-2245 or (719) 539-4051.**

Little River Ranch Motel Campground—Along the Little Arkansas River in Salida, seven wooded acres await. RV hookups (32) include water and electricity. Tent sites also available. Amenities include indoor jacuzzi, showers, trout ponds, etc. Twelve motel rooms ($$) with cable TV are also available. **7870 W. Hwy. 50, Salida, CO 81201; (719) 539-7607 or 1-800-727-0525.**

WHERE TO EAT

Casa del Sol—$$ to $$$

Most weekend hikers, river rafters, hunters and other frequent travelers through Buena Vista eventually discover the outstanding cuisine at Casa del Sol. Since 1974 Jeff Knox and his parents have been offering unusual and select dishes from various areas of Mexico. Even after so many years in the business, Jeff's enthusiasm and creativity show through in both his conversation and cuisine. Everything is made from scratch with prime ingredients, including red chili from the Espanola Valley of New Mexico and dark chili from Mexico. Dinners in this intimate spot feature such standards as rellenos and chicken enchiladas as well as specialties like chicken mole and shrimp quesadillas. Salad and soup come with dinner. If possible, try lunch on the attractive outdoor patio. Desserts also deserve special mention, especially the rum butter nut cake. No booze. Reservations in summer are a good idea. Lunch served 11:30 am–3 pm, dinner 4:30–9:30 pm. Open daily May–Oct. and on weekends in winter. **303 N. Hwy. 24, Buena Vista; (719) 395-8810.**

Grimo's—$$ to $$$

Grimo's recently opted to remove its rowdy bar area and concentrate on a small, romantic atmosphere for their tasty Italian food. The change works well. Hand-hewn wood beams, red table cloths and a number of other nice touches add greatly to the meal. Start off with a glass of wine. Veal, chicken and pasta dishes dominate the menu. In addition to baked eggplant parmigiana, Grimo's specialties include pesto dishes, veal and chicken marsala and Steak Sinatra, named in honor of "Ol' Blue Eyes." Dinners come with homemade soup and a trip to the salad bar. Open Tues.–Sat. 4–9 pm; 4–8 pm on Sun. **146 S. Main, Hwy. 285, Poncha Springs** located at the junction of 285 & 50; **(719) 539-2903.**

Delaney's Depot—$ to $$$

Conspicuously located along Hwy. 24 in Buena Vista, Delaney's does a booming business. Large portions of down-home food and the fast service keep the place packed with locals and vacationers stopping in for a quick bite. In keeping with its railroad theme, a train whistle blows when orders are ready in the kitchen. You'll find the breakfast items fairly standard, except for the "whistle stopper" steak and egg plate. A salad bar is available for lunch and dinner to go along with burgers, soups, ribs, steaks, chicken and fish. Open daily in summer 7 am–9 pm; in winter Delaney's closes one hour earlier. **605 Hwy. 24, Buena Vista, CO; (719) 395-8854.**

First Street Cafe—$ to $$$

A bit off the main drag, the First St. Cafe is worth a stop whether you want a meal or a freshly ground cup of coffee. Located in one of the oldest brick buildings in Salida's historic downtown section, the cafe is decorated with plants and latticed wood paneling. For breakfast try stuffed French toast, a breakfast burrito, an omelette or quiche. Lunch is the most popular meal here for salad bar, sandwiches and stir-fry. Dinners feature steaks, lemon garlic chicken and grilled trout topped with almonds. Great beer selection. Open in summer Mon.–Sat. 8 am–10 pm and on Sun from 11 am–4 pm; in winter Mon.–Thur. 8 am–7 pm and Fri.–Sat. 8 am–10 pm. **137 E. First St., Salida; (719) 539-4759.**

Gourmet Chef—$ to $$$

Although most Salida locals said the Gourmet Chef served the best Chinese food in the area, we were skeptical. After all, it serves the only Chinese food in the valley. But after eating there, we have to agree—it is good and reasonably priced. Located along Hwy. 50 in Salida, the Gourmet Chef is owned and operated by a Taiwanese family, and they know what they're doing. Along with a bar, the dining area has booths, tables and subdued lighting. Lunch specials are offered; main dishes include specialties from many different regions of the Chinese mainland. Open Mon.–Sat. 11 am–9:30 pm for lunch and dinner, and Sun. 5–9:30 pm for dinner (closed Sun. in winter). **710 Milford St., Salida; (719) 539-6600.**

Princeton Club Restaurant & Lounge—$ to $$$

Although the food is good, the Princeton Club's main attraction has to be its attractive dining environment and sweeping views. Located in the main lodge at Mt. Princeton Hot Springs Resort, the restaurant is accented by a large stone fireplace and local artwork hanging on the walls. Large picture windows provide views west to the Chalk Cliffs of Mt. Princeton. In summer months you can now enjoy meals on the immense two-level outside deck. Breakfast items include omelettes, spicy huevos rancheros and eggs bayou. Sandwiches and salads are featured for lunch. The Princeton Club's limited dinner menu focuses mainly on steaks. You might want to take a soak in the hot springs while you're here. Open 7 am–9 pm nightly; bar open til 10 pm (11 pm on weekends). From Buena Vista, drive south on Hwy. 24/285 to Nathrop and turn west on County Rd. 162. Drive about 5 miles to the lodge. **15870 County Rd. 162, Nathrop, CO 81236; (719) 395-2447.**

The Windmill—$ to $$$

When you first step into this false-front building, you'll think you're in an old country store. Knickknacks, including dozens of old signs, line the weathered wood walls. The building used to house a Ford car dealership, so there is plenty of room. Burgers, specialty salads and Tex-Mex dishes are lunch highlights. For dinner try a rib-eye steak or the popular chicken-fried steak. Soup, salad bar and potato come with all dinners. The Windmill has a good selection of beer and a separate bar area. Open 11 am–10 pm daily. **720 E. Hwy. 50, Salida; (719) 539-3594.**

Country Bounty—$ to $$

The consistently full parking lot at Country Bounty is no fluke. Located prominently along Hwy. 50 in Salida, this place serves up enormous portions of down-home cooking. The lengthy menu includes a full spectrum of standout dishes such as traditional breakfast items (like biscuits and gravy), homemade soups, burgers, chicken-fried steak and on and on. Those of you on a diet, consider yourselves warned: Country Bounty is famous for its homemade pies, including such specialties as Rocky Road and banana meringue. As it should be, the servers are extremely friendly and efficient. You may want to browse the gift shop that occupies a large portion of the interior floor space. Open 6 am–8 pm daily. **413 W. Rainbow Blvd. (Hwy. 50), Salida; (719) 539-3546.**

——— SERVICES ———

Greater Buena Vista Area Chamber of Commerce Visitor Center—
343 S. Hwy. 24, PO Box 2021, Buena Vista, CO 81211; (719) 395-6612.

Heart of the Rockies Chamber of Commerce—
406 W. Rainbow Blvd., Salida, CO 81201; (719) 539-2068.

Wet Mountain Valley

Though the phrase "off the beaten path" gets too much use these days, it does seem appropriate when describing the Wet Mountain Valley. This beautiful, remote location in the southern part of the state, wedged between the Wet Mountains to the east and the jagged peaks of the Sangre de Cristo Range to the west, remains unknown among many Coloradans. Quite a few people, however, find the valley by accident and end up returning by design. The surrounding San Isabel National Forest gets year-round use by fishermen, horseback riders, cross-country skiers and hikers. Steep trails into the Sangre de Cristos on the western side of the valley lead along many streams and to high alpine lakes. Some of the state's most rugged 14,000-foot peaks, including Crestone Needle, await those who want a difficult climbing challenge.

Though cattle ranching and farming are the mainstays, it was the silver boom in the late 1800s that attracted thousands of folks to the valley. Today Silver Cliff, the dominant mining town during the boom days, and nearby Westcliffe, the original rail town in the valley, are the supply centers providing the few services the area has to offer. Although all-important tourism is making its impact, many locals cherish the lack of development, doing whatever it takes to eke out a living. Many artistic, individualistic people are attracted here by the beauty and the simple, unadorned lifestyle that prevails. One local told us his biggest problem was the noise a herd of elk made while bugling out in his front yard. We should all have such problems.

HISTORY

Along with documented facts, many legends animate the early history of the valley. One, concerning a lost gold mine, has turned out to be partially true. Spanish conquistadors, while exploring the region from their territory to the south, discovered a deep cave located high on a mountain in the valley, which they used as a repository. The cave's entrance was reportedly marked with a Maltese Cross. In the late 1920s the existence of the cave was officially confirmed. Now known as Marble Cave or "La Caverna del Oro," it is located high up on Marble Mountain, southwest of Westcliffe. A number of speleologists have explored the vertical shafts, finding evidence of mining but, so far, no gold.

Ute Indians who inhabited the Wet Mountain Valley came into contact with trappers in the first half of the 1800s, but nothing changed much until the 1870s. In 1870 a group of 400 German immigrants arrived in the valley to establish Colfax, an ill-fated agricultural co-op, about 7 miles south of present-day Westcliffe. As it turned out, many of the colonists did not find communal living to their liking. On top of that, the cows ate garlic, which ruined the cheese! Within a few years many members of the group had left the valley; those remaining split up the land and started farming and cattle ranching.

About the time of Colfax's demise, interest of a much larger magnitude focused on the valley—the silver mining boom. In the winter of 1872–1873, Richard Irwin discovered rich silver deposits, and the rush was on to the new camp Rosita. For a short time, Rosita received recognition for being what the *Pueblo Chieftain* called "the liveliest mining town in the territory." Aside from another strike at Querida in 1877, the valley's real glory days began when horn silver was discovered in 1878—these chunks of black, greasy rock from a nearby cliff melted down to 75 percent silver. Thousands poured into the area and established the town of Silver Cliff. And what a town it was! Many considered it to rival the booming town of Leadville. When the decision was to be made concerning the location of the state capital, Silver Cliff was in the running along with Denver and Golden.

Hopes soared for the town in 1881 when the Denver & Rio Grande Railroad announced plans to lay tracks from Cañon City up Grape Creek to the area. But, much to the irritation of Silver Cliff residents, the train tracks stopped a mile from town—and as it had done so many other times throughout the state, the Denver & Rio Grande built its own community. Westcliffe became more important than Silver Cliff. When mining activity waned, prosperity in the valley took a sharp downturn and the Denver & Rio Grande Railroad discontinued service. Ranching and farming then became the dominant industries. When the Denver & Rio Grande Railroad laid tracks to the valley again in 1900, development and prosperity seemed a sure thing. But alas, the Denver & Rio Grande Railroad continued to lose money and ended service to Westcliffe in 1937, this time for good.

Today cattle ranching and hay farming are very important to the area's economy, as is slowly increasing tourism.

GETTING THERE

Westcliffe is located 150 miles southwest of Denver. From Denver drive south on Interstate 25 to Colorado Springs and take Hwy. 115 from the south end of town. Drive to Florence and head south on Hwy. 67 and then west on Hwy. 96.

FESTIVALS AND EVENTS

Rainbow Trail Round-Up Mountain Bike Race
mid-August

Among serious mountain bike racers, this race is considered one of the finest of its kind. Riders take off from the starting line in Westcliffe for a grueling loop ride south on the Rainbow Trail. For information about entering the race, contact the **Westcliffe Chamber of Commerce** at **(719) 783-9163.**

Jazz in the Sangres
second weekend in August

Come to Wet Mountain Valley for a weekend of great jazz performed by some of the best musicians in the Rocky Mountain West, including some nationally known performers. Styles range from fusion to blues to big band. This festival, which got its start in 1984, has been developing quite a reputa-tion among jazz lovers in the region. But you don't have to be a jazz lover to have a good time in this spectacular setting. Shows run during the day Sat. and Sun.; on Fri. night performers appear at local restaurants and bars. Make sure to book accommodations well in advance of the festival, unless you want to camp out. For information contact **PO Box 327, Westcliffe, CO 81252; (719) 783-2626 or 783-9163.**

——— OUTDOOR ACTIVITIES ———

BIKING
MOUNTAIN BIKING

Wet Mountain Valley offers many places to explore on a mountain bike. On the west side of the valley, jeep roads and na-tional forest trails are everywhere. Unfortu-nately, there are no rental shops in the area. For information about trail possibilities, in-quire locally and refer to the Hiking and Backpacking and Scenic Drives sections.

FISHING

It's not exactly a fisherman's paradise but many worthwhile fishing spots can be found in the Wet Mountain Valley area. Streams running down out of the Sangre de Cristos are, for the most part, steep and fast-moving. Most people have luck fish-ing the beaver ponds along smaller tribu-taries. For tackle and (if you're lucky) some advice about where the fish are biting, stop in at **Ace Valley Hardware** in Westcliffe.

Hermit Lake/Horseshoe Lake—
See Hermit Pass in the Four-Wheel-Drive Trips section.

Lakes of the Clouds—
To reach three lakes at an 11,200-foot elevation, you'll need a four-wheel-drive vehicle to get within a couple of miles or else you'll be in for a 5-mile hike. Below the lakes are beaver ponds that yield brook and cut-throat trout. The upper lake offers good rainbow and cutthroat fishing; the lower lake has mostly cutthroat. Don't bother with the middle lake because it's too shallow and often has winterkill. To reach the lakes from Westcliffe, head north on Hwy. 69 for about a mile and turn left on County Rd. 170. Proceed about 8 miles. From here either continue in your jeep or start hiking.

Lake Isabel—
Lake Isabel, heavily stocked with rain-bow and brook trout, is accessible by car. There are also a few browns in the lake that grow up to 15 pounds. A boat ramp is available. Many people try their luck ice fishing here in winter. To reach the lake from Westcliffe, drive east on Hwy. 96 and turn south on Hwy. 165 for 25 miles. The lake is on the right side of the road.

Middle Taylor Creek—
See Hermit Pass in the Four-Wheel-Drive Trips section.

FOUR-WHEEL-DRIVE TRIPS
Hermit Pass—
From the 13,000-foot summit of this road high in the Sangre de Cristo Range, you'll have beautiful views of the expan-sive San Luis Valley to the west and Wet Mountain Valley to the east. The road trav-els up Middle Taylor Creek past beaver dams, Hermit Lake and Horseshoe Lake; all provide decent fishing for brook, rain-bow and cutthroat trout. To reach the road from Westcliffe, head west on Hermit Lake Rd. (County Road 160) and keep going.

Medano Pass—
Once a route used by the Indians and even a few Spanish conquistadors, 9,950-

foot Medano Pass Rd. is a spectacular way to cross the Sangre de Cristos. From the summit of the pass, the road drops 6 miles along Medano Creek to **Great Sand Dunes National Monument** (see the Major Attractions section of the **San Luis Valley** chapter). When you reach the dunes, it's a 4-mile drive to the visitors center. You may want to let some air out of your tires to help you drive across the sand; refill at the air hose available at the monument's campground. To reach Medano Pass from Westcliffe, drive south on Hwy. 69 for 24 miles and turn right (west) on County Rd. 17. The summit of the pass is 9 miles west of Hwy. 69. Allow at least two hours for the trip.

HIKING AND BACKPACKING

Although Wet Mountain Valley remains undiscovered by many Colorado residents, it's fairly well known among active hikers and backpackers, especially those who like steep, challenging terrain. The Sangre de Cristo Range, which runs along the western edge of the valley, matches any mountain range in the state for rugged, high-altitude hikes—Crestone Needle, Crestone, Humboldt and Kit Carson peaks all top out above 14,000 feet. Among them, only Humboldt is considered a fairly easy climb; the other three have claimed their share of lives over the years. This eastern slope of the Sangre de Cristo Range, and much of the rolling Wet Mountains on the east edge of the valley, lie within **San Isabel National Forest**. Many well-marked trails crisscross the forests and valleys, but you should take along a good topographical map. For more specific information about trails in San Isabel National Forest, check with the **San Carlos Ranger District Office, 326 Dozier Ave., Cañon City, CO 81212; (719) 275-4119.**

Comanche/Venable Loop Trail—

Although this trail can get crowded in summer, the beauty of the area makes it worth trying. The fairly difficult, 10.5-mile loop begins at Alvarado Campground. Start the hike up the Comanche Trail (No. 1345). You'll climb steeply through the pine and aspen, eventually paralleling Hiltman Creek up to Comanche Lake. The trail then switchbacks up to the crest of the Sangre de Cristo Range, well above treeline. On extended trips many people continue west, down the western slope of the mountains to Crestone Creek. If you're not interested in this option, head north from the crest along the trail, which eventually drops down to Venable Lake and Venable Creek. Be on the lookout for the waterfall along Venable Creek, about 1.5 miles below the lake. Eventually you'll run into Rainbow Trail, a half mile north of your starting point. There is great camping and pretty good fishing along the entire route. To reach the trailhead from Westcliffe, head south on Hwy. 69 for 3 miles and turn right on Schoolfield Rd. Proceed 7 miles to Alvarado Campground.

Rainbow Trail—

This 100-mile-long trail is also very popular, with few uphill stretches. For the most part, it traverses the eastern slope of the Sangre de Cristos from Music Pass, about 15 miles southwest of Westcliffe, north by northwest to the Continental Divide near Marshall Pass. Take off for a day hike or a longer trip. There are many places to reach the well-marked trail. One of the easiest accesses from Westcliffe is at Alvarado Campground. See the previous entry for directions. For printed information about the Rainbow Trail, including maps and access points, contact the **San Carlos Ranger District Office** at **(719) 275-4119.**

HORSEBACK RIDING

Bear Basin Ranch—

Located on 3,000 acres about 11 miles east of Westcliffe, Bear Basin Ranch offers horseback trips to suit just about anyone. Ranging in duration from two hours to several days, trips head into the ranch property, 6,000 adjacent acres of the San Isabel National Forest and into the high mountains of the nearby Sangre de Cristos. Owner Gary Ziegler, a PhD in archaeology and accomplished mountaineer, has an obvious adventurous streak that he is willing to share. In addition to horseback trips,

Gary also arranges guided climbs of the Crestones, a couple of the most challenging 14,000-foot peaks in the state.

If you want to stay overnight, a bunkhouse ($) is available that sleeps 20; you'll need to bring your own sleeping bag. The ranch has no electricity but offers a solar shower and sauna. Meals can be arranged. Be sure to call for reservations. Contact **Bear Basin Ranch, Westcliffe, CO 81252; (719) 783-2519.**

LLAMA TREKKING
Wet Mountain Llamas—
Based at Trinity Ranch in Wetmore, this outfit offers reasonably priced day and weekend trips in the beautiful areas of the Greenhorn Mountains and the Sangre de Cristos. Paul Brown's operation comes highly recommended. **608 County Rd. 295, Wetmore, CO 81253; (719) 784-3220.**

SKIING
CROSS-COUNTRY SKIING
Cross-country skiing opportunities in the Wet Mountain Valley vicinity abound. Many trails lead up into the Sangre de Cristo Range west of Westcliffe. For information about trail possibilities, contact the **Custer County Chamber of Commerce, PO Box 81, Westcliffe, CO 81252; (719) 783-9163** or the **Sangre de Cristo Nordic Council, 102 Greenleaf Lane, Westcliffe, CO 81252; (719) 783-2487.** Additional information can be obtained at the **San Carlos Ranger District Office, 326 Dozier Ave., Cañon City, CO 81212; (719) 275-4119.**

Backcountry Trails—
Hermit Pass Trail—Many local cross-country skiers wax their skis and head for the 5-mile-long Hermit Pass Rd. A popular jeep road in summer, this road winds its way up Middle Taylor Creek, past Hermit Lake to the summit of the pass, just over 13,000 feet. From the summit, views west into the San Luis Valley and east to Wet Mountain Valley are stunning. To reach the trailhead, head west from Westcliffe on Hermit Lake Rd. Drive to where the plowing stops and begin skiing up the road.

Jackrabbit Trail System—Located at Lake DeWeese, this system of trails extends for a few forested miles along the lakeshore, into steep ravines and along a ridge with breathtaking views of the Sangre de Cristos. To get there from Westcliffe, head north for about 4 miles on County Rd. 241. Although the trails are at a fairly low elevation (7,500 feet), folks from the Sangre de Cristo Nordic Council consider it to be a natural refrigerator, which helps maintain a adequate snowpack. Organizers of the trails caution skiers against skiing out onto the iced-over lake. Contact the **Sangre de Cristo Nordic Council** for more information at **(719) 783-2487.**

Rainbow Trail—This 100-mile trail provides excellent cross-country skiing with fairly easy rolling terrain. See the Hiking and Backpacking section.

Groomed Trails—
Moon Shadow's Mountain Nordic Center—This small trail system, located at The Pines Ranch (see Where to Stay), offers 17 kilometers of mellow groomed trails adjacent to the San Isabel National Forest. Lessons and ski rentals are available at Moon Shadow's. For the more adventurous, try the "Over the Rainbow" guided tour, which starts 7 miles away at the top of Mountain Cliffe Ski Area and follows the Rainbow Trail back to the ranch. To reach the ranch from Westcliffe, head about 1 mile north on Hwy. 69 and then west for 10 miles on Pines Rd. **PO Box 311, Westcliffe, CO 81252; (719) 783-9261** or **1-800-446-WHOA.**

DOWNHILL SKIING
Mountain Cliffe—
Located at the base of the Sangre de Cristos, 5 miles west of Westcliffe, this small ski area caters mainly to families and groups. Mountain Cliffe (formerly Conquistador) offers four lifts and 1,200 vertical feet of skiing. Everything you'll need is available at the resort, including a restaurant, lodge (36 units), rentals, and even day care. In the past, snow conditions have been a bit spotty, so you should definitely call ahead before making the trip. **PO Box 775, Westcliffe, CO 81252; (719) 783-2100** or **1-800-472-1559.**

———— SEEING AND DOING ————

CEMETERIES

Silver Cliff Cemetery—

One night in 1882, as four drunken miners were walking by the Silver Cliff Cemetery, they saw blue lights darting around the gravestones. At first no one in town believed the stories of mysterious lights. Eventually many townsfolk also saw them. Over the years locals and visitors alike claim to have seen these lights at the graveyard. The phenomenon even attracted the attention of *National Geographic*. Whether you go to the graveyard at night to see the ghostly blue lights or roam around during the day to see this Victorian burial site, it's worth a trip. To reach the cemetery from Silver Cliff, head south on the road next to Clever's along Hwy. 96.

MUSEUMS AND GALLERIES

Bishop Castle—

About 27 miles southeast of Westcliffe, located among the thick pine trees of the Wet Mountains, lies one of Colorado's most bizarre attractions. Since 1969 Jim Bishop has been working single-handedly on his colossal stone and iron castle, which so far is a cross between Camelot and the Eiffel Tower. Not many who see it would argue Bishop's claim that the structure, billed as a monument to hard-working people, is the country's biggest one-man physical project. Jim describes it as "building by coincidence rather than design," which makes it more art than architecture. At the moment it consists of three stories of hand-set stone, topped with ornamental iron arches and an assortment of other wrought-iron flourishes. Other features include a 130-foot tower, flying buttresses and a spiral stone staircase to the top. On the front gable is perched a metal dragon whose nose serves as a chimney for a wood stove on the third floor.

As Bishop's wife, Phoebe, says, "The castle and Jim are one and the same."

Despite his devotion, Bishop is the first to admit that the project may never be finished, but he adds, "It ain't important that I get it done; it's important that I'm doing it." Future plans include a moat, a draw bridge and an onion dome, like the one on Saint Basil's Basilica in Russia, on top of the castle tower.

Admission is free but donations are appreciated. Visitors are free to explore the castle. To reach Bishop Castle from Westcliffe, drive 16 miles east on Hwy. 96 and turn right onto Hwy. 165. Proceed about 11 miles and look for the signs on the right side of the road. **HCR 75, Box 179, Rye, CO 81069; (719) 564-4366.**

Silver Cliff Museum—

Get a feel for the history of the valley at this small museum. Exhibits are housed in the old Silver Cliff Town Hall and Fire Station, which operated from 1879 to 1959. The museum is worth a look if you're in the area. Open Memorial Day–Labor Day, Thurs.–Sun., 1–4 pm. Located on **Hwy. 96** in Silver Cliff.

NIGHTLIFE

Silver Dome Dance Hall and Saloon—

Good times kick into high gear at this strange-looking geodesic dome, especially on weekends when live acoustic country and rock music are performed. Relax on one of two levels inside and choose from six beers on tap. Full bar service and munchies are also offered. Open Mon.–Sat. 11 am–2 am; Sun. from noon–midnight. Located on **Hwy. 96** in Silver Cliff—you can't miss it.

SCENIC DRIVES

Rosita/Junkins Park—

For spectacular scenery and a look at historical settlements around Wet Mountain Valley, take time to drive this 40-mile loop. From Westcliffe head east for 16.2

miles and turn right on County Rd. 358, just before the intersection with Hwy. 165. It takes you through Junkins Park with its interesting rock formations and remains of old cabins built by Czechoslovakian settlers. After passing through Junkins Park, you'll drop down a hill to Blumenau, originally settled in the late 1800s by German immigrants. The view of the Sangre de Cristos is fantastic from here. Further on you'll reach an intersection: County Rd. 347 heads to the right, back to Hwy. 96; County Rd. 328, on the left, leads to virtual ghost town of Rosita, which was the original silver mining settlement in the valley. Many old buildings still stand, including the general store and the Wet Mountain Rosita Fire Station. If you continue west from Rosita, you'll drive by Rosita Cemetery on the left. Established in 1870, there are still old tombstones as well as recent ones. From here proceed west to Hwy. 69, turn right and head back to Westcliffe.

WOLVES

Mission:Wolf—

Though difficult to find, Mission:Wolf rates as an extremely unique attraction. This sanctuary/refuge for wolves sits on 35 forested acres with sweeping views west to the Sangre de Cristos. Kent Weber and a number of dedicated volunteers have built large enclosures on the forested land to house approximately 30 pure and crossbred wolves. Most of these animals were raised elsewhere before being taken in as permanent residents. As Kent explains, "Many people who think having a wolf as a pet is a great idea quickly change their minds when they find out the animals can't be domesticated."

Try to visit during mealtime when the wolves' table manners are reminiscent of sharks in a feeding frenzy—you'll quickly understand the logical derivation of the term "wolfing your food."

The focus of Mission:Wolf, however, is education. Along with a few wolves, Kent spends a lot of time on the road during the school year. He travels the country educating students and teachers about the misconceptions connected with these beautiful, intelligent animals and their plight. An Ivy League swing a few years ago even included an interview on "Mr. Rogers' Neighborhood." Arrange a visit in advance by contacting Kent at **PO Box 211, Silver Cliff, CO 81249; (719) 746-2919 or 746-2370.**

WHERE TO STAY

ACCOMMODATIONS

During the jazz festival and hunting season, many of the accommodations are booked. The rest of the year you shouldn't have any trouble finding a place. For a complete rundown on all lodging opportunities in the area, contact the **Custer County Chamber of Commerce, PO Box 81, Westcliffe, CO 81252; (719) 783-9163.** Here are a few possibilities.

The Pines Ranch—$$$ to $$$$

First developed as a guest ranch way back in 1893 by Englishman, Reginald Cusack, The Pines enjoys a superb location at the edge of the Sangre de Cristo Range. Catering mainly to families, current owners Dean and Casey Rusk provide a number of activities to the guests, ranging from horseback rides (including overnight trips) to fishing to square dancing. Accommodations include rooms at the restored original lodge (shared baths) and modern cabins which include private baths. The ranch is open year-round; in winter activities shift toward cross country skiing at the ranch's Moon Shadow's Mountain Nordic Center (see the Skiing section) and sleigh rides. No matter what keeps you busy during the day, you can unwind in the Jacuzzi. Priority is given to guests who book week-long stays, but one- or two-night visits are encouraged (space permitting). Meals included. To reach the ranch from Westcliffe, drive about 1 mile north on Hwy. 69 and then west for about 10 miles on Pines Rd. **PO Box 311, Westcliffe, CO 81252; (719) 783-9261 or 1-800-446-WHOA.**

Rainbow Inn Bed & Breakfast—$$$

The Rainbow Inn is a welcome addition to lodging opportunities in the Wet Mountain Valley. Opened in the spring of 1993, this attractive, comfortable bed & breakfast offers three rooms (two with shared bath, one with private bath). All guests enjoy the common room upstairs with its pot-belly stove, large screen TV and excellent views out to the Sangre de Cristo Range. Full breakfast included. Guests who take their morning coffee seriously may want to stop in at the **Espresso Cafe** at the front of the building. They feature specialty coffee drinks, fresh muffins and cookies daily. **104 Main St., Westcliffe, CO 81252; (719) 783-2313.**

Alpine Lodge—$ to $$

For a more rustic stay in the Wet Mountain Valley, consider staying in one of the cabins at the Alpine Lodge. Located at the base of the Sangre de Cristos, the small, very rustic cabins have kitchenettes and sleep up to six people. Instead of cooking in your cabin, you may want to eat at the excellent restaurant at the lodge (see the Where to Eat section) considered by many to be the finest in the valley. Alpine Lodge is located 3 miles south of Westcliffe on Hwy. 69, and then 7 miles west on Schoolfield Rd. **6848 County Rd. 140, Westcliffe, CO 81252; (719) 783-2660.**

Bear Basin Ranch—$

See the Horseback Riding section for details.

Malachite—$ to $$

In these days of runaway environmental problems, rampant consumerism and giant agribusiness, a visit to Malachite is a refreshing break. Located in the Huerfano River Valley, with a spectacular view up the valley to Blanca Peak, this 260-acre nonprofit land-based learing center "practices, teaches and searches for respectful and sustainable ways of living and farming that are community responsible and environmentally sound," according to past director Kent Mace. Malachite focuses on family farm stays and providing an environment for individuals to connect with themselves as well as nature. By experiencing one of the programs, you can develop both the skills to become more self-sufficient and an awareness of our fragile green world.

Participate in organic gardening, beekeeping and farm chores; the extent of involvement is up to the individual. Families can spend a night or a week in this beautiful valley, join in with farm chores, take a hayride or go hiking. Many visitors to the farm camp out in tents, but beds are available in two solar-heated dorm rooms. Farm-fresh meals are provided three times a day. If you just want to stop by for a visit and take a tour, that's fine, too—just call ahead. Located about 45 miles south of Westcliffe. For more information about programs, costs, etc., contact Malachite, **8055 County Rd. 570, Gardner, CO 81040; (719) 746-2412.**

CAMPING

In San Isabel National Forest—

Alvarado Campground, located in the foothills of the Sangre de Cristo Range, is 10 miles from Westcliffe. From town head about 3 miles south on Hwy. 69 and then west on Schoolfield Rd. There are 47 sites and a fee is charged. **Lake Creek Campground** is located 12 miles northwest of Westcliffe on Hwy. 69 and 3 miles west from Hillside. It has 11 sites and a fee is charged.

In the Wet Mountains southeast of Westcliffe are a number of other campgrounds. From Westcliffe drive east on Hwy. 96 and turn south on Hwy. 165 for 18 miles to **Ophir Campground.** It has 31 sites; a fee is charged. A couple of miles farther south on Hwy. 165 takes you to **Davenport Campground** with 15 sites; a fee is charged. Five miles south from Davenport is the **Lake Isabel Recreation Area.** It has three campgrounds, including **Southside Campground** (8 sites), **St. Charles Campground** (15 sites) and **Cisneros Campground** (25 sites). All charge a fee.

Private Campgrounds—
Grape Creek RV Park—Thirty-four RV sites and numerous tent sites along Grape Creek await at this well-run campground that features its own fishing pond and sweeping views of the Sangre de Cristo range. Laundry and showers also available; handicapped-accessible. Located 1.5 miles south of Westcliffe on the west side of Hwy. 69. **PO Box 7, Westcliffe, CO 81252; (719) 783-2588, 783-2667 or 783-2694.**

WHERE TO EAT

Alpine Lodge—$$ to $$$
Located among the pines, 10 miles southwest of Westcliffe, the lodge offers fine dining in a attractive, rustic atmosphere. Sit by the stone fireplace and look out at the Wet Mountain Valley while enjoying one of the fine steak or seafood entrées. The Alpine Lodge has nightly specials, including prime rib, all-you-can-eat barbecue and chicken, and sirloin marinated in a honey bourbon sauce. A salad bar, sandwiches and homemade soups round out the lighter side of the menu. If you're not counting calories, try a slice of their excellent homemade pie or cheesecake. Open Wed.–Sun. 4:30–8:30 pm, Sun. brunch from 11 am–1:30 pm. Hours have been known to vary, so call ahead. **6848 County Rd. 140, Westcliffe, CO; (719) 783-2660.**

Mining Company Restaurant and Bar—$ to $$
Serving home-cooked meals all day, the Mining Company is a good bet. Menu standouts include pizza, specialty sandwiches, salad bar, homemade pies and soup that is prepared daily. Service is speedy and friendly. Open daily 7 am–9 pm. Located on the west edge of Silver Cliff at **1202 Main St.; (719) 783- 9144.**

Espresso Cafe & Art Gallery—$
See the Rainbow Inn B&B write up in the Where To Stay section.

Shining Mountains Food & Gifts—$ to $$
This pleasant southwestern-style cafe is the place to go in Westcliffe for healthful dishes made with fresh ingredients. Margaret and Sheila Davis, the owners offer homemade pastries and pies, deli sandwiches, veggie dishes and good Mexican food. The homemade green chili and the Mexican pita are definitely worth a try. When weather permits, the patio is a nice place for a meal or a cold beer. In summer the southwestern gift shop offers a selection of jewelry, pottery, rugs among other things. Open 9 am–6 pm daily in summer; winter from 11 am–3 pm. **212 Main St.; (719) 783-9143.**

SERVICES

Custer County Chamber of Commerce—
#2 Bassick Pl., PO Box 81, Westcliffe, CO 81252; (719) 783-9163.

Caboose Visitor Center—
Provides brochures and advice about what to do in the valley. Open Memorial Day–Labor Day at west end of Main St. in Westcliffe. Look for the old caboose.

Wet Mountain Valley Tribune—
Stop by the newspaper office for area information and a copy of the weekly paper that has been published every Thurs. since 1883. Open daily. **404 Main St., Westcliffe, CO 81252; (719) 783-2361.**

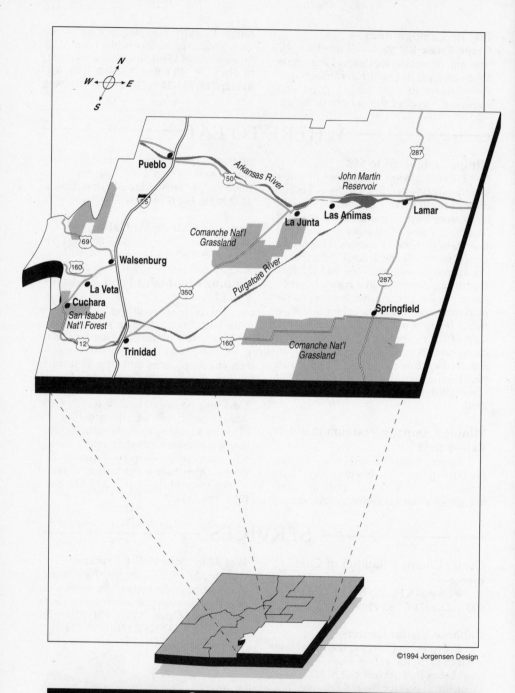

Southeast Region

SOUTHEAST REGION

Cuchara Valley

It's surprising that most Coloradans are unfamiliar with this little valley in the southern part of the state. Vacationers, primarily from Texas, Oklahoma and Kansas, have been coming to the Cuchara Valley since 1906, discovering early on what many natives continue to overlook. Nestled between the eastern slope of the southern Sangre de Cristo Range and the looming Spanish Peaks, the Cuchara Valley offers plenty of outdoor beauty along with an interesting history and a mix of Hispanic and Anglo cultures. Originally part of a Spanish land grant, the valley retains an Hispanic feel. In addition, working ranches give Cuchara a western flair. Texas longhorn cattle graze in some of the pastures along the road.

The expansive San Isabel National Forest runs through the central part of the valley, stretching west to east from the top of the Sangre de Cristo Range to the twin Spanish Peaks. These twins dominate the surrounding landscape, towering 7,000 feet above the nearby prairie. The national forest offers a number of outdoor activities, most notably hiking and cross-country skiing. One excellent way to enjoy this part of the state is to take a drive along a Scenic and Historic byway: the Highway of Legends.

At the northern entrance to the valley, the small town of La Veta serves as sentinel. In addition to local ranchers, an eclectic though friendly citizenry is largely made up of seniors, alternative lifestyle advocates, artists and expatriate southerners. If you're a golfer, a round at the Grandote Golf Club may cause you to stay longer than you thought. And Cuchara Valley Ski Area recently reopened following a three year hiatus. The Cuchara Valley is definitely worth looking into for its peace and quiet and stunning scenery.

HISTORY

Right from the beginning the Spanish Peaks have been inexorably tied to the history of southern Colorado and the Cuchara Valley. Called

Huajatolla ("Breasts of the Earth") by the Plains Indians, these two mammillary peaks were a source of significant religious wonder and, perhaps, mineral wealth. Gold on Aztec shrines in present-day Mexico was said to have come from "a double mountain far to the north." Despite reported sightings of ancient mines on the mountains, no significant mineral strikes have ever been recorded at the Spanish Peaks.

The Santa Fe Trail, which brought settlers across the prairie in the first half of the 1800s, relied heavily on the Spanish Peaks as a landmark. In 1862 the first settlement in the Cuchara Valley sprang up at the present site of La Veta. Col. John M. Francisco, with the help of Henry Daigre and Hiram W. Vasquez, built a fort that took on the name Fort Francisco and later Francisco Plaza. Francisco and his associates started a large sheep and cattle ranch, thereby enticing many sheep ranchers into the area during the next few years. But like many settlements in this part of the country, the real boost came in 1876 when the Denver & Rio Grande Railroad came to town on its way west. Farming and coal mining became the prominent industries for quite a while, but they eventually bowed to the rise of tourism.

GETTING THERE

From Denver the Cuchara Valley and the town of La Veta can be reached by driving 160 miles south on Interstate 25 to Walsenburg and then turning west on Hwy. 160. Drive about 11 miles and turn left (south) onto Hwy. 12. The town of La Veta is 4 miles down the road at the base of Cuchara Valley.

——————— OUTDOOR ACTIVITIES ———————

FISHING

Lathrop State Park—
See the write-up under Parks.

GOLF

Grandote Golf and Country Club—
Named for the Tarahumare Indian prophet who led his people to the Spanish Peaks from the south, this young but fine 18-hole course commands an excellent view of the nearby Spanish Peaks. Opened in the spring of 1986, the course was designed by Tom Weiskopf and planned in conjunction with a real estate development. The course may eventually go private, but not anytime in the near future.

Water hazards, including the Cucharas River and two lakes, come into play on 10 of the holes. The front nine is still open, but the back nine, with plentiful aspen and pine, looks much more mature than it really is. Moderately priced fees. Open May 1 to mid-Oct. Cart and club rentals available; full pro shop. **5540 Hwy. 12, PO Box 506, La Veta, CO 81055; (719) 742-3123.**

HIKING AND BACKPACKING

The southernmost parcel of San Isabel National Forest encompasses the Spanish

Peaks, Upper Cuchara Valley and the mountains immediately to the west, providing relatively undisturbed hiking and backpacking possibilities. The Spanish Peaks Wilderness Study Area protects the two famous mountains that have long helped explorers, pioneers and hikers find their way. There are a number of fine trails near these peaks.

North Fork Trail—

Beginning near Trinchera Peak and angling southeast, this 4.5-mile hike ranges in altitude from 9,800 to 10,800 feet. The trail begins along the four-wheel-drive road to Trinchera Peak near **Bear Lake Campground** (see Camping section) and ends at Purgatory Campground.

Peaks/Wahatoya Trail—

This highly recommended 10-mile hike takes you along the southern edge of the Spanish Peaks and then north through the saddle between the two peaks. Be on the lookout for deer and wild turkeys that thrive in this area. Reach the trailhead by taking the Cordova Pass Rd. (see Scenic Drives section). After crossing over the pass, continue down to the Apishapa Creek Picnic Ground. Look for the trailhead on the left (north) side of the road.

West Peak Trail—

Starting at about 11,000 feet, this trail is fairly easy up to treeline, then it's a steep rock scramble to the 13,626-foot summit of West Spanish Peak. Be sure to watch for thunderstorms. To reach the trailhead, drive to the top of Cordova Pass (see the Scenic Drives section) and look on the left (north) for the 2.5-mile trail.

HORSEBACK RIDING

Echo Canyon Outfitters—

Located a few miles south of La Veta off Hwy. 12, Echo Canyon Outfitters offers horseback rides ranging from two hours to multi-day pack trips. If you want the full experience, consider shelling out for the "Cowboy" breakfast or dinner rides as well.

For specific information contact **PO Box 328, La Veta, CO 81055; (719) 742-5524** or **(719) 742-5403.**

PARKS

Lathrop State Park—

If the summer heat is getting to you, head over to Lathrop State Park. Two lakes, Martin and Horseshoe, attract many area locals for swimming, boating and excellent lake fishing. Both reservoirs are stocked regularly and offer fishing for rainbow trout, wipers, channel catfish, bass, walleye, and the legendary (and predatory) tiger muskie. Plenty of fishing stories are told about these enormous monsters, including tales of muskies chasing boats and swallowing unsuspecting ducks.

Terrain at Lathrop is covered in juniper and piñon pine, with one of the best views to the Spanish Peaks in the area. Camping sites (96 sites; fee charged) are available with full hookups, laundry facilities and showers. Lathrop State Park also features a 9-hole golf course, open through much of the year. The **Walsenburg Golf Club (719) 738-2730)** overlooks Martin Reservoir and has a clubhouse restaurant, cart and club rentals.

For information about Lathrop, contact the **Park Ranger** at **70 County Rd. 502, Walsenberg, CO 81089; (719) 738-2376.** Campground reservations can be made by calling **1-800-678-CAMP.**

SKIING
CROSS-COUNTRY SKIING

For those who like to go out on their own, the San Isabel National Forest hiking trails make for good cross-country skiing in the winter. You might try skiing up the **Cordova Pass Road** (see Scenic Drives), accessed from the summit of Cuchara Pass. Another standout trail in winter is the **Old La Veta Pass Road**, originally a narrow-gauge railroad route built in the 1870s. A 3-mile ski up to the summit leads to a number of old buildings, including the old depot, listed on the National Register of Historic Places. A small fee is charged for access to surrounding private land. To reach the trail (road) from La Veta, take County Rd. 450 northwest for about 3 miles to Hwy. 160 and turn left (west). After 4 miles turn left onto Old La Veta Pass Rd. (County Rd. 443).

Cross-country and downhill ski rentals are available at **Seasons Sports** in the village of Cuchara; **(719) 742-3102.**

DOWNHILL SKIING
Cuchara Valley Resort—
It's back. After a three-year closing, Cuchara Valley Resort, with its spectacular slopeside views of the Spanish Peaks, has opened again. As the name implies, Cuchara Valley strives to be known as a resort destination, not just a ski area. Although it's not in the league with powerhouses like Steamboat and Vail, the area does have its own appeal. Small crowds, relatively inexpensive lift tickets and lodging, a general low-key family atmosphere, and, of course, the views are the main drawing cards. Skiers can take advantage of 1,600 vertical feet and four lifts. The resort caters largely to southerners, spawning such ski trail names as El Tejano (Spanish for "The Texan") and San Antonio.

Located just 25 miles from New Mexico, Cuchara is the southernmost ski area in Colorado. Its southern latitude is not a big factor in snow depths though, as the ski area averages over 200 inches annually. However, wind is a factor; it can whip the snow off a trail right down to the rock. Wind aside, when the snow conditions are good, it's a very pleasant place to ski. It features mainly beginner and intermediate terrain with a couple of expert runs thrown in for good measure. A new addition is the expert terrain found in The Burn, a high (though small) bowl.

At the base of the mountain the Baker Creek Village complex, offers shops and a restaurant ($$ to $$$). A large condominium complex (open year-round), located adjacent to the base area, offers the only lodging at the mountain. About 2 miles north of the ski area along Hwy. 12 in the village of Cuchara, the **Cuchara Inn** offers quality hotel accommodations. Ski rentals and lessons are available.

To reach the ski area, head south on Hwy. 12 from La Veta about 12 miles to the ski area entrance on the right. For information about the ski area and its accommodations, contact Cuchara Valley Resort, **946 Paradero Ave., Cuchara, CO 81055; (719) 742-3163** in state and **1-800-227-4436** out of state.

SEEING AND DOING

MUSEUMS
Fort Francisco Museum—
For such a small town, La Veta has put together an impressive museum that looks back nearly 130 years to the days of the first pioneers. The museum occupies the site of the Francisco Plaza, built in 1862 by the original La Veta settler, Col. John M. Francisco. Some of the original fort structures contain museum displays. The two main buildings have theme rooms focusing on clothing, pioneer ranching, Indian artifacts and furniture. Each room is packed full of an eclectic assortment of items, most of them donated locally. Read through letters written by settlers to the Territorial Governor in 1873 appealing for protection against the Indians. One letter was written in 1853 to a local attorney from a fellow attorney in Springfield, Illinois—Abraham Lincoln. Allow plenty of time to examine the large collection.

Also inspect the blacksmith shop, saloon, post office and schoolhouse that were all moved to the grounds from within the area. Admission fee is minimal. Open daily from Memorial Day–Labor Day 9 am–4:30 pm. Located in the center of La Veta just off Hwy. 12 (west side).

Walsenburg Mining Museum—
Located in Walsenburg, 15 miles northeast of La Veta, this small museum serves as an excellent information source about

southern Colorado's once-thriving coal mining industry. At the turn of the century, Walsenburg and the surrounding area of Huerfano and Las Animas counties supplied 60 percent of the coal mined in Colorado. But production began to fall off substantially by the 1950s. The museum features photographs and equipment donated by local families; also examine the simulated coal mine shaft (kids love it). Those wanting further information about southern Colorado coal mining should check the **Ludlow Monument** and **Highway of Legends** write-ups in the **Trinidad** chapter. Museum hours vary; call ahead. **101 E. 5th, Walsenburg, CO 81089; (719) 738-1107.**

NIGHTLIFE

La Veta Sports Pub & Grub—

If you're looking for a local hangout, this is it. Stop in for a beer and a burger and maybe watch a game on the tube; or drop a quarter in the CD jukebox and try some country swing on the small, makeshift dance area. The Sports Pub & Grub is open seven day a week, year round; 11 am–Midnight Sun. through Thurs., 11 am–2 am Fri.and Sat. Located near the golf course in La Veta at **923 S. Oak; (719) 742-3093.**

SCENIC DRIVES

Cordova Pass—

This road, built in 1934, can get rutted out and very bumpy, but it is one of the most beautiful in the area. Traveling just south of the Spanish Peaks, Cordova Pass winds a serpentine course to its summit at 11,000 feet and then down to the town of Aguilar near Interstate 25. After reaching the summit of Cordova Pass Rd. you drive through a tunnel blasted through one of the rock dikes radiating from the Spanish Peaks. Along the way, aspen groves and spectacular, unobstructed views of the adjacent Spanish Peaks vie for your attention. Just up the road a few miles is a well-marked trailhead for a fantastic quarter-mile wildflower identification trail, best seen in July and Aug. A brochure that will help you identify the flowers is available at the forest service office in La Veta.

Cordova Pass was originally known as Apishapa Pass. *Apishapa* means "stinky water" in Apache, possibly named after the nearby river which takes on a strong smell during the dry part of the year.

To reach the pass, drive south from La Veta on Hwy. 12 to Cucharas Pass. Just at the summit, turn left onto Cordova Pass Rd. (Forest Rd. 415). In addition to a picnic area, you'll find a number of good hiking trails along the road (see Hiking and Backpacking for some ideas).

Highway 12 south from La Veta—

Along this highly scenic route (known as the Highway of Legends), enjoy green pastures with grazing longhorn cattle, aspen and evergreen stands, and far-reaching views to the **Spanish Peaks** and their incredible geology. The two mountains are lava formations that popped up millions of years ago, causing cracks in the sedimentary layers on the surface. Lava flowed into these cracks, causing igneous intrusions. These intrusions, much more resistant to erosion than the surrounding sedimentary layers, remain now as lava dikes, radiating from the two peaks like bicycle spokes from the hub of a wheel. An amazing sight, many of them can be seen from Hwy. 12. Some of these dikes run unbroken as long as 13 miles, rising as high as 100 feet. Some of the better-known dikes along the highway include Devil's Stairstep, the Gap and Profile Rock (the profiles of George and Martha Washington and an Indian).

About 15 miles south of La Veta, the highway reaches the summit of **Cucharas Pass**. From here you can turn left up **Cordova Pass** (see previous entry) or continue down south, eventually reaching Trinidad (see Scenic Drives in the **Trinidad** chapter).

—————— WHERE TO STAY ——————

ACCOMMODATIONS

In addition to the fairly charming accommodation listed below, the town of Walsenburg, at the junction of Hwy. 50 and Interstate 25, offers numerous inexpensive motel rooms. Skiers and summer visitors may want to consider renting a condominium at the ski area. For information, see the Skiing section.

The 1899 Inn—$$ to $$$

This old stone home (actually built in 1909, not 1899) has seen a lot of changes over the years. Marilyn Schwarz Hall, the innkeeper, told us the building has been a residence, a hospital, a boarding house and finally a bed and breakfast. Hall, a New Englander, has renovated all the rooms and furnished them with antiques. With 18-inch-thick walls, the place is well insulated. Five bedrooms are available, some with private bath; a cottage out back has two beds, a private bath, kitchenette and fireplace. Full breakfast served each morning; Sun. breakfast includes popovers and eggs. No smoking. Only the cottage is open in winter. Located in La Veta next to the Fort Francisco Museum. **PO Box 372, 314 South Main St., La Veta, CO 81055; (719) 742-3576.**

CAMPING

Lathrop State Park—

See the Parks section for information.

In the San Isabel National Forest—

Four San Isabel National Forest campgrounds can be reached from Hwy. 12, starting just 2 miles south of the Cuchara Valley ski area turn-off. Turn right onto Forest Rd. 413, which follows Cucharas Creek up to Bear Lake and Blue Lake, nestled at 10,500 feet on the eastern flank of the Sangre de Cristo Range. The first campground is **Cuchara Campground,** with 31 sites; a fee is charged. Farther up Forest Rd. 413 are **Bear Lake Campground** (14 sites) and **Blue Lake Campground** (15 sites); fees are charged at both. Good views from these campgrounds southwest to 13,500-foot Trinchera Peak. Back on Hwy. 12, continue south over Cucharas Pass down to North Lake and turn right (west) onto Forest Rd. 411. Follow this road about 4 miles to **Purgatory Campground;** 23 sites, no water and no fee.

Private Campground—

Circle the Wagons RV Park—Located in La Veta, this place is not a wilderness experience; it has all of the amenities. In addition, small cabins ($$) are available. Circle the Wagons is well known in summer for its nightly square dances. **PO Box 122, 124 N. Main, La Veta, CO 81055; (719) 742-3233.**

—————— WHERE TO EAT ——————

Keep in mind that regular restaurant hours in the Cuchara area are very iffy; it's always best to call ahead.

La Veta Sports Pub & Grub—$ to $$

If you're looking for a local hangout, this is it. Stop in for a beer and a burger and maybe watch a game on the tube; or drop a quarter in the CD jukebox and try some country swing on the small, makeshift dance area. The Sports Pub & Grub is open

seven day a week, year round; 11 am–Midnight Sun. through Thurs., 11 am–2 am Fri. and Sat. Located near the golf course in La Veta at **923 S. Oak; (719) 742-3093.**

Timbers Restaurant—$$ to $$$

In marked contrast to a number of cafes and restaurants in the area, the Timbers Restaurant & Bar serves as a upscale and somewhat pricey dining experience for well-heeled resort visitors and locals. The cozy atmosphere of this attractive restaurant includes a high ceiling with hewn log beams and a stone fireplace. On a stage at one end of the room sits a guy at a grand piano playing a never-ending medley of show and pop tunes.

Timbers serves dinner only, and you will not leave hungry. Entrees include steaks, chicken, pasta and seafood such as trout almandine. The fajitas are absolutely great. Full bar. The Timbers is open 5-10 pm daily in summer; limited days in winter. Call ahead. Located in the village of Cuchara; **(719) 742-3838.**

The Bank—$ to $$

Located next to the old bank, this combination adobe cafe and gallery features local art and handicrafts as well as delicious wholesome food. Pat McMahon, the owner, cooks everything from scratch. All ingredients except the meat are grown or produced locally. For breakfast try a blintz, huevos rancheros or pancakes. At lunch-time her sandwiches are scrumptious, served on her stone-ground wheat bread. Dinners consistently feature rib-eye steak, chicken and seafood; other than that it's "chef's choice." The Chocolate Sin pie is well named. Patio seating available; farmers market in summer. Summer hours are 7 am–9pm daily, Sunday brunch 10 am–2 pm. Off-season hours vary, so call. **222 Main St., La Veta; (719) 742-5505.**

Ryus Avenue Bakery—$

The Ryus Avenue Bakery is definitely a bright spot if you hit La Veta hungry. Even if you aren't hungry, one whiff of the fresh baking bread will change your mind. Fresh breads, rolls, pastries and sandwiches are the featured treats at this small shop. Be sure to try a slice of homemade pie or perhaps a whole pie for the road. Alas, the Ryus Avenue Bakery is only open Tues., Thurs., and Sat. 8 am-1:30 pm. Located at **129 W. Ryus Ave., (719) 742-3830** or **742-3926.**

SERVICES

Huerfano County Chamber—
400 Main St., Walsenburg, CO 81089; **(719) 738-1065.**

La Veta/Cuchara Chamber of Commerce—
PO Box 32, La Veta, CO 81055; **(719) 742-3676.**

Pueblo

Once the butt of many jokes about its heavy industry and shabbiness, this town along the Arkansas River at the east edge of the Rockies has come a long way toward changing its image. Pueblo now has plenty of things to attract vacationers who previously were hard pressed to find reasons to come. Completion of the extremely popular Pueblo Reservoir (Lake Pueblo State Park), significant tapering off of pollution from the steel mill smokestacks, and a tenacious commitment to improving the economy have all helped to boost Pueblo's quality of life. These efforts have paid off. A few years ago, Pueblo was voted the best place to live in the United States by a University of Kentucky research team.

It's still debatable whether you will want to spend much of your precious vacation time in Pueblo. But by taking a few minutes to exit Interstate 25, you might be surprised by what you find. Pueblo, home to the University of Southern Colorado, has an amazing number of old neighborhoods with rows of nicely restored Victorian homes. At least drive by the immense Rosemount Victorian House Museum, or better yet, stop in for a tour. And for about three weeks each August, Pueblo packs them in for the Colorado State Fair.

Pueblo's people leave a lasting impression on any first-time visitor. Community pride and traditional hard-working ethics surface in everything from completed community projects to conversations in the local pubs. A diversity of ethnic groups, particularly Hispanics, populate the town. Up until the end of the Mexican War in the 1840s, the Arkansas River, which runs through the middle of town, served as the U.S.–Mexico border.

HISTORY

Over the years, Pueblo has been a natural crossroads for Indians, Spanish troops, traders/trappers and gold seekers, due to its prime location on the Arkansas River along the Front Range of the Rockies. Ute Indians long used the area as a camp when they traveled up the Arkansas Valley into the mountains. The first recorded visit to the Pueblo site was by Juan de Ulibarri, a Spaniard who came up from Santa Fe in 1706 looking for escaped Indian slaves.

In 1806 Lieutenant Zebulon Pike led an expedition into Colorado from St. Louis to "ascertain direction, extent, and navigation of the Arkansas and Red Rivers." As the result of some pretty bad information, Zeb wasn't too successful in finding the Red River (due to the minor fact that it's located in Texas, a few hundred miles to the south). But he did manage to find the Arkansas River and follow it west to the present site of Pueblo. Here he erected a log fort, said to be the first structure built by Americans in Colorado. It was from here that he set out on an unsuccessful attempt to scale the mountain that bears his name.

In 1822 fur trader Jacob Fowler and his party built a house on the Mexican side (south) of the Arkansas River. Twenty years later Jim Beckwourth, mountain man and "White Chief" of the Crow Indians, helped establish Fort Pueblo. It was a trading center for the mountain men and Indians. The fort was crude but relatively peaceful until the Christmas massacre of 1854, when 100 Utes and a few Apaches led by Tierra Blanca were allowed into the fort by a settler drunk on "Taos Lightning." The Indians nearly wiped out the entire settlement, sparing only a young Mexican woman, two children and a man named Romaldo. According to an account described in the *1930's WPA Guide to Colorado*, Romaldo lived long enough with a bullet hole through his tongue to tell the story, using Indian sign language.

Fort Pueblo remained largely uninhabited for the next few years. According to Lt. E.G. Beckwith, who passed by Fort Pueblo in 1855, mountain men avoided the site entirely, "because it was believed to be haunted by headless Mexican women." Others were concerned about the slightly more substantial threat of additional Indian attacks.

In 1858 prospectors began to enter the area, establishing Fountain City near Pueblo. The large gold strikes in the mountains the following year lured many a miner to the Pueblo area. In 1860 Pueblo City was established, absorbing the Fountain City overflow. Pueblo really picked up when the Denver & Rio Grande Railroad rolled into town in 1872. The railroad connection to the gold and silver mines in the mountains, along with access to nearby coal deposits at Trinidad and Walsenburg, made Pueblo the perfect workshop for the mines. Between 1870 and 1880 Pueblo's population grew by leaps and bounds, increasing eightfold to 24,588.

The Colorado Coal & Iron Company, later the Colorado Fuel & Iron Company (CF&I), opened its first blast furnace in 1881. Other companies opened smelters in 1882 and 1888. European immigrants, Mexicans and African-Americans responded to a need for workers by making Pueblo their home, thus giving the town a melting-pot image.

Early explorers had conflicting ideas about the agricultural potential of the Pueblo area. Ulibarri, the early visitor from Santa Fe, praised the valley for its beauty and fertility. But Major Stephen Long, whose expedition in 1820 brought him through the Pueblo area, had another opinion. He referred to the surrounding land as "dreary and disgusting, almost wholly unfit for cultivation." Ulibarri was closer to the mark, because in the late 1800s farmers moved into the valley in droves. With the help of irrigation, the land east of Pueblo soon became an agricultural center. Ranching got a big boost from Charles Goodnight, a pioneer of the range cattle industry who blazed 2,000 miles of cattle trails from Texas to Wyoming and headquartered his operation near Pueblo. Today Lake Pueblo State Park and the city zoo are located on parts of his ranch.

By 1902 CF&I steelworks was the biggest employer in town, and it continued to be for decades. As recently as the 1940s, Pueblo was the second largest town in Colorado. Unfortunately, in 1982, due to an industry downturn, CF&I was forced to lay off 4,000 workers. It was a devastating blow to the Pueblo economy. But in some ways it was a blessing in disguise. By shutting down the smokestacks, shedding its steel-town image and aggressively marketing itself, Pueblo has been successful in attracting new, cleaner industries.

GETTING THERE

Pueblo is located 110 miles south of Denver on Interstate 25. The town is serviced by **Greyhound Bus Lines. Continental Express (719) 948-2254 and United Express (719) 948-4423** fly into Pueblo Memorial Airport. **Airporter Inc. (719) 578-5232,** provides ground shuttle service between the Denver, Colorado Springs and Pueblo airports.

—————— MAJOR ATTRACTIONS ——————

Lake Pueblo State Park

Situated on the Arkansas River just a few miles west of town, Lake Pueblo State Park enjoys an impressive setting. Semi-arid plains surrounded by limestone cliffs and buttes contrast with mountain panoramas of Pikes Peak to the north and the Wet Mountains to the west. Completed in the early 1970s by the Bureau of Reclamation for flood control and water supplies, Lake Pueblo is one of the largest bodies of water in the state. Its cool, clean water, excellent fishing and sailing also make it one of the most popular places in the state for recreation.

Facts About the Reservoir—

At high water there are over 60 miles of twisting shoreline at the reservoir. Most of the northern shoreline is accessible by road, whereas getting to most of the southern shore involves a hike or access by boat. You have to pay an entrance fee. Here are some things to do once you get there.

Camping—

The state park has more than 400 sites available and a fee is charged. On summer weekends the sites can fill up quickly. For reservations up to 120 days in advance call **1-800-678-2267** or **(303) 470-1144** in Denver. Or write: **PO Box 231, Littleton, CO 80160.** Modern toilets, showers and trailer hookups available.

Fishing—

Most of the boats plying the waters of Pueblo Reservoir are out for a day of fishing. And with good reason. A recent *Denver Post* article stated that the reservoir "maintains its standing as the best all-around walleye, largemouth bass, smallmouth bass and wiper fishery in the state." People fish here year-round. According to park officials, trout (up to six pounds) are best caught in spring and fall. Walleyes strike often in winter; crappie, small- and largemouth bass, white bass and sunfish feed in the spring and summer. Large channel catfish also call these waters home. Tackle and minnows can be found at the Northshore and Southshore marina concessions.

Facilities for the Disabled—
The Rock Canyon Area, just below the dam, offers accessible fishing, camping and swimming areas as well as a half-mile, level nature trail suited for wheelchairs.

Swimming—
Swimming in the reservoir is not allowed. There is, however, a swimming area located just below the dam. A sandy beach down by the river is protected by limestone bluffs and shady cottonwood trees. **Rock Canyon Swim Area** has lifeguards. There is a small fee. Open in summer only 11am–7 pm daily; **(719) 561-2111.**

Watersports—
Boat ramps allow easy launching for power boats and sailboats. Both marinas offer boat slips and boat rentals. Wind at the reservoir is consistently strong in springtime, and the sailboaters and windsurfers love it. If you plan to windsurf, remember that the water in the reservoir comes from snow melt-off in the mountains. It's really cold in springtime. Most windsurfers wear a wet suit until at least mid-May. Although windsurfing is allowed all over the reservoir, a special launch area is set aside on the north shore.

If you want to sit back, relax, and let someone else show you around the reservoir, consider a cruise on the *Princess*, an attractively restored 1955 cruise boat that can accommodate over 30 people. Two-hour cruises are available Fri.–Wed., year round. Call **(719) 542-3615** for tour schedule and reservations.

Wildlife—
A State Wildlife area located adjacent to the northwest corner of the park serves as home to deer, badgers, bobcats, coyote, wild turkeys, quail, hawks, golden eagles and bald eagles. Below the dam to the east are the **Greenway and Nature Center of Pueblo** and the **Raptor Center of Pueblo**. You can hike or bike down from the reservoir or drive from town. For more information see the Riverfront section of Seeing and Doing.

For More Information—
The visitors center at Park Headquarters, located on the south shore, is open daily 8 am–4:30 pm year round. **Lake Pueblo State Park, 640 Pueblo Reservoir Rd., Pueblo, CO 81005; (719) 561-9320.**

———— EVENTS ————

Colorado State Fair
August
Each year at the end of August, Pueblo cuts loose when it hosts the Colorado State Fair. The town had its first annual fair back in 1872 and has been going strong ever since. Cowboys and city slickers alike crowd into the fairgrounds for the 17-day event which features stock shows, fiestas, top national rock and country music groups and, of course, a rodeo. It's hard not to have a good time no matter what your interests are. Be sure to make advance hotel reservations during the fair, as space gets very tight. The fairgrounds are located at the corner of **Prairie and Arroya Aves.; (719) 561-8484, 1-800-876-4567** or **1-800-444-FAIR.**

———— OUTDOOR ACTIVITIES ————

GOLF
The sun shines 73 percent of the year in Pueblo, making it a great climate for golfing. The best course in the area is probably the new Walking Stick course located on the northeast end of town near the University of Southern Colorado. **Walking Stick,** a city course that opened in summer of 1991, is a

challenging links-style course with plenty of undulating terrain. Walking Stick is located at **4301 Walking Stick Blvd; (719) 584-3400.** Another well-known course is the **Pueblo West Golf Club,** located about 8 miles west of town. Pueblo West carries a rating of 73.5. To reach it head west on Hwy. 50 to McCulloch Blvd. then turn left. **251 S. McCulloch Blvd.; (719) 547-2280.** In town try **City Park Golf Course,** located in City Park at **3900 Thatcher Ave.; (719) 561-4946.** The three courses are open all year.

RIVER FLOATING

The Arkansas River flowing through town is one of the most popular floating rivers in the state—though if you're a whitewater aficionado it isn't for you, because by the time the Arkansas exits its steep mountain canyon and arrives at Pueblo, most of its fight is gone. If you like tranquil water, rent a canoe at the **Pueblo Nature Center.** For a more secluded float, head upriver on Hwy. 50 to Swallow's Canyon, just below the town of Portland. This 10-mile stretch of the Arkansas is a mellow, peaceful float that snakes along through cottonwood groves. Look for blue herons, ospreys and eagles. It's perfect for an open canoe. You can float all the way down into the reservoir and get out at the Oasis Marina on the north shore or stop before the reservoir at any one of a number of fishing access roads.

For more challenging rafting and kayaking water located upriver, see the River Floating sections in the **Cañon City and Upper Arkansas Valley** chapters.

———— SEEING AND DOING ————

MUSEUMS AND GALLERIES

El Pueblo Museum—

Newly located on what is believed to be the original El Pueblo site in downtown Pueblo, this museum provides plenty of historical information about Pueblo and the Arkansas River. You'll also find some interesting artifacts, including some excavated from the original El Pueblo trading post built in 1842. Other exhibits provide information about the plains and mountain Indian tribes of Colorado. Check out the metal chest armor worn by a Spanish conquistador that visited the area hundreds of years ago. For a glimpse at frontier life prior to 1870, El Pueblo is quite good. The admission fee is minimal. Open year-round, Tues.–Sat. 10 am–3 pm; closed Sun.–Mon. **324 W. First St.; (719) 583-0453.**

Fred E. Weisbrod Aircraft Museum—

This collection of vintage military aircraft is still getting off the ground. Climb inside and inspect fighters, missiles, research vehicles and support equipment, like the 1942 Ford Refueler. A building in the south-west corner of the grounds houses a B-24 photo display. Located 6 miles east on Hwy. 50 at the **Pueblo Memorial Airport, 31475 Bryan Cir.** Open daily from 9 am to sunset. For special tours call **(719) 948-9219.**

Rosemount Victorian House Museum—

This palatial 24,000-square-foot mansion is easily one of the finest Victorian homes in Colorado. Rosemount was contracted in 1891 for John A. Thatcher, founder of the First National Bank of Pueblo, and was completed three years later. Serving as a monument to the finest designers and craftsmen of the era, Rosemount was built for about $100,000, an extravagant sum by Victorian standards. Thirty-seven rooms, 10 fireplaces, dual gas and electric lighting, a 1,500-gallon copper-lined tank in the attic for pressurized water, stunning woodwork throughout—it really has to be seen and experienced to be appreciated.

John Thatcher's son, Raymond, lived in the house until his death in 1968, at which time Rosemount was willed to a private museum foundation. Most of the original furniture and carpets remain. The mansion was named after Mrs. Thatcher's favorite flower. A rose theme appears in almost every room: from ceiling frescos to patterns on chamber pots. Even if you are just driving through Pueblo, make time to stop in for a tour. Knowledgeable guides are happy to take you on an hour-long tour through the mansion and fill you in on all the details. Special tours can be arranged.

Hours are June 1–Sept. 1: Tues.–Sat. 10 am–4 pm, Sun. 2–4 pm; Sept. 1–June 1: Tues.–Sat. 1–4 pm, Sun. 2–4 pm. The last tour begins at 3:30. Closed Mon. and Jan. Small admission fee charged, discount for seniors and children. Kids under 6 accompanied by adults are free. **419 W. 14th St.; (719) 545-5290.**

Sangre de Cristo Arts & Conference Center—

Located downtown, the arts center includes a permanent western art display, four galleries with changing exhibits, a theater for performing arts and the hands-on, participatory **Children's Museum**. On selected Fridays from 5–8 pm in summer, live music, food and good times can be had on the front steps. Galleries are free, and the Children's Museum admission is inexpensive. Galleries are open 11 am–4 pm Mon.–Sat.; Children's Museum is open until 5 pm. **210 N. Santa Fe Ave., Pueblo, CO 81003; (719) 543-0130** and box office at **(719) 542-1211.**

NIGHTLIFE

Here are some suggested spots where you can go to take the edge off.

Cavalcade Nite Club—

Folks come here to dance to hits from the 50s through today's top 40. on the enormous dance floor. Comedy night from 8:30–10 pm on Fri. Cover charge after 9 pm. Hours are Tues.–Sat. 7 pm–2 am; closed Sun. and Mon. **4109 Club Manor Dr.; (719) 542-8629.**

The Gold Dust Saloon—

Located on historic Union Ave., this corner bar with its hanging plants, large windows, high ceilings and postered walls is a relaxing nightspot. That is, unless you decide to sit back in their old barber's chair to shoot a kamikaze or an upside-down margarita. You get the picture. Throw peanut shells on the floor or order a burger and fries from their lunch menu (11 am–3 pm) or limited bar menu (3–8 pm). Open until 2 am, Mon.–Sat. **130 S. Union Ave.; (719) 545-0741.**

Gus' Place—

Gus' Place is a must for anyone who wants to get a feel for Pueblo's past as well as quaff a cheap beer. The memorabilia on the walls serve as a museum of sorts to the idle CF&I steel mill just a stone's throw from the front sidewalk. For decades, Gus' served as the watering hole of choice for steel workers coming off shift and looking for a cold one. And they must have been very thirsty—for three years Gus' held the record in Ripley's "Believe it or Not" for serving more beer per barstool than anywhere else in the world.

Nowadays urban professionals pack the place, changing the blue-collar atmosphere a bit. But it's still popular (standing room only on Friday nights). Just as the mill workers did, patrons still show up for a "Dutch Lunch" (the only menu item) and a schooner of beer. The "Dutch Lunch" is a do-it-yourself sandwich plate with meat, cheeses and veggies. Open daily 10 am–2 am; (until 8 p.m. on Sun.). **1201 Elm; (719) 542-0756.**

THE RIVERFRONT

Trails for hiking and bicycling follow the river through Rock Canyon, connecting 16 miles of trails in Pueblo Lake State Park with those in town. The meandering river is lined with tall cottonwood trees and limestone bluffs. This place where Indians used to camp is now a peaceful escape from town.

The Greenway and Nature Center of Pueblo—

The center offers nature trails and year-round events intended to educate children and adults alike about the prairie, desert and river valley ecosystems. It's a great place for family picnics. Bicycle rentals are available. Reach the Nature Center on foot by following the river trail just west of Pueblo Blvd. By car, turn west off Pueblo Blvd. just north of the Arkansas River, onto Nature Center Rd. Follow past the entrance to the Raptor Center of Pueblo to the end of the road. Open seven days a week, 9 am–5 pm. **5200 Nature Center Rd., Pueblo, CO 81003; (719) 545-9114.**

Raptor Center of Pueblo—

One of very few centers in the country that rehabilitates birds of prey and returns them to the wild. Feeding time varies; you'll be glad to know that the center accepts meat donations. Located next to the Greenway and Nature Center of Pueblo.

Open daily in summer from 9 am–5 pm; winter hours vary. **(719) 545-7117.**

Zoo at City Park—

Located just east of Rock Canyon, this is a great place to take the kids. Be sure to check out the new ecocenter exhibits including a tropical rain forest and the cooler (literally) coastline exhibit with black-footed penguins. The zoo has other regular exhibits as well as a kid's favorite called "Happy Time Ranch"—a farm re-creation complete with all the barnyard animals. Across from the zoo entrance is a recently restored carousel, built originally in 1911. After a trip to the zoo and a ride on the carousel, your kids will be so grateful they might even start eating their beets. Small fee. The zoo is open daily, 10 am–5 pm in summer and 9 am–4 pm in winter. **(719) 561-9664.**

WHERE TO STAY

Aside from the wonderful Abriendo Inn, lodging in Pueblo is limited to well-known motel/resort chains offering the latest in cable TV hookups and other standard comforts. However, an interesting bed and breakfast is located in Beulah, 26 miles west of the city.

BEULAH
K.K. Ranch—$$

Retired Navy Capt. Kay Keating runs a delightfully tight ship at the K.K. Ranch in Beulah. The guest house is a quaint, cozy Victorian, brimming with antiques and heated by wood stoves. International guests will feel at home since Keating can get by in Japanese, German and French, learned in her sailing days.

What gives K.K. its flair is Capt. Keating's avocation of restoring antique carriages. At the moment she owns 15 of the museum-quality vehicles, including a stagecoach and an eerie-looking hearse. She also restores antique sleighs, which she usually puts out in winter for dashes through nearby Pueblo Mountain Park.

Accommodations include three bedrooms upstairs and one bedroom down-

stairs. A hearty continental breakfast is served. Be sure to call for reservations and directions. **8987 Mountain Park Rd., Beulah, CO 81023; (719) 485-3250.**

PUEBLO
Abriendo Inn—$$$

With Pueblo's dozens of quiet, shady streets lined with beautiful old homes, it was only a matter of time before one of the homeowners got bitten by the entrepreneurial bug and opened up a bed and breakfast. Since the completion of its extensive restoration in August 1989, spearheaded by owner Kerrelyn McCafferty Trent, the Abriendo Inn offers what is quite easily one of the finest bed and breakfast experiences in the state. The massive four-square turn-of-the-century masterpiece, listed on the National Register of Historic Places, was built in 1906 for brewery giant Martin Walter and his eight children. Today the entire home is exquisite, from fine antiques in each of the seven rooms to the woodwork throughout. Kerrelyn, a former teacher and interior designer, explained that she wanted the inn to be elegant but not pretentious—a goal she has definitely achieved. The downstairs is highlighted by wooden wainscoting and a beautiful winding wooden staircase. Breakfast, including freshly brewed coffee and such taste treats as the egg sausage soufflé, is served on either of the two porches or in the sunny breakfast room adjacent to the kitchen. Kerrelyn is starting to offer special overnight packages that include art tours of local foundries and meetings with potters and sculptors. Highly recommended for honeymoons and other romantic getaways. Kids are not encouraged; no pets. **300 W. Abriendo Ave., Pueblo, CO 81004; (719) 544-2703.**

Best Western
The Inn at Pueblo West—$$ to $$$

Located north of Pueblo Reservoir in the planned community of Pueblo West, 10 miles west of Pueblo. Restaurant (popular Sun. brunch from 10 am–2 pm), cocktail lounge, room service, 80 rooms. The inn arranges tee times for guests at the nearby Pueblo West Golf Club. **201 S. McCulloch, Pueblo West, CO 81007; 1-800-448-1972 or (719) 547-2111.**

Holiday Inn—$$$

Boasting the only full-service hotel in Pueblo, the Holiday Inn offers 193 rooms, indoor pool, lounge and dining room. Free movies. **4001 N. Elizabeth, Pueblo, CO 81008; 1-800-HOLIDAY or (719) 543-8050.**

Youth Hostel—$

Located at the University of Southern Colorado dorms on the east side of town, the youth hostel is open only June–Aug. TV, gym facilities and a laundry room are offered. **2200 Bonforte Blvd., Pueblo, CO 81001-4901; (719) 549-2601.**

WHERE TO EAT

La Renaissance—$$$ to $$$$

La Renaissance is definitely a Pueblo dining highlight. Located in an old Presbyterian church built in the 1880s, the restaurant has been in operation since 1974. High ceilings and, of course, lots of stained glass provide a unique interior design element. The menu is primarily continental, offering prime rib, steaks, chicken and tempting seafood entrées. These are five-course dinners, so come hungry. A good selection of imported wines and beers awaits you. The diverse lunch menu ($$) contains pasta, sandwiches, seafood and salads. There is also a dessert cart. Compared to restaurants in Denver, La Renaissance is a good value. Lunch served Mon.–Fri. 11 am–2 pm, dinner Mon.–Sat. 5–9 pm. **217 E. Routt Ave.; (719) 543-6367.**

Cactus Flower—$$ to $$$

A bit more upscale than many other area Mexican restaurants, Cactus Flower breaks a bit with tradition, providing New Mexico style touches including blue corn tortillas and crab meat. You can still find many reliables such as rellenos and burritos. Attractive decor, with a definitive Mexican/New Mexican theme. Open 11 am–10 pm Mon. –Fri.; 4–10 pm Sat.; closed Sun. **2149 Jerry Murphy; (719) 545-8218.**

DJ's Steak House—$$ to $$$

If Charles Goodnight, the famous local cattle rancher, were alive today, he'd probably be eating his steak at DJ's. The restaurant has built a good reputation among the townsfolk for large portions of high-quality beef at reasonable prices. The prime rib is especially good. Seafood is also featured, as well as surf and turf combos. Open daily 4:30–10 pm. **4289 N. Elizabeth; (719) 545-9354.**

Lindy's at Rosemount—$$

This unique little lunch spot is located in the old carriage house at the Rosemount Victorian House Museum. Dine in a quiet, relaxed atmosphere with fine woodwork throughout. Sandwiches, salads and soups are served. Half portions are available for children under 12. Combine lunch or tea at

Lindy's with an afternoon tour of the mansion. Open Mon.–Fri., 11 am–2 pm. **419 W. 14th St.; (719) 544-9593.**

Ianne's Whisky Ridge—$ to $$$

Operated by a third generation of successful Pueblo restauranteurs, Ianne's is known for its fine Italian food. Their mouthwatering pasta dishes, veal and steaks highlight the menu. This semi-elegant eatery has the atmosphere of a suburban living room, with its stone fireplace, skylights and grey/blue carpeting. In the adjacent bar listen to live jazz on weekend nights and selected weeknights. Open 11 am–10 pm daily; bar is open until 2 am. **4333 Thatcher Ave., (719) 564-8551.**

Do-Drop-Inn—$ to $$

Ask the locals where the best pizza in town is and you'll get the Do-Drop-Inn for an answer. And it's great! They have recently installed a new oven to cut down the waiting time, which can stretch to as long as an hour and a half on a busy night. It's a small, very casual downtown bar that also serves up sandwiches and a pretty decent margarita. Belly up to the bar or sit in a booth. Take-out orders are available (add $1 per order). This joint is strictly cash-and-carry (no checks and leave your Gold Card at home). Open 11 am–2 am, Mon.–Sat.; 2 pm–10 pm on Sun. **1201 S. Santa Fe; (719) 542-0818.**

Grand Prix—$ to $$

This place gets the prize for the most randomly selected Mexican restaurant name. As co-owner Sadie Montoya explained, "My grandfather was part French, and since we wanted something a bit different than the typical 'Sombrero' or 'La Casa,' we chose 'Grand Prix.' " This family-run local favorite serves up spicy dishes including their popular combo plates, flautas and chili rellenos. The same chef has been cooking since opening day back in 1969, an aspect that has helped maintain a loyal clientele. All of the food is prepared from scratch, including the spicy green chili. The spacious restaurant is highlighted by the long wood bar and the bizarre collection of booze decanters placed throughout (be sure not to miss the Elvis statue collection behind the bar). Open Tues.–Thurs. 11 am–9:30 pm; Fri. 11 am–11:30 pm; Sat. 4–11:30 pm; closed Sun.–Mon. **615 E. Mesa Ave.; (719) 542-9825.**

Magpie's—$ to $$

Named after a pub in England, this comfortable lunch spot deserves special mention for its tasty sandwiches, baked goods and the "Magpie," an enormous cream puff with vanilla ice cream and chocolate sauce. Attention beer lovers...owner, Billy Coppola, has compiled an unusual list including micro-brewery offerings and plenty of imports. Open Mon.–Sat. 11 am–2 pm. **229 S. Union St.; (719) 542-5522.**

Liz's Old Town Cafe—$

This take-out Mexican cafe opens at 11 am and delivers anywhere in Pueblo until 3 am! Open daily. **1550 E. Evans Ave.; (719) 564-5476.**

SERVICES

The Pueblo Chamber of Commerce —

Visitor information is available Mon.–Fri. **302 N. Santa Fe Ave., Pueblo, CO 81003; 1-800-233-3446 or (719) 542-1704.**

Events Line—

Provides 24-hour recording of events in Pueblo. **(719) 542-1776.**

Southeast Plains

The southeastern section of Colorado with its miles of windswept plains isn't exactly a garden spot. Jackrabbits and rattlesnakes outnumber tourists by dizzying numbers. These high, somewhat barren plains, however, slope down to the fertile Arkansas Valley, which is one of the most intensely farmed areas in the state; miles of irrigation canals have made much of it possible. For 150 miles, from Pueblo to the Kansas border, the Lower Arkansas River makes its way east across the plains through fairly lush bottomland dotted with farms and ranches. The area's produce, especially the melons, is some of the best in the country.

What the southeast plains lack in outright tourist appeal is more than made up for by its fascinating history. The Native American, Hispanic and Anglo cultures have all left an indelible imprint on this part of Colorado. The Mountain Branch of the Santa Fe Trail, which brought so many pioneers west from Missouri in the 1800s, traveled through the heart of the Arkansas Valley before angling southwest at La Junta. Today Hwy. 50 follows the Santa Fe Trail west from the Kansas border through the Arkansas Valley toward the lofty Rockies.

For hearty hikers, naturalists, archaeologists and paleontologists, the immense Comanche National Grasslands provides many interesting opportunities, including an impressive variety of birdlife and what could be the longest set of fossilized dinosaur tracks in the world! (See the write-up under Lamar.)

Along Hwy. 50 you'll find a number of farming and ranching communities that offer accommodations, restaurants and a few attractions worth your time. One big draw to this corner of the state is the excellent bird hunting, especially for geese and pheasants. Springtime and early summer fishing in the warmwater reservoirs can also be quite worthwhile.

HISTORY

After Mexico declared independence from Spain in 1821, the Santa Fe Trail was established as a trade route between St. Louis, Missouri, and Santa Fe, Mexico. Along the Mountain Branch of the trail (the northern route), near present-day La Junta, Bent's Fort was established in 1833 and for years served as the most important trading center for the American western frontier (see the La Junta section for details on this excellent museum). Along with mountain men and travelers passing by on the Santa Fe Trail, the fort attracted the attention of Plains Indians. From the north side of the Arkansas River, bands of Arapaho and Cheyenne camped near the fort and traded their buffalo robes for food and goods.

Other tribes, such as the Kiowa, Prairie Apache and Comanche, camped along the south side of the river, also trading at the fort.

In the late 1840s, US troops spent time in the area during the war with Mexico. After the US victory, much land south of the Arkansas River previously claimed by Mexico became part of the US. With this part of Colorado (at the time the New Mexico Territory) under US jurisdiction and the allure of gold strikes in the Colorado mountains, settlers poured west along the Santa Fe Trail. Because of this huge influx, relations with the Plains Indians inevitably deteriorated.

In 1861 the Treaty of Fort Wise required the Plains Indians to cede much of their land in eastern Colorado. The Arapaho and Cheyenne refused to honor the treaty. After a band of renegades attacked the Hungate Ranch south of Denver in 1864, and settlers called for massive retaliations against the Indians, a group of Arapaho and Cheyenne, under the leadership of Chief Black Kettle, sued for peace. The Indians met with Gov. Evans in Denver and then traveled to Sand Creek, near Fort Lyon, where they were to be under the protection of US troops. Gov. Evans dispatched a battalion of Colorado Volunteers to southeastern Colorado, where the Indians were camped. What ensued was one of the most tragic episodes in American history.

The volunteer soldiers, led by Col. John M. Chivington, traveled to Fort Lyon, where they were told the Indians' location. They then traveled north to Sand Creek and, on the morning of Nov. 29, 1864, attacked the Indian camp. Here is Chivington's report on what happened: "I, at dawn this morning, attacked a Cheyenne village of one hundred and thirty lodges, from nine hundred to one thousand warriors strong. We killed Chief Black Kettle, White Antelope and Little Robe, and between four and five hundred other Indians ... " Later it was discovered that only about 150 Indians were in the camp. Chivington and his men killed approximately 120—mostly old men, women and children. Although anti-Indian sentiments ran high during this era, Chivington's act outraged many settlers. The Sand Creek Massacre dealt one of the most serious blows to the Plains Indians, who were eventually relocated to reservations in other states.

By 1870 cattlemen began to move into southeastern Colorado. The Chisholm, National and Goodnight trails brought huge herds of Texas longhorns up from the Lone Star State for summer grazing on the high grassy plains. Many head were sold to Colorado ranchers. One of the liveliest cattle towns was Trail City, located near the Kansas border. Edward Bowles, a rancher in northeastern Colorado, visited the town as a boy and recalls, "It was the toughest town God ever let live; nothing there but saloons and gambling houses, hotels and corrals." The Santa Fe Railroad arrived in the valley by the mid-1870s and proved to be a crucial link for moving cattle (and, later, produce) to market back east.

Cattle barons ruled this part of the state for a number of years, until encroaching homesteaders changed the balance of power. Farmers eager to carve a niche in this wild country snapped up agricultural land in the Arkansas Valley. Once irrigation canals were in place, land in the valley produced large crops of vegetables and, especially, melons, which became well known throughout the country.

Today this part of the state is still dominated by ranching and agriculture.

Highway 50—

This chapter describes towns that lie along Hwy. 50, beginning near the Kansas border and then heading west.

LAMAR

Touting itself as "Goose Hunting Capital of the Nation," Lamar rolls out the red carpet each fall for hunters who arrive from all around the country to hunt a variety of game birds and deer. Each fall, VIPs take part in the Two Shot Celebrity Goose Hunt.

Established in 1886, the town was named after L.Q.C. Lamar, the secretary of the interior under President Grover Cleveland. By naming the town in his honor, early developers hoped to sway the secretary to install the headquarters of the area land office in Lamar. The townsfolk must have successfully tapped into his ego because they got their wish.

In the 1890s Lamar suffered the devastation of a prolonged drought, a major fire and a catastrophic invasion of jackrabbits. The gentle beasts were eating up the farmers' crops, and finally action was taken. More than 100 hunters encircled a large area of land and converged on the horde of rabbits. When the dust cleared, more than 4,700 rabbits had been shot or clubbed to death. The rabbits were then strung up on wire for the whole town to see. This annual harvest went on for a few years until the problem was under control.

Today Lamar serves as a trade center for the region. There are plenty of services for travelers cruising through the area. For more information about the Lamar Area, contact the **Lamar Chamber of Commerce, PO Box 860, 109A. East Beech, Lamar, CO 81052; (719) 336-4379.**

Big Timbers Museum—

This museum takes its name from the 25-mile stretch along the Arkansas River where enormous cottonwood trees (some 18 feet in circumference) once lined both banks of the river. Indians, trappers, traders and pioneers traveling the Santa Fe Trail used to camp in Big Timbers, which provided a lush, wooded area in an otherwise barren region. William Bent (of Bent's Old Fort fame; see the La Junta section) maintained a couple of trading stations here. Unfortunately, settlers cut down virtually all of the trees for building material and fuel. Many of the area's original buildings were constructed with this wood.

Housed in this small museum is a collection of pioneer memorabilia, including a kitchen display, farm implements and period clothing. Check out the interesting collection of historic photos. No admission fee. Open 1:30–4:30 pm daily. Located on the north end of Lamar. **7515 Hwy. 50, PO Box 362, Lamar, CO 81052; (719) 336-2472.**

Comanche National Grassland—

Flat expanses of short grass prairie, twisting rocky canyons and scorching heat: all of these ingredients make up the harsh country in the Comanche National Grassland. Checkerboarded in sections of land that cover two primary areas (one 50 miles south of Lamar and the other southwest of La Junta on Hwy. 350), this barren country was the territory of the Comanche Indians until the early 1800s. When cattlemen entered southeastern Colorado in the 1870s, they allowed their herds to overgraze the fragile land. Eventually homesteaders settled in the area and, as required by the government, farmed at least 40 of their 160-acre tracts. The dry soil was ill-suited for cultivation techniques of the times, but the farmers stubbornly persisted. The destruction of the natural ground cover caused problems that eventually came home to roost in the Dust Bowl days of the 1930s. Beginning in 1938 the federal government began buying back the land to retire it from cultivation.

Though the forest service has successfully reclaimed much of these grasslands, on the whole they constitute a hot, dry, fairly inhospitable region visited by few. Archaeologists are an obvious exception. Several prehistoric Indian campsites and rock art provide fascinating clues about early Colorado residents. **Picture Canyon**, located near Springfield, provides an opportunity to view these petroglyphs. In recent years, some archaeologists have hypothesized that strange lines carved in some of Picture Canyon's caves are similar to Ogam writing used by the ancient Celts of Ireland. Could it be that Europeans visited the New World hundreds of years before Columbus? During the fall and spring equinox, festivals are held which attract visitors to these caves.

The grasslands also hold an appeal for those who enjoy desert hiking and wildlife. Antelope, mule deer, coyotes, badgers, foxes, raccoons and jackrabbits all inhabit the grasslands. The plentiful bird life includes raptors such as bald eagles, prairie falcons and red-tailed hawks; the endangered lesser prairie chicken can be spotted in spring. These colorful relatives of the grouse strut their stuff while performing a stomping courtship dance—it's quite a sight.

A few years ago, the US Army turned over a beautiful canyon area along the **Purgatoire River** to the Forest Service. Known as **Picket Wire Canyonlands**, this picturesque area south of La Junta is definitely worth a visit—wildlife, historic sites, and the main attraction ... over 1,300 fossilized dinosaur footprints. These dinosaur trackways, located in the ancient mudflats along the Purgatoire River, comprise the largest continuously mapped site in North America. Apatosaurus (Brontosaurus), Stegosaurus and Allosaurus prints are found at over 100 trackways. Due to the fragility and national importance of these prints, access to the canyon is limited. For up-to-date information about access, tours and directions, check with the **Comanche National Grasslands** office in La Junta.

If you visit the grasslands in summer, be sure to bring drinking water. For maps and information, stop in at the Comanche National Grassland Office, 46 miles south of Lamar on Hwy. 287. **27162 Hwy. 287, PO Box 127, Springfield, CO 81073; (719) 523-6591.** The northeastern tract is administered out of La Junta; the office is located at 3rd and Hwy. 50, **PO Box 817, La Junta, CO 81050; (719) 384-2181.**

Cow Palace Inn—$$$

Lamar's activities seem to center on this large motel, which caters to goose hunters, vacationers and businessmen. It also doubles as a popular place for local wedding receptions. One hundred comfortable rooms come with color TVs and king- and queen-sized beds. The motel has an indoor pool and a courtyard dining area with many tropical plants. The restaurant ($$ to $$$) is well known for its excellent steaks and salad bar. **1301 N. Main St., Lamar, CO 81052; 1-800-678-0344 or (719) 336-7753.**

Queens State Wildlife Area—

About 15 miles north of Hwy. 50 on Hwy. 287 sit four of the Plains' finest warmwater reservoir fisheries, all within a 5-mile radius of each other. Throwing a line from a boat on **Nee Noshe, Nee so Pah, Nee Grande** or **Nee Shaw** can yield walleye, perch, crappie, northern pike, channel catfish and bass. Nee Noshe is especially well known for excellent striped bass fishing. Nee Grande, the largest of the four reservoirs, was recently called "a veritable living bouillabaisse" by Charlie Meyers of the *Denver Post*. Springtime fishing is best here as water levels can drop dramatically by autumn due to irrigation needs. Boat ramps are available at every reservoir except Nee so Pah. The reservoirs also provide good bird hunting (especially for pheasants and geese). Goose pits are available on a first-come, first-served basis.

LAS ANIMAS

Founded in 1869 at the junction of the Arkansas and scenic Purgatoire rivers, Las Animas was originally an important cattle grazing area. The largest business was the Prairie Cattle Co., an English outfit that grazed 50,000 head of longhorn in the early 1880s. By 1916 the last major roundup was held. Today Las Animas serves as a trade center for farmers and ranchers. Accommodations and restaurants can be found in town. For additional information contact the **Las Animas/Bent County Chamber of Commerce, 332 Ambassador Thompson Blvd., Las Animas, CO 81054; (719) 456-0453.**

Bent's Fort Inn—$$ to $$$

This attractive and comfortable Best Western inn serves as an excellent base for exploring the sites of southwest Colorado or as an overnight stop while blasting through the area. In addition to the well-maintained rooms, you'll find a restaurant/lounge and a pool. Located near Bent's Old Fort National Historic Site. **10950 Hwy. 50; (719) 456-0011.**

Boggsville—

In 1862, Thomas Boggs and a number of other local pioneers settled at this site along the Purgatoire River. Until the arrival of the railroad in 1873, Boggsville was a regional center, even serving as the first county seat in Bent County.

Boggsville makes for an excellent historical glimpse of life in the 1860s and 70s. A number of original homes have been recreated or restored, including that of famous frontiersman, Kit Carson. Carson settled in Boggsville in 1867 with his wife and seven children. After the untimely deaths of both Carson and his wife (within weeks of each other) the Boggs family raised the Carson children. Open 9 am-4:30 pm Mon.–Fri. From La Junta, head south on Hwy. 101 for 1.8 miles; the entrance is on the left side. **PO Box 68, Las Animas, CO 81054; (719) 384-8113.**

John Martin Reservoir—

Surrounded by flat, treeless terrain, John Martin Reservoir is definitely not one of the most scenic bodies of water in the state. But when full it's one of the biggest. Located along the Arkansas River between Lamar and La Junta, it has a whopping capacity of 618,660 acre-feet, but usually sits at about 15,000 acre-feet. Even at this level, the reservoir provides enough water to support an impressive waterfowl population. Hunting can be quite good for geese, ducks and especially pheasant. Birdwatchers can be treated to sightings of white pelicans in summer and bald and golden eagles in winter.

In the past few years, the reservoir has also become a warmwater fishing destination, especially since the state record striped bass was taken here. The waters have been stocked with channel catfish, largemouth and smallmouth bass, crappie, walleye and sunfish. A couple of long cement boat ramps at the east end of the reservoir guarantee to get you into the water no matter what the level. Swimming and waterskiing are also popular.

Just below the dam at John Martin's eastern border is spring-fed, warmwater

Hasty Lake, stocked with rainbow trout, yellow perch, crappie, smallmouth and white bass, channel catfish, walleye and northern pike. Hasty Lake, like the reservoir, is administered by the Army Corp of Engineers and provides a wind-sheltered 150-acre campground laid out among mature stands of cottonwood and oak trees. Showers, RV hookups and other amenities provided; fee charged.

To reach John Martin Reservoir from Las Animas, head east toward Lamar on Hwy. 50 for about 15 miles to the town of Hasty and turn south on Hwy. 260. Proceed about 5 miles to the reservoir entrance. For more information stop in at the Army Corps information center at the dam or call **(719) 336-3406.**

Kit Carson Museum—

Housed in a building originally constructed to house German prisoners in WWII, the Kit Carson Museum provides an interesting look into the history of the area. Actually, the museum is really a complex of eight historic structures, including the main building, a stagecoach stop, a one-room steel jail, the original Bent County jail, the first Las Animas city jail, a carriage house, a one-room schoolhouse and a blacksmith shop. It's definitely worth a visit. Open 1–5 pm, Mon.–Fri. from Memorial Day –Labor Day. Located at 9th and Bent; **(719) 456-2005.**

LA JUNTA

La Junta (Spanish for "the junction") was probably named for its location at the convergence of the Santa Fe and Navajo trails. Today Hwys. 50 and 350 follow these same routes. Since the Santa Fe Railroad arrived in 1875, La Junta has served as the transportation hub for the lower Arkansas Valley. Today the town is home to the largest airport in southeastern Colorado. Amtrak trains running between Chicago and Los Angeles make daily stops. Produce and cattle are also shipped by train to every part of the country. For its setting on the windswept plains, La Junta is an attractive town, with parks and focal points, such as the Santa Fe Plaza and Otero Junior College. Although its population is predominately Anglo, the Hispanic influence is apparent. La Junta has a number of places to stay the night, along with a couple of good steak houses and Mexican restaurants. For more information contact the **La Junta Chamber of Commerce, 110 Santa Fe Ave., PO Box 408, La Junta, CO 81050; (719) 384-7411.**

Bent's Old Fort National Historic Site—

In 1834, brothers William and Charles Bent and Ceran St. Vrain completed a trading post along the Arkansas River in southeastern Colorado. It quickly became the most important hub for US trade with Mexico (which seceded from Spain in 1821) and the western territories all the way to the Pacific Ocean. Traders moved American-made goods along the Santa Fe Trail from Missouri to Santa Fe, where they traded for Mexican products to be brought back east. Mountain men also showed up to trade beaver pelts in exchange for supplies they needed to survive in the wilds.

The Bent brothers and St. Vrain were also very adept at trading with the Plains Indian tribes. Since the fort was located on southern Cheyenne hunting grounds, good relations with this tribe were especially important. To secure harmonious relations, William Bent married Owl Woman, the daughter of a Cheyenne priest, in 1837.

The immensely profitable Bent's Fort thrived until the late 1840s. After Charles Bent was killed in the Taos Revolt of 1847 and a cholera epidemic swept into the area from Missouri a few years later, William Bent abandoned the fort.

Today the immense adobe structure has been reconstructed to look exactly as it did in the 1840s when it was in its prime. This National Historic Site is furnished with a few antiques and many reproductions of other items. During living history programs, costumed employees provide a wealth of information about the way of life at Bent's Old Fort. This is a highly recommended stop for anyone interested in the settlement of Colorado and the American West. Small fee. Open daily 8 am–6 pm Memorial Day – Labor Day and 8 am–4:30 pm during the rest of the year. Located 8 miles east of La Junta on Hwy. 194. **35110 Hwy. 194 E., La Junta, CO 81050-9523; (719) 384-2596.**

Koshare Indian Museum—

What started as a Boy Scout troop's project in 1933 has grown into a nationally known Indian dance group and an excellent Indian museum. "Buck's Brats," as they were known for years, developed quite a reputation for their authentic Native American dances. Today the Koshare Indian Dance Group, from Explorer Scout Post 230, performs around the country as well as in their kiva at this museum. Though it takes a few minutes to get used to these blonde youngsters, they really can dance.

Generous donations have helped finance the attractive museum, which houses $5 million worth of Indian artifacts and art. The magnificent Koshare collection is beautifully displayed. If you're interested in Native American culture, dance and history, make a point to stop by. Open Mon.–Sat. 10 am–5 pm and 12:30–5 pm on Sun. June through Aug.; 12:30–4:30 pm during

the rest of the year. Dance performances Sat. at 8 pm during summer. For Christmas holiday performances and other selected show times, check with the museum. Located on the Otero Junior College campus at **115 W. 18th St., PO Box 580, La Junta, CO 81050; (719) 384-4411.**

Otero Museum—

Displays and artifacts of life from 1875, when the Santa Fe Railroad arrived, until the present are the focus of this fine historical museum. Housed in the old Sciumbato Grocery Store, the building dates back to the early 1900s and is listed on the National Register of Historic Places. Exhibits include early grocery store items, farming and ranching equipment, histories of the local sugar beet factories, and a Santa Fe Railroad room. The number of artifacts crammed into this place is impressive. Don't miss the old chuckwagon, the 1903 REO roadster and the 1857 stagecoach in which Horace Greeley is said to have traveled part of his famous journey west. Admission fee charged. Open daily 1–5 pm June–Sept. The museum is in the process of expanding and relocating behind a grocery store in town. Ask locally for directions or call **(719) 384-7500.**

Picket Wire Canyonlands—

For information about this beautiful and interesting area of the Comanche National Grasslands see the Lamar section.

ROCKY FORD

This small farming community gets its name from early pioneers who crossed the Arkansas River at this safe point in order to avoid quicksand along many other sections of the river. Rocky Ford really should be remembered for being the site of the first community irrigation canal in the lower Arkansas Valley. In 1874 settler George Swink convinced his neighbors to help dig a ditch. When it was finished, their hard work helped produce fantastic

crops. Swink went on to develop the sweet, juicy Rocky Ford cantaloupe, which is known throughout the country. If you are traveling through the area in Aug. or Sept., stop by one of the many roadside produce stands for a taste of this delicious treat as well as other fruit from the valley. Pick up a fruit stand brochure or seek further information at the **Rocky Ford Chamber of Commerce, 105 N. Main St., Rocky Ford, CO 81067; (719) 254-7483.**

Arkansas Valley Fair
mid-August

Coinciding with the melon harvest, this multi-day gathering of Arkansas Valley residents features events such as horse races, livestock shows, a carnival and a rodeo. Special theme days include Fiesta Day, which celebrates the area's Hispanic culture. You'll eat enough on Watermelon Day to keep you away from melons for a year. For more information about this annual event, contact the **Rocky Ford Chamber of Commerce, 105 N. Main St., Rocky Ford, CO 81067; (719) 254-7483.**

——— SERVICES ———

Colorado Welcome Center—
Provides one-stop information for this area as well as other destinations in Colorado. **109 E. Beech, Lamar, CO 81052; (719) 336-3483.**

La Junta Chamber of Commerce—
110 Santa Fe, P.O. Box 408, La Junta, CO 81050; (719) 384-7411.

Lamar Chamber of Commerce—
109 East Beech, Lamar, CO 81052; (719) 336-4379.

Las Animas/Bent County Chamber of Commerce—
332 Ambassador Thompson Blvd., Las Animas, CO 81054; (719) 456-0453.

Rocky Ford Chamber of Commerce—
105 N. Main St., Rocky Ford, CO 81067; (719) 254-7483

Trinidad

Located along Interstate 25, a mere 19 miles north of the New Mexico border, historic Trinidad lies under the shadow of nearby Fishers Peak. With a history dating back to the arduous days of the Santa Fe Trail, the Spanish and ranching influence on Trinidad is still palpable today: cobblestones cover the hilly streets of old downtown, designated the Corazon de Trinidad National Historic District. The Baca House and Bloom House museums, early Hispanic and Anglo residences, are also a major attraction. This small industrial city of about 10,000 bustled at the turn of the century when serving as a center to the nearby coal towns.

Coal mining is practically dormant today, but signs of the old days as well as beautiful scenery can be seen along the Scenic Highway of Legends—a designated Scenic and Historic Byway. Some may be interested in knowing that a local doctor's specialty has earned Trinidad a national reputation as an excellent place to get a sex change operation. Though you'd hardly want to spend your entire vacation in Trinidad, you might want to devote an afternoon to visiting some of the city's fine museums.

HISTORY

Trinidad's position at the confluence of the Purgatoire River and Raton Creek has always been a favored camping place—first for nomadic Indian tribes and then for trappers and traders. In the 1800s many Conestoga wagons passed through present-day Trinidad, heading south over Raton Pass on the "Mountain Branch" of the Santa Fe Trail. This pioneer path provided a fairly direct route between Santa Fe and trading centers along the Missouri River. In 1859 Gabriel Gutierrez and his nephew built a cabin, establishing Trinidad's first recorded permanent settlement.

As the town slowly grew, it maintained a tough reputation. Men of Spanish and Mexican descent mingled uncomfortably with those arriving from the eastern states. Fistfights were common, and tension reached a breaking point on Christmas Day 1867, when a friendly wrestling match turned into a free-for-all riot. Several were killed during this racially motivated "Battle of Trinidad."

The Trinidad area was a part of the Territory of New Mexico from 1850 until the Colorado Territory usurped the land in 1861. Over the years the town grew steadily as a sheep center and then a cattle center, until vast deposits of coal were mined from the nearby hills. For decades coal mining was the main source of employment for the people of

617

Trinidad. Though coal production has slowed considerably, the innocents killed in the nearby Ludlow Massacre on April 20, 1914, will never be forgotten (see the write-up under Museums).

GETTING THERE

Trinidad is located 197 miles south of Denver on Interstate 25.

———— SEEING AND DOING ————

MUSEUMS

A. R. Mitchell Memorial Museum of Western Art—

Arthur Roy Mitchell was one of the leading western-style painters of our century. During his lifetime (1889–1977) he painted more than 160 cover illustrations for popular "pulp" Westerns. In his later years he concentrated on painting accurate representations of early western life, gathering many awards for his style and expertise. Some 250 of his originals are on display in this large collection of western art. The gallery is also home to many other artists of the same genre. One part of the museum is dedicated to Hispanic folk art of Colorado and New Mexico. Rare bultos (wooden sculptures) and retablos (wooden altar pieces) are displayed in addition to a small replica of a morada—the meeting house of the Penitente brotherhood. A gift shop sells, among other items, jewelry, rugs and original paintings of southwestern artists. Free admission. Open Apr.–Sept., 10 am–4 pm daily, except Sun. and holidays. **150 East Main St.; (719) 846-4224.**

Baca House, Bloom Mansion and the Pioneer Museum—

This fascinating museum complex represents a decade-long span of tremendous change in the Colorado of the 1870s: from territory to state, from Santa Fe Trail to railroads, from sheep to cattle ranching, from natural gas to electricity, from adobe to brick Victorian. Side by side these imposing domiciles allow you to trace this dynamic phase of Colorado history. A knowledgeable tour guide in period dress will take you around. Small fee charged. Open 10 am–4 pm Mon.–Sat., 1–4 pm Sun., Memorial Day–Sept. Off-season open by appointment. **300 East Main St.; (719) 846-7217.**

Baca House—Built of adobe bricks in 1869 by John Hough, a merchant from Pennsylvania, this house was undoubtedly the finest in Trinidad at that time. It was purchased for $7,000 by Don Felipe Baca in 1870, complete with furnishings and dishes. Baca was a prosperous Spanish-American rancher and freighter who preferred a lifestyle of simplicity. Uneven wooden floors are covered by handwoven rugs, and the pie safe in the kitchen is built from recycled tins. Looking out of the second-floor windows you can see the path of the Mountain Branch of the Santa Fe Trail (now Main St.) through distorted hand-rolled glass.

Bloom Mansion—In 1881 the Victorian-styled Bloom Mansion was built next to the Baca House for Frank Bloom, a Colorado cattleman, merchant and banker. The differences between the two are startling. First off, the opulent Bloom Mansion was built for a mere $3,000, thanks to the establishment of the railroads and the accompanying infusion of cheap labor. Conveniences from the eastern United States were built into the elaborate three-story setting. The parlor features combination gas/electric fixtures, high ceilings, tasseled draperies and ornately carved furniture. The upstairs bedrooms all have massive bedsteads, quilts and lace curtains. Servants' quarters occupy the top floor. Behind the house, where a brick barn once stood, you'll enjoy a stroll through a carefully tended Victorian Cutting Garden, enhanced by the accompaniment of a splashing waterfall.

Pioneer Museum—Behind the Baca House, the adobe carriage house and sheepherders' quarters contain rooms full of interesting items from Trinidad's early days. Displays include Kit Carson's buckskin coat along with many Indian artifacts. Don't miss the bear trap, old photos of Bat Masterson and Doc Holliday and a gun collection dating from 1870. In addition to the large variety of exhibits in each room, carriages sitting idle outside await your inspection.

Louden-Henritze Archaeology Museum—

Our expectations were not exactly soaring as we proceeded to the ground floor of the Trinidad State Junior College library for a look at this museum. So it was a pleasant shock to be given a personal tour through the small but excellent collection of archaeology exhibits. The highlight was a diorama of nearby Trinchera Cave, which was occupied for thousands of years by prehistoric man. Other items range from fossilized shark teeth to an amazing collection of arrowheads. In 1962, before the construction of Trinidad Reservoir, the junior college directed the hurried excavation of more than 300 sites. Many of the artifacts that turned up are now on display at the museum, including a complete skeleton inside a bell-shaped burial pit. The now-defunct archaeological program at Trinidad State Junior College was initiated in 1951 by Hal Chase, a friend and contemporary of Jack Kerouac, William Burroughs and Allen Ginsburg. Chase appears in Kerouac's classic *On the Road* as the character Chad King. Free admission. 12–4 pm Mon.–Fri., May–early Sept. **Freudenthal Memorial Library, Trinidad State Junior College; (719) 846-5508.**

Ludlow Monument—

Twelve miles northwest of Trinidad, on April 20, 1914, a battle between striking coal workers and militiamen ended tragically. Seven months before the "Ludlow Massacre" took place, the United Mine Workers had encouraged the miners to strike for better working conditions and pay. Workers moved out of company-owned camps and established tent colonies to wait out the struggle. On the Ludlow prairie, not far from the mines, hundreds of miners and their families took residence.

Sporadic violence at Ludlow caused Gov. Elias Ammons to call out the state militia to quell the rising emotions. It might have been a good move except that the militia had been infiltrated by coal company strongmen. The "peacekeepers" were armed to the teeth, and it didn't take long for an accidental shot to prompt a volley of bullets. On April 20 several miners, along with an 18-year-old passerby and a young boy, were shot dead. On the same day, 11 children and two women suffocated while taking refuge in a makeshift cellar beneath a tent that went up in flames. This violent story of early American labor action is preserved in a granite monument erected by the United Mine Workers. To reach the monument from Trinidad, take Interstate 25 12 miles north to the Ludlow exit.

RECREATION AREA

Trinidad Lake State Park—

Only 4 miles west of Trinidad is a pleasant area for water sports, hiking and camping. Trinidad Lake covers a coal mining area that was heavily populated for decades around the turn of the century. Although water levels can fluctuate quite a bit, the reservoir is open for boating and fishing. Annual stocking includes rainbow trout, but warmwater species, including largemouth bass, catfish, walleye and crappie, can also be caught.

Over 9 miles of hiking trails lead into the surrounding hills, with excellent views of Fishers Peak. Sixty-two developed campsites on the north side of the lake provide flush toilets and showers. RV hookups and tent sites; fee charged. Campground reservations can be made by calling **1-800-678-CAMP**. To reach Trinidad Lake State Park, take Hwy. 12 west of Trinidad for 4 miles. For more information contact **32610 Hwy. 12, Trinidad, CO 81082; (719) 846-6951.**

SCENIC DRIVES

Scenic Highway of Legends—
This 120-mile loop has become one of the highlights of a trip to the Trinidad area. And the highway is well named, with history as a major component of the drive. The route offers a smattering of many things, including tiny Hispanic communities, geologic oddities, alpine forests and spectacular views of the lofty Sangre de Cristo Range and impressive Spanish Peaks.

To begin the route from Trinidad, drive west on Hwy. 12. About 8 miles out of town you'll see some large black slag piles on the north side of the highway left over from the coal processing at **Cokedale**. Now a National Historic District, Cokedale is perhaps the best-preserved example of the many Colorado coal mining camps that thrived in the early 1900s. On the south side of the highway are the remnants of the coke ovens.

As the road makes its way west through the **Purgatoire River Valley,** you'll pass through many small Hispanic plazas and communities, some of which date back to the 1860s. About 31 miles from Trinidad you'll pass through **Stonewall Gap,** an unusual narrow opening in an uplifted line of Dakota sandstone. Not long afterward, Hwy. 12 turns north as it continues to climb up through pine and aspens toward **Cucharas Pass.** Along this stretch you'll pass by Monument Lake, which offers fairly decent trout fishing, camping and accommodations at **Monument Lake Resort.**

From 9,941-foot Cucharas Pass, the view northeast to the Spanish Peaks is quite good. The highway drops from here down into the **Cuchara Valley,** winding its way north to La Veta, Hwy. 50 and Walsenburg. From Walsenburg return to Trinidad by heading south on Interstate 25 for 37 miles. Information on Cucharas Pass and the beautiful Cuchara Valley can be found in the Scenic Drives section of the **Cuchara Valley** chapter. An excellent map of the Highway of Legends containing historical and geological information about places along the way may be obtained in Trinidad at the **Colorado Welcome Center** and the **Trinidad Visitor Center.**

WHERE TO STAY

Trinidad lodging centers on motels. Many motels are easily visible from Interstate 25 as it winds through Trinidad. For specific listings and ideas contact the **Colorado Welcome Center** at **(719) 846-9512** or the **Trinidad Visitor Center** at **(719) 846-7244.**

WHERE TO EAT

La Fiesta—$
By many accounts, La Fiesta is the best Mexican restaurant in town. The two basement-level rooms in this Trinidad institution are nothing fancy, but the food is inexpensive and *all* homemade. This is made clear right off the bat with piping hot chips delivered to your table. Breakfast specialties include huevos rancheros. Lunch and dinner menus offer the full gamut of Mexican dishes plus a worthy Mexican hamburger. The salsa and gravies are great! La Fiesta's trademark daily specials are highly recommended. Open Mon.–Sat. 10 am–8 pm; closed Sun. **134 W. Main St.; (719) 846-8221.**

Nana & Nano's Pasta House—$ to $$
Opened in 1988 by the very Italian Monteleone family, this 20-table restau-

rant serves up tasty, inexpensive Italian dishes, especially pasta. The attractive decor hints of an Italian/Mexican mix but Perry Como tunes wafting through the air prepare you for spaghetti, mostoccioli, ravioli, fettucini or other dinner entrées. The lunch menu features sandwiches, pizza and soup or pasta of the day. All pasta dishes come with meatballs or Italian sausage. You'll like this place. Open in summer Mon.–Fri. 11:30 am–1:30 pm for lunch; Mon.–Fri. 4:30–8:30 pm for dinner; until 9:00 pm on Sat.; closed Sun.; in winter the restaurant closes a half hour earlier and is closed on Sun. and Mon. Exit 14A, **415 University; (719) 846-2696.**

SERVICES

Colorado Welcome Center—

This is a great source of information on Trinidad and other Colorado destinations. You'll see the signs on Interstate 25. Open daily. **309 N. Nevada Ave., Trinidad, CO 81082; (719) 846-9512.**

Trinidad Visitor Center—

Located across the bridge from the Colorado Welcome Center, the city visitor center is housed in a red caboose. Open Mon.–Fri. 9 am–5 pm. **135 N. Animas, Trinidad, CO 81082; (719) 846-7244.**

Trinidad Trolley—

Free hourly tours of the downtown historic district begin at the Colorado Welcome Center. Trolley tours available Memorial Day–Labor Day; 9:45 am–4:45 pm daily.

Index

About the Authors

Bruce Caughey has traveled in twenty-four foreign countries, and co-authored with his wife Naomi a walking guide entitled *Crete: Off the Beaten Track*. He is assistant coordinator of public information for Douglas County School District. He is also a contributing writer for the Rough Guide Series in London and *Southwest Traveler* magazine. His newest project in collaboration with Dean Winstanley is a yearly Colorado Guide Calendar available for the first time in 1995.

Dean Winstanley has spent most of his life studying and exploring Colorado. On returning from a teaching position in China in 1987, he joined forces with Bruce Caughey in conducting exhaustive research for this ultimate travel guide. Currently he is assistant to the director of Colorado State Parks working on state parks policy.